PALMYRENE ARAMAIC TEXTS

Publications of *The Comprehensive Aramaic Lexicon* Project

An Aramaic Bibliography, Part I
Old, Official, and Biblical Aramaic
Joseph A. Fitzmyer, S.J., and Stephen A. Kaufman

A Key-Word-in-Context Concordance
to Targum Neofiti
A Guide to the Complete Palestinian
Aramaic Text of the Torah
Stephen A. Kaufman and Michael Sokoloff

Palmyrene Aramaic Texts
Delbert R. Hillers and Eleonora Cussini

PALMYRENE ARAMAIC TEXTS

DELBERT R. HILLERS and

ELEONORA CUSSINI

THE JOHNS HOPKINS UNIVERSITY PRESS

Baltimore and London

Publication of this work was made possible in part by a grant from the
National Endowment for the Humanities, a Federal agency.

Printed in the United States of America on acid-free paper
05 04 03 02 01 00 99 98 97 96 5 4 3 2 1

The Johns Hopkins University Press
2715 North Charles Street, Baltimore, Maryland 21218-4319
The Johns Hopkins Press Ltd., London

Library of Congress Cataloging-in-Publication Data

Palmyrene Aramaic texts / Delbert R. Hillers and Eleonora Cussini
p. cm. — (Publications of the Comprehensive Aramaic Lexicon Project)
Aramaic and English.
Includes bibliographical references and indexes.
ISBN 0-8018-5278-1 (h : alk.paper)
1. Palmyrene language — Texts. I. Hillers, Delbert R.
II. Cussini, Eleonora. III. Series.
PJ5229.A1 1995 492'.2 — dc20 95-32142

A catalog record for this book is available from the British Library.

For Giovanni

E. C.

For Susan T. Strahan, in gratitude

D. R. H.

CONTENTS

PREFACE AND ACKNOWLEDGMENTS

> *And because ye shall not think that my travail and diligence in study is anything remitted or slackened, I give you knowledge that after great fervent labour with much watch and indefatigable travail I have learned both the Hebrew language and the Chaldean. ... These, my dear friend, be things which do appertain to a noble prince, I have ever thought and yet think.*
>
> *Giovanni Francesco Pico della Mirandola, trans. Sir Thomas More*

The present volume originates in the authors' work of gathering bibliography and entering, concording, and studying Palmyrene Aramaic texts for *The Comprehensive Aramaic Lexicon.* Since preparation of the major lexical work will inevitably take a long time, it seemed to us that other scholars, especially those who have not made a special study of Palmyrene inscriptions, would find it useful to have in hand now this preliminary synthesis of our work on Palmyrene Aramaic texts. The introductions to major sections of the work ("Bibliography," "Texts," "Glossary") provide additional explanation of our aims and editorial choices.

We wish to emphasize that the present volume does not represent the way Palmyrene Aramaic lexical material will ultimately be presented in *The Comprehensive Aramaic Lexicon,* with its greater scope and different purpose. We do hope that *Palmyrene Aramaic Texts* (within the work the acronym *PAT* is frequently used) will elicit from those who use it suggestions for additions, changes, and corrections, and that this process will enhance its value as a contribution to the larger Aramaic lexical project in progress.

From the beginning this has been a collaborative work of the two authors. Eleonora Cussini took the lead in gathering the bibliography and in collation and presentation of the texts and the data that accompany them, while Delbert Hillers took the lead in preparation of the Glossary. At all stages, however, we have been able to discuss and reach a consensus on issues major and minor.

The process of writing this book has made us aware of the need for a more nearly definitive and uniform reedition of these inscriptions, and we have made some steps toward this more ambitious goal. Although the textual basis for the inscriptions included is ordinarily the existing printed editions, with their photographs and drawings, in some cases circumstances have permitted the authors, especially E. Cussini, to collate a text or group of texts with the original. This is true, for example, for texts in the Istanbul Arkeoloji Müzesi, the Leiden Museum, the Metropolitan Museum of Art, New York, the Yale University Art Gallery, New Haven, the Art Museum, Princeton University, the Museo Capitolino, and the Museo Barracco, Rome; at Rome it proved possible to collate also those in the Collezione Federico Zeri. The acknowledgments immediately following, and notes to the texts, give a fuller notion of the fresh collations with the originals which have been made. In addition, in many cases we have been able to obtain museum photographs of inscribed Palmyrene sculptures, enabling a collation that went beyond use of existing editions. The acknowledgments that follow express our gratitude to the institutions and individuals that made this possible.

It is a pleasure to acknowledge at this point the generous assistance of those institutions and individuals who have contributed in special ways to our work.

Particular thanks are due to the Lucius N. Littauer Foundation and to its president, Mr. William Lee Frost, whose generous grant enabled the authors to work together in Baltimore at preparation of the final manuscript in summer, 1994. At an earlier time, in 1989, The Lutheran Church — Missouri Synod contributed funds to the Aramaic dictionary which in part were used specifically for work on the Palmyrene materials; we repeat our thanks to the Synod and to its then president, Dr. Ralph A. Bohlmann. Our thanks are due also to the Department of Near Eastern Studies of The Johns Hopkins University, and its chairman, Prof. Kyle McCarter, for essential support especially in the final stages of the work.

The debt we owe to previous scholars will be evident; we mention two works as of particular importance to us: *Personal Names in Palmyrene Inscriptions*, by Jürgen Kurt Stark, and the *Dictionnaire des inscriptions sémitiques de l'Ouest,* by Charles-F. Jean and Jacob Hoftijzer. The new, English edition by Hoftijzer and K. Jongeling, of 1995, *Dictionary of the North-West Semitic Inscriptions*, reached us too late to do more than note its publication here and in the bibliography.

Thanks are due to Stephen A. Kaufman and to Joseph A. Fitzmyer, S. J., the editors of *The Comprehensive Aramaic Lexicon*, for critical reading of the final manuscript, and for the many occasions on which they offered counsel in the preceding years.

We are indebted to Prof. Klaus Parlasca not only for his numerous exemplary contributions to Palmyrene studies, but for his exceptional generosity to us in giving of his time and expert knowledge; in the pages that follow, especially in the portion devoted to Texts, the reader will find references to specific contributions of Prof. Parlasca, but this only hints at the extent to which we are in his debt for encouragement, for helpful criticism and correction, and for specific information. We are grateful also to Prof. M. Gawlikowski, with whom we were able to discuss many Palmyrene matters, always with profit to us, during his stay at the Institute for Advanced Study, Princeton in 1994-95. Of course, in thanking these scholars or others, we wish it to be understood that we as authors are solely responsible for the errors and shortcomings of our book.

We gratefully acknowledge the cooperation of the following museums, collections, and libraries, and express thanks to the officials of these institutions who courteously and generously made their resources available to us, or offered other assistance: The Albright Institute in Jerusalem, Sy Gitin, Director; the American Academy in Rome; the American Schools of Oriental Research, for a grant in support of E. Cussini's work of collation; the Australian War Memorial, Canberra, Jean McAuslan, Acting Senior Curator of Art, and Laura Back; the Berkshire Museum, Pittsfield, Massachusetts, Tim Decker, Curator of Ancient Art; the Bible Lands Museum, Jerusalem, Alexis Hope Silverman, Assistant to the Curator; the Collezione Federico Zeri, in Rome, and Federico Zeri; the Studium Biblicum Franciscanum, Museum of the Flagellation Convent, Jerusalem, Fr. Michele Piccirillo, Director, and Fr. Massimo Pazzini; the Harvard University Art Museums, Amy Brauer, Assistant Curator; the State Hermitage Museum, St. Petersburg, E. V. Zeymal, Keeper of the Ancient East Section; the Indiana University Art Museum, in Bloomington, Indiana, and Kathy Henline; the Istanbul Arkeoloji Müzesi, Istanbul, Veysel Donbaz, Curator of the tablet collection; Şeniz Atik, Curator of the Classics collection, Nilüfer Atakan and Asuman Denker, Assistant Curators; the Metropolitan Museum of Art, New York, Prudence O. Harper, Curator, Ancient Near Eastern Art, and Kim Benzel, Curatorial Assistant; the Milton S. Eisenhower Library, The Johns Hopkins University, and especially to Mr. Pierre Berry of its staff; the Musée de Bethesda, Church of St. Anne in Jerusalem, the Curators and M. Arnaud Marion; the Museo Barracco di Scultura Antica, Rome, Maresita Nota Santi, Director, and Maria Gabriella Cimino; the Museo Capitolino, Rome, the Direzione and especially Daniela Velestino; the Pontifical Biblical Institute, Rome, Fr. James Swetnam and the Librarian, Fr. H. Bertels; the Art Museum, Princeton University, Princeton, New Jersey, Michael Padgett,

Curator of Ancient Art; the Arbeia Roman Fort Museum, South Shields, England, Clive Hart, Curator; the Toledo Museum of Art, Toledo, Ohio, Kurt Luckner, Curator of Ancient Art, and Lee Mooney, Registrarial Secretary; the Royal Ontario Museum in Toronto, Canada, Alison Easson; Sotheby's, New York, New York, Richard Keresey, Director, Department of Antiquities and Islamic Works of Art, and Coree Earle, Assistant to the Director; The Saint Louis Art Museum, St. Louis, Missouri, Pamela Paterson, Registrar's Office, and Diane Thomas, Photography Manager; the Walker Art Center, Minneapolis, Hank Dwyer, and Andrea Weiss, Registration Assistant; the Yale University Art Gallery, New Haven, Connecticut, Susan Matheson, Curator; the Beinecke Rare Book and Manuscript Library, Yale University, Robert Babcock, librarian.

In addition, we acknowledge with gratitude the special contributions of the following individuals: Maria Giulia Amadasi Guzzo; Annalisa Azzoni; Michael Barré of St. Mary's Seminary, Baltimore, Maryland; Stephan Bennett, who in his capacity as Associate Research Scholar with the CAL, assisted in countless ways, especially in computer matters; Simone C. Burger; Bella Greenfield, and Jonas Greenfield; Carolyn Higginbotham, of Muskingum College, especially for checking of text-references in the Glossary, but also for much other assistance; Harry Hoffner, of the Chicago Hittite Dictionary, for counsel and encouragement at an early stage; Jacob Hoftijzer, of the University of Leiden; Charles E. Jones, Research Archivist, The Oriental Institute of the University of Chicago; Georg Krotkoff, our teacher and colleague at The Johns Hopkins University, for translation of Russian materials, and advice on Arabic and Neo-Aramaic; Robert Lewis, of the Middle English Dictionary, University of Michigan; John Nitti, of the Dictionary of the Old Spanish Language, for early encouragement and generous giving of time and counsel; Dennis Pardee, of the University of Chicago; Palmira Piersimoni, who kindly made available to us a copy of her thesis of 1989; Ellen Reeder, of The Walters Art Gallery, Baltimore; Michael Sokoloff, of Bar Ilan University; Regina Soria, for assistance in consulting materials in Rome; Loren T. Stuckenbruck, who shared helpful information from his own study of bilingual inscriptions; Jan Verbruggen, of the Department of Near Eastern Studies, The Johns Hopkins University, especially for indispensable computer assistance.

This volume is one of the Publications of *The Comprehensive Aramaic Lexicon* Project. *The Comprehensive Aramaic Lexicon* has received support from the National Endowment for the Humanities. The National Endowment is a federal agency that funds the study of such fields as history, philosophy, literature, and languages.

ABBREVIATIONS AND TEXT SIGLA

Throughout this book, short references to items in the Bibliography have the form: author's name, date, thus B. Aggoula '79, with the "19" omitted. Such short references are not included in the following list. For the sake of economy, especially in the Glossary, the names of some authors cited with great frequency are frequently abbreviated. Such abbreviations are included in the present list, thus "Sta" for "Starcky." Text sigla, that is, abbreviations used to refer to publications of texts, are included below, distinguished by bold type. These text sigla are followed by a reference to the Bibliography, where fuller information will be found.

:: introduces contrasting opinion
? marks preceding letter in Aramaic text as damaged; definition as uncertain, etc
* in Glossary, after m or f: in body of article reference marked with * contains syntactic evidence for gender
< derived from, is a loanword from
1, 2, 3 first person, etc
AA Acta archaeologica
AA '30 Ingholt '30c
AA '32 Ingholt '32b
AAS *Les Annales archéologiques de Syrie*
AAS '53 Sabeh '53
AAS '65/2 Bounni and Saliby '65b
AAS '65 Bounni '65a
ab absolute
abbr abbreviation
acc. according (to)
ActH Ploug and Hvidberg-Hansen *Acta Hiperborea* '91
ad loc *ad locum*, on this passage
adj adjective
adv adverb
AfO *Archiv für Orientforschung*
AfO '53 Eilers '52-53
AHw von Soden '65 *(Akkadisches Handwörterbuch)*
AIΩN *Istituto Universitario Orientale di Napoli. Annali. Sezione di Archeologia e Storia Antica. Dipartimento di studi del mondo classico e del mediterraneo antico*
AIΩN '86a Vattioni '86
AIΩN '86b Callieri '86
AIA Kaufman *The Akkadian Influences on Aramaic*
AION *Istituto Universitario Orientale di Napoli. Annali*
AJA *American Journal of Archaeology*
Akk Akkadian
Anon Anonymous
ANRW *Aufstieg und Niedergang der Römischen Welt*
AP Cowley '23 (*Aramaic Papyri*)
Arab Arabic
Aram Aramaic
ARNA Milik and Starcky '70
AW *Antike Welt*
BA *Beiträge zur Assyriologie*
BASOR *Bulletin of the American Schools of Oriental Research*
Bd Band
Ber *Berytus*
Ber '34 Ingholt '34
Ber '35 Ingholt '35
Ber '36 Ingholt '36
Ber '38 Ingholt '38
Ber '70 Gawlikowski '70a
Ber '73 Winnett and Reed '73
BethSh Mazar '73
bib bibliography, bibliographical note
Bib Aram Biblical Aramaic
BibOr Biblica et Orientalia
BIFAO *Bulletin de l'Institut français d'archéologie orientale*
bis following number of inscription, the second text with this number
BJA Babylonian Jewish Aramaic
BJb *Bonner Jahrbücher des Landesmuseums in Bonn*
BJPES *Bulletin of the Jewish Palestine Exploration Society*
BJPES '47 Ben-Ḥayyim '47
BMB *Bulletin du Musée de Beyrouth*
BMB '55 Starcky '55
BO *Bibliotheca Orientalis*
Bou Bounni
BS III Dunant '71 (*Le sanctuaire de Baalshamin*, Vol III)
BS VI Fellmann and Dunant '75 (*Le sanctuaire de Baalshamin*, Vol VI)
c common, of common gender

C Afel, causative verbal conjugation
C as in C3901 *Corpus Inscriptionum Semiticarum* plus (number of text in Pars secunda, Tomus III: Inscriptiones palmyrenae); in Bibliography see J.B. Chabot '26
Ca Cantineau
CaGr Cantineau *Grammaire du palmyrénien épigraphique*
CAL Comprehensive Aramaic Lexicon
Caq Caquot
CatDam al-ʿUsh et al. *Catalogue du Musée National de Damas* '69
CatMD Abdul-Hak and Abdul-Hak *Catalogue illustré ... Musée National de Damas* '51
CE Catalogo epigrafico, Rome: Museo Capitolino
cf compare
Ch Chabot
Choix J.-B. Chabot *Choix d'inscriptions de Palmyre*
Christie's '94 Christie's, London, Auction Catalogue, Dec 7, 1994
CIS *Corpus Inscriptionum Semiticarum* (usually: Pars secunda, Tomus III: Inscriptiones palmyrenae)
cj conjunction
col, coll column(s)
Com Sem common Semitic occurrence
con construct
CPA Christian Palestinian Aramaic
CRAIBL *Comptes rendus des Séances de l'Académie des Inscriptions et Belles-Lettres*
CRAIBL '32 Chabot '32
CRAIBL '81 Teixidor '81
CRAIBL '85 Asʿad and Teixidor '85b
Ct Ettafal, reflexive-passive of Afel
D Pael, verb conjugation with doubling of middle radical
Dacia '70 Sanie '70b
DAIR Deutsches Archäologisches Institut Rom, Photographic archive
DaM *Damaszener Mitteilungen*
DaM '85 p 34 As'ad and Schmidt-Colinet '85
DaM '85 p 37- As'ad and Teixidor '85
DaM '92 Saliby '92
DBS *Dictionnaire de la Bible, Supplément*
Déd Milik '72 (*Dédicaces faites par des dieux*)
DISO Jean and Hoftijzer *Dictionnaire des inscriptions sémitiques de l'Ouest*
DJPA Sokoloff '90 (*Dictionary of Jewish Palestinian Aramaic*)
DN name of deity, divine name
DNWSI Hoftijzer and Jongeling, *Dictionary of the North-West Semitic Inscriptions* '93
Doura du Mesnil du Buisson *Inventaire des inscriptions palmyréniennes de Doura-Europos*
DuraPR '36 Rostovzeff et al., '36
DuraPR '39 Rostovzeff et al., '39
Dri Drijvers
Dri '82b Drijvers '82
Dt Etpaal, reflexive-passive of D
EaWe *East and West*
EaWe '67 Masson '67
EB *Enciclopedia biblica*
EblaDam Garroni and Parcu edd *Da Ebla a Damasco* '85
ed, edd editor, editors
em emphatic state
ESE Lidzbarski *Ephemeris für semitische Epigraphik*, I, II, III
esp. especially
et al. *et alii*
ETL *Ephemerides theologicae lovanienses*
exc no. excavation number
f feminine; name of female
fasc fascicle, fascicule
FévRel Février *La religion des Palmyréniens*
fig(s) figure(s)
fn footnote
FuB *Forschungen und Berichte der Staatlichen Museen* (Berlin)
G Peal, basic verb conjugation
Gaw M. Gawlikowski
Gaw ANRW Gawlikowski '90
Gk Greek
GLECS *Groupe linguistique d'études chamito-sémitiques*
GN geographical name
Gt Etpeel, reflexive-passive of Peal
Heb Hebrew
HNE Lidzbarski *Handbuch der nordsemitischen Epigraphik*
Hof Hoftijzer
HomVer Drijvers '78
IGLS *Inscriptions grecques et latines de la Syrie*
IH *Inventaire des inscriptions hatréennes* Aggoula '91
impf imperfect
Ing Ingholt

Interj Interjection
Inv *Inventaire des inscriptions de Palmyre*
Inv 1-9 Cantineau '30c
Inv 10 Starcky '49d
Inv 11 Teixidor '65
Inv 12 Bounni and Teixidor '75
IP Cantineau *Inscriptions palmyréniennes* '30a or b
Iraq '49 Starcky '49e
Iraq '87 al-Salihi '87
JA *Journal asiatique*
JA '18 Chabot '18b
JA '33 Cantineau '33
JANES *Journal of the Ancient Near Eastern Society* (formerly of Columbia University)
JAOS *Journal of the American Oriental Society*
Jastrow Jastrow *Dictionary of the Targumim, etc*
JBL *Journal of Biblical Literature*
JNES *Journal of Near Eastern Studies*
JRAS *Journal of the Royal Asiatic Society*
JRS *Journal of Roman Studies*
JSS *Journal of Semitic Studies*
JSS '88 Drijvers '88a
L-S Liddell and Scott *Greek-English Lexicon*
Lat Latin
Lidz Lidzbarski
loc location, present location of text
Lou Dentzer-Feydy and Teixidor '93
LS Brockelmann *Lexicon Syriacum*
LW loanword
m masculine
Maarav '87 Segal '87
Mand Mandaean
MDAIK Deutsches Archäologisches Institut, Kairo, Mitteilungen
Meisterwerke Jakob-Rost and Brandt '86
MélCol *Mélanges d'histoire ancienne et d'archéologie offerts à Paul Collart*
MélCol Dunant '76
MélDus *Mélanges syriens offerts à monsieur René Dussaud*
MélDus p 885 Levi della Vida '39
MélDus p 277 Cantineau '39
MélMich *Mélanges Offerts à Kazimierz Michalowski*
MélRob Starcky '56c
MélRob *Mélanges bibliques rédigés en l'honneur de André Robert*
Mes du Mesnil du Buisson
MF Gawlikowski *Monuments funéraires de Palmyre*
Mich Michalowski
MUSJ *Mélanges de l'Université Saint Joseph*
MUSJ '49 Starcky '49b
MUSJ '61 Starcky '61
MUSJ '62 Ingholt '62
MUSJ '66 Teixidor '66
MVAG *Mitteilungen der Vorderasiatischen Gesellschaft, Mitteilungen der Vorderasiatisch-ägyptischen Gesellschaft*
n noun
n phr noun phrase
NCE Nuovo catalogo epigrafico, Rome: Museo Capitolino
nf feminine noun
nm masculine noun
no. number
nom ag nomen agentis
Noth, IPN Noth *Die israelitischen Personennamen im Rahmen der gemeinsemitischen Namengebung*
NSI Cooke '03 *Text-book of North-Semitic Inscriptions*
num number
NyCG Hvidberg-Hansen '93
NyCG Hvidberg-Hansen '93
Obv. Obverse
Off Aram Official Aramaic
OLZ *Orientalistische Literaturzeitung*
OM *Oudheidkundige Mededelingen uit het Rijksmuseum van Oudheden te Leiden*
OM '88 Hoftijzer '88
Or *Orientalia*
OrLovAn *Orientalia Lovaniensia Analecta*
p, pp page, pages
Palm I, II etc = Michalowski, Palmyre: Fouilles polonaises 1960- .
Palm **III, IV, V:** Michalowski '63, '64, '66; **VIII:** Gawlikowski, '84
PalSb *Palestinskii Sbornik*
PapDura 152 Welles '59
Parl Parlasca
Parl '90b Parlasca '90b
Parl '90c Parlasca '90c
pass passive
PAT *Palmyrene Aramaic Texts* (this volume)
PEFQS *Palestine Exploration Fund Quarterly Statement*
Pers Persian
pf perfect
PGKK Ruprechtsberger ed '87

PGSc Ingholt '54
photo photograph
PJA Palestinian Jewish Aramaic
pl plural; plate(s)
PN personal name
PNO Schlumberger '51 (*La Palmyrène du Nord-Ouest*)
prb probably; problem/problematic
pred predicator
prep prepositon
pron pronoun
prov provenance
PS Ingholt '28 (*Studier over Palmyrensk Skulptur*)
PS Proto-Semitic
PSBA *Proceedings of the Society of Biblical Archaeology*
pt part
ptcp participle
PW Pauly-Wissowa, *Real-Encyclopädie der classischen Altertumswissenschaft*, 1893-
Quad Quadriliteral verb form
RA *Revue d'assyriologie*
RAR to be supplied; Starcky '74
RArch *Revue archéologique*
RB *Revue biblique*
RB '30 Cantineau '30d
RelAram Hof '68 (*Religio Aramaica*)
RES *Répertoire d'épigraphie sémitique*
rev. reverse
RevSém *Revue sémitique*
RHR *Revue de l'histoire des religions*
RIB Roman Inscriptions from Britain
Ros Rosenthal
RosAH Rosenthal *Aramaic Handbook*
RosSpr Rosenthal *Die Sprache der palmyrenischen Inschriften*
RSP Gawlikowski '74c (*Recueil d'inscriptions palmyréniennes*)
RTP Ingholt, Seyrig, and Starcky '55 (*Recueil de tessères de Palmyre*)
s singular
s ab singular, absolute state
Sam Samaritan
SBAW *Sitzungsberichte der Bayerischen Akademie der Wissenschaften*
ScPart Mathiesen '92
SEL *Studi epigrafici e linguistici*
Sem *Semitica*
Sem '50 Starcky '50
Sem '72 Starcky '72
Sem '73 Gawlikowski '73b
Sem '74 Starcky and Delavault '74
Sem '77 Drijvers '77a
Sem '77 p 117 Aggoula '77
Sem '79 Lozachmeur '79
Sem '86 Gawlikowski '86
Sem '91 Briquel-Chatonnet '91
sf suffix, with suffix
SFP Sadurska and Bounni '94
SKAWW *Sitzungsberichte der Kaiserlichen Akademie der Wissenschaften in Wien*
Soth Anon. *Sotheby's catalogue, issues of '86-'90 (with catalogue number)*
SPAW *Sitzungsberichte der Preussischen Akademie der Wissenschaften zu Berlin*
Sta Starcky
Stark PN Stark *Personal Names in Palmyrene Inscriptions*
Stieg Stieglitz Collection (text from private communication, K. Parlasca)
StSc Vermeule and Brauer '90
StudLdV *Studi orientalistici in onore di Giorgio Levi della Vida*
StudLdV 509-28 Starcky '56a
StudLdV 601-02 Walker '56
StudLitt Wuthnow '35
StudMiles Kouymjian, ed *Near Eastern Numismatics, Iconography, Epigraphy and History: Studies in Honor of George C. Miles*
StudMiles Ingholt '74
StudPalm '75 Gawlikowski '75
sub v. *sub voce*
Sumer '62 Teixidor '62
Sumer '64 Safar '64
Syr *Syria, Revue d'Art Oriental et d'Archéologie*
Syr '26 Ingholt '26
Syr '30 Ingholt '30b
Syr '31 Cantineau '31
Syr '33 Cantineau '33a
Syr '36 Cantineau '36
Syr '37 Seyrig
Syr '38 Cantineau '38
Syr '42-43 Dupont-Sommer '42
Syr '49 p 249 Seyrig and Starcky '49
Syr '49 35-41 Starcky '49f
Syr '50 Rodinson '50
Syr '59 Dunant '59
Syr '63 Starcky '63

Syr '70 Gawlikowski '70b
Syr '70 p 413 Caquot '70
Syr '71 Gawlikowski '71
Syr '85 p 257 Gawlikowski '85
Syr '85 p 271- As`ad and Teixidor '85
Syr '85 p 57- Caquot '85
Syr '90 Briquel-Chatonnet '90
t tome
Tad, Tadmorea See Cantineau *Syr* '33, '36, '38
TAD Porten and Yardeni '86 - (*Textbook of Aramaic Documents*)
Teix Teixidor
TeixPan Teixidor *The Pantheon of Palmyra*
ter following number of inscription, the third text with this number
TG Schmidt-Colinet '92, *Tempelgrab no. 36*
TMP du Mesnil du Buisson *Les tessères et les monnaies de Palmyre*
TP Gawlikowski '73 *Temple palmyrénien*
trans translation
Trf: — Tariff of Palmyra = C3913, see Trf(I): and Trf(II): below
Trf(I): — Tariff of Palmyra = C3913, first part (lines 1-14)
Trf(II): — Tariff of Palmyra = C3913, second part (lines 1-14); following lines of second part simply Trf:(line no.)
TribBou Matthiae et al., edd. *Resurrecting the Past: A Joint Tribute to Adnan Bounni*
TSBA *Transactions of the Society for Biblical Archaeology*
UF *Ugarit-Forschungen*
Ug Ugaritic
v verb
VA Vorderasiatisches
Vattioni, Hatra Vattioni '81 *(Le iscrizioni di Ḥatra)*
VDI *Vestnik drevnej istorii*
Verm '81 Vermeule '81
vol(s) volume(s)
VT *Vetus testamentum*
WdM Pope and Röllig "Syrien. Die Mythologie der Ugariter und Phönizier," in *Wörterbuch der Mythologie*, Stuttgart 1965
WZKM *Wiener Zeitschrift für die Kunde des Morgenlandes*
YCS *Yale Classical Studies*
YCS '55 Frye *et al. YCS* '55
ZA *Zeitschrift für Assyriologie*
ZAH *Zeitschrift für Althebraistik*
ZDMG *Zeitschrift der Deutschen Morgenländischen Gesellschaft*
ZPE *Zeitschrift für Papyrologie und Epigraphik*
⧐ in Glossary, = "See also", introducing reference to additional information
† article cites all occurrences in CAL corpus of Palmyrene texts

❖ ❖ ❖ ❖ ❖

BIBLIOGRAPHY

This Bibliography is restricted, though not rigidly, to relatively recent works in which Palmyrene Aramaic texts have been published or where the vocabulary and grammar of these texts is discussed. No effort has been made to include bibliography of the Greek or Latin inscriptions from Palmyra. For works prior to the publication of the relevant part of the ***Corpus inscriptionum semiticarum****, the reader is referred to the bibliographies there; here only a few collections of texts preceding the* ***Corpus*** *have been included, along with several other older books or articles of unusual importance. For recent bibliography of Palmyrene Aramaic, note especially F. Rosenthal,* ***Die aramaistische Forschung****, and the* ***Bulletin d'épigraphie sémitique****, of J. Teixidor in the journal* ***Syria*** *(beginning 1964), also gathered in his 1986 volume with the same title.*

*At the end of some entries in the Bibliography there is an abbreviation in bold type, thus after "Abdul-Hak, S., and A. Abdul-Hak. 1951. Catalogue illustré ... " comes "****CatMD****". This abbreviation is the text siglum, used especially in the sections "Texts" and "Glossary" to designate specific Aramaic texts contained in the publication listed.*

Abdul-Hak, S. 1952a. "L'hypogée de Taai à Palmyre," *AAS* 2 (1952) 193–250.

———. 1952b. "Madfan usra Tāʿī al-tudmurīya," (Arab: "The family tomb of Taai at Palmyra") *AAS* 2 (1952) 7-50.

Abdul-Hak, S., and A. Abdul-Hak. 1951. *Catalogue illustré du Département des antiquités greco-romaines au Musée de Damas I.* Publications de la Direction génerale des antiquités de Syrie: Damascus, 1951. **CatMD**

Aggoula, B. 1972. "Remarques sur les inscriptions hatréennes," *MUSJ* 47 (1972) 3-80. Pl I - III.

———. 1977. "Dédicace palmyrénienne à la Renommée et à la Miséricorde," *Sem* 27 (1977) 117–22. **Sem '77 p 117**

———. 1979. "Remarques sur l'inventaire des inscriptions de Palmyre, Fasc XI et XII," *Sem* 29 (1979) 109–18.

———. 1982. "Studia aramaica I," *Sem* 32 (1982) 101–16.

———. 1985. *Inscriptions et graffites araméens d'Assour.* *AION* Supp no. 43, vol 45 (1985), fasc 2. Naples: Istituto Universitario Orientale, 1985.

———. 1988. "Remarques sur les inscriptions hatréennes XIV," *Syr* 65 (1988) 193-96.

———. 1991. *Inventaire des inscriptions hatréennes.* Institut Français d'archéologie du proche-orient. Bibliothèque archéologique et historique tome CXXXIX. Paris: Geuthner, 1991.

Aharoni, Y. 1977. *Ktwbwt ʿrd.* (Heb: *Arad Inscriptions*) Jerusalem: Bialik, 1975.

Aimé-Giron, N. 1922. "Notes épigraphiques. Bague avec nom propre palmyrénien," *JA* 19 (1922) 65.

———. 1939. "Adversaria Semitica," *BIFAO* 38 (1939) 38 (No. 113).

Altheim, F. and R. Stiehl. 1953. *Das erste Auftreten der Hunnen. Das Alter der Jesaja-Rolle. Neue Urkunden aus Dura-Europos.* Baden-Baden: Verlag für Kunst und Wissenschaft, 1953.

———. 1970. *Geschichte Mittelasiens im Altertum.* Berlin: de Gruyter, 1970. Pp 704-09: two inscriptions, see M. Masson *EaWe* '67.

Amadasi Guzzo, M. 1982. "Il vocabolo m'ḫd/mḥz in ugaritico e in fenicio," in *Materiali lessicali ed epigrafici. I, Collezione di studi fenici*, 13. Rome: Consiglio nazionale delle ricerche, 1982. Pp 31-36.

Amy, R. 1933. "Premières restaurations à l'arc monumental de Palmyre," *Syr* 14 (1933) 396–411.

———. 1976. "Remarques sur la construction du temple de Bel," in *Palmyre, Bilan et Perspectives.* Strasbourg: AECR, 1976. Pp 53-68.

Amy, R. and H. Seyrig. 1936a. "Recherches dans la nécropole de Palmyre," *Syr* 17 (1936) 229–266.

———. 1936b. *Recherches dans la nécropole de Palmyre.* (Extrait de la Revue *Syria,* 1936, fasc.3). Paris: Geuthner, 1936.

Anon. 1980. *Palmyra: 1830-1980. 150 Jahre Staatlichen Museen zu Berlin.* Berlin: das Museum, 1980.

Anon. 1986. Sotheby's, New York, Auction Catalogue, Nov. 24, 1986. **Soth 5518**

Anon. 1988. Sotheby's, New York, Auction Catalogue, June 15, 1988. **Soth 5722**

Anon. 1988. Sotheby's, New York, Auction Catalogue, Dec. 2, 1988. **Soth 5788**

Anon. 1989. "Acquisitions/1988," *The J. Paul Getty Museum Journal* 17 (1989) "13. Funerary Stele" pp 110-11.

Anon. 1990. Sotheby's, London, Auction Catalogue, Dec. 13-14, 1990. **Soth 03472**

Anon. 1994. Christie's, London, Auction Catalogue, Dec. 7 1994. **Christie's '94**

Arnaud, D. 1982. "Emar et Palmyre," *AAS* 32 (1982) 83–88.

Arndt, P. n. d.. *La glyptothèque Ny-Carlsberg, fondée par Carl Jacobsen. Les monuments antiques.* Munich: F. Bruckmann, n. d.

Arnold, W. 1905. "Additional Palmyrene Inscriptions in the Metropolitan Museum of Art, New York," *JAOS* 26 (1905) 105-112.

al-Asʿad, K. 1968. "Mud̲akkira ḥawl al-maqbara al-bizanṭiya," (Arab: "Report on the Byzantine Cemetery discovered in the garden of the Palmyra Museum") *AAS* 18 (1968) 129-33.

———. 1987. "Das Museum von Palmyra," in *Palmyra: Geschichte, Kunst und Kultur der Oasenstadt*, ed E. Ruprechtsberger. Linzer archäeologische Forschungen, 16. Linz: Gutenberg, 1987. Pp 258-67.

al-Asʿad, K. and A. Bounni. 1982. *Palmyre: histoire, monuments et musée.* Damas: 1982.

al-Asʿad, K. and M. Gawlikowski. 1986. "New Honorific Inscriptions in the Great Colonnade of Palmyra," *AAS* 36 (1986) 164–71.

al-Asʿad, K. and A. Schmidt-Colinet. 1985. "Das Tempelgrab Nr. 36 in der Westnekropole von Palmyra. Ein Vorbericht," *DaM* 2 (1985) 17-35. **DaM '85**

al-Asʿad, K. and O. Taha. 1965. "Madfan Zabd-ʿAtah al-Tudmurî," (Arab: "The Palmyrene tomb of Zabd-ʿAtah") *AAS* 15/1 (1965) 29–46.

———. 1968. "Madfan Bûlhâ al-Tadmurî," (Arab: "The Palmyrene tomb of Bulha") *AAS* 18 (1968) 83–108.

al-Asʿad, K. and J. Teixidor. 1982. "Baʿḏ an-nuṣûṣ al-muktašafah hadît̲an fî Tudmur," (Arab: "Some of the recently discovered texts from Palmyra") *AAS* 32 (1982) 89–96.

———. 1985a. "Quelques inscriptions palmyréniennes inédites," *Syr* 62 (1985) 271–80. **Syr '85**

———. 1985b. "Un culte arabe préislamique à Palmyre d'après une inscription inédite," *CRAIBL* (1985) 286–92. **CRAIBL '85**

———. 1985c. "Votive and Funerary Inscriptions from Palmyra," *DaM* 2 (1985) 37-44. **DaM '85 p 37-**

Bäärnhielm, G. 1988. "Palmyra — en bakgrundsteckning," in *Palmyra. Öknens drottning*, edd P. Hellström, M. Nockert, S. Unge. Stockholm: Medelhavsmuseet & Statens historika museum, 1988. Pp 11-30.

Bagatti, B. 1939. *Guida al museo dello Studium Biblicum Franciscanum.* Jerusalem: Studium Biblicum Franciscanum, 1939.

Baldini, A. 1972. "Roma e Palmira: Note storico-epigrafiche," *Epigraphica* 34 (1972) 109-33.

———. 1975. "Problemi di storia palmirena: note sulla politica di Odenato," *Corsi di Ravenna* 13 (1975) 21-45.

Baratte, F. 1984. *Au pays du Baal et d'Astarté: 10.000 ans d'art en Syrie.* Paris: Ministère des Relations Extérieures, 1984.

Barthélemy, J. 1754. *Reflexions sur l'alphabet et sur la langue dont on se servoit autrefois à Palmyre.* Paris: Guérin, 1754.

———. 1759. "Réflexions sur l'alphabet et sur la langue dont on se servoit autrefois à Palmyre," *Mémoires de l'Académie des Inscriptions* 26 (1759) 577–97.

Bastet, F. L. 1979. *Duizendjarig dolen. Wandelingen door de antieke wereld.* Amsterdam: Querido, 1978. Pp 208-217 ("Een grande dame uit Palmyra").

Baur, P., M. Rostovtzeff and A. Bellinger. 1929. *Preliminary Report of the Excavations at Dura-Europos.* New Haven: Yale University, 1929-34.

Bellinger, A. 1938. *Coins from Jerash, 1928-1934.* Numismatic Notes and Monographs. New York: The American Numismatic Society, 1938.

Ben-Ḥayyim, Z. (W. Goldmann). 1935. *Die palmyrenischen Personennamen.* Leipzig: Teicher, 1935.

———. 1947. "Ktwbwt tdmwrywt," (Heb: "Palmyrene Inscriptions") *BJPES* 13 (1947) 141–48 [Hebrew]. **BJPES '47**

Bertinelli Angeli, M. 1970. *Nomenclatura pubblica e sacra di Roma nelle epigrafi semitiche*. Pubblicazioni dell'Istituto di Storia Antica e Scienze Ausiliarie dell'Università di Genova, 7. Genoa: Istituto di Storia Antica, 1970.

Blau, O. 1874. "Palmyrenisches Relief mit Inschrift," *ZDMG* 28 (1874) 73–76.

Böme, A. and W. Schottroff. 1979. *Palmyrenische Grabreliefs*. Liebighaus Monographie. Frankfurt/Main: 1979.

Bounni, A. 1958. "Taqrîr awwalî ʿan ḥafriyyât madfan šalam allât," (Arab: "Preliminary Report on excavations at the Tomb of Shalamallat") *Sumer* 14 (1958) 20–26.

———. 1961. "Inscriptions palmyréniennes inédites. 1. Inscriptions de l'hypogée de Šalamallât, Vallée des Tombeaux, Palmyre," *AAS* 11–12 (1961–62) 145–62.

———. 1965a. "Note sur un nouveau bas-relief palmyrénien," trans G. Saadé, *AAS* 15/I (1965) 87–98. **AAS '65**

———. 1965b. "Maḏkara ḥawl manḥûta tudmurîya jadîda," (Arab: "Note on a New Relief Sculpture from Palmyra") *AAS* 15/I (1965) 3-14. Pl I, II, III 1, III 2.

———. 1966. "Nouveaux bas-reliefs religieux de la Palmyrène." *Mélanges Offerts à Kazimierz Michalowski*, ed M.-L. Bernhard. Warsaw: Państwowe Wydawnictwo Naukowe, 1966. Pp 313–20.

———. 1967a. "Thalâth Manḥûtât dîniyya tadmuriyya jadîda min iqlîm tadmur," (Arab: "Three new Palmyrene religous sculptures from the region of Palmyra") *AAS* 17 (1967) 29–31.

———. 1967b. "En mission à Palmyre: Bilan de dix années de fouilles," *Archeologia* 16 (1967) 40–49.

———. 1970. "Antiquités palmyréniennes dans un texte arabe du Moyen Age," *MUSJ* 46 (1970–71) 329–39.

———. 1976. "Nabû palmyrénien," *Or* 45 (1976) 46–52.

———. 1985. "Palmyra: The Caravan City." *Ebla to Damascus: Art and Archaeology of Ancient Syria*, ed H. Weiss. Washington: Smithsonian Institution, 1985. Pp 380–85.

Bounni, A. and K. al-Asʿad. 1988. *Palmyra: History, Monuments & Museum*. 2nd edition, translated by A. Pardee. (for French edition see above, K. al-Asʿad and A. Bounni, 1982). Damascus: 1988.

Bounni, A. and N. Salibi. 1957. "Madfan šalam allât," (Arab: "The Tomb of Shalamallat") *AAS* 7 (1957) 25–52.

———. 1965a. "Al-tanqîb fî sittat mawâqiʿ jadîda fî Tadmur 1963–1964," (Arabic: "Six New Sites Dug at Palmyra 1963-1964") *AAS* 15/2 (1965) 35–58.

———. 1965b. "Six nouveaux emplacements fouillés a Palmyre," *AAS* 15/2 (1965) 121–38. **AAS '65 pt 2**

Bounni, A. and J. Teixidor. 1975. *Inventaire des inscriptions de Palmyre*. Fascicule XII. Damascus: Publications de la Direction Générale des Antiquités et Musées de la République Arabe Syrienne, 1975. **Inv 12**

Boyarin, D. 1981. "An Inquiry into the Formation of the Middle Aramaic Dialects." *Bono Homini Donum: Essays in Historical Linguistics in Memory of J. Alexander Kerns*, edd Y. Arbeitman and A. Bomhard. Amsterdam: J. Benjamins B. V., 1981 Pp 613–49.

Briquel-Chatonnet, F. 1990. "Un bas-relief de style palmyrénien inédit," *Syr* 67 (1990) 184-87. **Syr '90**

———. 1991. "Un petit autel votif palmyrénien," *Sem* 40 (1991) 83-87. **Sem '91**

Brockelmann, C. 1908. *Grundriss der vergleichenden Grammatik der semitischen Sprachen*. Berlin, 1908; repr. Hildesheim: Olms, 1961.

———. 1928. *Lexicon Syriacum*. Halle: Niemeyer, 1928.

Brock, S. 1975. "Some Aspects of Greek Words in Syriac," in *Synkretismus im syrisch-persischen Kulturgebiet*, ed A. Dietrich. Abhandlungen der Akademie der Wissenschaften in Göttingen, Phil.-hist. Klasse, 3. Folge, Nr. 96. Göttingen: Vandenhoeck & Ruprecht, 1975. Pp 80-108.

Brodersen, K. 1987. "Das Steuergesetz von Palmyra." *Palmyra, Geschichte, Kunst und Kultur der Syrischen Oasenstadt*, ed E. Ruprechtsberger. Linzer archäeologische Forschungen, 16. Linz: Gutenberg, 1987 Pp 153–62.

Bron, F. 1986. "Palmyréniens et chaldéens en Arabie du Sud," *SEL* 3 (1986) 95–98.

Browning, I. 1979. *Palmyra.* Parkridge: Noyes Press, 1979.

Buttrey, T. 1961. "'Old Aurei' at Palmyra and the Coinage of Pescennius Niger," *Ber* 14 (1961-63) 117-28.

Cagnat, R. 1884. "Remarques sur un tarif récemment découvert à Palmyre," *Revue de philologie* 8 (1884) 135–44.

———. 1906. *Inscriptiones Graecae ad Res Romanas Pertinentes.* Tomus III. Paris: *Académie des Inscriptions et Belles-lettres*, 1906; reprint Chicago: Ares, 1975.

———. 1911. *Inscriptiones Graecae ad Res Romanas Pertinentes.* Tomus I. Paris: *Académie des Inscriptions et Belles-lettres*, 1911.

Calasso, R. 1987. "La città della sceicca," *FMR* (Italian edition) 49 (March, 1987) 65-102

Callieri, P. 1980. "Il rilievo palmireno di BTMLKW e HYRN nel Museo Nazionale d'Arte Orientale di Roma," in *Arte Orientale in Italia*, V. Rome, 1980. Pp x - xx.

———. 1986. "Rilievi funerari palmireni nella Collezione Zeri," *AIΩN* 8 (Naples: 1986). Pp 223-44. **AIΩN '86b**

Cantineau, J. 1929. "Fouilles à Palmyre," *Mélanges de l'Institut français de Damas* (1929) 3–15.

———. 1930a. *Inscriptions palmyréniennes.* Châlon-sur-Saône: Bertrand, 1930. **IP**

———. 1930b. "Inscriptions palmyréniennes," *RA* 27 (1930) 27–51. **IP**

———. 1930c. *Inventaire des inscriptions de Palmyre.* Publications du Musée de Damas. Fascicules I-IX. Beyrouth: Institut Français d'archéologie de Beyrouth, 1930–36. **Inv 1-9**

———. 1930d. "Textes funéraires palmyréniens," *RB* 39 (1930) 520–51. **RB '30**

———. 1931. "Textes palmyréniens provenant de la fouille du temple de Bêl," *Syr* 12 (1931) 116–42. **Syr '31**

———. 1933a. "Tadmorea," *Syr* 14 (1933) 169-202.

———. 1933b. "Un *restitutor orientis* dans les inscriptions de Palmyre," *JA* 222 (1933) 217–33. **JA '33**

———. 1935. *Grammaire du palmyrénien épigraphique.* Cairo: Imprimerie de l'Institut français d'archéologie orientale, 1935.

———. 1936. "Tadmorea (suite)," *Syr* 17 (1936) 267–355. **Syr '36**

———. 1938. "Tadmorea (suite)," *Syr* 19 (1938) 72–82; 153-71. **Syr '38**

———. 1939. "La Susiane dans une inscription palmyrénienne." *Mélanges syriens offerts à monsieur René Dussaud.* Bibliothèque archéologique et historique. Paris: Geuthner, 1939. Vol I, pp 277–79. **MélDus p 277**

Caquot, A. 1952. "Chadrapha: a propos de quelques articles récents," *Syr* 29 (1952) 74–88.

———. 1955. "Remarques linguistiques sur les inscriptions des tessères de Palmyre," in *Recueil des tessères de Palmyre*, by H. Ingholt et al. Paris: Geuthner, 1955. Pp 139-83.

———. 1956. "Quelques nouvelles données palmyréniennes," *GLECS* 7 (1956) 77–78.

———. 1962. "Sur l'onomastique religieuse de Palmyre," *Syr* 39 (1962) 231–56.

———. 1970. Review of W. Oxtoby, *Some Inscriptions of the Safaitic Bedouin. Syr* 47 (1970) 413. **Syr '70 p 413**

———. 1985. "Un nouveau pyrée de Palmyre," *Syr* 62 (1985) 57–59. **Syr '85 57-59**

Caubet, A. 1990. *Aux sources du monde arabe: L'Islam avant l'Islam: Collections du Musée du Louvre* (Paris: Institut du Monde Arabe, Réunion des musées nationaux, 1990.

Chabot, J.-B. 1898. "Notes d'épigraphie et d'archéologie orientale. III Nouvelles inscriptions inédites de Palmyre," *JA* 9/12 (1898) 68–123.

———. 1900. *Répertoire d'épigraphie sémitique; publié par la commission du Corpus inscriptionum semiticarum.* Paris: Imprimerie Nationale, 1900-.

———. 1901a. "Nouvelles et mélanges. Sur quelques inscriptions palmyréniennes récemment publiées," *JA* 9/17 (1901) 346–49.

———. 1901b. "Notes d'épigraphie et d'archéologie orientale. IX Quelques nouvelles inscriptions palmyréniennes," *JA* 9/18 (1901).

———. 1906. "Notes sur quelques monuments épigraphiques araméens. III Dix inscriptions palmyréniennes," *JA* 10/7 (1906) 293–304.

———. 1918a. "Remarques sur le Tarif de Palmyre," *JA* 206 (1918) 301-17.
———. 1918b. "Glanures palmyréniennes," *JA* 12 (1918) 277–317. **JA '18**
———. 1922. *Choix d'inscriptions de Palmyre.* Paris: Imprimerie Nationale, 1922.
———. 1927. see *Corpus inscriptionum semiticarum.*
———. 1930. "Un *corrector totius orientis* dans les inscriptions de Palmyre," *CRAIBL* (1930) 312–18.
———. 1932. "Nouvelle inscription palmyrénienne d'Afrique," *CRAIBL* (1932) 265-69. **CRAIBL '32**
———. 1940. "Notes d'épigraphie sémitique," *CRAIBL* (1940) 345–349.

Chamay, J., and J.-L. Maier. 1989. *Art romain. Sculptures en pierre du Musée de Genève.* Tome II. Mainz am Rhein: Philipp von Zabern, 1989.

Champdor, A. 1953. *Ruines de Palmyre.* Paris: A. Guillot, 1953.

Chéhab, M. 1937 - 38. "Notice sur les fouilles de Ḥarbata," *MUSJ* 21 (1937-38) 74-85; (insert in S. Ronzevalle '37-38; 74-85; treats Palmyrene inscription p 76 (no. 8), Pl. XXII, 8).
———. 1962. "Tyr a l'époque romaine. Aspects de la cité à la lumière des textes et des fouilles," *MUSJ* 38 (1962) 11–40.

Chehade, J. 1987. "Zu Schmuckdarstellungen auf Palmyrenischen Grabreliefs." *Palmyra. Geschichte, Kunst und Kultur der Syrischen Oasenstadt*, ed E. Ruprechtsberger. Linzer archäeologische Forschungen, 16. Linz: Gutenberg, 1987. Pp 193–99. **PGKK**

Chwolson, D. 1876. "Ein Relief aus Palmyra mit zwei palmyrenischen Inscriften," *Mélanges asiatiques (St. Pétersbourg)* 7 (1876) 433–46.

Clermont-Ganneau, C. 1897. "Le calendrier palmyrénien d'après une nouvelle inscription," in Études d'archéologie orientale. Tome 2. Bibliothèque de l'École des Hautes Études, fasc 113. Paris: Buillon, 1897. Pp. 55-76. Pl I A.
———. 1898. "Notes d'épigraphie palmyrénienne," in *Recueil d'archéologie orientale*, tome 3 (Paris: Leroux, 1898). Pp 156-85.
———. 1906a. "Épigraphie palmyrénienne," in *Recueil d'archéologie orientale*, tome 7 (Paris: Leroux, 1906). Pp 1-38. Pl V. Relevant "Additions et rectifications" in tome 8 pp 303-04.
———. 1906b. "Épigraphie palmyrénienne," in *Recueil d'archéologie orientale*, tome 7 (Paris: Leroux, 1906). Pp 337-69. Relevant "Additions et rectifications" in tome 8 pp 303-04.
———. 1924. "Nouvelles inscriptions palmyréniennes," in *Recueil d'archéologie orientale*, tome 8 (Paris: Leroux, 1924). Pp 1-14. Pl I. Relevant "Additions et rectifications" p 304.

Collart, P. 1956. "Nouveau monument palmyrénien de Shadrafa," *Museum Helveticum* 13 (1956) 209-15.
———. 1957. "Le sanctuaire de Baalshamîn à Palmyre, Fouilles suisses 1954-1955-1956," *AAS* 1 (1957) 67–90.
———. 1961. "Le rôle de Palmyre à l'époque hellénistique et romaine d'après les découvertes récentes." *Atti del settimo congresso internazionale di archeologia classica, I.* Rome: "L'Erma" di Bretschneider, 1961. Pp 427–35.
———. 1962. "Réutilisation chrétienne d'un grand sanctuaire de Palmyre," *Rendiconti della Pontificia Accademia Romana di Archeologia* 35 (1962-63) 147–59.
———. 1963. "Quelques aspects de la vie économique de Palmyre à la lumière de découvertes récentes." *Mélanges d'histoire économique et sociale en hommage au professeur Antony Babel.* Genève: 1963. Pp 37–46.
———. 1966a. "Relief votiv de Palmyre." *Antike Kunst.* Bâle: 1966.
———. 1966b. "Aspects du culte de Baalshamîn à Palmyre." *Mélanges offerts à Kazimierz Michalowski*, ed M.-L. Bernhard. Warsaw: Państwowe Wydawnictwo Naukowe, 1966. Pp 325–37.
———. 1967. "Le sanctuaire de Baalshemên," *Archeologia* 16 (1967) 52–56.
———. 1976. "À propos de l'autel du sanctuaire de Nébo," in *Palmyre, Bilan et Perspectives.* Strasbourg: AECR, 1976. Pp 85-95.

Collart, P. and J. Vicari. 1969. *Le sanctuaire de Baalshamin à Palmyre, I-II: Topographie et architecture.* Bibliotheca helvetica romana. Neuchâtel: 1969.

Colledge, M. 1976a. *The Art of Palmyra.* London: Thames and Hudson, 1976.

———. 1976b. "Le temple de Bel à Palmyre: qui l'a fait, et pourquoi?" *Palmyre, Bilan et Perspectives.* Strasbourg: AECR, 1976. Pp 45-52.

Collingwood, R. and R. Wright. 1965. *The Roman Inscriptions of Britain.* Oxford: Clarendon Press, 1965.

Comstock, M. and C. Vermeule. 1976. *Sculpture in Stone. The Greek, Roman and Etruscan Collections of the Museum of Fine Arts, Boston.* Boston: Museum of Fine Arts, 1976.

Cooke, E. 1992. "Qumran Aramaic and Aramaic Dialectology," *Abr-Nahrain* Supplement 3 (Louvain: Peters, 1992) 1-21.

Cooke, G. 1903. *A Text-Book of North-Semitic Inscriptions.* Oxford: Clarendon Press, 1903. Pp 263–340.

———. 1922. "A Palmyrene Tessera," *JRAS* (1922) 271–73.

Cooney, J. 1966. "A Funerary Relief from Palmyra," *The Bulletin of The Cleveland Museum of Art* v. 53, no. 2 (1966) 34-37.

Corpus inscriptionum semiticarum. 1926. *Corpus inscriptionum semiticarum. Pars secunda. Tomus III: Inscriptiones palmyrenae*, ed J.-B. Chabot. Fasciculus primus: Paris: E reipublicae typographeo, 1926. Fasciculus secundus, 1947. Tabulae: Fasciculus primus, 1951; Fasciculus secundus, 1954.

Cowley, A. 1923. *Aramaic Papyri of the Fifth Century B.C.* Oxford: Clarendon, 1923; reprint Osnabrück: Zeller, 1967.

Crouch, D. 1972. "A Note on the Population and Area of Palmyra," *MUSJ* 47 (1972) 239–50.

Cumont, F. 1928. "L'autel palmyrénien du Musée du Capitole," *Syr* 9 (1928) 101–109.

Cussini, E. 1992a. *The Aramaic Law of Sale and the Cuneiform Legal Tradition.* (Ph. D. dissertation, Johns Hopkins, 1992).

———. 1992b. "Two Palmyrene Aramaic Inscriptions in American Collections," *Syr* 49 (1992) 423-29.

Dalman, G. 1905. *Grammatik des Jüdisch-Palästinischen Aramäisch.* 2nd ed. (Leipzig: Hinrichs, 1905; reprint Darmstadt: Wissenschaftliche Buchgesellschaft, 1960).

———. 1938. *Aramäisch-Neuhebräisches Handwörterbuch zu Targum, Talmud und Midrasch.* 3nd ed. (Göttingen: Pfeiffer, 1938).

Daniels, P. 1988. "'Shewing of Hard Sentences and Dissolving of Doubts': The First Decipherment," *JAOS* 108 (1988) 419–36.

Davis, M. and L. Stuckenbruck. 1992. "Notes on Translation Phenomena in the Palmyrene Bilinguals," in *Intertestamental Essays in Honour of Józef Tadeusz Milik*, Qumranica mogilanensia 6, ed. Z. Kapera. Cracow: Enigma, 1992.

Dawkins, H. and R. Wood. 1753a. *Les ruines de Palmyre autrement dite Tedmor au désert.* London: A. Millar, 1753.

———. 1753b. *The Ruins of Palmyra otherwise Tedmor in the Desart.* London: 1753.

Degen, R. 1972. Review of J. Stark, *Personal Names in Palmyrene Inscriptions, BO* 29 (1972) 210-16.

———. 1987. "Schrift und Sprache Palmyras," in *Palmyra. Geschichte, Kunst und Kultur der syrischen Oasenstadt*, ed E. Ruprechtsberger. Linzer Archäeologische Forschungen, 16. Linz: Gutenberg, 1987. Pp 27–31.

De Laet, S. 1949. *Portorium: Étude sur l'organisation douanière chez les romains, surtout a l'époque du haut-empire.* Rijksuniversiteit te Gent, Werken uitgeven door de Faculteit van de Wijsbegeerte en Letteren, no. 105. Brugge: de Tempel, 1949.

Del Chiaro, M. 1959. *Greek & Roman Portraits 470 BC — AD 500. Boston Museum of Fine Arts. 1959.* Boston: Museum of Fine Arts, 1959.

———. 1973. *Roman Art in West Coast Collections.* Santa Barbara: University of California, 1973.

Del Olmo Lete, G. 1984. "La 'capilla' o 'templete' (ḫmn) del culto ugaritico," *Aula Orientalis* II (1984) 277-80.

Dentzer-Feydy, J. and J. Teixidor 1993. *Les antiquités de Palmyre au Musée du Louvre.* Musée du Louvre, Département des antiquités orientales. Paris: Réunion des Musées Nationaux, 1993. **Lou**

Deonna, W. 1923. "Monuments orientaux du Musée de Genève," *Syr* 4 (1923) 224-33.

Derenbourg, J. 1868. "Nouvelles et mélanges. Notes épigraphiques. VIII Inscriptions palmyréennes," *JA* 6/13 (1868) 360–77.

Dessau, H. 1884. "Der Steuertarif von Palmyra," *Hermes* 19 (1884) 486–533.

Dhorme, P. 1924. "Palmyre dans les textes assyriens," *RB* N.S. 33 (1924) 106–8.

Díez Merino, L. 1971. "Influencias judía y cristiana en los signos e inscripciones palmirenas," *Studii Biblici Franciscani Liber Annuus* 21 (1971) 76–148 .

Dittenberger, W. 1903. *Orientis Graeci Inscriptiones Selectae.* 2 vols Leipzig, 1903; reprint Hildesheim: Olms, 1970). Vol 2, nos. 629-51, pp 323-58: "Palmyrene".

Dobiáš, J. 1931. "Nový nápis z Palmyreny," *Listy filologické* 58 (1931) 1–19.

Downey, S. 1970. "A Preliminary Corpus of the Standards of Hatra," *Sumer* 26 (1970) 195-225.

———. 1977. *The Stone and Plaster Sculpture.* Excavations at Dura-Europos. Final Report III, Part I, Fasc 2. Los Angeles: Yale University, 1977.

Drexhage, R. 1980. "Der Handel Palmyras in römischer Zeit," *Scripta Mercaturae* 2 (1980) 17–33.

Drijvers, H. 1972a. *Old-Syriac (Edessian) inscriptions.* Leyden: Brill, 1972.

———. 1972b. "The cult of Azizos and Monimos at Edessa," in *Ex orbe religionum, Studia Geo Widengren oblata.* Studies in the History of Religions (Supplements to *Numen*) vols 21, 22. Leiden: Brill, 1972. Vol 22, pp 355-371.

———. 1975. "Het Heilgdom van de Godin Allāt," *Phoenix* 21 (1975) 15-34.

———. 1976a. *The Religion of Palmyra.* Iconography of Religions. Leiden: Brill, 1976.

———. 1976b. "Das Heiligtum der arabischen Göttin Allât im westlichen Stadtteil von Palmyra," *AW* 7/3 (1976) 28–38.

———. 1977a. "Une main votive en bronze trouvée à Palmyre dédiée à Baʿalshamên," *Sem* 27 (1977) 105–16. **Sem '77**

———. 1977b. "Hatra, Palmyra und Edessa. Die Städte der syrisch-mesopotamischen Wüste in politischer, kulturgeschichtlicher und religionsgeschichtlicher Beleuchtung," *ANRW* II, 8 (1977). Pp 799–906.

———. 1978. "De matre inter leones sedente. Iconography and Character of the Arab goddess Allât," in *Hommages à Maarten J. Vermaseren*, ed M. de Boer et T. Edridge. Leiden: E. J. Brill, 1978. Pp 331–51. **HomVer**

———. 1982a. "After Life and Funerary Symbolism in Palmyrene Religion," in *La soteriologia dei culti orientali nell'Impero Romano. Atti del Colloquio Internazionale su La soteriologia dei culti orientali nell'Impero Romano. Roma 24-28 Settembre 1979*, edd U. Bianchi e M. J. Vermaseren. Études préliminaires aux religions orientales dans l'empire romain, , tome 92. Leiden: E. J. Brill, 1982. Pp 709-33.

———. 1982b. "Sanctuaries and Social Safety. The Iconography of Divine Peace in Hellenistic Syria," *Visible Religion* 1 (1982) 65–75. **Dri '82b**

———. 1988a. "Aramaic ḥmnʾ and Hebrew ḥmn: Their Meaning and Root," *JSS* 33 (1988) 165-80. **JSS '88**

———. 1988b. "Palmyras historia. En översikt," in *Palmyra. Öknens drottning*, edd P. Hellström, M. Nockert, S. Unge. Stockholm: Medelhavsmuseet & Statens historika museum, 1988. Pp 43-48.

Drouin, E. 1893. "Inscriptions funéraires palmyréniennes," *RevSém* 1 (1893) 270–272.

Dunant, C. 1956. "Nouvelle inscription caravanière de Palmyre," *Museum Helveticum* 13 (1956) 216–25.

———. 1959. "Nouvelles tessères de Palmyre," *Syr* 36 (1959) 102–10. **Syr '59**

———. 1971. *Le sanctuaire de Baalshamin à Palmyre.* Vol III: Les inscriptions. Bibliotheca Helvetica Romana. Rome: Institut Suisse de Rome, 1971. **BS III**

———. 1976. "Une inscription palmyrénienne au Musée de Genève," in *Mélanges d'histoire ancienne et d'archéologie offerts à Paul Collart*, edd P. Ducrey et al. Cahiers d'archéologie Romande. Lausanne: de Brocard, 1976. Pp 161–64. **MélCol**

Dupont-Sommer, A. 1942. "Un buste palmyrénien inédit," *Syr* 23 (1942-43) 78–85. **Syr '42-43**

———. 1966. "Remarques sur la prèmière campagne de fouilles à Palmyre," *CRAIBL* (1966) 188–190.

Duru, R. 1976. "Techniques de construction orientales (à propos du temple de Bel)," in *Palmyre, Bilan et Perspectives.* Strasbourg: AECR, 1976. Pp 69-74.

Dussaud, R. 1927. "La mention du vin dans un texte religieux palmyrénien," *RHR* (1927) 200–203.

———. 1929. "La Palmyrène et l'exploration de M. Alois Musil," *Syr* 10 (1929) 52–62 .
———. 1932a. "Le temple de Bêl à Palmyre," *Syr* 13 (1932) 313.
———. 1932b. "Bas-relief palmyrénien," *Bulletin des musées de France* 4/9 (1932) 149–51.
———. 1938. "Note additionelle," to R. du Mesnil, "Un bilingue araméen-grec de l'époque parthe a Doura-Europos," *Syr* 19 (1938) p 152.
Duval, R. 1883. "Nouvelles et mélanges. Communication sur la loi fiscale de Palmyre," *JA* 8/2 (1883) 537–39.
Eilers, W. 1952. "Eine Büste mit Inschrift aus Palmyra," *AfO* 16 (1952-53) 311–15. **AfO '53**
Eissfeldt, O. 1938. "Neue Belege für *ʾdt* ʿHerrin'," *OLZ* 41 (1938) cols. 489-91.
Euting, J. 1885. "Epigraphische Miscellen," *SPAW* 1885. Pp 669-88.
———. 1887. "Epigraphische Miscellen. Zweite Reihe," *SPAW* 1887. Pp 407-22.
Feissel, D. and J. Gascou. 1989. "Documents d'archives romains inédits du Moyen Euphrate (IIIe siècle aprés J.-C.)," *CRAIBL* (1989) 535-61.
Fellmann, R. 1976a. "Le 'Camp de Diocletien' à Palmyre et l'architecture militaire du Bas-Empire," in *Mèlanges d'histoire ancienne et d'archéologie offerts à P. Collart*, edd P. Ducrey et al. Cahiers d'archéologie Romande. Lausanne: de Brocard, 1976. Pp 173–91.
———. 1976b. "Le tombeau près du temple de Ba'ashamên, témoin de deux siècles d'histoire palmyrénienne," in *Palmyre, Bilan et Perspectives*. Strasbourg: AECR, 1976. Pp 213–31.
Fellmann, R. and C. Dunant. 1975. *Le sanctuaire de Baalshamin à Palmyre*. Vol VI: Kleinfunde — Objets divers. Bibliotheca Helvetica Romana. Rome: Institut Suisse de Rome, 1975. **BS VI**
Février, J. G. 1931a. *La religion des Palmyréniens*. Paris: J. Vrin, 1931.
———. 1931b. *Essai sur l'histoire politique et économique de Palmyre*. Paris: J. Vrin, 1931.
———. 1934a. "Les épithètes de Beelshamên," *Revue des études sémitiques* 1/1 (1934) 15-16.
———. 1934b. "À propos du panthéon palmyrénien," *Revue des études sémitiques* 1/3-4 (1934) 10-22.
———. 1934c. "Simia-Némésis," *JA* 224 (1934) 308–14.
Fiema, Z. 1986. "An Inscription from the Temple of Bel in Palmyra Reconsidered," *BASOR* No. 263 (Aug., 1986) 81–83.
Filarska, B. 1966. "Quelques remarques sur le caractère de l'art palmyrénien." *Mélanges Offerts à Kazimierz Michalowski*, ed M.-L. Bernhard. Warsaw: Państwowe Wydawnictwo Naukowe, 1966. Pp 389–96.
Fitzmyer, J. and S. Kaufman. 1992. *An Aramaic Bibliography: Part I*. Baltimore: Johns Hopkins, 1992.
Frézouls, E. 1976. "Questions d'urbanisme palmyrénien," in *Palmyre, bilan et perspectives*. Strasbourg: AECR, 1976.
Frye, R., J. Gilliam, H. Ingholt, C. Welles 1955. "Inscriptions from Dura-Europos," *YCS* 14 (1955) 127-201. Inscr. nos. 3 (pp 131-37) and 5 (pp 138-39) by Ingholt. Bilingual graffito no. 130 (p 177); parchment document 152 (p 414) by Welles. **YCS '55**
Furlani, G. 1962. "La religione dei Cananei e degli Aramei," in *Storia delle religioni*, ed P. Tacchi Venturi and G. Castellani. Torino: U.T.E.T., 1962. Pp 893–950.
Gabriel, A. 1926. "Recherches archéologiques à Palmyre," *Syr* 7 (1926) 71–92.
Garbini, G. 1968. "Divinità, confraternite e tribù a Palmira," *AION* 18 (1968) 74-89.
Garroni, G. and E. Parcu, edd. 1985. *Da Ebla a Damasco. Diecimila anni di archeologia in Siria. Roma, Campidoglio, Palazzo dei Conservatori 15 febbraio — 26 marzo 1985*, edd G. Garroni and E. Parcu. Milano: Electa, 1985. **EblaDam**
Gawlikowski, M. 1966. "Remarques sur l'usage de la fibule à Palmyre," in *Mélanges offerts à Kazimierz Michalowski*, ed M.-L. Bernhard. Warsaw: Państwowe Wydawnictwo Naukowe, 1966. Pp 411–19.
———. 1968. "Die pölnischen Ausgrabungen in Palmyra," *AA* (1968) 294.
———. 1970a. "Palmyrena," *Ber* 19 (1970) 65–86. **Ber '70**
———. 1970b. "Nouvelles inscriptions du Camp de Dioclétien," *Syr* 47 (1970) 313–25. **Syr '70**
———. 1970c. *Monuments funéraires de Palmyre*. Travaux du Centre d'archéologie méditerranéenne de l'Academie Polonaise des Sciences. Warsaw: Państwowe Wydawnictwo Naukowe, 1970.
———. 1970d. "Deux monuments funéraires palmyréniens en Pologne," (Polish: "Dwie Palmyreńskie rzeźby

nagrobne w zbiorach polskich") *Studia Palmyrenskie* 4 (1970) 87-92.

———. 1971. "Inscriptions de Palmyre," *Syr* 48 (1971) 407–26. **Syr '71**

———. 1973a. *Palmyre VI. Le temple palmyrénien. Étude d'épigraphie et de topographie historique.* Warsaw: Państwowe Wydawnictwo Naukowe, 1973.

———. 1973b. "Liturges et custodes sur quelques inscriptions palmyréniennes," *Sem* 23 (1973) 113–24. **Sem '73**

———. 1974a. "Les défenses de Palmyre," *Syr* 51 (1974) 231–42.

———. 1974b. "Le tadmoréen," *Syr* 51 (1974) 91–103.

———. 1974c. *Recueil d'inscriptions palmyréniennes provenant de fouilles syriennes et polonaises récentes à Palmyre* . Paris: Imprimerie Nationale and C. Klincksieck, 1974. **RSP**

———. 1975. "Trois inscriptions funéraires des camps de Dioclétien," *Studia Palmyrenskie* 6-7 (1975) 127–33. **StudPalm '75**

———. 1976a. "Le Camp de Dioclétien: bilan préliminaire," in *Palmyre, Bilan et Perspectives.* Strasbourg: AECR, 1976. Pp 153-63.

———. 1976b. "Allat et Baalshamîn," in *Mélanges d'histoire ancienne et d'archéologie offerts à Paul Collart*, edd P. Ducrey et al. Cahiers d'archéologie romande. Lausanne: Bibliothèque historique vaudoise, 1976. Pp 197–203.

———. 1983. "Réflexions sur la chronologie du sanctuaire d'Allat à Palmyre," *DaM* 1 (1983) 59-67.

———. 1984. *Palmyre VIII: Les principia de Dioclétien "Temple des Enseignes".* Warsaw: Państwowe Wydawnictwo Naukowe, 1984. **Palm VIII**

———. 1985. "Les princes de Palmyre," *Syr* 62 (1985) 251–61.

———. 1986. "Les comptes d'un homme d'affaires dans une tour funéraire à Palmyre," *Sem* 36 (1986) 87–99. **Sem '86**

———. 1990a. "Les dieux de Palmyre," in *Aufstieg und Niedergang der römischen Welt. Geschichte und Kultur Roms im Spiegel der neueren Forschung. II: Principat*, ed W. Haase. Berlin, New York: Walter de Gruyter, 1990. Pp 2605–58.

———. 1990b. "Le premier temple d'Allat," in *Resurrecting the Past: A Joint Tribute to Adnan Bounni*, edd P. Matthiae, M. van Loon, and H. Weiss. Istanbul: Nederlands historisch-archaeologisch Institut te Istanbul, 1990. Pp 101-108.

———. 1991. "Fouilles récentes à Palmyre," *CRAIBL* (1991) 399-410.

———. 1992. "Palmyra," in *The Anchor Bible Dictionary*, ed D. Freedman, Vol 5 (New York: Doubleday, 1992) 136-37.

———. 1995 (forthcoming). "Syrian Cults in the Graeco-Roman Period," in *Encyclopaedia of Religions in the Greek and Roman World*

———. 1995 (forthcoming). article (with new text) in *Mélanges Tram Tan Tinh*

———. 1995 (forthcoming). "Les arabes en Palmyréne,"

———. 1995 (forthcoming). article (with new text) in *Mélanges Ernest Will*

———. 1995 (forthcoming). "Palmyra as a Trading Centre,"

Gawlikowski, M. and K. al-Asʿad. 1993. "Le péage à Palmyre en 11 après J.-C.," *Sem* 41-42 (1993) 163-72. Fig 1 p 165. **Sem '93 p 164**

Gawlikowski, M. and M. Pietrzykowski. 1980. "Les sculptures du temple de Baalshamîn à Palmyre," *Syr* 57 (1980) 421–52.

Goldmann, W. 1935. *See Z. Ben-Ḥayyim*

Goldstein, J. 1966. "The Syriac Bill of Sale from Dura-Europos," *JNES* 25 (1966) 1-16.

Gostar, N. 1964. "Populaţia palmyreniana din Tibiscum în lumina monumentelor epigrafice," in *Arheologia Moldovei. Academia Republicii Socialiste Române, Filiala Iaşi, Institutul de Istorie şi Arheologie, Secţia de Istorie veche şi arheologie.* 1964, 2-3. Pp 299-309. (Romanian with Russian and French summaries; German abstract in *Bibliotheca Classica Orientalis* 12 (1967) cols. 147-48.

Gottheil, R. 1901. "Seven Unpublished Palmyrene Inscriptions," *JAOS* 21 (1901) 109-11. Pl with no. 1-7.

Greenfield, J. 1969. "The 'Periphrastic Imperative' in Aramaic and Hebrew," *IEJ* 19 (1969) 199-210.

Hajjar, J. 1990. "Divinités oraculaires et rites divinatoires en Syrie et en Phénicie à l'époque gréco-romaine," in *Aufstieg und Niedergang der römischen Welt. Geschichte und Kultur Roms im Spiegel der neueren Forschung. II: Principat*, ed W. Haase. Berlin, New York: Walter de Gruyter, 1990.

al-Hassani, D. and J. Starcky. 1953. "Autels palmyréniens découverts près de la source Efca," *AAS* 3 (1953) 145–64.

———. 1957. "Autels palmyréniens découverts près de la source Efca (suite)," *AAS* 7 (1957) 95–122.

Heichelheim, F. 1938. "Roman Syria," in *An Economic Survey of Ancient Rome*, ed T. Frank. Baltimore: Johns Hopkins, 1938; reprint New York: Octagon, 1975. Vol 4 pp 121-257.

Hellström, P., M. Nockert, and S. Unge, edd. 1988. *Palmyra. Öknens drottning*, edd P. Hellström, M. Nockert, S. Unge. Stockholm: Medelhavsmuseet & Statens historika museum, 1988.

Henning, W. 1954. Review of F. Altheim and R. Stiehl, *Asien und Rom* and *Das erste Auftreten der Hunnen*, *Gnomon* 26 (1954) 476-80.

Herzig, H. and A. Schmidt-Colinet. 1991. "Two recently discovered Latin inscriptions from Palmyra," *DaM* 5 (1991) 65-69, Pl. 29, 30. ("with the support of Khaled al-As'ad").

Hillers, D. 1972. "Paḥad Yiṣḥâq," *JBL* 91 (1972) 90–92.

———. 1995a*. "Palmyrene Aramaic Inscriptions and the Old Testament, especially Amos 2:8," *ZAH* ---. Cited as "Hillers, ZAH (forthcoming)".

———. 1995b*. "Notes on Palmyrene Aramaic Texts" (forthcoming). Cited as "Hillers, Notes (forthcoming)".

Hillers, D. and E. Cussini. 1992. "Two Readings in the Caravan Inscription Dunant, Baalshamin, No. 45," *BASOR* No. 286 (May, 1992) 35-37.

Hoftijzer, J. 1968. *Religio Aramaica: Godsdienstige Verschijnselen in Aramese Teksten.* Leiden: Ex Oriente Lux, 1968. Pp 25-50 "De Godsdienst van Palmyra.".

———. 1988. "A Palmyrene Bas-relief with Inscriptions," *Oudheidkundige Mededelingen uit het Rijksmuseum van Oudheden te Leiden* 68 (1988) 37-39. **OM '88**

Hoftijzer, J. and K. Jongeling 1995. *Dictionary of the North-West Semitic Inscriptions.* 2 vols. Leiden: Brill, 1995.

Hopkins, C. 1931. "The Palmyrene Gods at Dura-Europos," *JAOS* 51 (1931) 119–37.

———. 1934. "The Temple of Mithra at Dura-Europos," *Illustrated London News* 4990 (1934) 963–65.

van der Horst, P. 1991. *Ancient Jewish Epitaphs : An Introductory Survey of a Millenium of Jewish Funerary Epigraphy (300 BCE-700 CE).* Contributions to Biblical Exegesis and Theology, edd Tj. Barda and A. van der Woude, 2. Kampen, The Netherlands: Kok Pharos, 1991.

Houston, G. 1990. "The Altar from Rome with Inscriptions to Sol and Malakbel," *Syr* 67 (1990) 189-93.

Huart, C. 1929. "Inscriptions arabes de Palmyre," *Revue des études islamiques* 3 (1929) 237–44.

Hvidberg-Hansen, F. 1993. *Palmyra Samlingen: Katalog, Ny Carlsberg Glyptotek.* Copenhagen: Ny Carlsberg Glyptotek, 1993 **NyCG**

Ingholt, H. 1925. "Les thiases à Palmyre d'après une inscription inédite," *CRAIBL* (1925) 355-61.

———. 1926. "Un nouveau thiase à Palmyre," *Syr* 7 (1926) 128–41. **Syr '26**

———. 1928. *Studier over Palmyrensk Skulptur.* Copenhagen: C. A. Reitzels, 1928. **PS**

———. 1930a. "Some religious Monuments recently found in Palmyra," in *Actes du Ve congrès international d'histoire des religions à Lund, 17-29 août, 1929.* Lund: C. W. K. Gleerup, 1930. Pp 144–48.

———. 1930b. "Quatre bustes palmyréniens," *Syr* 11 (1930) 242–44. **Syr '30**

———. 1930c. "The Oldest Known Grave-Relief from Palmyra," *AA* 1 (1930) 191–94. **AA '30**

———. 1932a. "Deux inscriptions bilingues de Palmyre," *Syr* 13 (1932) 278–92.

———. 1932b. "Quelques fresques récemment découvertes à Palmyre," *AA* 3 (1932) 1–20. **AA '32**

———. 1934. "Palmyrene Sculptures in Beirut," *Ber* 1 (1934) 32–43. **Ber '34**

———. 1935. "Five Dated Tombs from Palmyra," *Ber* 2 (1935) 57–120. **Ber '35**

———. 1936. "Inscriptions and Sculptures from Palmyra I," *Ber* 3 (1936) 83–127. **Ber '36**

———. 1938. "Inscriptions and Sculptures from Palmyra II," *Ber* 5 (1938) 93–140. **Ber '38**

———. 1954. *Palmyrene and Gandharan Sculpture. An Exhibition Illustrating the Cultural Interrelations*

Between the Parthian Empire and its Neighbors West and East, Palmyra and Gandhara. New Haven: Yale University, 1954. **PGSc**

———. 1955. "Inscriptions from Dura-Europos" [Inscr. nos. 3 (pp 131-37) and 5 (pp 138-39) by Ingholt] in R. Frye, J. Gilliam, H. Ingholt, and C. Welles, *YCS* 14 (1955).

———. 1962. "Palmyrene Inscription from the Tomb of Malkū," *MUSJ* 38 (1962) 99–119. **MUSJ '62**

———. 1966. "Some Sculpures from the Tomb of Malkû at Palmyra." *Mélanges offerts à Kazimierz Michalowski*, ed M.-L. Bernhard. Warsaw: Pańśtwowe Wydawnictwo Naukowe, 1966. Pp 457–76.

———. 1967. "Palmyrene — Hatran — Nabataean," in *An Aramaic Handbook.*, ed F. Rosenthal. Porta Linguarum Orientalium, edd B. Spuler and H. Wehr, Neue Serie X. Wiesbaden: Harrassowitz, 1967. Part I/1 (Texts) pp 40-50; Part I/2 (Glossary) pp 42-51.

———. 1970. "The Sarcophagus of Beʿelai and Other Sculptures from the Tomb of Malkû, Palmyra," *MUSJ* 46 (1970–71) 171–200.

———. 1974. "Two Unpublished Tombs from the Southwest Necropolis of Palmyra Syria," in *Near Eastern Numismatics, Iconography, Epigraphy and History : Studies in Honor of George C. Miles*, ed D. K. Kouymjian. Beirut: American University of Beirut, 1974. Pp 37–54. **StudMiles**

———. 1976. "Varia Tadmorea," in *Palmyre, Bilan et perspectives*. Strasbourg: AECR, 1976. Pp 101–37.

Ingholt, H., H. Seyrig, and J. Starcky. 1955. *Recueil des tessères de Palmyre*. Institut Français d'Archéologie de Beyrouth. Bibliothèque archéologique et historique. Paris: Geuthner, 1955. **RTP**

Ingholt, H., J. Starcky, and G. Ryckmans. 1949. *Recueil épigraphique*. Paris: 1949.

Jakob-Rost, L. and E. Klengel-Brandt. 1986. *Meisterwerke aus Palmyra. Sonderausstellung aus der Syrischen Arabischen Republik Staatliche Museen zu Berlin Vorderasiatisches Museum. 3. Dezember 1986 — 11. Januar 1987*. Potsdam: "Märkische Volksstimme," 1986.

Janon, M. 1966. "Cultores dei Ierhobolis iuniores," *Bulletin d'archéologie algérienne* 2 (1966–67) 219–30.

Jastrow, M. 1903. *A Dictionary of the Targumim, the Talmud Babli and Yerushalmi, and the Midrashic Literature*. New York: Putnam, 1903.

Jean, C.-F. and J. Hoftijzer. 1965. *Dictionnaire des inscriptions sémitiques de l'Ouest*. Leiden: Brill, 1965.

Kádár, Z. 1955. "Monuments palmyréniens au Musée des Beaux-Arts de Budapest," *Acta Antiqua Academiae Scientiarum Hungaricae* 3 (1955) 105–21.

Kaibel, G. 1890. *Inscriptiones Graecae Siciliae et Italiae*. Vol 14. Berlin: Reimer, 1890.

Kaufman, S. 1974. The Akkadian Influences on Aramaic. Oriental Institute of the University of Chicago, Assyriological Studies no. 19. Chicago: Univ. of Chicago, 1974.

Kjellberg, E. 1921. "Ein Palmyrener Relief in Uppsala," *Le Monde Oriental* 15 (1921) 177–83.

Klíma, O. 1965. "Zum Palmyrenischen Zolltarif," in *Studia Semitica Ioanni Bakoš dicata*, ed S. Segert. Bratislava: Vydavatel'stvo Slovenskej Akadémie Vied, 1965. Pp 147-51.

Klugkist, A. 1983. "The Importance of the Palmyrene Script for Our Knowledge of the Development of the Late Aramaic Scripts," in *Aramaeans, Aramaic and the Aramaic Literary Tradition*, ed M. Sokoloff. Ramat Gan: Bar-Ilan University, 1983. Pp 57–74.

Kohlmeyer, K., et al. 1982. *Land des Baal: Syrien-Forum der Völker und Kulturen*. Mainz: P. von Zabern, 1982.

Legrain, L. 1927. "Tomb Sculptures from Palmyra," *The Museum Journal* 18 (1927) 325–50.

Levi della Vida, G. 1939. "Une bilingue gréco-palmyrénienne à Cos," in *Mélanges syriens offerts à Monsieur René Dussaud*. Bibliothèque archéologique et historique. Paris: Geuthner, 1939. Vol II, pp 883–86. **MélDus p 885**

Levy, M. 1858. "Einige Bemerkungen über altsyrische Schrift und über zwei in Nordafrika gefundene lateinisch-palmyrenische Inschriften," *ZDMG* 12 (1858) 209–219.

———. 1861a. "Zur semitischen Paläographie: I. Drei palmyrenische Inschriften," *ZDMG* 15 (1861) 615–23.

———. 1861b. "Epigraphische Beiträge zur Geschichte der Juden," *Jahrbuch für die Geschichte der Juden und des Judenthums* 2 (1861) 259–324.

———. 1864. "Die palmyrenischen Inschriften mit Beiträgen aus dem handschriftlichen Nachlasse von E. F. F. Beer," *ZDMG* 18 (1864) 65–117.

———. 1869. "Zu den palmyrenischen Inschriften," *ZDMG* 23 (1869) 282–91.

Liddell, H., R. Scott, and H. Jones. 1940. *A Greek - English Lexicon.* Oxford: Clarendon, 1958.

Lidzbarski, M. 1898. *Handbuch der nordsemitischen Epigraphik.* 2 vols Weimar: Felber, 1898.

Lidzbarski, M. 1902. *Ephemeris für semitische Epigraphik.* Vols 1-3. Giessen: Ricker'sche (Töpelmann), 1902, 1908, 1915.

Lidzbarski, M. 1927. "Epigraphisches," *OLZ* 30 (1927) coll 1043-44.

Lightfoot, C. and J. Naveh. 1991. "A North Mesopotamian Aramaic Inscription on a Relief in the Tigris Gorge," *Aram* 3 (1991) 319-37. Pl 3-12.

Lipiński, E. 1975. *Studies in Aramaic Inscriptions and Onomastics II.* OrLovAn 1. Louvain: Leuven University, 1975.

———. 1977. "La religion de Palmyre: Dix ans de travaux et d'études: 1967–1977," *Folia orientalia* 20 (1977) 205–20.

———. 1978. "The Greek — Aramaic Inscription from Ağaça Kale," *Türk Tarıh Kurumu Basimevi* (1978) 267-272.

———. 1985. "Le tarif de Palmyre," *Folia orientalia* 23 (1985–86) 227–36.

———. 1992. "*Maqlūta', qinīta'* et *plug qduš* à Palmyre," in *Intertestamental Essays in honour of Józef Tadeusz Milik*, ed Z. Kapera (Krakow: Enigma, 1992). Pp 305-11.

———. 1994. *Studies in Aramaic Inscriptions and Onomastics II.* OrLovAn 57. Louvain: Leuven University, 1994.

Littmann, E. 1901. "Deux inscriptions religieuses de Palmyre, le dieu šy' 'lqwm," *JA* 9/18 (1901) 374–90.

———. 1914. *Semitic Inscriptions.* Publications of the Princeton University Archaeological Expeditions to Syria in 1904-1905 and 1909. Division IV. Leiden: Brill, 1914.

———. 1934. *Semitic Inscriptions.* Publications of the Princeton University Archaeological Expeditions to Syria in 1904-5 and 1909. Division IV. Leiden: Brill, 1934.

———. 1943. *Semitic Inscriptions.* Publications of the Princeton University Archaeological Expeditions to Syria in 1904-5 and 1909. Division IV. Leiden: Brill, 1943.

———. 1949. *Semitic Inscriptions.* Publications of the Princeton University Archaeological Expeditions to Syria in 1904-5 and 1909. Division IV. Leiden: Brill, 1949.

Lozachmeur, H. 1979. "Relief palmyrénien," *Sem* 29 (1979) 105–7. **Sem '79**

Lukasiak, E. 1974. "Ikonografia Yarhibôla," *Studia Palmyrenskie* 5 (1974) 7–44.

Mackay, D. 1949. "The Jewellery of Palmyra and its Significance," *Iraq* 11 (1949) 160–87. Pls. LII-LXI. Appendix by J. Starcky pp 185-86.

Makowski, C. 1983. "Recherches sur le tombeau de A'ailamî et Zebîdâ," *DaM* 1 (1983) 175-87.

Maricq, A. 1959. "Classica et orientalia: 7. Vologésias, l'emporium de Ctésiphon," *Syr* 36 (1959) 264-76.

Martin, M. 1965. "Idioma palmireno," *EB* 4 (1965) 827–29.

Masson, M. 1967. "Two Palmyrene Stelae from the Merv Oasis," *EaWe* N.S. 17 (1967) 239-47. **EaWe '67**

Mathiesen H. 1992. *Sculpture in the Parthian Empire: A Study in Chronology.* 2 vols. Aarhus: Aarhus University, 1992. **ScPart**

Matthews, J. 1984. "The Tax Law of Palmyra: Evidence for Economic History in a City of the Roman East," *JRS* 74 (1984) 157–80.

Matthiae, P., M. van Loon, and H. Weiss, edd. 1990. *Resurrecting the Past: A Joint Tribute to Adnan Bounni.* Istanbul: Nederlands Historisch-Archeologisch Instituut te Istanbul, 1990.

Mazar, B. 1973. *Beth She'arim: Report on the Excavations during 1936–1940. Volume 1: Catacombs 1–4.* New Brunswick N. J.: Rutgers University, 1973. **BethSh**

du Mesnil du Buisson, R. 1936. "Inventaire des inscriptions palmyréniennes de Doura-Europos," *Études Sémitiques* (1936) 17–34.

———. 1938a. "Un bilingue araméen-grec de l'époque parthe a Doura-Europos," *Syr* 19 (1938) 147-52.

———. 1938b. "Inventaire des inscriptions palmyréniennes de Doura-Europos," *Etudes Sémitiques* (1938) 145–95.

———. 1939. *Inventaire des inscriptions palmyréniennes de Doura Europos (32 avant J.-C. à 256 après J.-*

C.). Paris: Geuthner, 1939. **Doura**
———. 1942-45. "Le service de garde dans le temple de Bêl à Palmyre," *Revue des Études Sémitiques* 1942-45 pp 76ff.
———. 1944. *Tessères et monnaies de Palmyre*. Planches. Paris: Bibliothèque nationale, 1944.
———. 1960. "Le vrai nom de Bôl prédécesseur de Bêl à Palmyre," *RHR* 158 (1960) 145–60.
———. 1962a. "De Shadrafa, dieu de Palmyre, à Bàal Shamīm dieu de Hatra, aux IIe et IIIe siècle après J.-C," *MUSJ* 38 (1962) 141–60.
———. 1962b. *Les tessères et les monnaies de Palmyre. Inventaire des collections du cabinet des médailles de la Bibliothéque nationale*. Paris: E. de Boccard, 1962. **TMP**
———. 1966. "Première campagne de fouilles à Palmyre," *CRAIBL* (1966) 158–90.
———. 1967a. "La découverte de la plus ancienne Palmyre," *BO* 24 (1967) 20–21.
———. 1967b. "Decouverte de la plus ancienne Palmyre ville amorite de la fin du IIIe millénaire," *Archeologia* 16 (1967) 50–51.
———. 1978. "Le dieu soi-disant anonyme à Palmyre," in *Hommages à Maarten J. Vermaseren*, edd M. B. de Boer and T. A. Edridge . Leiden: E. J. Brill, 1978. Pp 777–81.
Michalowski, K. 1960. *Palmyre: Fouilles Polonaises 1959*. Warsaw: Państwowe Wydawnictwo Naukowe, 1960.
———. 1961. "Fouilles polonaises à Palmyre 1961," *AAS* 11–12 (1961–62) 63–82.
———. 1962. *Palmyre: Fouilles Polonaises 1960*. Warsaw: Państwowe Wydawnictwo Naukowe, 1962.
———. 1963. *Palmyre: Fouilles Polonaises 1961*. Warsaw: Państwowe Wydawnictwo Naukowe, 1963. **Palm III**
———. 1964. *Palmyre: Fouilles Polonaises 1962*. Warsaw: Państwowe Wydawnictwo Naukowe, 1964. **Palm IV**
———. 1966. *Palmyre: Fouilles Polonaises 1963 et 1964*. Warsaw: Państwowe Wydawnictwo Naukowe, 1966. **Palm V**
———. 1967. "Lumières sur le camp de Dioclétien et la Vallée des Tombeaux," *Archeologia* 16 (1967) 57–63.
Milik, J. 1958. "Nouvelles inscriptions nabatéennes," *Syr* 35 (1958) 227-51.
———. 1960. "Notes d'épigraphie orientale," *Syr* 37 (1960) 94–8.
———. 1967. "Les papyrus araméens d'Hermoupolis et les cultes syro-phéniciens en Égypte perse," *Biblica* 48 (1967) 546-622.
———. 1972. *Dédicaces faites par des dieux (Palmyre, Hatra, Tyr) et des thiases sémitiques à l'époque romaine*. Recherches d'épigraphie proche-orientale. I. Paris: Geuthner, 1972. **Déd**
Milik, J. and J. Starcky. 1970. "III. Nabataean, Palmyrene, and Hebrew Inscriptions," in *Ancient Records from North Arabia*, ed F. Winnett and W. Reed. Toronto: University of Toronto, 1970. Pp 141–63.
Millar, F. 1993. *The Roman Near East, 31 B.C. — A.D. 337*. Cambridge, Mass.: Harvard University, 1993.
Mordtmann, A. 1875. *Neue Beiträge zur Kunde Palmyras*. SBAW Bd. II, Heft III. 1875.
Mordtmann, J. 1884. "Bemerkungen zu den palmyrenischen Inschriften," *ZDMG* 38 (1884) 584–89.
———. 1899. *Palmyrenisches*. Mitteilungen der Vorderasiatischen Gesellschaft, 1899, Heft 1.
Moreheart, M. 1956. "Early Sculpture at Palmyra," *Ber* 12/1 (1956-57) 53–83.
Mouterde, R. and A. Poidebard. 1931. "La voie antique des caravanes entre Palmyre et Hît au IIe siècle ap. J.-C. D'après une inscription retrouvée au S.-E. de Palmyre (Mars 1930)," *Syr* 12 (1931) 101–15.
Müller, D. 1884a. "Vier palmyrenische Grabinschriften im Besitze des Ministerial-Herrn Dr. J. C. Samson," *SKAWW* 108 (1884) 973–77.
———. 1884b. "Note additionelle aux inscriptions palmyréniennes," *Österreichische Monatsschrift für den Orient* 10 (1884) 124–26; 231-45.
———. 1885. *Österreichische Monatsschrift für den Orient* 11 (1885) 43–45.
———. 1892. "Palmyrenica aus dem British Museum," *WZKM* 6 (1892) 317–26.
———. 1894. "Palmyrenica aus dem British Museum II," *WZKM* 8 (1894) 11–16.
Musil, A. 1928. *Palmyrena. A Topographical Itinerary*. New York: American Geographical Society, 1928.

Nockert, M. 1988. "Vid Sidenvägens ände. Textilier från Palmyra till Birka," in *Palmyra. Öknens drottning*, edd P. Hellström, M. Nockert, and S. Unge. Stockholm: Medelhavsmuseet & Statens historika museum, 1988. Pp 77-105.

Nöldeke, T. 1870. "Beiträge zur Kenntniss der aramäischen Dialecte. 3. Ueber Orthographie und Sprache der Palmyrener," *ZDMG* 24 (1870) 85–109.

———. 1882. "Bemerkungen zu den von Sachau herausgegebenen palmyrenischen und edessenischen Inschriften," *ZDMG* 36 (1882) 664–68.

———. 1890. "Zu der lateinisch-palmyrenischen Inschrift von Karánsebes," *Archeologische Mittheilungen aus Oesterreich-Ungarn* 13 (1890) 180.

———. 1894. "Palmyrenische Inschrift," *ZA* 9 (1894) 264–67.

Noth, M. 1937. "*ʾdt* im Palmyrenischen," *OLZ* 40 (1937) coll 345-46.

O'Connor, M. 1984. "Northwest Semitic Designations for Elective Social Affinities," *JANES* 16-17 (1984-85) 41-54.

———. 1988a. "The Grammar of Finding Your Way in Palmyrene Aramaic and the Problem of Diction in Ancient West Semitic Inscriptions," in *Fucus. A Semitic/Afrasian Gathering in Remembrance of Albert Ehrman*, ed Y. Arbeitman. Amsterdam/Philadelphia: John Benjamins, 1988. Pp 353–69.

———. 1988b. "The Etymologies of Tadmor and Palmyra," in *A Linguistic Happening in Memory of Ben Schwartz: Studies in Anatolian, Italic, and Other Indo-European Languages*, ed Y. Arbeitman. Louvain-La-Neuve: Peeters, 1988. Pp 235-54.

Odenthal, J. 1982. *Syrien: Hochkulturen zwischen Mittelmeer und Arabischer Wüste — 5000 Jahre Geschichte im Spannungsfeld von Orient und Okzident.* Cologne: DuMont, 1982

Ostraz, A. 1967. "Note sur le plan de la partie médiane de la Rue Principale de Palmyre," *AAS* 16 (1967) 109–22.

Oxtoby, W. 1968. *Some Inscriptions of the Safaitic Bedouin.* American Oriental Series, Vol 50. New Haven: American Oriental Society, 1968. Pp 101-02 and Pl. XIX.

Parlasca, K. 1967. "Zur syrischen Kunst der frühen Kaiserzeit (Einflüsse italischer Skulptur im 1. Jh.," *Archaeologischer Anzeiger* 82 (1967) 547-68.

———. 1969 - 70. "A New Grave Relief From Syria," *The Brooklyn Museum Annual* XI (1969-70) 169-185.

———. 1976. "Probleme palmyrenischer Grabreliefs — Chronologie und Interpretation," in *Palmyre. Bilan et perspectives.* Strasbourg: AECR, 1976. Pp 33–43 1-8.

———. 1980. "Ein frühes Grabrelief aus Palmyra," in *Eikones. Studien zum griechishen und römischen Bildnis. Hans Jucker zum sechzigsten Geburtstag gewidmet.* Bern: Franke Verlag, 1980. Pp 149-152.

———. 1982. *Syrische Grabreliefs hellenistischer und römischer Zeit. Fundgruppen und Probleme (mit einem Exkursus von H. Heinen)*, Trierer Winckelmannsprogramme, Heft 3, 1981. Mainz am Rhein: Philipp von Zabern, 1982.

———. 1984a. "Die Stadtgöttin Palmyras," *BJb* 184 (1984) 167–76.

———. 1984b. "Probleme der palmyrenischen Sarkophage," *Marburger Winckelmann-Programm* (1984) 283-296.

———. 1985a. "Figürliche Stuckdekorationen aus Palmyra. Ältere Funde," *DaM* 2 (1985) 201-206.

———. 1985b. "Das Verhältnis der palmyrenischen Grabplastik zur römischen Porträtkunst," *Mitteilungen des deutschen Archaeologischen Instituts Roemische Abteilung* 92 (1985) 343-356.

———. 1987a. "Aspekte der palmyrenischen Skulpturen," in *Palmyra: Geschichte, Kunst und Kultur der Oasenstadt*, ed E. Ruprechtsberger. Linzer Archäologische Forschungen, 16. Linz: Gutenberg, 1987. Pp 276-82.

———. 1987b. "Ein antoninischer Frauenkopf aus Palmyra in Malibu," *Ancient Portraits in the J. Paul Getty Museum Volume 1.* Occasional Papers on Antiquities, 4. Malibu, California: J. Paul Getty Museum, 1987. Pp 107-114, .

———. 1988a. "Die Palmyrene — Ihr geographischer Rahmen im Lichte der bildenden Kunst und Epigraphik," *Géographie historique au Proche-Orient. Notes et Monographies Techniques n. 23.* Éditions du CNRS, Paris, 1988. Pp 241-248.

———. 1988b. "Ikonographische Probleme palmyrenischer Grabreliefs," *DaM* 3 (1988) 215-221.
———. 1989. "Beobachtungen zur palmyrenischen Grabarchitektur," *DaM* 4 (1989) 181-90.
———. 1990a. "Bemerkungen zur Topographie und kulturgeographischen Stellung Palmyras," in *Stuttgarter Kolloquium zur historischen Geographie des Altertums 2, 1984 und 3, 1987.* Bonn: Habelt, 1991. Pp 457-461.
———. 1990b. "Eine Dame aus Palmyra — Zu einem Büstenrelief in Privatbesitz," *Études et Travaux* XV (1990) 318-322. **Parl '90b**
———. 1990c. "Palmyrenische Skulpturen in Museen an der amerikanischen Westküste," pp 133-44, *Roman Funerary Monuments in the J. Paul Getty Museum Volume 1.* Occasional Papers on Antiquities, 6. Malibu: J. Paul Getty Museum,, California, 1990. **Parl '90c**
———. 1991. "Palmyrenisches im Donauraum?" *Römisches Österreich. Jahresschrift der österreichischen Gesellschaft für Archäologie. Jahrgang 17/18, 1989-1990.* Wien, 1991. Pp 203-205.
Parrot, A. 1939. *Malédictions et violations de tombes.* Paris: Geuthner, 1939.
Payne Smith, J. 1903. *A Compendious Syriac Dictionary.* Oxford: Clarendon Press, 1903.
Pfister, R. 1934. *Textiles de Palmyre.* Paris: Les Éditions d'art et d'histoire, 1934.
———. 1937. *Nouveaux textiles de Palmyre.* Paris, 1937.
———. 1940. *Textiles de Palmyre, III.* Paris, 1940.
Piersimoni, P. 1989. "Aramei e Arabi a Palmira: un'indagine onomastica." Unpublished thesis, University of Venice, 1989.
Piganiol, A. 1939. *Histoire de Rome.* Paris: Presses universitaires de France, 1939 Pp 385–90; 430ff.
———. 1945. "Observations sur le Tarif de Palmyre," *Revue Historique* 195 (1945) 10–24.
———. 1973. "Observations sur le tarif de Palmyra," *Scripta varia* 3 (1973) 149–62.
Ploix de Rotrou, G. and H. Seyrig. 1933. "Khirbet el-Sané," *Syr* 14 (1933) 12–19.
Ploug, G. and F. Hvidberg-Hansen. 1991. "A Dated Palmyrene Bust in the Danish National Museum," *Acta Hiperborea* 3 (1991) 365-78. **ActH**
Poidebard, A. 1937. *La trace de Rome dans le désert de Syria.* Haut-Commissariat de la République française en Syrie et au Liban, Service des Antiquités et des Beaux-Arts, Bibliothèque archéologique et historique, Tome 18. Paris: Geuthner, 1934.
Porten, B. and A. Yardeni. 1986-93. *Textbook of Aramaic Documents from Ancient Egypt.* Vols 1-3. Jerusalem: Hebrew University, 1986-93.
Porter, H. and C. Torrey. 1905-06. "Inscribed Palmyrene Monuments in the Museum of the Syrian Protestant College, Beirut," *AJSL* 22 (1905-06) 262-71.
Puech, E. 1984. " 'La crainte d'Isaac' en Genèse xxxi 42 et 53," *VT* 34 (1984) 356–61.
Quilici, L. 1969. "L'impianto topografico della città di Palmyra," *Archeologia Classica* 21 (1969) 246–57.
Raschke, M. 1978. "New Studies in Roman Commerce with the East," in *ANRW* II 9.2, edd H. Temporini and W. Haase. Berlin: de Gruyter, 1978. Pp 604-1378. Rich bibliography on Palmyra in footnotes, see index p 1277, s.v. 'Palmyra,' 'Palmyrene'.
Reckendorf, S. 1888a. "Palmyrenisches," *WZKM* 2 (1888) 325–27.
———. 1888b. "Der aramäische Theil des palmyrenischen Zoll-und Steuertarifs," *ZDMG* 42 (1888) 370–415.
Ridgway, B. 1972. *Classical Sculpture. Catalogue of the Classical Collection.* Museum of Art, Rhode Island School of Design. Providence, Rhode Island, 1972.
Rodinson, M. 1950. "Une inscription trilingue de Palmyre," *Syr* 27 (1950) 137–42. **Syr '50**
Ronzevalle, S. 1934a. "Sîma-Athéna-Némésis," *Or* 3 (1934) 121–46.
———. 1934b. "Notes et études d'archéologie orientale. Le prétendu 'char d'Astarté'," *MUSJ* 18 (1934) 109–47 II-VI.
———. 1937. "Notes et études d'archéologie orientale. Jupiter Héliopolitain, Nova et Vetera. Appendice I, Antiquités de Ḥarbata" *MUSJ* 21 (1937) 3–71.
Rosenthal, Franz. 1936. *Die Sprache der palmyrenischen Inschriften und ihre Stellung innerhalb Aramäischen.* Mitteilungen der Vorderasiatisch-Aegyptischen. Leipzig: J. C. Hinrichs'sche Buchhandlung, 1936.
———. 1937. Review of Cantineau, *Grammaire du Palmyrénien épigraphique. OLZ* 40 (1937) 31–34.

———. 1939. *Die aramaistische Forschung seit Th. Nöldeke's Veröffentlichungen.* Leiden: Brill, 1939.
———. 1967. *An Aramaic Handbook.* Porta Linguarum Orientalium, edd B. Spuler and H. Wehr, Neue Serie X. Wiesbaden: Harrassowitz, 1967.
Rostovtzeff, M. 1904. "Geschichte der Staatspacht in der römischen Kaiserzeit bis Diokletian," in *Philologus*, Supplement Band 9, 3. Heft (Leipzig: Dieterichs, 1904) 329-512.
———. 1932a. "The Caravan-Gods of Palmyra," *JRS* 22 (1932) 107–116.
———. 1932b. "The Caravan Cities of Petra and Palmyre," in *Out of the Past of Greece and Rome*, ed M. Rostovtzeff. New Haven: Yale University Press, 1932.
———. 1932c. "Les inscriptions caravanières de Palmyre," in *Mélanges Gustave Glotz.* 2 Paris: Les presses universitaires de France, 1932 Pp 793–811.
———. 1932d. "Seleucid Babylonia," *YCS* 3 (1932) 1-114. Pls. 1-11.
———. 1933. "Hadad and Atargatis at Palmyra," *AJA* 37 (1933) 58–63.
———. 1934. "Das Mithräum in Dura," *MDAIK* (1934) 180–207.
Rostovtzeff, M., A. Bellinger, C. Hopkins, and C. Welles 1936. *The Excavations at Dura-Europos: Preliminary Report of Sixth Season of work, October 1932 — March 1933.* New Haven: Yale University, 1936. **DuraPR '36**
Rostovtzeff, M., F. Brown, and C. Welles 1939. *The Excavations at Dura-Europos: Preliminary Report of the Seventh and Eighth Seasons of work, 1933 — 1934 and 1934 — 1935.* New Haven: Yale University, 1939. **DuraPR '39**
Ruprechtsberger, E., ed. 1987. *Palmyra: Geschichte, Kunst und Kultur der Oasenstadt.* Linzer archäeologische Forschungen, 16. Linz: Gutenberg, 1987. **PGKK**
Sabeh, J. 1953. "Sculptures palmyréniennes inédites du Musée de Damas," *AAS* 3 (1953) 17–26 I-II. **AAS '53**
Sachau, E. 1881. "Palmyrenische Inschriften," *ZDMG* 35 (1881) 728–48.
———. 1883. "Ueber den Palmyrenischen νόμος τελωνικός," *ZDMG* 37 (1883) 562-71.
Sadurska, A. 1975. "Une nouvelle tessère de Palmyre," *Studia Palmyrenskie* 6–7 (1975) 121–26.
———. 1976. "Nouvelles recherches dans la nécropole ouest de Palmyre," in *Palmyre, Bilan et Perspectives.* Strasbourg: AECR, 1976. Pp 11-32.
———. 1977. *Palmyra VII. Le tombeau de famille de ʿAlainê.* Warsaw: Państwowe Wydawnictwo Naukowe, 1977.
———. 1984. "Korpus rzeżb palmyrenskich w muzeach Syrii," *Studia archeologiczne* 2 (1984)
Sadurska, A. and A. Bounni. 1994. *Les Sculptures funéraires de Palmyre.* (En collaboration avec Khaled Al-Assʿad et Krzysztof Makowski.) Supplementi alla Rivista di Archeologia, 13. Rome: Bretschneider, 1994. **SFP**
Safar, F. 1964. "Inscriptions from Wadi Hauran," *Sumer* 20 (1964) 9-27. **Sumer '64**
Saliby, N. 1992. "L'hypogée de Sassan fils de Malê à Palmyre. Mit einem bibliographischen Anhang von Klaus Parlasca," *DaM* 6 (1992) 267-292. **DaM '92**
al-Salihi, W. 1987. "Palmyrene Sculptures Found at Hatra," *Iraq* 49 (1987) 53–61. **Iraq '87**
Samuel, A. 1972. *Greek and Roman Chronology: Calendars and Years in Classical Antiquity.* Müllers Handbuch der Altertumswissenschaft, Erste Abteilung, Siebenter Teil. Munich: Beck'sche, 1972.
Sanie, S. 1970a. "L'Onomastique orientale de la Dacie romaine," *Dacia* N.S. 14 (1970) 233-41.
———. 1970b. "Inscriptio bilinguis tibiscensis. A. Pars palmyrena," *Dacia* N.S. 14 (1970) 405-09. **Dacia '70**
Sauvaget, J. 1931. "Inscriptions arabes du temple de Bêl à Palmyre," *Syr* 12 (1931) 143–53.
Schlumberger, D. 1933. "Les formes anciennes du chapiteau corinthien en Syrie, en Palestine et en Arabie," *Syr* 14 (1933) 283–317.
———. 1937. "Réflexions sur la loi fiscale de Palmyre," *Syr* 18 (1937) 271–97.
———. 1942. "L'inscription d'Herodien, remarques sur l'histoire des princes de Palmyre," *Bulletin d'études Orientales* 9 (1942/43) 35–50.
———. 1951. *La Palmyrène du nord-ouest.* Paris: Geuthner, 1951. **PNO**

———. 1960. "Descendants non-méditerranéens de l'art grec," *Syr* 37 (1960) 253–318 XI, 1.
———. 1961. "Palmyre et la Mésène," *Syr* 38 (1961) 256-60.
———. 1962. "Le prétendu camp de Dioclétien à Palmyre," *MUSJ* 38 (1962) 77–97.
———. 1970. "Le prétendu dieu Gennéas," *MUSJ* 46 (1970–71) 207–22.
———. 1971. "Les quatre tribus de Palmyre," *Syr* 48 (1971) 121–33.
Schmidt-Colinet, A. 1985. "Neue deutsche Ausgrabungen in Palmyra. Das Tempelgrab einer Aristokratenfamilie," *Universitas* 40 (1985) 677–-89.
———. 1992. *Das Tempelgrab Nr. 36 in Palmyra. Studien zur Palmyrenisch Grabarchitektur und ihrer Ausstattung*. Damaszener Forschungen, Vol 4: Text; Tafeln, Beilagen und Pläne. Mainz am Rhein: Philipp von Zabern, 1992.
Schramm, J. 1962. *Beiträge zur Monographie von Palmyra (Syrien)*. Freiburg/Breisgau: 1962.
Schröder, P. 1884. "Neue palmyrenische Inschriften," *SPAW* (1884) 417–36.
Segal, A. 1981. "Tadmor/Palmyra," (Hebrew) *Qadmoniot* 14 (1981) 2–14.
Segal, J. 1987. "Five Ostraca Re-Examined," *Maarav* 4 (1987) 69-74. **Maarav '87**
Seyrig, H. 1931. "Antiquités syriennes 2. Notes épigraphiques," *Syr* 12 (1931) 321–23.
———. 1932a. "Antiquités syriennes 4. Monuments syriens du culte de Némésis," *Syr* 13 (1932) 50–64.
———. 1932b. "Antiquités syriennes 6. Hiérarchie des divinités de Palmyre," *Syr* 13 (1932) 190–95.
———. 1932c. "Antiquités syriennes 8. Trois bas-reliefs religieux de type palmyrénien," *Syr* 13 (1932) 258–66.
———. 1932d. "Antiquités syriennes 9. L'incorporation de Palmyre à l'empire romain," *Syr* 13 (1932) 266–77.
———. 1933a. "Des Heiligtum des Bel in Palmyre," *Archaeologische Anzeiger* (1933) 715–42.
———. 1933b. "Antiquités syriennes 12. Textes relatifs à la garnison romaine de Palmyre," *Syr* 14 (1933) 152–168.
———. 1933c. "Antiquités syriennes 13. Le culte de Bêl et de Baalshamîn," *Syr* 14 (1933) 238–52.
———. 1933d. "Antiquités syriennes 14. Nouveaux monuments palmyréniens des cultes de Bêl et de Baalshamîn," *Syr* 14 (1933) 253–82.
———. 1934. "Antiquités syriennes 17. Bas-reliefs monumentaux du temple de Bêl à Palmyre," *Syr* 15 (1934) 155–86.
———. 1936. "Notes sur les plus anciennes sculptures palmyréniennes," *Ber* 3 (1936) 137–40.
———. 1937a. "Antiquités Syriennes 21. Sur quelques sculptures palmyréniennes," *Syr* 18 (1937) 31–34. **Syr '37**
———. 1937b. "Antiquités syriennes 22. Iconographie de Malakbêl," *Syr* 18 (1937) 198–209.
———. 1937c. "Antiquités syriennes 23. Deux inscriptions grecques de Palmyre," *Syr* 18 (1937) 369–78.
———. 1941a. "Antiquités syriennes 34. Sculptures palmyréniennes archaïques," *Syr* 22 (1941) 31–48 .
———. 1941b. "Antiquiteés syriennes 36. Le statut de Palmyre," *Syr* 22 (1941) 155–75.
———. 1941c. "Antiquités syriennes 37. Postes romaines sur la route de Médine," *Syr* 22 (1941) 218–70.
———. 1941d. "Antiquités syriennes 38. Inscriptions grecques de l'agora de Palmyre," *Syr* 22 (1941) 223–70.
———. 1948. "Les tessères palmyréniennes et le banquet rituel," in *Mémorial Lagrange* 1940. Pp 51–58.
———. 1949. "Antiquités syriennes 41. Nouveaux monuments palmyréniens de Baalshamîn (avec un appendice épigraphique par J. Starcky)" *Syr* 26 (1949) 29–41.
———. 1951. "Le Repas des Morts et le 'Banquet funèbre' à Palmyre," *AAS* 1 (1951) 32–40.
———. 1963. "Les fils du roi Odainat," *AAS* 13 (1963) 159–72.
———. 1966. "Vhabalathvs Avgvstvs," in *Mélanges Offerts à Kazimierz Michalowski*, ed M.-L. Bernhard. Warsaw: Państwowe Wydawnictwo Naukowe, 1966. Pp 659–62.
———. 1970. "Antiquités syriennes 89. Les dieux armés et les Arabes en Syrie," *Syr* 47 (1970) 77–111.
———. 1971a. "Antiquités syriennes 93. Bêl de Palmyre," *Syr* 48 (1971) 85–114.
———. 1971b. "Antiquités syriennes 95. Le culte du soleil en Syrie à l'époque romaine," *Syr* 48 (1971) 337–73.

———. 1985. *Scripta Varia.* Mélanges d'archéologie et d'histoire. Institut français d'archéologie du proche-orient, Bibliothéque archéologique et historique. Tome 125. Paris: Geuthner, 1985.
Seyrig, H. and R. Amy and E. Will. 1975. *Le temple de Bêl à Palmyre.* Institut Français d'Archéologie de Beyrouth, Bibliothèque archéologique et historique. 2 Paris: Geuthner, 1975.
Seyrig, H. and J. Starcky. 1949. "Genneas," *Syr* 26 (1949) 230-57. **Syr '49 p 249**
Shiffmann, I. 1965. "The Property and Agrarian Relations in Palmyre According to the Inscriptions in the I-III Centuries A.D," (Russian; English abstract) *Palestinkij Sbornik* 13 (1965) 100–13.
———. 1974. "Miscellanea epigraphica palmyrena," *Palestinski Sbornik* 25 (1974) 87–94.
———. 1980. *Palmirskii poshlinnyi tarif.* Moskva: Izdvo Nauka, 1980.
———. 1984. "Collegium Statutes of the Worshippers of Bēlʿastōr in Palmyra," *VDI* 168 (1984) 60–77.
Simonsen, D. 1889. *Sculptures et inscriptions de Palmyre à la Glyptothèque de Ny Carlsberg.* Copenhagen: T. Lind, 1889.
Sobernheim, M. 1902. "Palmyrenische Inschriften," *BA* 4 (1902) 207-19.
———. 1905. "Palmyrenische Inschriften," *MVAG* 10 (1905), Heft 2. Pp 1-58.
von Soden, W. 1965. *Akkadisches Handwörterbuch.* 3 vols Wiesbaden: Harassowitz, 1965-81.
———. 1977. "Aramäische Wörter in neuassyrischen und neu- und spätbabylonischen Texten. Ein Vorbericht III," *Or* N.S. 46 (1977) 183-97.
Sokoloff, M. 1974. *The Targum to Job from Qumran Cave XI.* Ramat-Gan: Bar-Ilan, 1974.
———. 1990. *A Dictionary of Jewish Palestinian Aramaic of the Byzantine Period.* Ramat-Gan: Bar Ilan, 1990.
Spoer, H. 1905. "Palmyrene Tesserae," JAOS 26 (1905) 113-16. Pl preceding p 113.
Starcky, J. 1949a. "Les inscriptions palmyréniennes les plus anciennes," in *Actes du XXIe Congrés International des Orientalistes.* Paris: Société asiatique, 1949. Pp 111–14.
———. 1949b. "Trois inscriptions palmyréniennes," *MUSJ* 28 (1949–50) 45–58 XVI-XVII. **MUSJ '49**
———. 1949c. "Autour d'une dédicace palmyrénienne à Šadrafa et à Duʿanat," *Syr* 26 (1949) 43–85 III-IV.
———. 1949d. *Inventaire des inscriptions de Palmyre.* Fascicule X. Damascus: Imprimerie catholique de Beyrouth, 1949. **Inv 10**
———. 1949e. Appendix by J. Starcky pp 185-86 in D. Mackay, "The Jewellery of Palmyra and its Significance," *Iraq* 11 (1949) 160–87. Pls. LII-LXI. **Iraq '49**
———. 1949f. "Antiquités syriennes 41. Nouveaux monuments palmyréniens de Baalshamîn. Appendice. Les inscriptions," *Syr* 26 (1949) 35–41. **Syr '49 35-41**
———. 1950. "Bas-relief palmyrénien inédit dédié aux génies Šalmân et 'RGYʿ," *Sem* 3 (1950) 45–52. **Sem '50**
———. 1952. *Palmyre.* L'Orient ancien illustré. Paris: Maisonneuve, 1952.
———. 1955. "Inscriptions palmyréniennes conservées au Musée de Beyrouth," *BMB* 12 (1955) 29–44. **BMB '55**
———. 1956a. "Inscriptions archaïques de Palmyre," in *Studi orientalistici in onore di Giorgio Levi della Vida.* Rome: Istituto per l'Oriente, 1956. Pp 509–528. **StudLdV 509-28**
———. 1956b. "Palmyréniens Nabatéens et Arabes du Nord avant l'Islam," in *L'histoire des religions*, edd M. Brillant et R. Aigrain. Paris: Bloud et Gay, 1956. Pp 201–37.
———. 1956c. "Relief palmyrénien dédié au dieu Ilahay," in *Mélanges bibliques rédigés en l'honneur de André Robert.* Paris: Bloud et Gay, n.d. Pp 370–80. **MélRob**
———. 1960. "Palmyre," in *DBS* 6 (1960) coll 1066–1103.
———. 1961. "Deux inscriptions palmyréniennes," *MUSJ* 38 (1961) 121–39. **MUSJ '61**
———. 1963. "Une inscription palmyrénienne trouvée près de l'Euphrate," *Syr* 40 (1963) 47–55. **Syr '63**
———. 1966. Review of J. Cantineau, *Inventaire des inscriptions de Palmyre*, *RB* 73 (1966) 615-17.
———. 1967. "Les grandes heures de l'histoire de Palmyre," *Archeologia* 16 (1967) 30–39.
———. 1972. "Relief dédié au dieu Munʿîm," *Sem* 22 (1972) 57–65. **Sem '72**
———. 1973. See Winnett and Reed 1973.
———. 1974. "Le Sanctuaire de Baalshamîn à Palmyre d'après les inscriptions," *RAR* 1 (1974) 83–90.

———. 1975. "Stèle d'Elahagabal," *MUSJ* 49 (1975–76) 503–20.
———. 1976. "Reliefs de Palmyrène dédié à des Génies," in *Mélanges d'histoire ancienne et d'archéologie offerts à Paul Collart*, edd Pierre Ducrey et al. Cahiers d'archéologie romande. Lausanne: Bibliothèque historique vaudoise, 1976. Pp 327–34.
———. 1984. "Note sur les sculptures palmyréniennes du Musée de Grenoble," *Syr* 61 (1984) 37–44.
Starcky, J. and C.-M. Bennett. 1968. "Découvertes récentes au sanctuaire du Qasr à Pétra: III. Les inscriptions du téménos," *Syr* 45 (1968) 41–66 IX-X.
Starcky, J. and B. Delavault. 1974. "Reliefs palmyréniens inédits," *Sem* 24 (1974) 67–73. **Sem '74**
Starcky, J. and M. Gawlikowski. 1985. *Palmyre.* Édition revue et augmentée des nouvelles découvertes. Paris: Librairie d'Amérique et d'Orient, 1985.
Starcky, J. and S. Munajjed. 1948. *Palmyre.* Damas: Éditions de la Direction Générale des Antiquités, 1948.
Stark, J. 1971. *Personal Names in Palmyrene Inscriptions.* Oxford: Clarendon, 1971.
Stern, H. 1977. *Les mosaïques des maisons d'Achille et de Cassiopée à Palmyre.* Paris: Geuthner, 1977.
Stierlin, H. 1987. *Cités du désert. Pétra, Palmyre, Hatra.* L'art antique au Proche-Orient. Fribourg/Suisse: Seuil, 1987.
Stoneman, R. 1992. *Palmyra and Its Empire. Zenobia's Revolt against Rome.* Ann Arbor: The University of Michigan Press, 1992.
Suder, W. 1985. "Art et démographie. Quelques remarques sur la chronologie des portraits du tombeau de Bôlbarak à Palmyre," *DaM* 2 (1985) 291-95.
Swain, S. 1993. "Greek into Palmyrene: Odaenathus as 'Corrector Totius Orientis'?" *ZPE* 99 (1993) 157-64.
Swinton, J. 1754. "An Explication of all the Inscriptions in the Palmyrene," *Philosophical Transactions* 48 (1754) 690–756.
———. 1766. "Remarks on the Palmyrene Inscription at Teive," *Philosophical Transactions* 56 (1766) 4–9.
Taha, A. 1982. "Men's costume in Palmyra," *AAS* 32 (1982) 117–32.
Tanabe, K. 1986. *Sculptures of Palmyra, I.* Memoirs of the Ancient Orient Museum, vol I. Tokyo: Ancient Orient Museum, 1986.
Teixidor, J. 1962. "Three Inscriptions in the Iraq Museum," *Sumer* 18 (1962) 63–65. **Sumer '62**
———. 1963. "Deux inscriptions palmyréniennes du Musée de Bagdad," *Syr* 40 (1963) 33-46.
———. 1965. *Inventaire des inscriptions de Palmyre.* Fascicule XI. Beirut: Imprimerie Catholique, 1965. **Inv 11**
———. 1966. "Monuments palmyréniens divers," *MUSJ* 42 (1966) 177–79 I-II. **MUSJ '66**
———. 1977. *The Pagan God: Popular Religion in the Greco-Roman Near East.* Princeton: Princeton University Press, 1977.
———. 1979. *The Pantheon of Palmyra.* Études preliminaires aux religions orientales dans l'empire romain. Leiden: Brill, 1979.
———. 1980a. "L'Inscription palmyrénienne Inv. XII, 45," *Sem* 30 (1980) 61–62.
———. 1980b. "Cultes tribaux et religion civique à Palmyre," *RHR* 197 (1980) 277–387.
———. 1981. "Le thiase de Bêlastor et de Beelshamên d'après une inscription récemment découverte à Palmyre," *CRAIBL* (1981) 306–14. **CRAIBL '81**
———. 1982. "Cultes d'Asie Mineure et de Thrace à Palmyre," *Sem* 32 (1982) 97–100.
———. 1983a. "Palmyrene mḥwz and Ugaritic miḫd: A Suggestion," *UF* 15 (1983) 309–11.
———. 1983b. "Le Tarif de Palmyre: I. Un commentaire de la version palmyrénienne," *Aula Orientalis* 1 (1983) 235–52.
———. 1984. "Un port romain du désert: Palmyre et son commerce d'Auguste à Caracalla," *Sem* 34 (1984) 3–127.
———. 1985. "La religione della Siria in età ellenistica e romana," in *Da Ebla a Damasco. Diecimila anni di archeologia in Siria,* edd G. Garroni and E. Parcu. Milano: Electa, 1985. Pp 111–16.
———. 1986. *Bulletin d'épigraphie sémitique (1964-1980).* Institut Français d'Archéologie du Proche-Orient, Bibliothèque archéologique et historique, Tome 127. Paris: Geuthner, 1986.
———. 1987. "Religion und Kult in Palmyra," in *Palmyra: Geschichte, Kunst und Kultur der Oasenstadt,*

ed E. Ruprechtsberger. Linzer archäeologische Forschungen, 16. Linz: Gutenberg, 1987. Pp 32-43.

———. 1989. "Les derniers rois d'Edesse d'aprés deux nouveaux documents syriaques," *ZPE* 76 (1989) 219-22.

———. 1990. "Deux documents syriaques du IIIe siècle aprés J.-C., provenant du moyen Euphrate," *CRAIBL* 1990, pp 144-63 (observations of A. Guillaumont and E. Will, pp 163-66).

———. 1991. "Remarques sur l'onomastique palmyrénienne," *Studi epigrafici e linguistici* 8 (1991) 213-23.

———. 1993. "Un document syriaque de fermage de 242 après J.-C.," *Sem* 41-42 (1993) 195-208.

Torrey, C. 1904. "Four Palmyrene Epitaphs," *JAOS* 25 (1904) 320-323.

Trendall, A. 1942. *The Shellal Mosaic and Other Classical Antiquities in the Australian War Memorial in Canberra.* Canberra: Australian War Memorial, 1942.

Tudor, D. 1971. "Les Syriens en Dacie inférieure," *AAS* 21 (1971) 71-76.

Ustinova, Y. and J. Naveh. 1993. "A Greek-Palmyrene Aramaic Dedicatory Inscription from the Negev," *Atiqot* 22 (1993) 91-96. Fig 1 (drawing and photograph) **Atiqot '93 p 91**

al-ʿUsh, A., A. Joundi, and B. Zouhdi. 1969. *Catalogue du Musée National de Damas.* Damas: Publications de la Direction Générale des Antiquités et des Musée, 1969. **CatDam**

———. 1976. "Le plan de Palmyre," in *Palmyre, Bilan et Perspectives.* Strasbourg: AECR, 1976. Pp 165–73.

Van Berchem, D. 1970. "Le premier rempart de Palmyre," *CRAIBL* (1970) 231–37.

Van Rompay, L. 1990. "Palmyra, Emesa en Edessa: semitischen Steden in het Gehelleniseerde Nabije Osten," *Phoenix* 36 (1990) 73-84.

Vattioni, F. 1981. *Le iscrizioni di Ḥatra.* Istituto orientale di Napoli, Supplemento n. 28 agli Annali, vol 41 (1981), fasc. 3.

Vattioni, F. 1986. "Le iscrizioni sui rilievi palmireni nella Collezione Zeri," *AIΩN* 8 (1986) 245-48. **AIΩN '86a**

Vermeule, C. 1964. "Greek and Roman Portraits in North American Collections Open to Public," *Proceedings of the American Philosophical Society* 108 (1964) pp 99-134.

———. 1981. *Greek and Roman Sculpture in America. Masterpieces in Public Collections in the United States and Canada.* The J. Paul Getty Museum and University of California Press: Malibu, California-Berkeley, Los Angeles London, 1981. **Verm '81**

Vermeule, C. and A. Brauer. 1990. *Stone Sculptures: The Greek, Roman, and Etruscan Collections of Harvard University Art Museums.* Cambridge, Mass.: Harvard University Art Museums, 1990. **StSc**

Vicari, J. 1976. "Baalshamin, temple eustyle," in *Palmyre, Bilan et Perspectives.* Strasbourg: AECR, 1976. Pp 75-83.

Vinnikov, I. 1965. "More on Palmyran Inscriptions in the Soviet Union," *VDI* 1 (1965) 139–41.

de Vogüé, M. 1855a. "Note sur quelques inscriptions recueillies à Palmyre," *Bulletin archéologique de l'Athenaeum français* (1855) 34–38.

———. 1855b. "Lampe palmyrénienne," *Bulletin archéologique de l'Athenaeum français* (1855) 102–104.

———. 1868. *Syrie centrale. Inscriptions sémitiques.* Paris: J. Baudry, 1868.

———. 1883. *Inscriptions palmyréniennes inédites.* Extrait du Journal asiatique. Paris: Imprimerie Nationale, 1883.

———. 1883a. "Inscriptions palmyréniennes inédites," *JA* 8/1 (1883) 231–45.

———. 1883b. "Inscriptions palmyréniennes inédites," *JA* 8/2 (1883) 149–83.

———. 1883c. "Nouvelles et mélanges. Note additionnelle aux inscriptions palmyréniennes," *JA* 8/2 (1883) 549–50.

Wais, J. 1970. "Problemy ikonografii Malakbela," *Studia Palmyrenskie* 4 (1970) 5–62.

———. 1974. "Malakbel and Melqart," *Studia Palmyrenskie* 5 (1974) 97–101.

Walker, J. 1956. "A Palmyrene Tessera," in *Studi orientalistici in onore di Giorgio Levi della Vida.* Rome: Istituto per l'Oriente, 1956. Pp 601–2. **StudLdV 601-2**

Wartke, R.-B. 1991. "Palmyrenische Plastik im Vorderasiatischen Museum," *FuB* 31 (1991) 67-100.

Watzinger, C. 1949. "Palmyra," in *PW.* 36. Halbband, 2. Drittel. Stuttgart: Druckenmüller, 1949.

Welles, C., R. Fink, and J. Gilliam. 1959. *The Excavations at Dura-Europos. Final Report V, Part I The Parchments and Papyri.* New Haven: Yale, 1959. **PapDura 152**

Wiegand, T. 1932. *Palmyra. Ergebnisse der Expeditionen von 1902 und 1917.* Berlin: H. Keller, 1932.

Will, E. 1947. "La tour funéraire de Palmyre," *Syr* 26 (1947) 87– 116.

———. 1957. "Marchands et chefs de caravanes à Palmyre," *Syr* 34 (1957) 262–77.

———. 1966. "Le sac de Palmyre," in *Mélanges d'archéologie et d'histoire offerts à André Piganiol*, ed R. Chevallier. Paris: SEVPEN, 1966. Pp 1409–16.

———. 1983. "Le développement urbain de Palmyra: témoinages épigraphiques anciens et nouveaux," *Syr* 60 (1983) 69–81.

———. 1985a. "Pline l'ancien et Palmyre: Un problème d'histoire ou d'histoire littéraire?," *Syr* 62 (1985) 263–69.

———. 1985b. "Les problèmes iconographiques de la Syrie romaine," in *Actes du colloque sur les problèmes de l'image dans le monde méditerranéen classique. Château de Lourmarin en Provence: 2-3 septembre 1982.* Roma: Giorgio Bretschneider, 1985. Pp 41-48.

Winnett, F. and W. Reed. 1970. *Ancient Records from North Arabia.* Toronto: University of Toronto Press, 1970.

———. 1973. "An Archaeological-Epigraphical Survey of the Ḥāʾil Area of Northern Saʿudi Arabia," *Ber* 22 (1973) 89 (Palmyrene text and notes by J. Starcky), Pls. 12, 13. **Ber '73**

Wright, W. 1878. "Note on a Bilingual Inscription, Latin and Aramaic, Recently found at South Shields," *Transaction of the Society of Biblical Archaeology* 6 (1878) 436-40.

Wuthnow, H. 1935. "Eine palmyr. Büste." *Orientalistische Studien.* Festschrift E. Littmann. Leiden: Brill, 1935. Pp 63–69. **StudLitt**

Zahrnt, M. 1986. "Zum Fiskalgesetz von Palmyra und zur Geschichte der Stadt in hadrianischer Zeit," *ZPE* 62 (1986) 279–93.

Zouhdi, B. 1983. "La femme dans l'art de Palmyre," *DaM* 1 (1983) 315-16.

❖ ❖ ❖ ❖ ❖

TEXTS

The order of the texts is alphabetic, by sigla. Since many texts have appeared in more than one edition, preference is given in assigning sigla to certain major comprehensive collections, ranked in a fixed order. Primacy is given to the *Corpus inscriptionum semiticarum*, so if an inscription appears there, the siglum in this edition is "C3901," etc., and cross-references, bibliography, text, and so on are given at that point; next is the *Inventaire des inscriptions de Palmyre* ("Inv"), for texts not included in the *CIS*; then *Recueil d'inscriptions palmyréniennes ("RSP")*, and *Recueil des tessères de Palmyre ("RTP")*. Cross-referencing, the Bibliography and Abbreviations, and the Appendix "Concordances of Text References" will assist the reader in locating texts.

Note that, since published photographs are often insufficiently clear, no attempt has been made to mark as such letters that are partially effaced or otherwise uncertain, except that the notations of the editions followed is frequently given. In the Palmyrene script, *resh* and *daleth* are virtually identical; occasionally the scribes used a dot over *resh* to distinguish them. This distinction is preserved in our transliteration by printing dotted *resh* as ṙ, where this can be read from photographs, copies, or an editor's marks.

The following abridged and fictitious example illustrates and explains the types of data that may be given for an individual text in the present volume; not all these elements are appropriate for every text, of course. For bilinguals and trilinguals, Greek and Latin texts are printed for the reader's convenience; for practical reasons, most Greek texts are given as in the edition cited, leaving inconsistencies in editorial practice unchanged.

PAT 9999[a] **Ber '35 p 109**[b] I[c] **A.D. 142**[d]
Prov: Palmyra, S-W Necropolis, Tomb of Nasrallat[e]
Loc: Palmyra, *in situ*[f] *Funerary: Foundation.*[g] *On door-lintel.*[h] Group: Ber '35 pp 108-14.[i]
Bib: *Ingholt 1935, pl XLIV;*[j] MF Fondation no. 48.[k]

1 Τὸ σπήλαιον τοῦ ταφεῶνος etc. ... ἔτους τρίτου πεντηκοστοῦ υ Δαισίῳ etc. [l]

1 bt ʿlmʾ dnh ʿbd nṣrlt br mlkw ... etc. [m]
Gk uses numeral sign for 400, writes 53 in words[n]

a PAT (*Palmyrene Aramaic Texts*) number **b** In bold type, the text siglum **c** In this case the edition uses its own numbering system; for the possible convenience of users of *PAT*, where appropriate, this number is given (here a roman "I") **d** If the text contains an explicit and not too fragmentary date (according to the Seleucid era) the text heading gives the year in terms of our era; in exceptional cases, where there is peculiarity in the way the number is written, the year figure is enclosed in parentheses, thus "A.D. (106)". Texts without an explicit date are marked n.(ot) d.(ated)" even though usually at least an approximate date might be assigned **e** "Prov:" the provenance of the text; where no specific indication is given, the reader may assume that the text probably comes from Palmyra. **f** "Loc:" the present location of the text **g** In italics, the genre (type) of text is given, following certain broad designations **h** "On *such-and-such*": the position or kind of object on which the text is written. **i** Especially when a number of inscriptions are known to come from the same tomb, the texts that belong together are listed with the heading "Group:". **j** "Bib(liography):" introduces indications of literature about the text; where appropriate, the first information given, in italic print, specifies a plate or text-figure in the edition cited **k** Next, in roman type, other editions or relevant bibliography, with indications of figures of plates **l** For bilingual texts, the Latin or Greek **m** The Aramaic text **n** Occasionally, a textual or explanatory note follows, in smaller type. The word "Collated," unless otherwise qualified, means checked with the original stone inscription.

PAT 0001 **AA '30 p 192** **A.D. 65**
Prov: Palmyra. Loc: Ny Carlsberg Glyptothek, 2816. *Funerary. On relief.* Bib: *Ingholt '30c fig 1*; NyCG 1.

(On right)
1 ʾtt
2 brʿth
3 br ḥnbl
4 ʾʿby
5 šnt 3.100+
6 60+10+5+2
(On left)
1' b[...]

PAT 0002 **AA ’32 p 1** **A.D. (106)**

Prov: Palmyra, S-W Necropolis, Hypogeum. Loc: Palmyra, *in situ*. *Funerary: Foundation. On door lintel.* Group: AA ’32 p 1, p 4, p 6. Bib: *Ingholt ’32b fig 1 p 2;* MF Fondation 30.

1 lyqrh ʿbd ḥyrn br ydy br ḥyrn ḥntʾ lh wlbnth
šnt 10+5+3

Figure for hundreds omitted, as sometimes elsewhere; in this case, figure must be (4)18 of Seleucid era.

PAT 0003 **AA ’32 p 4**

Prov: Palmyra, S-W Necropolis. Loc: Palmyra, *in situ*. *Funerary. On wall, fresco.* Group: p 1, p 4, p 6. Bib: *Ingholt ’32 pl 2.*

1 ṣlm ḥyrn br
2 tymrṣw

PAT 0004 **AA ’32 p 6**

Prov: Palmyra, S-W Necropolis. Loc: Palmyra, *in situ*. *Funerary. On wall, fresco.* Group: p 1, p 4, p 6. Bib: *Ingholt ’32 fig 2 p 7.*

1 ṣlm
2 m[...]

PAT 0005 **AAS ’53 p 19** **A.D. 148**

Prov: Palmyra. Loc: Damascus, National Museum, 15028. *Funerary. On fragmentary relief from couch (klinè).* Bib: *Sabeh ’53 pl I, 2.*

(Right of male bust)
1 ḥbl
2 mqymw
3 ʾmnʾ
4 br nwrbl
5 br zbdʾ
(Right of female bust)
6 ḥbl
7 tdmr
8 ʾtt
9 mqymw
10 br nwrbl
11 br zbdʾ
12 ʾmnʾ
(Left of female bust)
13 mytt
14 ywm 20+5+4
15 bsywn
16 šnt 4.100+40+10+5+4

PAT 0006 **AAS ’53 p 22** **n. d.**

Prov: Palmyra. Loc: Damascus, National Museum, 15027. *Funerary. On relief.* Bib: *Sabeh ’53 pl II, 1.*

1 ḥbl
2 ʾḥyny
3 br ḥṭry

PAT 0007 **AAS ’53 p 24** **n. d.**

Prov: Palmyra. Loc: Damascus, National Museum, 15020. *Funerary. On relief.* Bib: *Sabeh ’53 pl II, 2.*

(On right)
1 blšwr
2 br ḥyrʾ
3 ʾkldy
4 ḥbl
5 ḥyʾ
6 šnyn 10+5+4
(On left)
1 mqymw
2 br ḥyrʾ
3 ʾkldy
4 ḥbl
5 ḥyʾ
6 šnyn 10+5+1

PAT 0008 **AAS ’65 p 90** **n. d.**

Prov: Palmyra, Temple of Nebo. Loc: Palmyra Museum. *Dedicatory. On relief.* Bib: *Bounni ’65a and ’65b, pl I*; Bounni ’65b pp 6-7.

1 mṣbʾ dn[h qrbw bwlḥ]zy br n[....... br]
ʾʿylmy
2 wtymʾ br zbd[.....br......... ʾš]trʾ ṭbtʾ

Text in French article improved by Bounni over that of Arab article following readings of Starcky

PAT 0009 **AAS '65/2 p 127** **A.D. 146**

Prov: Palmyra, Temple of Nebo. Loc: Palmyra, B 10/63. *Dedicatory. On statue base.* Bib: *Bounni and Saliby '65a, '65b pl 10.*

1 ṣlmʾ dnh dy mqymw br nbwzbd
2 br bryky ʿbšy dy ʾqymw lh
3 bnwhy lyqrh wʿbd mqymw [..]
4 ʿmwdʾ dnh wšryth wtṭlylh
5 dnbw ʾlhʾ ṭbʾ wškrʾ ʿl ḥywh
6 wḥyy bnwhy byrḥ nysn šnt
7 4.100+40+10+5+2

PAT 0009.2 **ActH '91** **A.D. 160**

Prov: not known. Loc: Copenhagen, Danish National Museum. *Funerary. On relief.*

1 zbdʿth
2 br brʿʾ
3 zbdʿth
4 ywm 20+5+2
5 bṭbt šnt 4.100+
6 20+20+20+10+1

PAT 0010 **AfO '53 p 312** **n. d.**

Prov: Palmyra. Loc: Canberra: Australian War Memorial, ART 00484. *Funerary. On relief.* Bib: *Trendall '42 pp 26-27, pl V*; Eilers '52-53 figs p 313.

1 ṣlmt hgr
2 brt zbydʾ
3 br mlʾ ʾtt
4 tymy br
5 blšwry
6 tymy ḥbl

AIΩN '86a p 246 (1) **n. d.**

Prov: Palmyra. Loc: Mentana (Rome), Federico Zeri Collection. *Funerary. On relief.* DAIR 77.4. Bib: *Vattioni '86 fig 68, 1*; Callieri '86 p 227, fig 66, 3.

1 ḥbl bʿ[ʾ]
2 brt ʿwy[dʾ]
3 br zbydʾ [....]
4 ʾtt yrḥy [....]
5 b[....]

Collated

AIΩN '86a p 247 (2) **n. d.**

Prov: Palmyra. Loc: Mentana (Rome), Federico Zeri Collection. *Funerary. On relief.* DAIR 77.1. Bib: *Vattioni '86 fig 68,2*; Callieri '86 pp 235-36, fig 64, 1.

1 ḥnynʾ
2 br mtny
3 ḥbl

Collated

AIΩN '86a p 247 (3) **n. d.**

Prov: Palmyra. Loc: Mentana (Rome), Federico Zeri Collection. *Funerary. On relief.* DAIR 84.831. Bib: *Vattioni '86 fig 69, 1*; Callieri '86 pp 236-38, fig 64,2.

1 ʿbdʾ br
2 šmʿwn
3 ḥbl

Collated

AIΩN '86a p 248 (5) **n. d.**

Prov: Palmyra. Loc: Mentana (Rome), Federico Zeri Collection. *Funerary. On relief.* DAIR 84.823. Bib: *Vattioni '86 fig 67, 2*; Callieri '86 p 241, fig 67, 1.

1 mlwkʾ br mlʾ ḥbl

Collated

PAT 0015 **AIΩN '86b p 231** **n. d.**

Prov: Palmyra. Loc: Mentana (Rome), Federico Zeri Collection. *Funerary. On relief.* DAIR 84.830. Bib: *Callieri '86 fig 63, 2.*

1' [ ]byn

Collated. Badly damaged inscription.

PAT 0016 **ARNA p 161** **A.D. (174)**
Prov: El-Qarqar, Wādī es-Sirḥān (Saudi Arabia). Loc: El-Qarqar. *Funerary. On stone slab.* Bib: *Milik and Starcky '70 pp 161-62 (Starcky) pl 31 (drawing).*

1 [byrḥ] sywn
2 [šnt] [4.100]+80+5
3 [dkyr] bgšw br
4 qmlʾ [br]
5 šʿd bṭb
6 p[s]l brh
7 5.100
8 +40+5+3

Figure for hundreds omitted or lost, (4)85 more probable than (3)85.

PAT 0017 **Atiqot '93 p 91** **n.d.**
Prov: Ḥaluẓa in Negeb, Israel. Loc: Israel Antiquity Authority Stores IAA 91-2354. *Dedicatory. On stone block.* Bib: *Fig 1 photo and drawing (Yardeni).*

1 θεῷ ὑψ
2 ίστῳ

1 dkryt

PAT 0018 **Ber '34 p 33** II **n. d.**
Prov: Palmyra. Loc: Beirut, American University Museum, 25.1. *Funerary. On relief.* Bib: *Ingholt '34 pp 33-36, pl VIII, 2* (Ber '34 1, p 32 = C4317).

1 yrḥbwlʾ
2 br nšʾ
3 ʿgʾ šlmʾ
4 ḥbl

PAT 0019 **Ber '34 p 36** III **A.D. 236**
Prov: Palmyra. Loc: Beirut, American University Museum, 32.25. *Funerary. On relief.* Bib: *Ingholt '34 pp 36-38, pl IX, 1.*

1 ḥgwr br
2 mlkw
3 mlk
4 bl
5 ḥbl
6 šnt

PAT 0020 **Ber '34 p 38** IV **n. d.**
Prov: Palmyra. Loc: Beirut, American University Museum, 32.56. *Funerary. On relief.* Bib: *Ingholt '34 pp 38-40, pl IX, 2.*

(On right)
1 ḥbl
2 bwrpʾ
3 br ʿtntn [br]
4 bwlḥʾ dy
5 ʿbd lh
6 bwlḥʾ
7 kldyʾ
8 brh
(On the left)
9 qbyr
10 bʾrʿ
11 gwmḥʾ ʿl
12 ymyn npšʾ
13 dh tḥwt
14 ʿlʾ brt
15 yrḥy

PAT 0021 **Ber '34 p 40** V **n. d.**
Prov: Palmyra. Loc: Beirut, American University Museum, 33.12. *Funerary. On relief.* Bib: *Ingholt '34 pp 40-42, pl X, 1.*

1 zbydʾ br
2 ydyʿbl
3 ḥbl
4 ʾmby
5 brt ʿgy
6 lw ʾmh
7 ḥbl

PAT 0022 **Ber '34 p 42** VI **A.D. 154**
Prov: Palmyra. Loc: Not known. *Funerary. On relief.* Bib: *Ingholt '34 pp 42-43, pl X, 2.*

1 whbʾ
2 ʿbdʿʾ
3 bwly
4 ḥbl

5 šnt 4.100
6 +60+5+1

PAT 0023 **Ber '35 p 59** I **A.D. 98**
Prov: Palmyra, S-W Necropolis, Tower of ʿAtenatan. Loc: Palmyra, *in situ. Funerary: Foundation. On stone tablet set in wall.* Group: Ber '35 pp 58-75. Bib: *Ingholt '35 pl XXIV, 1*; MF Fondation 25.

1 Τὸ σπήλαιον ἐποίησεν Αθηνα
2 θανος Ζαβδααθους τοῦ Ιαδδαιου
3 τοῦ Θαιμει εἴς τε αὐτὸν καὶ Αιρανην
4 τὸν ἀδελφὸν αὐτοῦ ἔτους ιυ'

1 mʿrtʾ dh ʿbd ʿtntn br zbdʿth
2 br ydy br tymy lh wlḥ[yr]n ʾḥwhy
3 byrḥ tšry 4.100+10 šlm

PAT 0024 **Ber '35 p 60** II **A.D. 229**
Prov: Palmyra, S-W Necropolis, Tower of ʿAtenatan. Loc: Palmyra, *in situ. Funerary: Foundation. On door lintel.* Group: Ber '35 pp 58-75. Bib: *Ingholt '35 pl XXIV, 2*; MF Fondation 62.

1 ʾksdrʾ dnh bt ʿlmʾ dy bgw mʿrtʾ mʿlyk mn bbʾ ʿl ymynʾ ʿbd mn kysh wbnʾ ywlys ʾwrlys mqy br zbdbwl mqy dwḥy lh wlbnwhy wlbnʾ
2 bnwhy dkrʾ lʿlmʾ byrḥ nysn šnt 5.100+40

PAT 0025 **Ber '35 p 64** III **n. d.**
Prov: Palmyra, S-W Necropolis, Tower of ʿAtenatan. Loc: Palmyra, *in situ. Funerary. On sarcophagus, with relief.* Group: Ber '35 pp 58-75. Bib: *Ingholt '35 pl XXVI.*

1 ṣlm mqy br zbdbwl dy bnʾ
2 ʾksdrʾ dnh

PAT 0026 **Ber '35 p 75** I **A.D. 109**
Prov: Palmyra, S-W Necropolis, Hypogeum of Julius Aurelius Male. Loc: Palmyra, *in situ. Funerary: Foundation(?). On door lintel.* Group: Ber '35 pp 75-89. Bib: *Ingholt '35 pl XXXVI*; MF Fondation 32.

1 byrḥ nysn šnt 4.100+20

PAT 0027 **Ber '35 p 76** II **A.D. 183**
Prov: Palmyra, S-W Necropolis, Hypogeum of Julius Aurelius Male. Loc: Palmyra, *in situ. Funerary: Cession. On door lintel.* Group: Ber '35 pp 75-89. Bib: *Ingholt '35 pl XXXVI, XXXVII, 1*; MF Concession 28.

1 ʾksdrʾ mʿlyk ʿl ymynk klh yhb wʾḥbr mlʾ br ḥyrn br ssn ltybwl br ʿbdʾ br tybwl qrybh
2 lh wlbnwhy wlbnʾ bnwhy lyqrhwn dy ʿlmʾ byrḥ ʾdr šnt 5.100+4

PAT 0028 **Ber '35 p 77** III. **A.D. 215**
Prov: Palmyra, S-W Necropolis, Hypogeum of Julius Aurelius Male. Loc: Palmyra, *in situ. Funerary: Cession. On door lintel.* Group: Ber '35 pp 75-89. Bib: *Ingholt '35 pl XXXVI, XXXVII, 1*; MF Concession 29.

1 ʾksdrʾ mʿlk ʿl smlk klh yhb wʾḥbr ywlys ʾwrlys mlʾ br ḥyrn br ssn lywlys ʾwrlys ḥyrn wlywlys ʾwrlys ʾbʾ
2 bny ywlys ʾwrlys mqy br yrḥy qrybwhy lhwn wlbnyhwn wlbny bnyhwn lyqrhwn dy ʿlmʾ byrḥ ʾyr šnt 5.100+20+5+1

PAT 0029 **Ber '35 p 78** IV **A.D. 223**
Prov: Palmyra, S-W Necropolis, Hypogeum of Julius Aurelius Male. Loc: Palmyra, *in situ. Funerary: Cession. On door lintel.* Group: Ber '35 pp 75-89. Bib: *Ingholt '35 pl XXXVI, XXXVII, 1*; MF Concession 30.

1 ywlyws ʾwrlys mlʾ br ḥyrn br ssn ʾḥbr wrḥq lywlys ʾwrlys ʿbsy br ḥnynʾ br ḥnynʾ br ʿgʾ yrq sṭrʾ
2 klh dy mʿlk ʿl ymynk mn qrnʾ dy ʾksdrʾ dy btr bnʾ wʿd zbwqtʾ dy sṭrʾ mqblʾ lh wlbnwhy wlbny bnwhy
3 lʿlmʾ byrḥ kslwl šnt 5.100+20+10+5

PAT 0030 **Ber '35 p 79** a **n. d.**
Prov: Palmyra, S-W Necropolis, Hypogeum of Julius Aurelius Male. Loc: Palmyra, *in situ*. *Funerary. On sarcophagus.* Group: Ber '35 pp 75-89.

1 ṣlm ʿbsy
2 br ḥnynʾ
3 ḥnynʾ yrq

This and the two following texts are engraved on the same sarcophagus.

PAT 0031 **Ber '35 p 79** b **n. d.**
Prov: Palmyra, S-W Necropolis, Hypogeum of Julius Aurelius Male. Loc: Palmyra, *in situ*. *Funerary. On sarcophagus.* Group: Ber '35 pp 75-89.

1 ḥbl ḥnynʾ br
2 ḥnynʾ ʿgʾ
3 yrq ʾbwn

PAT 0032 **Ber '35 p 79** c **n. d.**
Prov: Palmyra, S-W Necropolis, Hypogeum of Julius Aurelius Male. Loc: Palmyra, *in situ*. *Funerary. On sarcophagus.* Group: Ber '35 pp 75-89.

1 ṣlm mrty
2 brt yrḥbwlʾ
3 ʾtt ʿbsy

PAT 0033 **Ber '35 p 80** d **n. d.**
Prov: Palmyra, S-W Necropolis, Hypogeum of Julius Aurelius Male. Loc: Palmyra, *in situ*. *Funerary. On sarcophagus.* Group: Ber '35 pp 75-89.

1 ḥbl ḥnynʾ br
2 ḥnynʾ yrq

This and the two following texts are on the same sarcophagus

PAT 0034 **Ber '35 p 80** e **n. d.**
Prov: Palmyra, S-W Necropolis, Hypogeum of Julius Aurelius Male. Loc: Palmyra, *in situ*. *Funerary. On sarcophagus.* Group: Ber '35 pp 75-89.

1 ḥbl btšmyʾ
2 brt ʿbsy

PAT 0035 **Ber '35 p 81** f **n. d.**
Prov: Palmyra, S-W Necropolis, Hypogeum of Julius Aurelius, Male. Loc: Palmyra, *in situ*. *Funerary. On sarcophagus.* Group: Ber '35 pp 75-89.

1 ṣlm ʾqmt
2 brt šʿdy ʾmn

PAT 0036 **Ber '35 p 81** g **n. d.**
Prov: Palmyra, S-W Necropolis, Hypogeum of Julius Aurelius Male. Loc: Palmyra, *in situ*. *Funerary. On sarcophagus.* Group: Ber '35 pp 75-89.

1 ḥbl šʿdy
2 br ḥnynʾ
3 ḥnynʾ yrq

This and the two following texts are on the same sarcophagus

PAT 0037 **Ber '35 p 82** h **n. d.**
Prov: Palmyra, S-W Necropolis, Hypogeum of Julius Aurelius Male. Loc: Palmyra, *in situ*. *Funerary. On sarcophagus.* Group: Ber '35 pp 75-89.

1 ḥbl šʿdy br ʿbsy
2 br ḥnynʾ yrq

PAT 0038 **Ber '35 p 82** i **n. d.**
Prov: Palmyra, S-W Necropolis, Hypogeum of Julius Aurelius Male. Loc: Palmyra, *in situ*. *Funerary. On sarcophagus.* Group: Ber '35 pp 75-89.

1 ṣlm šlʾ brt
2 ḥnynʾ yrq

PAT 0039 **Ber ʾ35 p 82** V **A.D. 234**

Prov: Palmyra, S-W Necropolis, Hypogeum of Julius Aurelius Male. Loc: Palmyra, *in situ*. *Funerar: Cession. On door lintel.* Group: Ber ʾ35 pp 75-89. Bib: *Ingholt ʾ35 pl XXXVI, XXXVII, 1*; MF Concession 31.

1 gwmḥyʾ ʾln tltʾ mšlmnyn dy mn ʾksdrʾ mqblʾ mʿlyk bgwh dy ʾksdrʾ ʿl smlk mn qrqsʾ wlgw rḥq ywlys ʾwrlys mlʾ br
2 ḥyrn br mlʾ ḥyrn ssn lywlys ʾwrlys šyby br hrms mrqʾ lh wlbnwhy wlbny bnwhy lʿlmʾ byrḥ ʾyr šnt 5.100+40+5

line 1: *mlʾbr* at end added with Stark PN p 120

PAT 0040 **Ber ʾ35 p 84** VI **A.D. 235**

Prov: Palmyra, S-W Necropolis, Hypogeum of Julius Aurelius Male. Loc: Palmyra, *in situ*. *Funerary: Cession. On door lintel.* Group: Ber ʾ35 pp 75-89. Bib: *Ingholt ʾ35 pl XXXVI, XXXVII, 1*; MF Concession 32.

1 gwmḥyʾ ʾln tltʾ mšlmnyn dy bplṭyʾ mʿlyk bplṭyʾ ʿl smlk btr qrqsʾ qdmyʾ rḥq ywlys ʾwrlys mlʾ br ʾwrlys ḥyrn
2 br mlʾ ḥyrn ssn lywlys ʾwrlys ḥlptʾ br mqymw zbdʾ lh wlbnwhy wlbny bnwhy lʿlmʾ byrḥ šbṭ šnt 5.100+40+5+1

PAT 0041 **Ber ʾ35 p 85** VII **A.D. 235**

Prov: Palmyra, S-W Necropolis, Hypogeum of Julius Aurelius Male. Loc: Palmyra, *in situ*. *Funerary: Cession. On right doorjamb.* Group: Ber ʾ35 pp 75-89. Bib: *Ingholt ʾ35 pl XXXVIII, 1*; MF Concession 33.

1 byrḥ šbṭ dy šnt
2 5.100+40+5+1 ywlys
3 ʾwrlys mlʾ br ḥyrn
4 mlʾ rḥq lywlys
5 ʾwrlys zbdbwl br
6 zbdbwl khylw mn gwmḥyn
7 tryn dy bplṭyʾ btr
8 gwmḥyn tltʾ dy hnwn
9 lḥlptʾ dy lgw mn
10 qrqsʾ mʿlk ʿl smlʾ
11 wmn gwmḥ ʾḥrn dy bgw
12 [.....] lh wlbnwhy
13 wlbny bnwhy lyqrhwn
14 dy ʿlmʾ

PAT 0042 **Ber ʾ35 p 86** VIII **A.D. 237**

Prov: Palmyra, S-W Necropolis, Hypogeum of Julius Aurelius Male. Loc: Palmyra, *in situ*. *Funerary: Cession. On right doorjamb.* Group: Ber ʾ35 pp 75-89. Bib: *Ingholt ʾ35 pl XXXVIII, 2*; MF Concession 34.

1 ywlys ʾwrlys
2 ḥyrn br mqy yrḥy
3 rḥq lywlys ʾwrlys
4 ʾs[..] br ḥnynʾ šmʿwn
5 sṭrʾ mqblʾ dy
6 ʾksdrʾ ymnyʾ
7 mʿlyk mʿrtʾ dnh
8 ʿl smln qdmy wtwb
9 rḥq lh sṭrʾ mdnḥyʾ
10 mʿln ʾksdrʾ ʿl smln
11 sṭr mn gwmḥʾ ḥd
12 bryʾ dy by btrh
13 gwmḥʾ ḥd rḥq ḥyrn dnh
14 lḥlptʾ br mqymw
15 zbdʾ lhn wlbnyhwn
16 wlbny bnyhwn
17 lyqrhwn dy ʿlmʾ
18 byrḥ ʾyr šnt
19 5.100+40+5+3

line 4: Stark PN reads *ʾsy[.]*

PAT 0043 **Ber ʾ35 p 88** IX **A.D. 237**

Prov: Palmyra, S-W Necropolis, Hypogeum of Julius Aurelius Male. Loc: Palmyra, *in situ*. *Funerary: Cession. On right doorjamb.* Group: Ber ʾ35 pp 75-89. Bib: *Ingholt ʾ35 pl XXXVIII, 1*; MF Concession 35.

1 byrḥ kslwl šnt 5.100+40+5+4
2 ʾwrlys ḥyrn br mqy br
3 yrḥy ʾrḥq lʾwrlyʾ ṣmy
4 brt lšmš mn gwmḥyn trn
5 gwyyn mʿrbyyn dy hnwn
6 bʾksdrʾ ymnyʾ mʿlk
7 bbʾ ʿl smlk lh wlbnh
8 wlbny bnh lyqrhn lʿlmʾ

PAT 0044 **Ber '35 p 91** II **A.D. 186**
Prov: Palmyra, S-W Necropolis, Tomb of Malku. Loc: Palmyra, *in situ. Funerary: Cession. On door lintel.* Group: Ber '35 pp 90-108; Inv 8 60; MUSJ '62 p 104-19. Bib: *Ingholt '35 pl XXXIX, 2*; MF Concession 12.

1 nwrbl w'qmt ḥb' bny mlkw rb' br mlkw nwrbl 'ḥbr lnḥšṭb br ḥry ḥnṭ'
2 whby ḥlpt' wlrwḥbl br ḥry 'mtšlm' bt ḥry šgl brt zbyd' b'ksdr' grbyy'
3 m'lyk 'l ymyn' lhwn wlbnyhwn wlbny bnyhwn l'lm' byrḥ qnyn šnt 4.100+80+10+5+2
line 2: *'mtšlm'* with Stark PN p 120

PAT 0045 **Ber '35 p 93** III **A.D. 186**
Prov: Palmyra, S-W Necropolis, Tomb of Malku. Loc: Palmyra, *in situ. Funerary: Cession. On door lintel.* Group: see Ber '35 p 91. Bib: *Ingholt '35 pl XXXIX, 2, XL*; MF Concession 13.

1 nwrbl w'qmt ḥb' bny mlkw rb' br mlkw mlkw nwrbl šwtpt wrḥqt lb'ly br dywn mlkw dqrywn'
2 b'ksdr' tymn' m'lk 'l sml' lh wlbnwhy wlbn' bnwhy l'lm' byrḥ 'lwl mšlm šnt 4.100+80+10+5+2

PAT 0046 **Ber '35 p 95** IV **A.D. 188**
Prov: Palmyra, S-W Necropolis, Tomb of Malku. Loc: Palmyra, *in situ. Funerary: Cession. On door lintel.* Group: see Ber '35 p 91. Bib: *Ingholt '35 pl XXIX, 2, XL*; MF Concession 14.

1 b'ly br dywn br mlkw 'ḥbr lš'rn' br bly gwmḥyn tlt' bh b'ksdr' dh m'lk 'l ymn' lh wlbnwh wlbny bnwh lyqrhwn dy 'lm' byrḥ sywn šnt 4.100+80+10+5+4

PAT 0047 **Ber '35 p 96** V **A.D. 213**
Prov: Palmyra, S-W Necropolis. Tomb of Malku. Loc: Palmyra, *in situ. Funerary: Cession. On doorjamb.* Group: see Ber '35 p 91. Bib: *Ingholt '35 pl XLI, 1*; MF Concession 15.

1 byrḥ ṭbt šnt 5.100+20+4
2 'g' rḥqt l'ttn š'r
3 'ksdr' šḥym'

PAT 0048 **Ber '35 p 97** VI **A.D. 213**
Prov: Palmyra, S-W Necropolis, Tomb of Malku. Loc: Palmyra, *in situ. Funerary: Cession. On door lintel.* Group: see Ber '35 p 91. Bib: *Ingholt '35 pl XXXIX, 2, XL*; MF Concession 16.

1 ywlys 'wrlys nwrbl wml' bny mlkw rb' br mlkw mlkw nwrbl 'sy' rḥq lbs' wlrysq' bny š'rn' bly mn šṭr' ymny' dy bn' qrqsy' gwmḥyn
2 šṭ' dkn lhwn wlbnywhn wlbn' bnyhwn lyqrhwn dy 'lm' byrḥ tšry šnt 5.100+20+5

PAT 0049 **Ber '35 p 98** VII **A.D. 214**
Prov: Palmyra, S-W Necropolis, Tomb of Malku. Loc: Palmyra, *in situ. Funerary: Cession. On door lintel.* Group: see Ber '35 p 91. Bib: *Ingholt '35 pl XXXIX, 2, XL*; MF Concession 17.

1 ywlys 'wrlys nwrbl wml' [bny] mlkw rb' br mlkw br mlkw br nwrbl dy mqrh 'sy' rḥq mn šṭr' grbyy' dy hw m'lk bb' 'l ymyn' btr 'ksdr' btr bn' trn qrqsy' btr
2 gwmḥyn tlt' mdnḥy' gwmḥyn tlt' dkn m'rby' lywlys 'wrlys br 'prhṭ br ḥry zbdbwl br mlkw 'swyt lh wlbnwhy wlbn' bnyh l'lm' byrḥ 'b šnt 5.100+20+5

PAT 0050 **Ber '35 p 99** VIII **A.D. 213**
Prov: Palmyra, S-W Necropolis, Tomb of Malku. Loc: Palmyra, *in situ. Funerary: Cession. On door lintel.* Group: see Ber '35 p 91. Bib: *Ingholt '35 pl XXXIX, 2, XL*; MF Concession 19.

1 ywlys 'wrlys nwrbl wml' bny mlkw rb' br mlkw br mlkw br nwrbl dy mtqr' 'sy' rḥq mn šṭr' grbyy' dy hw m'lk mn bb' 'l ymyn' btr 'ksdr'
2 bn' trn qrqsy' gwmḥyn dkn tlt' mdnḥy' lywlys 'wrlys 'grp' br 'gtps br ḥry hlydyrs yrḥbwl' br ḥyrn bwn' lh wlbnwhy wlbn' bnyhn l'lm' šnt 5.100+20+5

PAT 0051 **Ber '35 p 100** IX **A.D. 241**
Prov: Palmyra, S-W Necropolis, Tomb of Malku. Loc: Palmyra, *in situ*. *Funerary: Cession. On doorway.* Group: see Ber '35 p 91. Bib: *Ingholt '35 pl XLI, 2*; MF Concession 20.

1 byrḥ ʾyr dy šnt
2 5.100+40+10+2 ywlys ʾwrlys ʿgʾ br rwḥbl
3 rḥq lywlys ʾwrlys lmlkʾ
4 br šlmn gpn mn ṭksys dy gwm
5 ḥyn trn dy hnwn bʾksdrʾ
6 mʿlyk bbʾ ʿl ymynk bzbwq
7 tʾ lh wlbnwhy wlbny bnwhy
8 lyqrhwn dy ʿlmʾ

PAT 0052 **Ber '35 p 102** X **A.D. 249**
Prov: Palmyra, S-W Necropolis, Tomb of Malku. Loc: Palmyra, *in situ*. *Funerary: Cession. On doorjamb.* Group: see Ber '35 p 91. Bib: *Ingholt '35 pl XLI, 1*; MF Concession 21.

1 byrḥ ʾb dy šnt 5.100+60
2 ʿgʾ br rwḥbl rḥq lmlkw br hrms
3 ʾbyhn mn gwmḥʾ ḥd dy hw gwʾ ʿl ymynʾ

PAT 0053 **Ber '35 p 102** XI **A.D. 267**
Prov: Palmyra, S-W Necropolis, Tomb of Malku. Loc: Palmyra, *in situ*. *Funerary: Cession. On inside of doorway.* Group: see Ber '35 p 91. Bib: *Ingholt '35 pl XLII, 1*; MF Concession 22.

1 gwmḥyʾ ʾln ʾrbʿʾ dy hnwn
2 bʾksdrʾ mʿrbyʾ bbʾ dy mʿrtʾ
3 ʿl smlʾ mnhwn trn mʿlyk ʾksdrʾ {ʿl}
4 ʿl ymynk gwyn dbqyn ʿrsʾ wtrn
5 mʿlyk ʾksdrʾ šrk ʿl smlʾ hnwn wqšṭyhwn
6 rḥq ddywn br ḥby br dygns lʾmw
7 brt bsʾ šʿrwnʾ lh wlbnh wlbny
8 byh l[yqrhwn dy ʿ]lmʾ
9 byrḥ šbṭ dy šnt
10 5.100+60+10+5+3

PAT 0054 **Ber '35 p 104** XII **A.D. 267**
Prov: Palmyra, S-W Necropolis, Tomb of Malku. Loc: Palmyra, *in situ*. *Funerary: Cession. On jamb.* Group: see Ber '35 p 91. Bib: *Ingholt '35 pl XLII, 2*; MF Concession 23.

1 gwmḥyʾ ʾln tr̊n dy bsṭr̊ʾ
2 ymnyʾ mʿlyk bbʾ dy mʿr̊tʾ
3 ʿl smlʾ dy mn btr̊ gwmḥʾ
4 qdmyʾ bynwt tr̊tn kpyʾ
5 pnn lsmlʾ wqsṭyhwn r̊ḥqt
6 ʾmw br̊t bsʾ šʿr̊wnʾ lywlyʾ
7 ʾwr̊lyʾ ʾgtwnʾ br̊ bsʾ gr̊mnʾ
8 wbʿly br̊ ʿbdy ʿdwn lhwn wlbnyhwn
9 wlbnʾ bnyhwn lyqr̊hwn dy ʿlmʾ
10 byr̊ḥ ʾdr̊ šnt 5.100+60+10+5+3

PAT 0055 **Ber '35 p 107** XIII **A.D. 274**
Prov: Palmyra, S-W Necropolis, Tomb of Malku. Loc: Palmyra, *in situ*. *Funerary: Cession. On doorway.* Group: see Ber '35 p 91. Bib: *Ingholt '35 pl XLII, 1*; MF Concession 24; Déd p 301.

1 gwmḥyʾ ʾln ḥmšʾ
2 tymnʾ mksdrʾ
3 mqbltʾ gwyʾ
4 rḥqt tmʾ brt
5 ʿbdʿswdr br
6 yrḥbwlʾ lʾbgr
7 br tymʾ br ʿnn
8 lh wlbnwhy wbny bn[why]
9 [dy] ʿlmʾ qmt šnt
10 5.100+80+5 byrḥ
11 sywn

PAT 0056 **Ber '35 p 109** I **A.D. 142**
Prov: Palmyra, S-W Necropolis, Tomb of Nasrallat. Loc: Palmyra, *in situ*. *Funerary: Foundation. On door lintel.* Group: Ber '35 pp 108-14. Bib: *Ingholt '35 pl XLIV*; MF Fondation 48.

1 Τὸ σπήλαιον τοῦ ταφεῶνος ἐποίησεν
Νασραλλαθος Μαλχου τοῦ Νασραλλαθου αὐτῷ
καὶ υἱοῖς ἄρσεσι καὶ υἱωνοῖς καὶ ἐγγόνοις αὐ-
2 τοῦ ὁμοίως ἄρσεσι ἔτους τρίτου πεντηκοστοῦ υ
Δαισίῳ

1 bt ʿlmʾ dnh ʿbd nṣrlt br mlkw br nṣrlt lh
wlbnwhy dkryʾ wlbnʾ bnwhy dkryʾ lyqrhwn dy
ʿlmʾ byrḥ sywn šnt 4.100+40+10+3

PAT 0057 **Ber '35 p 110** II **A.D. 263**
Prov: Palmyra, S-W Necropolis, Tomb of Nasrallat. Loc: Palmyra, *in situ*. *Funerary: Cession. On door lintel.* Group: Ber '35 pp 108-14. Bib: *Ingholt '35 pl XLIV*; MF Concession 46.

1 Ἐξεδρῶν δυεῖν ἐκ τοῦδε τοῦ σπηλαίου τοῦ ταφαιῶνος εἰσιόντων τὸ τοῦ σπηλαίου θύρωμα ἐν δεξίοις καὶ ἐωνίμοις σὺν δι-
2 καίοις πᾶσι ἐξεχώρησεν Ιούλιος Αὐρήλιος Ιεδειβηλος Αβισαμαια τοῦ Μαλχη Ιουλία Αυρηλία Αμαθη Βωλαζαιου τοῦ
3 Μοκιμου αὐτῇ τε καὶ υἱοῖς καὶ ὑωνοῖς εἰς τὸ παντελὲς μηνὶ Δαισίῳ τοῦ δοφ' ἔτους

1 'ksdryn trn mn m'rt' dh dy bt 'lm' m'lyk
bb' dy ymynk wdy smlk wqšṭyhwn rḥq ywlys
'wrlys ydy'bl br 'bdšmy' br mlk'
2 lywly' 'wrly' 'mt' brt bwlḥzy mqymw lh
wlbnh bnh lyqrhwn dy 'lm' byrḥ sywn dy šnt
5.100+60+10+4
line 2: *lywly' 'wrly' 'mt' brt* after Stark PN

PAT 0058 **Ber '35 p 112** III **A.D. 265**
Prov: Palmyra, S-W Necropolis, Tomb of Nasrallat. Loc: Palmyra, *in situ*. *Funerary: Cession. On doorjamb.* Group: Ber '35 pp 108-14. Bib: *Ingholt '35 pl XLIV, 1*; MF Concession 47.

1 ywlys 'wrlys ydy'bl
2 br 'bšmy' mlk' rḥq
3 mn gwmḥyn 'rb'' dy mnhwn
4 smlyn tlt' w'ḥrn'
5 m'rby wsmly mn 'ksdr'
6 mqbl' m'lyk hw 'ksdr'
7 'l ymynk wqšṭyhwn lywly'
8 'wrly' 'mt' brt bwlḥzy
9 mqymw lh wlbnh wlbn'
10 bnyhw lyqrhwn dy 'lm'
11 byrḥ 'dr šnt 5.100+60+10+5+1

PAT 0059 **Ber '35 p 115** **A.D. 186**
Prov: Palmyra, S-W Necropolis, Tomb of Bar'a. Loc: Palmyra, *in situ*. *Funerary: Foundation. On door lintel.* Group: Ber '35 pp 114-16. Bib: *Ingholt '35 pl XLV, 2*; MF Fondation 58.

1 Τὸ σπήλαιον τοῦ ταφεῶνος ὀρύξας ἐκαλλιέργησεν Βαρεας Βωννουρου τοῦ Βαρεα τοῦ Ζαβδααθους Θοσαβεβου αὐτῷ καὶ υἱοῖς καὶ
2 υἱωνοῖς εἰς τὸ παντελὲς ἔτους ζϘυ' μηνὸς Ξανδικοῦ

1 m'rt' dh bt 'lm' 'bd br'' br bnwr br
br'' zbd'th tšbb lh
2 wlbnwhy wlbn' bnwhy lyqrhn dy 'lm' byrḥ
nysn dy šnt 4.100+80+10+5+2

PAT 0060 **Ber '36 p 84** 1 **n. d.**
Prov: Palmyra, Temple of Bel, reemployed. Loc: Not known. *Dedicatory. On stone tablet.* Bib: *Ingholt '36 pl XVIII, 1.*

1 dkrn ṭb qdm br[yk]
2 šmh l'lm' ṭb'
3 wrḥmn' 'bd qbt'
4 dh wtṣbyth klh
5 [....]wl[....]

PAT 0061 **Ber '36 p 88** 2 **n. d.**
Prov: Palmyra, Temple of Bel, reemployed. Loc: Beirut, Musée National, 520. *Honorific. On column fragment.* Bib: *Ingholt '36 pl XX, 2*; BMB '55 p 43 (14); RosAH 19.

1 ṣlm ḥdwdn
2 br dkt' dy
3 twn' br ḥry
4 btprmwn

PAT 0062 **Ber '36 p 92** 3 **n. d.**
Prov: Palmyra. Loc: Beirut, Musée National. *Dedicatory. On altar fragment.* Bib: *Ingholt '36 pl XVIII, 3*; BMB '55 p 43 (15).

1 bryk šmh
2 l'lm' ṭb'
3 wrḥmn' mwd'
4 [...]

PAT 0063 **Ber ʾ36 p 94** 4 **n. d.**
Prov: Palmyra, Temple of Bel, reemployed. Loc: Palmyra, Museum, A 453. *Honorific. On stone slab.* Bib: *Ingholt ʾ36 pl XIX, 1.* (For Ber ʾ36 p 94 no. 5 see Inv 8 200).

1 wrwd ʾrgbṭʾ

PAT 0064 **Ber ʾ36 p 97** 6 **n. d.**
Prov: Palmyra. Loc: Palmyra, Museum, A 281. *Dedicatory. On stone jar fragment.* Bib: *Ingholt ʾ36 pl XX, 1.*

1 [...] wzbdʿth bny mlkw br ḥyrn

PAT 0065 **Ber ʾ36 p 99** 7 **n. d.**
Prov: Palmyra. Loc: Palmyra, Museum, 519. *Dedicatory. On stone plaque.* Bib: *Ingholt ʾ36 pl XIX, 2*; Déd p 182; BMB ʾ55 p 43 (16).

1 Ακαμαθη Μαλ[ης]
2 Ελαβηλου ἐυχήν

1 [l]ʾ[lhʾ rbʾ] m[r]ʾ nšmtʾ wlbryk
2 [šmh lʿlmʾ] mwdyʾ ʾqmt brt
3 [mlʾ br ʾ]lhbl dy qrth bḥškt!ʾ
4 [...]wtwb yʿnnh
5 [......]dyʾ lh dy bʿyrwth
6 [......]mn ṭlyw ʿd sybw
line 3: bḥškt!ʾ for bḥškkʾ

PAT 0066 **Ber ʾ38 p 94** (18 I) **A.D. 133**
Prov: Palmyra, S-W Necropolis, Hypogeum of Yarhai, ʿAtenuri, and Zabdibol ("Tomb of Three Brothers"). Loc: Palmyra, *in situ. Funerary. On door lintel.* Group: Ber ʾ38 pp 93-103; C4171-75; Syr ʾ36 p 355 = Tad 27. Bib: *Ingholt ʾ38 pl XXXIV, 2*; MF Fondation 43.

1 yrḥy br mqymw
2 ʿtnwry br mqymw
3 zbdbwl br̊ mqymw
4 ʿbd mʿr̊tʾ dnh
5 šnt 4.100+40+5
6 lbnyn wlbnʾ bnyn

PAT 0067 **Ber ʾ38 p 95** (18 II) **A.D. 194**
Prov: Palmyra, S-W Necropolis, Hypogeum of Yarhai, ʿAtenuri, and Zabdibol. Loc: Palmyra, *in situ. Funerary: Cession. On door lintel.* Group: see Ber ʾ38 p 94. Bib: *Ingholt ʾ38 pl XXXIV, 2*; MF Concession 36.

1 byr̊ḥ ʾyr̊ ywm ḥmštʾ dy
2 šnt 5.100+5 mqymw br̊ lšmš
3 br̊ ḥpr̊y wʾqmt bt yr̊ḥy br̊
4 mqymw ʾḥbr̊ lšlmn bṙ qlybw
5 br̊ ʾlhbl wltymw br̊ dbḥ br̊ ḥmyn
6 wʾr̊ḥq lhwn mn pnyn tr̊tn dy sṭr̊ʾ
7 gr̊byyʾ wtymnyʾ šḥymyʾ ʿd qwpyʾ
8 dy kptʾ mqbltʾ dy ʾksdr̊ʾ mʿr̊byʾ
9 dy yhwn ḥpr̊yn wbnn mqbr̊n hyk dy ṣbyn
10 lhwn wlbnyhwn wlbny bnyhwn lʿlmʾ

PAT 0068 **Ber ʾ38 p 101** (18 IIIa) **n. d.**
Prov: Palmyra, S-W Necropolis, Hypogeum of Yarhai, ʿAtenuri, and Zabdibol. Loc: Palmyra, *in situ. Funerary. On relief.* Group: see Ber ʾ38 p 94. Bib: *Ingholt ʾ38 pl XXXVII, 2, 3.*

1 ṣlm bsʾ
2 nqbʾ

PAT 0069 **Ber ʾ38 p 102** (18 IIIb) **n. d.**
Prov: Palmyra, S-W Necropolis, Hypogeum of Yarhai, ʿAtenuri, and Zabdibol. Loc: Palmyra, *in situ. Funerary. On relief.* Group: see Ber ʾ38 p 94. Bib: *Ingholt ʾ38 pl XXXVII, 4.*

1 ṣlm
2 mlwkʾ ḥbl

PAT 0070 **Ber ʾ38 p 102** (18 IIIc) **n. d.**
Prov: Palmyra, S-W Necropolis, Hypogeum of Yarhai, ʿAtenuri, and Zabdibol. Loc: Palmyra, *in situ. Funerary. On relief.* Group: see Ber ʾ38 p 94. Bib: *Ingholt ʾ38 pl XXXVII, 5.*

1 ṣlmt
2 ʾmtʾ
3 ʾtth

PAT 0071 **Ber ’38 p 104** (19) **A.D. 251**
Prov: Palmyra, S-W Necropolis, Tomb of Seleukos. Loc: Palmyra, *in situ. Funerary, cession. On door lintel.* Bib: *Ingholt ’38 pl XXXVIII, 2*; MF Concession 44.

1 slwqs br̊ typyls br̊ slwqs r̊ḥq gwmḥyn ʿsr̊ʾ dy bʾksdr̊ʾ
2 mʿlyk bbʾ lqblʾ lyr̊ḥbwlʾ br̊ sbynʾ wṭr̊nʾ br̊ tymʾ ḥlʾ lh
3 wlbnwhy wlb<n>y bnwhy lyqr̊hwn dy ʿlmʾ šnt 5.100+60+2 byr̊ḥ

PAT 0072 **Ber ’38 p 106** (20 I) **A.D. 186**
Prov: Palmyra, S-W Necropolis, Hypogeum of Lišamš. Loc: Palmyra, *in situ. Funerary, cession. On door lintel.* Group: Ber ’38 pp 106-19; C4194ff.. Bib: *Ingholt ’38 pl XL, 1*; MF Concession 9.

1 lšmš br lšmš br tymʾ wʾmdy br ydyʿbl bʿly ʾḥyn
2 bny ʾmʾ ḥbr wrdn br ḥry ʾnṭyks rpbwl br ʾnṭyks ʿtʿqb
3 br rpbwl wyhb lh sṭrʾ grbyyʾ dy hw ʾksdrʾ dy ʿl ymynʾ
4 wštt gwmḥwhy dy btrh byrḥ ʾyr šnt 4.100+80+10+5+2

PAT 0073 **Ber ’38 p 109** (20 I bis) **n. d.**
Prov: Palmyra, S-W Necropolis, Tomb of Lišamš. Loc: Beirut, Musée National. *Funerary, cession. On stone tablet.* Group: Ber ’38 pp 106-19. Bib: *Ingholt ’38 pl XL, 3*; BMB ’55 p 44 (18).

1 [lšm]š br̊ lšm[š br̊ tymʾ wʾmdy]
2 [br̊ ydy]ʿbl bʿly [ʾḥyn bnʾ ʾmʾ ḥbr̊]
3 [mn m]ʿr̊tʾ dh lwr̊dn [br̊ ḥr̊y ʾnṭyks]
4 [r̊pbw]l br̊ ʾnṭyks ʿt[ʿqb br̊ r̊pbwl]
5 [ʾks]dr̊ʾ dnh wgwm[ḥwhy wštʾ dy btr̊h]
6 [gwmḥ]why ʿd kptʾ [mqbltʾ]

Nearly exact replica of preceding inscription, Ber ’38 p 106 (20 I).

PAT 0074 **Ber ’38 p 109** (20 II) **A.D. 188**
Prov: Palmyra, S-W Necropolis, Tomb of Lišamš. Loc: Palmyra, *in situ. Funerary, cession. On doorjamb.* Group: Ber ’38 pp 106-19. Bib: *Ingholt ’38 pl XL, 2.*

1 byr̊ḥ knwn šnt 5.100
2 ʾḥbr̊ lšmš br̊ lšmš
3 br̊ tymʾ mn mʿr̊tʾ
4 dh lbwnʾ br̊ bwlḥʾ
5 br̊ bwnʾ br̊
6 yqr̊wr̊ ʾḥbr̊th
7 mn ʾksdr̊ʾ mqblʾ
8 gwmḥyn tmnyʾ mn
9 ymynk ʾr̊bʿʾ wmn
10 smlk ʾr̊bʿʾ

PAT 0075 **Ber ’38 p 110** (20 III) **A.D. 228**
Prov: Palmyra, S-W Necropolis, Tomb of Lišamš. Loc: Palmyra, *in situ. Funerary, cession. On doorjamb.* Group: Ber ’38 pp 106-19. Bib: *Ingholt ’38 pl XL, 2*; MF Concession 11.

1 byr̊ḥ ʾyr̊ šnt 5.100+20+10+5+4
2 ʾwr̊lys wr̊dn br̊ ḥr̊y ʾnṭykys
3 r̊pbwl br̊ ʿtʿqb r̊ḥq lʾwr̊lys
4 mlkw br̊ šlmn bnʾ mn ʾtr̊ʾ
5 šḥmʾ mʿr̊by ʾksdr̊ʾ bplṭyʾ
6 mʿlyk ʿl ymynk lh wlbnwhy wlbnʾ
7 bnwh lʿlmʾ

PAT 0076 **Ber ’38 p 114** (*sub* 20 III: a) **n. d.**
Prov: Palmyra, S-W Necropolis, Tomb of Lišamš. Loc: Palmyra, *in situ. Funerary, graffito. On tomb wall.* Group: Ber ’38 pp 106-19. Bib: *Ingholt ’38 pl XLI, 1.*

1 mlkw šlmn
2 mlkw šlmn
3 mlkw šlmn
4 mlkw šlmn
5 mlkw šlmn
6 mlkw šlmn
7 mlkw šlmn
8 mlkw šlmn
9 mlkw šlmn
10 mlkw šlmn

PAT 0077 **Ber ’38 p 114** (*sub* 20 III: b) **n. d.**
Prov: Palmyra, S-W Necropolis, Tomb of Lišamš. Loc: Palmyra, *in situ. Funerary, graffito. On tomb wall.* Group: Ber ’38 pp 106-19. Bib: *Ingholt ’38 pl XLI, 2.*

1 ʿzyzw ʾbyḥy
2 ʿzyzw ʾbyḥy

PAT 0078 **Ber ’38 p 114** (*sub* 20 III: c) **n. d.**
Prov: Palmyra, S-W Necropolis, Tomb of Lišamš. Loc: Palmyra, *in situ. Funerary, graffito. On tomb wall.* Group: Ber ’38 pp 106-19. Bib: *Ingholt ’38 pl XLI, 3.*

1 šky br mqy

PAT 0079 **Ber ’38 p 114** (*sub* 20 III: d) **n. d.**
Prov: Palmyra, S-W Necropolis, Tomb of Lišamš. Loc: Palmyra, *in situ. Funerary, graffito. On tomb wall.* Group: Ber ’38 pp 106-19. Bib: *Ingholt ’38 pl XLI, 4.*

ἀπέθανεν

1 mlkw šlmn
2 mlkw šlmn
3 mlkw šlmn
4 mlkw šlmn
5 mlkw šlmn
6 mlkw šlmn

PAT 0080 **Ber ’38 p 114** (*sub* 20 III: e) **n. d.**
Prov: Palmyra, S-W Necropolis, Tomb of Lišamš. Loc: Palmyra, *in situ. Funerary, graffito. On wall.* Group: Ber ’38 pp 106-19. Bib: *Ingholt ’38.*

1 tymnʾ brʿʾ

PAT 0081 **Ber ’38 p 114** (*sub* 20 III: f) **n. d.**
Prov: Palmyra, S-W Necropolis, Tomb of Lišamš. Loc: Palmyra, *in situ. Funerary, graffito. On wall.* Group: Ber ’38 pp 106-19.

1 brʿʾ br syry

PAT 0082 **Ber ’38 p 114** (*sub* 20 III: g) **n. d.**
Prov: Palmyra, S-W Necropolis, Tomb of Lišamš. Loc: Palmyra, *in situ. Funerary, graffito. On tomb wall.* Group: Ber ’38 pp 106-19.

1 sry wtymnʾ

PAT 0083 **Ber ’38 p 115** (*sub* 20 III) **n. d.**
Prov: Palmyra, S-W Necropolis, Tomb of Lišamš. Loc: Palmyra, *in situ. Funerary, graffito. On tomb wall.* Group: Ber ’38 pp 106-19. Bib: *Ingholt ’38 pl XLI, 5.*

1 kytwt
2 mzbnʾ
3 ʾtʿqb

PAT 0084 **Ber ’38 p 115** (*sub* 20 III) **n. d.**
Prov: Palmyra, S-W Necropolis, Tomb of Lišamš. Loc: Palmyra, *in situ. Funerary, graffito. On wall.* Group: Ber ’38 pp 106-19. Bib: *Ingholt ’38 fig 1 p 116.*

1 nsʾ
2 dkyr
3 bṭb
4 [...]
5 [...]
6 [...]
7 [...]
8 myt

PAT 0085 **Ber ’38 p 116** (*sub* 20 III) **n. d.**
Prov: Palmyra, S-W Necropolis, Tomb of Lišamš. Loc: Palmyra, *in situ. Funerary, graffito. On tomb wall.* Group: Ber ’38 pp 106-19. Bib: *Ingholt ’38 pl XLII, 1.*

1 sry brʿʾ sry

PAT 0086 **Ber ’38 p 116** (*sub* 20 III) **n. d.**
Prov: Palmyra, S-W Necropolis, Tomb of Lišamš. Loc: Palmyra, *in situ. Funerary, graffito. On wall.* Group: Ber ’38 pp 106-19.

1 tymnʾ brʿʾ
2 tymnʾ brʿʾ
3 tymnʾ brʿʾ
4 tymnʾ brʿʾ

PAT 0087 **Ber '38 p 116** (*sub* 20 III) **n. d.**
Prov: Palmyra, S-W Necropolis, Tomb of Lišamš. Loc: Palmyra, *in situ*. *Funerary, graffito. On tomb wall.* Group: Ber '38 pp 106-19.

1 tymnʾ brʿʾ

PAT 0088 **Ber '38 p 116** (*sub* 20 III) **n. d.**
Prov: Palmyra, S-W Necropolis, Tomb of Lišamš. Loc: Palmyra, *in situ*. *Funerary, graffito. On tomb wall.* Group: Ber '38 pp 106-19.

1 brʿʾ sry syry

PAT 0089 **Ber '38 p 116** (*sub* 20 III) **n. d.**
Prov: Palmyra, S-W Necropoli, Tomb of Lišamš. Loc: Palmyra, *in situ*. *Funerary, graffito. On tomb wall.* Group: Ber '38 pp 106-19.

1 kytwt mzbnʾ

PAT 0090 **Ber '38 p 116** (*sub* 20 III)
Prov: Palmyra, S-W Necropolis, Tomb of Lišamš. Loc: Palmyra, *in situ*. *Funerary, graffito. On tomb wall.* Group: Ber '38 pp 106-19.

1 mzbnʾ

PAT 0091 **Ber '38 p 116** (*sub* 20 III) **n. d.**
Prov: Palmyra, S-W Necropolis, Tomb of Lišamš. Loc: Palmyra, *in situ*. *Funerary, graffito. On tomb wall.* Group: Ber '38 pp 106-19.

1 kytwt mzbnʾ
2 kytwt mzbnʾ
3 kytwt mzbnʾ

PAT 0092 **Ber '38 p 117** (*sub* 20 III) **n. d.**
Prov: Palmyra, S-W Necropolis, Tomb of Lišamš. Loc: Palmyra, *in situ*. *Funerary. On stele.* Group: Ber '38 pp 106-19. Bib: *Ingholt '38 pl XLII, 2*; Starcky '55 p 44 (19).

1 ḥbl
2 lšmš br
3 rmy rpʾl

PAT 0093 **Ber '38 p 118** (*sub* 20 III) **n. d.**
Prov: Palmyra, S-W Necropolis, Tomb of Lišamš. Loc: Palmyra, *in situ*. *Funerary. On sarcophagus.* Group: Ber '38 pp 106-19. Bib: *Ingholt '38 pl XLIV, 1*.

1 šlm brt ʿgʾ ḥbl

PAT 0094 **Ber '38 p 120** (21 I)
Prov: Palmyra, S-W Necropolis, Hypogeum of ʿAbdʿastor. Loc: Palmyra, *in situ*. *Funerary, funerary. On stone tablet.* Group: Ber '38 pp 119-40. Bib: *Ingholt '38 pl XLVI, 2*; MF Fondation 26.

(Follows the Aramaic text)
4 ʾΑβδαασθῶ[ρο]ν Νουρβήλου
5 ὁ [ἰα]τρός

1 bt ʿlmʾ dnh ʿbd ʿbdʿstwr br nwrbl
2 ʾsyʾ br khylw br ʿtnwry ʾṣwly lh wlbnwhy
3 byrḥ nysn 4.100+10

PAT 0095 **Ber '38 p 124** (21 II)
Prov: Palmyra, S-W Necropolis, Hypogeum of ʿAbdʿastor. Loc: Palmyra, *in situ*. *Funerary: Cession. On door lintel.* Group: Ber '38 pp 119-40. Bib: *Ingholt '38 pl XLVII, 1*; MF Concession 41.

1 ʾksdrʾ smlyʾ mʿlyk
2 mʿrtʾ ʿl ymynʾ sṭr mn gwmḥyn trn bryyn ymnyyn
3 mqdšyn rḥq ywlyʾ ʾwrlyʾ šlmt brt ʿbdʿstwr br
4 yrḥbwlʾ wʾmdbw brt ḥry lwqys ʾwrlys brsmyʾ

5 mprnsytʾ dy bwnʾ br rbʾl brh lywlyʾ ʾwrlyʾ mlkw
6 br ʿgylw br šlmn gmḥyn tmnyʾ mdnḥyyn mʿlyk ʾksdrʾ
7 ʿl ymynʾ wlmʿynʾ brt bwnʾ br bwlḥʾ gwmḥyn mʿrbyyn
8 štʾ mʿlyk ʾksdrʾ ʿl smlʾ wmqblyn gwmḥyn tltʾ
9 dy plg bnyhwn lhwn wlbnyhwn wlbny bnyhwn lʿlmʾ byrḥ nysn
10 šnt 5.100+40+10

PAT 0096 **Ber ʾ38 p 127** **n. d.**
Prov: Palmyra, S-W Necropolis, Hypogeum of ʿAbdʿastor. Loc: Palmyra, *in situ*. *Funerary*. *On wall*. Group: Ber ʾ38 pp 119-40. Bib: *Ingholt ʾ38 pl XLVIII, 2*.

1 btšmyʾ brt nsʾ
2 ʾmh dy tymsʾ

PAT 0097 **Ber ʾ38 p 133** (21 III)
Prov: Palmyra, S-W Necropolis, Hypogeum of ʿAbdʿastor. Loc: Palmyra, *in situ*. *Funerary: curse*. *On door*. Group: Ber ʾ38 pp 119-40. Bib: *Ingholt ʾ38 fig 2 p 133, fig 3 p 134*; MFm(alédiction) 1.

1 mnw
2 dy
3 yzbn
4 ʿr̊bʾ
5 dy
6 qdm
7 mʿr̊tʾ
8 ʿl
9 npšh
10 ḥṭʾ
11 tdqrʿʾ
12 ʾš[..]h
13 ʾrḥ
14 ḥṭ[ʾ]

PAT 0098 **Ber ʾ38 p 134** (*sub* 21 III)
Prov: Palmyra, S-W Necropolis, Hypogeum of ʿAbdʿastor. Loc: Palmyra, *in situ*. *Funerary, graffito*. *On wall*. Group: Ber ʾ38 pp 119-40.

1 ḥbl brdwny

PAT 0099 **Ber ʾ38 p 135** (*sub* 21 III: a)
Prov: Palmyra, S-W Necropolis, Hypogeum of ʿAbdʿastor. Loc: Palmyra, *in situ*. *Funerary, graffito*. *On wall*. Group: Ber ʾ38 pp 119-40. Bib: *Ingholt ʾ38 pl XLIX, 2*.

1 dkyr ḥyrʾ br ʿwydlt br mqymw ʿlbn

PAT 0100 **Ber ʾ38 p 135** (*sub* 21 III: b)
Prov: Palmyra, S-W Necropolis, Hypogeum of ʿAbdʿastor. Loc: Palmyra, *in situ*. *Funerary, graffito*. *On wall*. Group: Ber ʾ38 pp 119-40.

1 mrty
2 ʿgylw
3 ḥbl

PAT 0101 **Ber ʾ38 p 135** (21 IVA)
Prov: Palmyra, S-W Necropolis, Hypogeum of ʿAbdʿastor. Loc: Palmyra, *in situ*. *Funerary, graffito*. *On wall*. Group: Ber ʾ38 pp 119-40.

1 ʾnʾ btmrṣw
2 wbnh
3 ḥbl

PAT 0102 **Ber ʾ38 p 135** (21 IVB) **n. d.**
Prov: Palmyra, S-W Necropolis, Hypogeum of ʿAbdʿastor. Loc: Palmyra, *in situ*. *Funerary, graffito*. *On wall*. Group: Ber ʾ38 pp 119-40.

1 ʾnʾ bt tymrṣw
2 ḥbl ʿgylw br ʾnʾ
3 ʾbʾ ḥbl

PAT 0103 **Ber ʾ38 p 135** (21 IVC) **n. d.**
Prov: Palmyra, S-W Necropolis, Hypogeum of ʿAbdʿastor. Loc: Palmyra, *in situ*. *Funerary, graffito*. *On wall*. Group: Ber ʾ38 pp 119-40.

1 bʿltgʾ
2 br ʿgʾ
3 ḥbl

PAT 0104 **Ber '38 p 135** (21 IVD) **n. d.**
Prov: Palmyra, S-W Necropolis, Hypogeum of ʿAbdʿastor. Loc: Palmyra, *in situ*. *Funerary*. *On wall*. Group: Ber '38 pp 119-40.

1 mwsʾ
2 br ʿgʾ
3 ḥbl

PAT 0105 **Ber '38 p 135** (21 IVE) **n. d.**
Prov: Palmyra, S-W Necropolis, Hypogeum of ʿAbdʿastor. Loc: Palmyra, *in situ*. *Funerary, graffito*. *On wall*. Group: Ber '38 pp 119-40.

1 bty
2 br ʿgʾ
3 ḥbl

PAT 0106 **Ber '38 p 135** (21 IVF) **n. d.**
Prov: Palmyra, S-W Necropolis, Hypogeum of ʿAbdʿastor. Loc: Palmyra, *in situ*. *Funerary*. *On wall*. Group: Ber '38 pp 119-40.

1 ʾhʾ
2 brt ʿgʾ
3 ḥbl

PAT 0107 **Ber '38 p 137** (*sub* 21 IV)
Prov: Palmyra, S-W Necropolis, Hypogeum of ʿAbdʿastor. Loc: Palmyra, *in situ*. *Funerary, graffito*. *On wall*. Group: Ber '38 pp 119-40.

1 dkyr
2 zbdʾ rp[..]
3 mqymw
4 bṭb

PAT 0108 **Ber '38 p 137** (*sub* 21 IV)
Prov: Palmyra, S-W Necropolis, Hypogeum of ʿAbdʿastor. Loc: Palmyra, *in situ*. *Funerary, graffito*. *On wall*. Group: Ber '38 pp 119-40.

1 dkyr
2 zb[dʾ]
3 bṭb

PAT 0109 **Ber '38 p 137** (*sub* 21 IV)
Prov: Palmyra, S-W Necropolis, Hypogeum of ʿAbdʿastor. Loc: Palmyra, *in situ*. *Funerary, graffito*. *On wall*. Group: Ber '38 pp 119-40.

1 dkyr

PAT 0110 **Ber '38 p 137** (*sub* 21 IV)
Prov: Palmyra, S-W Necropolis, Hypogeum of ʿAbdʿastor. Loc: Palmyra, *in situ*. *Funerary, graffito*. *On wall*. Group: Ber '38 pp 119-40.

1 dkyr
2 zbdʾ
3 rb[..]
4 bṭb

PAT 0111 **Ber '38 p 137** (*sub* 21 IV)
Prov: Palmyra, S-W Necropolis, Hypogeum of ʿAbdʿastor. Loc: Palmyra, *in situ*. *Funerary, graffito*. *On wall*. Group: Ber '38 pp 119-40.

1 dkyr
2 mqymw br
3 blšwry
4 bṭb

PAT 0112 **Ber '38 p 137** (*sub* 21 IV)
Prov: Palmyra, S-W Necropolis, Hypogeum of ʿAbdʿastor. Loc: Palmyra, *in situ*. *Funerary, graffito*. *On wall*. Group: Ber '38 pp 119-40.

1 mqy
2 ydyʿ
3 ʾḥwhy

PAT 0113 **Ber '38 p 137** (*sub* 21 IV)
Prov: Palmyra, S-W Necropolis, Hypogeum of ʿAbdʿastor. Loc: Palmyra, *in situ*. *Funerary, graffito*. *On wall*. Group: Ber '38 pp 119-40.

1 dkyr
2 zbdʿth
3 ydyʿ ʾḥwh ḥbl

PAT 0114 **Ber '38 p 138** (*sub* 21 IV)
Prov: Palmyra, S-W Necropolis, Hypogeum of ʿAbdʿastor. Loc: Palmyra Museum. *Funerary. On statue.* Group: Ber '38 pp 119-40. Bib: *Ingholt '38 pl XLIX, 3.*

1 [..]bʾ br
2 ʿtʿqb
3 ḥbl

PAT 0115 **Ber '70 p 66** (1) **A.D. (147)**
Prov: Palmyra, Temple of Bel. Loc: Palmyra Museum. *Honorific. On console of statue.* Bib: *Gawlikowski '70a fig 1.*

1 [... Σοαδου τοῦ Βηλιαδους τοῦ
2 Σ]οαδου τοῦ Θαιμισαμσου ἀνήγειρεν Ἰαρα[ιος]
3 Ὀγηλου τοῦ Θαιμαεους τοῦ Ἀειδααναυ Ἀσοραι-
4 ου τοῦ Ζαβδιβωλου τοῦ Ἀειδααναυ ὁ φίλος
5 αὐτοῦ τειμῆς χάριν μηνὸς Δύστρου ην[υ']

7 ṣlmʾ dnh dy šʿdw br blydʿ br šʿdw br
8 tymšmš dy ʾqym lh yrḥy br ʿgylw br
9 tymḥʾ br ʾydʿn ʾsry br zbdbwl br
10 ʾydʿn rḥmh lyqrh byrḥ ʾdr šnt
11 4.100+[4020+10]+5+3

PAT 0116 **Ber '70 p 67** (2) **A.D. (249)**
Prov: Palmyra, Temple of Bel. Loc: Palmyra Museum. *Honorific. On stone fragment, from wall.* Bib: *Gawlikowski '70a fig 2.* (No. 3, fig 3, is Gk.).

1 [. . . . .]ʾ ḥyrn
2 [. . . . .]ʾ [. .]
3 [. . . . .]ʾ dy
4 [. . . . .] br
5 [byrḥ ʾ]dr
6 [šnt 5.100]+60

PAT 0117 **Ber '70 p 69** (4) **A.D. 185**
Prov: Palmyra, near Transversal Colonnade (Tomb of Theodoros). Loc: Palmyra. *Funerary: Foundation. On door lintel.* Bib: *Gawlikowski '70a fig 4, 5.*

1 τὸ μνημεῖον τοῦ τα[φεῶνος ᾠκοδόμ]ησεν Θεοδῶ[ρος] ὁ [καὶ Μ]αρωνας Μακαρ[έως] τοῦ Θεοδώρο[υ τοῦ] καὶ [Ελ]αβ[ηλου]
2 ἑαυτῷ τε καὶ υἱοῖς καὶ υἱώνοις [ἔτους ζϘυ'] μηνὸς Δείου

2 [bt] ʿlmʾ b[nʾ .... ʾl]h[b]l dy [mt]qrʾ mrwnʾ br mqymw [br]
3 [ʾlh]bl lh wl[bnwhy wlbn]y b[n]why w[ly]qr mqymw br ʾlhbl ʾbwhy wlyqr mlkw br ʾlhbl ddh wḥmwhy byrḥ knwn šnt 4.100+80+10+5+2

PAT 0118 **Ber '70 p 71** (5) **A.D. 215**
Prov: Palmyra, Valley of Tombs, Jubwel al Ḥusayniyet, Tower 83 (Tomb of Julius Aurelius Moqimu). Loc: Palmyra, *in situ. Funerary, cession. On door lintel.* Bib: *Gawlikowski '70a (no photo or squeeze possible).*

1 ἔτους ἕκτου εἴκοστο[υ] φ' Περείτιου [τὸ μνημεῖον]
2 τοῦτο ἀπενείμεν Ἰου. Αὐρ. Μοκι[μος Ὀγηλου τοῦ]
3 Ἰαριβωλεους Ἀγγαμαλου Ἰουλίῳ Αὐρ[ήλιῳ ... τοῦ Λισαμσο]
4 υ τοῦ Ἰαραιου ἐξ ἀδελφῆ[ς] αὐτοῦ [αὐτῷ καὶ υἱοῖς κ]
5 αὶ υἱώνοις ἀ[ρσέσ]ιν εἰς τὸ παραπάν

5 [byrḥ šbṭ šnt 5.100+20+5+1 qbr]ʾ
6 [dnh rḥq ywlys ʾwrly]s mqymw br ʿgylw br yrḥbwlʾ ʾ[qm]l lywlys ʾwrlys
7 [.....] br lšmš br yrḥy br ʾḥth lh wlbnwh wlbnʾ bnwh dkryʾ
8 lʿlmʾ

PAT 0119 **Ber '70 p 74** (6) **A.D. 179**
Prov: Palmyra, Diocletian Camp, Hypogeum. Loc: Palmyra, *in situ. Funerary: Foundation. On door lintel.* Group: pp 73-77. Bib: *Gawlikowski '70a fig 6*; see also C3951= Inv 5 2.

1 mʿrtʾ dh dy bt ʿlmʾ ʿbdw ʿlynʾ br ḥyrn br ʿlynʾ
2 byrḥ [k]nwn šnt 4.100+40+10

See below, Honorific inscription CIS 3951 dedicated to same tomb founder.

PAT 0120 **Ber '70 p 76** (sub 6) **n. d.**
Prov: Palmyra, Diocletian Camp, Hypogeum. Loc: Palmyra Museum. *Funerary. On relief fragment.* Group: Pp 73-77. Bib: *Gawlikowski '70a.*

(On right)
1 [.....]
2 [b]r
3 [ʿ]g[y]lw
4 [srykw]
(On left)
1 [.....]
2 b[r]
3 ʿgyl[w]
4 sry[kw]

PAT 0121 **Ber '70 p 77** (7) **n. d.**
Prov: Palmyra. Loc: Palmyra Museum. *Funerary. On sarcophagus.* Group: Hypogeum 3 (Sarcophagus of Shoraiku and SFP 1 - 3). Bib: *Gawlikowski '70a fig 7 (general) and 8-11 (details)*; p 77 fig 7 = SFP 3 (1).

1 ʾwnʾ dnh dy ʿbdw šrykw br blḥzy mlkw [. . .]

Read ʾ<r>wnʾ ʿsarcophagusʾ ?; cf Syriac at Luke 7:14 (Sinaitic); on genealogy see improved version of SFP, Sadurska and Bounni '94 p 11

PAT 0122 **Ber '70 p 79** (sub 7) **n. d.**
Prov: Palmyra. Loc: Palmyra Museum. *Funerary. On sarcophagus.* Group: Hypogeum 3 (Sarcophagus of Shoraiku and SFP 1 -3). Bib: *Gawlikowski '70a fig 7, 10 ("9" in text p 79);* = SFP 3 (2).

1 bwlnʾ br
2 šrykw br
3 blḥzy
4 ḥbl

PAT 0123 **Ber '70 p 79** (sub 7) **n. d.**
Prov: Palmyra. Loc: Palmyra Museum. *Funerary. On sarcophagus.* Group: Hypogeum 3 (Sarcophagus of Shoraiku and SFP 1 -3). Bib: *Gawlikowski '70a 7, 11 ("10" text p 79);* = SFP 3 (3).

1 ydyʿbl br
2 blḥzy mlkw
3 ḥbl

PAT 0124 **Ber '70 p 79** (sub 7) **n. d.**
Prov: Palmyra. Loc: Palmyra Museum. *Funerary. On sarcophagus.* Group: Hypogeum 3 (Sarcophagus of Shoraiku and SFP 1 -3). Bib: *Gawlikowski '70a fig 7*; = SFP 3 (4).

1 blḥzy br
2 ml[k]w
3 tym[ḥʾ]
4 ḥbl

Reading of Makowski, SFP 3 (4)

PAT 0125 **Ber '70 p 80** (sub 7) **n. d.**
Prov: Palmyra. Loc: Palmyra Museum. *Funerary. On sarcophagus.* Group: Hypogeum 3 (Sarcophagus of Shoraiku and SFP 1 -3). Bib: *Gawlikowski '70a fig 7, 10 ("11" in text)*; = SFP 3 (6).

1 šrykw br
2 blḥzy ml[kw]
3 ḥbl

Reading of Makowski, SFP 3 (6)

PAT 0126 **Ber '70 p 80** (sub 7) **n. d.**
Prov: Palmyra. Loc: Palmyra Museum. *Funerary. On sarcophagus.* Group: Hypogeum 3 (Sarcophagus of Shoraiku and SFP 1 -3). Bib: *Gawlikowski '70a fig 7, 10 ("11" in text)*; = SFP 3 (7).

1 mrty brt
2 tymḥʾ mlkw
3 ḥbl

PAT 0127 **Ber ’70 p 82** (8 A) **n. d.**
Prov: Palmyra, Valley of Tombs, Umm Belqîs, Tower 67 (Tomb of Hairan). Loc: Palmyra, *in situ. Funerary. On relief.* Group: Tomb of Hairan. Bib: *Gawlikowski ’70a fig 12.*

1 [...... blšwry br] ḥyrn br
2 [blšwry...]h lyqr

Other tombs of same family: Towers 21 (Inv 4 26) and 68 (C4124).

PAT 0128 **Ber ’70 p 82** (8 B) **n. d.**
Prov: Palmyra, Valley of Tombs, Umm Belqîs, Tower 67. Loc: Palmyra Museum. *Funerary. On relief.* Group: Tomb of Hairan. Bib: *Gawlikowski ’70a fig 12.*

1 ṣlm
2 ḥyrn
3 brh

PAT 0129 **Ber ’70 p 82** (8 C) **n. d.**
Prov: Palmyra, Valley of Tombs, Umm Belqîs, Tower 67. Loc: Palmyra Museum. *Funerary. On relief.* Group: Tomb of Hairan. Bib: *Gawlikowski ’70a fig 12.*

1 ṣlm
2 šby
3 brh

PAT 0130 **Ber ’70 p 82** (8 D) **n. d.**
Prov: Palmyra, Valley of Tombs, Umm Belqîs, Tower 67. Loc: Palmyra Museum. *Funerary. On relief.* Group: Tomb of Hairan. Bib: *Gawlikowski ’70a fig 12.*

1 [......]yt

PAT 0131 **Ber ’73 p 89** 204
Prov: Ḥā’il (Saudi Arabia). Loc: Ḥā’il (Saudi Arabia). *Unclassified. On stone.* Bib: *Winnett and Reed ’73 p 89, pl 12 (drawing), 13 (photo).*

1 md‘
2 mddy (or: mrry)
3 ‘bd (or br) grm’l

Text and notes by Starcky; reading difficult at many points

PAT 0132 **BethSh p 198** (12) **n. d.**
Prov: Beth Shearim (Israel), Catacomb 1, hall C, room I. Loc: Beth Shearim, *in situ. Funerary. On wall.* Bib: *Mazar ’73 pl VIII, 4.*

1 bnpš’
2 dtm’
3 ’mš’

PAT 0133 **BethSh p 199** (17) **n. d.**
Prov: Beth Shearim (Israel), Catacomb 1, hall E, room III. Loc: Beth Shearim, *in situ. Funerary. On wall.*

1 tdrš

PAT 0134 **BethSh p 199** (18) **n. d.**
Prov: Beth Shearim (Israel), Catacomb 1, hall E, room III. Loc: Beth Shearim, *in situ. Funerary. On wall.*

1 tdrš
2 šlwm

PAT 0135 **BethSh p 202** (83) **n. d.**
Prov: Beth Shearim (Israel), Catacomb 1, hall K, room I. Loc: Beth Shearim, *in situ. Funerary. On wall.* Bib: *Mazar ’73 fig 10 p 99.*

1 btmlkw

PAT 0136 **BethSh p 203** (86) **n. d.**
Prov: Beth Shearim (Israel), Catacomb 1, hall K, room I. Loc: Beth Shearim, *in situ. Funerary. On wall.* Bib: *Mazar ’73 pl XV, 6.*

1 bt npš’ dnh
2 dbtmlkw mq[..]’
3 [......]št[..]

PAT 0137 **BethSh p 204** (94) **n. d.**

Prov: Beth Shearim (Israel), Catacomb 1, hall K, room III. Loc: Beth Shearim, *in situ*. *Funerary. On wall.* Bib: *Mazar '73 pl XV, 7.*

1 btmlkw

PAT 0138 **BethSh p 206** (126) **n. d.**

Prov: Beth Shearim (Israel), Catacomb 3, hall E, room VI. Loc: Beth Shearim, *in situ*. *Funerary. On wall.* Bib: *Mazar '73 pl XXVII.*

1 npš ʾstr

PAT 0139 **BethSh p 207** (130) **n. d.**

Prov: Beth Shearim (Israel), Catacomb 3, hall E, room VIII. Loc: Beth Shearim, *in situ*. *Funerary. On wall.*

1 [..........]
2 [d]wrn ḥbl

PAT 0140 **BethSh p 207** (132) **n. d.**

Prov: Beth Shearim (Israel), Catacomb 3, hall E, room VIII. Loc: Beth Shearim, *in situ*. *Funerary. On wall.* Bib: *Mazar '73 fig 19.*

1 whnpš whnpš d
2 ʿtḥn

PAT 0141 **BethSh p 207** (133) **n. d.**

Prov: Beth Shearim (Israel), Catacomb 3, arcosolium 2. Loc: Beth Shearim, *in situ*. *Funerary. On rock fragment in arch.*

1 ʿtḥn

BJPES '47 p 142 (I) **n. d.**

Prov: Palmyra. Loc: Israel, private collection. *Funerary. On relief.* Bib: *Ben-Ḥayyim '47 pp 141-42.*

(On left)
1 μοκιμε
2 μαλχου
3 αλυπαι
4 χαιρε

(On right)
1 ḥbl
2 mqymw
3 mlkw
4 br nṣrʾ

BJPES '47 p 145 (III) **n. d.**

Prov: Palmyra. Loc: Not known. *Funerary. On relief.* Bib: *Ben-Ḥayyim '47, pp 144-45.*

1 [ ]ḥʾ ʾmtbʿ[l]
2 brt srykʾ

PAT 0144 **BJPES '47 p 146** (IV) **n. d.**

Prov: Palmyra. Loc: Not known. *Funerary. On relief.* Bib: *Ben-Ḥayyim '47, pp 145-46.*

1 mlkw
2 br ʿtykʾ
3 ḥbl

BJPES '47 p 146 (V) **n. d.**

Prov: Palmyra. Loc: Jerusalem, Albright Institute. *Funerary. On relief.* Bib: *Ben-Ḥayyim '47, p 146.*

1 ʿty brt
2 ʿgʾ br
3 tybwl
4 yrḥbwlʾ
5 br tybwl
6 ḥbl
Collated

PAT 0146 **BMB '55 p 30** (1) **n. d.**

Prov: Palmyra. Loc: Beirut, Musée National, 2614. *Funerary. On relief.* Bib: *Starcky '55 pl XVII, 4.*

1 ḥbl
2 bly
3 ʿttn
4 zbdʿth

PAT 0147 **BMB '55 p 33** (2) **n. d.**
Prov: Palmyra. Loc: Beirut, Musée National, 692. *Funerary. On stele.* Bib: *Starcky '55 pl XVII, 3.*

1 mqymw
2 br š'dy
3 [...] ḥbl

PAT 0148 **BMB '55 p 34** (3) **n. d.**
Prov: Palmyra. Loc: Beirut, Musée National, 589. *Funerary. On relief fragment.* Bib: *Starcky '55 pl XVIII, 3.*

1 ḥbyb'
2 br šlmn
3 ḥbl

PAT 0149 **BMB '55 p 34** (4) **n. d.**
Prov: Palmyra. Loc: Beirut, Musée National, 696. *Funerary. On stele.* Bib: *Starcky '55 pl XVIII, 1.*

1 zbdbwl br bwrp'
2 ḥbl

PAT 0150 **BMB '55 p 35** (5) **n. d.**
Prov: Palmyra. Loc: Beirut, Musée National, 506. *Funerary. On stele.* Bib: *Starcky '55 pl XVIII, 2.*

1 'myt
2 brt zbd't'
3 ḥbl

PAT 0151 **BMB '55 p 36** (6) **A.D. (149)**
Prov: Palmyra. Loc: Beirut, Musée National, 587. *Funerary. On relief fragment.* Bib: *Starcky '55 pl XVIII, 5.*

1 ṣlmt 'mtbl
2 brt bgrt
3 ḥbl šnt (5.100)+60+1
In date, hundreds supplied by editor

PAT 0152 **BMB '55 p 38** (7) **n. d.**
Prov: Palmyra. Loc: Beirut, Musée National, 701. *Funerary. On relief fragment.* Bib: *Starcky '55 pl XVIII, 4.*

1 ṣ[lmt]
2 mzb[t']
3 brt
4 mlkw
5 ḥbl

PAT 0153 **BMB '55 p 38** (8) **n. d.**
Prov: Palmyra. Loc: Beirut, Musée National, 514. *Funerary. On relief.* Bib: *Starcky '55 pl XVII, 1* (No. 9 = C4406).

1 ḥbl
2 't'm
3 brt tly'
4 br yrḥy

PAT 0154 **BMB '55 p 41** (10) **n. d.**
Prov: Ḥarbata, North of Baalbek. Loc: Beirut, Musée National, 2625, 2626. *Funerary. On relief.* Bib: *Starcky '55 pl XIX.*

1 [..] tym' br bryky wh[...]

PAT 0155 **BMB '55 p 42** (11) **A.D. 130**
Prov: Palmyra. Loc: Beirut, Musée National, 515. *Funerary. On relief.* Bib: *Starcky '55 pl XX, 3*; PS 3 (for BMB '55 p 42 no. 12 see PS 28).

1 bryky br tym' br ml' gyr' ḥbl
2 nbwšy 'mh 'mbt' 'ḥth
3 ḥbl byrḥ nysn šnt 4.100+40+1

PAT 0156 **BMB '55 p 43** (13) **n. d.**
Prov: Palmyra. Loc: Beirut, Musée National, 689. *Funerary. On relief fragment.* Bib: *Starcky '55 pl XX, 2*; PS 391.

1 nwr[bl]

PAT 0157 **BS III p 10** **n. d.**
Prov: Palmyra, Temple of Baalshamîn. Loc: Private collection. *Tessera. On terracotta.* Bib: *Dunant '71 fig 1 p 10.*

(Face A)
1 bʿšmn
2 mlkbl
(Face B)
1 drḥlwn
2 ydy

PAT 0158 **BS III 1** **A.D. 67**
Prov: Palmyra, Temple of Baalshamîn, reemployed. Loc: Palmyra, Museum, exc no. 57. *Dedicatory. On door lintel.* Group: Portico of Yarhai. Bib: *Dunant '71 pl I, 1, 4.*

1 mṭltʾ dh klh ʿmwdyh wšryth wtṭlylh qrb yrḥy br lšmš br rʿy dy mn bny mʿzyn lbʿlšmn ʾlhʾ
2 ṭbʾ wškrʾ ʿl ḥywhy wḥyy bnwhy wʾḥwhy byrḥ ʾlwl šnt 3.100+60+10+5+3
Text identical to Inv 1 5 (= RA '30 p 45)

PAT 0159 **BS III 2** **n. d.**
Prov: Palmyra, Temple of Baalshamîn, reemployed. Loc: Palmyra, Museum, exc no. 96, 129, 254, 278, 161. *Dedicatory. On column drums.* Group: Portico of Yarhai. Bib: *Dunant '71 pl I, 5.*

(A, B, C: identical)
1 mṭltʾ dh klh
2 qrb yrḥy br
3 lšmš br rʿy
(D)
1 mṭlth dh klh
2 qrb yrḥy br
3 [lšmš br rʿ]y
(E)
1 mṭl[tʾ dh klh]
2 qr[b yrḥy br]
3 lš[mš br rʿy]

PAT 0160 **BS III 3** **n. d.**
Prov: Palmyra, Temple of Baalshamîn, reemployed. Loc: Palmyra, Museum, exc no. 42. *Dedicatory. On architrave block.* Group: Portico of Alaisha. Bib: *Dunant '71 pl II, 1, 2.*

1 mṭltʾ dh klh ʿmwdyh wšryth wtṭlylh ʿbd wqrb ʿlyšʾ br lš[.........]
2 lbʿlšmn ʾlhʾ ṭbʾ wškrʾ ʿl ḥywhy wḥyy [....]

PAT 0161 **BS III 4** **n. d.**
Prov: Palmyra, Temple of Baalshamîn, reemployed. Loc: Palmyra, Museum, exc no. 302. *Dedicatory. On column drums.* Group: Portico of Alaisha. Bib: *Dunant '71 pl II, 3.*

(A, B, C, D)
1 mṭltʾ dh klh
2 qrb ʾlyšʾ br
3 lšmš br zbdbl
(E same text, less well-preserved)
(F)
1 mṭltʾ dh kl[h]
2 qrb ʾlyšʾ br
3 lšmš br zbd[bl]

PAT 0162 **BS III 5** **n. d.**
Prov: Palmyra, Temple of Baalshamîn, reemployed. Loc: Palmyra, Museum, exc no. 90, 132, 227 (227 = A 1293). *Dedicatory. On column drums.* Group: Portico of Zabdilah. Bib: *Dunant '71 pl III, 1.*

(A, B, C identical)
1 mṭltʾ dh klh
2 qrb zbdlh br
3 zbdʿth mykʾ

PAT 0163 **BS III 6** **n. d.**
Prov: Palmyra, Temple of Baalshamîn, reemployed. Loc: Palmyra, Museum, exc no. 41. *Dedicatory. On column drum.* Group: Portico of Wahbai. Bib: *Dunant '71 pl III, 2.*

1 mṭltʾ dh klh
2 qrb whby br
3 ʿgʾ br whby

PAT 0164 **BS III 7** **A.D. 90**
Prov: Palmyra, Temple of Baalshamîn, reemployed. Loc: Palmyra, Museum, exc no. 109. *Dedicatory. On architrave.* Group: Portico of Malkû. Bib: *Dunant '71 pl III, 3.*

1 [mṭlt' dh mṣ'yt'] klh 'mwdyh wšryth wtṭlylh 'bd wqrb mlkw br 'g' br whby br blḥzy dy mn b[ny m'zyn]
2 [lb'lšmn wldrḥlwn 'lhy ṭ]by wškry' 'l ḥywhy wḥyy bnwhy byrḥ 'lwl šnt 4.100+1

PAT 0165 **BS III 8** **n. d.**
Prov: Palmyra, Temple of Baalshamîn, reemployed. Loc: Palmyra, Museum, exc no. 76 + 45. *Dedicatory. On fragment of architrave.* Bib: *Dunant '71 pl III, 4.*

1 mṭlt' d[h 'mwdy]h wšryth w[tṭlylh] qrb[.............]
2 [...........] 'l ḥywhy wḥyy bnwh[y] w'ḥwhy byrḥ [...] šnt

PAT 0166 **BS III 9** **n. d.**
Prov: Palmyra, Temple of Baalshamîn. Loc: Palmyra, Museum, exc no. 36. *Dedicatory. On fragment of architrave.* Bib: *Dunant '71 pl IV, 1.*

1 [mṭlt' dh] kl[h] w'mwdyh wktlh wtṭly[lh ...]

PAT 0167 **BS III 10** **A.D. 23**
Prov: Palmyra, Temple of Baalshamîn, reemployed. Loc: Palmyra, Museum, exc no. 283. *Dedicatory. On column drum.* Bib: *Dunant '71 pl IV, 2.*

1 byrḥ knwn šnt 3.100+20+10+5
2 qrbw 'ty wšbḥy bnt šḥr'
3 w'ṭ' brt prdš 'mwdy' 'ln
4 tryhwn lb'lšmyn 'lh' ṭb'
5 'l ḥyyhn wḥyy bnyhn w'ḥyhn

PAT 0168 **BS III 11** **A.D. 52**
Prov: Palmyra, Temple of Baalshamîn, reemployed. Loc: Palmyra, Museum, exc no. 277. *Dedicatory. On column drum.* Bib: *Dunant '71 pl V, 3.*

1 byrḥ ṭbt šnt 3.100+60+3
2 'mwd' dnh qrbt 'mtlt b[r]t
3 br'' br 'tntn dy mn bnt myt'
4 'tt tym' br blḥzy br zbdbl dy
5 mn pḥd bny m'zyn lb'lšmn 'lh'
6 ṭb' wškr' 'l ḥyyh wḥyy bnyh
7 w'ḥyh

PAT 0169 **BS III 12** **n. d.**
Prov: Palmyra, Temple of Baalshamîn, reemployed. Loc: Palmyra, Museum, exc no. 27. *Dedicatory. On column drum fragment.* Bib: *Dunant '71 pl IV, 4.*

1 [...............]
2 [dy] mn bn[y] m'zyn
3 [l]b'lš[mn] 'lh'
4 [...............]

PAT 0170 **BS III 14** **A.D. 67**
Prov: Palmyra, Temple of Baalshamîn, reemployed. Loc: Palmyra, Museum, exc no. 287. *Dedicatory. On architrave block.* Bib: *Dunant '71 pl V, 2.*

1 'mwdy' '[ln tlt]' wšrythwn wtṭl[ylhwn 'bd] wqrb ml[kw br 'lyš' br] mlkw 'ṣr' dy mn bny [m'zyn']
2 [l]b['lš]mn wldrḥlwn 'lhy' ṭby' wškry' 'l ḥ[yw]hy wḥyy bnwhn byrḥ 'lwl šnt 3.100+60+10+5+3

PAT 0171 **BS III 15** **n. d.**
Prov: Palmyra, Temple of Baalshamîn, reemployed. Loc: Palmyra, Museum, exc no. 288. *Dedicatory. On column drum.* Bib: *Dunant '71 pl V, 3.*

1 ['mwdy]' 'ln t[l]t'
2 [q]rb mlkw br 'lyš'
3 br mlkw 'ṣr'

PAT 0172 **BS III 16** **n. d.**
Prov: Palmyra, Temple of Baalshamîn. Loc: Palmyra, Museum, exc no. 346. *Dedicatory. On column drum.* Bib: *Dunant '71 pl V, 4.*

1 'mwdy' 'ln tlt' qrbw

2 ʿstwrgʾ wšmʿwn bny
3 zbydʾ qrqpn

7 šnt 4.100+60

PAT 0173 **BS III 17** **n. d.**
Prov: Palmyra, Temple of Baalshamîn, reemployed. Loc: Palmyra, Museum, exc no. 116. *Dedicatory. On column drum.* Bib: *Dunant '71 pl VI, 1.*

1 [ʿ]mwdyʾ ʾln tltʾ
2 šrythwn wtṯlylhw[n]
3 qrbw bny ʿgylw br
4 yrḥbwlʾ ʾspd/ʾspr

PAT 0174 **BS III 18** **n. d.**
Prov: Palmyra, Temple of Baalshamîn, reemployed. Loc: Palmyra, Museum, exc no. 282. *Dedicatory. On column drum.* Bib: *Dunant '71 pl VI, 2.*

1 ʿmwdyʾ ʾln ḥmšʾ qrb
2 nwrbl br zbdʿth br
3 nwrbl lbʿlšmn ʾlhʾ

PAT 0175 **BS III 19** **n. d.**
Prov: Palmyra, Temple of Baalshamîn. Loc: Palmyra, Museum, exc no. 87. *Dedicatory. On column drum.* See BS III 71, 72. Bib: *Dunant '71 pl VI, 3, 4.*

1 ʿmwdyʾ ʾln ʾrbʿʾ wṭpytʾ
2 wšrytʾ dy ḥṭrʾ wšrythwn
3 wtṯlylhwn gwyʾ ʿbdw ḥyrn
4 wymlʾ ʾḥwhy bny tymʾ
5 br ymlʾ lbʿlšmn wdrḥlwn
6 ʿl ḥyyhwn wḥyy bnyhwn

PAT 0176 **BS III 20** **A.D. 149**
Prov: Palmyra, Temple of Baalshamîn. Loc: Palmyra, Museum, exc no. 203. *Dedicatory. On shaft of column.* Bib: *Dunant '71 pl VI, 5.*

1 lbʿlšmn
2 wldwrḥln
3 ʿmdʾ wṭpytʾ
4 wšrytʾ wtṯlylʾ
5 ʿbd ṯtys plwys
6 prsqs byrḥ ʾlwl

PAT 0177 **BS III 21** **A.D. (67)**
Prov: Palmyra, Temple of Baalshamîn: *in situ.* Loc: Palmyra, Museum exc no. 89. *Dedicatory. On stone slab.* Group: Banquet Room. Bib: *Dunant '71 pl VI, 1.*

1 [by]rḥ ʾlwl šnt 3.100+60+10+[5+3] smkʾ dnh ʿbdw wqrbw bny m[rzḥʾ ʾln l]bʿ[lšm]n wldwr[ḥln ʾlhyʾ ṭ]b[y]ʾ lh[wn ...]

PAT 0178 **BS III 22** **n. d.**
Prov: Palmyra, Temple of Baalshamîn: *in situ.* Loc: Palmyra, Museum, exc no. 88. *Dedicatory. On stone slab.* Group: Banquet Room. Bib: *Dunant '71 pl VII, 2.*

1 šmʿw[n] wḥlptʾ br tymrṣw wʿgylw br zbdbl wb[ry]kw br zbdbwl wḥ[yr]n b[r] šʿdlt wtwry br nšʾ wḥyrn wnwrbl wydy[ʿblˀ] bny mlkw [w]blḥzy wzbdbl bny ʿlyy wmq[y]mw br[...]
2 wzbydʾ br tymw wy[..] br ḥyrn wʿgylw br mqymw wmlkw br kly wmlkw br m[qy]mw wyrḥy br mqy
Follows on previous inscription

PAT 0179 **BS III 23** **A.D. 62**
Prov: Palmyra, Temple of Baalshamîn, reemployed. Loc: Palmyra, Museum, exc no. 110. *Dedicatory. On altar.* Bib: *Dunant '71 pl VIII, 1.*

1 byrḥ [... šn]t 3.100+60+10+4 ʿltʾ dh
2 q[rb ... br ḥyr]n br ʿgylw ʾytybl dy mn bny
3 mʿzyn [l]bʿlšmyn wldwrḥlwn wlrḥm wlgdʾ dy
4 ydyʿ[b]l [... ʿ]l ḥywhy wḥyy bnwhy wʾ[ḥwhy]

PAT 0180 **BS III 24** **A.D. 73**
Prov: Palmyra, Temple of Baalshamîn, Banquet Room, *in situ.* Loc: Palmyra, Museum, exc no. 15. *Dedicatory. On altar.* Bib: *Dunant '71 pl VII, 3, 4.*

1 ʿlwtʾ ʾln qrbw mlkw wrʿyʾl bny

2 gdʾ br tymy dy mn bny mʿzyn lbʿlšmn
3 ʾlhʾ dy thwyn ʿlwtʾ ʾln ʿl bbʾ
4 rbʾ ʾtr dy yhwh byrḥ s[ywn] šnt
5 3.100+80+4

PAT 0181 **BS III 26** **n. d.**
Prov: Palmyra, Temple of Baalshamîn, reemployed. Loc: Palmyra, Museum, exc no. 231. *Dedicatory. On altar.* Bib: *Dunant '71 pl IX, 3 - 8.*

(In front)
1 mlkbl ṣlm mlkw
(On right)
2 ʾlt
(On left)
3 šʿdw/šʿrw

PAT 0182 **BS III 27** **A.D. 207**
Prov: Palmyra, Temple of Baalshamîn, reemployed. Loc: Palmyra, Museum, A 1303. *Dedicatory. On altar.* Bib: *Dunant '71 pl VIII, 5*; Gaw '73a, p 110.

1 b[ryk šm]h lʿlmʾ
2 ṭbʾ wrḥmnʾ ʿbd
3 wm[wd]ʾ ʿltʾ dh qrynw
4 [br m]lʾ qrynw ʿl ḥywhy
5 [wḥy]ʾ bnwhy byrḥ ʾlwl
6 šnt 5.100+10+5+3

PAT 0183 **BS III 28** **A.D. (113)**
Prov: Palmyra, Temple of Baalshamîn. Loc: Palmyra, Museum, A 1271. *Dedicatory. On altar fragment.* Bib: *Dunant '71 pl VIII, 6.*

1 [.......]
2 [....]byrḥ
3 [... š]nt 20+5

PAT 0184 **BS III 29** **n. d.**
Prov: Palmyra, sounding, N of Hotel Zenobia. Loc: Palmyra, exc no. 341. *Dedicatory. On altar fragment.* Bib: *Dunant '71 pl VIII, 2.*

1 [..........]
2 ṭbʾ [ʿbdw]
3 yrḥy br
4 wrdn wšby
5 [brt?] ʾwlʾ

PAT 0185 **BS III 32** **n. d.**
Prov: Palmyra, Temple of Baalshamîn. Loc: Palmyra, Museum, A 1268. *Dedicatory. On fragment of stone block.* Bib: *Dunant '71 pl X, 1.*

1 hyklʾ dnh dy [...]
2 lšmš wl[...]

PAT 0186 **BS III 33** **A.D. 385**
Prov: Palmyra, Temple of Baalshamîn, reemployed. Loc: Palmyra, Museum, exc no. 200. *Dedicatory. On fragment of stone block.* Bib: *Dunant '71 pl X, 2.*

1 [byrḥ] ʾlwl šnt 3.100+80+5
2 [mṣb]ʾ nṣb tymy br
3 [...]h lšmš

PAT 0187 **BS III 34** **n. d.**
Prov: Palmyra, Temple of Baalshamîn, reemployed. Loc: Palmyra, Museum, exc no. 99. *Unclassified. On fragment of architrave.* Bib: *Dunant '71 pl X, 3.*

1 [...]hn dy bny ydyʿbl klhn br bryky [...]
2 [...]w wʾḥydyn bh bštʾ dh ʿl b[...]
3 [.... ḥ]yrn br ʿgylw br ʾytyb[l ...]
4 [.....b]ny mʿzyn klhn lmn dy yḥdnh [...]
5 [.........] dy yhwh ʾrkwn mn [b]ny m[ʿzyn ...]

PAT 0188 **BS III 35** **n. d.**
Prov: Palmyra, Temple of Baalshamîn, reemployed. Loc: Palmyra, Museum, exc no. 156. *Dedicatory. On lintel fragment.* Bib: *Dunant '71 pl X, 4.*

1 [lbʿlšm]n wdrḥl[wn] wmrt mytʾ ʿbdw wqrbw
2 [..................] mtny br šmʿwn tryʾ šnt
3 [...]

PAT 0189 **BS III 36** **n. d.**

Prov: Palmyra, Temple of Baalshamîn, reemployed. Loc: Palmyra, Museum, A 1290 + A 1294. *Dedicatory. On lintel fragment.* Bib: *Dunant '71 pl X, 5, 6.*

1 [...] tṣby[................] zby[..] wbr[...]
1 [...]by br [...............]

PAT 0190 **BS III 37** **A.D. 32**

Prov: Palmyra, Temple of Baalshamîn, reemployed. Loc: Palmyra, Museum, exc no. 272. *Honorific. On statue console.* Bib: *Dunant '71 pl XI, 1.*

1 ṣlmʾ dnh dy zbdlh br bryky
2 br nwrbl qynw dy mn bny
3 mʿzyn dy ʾqymw lh bny
4 mʿzyn lyqrh byrḥ šbṭ
5 šnt 3.100+40+3

PAT 0191 **BS III 38** **A.D. 49**

Prov: Palmyra, Temple of Baalshamîn, reemployed. Loc: Palmyra, Museum, exc no. 8. *Honorific. On statue console.* Bib: *Dunant '71 pl XI, 2.*

1 byrḥ sywn šnt 3.100+60 ṣlmʾ
2 dnh dy zbʾ br tymnʾ br whby b[r]
3 blḥzy dy mn pḥd bny mʿzyn dy
4 ʾqymw lh kmryʾ dy bʿlš[mn]
5 [ʾl]hʾ mn dy špr lhwn ly[qrh]

PAT 0192 **BS III 39** **A.D. 61**

Prov: Palmyra, Temple of Baalshamîn, reemployed. Loc: Palmyra, Museum, exc no. 4. *Honorific. On statue console.* Bib: *Dunant '71 pl XI, 4.*

1 [.......] h 10+5+3 [.......] mwhywq[...]
2 btrʿw
3 ṣlmʾ dnh dy zbydʾ br ydy br mqymw
4 gbʾ dy mn bny mʿzyn dy ʾqymw lh
5 bny mʿzyn lyqrh dy špr lhwn
6 wlʾlhyhwn byrḥ tšry šnt
7 3.100+60+10+3

PAT 0193 **BS III 40** **A.D. 90**

Prov: Palmyra, Temple of Baalshamîn, reemployed. Loc: Palmyra, Museum, exc no. 30. *Honorific. On statue console.* Bib: *Dunant '71 pl XI, 3*; Déd p 95.

1 ṣlmʾ dnh dy mlkw br ʿgʾ
2 br whby br blḥzy dy mn bny
3 mʿzyn dy ʾqym lh bʿlšmn
4 wdrḥlwn wbny mʿzyn lyqrh
5 bdyl dy špr lhwn wlʾlhyhn
6 wʿbd mṭltʾ dh mṣʿytʾ klh
7 mn kysh byrḥ ʾlwl šnt 4.100+1

PAT 0194 **BS III 41** **A.D. 98**

Prov: Palmyra, Temple of Baalshamîn, reemployed. Loc: Palmyra, Museum, A 1285. *Honorific. On statue console.* Bib: *Dunant '71 pl XII, 1*; Déd p 101.

1' [...................]
2' [..........]πλ[.....]
3' [...ἔτους θυ' μην]ὸς Γορπ[ιαίου]

1 [ṣlmʾ dnh dy ...]ʾ br [...br...]šʾ dy ʿbd bʿlš[mn]
2 [wdrḥ]lwn wbny mʿzyn lyqrh bdyl dy špr lhwn
3 [wlʾlh]yhwn byrḥ ʾ[l]wl šnt 4.100+5+4

PAT 0195 **BS III 42** **A.D. (102)**

Prov: Palmyra, Temple of Baalshamîn, reemployed. Loc: Palmyra, Museum, exc no. 16. *Honorific. On statue console.* Bib: *Dunant '71 pl XII, 2.*

1 ṣl[mʾ dnh .....] br [.......] br
2 [...............]ʾ[............]
3 [.............. .]dkl[.......]
4 [...........] bdyl d[y š]pr l[h]wn
5 [byrḥ... šnt 4.100+]+10+4

PAT 0196 **BS III 43** **A.D. 103**

Prov: Palmyra, Temple of Baalshamîn, reemployed. Loc: Palmyra, Museum, exc no. 135. *Honorific. On statue console.* Bib: *Dunant '71 pl XII, 3.*

1 ṣlmʾ dnh dy blḥzy br ʿgʾ
2 br whby bwlḥzy dy ʿbdw lh
3 bny mʿzyn lyqrh wʿbd hw
4 wbnwhy mṭltʾ dh wʿmdyh
5 wtṭlylh šnt 4.100+10+5

PAT 0197 **BS III 45** **A.D. 132**

Prov: Palmyra, Temple of Baalshamîn, reemployed. Loc: Palmyra, Museum, exc no. 134. *Honorific. On statue console.* Bib: *Dunant '71 pl XIII, 1, 2, 3*; Déd p 2; Dunant '56; Hillers and Cussini '92.

1 Σοαδον Βωλιαδους τοῦ Σοαδου [εὐσεβῆ καὶ]
2 φιλόπατριν καὶ ἐν πολλοῖς καὶ [μεγάλοις]
3 καιροῖς γνησίως κ[αὶ φιλοτείμως]
4 παραστάντα τοῖς ἐμπό[ροις καὶ ταῖς]
5 συνοδί[α]ις καὶ τοῖς ἐν Οὐολογασιά[δι]
6 πολείταις, καὶ π[ά]ντοτε ἀφειδήσαντα
7 [ψ]υχῆς καὶ οὐσίας ὑπὲρ τῶν τῇ πατρίδι
8 διαφ[ε]ρόν[τ]ων καὶ διὰ τοῦτο δόγμασι
9 καὶ ψ[ηφίσ]μασι καὶ ἀνδριᾶσι δημοσίοις
10 καὶ ἐ[πιστολ]αῖς καὶ διατάγματι Πoβλικίου
11 Μαρκ[έλλου τοῦ διασ]ημοτάτου κυρίου
12 ὑπατικ[οῦ τετειμη]μένον, διασώσαντα
13 δὲ καὶ τὴν [προσφ]άτως ἀπὸ
Οὐολογαισιά[δος]
14 παραγενομέν[ην συν]οδίαν ἐκ τοῦ
15 περιστάντος αὐ[τ]ὴν μεγάλου κινδύνου,
16 ἡ αὐτὴ συνοδία, [ἀρετ]ῆς καὶ μεγαλο-
17 φροσύνης [καὶ εὐσεβείας ἕνεκ]α, αὐτοῦ
18 ἀνδρ[ιάντας τέσσαρας ἀνέστησ]ε, ἕν[α]
19 μὲ[ν ἐ]νταῦθ[α ἐν ἱερῷ Διός], ἕνα δὲ
20 [ἐ]ν ἱερῷ ἄλσει, ἕνα δὲ [ἐ]ν ἱε][ρῷ] Ἄρεος
21 καὶ τὸν τέταρτον ἐν ἱερῷ Ἀταργάτειος
22 διὰ Αγεγου Ιαριβωλεους καὶ Θαιμαρσου
23 τοῦ Θαιμαρσου συνοδιάρχων· ἔτους
24 [γ]μυʹ μηνὸς Περιτίου.

1 w[..............]
2 bd/rm[.........]
3 wb[.............]
4 wṭʾ[............]
5 mṣbt bšm bwlʾ [wdm]sʾ [..............]
6 wyqryn šgyʾyn wʾ[p pw]blwqyws mrql[ws]
7 hgmnʾ mrn bʾg[rtʾ] wbdy[ṭg]mʾ šhd lh
8 wšbḥh wbd[y] s[yʿ] šyr[tʾ] dy [sl]qt mn
9 ʾlgšyʾ bmdʿm [w]šwzbh mn qdns rb
10 d[y] hwt bh [h]nwn bny šyrtʾ dh ʿbdw lh
11 ṣlm[yʾ ʾln ʾrbʿ]ʾ lyqrh ʾḥd tnn bt
12 [bʿlšmn wʾḥd bt ʾr]ṣw wʾḥd bgntʾ ʾlym
13 [wʾrbʿtʾ [... bt ʿtrʿth brb]nwt šyrtʾ ḥ[ggw
b]r
14 [yrḥbwlʾ wtymr]ṣw br tymrṣw [byrḥ šbṭ]
15 [šnt 4.100+]40+3

PAT 0198 **BS III 46** **A.D. 138**

Prov: Palmyra, Temple of Baalshamîn, reemployed. Loc: Palmyra, Museum, exc no. 44. *Honorific. On statue console.* Bib: *Dunant '71 pl XIII, 4.*

1 ṣlmʾ dnh dy yrḥy br ʿgylw br
2 ḥyrn dwḥy dy ʾqym lh zbdʾ
3 br bryky br šmʿwn br brwky
4 bdyl dy špr lh lyqrh byrḥ
5 ṭbt šnt 4.100+40+5+4

PAT 0199 **BS III 47** **n. d.**

Prov: Palmyra, Temple of Baalshamîn. Loc: Palmyra, Museum, exc no. 160. *Honorific. On statue console.* Bib: *Dunant '71 pl XIII, 5, 6.*

1- 12 broken
13 [τε]ιμῆς χάριν

1 [...rḥym mdyt]h wdḥl ʾl[hy]ʾ [...]
2 [.............]ʾ lqys kyʾm[...]
3 [..................] wḥsr m[n kysh]
4 [................ k]mryʾ d[...]
5 [................] btwd/r[...]

PAT 0200 **BS III 51** **n. d.**

Prov: Palmyra, Temple of Baalshamîn, reemployed. Loc: Palmyra, Museum, exc no. 19. *Honorific. On statue console.* Bib: *Dunant '71 pl XIV, 5.*

1 byr[ḥ ... šnt] 5.100+[.. ṣlmʾ dnh dy]
2 zbʾ br mqyʾ br blḥzy [br ... br]
3 mqyʾ dy ʾqym lh pršyʾ bʾbr[ʾ]
4 dy gmlʾ wʿnʾ bdyl dy špr lhwn
5 lyqrh

PAT 0201 **BS III 53** **n. d.**
Prov: Palmyra, Temple of Baalshamîn. Loc: Palmyra, Museum, A 1310. *Honorific. On console fragment.* Bib: *Dunant '71 pl XIV, 6.*

1 ṣlm [...]

PAT 0202 **BS III 54** **n. d.**
Prov: Palmyra, Temple of Baalshamîn, reemployed. Loc: Palmyra, Museum, A 1280, A 1273. *Honorific. On statue base.* Bib: *Dunant '71 pl XV, 1, 2.*

On right:
1 [ṣl]m zbʾ br t[y]mnʾ whb[y]
On left:
1 ṣlm zbʾ br tym[nʾ whby]

PAT 0203 **BS III 55** **n. d.**
Prov: Palmyra, Temple of Baalshamîn. Loc: Palmyra, Museum, A 1274. *Honorific. On fragment of statue base.* Bib: *Dunant '71 pl XIV, 3, 4.*

1 ṣlm [... br tymnʾ] [ṣlm ... br ty]mnʾ

PAT 0204 **BS III 56** **n. d.**
Prov: Palmyra, Temple of Baalshamîn. Loc: Palmyra, Museum, B 1864. *Dedicatory. On relief.* Bib: *Dunant '71 pl XV, 7.*

1 blty

PAT 0205 **BS III 57** **n. d.**
Prov: Palmyra, Temple of Baalshamîn. Loc: Damascus, National Museum, 7459. *Dedicatory. On relief fragment.* Bib: *Dunant '71 pl XV, 5, 6.*

1 [...]kyd/r[...]

PAT 0206 **BS III 58** **n. d.**
Prov: Palmyra, Temple of Baalshamîn. Loc: Palmyra, Museum, A 1285. *Dedicatory. On relief fragment.* Bib: *Dunant '71 pl XV, 8.*

1 ʿbd ʾ?ʿ?l[..] br qr[ynw] or: ml[kw] or: ql[..]
2 lsdrpʾ ʾlhh wldʿnt

PAT 0207 **BS III 59** **n. d.**
Prov: Palmyra, Temple of Baalshamîn. Loc: Palmyra, Museum, exc no. 262. *Dedicatory. On plinth fragments.* Bib: *Dunant '71 pl XV, 9, 10.*

(A)
1 [d]kyr w[bryk]
(B)
1 [... ʿgy]lw br b[...]

PAT 0208 **BS III 60** **A.D. 11**
Prov: Palmyra, Temple of Baalshamîn. Loc: Palmyra, Museum, A 1302. *Funerary, unique type. On stone block.* Group: BS III 60-61. Bib: *Dunant '71 pl XVI, 1, 2*; Gaw 90b p 108, Pl 23b.

1 byrḥ ʾyr šnt 3.100+20+2
2 ptyḥ qbrʾ dnh
3 wʾbd/wʾbr wwhblt br mtny br gdrṣw
4 br mtny br qynw br ʿdty br
5 ydyʿbl ptḥh wʾbdh/wʾbrh
6 yhwh dkyr lʿlmʾ hw
7 wbnwhy bṭb wdkyr ʿgylw br
8 mlkw br ḥyrn dky[r]
9 ʿd ʿlmʾ [...]
10 br ydyʿbl rbʾ
11 ʾbwn rbʾ šlm
line 3: Gaw 90b p 104: (graphically possible) reading *ʿrty* excluded by form *ʿty* of RSP 143

PAT 0209 **BS III 61** **n. d.**
Prov: Palmyra, Temple of Baalshamîn. Loc: Palmyra. *Funerary, graffiti. On plaster.* See BS III 60. Bib: *Dunant '71 pl XVI, 2, 3, 4, 5.*

(A)
1 [d]kyr ʿbynw/ʿrynw/ʿdynw rb
(B)
1 dkyryn

2 wbrykyn
3 zbd[.]bwl
4 mqy mn
5 qdm
(C)
1 dkyr mšš br mtny
2 šnt 60+5+4
(D)
1 dkyr ml/bl[...]
(E)
1 dky[r]
2 ʿd ʿlmʾ [.....]
3 br ydyʿbl rbʾ
4 ʾbwn rbʾ šlm
(F)
1 yrḥy ʿgylw
2 ʾlhbl

PAT 0210 **BS III 62** **n. d.**
Prov: Palmyra, Temple of Baalshamîn, reemployed. Loc: Palmyra, Museum, B 1896. *Funerary. On fragment of stele.* Bib: *Dunant '71 pl XVII, 1.*

1 zbdbwl
2 br
3 zbdʿth
4 dnh

PAT 0211 **BS III 63** **n. d.**
Prov: Palmyra, Temple of Baalshamîn, reemployed. Loc: Palmyra, Museum, A 1277. *Funerary. On relief fragment.* Bib: *Dunant '71 pl XVII, 2.*

1 [ṣlmt ...]
2 bt wrg
3 dy ʿbd
4 bʿlh ḥbl

PAT 0212 **BS III 64** **n. d.**
Prov: Palmyra, Temple of Baalshamîn. Loc: Palmyra, Museum, B 1903. *Funerary. On relief fragment.* Bib: *Dunant '71 pl XVII, 3, 4.*

1 [zb]dlʾ
2 [br ʾ]bgl
3 [ḥb]l

PAT 0213 **BS III 65** **n. d.**
Prov: Palmyra, Temple of Baalshamîn. Loc: Palmyra, Museum, A 1297. *Funerary. On relief fragment.* Bib: *Dunant '71 pl XVII, 5.*

1 [ḥb]l šlmn
2 [w...]ly bny
3 [...] br šlm[n]

PAT 0214 **BS III 66** **n. d.**
Prov: Palmyra, Temple of Baalshamîn. Loc: Palmyra, Museum, A 1309. *Funerary. On relief fragment.* Bib: *Dunant '71 pl XVII, 6.*

1 ḥbtʾ [...]
2 ʿḋty [...]

line 2: dot over *r* may be accidental (Duant ad loc); see note ad BS III 60:3 above

PAT 0215 **BS III 67** **n. d.**
Prov: Palmyra, Temple of Baalshamîn, reemployed. Loc: Palmyra, Museum, A 1298. *Funerary. On relief fragment.* Bib: *Dunant '71 pl XVII, 7.*

1 [.............]
2 wlyrḥb[wlʾ]
3 ʾḥwhw

PAT 0216 **BS III 68** **n. d.**
Prov: Palmyra, Temple of Baalshamîn, *in situ.* Loc: Palmyra, *in situ*, exc no. 86. *Graffito. On stone.* Bib: *Dunant '71 pl XVIII, 1.*

1 ʾ[t]r ʾḥyd
2 [...]l lmlkw tymy

PAT 0217 **BS III 69** **n. d.**
Prov: Palmyra, Temple of Baalshamîn, *in situ.* Loc: Palmyra, *in situ*, exc no. 85. *Graffito. On stone.* Bib: *Dunant '71 pl XVIII, 1.*

1 lmlkw
2 tymy

PAT 0218 **BS III 70** **n. d.**
Prov: Palmyra, Temple of Baalshamîn, *reemployed.* Loc: Palmyra, *in situ*, exc no. 216. *Graffito. On stone.* Bib: *Dunant '71 pl XVIII, 2.*

1 ʾḥydʾ lbny

PAT 0219 **BS III 71** **n. d.**
Prov: Palmyra, Temple of Baalshamîn. Loc: Palmyra, Museum, exc no. 87. *Graffito. On column.* See BS III 19, 72. Bib: *Dunant '71 pl XVIII, 3.*

1 yrḥy
2 ymlky

PAT 0220 **BS III 72** **n. d.**
Prov: Palmyra, Temple of Baalshamîn. Loc: Palmyra, Museum, exc no. 87. *Graffito. On column.* See BS III 19, 71. Bib: *Dunant '71 pl XVIII, 4.*

1 yrḥy
2 [.........]

PAT 0221 **BS III 73** **n. d.**
Prov: Palmyra, Temple of Baalshamîn, reemployed. Loc: Palmyra, Museum, exc no. 273. *Graffito. On column drum.* Bib: *Dunant '71 pl XVIII, 5.*

1 šʿdw zbdʾ
2 mlkw brh

PAT 0222 **BS III 74** **n. d.**
Prov: Palmyra, Temple of Baalshamîn, reemployed. Loc: Palmyra Museum. *Graffito. On column drum.* Bib: *Dunant '71 pl XIX, 1.*

1 ṭ[.]

PAT 0223 **BS III 75** **n. d.**
Prov: Palmyra, Temple of Baalshamîn, reemployed. Loc: Palmyra Museum. *Graffito. On frame, temple thalamos.* Bib: *Dunant '71 pl XIX, 2.*

1 dkyr tymy

PAT 0224 **BS III 76** **n. d.**
Prov: Palmyra, Temple of Baalshamîn. Loc: Palmyra, *in situ. Graffito. On column.* Bib: *Dunant '71 pl XIX, 3.*

1 zbdby [...]

PAT 0225 **BS III 77** **n. d.**
Prov: Palmyra, Temple of Baalshamîn. Loc: Palmyra, *in situ. Graffito. On building stone.* Bib: *Dunant '71 pl XIX, 4.*

1 ʿbdʾ

PAT 0226 **BS III p 84** **n. d.**
Prov: Palmyra, Temple of Baalshamîn. Loc: Palmyra Museum. *Graffito. On relief.* Bib: *Dunant '71 p 84 (Note additionelle).*

1 dkyr wb[ryk...]

PAT 0227 **BS III 79** **n. d.**
Prov: Palmyra, Temple of Baalshamîn. Loc: Palmyra, Museum, A 1279. *Guide letter for assembly, graffito. On stone.*

b

PAT 0228 **BS III 80**
Prov: Palmyra, Temple of Baalshamîn. Loc: Palmyra, *in situ. Guide letters for assembly. On stone.* Bib: *Dunant '71 pl XIX, 6.*

(At various corners)
g b

PAT 0229 **BS III 81**
Prov: Palmyra, Temple of Baalshamîn. Loc: Palmyra, *in situ. Guide letter for assembly. On column drum.*

b

PAT 0230 **BS III 82** **n. d.**
Prov: Palmyra, Temple of Baalshamîn, reemployed. Loc: Palmyra, Museum, A 1295. *Dedicatory. On stone fragment.* Bib: *Dunant '71 pl XX, 1.*

1 [..................]
2 ʿl ḥywhy w[lḥyy bnwhy ...]

PAT 0231 **BS III 83** **n. d.**
Prov: Palmyra, Temple of Baalshamîn, reemployed. Loc: Palmyra, Museum, A 1301. *Unclassified. On stone fragment.* Bib: *Dunant '71 pl XX, 2.*

1 [...] ʾlhyʾ [...]

PAT 0232 **BS III 84** **n. d.**
Prov: Palmyra, Temple of Baalshamîn. Loc: Palmyra, Museum, A 1269. *Unclassified. On stone fragment.* Bib: *Dunant '71 pl XX, 3.*

1 bd/r[...]
2 wh[...]

PAT 0233 **BS III 85** **n. d.**
Prov: Palmyra, Temple of Baalshamîn. Loc: Palmyra, Museum, A 1287. *Unclassified. On stone fragment.* Bib: *Dunant '71 pl XX, 4.*

1 zbdʿt[h ...]

PAT 0234 **BS III 86** **n. d.**
Prov: Palmyra, Temple of Baalshamîn. Loc: Palmyra, Museum, A 1305. *Unclassified. On stone fragment.* Bib: *Dunant '71 pl XX, 7.*

1 [.....]r[...]
2 [.....]ʾb[...]
3 [...]bk

PAT 0235 **BS III 87** **n. d.**
Prov: Palmyra, Temple of Baalshamîn, reemployed. Loc: Palmyra, Museum, A 1307. *Unclassified. On stone fragment.* Bib: *Dunant '71 pl XX, 8.*

1 ʾrwnʾ dnʾ [...]
Dunant: other readings of first word possible, only this gives sense

PAT 0236 **BS III 88** **n. d.**
Prov: Palmyra, Temple of Baalshamîn, reemployed. Loc: Palmyra, Museum, A 1291. *Unclassified. On console fragment.* Bib: *Dunant '71 pl XX, 5.*

1 [...]tyh[...]

PAT 0237 **BS III 89** **n. d.**
Prov: Palmyra, Temple of Baalshamîn. Loc: Palmyra, Museum, A 1312. *Unclassified. On stone fragment.* Bib: *Dunant '71 pl XX, 6.*

1 [...]ʾš[...]

PAT 0238 **BS III 90** **n. d.**
Prov: Palmyra, Temple of Baalshamîn. Loc: Palmyra, Museum, A 1275. *Unclassified. On stone fragment.* Bib: *Dunant '71 pl XX, 10, 11.*

(A)
1 [...]ηκαι
2 [...]σ

(B)
1 [...]š dḥl
2 [......]n

PAT 0239 **BS VI p 113** (3) **n. d.**
Prov: Palmyra, Temple of Baalshamîn. Loc: Palmyra, Museum, exc no. 271. *Tessera. On terracotta.* Bib: *Fellmann and Dunant '75 pl 2.*

(Face A)
1 ʾgn
(Face B)
1 yrḥ

2 bwl

PAT 0240 **BS VI p 114** (4) **n. d.**
Prov: Palmyra. Loc: Palmyra, Museum, exc no. 238. *Tessera. On terracotta.* Bib: *Fellmann and Dunant '75 pl 2.*

(Face A)
1 yrḥbwl
2 wʿgḷbwl
3 nbw
(Face B)
1 bryky[n]
2 [t]ryʾ

PAT 0241 **BS VI p 114** (5) **n. d.**
Prov: Palmyra. Loc: Palmyra, Museum, exc no. 244. *Tessera. On terracotta.* Bib: *Fellmann and Dunant '75 pl 2.*

1 nbw
2 šbʿtʾ/šbʿtʾ

PAT 0242 **BS VI p 114** (6) **n. d.**
Prov: Palmyra. Loc: Palmyra, Museum, exc no. 123. *Tessera. On terracotta.* Bib: *Fellmann and Dunant '75 pl 2.*

1 [nbw]
2 [ʾbrykw]
Restored from RTP 303

PAT 0243 **BS VI p 115** (10) **n. d.**
Prov: Palmyra. Loc: Palmyra, Museum, exc no. 128. *Tessera. On terracotta.* Bib: *Fellmann and Dunant '75 pl 2.*

1 ʿgylw
2 bwnʾ

PAT 0244 **BS VI p 116** (12) **n. d.**
Prov: Palmyra. Loc: Palmyra, Museum, exc no. 133. *Tessera. On terracotta.* Bib: *Fellmann and Dunant '75 pl 2.*

1 ḥ[mr]
2 m[kl wpl]g
3 [qrš]
4 [bsmkʾ]

PAT 0245 **BS VI p 116** (16) **n. d.**
Prov: Palmyra. Loc: Palmyra, Museum, exc no. 13. *Tessera. On terracotta.* Bib: *Fellmann and Dunant '75 pl 2.*

1 [šmʿ]w[n]

PAT 0246 **C3901** **n. d.**
Prov: South Shields, Tyne and Wear (England). Loc: South Shields, Arbeia Roman Fort Museum, TWCMS T 765. *Funerary. On stele, below relief.* Bib: Wright 1878 (drawings); HNE p 482 d. γ 5, pl XLI, 13; RES 1612; RIB 1065 (drawing, bibliography for Latin inscription) cf. Latin inscription from Britain " [...]rathes Palmorenus"; possible identification discussed by R. Wright, with bibliography..

1 D(*is*) M(*anibus*). REGINA LIBERTA ET CONIUGE
2 BARATES PALMYRENUS NATIONE
3 CATUALLANA AN(*nnorum*) XXX

1 rgynʾ bt ḥry brʿtʾ ḥbl

PAT 0247 **C3902** **A.D. 236**
Prov: Rome, Giardino Mattei, Trastevere. Loc: Rome, Museo Capitolino, CE 6715 = NCE 2406. *Dedicatory. On stele.* Bib: HNE p 477 (Rome) 1, pl XLII, 9; RES 1612; NSI p 301, 1; Daniels '88.

1 Ἀγλιβώλῳ καὶ Μαλαχβήλῳ πατρῴοις θεοῖς
2 καὶ τὸ σίγνον ἀργυροῦν σὺν παντὶ κόζμῳ ἀνέθηκε
3 Τ. Αὐρ. Ἡλιόδωρος Ἀντιόχου Ἀδριανὸς Παλμυρηνὸς ἐκ τῶν ἰδίων ὑπὲρ
4 σωτηρίας αὐτοῦ καὶ τ(ῆς) συμβίου καὶ τ(ῶν) τέκνων, ἔτους ζμφʹ μηνὸς Περιτίου.

1 lʿglbwl wmlkbl wsmytʾ dy kspʾ wtṣbyth
ʿbd mn kysh yrḥy br ḥlypy br
2 yrḥy br lšmš šʿdw ʿl ḥywhy wḥyʾ bnwhy
byrḥ šbṭ šnt 5.100+40+5+2

C3902 to 3905 are from Rome; the first two were discovered already in the 15th century. See Daniels 1988 on their role in the decipherment of the Palmyrene script.

PAT 0248 **C3903** **n. d.**

Prov: Rome, near Acqua Acetosa. Loc: Rome, Museo Capitolino, CE 6721 = NCE 2402. *Dedicatory. On altar.* Bib: HNE p 477 (Rome) 2, pl XLII, 10; RES 1612; Houston '90 (bibliography esp. on the Latin text).

1 SOLI SANCTISSIMO SACRUM. TI(*berius*) CLAUDIUS FELIX ET CLAUDIA HELPIS ET TI(*berius*) CLAUDIUS ALYPUS FIL(*ius*) EORUM VOTUM SOLVERUNT LIBENS MERITO CALBIENSES DE COH(*orte*) III.

Consecrated to the most holy Sun. Tiberius Claudius Felix, Claudia Helpis, and their son, Tiberius Claudius Alypus, (thus) gladly have fulfilled a vow due to the Sun. Calbienses of the third cohort. (On the problematic last phrase see esp. Houston '90.

1 ʿltʾ dh lmlkbl wlʾlhy tdmr
2 qrb ṭbrys qlwdys plqs
3 wtdmryʾ lʾlhyhn šlm

PAT 0249 **C3904** **n. d.**

Prov: Rome, Syriac Sanctuary, Porta Portese. Loc: Rome, Museo Capitolino, CE 6707 = NCE 2398. *Dedicatory. On stele.* Bib: Déd p 266.

1 Θεοῖς πατρῴοις Βηλωι ʼΙαριβωλ[ωι ʼΑγλιβωλωι ...]
2 ἀνέθηκαν Μακκαιος Μαλη τ[οῦ Λισαμσου καὶ Σοαδος Θαιμεους τοῦ Λισαμσαιου, ἔτους ...]

1 [..... lšm]š wšʿdw br tymʾ lšmšy wqrbw

Gk text after Déd p 266; see Déd ad loc for restorations of Aram text

PAT 0250 **C3905** **n. d.**

Prov: Rome, via Appia. Loc: Rome, Museo Capitolino. *Funerary. On stele.* Bib: HNE p 481 d. γ 1, pl XLI, 1; Déd p 266.

1 D(*is*) M(*anibus*).
2 HABIBI . ANNU
3 BATHI F(*ilius*) PAL
4 MYRENUS . V(*ixit*) . AN(*n*)IS
5 XXXII . M(*ensibus*). V. D(*iebus*)
6 XXI . FECIT . HERES
7 FRATER.

1 npš ḥbyby br̊
2 mlkw ʾnbt ḥbl

PAT 0251 **C3906** **n. d.**

Prov: Karánsebes (Hungary). Loc: Timisioara (Rumania). *Funerary. On stele.* Bib: HNE p 482 d. γ 4; Déd p 266.

1 D(*is*) M(*anibus*) M
2 FL(*avius*) . GURAS . IIDDEI .
3 (*filius*) [OP]TIO . EX N(*umero*) PALMVR(*enorum*)
.
4 [VI]XIT . ANN(*is*) . XXXXII . MIL(*itavit*)
5 [AN]N(*is*) XXI . AEL(*ius*) . HABIBIS
6 [PON]TIF(*ex*) ET H(*eres*) B(*ene*).M(*erito*).P(*osuit*)

1 gwr̊ʾ̊ ydy hpṭyn

PAT 0252 **C3907** **n. d.**

Prov: Koestandje (Rumania). Loc: Bucharest (Rumania): Public Museum. *Funerary. On stele.* Bib: ESE III p 30, pl 4; RES 1038.

1 npšʾ dnyḥt ṭmʾ
2 brll bt
3 bkrw bt
4 bbt bt
5 ʾḥth
6 dʾrt ʾtt
7 mšlm br
8 ʿwb ʾbyh
9 dḥyrn
10 ḥbl

PAT 0253 **C3908**
Prov: al-Kantara (Algeria). Loc: Not known. *Funerary. On stele.* Bib: RES 1038; HNE p 482 d. γ 2, pl XLI, 11.

1 D(*is*) M(*anibus*) S(*acrum*)
2 SURICUS RUBATIS
3 PAL(*murenus*) SAG(*ittarius*) C(*enturia*) MAXIMI
4 (*vixit*) ANN(*is*) XLV MI(*lit*)
5 AVIT ANN(*is*) XIIII

1 npšʾ dnh dy
2 šr̊ykw br̊ r̊bt
3 tdmwr̊yʾ qšṭʾ
4 qṭr̊yʾ mksmws
5 br̊ šnt 40+[5]
6 ḥbl

PAT 0254 **C3908 bis** **A.D. 215**
Prov: al-Kantara (Algeria). Loc: Not known. *Funerary. On stele.* Bib: RES 1038.

1 npšʾ dnh dy rpʾl
2 br̊ nšʾ ty[m]y
3 5.100+20+5+2 ḥbl

PAT 0255 **C3909** **A.D. 149**
Prov: Lambesi (Algeria). Loc: Lambesi (Algeria), not known. *Funerary. On stele.* Bib: RES 1038; HNE p 482 d. γ 3, pl XLI, 12.

1 D(*is*) M(*anibus*) S(*acrum*)
2 MOCIMUS S
3 UMONIS FIL(*ius*)
4 PALMURENUS
5 VIXIT ANNIS
6 XXX. H(*aeres*) P(*osuit*).

1 npšʾ dnh
2 mqymw br̊
3 šmʿwn ḥbl
4 šnt 4.100+60+1

PAT 0256 **C3910** **n. d.**
Prov: Denderah (Egypt). Loc: Oxford, Ashmolean Museum, 1976.187. *Honorary. On stone tablet.* Bib: RES 488; Bernard '84, pl 30,1.

1' [Ἰού(λιον)] Αὐρ(ήλιον) [.........]
2' Μακκαί[ου .... οἱ .....]
3' καὶ ἔμπο[ροι.......]
4' τὸν παρα[κομίσαντα τὴν]
5' συν[οδίαν ....]

1' [...] mqy nḥ[t ...]

PAT 0257 **C3911** **A.D. 146**
Prov: Qaryaten (Syria). Loc: Not known. *Dedicatory. On stone tablet.* Bib: RES 449; Déd p 89.

1 b[š]nt 4.100+40+10+5+2
2 byrḥ qnyn ʿmwdʾ
3 dnʾ wttlylʾ dlʿl
4 mnh ʿbdw zbdbwl
5 wʿtnwr wmlkw wʿmrw
6 wydyʿbl bny bršmš
7 br zbdbwl tdmryʾ [dy]
8 bnzly lʾlhʾ rbʾ
9 dnzly ʿl ḥyyhn wḥ[yy]
10 bnyhn wḥyy blḥy
11 brt ʿmrw ʾmhn

PAT 0258 **C3912** **n. d.**
Prov: Tayyibeh (Syria), reemployed. Loc: London: British Museum, 125025. *Dedicatory. On stone tablet.* Bib: HNE p 477 c. 14, pl XL, 1; ESE I p 257; NSI p 296, 1; Déd p 177.

1 Διὶ Μεγίστῳ Κεραυν-
2 ίῳ ὑπὲρ σωτηρί-
3 ας Τρα(ιανοῦ) Ἀδριανοῦ Σεβ(αστοῦ)
4 τοῦ κυρίου Ἀγαθάνγε-
5 λος Ἀβιληνὸς τῆς Δεκα-
6 πόλεος τὴν καμάραν ᾠκο-
7 δόμησεν καὶ τὴν κλίνη(ν)
8 ἐξ ἰδίων ἀνέθηκεν
9 ἔτους εμυʹ μηνὸς Λώου.

1 lbʿlšmn mr̊ʾ ʿlmʾ qr̊b
2 kptʾ wʿr̊šʾ ʾgtgls

Discovered in 1616 by Pietro della Valle, who noted "...due versi di certe altre lettere strane, al mio parere un poco simili all'ebraiche e alle samaritane, delle quasi tutte presi e tengo copia."

PAT 0259 **C3913** **A.D. 137**

Prov: Palmyra. Loc: St. Petersburg, Hermitage, 4187. *Tariff. On stone slabs.* Bib: de Vogüé 1883 b; 1883c; Duval 1883; Sachau 1883; Dessau 1884; Reckendorf 1888; Lidzbarski HNE (1898) pp 463-73 b. pl XXXIX, 3 (photograph of squeeze); Rostovtzeff '02 pp 405-06; Dittenberger '03, vol.2, no 629, pp 323-39 (Gk text and commentary); Cooke NSI '03 147 pp 313-40; Chabot '18; Rostovtzeff '32 pp 75-76; Février '31 pp 39-42, 47-49; Schlumberger '37; Seyrig '41b; Piganiol '45; Inv x 143 ('49); Rostovtzeff '57; Jones '71; Teixidor 1983a, 1983b; Klíma 1965; RosAH '67 6; Déd '72, pp 209-11; Raschke '78 index p 1310; Shiffmann, '80; Matthews '84; Zahrnt '86. Text printed is that of CIS; some small changes reflect collation with photographs of 1901 kindly supplied by E. V. Zeymal of the Hermitage Museum.

[Heading of entire tariff]

1 [᾿Επὶ αὐτοκράτορος Καίσαρος θεοῦ Τρ]αιανο[ῦ Παρθι]κοῦ υἱο[ῦ, θε]ο[ῦ Νέρουα υἱωνοῦ, Τραιανοῦ ᾿Αδριανοῦ Σεβαστοῦ, ἀρχιερέως μεγίστου, δημαρχικῆς ἐξουσίας

2 τὸ κα', αὐτοκράτορος τὸ β', ὑπ]άτου τὸ γ', π[ατ]ρὸς πατρίδος, ὑπάτω[ν Λ. Αἰλίου Καί]σαρος [τὸ β' Πουβ]λίου Κοιλί[ου Βαλβίνου].

[First part, Greek text]

1 [῎Ετ]ους ημυ', μηνὸς Ξανδικοῦ ιη'. Δόγμα βουλῆς.
2 ᾿Επὶ Βωννέους Βωννέους τοῦ Αἰράνου προέδρου, ᾿Αλεξάνδρου ᾿Αλεξάνδρου τοῦ
3 Φιλοπάτορος γραμματέως βουλῆς καὶ δήμου, Μαλίχου ᾿Ολαιοῦς καὶ Ζεβείδου Νεσᾶ ἀρχόν-
4 των, βουλῆ[ς] νομίμου ἀγομένης, ἐψηφίσθη τὰ ὑποτεταγμένα. ᾿Επειδὴ [ἐν το]ῖς πάλαι χρόνοις
5 ἐν τῷ τε[λω]νικῷ νόμῳ πλεῖστα τῶν ὑποτελῶν οὐκ ἀνελήμφθη, ἐπράσ[σετο] δ[ὲ ἐ]κ συνηθείας, ἐν-
6 γραφομέ[νου] τῇ μισθώσει τὸν τελωνοῦντα τὴν πρᾶξιν ποιεῖσθαι ἀκολούθ[ω]ς τῷ νόμῳ καὶ τῇ
7 συνηθείᾳ, συνέβαινεν δὲ πλειστάκις περὶ τούτου ζητήσεις γενέσθ[αι με]ταξὺ τῶν ἐνπόρων
8 πρὸς τοὺς τελώνας· δεδόχθαι τοὺς ἐνεστῶτας ἄρχοντας καὶ δ[εκα]πρώτους διακρείνοντας
9 τὰ μὴ ἀνειλημμένα τῷ νόμῳ ἐνγράψαι τῇ ἔνγιστα μισθώσει καὶ ὑποτάξαι ἑκάστῳ εἴδει τὸ
10 ἐκ συνηθείας τέλος, καὶ ἐπειδὰν κυρωθῇ τῷ μισθουμένῳ, ἐνγραφῆναι μετὰ τοῦ πρώτου νό-
11 μου στήλῃ λιθίνῃ τῇ οὔσῃ ἀντικρὺς ἱερ[οῦ] λεγομένου ᾿Ραβασείρη, ἐπιμελεῖσθαι δὲ τοὺς τυγχά-
12 νοντας κατὰ καιρὸν ἄρχοντας καὶ δεκαπρώτους καὶ συνδίκο[υς τοῦ] μηδὲν παραπράσσειν
13 τὸν μισθούμενον. [Lines 14-15 follow 11 lines of Aramaic]
14 Γόμος καρρικὸς παντὸς γένους· τεσσάρων γόμων καμηλικῶν τέ-
15 λος ἐπράχθη.

[Third part of inscription, three columns of Greek: Column One]

1 Παρὰ τ[ῶν παῖδας εἰς Πάλμυρα]
2 ἢ εἰς τὰ ὅ[ρια Παλμυρηνῶν εἰσ-]
3 αγόντω[ν πράξει ἑκάστου σώματος X̶ κβ']
4 Παρ' οὗ δ[ὲ ....]
5 μ[.........ἑκάστ]ου σ[ώματος X̶ ιβ']
6 Παρ' οὗ [......]α οὐετραν[ὰ X̶ ι']
7 Κἂν τὰ σώμα[τα] .οτο[.......... ἐξ-]
8 άγηται ἑκάστου σώμα[τος πράξει X̶ ιβ']
9 ᾿Ο αὐτὸς δημοσιώνη[ς ξηροφόρτου]
10 πράξει ἑκάστου γόμο[υ καμηλικοῦ]
11 εἰσκομισ[θέ]ντος [X̶ γ']
12 ᾿Εκκομισθ[έντ]ος [γόμου καμηλικοῦ]
13 ἑκάστου [X̶ γ']
14 Γόμου ὀνικ[οῦ ἑκάστο]υ εἰ[σκομισθέντος X̶ β']
15 ᾿Εκκομισθέν[τος X̶ β']

16 Πορφύρας μηλωτῆ[ς], ἑκά[στου δέρμα-]
17 τος είσκομισθέν[τ]ος [πράξει ἀσσάρια η′]
18 ʼΕκκομισθ[έντο]ς [ἀσσάρια η′]
19 Γόμου κ[αμηλικοῦ] μύρου [τοῦ ἐν ἀλαβάσ-]
20 τροις ε[ἰσκομισθέντος πράξει ~~X~~ κε′]
21 Καὶ το [.....................]
22 ἐκ[κομισθέντος πράξει ~~X~~ ιγ′]
23 Γ[όμου καμηλικοῦ μύρου τοῦ ἐν ἀσκοῖς]
24 αἰγείοις [εἰσκομισθέντος πράξει ~~X~~ ιγ′]
25 [ʼΕκ]κ[ομισθέντος ~~X~~ ζ′]
26 [Γόμου ὀνικοῦ μύ]ρου τοῦ ἐ[ν ἀλαβάστροις]
27 εἰσ[κομισ]θέν[τος] πρά[ξει ~~X~~ ιγ′]
28 [ʼΕκκομισ]θέν[τος ~~X~~ ζ′]
29 Γόμου ὀνικοῦ μ[ύρου τοῦ ἐν ἀσκοῖς]
30 αἰγείοις εἰσκομ[ισθέντο]ς πρ[άξει ~~X~~ ζ′]
31 ʼΕκκομισθέντος π[ρ]άξ[ει ~~X~~ δ′]
32 Γόμου ἐλεηροῦ το[ῦ ἐν ἀσκο]ῖς [τέσσαρ-]
33 σι αἰγείοις ἐπὶ καμήλ[ου εἰσκομισθέν-]
34 τος [~~X~~ ιγ′]
35 ʼΕκκομισθέντο[ς ~~X~~ ιγ′]
36 Γόμου ἐλαιηροῦ τοῦ ἐ[ν ἀσκοῖς δυσὶ αἰ-]
37 γείοις ἐπὶ καμήλ[ου εἰσκομισθέντος]
38 πράξει [~~X~~ ζ′]
39 ʼΕκκομισθέντο[ς ~~X~~ ζ′]
40 Γόμου ἐλε[ηροῦ τοῦ ἐπ' ὄνο]υ ε[ἰσκομισθέν-]
41 τος π[ράξει ~~X~~ ζ′]
42 ʼΕκ[κομισθέντος ~~X~~ ζ′]
43 Γόμ[ου κ...... τοῦ ἐν ἀσκοῖς τ]έσσ[αρσι]
44 αἰγείοις [εἰσκομισθέντος πρά]ξει ~~X~~ ιγ′
45 ʼΕκκομι[σ]θέ[ντος] ~~X~~ ιγ.′
46 Γόμου κ[.....τοῦ ἐν] ἀ[σ]κοῖς δυσὶ αἰγείοις
47 ἐπὶ κ[αμήλου εἰσ]κομισθέντος πράξει ~~X~~ ζ′

[Column Two]

48 [ʼΕκκομισ]θέντος [~~X~~ ζ′]
49 [Γόμου ὀ]ν[ικοῦ κ...... εἰσκο-]
50 [μισθέντος πράξει ~~X~~ ζ′]
51 [ʼΕκκομισθ]έν[τος ~~X~~ ζ′]
52 [......]ο[.]κου[...........]
53 [ʼΕκκ]ο[μισθέντ]ο[ς πράξ]ει [~~X~~ .′]
[Lines 54-63 totally effaced]
64 [...........]φο[.............]
65 [..........................]
66 [.................]σ[........]
67 [..............]λλης[....]
68 [κα]μήλου το[......]κης [......]
69 [θ]ρέμματος [.]εσ[...]ενου[......]
70 [....]δ[.........]θ[....]
71 [..]νκαδ[..τ]εθυμένη[........]
72 ʼΟ αὐτὸς δ[ημ]οσιώνης ἑκάσ[του] μη[νὸς]
73 παρ' ἐκ[άστο]υ τῶ[ν τὸ] ἔλαιον κατα...
74 π[.]ον[.....ε]ις [πωλοῦ]ντων [.....]
75 ʼΟ αὐτ[ὸς δημοσιώνης] πρά[ξει ....]λει
76 [..τῶν ἑταιρ]ῶν ὅσαι[...............]
77 [..λαμβά]νουσιν π[.................]
78 [.......ἀ]σσάρια ὀκτώ [...........]αιη
79 [......ἀσ]σάρια ἓξ ἐν [...]καστ[......]ασσ ϛ′
80 [ʼΟ αὐτὸς δημ]οσιώνης πρ[άξ]ει ἐργαστηρίων
81 [...........]παντοπωλ[εί]ων σκυτικῶν
82 [........]ς ἐκ συνηθείας ἑκάστου μηνὸς
83 καὶ ἐργαστηρίου ἑκάστου, ~~X~~ α′
84 Παρὰ τῶν δέρματα εἰσκομιζόντ[ων ἢ πω-]
85 λούντων, ἑκάστου δέρματος ἀσσά[ρια β′]
86 ʼΟμοίως ἱματιοπῶλαι μετάβολοι πωλ[οῦν-]
87 τες ἐν τῇ πόλει τῷ δημοσιώνῃ τὸ ἱκανὸν
π[.]ι[...]
88 Χρήσεος πηγῶν β′ ἑκάστου ἔτους ~~X~~ ω′
89 ʼΟ αὐτὸς πρά[ξ]ει γόμου πυρικοῦ, οἰνικοῦ, ἀχύ-
90 ρων καὶ τοιούτου γένους, ἑκάστου γόμου
91 καμηλικοῦ καθ' ὁδὸν ἑκάστην ~~X~~ α′
92 Καμήλου ὃς κενὸς εἰσαχθῇ πράξει ~~X~~ α′
93 καθὼς Κίλιξ Καίσαρος ἀπελεύθερος ἔπραξεν.

[Column Three]

94 [..........................]
95 πο[......................]
96 τῆς γ[....................]
97 κο[.....................]
98 [........................]
99 [........................]
100 σ[........................]
101 Πορφ[........................]
102 [.....]εκ[....................]
[Of lines 103-113, little or nothing can be made out]
114 [..............]μ[..]η[.]γο[............]
115 [.........]εινέτω

116 Ὅς δ' ἂν ἅλα[ς ἔχ]ῃ ἐν Παλμύροις ἢ [ἐν ὅροις]
117 Παλμυρη[ν]ῶν παραμετρησάτω [τῷ δημο-]
118 σιώνῃ ε[ἰς ἕκ]αστον μόδιον, ἀσσά[ριον_]
119 ὃς δ' ἂν οὐ [....]ν παραμετρήσ[ῃ......]
120 σῃ ἔχων το [.....] δημο[σιών....]
121 Παρ' οὗ ἂν ὁ δ[ημοσι]ώνης [......... ἐνέ-]
122 χυρα λά[βῃ ....]
123 ἀποδο[θῶ]σιν ο[..............]αβρει
124 δημο[σιώνῃ] τοῦ διπ[λοῦ] τὸ ἱκανὸν λαμβα-
125 νέτω· περὶ τ[ο]ύτου πρὸς τὸν δημοσιώνην
126 τοῦ διπλοῦ ε[ἰσα]γέσθω
127 Περὶ οὗ ἂν ὁ δημ[ο]σιώνης τινὰ ἀπαιτῇ, περί τε
128 οὗ ἂν ὁ δημοσιώ[νης ἀ]πό τινος ἀπαιτῆται, περὶ
129 τούτου δικαιοδο[τείσ]θω παρὰ τῷ ἐν Παλμύ-
130 ροις τεταγμένῳ
131 Τῷ δημοσιώνῃ κύρι[ον] ἔ[σ]τω παρὰ τῶν μὴ ἀπο-
132 λ[υόντων ἐν]έχυρα [λ]α[μβάνει]ν δι' ἑαυτοῦ ἢ δι[ὰ]
133 [τῶν ὑπη]ρ[ετῶν· κἂν τα]ῦτα τὰ [ἐνέ]χυρα ἡμέραις
134 [τρισίν μὴ λυθῇ, ἐξέστω τῷ δημ]οσιώνῃ πωλεῖν
135 [............ ἐν τόπῳ δημ]οσίῳ χωρὶς
136 δόλου πο[νηροῦ.......]ω[......] ἐπράθη
137 ἢ δοθῆναι ἔδει π[ράσσ]ειν τῷ δη[μοσιώνῃ] καθὼς
138 καὶ [.....]στιν [.....] τοῦ νόμου [ἐξέσ]τω
139 Λιμένος π[........ πη]γῶν ὑδάτων Καίσαρος
140 τῷ μισθωτῇ [......]εντος [........] παρασχέσ[θαι]

[Fourth part, Column One]

141 ἄλλῳ μηδενὶ πράσσειν διδόναι λαμ[βάνειν]
142 ἐξέστω μήτε τ[...]ε[....]νωφο[..] ἀνθρ[ωπ.. μή]
143 τε τινι [ὀν]όματι το στ[....]οε[..]υπ[......]ν
144 τούτων εἰ ποιήσῃ ἢ ε[.......... πραχ-]
145 [θήτω τὸ] διπλοῦν [....... ....]
146 [..........]ητε[..................]οι[..]
147 [................................]
148 Κ[................................]
149 κα[..............................]
150 Γαιο[..............................]
151 αντι[............................]
152 Μεταξὺ Παλ[μυρηνῶν ....]
153 γνους ἐστι[.... ....]
154 γείνεσθαι καθ' οι[...................]
155 εὐ[....] σατο μ[.....................]
156 [......]οσα δὲ ἐξ[..................]
157 [.......]ως
158 Αὐτό[ῖ]ς [...]τα[....]λεισπ[.............]
159 τω[ν τ]α[......]ωνυ[................]
160 τῷ τελών[ῃ διδόσ]θω
161 οἵ δ' ἂν ε[..]α[...]ασω[....]ἐξα[γ........]
162 [....]ει[..........................]
163 [.]εο[..............]δο[...]
164 Καθ' ἣν ἀναλο[....................]
165 Τοῦ δὲ ἐξαγω[................]αι[.....]
166 αδωσε[...]νο[..............]
167 Ἐρίων[...............................]
168 θαρ[...............................]
169 π[..................]ειμ[..............]
170 [.]ρ[..................]διαγ[..............]
171 [.....]φορον[.........]ματουμεν[......]φορι[..]
172 [....]αγωγη [........]ι ~~X~~ ς' τοῦ δὲ [........~~X~~] θ'
173 ἀξιοῦντος το[.....]νου εἰ καὶ μὴ [........]
174 [ἰτ]αλικῶν ἐξαγ[ομένω]ν πράσσειν ὕστ[ερον ὡς συν-]
175 εφωνήθη μ[ὴ ἀπὸ τ]ούτων ἐξαγο[μένων τὸ τέλος δί-]
176 δοσθαι
177 Μύρου τοῦ ἐν ἀσκο[ῖς αἰγεί]οις πρά[ξει ὁ τελώνης]
178 κατὰ τὸν νόμο[ν ....] οὔτε[...........]άμ[άρ-]
179 τημα γέγονεν τῷ προτεθέντι [.]εικ[...... ἐν τῷ συν-]
180 εσφραγισμένῳ νόμῳ τέτακται
181 Τὸ τοῦ σφάκτρου τέλος εἰς δηνάριον ὀφείλει λο[γεύεσθαι]
182 καὶ Γερμανικοῦ Καίσαρος διὰ τῆς πρὸς Στατείλι[ον ἐπισ-]
183 τολῆς διασαφήσαντος ὅτι δεῖ πρὸς ἀσσάριον ἰτα[λικόν]
184 τὰ τέλη λογεύεσθαι· τὸ δὲ ἐντὸς δηναρίου τέλο[ς]

185 συνηθείᾳ ὁ τελώνης πρὸς κέρμα πράξει· τῶ[ν δὲ]
186 διὰ τὸ νεκριμαῖα εἶναι ρ(ειπτουμένων τὸ τέλο[ς οὐκ
186 ὀφείλεται.]
187 Τῶν βρωτῶν τὸ κα(τὰ) τὸν νόμον τοῦ γόμου δην[άριον]
188 εἴστημι πράσσεσθαι ὅταν ἔξωθεν τῶν ὅρων εἰσά[γηται]
189 ἢ ἐξάγηται.Τοὺς δὲ εἰς χωρία ἢ ἀπὸ τῶν [χω-]
190 ρίων κατακομίζοντας ἀτελεῖς εἶναι, ὡς καὶ συνεφώ-
191 νησεν αὐτοῖς. Κώνου καὶ τῶν ὁμοίων ἔδ[ο-]
192 ξεν ὅσα εἰς ἐμπορείαν φέρεται τὸ τέλος εἰς τὸ ξη-
193 ρόφορτον ἀνάγεσθαι, ὡς καὶ ἐν ταῖς λοιπαῖς γείνεται πόλεσι.
194 Καμήλων ἐάν τε κεναὶ ἐάν τε ἔνγομοι εἰσάγωνται ἔξωθεν
195 τῶν ὅρων ὀφείλεται δηνάριον ἑκάστης κατὰ τὸν
196 νόμον ὡς καὶ Κουρβούλων ὁ κράτιστος ἐσημι-
197 ώσατο ἐν τῇ πρὸς Βάρβαρον ἐπιστολῇ.

[Column Two]
198 [............]ρλ[...................]
199 [...]οι[........]νο[.........]οξη[........]
200 ἀγεσ[θαι......]τ(α)[.......]οποστ[......]
201 [...........]π[ρ]οσ[..................]
202 [....]υσ[...]π[..............]
203 [Παρὰ τῶν] ἑταιρῶ[ν αἳ δηνάριον ἢ πλέον λαμβά-]
204 [νουσιν ..ἑ]κάστης[..................]α[.]αν
205 [...........]εου[...................]ναλα
206 [............]οσ[............πρ]άσσειν
207 [.........................]τον θ[...]αν
208 [....................]ντος ο[......]
209 [.....................]του[....]
210 [....................]ι[.......]
211 [................................]
212 [..................]νιτ[...]ον[....]
213 [................]μενοιτ[.........]
214 [.]ειποι[..........................]
215 νόμον [.]τ[...... ....]
[In lines 216-227 only a few letters can be made out]
228 [.....]πατ[.......................]
229 [.......]ω[.......................]
230 [...]πας συνφων [...................]
231 τελώ[ν]ην γείνεσθαι· επει[......τὸ ἐκ τοῦ]
232 νόμο[υ] τέλος πρὸς δηνά[ρ]ιον φ[έρειν.]
233 ʽΕννόμιον συνεφωνήθη μὴ δεῖν πράσσε[ιν ἐκτὸς τῶν]
234 τελῶν· [τ]ῶν δὲ ἐπὶ νομὴν μεταγομένων [εἰς Παλ-]
235 μυρηνὴν θρεμμάτων ὀφείλεσθαι· χαρα[κτη-]
236 ρίσασθαι τὰ θρέμματα ἐὰν θέλῃ ὁ δημο[σιώνης,]
237 ἐξέστω.

I

1 dgmʾ dy bwlʾ byrḥ nysn ywm 10+5+3 šnt 4.100+40+5+3 bplhdrwtʾ dy bwnʾ br
2 bwnʾ br ḥyrn wgrmṭyʾ dy ʾlksdrs br ʾlksdrs br plpṭr grmṭws dy bwlʾ wdms wʾrkwnyʾ
3 mlkw br ʿlyy br mqymw wzbydʾ br nšʾ kd hwt bwlʾ knyšʾ mn nmwsʾ ʾšrt
4 mdy ktyb mn lṯht bdyl dy bzbnyʾ qdmyʾ bnmwsʾ dy mksʾ ʿbydn šgyn ḥybn
5 mksʾ lʾ ʾsqw whww mtgbyn mn ʿydʾ bmdʿn dy hwʾ mtktb bʾgwryʾ dy
6 mksʾ whwʾ gbʾ hyk bnmwsʾ wbʿydʾ wmṯl kwt zbnyn šgyn ʿl ṣbwtʾ ʾln
7 srbnyn hww byny tgrʾ lbyny mksyʾ ʾṯzy lbwlʾ dy ʾrkwnyʾ ʾln wlʿšrtʾ
8 dy ybn[w]n mdʿm dy lʾ msq bnmwsʾ wyktb bšṭr ʾgryʾ ḥdtʾ wyktb lmdʿmʾ
9 mdʿmʾ mksh dy mn ʿydʾ wmdy ʾšr lʾgwrʾ wktb ʿm nmwsʾ qdmyʾ bgllʾ
10 dy lqbl hyklʾ dy rbʾsyrʾ wyhwʾ mbṭl lʾrkwnyʾ dy hwn bzbn zbn wʿšrtʾ
11 wsdqyʾ dy lʾ yhwʾ gbʾ ʾgwrʾ mn ʾnš mdʿm ytyr
[An insertion in Gk (lines numbered 14-15 above, with Gk text) occurs at this point]
12 Γόμος καρρικὸς παντὸς γένους· τεσσάρων γόμων καμηλικῶν τέ-

13 λος ἐπράχθη. [Aramaic resumes] ṭʿwn qrs dy klmʾ gns klh lʾrbʿʾ ṭʿwnyn dy gmlyn
14 mksʾ gby

II [Line 1 above columns 1-3]
1 nmwsʾ dy mksʾ dy lmnʾ dy hdrynʾ tdmr wʿyntʾ dy myʾ [dy ʾy]ls qysr
[Part II, Column 1]
2 mn mʿly ʿlymyʾ dy mtʾʿlyn ltdmr
3 ʾw [ltḥwmyh ygbʾ mks]ʾ lkl rgl[y] [..] d<ynr> 20+2
4 mn ʿlm dy y[zb]n b[mdy]t[ʾ..] [d]<ynr> 10+2
5 mn ʿlm wtr[n] dy yzbn [...] [d]<ynr> [...]
6 whn zbwnʾ [ypq] ʿlymyn ytn lkl rgly [d]<ynr> 10+2
7 hw m[ksʾ yg]bʾ [m]n ṭʿwn gmlʾ dy yby[šyn]
8 lmʿlnʾ [......] dy ṭʿwn gmlʾ d<ynr> [3]
9 mn [ṭʿwn gmlʾ] lm[pqnʾ] d<ynr> 3
10 mn ṭ[ʿwn] ḥmrʾ lmʿlnʾ w[lmpqnʾ d<ynr> 2]
11 mn ʾ[rg]wnʾ mlṭʾ lkl m[šk lmʿlnʾ]
12 wlm[p]qnʾ ʾsryn 5+3
13 mn ṭʿ[wn g]ml[ʾ] dy mšḥʾ bšymʾ [dy]
14 mtʾʿl [b]š[typt]ʾ d<ynr> 20+5
15 wlmʾ d[... mšḥ]ʾ dnh
16 lmpqn[ʾ ......] gml lṭʿwnʾ d<ynr> 10+3
17 mn ṭʿwn gmlʾ dy [m]šḥʾ bšymʾ [dy ytʾʿl]
18 bzqy[n dy] ʿ[z l]m[ʿl]nʾ d<ynr> 10+3 wlmpq[nʾ d<ynr> 5+2]
19 mn ṭ[ʿwn ḥmr dy m]šḥʾ bš[ymʾ d]y ytʾʿl
20 bš[ṭyp]yʾ [d]<ynr> 10+3 wlmpqnʾ d<ynr> 5+2
21 mn ṭʿwn ḥm[r d]y mšḥʾ b[šy]mʾ dy
22 ytʾʿl bzqy[n dy ʿ]z d<ynr> 5+2 [wlm]pqnʾ d<ynr> 4
23 mn ṭʿwn dy mš[ḥʾ dy bzq]yn ʾrbʿ
24 dy ʿz lmʿln ṭʿwn g[m]lʾ d<ynr> 10+3
25 wlmpqnʾ d<ynr> [10+3]
26 mn ṭʿwn dy mš[ḥʾ] dy bzqyn trtn dy ʿz
27 lmʿl[n] ṭ[ʿwn]ʾ dy gmlʾ d<ynr> [5+2] wlmpqnʾ d<ynr> [5+2]
28 mn ṭʿw[n] ḥmr dy mšḥ lmʿ[lnʾ] d<ynr> 5+2 wl<m>pqnʾ [d<ynr> 5+2]
29 mn ṭʿwn dhnʾ dy bzqyn ʾ[rbʿ] dy ʿz dy
30 ṭʿwn gml <l>mʿlnʾ d<ynr> 10+3 wl[mpq]nʾ d<ynr> 10+3
31 mn ṭʿwn dhnʾ dy bzqyn t[rtn dy] ʿz
32 lṭʿwn gml lmʿlnʾ d<ynr> 5+2 wlm[pqnʾ d]<ynr> 5+2
33 mn ṭʿwn [dh]nʾ dy ḥmr lmʿlnʾ [d<ynr> 5+2 wlmpqnʾ d<ynr> 5+2]
34 mn ṭʿwn n[wny]ʾ mlyḥyʾ lṭʿwnʾ dy [gmlʾ]
35 [lmʿ]lnʾ d]<ynr> wmn mpq mnhwn [...]
36 [.........]ʾ lṭʿwnʾ dy gmlʾ lm[....]
37 [......]ʾ dy ṭʿwn ḥmrʾ lmʿln[ʾ] d[..]
38 [.............]nʾ ygbʾ mksʾ d<ynr> 3
39 mn [..........]yʾ d<ynr> wlkwdn[ʾ ..]
40 [................]l mn [...]ʾm[..]ʾ[...]
41 [............]yʾ[... ʾs]ryn 2
42 m[......] ʾmryʾ lmʿ[ln wlmpqn] lršʾ ḥd ʾsrʾ ḥd
43 mn[..]ʾ gmlʾ ʾ[sry]n 3
44 mn[..]ʾ rbʾ [......] [ʾ]sryn 2
45 mn[..]w[.]d[n m]k[sʾ ʾsr]ʾ ḥd
46 ʾp [y]g[b]ʾ mk[sʾ lkl yr]ḥ mn dy yh[wʾ] mzbn mšḥʾ
47 bšymʾ ʾsryn 2 ʾp ygbʾ mksʾ mn znytʾ mn
48 mn dy šqlʾ dynr [ʾw] ytyr dnrʾ ḥd mn ʾtʾ
49 wmn mn dy šqlʾ ʾsryn tmnyʾ
50 ygbʾ ʾsryn tmnyʾ
[Part II, Column 2]
51 wmn mn dy šql[ʾ] ʾsry[n š]tʾ
52 ygbʾ ʾsryn [štʾ]
53 ʾp ygbʾ [mksʾ mn .....]yw[..]
54 [..]ypʾ[...]ḥ[...]ʾ hyk ʿdʾ
55 [lkl] yr[ḥ] mn ḥnwtʾ d<ynr> 1
56 [mn k]l mšk dy [y]tʾʿl ʾw yzbn lmškʾ ʾsryn 2
57 [mzbn]y nḥtyʾ dy hpkyn bmdytʾ yhn mwṭ mksʾ
58 [ltš]myš ʿynn trtn dy m[y] dy bmdytʾ d<ynr> 8.100
59 [y]gbʾ mksʾ lṭʿwnʾ dy ḥṭʾ wḥmrʾ wtbnʾ
60 w[k]l mdy dmʾ [lhwn lk]l gml lʾrḥ ḥdʾ d<ynr> 1
61 lgmlʾ kdy ytʾyʿl sryq ygbʾ d<ynr> 1
62 hyk [dy gbʾ] qlqys br ḥry qysr
63 nm[ws dy mk]sʾ dy tdmr wʿyntʾ dy myʾ
64 wml[ḥʾ d]y b[m]dytʾ wtḥwmyh hyk
65 ʾ[gwryʾ d]y ʾ[t]ʾgr qdm mryns hygmwnʾ

66 m[n ......]lk[l] ṭ‘wn dy gml m‘ln d<ynr> 4 wmpqn d<ynr> 4
67 m[n ’]r[gwn’] mlṭ’ lkl mšk lm‘ln’ d<ynr> 4 wlmpqn’ d<ynr> 4
68 ’p ygb’ [mks]’ mn gnsy’ klhwn hyk dy ktyb mn l‘l
69 [mlḥ] ṭb [ytg]b’ ’sr’ ḥd lmdy’ dy qsṭwn
70 ‘šr w[š]t [w]m’ dy ytb‘’ ytn [lh]n ltšmyš’
71 w[dy] l’ y[...y]pr‘ lkl md’ mn nm[ws]’ dnh ssṭrṭyn [trn]
72 mn dy yhw’ lh mlḥ btd[mr ’w btḥw]m’ d[y]
73 t[dmry]’ ykylnh l[mks]’ [’]py mdy’ b’sr’ ḥd
74 m[....]gys[......]qy hygmwn’
75 [..] ḥšbn mk[.....]bny tdmry’ l[....]
76 [..]q[.]t mks[ms] qy[sr] dy [..] [m]ks’
77 ḥyb lmhw’ [....]s’ [dy] ’gr bh
78 ’lqms wḥ[....] nmws’ md‘m lhn
79 mšttp wm[....]’ dy [..] yhw’
80 pr‘ lmks’ mn dy m‘l rglyn ltdmr
81 [’]w ltḥ[wm]yh wmpq lkl rgly d<ynr> 20+2
82 w[m]n dy [........ m]pq ypr‘ lmk[s’ d]<ynr> 10+2
83 w[mn] dy y[zbn ‘l]m wṭrn ypr‘ d<ynr> 5+3
84 [...]l kl [....]my’ dnh [....]
85 w[d]y m‘l[....]hw d<ynr> wmpq [d]<ynr> 10+2
86 [...............] mn dy mpq ‘lm wṭrn
87 [..] ḥšb[n] [........hyk dy] ktyb bnmws’
88 [mn] dy yz[bn ....] ypr‘ d<ynr> 5+4
89 w[dy m]pq [...]l’ ktyb bdyl [dy]
90 md‘m l’ [..]’ wk[.........]
91 l’ dmy’ [..........]y[....]
92 wm‘ln mk[....]b[....]y m[..]
93 wdy ‘mr’ [........]s’ dy ’p m[...]
94 tdm[r] l[’ m]ks[.....] pr‘’ thw’ ‘mr’
95 dy ’yṭ[ly’ .....] mks’ lmpqn’ btr
96 kwt hww spw[n ...]l’ ‘mr’ ’yṭlyq[’]
97 [t]hw’ pr‘’ [mk]s[’] lmpq<n>’
98 mšḥ’ b[šym’ dy] bzqyn dy ‘z yhw’ mks’
99 mt[gb’ hyk nmws]’ bdyl dy bṭ‘wn dy

[Part II, Column 3]

100 ktb dy ṭ‘’ mks[’ ..]bl[......]
101 [.]k[..]š wbnmws’ rṣyp d<ynr> 10+3
102 mks’ dy qṣb’ ’py dnr ḥyb
103 lmtḥšbw hyk dy ’p grmnqws qysr
104 b’grt’ dy ktb lsṭṭyls pšq dy
105 h’ kšr dy [yh]n mksy’ ’py ’sr ’yṭlq[’]
106 gbn wmdy gw mn dnr ḥyb mks’ hyk
107 ‘dt’ ‘[r]pn yh’ gb’
108 pgryn dy mštdn mks l’ ḥybyn
109 lṭ‘mt’ hy<k> bnm[w]s’ lṭ‘wn’ ’qymt
110 dy yhw’ [mtgb]’ dnr
111 mdy yhw’ mt[’‘]l br mn tḥwm’ ’w m’pq
112 mn dy mpq l[qry]’ [’w m]’‘l mn qry’
113 mks l’ ḥyb hyk dy ’p hww spwn
114 ’sṭrbyly’ wmdy dm’ lhwn ’tḥzy dy
115 lkl dy ‘ll lḥšbn tgr’ yhw’ mks’
116 hyk lybyš hyk dy hw’ ’p bmdynt’
117 ’ḥrnyt’
118 gmly’ hn ṭ‘ynyn whn sryqyn yhn
119 mt’‘lyn br mn tḥwm’ ḥyb kl
120 gml dnr hyk bnmws’ whyk dy ’šr
121 qrblwn kšyr’ b’grt’ dy ktb lbrbrs
122 ‘l gldy’ dy gmly[’] ’p ’ln kprw dy mks
123 l’ gbn ‘šb[y]’ w[nt]yrt’ ’tḥzy dy yhwn
124 yhbyn mk[s’] bdyl dy ’yt bhwn tgrt’
125 mks’ dy ‘lymt’ hyk dy nmws’ mwḥ’ pšqt
126 hw mks’ yg[b’ mk]s’ mn ‘lymt’ dy šqln dnr
127 ’w ytyr l’t[t’ dn]r whn ḥsyr thwh šql’
128 mdy hy šq[l’ ygb’ ‘l] ṣlmy nḥš’ ’drṭy’
129 ’tḥzy dy ytgb[wn] hyk [nḥ]š’ wyhw’ pr‘ ṣlm
130 bplgwt [ṭ‘w]n wṣlmyn trn ṭ‘wn ‘l mlḥ’
131 qšṭ[’ ’]tḥzy ly dy b’tr dy dms thw’
132 mtzbn’ b’tr dy mtknšyn wmn mn tdmry’
133 yzbn lḥš[ḥ]th yhw’ yhb lmdy’ ’sr ’yṭlq[’]
134 hyk bnmws’ w’p mks’ [m]lḥ’ dy hwy’
135 btdmr hyk bh[. ...] ’py ’sr yhw’
136 mtqbl wl[tdmry]’ yhw’ mzbn hyk ‘yd’
137 [....... mk]s’ dy ’rgwn’ bdyl dy
138 [......] ’rb‘’ wplgw [...]b[..]
139 [........] m[h]lkyn b[md]yt wḥyṭ’
140 [.......]d dy yhw’
141 [..]’[..............] yhw’ mtgb’
142 mks’ hyk dy k[tyb mn l]‘l lm‘ln šlḥ’
143 ’sryn 2 ’šl[.....] mtgb’ wlmmpqn’
144 lṭ‘wn[’...]’ [hyk dy ’]p hww spwn
145 ‘n’ t[h]w[’ m]t’‘l’ m[n br] mn tḥwm’ ’p hn
146 [....... mt]’‘l’ mks’ ḥyb’ whn lgw mn
147 [....... mt]’‘l’ lmdyt’ lmgz mks l’ ḥyb[’]
145 ‘n’ t[h]w[’ m]t’‘l’ m[n br] mn tḥwm’ ’p hn
146 [....... mt]’‘l’ mks’ ḥyb’ whn lgw mn
147 [.......] mt’‘l’ lmdyt’ lmgz mks l’ ḥyb[’]
148 m[.........]nwt’ wmn dy hyk <d>y hwn hwn

[last line, below other columns]
149 [s]pwn mks' [.....]' hyk bnmws' dnr yhw' mtgb' ['p] mn[....] mdy pr' mks' l' yhw' mtgb' 'l' l'n dy thw' m''l' l[.... tḥw]m tdmr 'n yṣb' mks' yhw' [...]' lh

----

PAT 0260 **C3914** **A.D. 175**

Prov: Palmyra, Temple of Bel, Propylaeum. Loc: Palmyra, *in situ. Honorific. On stone tablet.* Bib: RES 2127; Inv 9 25; Déd p 34.

1 Ἡ βουλὴ καὶ ὁ δῆμος
2 [ἀνέστησαν το]ὺς ἀνδριάντας Ἰαριβωλῇ Σεγῇ καὶ Ἀουεί-
3 [δῳ Ἀδδουδάν]ου, ὑωνοῖς Ἰαριβωλέους τοῦ Ἀδδουδά-
4 [νου τοῦ Ζα]βδιβώλου Ἀδδουδάνου Φίρμωνος, εὐσε-
5 [βέσι καὶ φ]ιλοπάτρισι καὶ φιλοτείμοις ἐν πολλοῖς
6 [πράγ]μασι, ποιήσασι τὰς θύρας ταύτας τὰς αὐρο-
7 [χαλκ]είους ἐξ ἰδίων, τὰς ἐν τῇ μεγάλῃ βασιλικῇ
8 τοῦ Βήλου· ἔτους ϛπυ', Δύστρου.

1 bwl' wdms 'qymt ṣlmy' 'ln trwyhwn dy yrḥbwl' [br]
2 'g' w'wyd' br ḥdwdn bny yrḥbwl' br ḥdwdn br zbdbwl br ḥdw[dn]
3 prmwn dḥl' 'lhy' wrḥym' mdythwn wnhryn bmgdyhwn šgy'[y']
4 'ḥrn' 'bdw tr'y' 'ln šttyhn dy plz' dy bbslq' rbt'
5 dy bt bl mn kyshwn byrḥ 'dr šnt 4.100+80+5+1

PAT 0261 **C3915** **A.D. 21**

Prov: Palmyra, Temple of Bel. Loc: Palmyra, *in situ. Honorific. On column console.* Bib: HNE p 457 a. 1, pl XXXVII, 1; Inv 9 13; RES 451.

1 ṣlm ḥšš br nš' br bwlḥ' ḥšš dy
2 'bdw lh bny kmr' wbny mtbwl mn [dy] qm
3 bršhwn w'bd šlm' bynyhwn wprns
4 brmnhwn bkl [ṣ]bw klh rb' wz'r'
5 lyqrh byrḥ knwn šnt 3.100+20+10+3

On Greek of CIS see at Inv 9 11; Aram text was more damaged by time of edition in Inv 9 13

PAT 0262 **C3916** **A.D. 142**

Prov: Palmyra, Temple of Bel. Loc: Palmyra, *in situ. Honorific. On column-console.* Bib: Inv 9 14a; RES 452.

(In larger script, at top)
1 Νεσῆ Ἀλᾶ τοῦ Νεσῆ?
(main text, below)
1 Νεσῆ Ἀλᾶ τοῦ Νεσῆ τοῦ Ἀλᾶ τοῦ Ῥεφαέλου
2 τοῦ Ἀβισσέου συνοδιάρχην, οἱ συναναβάν
3 τες μετ' αὐτοῦ ἔμποροι ἀπὸ Φοράθου κὲ
4 Ὀλαγασιάδος, τειμῆς καὶ εὐχαριστείας
5 ἕνεκεν, ἔτους γνυ', μηνὸς Ξανδ[ι]κοῦ.

1 ṣlm' dnh dy ns' br ḥl' br ns' br ḥl' br
2 rp'l br 'bsy dy 'qym lh bny šyrt' dy slq
3 'mh mn prt wmn 'lgšy' bdyldy špr lhwn
4 wqm bršhwn w'drnwn bkl ṣbw klh [lyqrh]
(lower margin)
5 byrḥ nysn [šn]t 4.100+40+10+3
Text of Inv 9 14a

PAT 0263 **C3917** **A.D. 108**

Prov: Palmyra, Temple of Bel. Loc: Palmyra, *in situ. Honorific. On column console.* Bib: RES 2128; Inv 9 15; Déd p 307; RosAH 5; Dri '88 p 168.

1 Ἄκκεον Νοαραίου τοῦ Ἀκκαέου
2 οἱ Γαδδειβώλιοι τειμῆς χάριν.

1 ṣlm' dnh dy 'qyḥ b[r n'r]y br 'qyḥ
2 dy 'bdw lh bny gdybwl bdyldy 'bd lhn
3 bb' wtr'why w'p 'bd b'lgšy' ḥmn'
4 klh hw w'trh w'p ṭll 'drwn'
5 klh wšpr lhwn bkl ṣbw klh
6 bdylkwt 'bdw lh ṣlm' dnh lyqrh
7 byrḥ knwn šnt 4.100+20

PAT 0264 **C3918** **n. d.**
Prov: Palmyra, Temple of Bel. Loc: Palmyra, *in situ*. *Honorific. On column console.* Bib: Inv 9 18.

1 [....] br ḥyr[n ...]
Text of Inv 9 18

PAT 0265 **C3919** **A.D. 117**
Prov: Palmyra, Temple of Bel. Loc: Palmyra, *in situ*. *Honorific. On column console.* Bib: RES 2129; Inv 9 19; Déd p 229.

1 ṣlmʾ dnh dy zbydʾ br šʿdw
2 tymšmš dy ʿbdt lh bwlʾ
3 [ly]qrh wshd lh yrḥbwl ʾlhʾ
4 brbnwt mrzḥwth dy kmry bl
5 byrḥ nysn šnt 4.100+20+5+3

PAT 0266 **C3920** **A.D. 127**
Prov: Palmyra, Temple of Bel, reemployed in Muslim wall. Loc: Palmyra, *in situ*. *Honorific. On column console.* Bib: RES 2130; Inv 9 32; Déd p 267.

1 Θαιμῆν Λισαμσαίου τοῦ ᾿Ογήλου
2 τοῦ ᾿Ιεδειβήλου Σόαδος ὁ υἱὸς αὐτοῦ
3 μετὰ τὴν τελευτὴν τειμῆς χάριν ἔτο[υς]
4 θλυ′ μηνὸς ῾Υπερβερεταίου

1 ṣlmʾ dnh
2 dy tymʾ br lšmšy br ʿgʾ ydyʿbl dy ʿbd
3 lh šʿdw brh btr dy myt lyqrh byrḥ
4 tš[ry] šnt 4.100+20+10+5+4

PAT 0267 **C3921** **A.D. 120**
Prov: Palmyra, Temple of Bel, reemployed in Muslim wall. Loc: Palmyra, *in situ*. *Honorific. On column console.* Bib: RES 2131; Inv 9 31.

1 ῾Η βουλὴ καὶ ὁ δῆμος Μάλιχον
2 Οὐαβαλλάθου τοῦ Μανναίου,
3 τειμῆς χάριν.

1 ṣlmʾ dnh dy mlkw br whblt br mʿny dy
2 ʿb[d]w lh bwlʾ wdms lyqrh qm ṣlmʾ dnh
3 b[yrḥ .....] šnt 4.100+20+10+2
line 2: *ʿb[d]w* with Cantineau Inv 9 31 :: CIS

PAT 0268 **C3922** **A.D. 28**
Prov: Palmyra, Temple of Bel. Loc: Palmyra, *in situ*. *Honorific. On column console.* Bib: Inv 9 9; RES 809.

1 ṣlmʾ dnh dy ʿgylw br tymy b[r]
2 zbdbwl dy m[n] bny kmrʾ dy ʾqym
3 lh bnwhy lyqrh šnt 3.100+40

PAT 0269 **C3923** **A.D. 51**
Prov: Palmyra, Temple of Bel. Loc: Palmyra, *in situ*. *Honorific. On column console.* Bib: Inv 9 8; Déd p 154; RES 810; cf Inv 11 35.

1 [Παλμυρη]νῶν ἡ [π]ό[λις Μόκειμον ᾿Ογήλου τοῦ
2 [καὶ] ᾿Οχχαίσου ἀρέσ[αντ]α αὐ(τ)ῇ τε καὶ τοῖς θεο[ῖς]
3 διδόντα ἐξ ἰδίων εἰς [τὸ ἱε]ρὸν σπονδοφό[ρ]ο[ν]
4 καὶ θυμιατήριν χρυσᾶ ἐγ δηναρίων ρν′ καὶ το[.....]
5 [..]αλια τέσσαρα χρυσᾶ ἐγ δη. ρκ′ καὶ τ[ραπεζ]ώ[ματα]
6 [κ]αὶ [π]ρ[οσ]κεφαλάδιον εἰς τὴν[...........]
7 [κ]λείνην ἠγορασμένα ἀργυρίου δηναρ[ίων ...]
8 [τειμῆ]ς κ[αὶ εὐνοί]ας ἕνεκεν· ἔτους β[ξ]τ′ μηνὸς [Δύστρου].

1 ṣlmʾ dnh dy mqymw br ʿgylw br pṣyʾ[l]
2 br tymy dy mtqrh ḥkyšw dy mn bny zb[d]b[wl]
3 [dy ʾ]qymw lh gbl tdmryʾ klhn mndy špr [lhn]
4 [wq]rb lbt ʾlhyhn mn [....]w[.....]qr[...
5 [byrḥ ʾ]dr [šnh] 3.100+[60]+2
Text of CIS based on first squeezes on now-damaged inscription, cf Inv 9 8

PAT 0270 **C3924** **A.D. 19**
Prov: Palmyra, Temple of Bel, reemployed. Loc: Palmyra, A 34. *Honorific. On stone tablet.* Bib: Inv 9 6A; RES 811.

1 [....................]
2 [....ἔμπ]ο[ρ]οι Πα[λμυρηνοὶ]
3 [καὶ Ἕλλην]ες ἀνέσ[τη]σ[αν]
4 [τὸν ἀνδριάν]τα Ἰεδειβ[ήλῳ]
5 [Ἀζίζου Παλ]μυρηνῷ φ[υλῆς]
6 [Μανθαβω]λείων ἐπεὶ
7 [κατεσπο]ύδασεν εἰς τὴν
8 [κτίσιν τ]οῦ ναοῦ Βήλου.

1 byrḥ ʾb šnt 3.100+20+10 [ṣlmʾ dnh dy]
2 ydyʿbl br ʿzyzw br ydyʿ[?][bl dy mn]
3 bny mtbw[l dy] ʾqym[w lh tdmryʾ]
4 wywnyʾ dy bslwkyʾ [bdyldy]
5 qm wšmš bmgdʾ r[bʾ lbt bl]

Originally on same tablet as text C3925, on left; text of Inv 9 6A; see there for further restorations of Gk

PAT 0271 **C3925** **A.D. 17**

Prov: Palmyra, Temple of Bel, reemployed. Loc: Palmyra, A 34. *Honorific. On stone tablet.* Bib: Inv 9 6B; RES 812.

1 [Ἀζειζον Ἰεδειβήλου τοῦ]
2 [Βαρ]χαίου Παλμυρηνὸν
3 φυλῆς Μανθβωλείω[ν]
4 Ἰεδείβηλος ὁ υἱὸς ἔτ[ους]
5 ηκ[τʹ,] μηνὸς Γορπιαί[ου]

1 [byrḥ] ʾlwl šnt 3.100+20+5+3 ṣl[mʾ]
2 [d]y ʿzyzw b[?]r ydyʿbl brky dy m[n]
3 [b]ny mtbwl dy ʾqym lh ydy[ʿbl]
4 [b]rh

Originally on same tablet as text C3924, on right

PAT 0272 **C3926** **A.D. 135**

Prov: Palmyra, Temple of Bel. Loc: Palmyra. *Honorific. On stone tablet.* Bib: RES 813.

1 [.................]
2 [.....λειτ]ηνταιναιαν
3 [.....]ίῳ τοῦ ζμυʹ ἔτους

1 ṣlm mlkw br m[...]
2 [dy] ʿbdw lh km[ry ...]
3 [....]hwn wy[.....]

PAT 0273 **C3927** **A.D. 140**

Prov: Palmyra, Temple of Bel, reemployed. Loc: Palmyra. *Honorific. On stone tablet.* Bib: Photo Déd pl I, 3.

1 Ἡ βουλὴ Ἀο[φ]άλειν Αἱράνου τοῦ Σαβᾶ τοῦ
2 [Αἱρ]άνου τοῦ Βωννέους ἐπανγει-
3 λάμενον αὐτῇ ἐπίδοσιν αἰωνίαν
4 [κα]ὶ Θυσίαν καὶ ἕτ[ε]ρα ἀναθέματα
5 [Μα]λαχβήλῳ καὶ Τύχῃ Θαιμεῖος καὶ
6 [Ἀτε]ργάτει, πατρῴοις θεοῖς, τειμῆς καὶ
7 μνήμης χάριν. Ἔτους ανυʹ, Πανήμου

1 ṣlmʾ dnh dy ʾḥply br ḥyrn šbʾ br
2 ḥyrn bwnʾ š[ʿ]t dy ʿbdt lh bwlʾ dy
3 mgd lh ḥr[m]ʾ lʿlmʾ w[m]qlwtʾ wʾqm
4 [m]ḥr[m]n lmlkb[l] wgdtymy wlʿtrʿth
5 ʾlh[yʾ] ṭb[yʾ] btr dy myt lyqrh byrḥ
6 [qnyn] šnt 4.100+40+10+1

PAT 0274 **C3928** **A.D. 155**

Prov: Palmyra, Temple of Bel, reemployed. Loc: Palmyra. *Honorific. On stone tablet.*

1 [Μᾶρκον Οὔλπιον Ἰαραῖον Αἱ-]
2 [ράνου τοῦ Ἀβγάρου ἡ τῶν ...]
3 [.............. ἀπὸ Σπασί-]
4 [νου] Χάρακος συνοδία βο[ηθή-]
5 σαντα αὐτῇ παντὶ τρόπῳ διὰ
6 Ζαβδεάθους Ζαβδελᾶ τοῦ
7 Ἰα[δδαίου] συνοδιάρχου,
8 ἔτους ζξυʹ, μηνὸς Λῴου.

1 [ṣl]m mrqs ʾlp[?]y[s] yr[ḥy br ḥyrn]
2 [br ʾ]<b>gr dy ʾqymw lh bny šyrtʾ dy
3 [slq]t[?] mn krk ʾspsnʾ bdyldy ʿdrh
4 [bkl ṣb]w [kl]h lyqrh brbnwt šyrt[ʾ]
5 [dy zbdʿ]tʾ br zbdlʾ ydy byrḥ ʾb šnt
6 4.100+60+5+1

PAT 0275 **C3929** **n. d.**

Prov: Palmyra. Loc: Istanbul Arkeoloji Müzesi, 3711 T?. *Honorific. On pedestal.* Bib: RES 422, 2515; Déd p 85.

1 ṣlmʾ dnh dy [blš]wry
2 br ḥggw br blšwry bʿʾ [dy]
3 ʾqymw lh š[m]rpʾ/šdʾrpʾ wkmrʾ
4 lyqrh mndy špr lhn
5 wl ʾlhyhwn byrḥ knwn š[nt]
6 [3..]

Could not be located in Istanbul for collation ('93).

PAT 0276 **C3930** **A.D. 139**

Prov: Palmyra. Loc: Palmyra, *in situ*. *Honorific. On column.* Bib: HNE p 458 a. 2, pl XXXIX, 4; Inv 2 2.

1 Ἡ βουλὴ καὶ ὁ δῆμος Ἀαιλάμειν Αἰράνου
2 τοῦ Μοκίμου τοῦ Αἰράνου τοῦ Μαθθᾶ, καὶ
3 Αἰράνην τὸν πατέρα αὐτοῦ, εὐσεβεῖς
4 καὶ φιλοπάτριδας καὶ παντὶ τρόπῳ φιλο-
5 τείμως ἀρέσαντας τῇ πατρίδι καὶ
6 τοῖς πατρίοις θεοῖς, τειμῆς χάριν,
7 ἔτους νυʹ, μηνὸς Ξανδικοῦ.

1 bwlʾ wdms ʿbdw ṣlmyʾ ʾln trwyhwn
2 lʾʿylmy br ḥyrn br mqymw br ḥyrn mtʾ
3 wlḥyrn ʾbwhy rḥymy mdythwn wdḥly ʾlhyʾ
4 bdyldy šprw lhwn wlʾlhyhwn bkl ṣbw klh
5 lyqrhwn byrḥ nysn šnt 4.100+40+10

PAT 0277 **C3931** **A.D. 139**

Prov: Palmyra. Loc: Palmyra, *in situ*. *Honorific. On column.* Bib: Inv 2 3.

1 Ἡ βουλὴ καὶ ὁ δῆμος Βαρείχειν
2 Ἀμρισάμσου τοῦ Ἰαριβωλέους
3 καὶ Μόκιμον υἱὸν αὐτοῦ, εὐσεβεῖς
4 καὶ φιλοπάτριδας, τειμῆς χάριν.

1 bwlʾ wdms ʿbdw ṣlmyʾ ʾln
2 trwyhn lbryky br ʾmršʾ br
3 yrḥbwlʾ wlmqym[w] brh rḥymy
4 mdythwn wdḥly ʾ[lh]yʾ lyqrhwn
5 byrḥ nysn šnt 4.100+40+10

PAT 0278 **C3932** **A.D. 242**

Prov: Palmyra, Great Colonnade. Loc: Palmyra, *in situ*. *Honorific. On column.* Bib: HNE p 459 a. 5, pl XXXVII, 3; RES 841; Inv 3 22; RosAH 12.

1 Ἡ βουλὴ καὶ ὁ δῆμος
2 Ἰούλιον Αὐρήλιον Ζηνόβιον
3 τὸν καὶ Ζαβδίλαν, δὶς Μάλ-
4 χου τοῦ Νασσούμου, στρατη-
5 γήσαντα ἐν ἐπιδημίᾳ θεοῦ
6 Ἀλεξάνδρου καὶ ὑπηρετή-
7 σαντα παρουσίᾳ διηνεκεῖ
8 Ῥουτιλλίου Κρισπείνου τοῦ
9 ἡγησαμένου καὶ ταῖς ἐπιδη-
10 μησάσαις οὐηξιλλατίοσιν, ἀ
11 γορανομήσαντα τε καὶ οὐκ ὀλί-
12 γων ἀφειδήσαντα χρημάτων
13 καὶ καλῶς πολειτευσάμενον,
14 ὡς διὰ ταυτὰ μαρτυρηθῆναι
15 ὑπὸ θεοῦ Ἰαριβώλου καὶ ὑπὸ Ἰου-
16 λίου [Πρείσκου] τοῦ ἐξοχωτάτου
17 ἐπάρχου τοῦ ἱεροῦ πραιτω-
18 ρίου, καὶ τῆς πατρίδος τὸν φιλό
19 πατριν, τειμῆς χάριν. ἔτους δνφʹ

1 ṣlm ywlys ʾwr̊lys zbdlʾ br̊ mlkw br̊ mlkw
2 nšwm dy hwʾ ʾsṭr̊tg lqlnyʾ bmytwytʾ dy
3 ʾlhʾ ʾlksndr̊ws qsr wšmš kdy hwʾ tnn
4 q[r]spynws hygmwnʾ wkdy ʾty lkʾ yt lgynyʾ
5 zbnyn sgyʾn whwʾ r̊b šwq wḥsk r̊zʾyn šgyʾyn
6 wdbr̊ ʿmr̊h škytyt mṭlkwt shd lh yr̊ḥbwl
7 ʾlhʾ wʾp ywlys [prysqws rbʾ?] dy spʾ wr̊ḥym mdth
8 dy ʾqym lh bwlʾ wdmws lyqr̊h šnt 5.100+40+10+4

Line 7: restoration of *rbʾ* after Inv 3 22

PAT 0279 **C3933** **A.D. 247**

Prov: Palmyra, Great Colonnade. Loc: Palmyra, *in situ*. *Honorific. On column.* Bib: HNE p 459 a. 6, pl XXXVII, 4; Inv 3 21.

1 Ἰούλιον Αὐρηλιον Ζεβείδαν
2 Μοκίμου τοῦ Ζεβείδου
3 Ἀσθώρου Βαιδᾶ οἱ σὺν αὐτῷ
4 κατελθόντες εἰς Ὀλογεσι-

5 ἀδα ἔνποροι ἀνέστησαν ἀρ-
6 έσαντα αὐτοῖς, τειμῆς χάριν·
7 Ξανδικῷ τοῦ ηνφ' ἔτους

1 ṣlmʾ dnh dy ywlys ʾwr̊lys
2 zbydʾ br̊ mqymw br̊ zbydʾ ʿštwr̊
3 bydʾ dʾ$^{?}$yʾ$^{?}$ ʾqym lh tgr̊ʾ bny šyr̊tʾ
4 dy nḥt ʿmh lʾlgšyʾ lyqr̊h bdyl
5 dy špr̊ lhwn byr̊ḥ nysn šnt 5.100
6 +40+10+5+3

PAT 0280 **C3934** **A.D. 254**

Prov: Palmyra, Great Colonnade. Loc: Palmyra, *in situ. Honorific. On column.* Bib: HNE p 460 a. 7, pl XXXVII, 5; Inv 3 14.

1 Ἡ β[ουλὴ καὶ ὁ δῆμος Ἰ]ούλιον
2 Αὐρή[λιον Ὄγγαν τὸν καὶ] Σέλευ-
3 κον [δὶς τοῦ Ἀζίζο]υ τοῦ Σεείλα
4 δυα[νδρικὸν φιλοτεί]μως
5 στρατ[ηγήσαντα κ]αὶ μαρτυ-
6 ρηθέν[τα καὶ φιλ]οτειμη-
7 σάμεν[ον τῇ] κρατίστῃ
8 βουλῇ ἀτ[τικὰς] μυρίας,
9 τειμῆς ἕνεκεν, ἔτους
10 ζξφ', Ὑπερβερεταίῳ.

1 bwlʾ wdmws lywlys ʾwr̊lys
2 ʿgʾ dy mtqr̊ʾ slwqws br̊
3 ʿzyzw ʿzyzw šʾylʾ dy šmš wšpr̊
4 lhwn bʾstr̊ṭgwth wmgd lbwlʾ
5 zwzyn r̊bw lyqr̊h byr̊ḥ tšr̊y šnt
6 5.100+60+5+1

Gk text restored differently in Inv 3 14; little is certain

PAT 0281 **C3935** **A.D. 259**

Prov: Palmyra, Great Colonnade. Loc: Palmyra, *in situ. Honorific. On column.* Bib: Inv 3 15.

1 Ἡ βου[λὴ καὶ ὁ δῆ]μος
2 Σ[έ]λ[ευκον Ὄγηλον]
3 [δὶς Ἀζίζου τοῦ Σεείλα]
4 [ἱππέα Ῥ]ωμαίων
5 (εὐ)ν[οίας καὶ τει]μῆς
6 χάριν, [ἔτους οφ' μ]ηνεὶ
7 [Ξανδικῷ]

1 ṣlm [slwqws] ʿgʾ br̊
2 ʿzyzw ʿz[yzw br̊] šʾylʾ
3 dy ʾqym l[h b]wlʾ wdmws
4 lyqr̊h mn r̊ḥmʾ byr̊ḥ nysn
5 dšnt 5.100+60+10

Line 1: with Stark PN p 119

PAT 0282 **C3936** **A.D. 257**

Prov: Palmyra, Great Colonnade. Loc: Palmyra, *in situ. Honorific. On column.* Bib: HNE p 460 a. 8, pl XXXVII, 6; Inv 3 13.

1 Ἡ βουλ[ὴ καὶ ὁ δῆμος Ἰ]ούλιον
2 Αὐρήλιο[ν Σαλαμάλ]λαθον
3 Μαλῆ τοῦ [Ἀβδαίου ἀ]ρχέμπορον
4 ἀνακομίσα[ντα τὴν] συνοδίαν
5 προῖκα ἐξ ἰδίων τειμῆς χάριν
6 ἔτους θξφ'

1 ṣlmʾ dnʾh dy ywlys ʾwr̊lys
2 šlmlt br̊ mlʾ ʿbdy r̊b šyr̊tʾ
3 dy ʾqymt lh bwlʾ wdms lyqr̊h
4 dy ʾsq šyr̊tʾ mgn mn kysh
5 šnt 5.100+60+5+4

Gk after Inv 3 13

PAT 0283 **C3937** **A.D. 258**

Prov: Palmyra, Great Colonnade. Loc: Palmyra, *in situ. Honorific. On column.* Bib: Inv 3 12.

1 Αὐρήλιον Οὐορώδην
2 ἱππικὸν καὶ βουλευτὴν
3 Παλμυρηνὸν Βηλά
4 καβος Ἀρσᾶ τὸν φί
5 [λον τ]ειμῆς χάριν
6 ἔτους οφ'.

1 lʾwr̊lys [w]r̊wd hpqʾ
2 wbylwṭʾ tdmr̊yʾ ʿbd
3 blʿqb br̊ ḥr̊šʾ lyqr̊h
4 šnt 5.100+60+10

PAT 0284 **C3938** **A.D. 262**

Prov: Palmyra, Great Colonnade. Loc: Palmyra, *in situ*. *Honorific*. *On column*. Bib: HNE p 461 a. 11, pl XXXVII, 9; RES 841; Inv 3 11.

1 ʾΗ βουλὴ καὶ ὁ δῆμος Σεπτίμιον
2 Οὐορώδην τὸν κράτιστον ἐπί-
3 τροπον [Σεβ]αστο[ῦ τοῦ κυρίου]
4 δου[κηνάριον ..... τειμῆς]
5 χάριν [ἔτους γοφʹ μηνεὶ]
6 [Ξ]αν[δικῷ].

1 ṣlmʾ dnh dy spṭmyws
2 wr̊wd ʾpṭr̊pʾ dwqnr̊ʾ dy
3 qsr̊ mr̊n dy ʾqym lh
4 bwlʾ wdmws lyqr̊h
5 byr̊ḥ nysn dy šnt 5.100+60+10+3

Gk text after Inv 3 11; C3938 shows more damaged text

PAT 0285 **C3939** **A.D. 262**

Prov: Palmyra, Great Colonnade. Loc: Palmyra, *in situ*. *Honorific*. *On column*. Bib: HNE p 461 a. 10, pl XXXVII, 8; RES 841; Inv 3 10.

1 Σεπτί[μιον Οὐορώδην τὸν κράτιστ]ον
2 ἐπίτρο[πον Σεβαστοῦ δ]ουκηνάριον
3 ʾΙούλιος Αὐρή[λιος Νεβούζ]αβα[δ]ος Σοά
4 δου τοῦ Αἱρῆ [στρατ]ηγὸς [τῆς] λαμπροτά
5 της κολωνείας [τ]ὸν ἑαυτοῦ φίλον
6 τειμῆς ἕνεκεν ἔτους δοφʹ μηνεὶ
7 ʾΑπελλαίῳ

1 spṭmys wr̊wd qr̊ṭsṭ?s ʾpṭr̊pʾ
2 dwqnr̊ʾ dy ʾqym lyqr̊h
3 ywlys ʾw<r̊>lys nbw?[z]bd br̊ šʿdw ḥyr̊ʾ
4 ʾsṭr̊<ṭ>gʾ dy qlnyʾ r̊ḥmh
5 šnt 5.100+60+10+4 byr̊ḥ kslwl

Gk text of Inv 3 10

PAT 0286 **C3940** **A.D. (262)**

Prov: Palmyra, Great Colonnade. Loc: Palmyra, *in situ*. *Honorific*. *On column*. Bib: HNE p 461 a. 12, pl XXXVIII, 2; Inv 3 9.

1 Σεπτίμιο[ν] Οὐορώδην
2 τὸν κράτιστον ἐπίτρο
3 πον Σεβαστοῦ δουκη
4 νάριον καὶ ἀργαπέτην
5 ʾΙούλιος Αὐρήλιος
6 Σεπτίμιος ʾΙαδῆς ἱπ
7 πικός Σεπτιμίου ʾΑλε
8 [ξά]νδρου τοῦ ʾΗρώδου
9 ἀπὸ στρατιῶν τὸν φί
10 λον καὶ προστάτην
11 τειμῆς ἕνεκεν ἔτους
12 ηοφʹ, μηνεὶ Ξανδικῷ

1 spṭmyws wr̊wd qr̊ṭsṭws ʾpṭr̊pʾ
2 dqnr̊ʾ wʾr̊gbṭʾ ʾqym ywlys
3 ʾwr̊lys s[p]ṭmyws ydʾ hpqws
4 br̊ ʾlks[nd]r̊ws ḥyr̊n sr̊ykw lyqr̊
5 r̊ḥmh wqywmh byr̊ḥ sywn dy
6 šnt 5.100+60+10+5

PAT 0287 **C3941** **n. d.**

Prov: Palmyra, Great Colonnade. Loc: Palmyra, *in situ*. *Honorific*. *On column*. Bib: Inv 3 8; RES 819.

1 Σεπτίμ[ιον Οὐορώδη]ν
2 τὸν κράτ[ιστον ἐπίτρο]
3 πον Σεβα[στοῦ δουκ]η
4 νάριον καὶ ἀ[ργαπ]έτην
5 ʾΙούλιος Αὐρήλιος Σε
6 π[τίμι]ος Μάλχος Μαλω
7 χᾶ Νασσούμου ὁ κράτι
8 στος τὸν φίλον καὶ προ
9 στάτην τειμῆς ἕνεκεν
10 ἔτους ζοφʹ, μηνεὶ Ξανδικῷ

1 spṭ[myws wrw]d qr[ṭsṭ]ws
2 ʾ[p]ṭ[rpʾ dqnrʾ wʾrg]bṭʾ
3 [ʾqym ywlys ʾwrlys spṭmy]ws
4 mlk[w br mlwkʾ nšwm qrṭsṭs lyqr]
5 rḥm[h wqywmh byrḥ ny]sn
6 [šnt [5.100+60+10+5+1]

Text after Inv 3 8

PAT 0288 **C3942** **A.D. 267**

Prov: Palmyra, Great Colonnade. Loc: Palmyra, *in*

situ. Honorific. On column. Bib: RES 818; Inv 3 7.

1 ῾Η βου[λὴ καὶ ὁ δῆ]μος
2 Σεπτίμ[ιον Οὐορώδην] τὸν κρά
3 τιστον ἐ[πίτροπον] Σεβαστοῦ
4 δουκην[άριον, δι]κεοδότην
5 τῆς μητρ[οκολω]νείας, καὶ ἀ
6 νακομίσαν[τα τ]ὰς συνοδίας
7 ἐξ ἰδίων, καὶ μαρτυρηθέντα
8 ὑπὸ τῶν ἀρχεμπόρων
9 καὶ λαμπρῶς στρατηγήσαντα
10 καὶ ἀγορανομήσαντα τῆς αὐτῆς
11 μητροκολωνείας, καὶ πλεῖστα
12 οἴκοθεν ἀναλώσαντα, καὶ ἀρέσαν
13 τα τῇ τε αὐτῇ βουλῇ καὶ τῷ δήμῳ̣
14 καὶ νυνεὶ λαμπρῶς συμποσίαρ
15 χον τῶν το[ῦ θεοῦ] Διὸς Βήλου ἱε
16 ρέων, ἀ[γνείας καὶ] τειμῆς ἕνε
17 κεν, ἔτ[ους ζοφ′ μη]νεὶ Ξανδικῷ̣

1 [....] qr̊ṭsṭs
2 [....]q.ʾ[.....]
3 [....]s[....]
4 [....]w[.]wdy[....]

PAT 0289 **C3943** **A.D. 267**

Prov: Palmyra, Great Colonnade. Loc: Palmyra, *in situ. Honorific. On column.* Bib: Inv 3 6.

1 Σεπτίμιον Οὐορώδην
2 τὸν κράτιστον ἐπίτρο-
3 πον Σεβαστοῦ δουκη-
4 νάριον καὶ ἀργαπέτην
5 ᾽Ιούλιος Αὐρήλιος Σάλμης
6 Κασσιανοῦ τοῦ Μαεναίου
7 ἱππεὺς ῾Ρωμαίων τὸν φίλον
8 καὶ προστάτην, ἔτους ηοφ′,
9 μηνεὶ Ξανδικῷ̣.

1 spṭmyws wr̊wd qr̊ṭsṭws
2 ʾpṭr̊pʾ dqnˀr̊ˀʾ wʾr̊gbṭʾ
3 ʾqym ywlys ʾwr̊lys šlmʾ
4 br̊ qsynʾ br̊ mʿny hˀpqʾ
5 lyqr̊ r̊ḥmh wqyw[mh]

6 byr̊ḥ nysn šnt 5.100+60+10+5+3
line 5: Inv 3 6 *qywmh* (no lacuna)

PAT 0290 **C3944** **A.D. 251**

Prov: Palmyra, Great Colonnade. Loc: Palmyra, *in situ. Honorific. On column.* Bib: HNE p 460 a. 9, pl XXXVII, 7; Inv 3 16.

1 Σεπτίμιον Αἱράνην ᾽Ο-
2 δαινάθου τὸν λαμπρό-
3 τατον συνκλητικόν,
4 ἔξα[ρχον Παλμυ]ρηνῶν
5 Αὐρήλι[ος Φιλεῖνο]ς Αὐρ. ῾Ηλι-
6 οδώρου [τοῦ ῾Ρααίου] στρατιώ-
7 της λεγ[εῶνος Κυρηνα]ϊκῆς τὸν
8 πάτρω[να, τει]μῆς καὶ εὐχα-
9 ριστίας χάριν, ἔτους γξφ′.

1 ṣlmʾ dnh dy spṭmyws ḥyr̊n br̊
2 ʾdynt snqlṭyqh nhyr̊ʾ wr̊š
3 tdmwr̊ dy ʾqym lh ʾwr̊lys
4 plynws br̊ mr̊yʾ plynʾ r̊ʿy plḥʾ
5 dblgywnʾ dy bṣr̊ʾ lyqr̊h byr̊ḥ
6 tšr̊y dy šnt 5.100+60+3
Gk after Inv 3 16

PAT 0291 **C3945** **A.D. 258**

Prov: Palmyra, Great Colonnade. Loc: Palmyra, Room I, S wall. *Honorific. On column.* Bib: HNE p 462 a. 13, pl XXXVIII, 1; Inv 3 17; Bounni and Asʿad '82 p 107.

1 Σεπ[τίμιον ᾽Οδαίναθον]
2 τὸν λαμ[πρότατον ὑπατικ]ὸν
3 συντέ[λεια τῶν χρυσοχ]όων
4 καὶ ἀργυ[ροκόπων, τ]ὸν δεσπότην
5 τειμῆς χάριν, [ἔτ]ους θξφ′
6 μηνεὶ Ξανδικῷ̣.

1 ṣlm spṭmyws ʾdynt
2 nhyr̊ʾ hpṭyqʾ mr̊n dy
3 ʾqym lh tgmʾ dy qynyʾ
4 ʿbdʾ dhbʾ wkspʾ lyqr̊h
5 byr̊ḥ nysn šnt 5.100+60+5+4

PAT 0292 **C3946** **A.D. 271**

Prov: Palmyra, Great Colonnade. Loc: Palmyra, *in situ. Honorific. On column.* Bib: HNE p 462 a. 14, pl XXXVIII, 3; Inv 3 19; RosAH 16.

1 ṣlm spṭmyws ʾdy[nt] mlk mlkʾ
2 wmtqnnʾ dy mdn?ḥʾ klh spṭmyʾ
3 zbdʾ r̊b ḥylʾ r̊bʾ wzby r̊b ḥylʾ
4 dy tdmwr̊ qr̊ṭsṭʾ ʾqym lmr̊hwn
5 byr̊ḥ ʾb dy šnt 5.100+80+2

PAT 0293 **C3947** **A.D. 271**

Prov: Palmyra, Great Colonnade. Loc: Palmyra, *in situ. Honorific. On column.* Bib: HNE p 462 a. 15, pl XXXVIII, 4; Inv 3 20; RosAH 17.

1 Σεπτιμίαν Ζηνοβίαν τὴν λαμ
2 προτάτην εὐσεβῆ βασίλισσαν
3 Σεπτίμιοι Ζάβδας ὁ μέγας στρα
4 τηλάτης καὶ Ζαββαῖος ὁ ἐνθάδε
5 στρατηλάτης, οἱ κράτιστοι, τὴν
6 δέσποιναν, ἔτους βπφ', μηνεὶ Λώῳ

1 ṣlmt spṭmyʾ btzby nhyr̊tʾ wzdqt[ʾ]
2 mlktʾ spṭmywʾ zbdʾ r̊b ḥylʾ
3 r̊bʾ wzby r̊b ḥylʾ dy tdmwr̊ qr̊ṭsṭwʾ
4 ʾqym lmr̊thwn byr̊ḥ ʾb dy šnt 5.100+80+2

line 1: Inv 3 20 *wzdqtʾ*

PAT 0294 **C3948** **A.D. 193**

Prov: Palmyra, Great Colonnade. Loc: Palmyra, *in situ. Honorific. On column.* Bib: HNE p 458 a. 4, pl XXXIX, 5; Inv 3 28; Buttrey '61-'63 pp 117-21.

1 Τὸν ἀνδρ[ιάντα] ἀνέστησαν [Θαι]μαρ-
2 σᾷ Θαιμῆ τοῦ [Μο]κίμου τοῦ Γαβ[β]ᾶ σ[υν-]
3 οδιάρχῃ, οἱ σὺν [αὐτῷ ἀ]ναβάντε[ς ἀπὸ]
4 Σπασίνου Χάρ[ακος κουφίσαν-]
5 τι αὐτοὺς χρυσᾶ παλαιὰ δηνάρι[α]
6 τριακόσια ἀναλ[ωμ]άτω[ν καὶ ἀρέ-]
7 σαντι αὐτοῖς, εἰς τειμὴν [αὐτοῦ]
8 καὶ ʾΙαδδαίου καὶ Ζαβδιβώλου υἱῶν
9 αὐτοῦ, ἔτους δφ' Ξανδικοῦ.

1 ṣlmʾ dnh dy tymr̊ṣw br̊ tymʾ br̊ mqymw
2 gr̊bʾ r̊b šyr̊tʾ dy ʿbdw lh bny šyr̊tʾ dy slqw
3 ʿmh mn kr̊kʾ bdyldy ḥsknwn nwr̊ dnr̊yn dy dhb
4 ʿtyqyn tlt mʾh wšpr̊ lhwn lyqr̊h wlyqr̊ ydy
5 [wz]bdbwl bnwhy byr̊ḥ nysn šnt 5.100+4

Gk line 2: Inv 3 28 *Γαρ[βᾶ]* but see CIS ad loc; Gk text of Buttrey varies at several points

PAT 0295 **C3949** **A.D. 210**

Prov: Palmyra, Great Colonnade. Loc: Palmyra, *in situ. Honorific. On column.* Bib: RES 2191; Inv 3 29.

1 ʾΙαδδαῖον Θαιμ[αρσᾶ τοῦ Θαιμῆ τοῦ]
2 Μοκίμου τοῦ [Γαββᾶ συνοδιάρχην]
3 τῶν ἐμπόρων κα[ὶ ἀρέσαντα]
4 αὐτοῖς πανταχοῦ [.......
5 καὶ Οὐολογαισιά[δος .....]
6 αὐτοὺς κουφίσ[αντα ἡ σὺν αὐτῷ]
7 κατελθοῦσα συν[οδία τειμῆς]
8 χάριν, ἔτους βκ[φ', μηνεὶ Δύστρῳ]

1 [ṣlmʾ.. ..gr]b?ʾ dy ʾqym lh
2 [.....] wʾlgšyʾ wmwdn
3 [.... z]b?nyn šgyʾn
4 [....] wbklʾtr klh
5 [...]hwn wʾr/dz[....] bzʿyd/r bkl
6 ʾnwklʾ [.....]wlʾ ʾ[t]r klʾ
7 [...] byrḥ ʾdr
8 šnt 5.100+20+2

Gk and Aram present many uncertainties; our texts after C3949

PAT 0296 **C3950** **A.D. 179**

Prov: Palmyra, Transversal Colonnade. Loc: Palmyra, *in situ. Honorific. On column console.* Bib: Inv 5 1.

1 ʾΙαδῆν Σοραίχου
2 τοῦ Αἱράνου τοῦ ʾΑλαινῆ
3 Σεφφερᾶ οἱ ἐγ γένους
4 Ζαβδιβωλείων τειμῆ[ς]
5 ἕνεκεν. μηνὶ Δύστρῳ το[ῦ]
6 ϙυ' ἔτους

1 ṣlmʾ dnh dy ydʾ br̊ šr̊ykw br̊ ḥy[r̊n br̊]

2 ʿlynʾ ṣpr̊ʾ dy ʾqymw lh bny zbdb[wl]
kl[hwn]
3 lyqr̊ šr̊y[kw] ʾbwhy byr̊ḥ ʾdr̊ šnt 4.[100]+
4 80+10

Gk after Inv 5 1; Aram of CIS

PAT 0297 **C3951** **A.D. 179**
Prov: Palmyra, Transversal Colonnade. Loc: Palmyra, *in situ*. *Honorific*. *On column console*.
Bib: Inv 5 2; Gaw '70a, pp 74-75.

1 ʿΑλαι[ν]ῆν Αἰράνου το[ῦ
2 ʿΑλα[ι]νῆ Σεφφερᾶ
3 ο[ἱ] ἐγγ[έ]νους Ζαβδιβω-
4 λείων τειμῆς ἕνεκεν
5 μη[νὶ Δ]ύστρ[ῳ] τοῦ [Ϙυʹ ἔτους.

1 ṣlmʾ dnh dy ʿl[y]nʾ br ḥyrn br [ʿ]lynʾ
2 ṣ[prʾ] dy ʾqymw lh bny zbdbwl k[lhw]n
3 bdyldy špr lhwn lyq[r]h byrḥ ʾdr
4 šnt 4.100+80+10
5 wʿbd qlstr[ʾ dy] kspʾ qd[m] šmš ʾlh[ʾ]

Gk text of Gaw '70a; for tomb foundation by same person, see Ber '70 p 74.

PAT 0298 **C3952** **A.D. 179**
Prov: Palmyra, Transversal Colonnade. Loc: Palmyra, *in situ*. *Honorific*. *On column console*.
Bib: HNE p 458 a. 3, pl XXXVII, 2; Inv 5 3.

1 ʿΗ βουλὴ
2 Σόραιχον Αἰράνου τοῦ
3 ʿΑλαινῆ Σεφφερᾶ εὐσεβῆ
4 καὶ φιλόπατριν καὶ φιλό-
5 τειμον τειμῆς καὶ εὐ-
6 νοίας χάριν,
7 μηνὶ Δύστρῳ Ϙυʹ ἔτους

1 ṣlmʾ dnh dy šrykw br ḥyrn br ʿlynʾ
2 ṣprʾ dy ʾqymt lh bwlʾ lyqrh
3 wʿbd bslqʾ dnh ʿmwdyn šbʿʾ
4 wtṣbythwn klh wʿbd knwnʾ dy nḥšʾ
5 byrḥ ʾdr šnt 4.100+80+10

PAT 0299 **C3953** **A.D. 179**
Prov: Palmyra, Transversal Colonnade. Loc: Palmyra, *in situ*. *Honorific*. *On column console*.
Bib: Inv 5 4.

1 ʿΗρώδην τὸν καὶ
2 Αἰράνην Σοραίχου τοῦ
3 Αἰράνου τοῦ ʿΑλαινῆ
4 Σεφφερᾶ οἱ ἐγ γένους
5 Ζαβδιβωλείων τειμῆς
6 ἕνεκεν, μηνὶ Δύστρῳ τοῦ
7 Ϙυʹ ἔτους

1 ṣlmʾ dnh dy ḥyr̊n br šrykw br
2 ḥyrn br ʿlynʾ ṣprʾ d[y] ʾʔqymw lh
3 bny [zb]dbwl klhwn ly[qr] šʔr[y]kw ʾbwh[y]
4 byr[ḥ] ʾdr̊ šnt 4.100+80+10

Text after Inv 5 4

PAT 0300 **C3954** **A.D. 179**
Prov: Palmyra, Transversal Colonnade. Loc: Palmyra, *in situ*. *Honorific*. *On column console*.
Bib: Inv 5 5.

1 Μάρθειν ʿΑλεξάνδρου τοῦ
2 καὶ ʿΙαδῆ τοῦ Οὐαβαλλάθου
3 τοῦ Συμώνου, Σόραιχος
4 Αἰράνου ἀνὴρ αὐτῆς μνή-
5 μης ἕνεκεν, μηνὶ Δύστρῳ
6 τοῦ Ϙυʹ ἔτους

1 ṣlmtʾ dnh dy mr̊ty br̊t yd[ʾ br̊ whblt]
2 br̊ šmʿwn dy ʾqym lh šr̊ykʔ[w bʿlh btr̊]
3 dy mytt lyqr̊h byr̊ḥ ʾdr̊ š[nt 4.100+]
4 80+10

PAT 0301 **C3955** **A.D. 129**
Prov: Palmyra, Transversal Colonnade. Loc: Palmyra, *in situ*. *Honorific*. *On column console*.
Bib: Inv 5 8; Déd p 115.

1 [....]
2 [....]
3 klhwn lyqrh bdyld[y špr lhwn]
4 wʿbd hw wlšmš ʾḥwhy bʾsṭ[wʾ]
5 dnh ʿmwdyn šṭʾ wšrythwn

6 [wt]ṯlylhwn mn kyshwn lyqr šmš
7 wʾlt wrḥm ʾlhyʾ ṭbyʾ byrḥ
8 ʾdr šnt 4.100+40

For restorations at beginning, see Déd p 115

PAT 0302 **C3956** **A.D. 166**

Prov: Palmyra, Transversal Colonnade. Loc: Palmyra, *in situ*. *Honorific*. *On column console.* Bib: Inv 5 7; Déd p 116.

1 ṣl[m] ḥ$^{?}$lypy br ʾtpny br ḥlypy
2 [dy] ʿbd lh ḥlypy [b]r$^{?}$ ḥggw br mlkw
3 [bdy]ldy š$^{?}$pr lh lyqrh wʾšlṭh
4 [šmš...] bʿmwdʾ dnh lmqmw ʿlwhy
5 [ṣlm]yn trn dy yḥ[l]ʾ byrḥ ʾdr šnt
6 4.100+60+10+3

Text after Déd p 116

PAT 0303 **C3957** **A.D. (229)**

Prov: Palmyra, Transversal Colonnade. Loc: Palmyra, *in situ*. *Honorific*. *On column console.* Bib: Inv 5 6.

1 ṣlmʾ dnh dy mlkw br̊ mqym$^{?}$[w]
2 br̊ m$^{ʿ?}$y$^{?}$ty br̊ ḥlypy dy ḥdt l[h]
3 br̊ʿth br lšmš mlkw
4 br̊h byrḥ ʾdr̊ šnt [...] 5.100+40+[...]

Text after CIS

PAT 0304 **C3958** **A.D. (181)**

Prov: Palmyra, Temple of Baalshamîn. Loc: Palmyra, *in situ*. *Honorific*. *On column console.* Bib: RES 2133; Inv 1 3.

1 [....]
2 [....]
3 [....]
4 mʿzyn lʾ [...]
5 [...]d/rmyʾ [ʿ]tyqʾ [....]
6 wt$^{?}$r$^{?ʿ?}$w$^{?}$hy byrḥ ʾ[...]
7 [4].100+80+10+2

Text after Inv 1 3; line 7: Stark PN [3].100

PAT 0305 **C3959** **A.D. (131)**

Prov: Palmyra, Temple of Baalshamîn. Loc: Palmyra, *in situ*. *Honorific*. *On column console.* Bib: RES 2162; BS III 44; Inv 1 2; Déd p 10.

1 Ἡ βουλὴ καὶ ὁ δῆμος
2 Μαλῆν τὸν καὶ Ἀγρίππαν
3 Ἰαραίου τοῦ Ῥααίου, γραμμα-
4 τέα γενόμενον τὸ δεύτε-
5 ρον ἐπιδημ[ίᾳ] θεοῦ Ἀδρι-
6 ανοῦ ἄλιμμα παρα(σ)χόν-
7 τα ξένοις τε καὶ πολείται[ς,]
8 ἐν πᾶσιν ὑπηρετήσαντα
9 τῇ τ[ῶν] στρατευμάτων
10 ὑπο[δοχ]ῇ καὶ τὸν ναόν
11 τὸν [τοῦ] Διὸς σὺν τῷ π[ρο-]
12 ναίῳ [καὶ σὺν] ταῖς ἄλλαι[ς α]ὐτ[οῦ στοαῖς ....]
13 ....

1 mn twḥyt bwlʾ wdmws [ṣlmʾ dnh dy mlʾ]
2 br yrḥy l[šmš] rʿy dy hwʾ grmṭws dy trtyʾ
3 wkdy ʾt[ʾ mr]n hdry[nʾ] ʾlhʾ yhb mšḥʾ
4 lbny md[yntʾ wl]ʾsṭr[ṭwmʾ] wlʾksnyʾ dy ʾtʾ
5 ʿmh [wprns lmš]ryth b[k]l mdʿn wbnʾ hyklʾ
6 wprnʾ[yn [wtṣb]yth k[l]h mn kysh lbʿlšmn
7 wldrḥ$^{?}$[lwn]h d$^{?}$[...]mn bny ydyʿbl
8 byr[ḥ ...]n šnt 1+[3].100+40+2

Gk text after CIS; Aram after BS III; see there for previously suggested restorations

PAT 0306 **C3960** **A.D. 157**

Prov: Palmyra, Agora. Loc: Palmyra, *in situ*. *Honorific*. *On column console.* Bib: IP 9; Inv 10 87 (Aram); Inv 10 88 (Gk).

1 Μάρκον Οὔλπιον Ἰαραῖον Αἰ-
2 ράνου τοῦ Ἀβγάρου οἱ ἀναβά-
3 ν[τε]ς [ἀπὸ Χ]ου[μ]άνων ἐνπ-
4 [οροι..................
5 [................] τειμῆ[ς]
6 [ἕνεκε, ἔτ]ο[υς ηξ]υ', (μ)ηνὸ[ς]
7 [Δύστρου]

1 ṣlmʾ dnh dy mrqs ʾlps
2 yrḥy br ḥyrn ʾbgr dy
3 ʾqymw lh ḥyrn br yrḥy

4 br tymʾ wḥbyby br
5 yrḥy br ḥyrn bny ʾnwbt
6 rḥmwhy wtgryʾ dy slq
7 ʿmhwn lyqrh by<r>ḥ ʾdr
8 šnt 4.100+60+5+3

See ad Inv 10 87 on complex textual situation

PAT 0307 **C3961** **n. d.**

Prov: Palmyra, Agora. Loc: lost. *Honorific. On column console.* Bib: Inv 10 89.

1 [ṣl]m m[rqs] ʾlp[ys] yrḥy br
2 [ḥyrn ʾbgr dy ʿ]b$^{?}$d$^{?}$w$^{?}$ l[h tg]r$^{?}$yʾ dy
3 [slqw ʿmh mn .....]
4 [....]

Text of Inv 10 89

PAT 0308 **C3962** **n. d.**

Prov: Palmyra, Agora. Loc: Palmyra, *in situ. Honorific. On column console.* Bib: Inv 10 17; Déd p 245.

1 [..................]OH I GEBASIS
2 [.....]VPRAVI[.....]T HIERAPOLI
3 ELABELUSQVIETSATVRNINVSMALICHI F

1 ṣlm qlstqs qṭrywnʾ
2 dy mn lgywnʾ dy ʾrbʿtʾ dy ʿbd
3 [l]h ʾlhb[l ...]
4 [.....]

PAT 0309 **C3963** **n. d.**

Prov: Palmyra, Agora. Loc: Palmyra, *in situ*, S 1707. *Honorific. On wall console.* Bib: Inv 10 47.

1 Θαιμαρσᾶν Λισάμσου τοῦ Μαλί[χου]
2 τοῦ ʼΑαβεῖ εὐσεβῆ καὶ φιλόπατρ[ιν]
3 [..............]

1 [ṣ]lm tymrṣw br l$^{?}$šmš br mlkw ʾʿby dy
2 [ʾqy]m$^{?}$w lh bny šyrtʾ dy [slq]w [ʿ]m[h
3 [.... b]dyldy špr lhwn wʿdr[nwn bkl]
4 [ṣbw klh by]rḥ nysn šnt 4.100+[..] .]

PAT 0310 **C3964** **n. d.**

Prov: Palmyra, Agora. Loc: Palmyra, *in situ. Honorific. On column console.*

1 ṣlm mʿny br mlkw [br .....]ʾ ʾ$^{?}$t$^{?}$[..]

PAT 0311 **C3965** **n. d.**

Prov: Palmyra, Agora. Loc: Palmyra, *in situ. Honorific. On column console.*

1 ṣlm ʿzyzy br ml$^{?}$[kw ..]

PAT 0312 **C3966** **A.D. 64**

Prov: Palmyra, Diocletian Camp. Loc: Palmyra, *in situ. Honorific. On column.* Bib: RES 2142; Inv 2 1; Photo of squeeze: Inv 6 opposite p 6; Déd pp 82-85, pl IV 2, 3; TP pp 61-62; RSP 156; Gaw '83 pp 61-62.

1 [.....]ισμον [...................]
2 [......]τασ μ[..................]
3 [Σαλαμ]άλλαθον· [ʼΙαριβωλέους τοῦ]
4 [Νουρ]βήλου· τοῦ· ἐπικαλ[ουμένο]υ· [.]α[.]ι·
5 [Παλ]μυρηνὸν· φυλῆς τῆς αὐτῆς εὐσεβῆ καὶ
6 [ἀρέ]σαντα· αὐτοῖς ἐν· πολλοῖς πράγμασιν·
7 [ἐ]ν τε· κτίσμασιν καὶ· ἀναθήμασιν·
8 ἀναλώμασι· τε· οὐκ ὀλίγοις τειμῆς
9 ἕνεκεν (ἔ)το(υ)ς εοτʹ μηνὸς Περειτίου·

1 ṣl[m]ʾ dnh dy šlmlt br
2 [yrḥbw]lʾ br nwrbl dy mtqrh
3 ʾ[.....] br ydyʿbl tdmryʾ dy mn
4 [bny] mʿzyn dy ʾqymw lh ʾlt
5 [wbny mʿzyn] bdyldy qm wbnʾ wqrb
6 [.... wšpr l]hn bkl gns klh
7 [bdylkwt ʾqymw lh ṣ]lmʾ dnh wʿmwdʾ
8 [dnh lyqrh byrḥ šbṭ] šnt 3.100+60+10+[5]

Text mostly after RSP 156 and TP (73a); Déd differs in detail

PAT 0313 **C3967** **A.D. 150**

Prov: Palmyra, Diocletian Camp, "Temple des Enseignes". Loc: Palmyra, 41 and 45/62. *Honorific. On stone fragments.* Bib: RES 2147; Inv 6 7; Déd p 266; RSP 158.

1 [...ἀδ]ελφο[ί...]
2 [...]α[ξ]υ'[...]

1 ṣlmʾ dnh dy ymlkw br [ʿgʾ] yʿty dy [ʾqymw]
2 [l]h ḥgy br ʿgʾ ḥgy wʾḥwhy lyqr[h]
3 byrḥ ʾb šnt 4.100+60+1
Text of RSP 158

PAT 0314 **C3968** **A.D. 135**
Prov: Palmyra, Diocletian Camp, "Temple des Enseignes". Loc: Palmyra, *in situ*, TE 36. *Honorific. On statue base.* Bib: RES 2148; Inv 6 6; Déd p 7; RSP 157; Sem '73 p 119..

1 [τὸν δεῖνα οἱ ἱερεῖς Αγλιβωλου καὶ]
2 [Μαλαχ]βηλου θεων ἱεροῦ ἄλσο[υς ...]

1 [ṣlmʾ dnh dy ...]qlys hgm[w]nʾ ʿbdw kmry ʿglbwl
2 [wmlkbl ʾlhy] hlss bʾpmlṭwt yrḥbwlʾ br
3 [....] wmlkw br ʿwydʾ ʾnqyr br ʿgʾ br
4 [............] nṣry ḥby br ʿgʾ nṣry ḥby ʾrṭbn
5 [.....] mqy wrbʾl br ḥyrn bgšw
6 [.....] 4.100+40+5+1
Text after Gaw RSP 157; Gk and line 2 after Déd

PAT 0315 **C3969** **(17) B.C.**
Prov: Palmyra. Loc: Palmyra Museum?. *Honorific. On statue base.* Bib: RES 2450; Inv 11 84; Déd p 62.

1 ṣlmtʾ dh dy ʿtʾm b[rt...]
2 ʾwšy ʾtt bwlḥʾ [br ...]
3 dy ʾqym lh ʿglbwl w?[mlkbl]
4 wbny kmrʾ byrḥ ʾdr š[nt 2.100]
5 80+10+4
Text of Déd p 62

PAT 0316 **C3970** **A.D. 203**
Prov: Palmyra, reemployed in Byzantine church. Loc: Palmyra. *Honorific. On door lintel.* Bib: RES 2152; Herzig and Schmidt-Colinet '91 p 68.

1 Αὐτοκράτορα Καίσαρα Λ. Σεπτίμιον Σεουῆρον Εὐσεβῆ Περτίνακα Σεβαστὸν ʾΑραβικὸν ʾΑδιαβηνικὸν Παρθικὸν μέγιστον
2 κα[ὶ Αὐ]τοκ[ράτορα Καίσαρα Μάρκ]ον [Αὐ]ρ[ή]λι[ον] ʾΑντωνεῖνον Εὐσεβῆ Σεβαστὸν [......................] καὶ ʾΙουλίαν Δό-
3 μν[αν] Σεβαστὴν Μητέρα τῶν ἱ[ερῶν στρατ]οπέδων καὶ [Αὐτοκράτορα Καίσαρα Π. Σεπτίμιον Γέτα Σεβαστὸ]ν, δεσπότας γῆς καὶ θαλάσσης καὶ
4 [παντὸς ἀνθρώπ]ων γέ[ν]ους Σά[λμης Μα]λίχου τ[οῦ Βω]λιάδους ἀρχιερεὺς καὶ συ[μποσία]ρχος ἱερέων μεγίστου θεοῦ Διὸς Βή-
5 [λου........] ἐξ ἰδίων ἀνέστησεν ἔτους [δ]ιφʹ μηνὸς Ξανδικοῦ

1 bṛbnwt mṛzḥwt šlmʾ bṛ mlkw bṛ blydʿ [ʿbd ṣlmy]ʾ ʾln šṭʾ
2 mn kysh byrḥ nysn šnt 5.100+10+4

PAT 0317 **C3971** **n. d.**
Prov: Palmyrene: el Kerasi. Loc: Palmyra?. *Honorific. On pillar.*

reading of fragments of Latin text uncertain, see CIS ad loc

1' [......]
2' [..... κ]α[ὶ ὑπὲρ σω-]
3' τηρίας Σεπτιμίας Ζηνο-
4' βίας τῆς λαμπροτάτης
5' βασιλίσσης μητρὸς τοῦ
6' βασιλέως, [...]υ[...]

1 ʿl ḥ[ywh] wz[kwth dy] sptymyws
2 whblt ʾtndr[ws nhy]rʾ mlk mlkʾ
3 wʾpnrtṭʾ dy mdnḥʾ klh br
4 spṭ[ymy]ws [ʾdynt mlk] mlkʾ wʿl
5 ḥyh dy spṭymyʾ btzby nhyrtʾ
6 mlktʾ ʾmh dy mlk mlkʾ
7 bt ʾnṭywkws m<yl> 10+4

PAT 0318 **C3972** **A.D. 55**
Prov: Palmyra. Loc: London, British Museum, 125206. *Dedicatory. On pillar.* Bib: Déd p 224; PS 1.

1 byrḥ ʾyr šnt 3.100+60+5+1 mṣbʾ
2 dnh nṣb ʿtntn br zbdʿth tšbb
3 lšdrpʾ ʾlhʾ ṭbʾ dy yhʾ
4 gyr bh hw wbny byth klhn

PAT 0319 **C3973** **A.D. 132**
Prov: Palmyra. Loc: Palmyra Museum?. *Dedicatory. On altar.* Bib: RES 285; RES 815.

1 [t]rtn ʿlwtʾ ʾln ʿbd ʿbydw br ʿnmw
2 [br] šʿdlt nbṭyʾ rwḥy[ʾ] dy hwʾ prš
3 [b]ḥyrtʾ wbmšrytʾ dy ʿnʾ
4 lšyʿʾlqwm ʾlhʾ ṭbʾ wškrʾ dy lʾ
5 štʾ ḥmr ʿl ḥywhy wḥyy mʿyty
6 wʿbdw ʾḥwhy wšʿdlt brh byrḥ
7 ʾlwl šnt 4.100+40+3 wdkyr zbydʾ br
8 [š]mʿwn br blʿqb gyrh wrḥmh qdm
9 šyʿʾlqwm ʾlhʾ ṭbʾ wdkyr kl
10 mʿyd ʿlwtʾ ʾln wʾmr dkyryn
11 [h]ʾ ʾln klhwn bṭb

PAT 0320 **C3974** **A.D. (113)**
Prov: Palmyra. Loc: Damascus, National Museum, 164 (248). *Dedicatory. On stone tablet.* Bib: Déd p 22; PS 22; RES 30; RES 817.

1 lʾrṣw wlʿzyzw ʾlhyʾ ṭbyʾ wskryʾ ʿbd
bʿly
2 br yrḥbwlʾ ʾpklʾ dy ʿzyzw ʾlhʾ ṭbʾ
3 wrḥmnʾ ʿl ḥywhy wḥyʾ ʾḥwhy byrḥ tšr[y]
4 šnt 20+5 dkyr yrḥy glwpʾ
line 4 dkyr - end: written separately and smaller

PAT 0321 **C3975** **n. d.**
Prov: Palmyra. Loc: Palmyra Museum?. *Dedicatory. On altar fragment.* Bib: Déd p 19.

1 qrb rbʾl br ʾmršʾ
2 dy mn bny mtbwl
3 ʿltʾ dh l[ʾ]rṣw
4 [ʾ]lhʾ

PAT 0322 **C3976** **n. d.**
Prov: Palmyra. Loc: Istanbul Arkeoloji Müzesi, 160. *Dedicatory. On altar.* Bib: HNE p 476 c. 11, pl XL, 5

1 lgdʾ dy ʿynʾ bryktʾ ʿb[d]
2 bʾpml{wṭ}<ṭw>n tr̊tn bwlnʾ br̊
3 ʿzyzw br ʿzyzw br šʾylʾ dy
4 ʾšlmt ʿl ydwh
Collated 19-24/10/93

PAT 0323 **C3977** **n. d.**
Prov: Palmyra, Diocletian Camp, in "Temple des Enseignes". Loc: lost, see RSP ad loc. *Dedicatory. On stone fragments.* Group: C3977=Inv 6 11; Inv 6 11 fragments a, b. Bib: Inv 6 11; RSP 132.

(A)
1 [....]lwn
2 [....]dh dy ṣlmʾ [.....]
3 [....] lmrt bytʾ d[.....]
4 [....]lh l[bt b]l nsyb knwnʾ dnh
(B)
1 [...] ʾlhyʾ wnksyhwn [...]
2 [...] wzbnwhy dy ʿw?šy?
Text of RSP 132

PAT 0324 **C3978** **A.D. (85)**
Prov: Palmyra. Loc: Oxford, Ashmolean Museum, C2-9. *Dedicatory. On altar.* Bib: HNE p 474 c. 2, pl XXXVIII, 6; Déd pp 115, 306; Gaw '76b pp 198-200; Gaw '83 p 65.

1 [b]yrḥ ʾlwl šnt 3.100+60+[20]+
2 10+5+1 ḥmnʾ dnh wʿltʾ dh
3 [ʿ]bdw wqrbw lšmš wzbydʾ
4 bny mlkw br ydyʿbl br nšʾ
5 dy mtqrʾ br ʿbdbl dy mn
6 pḥd bny mgdt lšmš
7 ʾlh byt ʾbwhn ʿl
8 ḥyyhwn wḥyy ʾḥyh[wn]
9 wbnyhwn

PAT 0325 **C3979** **n. d.**
Prov: Palmyra. Loc: Palmyra Museum?. *Dedicatory. On altar.*

1 Ἡλίῳ πατρῴῳ καὶ ἐπηκόῳ θεῷ

1 [....]ʾ

2 [...]šw br [... br z]bdbwl [...]š᾽ lšmš ᾽lh᾽ ṭb[᾽]

PAT 0326 **C3980** **A.D. 34**
Prov: Palmyra. Loc: Palmyra Museum?. *Dedicatory. On altar.* Bib: Déd p 119; RES 284; RES 814.

1 [byrḥ] šbṭ šnt 3.100+40+5 ʿlt᾽ dh [ʿbdw]
2 [bny m]rzḥ᾽ ᾽ln lʿglbwl wlmlkbl ᾽lh[y᾽]
3 [wh]by br ʿtnwry ʿwdw wḥggw br zbdlh kmr᾽
4 [wn]bwzbd br mlkw mtn᾽ wtymw br ʿgylw rbbt
5 [w]mlkw br yrḥbwl᾽ ḥty wyrḥbwl᾽ br tymrṣw
6 ᾽brwq wzbdbwl br ydyʿbl ᾽lhw wʿgylw br
7 nwry zbdbl wmlkw br mqymw tymʿmd

PAT 0327 **C3981** **A.D. 188**
Prov: Palmyra. Loc: Palmyra Museum?. *Dedicatory. On altar.* Bib: HNE p 475 c. 9, pl XXXVIII, 9

1 mwdn kl ywm zbdbwl
2 wmqymw bny gd᾽ br
3 mqymw rp᾽l lrḥm<n>᾽
4 ṭb᾽ wtyr᾽ ʿl ḥyyhwn
5 wḥy᾽ bnyhwn wbythwn
6 klh kdy lʿglbwl wmlkbl ᾽l[...]
7 by[r]ḥ [k]slwl d[y] šnt 5.100

PAT 0328 **C3982** **A.D. (119)**
Prov: Palmyra. Loc: Palmyra?. *Dedicatory. On stone tablet.*

(Above, on right) 1 [ʿ]glbwl
(Above female figure) 1 [...]l
(Below)
1' [...]᾽ br mlkw [ʿš]twrg᾽ byrḥ ṭbt šnt [4.100]+20+10/[5.100]+20+10

1': *+20+10* written above line

PAT 0329 **C3983** **A.D. 67**
Prov: Palmyra, Temple of Baalshamîn. Loc: Palmyra Museum. *Dedicatory. On stone tablet.* Bib: HNE p 473 c. 1 XXXVIII, 5; Inv 1 4; RES 390.

1 ʿmwdy᾽ ᾽ln ḥmš᾽ wšrythwn wtṯlylhwn qrb zbdy br zbdnbw qḥzn dy mn bny mʿzyn lbʿlšmn ᾽lh᾽ ṭb᾽
2 wškr᾽ ʿl ḥywhy wḥyy bnwhy w᾽ḥwhy byrḥ ᾽lwl šnt 3.100+60+10+5+3

Inv 1 4 notes that text already then partly effaced; intact when discovered

PAT 0330 **C3984** **A.D. (110)**
Prov: Palmyra, Transversal Colonnade. Loc: Palmyra Museum. *Dedicatory. On column.* Bib: Inv 5 9.

1 qrb ʿmwdy᾽ ᾽ln tryhwn
2 wšrythwn wtṯlylhn mlk᾽
3 br tym᾽ br mlk᾽ tym᾽
4 byrḥ knwn šnt 4.100+20+[2]

Text of Inv 5 9

PAT 0331 **C3985** **A.D. (148+)**
Prov: Palmyra, Diocletian Camp, Temple of Allat. Loc: Palmyra, *in situ*. *Dedicatory: dedication of Allat temple. On door lintel.* Bib: de Vogüé 1868 p 17 14, pl 2 14; Inv 6 1; RSP 152; Gaw '70a p 75; Gaw '73a p 92; Gaw '88 p 61.

1 [...] ʿbd [...] qrb [...l᾽lt] ᾽s[t]r᾽ [ṭbt᾽...]
2 [..ʿ]l ḥywhy wḥy᾽ bnwhy w᾽ḥwhy [...]r/dwt šnt 4.100+60+[.]
3 [...p]rnyn wtṣbyth klh mn kys ᾽lt

Text of RSP 152 (inscription now almost obliterated); line 1: some restorations by DRH

PAT 0332 **C3986** **A.D. 114**
Prov: Palmyra. Loc: Palmyra Museum?. *Dedicatory. On altar.* Bib: HNE p 474 c. 4 pl XL, 2

1 lbʿlšmn mr᾽ ʿlm᾽ ʿbdw
2 nbwzbd wyrḥbwl᾽ bny brnbw
3 br nbwzbd br zbdl᾽ ᾽knby ʿl
4 [ḥ]yyhwn wḥyy bnyhwn w᾽ḥyhwn
5 byrḥ ᾽b šnt 4.100+20+5

PAT 0333 **C3987** **A.D. 132**

Prov: Palmyrene. Loc: Palmyra Museum?. *Dedicatory. On altar.*

1 dkrn ṭb lbʿlšmn ʿ$^?$bd ʿgylw br mlkw
2 [b]r mqymw qšṭy ʿl ḥywhy wḥyy bnwhy
3 [by]r$^?$ḥ šbṭ šnt 4.100+40+3 ywm šbʿtʾ

PAT 0334 **C3988** **A.D. 89**

Prov: Palmyra, Diocletian Camp, reemployed in “Temple des Enseignes”. Loc: Palmyra, *in situ*, TE 320. *Dedicatory. On stele.* Bib: Inv 6 3; RSP 128.

1 [ʿl]tʾ dh lbʿlšmn rbʾ wrḥmnʾ ʿbdt ʿt[... brt]
2 [m]lkw br whblt br ʿrgn ʾtt mlkw br ʿgʾ ʾʿ[by]
3 [ʿ]l ḥyyh wḥyy bnyh wʾḥyh byrḥ šbṭ šnt 4.100+[...]

Text after RSP

PAT 0335 **C3989** **A.D. 135**

Prov: Palmyra, Diocletian Camp, in “Temple des Enseignes”, S-E corner. Loc: Palmyra, *in situ*, TE 1. *Dedicatory. On stele.* Bib: Inv 6 9; RSP 131.

1 lmrʾ ʿlmʾ ṭbʾ wrḥmnʾ
2 mwdʾ mʿny br mlkw rb$^{ʾ?}$ br mʿny
3 rʾwmʾ ʿl ḥ[y]why wḥy[y] b[n]why wʾḥwhy
4 byrḥ šbṭ šnt [4].100+40+5+1

After RSP 152 esp for date

PAT 0336 **C3990** **n. d.**

Prov: Palmyra. Loc: Palmyra Museum. *Dedicatory. On altar.*

1 lmrʾ ʿlmʾ ʿbd ḥyr$^?$[n]
2 b$^?$r blḥzy br blḥʾ
3 [m]q$^?$y [ʾʿb]y ʿl ḥywhy
4 [w]ḥyʾ [ʿgy]lw brh šbṭ
5 š$^?$[nt ...]

PAT 0337 **C3991** **n. d.**

Prov: Palmyra. Loc: Palmyra Museum. *Dedicatory. On altar.* Bib: Déd p 211.

1 ʿbd whblt
2 br̊ ʾbmr̊t
3 [l]ʾlh ṣʿb[w]
4 dy mqrʾ gdʾ
5 [ʾ]nbṭ ʿl ḥywh
6 [wḥy]y$^?$ brh$^?$ [...]

PAT 0338 **C3992** **A.D. (3? or 103?)**

Prov: Palmyra. Loc: Palmyra Museum. *Dedicatory. On altar.*

1 lbryk šmh lʿlmʾ ʿbd
2 zbdlh br mqym!w ṭm[ys]
3 ʿl [ḥywh] w[ḥy]y b[nw]h byrḥ
4 ʾyr šnt 3.100+10+4

line 2 *mqym!w:* text copy in CIS: *mqynw*

PAT 0339 **C3993** **A.D. 111**

Prov: Palmyra. Loc: Palmyra Museum. *Dedicatory. On altar.* Bib: Syr ’33 p 192 (Tad 13).

1 [ʿ]ltʾ dh dkrn lbryk šmh [lʿl]mʾ
2 wlʿdnʾ ṭbʾ ʿbd
3 [ḥl]dʾ br zbdʿth br ḥld[ʾ ʿl]
4 [ḥ]ywhy wḥyy bnwhy byrḥ t[šry]
5 šnt 4.100+20+3

line 2 CIS: wl[rḥm]nʾ; corrected by Cantineau ’33a p 192 from copy and photograph of Waddington

PAT 0340 **C3994** **A.D. 114**

Prov: Palmyrene, al-Karasi. Loc: al-Karasi, *in situ*. *Dedicatory. On 3 altars.* Bib: HNE p 474 c. 3; Déd p 211.

(Above)

1 Διὶ ὑψίστῳ καὶ ἐπηκόῳ ἡ πόλις εὐχήν.

(Below)

1 Ἔτους εκυʹ Δύστρου ακʹ, ἐπὶ ἀργυροταμιῶν Ζεβείδου Θαιμοαμέδου, καὶ Μο-
2 κίμου Ἰαριβωλέους καὶ Ἰαραίου Νουρβήλου, καὶ Ανάνιδος Μαλίχου.

(A)

1 ʿbdt mdyntʾ lbryk
2 šmh lʿlmʾ mn ksp

3 ʿnwštʾ bʿnwšt zbyd[ʾ]
4 br tymʿmd mškw wmqy[mw]
5 br yrḥbwlʾ gmlʾ wyrḥ[y]
6 br nwrbl šgry wʿnnw br ml[kw]
7 ʿnnw byrḥ ʾdr ywm 20+1
8 šnt 4.100+20+5
(B)
1 ʿbdt mdyntʾ lbryk
2 šmh lʿlmʾ mn ksp
3 ʿnwštʾ bʿnwšwt zby[dʾ]
4 br tymʿmd mškw wmq[ymw]
5 br yrḥbwlʾ gmlʾ wyr[ḥy]
6 br nwrbl šgry wʿnny [br]
7 mlkw ʿnny byrḥ ʾ[dr]
8 ywm 20+1 šnt 4.100+20+5
(C)
1 [ʿ]bdt mdyntʾ lbryk
2 šmh lʿlmʾ mn ksp
3 ʿnwštʾ bʿnwšt zbydʾ
4 br tymʿmd mškw wmqymw
5 br yrḥbwlʾ gmlʾ wyrḥy
6 br nwrbl šgry wʿnny br
7 mlkw ʿnny byrḥ ʾdr ywm 20+1 šnt
4.100+20+5

PAT 0341 **C3995** **A.D. 155**
Prov: Palmyrene. Loc: Palmyra Museum. *Dedicatory. On altar.*

1 lbryk šmh lʿlmʾ ʿbdw
2 blydʿ wʿtnwry wmʿnw$^{?}$ [bny]
3 tymʿmd br blydʿ ʿl m[...]
4 ʾḥwhn ywm 20+2 bšb[ṭ šnt]
5 4.100+20+5+1

PAT 0342 **C3996** **A.D. 125**
Prov: Palmyra, Temple of Bel. Loc: Palmyra Museum. *Dedicatory. On altar.* Bib: HNE p 474 c. 5, pl XXXVIII, 8.

1 lbryk š[m]h l[ʿ]lmʾ
2 ṭbʾ wr[ḥ]mnʾ
3 ʿbd prn<k> brḥry
4 lšmš br šmšgrm
5 nrqys brḥry mlʾ
6 brpʾ ʿl ḥyyhn wḥyy
7 bnyhn byrḥ kslwl
8 šnt 4.100+20+10+5+2

PAT 0343 **C3997** **A.D. 129**
Prov: Palmyra. Loc: Palmyra Museum. *Dedicatory. On altar.*

1 [l]bryk šmh [lʿ]lmʾ ʿbd zbyd[ʾ]
2 b$^{?}$r zbdbl ydyʿbl ʿl byth
3 byrḥ ʾlwl šnt 4.100+40

PAT 0344 **C3998** **A.D. 132**
Prov: Palmyra, Diocletian Camp, reemployed in "Temple des Enseignes". Loc: Palmyra, *in situ*, TE 220. *Dedicatory. On stele.* Bib: Inv 6 5; RSP 130.

1 Διὶ ὑψίστῳ καὶ ἐπηκ[όῳ τὸν βωμὸν]
2 ἀνέθηκεν Ζαβδίβω[λος ʼΙαριβωλέους]
3 τοῦ Λισαμσαίου τοῦ Αἰρ[άνου ὑπὲρ τῆς]
4 ὑγείας αὐτοῦ καὶ τέκνω[ν καὶ]
5 ἀδελφῶν, ἔτους δμυʹ ʼΥπ[ερβερεταίου]

1 [qrb ldk]rn qdm bryk šmh lʿlmʾ
2 [zbdbwl] br yrḥbwlʾ br lšmšy
3 [ḥyrn ʿl] ḥywhy wḥyy bnwhy wʾḥwhy
4 [byrḥ tš]ry šnt 4.100+40+4
5 [lbryk šm]h$^{?}$ lʿlmh mrʾ kl
6 [ʿlmʾ] mwdʾ zbdbwl br
7 [...mql]wtʾ dy ʾnšw$^{?}$h$^{?}$
8 [bkl šnʾ ywm ṭbʾ bny]sn lʿlmʾ
9 [......]s zbdbwl br zbdbwl
10 [.........] ktbʾ dnh
For text consult especially RSP 130

PAT 0345 **C3999** **A.D. 136**
Prov: Palmyra. Loc: Palmyra Museum. *Dedicatory. On altar.*

1 lbryk šmh lʿlmʾ ʿbd šlmn br nšʾ br
2 ḥyrʾ brq ʿl ḥywhy wḥyy bnwhy
3 byrḥ nysn šnt 4.100+40+5+2

PAT 0346 **C4000** **A.D. 143**
Prov: Palmyra. Loc: Palmyra Museum. *Dedicatory. On altar.*

1 dkr̊n ṭb lbr̊yk

2 šmh lʿlmʾ
3 ʿbd ʿbnr̃gl br̃
4 ḥr̃y tymʾ br̃ ʿnn
5 ʿl ḥywh wḥyʾ
6 ʿnn br̃h byr̃ḥ
7 ʾb? šnt
8 4.100+40+10+4

PAT 0347 **C4001** **A.D. 161**
Prov: Palmyra. Loc: Palmyra Museum.
Dedicatory. On altar. Bib: Syr '31 15; Déd p 178.

1 dkrn ṭb lbryk šmh lʿlmʾ
2 ṭbʾ wrḥmnʾ
3 wltrn ʾ[ḥy]ʾ qdyšʾ
4 ʿbd w[qr]b ʾ[...]
5 br ḥr[y ..... br]
6 ʿlbn[.]m/q [...]
7 [.....]
8 [.....]ʿ[..]
9 [wʿl] ḥyy h[r]ms [.
10 ʾ]tth byrḥ s<y>wn
11 šnt 4.100+60+10+2
12 wʿbd tṣbyt[h k]lh

PAT 0348 **C4002** **n. d.**
Prov: Palmyra. Loc: Palmyra Museum.
Dedicatory. On altar.

1 lbryk šmh lʿlmʾ ṭbʾ wrḥmnʾ
2 [w]l[trn ʾḥ]yʾ qdšʾ ʿbd ʿlw[t]ʾ
3 [.......] dny w[ʿ]lyw bny ʿšt[rg]ʾ
4 br dny [...]yḥ[... ʿl ḥyyhwn]
5 wḥyy bnhw[n byrḥ ......]
6 šnt 3.100[+1.100....]
line 5: CIS bn<y>hw[n]

PAT 0349 **C4003** **A.D. 173**
Prov: Palmyra. Loc: Palmyra Museum.
Dedicatory. On stone tablet.

1 [Διὶ ὑ]ψίστῳ καὶ ἐπηκό[ῳ ...]
2 [....]σ[.]ῳ Κα[σι]ανὸς Ζη[νοβίου]
3 [το]ῦ Φιλοπάτορος ὑπ[ὲρ ὑγείας]
4 [αὐ]τοῦ καὶ ἀδελφῶ[ν αὐτοῦ]
5 [ἔ]τους δπυ' Π[εριτίου]

1 [mwdʾ ....]ʾ br zbydʾ ʾpyn ʿl ḥywh
2 [wḥyʾ ʾḥwhy] b[y]r[ḥ] šbṭ šnt 4.100+80+4

PAT 0350 **C4004** **A.D. 176**
Prov: Palmyra. Loc: Palmyra Museum.
Dedicatory. On altar.

1 [mwd]ʾ ḥyrn br
2 [m]q?y?[mw] br yrḥy
3 qdm [b]ryk šmh lʿlmʾ
4 ʾlh[ʾ ṭ]bʾ
5 š?nt 4.100+80+5+3
6 [byr]ḥ kn[wn] ywm 10+5+4
7 [ʿ]l ḥywhy wḥyʾ bnwh[y]

PAT 0351 **C4005** **A.D. (179)**
Prov: Palmyra. Loc: Palmyra Museum.
Dedicatory. On altar.

1 [bryk šmh l]ʿlmʾ
2 [ʿbd wmwdʾ] šlmʾ
3 [br ... by]rḥ ʾdr
4 [šnt] [4.100]+80+10

PAT 0352 **C4006** **A.D. 178**
Prov: Palmyra. Loc: Palmyra Museum.
Dedicatory. On altar.

1 lbr̃y[k šmh] l[ʿlm]ʾ
2 mwdyʾ ḥ?[nt]ʾ? br̃t
3 [ʿw]yd lh wltymr̃ṣw
4 wlbwr̃pʾ šnt
5 4.100+80+10

PAT 0353 **C4007** **A.D. 190**
Prov: Palmyra. Loc: Palmyra Museum.
Dedicatory. On altar.

1 bryk šmh lʿlmʾ ṭbʾ
2 wr̃ḥmnʾ ʿbd wmwdʾ
3 ydyʿbl br zb?[d]ʾ lšmš
4 myšn ʿl ḥyw[hy] wḥyy bny
5 [ʾ]ḥwhy byrḥ nysn
6 šnt 5.100+1

PAT 0354 **C4008** **A.D. 191**

Prov: Palmyra. Loc: Ny Carlsberg Glyptotek, 1081. *Dedicatory. On altar.* Bib: PS 85; NyCG 9.

1 ʿltʾ dh ʿbd wh?[bʾ]
2 br̊ mlkw mlʾ lbr̊yk
3 šmh lʿlmʾ ʿl ḥyw[h]
4 wḥyʾ ʾḥwhy byr̊ḥ
5 sywn šnt 5.100+2

PAT 0355 **C4009** **A.D. 191**

Prov: Palmyra. Loc: Palmyra Museum. *Dedicatory. On altar.* Bib: Inv 11 8, pl I.

1 lb[ryk] š[mh]
2 lʿlmʾ wr̊[ḥmnʾ]
3 ṭbʾ mwdʾ [ḥl]pw
4 nʾ br̊ zbdʾ wb
5 [..]y ʿl ḥyw [w]ḥyʾ
6 byth klh [.]b[..]
7 šnt 5.100+3

Text abraded at points; consult Inv 11 8 (probably same text) for possible alternate readings

PAT 0356 **C4010** **n. d.**

Prov: Palmyra. Loc: Palmyra, A 249. *Dedicatory. On altar.* Bib: Inv 11 23 pl XIII.

1 ʿltʾ dh lbryk šmh lʿlmʾ
2 ʿbdt wmwdyʾ
3 ʿlʾ brt zbydʾ br ʿtʿy
4 rpʾ ʿl ḥyh wʿl ḥyʾ ydy
5 br tymrṣw ydy bʿlh
6 wʿl ḥ[y]ʾ b[...] lʿlmʾ
7 ywm tšʿʾ byrḥ ʾb šnt
8 5.100+[x]

Text of Inv 11 23

PAT 0357 **C4011** **A.D. (199)**

Prov: Palmyra. Loc: Palmyra Museum. *Dedicatory. On altar.*

1 [....]m[.]dʾ[...]
2 bry[k šmh] lʿlmʾ [rḥmnʾ]
3 ṭb[ʾ ʿbd wmwdʾ t]ymʾ [.....]
4 bryk šmh lʿlm[ʾ] r[ḥmnʾ]
5 qryh bkwl ʾtr wʿnyh [...]
6 [l]h ʿl ḥywh wḥy mrwhy w[...]
7 byrḥ ʾb dy šnt 5.100+10

PAT 0358 **C4012** **A.D. 203**

Prov: Palmyra. Loc: Palmyra Museum. *Dedicatory. On altar.*

1 [lb].yk šmh l[ʿlmʾ]
2 [ʿbd] wmwdʾ [......]
3 [b.] ʿwdʾl ʿl ḥywh
4 [w]ḥyʾ bnwh by.ḥ
5 qnyn šnt 5.100+10+4

PAT 0359 **C4013** **A.D. 205**

Prov: Palmyra. Loc: Palmyra Museum. *Dedicatory. On altar.*

1 [lb].yk šmh lʿlmʾ
2 [ʾl]hʾ ṭbʾ wsk.ʾ ʿbd
3 ʿltʾ dnh h.ms bsm
4 [b]. ḥ.y mlkw b. whbʾ
5 [ʿ]l ḥywhy wḥyʾ bnwhy
6 [b]y.ḥ sywn ywm 20+4
7 šnt 5.100+10+5+1

PAT 0360 **C4014** **A.D. 207**

Prov: Palmyra. Loc: Strassburg, University Library?. *Dedicatory. On altar.* Bib: HNE p 475 c. 6 XL, 3; RES 391.

1 lb.yk šmh lʿlmʾ
2 ṭbʾ w.ḥmnʾ ʿltʾ
3 dnh ʿbdt mky b.t
4 ʿgʾ ʾtt mlʾ b.
5 mlkw lḥyh wlḥyʾ
6 b.th by.ḥ ṭbt
7 šnt 5.100+10+5+3

PAT 0361 **C4015** **A.D. 207**

Prov: Palmyra, reemployed in private house. Loc: Palmyra Museum. *Dedicatory. On altar.* RES 2132

1 [...]l br [....]

2 [n]bwz’ br nš’
3 [ʿ]l ḥywh wʿl ḥ[y]’
4 rbn’ wn[....]
5 bnw byrḥ nysn
6 šnt 5.100+10+5+3

PAT 0362 **C4016** **A.D. 212**

Prov: Palmyra, reemployed in private house. Loc: Palmyra Museum. *Dedicatory. On altar.*

1 lbryk šmh lʿlm’
2 ṭb’ wrḥmn’ ʿbd
3 wmwd’ rdwn br hrmsyn’
4 btšry šnt 5.100+20+4

PAT 0363 **C4017** **A.D. 216**

Prov: Palmyra, reemployed in private house. Loc: Palmyra Museum. *Dedicatory. On altar.*

1 [lbry]k$^{?}$ šmh lʿlm’ ṭb’
2 ẉḥmn’ ʿbd wmwd’
3 bwṭ’ ḅ šmšgṃ ʿl
4 [ḥy]w$^{?}$hy wḥy’ ’mh wḥy[’]
5 ’ḥwhy wḥy’ bnyhwn
6 by̩ḥ ’lwl šnt
7 5.100+20+5+2

PAT 0364 **C4018** **A.D. 219**

Prov: Palmyra. Loc: Palmyra Museum. *Dedicatory. On altar.*

1 [b]r$^{?}$yk šmh drḥ$^{?}$[mn’]
2 [ṭ]b’ ʿbd mqy
3 [w]’ḥwh bn’$^{?}$
4 yrḥy br zbyd[’]
5 ’lpy ʿly ḥy’
6 dy ’mhwn wʿl
7 ḥyyhwn wdy
8 ’ḥthwn byrḥ
9 ’b šnt 5.100+20+10

Line 5 *ʿly ḥy’*: see Chabot ad loc on odd writing of formulaic expression

PAT 0365 **C4019** **A.D. 220**

Prov: Palmyra. Loc: Palmyra Museum. *Dedicatory. On altar fragment.* Bib: Inv 11 14.

1 [bryk] šm[h]
2 [.....]
3 [.....]
4 [....] brsmy$^{?}$
5 ʿl ḥywhy wḥy
6 šlmt ’m[h]
7 byrḥ ’yr š[nt]
8 5.100+20+10+1

Text after Inv 11 14

PAT 0366 **C4020** **A.D. 220**

Prov: Palmyra. Loc: Istanbul Arkeoloji Müzesi, 3703 T. *Dedicatory. On altar.*

(A)
1 bryk šmh lʿlm’
2 mwdy’ dwmnyn’ brt
3 [y]dyʿbl br yrḥy dʿ[n]h
4 [šnt] 5.100+20+10+2
(B)
1 bryk šmh lʿlm’ ṭb’
2 wrḥmn’ mwdy’
3 dwmny[n’ br]t ydyʿbl

Collated 19-24/10/93

PAT 0367 **C4021** **A.D. 221**

Prov: Palmyra. Loc: Oxford, Asmolean Museum, C2-10. *Dedicatory. On altar.*

1 lbryk šmh lʿlmh ṭb’ wrḥmn’
2 mwd’ mrywn br zbdbwl br mlkw ʿl
3 ḥywhy wḥy’ ’ḥwh!y byrḥ tšry
4 šnt 5.100+20+10+3

line 3 *ḥwh!y* for *ḥwḥy*

PAT 0368 **C4022** **A.D. 225**

Prov: Palmyra. Loc: Palmyra Museum. *Dedicatory. On stone tablet.* Cf PNO no. 73.

1 ’Αββαθα καὶ ’Αγγάθ
2 ’Ραββήλου τοῦ ’Ειά
3 θου εὐξάμενοι
4 ἀνέθηκαν

1 [.....]
2 [.... bryk šmh] [l]ʿ$^{?}$l$^{?}$m
3 rḥmn’ ṭb’

4 [d]y ʿnh byrḥ ṭbt
5 š$^?$nt 5.100+20+10+5+1
PNO no. 73 may provide beginning

PAT 0369 **C4023** **A.D. 226**
Prov: Palmyra. Loc: Palmyra Museum. *Dedicatory. On altar.*

1 [........]
2 ṭbʾ b.šmš
3 wʾdynt b.h
4 [w]m.ym ʾtt$^?$[h]
5 šnt 5.100+20+[10]+5+3

PAT 0370 **C4024** **A.D. 228**
Prov: Palmyra. Loc: Palmyra Museum. *Dedicatory. On altar.*

1 b.k šmh lʿlm[.$^?$]
2 ʿbd wmwdʾ
3 mqymw b. gy$^?$
4 ʿl ḥywh wḥyʾ$^?$
5 ʾmh wʾḥw
6 by.h ʾb
7 šnt 5.100+
8 20+10+5+4

PAT 0371 **C4025** **A.D. 227**
Prov: Palmyra. Loc: Palmyra Museum. *Dedicatory. On altar?.*

4 ʿbd wmwdʾ
3 y.ḥy wydʿ b.h
2 l.ḥmnʾ šnt
1 5.100+20+10+5+4
On stone, line 1 at top, etc.

PAT 0372 **C4026** **A.D. (229)**
Prov: Palmyra. Loc: Palmyra Museum. *Dedicatory. On altar.*

1 [bryk šm]h lʿlmʾ ṭbʾ
2 [wrḥ]mnʾ mwdʾ t[ymrṣw]
3 [b]r whblt br tymrṣ[w ʿl]
4 [ḥ]ywhy$^?$ wḥyʾ ʾḥwhy w[bny]
5 byt$^?$h$^?$ byrḥ ʾdr šnt

6 [5].100+40

PAT 0373 **C4027** **A.D. 230**
Prov: Palmyra. Loc: Louvre, AO 4998. *Dedicatory. On altar.* Bib: HNE p 475 c. 7 XXXVIII, 10; Lou 148.

1 lb.yk šmh lʿlmʾ ṭbʾ
2 w.ḥm<n>) ʿbdt btzbydʾ
3 b.t gd.sw ʿl ḥyh wḥyʾ
4 ʿbydw bʿlh by.ḥ ʾb šnt
5 5.100+40+1

PAT 0374 **C4028** **A.D. 231**
Prov: Palmyra. Loc: Leipzig? *Dedicatory. On altar.* Bib: RES 1040.

1 br̊yk šmh dy
2 r̊ḥmnʾ ṭbʾ
3 wtyr̊ʾ ʿbd
4 wmwdʾ whblt br̊
5 sr̊ykw ʿl ḥywh
6 wḥyʾ bnwhy
7 by<r̊>ḥ ʾdr̊ dš
8 nt 5.100+40+2

PAT 0375 **C4029** **A.D. 231**
Prov: Palmyra, Temple of Bel. Loc: Palmyra Museum. *Dedicatory. On altar.* Bib: HNE p 475 c. 8 XXXVIII, 9

1 br̊yk šmh lʿlmʾ ṭbʾ
2 wr̊ḥmnʾ ʿltʾ dnh ʿbd
3 wmwdʾ kyly br̊ yʿqwb
4 tymr̊ṣw dbyḥtʾ ʿl ḥy[wh]
5 wḥyy ʾḥywh šnt 5.100+40+2

PAT 0376 **C4030** **A.D. 232**
Prov: Palmyra. Loc: New York, Metropolitan Museum of Art, MMA 95.28. *Dedicatory. On altar.* Bib: Clermont-Ganneau 1897 pp 58-60, pl I A; HNE p 476 c. 10, pl XL, 8; Chabot '22 p 83, pl XXIV, 10; Arnold '05 p 110 no. VIII, pl VIII; RES 761.

1 br̊yk šmh lʿlmʾ

2 ṭbʾ wr̊ḥmnʾ ʿbd
3 wmwdʾ ḥggw br̊
4 yhybʾ br̊ yr̊ḥy
5 dkʾ ʿl ḥywhy
6 wḥyʾ ʾbwhy
7 wʾḥwhy byr̊ḥ
8 qnyn šnt 5.100
9 +40+3

Collated E. C., 8/25/94; traces of rubrication; cf C4050

1 lbryk šmh lʿlmʾ
2 rḥmnʾ
3 ṭbʾ ʿbd wmwdʾ
4 zbydʾ br mlkw
5 zbydʾ ʿbʾ ʿl
6 ḥywhw wbny byth
7 byrḥ nysn šnt
8 5.100+40+5+2

line 6 *ḥywhw: sic*

PAT 0377 **C4031** **A.D. 233**

Prov: Palmyra. Loc: Oxford, Ashmolean Museum, C2-11. *Dedicatory. On altar.*

1 Διὶ ὑψίστῳ καὶ [ἐ]
2 πηκόῳ Ἰού(λιος) Αὐρ(ήλιος) Ἀ-
3 ντίπατρος ὁ καὶ
4 Ἀλαφώνας Ἀαιλ-
5 αμει τοῦ Ζηνοβί-
6 ου τοῦ Ἀκοπάου
7 εὐξάμενος ἀνέ-
8 θηκεν ἔτους δμφʹ
9 Αὐδυναίου κδʹ

1 [m]wdʾ lbryk šmh lʿlmʾ
2 ywl<ys> ʾwr<lys>
3 ḥlpwnʾ br̊ ʾʿylmy
4 zbydʾ ʾqwpʿ
5 byr̊ḥ ṭbt
6 ywm 20+4
7 šnt 5.100+40+4

PAT 0378 **C4032** **A.D. 235**

Prov: Palmyra. Loc: Palmyra Museum. *Dedicatory. On altar.*

1 [bry]k? šmh lʿlmʾ ṭbʾ
2 [wr]ḥmnʾ mwdʾ mqym?[w]
3 br̊ ymlʾ ʿl ḥywh wḥyʾ?
4 [ḥ]yr̊n ʾḥwhy byr̊ḥ tšry
5 šnt 5.100+40+5+2

PAT 0379 **C4033** **A.D. 236**

Prov: Palmyra. Loc: Palmyra Museum. *Dedicatory. On altar.*

PAT 0380 **C4034** **A.D. 238**

Prov: Palmyra. Loc: Palmyra Museum. *Dedicatory. On altar.*

1 br̊yk šmh lʿlmʾ
2 ṭbʾ wlr̊ḥmnʾ
3 mwdʾ mzbnʾ b[r̊]
4 yr̊ḥy kyly r̊bʾ dy
5 dy qr̊ lh wʿnyh
6 šnt 5.100+40+10

Lines 4-5 *dy*: dittography

PAT 0381 **C4035** **A.D. 238**

Prov: Palmyra. Loc: Palmyra, A 255. *Dedicatory. On altar.* Bib: Inv 11 15 pl I.

1 bryk šmh lʿlmʾ
2 ʿbd gdʾ wmwdʾ br
3 ḥlyʾ ʿl ḥywh wḥyʾ
4 bnwh wgrh dypyn
5 šnt 5.100+40+10

line 4: text of Inv 11 15 differs in detail

PAT 0382 **C4036** **A.D. 240**

Prov: Palmyra. Loc: Palmyra Museum. *Dedicatory. On altar.*

(On front)
1 bryk šmh lʿlmʾ ṭbʾ wrḥmn[ʾ]
2 ʿbd wmwdʾ zbdbwl br mlkw
3 zbdbwl ʾtr̊msyn ʿl ḥywhy
4 wḥyʾ bnwhy wbny byth klhn
5 byrḥ nysn šnt 5.100+40+10+1
(On left side)
1 mwdʾ mlkw br̊ zbdbwl
2 br̊ mlkw ʾtrmsyn
3 ʿl ḥywh wḥyʾ ʾbyh

PAT 0383 **C4037** **A.D. 240**

Prov: Palmyra. Loc: Strassburg, University Library. *Dedicatory. On altar.* Bib: RES 392; Seyrig '33.

1 mwdʾ bwr̊pʾ
2 br̊ ḥ[lpt]ʾ [br̊]
3 [....]t šnt
4 5.100+40+10+1
5 byr̊ḥ ʾyr̊

PAT 0384 **C4038** **A.D. 240**

Prov: Palmyra. Loc: Palmyra Museum. *Dedicatory. On altar.*

1 br̊yk šmh lʿlmʾ r̊ḥmnʾ
2 ṭbʾ wtyr̊ʾ ʿbd wmwdʾ
3 šʿdw br̊ mlkw ḥss ʿl ḥywhy
4 wḥyʾ bnwhy dy qr̊ lh wʿny
5 byr̊ḥ ʾlwl dy šnt 5.100+40+10+1

PAT 0385 **C4039** **A.D. 240**

Prov: Palmyra. Loc: Palmyra Museum. *Dedicatory. On altar.*

1 [ʿl]tʾ [......]
2 lbryk š[mh lʿlmʾ ṭbʾ]
3 wrḥmnʾ yrḥb[wlʾ br]
4 [yr]ḥbwlʾ ḥyq[...]
5 ʿl ḥyʾ yrḥy [brh wḥyy]
6 ʾḥwhy byrḥ ʾ[b šnt]
7 5.100+40+10+2

PAT 0386 **C4040** **A.D. (240)**

Prov: Palmyra. Loc: Palmyra Museum. *Dedicatory. On altar.*

1 bryk šmh lʿlmʾ
2 [mwdʾ t]ymy br ʿbdy
3 [......]
4 [......]
5 [....... šnt]
6 [5.100]+40+10+2

PAT 0387 **C4041** **A.D. 245**

Prov: Palmyra. Loc: Palmyra Museum. *Dedicatory. On altar.*

1 br̊yk šmh lʿlmʾ
2 ṭbʾ wtyr̊ʾ
3 ʿbd wmwdʾ nḥyʿzyz
4 [ʿ]r̊by byr̊ḥ ʾb
5 šnt 5.100+40+10+5+1

PAT 0388 **C4042** **A.D. (247)**

Prov: Palmyra. Loc: Palmyra Museum. *Dedicatory. On altar.*

1 bryk šmh
2 [r̊]ḥmnʾ ṭbʾ wtyr̊[ʾ]
3 ʿbdt sr̊ʾ wmw[dyʾ]
4 byr̊ḥ ʾyr̊ šnt
5 [5.100]+40+10+5+3

PAT 0389 **C4043** **A.D. 248**

Prov: Palmyra. Loc: Palmyra, A 357. *Dedicatory. On altar.* Bib: Inv 11 18, pl II.

1 [mwd]ʾ m[l]ʾ br bwṭn
2 ʿl ḥywh wḥyʾ bnw[h]
3 byrḥ šbṭ šnt 5.100+40+10
4 5+4

Text of Inv 11 18

PAT 0390 **C4044** **A.D. 249**

Prov: Palmyra. Loc: Palmyra Museum. *Dedicatory. On altar.*

1 bryk šmh lʿlmʾ
2 ṭbʾ ʿbd wmwdʾ
3 ʿgylw br ʿbdlt
4 br ʿrby ʿl ḥywh
5 wḥyʾ ʾbwh wḥyʾ
6 ʾḥwh byrḥ ʾdr
7 šnt 5.100+60

PAT 0391 **C4045** **A.D. 249**

Prov: Palmyra. Loc: Palmyra Museum. *Dedicatory. On altar.*

1 [lbryk šmh lʿl]mʾ
2 [rḥmnʾ ṭb]ʾ mwdʾ
3 [...]ʾ br zbwd ʿl
4 [ḥ]yw[hy wḥ]y[y] ʾbwhy
5 [wʾḥw]hy šnt 5.100+60
6 b[yrḥ n]ysn

PAT 0392 **C4046** **A.D. 253**
Prov: Palmyra. Loc: Palmyra Museum. *Dedicatory. On altar.* Bib: HNE p 476 c. 13, pl XL, 6

1 lbr̊k šmh lʿlmʾ
2 ṭbʾ
3 wr̊ḥmnʾ wtyr̊
4 ʿbd wmwdʾ
5 mqy br̊ lšmš
6 lḥyʾ br̊h dy
7 qr̊ lh wʿ[ny]hy
8 byr̊ḥ ʾb dy
9 5.100+60+4
10 šnt

PAT 0393 **C4047** **A.D. 256**
Prov: Palmyra. Loc: Palmyra Museum. *Dedicatory. On altar.* Bib: RosAH 15.

1 bryk šmh lʿlmʾ [ṭ]bʾ
2 wr̊ḥmnʾ mwdʾ mhr̊yt
3 lšmš lr̊ḥmnʾ dy qr̊ lh
4 bymʾ wbybšʾ wʿnh [bk]l
5 dy qr̊h hw w[bny by]th
6 byr̊ḥ ʾlwl šnt [5.100]+60+5+2

PAT 0394 **C4048** **A.D. 263**
Prov: (Palmyra) found in Damascus. Loc: Not known. *Dedicatory. On altar.* Bib: RES 672.

1 mwdʾ yrḥy br
2 nbwdʿ br̊ mqy
3 [w]qwšy br̊t slwqʾ
4 wšbty br̊t whblt
5 wbny <by>tʾ kwlhwn
6 dy qryny wʿnn
7 šnt 5.100+60+10+5

PAT 0395 **C4049** **A.D. 258**
Prov: Palmyra. Loc: Palmyra Museum. *Dedicatory. On altar.*

1 lbryk šmh lʿlmʾ
2 ʿbd [ʾ]spydn [b]r
3 [..... m]lkw br n[sʾ]
4 [.....]ʾ [dy] q[...]
5 [.....]
6 [...... yw]m 10
7 [šnt 5].100+60+10

PAT 0396 **C4050** **A.D. 261**
Prov: Palmyra, Temple of Bel, reemployed. Loc: Palmyra Museum. *Dedicatory. On altar.*

1 br̊yk šmh lʿlmʾ ṭbʾ
2 [w]r̊ḥmnʾ ʿbd wmwdʾ
3 [ḥ]ggw br̊ yhybʾ yr̊ḥy
4 dkʾ ʿl ḥywhy wḥyʾ
5 ʾbwhy wḥyʾ ʾḥwhy
6 wḥyʾ bnyhwn byr̊ḥ
7 [n]ysn šnt 5.100+20+[20]+20+10+2
8 [...]ʾ wqbyl l[r̊ḥ]mnʾ
9 ʾl[..] wdy ysb ʿltʾ
10 [....]ʾ[.]wʿʾ [w]qbyl
11 [......]ʾ ʿ[l]m[...]y
12 [...]l[..]yh

PAT 0397 **C4051** **A.D. 262**
Prov: Palmyra. Loc: Palmyra Museum. *Dedicatory. On altar.* Bib: HNE p 476 c. 12, pl XL, 4

1 ʿbd wmwdʾ bʿly
2 wbnwhy wbnyh [dy]
3 byth klhn
4 lr̊ḥmnʾ ṭbʾ
5 wtyr̊ʾ dy qr̊ lh
6 wʿnyh šnt 5.100+60+10+4

PAT 0398 **C4052** **A.D. 263**
Prov: Palmyra. Loc: Palmyra Museum. *Dedicatory. On altar.*

1 [....]
2 [...... ʿbd] wmwd[ʾ]

3 [.... br d]yny b[r]
4 [.... ʿl] ḥywhy
5 [wḥyʾ] ʾḥwhy wʿl
6 ḥyʾ ʿgylw ḥlh
7 wbnwhy byrḥ sywn
8 šnt 5.100+[20]+40+10+4

PAT 0399 **C4053** **A.D. 268**
Prov: Palmyra. Loc: Palmyra Museum. *Dedicatory. On altar.*

1 ʿltʾ dnh ʿbd zb[dʾ]
2 br ḥlʾ wbʿltgʾ bt
3 ʿgʾ wbnh byrḥ nysn
4 dy šnt ḥmš mʾh
5 wšbʿyn wtšʿ dy
6 qr̊w lh lʾlhʾ
7 wʿnnwn ṭbʾ

PAT 0400 **C4054** **n. d.**
Prov: Palmyra. Loc: Istanbul?. *Dedicatory. On altar.*

1 bryk šmh lʿlmʾ
2 mwdʾ ʾspdyn wʾ[...]
3 wbnʾ byth [klhwn]
4 šnt 5.[100]

Location according to CIS. Not in Istanbul Arkeoloji Müzesi today.

PAT 0401 **C4055** **n. d.**
Prov: Palmyra. Loc: Palmyra Museum. *Dedicatory. On altar.*

1 bryk šm[h]
2 lʿlm[ʾ] mwdʾ
3 ʾd[.......]
4 dy q[......]
5 šnt 5[.100...]

PAT 0402 **C4056** **n. d.**
Prov: Palmyra. Loc: Palmyra Museum. *Dedicatory. On altar.*

1 bryk šmh [lʿlmʾ]
2 ṭbʾ wr̊ḥmn[ʾ]
3 ʿbd ydy br̊ ḥ[...]
4 [w]lšmš br̊ š[...]
5 ʾ[ḥ]wh ʿl ḥyy[hwn]
6 wḥyy ʾmhwn
7 wbnwhwn byr̊ḥ
8 ʾ[d]r šnt 5[..]

PAT 0403 **C4057** **n. d.**
Prov: Palmyra. Loc: Palmyra Museum. *Dedicatory. On altar.*

1 br̊yk šmh lʿlmʾ
2 [ṭ]bʾ wrḥmnʾ ʿbd
3 [w]mwdʾ swsʾ br
4 [l]šmš br ʿgylw [br]
5 [ty]mʾ ʿl ḥywhy
6 [.......]r[....]

PAT 0404 **C4058** **n. d.**
Prov: Palmyra. Loc: Istanbul?. *Dedicatory. On altar.* Bib: Déd p 181.

1 [lbryk] šmh lʿlmʾ ṭbʾ
2 [wrḥmn]ʾ ʿltʾ dh ʿbd
3 [mqy]mw br̊ yr̊ḥbwlʾ br̊
4 [gmlʾ ʿl] ḥyʾ šgl br̊th dy
5 [.......]lh r̊wḥʾ šnyn
6 [.... y]dh wr̊glh wlʾ
7 [.....]wblnh lwt
8 [....]lʾ hw
9 [......]

Location according to CIS. Not in Istanbul Arkeoloji Müzesi today.

PAT 0405 **C4059** **n. d.**
Prov: Palmyra. Loc: Palmyra Museum. *Dedicatory. On altar.*

1 br[yk] š[m]h lʿ[lmʾ]
2 ṭbʾ wrḥ[mn]ʾ [tyrʾ]
3 ʿ[bd wmwdʾ] nsʾ b[r]
4 [n]sʾ [br r]p[ʾ]l [ʿl]
5 [ḥywh wḥ]yʾ [...]

PAT 0406 **C4060** **n. d.**

Prov: Palmyra. Loc: Palmyra Museum. *Dedicatory. On altar.* Bib: Syr '31 16.

1 [lb]ryk šmh wlmlk
2 [...]hy mwdʾ ydʿw br
3 [ʿg]ylw br ydʿw ʿl
4 ḥywhy wḥyʾ bnwhy
5 byrḥ tšry šnt
6 [.....]

PAT 0407 **C4061** **n. d.**

Prov: Palmyra. Loc: Palmyra Museum. *Dedicatory. On altar.*

1 lbr̊yk šmh
2 lʿlmʾ ʿbd
3 wmwdʾ mr̊wnʾ
4 [b]r̊ ḥdwdn br̊
5 [mr̊]wnʾ lḥywh
6 [wḥy]ʾ ʾbwh
7 [wʾḥw]h wr̊ḥmwh
8 [byr̊ḥ t]šr̊y
9 [šnt ...]

PAT 0408 **C4062** **n. d.**

Prov: Palmyra. Loc: Palmyra Museum. *Dedicatory. On altar.*

1 dkrn ṭb lbryk
2 šmh lʿlmʾ ʿbd
3 ʿbydw ʿsty br
4 gwr̊ʾ br̊ nšm
5 ʾmṣr

PAT 0409 **C4063** **n. d.**

Prov: Palmyra. Loc: Istanbul Arkeoloji Müzesi, 3704 T. *Dedicatory. On altar.*

1 ʿbd wmwdʾ
2 lbryk šmh
3 lʿlmʾ mktš
4 br [w]hblt br
5 [.]ʿ[.....]bʾ
6 [....]ʿl ḥwh
7 wḥyy ʾḥwhy

Collated 19-24/10/93

PAT 0410 **C4064** **n. d.**

Prov: Palmyra. Loc: Palmyra Museum. *Dedicatory. On altar.*

1 bryk š[mh lʿl]mʾ ṭ[bʾ]
2 wrḥmnʾ ʿbd wmw[dʾ ...]
3 br mqy ʿl ḥywhy w[ḥyʾ]
4 bnwhy byrḥ sywn š[nt ...]
5 bd ʾmlk ʾpkl[ʾ dy]
6 mṣb ʿynʾ

PAT 0411 **C4065** **n. d.**

Prov: Palmyra. Loc: Palmyra Museum. *Dedicatory. On altar.*

1 [lbryk šmh]
2 lʿlmʾ ʿltʾ dh
3 ʿbd [pṣ]yʾl br zm[.]
4 ʾ[pk]lʾ dy mṣb ʿynʾ
5 ʿl ḥywh [wʿ]l [ḥy]ʾ
6 [.....]

PAT 0412 **C4066** **n. d.**

Prov: Palmyra. Loc: Palmyra Museum. *Dedicatory. On altar.*

1 Διὶ ὑψίστῳ καὶ ἐπη-
2 κόῳ τὸν βωμὸν ἀν-
3 [ἔθηκεν] εὐχαρίστ[ως]
4 [....]

1 bryk šmh lʿlmʾ ṭbʾ
2 wrḥ[mnʾ ʿlt]ʾ dh ʿbd
3 wmw[dʾ ḥyrn] br srykw
4 ḥy[rn ʿl ḥywhy w]ḥyʾ
5 [.....]ny[.]

PAT 0413 **C4067** **n. d.**

Prov: Palmyra. Loc: Palmyra Museum. *Dedicatory. On altar.*

1 mzbʾ brt mzbnʾ
2 mwd[yʾ] <l>bryk šmh lʿlmʾ
3 dʿnh
4 [w]ʾbwh wʾḥh

PAT 0414 **C4068** **n. d.**
Prov: Palmyra. Loc: Istanbul?. *Dedicatory. On altar.*

1 bryk šmh lʿlmʾ ṭbʾ
2 wrḥmnʾ [ʿb]d ʾsṭ[.]
3 ʿl ḥywh [wḥyy] sr̊ykw
4 m[.]w[.....]ʾ
5 [.....] šnt
6 [.....]

Location according to CIS. Not in Istanbul Arkeoloji Müzesi today.

PAT 0415 **C4069** **n. d.**
Prov: Palmyra. Loc: Palmyra Museum. *Dedicatory. On altar.*

1 [lbryk] šmh lʿlmʾ ṭbʾ
2 [ʿ]bd [w]mwdʾ m[qy] ṭbḥʾ
3 [ʿ]l ḥywh w[ḥyʾ ʾt]th
4 [wb]nwh [......]

PAT 0416 **C4070** **n. d.**
Prov: Palmyra. Loc: Palmyra Museum. *Dedicatory. On altar.*

1 bryk šmh lʿlmʾ
2 mwdʾ zby br
3 zbdʾ zbd

PAT 0417 **C4071** **n. d.**
Prov: Palmyra. Loc: Palmyra Museum. *Dedicatory. On altar.*

1 lbryk šmh lʿlmʾ
2 ʿbd mlʾ br šmʿwn
3 h[......]
4 š[......]

PAT 0418 **C4072** **n. d.**
Prov: Palmyra. Loc: Palmyra Museum. *Dedicatory. On altar.*

1 [lbryk šmh] lʿlmʾ
2 ṭbʾ wrḥmnʾ ʿbd
3 wmwdʾ m$^{?}$lkw wyrḥb[wlʾ]
4 brh dy ʾḥwhy [...]
5 ʿl ḥywhy wḥyʾ
6 ʾḥwh byrḥ ʾdr
7 [šnt ....]

PAT 0419 **C4073** **n. d.**
Prov: Palmyra. Loc: Istanbul?. *Dedicatory. On altar.*

1 bryk šmh [lʿlm]ʾ
2 ṭbʾ r̊ḥmn[ʾ mwdʾ]
3 syʿnʾ br̊ zb[y]dʾ

Location according to CIS. Not in Istanbul Arkeoloji Müzesi today.

PAT 0420 **C4074** **n. d.**
Prov: Palmyra. Loc: Ny Carlsberg Glyptotek, 1080. *Dedicatory. On pillar.* Bib: NyCG 129.

1 lbr̊yk šmh lʿlmʾ ʿbd[t$^{?}$]
2 [r̊]mlhʾ whr̊mz ʿl ḥyʾ br̊h

line 1: *ʿbd[t$^{?}$]* Chabot CIS sees traces of *t;* read *ʿbd[w]?*

PAT 0421 **C4075** **n. d.**
Prov: Palmyra. Loc: Palmyra, Museum, A 417. *Dedicatory. On altar.* Bib: Inv 11 29, pl XIII.

1 bryk šmh lʿlmʾ
2 [ṭ]bʾ wrḥmnʾ
3 [w]tyrʾ mwdʾ kl
4 [y]wm kytwt br
5 kytwt ʿl ḥy br
6 [..]wḥ[..]

Text of Inv 11 29

PAT 0422 **C4076** **n. d.**
Prov: Palmyra. Loc: Palmyra Museum. *Dedicatory. On altar.* Bib: Inv 11 9.

1 bryk šmh lʿlmʾ ṭ[b]ʾ wrḥmn[ʾ]
2 [wtyrʾ ʿ]ltʾ dh [mw]dʾ gdyʾ b[r]
3 ḥ[yrn b]gdn wlb[ryk]
4 [...]r[...]y[....]

PAT 0423 **C4077** **n. d.**

Prov: Palmyra. Loc: Istanbul Arkeoloji Müzesi, 3708 T. *Dedicatory. On altar.*

1 bryk šmh lʿlmʾ
2 wrḥmnʾ ṭbʾ ʿbd
3 wmwdʾ ʿgylw br ḥyr[ʾ]
4 [ʿl ḥy]why wḥy]ʾ [...]

Collated 19-24/10/93

PAT 0424 **C4078** **n. d.**

Prov: Palmyra. Loc: Palmyra Museum. *Dedicatory. On altar.*

1 bryk š[mh lʿ]lmʾ ṭb[ʾ]
2 wr̊ḥmnʾ ʿbd wmwdʾ
3 mqymw br̊ zbd[b]wl b[r]
4 ḥbry ʿl [ḥy]why wḥyʾ
5 [bn]why byrḥ n[ysn šnt ...]

PAT 0425 **C4079** **n. d.**

Prov: Palmyra. Loc: Palmyra Museum. *Dedicatory. On altar.*

1 bryk šmh lʿlmʾ ṭbʾ
2 [wr]ḥmnʾ ʿbd wmwdʾ ʿltʾ
3 [dh ʿ]gʾ br̊ zbdbwl br
4 [.....]my ʿl ḥywhy wḥyʾ
5 [...]y[....]

PAT 0426 **C4080** **n. d.**

Prov: Palmyra. Loc: Not known. *Dedicatory. On altar.* Bib: RES 720.

1 lbryk šm[h lʿlmʾ]
2 ṭbʾ wrḥm[nʾ .....]
3 hdyrʾ brt [.......]
4 mrqlʾ mwdyʾ [...]
5 wšmʿ bqlh mwʾ[lʾ br]
6 ʾtpny br mrqlʾ
7 wrwḥʾ bt mqy
8 wmrqlʾ b[r] [.....]
9 wrpʾ[l br] [.....]
10 w[....]

line 5: after bqlh, punctuation ∧

PAT 0427 **C4081** **n. d.**

Prov: Palmyra, Temple of Bel, reemployed. Loc: Palmyra Museum. *Dedicatory. On altar.*

1 br̊yk šmh lʿlmʾ ṭbʾ
2 mwdʾ hr̊ms wʾmtbl
3 lr̊ḥm[nʾ] ʿl ḥyʾ tymrṣw
4 wʾtʿmn wymlʾ bnh
5 lʿlmʾ ṭbʾ

PAT 0428 **C4082** **n. d.**

Prov: Palmyra. Loc: Palmyra Museum. *Dedicatory. On altar.*

1 br̊yk šmh lʿlmʾ
2 ṭbʾ wr̊ḥmnʾ ʿb[d]
3 wmwdʾ [ʾ]l[hb]l b[r]
4 [.....]

PAT 0429 **C4083** **n. d.**

Prov: Palmyra. Loc: Palmyra Museum. *Dedicatory. On altar.*

1 bryk šmh lʿlm[ʾ]
2 mwdyʾ šlm[t bt]
3 ʾlh dy qr lh
4 wʿnh

PAT 0430 **C4084** **n. d.**

Prov: Palmyra. Loc: Palmyra Museum. *Dedicatory. On altar.*

1 lbr̊yk šmh lʿlmʾ
2 r̊ḥmnʾ wḥnnʾ
3 wtyr̊ʾ mwdʾ dwr̊ʾ
4 br̊ zbdbwl mlkʾ
5 ʾtndwr̊ʾ ʾpwqḥ
6 [dy] qr̊ lh [..]b[..]
7 wb[...]ʾ[...]

PAT 0431 **C4085** **n. d.**

Prov: Palmyra. Loc: Palmyra Museum. *Dedicatory. On altar.*

1 lbr̊yk šmh lʿlmʾ
2 ṭbʾ

3 wr̊ḥmnʾ ʿbd
4 nšr̊y wnyqʾ
5 [d]y qr̊w lh
6 [wʿnw]nn šnt
7 [...]

PAT 0432 **C4086** **n. d.**
Prov: Palmyra, Temple of Bel, reemployed. Loc: Palmyra Museum. *Dedicatory. On altar.*

1 lbryk šmh lʿlmʾ
2 ʿbd
3 sbyns br
4 yrḥbwlʾ
5 yrḥy

PAT 0433 **C4087** **n. d.**
Prov: Palmyra. Loc: Palmyra Museum. *Dedicatory. On altar.*

1 [b]r̊yk šmh [l]ʿlm
2 ʿbdt
3 [..]r̊bnʾ ʿl
4 ḥyh wḥyʾ
5 [..]yh

PAT 0434 **C4088** **n. d.**
Prov: Palmyra. Loc: Palmyra Museum. *Dedicatory. On altar.*

1 lbry[k] šm[h]
2 rḥmnʾ [mwd]ʾ
3 pṣyʾ[l br ty]m[ʾ]
4 b[r .....]
5 ʿl ḥywh wḥyʾ
6 ʾḥwh [.....]
7 b[yr]ḥ [...] šnt

PAT 0435 **C4089** **n. d.**
Prov: Palmyra. Loc: Ny Carlsberg Glyptotek, 1161. *Dedicatory. On altar.* Bib: NyCG 128.

1 [l]br̊yk šmh lʿlmʾ
2 [ʿ]bd šmʿwn br̊
3 gdyʾ mwdʾ

PAT 0436 **C4090** **n. d.**
Prov: Palmyra. Loc: Palmyra Museum. *Dedicatory. On altar.*

1 εὐχή

1 [m]wdʾ zbd[bw]l [br]
2 [b]r̊ʿth [....]

PAT 0437 **C4091** **n. d.**
Prov: Palmyra. Loc: Palmyra Museum. *Dedicatory. On altar.*

1 [ε]ὐχή

1 [m]wdʾ yr̊ḥy br [........]
2 br̊yk lrḥmnʾ [..........]

PAT 0438 **C4092** **n. d.**
Prov: Palmyra. Loc: Palmyra Museum. *Dedicatory. On altar.*

1 mwdʾ lr̊ḥmnʾ ṭbʾ
2 nʿm br̊ gdylt
3 dy qr̊ lh wʿny

PAT 0439 **C4093** **n. d.**
Prov: Palmyra. Loc: Palmyra Museum. *Dedicatory. On altar.*

1 [mwdʾ] lrḥmnʾ ṭbʾ
2 [..]yt wnbyʿt wzkrt

PAT 0440 **C4094** **A.D. (238)**
Prov: Palmyra. Loc: Palmyra Museum. *Dedicatory. On altar.*

1 mwdʾ slwq[ʾ]
2 br mqwlʾ [br]
3 tydwrʾ br
4 [.]lgwrʾ[....]ʾ
5 [... [5].100+40+10

PAT 0441 **C4095** **n. d.**
Prov: Palmyra. Loc: Palmyra Museum. *Dedicatory. On altar.*

1 mwdʾ wh[.....]

PAT 0442 **C4096** **n. d.**
Prov: Palmyra. Loc: Palmyra Museum. *Dedicatory. On altar.*

1 mwdʾ zbwd
2 lbryk šmh lʿl
3 mʾ ṭbʾ

PAT 0443 **C4097** **n. d.**
Prov: Palmyra. Loc: Palmyra Museum. *Dedicatory. On altar.*

1 [m]wdʾ šlmn
2 br ʿgylw

PAT 0444 **C4098** **n. d.**
Prov: Palmyra. Loc: Palmyra Museum. *Dedicatory. On altar.*

1 [m]wdʾ ḥyr̊ʾ
2 [b]r̊ zbydʾ ʿl
3 [......]b[.]

PAT 0445 **C4099** **n. d.**
Prov: Palmyra. Loc: Palmyra Museum. *Dedicatory. On alar.*

1 mwdʾ ʿšy lrḥmn[ʾ]
2 ṭbʾ <d>y qr lh w[ʿnh]
line 2 *<d>y*: stone has *r̊y*

PAT 0446 **C4100** **n. d.**
Prov: Palmyra. Loc: Palmyra Museum. *Dedicatory. On altar.*

1 [t]šʿʾ ṭbʾ wšmyʿʾ [...]
2 [....]w[....]
3 [.....]h dy qr̊w lh
4 bʿqʾ wʿnnwn
5 br̊wḥʾ byr̊ḥ
6 [... šnt ...]

PAT 0447 **C4101** **n. d.**
Prov: Palmyra. Loc: Palmyra, A 269. *Dedicatory. On pillar.*

1 ʿltʾ dnh
2 ʿbd ʿbʾ
3 br [ky]ly b[r]
4 [ʿ]bʾ

PAT 0448 **C4102** **n. d.**
Prov: Palmyra, Diocletian Camp, vicinity of "Temple des Enseignes". Loc: lost. *Dedicatory. On altar fragment.* Bib: Inv 6 12; RSP 133.

1 ʿltʾ dh l[...]
2 wdkyr wbr[yk...]
Text of RSP 133

PAT 0449 **C4103** **n. d.**
Prov: Palmyra. Loc: Palmyra Museum. *Dedicatory. On altar fragment.*

1 [d]kyr̊ ʾwṭkʾ
2 [d]ʿbd ʿltʾ dh

PAT 0450 **C4104** **n. d.**
Prov: Palmyra. Loc: Palmyra Museum. *Dedicatory. On altar fragment.*

1 [...]w tymʾ br[...]
2 [..]ʿ[....]

PAT 0451 **C4105** **n. d.**
Prov: Palmyra. Loc: Palmyra Museum. *Dedicatory. On altar.*

1 dkyr bʿly wrḥm[why] klhw[n]
2 wdkyr [k]l [....]

PAT 0452 **C4105bis** **n. d.**
Prov: Palmyra. Loc: Palmyra Museum. *Dedicatory. On altar.*

1 [...]mn'[....]
2 [....]'r[....]

PAT 0453 **C4105ter** **n. d.**
Prov: Palmyra. Loc: Palmyra, A 453. *Dedicatory. On pillar.*

1 [...] wr̊wd 'r̊gbṭ'

PAT 0454 **C4106** **n. d.**
Prov: Palmyra. Loc: Palmyra Museum. *Dedicatory. On pillar.* Bib: Mordtmann 1875, 25.

1 [d]k[r]n ṭb lb[ryk]
2 [š]mh l[ʿl...]
3 [.....]
4 byr[ḥ .... šnt]
5 4[..]

PAT 0455 **C4107** **n. d.**
Prov: Palmyra. Loc: Palmyra Museum. *Dedicatory. On pillar.* Bib: Mordtmann 1875, 29.

1 bryk šmh lʿlm'
2 mwd' gd' br
3 [.....]
4 [.....]
5 [.....]

PAT 0456 **C4108** **n. d.**
Prov: Palmyra. Loc: Palmyra Museum. *Dedicatory. On pillar.* Bib: Mordtmann 1875, 30.

1 [.....]
Text much effaced

PAT 0457 **C4109** **9 B.C.**
Prov: Palmyra, Valley of Tombs, Tower 7. Loc: Palmyra,*in situ. Funerary: Foundation. On stone tablet.* Group: 4109, 4110, 4111. Bib: HNE p 478 d. α 1, pl XL, 11; Inv 4 28; MF Fondation 1.

(A)
1 qbr' dnh dy
2 ʿtntn br khylw dy
3 bnw ʿlwhy bnwhy
4 khylw wḥyrn bnwhy
5 dy mn bny myt'
6 byrḥ knwn šnt 3.100+4
(B)
1 qbr' dnh dy ʿtntn
2 br khylw dy bnw ʿlwhy
3 bnwhy khylw wḥyrn
4 bnwhy dy mn bny myt'
5 byrḥ knwn šnt 3.100+4
Text of Inv 4 28

PAT 0458 **C4110** **n. d.**
Prov: Palmyra, Valley of Tombs. Loc: Palmyra, *in situ. Funerary. On tomb wall.* See 4109.

1 ʿbdbl[.]
2 khylw

PAT 0459 **C4111** **n. d.**
Prov: Palmyra, Valley of Tombs. Loc: Palmyra, *in situ. Funerary. On tomb wall.* See 4109.

1 ḥbl khylw wḥyrn
2 wḥyrn bny ʿtntn
3 wbn[....]

PAT 0460 **C4112** **(4) B.C.**
Prov: Palmyra, Valley of Tombs. Loc: Louvre, AO 2205. *Funerary: Foundation. On stone tablet.* Bib: RES 1073; MF Fondation 2; Lou 190.

1 [byrḥ] nysn šnt
2 [3].100+5+3 qbr'
3 [dnh] dy zbdbwl br
4 [....]h br ʿtršwry
5 [dy mn] bny kmr' dy
6 [ʿbd] lh wlbnwhy

PAT 0461 **C4113** **A.D. 9**
Prov: Palmyra, reemployed in Islamic house. Loc: Palmyra Museum. *Funerary: Foundation. On*

stone tablet. Bib: HNE p 478 d. α 2, pl XL, 9; Inv 8 56; MF Fondation 3.

1 byrḥ ʾdr šnt
2 3.100+20 qbrʾ
3 dnh dy šlmn
4 br tymrṣw br
5 škyy dy mn pḥd
6 bny mtbwl

PAT 0462 **C4114** **A.D. 33**

Prov: Palmyra, Valley of Tombs, Umm Belqîs, Tower 67. Loc: Palmyra, *in situ. Funerary: Foundation. On stone tablet.* Group: C4114 (Inv 4 4a), Inv 4 4b. Bib: RES 2186; Inv 4 4a, photo of squeeze following p 10; MF Fondation 5; Déd p 86.

1 byrḥ knwn šnt 3.100+40+5
2 qbrʾ dnh dy ḥyrn br blšwry
3 br g[d]rṣw [dy] mtqrh br bʿʾ
4 d[y mn] pḥd bny knbt wdkyr
5 blš[w]ry b[r]h dy ḥyrn
6 dnh b[t]b ʿ[d] ʿlmʾ

Text after Inv 4 4a (pl 1 following p 10)

PAT 0463 **C4115** **A.D. (41)**

Prov: Palmyra, Valley of Tombs, *Gubwel al Husayniyet*, Tower 44. Loc: lost. *Funerary: Foundation. On stone tablet.* Group: 4115, 4115bis. Bib: Inv 4 18a; MF Fondation 6.

1 byrḥ sywn šnt 3.[100+40+10+2] qbrʾ dnh dy kytwt
2 br tymrṣw br kytwt br tymʾ rbʾ dy mn pḥd bny
3 [mt]bwl dy ʿbd lh wlbnwhy lʿlmʾ

Texts was missing already before 1930, see Inv 4 18a

PAT 0464 **C4115bis** **A.D. 41**

Prov: Palmyra, Valley of Tombs, *Gubwel al Husayniyet*, Tower 44. Loc: Palmyra, *in situ. Funerary Foundation. On stone tablet.* See 4115. Bib: Inv 4 18b; MF Fondation 6.

1 [byrḥ sywn] šnt 3.100+40+10+2
2 [ṣlmyʾ ʾln] dy kytwt br
3 [tymrṣw wdy myš]ʾ brt
4 [mlkw ʾtt]h wdy lšmš
5 [brh wdy šlmn] brh wdy
6 mlkw ʿlymh

Text lost already by time of Inv 4 (1930); editors rely on old copies of Waddington and de Vogüé

PAT 0465 **C4116** **A.D. 56**

Prov: Palmyra, unidentified tomb. Loc: Not known. *Funerary: Foundation. On stone tablet.* Group: 4116, 4117, 4118. Bib: HNE p 478 d. α 3, pl XL, 10; MF Fondation 8.

1 qbrʾ dnh bt ʿlmʾ
2 dy ʿtʿqb br gdyʾ
3 br ʿtʿqb dy mn pḥd
4 bny mytʾ dy bnʾ
5 bḥywhy lyqrh wlyq[r]
6 bnwhy ʿl gdyʾ ʾbw[h]
7 byrḥ nysn šnt 3.100+60+5+2

PAT 0466 **C4117** **n. d.**

Prov: Palmyra. Loc: New York, Metropolitan Museum of Art, MMA 98.19.1. *Funerary. On relief.* See 4116. Bib: Gottheil '01 p 111 no. 7, pl 7; Chabot '01a p 348; ESE I p 215; Chabot '22 p 129, pl XXXI, 11; PS 204; RES 160.

1 ʿqybʾ
2 br ʿtʿqb
3 gdyʾ
4 ḥbl

Collated E. C., 8/25/94

PAT 0467 **C4118** **n. d.**

Prov: Palmyra. Loc: London, British Museum, 1250. *Funerary. On relief.* See 4116. Bib: PS 151; RES 1624.

1 mqymw
2 br gdyʾ
3 ʿtʿqb
4 [z]bdʾ
5 [r]bʾ

PAT 0468 **C4119** **A.D. 57**

Prov: Palmyra. Loc: Louvre, AO 2203. *Funerary: Foundation. On stone tablet.* Bib: MF Fondation 9; RES 1072; Lou 188.

1 byrḥ nysn dy šnt
2 3.100+60+5+3 bt ʿlmʾ
3 dnh dy ʿgylw br ʾwšy
4 br khylw tdmryʾ dy
5 mn pḥd bny mytʾ dy
6 ʿbd lh bḥywhy lbt
7 ʿlmh lyqrh wlyqr
8 bnwhy wʾḥwhy lbt ʿlmʾ

PAT 0469 **C4120** **A.D. 59**

Prov: Palmyra. Loc: Palmyra, A 189. *Funerary: Foundation. On stone tablet.* Bib: Inv 8 75; MF Fondation 11; Déd p 305.

1 Τὸ μνῆμα τοῦτο καὶ τὸ σπήλαιο(ν) ᾠ-
2 κοδόμησεν [..........] τοῦ Νου-
3 ρβήλου τοῦ ʼΑκ[....]μου φ[υλῆ]ς
4 Μαγερηνῶν εἰς τὴν ἑαυτοῦ τει-
5 μὴν καὶ ʼΟγήλου τοῦ ἀδελφοῦ αὐ-
6 τοῦ καὶ τῶν υἱῶν αὐτῶν, εἰς τὸν
7 αἰῶνα· μηνὸς Ξανδικοῦ ἔτους οτʹ.

1 wlyq[r ...]
2 byrḥ nysn šnt 3.100+20+[40+10]

PAT 0470 **C4121** **A.D. 79**

Prov: Palmyra, Valley of Tombs, *Umm Belqîs*, Tower 63. Loc: Palmyra, *in situ. Funerary: Foundation. On door lintel.* Bib: Inv 4 5; MF Fondation 14.

1 qbrʾ dnh ʿbd bny wʾlhšʾ wʾrʾwm bny tymšʾ br bny dy mtqrh ʾrwnʾ lhwn wlbnyhwn
2 lyqrhwn dy bt ʿlmʾ byrḥ nysn šnt 3.100+80+10

line 1 ʾrwnʾ: or ʾdwnʾ see Stark PN

PAT 0471 **C4122** **A.D. 79**

Prov: Palmyra, N-W Necropolis, Tower 155. Loc: Palmyra, *in situ. Funerary: Foundation. On stone tablet.* Bib: HNE p 478 d. α 4, pl XXXIX, 1; Inv 7 6a; MF Fondation 15.

1 Τὸ μνημ[ε]ῖον τοῦτο καὶ τὸ σπήλεον
2 αὐτοῦ ᾠκοδόμησεν Μάλιχος Μοκείμου
3 τοῦ Βωλβαράχου φυλῆς Κλαυδιάδος
4 αὐτῷ καὶ υἱοῖς αὐτοῦ καὶ ἀδελφοῖς
5 εἰς τειμὴν αἰωνίαν, ἔτους αϙτʹ.

1 qbrʾ dnh wmʿrtʾ dy bnʾ
2 mlkw br mqymw b[r] b[wlbr]k ḥwml
3 lh wlbnwhy wlʾḥwhy lyqrhn
4 dy ʿlmʾ šnt 3.100+80+10+1

Text of Inv 7 6a

PAT 0472 **C4123** **A.D. 83**

Prov: Palmyra, Valley of Tombs, Umm Belqîs, Tower 51 (Tomb of Yamliku). Loc: Palmyra, *in situ. Funerary: Foundation. On door lintel.* Group: 4123, 4123bis, 4187, 4188, 4189, 4190, 4191. Bib: Inv 4 6b; MF Fondation 17b; Déd p 222.

1 Μνημεῖον αἰώνιον γέρας ᾠκοδόμησεν ʼΙάμλιχος Μοκείμου τοῦ καὶ ʼΑκκαλείσου τοῦ Μαλί
2 χου εἰς τε ἑαυτὸν καὶ υἱοὺς καὶ ἐγγόνους ἔτους δϙτʹ μηνὶ Ξανδικῷ

1 dkrnʾ dnh dy hw yqr bt ʿlmʾ bnʾ ymlkw br mqymw dy mtqrh ʾqlyš br mlkw br blʿqb
2 tdmryʾ lyqrh wlyqr bnwhy wbny bnwhy ʿd ʿlmʾ byrḥ nysn šnt 3.100+60+[20+10+4]

Texts after CIS

PAT 0473 **C4123bis** **A.D. 83**

Prov: Palmyra, Valley of Tombs, Umm Belqîs, Tower 51. Loc: Palmyra, *in situ. Funerary: Foundation. On stone tablet.* See 4123. Bib: Inv 4 6a; MF Fondation 17a.

1 Μνημεῖον αἰώνιον γέρας ᾠκοδόμ-
2 ησεν ʼΙάμλιχος Μοκείμου τοῦ καὶ
3 ʼΑκκαλείσου τοῦ Μαλίχου εἰς
4 τε ἑαυτὸν καὶ υἱοὺς καὶ ἐγγόνους ἔτους δϙτʹ
5 μηνὶ Ξανδικῷ

1 byrḥ nysn šnt 3.100+80+10+4

2 qbrʾ dnh bnʾ ymlkw br mqymw ʾqlyš br mlkw
3 ʾbnyt br blʿqb br mykʾ br mtʾ tdmryʾ lh
4 wlbnwhy wlbny bnwhy lyqrhwn ʿd ʿlmʾ

PAT 0474 **C4124** **A.D. 83**
Prov: Palmyra, Valley of Tombs, Umm Belqîs, Tower 68. Loc: Palmyra, *in situ*. *Funerary: Foundation. On door lintel.* Group: 4124, 4125, (apparently) 4126, 4127a-c, 4128, 4129. Bib: Inv 4 3; MF Fondation 18; Déd p 87.

1 Τὸ μνημεῖον καὶ τὸ σπήλαιον ᾠκοδόμησ[αν]
2 Σαβεῖς Νεβουζάβαδος Θαιμαῖος καὶ Νεβούλας ο[ἱ]
3 Βηλσούρου Αἱράνου τοῦ Βηλσούρου τοῦ Γαδδάρ-
4 [σ]ου τοῦ ἐπικαλουμένου Βαά· εἰς τε ἑαυτοὺς καὶ
5 [υἱ]οὺς [καὶ] ἐκγόνους. Μηνὶ Ξανδικῷ τοῦ δϙτʹ ἔτους.

1 qbrʾ dnh wmʿrtʾ bnw šby wnbwzbd wt[ymy wnbwlʾ]
2 bny blšwry br ḥyrn br blšwry br gdrṣw dy mtqrn bny
3 bʿʾ lhwn wlbnyhwn lyqrhwn dy bt ʿlmʾ šlm
4 byrḥ nysn šnt 3.100+80+10+4

Texts after Inv 4 3; other tombs of same family: Tower 67 (Ber '70 p 82)

PAT 0475 **C4125** **n. d.**
Prov: Palmyra, Valley of Tombs, Umm Belqîs, Tower 68. Loc: Palmyra, Museum, A 177. *Funerary. On group relief.* See 4124. Bib: Inv 8 160.

1 [ṭ]lyʾ ʾln bny [b]l[š]wry br šby br blšwry
(At heads of figures of children)
2 šby šby šby

Text of Inv 8; CIS line 1: *ṣlmyʾ* not materially possible

PAT 0476 **C4126** **n. d.**
Prov: Palmyra, Valley of Tombs, Umm Belqîs, Tower 68. Loc: Palmyra, Museum, A 215. *Funerary. On group relief.* See 4124. Bib: Inv 8 161a.

1 [....]n[...]
2 [...]r[....]
3 [ḥ]yr[n]
4 br blšwry

Text of Inv 8 for this and through C4127c

PAT 0477 **C4127a** **n. d.**
Prov: Palmyra, Valley of Tombs, Umm Belqîs, Tower 68. Loc: Palmyra, Museum, A 215. *Funerary. On group relief.* See 4124. Bib: Inv 8 161b.

1 b[....]
2 šb[y] br
3 blšwry

PAT 0478 **C4127b** **n. d.**
Prov: Palmyra, Valley of Tombs, Umm Belqîs, Tower 68. Loc: Palmyra, Museum, A 215. *Funerary. On group relief.* See 4124. Bib: Inv 8 161c.

1 b[...]
2 ḥ[bl]

PAT 0479 **C4127c** **n. d.**
Prov: Palmyra, Valley of Tombs, Umm Belqîs, Tower 68. Loc: Strassburg?. *Funerary. On relief fragment.* See 4124.

1 [...w]s
2 [ḥ]bl

Fragment from C4127b. Brought to Strassburg by J. Euting

PAT 0480 **C4128** **n. d.**
Prov: Palmyra, Valley of Tombs, Umm Belqîs, Tower 68. Loc: Strassburg?. *Funerary. On relief fragment.* See 4124. Bib: RES 393.

1 [...]
2 br š[by]
3 br blš[wry]
4 br ḥyrn
5 blšwry ḥbl

PAT 0481 **C4129** **A.D. 114**
Prov: Palmyra, Valley of Tombs, Umm Belqîs, Tower 68. Loc: St. Petersburg: Hermitage Museum, 4177. *Funerary. On group relief.* See 4124. Bib: PS 2.

(Between heads of figures)
1 ḥbl
2 bʿltgʾ
3 wʿlyšʾ
4 bny bwnʾ br
5 šby
(In lower margin)
1 byrḥ knwn šnt 4.100+20+5+1 ṣlmyʾ ʾln trwyhn
2 dy ʿlyšʾ wbʿltgʾ bny bwnʾ br šby br
3 blšwr br ḥyrn ḥbl

PAT 0482 **C4130** **A.D. 95**
Prov: Palmyra. Loc: Qaryatein. *Funerary: Foundation. On stone tablet.* Group: 4130, 4131, (apparently) 4132, 4133. Bib: HNE p 478 d. α 5; MF Fondation 24; RES 1079.

1 bt ʿlmʾ dnh ʿbd mtny br nwrbl br mlkw
2 br tymḥʾ ʿl nwrbl ʾbwhy wʿl nby ʾmh lyqrhn
3 wlyqr bnwhy dy ʿlmʾ ṣlmyʾ ʾln dy mtny br
4 nwrbl br mlkw br tymḥʾ br mtny br bwnʾ br
5 mtny dy mtqrh mhwy wdy nwrbl ʾbwhy wdy
6 nby ʾmh byrḥ ʾb šnt 4.100+5+1

PAT 0483 **C4131** **n. d.**
Prov: Palmyra. Loc: Istanbul Arkeoloji Müzesi, 3759 T. *Funerary. On relief.* See 4130. Bib: PS 340; RES 356.

1 tmʾ brt
2 ḥršʾ
3 ʾtt mtny
4 br nwrbl
5 mhwy ḥbl
Collated 19-24/10/93

PAT 0484 **C4132** **n. d.**
Prov: Palmyra. Loc: Not known. *Funerary. On relief.* See 4130. Bib: RES 1618.

1 tmʾ
2 brt tymy
3 mhwy

PAT 0485 **C4133** **n. d.**
Prov: Palmyra. Loc: Ny Carlsberg Glyptotek, 1147. *Funerary. On relief.* See 4130. Bib: PS 518; RES 728; NyCG 69.

1 ḥbl
2 nwrbl
3 br tymy
4 mtny

PAT 0486 **C4134** **A.D. 103**
Prov: Palmyra, Valley of Tombs, Tower 13 (Tomb of Elahbel). Loc: Palmyra, *in situ. Funerary: Foundation. On stone tablet.* Group: 4134, 4135 through 4157. Bib: Inv 4 27a; MF Fondation 28.

1 Τὸ μνημεῖον ἔκτισαν ʾΕλάβηλος Μ-
2 ανναῖος Σοχαίεις Μάλιχος Οὐαβαλ-
3 λάθου τοῦ Μανναίου τοῦ ʾΕλαβήλου αὐτ-
4 οῖς καὶ υἱοῖς ἔτους διυʹ μηνὸς Ξανδικοῦ.

1 qbrʾ dnh bnʾ ʾlhbl wmʿny wškỵy
2 wmlkw bny whblt br mʿny ʾlhbl
3 lhwn wlbnyhwn byrḥ nysn šnt 4.100+10+4

PAT 0487 **C4135** **n. d.**
Prov: Palmyra, Valley of Tombs, Tower 13. Loc: Palmyra, *in situ. Funerary. On wall.* See 4134. Bib: Inv 4 27h.

1 ṣlm ʾtpny br
2 [m]ʿny br whblt
Relief is missing

PAT 0488 **C4136** **n. d.**
Prov: Palmyra, Valley of Tombs, Tower 13. Loc: Palmyra, *in situ*. *Funerary*. *On wall*. See 4134.
Bib: Inv 4 27i.

1 ṣlm whblt br
2 škyy br whblt
Relief is missing

PAT 0489 **C4137** **n. d.**
Prov: Palmyra, Valley of Tombs, Tower 13. Loc: Palmyra, *in situ*. *Funerary*. *On wall*. See 4134.
Bib: Inv 4 27j.

1 ṣlm ʾlhbl br
2 škyy br whblt
Relief is missing

PAT 0490 **C4138** **n. d.**
Prov: Palmyra, Valley of Tombs, Tower 13. Loc: Palmyra, *in situ*. *Funerary*. *On wall*. See 4134.
Bib: Inv 4 27k.

1 ṣlm mʿny br
2 ʾlhbl br whblt
Relief is missing

PAT 0491 **C4139** **n. d.**
Prov: Palmyra, Valley of Tombs, Tower 13. Loc: Palmyra, *in situ*. *Funerary*. *On wall*. See 4134.
Bib: Inv 4 27l.

1 ṣlm mʿny ṭlyʾ
2 br whblt br [....]
Relief is missing

PAT 0492 **C4140** **n. d.**
Prov: Palmyra, Valley of Tombs, Tower 13. Loc: Palmyra, *in situ*. *Funerary*. *On wall*. See 4134.
Bib: Inv 4 27c.

1 ṣlm ʾlhbl br
2 mʿny br ʾlhbl
Relief is missing

PAT 0493 **C4141** **n. d.**
Prov: Palmyra, Valley of Tombs, Tower 13. Loc: Palmyra, *in situ*. *Funerary*. *On wall*. See 4134.
Bib: Inv 4 27d.

1 ṣlm whblt br
2 ʾlhbl br whblt
Relief is missing

PAT 0494 **C4142** **n. d.**
Prov: Palmyra, Valley of Tombs, Tower 13. Loc: Palmyra, *in situ*. *Funerary*. *On wall*. See 4134.
Bib: Inv 4 27e.

1 ṣlm whblt br
2 mlkw br whblt
Relief is missing

PAT 0495 **C4143** **n. d.**
Prov: Palmyra, Valley of Tombs, Tower 13. Loc: Palmyra, *in situ*. *Funerary*. *On wall*. See 4134.
Bib: Inv 4 27f.

1 ṣlm blʿqb br
2 ʾlhbl br whblt
Relief is missing

PAT 0496 **C4144** **n. d.**
Prov: Palmyra, Valley of Tombs, Tower 13. Loc: Palmyra, *in situ*. *Funerary*. *On wall*. See 4134.
Bib: Inv 4 27g.

1 ṣlm whblt br
2 mʿny br whblt
Relief is missing

PAT 0497 **C4145** **n. d.**
Prov: Palmyra, Valley of Tombs, Tower 13. Loc: Palmyra, *in situ*. *Funerary*. *On relief*. See 4134.
Bib: Inv 4 27m.

1 ʾmtʾ brt
2 ʾlhbl br whblt
3 ʾtt škyy br
4 whblt

PAT 0498 **C4146** **n. d.**
Prov: Palmyra, Valley of Tombs, Tower 13. Loc: Palmyra, *in situ*. *Funerary*. *On relief*. See 4134.
Bib: Inv 4 27n.

1 ʿty brt šlmlt
2 br mʿny ʾtt mlkw
3 br whblt

PAT 0499 **C4147** **n. d.**
Prov: Palmyra, Valley of Tombs, Tower 13. Loc: Palmyra, *in situ*. *Funerary*. *On relief*. See 4134.
Bib: Inv 4 27o.

1 hdyrt brt mʿny
2 br whblt

PAT 0500 **C4148** **n. d.**
Prov: Palmyra, Valley of Tombs, Tower 13. Loc: Palmyra, *in situ*. *Funerary*. *On relief*. See 4134.
Bib: Inv 4 27p.

1 šgl brt šky[y br]
2 whblt ʾtt bl[ʿqb]
3 br ʾlhbl whblt

PAT 0501 **C4149** **n. d.**
Prov: Palmyra, Valley of Tombs, Tower 13. Loc: Palmyra, *in situ*. *Funerary*. *On relief*. See 4134.
Bib: Inv 4 27q.

1 šgl brt škyy br šlmn br tymr[ṣw]
2 r[bʾ] ʾtt whblt br mʿny

PAT 0502 **C4150** **n. d.**
Prov: Palmyra, Valley of Tombs, Tower 13. Loc: Palmyra, *in situ*. *Funerary*. *On relief*. See 4134.
Bib: Inv 4 27r.

1 [ʾq]mt brt whblt br mʿny

PAT 0503 **C4151** **n. d.**
Prov: Palmyra, Valley of Tombs, Tower 13. Loc: Palmyra, *in situ*. *Funerary*. *On relief*. See 4134.
Bib: Inv 4 27s.

1 ʾmtḥʾ brt blʿqb br nšʾ
2 ʾtt ʾlhbl br [whbl]t

PAT 0504 **C4152** **n. d.**
Prov: Palmyra, Valley of Tombs, Tower 13. Loc: Palmyra, *in situ*. *Funerary*. *On relief*. See 4134.
Bib: Inv 4 27t.

1 bltyḥn brt ʾtpny ʾtt
2 mʿny br whblt

PAT 0505 **C4153** **n. d.**
Prov: Palmyra, Valley of Tombs, Tower 13. Loc: Palmyra, *in situ*. *Funerary*. *On relief*. See 4134.
Bib: Inv 4 27u.

1 ʾmtʾ brt
2 škyy br
3 whblt
4 ʾtt
5 whblt
6 br
7 mʿny

PAT 0506 **C4154** **n. d.**
Prov: Palmyra, Valley of Tombs, Tower 13. Loc: Palmyra, *in situ*. *Funerary*. *On relief*. See 4134.
Bib: Inv 4 27v.

1 hdyrt brt
2 ʾlhbl br
3 whblt br
4 mʿny

PAT 0507 **C4155** **n. d.**
Prov: Palmyra, Valley of Tombs, Tower 13. Loc: Palmyra, *in situ*. *Funerary*. *On relief*. See 4134.
Bib: Inv 4 27w.

1 šgl brt
2 ʾlhbl

3 whblt
4 ʾtt whblt
5 br mlkw
6 br whblt

PAT 0508 **C4156** **n. d.**

Prov: Palmyra, Valley of Tombs, Tower 13. Loc: Palmyra, *in situ*. *Funerary*. *On relief*. See 4134. Bib: Inv 4 27x.

1 šgl brt mlkw br
2 whblt br mʿny

PAT 0509 **C4157** **n. d.**

Prov: Palmyra, Valley of Tombs, Tower 13. Loc: Palmyra, *in situ*. *Funerary*. *On relief*. See 4134. Bib: Inv 4 27b.

1 ṣlm blʿqb br ʾlhbl
2 br whblt br mʿny
3 ʾpmlṭʾ dy nmšʾ dh

PAT 0510 **C4158** **A.D. 121**

Prov: Palmyra, Valley of Tombs, Tower 13. Loc: Palmyra, *in situ*. *Funerary*. *On door lintel*. See 4134. Bib: Inv 4 27y.

1 byrḥ tšry šnt 4.100+20+10+3 ywm 20+10 ḥbl mʿny br ʾḥd mn
2 ʾrbʿʾ ʾḥyʾ dy bnw qbrʾ dnh wbltyḥn brt ʾtpny br mlkw
3 ʿtršwry ʾtth

PAT 0511 **C4159** **A.D. 114**

Prov: Palmyra, S-W Necropolis, Hypogeum. Loc: Palmyra Museum. *Funerary: Foundation*. *On stone tablet*. Bib: MF Fondation 33; RES 369; RES 816.

1 mʿr̊tʾ dh ḥpr̊ mn kyshwn bt ʿlmʾ
2 zbdʿth br̊ ʾtʿqb br̊ zbdʿth br̊ sr̊y br̊
3 zbdʿth br̊ mlkw dy mtqr̊ʾ̊ ʾr̊ʾ̊š wmqymw
4 br̊ zbdʾ br̊ mqymw br̊ ʿtʿqb br̊ mqymw br̊
5 mlkw dy mtqr̊ʾ̊ ʾr̊ʾ̊š lhwn wlbnyhwn wlbnʾ
6 bnyhwn dkr̊yʾ lʿlmʾ byr̊ḥ nysn dy šnt
7 4.100+20+5

PAT 0512 **C4160** **A.D. 114**

Prov: Palmyra, S-W Necropolis, Hypogeum. Loc: Palmyra, *in situ*. *Funerary: Foundation*. *On door lintel*. Bib: MF Fondation 35; RES 29.

1 Συμώνης Φειλᾶ τοῦ Συμώνου
2 τοῦ Μοφλέου τὸν ταφεῶνα
3 κατεσκεύασεν εἰς τειμὴν Φειλᾶ
4 τοῦ πατρὸς αὐτοῦ· ἔτους ζκυʹ.

1 bt qbwrʾ dnh ʿbd šmʿwn br pylʾ
2 br šmʿwn mpl[ys] lh wlbnwhy
3 lyqr pylʾ ʾbwhy dy ʿlmʾ bšnt 4.100+20+5+1

PAT 0513 **C4161** **A.D. 115**

Prov: Palmyra, Diocletian Camp, reemployed. Loc: Palmyra Museum. *Funerary: Foundation*. *On door lintel*. Bib: MF Fondation 34.

1 [qbrʾ d]nh [ʿb]d nšʾ wbw[nʾ bn]y
2 nšʾ br tym[ʾ lhwn wlb]nyhwn
3 byrḥ nysn šnt 4.100+20+5+1

PAT 0514 **C4162** **A.D. 118**

Prov: Palmyra, N-W Necropolis, Tower 164. Loc: Palmyra Museum. *Funerary: Foundation*. *On door lintel*. Bib: IP 65; RB '30 2 A/B; Inv 7 1a; MF Cession 50; MF Fondation 36.

1 Πόπλιος Αἴλιος ʾΟβαιαν[ός .... το]ῦ Νουρβήλου τὸ μνημεῖον ἔ[κτι-]
2 σεν καὶ ἀφιέρωσεν [ἑαυτῷ καὶ τοῖς υἱ]οῖς ἔτους θκυʹ μηνὸς Ξανδ[ικοῦ].

1 [qbr]ʾ dnh bnʾ wʾqdš ʾb[yhn br šmʿ]wn br ʾbyhn br wlbnwhy wlbnʾ bnwhy lyqrhwn lʿlmʾ
2 [byr]ḥ nysn šnt 4.100+20+5+4

Text of Inv 7 1a

PAT 0515 **C4163** **A.D. 119**

Prov: Palmyra, Temple of Bel, reemployed. Loc: Palmyra, A 152. *Funerary: Foundation*. *On stone tablet.* Bib: CIS pp 481-82 no. 4163; Inv 8 61; MF Fondation 38; Syr '38 p 160 39.

1 ἔτους λυ' μηνὸς Δύστρου σπή-
2 λαιον ταφεῶνος ὤρυξαν Βαρὲ-
3 -ας καὶ Βωρόφας οἱ Ραββήλου
4 [τοῦ Βαρὲα ἑ]αυτοῖς καὶ υἱοῖς <κ>αὶ υ-
5 -ἱωνοῖς εἰς τὸν ἅπαντα χρόνον.

1 byrḥ ʾdr šnt 4.100+20+10 bt
2 qbwrʾ dnh ʿbdw brʿʾ wbwrpʾ
3 bny rbʾl br brʿʾ lhwn
4 wlbnyhn wlbny bnyhwn lyqrhwn dy ʿlmʾ

Inscription a combination of pieces published at various times

PAT 0516 **C4164** **A.D. 128**

Prov: Palmyra, Valley of Tombs, Tower 34. Loc: Palmyra, *in situ. Funerary: Foundation. On door lintel.* Bib: HNE p 479 d. α 6, pl XL, 12; Inv 4 19; MF Fondation 42.

1 npšʾ dh dy bnʾ mqymw br zbydʾ br yrḥy dy mn bny ḥṭry lh wlbnwhy wlbny bnwhy lyqrhwn lʿlmʾ byrḥ knwn šnt 4.100+40

PAT 0517 **C4165** **A.D. 138**

Prov: Palmyra, S-W Necropolis, Tower of Kitot (Qasr el-Madrus). Loc: Palmyra, *in situ. Funerary: Foundation. On door lintel.* Bib: MF Fondation 44; RES 28, 1649.

1 bt qbwrʾ dnh ʿbd ḥdw[dn] br ṣpry
2 brʿth lh wlbnwhy lyqrhwn dy ʿlmʾ
3 byrḥ ʾb šnt 4.100+40+5+4

PAT 0518 **C4166** **A.D. 139**

Prov: Palmyra, Diocletian Camp, reemployed. Loc: Palmyra, 1403. *Funerary: Foundation. On stone tablet.* Bib: Inv 12 16; MF Fondation 46.

1 mʿrtʾ dh dy bt
2 qbwrʾ ʿbd mʿytw [....]
3 br ḥlptʾ br mrywn lh
4 wlbnwhy wlb[ny] bnwhy
5 lʿlmʾ byrḥ [ny]sn šnt
6 4.100+40+10+4

Text of Inv 12 16

PAT 0519 **C4167** **(A.D. 143)**

Prov: Palmyra, S-E Necropolis, Funerary temple 188. Loc: Palmyra, *in situ. Funerary: Foundation. On door lintel.* Bib: RES 1643; MF Fondation 49; Déd p 305.

1 Μημεῖον ταφεῶνο[ς ᾠκοδόμησεν κ]α[ὶ] ἀφιέ[ρωσεν κ]αὶ [......... Λίσαμσος Νου]ρβήλου τοῦ Μο[κεί]μου [το]ῦ ʼΟγήλου τοῦ ʼΑκ-
2 κιμ[άλ]ου εἰ[ς τειμὴν] αὐτ[οῦ] τε καὶ Μάλχου υειοῦ α[ὐτο]ῦ κ[αὶ υ]ἱῶν α[ὐτῶ]ν καὶ ἐκγόνων· μηνὶ Δαισίῳ τοῦ δνυ' ἔτους

1 qbrʾ dnh bnʾ lšmš br nwrbl br mqymw br ʿgylw ʾqml lyqrh wlyqr mlkw brh wlbnyhwn wlbnʾ bnyhwn lʿlmʾ byrḥ sywn
2 [šnt 4.100+40+10+4]

Line 2: conjectural restoration of editors, probably correct

PAT 0520 **C4168** **A.D. 149**

Prov: Palmyra, Valley of Tombs, Funerary temple 85b (Tomb of Aʿailamī and Zebīdā). Loc: Palmyra, *in situ. Funerary: Foundation. On door lintel.* Group: Watzinger 85b, C4168, C4169, C4243, C4244; Inv 4 9a, (=C4168), Inv 4 9b; IP pp 13-18, nos. 12bis-23. Bib: Sobernheim 46; de Vogüé 1868 p 6 (sub 1); IP pp 13-18, nos. 12-23; Inv 4 9a; MF pp 135-36, fig 81: Fondation 51; Déd p 249-52; Makowski '83 pp 175-87, Pl. 48-53.

1 ʼΑαιλάμεις καὶ Ζηνόβιος οἱ Αἱράνου Μοκίμου τοῦ Αἱράνου τοῦ Μαθθᾶ <ε> ταφὴν αἰώνιον αὑτῶν καὶ υἱῶν καὶ ἐγγόνων ἔκτισαν.
2 ἔτους [ξυ'] μηνὸς Ξανδικοῦ

1 qbrʾ dnh bt ʿlmʾ wʾsṭwʾ dy qdmwhy bnw ʾʿylmy wzbydʾ br mqymw br ḥyrn mtʾ lhwn wlbnyhwn wlbny bnyhwn lʿlmʾ
2 byrḥ nysn šnt 4.100+60

PAT 0521 **C4169** **n. d.**
Prov: Palmyra, Temple of Bel, reemployed. Loc: Palmyra Museum. *Funerary. On stone fragment.* Group: Tomb of Aʿailamī and Zebīdā, Watzinger 85b, C4168, C4169, C4243, C4244; Inv 4 9a, (=C4168), Inv 4 9b. Bib: IP pp 13-18, nos. 12-23.

1 [....] br zbydʾ br ḥyrn mtʾ dy bnʾ ʾbwhy
qbrʾ dnh

PAT 0522 **C4170** **A.D. 149**
Prov: Palmyra, Valley of Tombs, Funerary temple 38a. Loc: Palmyra, *in situ. Funerary: Foundation. On door lintel.* Bib: Inv 4 23; MF Fondation 52.

1 bt mqbrtʾ dh bnʾ zbydʾ br mqymw zbydʾ
[.........]m lh wlbnwhy wlbnʾ bnwhy
2 lʿlmʾ byrḥ knwn šnt 4.100+60+1

PAT 0523 **C4171** **A.D. 160**
Prov: Palmyra, S-W Necropolis, Hypogeum of Yarhai, ʿAtenuri, and Zabdibol ("Tomb of the Three Brothers"). Loc: Palmyra, *in situ. Funerary: Cession. On door lintel.* Group: Ber '38 pp 102ff; C4171-86; Syr '36 p 355 = Tad 27. Bib: MF Cession 2; RES 1041.

1 nʿmʿyn wmlʾ wṣʿdy bny ṣʿdy br̊ mlʾ ʾln
dy ḥpr̊ mʿr̊tʾ dh wbnw r̊ḥq lḥdwdn br̊ šlmn br̊
zbdbwl mn gmḥyn ʾr̊bʿʾ mn
2 štr̊ʾ mʿr̊byʾ dy ʾkšdr̊ʾ tymnyʾ dy hnn btr̊
gmḥyn tr̊n qdmyn wmn štr̊ʾ klh mqblʾ tymnyʾ
dydh dy ʾkšdr̊ʾ
3 dy bh ṭksys dy gmḥyn ʾr̊bʿʾ lh wlbnwh
wlbny bnwh lʿlmʾ byr̊ḥ tšr̊y šnt 4.100+60+10+2

PAT 0524 **C4172** **A.D. 160**
Prov: Palmyra, S-W Necropolis. Loc: Palmyra, *in situ. Funerary: Cession. On door lintel.* See 4171. Bib: MF Cession 1; RES 1042.

1 nʿmʿyn wmlʾ wṣʿdy bny ṣʿdy br̊ mlʾ br̊
ṣʿdy dy ḥ r̊ḥq lʿbdṣyr̊ʾ br̊ ḥr̊y ʿtʿqb br̊ r̊pbwl
mn ʾksdr̊ʾ smlyʾ dy hw pnʾ
2 lymynʾ dy hw mʿl bbʾ ʿl ymynʾ dy bh
gwmḥyn pnn ʿsr̊yn wmn gwmḥyn ʾr̊bʿʾ dy lbr̊
mn kptʾ mʿl bbʾ ʿl ymynk tr̊n dy mwln twpr̊ʾ
3 lh wlbnwhy wlbny bnwhy dkr̊yʾ lyqr̊hwn dy
ʿlmʾ byr̊ḥ knwn dy šnt 4.100+60+10+2

PAT 0525 **C4173** **n. d.**
Prov: Palmyra, S-W Necropolis. Loc: Palmyra, *in situ. Funerary: Cession. On door lintel.* See 4171. Bib: MF Cession 4; RES 1043.

1 byr̊ḥ ʾyr̊ šnt ḥmš mʾh wtr̊tn zbdbwl br̊ kptwt
br̊ br̊ʾ br̊ ḥr̊y ʿgylw br̊ mlkw mn str̊ʾ mdnḥyʾ
dy ʾksdr̊ʾ
2 tymnyʾ dy bh ṭksys dy gmḥyn tmnyʾ wmn
gmḥyn ʾḥr̊nyn tltʾ dy hnn mʿlyk ʿl šmlʾ ʿqr̊
twpr̊ʾ lh wlbnwhy wlbny
3 bnwhy lʿlmʾ dy r̊ḥq lh lzbdbwl dnh nʿmʿyn
wmlʾ wṣʿdy bny ṣʿdy ʾln dy ḥpr̊ wṣbt mʿr̊tʾ
dh

PAT 0526 **C4174** **A.D. 191**
Prov: Palmyra, S-W Necropolis. Loc: Palmyra, *in situ. Funerary: Cession. On door lintel.* See 4171. Bib: MF Cession 3; RES 1044.

1 nr̊qys br̊ ḥr̊y ʿgylw r̊ḥq
2 lšmʿwn br̊ ʾbʾ br̊ ḥnynʾ mn
3 gwmḥyn ʾr̊bʿʾ gwyyn tymnyyn dy bstr̊ʾ
4 mdnḥyʾ <dy> ʾksdr̊ʾ dy mʿl mʿr̊tʾ dh
5 ʿl smlk wmn gwmḥyn tr̊n dy mn ʿqr̊
6 twpr̊ʾ dkn lh wlbnwhy wlbny bnwhy
7 lyqr̊hwn dy ʿlmʾ byr̊ḥ qnyn šnt
8 ḥmš mʾh wtr̊tn

PAT 0527 **C4175** **A.D. 241**
Prov: Palmyra, S-W Necropolis. Loc: Palmyra, *in situ. Funerary: Cession. On door side.* See 4171. Bib: MF Cession 5; RES 1045.

1 byr̊ḥ ʾlwl šnt 5.100+40+10+2
2 ywlyʾ ʾwr̊lyʾ btmlkw br̊t
3 zbdbwl br̊ šʿdy r̊ḥqt lywlys
4 ʾwr̊lys mlʾ br̊ ydʿw br̊ ydyʿbl
5 mn gwmḥyn ʾr̊bʿʾ dy bstr̊ʾ
6 šmlyʾ btr̊ ʾksdr̊ʾ
7 mqbltʾ mʿr̊bytʾ dy ʾyt bgwmḥʾ
8 mqbr̊n št lh wlbnwhw
9 wlbny bnwh lʿlmʾ

PAT 0528 **C4176b** **n. d.**
Prov: Palmyra, S-W Necropolis. Loc: Palmyra, *in situ*. *Funerary*. *On wall*. See 4171.

1 btmlkw bt zbdbwl
2 br̊ zbdbwl br̊ ṣʿdy
3 wr̊št̊ʾ dy bytʾ wmʿr̊tʾ

PAT 0529 **C4176c** **n. d.**
Prov: Palmyra, S-W Necropolis. Loc: Palmyra, *in situ*. *Funerary*. *On wall*. See 4171.

1 btmlkw bt zbdbwl wrštʾ
2 br zbdbwl br ṣʿdy dy bytʾ wmʿrtʾ

PAT 0530 **C4176e** **n. d.**
Prov: Palmyra, S-W Necropolis. Loc: Palmyra, *in situ*. *Funerary*. *On wall*. See 4171.

1 [btmlkw] b[t] zbdbwl
2 [br zbd]bwl br ṣʿdy

PAT 0531 **C4177b** **n. d.**
Prov: Palmyra, S-W Necropolis. Loc: Palmyra, *in situ*. *Funerary*. *On wall*. See 4171. Bib: RES 31.

1 mlʾ br̊ ydʿw ydyʿbl
C4177a (on right, b is on left) is said to be same as b

PAT 0532 **C4177c** **n. d.**
Prov: Palmyra, S-W Necropolis. Loc: Palmyra, *in situ*. *Funerary*. *On wall*. See 4171.

1 [..y]dʿw ydyʿbl

PAT 0533 **C4178** **n. d.**
Prov: Palmyra, S-W Necropolis. Loc: Palmyra, *in situ*. *Funerary*. *On wall*. See 4171.

1 ṣlmt
2 btʿʾ brt
3 mlʾ ḥbl

PAT 0534 **C4179a** **n. d.**
Prov: Palmyra, S-W Necropolis. Loc: Palmyra, *in situ*. *Funerary*. *On wall*. See 4171. Bib: RES 32.

1 ṣlmt b[t]ʿʾ
2 br̊t
3 šmʿwn
4 ḥbl

PAT 0535 **C4179b** **n. d.**
Prov: Palmyra, S-W Necropolis. Loc: Palmyra, *in situ*. *Funerary*. *On wall*. See 4171.

1 tdmr̊yʾ ʾ[.]t[.]w
2 ʾnʾ[.]pʾ[......]
3 nmnʿy

PAT 0536 **C4180** **n. d.**
Prov: Palmyra, S-W Necropolis. Loc: Palmyra, *in situ*. *Funerary*. *On wall*. See 4171. Bib: RES 33.

1 dkr̊n
2 šmʿwn
3 br̊ ʾbʾ
4 ʾbr̊mʾ

PAT 0537 **C4181c** **n. d.**
Prov: Palmyra, S-W Necropolis. Loc: Palmyra, *in situ*. *Funerary*. *On wall*. See 4171.

1 mlʾ br ydʿw ydyʿbl
A, B, D, E practically illegible

PAT 0538 **C4182** **n. d.**
Prov: Palmyra, S-W Necropolis. Loc: Palmyra, *in situ*. *Funerary*. *On wall*. See 4171. Bib: RES 37.

1 šmʿwn br̊ ʾbʾ

PAT 0539 **C4183** **n. d.**
Prov: Palmyra, S-W Necropolis. Loc: Palmyra, *in situ*. *Funerary*. *On wall*. See 4171. Bib: RES 38.

1 mlkw ḥdwdn

PAT 0540 **C4184** **n. d.**
Prov: Palmyra, S-W Necropolis. Loc: Palmyra, *in situ*. *Funerary*. *On wall.* See 4171. Bib: RES 34.

1 btmlkw bt zbdbwl
2 br zbdbwl br ṣʿdy
3 wrštʾ dy bytʾ wmʿrtʾ

PAT 0541 **C4185** **n. d.**
Prov: Palmyra, S-W Necropolis. Loc: Palmyra, *in situ*. *Funerary*. *On wall.* See 4171. Bib: RES 36.

1 nr̊qys ʿgylw

PAT 0542 **C4186** **A.D. 259**
Prov: Palmyra, S-W Necropolis. Loc: Palmyra, *in situ*. *Funerary*. *On wall.* See 4171. Bib: RES 39.

1 mqbrn
2 klh byrḥ
3 ʾdr šnt 5.100+60+10
Fragmentary text; gaps not marked here

PAT 0543 **C4187** **A.D. (166)**
Prov: Palmyra, Valley of Tombs, Umm Belqîs, Tower 51 (Tomb of Yamliku). Loc: Palmyra, *in situ*. *Funerary*. *On door lintel.* Group: 4123, 4123bis, 4187, 4188, 4189, 4190, 4191. Bib: Inv 4 2; Déd p 27.

1 Αἱ ἐν τῇ ψαλίδι εἰκόνες Μο[κείμου καὶ Θαιμισᾶ καὶ Ζεβείδου τῶν] Ἑλασσᾶ τοῦ Σαεδεῖ τοῦ Ἑλ[ασσᾶ, καὶ]
2 Ἑλασσᾶ καὶ Ὀγήλου καὶ Σαεδε[ῖ [τῶν υἱῶν τοῦ Μοκείμου τούτου] καὶ Ἑλασσᾶ τούτου Θαι[μισᾶ]
3 [τοῦ υ]είου, [καὶ] Μοκείμου [τούτου Ζεβείδου τοῦ υείου φυλῆς Μαθθαβωλ]ίων, μηνὸς Δείου τοῦ η[ου′] ἔτου[ς]

1 ṣ[lmyʾ dy] bkptʾ dy mqymw wtymš[ʾ wzbydʾ bny ʾlhš]ʾ br ṣʿdy br ʾlhšʾ wdy ʾlhšʾ wʿgylw
2 wṣ[ʿdy bny mqy]mw dnh wdy ʾlhšʾ br [tymšʾ dnh wdy mqymw b]r zbydʾ dnh dy mn pḥ[d bny mtbw]l
Gk text after Déd p 27; Aram line 1: tymš[ʾ] with Stark PN p 119; see Inv 4 2 on deteriorated condition of stone; text after C4187

PAT 0544 **C4188** **n. d.**
Prov: Palmyra, Valley of Tombs, Umm Belqîs, Tower 51. Loc: Ny Carlsberg Glyptotek, 1137. *Funerary*. *On relief fragment.* See 4123. Bib: RES 2207; Déd p 28; NyCG 134.

1 ḥbl ʾlhšʾ
2 rbʾ br mqymw
3 zbydʾ ʾlhšʾ
4 ṣʿdy

PAT 0545 **C4189** **n. d.**
Prov: Palmyra, Valley of Tombs, Umm Belqîs, Tower 51. Loc: Ny Carlsberg Glyptotek, 1136. *Funerary*. *On relief fragment.* See 4123. Bib: RES 2208; Déd p 28; NyCG 133.

1 ʾtt mqymw
2 br ʾlhšʾ
3 br mqymw
4 ṣʿdy

PAT 0546 **C4190** **n. d.**
Prov: Palmyra, Valley of Tombs, Umm Belqîs, Tower 51. Loc: Ny Carlsberg Glyptotek. *Funerary*. *On relief fragment.* See 4123. Bib: Déd p 28; RES 402.

1 ḥbl [h]dʾ
2 brt mqymw
3 br ṣʿdy ʾmh
4 dy ʾqmt dh
5 dy mn lʿl

PAT 0547 **C4191** **n. d.**
Prov: Palmyra, Valley of Tombs, Umm Belqîs, Tower 51. Loc: Istanbul Arkeoloji Müzesi, 3716 T. *Funerary*. *On relief.* See 4123. Bib: Déd p 28; PS 147; RES 2211.

1 ḥbl
2 ʾlhšʾ
3 br
4 tymšʾ
5 dy ʿbd lh
6 ʾlhšʾ
7 br tymšʾ
8 br šmšgrm
9 [ḥ]bzy
Collated 19-24/10/93

PAT 0548 **C4192** **A.D. 181**

Prov: Palmyra, Valley of Tombs, Funerary Temple 38. Loc: Palmyra, *in situ*. *Funerary: Foundation. On door lintel.* Bib: Inv 4 22; MF Fondation 56.

1 Τὸ κτίσμα τοῦτό ἐστιν αἰώνιος τειμὴ, τάφος ἔκτισεν Ζαβδαάθης Ζαβδιλᾶ τοῦ ʼΙαδδαίου εἰς τειμὴν αὐτοῦ καὶ
2 υἱῶν καὶ υἱωνῶν εἰς τὸ παντελές, μηνὶ Δείῳ τοῦ γπυʹ ἔτους.

1 [dkrnʾ] dnh dy hw yqr bt ʿlmʾ qbrʾ dnh dy bnʾ zbdʿth br ydy lyqrh wl<q>r bnwhy wb<n>ʾ b[n]why lʿlmʾ byrḥ knwn šnt
2 4.100+80+10+3

PAT 0549 **C4193** **A.D. (73)**

Prov: Palmyra, S-E Necropolis, Funerary Tower 194. Loc: Palmyra Museum. *Funerary: Foundation. On stone tablet.* Bib: RB '30 5; MF Fondation 13.

1 ṣlmyʾ ʾln dy ʿgylw br ʿgʾ br mqymw
2 br ḥdwdn wdy ʾmtḥʾ brt bwnʾ ʾtth
3 tdmry[ʾ] wdy ʿgʾ brh dy bnʾ [b]ḥywhy lyqrh
4 wly[qr b]nwhy dy bt ʿlmʾ byrḥ nysn šnt
5 [3].100+80+4

PAT 0550 **C4194** **A.D. 181**

Prov: Palmyra, S-W Necropolis, Hypogeum of Lišamš. Loc: Qaryatein. *Funerary: Cession. On stone tablet.* Group: Ber '38 p 106ff; C4194.. Bib: HNE p 479 d. α 7; MF Cession 8; RES 1605.

1 byrḥ ʾdr šnt 4.100+80+10+2
2 ʾḥbr lšmš
3 br lšm̱š br tymʾ mn
4 mʿrtʾ dh lsry br zbdʿth
5 br ʿtʿqb ʾksdrʾ dnh
6 wgwmḥyʾ dy btrh štʾ
7 ʿd kptʾ mqbltʾ

PAT 0551 **C4195** **A.D. 188**

Prov: Palmyra, S-W Necropolis, Hypogeum of Lišamš. Loc: Istanbul Arkeoloji Müzesi, 3742 T. *Funerary: Cession. On stone tablet.* Bib: HNE p 479 d. α 8, XL, 7; MF Cession 10; RES 1606.

1 byrḥ knwn šnt 5.100
2 ʾḥbr lšmš br lšmš
3 br tymʾ mn mʿrtʾ
4 <d>h lbwnʾ br bwlḥʾ
5 br bwnʾ br yqrwr
6 ʾḥbrth mn ʾksdrʾ mqblʾ
7 gmḥyn tmnyʾ mn ymynk
8 ʾrbʿʾ wmn smlk ʾrbʿʾ
Collated 19-24/10/93

PAT 0552 **C4196** **A.D. 184**

Prov: Palmyra, S-E Necropolis, Funerary temple 191. Loc: Palmyra, *in situ*. *Funerary: Foundation. On door lintel.* Bib: MF Fondation 57.

1 Τὸ μνημεῖν ἔκτισεν ʼΑουίδης ʼΙαραίου τοῦ Μαλῆ τοῦ ʼΑφφούσου αὐτῷ τε [καὶ υἱοῖς αὐτοῦ καὶ υἱωνοῖς ἄρσεσιν εἰς τειμὴν αἰώνιον]
2 ἔτους ϛϙυʹ δείου

1 [......lh wlbn]why wlbnʾ bnwhy dkryʾ lyqrhwn lʿlmʾ b
2 [........ šnt [4.100+80]+10+5+1

PAT 0553 **C4197** **n. d.**

Prov: Palmyra, N-W Necropolis, reemployed. Loc: Palmyra Museum. *Funerary: Foundation. On door lintel.* Bib: Group: C4197 = Inv 7 15a, b; Inv 7 15c.

A (Foundation)

1 m[ʿrtʾ d]h bt [ʿlmʾ ...]mn bny mʿ[zy]n lhwn [wlbnyhwn wlbny bnyhwn]
2 lʿlmʾ šnt 3.100+20+20+20+20+10+3 wḥdt bbʾ dnh mlʾ br ʿgʾ br [ml]ʾ br ʿgylw ʾ[ytyb]l wʿgʾ br šlmʾ [šm]šgrm br br [...]ʿgʾ[...]
3 ʾytybl lh[wn] wlbnyhwn wlbny bnyhwn lʿlmʾ [...] šnt 5.100+[...]
B (For Cession see Inv 7 15C)

PAT 0554 **C4198** **A.D. 204**
Prov: Palmyra. Loc: Palmyra Museum. *Funerary. On stone tablet.*

(Upper inscription)
1 byrḥ tšry šnt 5.100[.....]
2 lšmš br qm[...............]
3 [.........................]
(Lower inscription)
1 byrḥ ʾb šnt 5.100+10+5 qwpʾ ḥlpʾ br ṣpry br [....
2 [l]šmš br [..]qwp[..rḥ]q l[...]d[.]br šlmny br ʿbšlmʾ mn
3 [....] mʿrbyʾ [...]ʾ mʿrt[ʾ] dh

PAT 0555 **C4199** **A.D. 193**
Prov: Qaryatein: reemployed from hypogeum. Loc: Qaryatein. *Funerary: Foundation, reference to Cession. On door lintel.* Group: 4199, 4200. Bib: HNE p 479 d. α 9; MF Cession 27; MF Fondation 59; RES 1604.

1 mʿrtʾ dh dy bt ʿlmʾ ʿbd
2 pṣyʾl br ʿstwrgʾ br ʿwyd
3 br lšmš br lšmš lh šqqn
4 trtn ḥdʾ ʿl ymynʾ kdy ʾnt
5 ʿll wʾḥrtʾ mqblʾ
6 wzbydʾ br mʿn br bwlnwr <nwr>ʿth
7 šqqʾ kdy ʾnt ʿll ʿl šmlʾ
8 ʾksdrʾ dnh mqblʾ dy
9 mʿrtʾ dy mqbl bbʾ ḥpr
10 wṣbt šyʿn br tymʾ br
11 ʾbgr lh wlbnwhy wlbny
12 bnwhy h<yk> dy rḥqt lh šgl
13 brt lšmš br ʿštwrgʾ br
14 pṣyʾl byrḥ ʾdr šnt ḥmš
15 mʾh wʾrbʿ

PAT 0556 **C4200** **n. d.**
Prov: Palmyra. Loc: London, British Museum, 102612. *Funerary. On relief.* See 4199. Bib: PS 412; RES 1616.

1 ʾqmt brt
2 ḥggw zbydʾ
3 mʿn ḥbl

PAT 0557 **C4201** **A.D. 212**
Prov: Palmyra, N Necropolis, Funerary temple 175. Loc: Palmyra, *in situ. Funerary: Foundation. On door lintel.* Bib: Inv 7 4; MF Fondation 60.

1 [Τὸ μνημεῖον τοῦ ταφε]ῶνος ᾠκοδόμησαν Ζηνόβιος καὶ Σαμουῆλος Ληουὶ τοῦ Ἰακούβου
2 [τοῦ Σαμουήλου εἰς τειμὴ]ν Ληουὶ πατρὸς αὐτῶν, αὐτοῖς καὶ ἀδελφοῖς καὶ υἱοῖς καὶ ὑωνοῖς καὶ
3 [ἐγγόνοις εἰ]ς τὸν ἅπαντα χρόνον, μηνὶ Ξανδικῷ τοῦ γκφʹ ἔτους.

1 qbrʾ dnh bt ʿlmʾ
2 [w]tṣbyth kl[h] ʿbdw mn kyshwn zbyd[ʾ wš]mwʾl bn[y] lwy br
2 yʿqwb br šmwʾl lyqr lwy ʾbwh[wn lhwn]
3 [wlbnyhwn wlbnʾ bnyhwn lʿlmʾ b]yrḥ nysn šnt 5.100+20+3

PAT 0558 **C4202** **n. d.**
Prov: Palmyra. Loc: Palmyra Museum. *Funerary: Foundation. On door lintel.* Bib: HNE p 480 d. α 10, XXXIX, 2; Inv 8 55; MF Fondation 68; Déd p 317.

1 Τὸ μνημῖον τοῦ ταφεῶνος ἔκτισεν ἐξ ἰδίων Σεπτίμιος Ὀδαίναθος, ὁ λαμπρότατος συνκλητ[ικός,]
2 Αἱράνου Οὐαβαλλάθου τοῦ Νασώρου, αὐτῷ τε καὶ υἱοῖς αὐτοῦ καὶ υἱωνοῖς εἰς τὸ παντελὲς, αἰώνιον τειμήν.

1 [qbrʾ dn]h bnʾ ʾdynt sqltyqʾ br̊ ḥyr̊n whblt nṣwr̊ wlbnʾ bnwhy lʿlmʾ

PAT 0559 **C4203** **A.D. 218**

Prov: Palmyra. Loc: Palmyra Museum. *Funerary: Foundation. On door lintel.* Bib: MF Fondation 61.

1 [Τὸ μνημεῖον ἔκτισεν ʼΙούλιος] Αὐρήλιος ʼΡεφάβωλος ʼΑθηακάβου ʼΡεφαβώλου τοῦ ʼΑθηακάβου τοῦ ἐπικαλουμένου Ν[εβουζαβάδου]

2 [...............ἑαυτῷ καὶ υἱοῖς] καὶ υἱωνοῖς καὶ ἐγγόνοις εἰς τὸ παράπαν, Αὐδυναίῳ τοῦ θκφʹ ἔτους

1 [qbrʾ dn]h bnʾ mn [kysh]
2 [ywlys] ʾwr[lys] rp[bwl b]r ʿtʿqb [br] rpbwl br ʿtʿ[qb] dy mtqrʾ nb[wzbd]
3 [byrḥ ṭ]bt šnt 5.100+20+5+4

PAT 0560 **C4204** **A.D. 226**

Prov: Palmyra, S-E Necropolis, Hypogeum. Loc: Palmyra, *in situ. Funerary: Cession. On stone tablet.* Bib: MF Cession 37.

1 sṭrʾ dnh mʿrbyʾ mʿlyk bbʾ ʿl smlk bʾksdrʾ tymnyʾ
2 mʿlyk ʾksdrʾ ʿl ymynʾ wtṣbwth klh rḥq ywlyʾ ʾwrlyʾ
3 šlmn wškny bny yrḥy šlmn br ydʾ lywlys ʾwrlys yrḥbwlʾ br
4 mqymw npry lh wlbnwhy wlbny bnyhwn lʿlmʾ byrḥ knwn
5 šnt 5.100+20+10+5+3

PAT 0561 **C4205** **n. d.**

Prov: Palmyra. Loc: Palmyra Museum?. *Funerary. On sarcophagus.* See 4204.

1 ṣlm
2 ʿgʾ
3 br
4 mtnw
5 ḥbl

Possibly same as PS 124, see Stark '71 p 130 (name there read, after Ingholt, mtny)

PAT 0562 **C4206** **A.D. 229, 234**

Prov: Palmyra, Valley of Tombs, Umm Belqîs, Tower 70. Loc: Palmyra, *in situ. Funerary, Cessions. On door lintel.* Group: 4206, 4207, 4208, Sem '86 p 89. Bib: Inv 4 1a; MF Cession 38; MF Cession 39.

1 byrḥ ṭbt šnt 5.100+40 ywlys ʾwrlys bwlmʾ br zbdbwl br bwlmʾ nynyʾ rḥqt lywlʾ ʾwr̄lyʾ ʿgʾ wšlmʾ
2 bny šlmʾ br tymʾ br nbwmr̄ bny ḥlh mn mnth plgh dqbrʾ wmʿrtʾ dy bgwh lhwn wlbnyhn wlbny bnyhwn ly[qrhwn lʿlmʾ]
3 [.....] klh byrḥ šbṭ dy šnt 5.100+40+5 ywlys ʾwrlys bwlmʾ br zbdbwl b[r bwlmʾ nynyʾ]
4 [rḥq .....l..... br]t nbwʾ?zʾ? br̄ ty[m]ʾ br nbwm<r> wʾ[..]n bt ḥlh mn rbʿwt qbrʾ dnh wmn [....]

Text of Inv 4 1a

PAT 0563 **C4207** **n. d.**

Prov: Palmyra, Valley of Tombs, Umm Belqîs, Tower 70. Loc: Palmyra, *in situ. Funerary. On wall.* See 4206. Bib: Inv 4 1b.

1 bl dkyr yrḥy br nšʾ mky bṭb wlʿlmʾ

PAT 0564 **C4208** **n. d.**

Prov: Palmyra, Valley of Tombs, Umm Belqîs, Tower 70. Loc: Palmyra, *in situ. Funerary. On wall.* See 4206. Bib: Inv 4 1c; RES 450.

1 [..] dkyr yr[ḥ]y [m]ky bṭb

PAT 0565 **C4209** **A.D. 236 (Gk.)**

Prov: Palmyra, Valley of Tombs, Umm Belqîs, Funerary temple 150. Loc: Palmyra; *in situ. Funerary: Foundation, with Cession. On door lintel.* Bib: MF Cession 49; MF Fondation 65; RES 1644.

1 Τὸ μνημεῖον τοῦτο σὺν ὑπογείῳ ἐξ ἰδίων ᾠκοδόμησεν ʼΙούλιος Αὐρή[λιος Μ]άρωνα [Μαλῆ τοῦ κα]ὶ Μεζαββαν[ᾶ τοῦ]

2 ʼΑδριανοῦ εἰς τειμὴν αὐτοῦ καὶ υἱῶν καὶ υἱωνῶν εἰς τὸ παντελὲς, ἔτ[ους ζμφʹ] μηνεὶ Δύστρῳ

3 ʽΙούλιος Αὐρήλιος Ζηνόβιος ʽΑσθώρου τοῦ Ζεβείδου ἐξ[εστήσατο τούτου τοῦ μ]νημείου σὺν ὑπογείῳ αὐτοῦ κ[αὶ σὺν παντὶ κόσ-]
4 μῳ καὶ δικαίοις πᾶσι ʽΙουλίῳ Θεοδώρῳ ʼΑγρίπου τοῦ Μαρκέλλου, [αὐτῷ καὶ υἱοῖς] καὶ υἱωνοῖς εἰς τὸ παντελὲς, [ἔτους..φ' μηνεὶ ....]

1 [qbrʼ dnh wmʽr]tʼ dy
2 [bnʼ mn kysh] ywlys ʼwrlys mrwnʼ br mlʼ dy [mtqrʼ mzbn]ʼ br ʼdrynws lyqrh wlbnwh wbnʼ bnwh lʽlmʼ šnt 5.100+40+5+2 byrḥ ʼdr
3 [ywlys ʼwrlys zbydʼ] br ʽštwr zbydʼ [rḥq mn qbrʼ dnh wmʽrtʼ] dh wtṣbyth wqš[ṭ]h lywlys ʼwrlys tydrws br [ʼgrpʼ br]
4 [mrqlʼ lh wlbnwh wbnʼ bnwh lʽlmʼ byrḥ .... šnt 5 ..]

PAT 0566 **C4210** A.D. 237

Prov: Palmyra. Loc: Not known. *Funerary. On stone tablet.* Bib: RES 718.

1 npšʼ dnh dy ḥlʼ br
2 nbwzbd br kyly ḥbl
3 bšnt 5.100+40+5+3
4 byrḥ sywn ywm 10+5+3

PAT 0567 **C4211** A.D. 237

Prov: Palmyra. Loc: Ny Carlsberg Glyptotek, 1135. *Funerary: Cession. On stone tablet.* Bib: MF Cession 40; NyCG 132.

1 [ʽΙούλιος Αὐ]ρήλιος [Εὐτύχης]
2 [ʼΑγγαίο]υ κοινωνὸν [προσ-
3 ελάβε]το, ἐν τῷ ἀναγαί[ῳ]
4 [.....]ετου μνημείο[υ]
5 [Γάϊο]ν ʽΙούλιον ʽΕρμείαν, ἀ-
6 δελφὸν αὐτοῦ, ὃ ἀμφό-
7 τεροι οἰκοδομήσαντες
8 ἀνενέωσαν ἐξ ἰδίων, ἑαυ-
9 τοῖς καὶ υἱοῖς καὶ υἱωνοῖς,
10 καὶ εἰς τειμὴν υἱῶν Μαε-
11 νᾶ ἀδελφοῦ αὐτῶν. Μη-
12 νὶ Λώῳ ημφ' ἔτους.

1 ywlys ʼwrlys ʼwṭkʼ ḥgy ʼḥ[br]
2 bʽly[tʼ dy] qbrʼ dnh l[gys]
3 [yw]ly[s hrmys ʼ]ḥwhy dy [.....]

C4212 A.D. 252

Prov: Palmyra, N Necropolis, Tower 118. Loc: Palmyra, *in situ. Funerary. On door lintel.* Bib: IP 39; Inv 7 13; MF Cession 45; MF Fondation 74.

(Greek, to right of Aramaic)
1 Βαρέχ[ει........]τοῦ μακκ[αίου...]αι ασυμ[........ἀ-]
2 δελφῷ αυτου και μουκιάνῳ αδελφῷ αὐτοῦ ε<ἰ>ς τειμ[ὴν αυτῶν κ-]
3 αὶ υιῶν καὶ <υἱ>ωνῶν και ἐγγόνων εἰς τὸ παντελές μηνὶ γ[ορπιαίῳ το-]
4 ῦ γψφ' ἔτους
Gk text after Inv 7 13

(Left of Greek)
1 lhwn wlbnyhwn wlbny bnyhwn lʽlmʼ
(Below Greek, on right:
2 ʼdy
(below Greek, central)
3 qbrʼ dnh wgwmḥyn ʼrbʽʼ dy ʽlytʼ
2 mqymw brt zbdʽth wʼqmʼ brt blṭy wr̊mnws br mlʼ
3 bryky br [.....]5.100+20+20[...]

PAT 0569 **C4213** A.D. 253

Prov: Palmyra, N Necropolis, Funerary temple 144. Loc: Palmyra, *in situ. Funerary. On door lintel.* Bib: RES 1642; Inv 7 11; MF Fondation 66.

1 [Τὸ μνημεῖον τοῦτο ἔκτ]ισαν ʼΑδδουδάνης καὶ ʼΑλαίσα[ς.......]
2 [ἑαυτοῖς καὶ υἱοῖς καὶ ε]γγόνοις. ἔτους τετάρτου ἑξ[ηκοστοῦ....]

1 [... b]nʼ bnh lʽlmʼ bʼlwl šnt 5.100+[60+4]
(Gk text written between these two lines)
2 [....] br tymʼ ʼzrzyrt lhwn wl[bn]yh[wn ...]
Text after Inv 7 11

PAT 0570 **C4214** **n. d.**
Prov: Palmyra, N Necropolis, Funerary temple 173d. Loc: Palmyra, *in situ*. *Funerary*. *On door lintel*. Bib: Inv 7 2; MF Fondation 67; Déd p 242.

1 [Tὸ μνημεῖον τοῦτο ἔκτισα καὶ] ἀφιέρωσα υἱοῖς καὶ ὑωνοῖς ἄρσεσι, ἐπὶ τῷ κατὰ μηδένα τρόπον κοινωνὸν αὐτοῦ προσλαβείν, καθ[ὰ ἔγραψα].

1 [... qb]r' dnh dbnt! w'qdšt lbnyn wlbny bn yhwn[....]wr 'w lmb'd 'w l'ḥbwr' bh 'yš hyk dy ktbt [......]

For *dbnt*! '(is) what I built' text has *dnbt* (correction by Nöldeke); division of words after *'w* follows Chabot :: Cantineau Inv 7 2

PAT 0571 **C4215** **n. d.**
Prov: Palmyra, S-E Necropolis, Funerary temple 187. Loc: Palmyra, *in situ*. *Funerary: Foundation. On door lintel*. Bib: RES 2189; MF Fondation 77.

1 [Tὸ μνημεῖον τοῦτο ἔκτι]σαν Ὄγηλος Σαλαμαλλάθου τοῦ Νεσᾶ καὶ Ἰαρ(ι)βωλῆς Σάλμης Νέσης Νέσας Μαεναῖος Ὄγηλος καὶ Βάρσαδος υἱοὶ
2 [αὐτοῦ εἰς τειμὴν ἑαυτῶν καὶ υἱῶν] καὶ υἱωνῶν καὶ ἐγγονῶν εἰς τὸ παντελὲς ἀφειερώσαντες αὐτό ἀιΐδιον ὡς μὴ ἐξεῖναί τινι ἀπαλλοτριοῖν
3 [αὐτὸ κατὰ μηδένα τρόπον ἢ] τὸν τοιοῦτον ἐνέχασ[θαι ....]τῷ ταμείῳ ~~X~~ ε

1 qbr' dnh dy bn'
2 [....]

C4215 fills lacuna on basis of Gk; Βάρσαδος = *brš'd* of other texts, see "Personal Names" below

PAT 0572 **C4216** **n. d.**
Prov: Palmyra, Valley of Tombs, Funerary temple 36. Loc: Palmyra, *in situ*. *Funerary: Foundation. On door lintel*. Group: C4216 + C4217, DaM '85 p 34. Bib: IP 71; Inv 4 21; MF 79; As'ad and Schmidt-Colinet '85 pp 34-35, Taf. 7a; Schmidt-Colinet '92 (TG) pp 41-42; pl 15; Beilage 17; PGKK p 239 Abb. 15, 16.
(from C4217)

1 [..]
2 [........υἱ]οῖς καὶ υἱωνοῖς καὶ ἐγγόνοις ἄρσεσι[..........]
3 παρὰ τὸ ἐξὸν ο[ἱῳδ]ήποτε τρόπῳ ἀπαλλοτριῶσαι τὸ σ[.....
4 [.............τοῦ τ]άφου σι[.....................]

1 qbr' dnh bt 'lm' [......]
2 [......] 'nš mn wrw[d....]
3 [....]wšn[...]

Combined Greek and Aramaic texts following Inv 4 21 (= C4216 and C4217) and As'ad and Schmidt-Colinet '85; the latter, following Starcky (private communication), read *knwn* 'November', in the Aram. portion

PAT 0573 **C4217** **n. d.**
Prov: Palmyra, Valley of Tombs, Funerary temple 36. Loc: Palmyra Museum. *Funerary: Foundation. On door lintel*. Group: C4216, C4217, DaM '85 p 34; Schmidt-Colinet TG '92. Bib: See above at C4216.

Greek text: see above at C4216

Palmyrene text: see above at C4216
following Inv 4 21, see C4216 above

PAT 0574 **C4218** **n. d.**
Prov: Palmyra. Loc: Louvre, AO 2204. *Funerary: contains curse. On stone tablet*. Bib: HNE p 480 d. α 11, pl XLI, 2; RES 1071, 1656; MF Malédictions 3; Lou 189.

1 ḥbl šmšgrm br nwrbl
2 mr'gr' whw bn' qbr' dnh
3 w'nš l' ypth 'lwhy gwmḥ'
4 dnh 'd 'lm' l' yhw' lh
5 zr' wgr 'd 'lm' wl' yqšṭ
6 lmn dy ypthyhy 'd 'lm'
7 wlḥm wmn lm' yšb'

PAT 0575 **C4219** **n. d.**
Prov: Palmyra, Tower. Loc: Palmyra Museum. *Funerary. On stone tablet*. Group: 4219-4226. Bib: RES 395.

1 ḥbl psy'l

2 br̊ šdy br̊
3 r̊pbwl ʾr̊ʾš

PAT 0576 **C4220** **n. d.**
Prov: Palmyra. Loc: Not known. *Funerary. On stone tablet.* See 4219. Bib: RES 396.

1 šlmʾ br̊t
2 ʾqm[l br]
3 šdy ḥbl
4 ḥbl šlmy
5 br̊t pṣyʾ

PAT 0577 **C4221** **n. d.**
Prov: Palmyra. Loc: Palmyra, *in situ. Funerary. On wall.* See 4219. Bib: RES 399

1 ḥbl šlmʾ
Prb. not identical to PS 234 :: Stark '71 p 130

PAT 0578 **C4222** **n. d.**
Prov: Palmyra. Loc: Palmyra, *in situ. Funerary. On wall.* See 4219. Bib: RES 397.

1 [......]
2 brt
3 [š]dy ʾrʾš

PAT 0579 **C4223** **n. d.**
Prov: Palmyra. Loc: Palmyra, *in situ. Funerary. On wall.* See 4219. Bib: RES 398.

1 ʾlhbl

PAT 0580 **C4224** **n. d.**
Prov: Palmyra. Loc: Palmyra, *in situ. Funerary. On wall.* See 4219. Bib: RES 400.

1 ḥbl [t]mʾ
2 brt ʿtʿqb
3 [zbd]ʿth
4 [ʿt]ʿqb
5 ḥbl

PAT 0581 **C4225** **n. d.**
Prov: Palmyra. Loc: Palmyra, *in situ. Funerary. On wall.* See 4219. Bib: HNE p 481 d. β 9, pl XLI, 9; RES 401.

1 ḥbl r̊pbwl br̊ ʿtʿqb
2 br̊ {zbd} zbdʿth ʾr̊ʾš
3 ḥbl

PAT 0582 **C4226** **n. d.**
Prov: Palmyra. Loc: Palmyra, *in situ. Funerary. On wall.* See 4219.

1 bl[....]
2 br [...] bṭb

PAT 0583 **C4227** **n. d.**
Prov: Palmyra, Hypogeum. Loc: Not known. *Funerary. On wall.* Group: 4227-4230. Bib: RES 1629.

1 mṭʾ lʿty br̊ ʿtntn
2 ʿwydʾ tybwl gwmḥʾ
3 gwyʾ d[..]h wplgh
4 dy ʾksdr̊ʾ dnh
5 [.]ʾ[.]hy[.] bny bnyn
6 d[..]mʾ btʾ[..]ʾ

PAT 0584 **C4228** **n. d.**
Prov: Palmyra. Loc: Not known. *Funerary. On wall.* See 4227. Bib: RES 1628.

1 lʿty br̊ ʿ[tntn]
2 ʿwydʾ gmḥyn
3 ʾr̊bʿʾ

PAT 0585 **C4229** **n. d.**
Prov: Palmyra. Loc: Not known. *Funerary. On wall.* See 4227. Bib: RES 1627.

1 [..]yt[..]š[...]hwn
2 gmḥyn tšʿʾ

PAT 0586 **C4230** **n. d.**

Prov: Palmyra. Loc: Not known. *Funerary. On wall.* See 4227. Bib: RES 1630.

1 ḥby br̊ ʿwydʾ
2 ḥbl

PAT 0587 **C4231** **n. d.**

Prov: Palmyra. Loc: Palmyra, A 218. *Funerary. On group relief.* Bib: PS 61; RES 1070a; Seyrig '34 p 174 and Pl. 24; Inv 8 194.

(A)
1 ṣlm brʿth
2 br brnbw br
3 brnbw
(B)
1 brʿth br
2 brnbw ʾḥwhy
(C)
1 brnbw br brnbw
2 ʾḥwhy
(D)
1 nbwgdy br
2 brnbw ʾḥwhy
(E)
1 ʿtmʾ [bt]
2 mqymw
3 gdybwl
4 ʾmhn

PAT 0588 **C4232** **n. d.**

Prov: Palmyra, Valley of Tombs, Jubwel al Husayniyet. Loc: Palmyra, 218. *Funerary. On sarcophagus.* Bib: Inv 4 17.

(A)
1 mlkw br
2 ḥggw whblt
(B)
1 pṣyʾl br [...]
2 ḥggw br mlʾ
3 whblt ḥbl
(C)
1 pṣʾ br[t]
2 nšʾ ḥggw
3 ʾmh ḥbl
(D)
1 ḥggw [br ml]ʾ
(E)
1 p[ṣ]ʾ b[.....]
2 ḥg[gw]
3 m[lʾ]

PAT 0589 **C4233** **n. d.**

Prov: Palmyra. Loc: Palmyra Museum. *Funerary. On sarcophagus.*

1 bwnʾ brh
2 khylw brh
3 ʾm[tʾ] brt
4 brʿth ʾ[t]th
5 mlkw brh

Lines 1, 2, 3-4, 5 separate texts between heads of reliefs

PAT 0590 **C4234** **n. d.**

Prov: Palmyra. Loc: Palmyra Museum. *Funerary. On sarcophagus fragment.*

1 ḥbl šlmt brt yrḥy ʾtt šḥrw br ḥyrn ḥbl

PAT 0591 **C4235** **A.D. 58**

Prov: Palmyra, Temple of Bel, reemployed. Loc: Palmyra Museum. *Funerary. On stone tablet.* Bib: Inv 8 57; MF Fondation 10.

1 [L*(ucius)* S]PEDIUS CHRYSANTHUS
2 [VI]VOS FECIT SIBI ET SUIS

1 Λούκιος Σπέδιος Χρύσανθο[ς]
2 ζῶν ἐποίησεν ἑαυτῷ καὶ τ[οῖς]
3 ἰδ[ίοι]ς, ἔτους θξτʹ μηνὸς Γ[ορ]π[ιαίου].

1 byrḥ ʾlwl šnt 3.100+60+5+2+[2] bnh [lwqy]ws
2 ʾspdy[s] krystws mksʾ bḥywhy [qbrʾ dnh]
3 lh wlbnwhy wlbny byth ly[q]rh[wn]

PAT 0592 **C4236** **A.D. 169**

Prov: Palmyra, Valley of Tombs, Umm Belqîs, Tower. Loc: Palmyra, *in situ. Funerary. On door lintel.* Bib: RES 1611; Inv 7 6b.

1 ṣlm yrḥy br mlkw br yrḥy ḥwml byrḥ ʾdr šnt 4.100

PAT 0593 **C4237** **n. d.**

Prov: Palmyra, Valley of Tombs, near Umm Belqîs. Loc: Palmyra Museum. *Funerary. On sarcophagus.* Bib: RES 1638; Inv 7 8; Déd p 113.

(On right)
1 mlkw br mlkw
2 mqymw ḥbl
(On left)
1 ʾqmʾ bt
2 bwlmʾ ʾtth
3 ḥbl

PAT 0594 **C4238** **n. d.**

Prov: Palmyra. Loc: Palmyra Museum? *Funerary. On stone tablet.* Bib: RES 1610, 1623; Déd p 113.

1 mrthwn [br]t lšmš br yrḥbwlʾ
2 škybl ʾ[t]t ml[k]w rbʾ br [ʿn]nw
3 mqym[w] ḥbl

PAT 0595 **C4239** **n. d.**

Prov: Palmyra, Valley of Tombs, near Temple 85b (Tomb of Aʿailamī and Zebīdā). Loc: Palmyra, A 217. *Funerary. On stone tablet with relief.* Bib: Inv 8 193.

1 ṣlm ʾprhṭ gwyʾ mhymnʾ ḥbl

PAT 0596 **C4240** **n. d.**

Prov: Palmyra. Loc: Palmyra Museum? *Funerary. On sarcophagus.*

1 whblt br
2 bryky br
3 zbdbwl

PAT 0597 **C4241** **A.D. 156**

Prov: Palmyra, Valley of Tombs. Loc: Palmyra Museum. *Funerary. On stone tablet fragment.* Bib: Inv 8 100; Déd p 113.

1 ʿmr?t?
2 brt lšmš
3 br yrḥbwl[ʾ]
4 ḥbl byrḥ
5 ʾlwl šnt
6 4.100+
7 20+20+20+5+2
Text of Inv 8 100

PAT 0598 **C4242** **n. d.**

Prov: Palmyra. Loc: Palmyra Museum. *Funerary. On relief fragment.*

1 ḥb[l]
2 lšm[š]
3 br
4 yrḥbwl[ʾ]
5 b[r]h

PAT 0599 **C4243** **A.D. 231**

Prov: Palmyra, Valley of Tombs, Funerary Temple 85b (Tomb of Aʿailamī and Zebīdā). Loc: Damascus, National Museum, 22. *Funerary. On relief.* Group: (Watzinger 85b) C4168(=Inv 4 9a), C4169; C4243, C4244; C4245; Inv 4 9b. Bib: RES 143, 1082; RES 1082; PS 24.

1 zbydʾ br̊
2 mqymw br̊
3 ḥyr̊n ʾʿylm[y]
4 ḥbl šnt
5 5.100+40+2

PAT 0600 **C4244** **A.D. 226**

Prov: Palmyra, Valley of Tombs, Funerary Temple 85b. Loc: Damascus, National Museum, 9. *Funerary. On relief.* See 4243. Bib: RES 142; PS 51.

(On right)
1 ṣlmt bt
2 ḥby brt
3 zbydʾ
4 ḥbl
(On left)
5 šnt
6 5.100+

7 20+10+5+3

PAT 0601 **C4245** **n. d.**

Prov: Palmyra, Valley of Tombs, Funerary Temple 85b. Loc: Mainz, Prinz Johann Georg Sammlung der Universität, 835. *Funerary. On relief.* See C4243. Bib: RES 1631, 1085; PS 271; RES 1085.

(On right)
1 mqy br zbydʾ
2 mqymw ḥbl
(On left)
1 br[k]ʾ br zbydʾ
2 mqymw ḥbl

PAT 0602 **C4246** **n. d.**

Prov: Palmyra. Loc: Not known. *Funerary. On relief.* Bib: RES 1608; PS 5.

1 brʿʾ br
2 zbdʿth
3 br zbdʿth
4 brʿʾ šnt
5 40+5 ḥbl

Texts 4246-4256 seems to refer to same family, see CIS p 346

PAT 0603 **C4247** **A.D. 125**

Prov: Palmyra. Loc: Ny Carlsberg Glyptotek, 1155. *Funerary. On relief.* Bib: RES 725; PS 34; NyCG 4.

(On left)
1 ḥbl hdʾ
2 brt bwlḥʾ
3 br zbdlʾ
(On right)
4 ʾtt brʿʾ
5 br zbdʿtʾ
6 šnt
7 4.100
8 +20+10+5+2

PAT 0604 **C4248** **A.D. 134**

Prov: Palmyra. Loc: Beirut, American University Museum, 2740. *Funerary. On relief.* Bib: RES 737, 1020; PS 35.

1 ḥbl ʾmby
2 brt brʿʾ
3 zbdʿth
4 šnt
5 4.100+40+5+1

PAT 0605 **C4249** **A.D. 145**

Prov: Palmyra. Loc: Rome, Vatican Museums? *Funerary. On relief.* Bib: RES 515; PS 36.

(On left)
1 [ḥb]l šlm[t]
2 brt brʿʾ
3 zbdʿth
4 ʾtt
5 nbwlʾ
6 nbwzʾ
(On right)
7 [byrḥ]
8 tšry šnt
9 4.100+40+10+5+2

PAT 0606 **C4250** **A.D. 176**

Prov: Palmyra. Loc: Louvre, AO 2200. *Funerary. On relief.* Bib: RES 1074; PS 14; Lou 185.

1 ḥbl
2 zbdlh br
3 brʿʾ br
4 zbdʿth
5 byrḥ ʾdr šnt
6 4.100+80
7 +5+2

PAT 0607 **C4251** **A.D. 155**

Prov: Palmyra. Loc: Louvre, AO 2201. *Funerary. On relief.* Bib: RES 1080; PS 10; Lou 186.

(On right)
1 bnwr br
2 brʿʾ
3 zbdʿth

4 ḥbl
(On left)
5 byrḥ
6 ṯbt
7 šnt
8 4.100
9 +60+5+1

PAT 0608 **C4252** **n. d.**
Prov: Palmyra. Loc: Beirut? *Funerary. On relief.* Bib: RES 46, 1655.

(On left)
1 tdmr brt
2 zbydʾ
3 ʾtt
4 bnwry
5 br brʿʾ
6 ḥbl
(On right)
1 zbydʾ
2 brh

PAT 0609 **C4253** **n. d.**
Prov: Palmyra. Loc: Beirut? *Funerary. On relief.* Bib: RES 139, 995; PS 280; RES 139.

1 zbdʿth
2 br bnwr
3 brʿʾ
4 ḥbl

PAT 0610 **C4254** **A.D. 150**
Prov: Qaryatein. Loc: Beirut, American University Museum, 2739. *Funerary. On relief.* Bib: RES 1069; PS 43.

(On left)
1 ḥbl
2 ʾḥʾ brt
3 ḥlptʾ
4 br brʿʾ
5 zbdʿth
(On right)
6 byrḥ
7 ʾlwl
8 šnt
9 4.100+60+1

PAT 0611 **C4255** **A.D. 169**
Prov: Palmyra. Loc: Damascus, National Museum. *Funerary. On relief.* Bib: RES 144; PS 44.

1 hdyrt
2 ʾḥʾ brt
3 bwlḥʾ
4 br brʿʾ
5 br zbdʿth
6 ḥbl
7 byrḥ
8 nysn
9 šnt
10 4.100+80

PAT 0612 **C4256** **A.D. 181**
Prov: Palmyra. Loc: Beirut, American University Museum, 2733. *Funerary. On relief.* Bib: RES 738, 1020; PS 15.

(In lower margin)
1 šlmt wnbwlʾ bny mlkw br nbwlʾ ḥbl
(Between sculptured heads)
1 byrḥ
2 qnyn
3 šnt 4.100+80+10+2

PAT 0613 **C4257** **A.D. (4)50**
Prov: Palmyra. Loc: Brussels, Musées Royaux d'Art et d'Histoire, A 1620. *Funerary. On relief.* Bib: RES 1607; PS 6.

1 rmʾ br
2 zbdlh br
3 bwlḥʾ
4 šnt 40+10
5 ḥbl

PAT 0614 **C4258** **A.D. 146**
Prov: Palmyra. Loc: New York, Metropolitan Museum of Art, MMA 02.29.3. *Funerary. On relief.* Bib: Arnold '05 p 105 I, pl I (precedes p 105); Clermont-Ganneau '06b pp 355-56; Chabot '22 p 113, pl XXVII 2; RES 754; PS 37.

(On right)
1 ḥbl tdmr
2 ʾtt
3 mqymw br
4 nwrbl
5 ʾmnʾ
6 mytt yw!m
7 20+5+4
(On left)
8 bsyw!n
9 šnt 4.[100]
10 +40+10+5+2

Collated E. C., 8/25/94; line 6: text clearly *yym*, line 8 *bsyyn*; traces of rubrication.

PAT 0615 **C4259** **n. d.**

Prov: Palmyra. Loc: New York, Metropolitan Museum of Art, MMA 02.29.1. *Funerary. On group relief.* Bib: Arnold '05 p 106 no. II, pl II; Clermont-Ganneau '06 pp 356-57; Chabot '22 pp 112-13, pl XXVII, 11; RES 755; PS 67; Ingholt '54 Pl. 6: Photo.

(A. On left of male figure)
1 zbdbwl
2 br mqymw
3 br nwrbl
4 br zbdʾ
5 [b]r ʿbdy
6 [zbd]bwl
(B. By girl on right)
1 tdmwr
2 brth
(C. By head of boy)
1 mqymw
2 brh
(D. By girl on left)
1 ʿlyt
2 brth

Collated E. C., 8/25/94

PAT 0616 **C4260** **n. d.**

Prov: Palmyra. Loc: New York, Metropolitan Museum of Art, MMA 02.29.5. *Funerary. On relief.* Bib: Arnold '05 p 107 no. III, pl III; Chabot '22 p 113, pl XXVII, 7; RES 756; PS 420.

1 ʿlyt
2 brt
3 zbdbwl

Collated E. C., 8/25/94; traces of rubrication.

PAT 0617 **C4261** **A.D. 172**

Prov: Palmyra. Loc: Not known. *Funerary. On relief.* Bib: RES 49.

(On right)
1 ḥbl šʿdʾl
2 br zbdbwl
3 br mqymw
4 ʾmnʾ
(On left)
5 myt ywm
6 3 bknwn
7 šnt
8 4.100+80+4

PAT 0618 **C4261bis** **A.D. 172**

Prov: Palmyra. Loc: New York, Metropolitan Museum of Art, MMA 02.29.6. *Funerary. On relief.* Bib: Arnold '05 p 108 no. V, pl V; Clermont-Ganneau '06b p 358; Chabot '22 p 113, pl XXVII, 1; RES 758; PS 13.

1 ḥbl
2 šʿdʾl
3 br zbdbwl
4 br mqymw
5 ʾmnʾ
6 myt ywm 3
7 bknwn šnt
8 4.100+80
9 +4

Collated E. C., 8/25/94

PAT 0619 **C4262** **n. d.**

Prov: Palmyra. Loc: Not known. *Funerary. On relief.*

1 tdm[wr]
2 brt
3 mqymw
4 br nwrb[l]
5 ʾtt
6 zbdb[wl]

PAT 0620 **C4263** **A.D. 181**

Prov: Palmyra. Loc: New York, Metropolitan Museum of Art, MMA 02.29.4. *Funerary. On relief.* Bib: Arnold '05 p 107, pl IV; Chabot '22 p 113, pl XXVII, 8; RES 757; PS 16.

1 ḥbl
2 nwrbl br
3 mqymw nwrbl
4 bqnyn šnt
5 4.100
6 +80
7 +10+2
Collated E. C., 8/25/94

PAT 0621 **C4264** **n. d.**

Prov: Palmyra. Loc: Istanbul Arkeoloji Müzesi, 3822 T. *Funerary. On relief.* Bib: RES 1001; PS 222.

1 mqymw
2 br n<w>rbl
3 br m[q]ymw
4 [ḥb]l
Collated 19-24/10/93

PAT 0622 **C4265** **n. d.**

Prov: Palmyra. Loc: Geneva, Musée d'Art et d'Histoire, 8195. *Funerary. On relief.* Bib: RES 258; PS 99.

1 tymʾ
2 br ḥlp
3 tʾ
4 br
5 tymʾ
6 ḥbl

PAT 0623 **C4266** **n. d.**

Prov: Palmyra. Loc: Bloomington, Indiana University Art Museum, 61.16. *Funerary. On relief.* Bib: RES 268.

1 zbydʾ br
2 tymʾ br
3 ḥlptʾ
4 ḥbl
Collated with museum photograph

PAT 0624 **C4267** **n. d.**

Prov: Palmyra. Loc: Not known. *Funerary. On relief.* Bib: RES 48.

1 ḥlptʾ
2 br tymʾ
3 ḥlptʾ
4 ḥbl

PAT 0625 **C4268** **A.D. 150**

Prov: Palmyra. Loc: Berlin, Staatliche Museen, Vorderasiatisches Sammlung, VA 3032. *Funerary. On relief.* Bib: RES 987; PS 40.

(On right)
1 nʿmy brt
2 zbdʾ br
3 tymʾ br
4 ḥlptʾ ḥbl
5 ʾtt ḥlptʾ
6 br zbydʾ br
7 tymʾ ḥlptʾ
8 zbydʾ
9 brh ḥbl
(On left)
10 byrḥ ks[lw]l
11 šnt 4.100
12 +60+2

PAT 0626 **C4269** **n. d.**

Prov: Palmyra. Loc: Berlin, Staatliche Museen, Vorderasiatisches Sammlung, VA . *Funerary. On relief.* Bib: RES 256; PS 298; Wartke '91 13.

1 ḥbl
2 tymʾ
3 br mlʾ
4 tymʾ

PAT 0627 **C4270** **n. d.**

Prov: Palmyra. Loc: Geneva, Musée d'Art et d'Histoire, 8191. *Funerary. On relief.* Bib: RES 261.

1 mzbtʾ
2 brt
3 tymʾ
4 ḥbl

PAT 0628 **C4271** **n. d.**
Prov: Palmyra. Loc: Palmyra Museum? *Funerary. On relief.* Bib: RES 47

1 ḥbl
2 mlʾ br
3 tymʾ

PAT 0629 **C4272** **n. d.**
Prov: Palmyra. Loc: Beirut, American University Museum, 2732. *Funerary. On relief.* Bib: RES 742, 1020; PS 212.

1 šʾylʾ
2 br ḥlptʾ
3 qwqḥ
4 ḥbl

PAT 0630 **C4273** **n. d.**
Prov: Palmyra. Loc: Not known. *Funerary. On relief.* Bib: RES 267; PS 228.

1 nšʾ br
2 ḥlptʾ
3 qwqḥ
4 ḥbl

PAT 0631 **C4274** **n. d.**
Prov: Palmyra. Loc: Istanbul Arkeoloji Müzesi, 3747 T. *Funerary. On relief.* Bib: RES 346; PS 165.

1 nšʾ br
2 qwqḥ
3 ḥlptʾ
4 ḥbl
Collated 19-24/10/93

PAT 0632 **C4275** **n. d.**
Prov: Palmyra. Loc: Beirut, American University Museum, 2737. *Funerary. On relief.* Bib: RES 740; PS 200.

1 qwqḥ b[r]
2 šmʿwn
3 br qwqḥ
4 ḥb[l]

PAT 0633 **C4276** **n. d.**
Prov: Palmyra. Loc: Jerusalem, Musée biblique de Bethesda, PB 2669. *Funerary. On relief.* Bib: RES 277; PS 398.

1 ṣprʾ
2 brt
3 ḥnynʾ
4 qwqḥ
5 ḥbl
Collated

PAT 0634 **C4277** **n. d.**
Prov: Palmyra. Loc: Geneva, Musée d'Art et d'Histoire, 8188. *Funerary. On relief.* Bib: RES 257; PS 79.

1 tymʾ
2 br ḥlptʾ
3 br tymrṣw
4 br ḥlptʾ
5 br šmʿwn
6 dy mtqrh
7 qwqḥ
8 rbʾ

PAT 0635 **C4278** **n. d.**
Prov: Palmyra. Loc: Beirut, American University Museum, 2734. *Funerary. On relief.* Bib: RES 739; PS 402.

1 tmʾ
2 brt
3 ḥlptʾ
4 ḥbl

PAT 0636 **C4279** **n. d.**
Prov: Palmyra. Loc: Aleppo Museum? *Funerary. On relief.* Bib: RES 2171; PS 108.

1 ḥbl
2 mlkw br
3 bwrpʾ
4 ʾḥytwr

PAT 0637 **C4280** **n. d.**
Prov: Palmyra. Loc: Ny Carlsberg Glyptotek, 1046. *Funerary. On relief.* Bib: PS 218; NyCG 50.

1 ʿtntn
2 br mlkw
3 ʾḥytwr
4 ḥbl

PAT 0638 **C4281** **A.D. 133**
Prov: Palmyra. Loc: Ny Carlsberg Glyptotek, 1049. *Funerary. On relief.* Bib: HNE p 481 d. β 3, pl XLI, 6; PS 4.

1 ḥbl
2 ʿtntn
3 gwry br
4 bwrpʾ
5 ʿtntn ʾḥytwr
6 šnt 4.100+40+5

PAT 0639 **C4282** **n. d.**
Prov: Palmyra. Loc: London, British Museum, 125038. *Funerary. On relief.* Bib: RES 1028, 2200; PS 95; PS 103.

(On right)
1 ḥbl whblt
2 br bwlḥʾ
(On left)
3 br bwrpʾ
4 ʾḥytwr

PAT 0640 **C4283** **n. d.**
Prov: Palmyra. Loc: Ny Carlsberg Glyptotek, 1028. *Funerary. On relief.* Bib: HNE p 481 d. β 4, XLI, 4; PS 57; NyCG 29.

1 ʿtntn br
2 bwlḥʾ
3 ḥbl šlmt
4 ʾtth ḥbl
5 ʿbd yrḥy
6 brhwn

line 3: šlmt :: Stark šlmy

PAT 0641 **C4284** **n. d.**
Prov: Palmyra. Loc: Louvre, AO 1757. *Funerary. On relief.* Bib: RES 1056; Lou 172.

1 ʿty brt
2 ʿtntn
3 ḥbl dy
4 ʿbd lh
5 yrḥy
6 ʾḥwh

PAT 0642 **C4285** **n. d.**
Prov: Palmyra. Loc: Ny Carlsberg Glyptotek, 1032. *Funerary. On relief.* Bib: RES 2199; PS 142; NyCG 20.

1 ḥbl
2 [b]wlḥʾ
3 [br] ʿtntn
4 [bw]lḥʾ
5 ʾḥytwr

PAT 0643 **C4286** **n. d.**
Prov: Palmyra. Loc: Ny Carlsberg Glyptotek, 1037. *Funerary. On relief.* Bib: RES 2200; PS 95; NyCG 17.

1 bwrpʾ
2 br bwlḥʾ
3 ʿt<n>tn
4 ḥbl

PAT 0644 **C4287** **n. d.**
Prov: Palmyra. Loc: Louvre, AO 1558. *Funerary. On relief.* Bib: RES 1055; PS 337; Lou 168.

1 ḥbl ḥgt
2 brt bwlḥʾ
3 ʿtntn
4 ʾḥytwr
5 ʾm ʾqmʾ
6 brt dynys
7 ṣʿdy wʾm
8 ʿtʿqb
9 br šdy

PAT 0645 **C4288** **n. d.**
Prov: Palmyra. Loc: London, British Museum, 125201. *Funerary. On relief.* Bib: RES 1029; PS 251.

1 tybwl br
2 lšmš tybwl
3 rbʾ ḥbl
4 dy ḥdt ʿzyz br
5 tybwl dy
6 mtqrʾ
7 [ʿ]bdʾ

PAT 0646 **C4289** **n. d.**
Prov: Palmyra. Loc: Louvre, AO 1197. *Funerary. On relief.* Bib: RES 1027; Lou 163.

1 ḥlpw
2 brt ḥlpʾ
3 [br] lšmš
4 [tybwl] rbʾ

PAT 0647 **C4290** **n. d.**
Prov: Palmyra. Loc: Cuba, Museo Nacional de l'Havana. *Funerary. On relief.* Bib: RES 1019.

1 ḥbl šlmʾ
2 brt bwrpʾ
3 ʾtt ḥyrn
4 br tybwl

PAT 0648 **C4291** **n. d.**
Prov: Palmyra. Loc: Cambridge, Mass., Harvard University Art Museums, 1975.41.116. *Funerary. On relief.* Bib: RES 984; PS 482; Vermeule and Brauer '90 n. 150.

1 rʿtʾ
2 brt ḥyrn
3 tybwl
4 ḥbl

PAT 0649 **C4292** **A.D. 189**
Prov: Palmyra. Loc: Hermitage, 8840. *Funerary. On relief.* Bib: RES 1046; PS 19.

(On right)
1 ḥbl ḥyrn
2 bnpqyrʾ
3 br bwrpʾ
4 br ḥyrn br
5 tybwl byrḥ
6 ṭbt šnt 5.100
(On left)
7 hw wʾbwhy
8 bgwmḥʾ
9 dnh

PAT 0650 **C4293** **n. d.**
Prov: Palmyra. Loc: São Paulo (Brasil), São Paulo University Museum, 69/3.1. *Funerary. On relief.* Bib: RES 252; PS 29.

(On right)
1 ḥbl
2 mlkw
3 br ʿgʾ
4 tybwl
5 zwrw
(On tessera held in left hand)
1 mlkw

PAT 0651 **C4294** **A.D. 201**
Prov: Palmyra. Loc: Aleppo Museum? *Funerary. On relief.* Bib: RES 274; PS 20.

1 ʿgʾ br
2 tybwl

3 zwr ḥbl
4 šnt 5.100+10
5 +3

PAT 0652 **C4295** **n. d.**
Prov: Palmyra. Loc: Aleppo Museum? *Funerary. On relief.* Bib: RES 275.

1 [ʿ]gʾ br
2 mlkw ʿgʾ
3 zwr ḥbl

PAT 0653 **C4296** **n. d.**
Prov: Palmyra. Loc: London, British Museum, 125036. *Funerary. On relief.* Bib: PS 49.

(Between sculptured heads)
1 mrty brt
2 ʾlhbl br
3 mrywn ḥbl
4 bʿlt[g]ʾ brt
5 ʿwydʾ b[r]
6 tymrṣw
7 ḥbl
(On right)
1 ʾtt
2 mrywn
3 br
4 ʾlhbl

PAT 0654 **C4297** **n. d.**
Prov: Palmyra. Loc: London, British Museum, 125032. *Funerary. On relief.*

1 ḥbl ḥyr[n]
2 br mry[wn]
3 br ʾ[lhbl]

PAT 0655 **C4298** **n. d.**
Prov: Palmyra. Loc: Ny Carlsberg Glyptotek, 1033. *Funerary. On relief.* Bib: RES 406; PS 302; NyCG 76.

1 ḥbl
2 mrywn
3 br
4 ʾlhbl

PAT 0656 **C4299** **n. d.**
Prov: Palmyra. Loc: Istanbul Arkeoloji Müzesi, 3837 T. *Funerary. On relief.* Bib: RES 1609; PS 175.

1 mrywn br
2 ʾlh[b]l
3 ḥyrn ḥbl
4 dy ʿbd lh
5 ḥggw brh
Collated 19-24/10/93

PAT 0657 **C4300** **A.D. (226)**
Prov: Palmyra. Loc: Dresden, Staatliche Skulpturensammlung, ZV 846. *Funerary. On relief.* Bib: RES 385; PS 50.

1 [ṣ]lmt nhr̊ʾ
2 bt šlmn dy
3 ʿb<d> lh syʿwnʾ
4 ʾḥwh šnt
5 [5].100+20+10+5+3

PAT 0658 **C4301** **A.D. 234**
Prov: Palmyra. Loc: Berlin, Staatliche Museen, Vorderasiatisches Sammlung, VA 2660. *Funerary. On relief.* Bib: RES 358; PS 52.

(On right of female figure)
1 ṣlmt lwyʾ
2 ʾtt syʿwnʾ
3 br šlmn ḥbl
4 šnt 5.100+40+5+1
(By child, on left)
5 šlmn

PAT 0659 **C4302** **A.D. 240**
Prov: Palmyra. Loc: Germany, private collection. *Funerary. On relief.* Bib: RES 381; PS 25.

(On left)
1 syʿwnʾ br
2 šlmn ḥbl
(On right)

3 šnt 5.100
4 +40+10+2

PAT 0660 **C4303** **n. d.**
Prov: Palmyra. Loc: Istanbul Arkeoloji Müzesi, 3758 T. *Funerary. On relief.* Bib: RES 375; PS 289.

1 ʿgʾ br
2 syʿwnʾ br
3 tymʾ ḥbl

PAT 0661 **C4304** **n. d.**
Prov: Palmyra. Loc: Brussels, Musées Royaux d'Art et d'Histoire, O 3633. *Funerary. On relief.* Bib: RES 1010.

1 ydyʿt
2 brt syʿnʾ
3 ḥbl

PAT 0662 **C4305** **A.D. 242**
Prov: Palmyra. Loc: Aleppo Museum? *Funerary. On relief.* Bib: RES 2165; PS 26.

(On right)
1 ʾlhbl
2 br tymʾ
3 br ḥyrn šnt
4 5.100+20+10 (A.D. 228)
(On left)
5 ʿbd lh
6 ḥyrn ʾḥyh
7 šnt 5.100+40+10+4

PAT 0663 **C4306** **A.D. 218**
Prov: Palmyra. Loc: Istanbul Arkeoloji Müzesi, 3783 T. *Funerary. On relief.* Bib: RES 1004; PS 23.

(A. Between heads)
1 5.100
2 +20+10+[x]
(B. Below images)
1 ḥ[yr]n br tymʾ
2 br ḥyrn twpʾ
3 ʾbnʾ brt
4 šmʿwn šqn
Collated 19-24/10/93

PAT 0664 **C4307** **A.D. 240**
Prov: Palmyra. Loc: Oslo, National Gallery (former Ustinow-Samling). *Funerary. On relief.* Bib: RES 370; PS 53.

(On right)
1 mzbtʾ
2 brt ḥyrn
3 tymʾ ḥbl
4 šnt 5.100+40+10+2
(On left)
5 šnt 5.100+40
6 +10+2

PAT 0665 **C4308** **A.D. 233**
Prov: Palmyra. Loc: Oslo, National Gallery (former Ustinow-Samling). *Funerary. On relief.* Bib: RES 371; PS 27.

(On right)
1 šmʿwn
2 br ḥyrn
3 ḥbl
(On left)
4 šnt
5 5.100
6 +40+5

PAT 0666 **C4309** **n. d.**
Prov: Palmyra. Loc: Geneva, Musée d'Art et d'Histoire, 8194. *Funerary. On relief.* Bib: RES 734.

1 ḥbyby
2 br nšʾ
3 ʿlbn
4 ḥbl

PAT 0667 **C4310** **n. d.**
Prov: Palmyra. Loc: Geneva, Musée d'Art et d'Histoire, 8194. *Funerary. On relief.* Bib: RES 260; PS 263.

(On right)
1 ḥbyby
2 br ḥbyby
3 nšʾ ḥbl
(On left)
1 ḥbyby br ḥbyby

PAT 0668 **C4311** **n. d.**
Prov: Palmyra. Loc: Not known. *Funerary. On relief.* Bib: RES 44.

(A)
1 ḥbyby br
2 ḥbyby
3 nsʾ ḥbl
(B)
1 brwqʾ
2 br nsʾ
3 ʿlbn ḥb[l]

PAT 0669 **C4312** **n. d.**
Prov: Palmyra. Loc: Princeton, The Art Museum, Princeton University, 1946-109. *Funerary. On relief.* Bib: RES 43.

1 ydyʿbl br
2 mzbnʾ
3 brwqʾ
4 ḥbl
Collated, 1/11/95

PAT 0670 **C4313** **n. d.**
Prov: Palmyra. Loc: Pittsfield, Mass., Berkshire Museum, 1903.7.3. *Funerary. On relief.* Group: C4313, C4315 (on same relief). Bib: RES 752, 1021; PS 433.

1 nʿm[y]
2 bt gd[r]
3 ṣw ʾtt
4 ḥnynʾ
5 [y]rḥy
6 ḥbl

PAT 0671 **C4314** **n. d.**
Prov: Palmyra. Loc: Oslo, National Gallery (former Ustinow-Samling). *Funerary. On relief.* Bib: RES 372; PS 217.

1 ḥbl
2 yrḥy
3 br
4 ḥnynʾ

PAT 0672 **C4315** **n. d.**
Prov: Palmyra. Loc: Pittsfield, Mass., Berkshire Museum 1903.7.3. *Funerary. On relief.* Group: C4313, C4315 (on same relief). Bib: RES 751.

1 ḥbʾ bt
2 ḥnynʾ
3 ḥbl

PAT 0673 **C4316** **n. d.**
Prov: Palmyra. Loc: New York, Metropolitan Museum ofArt? *Funerary. On relief.* Bib: RES 749.

1 gdrṣw br
2 mlʾ br
3 ḥnynʾ
4 ḥbl
Relief seems not to be at MMA

PAT 0674 **C4317** **n. d.**
Prov: Palmyra. Loc: Beirut, American University Museum, 30.11. *Funerary. On relief.* Bib: RES 253; Ingholt 1934 p 32, Pl. VIII, 1.

1 ḥbl
2 mlkw
3 br gdrṣw
4 ḥnynʾ

PAT 0675 **C4318** **n. d.**
Prov: Palmyra. Loc: Ny Carlsberg Glyptotek, 1029. *Funerary. On relief.* Bib: RES 2194; PS 83; AA '32 p 10, fig 3; NyCG 45.

(By male head)

1 ḥbl
2 mlkw br
3 zbdbwl
4 br mlkw
5 ʾʿwyd
(By girl's head)
6 brth

PAT 0676 **C4319** **n. d.**
Prov: Palmyra. Loc: Not known. *Funerary. On relief.* Bib: RES 992; PS 87.

1 ḥbl
2 ʿgylw br
3 mqymw
4 br mlkw
5 ʾʿwyd

PAT 0677 **C4320** **n. d.**
Prov: Palmyra. Loc: Ny Carlsberg Glyptotek, 1030. *Funerary. On relief.* Bib: RES 2193; PS 379; AA '32 p 10, fig 4; NyCG 44.

1 ḥbl
2 rʿth
3 brt
4 mqymw
5 ʾʿwyd

PAT 0678 **C4321** **n. d.**
Prov: Palmyra. Loc: Louvre, AO 1557. *Funerary. On relief.* Bib: RES 1032; PS 338; Lou 167.

1 ḥbʾ brt
2 mqymw
3 ʾʿwyd
4 ḥbl

PAT 0679 **C4322** **n. d.**
Prov: Palmyra. Loc: Ny Carlsberg Glyptotek, 1024. *Funerary. On relief.* Bib: RES 1031; PS 303; NyCG 126.

1 ḥb[l]
2 yrḥy
3 br yrḥy
4 br yrḥy
5 ydyʿbl
6 yʿt

PAT 0680 **C4323** **n. d.**
Prov: Palmyra. Loc: London, British Museum, 125020. *Funerary. On relief.* Bib: PS 246.

(By head of male)
1 ḥbl
2 ʿgʾ br
3 yrḥy
4 yʿt
(On tessera in left hand)
5 ḥbl ʿgʾ

PAT 0681 **C4323 bis et ter** **n. d.**
Prov: Palmyra. Loc: Louvre, AO 2199. *Funerary. On relief.* Similar to C4323. Bib: Lou 184.

(By head of male)
1 ḥbl
2 ʿgʾ br
3 yrḥy
4 yʿt
(On tessera)
5 ḥbl ʿgʾ

PAT 0682 **C4324** **n. d.**
Prov: Palmyra. Loc: London, British Museum, 125202. *Funerary. On relief.* Bib: PS 249.

1 [.......]
2 [ydyʿ]bl
3 br ʿgʾ
4 yʿt

line 4: possibly yʿtw, see Chabot ad loc

PAT 0683 **C4325** **n. d.**
Prov: Palmyra. Loc: Ny Carlsberg Glyptotek, 1061. *Funerary. On relief.* Bib: PS 400; NyCG 52.

1 [.....]
2 [lšm]š
3 [.....]

4 [ʾt]t yrḥy
5 br ʿgʾ
6 yʿt

PAT 0684 **C4326** **n. d.**
Prov: Palmyra. Loc: London, British Museum, 125019. *Funerary. On relief.* Bib: RES 1031; PS 483.

1 [ḥbl ḥr]
2 tʾ brt
3 ʿgylw šl
4 mwy ʾtt
5 rbʾl yrḥ
6 y yʿt

PAT 0685 **C4327** **n. d.**
Prov: Palmyra. Loc: New York, Metropolitan Museum of Art, MMA 98.19.3. *Funerary. On relief.* Bib: Gottheil '01 no. 3, p 110; Chabot '01 p 347; ESE I p 215; Chabot '22 p 129 Pl. XXXI, 1; RES 157; PS 282; Ingholt '54 pl 9.

1 zbdʿth
2 br̊ whbʾ
3 br̊ zbdʿth
4 dy ʿbd lh wh
5 bʾ brh

Collated, E. C., 8/25/94; traces of rubrication

PAT 0686 **C4328** **n. d.**
Prov: Palmyra. Loc: New York, Metropolitan Museum of Art, MMA 98.19.2. *Funerary. On relief.* Bib: Gottheil '01 p 110 no. 4, pl 4; Chabot '01a p 348; Chabot '22 p 129, pl XXXI, 1; RES 158; PS 202.

1 npšʾ
2 dnh
3 zbdʿth
4 br zbdʿth
5 dy ʿbd lh
6 whbʾ
7 ʾḥwhy
8 ḥbl

Collated E. C., 8/25/94

PAT 0687 **C4329** **n. d.**
Prov: Palmyra. Loc: Jerusalem, Musée biblique de Bethesda, PB 2670. *Funerary. On relief.* Bib: RES 276; PS 183.

(On right)
1 ḥbl
2 yr̊ḥ
3 bwlʾ
4 br̊
5 zbdʿth

(Between heads)
1 dy ʿbd
2 lh
3 whbʾ
4 ʾḥwhy

(On left)
1 ḥ[bl]
2 mqy[mw]
3 br zbdʿt[ʾ]
4 dy ʿbd lh
5 whbʾ ʾḥwhy

Collated.

PAT 0688 **C4330** **n. d.**
Prov: Palmyra. Loc: New York, Metropolitan Museum of Art, MMA 98.19.4. *Funerary. On relief.* Bib: Gottheil '01 no. 5, 6, pl 5, 6; Chabot '01a p 349; Chabot '22 p 129, pl XXXI, 2; ESE I p 215; Torrey '05 p 111; RES 159, 762; PS 169.

(On right)
1 ḥbl
2 [ʿ]gʾ
3 [br] zbdʿt
4 h

(On left, written perpendicularly)
1 whbʾ
2 dy ʿbd
3 ʾḥwhy

Collated E. C., 8/25/94; traces of rubrication

PAT 0689 **C4331** **n. d.**
Prov: Palmyra. Loc: Louvre, AO 5005. *Funerary. On relief.* Bib: PS 299; Lou 207.

1 ṣlm
2 bnr̊ʾ

3 ḥbl

PAT 0690 **C4332** **n. d.**
Prov: Palmyra. Loc: Ny Carlsberg Glyptotek, 1039. *Funerary. On relief.* Bib: RES 2197; PS 91; NyCG 11.

1 ʿgylw
2 br mlkw
3 br mqym[w]
4 ḥbl

PAT 0691 **C4333** **n. d.**
Prov: Palmyra. Loc: Louvre, AO 22254. *Funerary. On relief.* Bib: RES 1658; PS 229; Caubet '90 no. 36; Lou 230.

(On left of male)
1 yrḥbwlʾ
2 br mlkw
3 ḥbl
(By child)
1 bwnʾ brh
2 ḥbl

PAT 0692 **C4334** **n. d.**
Prov: Palmyra. Loc: Louvre, AO 22253. *Funerary. On relief.* Bib: RES 1657; PS 214; Lou 229.

1 mtnʾ br
2 br bwnʾ
3 br yrḥbwlʾ
4 šlmwy br
5 bwnʾ ḥbl

PAT 0693 **C4335** **n. d.**
Prov: Palmyra. Loc: London, British Museum, 125203. *Funerary. On relief.* Bib: PS 333.

1 ṣlmt
2 mrtʾ
3 brt
4 mlkw
5 yrḥbwlʾ
6 ḥbl

PAT 0694 **C4336** **n. d.**
Prov: Palmyra. Loc: Istanbul Arkeoloji Müzesi? *Funerary. On relief.*

1 ʾqmt brt
2 zbdbwl br
3 ʿgʾ ʾtt
4 yrḥbwlʾ
5 br lšmšy
6 br tymʾ
7 ḥbl

PAT 0695 **C4337** **n. d.**
Prov: Palmyra. Loc: London, British Museum (580). *Funerary. On relief.*

1 yrḥbwlʾ
2 br rbʾl
3 šlmʾ ḥbl

PAT 0696 **C4338** **n. d.**
Prov: Palmyra. Loc: London, British Museum, 125024. *Funerary. On relief.* Bib: RES 1639; PS 488.

1 ʾqmʾ
2 brt
3 ḥbzy
4 ḥbl

PAT 0697 **C4339** **n. d.**
Prov: Palmyra. Loc: Strassburg, University Library. *Funerary. On relief.* Bib: RES 394; PS 485.

1 ḥbl
2 [l]wyʾ bt
3 [ḥ]ry ʾqm[ʾ]
4 [....]y

PAT 0698 **C4340** **n. d.**
Prov: Palmyra. Loc: Louvre, AO 1144. *Funerary. On relief.* Bib: RES 1640; PS 428; Lou 162.

1 šlmt

2 bt
3 ḥry
4 bgdn
5 ḥbl

PAT 0699 **C4341** **n. d.**
Prov: Palmyra. Loc: Ny Carlsberg Glyptotek, 1055. *Funerary. On relief.* Bib: RES 967; PS 349; NyCG 24.

1 ʿtšʾ
2 brt
3 zbdb<w>l
4 ḥbl

PAT 0700 **C4342** **n. d.**
Prov: Palmyra. Loc: Not known (formerly, collection de Clerq). *Funerary. On relief.* Bib: RES 1659; Parlasca '67 p 560.

1 ḥbl
2 mlʾ br
3 mlʾ br
4 ḥlʾ

PAT 0701 **C4343** **n. d.**
Prov: Palmyra. Loc: Ny Carlsberg Glyptotek, 1139. *Funerary. On relief.* Bib: RES 403; NyCG 136.

1 ṣlmt
2 [ʿ]lyy brt
3 whbʾ
4 ʿštwr
5 ḥbl

PAT 0702 **C4344** **n. d.**
Prov: Palmyra. Loc: Ny Carlsberg Glyptotek, 1044. *Funerary. On relief.* Bib: RES 404; PS 126; NyCG 19.

1 [... b]r šmʿw[n]
2 [...] qbrʾ dnh

PAT 0703 **C4345** **n. d.**
Prov: Palmyra. Loc: Istanbul Arkeoloji Müzesi, 3713 T. *Funerary. On relief.* Bib: RES 2210; PS 341.

1 šgl brt
2 [ʿ]tnwry br
3 mqymw ḥbl
Collated 19-24/10/93

PAT 0704 **C4346** **n. d.**
Prov: Palmyra. Loc: Istanbul Arkeoloji Müzesi, 3712 T. *Funerary. On relief.* Bib: RES 2212; PS 361.

1 ʾqmt brt
2 ʿgylw ʾtt
3 ydyʿbl br
4 yrḥy ḥbl
Collated 19-24/10/93

PAT 0705 **C4347** **n. d.**
Prov: Palmyra. Loc: Istanbul Arkeoloji Müzesi, 3719 T. *Funerary. On relief.* Bib: RES 2213; PS 154.

1 ḥbl mqymw
2 br ḥlypy

PAT 0706 **C4348** **n. d.**
Prov: Palmyra. Loc: Istanbul Arkeoloji Müzesi, 3714 T. *Funerary. On relief.* Bib: RES 2214; PS 227.

1 whblt
2 br mlʾ
3 br whblt
4 gwrʾ
5 ḥbl
Collated 19-24/10/93

PAT 0707 **C4349** **n. d.**
Prov: Palmyra. Loc: Vienna, Kunsthistorisches Museum, I 1525. *Funerary. On relief.*

1 ḥbl

2 yrḥbw
3 lʾ
4 br whblt
5 [gw]rʾ

PAT 0708 **C4350** **n. d.**
Prov: Palmyra. Loc: Istanbul Arkeoloji Müzesi, 3715 T. *Funerary. On relief.* Bib: RES 2215; PS 88.

1 ʿgʾ
2 br ḥyrn
3 [br] ʿgʾ ḥ[bl]
Collated 19-24/10/93

PAT 0709 **C4351** **n. d.**
Prov: Palmyra. Loc: Vienna, Kunsthistorisches Museum, I 1526. *Funerary. On relief.*

1 ṣlm šlmlt
2 br zbdʾ ḥb[l]

PAT 0710 **C4352** **n. d.**
Prov: Palmyra. Loc: Vienna, Kunsthistorisches Museum, I 1524. *Funerary. On relief.* Bib: PS 63.

(On left)
1 ʾ[.....]
2 br ydy
3 ʿbl
4 ḥbl
(On right)
1 ʿt[...]
2 brt
3 ydyʿbl
4 ḥbl

PAT 0711 **C4353** **n. d.**
Prov: Palmyra. Loc: Vienna, Kunsthistorisches Museum, I 1523. *Funerary. On relief.* Bib: PS 70.

(On right)
1 rbt
2 br
3 blʿqb
4 ḥbl
(On left)
1 mqy ʾtth
2 ḥbl

PAT 0712 **C4354** **A.D. 196**
Prov: Palmyra. Loc: Ny Carlsberg Glyptotek, 1057. *Funerary. On relief.* Bib: PS 30; NyCG 2.

(On right)
1 [ʾ]bnʾ brt
2 šlmn br
3 šlmn br
4 tymrṣw
5 ḥbl bʾdr
6 [š]nt
7 5.100+5+2
(On left)
8 ʾt[t...]
9 br ʿgy[lw]
10 whby

PAT 0713 **C4355** **n. d.**
Prov: Palmyra. Loc: Ny Carlsberg Glyptotek, 1138. *Funerary. On relief.* Bib: Déd p 43; NyCG 135.

1 ṣlm y<d>yʿ
2 bl br ḥ
3 bwlʾ

PAT 0714 **C4356** **n. d.**
Prov: Palmyra. Loc: London, British Museum, 125048. *Funerary. On relief.* Bib: PS 517.

1 [mʿ]ny br [y]
2 [r]ḥbwlʾ
3 [..]y
4 [ḥ]bl

PAT 0715 **C4357** **n. d.**
Prov: Palmyra. Loc: Ny Carlsberg Glyptotek, 1040. *Funerary. On relief.* Bib: HNE p 481 d. β 2, pl XLI, 3; PS 177; NyCG 49.

1 zbydʾ
2 br
3 ʾwṭkʾ
4 dy bwrpʾ
5 kldy
6 ḥbl

line 4: bwrpʾ with aleph written underneath. Line 5: kldy :: Stark ʾkldy

PAT 0716 **C4358** **n. d.**

Prov: Qaryatein. Loc: Not known. *Funerary. On relief.* Bib: RES 25.

(By female figure)
1 btʿgʾ
2 brt
3 ḥyrʾ blšwr
4 ḥbl
(By male figure)
1 blšwr
2 br ḥyrʾ
3 ʾkldy
4 ḥbl
5 ḥyʾ
6 šnyn
7 10+5+3

PAT 0717 **C4359** **n. d.**

Prov: Palmyra. Loc: Damascus, National Museum, 6340 (15029). *Funerary. On relief.* Bib: RES 26.

1 mqymw
2 br ḥyrʾ
3 ʾkldy
4 ḥbl
5 ḥyʾ
6 šnyn
7 10+5+1

PAT 0718 **C4360** **n. d.**

Prov: Palmyra. Loc: Ny Carlsberg Glyptotek, 1038. *Funerary. On relief.* Bib: PS 90; NyCG 10.

1 ḥyrn br
2 šlmn br
3 ʿgʾ ḥbl

PAT 0719 **C4361** **n. d.**

Prov: Palmyra. Loc: Ny Carlsberg Glyptotek, 1041. *Funerary. On relief.* Bib: PS 285; NyCG 74.

1 ʿwtn br
2 lšmš
3 ʾwšy

PAT 0720 **C4362** **n. d.**

Prov: Palmyra. Loc: Not known. *Funerary. On relief.* Bib: PS 519.

1 ʿgylw
2 br
3 ʾwšy
4 ḥbl

PAT 0721 **C4363** **A.D. (251)/(151)**

Prov: Palmyra. Loc: Beirut, American University Museum, 2738. *Funerary. On relief.* Bib: RES 745, 1020; PS 41; Déd p 63.

(On right)
1 ḥbl
2 šlwm
3 brt
4 ʾwšy
5 ʾwšy
(On left)
6 ywm 1
7 btšrn
8 šnt
9 60+3

PAT 0722 **C4364** **n. d.**

Prov: Palmyra. Loc: Ny Carlsberg Glyptotek, 1034. *Funerary. On relief.* Bib: PS 305; NyCG 75.

1 ḥbl yrḥy
2 br ydyʿbl
3 br šmʿwn
4 ʿrgn

PAT 0723 **C4365** **n. d.**
Prov: Palmyra. Loc: Ny Carlsberg Glyptotek, 1025. *Funerary. On relief.* Bib: NyCG 86.

1 šlmt ḥbl
2 ʿktʾ ʾmh

PAT 0724 **C4366** **n. d.**
Prov: Palmyra. Loc: Ny Carlsberg Glyptotek, 1140. *Funerary. On relief.* Bib: NyCG 43.

1 ḥbl ʾḥʾ [b]rt zbdb[wl]

PAT 0725 **C4367** **n. d.**
Prov: Palmyra. Loc: Ny Carlsberg Glyptotek, 1059. *Funerary. On relief.* Bib: PS 479; NyCG 79.

1 ʾmtlt
2 brt mzbnʾ
3 ḥbl

PAT 0726 **C4368** **n. d.**
Prov: Palmyra. Loc: Not known. *Funerary. On relief.* Bib: RES 408; PS 525; Déd p 64.

1 ʿbsʾ
2 [b]r šlwm
3 [w]ʾmtʾ
4 ḥbl

PAT 0727 **C4369** **n. d.**
Prov: Palmyra. Loc: Copengagen, Ny Carlsberg Glyptotek, 2776. *Funerary. On relief.* Bib: RES 412; PS 514; NyCG 46.

(On right)
1 tymḥʾ
2 br whblt
3 br tymʾ
4 ḥbl
(Between heads of figures)
1 plns
2 ʾḥwhy
3 ḥbl

PAT 0728 **C4370** **n. d.**
Prov: Palmyra. Loc: Not known. *Funerary. On relief.* Bib: RES 411.

1 [ḥ]b[l]
2 mlkw b[r]
3 mlkw
4 šʿdy

Relief not in Istanbul Arkeoloji Müzesi.

PAT 0729 **C4371** **n. d.**
Prov: Palmyra. Loc: Not known. *Funerary. On relief.* Bib: RES 413; PS 118.

1 š[ʿ]dʾ br
2 rmy rbwty
3 ḥbl

PAT 0730 **C4372** **n. d.**
Prov: Palmyra. Loc: Haifa. *Funerary. On relief.* Bib: RES 409; PS 98; Ben-Ḥayyim '47, pp 143-44.

(On right)
1 ḥbl tymrṣ[w]
2 br zbdbwl
3 brh
(In middle)
1 ḥbl zbdbwl
2 br mlkʾl rmy
(On left)
1 ḥbl mlkʾl br
2 zbdbwl brh

PAT 0731 **C4373** **n. d.**
Prov: Palmyra. Loc: Beverly Hills (CA), Donald Simon Collection. *Funerary. On relief.* Bib: RES 410; PS 440; Parl '90c 16.

(Between heads of figures)
1 s[...]
2 brt
3 mqymw
4 ḥbl
(On left)
1 ḥbʾ br[t]
2 ʿtʿqb tymʾ brh

PAT 0732 **C4374** **A.D. 113**

Prov: Palmyra. Loc: London, British Museum, 125695. *Funerary. On relief.* Bib: RES 1030; PS 31.

(On right)
1 ḥbl
2 ʿlʾ
3 brt
4 yrḥy
5 ʾbb
(On left)
6 šnt
7 4.100
8 +20+5

PAT 0733 **C4374bis** **A.D. 113**

Prov: Palmyra. Loc: Ny Carlsberg Glyptotek, 1079. *Funerary. On relief.* Bib: PS 32; NyCG 3.

1 ḥbl
2 ʿlʾ brt
3 yrḥy ʾbb
4 šnt 4.100
5 +20+5

PAT 0734 **C4375** **n. d.**

Prov: Palmyra. Loc: Louvre, AO 5006. *Funerary. On stele.* Bib: RES 1053; Lou 208.

1 ṣlm mtbwl br[h ...]

PAT 0735 **C4376** **n. d.**

Prov: Palmyra. Loc: Louvre, AO 5004. *Funerary. On relief.* Bib: RES 1052; PS 359; Lou 206.

1 ḥbl ʾnʾ
2 brt rzy
3 ṣyḥ ʾtt
4 gdyʾ

PAT 0736 **C4377** **n. d.**

Prov: Palmyra. Loc: Louvre, AO 5000. *Funerary. On sarcofagus fragment.* Bib: RES 1641; PS 323; Lou 202.

1 mlkʾ br [...]

PAT 0737 **C4378** **n. d.**

Prov: Palmyra. Loc: Strassburg, University Library. *Funerary. On relief.* Bib: RES 394.

1 [....] br
2 [..]ʾ šdy
3 ḥbl

PAT 0738 **C4379** **n. d.**

Prov: Palmyra. Loc: Damascus, National Museum? *Funerary. On relief.* Bib: RES 990.

1 rpbwl
2 br
3 rstqʾ
4 šdy
5 ḥbl

PAT 0739 **C4380** **n. d.**

Prov: Palmyra. Loc: Ny Carlsberg Glyptotek, 1063. *Funerary. On relief.* Bib: RES 405; NyCG 124.

1 btwhby
2 bt ʿdn

PAT 0740 **C4381** **n. d.**

Prov: Palmyra. Loc: Louvre, AO 2398. *Funerary. On relief.* Bib: RES 407; PS 221; Lou 191.

1 yrḥy br
2 ʾlhbl
3 ḥbl

PAT 0741 **C4382** **n. d.**

Prov: Palmyra. Loc: Berlin, Staatliche Museen, Vorderasiatisches Sammlung, VA 51. *Funerary. On relief.* Bib: RES 439; PS 378; Wartke '91 2; AA '32 p 10 and p 11, fig 5.

1 šbḥy brth tmʾ brt zbyd[ʾ]

PAT 0742 **C4383** **n. d.**
Prov: Palmyra. Loc: Berlin, Staatliche Museen, Vorderasiatisches Sammlung, VA 47. *Funerary. On relief.* Bib: RES 440; Wartke '91 5.

1 bty brt
2 yrḥy br
3 yrḥy ḥbl

PAT 0743 **C4384** **n. d.**
Prov: Palmyra. Loc: Ny Carlsberg Glyptotek, 1053. *Funerary. On relief.* Bib: HNE p 481 d. β 5, XLI, 5; RES 2195; Colledge '76 p 72 and Pl. 91; NyCG 84.

1 ṣlmt bty
2 brt yrḥy
3 ḥbl
Statue of a girl, not a eunuch :: Colledge

PAT 0744 **C4385** **n. d.**
Prov: Palmyra. Loc: Berlin, Staatliche Museen, Vorderasiatisches Sammlung, VA 50. *Funerary. On relief.* Bib: RES 441; PS 279; Wartke '91 12.

1 ʾwṭkʾ br̊
2 ḥry mlkwsʾ
3 ḥbl

PAT 0745 **C4386** **n. d.**
Prov: Palmyra. Loc: Basel, Antikenmuseum, 1906/57. *Funerary. On Palmyra.* Bib: RES 442.

1 ʾtt ḥ[....]

PAT 0746 **C4387** **n. d.**
Prov: Palmyra. Loc: Strassburg, University Library. *Funerary. On relief.*

1 ḥbl

PAT 0747 **C4388** **n. d.**
Prov: Palmyra. Loc: Ny Carlsberg Glyptotek, 1056. *Funerary. On relief.* Bib: RES 2196; PS 406; NyCG 56.

1 ḥntʾ
2 brt
3 bwrpʾ
4 ḥbl

PAT 0748 **C4389** **n. d.**
Prov: Palmyra. Loc: Ny Carlsberg Glyptotek, 1045. *Funerary. On relief.* Bib: RES 2198; PS 97; NyCG 18.

1 ʿtʿqb
2 mlkw
3 mly ḥbl

PAT 0749 **C4390** **n. d.**
Prov: Palmyra. Loc: Ny Carlsberg Glyptotek, 1052. *Funerary. On relief.* Bib: PS 176; NyCG 48.

1 mlkw
2 br
3 ʿtyʿ
4 qb
5 ḥbl

PAT 0750 **C4391** **n. d.**
Prov: Palmyra. Loc: Ny Carlsberg Glyptotek, 1060. *Funerary. On relief.* Bib: RES 2201; PS 437; NyCG 58.

1 mrty
2 brt šlmlt
3 ʾkrn
4 ʾtth
5 ḥbl

PAT 0751 **C4392** **n. d.**
Prov: Palmyra. Loc: Ny Carlsberg Glyptotek, 1042. *Funerary. On relief.* Bib: RES 2202; PS 96; NyCG 13.

1 ḥbl
2 zbdbl b[r]
3 mqymw
4 ḥbʾ

PAT 0752 **C4393** **n. d.**
Prov: Palmyra. Loc: Ny Carlsberg Glyptotek, 1054. *Funerary. On relief.* Bib: RES 2203; PS 465; NyCG 82.

1 [š]lm[t]
2 brt
3 tymʾ
4 ḥbl

PAT 0753 **C4394** **n. d.**
Prov: Palmyra. Loc: Ny Carlsberg Glyptotek, 1058. *Funerary. On relief.* Bib: HNE p 481 d. β 6, pl XLI, 7; RES 2205; PS 476; NyCG 81.

(On right)
1 [ṣ]lmt
2 [b]wlʿʾ bt
3 [ʿ]qybʾ
4 ḥbl
(On left)
1 ṣlmt
2 ḥrtʾ bt
3 ʿgʾ ḥbl

PAT 0754 **C4395** **n. d.**
Prov: Palmyra. Loc: Ny Carlsberg Glyptotek, 1031. *Funerary. On relief.* Bib: RES 2206; PS 145; NyCG 21.

1 mlʾ br
2 mqymw
3 bgš ḥbl

PAT 0755 **C4396** **n. d.**
Prov: Palmyra. Loc: Not known. *Funerary. On relief.*

1 zbdbwl
2 br šmʿwn
3 ḥbl

PAT 0756 **C4397** **n. d.**
Prov: Palmyra. Loc: Grenoble, Musée des Beaux Arts, 1582. *Funerary. On relief.* Bib: RES 137; PS 219.

1 tymḥʾ
2 br
3 šmʿwn
4 ḥbl

PAT 0757 **C4398** **n. d.**
Prov: Palmyra. Loc: Louvre, AO 1555. *Funerary. On stele.* Bib: RES 1034; PS 516; Lou 165.

1 ḥbl
2 yrḥ<b>wlʾ
3 br šmʿwn

PAT 0758 **C4398bis** **n. d.**
Prov: Palmyra. Loc: Not known. *Funerary. On relief.*

1 ḥbl
2 yrḥbwlʾ
3 br šmʿwn

PAT 0759 **C4399** **n. d.**
Prov: Palmyra. Loc: Louvre, AO 1562. *Funerary. On relief.* Bib: RES 1033; PS 372; Lou 169.

1 ḥbbt
2 brt mlkw
3 ḥbl

PAT 0760 **C4400** **n. d.**
Prov: Palmyra. Loc: Ny Carlsberg Glyptotek, 1035. *Funerary. On relief.* Bib: PS 76; NyCG 16.

1 [bw]lḥʾ
2 [br] mlkw
3 ḥbl

PAT 0761 **C4401** **n. d.**
Prov: Palmyra. Loc: Louvre, AO 1556. *Funerary. On relief.* Bib: RES 1054; Lou 166.

1 Μάρκος
2 Ἰούλιος
3 Μάξιμος

4 Ἀριστείδης
5 κολῶν
6 Βηρύτιος
7 πατὴρ Λου-
8 κίλλης γυ-
9 ναικὸς Περ-
10 τίνακος.

1 mr̊qws ywlyws mksmws
2 ʾr̊sṭyds qwlwn
3 brtyʾ ʾb<w>h dy
4 lwqlʾ ʾtt pr̊tnks

PAT 0762 **C4402** **n. d.**

Prov: Palmyra. Loc: Louvre, AO 4086. *Funerary. On relief.* Bib: RES 1634; PS 144; Déd p 245; Parlasca 85b, p 353; Lou 196.

(On left)
1 [Ἀ]πολλό-
2 [δ]ωρος
3 Ἐλαβή-
4 λου. Ἅλυ-
5 πε χαῖρε.

(On right)
1 bgdn br̊
2 ʾlhbl br
3 mlkw ḥbl

PAT 0763 **C4403** **n. d.**

Prov: Qaryatein. Loc: Berlin, Friedrich Sarre Collection? *Funerary. On relief.* Bib: HNE p 480 d. β 1, pl XLI, 8; PS 254; Parlasca '85b, p 352.

1 Νασράλ-
2 λαθε Μάλ-
3 χου, ἄλυπε
4 χαῖρε.

1 nṣrʾ br
2 mlkw br
3 nṣrʾ ḥbl

PAT 0764 **C4404** **n. d.**

Prov: Palmyra. Loc: London, British Museum, 104460. *Funerary. On relief.*

1 [.....] <ṣ>lm zbydʾ
2 [....]l br nṣrʾ br
3 [....]ʾ mlkʾ zbydʾ

PAT 0765 **C4405** **n. d.**

Prov: Palmyra. Loc: Ny Carlsberg Glyptotek, 1027. *Funerary. On relief.* Bib: RES 1035; PS 168; NyCG 61.

(A. By left male head)
1 yrḥbwlʾ
2 br mlʾ
3 ḥbl
(By side of girl)
1 bltʾ
2 brth
3 ḥbl

PAT 0766 **C4406** **n. d.**

Prov: Palmyra. Loc: Beirut, National Museum, 516. *Funerary. On relief.* Bib: BMB '55 p 40 9, Pl. XVII, 2; PS 258, p 120 note 5.

1 ḥbl
2 yrḥbwlʾ
3 br mlʾ

PAT 0767 **C4407** **n. d.**

Prov: Palmyra. Loc: Vienna, Kunsthistorisches Museum, 1503. *Funerary. On relief.* Bib: RES 1647; PS 397.

1 [......]
2 [brt]
3 yrḥbwlʾ
4 br mlʾ

PAT 0768 **C4408** **n. d.**

Prov: Palmyra. Loc: Ny Carlsberg Glyptotek, 1074. *Funerary. On relief.* Bib: RES 1036; PS 445; NyCG 1074.

1 kspʾ brt
2 ṭm<y>s
3 ḥbl

PAT 0769 **C4409** **n. d.**
Prov: Palmyra. Loc: Ny Carlsberg Glyptotek, 1073. *Funerary. On relief.* Bib: RES 1782; PS 475; NyCG 80.

1 ṣlmtʾ
2 dy mrʾ bt
3 yrḥb<w>lʾ
4 ṭmys br
5 ydyʿbl
6 ḥbl

PAT 0770 **C4410** **n. d.**
Prov: Palmyra. Loc: Louvre, AO 2630. *Funerary. On relief.* Bib: RES 1633; Lou 192.

1 [.....]bwl ṭms ʾtth

PAT 0771 **C4411** **n. d.**
Prov: Palmyra. Loc: Louvre, AO 1758. *Funerary. On relief.* Bib: RES 1057; PS 497; Lou 173.

1 ʿly[t bt]
2 yrḥb[wlʾ]
3 ʾtt
4 yrḥb[wlʾ]
5 nšʾ
6 ʿgʾ
7 ḥbl

PAT 0772 **C4412** **n. d.**
Prov: Palmyra. Loc: Louvre, AO 5007. *Funerary. On relief.* Bib: PS 56; Lou 209.

1 ʿlyt
2 brt
3 zbdbwl
4 ʾtt
5 tymy
6 ḥbl

PAT 0773 **C4413** **n. d.**
Prov: Palmyra. Loc: Rome, Museo Nazionale d'Arte orientale, 6011. *Funerary. On relief.* Bib: RES 136; PS 462.

(On right of female)
1 btmlkw
2 bt mlʾ
3 ḥbl
(Between woman and child)
1 ḥyrn
2 br qrdʾ
3 ḥbl

PAT 0774 **C4414** **n. d.**
Prov: Palmyra. Loc: Damascus, National Museum, 2. *Funerary. On relief.* Bib: RES 150; PS 268.

1 ḥyrn br
2 qrdʾ
3 br ydy
4 ḥbl

PAT 0775 **C4415** **n. d.**
Prov: Palmyra. Loc: Damascus, National Museum? *Funerary. On relief.* Bib: RES 1612.

1 ḥbl
2 ḥyrn b[r]
3 qrdʾ

PAT 0776 **C4416** **n. d.**
Prov: Palmyra. Loc: Istanbul Arkeoloji Müzesi, 3750 T. *Funerary. On relief.* Bib: RES 350; PS 481.

1 btʿʾ
2 brt
3 qrdʾ
Collated 19-24/10/93

PAT 0777 **C4417** **n. d.**
Prov: Palmyra. Loc: Mainz, Prinz Johann Georg Sammlung der Universität, 834. *Funerary. On relief.* Bib: RES 1646.

1 šlm
2 nʾ brh
3 bʿltg[ʾ]
4 brt
5 yrḥbw[lʾ]
6 ḥbl

PAT 0778 **C4418** **n. d.**
Prov: Palmyra. Loc: Istanbul Arkeoloji Müzesi? *Funerary. On relief.* Bib: RES 376.

1 ʿbdʿstwr
2 br
3 zbdʿth
4 [ḥ]bl

PAT 0779 **C4419** **n. d.**
Prov: Palmyra. Loc: Istanbul Arkeoloji Müzesi, 3753 T. *Funerary. On relief.* Bib: RES 352; PS 350; Ber '38 p 123 Pl. XLVI, 3.

1 bʿltgʾ brt
2 ʿbdʿstwr
3 nwrbl ḥbl
Collated 19-24/10/93

PAT 0780 **C4420** **n. d.**
Prov: Palmyra. Loc: Beirut, American University Museum, 2763. *Funerary. On relief.* Bib: RES 1020, 1082; PS 196; RES 743.

1 ydyʿbl
2 br bwnʾ
3 br ʿbdʿstwr
4 ḥbl

PAT 0781 **C4421** **n. d.**
Prov: Palmyra. Loc: Istanbul Arkeoloji Müzesi, 3725 T. *Funerary. On relief.* Bib: RES 377; PS 468; Ber '38 p 126, Pl. XLVII, 2.

(A. On left, by head of younger woman, perpendicularly written)
1 šlmt brt ʿbdʿstwr
2 yrḥbwlʾ ʾmh
(B. Between heads)
1 ḥgʾ brt
2 zbydʾ
3 brth
Collated 19-24/10/93

PAT 0782 **C4422** **n. d.**
Prov: Palmyra. Loc: Istanbul Arkeoloji Müzesi, 3745 T. *Funerary. On relief.* Bib: RES 344; PS 276; Ber '38 p 126, Pl. XLVIII, 1.

1 ʿbdʿstwr̊
2 br̊ yr̊ḥbwlʾ
3 wmqy br̊h ḥbl
Collated 19-24/10/93

PAT 0783 **C4423** **n. d.**
Prov: Palmyra. Loc: Istanbul Arkeoloji Müzesi, 3730 T. *Funerary. On relief.* Bib: RES 378; PS 127.

1 ḥbl
2 nšʾ br
3 ʿgʾ
4 nšʾ
Collated 19-24/10/93

PAT 0784 **C4424** **n. d.**
Prov: Palmyra. Loc: Istanbul Arkeoloji Müzesi, 3801 T. *Funerary. On relief.* Bib: RES 379; PS 401.

1 ḥbl
2 [ʿ]ty b[t]
3 [mqy]mw
4 [nwr]bl
5 [......]
Collated 19-24/10/93

PAT 0785 **C4425** **n. d.**
Prov: Palmyra. Loc: Not known. *Funerary. On relief.* Bib: RES 380.

1 ḥbl
2 ḥdwdn
3 br mzbnʾ

PAT 0786 **C4426** **n. d.**
Prov: Palmyra. Loc: Damascus, National Museum? *Funerary. On relief.* Bib: RES 991.

1 [t]ym'
2 br̊
3 [m]zbn'
4 ḥbl

PAT 0787 **C4427** **n. d.**
Prov: Palmyra. Loc: Istanbul Arkeoloji Müzesi, 3828 T. *Funerary. On relief.* Bib: RES 998.

1 ḥlpt'
2 br mzbn'
3 ḥbl
Collated 19-24/10/93

PAT 0788 **C4428** **n. d.**
Prov: Palmyra. Loc: Louvre, AO 2196. *Funerary. On relief.* Bib: RES 1075; PS 403; Lou 181.

1 'myt
2 brt
3 yrḥy
4 ḥbl

PAT 0789 **C4429** **n. d.**
Prov: Palmyra. Loc: Istanbul Arkeoloji Müzesi, 3794 T. *Funerary. On relief.* Bib: RES 1007; PS 463.

1 mrty brt
2 yrḥy ḥbl
Collated 19-24/10/93

PAT 0790 **C4430** **n. d.**
Prov: Palmyra. Loc: Geneva, Musée d'Art et d'Histoire, 8196. *Funerary. On relief.* Bib: RES 259; PS 294.

1 'gylw
2 br
3 yrḥy
4 ḥbl

PAT 0791 **C4431** **n. d.**
Prov: Palmyra. Loc: Geneva, Musée d'Art et d'Histoire, 8193. *Funerary. On relief.* Bib: RES 262; PS 399.

1 bt'ty
2 brt
3 yrḥy br
4 ḥyrn
5 ḥbl

PAT 0792 **C4432** **n. d.**
Prov: Palmyra. Loc: London, British Museum, 125156. *Funerary. On relief.* Bib: PS 179.

1 ṣlm
2 't'qb
3 br̊ 'by'
4 ḥbl
line 3: *b̊y'* with Stark PN p 120: CIS *'̊sy'*

PAT 0793 **C4433** **n. d.**
Prov: Palmyra. Loc: London, British Museum, 125125. *Funerary. On relief.* Bib: PS 365.

1 'ty
2 brt
3 '[..]'
4 ḥbl

PAT 0794 **C4434** **n. d.**
Prov: Palmyra. Loc: Damascus, National Museum. *Funerary. On relief.* Bib: RES 140, 1082; PS 206; RES 140.

1 bny br
2 ḥyrn ḥbl

PAT 0795 **C4435** **n. d.**
Prov: Palmyra. Loc: Damascus, National Museum. *Funerary. On relief.* Bib: RES 145; PS 207.

1 bny br
2 tymy ḥbl

PAT 0796 **C4436** **n. d.**
Prov: Palmyra. Loc: Damascus, National Museum. *Funerary. On relief.* Bib: RES 1086, 1631; PS 522; RES 1086.

1 ḥbl [ʾb]bʾ
2 brt tymy
3 br bn[y]

PAT 0797 **C4437** **n. d.**
Prov: Palmyra. Loc: Mainz, Prinz Johann Georg Sammlung der Universität, 833. *Funerary. On relief.* Bib: RES 141.

1 ṣlmt
2 ʾmtʾ brt
3 mqy brt
4 ʾmršʾ ḥbl

PAT 0798 **C4438** **n. d.**
Prov: Palmyra. Loc: Mainz, Prinz Johann Georg Sammlung der Universität? *Funerary. On relief.* Bib: RES 146.

1 hgr̊ br̊t
2 bwr̊pʾ br̊
3 ʿtykʾ ḥb[l]

PAT 0799 **C4439** **Nov. 20, A.D. 200**
Prov: Palmyra. Loc: Poznan, Schloß Gołuchów. *Funerary. On relief.* Bib: RES 1615; PS 21; Gaw 70d.

1 ʿtykʾ
2 br mlkw
3 ḥbl šnt
4 5.100+10+2 bknwn
5 ywm 20

May belong with BJPES '47 p 146 IV (Parlasca, private communication)

PAT 0800 **C4440** **n. d.**
Prov: Palmyra. Loc: Aleppo Museum? *Funerary. On relief.* Bib: RES 2184; PS 68.

1 blydʿ br
2 ʿtykʾ
3 ʾḥʾ brt
4 bwrpʾ ʾtth
5 ḥbl

PAT 0801 **C4441** **n. d.**
Prov: Palmyra. Loc: Not known. *Funerary. On relief.* Bib: RES 1012.

1 nwrbl br
2 mlwkʾ
3 ʿtykʾ
4 ḥbl

PAT 0802 **C4442** **n. d.**
Prov: Palmyra. Loc: Damascus, National Museum. *Funerary. On relief.* Bib: RES 1084; PS 491.

1 ṣlmt
2 ḥlyw
3 brt
4 [m]lwk[ʾ]
5 ʿtykʾ
6 ḥbl

PAT 0803 **C4443** **n. d.**
Prov: Palmyra. Loc: Damascus, National Museum. *Funerary. On relief.* Bib: RES 2180; PS 432.

1 hgr̊ bt
2 mlʾ
3 ḥbʾ bt
4 mlwkʾ
5 ḥbl

PAT 0804 **C4444** **n. d.**
Prov: Palmyra. Loc: Damascus, National Museum, 7. *Funerary. On relief.* Bib: RES 1083; Colledge '76 p 72 and Pl. 95.

1 ṣlm hgr̊
2 bt zbydʾ br̊
3 ʿtykʾ ḥbl

zbydʾ: text has zbyr̊ʾ, scribe marks both resh and daleth with dot; statue of a woman and child, not a eunuch and siren:: so Colledge

PAT 0805 **C4445** **n. d.**
Prov: Palmyra. Loc: Damascus, National Museum? *Funerary. On relief.* Bib: RES 151, 1082; PS 105.

1 ḥbl
2 khylw
3 br
4 mškw
5 br ymlk[w]
6 ḥbl

PAT 0806 **C4446** **n. d.**
Prov: Palmyra. Loc: Damascus, National Museum? *Funerary. On relief.* Bib: RES 152, 1082; PS 93.

1 mlkw br
2 ydy br
3 ptyḥb
4 ḥbl

PAT 0807 **C4447** **n. d.**
Prov: Palmyra. Loc: Istanbul Arkeoloji Müzesi, 3749 T. *Funerary. On relief.* Bib: RES 348; PS 119.

1 ydʿw br
2 mlkw br ydy
3 ḥbl
Collated 19-24/10/93

PAT 0808 **C4448** **n. d.**
Prov: Palmyra. Loc: Damascus, National Museum. *Funerary. On relief.* Bib: RES 153, 1082; PS 358.

1 ḥbl [bt]
2 štgʾ b[r]
3 t ymlʾ
4 [..]pgʾ

PAT 0809 **C4449** **n. d.**
Prov: Palmyra. Loc: Damascus, National Museum, 12. *Funerary. On relief.* Bib: RES 154, 1082; PS 453.

(By female figure)
1 ḥsd brt
2 brʿth
3 ḥggw
4 ḥbl
(In hand of female)
1 bt ʿlmʾ

PAT 0810 **C4450** **n. d.**
Prov: Palmyra. Loc: Jerusalem, Studium Biblicum Franciscanum. *Funerary. On relief.* Bib: RES 2168; PS 287; Bagatti '39 pp 33-34.

1 ʿqrbn
2 brh
3 dbršmš
4 ḥbl

PAT 0811 **C4451** **n. d.**
Prov: Palmyra. Loc: Jerusalem, Studium Biblicum Franciscanum. *Funerary. On relief.* Bib: RES 2167; Bagatti '39, pp 33-34.

1 ḥbl
2 mlkw
3 br mlkw

PAT 0812 **C4452** **n. d.**
Prov: Palmyra. Loc: Not known. *Funerary. On relief.* Bib: RES 2170; PS 195.

1 ṣlm
2 šlmlt b[r]
3 mʿny
4 ḥbl
(On tessera in hand of figure)
5 ḥbl

PAT 0813 **C4453** **A.D. 154**
Prov: Palmyra. Loc: Aleppo Museum? *Funerary. On relief.* Bib: RES 2172; PS 42.

1 byrḥ
2 ʾyr
3 šnt
4 4.100
5 +60+5

PAT 0814 **C4454** **n. d.**
Prov: Palmyra. Loc: Not known. *Funerary. On relief.* Bib: RES 2173; PS 107.

1 [.... br]
2 [ʿ]wydʾ
3 bgdn
4 ḥbl

PAT 0815 **C4455** **n. d.**
Prov: Palmyra. Loc: Text seems not to be in The Art Museum, Princeton University, as reported by CIS. *Funerary. On relief fragment.* Bib: RES 821.

1 ʿty brt
2 rbʾl br
3 ḥyrn bg[dn]
4 ḥbl
5 ʾtt
6 b[....]

PAT 0816 **C4456** **n. d.**
Prov: Palmyra. Loc: Aleppo Museum. *Funerary. On relief.* Bib: RES 2174; PS 153 A.

1 mzbnʾ
2 br mlkw
3 tymrṣw
4 ʾʿby

PAT 0817 **C4457** **n. d.**
Prov: Palmyra. Loc: Louvre, AO 5972. *Funerary. On relief.* Bib: PS 115; Lou 211.

1 tymrṣw
2 br mlkw
3 br tymrṣw
4 ʾʿby

PAT 0818 **C4458** **A.D. (147)**
Prov: Palmyra. Loc: Ny Carlsberg Glyptotek, 1159. *Funerary. On sarcophagus fragment.* Group: Sarcophagus, C4458, C4458bis. Bib: RES 726; RES 727; PS 8; PS 38; Déd p 235; NyCG 8.

1 [....] mlkw br lšmš br ḥnbl ʾʿby [.....] šnt 40+10+5+3

PAT 0819 **C4458bis** **A.D. (147)**
Prov: Palmyra. Loc: Ny Carlsberg Glyptotek, 1160. *Funerary. On sarcophagus fragment.* Group: Sarcophagus, C4458, C4458bis. Bib: See C4458 above; NyCG 8.

1 [....] šmʿwn br ḥyrn prdšy ʾtth

PAT 0820 **C4459** **n. d.**
Prov: Palmyra. Loc: Milan, Vitali Collection. *Funerary. On relief.* Bib: RES 2178; PS 513.

1 [.....]
2 mlkw

PAT 0821 **C4460** **A.D. 241**
Prov: Palmyra. Loc: Washington, Freer Art Gallery, 08.236. *Funerary. On relief.* Bib: RES 2175; PS 54; Parlasca '85b, p 355.

(On left)
1 ṣlm[t]
2 ḥl
3 ypt b
4 r̊t ʿt
5 tn br̊
6 gr̊ymy
7 ḥbl
(On right)
1 šnt
2 5.100
3 +20+20+10+3

PAT 0822 **C4461** **n. d.**
Prov: Palmyra. Loc: Erlangen (Germany), Archäologisches Institut der Universität, I 1156. *Funerary. On relief.* Bib: RES 2176; PS 335; Parlasca '76 Pl. 2.

1 ḥbl
2 ʿytʾ
3 brt
4 ʾʿylmy

5 yrḥy

PAT 0823 **C4462** **n. d.**
Prov: Palmyra. Loc: Not known. *Funerary. On relief.* Bib: RES 2177; PS 495; PS 524.

1 ʾbbʾ brt ḥyrn br
2 khyly ḥbl
3 šyštʾ
4 ʾḥth
5 ḥbl

PAT 0824 **C4463** **n. d.**
Prov: Palmyra. Loc: Not known. *Funerary. On relief.* Bib: RES 2179; PS 357.

1 nby brt
2 khyly br
3 ydyʿbl
4 ḥbl

PAT 0825 **C4464** **n. d.**
Prov: Palmyra. Loc: Damascus, National Museum, 10. *Funerary. On relief.* Bib: RES 147.

1 ḥbl
2 ʾqmt
3 brt blḥzy
4 nwry

PAT 0826 **C4465** **n. d.**
Prov: Palmyra. Loc: Louvre, AO 4085. *Funerary. On relief.* Bib: RES 1635; PS 146; Lou 195.

1 ḥbl
2 zbdbwl br
3 ḥyrn nwry

PAT 0827 **C4466** **n. d.**
Prov: Palmyra. Loc: Not known. *Funerary. On relief.* Bib: RES 2181; PS 354.

1 ʾqmʾ
2 brt
3 mqymw

4 ḥbl

PAT 0828 **C4467** **n. d.**
Prov: Palmyra. Loc: Not known. *Funerary. On relief.* Bib: RES 2182.

1 mlkw
2 br yrḥy
3 ʾšʿ[..]r
4 ḥbl

PAT 0829 **C4468** **n. d.**
Prov: Palmyra. Loc: Not known. *Funerary. On relief.* Bib: RES 2183; PS 230.

1 ḥggw
2 br ʿgʾ
3 br ydyʿb[l]
4 ḥbl

PAT 0830 **C4469** **A.D. 211**
Prov: Palmyra. Loc: Warsaw, Muzeum Narodowe, 199576. *Funerary. On relief.* Bib: Lidzbarski '27 (improves some readings of F. Peiser MVAG 2 (1897) 315; Gaw '70d.

1 hgy brt
2 tymw ḥbl
3 šnt 5.100
4 +20+3 byrḥ
5 knwn 1

PAT 0831 **C4470** **n. d.**
Prov: Palmyra. Loc: Louvre, AO 4449. *Funerary. On relief.* Bib: RES 1632; PS 69; Lou 199.

(Between heads)
1 hgy
2 brt
3 ḥdwdn
4 ḥbl
(By head of male figure)
1 zbdbwl
2 br šlmn
3 ḥbl

PAT 0832 **C4471** **n. d.**
Prov: Palmyra. Loc: Istanbul Arkeoloji Müzesi, 3839 T. *Funerary. On relief.* Bib: RES 1603; PS 114.

1 ḥbl yrḥy
2 br mtny
3 br ʿgʾ
Collated 19-24/10/93

PAT 0833 **C4472** **n. d.**
Prov: Palmyra. Loc: Not known. *Funerary. On relief.* Bib: RES 986.

1 ʾqmʾ
2 brt ʿ[g]ʾ
3 br [mt]ny
4 [ḥb]l

PAT 0834 **C4473** **n. d.**
Prov: Palmyra. Loc: Damascus, National Museum, 21. *Funerary. On relief.* Bib: RES 148, 149; PS 297.

(On right)
1 ḥgwgʾ
2 br brʿth
3 ḥbl
(On tessera in hand of figure)
4 bt ʿlmʾ

PAT 0835 **C4474** **n. d.**
Prov: Palmyra. Loc: Mainz, Prinz Johann Georg Sammlung der Universität, 721. *Funerary. On relief.* Bib: RES 1613; PS 523.

1 ʾbbʾ
2 br̊t
3 whblt
4 ḥbl

PAT 0836 **C4475** **n. d.**
Prov: Palmyra. Loc: Not known. *Funerary. On relief.* Bib: RES 1614.

1 ʿgʾ br
2 bwnʾ ḥbl

PAT 0837 **C4476** **n. d.**
Prov: Palmyra. Loc: Istanbul Arkeoloji Müzesi, 3816 T. *Funerary. On relief.* Bib: RES 1009; PS 355.

(A. On left)
1 [....]t
2 brt
3 ʾšd
4 ḥbl
(B. On right)
1 [....]
2 br
3 zbd
4 brh
Collated 19-24/10/93

PAT 0838 **C4477** **n. d.**
Prov: Palmyra. Loc: Not known. *Funerary. On relief.* Bib: RES 1617.

1 ḥbl
2 mlkw
3 br ʾšd

PAT 0839 **C4478** **n. d.**
Prov: Palmyra. Loc: Pittsfield, Mass., Berkshire Museum, 1903.7.5. *Funerary. On relief.* Bib: RES 993; PS 415; Ber '38 p 131, Pl. XLVII, 4.

(On right)
1 ḥbl
2 šlmt
3 brt
4 ʾšd
(On left)
1 lšmš b[r]
2 šʿd ʿb[d]
3 mrbynh
4 lyqrh
Collated with museum photograph

PAT 0840 **C4479** **n. d.**

Prov: Palmyra. Loc: Berlin, Staatliche Museen, 27/65 . *Funerary. On relief.* Bib: RES 1011; PS 261.

(On tablet in hand of male figure)
1 yrḥy br
2 bwnʾ dy
3 ʿbd lh
4 mrbyth
(By female figure)
1 mʿynt brt
2 bwnʾ ḥbl

PAT 0841 **C4480** **n. d.**

Prov: Palmyra. Loc: Not known. *Funerary. On relief.* Bib: RES 994.

1 ḥgt brt
2 yrḥy br
3 zbdlh
4 krḥ

PAT 0842 **C4481** **n. d.**

Prov: Palmyra. Loc: Damascus, National Museum? *Funerary. On relief.* Bib: RES 1619.

1 [...yr]
2 [ḥ]y kr[ḥ]
3 br nṣrʾ
4 ḥbl

PAT 0843 **C4482** **n. d.**

Prov: Palmyra. Loc: Damascus, National Museum? *Funerary. On relief.* Bib: RES 1620.

1 ṣlm ʿbd[ʾ]
2 br ḥrʾ
3 ʾqmʾ

PAT 0844 **C4483** **n. d.**

Prov: Palmyra. Loc: Qaryatein. *Funerary. On relief.* Bib: RES 1622; IP 1.

(On right)
1 šlʾ brt
2 ḥṭry br
3 yrḥy ḥbl
(On left)
4 ʾtt
5 yrḥy b[r]
6 ḥlptʾ

PAT 0845 **C4484** **n. d.**

Prov: Palmyra. Loc: Not known. *Funerary. On relief.*

1 ḥṭry br
2 yrḥy br
3 ḥlptʾ
4 ḥbl

PAT 0846 **C4485** **n. d.**

Prov: Palmyra. Loc: Not known. *Funerary. On relief.* Bib: Chabot '18b p 285.

1 rʿtʾ
2 brt
3 ym[lʾ]
4 ʾtt
5 ḥṭry
6 br yrḥy
7 [ḥ]bl

PAT 0847 **C4486** **n. d.**

Prov: Palmyra. Loc: Qaryatein. *Funerary. On stone tablet.* Bib: RES 1621; IP 3.

(On right)
1 ḥbl
2 mqymw br
3 tmʾ byšt
4 gdʾ
(On left)
5 ḥbl
6 mlkw br
7 tmʾ byšt
8 gdʾ

PAT 0848 **C4487** **n. d.**

Prov: Palmyra. Loc: Palmyra Museum. *Funerary. On stone tablet.* Bib: RES 820; Parlasca '76 p 35.

1 ḥbl mlʾ br
2 nšʾ ḥbl

PAT 0849 **C4488** **n. d.**
Prov: Palmyra. Loc: Ny Carlsberg Glyptotek, 1064. *Funerary. On relief.* Bib: PS 348; NyCG 23.

1 [.......]
2 [brt ....]th
3 [br m]qymw
4 [b]r bwlḥʾ
5 qwpyn ʾtt
6 mqymw

PAT 0850 **C4489** **n. d.**
Prov: Palmyra. Loc: Ny Carlsberg Glyptotek, 1062. *Funerary. On relief.* Bib: PS 444; NyCG 55.

1 [.... bt]
2 [br]ʿth
3 [b]r
4 [m]lkw
5 ḥbl

PAT 0851 **C4490** **n. d.**
Prov: Palmyra. Loc: Ny Carlsberg Glyptotek, 1065. *Funerary. On relief.* Bib: Dri '82a; NyCG 89.

On first and third keys in hand of female figure. Reading difficult or impossible

(On second of three keys)
1 bt ʿlmʾ

PAT 0852 **C4491** **n. d.**
Prov: Palmyra. Loc: Not known. *Funerary. On relief.* Bib: RES 1022; PS 213.

Enigmatic AIOΨ on two keys held by figure

1 ydyʿb
2 l br yd
3 bw ḥbl
lines 2-3 *ydbw*: or, *yrbw*

PAT 0853 **C4492** **n. d.**
Prov: Palmyra. Loc: Ny Carlsberg Glyptotek, 1050. *Funerary. On relief.* Bib: PS 89; NyCG 14.

1 mlkw br
2 mlʾ br
3 mky
4 ḥbl

PAT 0854 **C4493** **n. d.**
Prov: Palmyra. Loc: Ny Carlsberg Glyptotek, 1072. *Funerary. On relief.* Bib: PS 344; NyCG 26.

1 [ṣlm]t ḥnʾ brt mqymw br
2 [tyb]wl [ʾtt] lšmš škybl ḥbl

PAT 0855 **C4494** **n. d.**
Prov: Palmyra. Loc: Ny Carlsberg Glyptotek, 1051. *Funerary. On relief.* Bib: PS 75; NyCG 15.

1 bwrpʾ br
2 mlkw
3 ḥbl

PAT 0856 **C4495** **n. d.**
Prov: Palmyra. Loc: Ny Carlsberg Glyptotek, 1077. *Funerary. On relief.* Bib: PS 423; NyCG 53.

1 šgl brt
2 ʿttn
3 mly ḥbl
Line 2: CIS ʿt<n>tn

PAT 0857 **C4496** **n. d.**
Prov: Palmyra. Loc: Ny Carlsberg Glyptotek, 1078. *Funerary. On relief.* Bib: PS 367; NyCG 27.

(On right)
1 qbwdʾ
2 brt mlʾ

3 mtny
4 ḥbl
(On left)
1 d[....]
2 ml'

PAT 0858 **C4497** **n. d.**
Prov: Palmyra. Loc: Louvre, AO 2069. *Funerary. On relief.* Bib: RES 1067; PS 253; Lou 179.

1 ṣlm
2 ʿgylw
3 br
4 ʿtnwry

PAT 0859 **C4498** **n. d.**
Prov: Palmyra. Loc: Louvre, AO 2067. *Funerary. On relief.* Bib: RES 1068; Lou 177.

1 ḥbl ʿtnwry br ʿgylw

PAT 0860 **C4499** **n. d.**
Prov: Palmyra. Loc: Louvre, AO 2068. *Funerary. On relief.* Bib: PS 231; Lou 178.

1 [... l]t
2 [br nw]rbl
3 ḥbl

PAT 0861 **C4500** **n. d.**
Prov: Palmyra. Loc: Louvre, AO 2198. *Funerary. On relief.* Bib: RES 1060; PS 436; Lou 183.

1 šʿd'
2 brt
3 ʿlyt
4 ḥbl

PAT 0862 **C4501** **n. d.**
Prov: Palmyra. Loc: Louvre, AO 2000. *Funerary. On relief, tabula ansata.* Bib: HNE p 481 d. β 8, pl XLI, 10; RES 1058; PS 73; Caubet '90 no. 35; Lou 175.

1 ṣlm mlkw br ḥggw br
2 mlkw qšyš' dy
3 dyr' ḥbl whdyr'
4 'tth ḥbl

PAT 0863 **C4502** **n. d.**
Prov: Palmyra. Loc: Louvre, AO 2093. *Funerary. On relief, tabula ansata.* Bib: HNE p 481 d. β 7; RES 1059; PS 74; Lou 180.

1 ṣlm tym' br mlkw br
2 ḥggw ḥbl whdyr'
3 'mh ḥbl

Line 2 *whdyr'*: Lou (text) has *wḥdyr'* by typographical error.

PAT 0864 **C4503** **n. d.**
Prov: Palmyra. Loc: Louvre, AO 1998. *Funerary. On relief.* Bib: RES 1037; PS 409; Lou 174.

1 tbnn
2 brt
3 ḥggw
4 mlkw
5 ḥbl

PAT 0865 **C4504** **n. d.**
Prov: Palmyra. Loc: Not known. *Funerary. On relief.* Bib: RES 155; PS 301.

1 mlkw br̊
2 ḥggw
3 ḥbl

PAT 0866 **C4505** **n. d.**
Prov: Palmyra. Loc: Not known. *Funerary. On relief.* Bib: RES 1014.

(On left)
1 mqyḥy
2 br mqy
(On right)
3 ḥbl

PAT 0867 **C4506** **n. d.**
Prov: Palmyra. Loc: Dresden, Staatliche Skulpturensammlung, ZV 845. *Funerary. On relief.* Bib: RES 384; PS 226.

(On right)
1 [m]lwk[ʾ]
(On left)
2 mqyḥy

PAT 0868 **C4507** **A.D. 184**
Prov: Palmyra. Loc: London, British Museum, 125150. *Funerary. On relief.* Bib: PS 46.

1 ḥbl šlmt
2 ʾmh ḥbl
3 šlmt br̊t
4 šmšgr̊m
5 byr̊ḥ ʾlyl
6 šnt 4.100
7 +80+10+5
(On left of child)
1 ḥyr̊n br̊h

PAT 0869 **C4508** **n. d.**
Prov: Palmyra. Loc: London, British Museum, 125204. *Funerary. On relief.* Bib: PS 376.

1 tmʾ brt
2 šmšgrm
3 br mlkw
4 br nšwm
5 ḥbl

PAT 0870 **C4509** **n. d.**
Prov: Palmyra. Loc: London, British Museum, 125017. *Funerary. On relief.*

1 ṣlm
2 ḥbyby br
3 mlkw
4 bly[dʿ] ḥbl

PAT 0871 **C4510** **n. d.**
Prov: Palmyra. Loc: Berlin, Staatliche Museen, Vorderasiatisches Sammlung, VA 2015. *Funerary. On relief.* Bib: RES 357; Wartke '91 1.

1 ḥbl
2 tymšʾ
3 br
4 mlʾ

PAT 0872 **C4511** **n. d.**
Prov: Palmyra. Loc: Berlin, Staatliche Museen, Vorderasiatisches Sammlung, VA 2661. *Funerary. On relief.* Bib: RES 359; PS 172; Wartke '91 11.

1 ḥbl
2 tymʾ br
3 mlkw [...]

PAT 0873 **C4512** **n. d.**
Prov: Palmyra. Loc: Istanbul Arkeoloji Müzesi, 3740 T. *Funerary. On relief.* Bib: RES 353; PS 446.

(On right)
1 ṣlmt
2 ḥbʾ brt
3 bwnʾ
4 ḥbl
(Between heads of figures)
1 [ṣl]mt mrthwn
2 brt
3 [ḥ]lypʾ
4 bwnʾ
Collated 19-24/10/93

PAT 0874 **C4513** **n. d.**
Prov: Palmyra. Loc: Istanbul Arkeoloji Müzesi, 3741 T. *Funerary. On relief.* Bib: RES 354; PS 418.

(On right)
1 ḥbʾ brt
2 mlʾ ʾsyʾ
3 ḥbl
(On left)
1 ḥbʾ brt

2 ml' ḥbl
Collated 19-24/10/93

PAT 0875 **C4514** **n. d.**
Prov: Palmyra. Loc: Istanbul Arkeoloji Müzesi, 3743 T. *Funerary. On relief.* Bib: RES 342; PS 277.

1 hrqlyd'
2 br sbyn'
3 ḥbl
Collated 19-24/10/93

PAT 0876 **C4515** **n. d.**
Prov: Palmyra. Loc: Istanbul Arkeoloji Müzesi, 3744 T. *Funerary. On relief.* Bib: RES 343; PS 166.

1 'lqm'
2 br
3 šm'wn
4 br
5 hn'y
6 ḥbl
Collated 19-24/10/93

PAT 0877 **C4516** **n. d.**
Prov: Palmyra. Loc: Istanbul Arkeoloji Müzesi, 3748 T. *Funerary. On relief.* Bib: RES 347; PS 102.

(On right)
1 ṣlm 'tntn
2 br zbd'th
3 dy 'bdt lh
4 'ḥ' brt nš'
5 'tth ḥbl
(On left)
1 'qmt
2 brth
Collated 19-24/10/93

PAT 0878 **C4517** **n. d.**
Prov: Palmyra. Loc: Istanbul Arkeoloji Müzesi, 575 T. *Funerary. On relief.* Bib: RES 349; PS 364.

1 kdnny brt
2 mlkw bqy
3 ḥbl
Collated 19-24/10/93

PAT 0879 **C4518** **n. d.**
Prov: Palmyra. Loc: Istanbul Arkeoloji Müzesi, 3751 T. *Funerary. On relief.* Bib: RES 351; PS 363.

(A. Beneath figure of woman)
1 ḥbl 'qm'
2 brt mlkw br dynys dy 'bd lh bnwry
3 b'lh lyqrh dy 'wqrt mlkw 'ḥwh
4 wbnwhy
(B. On left)
1 šrykw
2 brh
3 ḥbl
(C. On right)
1 btḥw
2 brth
3 ḥbl
Collated 19-24/10/93

PAT 0880 **C4519** **n. d.**
Prov: Palmyra. Loc: New York, Metropolitan Museum of Art, MMA 01.25.2. *Funerary. On relief.* Bib: Clermont-Ganneau 1898 pp 184-85 (drawing); ESE I p 85; Chabot '22 p 129, pl XXXI, 3; RES 355; PS 216.

1 zbyd' br
2 dyny br
3 ml'
4 ḥbl
Collated E. C., 8/25/94; rubricated

PAT 0881 **C4520** **n. d.**
Prov: Palmyra. Loc: Not known. *Funerary. On relief.* Bib: RES 1645; PS 80.

1 dyny br
2 brp'
3 ḥbl

PAT 0882 **C4521**

Prov: Palmyra. Loc: Not known. *Funerary. On relief.* Bib: RES 40.

1 ʿty
2 brt
3 mʿny
4 ḥbl

PAT 0883 **C4522** **n. d.**

Prov: Palmyra. Loc: Not known. *Funerary. On relief.* Bib: RES 41.

1 [n]by brt
2 yrḥy br
3 zgwg ḥbl

PAT 0884 **C4523** **n. d.**

Prov: Palmyra. Loc: Not known. *Funerary. On relief.* Bib: RES 42.

1 ʾmtʾ
2 brt
3 whblt

PAT 0885 **C4524** **n. d.**

Prov: Palmyra. Loc: Not known. *Funerary. On relief.* Bib: RES 45.

(On right)
1 mrthwn
2 brt
3 tymrṣw
4 br ydy
5 grbʾ
6 ḥbl
(On left)
7 ʾtt
8 mʿny
9 br
10 brʿʾ

PAT 0886 **C4525** **n. d.**

Prov: Palmyra. Loc: Palmyra Museum. *Funerary. On stone fragment.* Bib: RES 27, 1648; Inv 8 93.

1 ḥyrʾ br zbdbwlʾ ḥyrʾ ḥ]bl

Text eclectic; reading and line-division partly conjectural

PAT 0887 **C4526** **A.D. 211**

Prov: Palmyra. Loc: Not known. *Funerary. On relief.* Bib: RES 156; PS 47.

1 ʿty
2 brt
3 ʿtšwr
4 ḥbl
5 šnt
6 5.100+20+2
7 byrḥ
8 ṭbt

PAT 0888 **C4527** **A.D. (181)/(281)**

Prov: Palmyra. Loc: Ny Carlsberg Glyptotek, 2774. *Funerary. On relief.* Bib: PS 45; Chabot '18b p 283 B; NyCG 7.

1 ṣlmtʾ
2 dy ʿty br̊t
3 ʿtšwr br
4 klby br
5 lšmš br
6 [...]y ḥbl
7 byrḥ ʾdr̊
8 šnt 80
9 +10+2

line 6: Stark PN *kyly*

PAT 0889 **C4528** **n. d.**

Prov: Palmyra. Loc: Not known. *Funerary. On relief.* Bib: PS 439; Chabot '18b p 283 A.

1 šlmt
2 brt tymʾ
3 ḥbl

PAT 0890 **C4529** **n. d.**

Prov: Palmyra. Loc: Not known. *Funerary. On relief.* Bib: RES 266.

1 ḥbl gdyʾ

2 br tybwl
3 nwrʿth

PAT 0891 **C4530** **n. d.**

Prov: Palmyra. Loc: Louvre, AO 14926. *Funerary. On relief.* Bib: Chabot '18b p 289; Lou 219.

1 syʿt
2 brt
3 ḥlypʾ
4 ḥbl

PAT 0892 **C4531** **n. d.**

Prov: Palmyra. Loc: Not known. *Funerary. On relief.* Bib: RES 270.

1 yrḥy
2 br zbdʿtʾ
3 pzgʾ ḥbl

PAT 0893 **C4532** **n. d.**

Prov: Palmyra. Loc: Not known. *Funerary. On relief.* Bib: RES 271; Chabot '18b p 288.

1 ṣlmt lwyʾ
2 [b]rt yrḥy br
3 ʿgyly ḥbl
4 mlkw
5 wzbydʾ
6 ʾḥh
7 ḥbl

PAT 0894 **C4533** **n. d.**

Prov: Palmyra. Loc: Not known. *Funerary. On relief.* Bib: RES 272.

1 bwly br ʿgylw
2 ḥbl

PAT 0895 **C4534** **n. d.**

Prov: Palmyra. Loc: Istanbul Arkeoloji Müzesi, 3808 T. *Funerary. On relief.* Bib: RES 1026; PS 290; RES 273.

1 tymrṣw
2 br bryky
3 ḥbl

Collated 19-24/10/93. Dotted resh

PAT 0896 **C4535** **n. d.**

Prov: Palmyra. Loc: Portland (OR), Portland Art Museum, 54.2. *Funerary. On relief.* Bib: RES 968; Parl '90 5; Cussini '92 pp 425-26, figs 1, 2..

(On right)
1 mkbl
2 br yrḥ
3 bwlʾ
4 ḥbl
(On left)
1 yrḥbwlʾ
2 br tmʾ
3 ʾḥth
4 ḥbl

PAT 0897 **C4536** **n. d.**

Prov: Palmyra. Loc: Not known. *Funerary. On relief.* Bib: RES 969; PS 220.

1 ʿbdʿtʾ
2 br šlmn
3 ḥbl

PAT 0898 **C4537** **n. d.**

Prov: Palmyra. Loc: Portland (OR): Portland Art Museum, 54.3. *Funerary. On relief.* Bib: RES 970; PS 65; photo: Vermeule '81 p 384 333; photo: Del Chiaro '73 p 76 37; Parl '90c 6.

(By male figure)
1 yrḥy
2 br ʿgʾ
3 ḥbl
(By female figure)
1 blyʾ
2 brth
3 ḥbl

PAT 0899 **C4538** **n. d.**
Prov: Palmyra. Loc: Louvre, AO 4147. *Funerary. On relief.* Bib: RES 1636; PS 512; Lou 197.

1 ḥbl
2 ḥb᾽
3 brt ʿg᾽
4 yrḥy

PAT 0900 **C4539** **n. d.**
Prov: Palmyra. Loc: Strassburg, University Library. *Funerary. On relief.* Bib: RES 394C.

1 ʿ[ty]
2 b[rt]
3 yr[ḥy]
4 ḥbl

PAT 0901 **C4540** **n. d.**
Prov: Palmyra. Loc: Berlin, Staatliche Museen, Vorderasiatisches Sammlung, VA 3098. *Funerary. On relief.* Bib: RES 255; Wartke '91 14.

1 mqy br
2 šmšgrm
3 ḥbl ʿbdt
4 lh ʿlmth
5 wbrth
6 dkrn

PAT 0902 **C4541** **n. d.**
Prov: Palmyra. Loc: Geneva, Musée d'Art et d'Histoire. *Funerary. On relief.* Bib: RES 263; PS 425.

1 nn᾽
2 brt
3 nwrbl
4 ḥbl

PAT 0903 **C4542** **n. d.**
Prov: Palmyra. Loc: Geneva, Musée d'Art et d'Histoire. *Funerary. On relief.* Bib: RES 264; PS 366.

1 ᾽ḥt᾽ brt šl᾽ ḥbl
2 dy ʿ[bd] brny lyqrh

PAT 0904 **C4543** **n. d.**
Prov: Palmyra. Loc: Geneva, Musée d'Art et d'Histoire. *Funerary.* On relief. Bib: RES 265; PS 291.

1 yrḥy
2 br sbn᾽
3 ḥbl

PAT 0905 **C4544** **n. d.**
Prov: Palmyra. Loc: Text seems not to be in The Art Museum, Princeton University, as reported by CIS. *Funerary. On relief fragment.* Bib: RES 822.

1 foršʿd br
2 [š]ṭ᾽ ḥbl

PAT 0906 **C4545** **n. d.**
Prov: Palmyra. Loc: Strassburg, Museum, S 236 (formerly: Schlumberger Collection). *Funerary. On relief.* Bib: PS 163.

1 tym᾽ br
2 zbyd᾽
3 ḥbl

PAT 0907 **C4546** **n. d.**
Prov: Palmyra. Loc: Strassburg, Museum? (formerly: Schlumberger Collection). *Funerary. On relief.* Bib: PS 480.

1 ḥbl
2 ᾽mtḥ᾽
3 brt zbyd᾽
4 ywnyt

PAT 0908 **C4547** **n. d.**
Prov: Palmyra. Loc: New Haven, Yale University Art Gallery, 1954.30.1. *Funerary. On relief.* Bib: RES 1082; PS 424; RES 721.

1 ḥbl

2 šgl
3 brt bwrpʾ
4 mṣryt
Collated, 1/19/95

PAT 0909 **C4548** **n. d.**
Prov: Palmyra. Loc: New Haven, Yale University Art Gallery, 1954.30.2. *Funerary. On relief.* Bib: RES 722.

1 ḥrtʾ brt
2 bydʾ šgl
3 bt ḥbʾ ḥbl
Collated, 1/19/95

PAT 0910 **C4549** **A.D. 187**
Prov: Palmyra. Loc: New Haven, Yale University Art Gallery, 1954.30.3. *Funerary. On relief.* Bib: RES 723; PS 17; PGSc 7.

(On right)
1 [ḥb]l
2 [..]ʾ br
3 [ty]m[ḥʾ]
4 br [mlkw]
(On left)
5 byrḥ
6 sywn
7 šnt
8 4.100
9 +80+10+5+3
Collated, 1/18/95. Text less readable than at time of CIS edition

PAT 0911 **C4550** **n. d.**
Prov: Palmyra. Loc: New Haven, Yale University Art Gallery, 1954.30.4. *Funerary. On relief.* Bib: RES 724; PS 173.

1 ʿb[dʾ]
2 br
3 mrh
4 ḥbl
Collated, 1/18/95. Relief suffered damages, left upper corner now missing :: fuller text of CIS

PAT 0912 **C4551** **n. d.**
Prov: Palmyra. Loc: New York, Metropolitan Museum of Art, MMA 01.25.3. *Funerary. On relief.* Bib: Arnold '05 p 109 no. VI, pl VI; Clermont-Ganneau '06b p 358; Chabot '22 p 129, pl XXVII, 3; RES 759; PS 283.

(on right)
1 mtny br
2 zbyʾdʾ ḥbl
(on left)
one or several illegible lines
line 2 letter *y* not visible on plates; Arnold read *zbdʾ* :: Chabot CIS

PAT 0913 **C4552** **n. d.**
Prov: Palmyra. Loc: New York, Metropolitan Museum of Art, MMA 01.25.5. *Funerary. On relief.* Bib: Arnold '05 p 110 no. VII, pl VII; Clermont-Ganneau '06b p 358; Chabot '22 p 129, pl XXXI, 5; RES 760; PS 187.

1 mlkw b[r]
2 zbʾ br[ʿth]
Collated, 8/25/94

PAT 0914 **C4553** **n. d.**
Prov: Palmyra. Loc: Antioch: Private collection? *Funerary. On relief.* Bib: RES 763; PS 434.

1 ʾmby
2 brt
3 ṣprʾ
4 ḥbl

PAT 0915 **C4554** **A.D. (215)/(115)**
Prov: Palmyra. Loc: Antioch: Private collection? *Funerary. On relief.* Bib: RES 764; PS 48.

(On right)
1 mrty brt
2 tymrṣ[w]
3 dy ʿbd l[h]
4 šgl ʾḥt[h]
5 ḥbl
(On left)
6 byrḥ tšry

7 šnt 20+5+2

PAT 0916 **C4555** **n. d.**

Prov: Palmyra. Loc: Ny Carlsberg Glyptotek, 1146. *Funerary. On relief.* Group with 4556. Bib: RES 729 a; PS 211; NyCG 51.

(On right)
1 [ydy]ʿbl br
2 [m]qymw klb[w]
3 ḥbl

PAT 0917 **C4556** **n. d.**

Prov: Palmyra. Loc: Ny Carlsberg Glyptotek, 1146. *Funerary. On relief.* Group with C4555. Bib: RES 729 a; PS 211; NyCG 51.

(On left)
1 mlkw [br]
2 pṣyʾl
3 [ydy]ʿbl

PAT 0918 **C4557** **n. d.**

Prov: Palmyra. Loc: Not known. *Funerary. On relief.* Bib: RES 730; PS 275.

1 ḥbl
2 ḥnynʾ
3 br ḥnynʾ
4 ʿgʾ yrq

PAT 0919 **C4558** **n. d.**

Prov: Palmyra. Loc: Not known. *Funerary. On relief.* Bib: RES 731; PS 272.

1 yr̊ḥy br
2 nšʾ[..]
3 [m]q[y]m[w]

PAT 0920 **C4559** **n. d.**

Prov: Palmyra. Loc: Not known. *Funerary. On relief.* Bib: RES 732; PS 117.

1 ḥbl
2 bl[ḥʾ]
3 br nšʾ
4 ḥšš

PAT 0921 **C4560** **n. d.**

Prov: Palmyra. Loc: New York, Metropolitan Museum of Art, MMA L 1994.1 (formerly L. 66.9.12), from the collection of Armida B. Colt. *Funerary. On relief.* Bib: ESE III p 144 (drawing, reproduced in CIS ad loc); RES 1018.

(Relief with two figures, originally; right figure now missing; first inscription (A) with missing figure; second (B) with surviving figure)
(A)
1 nšʾ
2 br
3 [...]
(B)
1 blḥʾ
2 ḥšš
3 ḥbl

Collated E. C., 8/25/94

PAT 0922 **C4561** **A.D. 141**

Prov: Palmyra. Loc: St. Louis (MI), The St. Louis Art Museum, 24:60. *Funerary. On relief.* Bib: RES 733; PS 7.

(On right)
1 ḥbl
2 ydyʿbl
3 br ʿtʿqb
4 ydyʿbl
5 ʿtʿqb
6 ʿqby
(On left)
7 ywm 10+5+2
8 bknwn
9 šnt 4.100
10 +40+10+3

PAT 0923 **C4562** **A.D. (162)**

Prov: Palmyra. Loc: Not known. *Funerary.* On relief. Bib: RES 996; PS 12; RES 736.

(On right)
1 [ty]mrṣw

2 rbʾ br ʿtʿqb
3 br ydyʿbl
4 br ʿtʿqb
5 ʿqby
(On left)
6 ḥyʾ šnyn
7 60+10+5+1
8 myt ywm 4
9 bʾdr šnt
10 60+10+3

PAT 0924 **C4563** **n. d.**
Prov: Palmyra. Loc: Beirut, American University Museum. *Funerary. On relief.* Bib: RES 1024; PS 199.

1 [z]bdʿth
2 br mʿny
3 ḥbl

PAT 0925 **C4564** **n. d.**
Prov: Palmyra. Loc: Beirut, American University Museum, 2745. *Funerary. On relief.* Bib: RES 741, 1020; PS 223.

1 [....] br
2 [z]bdʾ br
3 yrḥy ḥbl

PAT 0926 **C4565** **n. d.**
Prov: Palmyra. Loc: Beirut, American University Museum, 2742. *Funerary. On relief.* Bib: RES 1025; PS 269.

1 qlsṭʾ
2 br šlm[n]
3 dy mrqlʾ
4 ḥbl

PAT 0927 **C4566** **n. d.**
Prov: Palmyra. Loc: Beirut, American University Museum, 2754. *Funerary. On relief.* Bib: RES 747; PS 295.

1 [ṣ]lm nrq<y>s
2 br šlmn
3 mrqlʾ ḥbl
4 dy ʿbd lh
5 tymʾ br
6 qlsṭʾ
7 ʾḥwhy

PAT 0928 **C4567** **n. d.**
Prov: Palmyra. Loc: Beirut, American University Museum, 2748. *Funerary. On relief.* Bib: RES 748; PS 273.

1 ṣlm mʿnʾ
2 br ḥry bwrpʾ
3 br mrqlʾ
4 ḥbl

PAT 0929 **C4568** **n. d.**
Prov: Palmyra. Loc: Beirut, American University Museum, 2753. *Funerary. On relief.* Bib: RES 744; PS 447.

(On left)
1 ḥbl
2 btḥyrn
3 brt
4 mlʾ
(Between heads of figures)
5 ʾḥth

PAT 0930 **C4569**
Prov: Palmyra. Loc: Erlangen, Archäologisches Institut der Universität, I 1184. *Funerary. On relief.* Bib: RES 746, 1082.

1 mqymw
2 br tymrṣw
3 tymʿʾ
4 ḥbl

PAT 0931 **C4570** **n. d.**
Prov: Palmyra. Loc: Los Angeles County Museum of Art, M.79.147 (formerly: Minneapolis, Walker Art Center X.1495). *Funerary. On relief.* Bib: RES 750; PS 347; Parl '90 9.

1 ʾqmʾ brt

2 mqy ḥbl

PAT 0932 **C4571** **n. d.**

Prov: Palmyra. Loc: Minneapolis, Minneapolis Institute of Art. *Funerary. On relief.* Bib: RES 753; PS 55.

(A)
1 ḥbl
2 ʾbrwq ḥbn [ʿg]
3 ʾ wšlmt bnwhy
(B)
1 ḥbl ʿgʾ
2 wšlmt bn[y]
3 ʾbrwq ḥbn

PAT 0933 **C4572** **n. d.**

Prov: Palmyra. Loc: Louvre, AO 7476. *Funerary. On relief.* Bib: RES 735; PS 373; Lou 216.

1 rʿtʾ
2 brt
3 mqymw
4 ḥbl

PAT 0934 **C4573** **n. d.**

Prov: Palmyra. Loc: Berlin, Private collection. *Funerary. On relief.* Bib: RES 801; PS 252.

(On right of male figure)
1 mlʾ br tybwl br mlʾ ḥbl
(On right of female figure)
1 ʾqmʾ ʾmh

PAT 0935 **C4574** **n. d.**

Prov: Palmyra. Loc: Hermitage, 8844. *Funerary. On relief.* Bib: RES 1047; PS 346.

1 ʾqmt
2 brt yrḥy
3 šgʾ ʾtth

PAT 0936 **C4575** **n. d.**

Prov: Palmyra. Loc: Hermitage, 8842. *Funerary. On relief.* Bib: RES 1048; PS 161.

1 zbdbwl br
2 zbdlh br
3 bwrpʾ br
4 zbdlh
5 ḥbl

PAT 0937 **C4576** **n. d.**

Prov: Palmyra. Loc: Damascus, National Museum, 26. *Funerary. On relief.* Bib: RES 1016.

1 ṣlm
2 zbdlh
3 br bwrpʾ

PAT 0938 **C4577** **n. d.**

Prov: Palmyra. Loc: Hermitage, 8843. *Funerary. On relief.* Bib: RES 1049; PS 140.

1 ṣlm
2 whblt
3 br bwrpʾ

PAT 0939 **C4578** **A.D. 152**

Prov: Palmyra. Loc: Hermitage, 8841. *Funerary. On relief.* Bib: RES 1050; PS 9.

1 š[nt]
2 4.100
3 +60+5+1

PAT 0940 **C4579** **n. d.**

Prov: Palmyra. Loc: Hermitage, 8839. *Funerary. On relief.* Bib: RES 1051; PS 64.

1 bwšʾ
2 br tymʾ
3 šlmʾ ḥbl
4 brt mlkw ʾtth
5 ḥbl

PAT 0941 **C4580** **n. d.**

Prov: Palmyra. Loc: London, British Museum, 125031. *Funerary. On relief.* Bib: RES 1625; PS 208.

1 ḥbl
2 mqymw
3 br mqymw

PAT 0942 **C4581** **n. d.**
Prov: Palmyra. Loc: London, British Museum, 125023. *Funerary. On relief.* Bib: RES 1626; PS 404.

1 mlkt brt
2 ʾydʿn
3 ḥbl

PAT 0943 **C4582** **n. d.**
Prov: Palmyra. Loc: Not known. *Funerary. On relief.* Bib: RES 1039.

1 zbydʾ
2 [br]
3 ḥlypt [dy]
4 mtqr̊yʾ
5 [......]

PAT 0944 **C4583** **n. d.**
Prov: Palmyra. Loc: Not known. *Funerary. On relief.* Bib: RES 971.

1 ḥbl mqymw br
2 ʿtʿqb

PAT 0945 **C4584** **n. d.**
Prov: Palmyra. Loc: Strassburg, Museum, S 233 (formerly: Schlumberger Collection). *Funerary. On relief.* Bib: RES 972; PS 426.

1 ʾqmt
2 brt
3 ydy
4 ḥbl

PAT 0946 **C4585** **n. d.**
Prov: Palmyra. Loc: Strassburg, Museum, S 234 (formerly: Schlumberger Collection). *Funerary. On relief.* Bib: PS 431.

1 šgl
2 brt
3 ydy
4 ḥbl

PAT 0947 **C4586** **n. d.**
Prov: Palmyra. Loc: Istanbul Arkeoloji Müzesi, 3746 T. *Funerary. On relief.* Bib: RES 345; PS 77.

1 ḥbl
2 bny br
3 ydy
Collated 19-24/10/93

PAT 0948 **C4587** **n. d.**
Prov: Palmyra. Loc: Mentana (Rome), Federico Zeri Collection. *Funerary. On relief.* DAIR 84.827. Bib: RES 973; Callieri '86, p 239; Vattioni '86, p 247.

1 ṣlmt
2 rwmy ʾtt
3 yrḥy br
4 ʿgnʾ ḥbl
Collated

PAT 0949 **C4588** **n. d.**
Prov: Palmyra. Loc: Louvre, AO 3984. *Funerary. On stele.* Bib: RES 974; PS 515; Lou 193.

1 kwmy
2 br šlmlt
3 ḥbl

PAT 0950 **C4589** **n. d.**
Prov: Palmyra. Loc: Damascus, National Museum, 31. *Funerary. On relief.* Bib: RES 975.

1 ymlʾ br
2 tymlt br
3 ymlkw kwmy

PAT 0951 **C4590** **n. d.**
Prov: Palmyra. Loc: Istanbul Arkeoloji Müzesi, 3824 T? *Funerary. On relief.* Bib: RES 976.

1 ḥbl lšmš
2 br tymlt
3 br ymlkw
4 kwmy

PAT 0952 **C4591** **n. d.**
Prov: Palmyra. Loc: Istanbul Arkeoloji Müzesi, 3824 T. *Funerary. On relief.* Bib: RES 1003; PS 84.

(Between heads of figures)
1 mlkw wyrḥy
2 bny ymlkw
3 br whblt
4 ḥbl
(On table, below)
1 ḥbl mlkw wyrḥy bny ymlkw br
2 whblt ḥbl
Collated 19-24/10/93

PAT 0953 **C4592** **n. d.**
Prov: Palmyra. Loc: Not known. *Funerary. On relief.* Bib: RES 980.

1 ʿzyz br
2 ʾbyḥy
3 mqy

PAT 0954 **C4593** **n. d.**
Prov: Palmyra. Loc: Munich, Glyptotek König Ludwigs I, Gl. 469. *Funerary. On relief.* Bib: RES 1023; PS 345.

1 gbl brt
2 tybwl ḥbl

PAT 0955 **C4594**
Prov: Palmyra. Loc: Not known. *Funerary. On relief.* Bib: RES 981.

(Between figures of woman and child)
1 ʿty brt
2 ʾdynt
3 ḥbl
4 ʾmyʾ
5 brth
(Between figures of woman and child)
1 yrḥy
2 brh

PAT 0956 **C4595** **n. d.**
Prov: Palmyra. Loc: Portland (OR), Portland Art Museum, 54.1. *Funerary. On relief.* Bib: RES 982; Del Chiaro 38, photo p 77 38; Parl '90c 4.

1 pzl br zbdʾ
2 br zbdʾ pzl
3 ḥbl
Degen (Parl '90c): *pwl*; read *pkl* ?

PAT 0957 **C4596** **n. d.**
Prov: Palmyra. Loc: Not known. *Funerary. On relief.* Bib: RES 983.

1 ʿtntn br
2 kyly br
3 mškw b[r]
4 ʿtdt br
5 ḥyrn ḥbl

PAT 0958 **C4597** **n. d.**
Prov: Palmyra. Loc: Not known. *Funerary. On relief.* Bib: RES 985.

1 npš bwrpʾ
2 ʿgʾ zbydʾ
3 mytqʾ

PAT 0959 **C4598** **n. d.**
Prov: Palmyra. Loc: Omaha (NB), Joslyn Art Museum, 1960.266. *Funerary. On relief.* Bib: RES 988.

1 šlmt
2 ʿbdʾ
3 ʿtʿy
4 šydn ʾtt

5 tyrdt yrḥy
6 ḥbl

PAT 0960 **C4599** **n. d.**
Prov: Palmyra. Loc: Not known. *Funerary. On relief.* Bib: RES 989.

1 [ʾ]mt[ʾ]
2 brt
3 [ty]rdt
4 ḥbl

PAT 0961 **C4600** **n. d.**
Prov: Palmyra. Loc: Istanbul Arkeoloji Müzesi, 3820 T. *Funerary. On relief.* Bib: RES 997; PS 109; Ber '38 Pl XLII 3.

1 [ṣl]m
2 whblt
3 br rmy
4 br rpʾl
Collated 19-24/10/93

PAT 0962 **C4601** **n. d.**
Prov: Palmyra. Loc: Istanbul Arkeoloji Müzesi, 3796 T. *Funerary. On relief.* Bib: RES 999; PS 264.

1 ḥbl šmʿwn
2 br zbydʾ
3 mwʾlʾ
Collated 19-24/10/93

PAT 0963 **C4602** **n. d.**
Prov: Palmyra. Loc: Istanbul Arkeoloji Müzesi, 3821 T. *Funerary. On relief.* Bib: RES 1000; PS 190.

1 ymlʾ br
2 yrḥy br
3 ymlʾ
4 ḥbl
Collated 19-24/10/93

PAT 0964 **C4603** **n. d.**
Prov: Palmyra. Loc: Istanbul Arkeoloji Müzesi, 3823 T. *Funerary. On relief.* Bib: RES 1002; PS 259.

1 ydyʿbl
2 br
3 zbdʿth
4 zbdʿth
5 br ydyʿbl
6 ḥbl
Collated 19-24/10/93

PAT 0965 **C4604** **n. d.**
Prov: Palmyra. Loc: Istanbul Arkeoloji Müzesi, n. 3805 T. *Funerary. On relief.* Bib: RES 1005; PS 260.

(By female figure)
1 gtmy
2 brt
3 mʿn
(By figure of youth)
1 mʿn
2 br
3 gtmy
4 brt
5 mʿn
6 ḥbl
Collated 19-24/10/93

PAT 0966 **C4605** **n. d.**
Prov: Palmyra. Loc: Istanbul Arkeoloji Müzesi, 3818 T. *Funerary.* On relief. Bib: RES 1006.

(On right)
1 ʾqmt
2 brt
3 zbdʿth
4 ḥbl
(On left)
5 zbdbwl
6 brh
7 ʿbd lh
Collated 19-24/10/93

PAT 0967 **C4606** **n. d.**

Prov: Palmyra. Loc: Istanbul Arkeoloji Müzesi, 3784 T? *Funerary. On relief.* Bib: RES 1008; PS 352.

1 ʾqmʾ
2 brt
3 mtny br
4 ḥyrn ḥbl

Relief cannot be located.

PAT 0968 **C4607** **n. d.**

Prov: Palmyra. Loc: Louvre, AO 5991. *Funerary. On relief.* Bib: RES 135; PS 245; Lou 213.

(On right)
1 ṣlm
2 [y]rḥy br
3 [yr]ḥy ḥbl
(On tablet in hand of male figure)
4 lyrḥy
5 yrḥy ḥbl

PAT 0969 **C4608** **n. d.**

Prov: Palmyra. Loc: New York, Columbia University? *Funerary. On relief.* Bib: RES 1013.

1 šmʿwn
2 br ḥyrn
3 ḥbl

PAT 0970 **C4609** **n. d.**

Prov: Palmyra. Loc: Not known. *Funerary. On relief.* Bib: RES 1015.

1 ʾmtlt
2 brt
3 ḥyrʾ
4 ḥbl

PAT 0971 **C4610** **n. d.**

Prov: Palmyra. Loc: Damascus, National Museum, 15. *Funerary. On relief.* Bib: RES 1017; PS 300.

1 ḥyrn br bltʾ
2 br ḥyrn ḥbl

PAT 0972 **C4611** **n. d.**

Prov: Palmyra. Loc: Ny Carlsberg Glyptotek, 1043. *Funerary. On relief.*

1 [ḥb]l

PAT 0973 **C4612** **n. d.**

Prov: Palmyra. Loc: Ny Carlsberg Glyptotek, 1036. *Funerary. On relief.* Bib: PS 266; NyCG 71.

1 ḥbl

Rest of text illegible

PAT 0974 **C4613** **n. d.**

Prov: Palmyra. Loc: Qaryatein. *Funerary. On relief.* Bib: IP 4.

1 šlmt brt
2 šrykw
3 ḥbl

PAT 0975 **C4614** **n. d.**

Prov: Palmyra. Loc: Not known. *Funerary. On relief.* Bib: IP 2; PS 360.

1 ḥbl tʿyd
2 wšlmʾ
3 brth

PAT 0976 **C4615** **n. d.**

Prov: Palmyra. Loc: Paris, Nitot Collection. *Funerary. On relief.* Bib: PS 164.

1 mlʾ br
2 ḥnbl
3 ḥbl
4 ḥrʾ
5 ʾmhwn
6 ʾqyḥ
7 ʾḥwhy
8 ḥbl

PAT 0977 **C4616** **A.D. 157**
Prov: Palmyra. Loc: Istanbul Arkeoloji Müzesi, 3840 T. *Funerary. On relief.* Bib: PS 11.

(On right)
1 ḥbl
2 ʿtʿqb
3 br ydyʿbl
4 br ʿtʿqb
5 ydyʿbl
6 ʿqby
(On left)
7 ḥyʾ šnyn
8 40+10+5+1
9 wmyt ywm
10 10+3 bʾyr
11 šnt 4.100
12 +60+5+3
Collated 19-24/10/93

PAT 0978 **C4617** **n. d.**
Prov: Palmyra. Loc: Brussels, Musées Royaux d'Art et d'Histoire, A. 1621. *Funerary. On relief.* Bib: PS 224; Chabot 18b p 290.

1 zbdʿt
2 ʾ br ym
3 lkw nšʾ
4 ḥbl

PAT 0979 **C4618** **n. d.**
Prov: Palmyra. Loc: Not known. *Funerary. On lost object of unknown nature*

1 [Μάλ]ιχος Ἰαριβωλέους τοῦ Βωροφᾶ τοῦ Μαλίχου τοῦ Ὀ[σ]αι[λ]άθου.

1 ṣlmʾ dnh dy ml[kw] br yrḥbwlʾ br bwrpʾ br ml[k]w

PAT 0980 **C4619** **n. d.**
Prov: Palmyra. Loc: Strassburg, University Library. *Funerary. On relief.*

1 [m]l[w]kʾ

PAT 0981 **C4620** **n. d.**
Prov: Palmyra. Loc: Louvre, AO 4148. *Funerary. On relief.* Bib: RES 1637; PS 422; Lou 198.

1 ḥbl
2 twʾl
3 brt
4 tymʾ

PAT 0982 **C4621** **n. d.**
Prov: Palmyra. Loc: Louvre, AO 14925. *Funerary. On relief.* Bib: Lou 218.

1 btʿgʾ
2 brt
3 ḥyrʾ
4 blšwr
5 ḥbl

PAT 0983 **C4622** **n. d.**
Prov: Palmyra. Loc: Istanbul Arkeoloji Müzesi, 3833 T. *Funerary. On relief.* Bib: PS 496.

1 ḥbl
2 ʿtrn
3 brt
4 ymlʾ
Collated 19-24/10/93

PAT 0984 **C4623** **n. d.**
Prov: Palmyra. Loc: Not known. *Funerary. On relief.*

1 ḥbl
2 ḥyrʾ br
3 ḥyrn br
4 ḥyrn br
5 ʿgylw

PAT 0985 **C4624** **n. d.**
Prov: Palmyra. Loc: New York, private collection. *Funerary. On relief.* Bib: Sotheby's, New York, Auction catalog, Jun. 23, '89, sale 5882 no. 24.

1 yrḥy br
2 šlmn

PAT 0986 **CatDam p 123** **n. d.**

Prov: Palmyra, Tomb of Malku. Loc: Damascus, National Museum, 4947 (10941). *Funerary. On sarcophagus.* Group: Tomb of Malku, see Ber ’35 p 91. Bib: al-‘Ush, Joundi, and Zouhdi ’69 p 123.

1 hrms ḥbl

Reading deduced from translation

PAT 0987 **CatMD** 11 **n. d.**

Prov: Palmyra. Loc: Damascus, National Museum, 4522. *Funerary. On relief.* Bib: *Photo.*

1 ḥbl
2 ‘g’
3 br m‘ny
4 br ‘g’

Text from Abdul-Hak’s transcription; photo illegible

PAT 0988 **CatMD** 25 **n. d.**

Prov: Palmyra. Loc: Damascus, National Museum, 8832. *Funerary. On relief.*

1 lšmš br
2 ḥrwṣ

Text from Abdul-Hak’s transcription

PAT 0989 **CatMD** 28 **n. d.**

Prov: Palmyra. Loc: Damascus, National Museum, 5318. *Funerary. On relief.*

1 ḥbl nby brt ’šbr
2 wzbdbwl w’šbr bnyh

Text from Abdul-Hak’s transcription

PAT 0990 **CRAIBL ’32 p 266** **n. d.**

Prov: El-Kantara (Algeria). Loc: El-Kantara?. *Funerary. On stele.*

1	IERHOBO	ʌ//////[..]
2	LES•IEDD	GʌFI[......]
3	EI•MIL•PAL	MII[.......]
4	VIX•AN•XLV	V[.........]

(A)
1 npš’ dh dy
2 yrḥbwl’ ydy
3 ḥbl
(B)
1 npš’ dh dy
2 ‘stwrg’ brh
3 ḥbl

PAT 0991 **CRAIBL ’81 p 306** **n. d.**

Prov: Palmyra, reemployed in Justinian Wall. Loc: Palmyra Museum. *Legal: Rules for a symposium. On stone block.* Bib: *Photo, fig 1.*

1 byrḥ ’dr šnt 3.100+[...]
2 kmry’ dy bl‘str wb‘l[šmn .....]
3 ’nš mnhwn ywm’ dy yhwn sm[ky .... gbr’ dy]
4 mrzḥ dy yh’ bršhwn lmql[wt’ ....]
5 ’l’ gbr dy yhw’ ’ḥyd brš[hwn .....]
6 s<l‘n> 3 ṣry ldhb’ wmn mnhwn[......]
7 b’drwn’ ’w ywšṭ ydh ‘l[...]
8 wmn dy y‘d šbynyhwn yḥw l[..... ....]
9 dy yhw’ ’ḥyd ‘l dhb’ wyhym[n .....]
10 dy hymn bšth w’p ’šrw [dy l]’ yšlṭ ’nš [....]
11 mwm’ b’drwn’ wmn dy ym’ [l]ḥmn yḥwb ḥty’ dd[ynrn ... w’p]
12 ’šrw dy kl gbr mn bny ‘t‘qb dy ygnb mn bt b[l‘str ....]
13 ‘lwhy dy yḥwb ḥṭy’ ddynrn ldhb’ w’ḥr šb‘[.....]
14 yh’ šlyṭ gbr’ dy yg[wr] lmšt’ b’drwn’ ‘d dy[.....]
15 dy hn yḥšḥ ’pr ‘l b[y]t bl wbny ‘t‘qb kmry[’ ...]
16 ’w lmntn lbl‘str md‘n dy ymd lgbr’ dy [mrzḥ .....]
17 ymd mṣ‘t gw’ ‘l [ḥš]bn’ wmd‘n ’ḥrn l’ym[....]
18 lmbqrw wlmw[d‘ mn dy] ḥṭyw wlm‘bd pt[......]
19 ’nš’ dy šn[.....]r/d wmn mn dy ’zl[...]
20 mn mn dy y[....]’ qdmy’ dy b[....]
21 wdy yhw[.....]’ky yn[....]
22 ’‘l[...]
23 hy[...]
24 l[....]

Word-division at various points uncertain, thus line 8, perhaps better *wmn dy y‘d/rš bynyhwn* whoever does X among them

PAT 0992 **CRAIBL '85** **A.D. 63**

Prov: Palmyra, Temple of Arṣu. Loc: Palmyra, 1471/8834. *Dedicatory. On altar.* Bib: *Photo, fig 1.*

1 byrḥ ʾlwl šnt 3.100
2 +20+20+20+10+5 ʿlwtʾ ʾl[n]
3 qrb brʿʾ br mqymw br
4 twry br brʿʾ dy mn bny
5 mtbwl lʾrṣw wlqsmyʾ
6 [w]lbntʾl ʾlhyʾ ṭbyʾ ʿl
7 ḥyy mqymw ʾbwhy wḥywhy
8 wḥyy bnwhy [wḥyy] wʾḥwhy

Line 8 *[wḥyy]*: photo unclear but space seems to demand this or other restoration.

PAT 0993 **Christie's '94** **n.d.**

Prov: Palmyra. Loc: Not known. *Funerary. On relief.* Bib: *Photo*, Christie's, London, Auction catalog, p 56.

1 yrḥbwlʾ
2 br mqy
3 ḥbl
4 ḥgt brt
5 mqymw
6 ʾtth ḥbl

Reading from photo. London, Christie's, Dec. 7, 1994

PAT 0994 **Dacia '70 p 405** **A.D. 158**

Prov: Tibiscum (Rumania). Loc: Not known. *Funerary. On stele.* Bib: Sanie '70a pp 233-41.

1 D(*is*) M(*anibus*)
2 N[E]SES IERHEI [F(*ilius*)]
3 [7$^?$] N(*umeri*) PAL(*myrenorum*) VIXIT
4 [A]N(*nis*) XXV MALCHUS ET IER
5 F(*ratri*) B(*ene*) M(*erenti*) P(*osuerunt*)

1 ʿbd mlkw
2 lnšʾ [....] [ʾ$^?$ḥ$^?$]w$^?$h$^?$
3 šnt 4.100+60+10
4 byrḥ ṭbt

Latin text conjectural at many points

PAT 0995 **DaM '85 p 34** **n. d.**

Prov: Palmyra, W necropolis, Funerary temple 36. Loc: Palmyra, *in situ. Graffito. On niche.* Group: Funerary temple 36, see C4216. Bib: Asʾad and Schmidt-Colinet report interpretation of J. Teixidor in private communication.

1 mš

Mason's mark: Teixidor: *m<n> š<ml>* "to the left, north"

PAT 0996 **DaM '85 p 37** 1 **n. d.**

Prov: Palmyra, near spring Afqa. Loc: Palmyra, A 1415/8423. *Dedicatory. On altar.* Bib: *Pl 13, 1.*

1 bryk šmh lʿlmʾ
2 ṭbʾ wrḥmnʾ
3 mwdʾ blʿqb br
4 ʾbgl br nwrbl

PAT 0997 **DaM '85 p 37** 2 **A.D. 259**

Prov: Palmyra, near spring Afqa. Loc: Palmyra, A 1416/8424. *Dedicatory. On altar.* Bib: *Pl 13, 2.*

1 mwdʾ šʿdw br
2 ṭʿnw lrḥmnʾ
3 ʿl ḥywhy wḥyʾ
4 ʾnšwhy byrḥ
5 ṭbt šnt 5.100
6 +20+20+20+10

PAT 0998 **DaM '85 p 38** 3 **n. d.**

Prov: Palmyra, near spring Afqa. Loc: Palmyra, A 1417/8425. *Dedicatory. On altar.* Bib: *Pl 13, 3.*

1 bryk šmh
2 lʿlmʾ ʿbd
3 wmwdʾ mryʾ
4 kl ywm
5 lrḥmnʾ
6 ṭbʾ

PAT 0999 **DaM '85 p 38** 4 **n. d.**

Prov: Palmyra, near spring Afqa. Loc: Palmyra, A 1415/8426. *Dedicatory. On altar.* Bib: *Pl 13, 4.*

1 lqdm bryk šmh
2 lʿlmʾ ʿbd
3 mlʾ ʿl ḥywhy
4 bṭb

PAT 1000 **DaM '85 p 39** 5 **n. d.**
Prov: Palmyra, near spring Afqa. Loc: Palmyra, A 1419/8427. *Dedicatory. On altar.* Bib: *Pl 13, 5.*

1 bwnʾ br ʿlyšʾ
2 br tymʾ mwdʾ

PAT 1001 **DaM '85 p 39** 6 **A.D. 233**
Prov: Palmyra, near spring Afqa. Loc: Palmyra, A 1420/8428. *Dedicatory. On altar.* Bib: *Pl 13, 6.*

1 bryk šmh lʿlmʾ
2 [ṭ]bʾ wrḥmnʾ ʿbd
3 wmwdʾ yrḥbw[lʾ]
4 br [.]wly [...]ty
5 wšlwm brth ʿl
6 ḥyyhwn byrḥ ʾb
7 šnt 5.100+20+20+4

PAT 1002 **DaM '85 p 39** 7 **A.D. 213**
Prov: Palmyra, near spring Afqa. Loc: Palmyra, A 1422/8423. *Dedicatory. On altar.* Bib: *Pl 14, 7.*

1 bryk šmh lʿlmʾ
2 ṭbʾ wrḥmnʾ ʿbd
3 wmwdʾ šmʿwn br
4 [ʾw]šy ʿl ḥywhy wḥyʾ
5 [ʾ]byhy wʾmh wʾḥwh
6 y byrḥ nysn šnt 5.100
7 +20+4

PAT 1003 **DaM '85 p 40** 8 **n. d.**
Prov: Palmyra, at N. Wall. Loc: Palmyra, A 1474/8842. *Dedicatory. On altar.* Bib: *Pl 14, 8.*

1 ʿbd wmwdʾ ʿbdbl
2 lrḥmnʾ ṭbʾ

PAT 1004 **DaM '85 p 40** 9 **n. d.**
Prov: Palmyra, at N. Wall. Loc: Palmyra, A 1473/8841. *Dedicatory. On altar.* Bib: *Pl 14, 9.*

1 bryk šmh lʿlm[ʾ]
2 ʿbd wmwdʾ šlm[n?/ʾ]
3 br rwmnʾ lḥy[why]
4 [wl]ḥyʾ bnw[hy...]

PAT 1005 **DaM '85 p 40** 10 **A.D. 189**
Prov: Palmyra, at N. Wall. Loc: Palmyra, A 1472/8840. *Dedicatory. On altar.* Bib: *Pl 14, 10.*

1 bryk šmh
2 lʿlmʾ mwdʾ
3 ʾytybl br ʿgʾ
4 br tymrṣw ʿrgn
5 byrḥ ʾb šnt
6 5.100

PAT 1006 **DaM '85 p 40** 11 **A.D. 163**
Prov: Palmyra, at N. Wall. Loc: Palmyra, A 1465/8772. *Dedicatory. On altar.* Bib: *Pl 15, 11.*

1 bryk šmh lʿlmʾ
2 ṭbʾ wrḥmnʾ ʿlt zh
3 ʿbd mhr byrḥ sywn
4 šnt 4.100+20+20+20+10+4

PAT 1007 **DaM '85 p 41** 12 **n. d.**
Prov: Palmyra, at N. Wall. Loc: Palmyra, A 1475/8843. *Funerary. On stele.* Bib: *Pl 15, 12.*

1 ḥgwgʾ
2 ḥbyby
3 bwnʾ
4 ḥbl

PAT 1008 **DaM '85 p 41** 13 **n. d.**
Prov: Palmyra, at N. Wall. Loc: Palmyra, A 1475/8843. *Funerary. On stele.* Bib: *Pl 15, 13.*

1 ḥbl ḥgt
2 brt ʾydʿn
3 br lšmš
4 ʾtt zbdbl

5 br blyḥ

PAT 1009 **DaM '85 p 42** 14 **n. d.**
Prov: Palmyra, at N. Wall. Loc: Palmyra, A 1441/8599. *Dedicatory. On altar.* Bib: *Pl 13, 14.*

1 bwlmʾ
2 ʾtt
3 yrḥbwlʾ
4 br zbdbl
5 blyḥ

PAT 1010 **DaM '85 p 42** 15 **A.D. 183**
Prov: Palmyra, at N. Wall. Loc: Palmyra, A 1454/8654. *Funerary. On stele.* Bib: *Pl 16, 15.*

1 [ʾ]qmʾ
2 brt ʿgylw
3 byrḥ knwn
4 šnt 4.100
5 +20+20+20+20+10+5
6 ḥbl

PAT 1011 **DaM '85 p 42** 16 **n. d.**
Prov: Palmyra, at N. Wall. Loc: Palmyra, A 2471/8710. *Funerary. On stele.* Bib: *Pl 16, 16.*

1 ḥggw br
2 tymrṣw
3 br ḥggw
4 qwzʾ

PAT 1012 **DaM '85 p 43** 17 **n. d.**
Prov: Palmyra, at N. Wall. Loc: Palmyra, A 1453/8646. *Funerary. On stele.* Bib: *Pl 16, 17.*

1 šy[...]
2 bt ʿlm[ʾ]
3 wpylʾ wʾy[.]
4 br gdʾ br[.]
5 ʾ ʿrg[n]
6 lyqr[hn]

PAT 1013 **DaM '85 p 43** 18 **n. d.**
Prov: Palmyra, at N. Wall. Loc: Palmyra, A 1460/8690. *Funerary. On stele.* Bib: *Pl 16, 18.*

[............]
1' gwmḥyʾ dy b[....]
2' ʿsryn wtl<t>ʾ ʿbdw [.]
3' br bl[y] w$^{?}$w$^{?}$h$^{?}$[b]ʾ mlkw [.]
4' yr/d[..] br ʾyt[ybl]

PAT 1014 **DaM '85 p 44** 19 **n. d.**
Prov: Palmyra, at S. Wall. Loc: Palmyra, 38 (?). *Dedicatory. On relief fragment.* Bib: *Pl 16, 19.*

1 mlkw br ʿzyz wʾmn[.]
2 mwdn wbnyhwn[.]

PAT 1015 **DaM '92 2** **n. d.**
Prov: Palmyra, S-E necropolis, hypogeum no. 6. Loc: Palmyra, 1937/7029. *Funerary. On bust.* Group: Hypogeum of Sassan son of Male (cf SFP 44-94). Bib: *Pl 45b*; SFP 45 fig 183.

1 nby brt
2 ʾʿylmy
3 br lšmš
4 ḥbl

Pl and fig seem to show line-division as above :: DaM '92; in this group as a whole line division of SFP is followed

PAT 1016 **DaM '92 3** **n. d.**
Prov: Palmyra, S-E necropolis, hypogeum no. 6. Loc: Palmyra, 1938/7030. *Funerary. On bust.* Group: Hypogeum of Sassan son of Male (cf SFP 44-94). Bib: *Pl 45c*; SFP 46 fig 33; Tanabe '82 pl 304.

Inscription "mutilated" (Saliby DaM '92 :: SFP "anépigraphique")

PAT 1017 **DaM '92 4** **n. d.**
Prov: Palmyra, S-E necropolis, hypogeum no. 6. Loc: Palmyra, 1939/7031. *Funerary. On bust.* Group: Hypogeum of Sassan son of Male (cf SFP 44-94). Bib: *Pl 45d*; SFP 47 fig 69.

1 ḥb[l]

2 m[...]
3 br[...]
4 s[sn]

Text is from SFP p 46; not visible on pl and fig; no inscription mentioned in DaM '92

PAT 1018 **DaM '92 5** **n. d.**
Prov: Palmyra, S-E necropolis, hypogeum no. 6. Loc: Palmyra, 1940/7032. *Funerary. On bust.* Group: Hypogeum of Sassan son of Male (cf SFP 44-94). Bib: *Pl 46a*; SFP 48 fig 147.

1 nby
2 brt
3 blšwry
4 ḥbl

PAT 1019 **DaM '92 6** **n. d.**
Prov: Palmyra, S-E necropolis, hypogeum no. 6. Loc: Palmyra, 1941/7033. *Funerary. On bust.* Group: Hypogeum of Sassan son of Male (cf SFP 44-94). Bib: *Pl 46b*; SFP 49 fig 60.

1 ḥbl
2 ssn
3 br̊
4 ml’
5 r̊b’

PAT 1020 **DaM '92 8** **n. d.**
Prov: Palmyra, S-E necropolis, hypogeum no. 6. Loc: Palmyra, 1943/7035. *Funerary. On bust.* Group: Hypogeum of Sassan son of Male (cf SFP 44-94). Bib: *Pl 46d*; SFP 51 fig 55.

Inscription "mutilated" (Saliby DaM '92 :: SFP "anépigraphique")

PAT 1021 **DaM '92 9** **n. d.**
Prov: Palmyra, S-E necropolis, hypogeum no. 6. Loc: Palmyra, 1944/7036. *Funerary. On bust.* Group: Hypogeum of Sassan son of Male (cf SFP 44-94). Bib: *Pl 47a*; SFP 52 fig 22.

1 ml’ br
2 ssn
4 ḥbl

PAT 1022 **DaM '92 10** **n. d.**
Prov: Palmyra, S-E necropolis, hypogeum no. 6. Loc: Palmyra, 1945/7037. *Funerary. On bust.* Group: Hypogeum of Sassan son of Male (cf SFP 44-94). Bib: *Pl 47b*; SFP 53 fig 51.

1 ḥbl
2 ml’
3 br
4 yrḥbwl’
5 ssn

PAT 1023 **DaM '92 11** **n. d.**
Prov: Palmyra, S-E necropolis, hypogeum no. 6. Loc: Palmyra, 1946/7038. *Funerary. On bust.* Group: Hypogeum of Sassan son of Male (cf SFP 44-94). Bib: *Pl 47c*; SFP 54 fig 52; PGKK no. 16 pp 280 (Parlasca); 296-97 (Gawlikowski).

1 ḥbl
2 ‘ġ’
3 br ssn
4 br ml’

PAT 1024 **DaM '92 12** **n. d.**
Prov: Palmyra, S-E necropolis, hypogeum no. 6. Loc: Palmyra, 1947/7039. *Funerary. On bust.* Group: Hypogeum of Sassan son of Male (cf SFP 44-94). Bib: *Pl 47d*; SFP 55 fig 168.

1 ḥbl
2 ḥly
3 brt
4 yml’

PAT 1025 **DaM '92 13** **A.D. 181**
Prov: Palmyra, S-E necropolis, hypogeum no. 6. Loc: Palmyra, 1948/7040. *Funerary. On bust.* Group: Hypogeum of Sassan son of Male (cf SFP 44-94). Bib: *Pl 48a*; SFP 56 fig 99.

1 zbd’ br
2 zbdbwl
3 br ssn ḥbl

4 mplwn br
5 zbdbwl br ssn
6 ḥbl šnt 4.100+
7 80+10+3

PAT 1026 **DaM '92 14** **n. d.**

Prov: Palmyra, S-E necropolis, hypogeum no. 6. Loc: Palmyra, 1949/7041. *Funerary. On bust.* Group: Hypogeum of Sassan son of Male (cf SFP 44-94). Bib: *Pl 48b*; SFP 57 fig 53; Tanabe '82 pl 295.

(Over shoulder of father)
1 ḥbl
2 yrḥbwl'
3 br ssn
(Over shoulder of son, small figure)
4 ḥbl
5 yrḥy
6 brh

Inscription with figure of son from Tanabe '82; text in Saliby DaM '92 very confused

PAT 1027 **DaM '92 15** **n. d.**

Prov: Palmyra, S-E necropolis, hypogeum no. 6. Loc: Palmyra, 1950/7042. *Funerary. On bust.* Group: Hypogeum of Sassan son of Male (cf SFP 44-94). Bib: *Pl 48c*; SFP 58 fig 75; Tanabe '82 pl 296.

1 ḥbl
2 ml' br
3 'g' br
4 ssn

PAT 1028 **DaM '92 16** **n. d.**

Prov: Palmyra, S-E necropolis, hypogeum no. 6. Loc: Palmyra, 1951/7043. *Funerary. On bust.* Group: Hypogeum of Sassan son of Male (cf SFP 44-94). Bib: *Pl 48d*; SFP 59 fig 114.

1 mplwn
2 br 'g'
3 ssn
4 ḥbl

PAT 1029 **DaM '92 17** **n. d.**

Prov: Palmyra, S-E necropolis, hypogeum no. 6. Loc: Palmyra, 1952/7044. *Funerary. On bust.* Group: Hypogeum of Sassan son of Male (cf SFP 44-94). Bib: *Pl 49a*; SFP 60 fig 87.

1 'g' br
2 blšwry
3 ssn ḥbl

PAT 1030 **DaM '92 18** **n. d.**

Prov: Palmyra, S-E necropolis, hypogeum no. 6. Loc: Palmyra, 1953/7045. *Funerary. On bust.* Group: Hypogeum of Sassan son of Male (cf SFP 44-94). Bib: *Pl 49b*; SFP 61 fig 165.

1 nby brt
2 'g' ssn
3 ḥbl

PAT 1031 **DaM '92 19** **n. d.**

Prov: Palmyra, S-E necropolis, hypogeum no. 6. Loc: Palmyra, 1954/7046. *Funerary. On bust.* Group: Hypogeum of Sassan son of Male (cf SFP 44-94). Bib: *Pl 49c*; SFP 62 fig 164.

1 ḥbl
2 mlkt
3 brt 'g'
4 br ssn

PAT 1032 **DaM '92 21** **n. d.**

Prov: Palmyra, S-E necropolis, hypogeum no. 6. Loc: Palmyra, 1956/7048. *Funerary. On bust.* Group: Hypogeum of Sassan son of Male (cf SFP 44-94). Bib: *Pl 50a*; SFP 64 fig 101.

1 ssn
2 br
3 yrḥbwl'
4 ḥbl

PAT 1033 **DaM '92 22** **n. d.**

Prov: Palmyra, S-E necropolis, hypogeum no. 6. Loc: Palmyra, 1957/7049. *Funerary. On bust.* Group: Hypogeum of Sassan son of Male (cf SFP

44-94). Bib: *Pl 50b*; SFP 65 fig 169.

1 nby
2 brt
3 yrḥbwlʾ
4 ḥbl

PAT 1034 **DaM '92 23** **n. d.**
Prov: Palmyra, S-E necropolis, hypogeum no. 6. Loc: Palmyra, 1958/7050. *Funerary. On bust.* Group: Hypogeum of Sassan son of Male (cf SFP 44-94). Bib: *Pl 50c*; SFP 66 fig 170.

1 ḥbl
2 ʾmtʾ
3 brt
4 ssn
5 šmʾ
6 brth

PAT 1035 **DaM '92 24** **n. d.**
Prov: Palmyra, S-E necropolis, hypogeum no. 6. Loc: Palmyra, 1959/7051. *Funerary. On bust.* Group: Hypogeum of Sassan son of Male (cf SFP 44-94). Bib: *Pl 50d*; SFP 67 fig 24.

1 brwqʾ
2 br ʿgʾ
3 br mlʾ
4 ḥbl

PAT 1036 **DaM '92 25** **n. d.**
Prov: Palmyra, S-E necropolis, hypogeum no. 6. Loc: Palmyra, 1960/7052. *Funerary. On bust.* Group: Hypogeum of Sassan son of Male (cf SFP 44-94). Bib: *Pl 51a*; SFP 68 fig 67.

1 ḥbl bryky
2 br brw[qʾ]

PAT 1037 **DaM '92 26** **n. d.**
Prov: Palmyra, S-E necropolis, hypogeum no. 6. Loc: Palmyra, 1961/7053. *Funerary. On bust.* Group: Hypogeum of Sassan son of Male (cf SFP 44-94). Bib: *Pl 51b*; SFP 69 fig 56; Tanabe '82 pl 402.

(On right)
1 ḥbl
2 ḥlptʾ
3 brwqʾ
(On left)
4 ḥbl
5 zbdlʾ
6 brwqʾ
(Below figures)
7 ḥbl zbdʾ ḥlptʾ

PAT 1038 **DaM '92 27** **n. d.**
Prov: Palmyra, S-E necropolis, hypogeum no. 6. Loc: Palmyra, 1962/7054. *Funerary. On bust.* Group: Hypogeum of Sassan son of Male (cf SFP 44-94). Bib: *Pl 51c*; SFP 70 fig 102.

1 mqymw
2 br
3 ʿgʾ
4 mqymw
5 ḥbl

PAT 1039 **DaM '92 28** **n. d.**
Prov: Palmyra, S-E necropolis, hypogeum no. 6. Loc: Palmyra, 1963/7055. *Funerary. On bust.* Group: Hypogeum of Sassan son of Male (cf SFP 44-94). Bib: *Pl 51d*; SFP 71 fig 184.

1 ʾmtʾ
2 brt
3 mlkʾl
4 mqymw
5 ḥbl

PAT 1040 **DaM '92 30** **n. d.**
Prov: Palmyra, S-E necropolis, hypogeum no. 6. Loc: Palmyra, 1965/7057. *Funerary. On bust.* Group: Hypogeum of Sassan son of Male (cf SFP 44-94). Bib: *Pl 52b*; SFP 73 fig 146.

1 [ḥbl]
2 [ʾmtʾ]
3 [brt]
4 [m]lkw
5 [ʾ]tt
6 [blš]wry

7 [br] ssn

Broken inscription, text given as visible from photo. In lacunae complete text as given by DaM '92 and SFP

PAT 1041 **DaM '92 31** **n. d.**

Prov: Palmyra, S-E necropolis, hypogeum no. 6. Loc: Palmyra, 1966/7058. *Funerary. On bust.* Group: Hypogeum of Sassan son of Male (cf SFP 44-94). Bib: *Pl 52c*; SFP 74 fig 144.

(On left)
1 ḥbl
2 ʾqmʾ
3 brt
4 sygʾ
(On right)
5 brt
6 blš
7 wry

line 2 ʾqmʾ! :: DaM '92 and SFP tmʾ

PAT 1042 **DaM '92 32** **n. d.**

Prov: Palmyra, S-E necropolis, hypogeum no. 6. Loc: Palmyra, 1967/7059. *Funerary. On bust.* Group: Hypogeum of Sassan son of Male (cf SFP 44-94). Bib: *Pl 52d*; SFP 75 fig 103; Tanabe '82 pl 369.

(With male figure)
1 ḥbl
2 mlʾ br brqʾ
3 br ʿgʾ ssn
(With female figure)
4 ḥbl
5 mlptʾ
6 bt brqʾ
7 ʿgʾ
8 ssn

Lines 2, 6 brqʾ from pl and fig; DaM '92 and SFP: brmʾ

PAT 1043 **DaM '92 33** **n. d.**

Prov: Palmyra, S-E necropolis, hypogeum no. 6. Loc: Palmyra, 1968/7060. *Funerary. On bust.* Group: Hypogeum of Sassan son of Male (cf SFP 44-94). Bib: *Pl 53a*; SFP 76 fig 131.

1 ʾqmt
2 brt brwq[ʾ]
3 br tymšʾ
4 ʾtt blšwry
5 br mṭy rbʾ
6 ḥbl

PAT 1044 **DaM '92 34** **n. d.**

Prov: Palmyra, S-E necropolis, hypogeum no. 6. Loc: Palmyra, 1969/7061. *Funerary. On bust.* Group: Hypogeum of Sassan son of Male (cf SFP 44-94). Bib: *Pl 53b*; SFP 77 fig 145.

(On left)
1 ḥbl
2 šlmt
3 brt
4 mlk[w]
5 mṭy
6 ḥbl
(On right)
7 šlm[t]
8 ʾtt
9 tymʿ
10 md
11 br
12 zbydʾ

PAT 1045 **DaM '92 35** **n. d.**

Prov: Palmyra, S-E necropolis, hypogeum no. 6. Loc: Palmyra, 1970/7062. *Funerary. On stele.* Group: Hypogeum of Sassan son of Male (cf SFP 44-94). Bib: *Pl 53d, 58c*; SFP 78 fig 10.

1 mlkw br
2 tymʿmd
3 ḥbl

PAT 1046 **DaM '92 36** **n. d.**

Prov: Palmyra, S-E necropolis, hypogeum no. 6. Loc: Palmyra, 1971/7063. *Funerary. On stele.* Group: Hypogeum of Sassan son of Male (cf SFP 44-94). Bib: *Pl 53d, 58c*; SFP 79 fig 8.

1 ḥbl
2 brwqʾ
3 br

4 mṭy br
5 blš
6 wry

line 4: mṭy; Dam '92, SFP mty

PAT 1047 **DaM '92 37** **n. d.**

Prov: Palmyra, S-E necropolis, hypogeum no. 6. Loc: Palmyra, 1972/7064. *Funerary. On bust.* Group: Hypogeum of Sassan son of Male (cf SFP 44-94). Bib: *Pl 54a, 58c*; SFP 80 fig 20; Tanabe '82 pl 368.

1 ḥbl
2 mlkw br
3 mṭy
4 wʾbrnyq
5 brt rbʾl
6 ʾtt<h> ḥbl

line 4: wʾbrnyq! "and Berenice" :: DaM '92, SFP wʾ brnym; cf DaM '92 41:1 below. Line 6: SFP has wrong layout, cf photo

PAT 1048 **DaM '92 38** **n. d.**

Prov: Palmyra, S-E necropolis, hypogeum no. 6. Loc: Palmyra, 1973/7065. *Funerary. On bust.* Group: Hypogeum of Sassan son of Male (cf SFP 44-94). Bib: *Pl 54b, 58c*; SFP 81 fig 9.

1 zbydʾ
2 br ty
3 mʿm
4 dw zby
5 dʾ
6 ḥbl

lines 2-4: tymʿmdw! :: DaM '92, SFP tymʿmd

PAT 1049 **DaM '92 39** **n. d.**

Prov: Palmyra, S-E necropolis, hypogeum no. 6. Loc: Palmyra, 1974/7066. *Funerary. On stele.* Group: Hypogeum of Sassan son of Male (cf SFP 44-94). Bib: *Pl 54c*; SFP 82 fig 14; Tanabe '82 pl 265; PGKK '87 no. 19 p 299.

1 khylw
2 br mlʾ
3 khylw
4 ḥbl

Lines 1, 3 khylw: or khyly, w and y practically identical, distinct only perhaps in line 3; see DaM '92, SFP :: Gawlikowski PGKK p 299

PAT 1050 **DaM '92 40** **n. d.**

Prov: Palmyra, S-E necropolis, hypogeum no. 6. Loc: Palmyra, 1975/7067. *Funerary. On bust.* Group: Hypogeum of Sassan son of Male (cf SFP 44-94). Bib: *Pl 54d*; SFP 83 fig 23.

1 ḥbl
2 yrḥy
3 br ʿgʾ
4 ʾʾrg

line 4: DaM '92, SFP ʿʿrg

PAT 1051 **DaM '92 41** **n. d.**

Prov: Palmyra, S-E necropolis, hypogeum no. 6. Loc: Palmyra, 1976/7068. *Funerary. On bust.* Group: Hypogeum of Sassan son of Male (cf SFP 44-94). Bib: *Pl 55a*; SFP 84 fig 179; Tanabe '82 pl 344.

1 ʾbrnyq
2 brt
3 ssn
4 br
5 bwrpʾ
6 ḥbl
7 dy ʿbd
8 lh
9 bwlmʾ
10 brh

line 1: q of ʾbrnyq (see above no. 38) above line; DaM '92, SFP brnym; line 9: ʾ below line

PAT 1052 **DaM '92 42** **n. d.**

Prov: Palmyra, S-E necropolis, hypogeum no. 6. Loc: Palmyra, 1977/7069. *Funerary. On bust.* Group: Hypogeum of Sassan son of Male (cf SFP 44-94). Bib: *Pl 55b*; SFP 85 fig 66; Tanabe '82 pl 297.

1 ssn br
2 bwrpʾ
3 ḥbl

PAT 1053 **DaM '92 43** **n. d.**
Prov: Palmyra, S-E necropolis, hypogeum no. 6. Loc: Palmyra, 1978/7070. *Funerary. On bust.* Group: Hypogeum of Sassan son of Male (cf SFP 44-94). Bib: *Pl 55c*; SFP 86 fig 68; Tanabe '82 pl 302.

1 ḥbl bwrpʾ
2 br ssn br
3 bwrpʾ

PAT 1054 **DaM '92 44** **n. d.**
Prov: Palmyra, S-E necropolis, hypogeum no. 6. Loc: Palmyra, 1979/7071. *Funerary. On bust.* Group: Hypogeum of Sassan son of Male (cf SFP 44-94). Bib: *Pl 55d*; SFP 87 fig 74.

1 mqymw
2 br
3 šsn
4 ḥbl
line 3: SFP šsn "sic!"; photographs confirm reading

PAT 1055 **DaM '92 45** **n. d.**
Prov: Palmyra, S-E necropolis, hypogeum no. 6. Loc: Palmyra, 1980/7072. *Funerary. On bust.* Group: Hypogeum of Sassan son of Male (cf SFP 44-94). Bib: *Pl 56a*; SFP 88 fig 76.

1 [...]ʾ
2 br ssn
3 br bwrpʾ
4 ḥbl
line 2 ssn: clear on pl; DaM '92, SFP ssʾ

PAT 1056 **DaM '92 46** **n. d.**
Prov: Palmyra, S-E necropolis, hypogeum no. 6. Loc: Palmyra, 1981/7073. *Funerary. On bust.* Group: Hypogeum of Sassan son of Male (cf SFP 44-94). Bib: *Pl 56b*; SFP 89 fig 54; Tanabe '82 pl 301.

1 ḥbl
2 pṣyʾl
3 br bwlmʾ
4 br mqy

PAT 1057 **DaM '92 47** **n. d.**
Prov: Palmyra, S-E necropolis, hypogeum no. 6. Loc: Palmyra, 1982/7074. *Funerary. On bust.* Group: Hypogeum of Sassan son of Male (cf SFP 44-94). Bib: *Pl 56c*; SFP 90 fig 100; Tanabe '82 pl 299.

1 zbydʾ
2 br
3 zbydʾ
4 lšmš
5 ḥbl

PAT 1058 **DaM '92 48** **n. d.**
Prov: Palmyra, S-E necropolis, hypogeum no. 6. Loc: Palmyra, 1983/7075. *Funerary. On bust.* Group: Hypogeum of Sassan son of Male (cf SFP 44-94). Bib: *Pl 56d*; SFP 91 fig 156; Tanabe '82 pl 354.

1 bylt
2 brt
3 ʾlhbl
4 ḥbl
5 [.]ḥr?
line 5: reading very uncertain

PAT 1059 **DaM '92 49** **n. d.**
Prov: Palmyra, S-E necropolis, hypogeum no. 6. Loc: Palmyra, 1984/7076. *Funerary. On stele.* Group: Hypogeum of Sassan son of Male (cf SFP 44-94). Bib: *Pl 57a*; SFP 92 fig 18; Tanabe '82 pl 264.

1 nwrbl
2 br brnbw
3 ḥbl

PAT 1060 **DaM '92 50** **n. d.**
Prov: Palmyra, S-E necropolis, hypogeum no. 6. Loc: Palmyra, 1985/7077. *Funerary. On bust.* Group: Hypogeum of Sassan son of Male (cf SFP 44-94). Bib: *Pl 57b*; SFP 93 fig 166.

1 mrʾ
2 brt
3 brʿtʾ

4 ḥbl

PAT 1061 **DaM '92 51** **n. d.**
Prov: Palmyra, S-E necropolis, hypogeum no. 6. Loc: Palmyra, 1986/7078. *Funerary. On bust.* Group: Hypogeum of Sassan son of Male (cf SFP 44-94). Bib: *Pl 57c*; SFP 94 fig 17; Tanabe '82 pl 271.

1 ḥbybtʾ
2 brt mqy
3 br nwrbl
4 ḥbl

PAT 1062 **Déd p 13** **A.D. 145**
Prov: Palmyrene: Umm el-ʿAmad, 22 km. from Palmyra. Loc: Umm el-ʿAmad, *in situ. Honorific. On column drum.* Poidebard '34 p 107 and Pls. 101 (photo), 102 (squeeze); Mouterde et Poidebard '31 pp 101-115 for Greek.

1 Ἔτο[υς ...]
2 ἡ βουλὴ [κ]αὶ ὁ δῆμος [Σόαδ]ον Βωλιάδους
3 τοῦ Σ[ο]άδου τοῦ Θαιμισάμσου, εὐσεβῆ καὶ
4 φθιλόπατριν, καὶ ἐν πολλοῖς καὶ μεγάλοις καιροῖς
5 γν[η]σίως καὶ φιλοτείμως παραστάντα τοῖς
6 ἐ[μπόρ]οις καὶ ταῖς συνοδίαις καὶ τοῖς ἐν Ὀλογασιάδι
7 πολείταις, καὶ επὶ τούτοις [ἐπισ]τολ[ᾳ̣] θεοῦ
8 [Ἁ]δριανοῦ καὶ τοῦ θειοτάτου α[ὐ]τοκράτορος
9 Ἀντωνεινοῦ υἱοῦ αὐτοῦ μαρτυρεθέντα,
10 ὁμοίως καὶ διατάγματι Ποβλικίου Μαρκέλλου
11 καὶ ἐπιστολᾳ̣ αὐτοῦ καὶ τῶν ἑξῆς ὑπατικῶν,
12 καὶ ψηφίσμασι καὶ ἀνδριᾶσι τειμηθέντα ὑπὸ
13 βουλῆς καὶ δήμου καὶ τῶν κατὰ καιρὸν συν-
14 οδιῶν καὶ τῶν καθ'ἕνα πολειτῶν, καὶ νῦν τοῦτον
15 πατρίδος διὰ τὰς συνεχεῖς καὶ ἐπ' ἀλ[λ]ήλους
16 εὐποίας τεσσάρων ἀνδριάντων ἐν τῷ
17 τετραδείῳ τῆς πόλεος ἐπὶ κειόνων δημοσίοις
18 ἀναλώμασι κατηξιωμένον, καὶ ἄλλων
20 ἀνδριάντων τριῶν ἕν τε Σαπασίνου Χάρακι
21 [κα]ὶ ἐν Ὀλ[ο]γασιά[δι] καὶ ἐ[ν] Γεννάη καταλύματι συν-
22 <συν>οδιῶν ὑπὸ β[ουλ]ῆς καὶ δήμου. καὶ κτίσαντα
23 [ἐ]ν Ὀλογα[σιάδι ναὸν τῶν Σε]βαστῶν κ[αὶ] κ[α]θι-
24 [ερώ]σαν[τα ...]

B

1 [καὶ (?) πίστε]ω[ς (?) κ]αὶ μεγαλοφ[ρ]οσύνης ἕ[νεκα] (?)
2 πά[νυ (?) πᾶσα]ν ἐνχειρισθέντα δυναστείαν
3 [. . . . . .]στωτο[. . . . .]ειρω
4 [. . . . . .]σ στασι[. . . .]

1 [byrḥ . . .] šn[t] 4.100+40+10+5+2
2 b[wl]ʾ wdms [l]šʿdw br [bl]ydʿ br šʿd[w]
3 tymšmš dḥl ʾl[hyʾ wrḥym] mdynth wbzb[nyn]
4 šgyʾn wrbrbn ... yb.[........] nhw[ryt]
5 [....] tgryʾ wšy[rt]ʾ wb[ny mdyn]th d[y]
6 [bʾlgšyʾ ....]
7 [..............................]
8 [..........] ... [...............]
9 whgmnyn dy bʾ[trh ....]
10 wbdgmyn wyqryn wṣ[l]myn [........]
11 [l]šyryn [bkl ṣb]w klh
12 [..............................]
13 [..............................]
14 [..............................]
15 [ʾḥ]d ṣlm [bkrkʾ dy myšn wʾḥd ṣlm]
16 bʾlg[šy ....]
17 bwlʾ wdms dm[h l]ʾqmw[...........]
18 [...]. yhk [....................]
19 mn bny šyr[tʾ ....]

PAT 1063 **Déd p 36** **A.D. 198**
Prov: Palmyra. Loc: Palmyra, A 11. *Honorific. On stone tablet.* Bib: *Déd pl III, 1 and 2*; Ing '32a p 279 Greek text.

[...................]
[...................]
[...................]
1' εἰρηνης κατασταθέντα ὑπό τε
2' Μανειλίου Φούσκου καὶ Οὐενιδίου
3' Ῥούφου ὑπατικῶν καὶ ὑπό τῆς πα-
4' τρίδος καὶ πολλὴν σπουδὴν καὶ ἀνδρεί-

5' αν ἐνδειξάμενον καὶ στρατηγήσαντα
6' πλειστάκις καὶ τὴν αὐτὴν ἀνδρείαν
7' καὶ ἀρετὴν σώσαντα καὶ ἐπ' οὕτοις (sic) μαρ-
8' τυρηθέντα ὑπό τε Ἰαριβώλου τοῦ πατ-
9' ρίου θεοῦ καὶ τῶν ἡγησαμένων καὶ ὑπὸ
10' τῆς πατρίδος ψηφίσμασι, ἐφ' οἷς ἀμειβομέ-
11' νη αὐτὸν ἡ πατρίς τὰς πρέπουσας αὐτῷ
12' τειμὰς ἐψηφίσατο ἔφιππον ἀνδριάντα καὶ
13' αἱ τέσσαρες φυλαὶ ἐν ἰδίοις ἱεροῖς ἐξ ἰδίων
14' ἀνδριάντας τέσσαρες, ὧν τοῦτον Χωνει-
15' τῶν φυλή, ἀρετῆς καὶ ἀνδρείας ἕνεκεν. ἔτ-
16' ους ΘΦ Περειτίου ΚΕ

1 mn twḥyt bwlʾ wdms ṣlmʾ dnh dy ʾlys
2 bwrʾ br ṭyṭs ʾlys ʿgylw ʾsṭrṭgʾ dy
3 ʿbd šlmʾ btḥwmy mdytʾ wlʾ ʾḥ[y]s npšh
4 ʿl mdyth dy ʾqymw lh bny kmrʾ nwyt šʾwr
5 pḥzʾ bt ʾlhyhwn lyqrh byrḥ šbṭ šnt 509

PAT 1064 **Déd p 43** = PS 498
Prov: Palmyra. Loc: Rome, Museo Barracco di scultura antica, 249. *Funerary. On relief.* Bib: PS 498.

1 ḥbʾ
2 brt
3 ʿgʾ
4 ʾtt
5 nšʾ
6 ʾmwn
collated

PAT 1065 **Déd p 43** = PS 467
Prov: Palmyra. Loc: Rome, Museo Barracco di scultura antica, 206. *Funerary. On relief.* Bib: PS 467.

1 [...]ʾ
2 [br]t
3 mhr
4 ʿnzʾ
collated

PAT 1066 **Déd p 217** **A.D. 204**
Prov: Palmyra. Loc: Paris, Institut Catholique, Musée Bible et Terre Sainte. *Honorific. On stone tablet.* Bib: *Pl VIII*, 2.

1 [ʾln ʾ]nšyʾ dy ḥdt bt ʾlh?[ʾ]
2 [dnh z]bdbl mqymw wr/dbḥ/ṣ
3 [ ]r/dh šlmn ʾbʾ
4 [lbl] yrḥbwl ʿglbwl
5 [byrḥ] sywn
6 šnt 5.100+10+5

PAT 1067 **Doura 1** **32 B.C.**
Prov: Dura Europos, necropolis. Loc: . *Dedicatory. On stone slab.*

1 byrḥ sywn šnt
2 2.100 +60+10+5+4 hw zbdbwl
3 br bʿyḥw dy mn bny
4 gdybwl wmlkw br
5 rmw dy mn bny kmrʾ
6 ʿbdw hyklʾ lbl
7 wyrḥbwl

PAT 1068 **Doura 2** **n. d.**
Prov: Dura Europos, necropolis, tomb XII. Loc: . *Unclassified. On vase.*

1 kn[...] gdʾ br [...]
2 bl wʾrṣʾ

PAT 1069 **Doura 3** **n. d.**
Prov: Dura Europos, Palmyra Gate. Loc: Dura Europos, *in situ*. *Graffito. On Wall.*

1 ʿwydy

PAT 1070 **Doura 4** **n. d.**
Prov: Dura Europos, Palmyra Gate. Loc: Dura Europos, *in situ*. *Graffito. On wall.*

1 ʿwydy

PAT 1071 **Doura 5** **n. d.**
Prov: Dura Europos, Palmyra Gate, Tower 15. Loc: Dura Europos, *in situ*. *Graffito. On wall.*

1 ʿwydy

2 br tymy
3 ʾyth

PAT 1072 **Doura 6** **n. d.**
Prov: Dura Europos, between Palmyra Gate and Tower 18. Loc: Dura Europos, *in situ*. *Graffito*. *On wall.*

1 ʿwydy

PAT 1073 **Doura 7** **n. d.**
Prov: Dura Europos, Wall. Loc: Dura Europos, *in situ*. *Graffito*. *On wall.*

1 bny

PAT 1074 **Doura 8** **n. d.**
Prov: Dura Europos, rampart, tower 2. Loc: Dura Europos, *in situ*. *Graffito*. *On wall.*

1 bny
2 ʾtm[.]
3 škm

PAT 1075 **Doura 9** **n. d.**
Prov: Dura Europos, rampart, tower 2. Loc: Dura Europos, *in situ*. *Unclassified*. *On wall.*

1 mqymw
2 br ḥy[m]

PAT 1076 **Doura 10** **n. d.**
Prov: Dura Europos, rampart, inside tower 2. Loc: Dura Europos, *in situ*. *Graffito*. *On wall.*

1 mqymw
2 [.]qṭn
3 [..]

PAT 1077 **Doura 11** **n. d.**
Prov: Dura Europos, rampart, inside tower 2. Loc: Dura Europos, *in situ*. *Graffito*. *On wall.*

1 mqymw

PAT 1078 **Doura 12** **A.D. 244**
Prov: Dura Europos, Palmyra Gate. Loc: New Haven (CT), Yale University Art Gallery, 1938.5312. *Dedicatory*. *On stele.* Bib: Downey '77 9.

1 Θεᾷ Νεμέσι Ιούλιος Αὐρήλιος Μαλωχὰς
2 Σουδαίου Παλμυρηνὸς ἀνέθηκεν

1 ʿbd wmwdʾ mlwkʾ br šwdy tdmryʾ lnmsys
2 šnt 5.100+40+10+5+1
Collated. Line 3: added to date +10+5+1

PAT 1079 **Doura 13** **n. d.**
Prov: Dura Europos, Palmyra Gate. Loc: . *Dedicatory*. *On altar.*

1 ʿbd
2 mqymw
3 br
4 yrḥbwlʾ
5 lgdʾ

PAT 1080 **Doura 14** **n. d.**
Prov: Dura Europos, Palmyra Gate. Loc: . *Dedicatory*. *On stele.*

1 [.....]
2 br
3 zbdʿth
4 br bbʾ

PAT 1081 **Doura 15** **n. d.**
Prov: Dura Europos, Temple of Palmyrene Gods. Loc: Dura Europos, *in situ*. *Dedicatory*. *On column.*

1 dkyr mlkw br whblt
2 qdm yrḥbwl w[....]
3 wrṣʾ wʿbd d[...]
4 ṭb wskrʾ lh[wn]
5 bknn ktb

PAT 1082 **Doura 16** **n. d.**
Prov: Dura Europos, Temple of Palmyrene Gods. Loc: Dura Europos, *in situ. Unclassified. On column.*

1 [...] br bbʾ br
On same column where text Dura 15 is.

PAT 1083 **Doura 17** **n. d.**
Prov: Dura Europos, Temple of Palmyrene Gods, *pronaos*. Loc: Dura Europos, *in situ. Graffito. On wall.*

1 tymrṣw ḥrtʾ
2 tymʾ

PAT 1084 **Doura 18** **n. d.**
Prov: Dura Europos, Temple of Palmyrene Gods, *pronaos*, N wall. Loc: Dura Europos, *in situ. Graffito. On wall.*

1 ywm 10+1 [....]
2 [....] 10
3 ywm 10+3 [...] 2 dkrn
4 [....] 10+5+1 [.......]
5 ywm 10+5+4 [......] 5+1 [....]
6 ywm [.....]
7 [.....] 10+1
8 [.....]

PAT 1085 **Doura 19** **A.D. 168**
Prov: Dura Europos, Temple of Palmyrene Gods, *naos* (Mithraeum). Loc: New Haven (CT), Yale University Art Gallery, 1935.97. *Dedicatory. On wall.* Bib: Downey '77 7; ScPart 172 fig 52.

1 Θεᾷ Νεμέσι Ἰούλιος Αὐρήλιος Μαλωχᾶς
2 Σουδαίου Παλμυρηνὸς εὐξάμενος ἀνέθηκεν

1 dkrn ṭb ʿbd ʾtpny ʾsṭr[ṭg]ʾ
2 br zbdʿʾ dy ʿl qšṭʾ dy bdwrʾ
3 byrḥ ʾdr šnt 4.100+80
Collated. Line 2: dy! ʿl qšṭʾ

PAT 1086 **Doura 20** **n. d.**
Prov: Dura Europos, Wall Street, near tower 18. Loc: Damascus, National Museum, 10948. *Dedicatory. On stele.* Bib: Déd p 342; Downey '77 45; ScPart 181 fig 59.

1 dkrn ṭb lʾšrw wšʿd
2 gnyʾ ʿbd bnyšm mṭʾ

PAT 1087 **Doura 21** **n. d.**
Prov: Dura Europos, *insula* L 7, section W 28. Loc: . *Dedicatory. On stele fragment.* Bib: Déd p 342.

1 dkrn ṭb
2 lʾšr
3 [..]ʿ[..]

PAT 1088 **Doura 22** **n. d.**
Prov: Dura Europos, Temple of Adonis. Loc: . *Graffito. On plaster fragment.*

1 dkyr [.....]
2 br bz[..]

PAT 1089 **Doura 23** **A.D. 31**
Prov: Dura Europos, Temple of Zeus Kyrios-Baalshamîn. Loc: New Haven (CT), Yale University Art Gallery, 1935.45. *Dedicatory. On relief.* Bib: Downey '77 10.

1 Σέλευκος Λευκίου ἐδώρησ
2 α τό[ν] ἀνδριάντα [τ]ῷ Δεῖ κυρ
3 ίῳ καὶ Ἀβαβοῦις υἱός αὐτοῦ
4 ἔτους γμτ' μηνὸς Ἀπελλ
5 αίου. μνησθῇ Ἰαραῖος .[.]ΛΑΦΤΕΣ

1 byr[ḥ] tšry šnt 3.100+40+3
2 mṣbʾ dnh nṣb b[..]th br
3 lwqy wʾbbwhy brh
4 lbʿlšmyn ʾlhʾ
Collated. Greek, line 5: "Last word presents difficulties." Various conjectures involving an odd form of Gk 'sculptor' *glyptēs* have been offered by Torrey and Downey. Perhaps a form of the Palmyrene PN ḥlptʾ ? Palmyrene, line 4: lbʿlšmyn!

PAT 1090 **Doura 24** **n. d.**
Prov: Dura Europos, "Banquet Fresco" House, S wall. Loc: . *Graffito. On wall.*

(With figure of archer)
1 b[w]lḥzy
(Below horse's belly)
2 hr̊[...]

PAT 1091 **Doura 25** **A.D. 194**
Prov: Dura Europos, "Banquet Fresco" House, S wall. Loc: . *Honorific. On wall.*

1 dkyryn wbrykyn
2 ʾnšyʾ dṣyry[n]
3 tnn qdm bl wyrḥbwl
4 wʿglbwl wʾrṣw
5 [w]dkyryn ʾlhšmš
6 br ṣlt wtʾ[m]ʾ bnyh
7 dy ṣrw ṣwrtʾ hd[ʾ]
8 bṭb[t] šnt 5.100+5

PAT 1092 **Doura 26** **n. d.**
Prov: Dura Europos, "Banquet Fresco" House, W wall. Loc: . *Graffito. On wall.*

1 tmlʾ
2 ʾhryʾ
3 btʾ

PAT 1093 **Doura 27** **n. d.**
Prov: Dura Europos, "Banquet Fresco" House. Loc: . *Graffito. On wall.*

1 brʿtʾ
2 ʾbyhn
3 mlkw
4 gdʾ/grʾ
5 bʿly

PAT 1094 **Doura 28** **A.D. 159**
Prov: Dura Europos, *Naos* 3, Temple of Gaddé. Loc: New Haven (CT), Yale University Art Gallery, 1938.5314. *Dedicatory. On relief.* Group: Doura 28-30. Bib: Downey '77 4.

(On center)
1 gdʾ dy dwrʾ ʿbd ḥyrn br
2 mlkw br nṣwr byrḥ nysn
3 šnt 4.100+60+10
Collated

PAT 1095 **Doura 29** **n. d.**
Prov: Dura Europos, *Naos* 3, Temple of Gaddé. Loc: New Haven (CT), Yale University Art Gallery, 1938.5314. *Dedicatory. On relief.* Group: Doura 28-30. Bib: Downey '77 4.

(On right)
1 slwqws
2 nyqṭwr
Collated

PAT 1096 **Doura 30** **n. d.**
Prov: Dura Europos, *Naos* 3, Temple of Gaddé. Loc: New Haven (CT), Yale University Art Gallery, 1938.5314. *Dedicatory. On relief.* Group: Doura 28-30. Bib: Downey '77 4.

(On left)
1 ṣlm ḥyrn br
2 mlkw br nṣwr
Collated

PAT 1097 **Doura 31** **n. d.**
Prov: Dura Europos, *Naos* 3, Temple of Gaddé. Loc: New Haven (CT), Yale University Art Gallery, 1938.5314. *Dedicatory. On relief.* Group: Doura 31-32. Bib: Downey '77 5.

(On center)
1 gdʾ dy tdmwr ʿbd ḥ[yrn]
2 br mlkw br nṣwr
Collated

PAT 1098 **Doura 32** **A.D. 159**
Prov: Dura Europos, *Naos* 3, Temple of Gaddé. Loc: New Haven (CT), Yale University Art Gallery, 1938.5314. *Dedicatory. On relief.* Group: Doura 31-32. Bib: Downey '77 5.

(On left)

1 byrḥ nysn šnt 4.100+60+10
Collated

PAT 1099 **Doura 33** **n. d.**
Prov: Dura Europos, *Naos* 3, Temple of Gaddé. Loc: New Haven (CT), Yale University Art Gallery, 1938.5301. *Dedicatory. On relief.* Bib: Déd p 74; RosAH 21; Downey '77 47; ScPart 183 fig 60.

1 yrḥbwl ʾlhʾ
2 ṭbʾ mṣbʾ dy
3 ʿynʾ ʿbd bny
4 mytʾ qšṭʾ
Collated

PAT 1100 **Doura 34** **n. d.**
Prov: Dura Europos, *Naos* 3, Temple of Gaddé. Loc: New Haven (CT), Yale University Art Gallery, 1938.5304. *Dedicatory. On statue base.* Bib: Downey '77 48; ScPart 184 fig 61.

1 nbw ʿbd zbdʾ
2 br zblʾ
Collated

PAT 1101 **Doura 35** **n. d.**
Prov: Dura Europos, *insula* L 8, section W 106. Loc: . *Unclassified. On jar fragment.*

1 b[r l]šmš br bly br br bnkmyn

PAT 1102 **Doura 36** **n. d.**
Prov: Dura Europos, *insula* L 8, section W 106. Loc: . *Unclassified. On jar fragment.*

1 bbw

PAT 1103 **Doura 37** **n. d.**
Prov: Dura Europos, *insula* L 8, section W 106. Loc: . *Unclassified. On jar fragment.*

1 ʾb

PAT 1104 **Doura 38** **n. d.**
Prov: Dura Europos, "Funduq of the Palmyrenians", temple niche. Loc: . *Dedicatory. On wall.*

1 ʿbd mlkw br [n]ṣwr
2 nṣwr

PAT 1105 **Doura 39** **n. d.**
Prov: Dura Europos, "Funduq of the Palmyrenians", temple *pronaos, S wall.* Loc: . *Graffito. On wall.*

1 dkyr ʿzyz brḥ
2 bb[ʾ] wbṭb
3 whdy nṭryn ʾp bbʾ

PAT 1106 **Doura 40** **n. d.**
Prov: Dura Europos, "Funduq of the Palmyrenians", temple *pronaos, S wall.* Loc: . *Graffito. On wall.*

1 ʿl ʿbdy m[.....]
2 ʿl n[ṭ]ry mlkʾ wmqṣ
3 rnnyʾ m<kl> 5
4 ʿl blʿm [...] dmʿṣ[...]
5 ʿl kmry m[..] 5
6 ʿl[....]

PAT 1107 **Doura 41** **n. d.**
Prov: Dura Europos, "Funduq of the Palmyrenians", temple *pronaos, W wall.* Loc: . *Graffito. On wall.*

1 [...]r
2 rb mrw/mdw
3 zbd[bw]l

PAT 1108 **Doura 42** **n. d.**
Prov: Dura Europos, "Funduq of the Palmyrenians", temple *pronaos, W wall.* Loc: . *Graffito. On wall.*

1 [...] yḥy[..]
2 brb[.....]
3 b[.]g[...]n
4 hnb[....]
5 yr/d[.]šw[...]b[..]
6 d[.]lh bṭb

PAT 1109 **Doura 43** **n. d.**
Prov: Dura Europos, "Funduq of the Palmyrenians", temple *pronaos, W wall.* Loc: . *Dedicatory, Graffito. On wall.*

1 dkyr brkh
2 zb[d]bwl

PAT 1110 **Doura 44** **n. d.**
Prov: Dura Europos, "Funduq of the Palmyrenians", temple soundings. Loc: . *Graffito. On plaster fragment.*

1 šlwtʾ

PAT 1111 **Doura 45** **n. d.**
Prov: Dura Europos, "Funduq of the Palmyrenians", temple soundings. Loc: . *Graffito. On plaster fragment.*

1 tymwʾ br [....]

PAT 1112 **Doura 46** **n. d.**
Prov: Dura Europos, "Funduq of the Palmyrenians", temple soundings. Loc: . *Graffito. On plaster fragment.* Bib: RosAH 20.

1 [.....]rq
2 [.....]wz
3 br w[.....]
4 brtʾ[..]
5 brʿ[....]

PAT 1113 **Doura 47** **n. d.**
Prov: Dura Europos, Temple of Zeus Megistos, *insula* C 4, 11. Loc: New Haven (CT), Yale University Art Gallery, 1938.5311. *Dedicatory. On relief.* Bib: Ing YCS '55 p 138; Downey '77 42; ScPart 178 fig 57.

1 ʾrṣw wmtyʾ ʿbd ʿgʾ glpʾ lḥy brh
Collated

PAT 1114 **Doura 48** **n. d.**
Prov: Dura Europos, Temple of Aphlad. Loc: . *Graffito. On wall.*

1 gdr hrbz

PAT 1115 **Doura 49** **n. d.**
Prov: Dura Europos, Temple of Palmyrene Gods. Loc: Dura Europos, *in situ. Graffiti. On column.*

1 whblth
2 qdm yr[ḥybwl]
This and Doura 50 are written on same column.

PAT 1116 **Doura 50** **n. d.**
Prov: Dura Europos, Temple of Palmyrene Gods. Loc: Dura Europos, *in situ. Graffito. On column.*

1 [d]kyr ʿyb
This and Doura 49 are written on same column.

PAT 1117 **Doura 51** **n. d.**
Prov: Dura Europos, Temple of Palmyrene Gods, *pronaos*, S wall. Loc: . *Dedicatory, Graffito. On wall.*

1 θαρθηνγοβνινδααβαβιδσαλμα
2 βανινξαναaβαρακικη

Greek letters transcribing an Aramaic text.

PAT 1118 **Doura 52** **n. d.**
Prov: Dura Europos, House of Lysias. Loc: . *Graffito. On wall.*

1 ʿwpl
2 [...]m bbyʾ ṭmš qmzyn

PAT 1119 **Doura 53** **n. d.**
Prov: Dura Europos, N of main street, Street D. Loc: . *Graffito. On plaster fragment.*

1 [..] br lbn

PAT 1120 **Doura 54** **n. d.**
Prov: Dura Europos, rampart. Loc: Dura Europos, *in situ. Dedicatory. On stone block.*

1 dkyr brʿbʾ
2 kmyn

PAT 1121 **Doura 55** **n. d.**
Prov: Dura Europos, rampart, tower 14 (or S-W tower). Loc: Dura Europos, *in situ. Graffito. On wall.*

1 db

PAT 1122 **Dri '82 p 65** **n. d.**
Prov: Palmyra, Temple of Allat, reemployed. Loc: Palmyra, entrance. *Unclassified. On orthostat (3.60 m. by 1.60 m.).* Bib: *Pls. 1, 2*; Gaw '83, Pl 14 b.

1 tbrk ʾ[lt]
2 mn dy lʾ yšd
3 dm ʿl ḥgbʾ

Lion with small antelope between front legs. See Dri '82 for an analysis of the motif.

PAT 1123 **EaWe '67** Fig. 1 **n. d.**
Prov: Uncertain. Loc: Tashkent (Turkmenistan), State University Archaeological Collection. *Funerary. On relief.* Bib: PS 521. *figs 1, 3, bibliog. p 247*; Altheim and Stiehl '70 pp 704-709.

1 bʿyt
2 brt
3 ḥyrn
4 tymr
5 ṣw
6 ḥbl

PAT 1124 **EaWe '67** Fig. 2 **n. d.**
Prov: Uncertain. Loc: Tashkent (Turkmenistan), State University Archaeological Collection. *Funerary. On relief.* Bib: PS 288; Altheim and Stiehl '70 pp 704-709.

1 ṣlm
2 mzbnʾ
3 br brʿʾ
4 mtʾ
5 ḥbl

PAT 1125 **EblaDam p 290** 184 **n. d.**
Prov: Palmyra, S-W necropolis, hypogeum no. 6 (Tomb of Sasan). Loc: Palmyra, B 7078. *Funerary. On relief.* Group: EblaDam p 290, PGKK p 296, PGKK p 299. Bib: *Photo p 291 184, bibliography.*

1 ḥbybtʾ
2 brt mqy
3 br nwrbl
4 ḥbl

PAT 1126 **EblaDam p 295** 188 **n d.**
Prov: Palmyra. Loc: Damascus, National Museum, 2793 (7864). *Funerary. On relief.* Bib: *Photo. bibliog.*

1 [.....]ḥʾ
2 [brt] ʾbnt?
3 [br ʾl]hbl
4 [..ḥ]bl

Text from photo, not totally clear

PAT 1127 **EblaDam p 296** 190 **n. d.**
Prov: Palmyra, S-E necropolis, hypogeum no. 3. Loc: Damascus, National Museum, 7444. *Funerary. On relief.* Bib: *Bibliography p 296, photo p 297*; Land des Baal 181; Pays du Baal et d'Astarté 303.

1 ḥbl
2 ʿlyt brt
3 tymrṣw
4 mnʿm

PAT 1128 **HomVer** (p) **n. d.**
Prov: Palmyra, Diocletian Camp, Temple of Allat, cella. Loc: Palmyra, CD 147/75. *Dedicatory. On relief.* Bib: Pl 73; PGKK p 309 31.

1 mṣbyʾ ʾln ʿbd smgʾ br yrḥy mn kysh

wṣb[.]
2 brbnwt mrzḥwth byrḥ ʾ[yr] ywm 10+6 lʿlmʾ
ʿl ḥyw[hy]

PAT 1129 **HomVer** (q) **n. d.**
Prov: Palmyra, Diocletian Camp, Temple of Allat, cella. Loc: Palmyra, CD 38/76. *Dedicatory. On relief.* Bib: Pl 74.

1 ʾlt

PAT 1130 **Inv 1 5** **A.D. 67**
Prov: Palmyra, Temple of Baalshamîn. Loc: Palmyra, *in situ. Dedicatory. On column console.* Bib: IP 30.

1 mʿltʾ dh klh ʿmwdyh wšryth wtṯlylh qrb
yrḥy br lšmš br rʿy dy mn bny mʿzyn lbʿlšmn
2 ʾlhʾ ṭbʾ wškrʾ ʿl ḥywhy wḥyy bnwhy
wʾḥyhy byrḥ ʾlwl šnt 3.100+60+10+5+3

PAT 1131 **Inv 3 2** **n. d.**
Prov: Palmyra, Great Colonnade. Loc: Palmyra, *in situ. Dedicatory. On stone block.* Bib: IP 47; Inv 12 19; Déd p 240; Gaw '73 pp 80-81.

1 [.........] Βαγεσος [Α]ββ[ε]ους τοῦ Β[αγ]εσου τοῦ
[Ζαβδι]βω[λου]
2 [..........κ]αι ἐποί[ησ]εν ἐξ ἰδί[ων τὴν ὀ]πὴν τῆς
τοῦ ἀνδρων[ος]
3 [.........]ιου

1 [.......]h wtṣbyth klh ʿd lʿl ʿbd wqrb mn
kysh [...]
2 [....] br [...]ʾ[..]q[.]l[...]
Gk text after Inv 12 19; for more reconstruction see Déd p 240; Gaw '73 pp 80-81

PAT 1132 **Inv 3 25** **n. d.**
Prov: Palmyra, Great Colonnade. Loc: Palmyra, *in situ. Unclassified. On entablature fragment.*

1 [....]tʾwhy[...............]mʾhd/rwmhʾym[.....]

PAT 1133 **Inv 4 4b** **A.D. 129**
Prov: Palmyra, Valley of Tombs, Umm Belqîs, Tower 67. Loc: Palmyra, *in situ. Funerary. On wall.* Tomb Group: C4114; Inv 4 4b.

1 [ḥ]bl zqʾ
2 [š]mh šnt
3 4.100+40+1

PAT 1134 **Inv 4 7a** **A.D. 67**
Prov: Palmyra, Valley of Tombs, Umm Belqîs, reemployed in later hypogeum. Loc: Palmyra, *in situ. Funerary: Foundation. On door lintel.* Tomb Group: Inv 4 7a, b; 8. Bib: *Retouched photo of squeeze follows p 24*; RB '30 4; Gaw '70c MF Fondation 12; Déd p 39.

1 Τὸ σπήλαιον καὶ τὸ ἐπὶ τούτῳ μνημεῖον
ῳκοδόμησεν
2 ʾΙεδείβηλος Θαιμάη τοῦ ʾΑγγόδομος φυλῆς
Χομαρηνῶν ἐξ ἰδίων ἐπὶ Θαιμάῃ
3 τῷ πατρὶ αὐτοῦ καὶ Μαίσᾳ Θαιμίσα τοῦ
Τείμωνος τῇ μητρὶ καὶ ʾΟγήλῳ Θαιμάῃ καὶ
4 ʾΑθθαίᾳ τοῖς ὁμομητρίοις αὐτοῦ ἀδελφοῖς
αἰώνιον γέρας ἔτους ηοτ'

1 npšʾ dh wmʿrtʾ ʿbd ydyʿbl br tymḥʾ br
ydyʿbl br
2 ʾgdm ʿl tymḥʾ ʾbwhy wʿl myšʾ brt tymšʾ
br ydyʿbl ṭymwn ʾmh
3 wʿl ʿgylw wtymḥʾ wʿty bny ḥyrn br
ʿbdʿth ʾgdm ʾḥwhy bny myšʾ dh
4 dy mn pḥz bny kmrʾ lyqrh dy ʿlmʾ byrḥ ṭbt
šnt 3.100+60+10+5+3

PAT 1135 **Inv 4 7b** **A.D. 191**
Prov: Palmyra, Valley of Tombs, Umm Belqîs, reemployed in later hypogeum. Loc: Palmyra, *in situ. Funerary: Cession. On door lintel.* Group: See Inv 4 7a. Bib: *Retouched photo of squeeze follows p 24*; Gaw '70c MF Cession 25.

1 Μηνὶ Ξανδικῷ τοῦ βφ' ἔτους
2 ʾΑλέξανδρος ʾΑλεξάνδρου τοῦ
3 ʾΑπολλωνίου τοῦ Νεβουζαβάδου
4 τοῦ Θαιμάη τοῦ ʾΑγγοδόμου

5 ἐξεχώρησεν Βαγγαίῳ ᾿Αζεί-
6 ζου τοῦ Μαλίχου ἀρκτικοῦ
7 πλευροῦ τῆς ἐσωτέρας ἐξέδρας
8 τάξεις νεκροθή<κ>ων πέντε
9 αὐτῷ καὶ υἱοῖς. καὶ υἱωνοῖς
10 καὶ ἐγγόνοις εἰς τὸ παράπαν

1 byrḥ nysn šnt 5.100+2 ʾlkdrys br ʾlkdrys br ʾplny tymʿʾ
2 br ʾgdm ʾḥbr bgy br ʿzyzw br mlkw bsṭrʾ gbʾ dy smlʾ dy ʾksdrʾ gwyʾ
3 ṭksys dy gwmḥyʾ ḥmšʾ lh wlbnyh wlbnʾ bnyh lʿlmʾ

PAT 1136 **Inv 4 8a** **n. d.**
Prov: Palmyra, Valley of Tombs, Umm Belqîs, reemployed in beduin tomb. Loc: Palmyra, *in situ*. *Funerary*. *On relief*. Group: See Inv 4 7a. Bib: IP 68; Déd p 28.

1 tymṣʾ br
2 ʾlhšʾ
3 ʿgylw ḥbl

This text and the following are written on the same relief.

PAT 1137 **Inv 4 8b** **n. d.**
Prov: Palmyra, Valley of Tombs, Umm Belqîs, reemployed in beduin tomb. Loc: Palmyra, *in situ*. *Funerary*. *On relief*. Group: See Inv 4 7a.

1 tymṣʾ br ʾlhšʾ [.....]
2 ḥbl

PAT 1138 **Inv 4 9b** **A.D. 149**
Prov: Palmyra, Valley of Tombs, Funerary Temple 85b. Loc: Palmyra, *in situ*. *Funerary: Foundation*. *On lintel*. Group: Tomb of Aʿailamī and Zebīdā, Watzinger 85b, C4168, C4169, C4243, Inv 4 9a, (=C4168), Inv 4 9b-f; IP pp 13-18, nos. 12-23.

1' [...]υἱῶν καὶ ἐγγόνων ἔκτισαν, ἔτους ξυ' μηνὸς [...]

1 qbrʾ dnh bt ʿlmʾ wʾsṭwʾ [.....]
2 byrḥ nysn šnt 4.100+60

PAT 1139 **Inv 4 9d** **n. d.**
Prov: Palmyra, Valley of Tombs, Funerary Temple 85b. Loc: Palmyra Museum. *Funerary*. *On relief*. See Inv 4 9b. Bib: IP 15; Makowski '83 p 186 5, Pl 51b.

1 ṣlm ʾʿylmy br zbydʾ
2 ḥyrn ḥbl

PAT 1140 **Inv 4 9e** **n. d.**
Prov: Palmyra, Valley of Tombs, Funerary Temple 85b. Loc: Palmyra Museum?. *Funerary*. *On relief*. Group: See Inv 9b. Bib: IP 17; DaM '83 p 186 3, and Pl 50c.

1 [.......]nwr/d zbydʾ
2 byr/d[....]

PAT 1141 **Inv 4 12** **A.D. (164)**
Prov: Palmyra, Valley of Tombs, Gubwel al Husayniyet. Loc: Palmyra Museum. *Funerary: Foundation*. *On door lintel*. Bib: RB '30 3; Gaw '70c MF Fondation 54.

1 [..... αὐ]τῷ καὶ [υἱω]νοῖς καὶ ἐγγόνοις εἰς τὸ παντελὲς,
1 ἔτους εξ[υ', μηνὸς Ξανδικοῦ].

1 qbrʾ dnh ʿbd ʾlhbl br mlkw br zbdbwl brtʾ lh wlb bnwhy lʿlmʾ byrḥ]
2 nysn šnt 4.100+60+10+[5]

PAT 1142 **Inv 4 13** **A.D. 232**
Prov: Palmyra, Diocletian Camp, Hypogeum. Loc: Palmyra, *in situ*. *Funerary: Foundation*. *On door lintel*. Bib: IP 40; Gaw '70c MF Fondation 63; Gaw '75 pp 127-33.

1 [Τὸ σπήλαιον τοῦ ταφεῶνος ὤρυξεν ἐξ ἰδίων καὶ ᾠκοδόμησεν σὺν] κόσμῳ
2 [᾿Ιούλιος Αὐρήλιος ῾Ερμῆς ἀπελεύθερος Αὐρηλίου .....]ου ἑαυτῷ κ[αὶ ᾿Ι]ουλίᾳ Αὐρηλίᾳ [Θαιμῇ, ἀπελευθέρᾳ Αὐρηλίας ᾿Ακμῆς ᾿Αντ]ιόχου τοῦ καὶ
3 ᾿Ολαίφει ἑαυτοῖς καὶ υἱοῖς αὐτῶν

4 [καὶ ἐγγόνοις μηνὶ 'Αρτεμισίῳ γμφ' ἔτ]ους.

1 mʿrtʾ dnh dy bt ʿlmʾ ḥpr wbnʾ wṣbt
2 mn kysh ywlys ʾwrlys hrms br ḥry ʾwrl[ys .....]
3 [w]prymʾ brt ḥry ʾwrlyʾ ʾqmʾ brt ʾn[ṭy?ks ḥlypy byrḥ]
4 ʾyr šnt 5.100+40+3
Text after Gaw '75 p 128

PAT 1143 **Inv 4 14** **A.D. 179**
Prov: Palmyra, Valley of Tombs, Gubwel al Husayniyet, hypogeum no. 81. Loc: Palmyra, *in situ. Funerary: Foundation. On door lintel.* Bib: IP 41; Gaw '70c MF Fondation 55.

1 Τὸ σπήλαιον τοῦ ταφαιῶνος ὤρυξεν καὶ ᾠκοδόμησεν ἐξ ἰδίων [Σά]εδος Βαράθου[ς] τοῦ Σαέδου τοῦ Βαράθ[ους .....]
2 τε καὶ υἱοῖς καὶ υἱωνοῖς καὶ ἐκγόνοις μηνὶ Ξανδικῷ τοῦ Ϙυ' ἔτους

1 mʿ[rtʾ dh bt ʿlmʾ ḥpr wbnʾ mn kysh ṣʿdw br brʿth brʿ[th dy] mn pḥd bny ʿtr lyqr b[..... bnw]hy byrḥ nysn
2 šnt 4.100+80+10

PAT 1144 **Inv 4 15a** **n. d.**
Prov: Palmyra, Valley of Tombs, Gubwel al Husayniyet. Loc: Palmyra Museum. *Funerary. On sarcophagus fragment.* Group: Inv 15a, b, c.

1 ṣlm ḥggw
2 brnbw brʿth

PAT 1145 **Inv 4 15b** **n. d.**
Prov: Palmyra, Valley of Tombs, Gubwel al Husayniyet. Loc: Palmyra Museum. *Funerary. On sarcophagus fragment.* Group: Inv 15a, b, c.

1 ʾḥybl?
2 br
3 mqymw

PAT 1146 **Inv 4 15c** **n. d.**
Prov: Palmyra, Valley of Tombs, Gubwel al Husayniyet. Loc: Palmyra Museum. *Funerary. On sarcophagus fragment.* Group: Inv 15a, b, c.

1 ṣlm mqymw
2 br brnbw
3 brʿth

PAT 1147 **Inv 4 16** **n. d.**
Prov: Palmyra, Valley of Tombs, Gubwel al Husayniyet. Loc: Palmyra Museum. *Unclassified. On stone tablet.* Bib: IP 59; Déd p 148.

1 [..........]
2 [...]ου Μαλίχου
3 [...] 'Α[δ]δου[δ]άνου
4 [... ἔκτ]ισεν
5 [......]υ

1 ml[kw ......]
2 [......]
3 [......]
4 by[rḥ ......]

PAT 1148 **Inv 4 24** **n. d.**
Prov: Palmyra, Valley of Tombs. Loc: Palmyra Museum. *Funerary. On relief.*

1 tymlt
2 ʿwydlt
3 ʾmrsʿ

PAT 1149 **Inv 4 25** **A.D. (8)**
Prov: Palmyra, Valley of Tombs. Loc: Palmyra, *in situ. Funerary: Foundation. On door lintel.*

1 [Τὸ σπ]ήλα[ιο]ν ταφαιῶνο[ς.....]
2 [.....κα]ὶ ἐγγό[νοις......]νος[...]

1 [....]ʾ dnh dy ʿlmʾ [.....]

PAT 1150 **Inv 4 26** **A.D. 24**
Prov: Palmyra, Valley of Tombs, Umm Belqîs,

Tower 21. Loc: Palmyra, *in situ*. *Funerary*. *On wall.*

(A)
1 mqymw br
2 [ḥg]gw šlm lh
3 [šnt] [3.100+]20+10
(B)
1 blšwry br ḥggw šlm lh
2 šnt 3.100+20+10+5+1

Other tombs of same family: Towers 67 (Ber '70 p 82) and 68 (C4124).

PAT 1151 **Inv 5 10** **n. d.**
Prov: Palmyra, Transversal Colonnade. Loc: Palmyra, *in situ*. *Dedicatory*. *On column*. Bib: *Drawing with text*; IP 35.

1 qrb ʿtʿqb wrpbwl wšdy
2 bny brʿth br ʿtʿqb br
3 zbdʿth ʾrʾš

PAT 1152 **Inv 6 4** **n. d.**
Prov: Palmyra, Diocletian Camp, reemployed in "Temple des Enseignes". Loc: Palmyra, *in situ*, TE 243. *Dedicatory*. *On stele*. Bib: Palm V '63-'64 pp 117-18, 174, fig 226; RSP 129.

1 [lbr]yk šm[h .....]
2 tymʾ b[r ...... p]ṭmh
3 dy pṭm [.....]
4 zbdʾ [....... bry]k šmh

Text after RSP 129

PAT 1153 **Inv 7 1b** **n. d.**
Prov: Palmyra, N-W necropolis, Tower 164. Loc: Palmyra, *in situ*. *Funerary: Cession*. *On door lintel*. Tomb Group: C4162; Inv 7 1b. Bib: Gaw MF Concession 50.

1 ywlyʾ ʾwrlyʾ ʾbyhn wmlkw
2 [............. ty]mrṣw br pplws ʾlys ʾbyhn br šmʿwn rḥq
2 lywlyʾ ʾwrlyʾ tymrṣ[w]
3 [....] br ʿwydʾ br mlkw mn gwmḥyn trn tḥt [...] wtḥwt twprʾ dy
3 ptyḥ lʾpʾ [....]

See above, C4162, tomb foundation.

PAT 1154 **Inv 7 5** **A.D. 159**
Prov: Palmyra, N-W necropolis, Funerary temple 149. Loc: Palmyra, *in situ*. *Funerary: Foundation*. *On door lintel*. Bib: RB '30 1; Gaw '70c MF Fondation 53.

1 Τὸ μνημεῖον ταφέωνα ἔκτισεν Θαιμάρσας Βωρόφα τοῦ Μαλίχου τοῦ ʿΟσαιλάθους αὐτῷ καὶ υἱοῖς.
2 καὶ υἱωνοῖς καὶ ἐγγόνοις εἰς τὸν αἰῶνα, ἔτους αου' μηνὸς Δείου.

1 qbrʾ dnh bt ʿlmʾ bnʾ tymrṣw br bwrpʾ br mlkw br ʿšylt br pḥwz bny mtbwl lh wlbnwhy wlbny bnwhy dy
2 ʿlmʾ byrḥ knwn šnt 4.100+60+10+1

PAT 1155 **Inv 7 7** **n. d.**
Prov: Palmyra, N-W necropolis, Tower. Loc: Palmyra, *in situ*. *Funerary*. *On stone tablet*. Bib: IP 64.

1 qr[......]bwl
2 šk[......]by
3 mq[......]

PAT 1156 **Inv 7 9** **n. d.**
Prov: Palmyra, N-W necropolis. Loc: Palmyra, *in situ*. *Funerary*. *On relief*. Bib: IP 63.

1 ṣlm [ ]
2 br ʿz[yzw]

Text of IP 63. Tomb became part of Justinian wall.

PAT 1157 **Inv 7 10** **n. d.**
Prov: Palmyra, N-W necropolis, Tower 145. Loc: Palmyra, *in situ*. *Funerary: Foundation*. *On door lintel*. Bib: *Drawing with text*; Gaw '70c MF Fondation 73.

1 [qbr]ʾ dnh ʿbd šlmlt br ydʿw br šlmlt lh wlbnwhy lʿlmʾ

PAT 1158 **Inv 7 12** **n. d.**

Prov: Palmyra, N-W necropolis. Loc: Palmyra, *in situ*. *Funerary*. *On door lintel.*

1 [...]l[.]lt[...]r[.. lh wlbnwhy

Tomb became part of Justinian wall.

PAT 1159 **Inv 7 14** **n. d.**

Prov: Palmyra, N-W necropolis. Loc: Palmyra Museum. *Funerary*. *On sarcophagus.*

1 ḥbl bgšw br šḥrw ḥnyny

PAT 1160 **Inv 7 15c** **A.D. 265**

Prov: Palmyra, N-W necropolis. Loc: Palmyra Museum. *Funerary: Cession*. *On door lintel.* Tomb Group: C4197 = Inv 7 15a, b; Inv 7 15c.

1 [...]
2 [...]nʾ br [...]ynt l[...] wlbnyhwn wlbny
3 [bnyhwn lʿlmʾ] byrḥ sywn dy šnt
5.100+60+10+5+1

PAT 1161 **Inv 8 1** **n. d.**

Prov: Palmyra. Loc: Palmyra Museum. *Funerary*. *On stele.* Bib: *Drawing.*

1 [zbd]ʿth br
2 [ʿ]tntn
3 ḥbl

PAT 1162 **Inv 8 2** **A.D. 140**

Prov: Palmyra. Loc: Palmyra Museum. *Funerary*. *On stele.* Bib: *Drawing.*

1 ḥbtʾ brt
2 ḥlptʾ br
3 ḥ[l]p [...] br
4 tymrṣw ʾtt
5 zbdʾ br tymʾ
6 br ḥlptʾ šnt
7 4.100+40+10+2
8 ḥbl

PAT 1163 **Inv 8 3** **n. d.**

Prov: Palmyra. Loc: Palmyra Museum. *Funerary*. *On stele.* Bib: *Drawing.*

1 ḥbl tmh brt
2 mqymy br šgdy

PAT 1164 **Inv 8 4** **n. d.**

Prov: Palmyra. Loc: Palmyra Museum. *Funerary*. *On stele.* Bib: *Drawing.*

1 ḥbl
2 ʾytybl
3 br tymʾ br
4 ʾytybl br
5 ʿgylw

PAT 1165 **Inv 8 5** **n. d.**

Prov: Palmyra. Loc: Palmyra Museum. *Funerary*. *On stele.* Bib: *Drawing.*

1 ḥbl mky brt
2 tymw ʿlybʿl

PAT 1166 **Inv 8 6** **n. d.**

Prov: Palmyra. Loc: Palmyra Museum. *Funerary*. *On stele.* Bib: *Drawing.*

1 ḥbl yrḥy br
2 blšwr ḥbl
3 whʾ npšʾ
4 dh mwlyʾ b
5 šmš

PAT 1167 **Inv 8 7** **n. d.**

Prov: Palmyra. Loc: Palmyra Museum. *Funerary*. *On stele.* Bib: *Drawing.*

1 ḥbl mlkw br
2 zbdʿy rbʾ ḥbl

PAT 1168 **Inv 8 8** **n. d.**

Prov: Palmyra. Loc: Palmyra Museum. *Funerary*. *On stele.* Bib: *Drawing.*

1 ḥbl ḥyrn b[r]
2 yrḥy ḥbl
3 wh npšʾ dh
4 mwlyʾ bšmš

PAT 1169 **Inv 8 9** **n. d.**
Prov: Palmyra. Loc: Palmyra Museum. *Funerary.* *On stele.* Bib: *Drawing.*

1 ḥbl zbdbw!l
2 br mtnʾ br
3 zbdlh br blʿqb
4 dy mtqrh ʾṣrʿ
5 [ḥ]bl
line 1: *zbdbw!l* with Stark PN

PAT 1170 **Inv 8 10** **n. d.**
Prov: Palmyra. Loc: Palmyra Museum. *Funerary.* *On stele.* Bib: *Drawing.*

1 ḥbl mtny
2 br bryky
3 btʾ ḥbl

PAT 1171 **Inv 8 11** **n. d.**
Prov: Palmyra. Loc: Palmyra Museum. *Funerary.* *On stele.* Bib: *Drawing.*

1 ḥbl
2 tmʾ brt ʿgʾ
3 ʾṣdny/ʾṣrny ḥbl

PAT 1172 **Inv 8 12** **n. d.**
Prov: Palmyra. Loc: Palmyra Museum. *Funerary.* *On stele.* Bib: *Drawing.*

1 ʾbyšy brt zbdbl
2 br mlkw ḥbl

PAT 1173 **Inv 8 13** **n. d.**
Prov: Palmyra. Loc: Palmyra Museum. *Funerary.* *On stele fragment.* Bib: *Drawing.*

1 [....]wry br
2 [....] ḥbl

PAT 1174 **Inv 8 14** **n. d.**
Prov: Palmyra. Loc: Palmyra Museum. *Funerary.* *On stele fragment.* Bib: *Drawing.*

1 ḥbl
2 [... t]ymy br

PAT 1175 **Inv 8 15** **n. d.**
Prov: Palmyra. Loc: Palmyra Museum. *Funerary.* *On stele.* Bib: *Drawing.*

1 ḥbl
2 šbty brt
3 ʿnny br
4 mqymy ḥlʾ
5 ḥbl

PAT 1176 **Inv 8 16** **n. d.**
Prov: Palmyra. Loc: Palmyra Museum. *Funerary.* *On stele.* Bib: *Drawing.*

1 ḥbl
2 nšry br šmy
3 ḥbl

PAT 1177 **Inv 8 17** **n. d.**
Prov: Palmyra. Loc: Palmyra Museum. *Funerary.* *On stele.* Bib: *Drawing.*

1 ḥbl
2 mlkw br tym[...]
3 br ʾmšy[...] [...]

PAT 1178 **Inv 8 18** **n. d.**
Prov: Palmyra. Loc: Palmyra Museum. *Funerary.* *On stele.* Bib: *Drawing.*

1 tbll brt
2 ydy ḥbl

PAT 1179 **Inv 8 19** **n. d.**
Prov: Palmyra. Loc: Palmyra Museum. *Funerary.* *On stele.* Bib: *Drawing.*

1 ḥbl ʿwydlt
2 [b]r yrḥy nṣrʾ
May be same as IP 76

PAT 1180 **Inv 8 20** **n. d.**
Prov: Palmyra. Loc: Palmyra Museum. *Funerary.*
On stele fragment. Bib: *Drawing.*

1 [...] mtny [...]

PAT 1181 **Inv 8 21** **n. d.**
Prov: Palmyra. Loc: Palmyra Museum. *Funerary.*
On stele. Bib: *Drawing.*

1 tym[...]
2 mqymw A (Gk letter)
3 tymy ḥbl

PAT 1182 **Inv 8 22** **n. d.**
Prov: Palmyra. Loc: Palmyra Museum. *Funerary.*
On stele. Bib: *Drawing.*

1 zbdbwl br brwqʾ
2 br ʾknt ḥbl

PAT 1183 **Inv 8 23** **n. d.**
Prov: Palmyra. Loc: Palmyra Museum. *Funerary.*
On stele. Bib: *Drawing.*

1 ḥbl rmy br tymnʾ
2 br zbʾ ḥbl

PAT 1184 **Inv 8 24** **n. d.**
Prov: Palmyra. Loc: Palmyra Museum. *Funerary.*
On stele. Bib: *Drawing.*

1 ḥbl mlkw br
2 tymnʾ bzy ḥbl

PAT 1185 **Inv 8 25** **n. d.**
Prov: Palmyra. Loc: Palmyra Museum. *Funerary.*
On stele. Bib: *Drawing.*

1 ḥbl
2 ʾbrwq br
3 brʿth
4 gḥynt ḥ?bl

PAT 1186 **Inv 8 26** **n. d.**
Prov: Palmyra. Loc: Palmyra Museum. *Funerary.*
On stele. Bib: *Drawing.*

1 ḥbl
2 blḥzy br
3 tymnʾ whby
4 ʾd/ry[..] ḥb[l]

PAT 1187 **Inv 8 27** **n. d.**
Prov: Palmyra. Loc: Palmyra Museum. *Funerary.*
On stele. Bib: *Drawing.*

1 ḥbl ʾbnʾ
2 ʾtt zbydʾ
3 ʾṣrʿ ḥbl

PAT 1188 **Inv 8 28** **n. d.**
Prov: Palmyra. Loc: Palmyra Museum. *Funerary.*
On stele. Bib: *Drawing.*

1 [ḥb]l nbwydʿ br
2 [b]rʿth nbwydʿ ḥ[bl]

PAT 1189 **Inv 8 29** **n. d.**
Prov: Palmyra. Loc: Palmyra Museum. *Funerary.*
On stele. Bib: *Drawing.*

1 ḥbl tymlt br
2 ymlkw ḥbl

PAT 1190 **Inv 8 30** **n. d.**
Prov: Palmyra. Loc: Palmyra Museum. *Funerary.*
On stele. Bib: *Drawing.*

1 ḥbl mqymw br [...]
2 ḥbl

PAT 1191 **Inv 8 31** **n. d.**
Prov: Palmyra. Loc: Palmyra Museum. *Funerary. On stele.* Bib: *Drawing.*

1 ḥbl
2 yrḥbwl'
3 br tym' br
4 'zmr/d ḥbl

PAT 1192 **Inv 8 32** **n. d.**
Prov: Palmyra. Loc: Palmyra, A 72. *Funerary. On stele.* Bib: *Drawing;* Parl '76, pl 1-1; Tanabe '86, pl 258.

1 ḥbl
2 mlkw br
3 mtny pyl'
4 ḥbl

PAT 1193 **Inv 8 33** **n. d.**
Prov: Palmyra. Loc: Palmyra Museum. *Funerary. On stele.* Bib: *Drawing;* Tanabe '86, pl 257.

1 ḥbl tymrṣw
2 'yd'n br lšmš
3 br šwḥbw

PAT 1194 **Inv 8 34** **n. d.**
Prov: Palmyra. Loc: Palmyra Museum. *Funerary. On stele.* Bib: *Drawing.*

1 ḥbl mqymw br mrqy

PAT 1195 **Inv 8 35** **n. d.**
Prov: Palmyra. Loc: Palmyra Museum. *Funerary. On stele.* Bib: *Drawing.*

1 ḥbl
2 gd' br
3 tymy ḥbl

PAT 1196 **Inv 8 36** **n. d.**
Prov: Palmyra. Loc: Palmyra Museum. *Funerary. On stele.* Bib: *Drawing.*

1 ḥbl rmy br k?'b[w]
2 nwrbl

PAT 1197 **Inv 8 37a** **n. d.**
Prov: Palmyra. Loc: Palmyra Museum. *Funerary. On stele.* Bib: *Drawing.*

1 ḥbl
2 mqy[mw]
3 yrḥy

PAT 1198 **Inv 8 37b** **n. d.**
Prov: Palmyra. Loc: Palmyra Museum. *Funerary. On stele.* Bib: *Drawing.*

1 wh' npš' dh
2 mwly' bšmš

PAT 1199 **Inv 8 38** **n. d.**
Prov: Palmyra. Loc: Palmyra Museum. *Funerary. On stele fragment.* Bib: *Drawing.*

1 ḥbl 'm[...]
2 'gy[l]w [...]

PAT 1200 **Inv 8 39** **n. d.**
Prov: Palmyra. Loc: Palmyra Museum. *Funerary. On stele.* Bib: *Drawing.*

1 whblt br 't'qb
2 br ḥšy ḥbl

PAT 1200.02 **Inv 8 40** **n. d.**
Prov: Palmyra. Loc: Palmyra Museum. *Funerary. On stele fragment.* Bib: *Drawing.*

1 [...]t? brt [...]

PAT 1201 **Inv 8 41** **n. d.**
Prov: Palmyra. Loc: Palmyra Museum. *Funerary. On stele fragment.* Bib: *Drawing.*

1 ḥbl

2 [...]th br
3 [... m]qymw

PAT 1202 **Inv 8 42** **n. d.**
Prov: Palmyra. Loc: Palmyra Museum. *Funerary.*
On stele fragment. Bib: *Drawing.*

1 ʿmt br mq?[ymw]
2 ḥbl

PAT 1203 **Inv 8 43** **n. d.**
Prov: Palmyra. Loc: Palmyra Museum. *Funerary.*
On stele fragment. Bib: *Drawing.*

1 ḥbl m[...]
2 br yrḥ [...]
3 ḥ?[bl]

PAT 1203.02 **Inv 8 44** **n. d.**
Prov: Palmyra. Loc: Palmyra Museum. *Funerary.*
On stele fragment. Bib: *Drawing.*

1 ḥbl

PAT 1204 **Inv 8 45** **n. d.**
Prov: Palmyra. Loc: Palmyra Museum. *Funerary.*
On stele fragment. Bib: *Drawing.*

1 ḥbl
2 šʿdy br
3 tymʾ ḥbl

PAT 1205 **Inv 8 46** **n. d.**
Prov: Palmyra. Loc: Palmyra Museum. *Funerary.*
On stele fragment. Bib: *Drawing.*

1 ty[...]
2 br ty[...]
3 tymʾ[...]

PAT 1206 **Inv 8 47** **n. d.**
Prov: Palmyra. Loc: Palmyra Museum. *Funerary.*
On stele. Bib: *Drawing.*

1 ḥbl y[d]yʿ[bl]
2 br tmʾ tymnʾ

PAT 1207 **Inv 8 48** **n. d.**
Prov: Palmyra. Loc: Palmyra Museum. *Funerary.*
On stele. Bib: *Drawing.*

1 mqymw
2 bry ḥbl

PAT 1208 **Inv 8 49** **n. d.**
Prov: Palmyra. Loc: Palmyra Museum. *Funerary.*
On stele. Bib: *Drawing.*

1 [......]
2 br šmʿwʾ
3 br tdmrʾ
4 ḥbl

Line 4 tdmrʾ: probably correct reading; text as a whole not very legible

PAT 1209 **Inv 8 50a** **n. d.**
Prov: Palmyra. Loc: Palmyra Museum. *Funerary.*
On stele. Bib: *Drawing.*

1 ḥbl whby
2 ʾ[...]tʾbny
3 ḥbl

PAT 1210 **Inv 8 50b** **n. d.**
Prov: Palmyra. Loc: Palmyra Museum. *Funerary.*
On stele. Bib: *Drawing.*

1 ḥbl ʿgyl[w]
2 br tymnʾ

PAT 1211 **Inv 8 51** **n. d.**
Prov: Palmyra. Loc: Palmyra, A 91. *Funerary.*
On stele. Bib: *Drawing.* Bib: Tanabe '86, pl 259.

1 ḥbl
2 ʾyty
3 bl br
4 zbdʾ

PAT 1212 **Inv 8 52** **n. d.**
Prov: Palmyra. Loc: Palmyra Museum. *Funerary. On stele.* Bib: *Drawing.* Bib: Tanabe '86, pl 269.

1 ḥbl ʾqmt brt šm[.]

PAT 1213 **Inv 8 53a** **n. d.**
Prov: Palmyra. Loc: Palmyra Museum. *Funerary. On stele.* Bib: *Drawing.*

1 ʿlyt
2 ḥbl

PAT 1214 **Inv 8 53b** **n. d.**
Prov: Palmyra. Loc: Palmyra Museum. *Funerary. On stele.* Bib: *Drawing.* Bib: Parl '76, pl 4-1; Tanabe '86, pl 267.

1 ḥbl ʿlyt brt ʿlyšʾ

PAT 1215 **Inv 8 54** **n. d.**
Prov: Palmyra. Loc: Palmyra Museum. *Funerary. On stele.* Bib: *Drawing.*

1 ḥbl
2 ʾmtʾ
3 brt
4 ʾyty
5 bl

PAT 1216 **Inv 8 58** **n. d.**
Prov: Palmyra, near Hotel Zenobia. Loc: Palmyra Museum. *Funerary: Foundation. On door lintel.* Bib: *Drawing*; Gaw '70c MF Fondation 69.

1 [Τὸ μνημεῖον τοῦτο ᾠ]κοδόμησα[ν ἐξ ἰδίω]ν Αὐρήλιοι Νούρ[εος καὶ] Ζαβδίβωλος καὶ ʼΟγηλος οἱ Μακκ[αίου......]
2 ʼΑβαζέου αὐτοῖς τε καὶ υἱοῖς καὶ υἱωνοῖς ἄ[ρσε]σι εἰς τὸ παντελὲς μηνὶ (written μνηι) Ξανδικῷ[......]

1 qbrʾ dnh bt ʿlmʾ bnw mn k[ys]hwn ywlyʾ ʾwrlyʾ nwry wzbdbwl w[ʿgylw] bny m[qy ......]
2 ḥbzy lyqr mqy ʾbhwn l[hwn w]lbnyhwn wlbny bnyhwn dkryn

PAT 1217 **Inv 8 59** **A.D. 104**
Prov: Palmyra, S-W necropolis. Loc: Palmyra, A 105. *Funerary: Foundation. On stone tablet.* Bib: *Drawing;* Gaw '70c MF Fondation 29.

1 Τὸ μνημεῖον ἀνωκοδ-
2 όμησαν Βωλέης Μοκε-
3 [ί]μαιος Λίσαμσος Αἱράνης κ-
4 αὶ Βεέλαιος οἱ Οὐαβαίου τοῦ
5 Βωλαζαίου ἐπὶ τοῖς γον-
6 εῦσι αὐτῶν εἴς τε ἑαυτοὺς
7 καὶ υἱοὺς αὐτῶν καὶ ἐγγόνου-
8 ς μηνὶ Ξανδικῷ τοῦ ειυ' ἔτους

1 byrḥ nysn šnt 4.100+00+10+5 qbrʾ dnh
2 bnʾ bwlḥʾ wmqymy wḥyrn wlšmš wbʿl[y]
3 bny whby br bwlḥzy ʿl ʾbhthwn
4 lyqrhwn l[hwn wlbnyhwn wlbny bnyhwn lʿlmʾ lʿlmʾ]

PAT 1218 **Inv 8 60** **A.D. 120**
Prov: Palmyra, S-W necropolis, hypogeum of Malku. Loc: Palmyra, A 153. *Funerary: Foundation. On stone tablet.* Tomb Group: see Ber '35 pp 90-108; Inv 8 60; MUSJ '62 pp 104-19. Bib: *Drawing;* Gaw '70c MF Fondation 40.

1 mʿrth dh dy ʿbd mlkw br
2 mlkw br nwrbl ʾsyʾ lh
3 wlbnwhy wlbny bnwhy lyqrhn
4 dy ʿlmʾ bnysn šnt 4.100+20+10+2

PAT 1219 **Inv 8 62** **A.D. 119**
Prov: Palmyra. Loc: Palmyra, A 99. *Funerary: Foundation. On stone tablet.* Bib: *Drawing;* Gaw '70c MF Fondation 39.

1 bt qbwrʾ dh ʿbd ḥlyšy
2 br bryky br blḥzy wšʿd
3 br ʿgʾ br ʿwydy lhwn wlbnyhwn
4 lʿlmʾ byrḥ nysn šnt
5 4.100+20+10

PAT 1220 **Inv 8 63** **n. d.**
Prov: Palmyra. Loc: Palmyra, A 106. *Funerary. On stone tablet.* Bib: *Drawing.*

1 ḥbl tymsʾ br
2 zbdʿth qysʾ
3 wbnwhy pzbdʿth
4 brh wḥbl tymʾ
5 brh wḥbl ʿtʿqb
6 brh wḥbl ʾqmt
7 brt tymʾ ʾmhwn
8 wḥbl šlmt
9 mrbythwn

PAT 1221 **Inv 8 64** **n. d.**
Prov: Palmyra, N necropolis. Loc: Palmyra, A 521. *Funerary. On stone slab.* Bib: *Drawing;* IP 77??.

1 Μνημῖον
2 ʼΑθησώβα
3 ʼΙαρεος

1 npšʾ
2 dʿtšbʾ
3 bt yrḥy
4 mlkw

PAT 1222 **Inv 8 65** **n. d.**
Prov: Palmyra. Loc: Palmyra, A 38. *Funerary: Foundation. On stone tablet.* Bib: *Drawing;* IP 77; Gaw ʾ70c MF Fondation 70.

1 qbrʾ dnh wm[ʿrtʾ .....]
2 [d]y bgwh bnh[y . br ...]
3 [.l]wy br zbdl[h ....]
4 [td]mryʾ by[rḥ .....]
5 [šnt ...] 120[......]

PAT 1223 **Inv 8 66** **n. d.**
Prov: Palmyra. Loc: Palmyra, A 100. *Funerary. On stone tablet fragment.* Bib: *Drawing.*

1 [....] br mqymw br whbl[t] br [..]
2 [....] ʿlmʾ by[rḥ ...]

PAT 1224 **Inv 8 67** **n. d.**
Prov: Palmyra. Loc: Palmyra, A 158. *Funerary. On stone slab fragment.* Bib: *Drawing;* Gaw ʾ70c MF Fondation 71.

1 qbrʾ dnh wmʿrtʾ d[......]
2 ʾdwnʾ br šʿdy br [......]
3 [ʾ]qml [....]
line 2: or: *ʾrwn'*

PAT 1225 **Inv 8 69** **n. d.**
Prov: Palmyra. Loc: Palmyra, A 98. *Funerary: Cession. On stone tablet fragment.* Bib: *Drawing.*

1 bt qb[wrʾ .....]
2 blnwr[y]
3 [l]h w[...]

PAT 1226 **Inv 8 70** **n. d.**
Prov: Palmyra. Loc: Palmyra, A 191. *Funerary. On stone tablet fragment.* Bib: *Drawing.*

1 [.... m]ʿrtʾ dy tḥ[... ....]
2 [...... wlbnw]hy w[.....]

PAT 1226.02 **Inv 8 71** **n. d.**
Prov: Palmyra. Loc: Palmyra Museum. *Funerary. On stone tablet fragment.* Bib: Cantineau Syr ʾ33 Tad 12b with drawing; Déd p 233.

1 [...]
2 [..]wʿzq b?[ytʾ d]nh [dy]
3 bnhy mqym[w b]r zbdb[wl]
4 br ʿrymʾ dy mn? pḥd bn[y]
5 ʿgrwd lh wlbnwhy
6 wlʾḥwhy wʿl zbdbwl
7 ʾbwhy lyqrhwn
Text after Déd p 233; Milik collated with photographs

PAT 1227 **Inv 8 72** **n. d.**
Prov: Palmyra. Loc: Palmyra, A 180. *Funerary: Cession. On door lintel fragments.* Bib: *Drawing;* Gaw ʾ70c MF Cession 52.

1 [.... tḥ]wth rḥq[....]s mn mntʾ [.....]
2 [....] mn smly [.......] ʿlmʾ [.....]

PAT 1228 **Inv 8 73** **n. d.**
Prov: Palmyra. Loc: Palmyra, A 283. *Funerary. On stone tablet.* Bib: *Drawing;* Gaw '70c MF Fondation 75.

1 [bt] qbwr᾽ d[nh ....]
2 [....] br zbdbl [...]
3 [....]n᾽ wmlkw b[r ....]
4 [ml]kw br mqym[w ....]
5 [b]r mzy/qzy lhn
6 [ʿlm]᾽ byrḥ sy[wn ...]

PAT 1229 **Inv 8 74** **n. d.**
Prov: Palmyra. Loc: Palmyra, A 182. *Funerary. On stone tablet.* Bib: *Drawing.*

1 bt ʿl[m᾽ .....]
2 ḥyrn [........]
3 ḥ[......]
4 b[......]

PAT 1230 **Inv 8 75** **A.D. (59)**
Prov: Palmyra. Loc: Palmyra, A 189. *Funerary. On stone tablet fragments.* Bib: *Drawing.*

Fragment A:
1 [....] μνῆμα [τοῦ]το [......... ᾠ-]
2 κοδόμησεν [..............]
3 ιβήλου τοῦ ᾿Ακι[...........]
Fragment B:
1 [...........] τοῦ ἀδελφοῦ [αὐ-
2 τοῦ κα[ὶ τ]ῶν υἱῶν αὐτῶν εἰς τὸ[ν
3 αἰῶνα μηνὸς Ξανδικοῦ ἔτους ο[......]

1 [...... šn]t . . . [.......]300 . . .

PAT 1231 **Inv 8 76** **n. d.**
Prov: Palmyra. Loc: Palmyra, A 190. *Unclassified. On stone fragment.* Bib: *Drawing.*

1 ᾽[.......]bwn᾽ brh [.....]
2 lyqr[hwn] dy ʿlm᾽ šnt [.....]

PAT 1232 **Inv 8 77** **n. d.**
Prov: Palmyra. Loc: Palmyra, A 315. *Unclassified. On stone tablet fragment.* Bib: *Drawing.*

1 [....]᾽ br zbdb[wl .....]
2 [....] ḥy᾽ lyqr[h ....]

PAT 1233 **Inv 8 78** **A.D. (118)**
Prov: Palmyra. Loc: Palmyra, A 316. *Funerary. On stone tablet fragment.* Bib: *Drawing.*

1 [.....]ασεν Βογράνης Ζ[αβδααθους ....]
2 [... μηνὶ Ξανδ]ικῷ τοῦ θκ[υ' ἔτους .....]

1 [........ bgr]n br zbdʿth [......]

PAT 1234 **Inv 8 79** **n. d.**
Prov: Palmyra. Loc: Palmyra, A 264. *Unclassified. On stone tablet fragments.* Bib: *Drawing.*

1 [......]thwn[...... b]rt lšmš br yd[......]
2 [.......]ybl ᾽[....]ml[...]rb᾽ br [......]
3 [....]my[.....]

PAT 1235 **Inv 8 81** **n. d.**
Prov: Palmyra. Loc: Palmyra, A 320. *Unclassified. On stone tablet.* Bib: *Drawing.*

1 [....]ḥry
2 [...]mš᾽
3 [........] plgwt
4 [.........] lšm[...]
5 [......]

PAT 1236 **Inv 8 82** **n. d.**
Prov: Palmyra. Loc: Palmyra, A 321. *Unclassified. On stone tablet fragment.* Bib: *Drawing.*

1 [......].
2 [..... d]y bnw
3 [.........] br
4 [.....]dyn[.]

5 [.........]l nš'?
6 [....] d]y ʿlmʾ

PAT 1237 **Inv 8 83** **n. d.**
Prov: Palmyra. Loc: Palmyra, A 322. *Unclassified. On stone tablet fragment.* Bib: *Drawing.*

1 knwn šnt [...]

PAT 1238 **Inv 8 84** **n. d.**
Prov: Palmyra. Loc: Palmyra, A 323. *Unclassified. On stone tablet fragment.* Bib: *Drawing.*

1 [...]n dy
2 [...]55
3 [...]y

PAT 1239 **Inv 8 85** **n. d.**
Prov: Palmyra. Loc: Palmyra, A 325. *Unclassified. On stone tablet fragment.* Bib: *Drawing.*

1 [...]
2 [...]
3 šlm

PAT 1240 **Inv 8 86** **n. d.**
Prov: Palmyra. Loc: Palmyra, A 326. *Funerary. On stone fragment.* Bib: *Drawing;* Gaw '70c MF Malédictions 2.

1 [..]nk[..]m[..]m
2 ygnb wlʾ ypt̲ḥ ʾyš
3 [.... y]qrh

PAT 1241 **Inv 8 88** **n. d.**
Prov: Palmyra. Loc: Palmyra, A 328. *Unclassified. On stone tablet fragment.* Bib: *Drawing.*

1 [....]dnh ʿ[bd ...]
2 [...]ḥyb[...]

PAT 1242 **Inv 8 89** **n. d.**
Prov: Palmyra. Loc: Palmyra, A 329. *Funerary. On stone fragment.* Bib: *Drawing.*

1 [.... bt] ʿlmʾ dnh [...]

PAT 1243 **Inv 8 90** **n. d.**
Prov: Palmyra. Loc: Palmyra, A 330. *Funerary. On door lintel fragment.* Bib: *Drawing.*

1 [....] dnh bn[...]
2 [....] wlbnyh [...]
3 [...]dy[.....]

PAT 1244 **Inv 8 91** **A.D. (185)**
Prov: Palmyra. Loc: Palmyra, A 95. *Unclassified. On statue-base fragment.* Bib: *Drawing.*

1 [...4]97[...]

PAT 1245 **Inv 8 92** **n. d.**
Prov: Palmyra. Loc: Palmyra, A 96. *Funerary. On statue base.* Bib: *Drawing.*

1 ṣlmtʾ ʾbyšy [...]

PAT 1246 **Inv 8 93** **n. d.**
Prov: Palmyra. Loc: Palmyra, A 97. *Funerary. On stone fragment.* Bib: *Drawing.*

1 ḥyrʾ br zbdbw[l]

PAT 1247 **Inv 8 94** **n. d.**
Prov: Palmyra. Loc: Palmyra, A 101. *Funerary. On relief fragment.* Bib: *Drawing.*

1 [ʿ]gylw
2 br yrḥy
3 br ḥry ḥy[rn]
4 ḥbl

PAT 1248 **Inv 8 95** **n. d.**
Prov: Palmyra. Loc: Palmyra, A 103. *Funerary.*

On relief fragment. Bib: *Drawing.*

1 ʿtʿ
2 qb
3 mqym
4 w gdyʾ
5 ḥbl

PAT 1249 **Inv 8 96** **n. d.**
Prov: Palmyra. Loc: Palmyra, A 104. *Funerary. On relief fragment.* Bib: *Drawing.*

1 [mq]ymt
2 brt mʿnw
3 br mqymw
4 ḥbl
5 mqymt
6 br mlkw
7 ḥbl

PAT 1250 **Inv 8 97** **n. d.**
Prov: Palmyra. Loc: Palmyra, A 107. *Funerary. On relief fragment.* Bib: *Drawing.*

1 ḥyrn br škyb[l ....]
2 lṣḥt ḥbl

PAT 1251 **Inv 8 98** **n. d.**
Prov: Palmyra. Loc: Palmyra, A 108. *Funerary. On relief fragment.* Bib: *Drawing.*

1 ʾmtʾ br[t ...]
2 blḥzy ʾ[....]
3 mlkw [......]
4 šlm [.....]

PAT 1252 **Inv 8 99** **n. d.**
Prov: Palmyra. Loc: Palmyra, A 109. *Funerary. On relief fragment.* Bib: *Drawing.*

1 wrwd
2 br
3 gʿl
4 ḥ[bl]

PAT 1254 **Inv 8 101** **n. d.**
Prov: Palmyra. Loc: Palmyra, 111. *Funerary. On relief fragment.* Bib: *Drawing.*

1 ʾʿy[.....]
2 ʾtt
3 ḥyrn

PAT 1255 **Inv 8 102** **n. d.**
Prov: Palmyra. Loc: Palmyra, 112. *Funerary. On relief fragment.* Bib: *Drawing.*

1 [... ʿ]gylw
2 [....]ḥlynmʾ
3 [...] ḥbl

PAT 1256 **Inv 8 103** **n. d.**
Prov: Palmyra. Loc: Palmyra, 113. *Funerary. On relief fragment.* Bib: *Drawing.*

1 ḥyrn br
2 mqymw
3 mlkw ḥbl

PAT 1257 **Inv 8 104** **n. d.**
Prov: Palmyra. Loc: Palmyra, A 114. *Funerary. On relief fragment.* Bib: *Drawing.*

1 mlkw br
2 nḥšṭb

PAT 1257.02 **Inv 8 105** **n. d.**
Prov: Palmyra. Loc: Palmyra Museum. *Funerary. On relief fragment.* Bib: *Drawing.*

1 ḥbl[...]
2 br mq[...]
3 [.]ʾ[...]

PAT 1258 **Inv 8 106** **n. d.**
Prov: Palmyra, near Hotel Zenobia. Loc: Palmyra, A 116. *Funerary. On relief fragment.* Bib: *Drawing.*

1 ḥbl
2 ḥyrn [....]
3 br mlk[......]
4 br ḥ[.....]
5 [..]ʾ[.....]

PAT 1259 **Inv 8 107** **n. d.**
Prov: Palmyra. Loc: Palmyra, A 117. *Funerary.*
On relief fragment. Bib: *Drawing.*

1 ḥbl
2 šbʾ brt
3 ʿttn
4 br ʿtʾ
5 [....]r[.....]

PAT 1260 **Inv 8 108** **n. d.**
Prov: Palmyra. Loc: Palmyra, A 118. *Funerary.*
On relief fragment. Bib: *Drawing.*

1 ṣlm
2 ḥgy
3 br yrḥy
4 br ʿgʾ
5 ydyʿbl
6 ḥbl

PAT 1261 **Inv 8 109** **n. d.**
Prov: Palmyra. Loc: Palmyra, A 119. *Funerary.*
On relief fragment. Bib: *Drawing;* IP 75.

1 blydʿw
2 br
3 mqymw
4 br mlkw
5 [......]

PAT 1262 **Inv 8 110** **n. d.**
Prov: Palmyra. Loc: Palmyra, A 120. *Funerary.*
On relief fragment. Bib: *Drawing.*

1 ḥbyby
2 mqymw
3 br ʿlyy
4 ḥbl

PAT 1263 **Inv 8 111** **n. d.**
Prov: Palmyra. Loc: Palmyra, A 121. *Funerary.*
On relief fragment. Bib: *Drawing.*

1 [..] m/q[..] brt
2 [..] ʿlyʾ ḥbl

PAT 1264 **Inv 8 112** **A.D. (128/148)**
Prov: Palmyra. Loc: Palmyra, A 122. *Funerary.*
On relief fragment. Bib: *Drawing.*

1 [š]nt
2 4.100+[.]40 ḥbl

PAT 1265 **Inv 8 113** **n. d.**
Prov: Palmyra. Loc: Palmyra, A 124. *Funerary.*
On relief fragment. Bib: *Drawing.*

1 [....]ṣ?k?y
2 brh

PAT 1266 **Inv 8 114** **A.D. 175**
Prov: Palmyra. Loc: Palmyra, A 125. *Funerary.*
On relief fragment. Bib: *Drawing.*

1 šgl
2 brt ḥry yrḥy
3 ḥbl
4 šnt 4.100
5 +80+5+2

PAT 1267 **Inv 8 115** **n. d.**
Prov: Palmyra. Loc: Palmyra, A 126. *Funerary.*
On relief fragment. Bib: *Drawing;* Déd p 25.

1 [.... yr]ḥbwlʾ šwyrʾ [....]
2 mzbtʾ br yr[....]

PAT 1268 **Inv 8 116** **n. d.**
Prov: Palmyra. Loc: Palmyra, A 128. *Funerary.*
On relief. Bib: *Drawing.*

1 šlmt
2 brt zbʾ

3 ḥbl

PAT 1269 **Inv 8 117** **n. d.**
Prov: Palmyra. Loc: Palmyra, A 129. *Funerary.* *On relief.* Bib: *Drawing.*

1 ʿwydt
2 brth ḥbl

PAT 1270 **Inv 8 118** **n. d.**
Prov: Palmyra. Loc: Palmyra, A 130. *Funerary.* *On relief.* Bib: *Drawing.*

1 ʿtšbʾ
2 wbnth
3 br mlkw
4 ḥbl

PAT 1271 **Inv 8 119** **n. d.**
Prov: Palmyra. Loc: Palmyra, A 131. *Funerary.* *On relief.* Bib: *Drawing.*

1 ḥbl
2 ḥnynʾ
3 br ʿgylw
4 nbwlʾ

PAT 1272 **Inv 8 121** **n. d.**
Prov: Palmyra. Loc: Palmyra, A 134. *Funerary.* *On relief fragment.* Bib: *Drawing.* Bib: *Drawing;* Seyrig '37 Pl III 3.

1 tymrṣw
2 br
3 zbdbwl
4 qšt
5 ḥbl

PAT 1273 **Inv 8 122** **n. d.**
Prov· Palmyra. Loc: Palmyra, A 135. *Funerary.* *On relief fragment.* Bib: *Drawing.*

1 m$^?$[.....]
2 mks[...]
3 ms[....]
4 ʾl[....]
5 md[....]

PAT 1274 **Inv 8 123** **n. d.**
Prov: Palmyra. Loc: Palmyra, A 136. *Funerary.* *On relief fragment.* Bib: *Drawing;* Déd p 28.

1 [......]
2 ʾlh[bl]
3 ṣʿdy

PAT 1275 **Inv 8 124** **n. d.**
Prov: Palmyra. Loc: Palmyra, A 137. *Funerary.* *On relief fragment.* Bib: *Drawing;* Déd p 246.

1 ḥyrn br mqym[...]
2 br mlkw mqym[...]
3 ḥbl
4 dy ʿbd l[h .....]
5 mʿny [....]
6 šš[....]

PAT 1276 **Inv 8 125** **n. d.**
Prov: Palmyra. Loc: Palmyra, A 138. *Funerary.* *On relief.* Bib: *Drawing.*

1 [z]bdl
2 nš[ʾ] brh

PAT 1277 **Inv 8 126** **n. d.**
Prov: Palmyra. Loc: Palmyra, A 139. *Funerary.* *On relief.* Bib: *Drawing.*

1 [......]n šnt
2 [.........]5+4

PAT 1278 **Inv 8 127** **n. d.**
Prov: Palmyra. Loc: Palmyra, A 140. *Funerary.* *On relief.* Bib: *Drawing;* Déd p 28.

1 ʾlhšʾ br
2 mqymw br
3 ʾlhšʾ ṣʿdy
4 ḥbl

PAT 1279 **Inv 8 128** **n. d.**

Prov: Palmyra. Loc: Palmyra, A 141. *Funerary.* *On relief.* Bib: *Drawing.*

1 [.....]ny br̊
2 [.....]ymʾ
3 ḥbl

PAT 1280 **Inv 8 129** **n. d.**

Prov: Palmyra. Loc: Palmyra, A 142. *Funerary.* *On relief fragment.* Bib: *Drawing.*

1 mlkw br [....]
2 ḥyrn q[....]
3 ḥbl

PAT 1281 **Inv 8 130** **n. d.**

Prov: Palmyra. Loc: Palmyra, A 143. *Funerary.* *On relief.* Bib: *Drawing;* PS 410.

1 ṣlmt
2 ʾḥtʾ
3 brt ʿqybʾ
4 ḥbl

PAT 1282 **Inv 8 131** **n. d.**

Prov: Palmyra. Loc: Palmyra, A 144. *Funerary.* *On relief.* Bib: *Drawing.*

1 mqym[..]
2 br
3 mqym[..]

PAT 1283 **Inv 8 132** **n. d.**

Prov: Palmyra. Loc: Palmyra, A 145. *Funerary.* *On relief.* Bib: *Drawing.*

1 ḥyrn br
2 ydy[...]nt
3 ḥbl

PAT 1284 **Inv 8 133** **n. d.**

Prov: Palmyra. Loc: Palmyra, A 146. *Funerary.* *On relief.* Bib: *Drawing.*

1 mšk[w]
2 br
3 bwlḥzy
4 ḥbl

PAT 1285 **Inv 8 134** **n. d.**

Prov: Palmyra. Loc: Palmyra, A 147. *Funerary.* *On relief fragment.* Bib: *Drawing.*

1 ḥnʾ
2 brt
3 yrḥy
4 ḥlpt[ʾ]
5 brh
6 ḥbl

PAT 1286 **Inv 8 135** **n. d.**

Prov: Palmyra. Loc: Palmyra, A 148. *Funerary.* *On relief fragment.* Bib: *Drawing.*

1 mqy n[...]
2 mksm[...]
3 ḥ[......]

PAT 1287 **Inv 8 136** **n. d.**

Prov: Palmyra. Loc: Palmyra, A 149. *Funerary.* *On relief.* Bib: *Drawing.*

1 ʿly br
2 tymlt
3 br bydn
4 ḥbl

PAT 1288 **Inv 8 137** **n. d.**

Prov: Palmyra. Loc: Palmyra, A 150. *Funerary.* *On relief.* Bib: *Drawing.*

1 mqy
2 br šʿdy
3 br mqy
4 ḥbl
5 dy ʿbd lh
6 bʿly
7 ššbynh
8 lyqrh

PAT 1289 **Inv 8 138** **n. d.**
Prov: Palmyra. Loc: Palmyra, A 151. *Funerary.* *On relief.* Bib: *Drawing.*

(On right)
1 ṣlmt
2 ḥgʾ
3 brt
4 zbdʾ
5 br mʿny
6 ʾtt
(On left)
7 whby
8 br rmy

PAT 1290 **Inv 8 139** **n. d.**
Prov: Palmyra. Loc: Palmyra, A 154. *Funerary.* *On relief fragment.* Bib: *Drawing.*

1 dy m[....]

PAT 1291 **Inv 8 140** **A.D. 189**
Prov: Palmyra. Loc: Palmyra, A 155. *Funerary.* *On relief fragment.* Bib: *Drawing.*

1 byrḥ
2 šbṭ
3 20+5+[.]
4 šnt
5 5.100

PAT 1292 **Inv 8 141** **n. d.**
Prov: Palmyra. Loc: Palmyra, A 156. *Funerary.* *On relief fragment.* Bib: *Drawing.*

1 [.....]
2 [....]bwl br
3 [.]qyʾ ḥbl

PAT 1293 **Inv 8 142** **n. d.**
Prov: Palmyra. Loc: Palmyra, A 157. *Funerary.* *On statue-base fragment.* Bib: *Drawing.*

1 [ ]
2 pnymn[ ]
3 ḥbl

PAT 1294 **Inv 8 143** **n. d.**
Prov: Palmyra. Loc: Palmyra, A 159. *Funerary.* *On relief fragment.* Bib: *Drawing;* Déd p 173.

1 ḥbl nwrb[l .....]
2 nʿbʾ br n[.....]

PAT 1295 **Inv 8 144** **n. d.**
Prov: Palmyra. Loc: Palmyra, A 160. *Funerary.* *On relief fragment.* Bib: *Drawing;* IP 24; Déd p 251.

1 ḥn[?]wnyʾ[?]
2 ḥbl

PAT 1296 **Inv 8 145** **n. d.**
Prov: Palmyra. Loc: Palmyra, A 161. *Funerary.* *On relief fragment.* Bib: *Drawing;* IP 22.

1 zb[...]
2 ʾl[...]

PAT 1297 **Inv 8 146** **n. d.**
Prov: Palmyra, Valley of Tombs, Funerary Temple 85b (Tomb of Aʿailamī and Zebīdā). Loc: Palmyra, A 162. *Funerary.* *On relief fragment.* Tomb Group: see C4168. Bib: *Drawing;* Déd p 252.

1 ḥbl
2 ʾmš[mš ...]
3 md/r[....]
4 r/d[....]

PAT 1298 **Inv 8 147** **n. d.**
Prov: Palmyra. Loc: Palmyra, A 163. *Funerary.* *On relief fragment.* Bib: *Drawing.*

1 [.....]ṣlmt
2 [...]mt[...]
3 [...]ʿyʾ[...]
4 [...]lh[...]n

PAT 1299 **Inv 8 148** **n. d.**
Prov: Palmyra. Loc: Palmyra, A 165. *Funerary.* *On relief fragment.* Bib: *Drawing.*

1 [.........]
2 ḥbl

PAT 1300 **Inv 8 149** **n. d.**
Prov: Palmyra. Loc: Palmyra, A 166. *Funerary.* *On relief fragment.* Bib: *Drawing.*

1 [....]mbw
2 brt
3 šʿdy
4 ʾtt
5 tymʾ

PAT 1301 **Inv 8 150** **n. d.**
Prov: Palmyra. Loc: Palmyra, A 167. *Funerary.* *On relief fragment.* Bib: *Drawing.*

1 [...] br
2 [...] byrḥ
3 [.. šn]t 4.100
4 +[..]18

PAT 1302 **Inv 8 151** **n. d.**
Prov: Palmyra. Loc: Palmyra, A 168. *Funerary.* *On relief fragment.* Bib: *Drawing.*

1 [....]s
2 [.....]ygʾ

PAT 1303 **Inv 8 152** **n. d.**
Prov: Palmyra. Loc: Palmyra, A 169. *Funerary.* *On relief fragment.* Bib: *Drawing.*

1 ḥggw
2 br
3 [...] ḥbwb?[..]
4 [....]š

PAT 1304 **Inv 8 153** **n. d.**
Prov: Palmyra. Loc: Palmyra, A 170. *Funerary.* *On relief fragment.* Bib: *Drawing.*

1 [...]y br
2 [.....]mʾ

PAT 1305 **Inv 8 154** **n. d.**
Prov: Palmyra. Loc: Palmyra, A 171. *Funerary.* *On relief fragment.* Bib: *Drawing.*

1 [...]br ʿg[....]
2 ḥbl

PAT 1306 **Inv 8 155** **n. d.**
Prov: Palmyra. Loc: Palmyra, A 172. *Funerary.* *On relief fragment.* Bib: *Drawing.*

1 nbwzbd
2 br nbwzbd
3 br nbwzbd
4 ḥbl lʾwm[.....]
5 [..]t ʿg[......]

PAT 1307 **Inv 8 156** **n. d.**
Prov: Palmyra, Tell ez-Zor, near S-W necropolis. Loc: Palmyra, A 173. *Funerary.* *On relief fragment.* Bib: *Drawing.*

(On left)
1 hgy
2 brt
3 yrḥbwlʾ
4 ḥbl
(On right)
1 [....... yrḥb]wlʾ
2 [.......... ḥb]l

PAT 1308 **Inv 8 157** **n. d.**
Prov: Palmyra. Loc: Palmyra, A 174. *Funerary.* *On relief fragment.* Bib: *Drawing.*

1 ntny br
2 šlmlt br
3 lšmš

PAT 1309 **Inv 8 158** **n. d.**
Prov: Palmyra. Loc: Palmyra, A 175. *Funerary.*
On relief fragment. Bib: *Drawing.*

1 šlmʾ brt[......]

PAT 1310 **Inv 8 159** **n. d.**
Prov: Palmyra. Loc: Palmyra, A 176. *Funerary.*
On relief fragment. Bib: *Drawing;* IP 66.

1 [......]r/dn br ʾply
2 [......]šmn

PAT 1311 **Inv 8 162** **n. d.**
Prov: Palmyra. Loc: Palmyra, A 179. *Funerary.*
On statue base. Bib: *Drawing.*

1 bʿšmn br ty[.....]
2 ʾwdr̊nytʾwdr̊
3 [....] ḥbl

PAT 1312 **Inv 8 163** **n. d.**
Prov: Palmyra. Loc: Palmyra, A 181. *Funerary.*
On moulding fragment. Bib: *Drawing.*

1 [ ] ḥbl

PAT 1313 **Inv 8 165** **n. d.**
Prov: Palmyra. Loc: Palmyra, A 184. *Funerary.*
On relief fragment. Bib: *Drawing.*

1 whblt br
2 ʿgylw br
3 yrḥbwlʾ

PAT 1314 **Inv 8 166** **n. d.**
Prov: Palmyra. Loc: Palmyra, A 185. *Funerary.*
On relief fragment. Bib: *Drawing.*

1 mzbt[ʾ]
2 bt ḥlʾ
3 ḥbl

PAT 1315 **Inv 8 167** **n. d.**
Prov: Palmyra. Loc: Palmyra, A 186. *Funerary.*
On relief fragment. Bib: *Drawing.*

1 [....]l mlʾ b[r]
2 [....]ʾ ḥbl

PAT 1316 **Inv 8 168** **n. d.**
Prov: Palmyra. Loc: Palmyra, A 187. *Funerary.*
On relief fragment. Bib: *Drawing.*

1 ḥbl
2 zbdʾ br
3 mlʾ br wly
4 br šnyn 5+4

PAT 1317 **Inv 8 169** **A.D. 155**
Prov: Palmyra. Loc: Palmyra, A 188. *Funerary.*
On relief fragment. Bib: *Drawing;* IP 29.

1 šnt
2 4.100
3 +60+5+2

PAT 1318 **Inv 8 170** **n. d.**
Prov: Palmyra. Loc: Palmyra, A 192. *Funerary.*
On relief fragment. Bib: *Drawing.*

1 ḥbl brm[....]
2 brt ym[.....]
3 mškw ḥ[....]

PAT 1319 **Inv 8 171** **n. d.**
Prov: Palmyra. Loc: Palmyra, A 193. *Funerary.*
On relief fragment. Bib: *Drawing.*

(A)
1 nšʾ br tymʾ
2 ḥbl
(B)
1 ʾg/ʾḥ

PAT 1320 **Inv 8 172** **n. d.**
Prov: Palmyra. Loc: Palmyra, A 194.

Unclassified. On relief fragment. Bib: *Drawing.*

1 mn kl byšʾ klh

PAT 1321 **Inv 8 173** **n. d.**
Prov: Palmyra. Loc: Palmyra, A 195. *Funerary. On relief fragment.* Bib: *Drawing.*

1 ʾmtʾ
2 brt
3 mʿny

PAT 1322 **Inv 8 174** **n. d.**
Prov: Palmyra. Loc: Palmyra, A 196. *Funerary. On relief fragment.* Bib: *Drawing.*

1 ḥyrn
2 br
3 yrḥbwl[ʾ]

PAT 1323 **Inv 8 175** **n. d.**
Prov: Palmyra. Loc: Palmyra, A 197. *Funerary. On stele.* Bib: *Drawing.*

1 ḥbl
2 ʾšdw
3 br pṣy
4 ʾl

PAT 1324 **Inv 8 176** **n. d.**
Prov: Palmyra. Loc: Palmyra, A 198. *Funerary. On relief fragment.* Bib: *Drawing.*

1 [......]šʾ
2 [.... b]r
3 [... yr]ḥbwlʾ
4 [... m]qymw
5 [ḥ]bl

PAT 1325 **Inv 8 177** **n. d.**
Prov: Palmyra. Loc: Palmyra, A 199. *Funerary. On relief.* Bib: *Drawing.*

1 mqymw b[r]
2 mky br
3 mqymw ḥbl

PAT 1326 **Inv 8 178** **n. d.**
Prov: Palmyra, modern village. Loc: Palmyra, A 200. *Funerary. On relief.* Bib: *Drawing.*

1 [....]bly
2 [....] ḥbl

PAT 1327 **Inv 8 179** **n. d.**
Prov: Palmyra, modern village. Loc: Palmyra, A 201. *Funerary. On relief.* Bib: *Drawing.*

1 ʿgylw br
2 mqymw br
3 rpbwl br
4 nṣrlt ḥbl

PAT 1328 **Inv 8 180** **n. d.**
Prov: Palmyra, near Temple of Bel. Loc: Palmyra, A 202. *Funerary. On relief.* Bib: *Drawing.*

1 šky br̊ whby br̊ mlʾ
2 rḥymʾ ʾdyʾ ḥbl

PAT 1329 **Inv 8 181** **n. d.**
Prov: Palmyra. Loc: Palmyra, A 203. *Funerary. On relief.* Bib: *Drawing;* Seyrig Syr ʾ37 p 22 fig 13 (copy).

1 [....]ʾ
2 [....]t
3 [....]ʿwʾ
4 [....]t
5 [....]bwl
6 [....]my
7 [..... ḥ]bl

PAT 1330 **Inv 8 182** **n. d.**
Prov: Palmyra. Loc: Palmyra, A 204. *Funerary. On relief.* Bib: *Drawing;* Syr ʾ37 p 22 fig 13 (copy).

1 [....]bʾ

PAT 1331 **Inv 8 183** **n. d.**
Prov: Palmyra. Loc: Palmyra, A 205. *Funerary. On relief.* Bib: *Drawing;* Syr '37 p 22 fig 13 (copy).

(A)
1 [....]br
2 'plnys
3 ḥbl
(B)
1 [....]t ḥb'
2 [....]ydy brh

PAT 1332 **Inv 8 184** **n. d.**
Prov: Palmyra. Loc: Palmyra, A 206. *Funerary. On relief.* Bib: *Drawing.*

1 mlkw
2 ḥl'
3 ḥbl

PAT 1333 **Inv 8 185** **n. d.**
Prov: Palmyra. Loc: Palmyra, A 207. *Funerary. On relief.* Bib: *Drawing.*

(A)
1 'qm'
2 brt
3 'g'
(B)
1 '[....]
2 '[....]
3 m[....]

PAT 1334 **Inv 8 186** **n. d.**
Prov: Palmyra. Loc: Palmyra, A 208. *Funerary. On relief.* Bib: *Drawing.*

1' [...]δης[...]

1 [....]ṭly'
2 [....]bynh

PAT 1335 **Inv 8 187** **n. d.**
Prov: Palmyra. Loc: Palmyra, A 209. *Funerary. On relief.* Bib: *Drawing.*

1 ḥbl

PAT 1336 **Inv 8 188** **n. d.**
Prov: Palmyra. Loc: Palmyra, A 210. *Funerary. On relief.* Bib: *Drawing.*

1 [...] br [.....]

PAT 1337 **Inv 8 189** **n. d.**
Prov: Palmyra. Loc: Palmyra, A 211. *Funerary. On relief.* Bib: *Drawing.*

1 [.....]ḥy't[.....]

PAT 1338 **Inv 8 190** **n. d.**
Prov: Palmyra, Tell ez-Zor, near S-W necropolis. Loc: Palmyra, A 212. *Funerary. On relief.* Bib: *Drawing.*

1 ṣlm bwn'
2 br bwn'
3 ḥbl

PAT 1339 **Inv 8 191** **n. d.**
Prov: Palmyra. Loc: Palmyra, A 213. *Funerary. On relief.* Bib: *Drawing.*

1 [......]bw
2 [......] dnt
3 [... yr]ḥbwl'
4 [.........]

PAT 1340 **Inv 8 192** **n. d.**
Prov: Palmyra. Loc: Palmyra, A 178. *Funerary. On relief.* Bib: *Drawing.*

1 [......]ḥ
2 [......]ḥt
3 [...] br
4 [..]' ḥbl

PAT 1341 **Inv 8 195** **n. d.**
Prov: Palmyra, necropolis, S of Jebel Qalaᶜat ibn

Maᶜan. Loc: Palmyra, A 219. *Funerary. On klinè fragment.* Bib: *Drawing.*

(A)
1 [.......] br
2 [.......]r
3 [......]bʾ
(B)
1 ʾqm[t]
2 ʾtth

PAT 1342 **Inv 8 196** **n. d.**
Prov: Palmyra. Loc: Palmyra, A 224. *Funerary. On relief.* Bib: *Drawing.*

1 [......] br
2 [...] mlkw

PAT 1343 **Inv 8 197** **n. d.**
Prov: Palmyra. Loc: Palmyra, A 225. *Funerary. On relief.* Bib: *Drawing.*

1 [....] br
2 ḥbl

PAT 1344 **Inv 8 198** **n. d.**
Prov: Palmyra. Loc: Palmyra, A 451. *Funerary. On relief.* Bib: *Drawing.*

1 ḥbl
2 ḥ[l]ptʾ
3 br qwqʾ
4 ḥlptʾ

PAT 1345 **Inv 8 199** **n. d.**
Prov: Palmyra. Loc: Palmyra, A 342. *Funerary. On relief.* Bib: *Drawing.*

1 [......]
2 ḥbl

PAT 1346 **Inv 8 200** **n. d.**
Prov: Palmyra, E of village. Loc: Palmyra, A 454. *Honorific. On column.* Bib: *Drawing;* IP 45; Ber '36 5; Déd p 325.

(A)
1 [ṣlmt...]ʾ brt mqy
2 [ʾmby dy] ʿbd lh mʿny
(B)
1 ṣlmt hgr brt mqy
2 ʾmby dy ʿbd lh mʿny
(C)
1 ʾḥwh

IP and Inv 8 text incomplete; Ber '36 5 gives whole text

PAT 1347 **Inv 9 1** **A.D. 32**
Prov: Palmyra, Temple of Bel, reemployed. Loc: Palmyra, A 26. *Honorific. On statue base.* Bib: Syr '33 1; RosAH 4.

1 byrḥ tšry šnt 3.100+40+10+5+2
2 ṣlmʾ dnh dy lšmš br tybwl
3 br škybl dy mn bny kmrʾ dy
4 ḥnk hyklʾ dy bl wyrḥbwl
5 wʿglbwl ʾlhyʾ bqdšwhy
6 ywm šttʾ bnysn šnt 3.100+40+3
7 dy ʾqymw lh bnwhy lyqrh

PAT 1348 **Inv 9 3** **n. d.**
Prov: Palmyra, Temple of Bel. Loc: E wall. *Graffito. On wall.* Bib: *Drawing.*

1 hlyd/rn

PAT 1349 **Inv 9 4a, 4b** **n. d.**
Prov: Palmyra, Temple of Bel. Loc: Palmyra, *in situ. Honorific. On stone slab.* Bib: *Drawing.*

1 Μνησθῇ ʽΑντίοχος
2 καθηγητῆς.

Gk goes with (A)

(A)
1 dkyr ʾṭykʾ
2 sbrʾ
(B)
1 dkyr ʾlhšʾ
2 br dynys

PAT 1350 **Inv 9 5a** **n. d.**
Prov: Palmyra, Temple of Bel, S peristyle of cella. Loc: Palmyra, *in situ. Honorific. On column drum.* Bib: *Drawing.*

1 dkyr zbdʾ
2 [br]ʿdl b[r] zbd[ʾ]
line 2: with Stark PN p 120

PAT 1351 **Inv 9 7** **A.D. (328)**
Prov: Palmyra, Temple of Bel. Loc: Palmyra, 220. *Honorific. On satue base.* Bib: *Drawing.*

1 byrḥ šbṭ šnt 3.100+20+10+5 ṣlmʾ dnh dy
2 [yd]y br mlkw br gylw br ʿbdʿstwr br ʿtzʾ
3 [dy] mn bny zbwd dy ʾqymw lh gylw wydy
4 bnwhy

PAT 1352 **Inv 9 11** **A.D. 24**
Prov: Palmyra, Temple of Bel. Loc: Palmyra, *in situ. Honorific. On column console.* Bib: Syr '31 4; RosAH 3.

1 Μάλιχον Νεσᾶ τοῦ Βωλάα τοῦ ἐπικαλ-
2 ουμένου ʽΑσάσου, φυλῆς Χομαρηνῶν, Παλ-
3 μυρηνῶν ὁ δῆμος, εὐνοίας ἕνεκα.

1 b[yr]ḥ knwn šnt 3.100+20+10+5+1 ṣlmʾ dnh dy mlkw
2 br nšʾ br bwlḥʾ dy mtqrʾ ḥšš dy mn bny
3 kmrʾ dy ʾqymw lh t[g]ryʾ klhwn dy bmdynt
4 bbl mn dy špr lhwn bkl gns klh wʿ[d]r bnynʾ
5 dy h[y]klʾ dy bl wyhb mn kysh dy lʾ ʿbdh
6 ʾnš bdyl kwt ʾqymw lh ṣlmʾ dnh lyqrh

PAT 1353 **Inv 9 12** **A.D. 35**
Prov: Palmyra, Temple of Bel. Loc: Palmyra, *in situ. Honorific. On column console.* Bib: Syr '31 5.

1 Μάλιχον Νεσᾶ τοῦ Βωλάα τοῦ ʽΑσά-
2 σου, φυλῆς Χομαρηνῶν, οἱ ἀργυρο-
3 τομίαι καὶ Παλμυρηνῶν ὁ δῆμος,
4 εὐνοίας ἕνεκα.

1 [b]yrḥ sywn šnt 3.100+20+10+5+1 ṣlmʾ dnh dy
2 [ml]kw br nšʾ br bwlḥʾ ḥšš dy mn bny kmrʾ
3 [dy] ʾqymw lh ʾnwš ʿnwštʾ wgbl tdmryʾ
4 [mn d]y špr lhwn wlmḥwzhwn wlbt ʾlhyhwn

PAT 1354 **Inv 9 14b** **n. d.**
Prov: Palmyra, Temple of Bel. Loc: Palmyra, *in situ. Honorific. On column console.*

1 nsʾ br ḥlʾ
2 br nsʾ ʾḥmr

PAT 1355 **Inv 9 16** **n. d.**
Prov: Palmyra, Temple of Bel. Loc: Palmyra, *in situ. Honorific. On column console.* Bib: Syr '31 7.

1 [ṣlmʾ dnh] dy tymʿmd br nšʾ br [.....]
2 [...... d]y mn pḥd bny šmʿr/šmʿd

PAT 1356 **Inv 9 20** **A.D. 56**
Prov: Palmyra, Temple of Bel. Loc: Palmyra, *in situ. Honorific. On column console.* Bib: *Drawing*; Déd p 72.

1 [Αἱράνην Βωννέ]ους [τοῦ ʽΡαβ]βήλου [τοῦ Βων-]
2 [νέους] τοῦ ʼΑθηναθάνου τοῦ ἐπικαλουμέ[νου Βαρ-]
3 [σαά]θου, φυλῆς Μιθηνῶν, ἱερεῖς θεοῦ μεγίσ[του Διὸς]
4 [Βήλου], τειμῆς καὶ εὐνοίας ἕνεκεν, ἔτους ζξτʹ, μη[νὸς]
5 Ξανδικοῦ ηʹ

1 byrḥ nysn šnt 3.100+60+10+1 ṣlmʾ dnh d[y]
2 ḥyrn br bwnʾ br rbʾl br bwnʾ br ʿtntn dy
3 [mt]qrʾ buršʿt dy mn bny mytʾ dy ʾqym[w]
4 [lh k]mryʾ dy bl

PAT 1357 **Inv 9 26** **A.D. 193**
Prov: Palmyra, Temple of Bel, Propylaeum. Loc: Palmyra, *in situ. Honorific. On stone tablet.* Bib:

Drawing; Syr '31 3; Déd p 254.

1 [..........................]
2 [..........................]
3 καὶ Μεζαββ[άνη.....] τοῦ Μαλίχου
4 τοῦ Ζεβει [..........ἀ]ρχιερεὺς κ[αὶ]
5 [σ]υμποσιάρχ[ης ἱερέων με]γίστου θεοῦ
6 Διὸς Βήλ[ου......... ἔτ]ους δφ' Λώου.

1 [ʾw]ṭqrṭwr qs[r .....]
2 [....] dy ʾqym lh mlk[w ...]
3 mtqr̊ʾ mzbnʾ br b[.....]
4 bmr̊zḥwth dy km[rʾ dy bl....] byrḥ ʾb šnt 5.100+[4]

PAT 1358 **Inv 9 28** **A.D. 272**
Prov: Palmyra, Temple of Bel, Propylaeum. Loc: Palmyra, *in situ*. *Honorific*. *On stone tablet*. Bib: IP 31; Syr '71 pp 413-21; Déd p 270; RosAH 18.

1 brbnwt mrzḥwt ḥdwdn snqlṭyqʾ
2 br ʿgylw mqy dkyryn wbrykyn ʾnšʾ dy
3 hww mhrqryn b[bt bl m]lʾ br yrḥy mlʾ
4 dy hwʾ[...]šʿʾ brʾtʿqb šʿʾ
5 dy hwʾ ʿ[l ...ʾd]r?wnʾ wʾtʿqb br yrḥy ʿl
6 twnʾ [......] ʿgylw dy hwʾ ʿl ʿmwdʾ
7 wnrqys wʿgylw br mhrdd dhwʾ qym ʿl
8 ṭlyʾ wʿgylw br wrwd dhwʾ qym ʿl ʿmwdʾ (or: ʿmwrʾ)
9 wbt nṭrʾ wšmʿ ṭbyt byrḥ ʾdr šnt 5.100+80+3

line 7: *wnrqys* with Stark PN p 120; text after Déd p 270 (Milik collated with photo and stone)

PAT 1359 **Inv 9 29** **A.D. (239+)**
Prov: Palmyra, Temple of Bel, reemployed. Loc: Palmyra, *in situ*. *Honorific*. *On stone block*. Bib: IP 32; Déd p 103.

1 [ṣlmʾ dnh dy ......] brʿth br zbydʾ br [.....]
2 [.....]ʾ bydʾ rḥym mdyth [wdḥyl ʾlhyʾ]
3 [..... dy ʾqymw] lh bwlʾ wdmws lyqrh
4 [....... byrḥ] ʾb šnt ḥmš mʾh wḥmšyn [........]

Text of Inv 9 29; more reconstruction Déd p 203

PAT 1360 **Inv 9 30** **n. d.**
Prov: Palmyra, Temple of Bel, reemployed. Loc: Palmyra, A 222. *Honorific*. *On column drum*. Bib: *Drawing*.

1 Ἡ βουλὴ [καὶ ὁ δῆμο]ς
2 Ἰούλιον Αὐρήλιον [Ν]ε[β]ού-
3 μαιον Θαι[μισάμ]σο[υ τ]οῦ
4 Βωννέο[υ]ς [Σ]αβεῖ συνοδι-
5 άρχην ἀνακο[μ]ίσ[αντ]-
6 α τὴν [συ]νοδίαν [κ]αὶ ἀρέ-
7 σαν[τα] τῇ πόλει· [τειμῆς]
8 χάριν [........]

1 [ṣlmʾ dnh dy ywlys] ʾwrlys
2 [nbwmy br tymšm]š bwnʾ
3 [šby... dy ʾqym]t lh
4 [....]

PAT 1361 **Inv 9 33** **A.D. 128**
Prov: Palmyra, Temple of Bel, reemployed in Muslim wall. Loc: Palmyra, *in situ*. *Honorific*. *On column console*. Bib: Syr '31 9, fig 9.

1 ṣlmʾ dy ḥbʾ br bgšw
2 br zbdbwl dy ʾqymw lh
3 bny ḥšš lyqrh byrḥ
4 ʾyr šnt 4.100+20+10+5+4

PAT 1362 **Inv 9 34** **n. d.**
Prov: Palmyra, Temple of Bel, reemployed in Muslim wall. Loc: Palmyra, *in situ*. *Honorific*. *On column console*. Bib: Syr '31 10, fig 10.

1 ṣlmʾ dnh dy bgšw br ḥb[ʾ br]
2 bgšw dy ʾqymw lh bny ḥ[šš]
3 [lyq]rh byr[ḥ .....] šnt [.....]

PAT 1362.02 **Inv 9 35bis** **n. d.**
Prov: Palmyra. Loc: Palmyra Dépôt A233. *Unclassified*. *On fragment*. Bib: *Drawing*.

1' [...]ʾwym 4 b[...]

PAT 1363 **Inv 10 3** **n. d.**
Prov: Palmyra, Agora. Loc: Palmyra, *in situ*.

Graffito. On door frame.

1 dkyr whblt

PAT 1364 **Inv 10 4** **n. d.**
Prov: Palmyra, Agora. Loc: Palmyra, *in situ*, S 1911. *Honorific. On double console.* Bib: *Pl V, 4.*

(On right)
1 ṣlm yrḥy br mq[y]mw
2 br zbdʿth dkʾ
(On left)
1 [wṣlm ... ʾḥwhy]
2 dy [ʿbd] lh[wn] mqymw ʾbwhn
3 btr dy myt lyqrhwn byrḥ
4 tšry šnt 4.100+80+10+4/4.100+80+10+3

PAT 1365 **Inv 10 6** **n. d.**
Prov: Palmyra, near Agora. Loc: Palmyra, *in situ*, S 1962. *Unclassified. On door lintel.* Bib: *Pl V, 1.*

1 [...]tyḥwt
2 [...]šlmn[....]

PAT 1366 **Inv 10 7** **A.D. (before 88)**
Prov: Palmyra, Agora. Loc: Palmyra, *in situ*, S 1910. *Unclassified. On console.* Bib: *Pl V, 12.*

1 [......οἱ ἀνα-]
2 βάντες ἀπὸ Σπασινο[υ Χαρακ-]
3 ος Παλμυρηνῶν ἔμ[ποροι....]

1 [.... tgry]ʾ dy tdm[wr dy slqw]
2 [ʿmh mn krkʾ] dy myšn lyq[rh]
3 [byrḥ ...] šnt 3.100+20+[.] [...]

PAT 1367 **Inv 10 8** **A.D. (before 88)**
Prov: Palmyra, outside Agora. Loc: Palmyra, A 1057. *Unclassified. On console fragment.* Bib: *Pl V, 9.*

1 [... šn]t 300[...]

PAT 1368 **Inv 10 11** **n. d.**
Prov: Palmyra, Agora. Loc: Palmyra, A 1057. *Unclassified. On console fragment.* Bib: *Pl II, 3.*

1 [bwlʾ] wdmws

PAT 1369 **Inv 10 12** **n. d.**
Prov: Palmyra, Agora. Loc: Palmyra, A 972. *Honorific. On wall console.* Bib: *Pl VIII, 7.*

1' [.....]
2' [Π]αλμύρα[ς μητρο]κολων[ε]ίας τιμ[ῆς]
3' χάρι[ν, ἔτους...] μην[ὸς 'Απελ]λαίο[υ].

1' [...]h lyq[rh ...]

PAT 1370 **Inv 10 13** **A.D. 218**
Prov: Palmyra, Agora. Loc: Palmyra, *in situ*. *Honorific. On column.* Bib: *Pl II, 4.*

1 [ṣ]lm[ʾ] dnh dy tybwl br
2 [....] br[.]b[.....]
3 [... dy ʿ]bdw lh bw[lʾ wd]mws
4 bgrmṭyʾ dydh b[d]yl dy [š]pr
5 lh[n w]m[g]d lbnynʾ dy b[....]
6 [.....]mlw[.]ʾ q[...]
7 [ḥm]š mʾ[h] lyqrh byrḥ
8 nysn šnt 5.100+20+5+4

PAT 1371 **Inv 10 16** **n. d.**
Prov: Palmyra, Agora. Loc: Palmyra, A 993. *Honorific. On console fragment.* Bib: *Pl II, 2.*

1 [.......]λλαθου τοῦ
2 [...τειμῆ]ς ἕνεκεν

1 ṣlmʾ dnh d[y....lt]
2 [br] b?n?y dy ʿb?[d lh...]

PAT 1372 **Inv 10 24** **A.D. 164**
Prov: Palmyra, Agora. Loc: Palmyra, *in situ*. *Honorific. On pillar.* Bib: *Pl II,7*; Déd p 275.

1 [τὸν ἀ]νδριά[ντα Αδδουδ]ανου Αγεγου [τοῦ

Λισαμσου]
2 [τοῦ] Ζαρζιραθου ἀνέστησεν Αλαισας ἀδελφὸς
3 [αὐτο]ῦ ἱεράσαντα Βήλω θεῷ ἐξ ἰδίων Αδδουδανην
4 [υἱὸν αὐτοῦ, μηνὸς Ξανδι]κοῦ τοῦ εου' ἔτ[ο]υς.

1 [ṣ]lmʾ dn[h dy] ḥ[d]wdn br ḥggw lš[mš]ʾ zrzyrt dy ʾqym l[h]
2 ʿlyšʾ ʾḥ[w]hy lyqrh bdyl dy qdš lh ḥdwdn brh mn
3 [k]ysh l[...]h byrḥ nysn šnt 4.100+60+10+5

2 [...]
(On right side of statue)
1 lyqr[h]
2 [byrḥ nysn šn]t? [4.100+40+2]

PAT 1373 **Inv 10 29** **A.D. 161**
Prov: Palmyra, Agora. Loc: Palmyra, *in situ,* S 1737. *Honorific. On column console.*

1 Μᾶρκον Αἰμίλιον Μαρκιανὸν
2 Ἀσκληπιάδην, Ἀντιοχέων βου-
3 λευτήν, τεταρτώνην, οἱ ἀναβάν-
4 τες ἀπὸ Σπασινου Χαρακος ἔμπο-
5 ροι, προηγουμένου αὐτῶν Νεση Βωλι-
6 αδους, ἔτους βου', μηνὶ Πανήμωι.

1 mrqs ʾmlyws mrqynws
2 ʾsqlpydʾ blwṭ bʾnṭkyʾ dy rbʿʾ
3 ʿbdw lh tgryʾ dy slq mn krkʾ
4 dy slq bhwn ršʾ šyrʾ nšʾ br blydʿ
5 byrḥ qnyn šnt 4.100+60+10+4

PAT 1374 **Inv 10 38** **A.D. 131**
Prov: Palmyra, Agora. Loc: Palmyra, *in situ,* S 1494. *Honorific. On column console.* Bib: *Pl III, 1.*

1 Ιαραιον Νεβο[υζαβαδ]ου τοῦ
2 [Σ]αλαμαλλαθου [τοῦ] Αχχαδανου
3 [Ἀδ]ριανὸν Παλμυρηνόν, σατρά-
4 [π]ην Θιλουανων Μεερεδατου
5 βασιλέως Σπασινου Χαρακος
6 οἱ ἐν (Σ)πασινου Χαρακι ἔνποροι,
7 τειμῆς χάριν. ἔτους βμυ', μη[νὶ]
8 Ξανδικῷ

(Under Greek text)
1 [ṣlmʾ dnh] dy yrḥy br nbwzbd br

PAT 1375 **Inv 10 39** **A.D. 75**
Prov: Palmyra, Agora. Loc: Palmyra, *in situ,* S 1307. *Honorific. On column console.* Bib: *Pl II, 5*; IP 6.

1 [ἡ βουλὴ]
2 Ζαβδιλαν Σαμσιγεραμου Ιο[υ]σα γραμματέα πᾶσαν φιλοτειμ[ίαν] ἐνδειξάμενον ἐν τοῖς τῆς πό-
3 λεος [πρ]άγμασι [κ]αὶ ἁγνῶς γραμματ[εύσα]ντα, τειμῆς χάριν, ἔτους ζπτ'.

1 ṣlmʾ dnh dy zb[d]lh br šmšgrm ʾyšʾ
2 grmṭws rḥym mḥwzh wbkl ṣ[b]w klh
3 špr lmdyth wʾp bgrmṭyʾ dy lh hlk
4 [špy]r wbdylkwt bwlʾ ʾqymt lh
5 ṣlmʾ dn[h] lyq[rh byrḥ ... šn]t
6 3.100+[80+5+2]

PAT 1376 **Inv 10 40** **A.D. (81)**
Prov: Palmyra, Agora. Loc: Palmyra, *in situ,* S 1308. *Honorific. On console.* Bib: *Pl II, 1*; IP 7.

1 [Ζ]αβδιβωλον Ο[γ]ηλου το[ῦ Αμ-]
2 μαθου τοῦ Λαχει Παλμυρην[ον]
3 οἱ ἀπὸ Σπασίνου Χάρακος ἀν[αβ]άντες Παλμυρηνοὶ ἔμπορο[ι]
4 τειμῆς χάριν.

1 ṣlmʾ dnh d[y] zbdbwl
2 [br] ʿgylw br [ʿm]t br ʿ[.....]
3 [d]y mn bny mʿzyn dy ʾqymw lh tgryʾ
4 [tdmryʾ dy s]lqw mn krk my[šn]
5 [lyqrh byrḥ ʾ]b [šn]t 3.100+[80+10+2]

PAT 1377 **Inv 10 42** **n. d.**
Prov: Palmyra, Agora. Loc: Palmyra, A 1023. *Honorific. On console fragment.*

1' [....] ωαπο

1' [... mn] pḥz

PAT 1378 **Inv 10 44** **A.D. 199**
Prov: Palmyra, outside Agora. Loc: Palmyra, *in situ,* S 1861. *Honorific. On wall console.* Bib: *Pl V, 3*; Déd pp 23-27 and pl II, 1.

1 Προστάγματι βουλῆς καὶ δήμου,
2 αἱ τέσσαρες φυλαὶ Ογηλον Μακκαιου τοῦ Ογηλου τοῦ Αγεγου
3 τοῦ Σεουιρα δι' ἀρετὴν πᾶσαν καὶ ἀνδρείαν καὶ διὰ τὰς συνεχεῖς τὰς
4 κατὰ τῶν νομάδων στρατηγίας συναράμενον καὶ τοῖς ἐν-
5 πόροις καὶ ταῖς συνοδίαις ἀεὶ τὴν ἀσφάλιαν παρασχόντα ἐν πάσαις
6 συνοδιαρχίαις καὶ πολλὰ καὶ διὰ ταῦτα ἐξ ἰδίων ἀναλώσαντα καὶ πᾶ
7 σαν πολειτίαν λαμπρῶς καὶ ἐνδόξως ἐκτε[λέσαντα], τειμῆς χάριν, ἔτους ι[φ]'.

1 btwḥyt bwl' wdms
2 ṣlmy' 'ln 'rb'tyhwn dy 'gylw br mqy 'gylw
3 šwyr' dy 'bd lh 'rb' pḥzy' lyqrh bdyl dy špr
4 lhwn b'sṭrṭgwn šgy'n wbṣryḥyn
5 wšyryn dy slq bhn 'qly dy 'pq mn kysh
6 npqn rbrbn wsy' tgry' bkl ṣbw klh
7 w'bd plṭy' šbyḥyt wnhwryt byrḥ
8 ṭbt šnt 5.100+10

PAT 1379 **Inv 10 48** **n. d.**
Prov: Palmyra, Agora, N-E corner. Loc: Palmyra, A 1033. *Honorific. On console fragment.* .

1' [....]
2' [dy ']qymw [lh ....]r' bd?[yl dy .....]
3' [byr]ḥ 'd[r šnt ......]

PAT 1380 **Inv 10 49** **n. d.**
Prov: Palmyra, Agora, N-E corner. Loc: Palmyra, A 1039. *Honorific. On console fragment.*

1 [.....]
2 [']w?rly' [.....]
3 w?lb[.....]

PAT 1381 **Inv 10 53** **A.D. 211**
Prov: Palmyra, Agora. Loc: Palmyra, *in situ,* S 565. *Honorific. On stone tablet.* Bib: *Pl VIII, 4.*

1 ṣlm' dnh dy yrḥbwl' br
2 mqymw br šrykw dy 'qym
3 lh ymlkw br whblt gwrny btr
4 mwt' dy whblt 'bwhy lyqrh
5 bdyl dy hlk 'mh špr byrḥ
6 'b šnt 5.100+20+2

PAT 1382 **Inv 10 54** **A.D. 122**
Prov: Palmyra, Agora. Loc: Palmyra, *in situ,* S 1170. *Honorific. On wall console.* Bib: *Pl II, 8.*

1 [...........]
2 Μαλιχον Χειλου τοῦ καὶ Καιε-
3 μου τοῦ Νουρβηλου τοῦ Χει-
4 λου τὸν φιλόπατριν καὶ φιλό-
5 τειμον, τε[ιμῆς χά]ριν, ἔτους
6 γλυ', μηνὸς Δύστρου.

1 [ṣlmh] d[nh dy m]l?k?w br khylw qymw
2 [br nwrbl br khy]l?w rḥym mdyth dy
3 [......]l[.......] lh bdyl
4 [kwt 'qymw .....] l?ḥ?lqh kl
5 [...............]q? ywm
6 [......] b'lwl lyqrh šnt
7 [... tltyn] wtlt byrḥ 'dr

PAT 1383 **Inv 10 56** **n. d.**
Prov: Palmyra, Agora. Loc: Palmyra, A 1009. *Unclassified. On stone fragments.*

1' [...Σ]οαδον Β[ωλιαδους...]
2' [.....]ουτ[..........]

1 [... š'd]w br bl[yd']

PAT 1384 **Inv 10 57** **n. d.**
Prov: Palmyra, Agora. Loc: Palmyra, *in situ,* S 1782. *Honorific. On wall console.* Bib: *Pl IV, 1;*

VIII, 3.

1 Ἡ βουλὴ
2 [.......]ον Θαιμαρσου τοῦ Μα-
3 [λιχου του Λι-]
4 σα[μσου τ]ὸ[ν] ε[ὐ]σεβῆ
5 [καὶ φιλότειμ]ον [σ]ύνεδρον αὐτῆ-
6 [ς, ἔτους ...]

1' [........]' br tymrṣw br mlkw [......]
2' [........] dy ʿbdt lh bwlʾ lyqrh

PAT 1385 **Inv 10 61** **n. d.**
Prov: Palmyra, Agora. Loc: Palmyra, A 1013. *Honorific. On stone fragment.* Bib: *Pl V, 10.*

1 [.....]w?n[...]
2 [..... dy] ʾqymw [...]
3 [.... t]lt pḥzyʾ[.........] 10+[.]+3 (or: 1.100+[.]+3)

PAT 1386 **Inv 10 62** **A.D. 111**
Prov: Palmyra, Agora. Loc: Palmyra, A 1015, A 1003. *Honorific. On console fragments.* Bib: *Pl VI, 4.*

1 ṣlmʾ dnh dy mlʾ br tym[.........]
2 dḥl ʾlhyʾ wrḥym m?d?y?n?t?[h dy ʾqy]m l?h? [...]
3 [... byr]ḥ ʾdr šnt 4.100+20+2

PAT 1387 **Inv 10 63** **n. d.**
Prov: Palmyra, Agora. Loc: Palmyra, *in situ,* S 1781. *Honorific. On console.* Bib: *Pl VI, 1.*

1 ἡ βουλὴ
2 Ελαβηλον Ε(λ)αβηλου τοῦ [Ζαβδιβωλο]υ
3 Αεουαδου, εὐσ[εβῆ........]

1 ṣlm ʾlhbl br ʾlhbl br
2 zbdbwl ʾh?w?d dy ʿbdt lh
3 bwlʾ bmwtbh lyqrh

PAT 1388 **Inv 10 65** **n. d.**
Prov: Palmyra, Agora. Loc: Palmyra, A 999. *Honorific. On stone fragment.*

1 [...]ḥ?lʾ[....]
2 [...]lʾl?[....]

PAT 1389 **Inv 10 69** **A.D. (112)**
Prov: Palmyra, Agora, S-W wall. Loc: Palmyra, *in situ,* S 1209. *Honorific. On wall console.* Bib: *Pl III,* 2; Déd p 266.

1 ἡ βουλὴ
2 Αγεγον Ιαραιου τοῦ Ογα, εὐσε[β]ῆ καὶ
3 φιλότειμον σύνεδρον αὐτῆ[ς, τειμῆς]
4 χάριν, ἔτους γκυʹ, μηνὸς Λώ[ου].

1 [ṣlmʾ] dnh dy ḥggw br yrḥy br ʿgʾ ydyʿbl
2 [dḥl ʾl]hyʾ wrḥ[ym mdyth] d[y] ʿbdt lh
3 [bwlʾ lyqrh b]yrḥ ʾb šnt 4.100+[20+3]
1 [......]lkb[..]

Line 4 Gk: γκυʹ conjecture for ικυʹ of text.

PAT 1390 **Inv 10 70** **n. d.**
Prov: Palmyra, Agora, S corner. Loc: Palmyra, A 1008. *Unclassified. On stone fragment.* Bib: *Pl IV, 4.*

1 [......]lkb[..]

PAT 1391 **Inv 10 72** **n. d.**
Prov: Palmyra, Agora. Loc: Palmyra, A 1017. *Unclassified. On stone fragment.*

1 ms/qṭt[...]

PAT 1392 **Inv 10 74** **n. d.**
Prov: Palmyra, Agora. Loc: Palmyra, A 1004. *Honorific. On console fragment.* Bib: *Pl V, 11.*

1 [.....μηνὸς Λώ]ου

1 ṣlmʾ d[nh dy .....]
2 dḥl ʾl[hyʾ ....]
3 bwlʾ lyqrh b[yrḥ ʾb šnt ...]

PAT 1393 **Inv 10 75** **n. d.**
Prov: Palmyra, Agora. Loc: Palmyra, A 1005. *Honorific. On stone fragment.* Bib: *Pl V, 5.*

1 [.. ʿb]dt ṣlm[.....]
2 [... l]ḥyy ʾt[th ...]
3 [....]lyqr[....]

PAT 1394 **Inv 10 76** **n. d.**
Prov: Palmyra, Agora. Loc: Palmyra, A 1001. *Unclassified. On stone fragment.* Bib: *Drawing (reversed).*

1 [....]lḥyʾ[....]
2 [.. lyq]rh b[yrḥ ...]

PAT 1395 **Inv 10 77** **A.D. 157**
Prov: Palmyra, Agora. Loc: Palmyra, A 997. *Honorific. On console.* Bib: *Pl VI, 7.*

1 Μᾶρκον Οὔλπιον Ιαραιον
2 Αιρανου τοῦ Αβγαρου υἱὸν, Θαιμεις
3 Θαιμαρσου τοῦ Λισαμσου τοῦ Γουρ-
4 ονναιου τὸν ἑαυτοῦ εὐεργέτην,
5 τειμῆς χάριν, ἔτους ηξυʹ, μηνὸς Ξ-
6 ανδικοῦ.

1 [ṣlm mrqs ʾlpys yrḥy br ḥyrn] ʾbgr dy
2 [ʾqym lh tymʾ br] tymrṣw lšmš gwrny
3 [....... bk]l ṣbw klh lyqrh bnysn šnt
4 [4.100+40]+20+5+3

PAT 1396 **Inv 10 78** **A.D. 157**
Prov: Palmyra, Agora. Loc: Palmyra, *in situ,* S 760. *Honorific. On console.* Bib: IP 8.

1 Μᾶρκο[ν] Οὔλ[πιον Ι]αραιο{ς}<ν> Αιρα-
2 νου τοῦ Αβ[γαρου Β]ηλσουρος
3 Ιαραιου τοῦ θιξη τὸν αἰαυτοῦ (sic)
4 φίλον τειμῆ[ς] χάριν, ἔτους θξυʹ.

1 ṣlm mrq[s ʾlpys yrḥy] br
2 ḥy[rn ʾbgr dy ʾqym lh]
3 blšwr b[r yr]ḥy [br tym]ʾ
4 rḥmh lyq[rh byrḥ]
5 [... šnt 4.100+60+5+4]

line 3: *[tym]ʾ* with Stark PN; published Gk text questionable at this point

PAT 1397 **Inv 10 81** **A.D. 135**
Prov: Palmyra, Agora. Loc: Palmyra, *in situ,* S 1903. *Honorific. On wall console.*

1 [ʾΙούλιον Μάξιμον (ἑκατόνταρχον) λεγ(ιῶνος) ..]
2 Μᾶρκος Οὔλπιος Αβγαρος
3 Αιρανου υἱὸς καὶ οἱ ἀπὸ Σπασινου
4 Χαρακος, τειμῆς χάριν.

1 ṣlmʾ dnh
2 dy ywlys mksms qṭrynʾ dy lgywnʾ
3 dy ʿbdw lh mrqs ʾlpys ʾbgr br
4 ḥyrn ʾbgr wbny šyrtʾ dy slqt ʿmh
5 mn krk myšn lyqrh bkslw šnt <4.100+>40+5+2

PAT 1398 **Inv 10 85** **A.D. 193**
Prov: Palmyra, (Agora?) reemployed in wall. Loc: Palmyra, A 1056. *Honorific. On column console.* Bib: *Pl VI, 2.*

1 [......] ʼΑ[..]ε(or σ)[....]ν [στ-]
2 [ρατηγή]σαντα ἐπισήμως κα[ὶ ἀ-]
3 γορανομήσαντα ἁγνῶς καὶ ἐπ[ι-]
4 μελῶς, ὡς καὶ ὑπὸ ʼΙαριβ[ω]λου
5 [τοῦ π]ατρ[ώ]ου θ[ε]οῦ μαρτ[υ-]
6 ρηθῆναι, τειμῆς ἕνεκα, μ[ηνὶ]
7 [Δαισ]ίω (or [Δ]ίω) τοῦ φʹ ἔτους.

1 [....]
2 b[...]
3 lqrh[....]
4 shd lh byrḥ s?[ywn šnt 5.100+4]

PAT 1399 **Inv 10 90** **(A.D. 157)**
Prov: Palmyra, Agora. Loc: Palmyra, S 118 (A 969). *Honorific. On column console.* Bib: *Pl III, 7.*

1 Μᾶρκον Οὔλπιον Ιαραιο-
2 ν Αιρανου τοῦ Αβγαρου
3 υἱὸν, ἡ ἀναβᾶσα ἀπὸ Σπ-

4 ασινου Χαρακος συνο-
5 δία, διὰ <Ια>δδαιου Ζαβδιλα
6 τοῦ Ιαδδαιου, τειμῆς
7 χάριν, ἔτους ηξυʹ,
8 [μ]ηνὸς Αυδναίου

1 ṣlm mrqws ʾlpys yrḥy br ḥyrn
2 ʾbgr dy ʾqymt lh šyrtʾ dy
3 slqt mn krkʾ bšyrt yd?y br zbdl?[h]
4 ydy lyqrh byrḥ ṭb?t šnt? [468]

PAT 1400 **Inv 10 91** **n. d.**
Prov: Palmyra, Agora. Loc: Palmyra, A 1075. *Honorific. On console fragment.* Bib: Déd p 32. Bib: *Drawing (reversed).*

1 ʾ?l?p?y?s?
Déd p 32: perhaps belongs with Syr '33 p 187 and Inv 10 95 (Gk text)

PAT 1401 **Inv 10 93** **n. d.**
Prov: Palmyra, Agora, rampart. Loc: Palmyra, A 1083. *Unclassified. On relief fragment.*

1 [...]
2 mʿny ʾt[th]

PAT 1402 **Inv 10 94** **n. d.**
Prov: Palmyra, Agora, rampart. Loc: Palmyra, A 1076. *Unclassified. On stone fragment.* Bib: *Pl V, 6.*

1 [...]ʾ wʿgy?l[w ...]

PAT 1403 **Inv 10 96** **n.d.**
Prov: Palmyra, Agora, rampart. Loc: Palmyra, A 964. *Honorific. On console fragment.* Bib: *Pl IV, 5.*

1 Μᾶρκον Οὔλπ[ιο]ν Ιαραιον Αιρα[νου]
2 τοῦ Αβγαρου υ[ἱὸν] τὸν φιλόπατριν·
3 [ἔ]μποροι οἱ ἀν[αχ]θέντες ἀπὸ Σκυθ[ίας]
4 [ἐν] πλύω Ονα[ιν]ου Αδδουδανου τοῦ
5 [....., πάσῃ προ]θυμίᾳ βοηθήσαντα
6 αὐτοῖς καὶ συνλαβόμενον, τειμῆς
7 χάριν. Δύστρω τοῦ ηξυʹ ἔτους

1 ṣlmʾ dnh dy [mrqs ʾlpys yrḥy br ḥyrn ʾbgr]
2 dy ʾqymw l[h tgryʾ dy ...]
3 [..] ḥ?n?ynw br?[ḥdwdn .....]
4 [ly]qrh by[rḥ ʾdr šnt 4.100+60+5+3]

PAT 1404 **Inv 10 98** **A.D. (109+)**
Prov: Palmyra, Agora. Loc: Palmyra, A 966. *Honorific. On console fragment.* Bib: *Pl VI, 5.*

1 [.... r]ḥym m[dyt]h dy ʿbdt lh
2 bwlʾ lyqrh? šnt? 4.100+20+[.]

PAT 1405 **Inv 10 99** **A.D. 141**
Prov: Palmyra, Agora, rampart. Loc: Palmyra, A 968+A 1037+A 1030. *Honorific. On console fragments.* Bib: *Pl IV, 7 a and b.*

1 [Μ]ᾶρκον Οὔλπιο[ν Αβγα]ρον, ἔπαρχον
2 Παλμυρηνῶ[ν το]ξοτῶν καὶ γερ
3 [......]
4 [Μᾶρ]κοι Οὔλπιοι Ο[.....]
5 [.........]ων ἑκατόντ[αρχος]
6 [.........] οἱ υἱοὶ αὐτοῦ, τε[ιμῆς]
7 [χάριν, ἔ]τους βνυʹ, Αὐδυναίο[υ].

1 ṣ?lm? ʾbgr br tymr?[ṣw ......]
2 [... dy] ʿ?bd lh [......]

PAT 1406 **Inv 10 102** **n. d.**
Prov: Palmyra, Agora, rampart. Loc: Palmyra, A 1040. *Honorific. On console fragment.* Bib: *Pl VI, 3.*

[...]MHMO[...]

1 [... qr]ṭsṭs wgmnsyrks?[....]
2 [.. ʾwṭ]q?rṭwr ʾṭnynys q[sr ...]
3 [.... y]qrh bʾrgwnʾ [....]
4 [.....] rḥym m?d?[yth ...]
5 [.....]

PAT 1407 **Inv 10 105** **n. d.**
Prov: Palmyra, Agora. Loc: Palmyra, *in situ,* S 13 (A 633). *Honorific. On column console.* Bib: Syr '38 30.

1 [ἡ βουλὴ καὶ ὁ δῆμος]
2 Μαλιχον Μοκ[ειμου τοῦ]
3 Αιρανου τοῦ Βαραθ[ους]
4 εὐσεβῆ καὶ φιλόπατριν κ[αὶ]
5 φιλότειμον, τειμῆς χάριν,
6 ἔτους πλυ'

1 [ṣlm]ʾ dnh dy mlkw br mqymw
2 [br ḥyrn br] brʿy dḥl ʾlhyʾ
3 [....]

PAT 1408 **Inv 10 106** **A.D. 119**
Prov: Palmyra, Agora. Loc: Palmyra, *in situ,* S 1854. *Honorific. On wall console.* Bib: *Pl VII, 4.*

1 [....] br mlkw nšwm
2 [dy ... lh b]wlʾ bmwtbh
3 [lyqrh byr]ḥ ʾyr šnt 4.100+20+10

Line 2 *bmwtbh*: *w* omitted by typographical error in Inv 10 106.

PAT 1409 **Inv 10 107** **A.D. 159**
Prov: Palmyra, Agora. Loc: Palmyra, A 621. *Honorific. On column console.* Bib: Syr '38 28A. Bib: *Pl VIII, 1.*

1 [Μᾶρκον Οὔλπιον Ιαραιον] Αιρα[νου τ]οῦ Αβγαρο[υ]
2 [ἡ] ἀναβᾶσα ἀπὸ Σπασινου Χαρακο[ς]
3 συνοδία ἧς ἡγήσατο Αβγαρος υἱὸ[ς]
4 αὐτοῦ, βοηθήσαντα αὐτῇ παντὶ
5 τρόπω, τειμῆς χάριν, ἔτους ου'
6 μηνὸς ʼΑρτεμεισίου.

1 ṣlm mrqs ʾlpys yrḥy br ḥyrn
2 ʾbgr dy ʾqymw lh šyrtʾ dy slqt
3 mn krk ʾspsnʾ ʿm ʾbgr brh bdyl
4 dy ʿdrh bkl ṣbw klh lyqrh
5 byrḥ ʾyr šnt 4.100+60+10

PAT 1410 **Inv 10 110** **n. d.**
Prov: Palmyra, Agora. Loc: Palmyra, A 1054. *Unclassified. On capital.*

1 [....]
2 ʾb[..]
3 glwp$^{?}$[ʾ]

PAT 1411 **Inv 10 111** **A.D. 156**
Prov: Palmyra, Agora. Loc: Palmyra, A 603. *Honorific. On column console.* Bib: *Pl VII, 5*; Syr '38 28B.

1 [ṣlm mr]qs ʾlpys yrḥy b[r]
2 [ḥyr]n ʾbgr dy ʾqmt l[h]
3 šyrtʾ dy nḥtt lkrkʾ
4 bdyl dy qm wʿdrnn bkl ṣbw
5 klh lyqrh by[r]ḥ ʾb šnt
6 4.100+60+5+2

PAT 1412 **Inv 10 112** **A.D. 140**
Prov: Palmyra, outside Agora. Loc: Palmyra, A 1055=A 1070. *Honorific. On console fragments.* Bib: *Pl VII, 2.*

1 [.....................]
2 [τοῦ ʼΑ]λεξάνδ[ρου, ἄρχοντα $^{?}$
3 [Φορ]αθων τῆς περ[ὶ Σπασινου]
4 [Χα]ρακα· ἡ μετὰ Μαλχο[υ τοῦ]
5 [Αζ]ειζου παραγενομένη
6 ἀπ[ὸ τ]οῦ Χαρακος εἰς Παλμυρα
7 <καὶ> Ολογαισίαν συνοδία, τειμῆς
8 ἕνεκεν, ἔτ[ο]υς ανυ',
9 μηνὸς Γορπιαίου.

1 [ṣlmʾ dnh dy...]py[.]
2 [...br ʾlksndrs ... prt]m$^{?}$yšn
3 [dy ʾqymw lh bny šyrtʾ]
4 [dy] slqw ʿm [mlkw br ʿzyzw] mn krk[ʾ]
5 d$^{?}$y$^{?}$ myšn lʾlgšyʾ wltdmr bdyl dy
6 [špr lhn bkl] ṣbw klh lyqrh
7 [byrḥ ʾlwl šnt 4.100+]40+10+1

PAT 1413 **Inv 10 113** **A.D. 174**
Prov: Palmyra, Agora. Loc: Palmyra, *in situ,* S

1990. *Honorific. On wall console.*

1 L(*vcio*) ANTONIO CALLIS
2 TRATO MANC(*ipi*) IIII MER(*catvrae*)
3 GALENVS ACTOR

1 Λ. Ἀντωνίῳ Καλ-
2 λιστράτῳ τεταρτώ-
3 νῃ, Γαληνὸς πραγ-
4 ματευτὴ[ς] ἴδιο[ς].

1 ṣlm' dnh dy {b}<l>wqys 'nṭwnys
2 qlsṭrṭs dy rb'' dy
3 'qym lh lyqrh glnws
4 prgmṭṭ' dydh byrḥ 'b šnt 4.100+80+5

PAT 1414 **Inv 10 114** **A.D. 138**
Prov: Palmyra, Agora. Loc: Palmyra, A 618. *Honorific. On console fragments.* Bib: *Pl IV 8 a, b, c, d*; Seyrig '37c pp 369-70; Cantineau '39 pp 277-79, drawing p 278 (see MelDus p 277 below).

1 ἡ βουλὴ Ιαριβωλην Λισαμσο[υ τοῦ ......]
2 Ααβει τὸν φιλόπατριν καὶ φ(ι)λότ[ειμον, τειμῆς]
3 χάριν, ἐν παντὶ καιρῷ προ[θύμως συνερ-]
4 γοῦντα ἐμπόροις τοῖς ἐ[ν Σπασινου Χα-]
5 [ρακι] καὶ [συναρ]άμενον αὐ[τοῖς .....]
6 [..]ε ἀφειδήσ[α]ντα ψυχῆς κα[ὶ χρημα-]
7 [τ]ων καὶ π[ρεσβεύσαντα] αὐθαιρέτως
8 [πρὸς Ὀρώδην τὸν β]ασιλέα τῆς Αἰλ[υ-]
9 [μήνης ....]κῶν δωρη-
10 [.....................]
11 [.....................]
12 [......................]
13 [.........] τῇ Αἰλυμήνῃ [................]
14 [.........] ποτωναποι [..........] ευ[χα-]
15 ριστηθῆναι αὐτὸν [............ ἐ]πὶ τῆς
16 κρατίστης βουλῆ[ς ....] αὐτοῦ τὸ
17 πρὸς τὴν πατρί[δα ....με]μαρ-
18 [τύ]ρηκεν [κατ]ὰ καιροὺς διὰ ψηφισμάτων παρὰ[...]
19 [..........] καὶ Βρουττίῳ Πραίσεντι καὶ Ἰουλίῳ Μ[...]
20 [.........ὑ]πατικοῖς, ἔτους θμυ', Ξανδικοῦ.

1 ṣlm yrḥbwl' br lšmš[....]
2 [....]
3 [..]kktbw tgry' tdmry' [....]
4 [zb]nyn wl' z'wrn 'wdw lbwl' [...]
5 [....]t[...]
6 [.....bdy]l dy
7 [.....] bšwšn
8 [.....] wrwd mlk
9 [......]

PAT 1415 **Inv 10 115** **n. d.**
Prov: Palmyra, Agora, rampart. Loc: Palmyra, *in situ*, S 1872. *Honorific. On double console.* Bib: *Pl VII, 1a, b, c.*

1 [ἡ βουλὴ καὶ ὁ δῆμος Ἰούλιον Αὐρήλιον Μαλι? χον] Ουασεου Μαλιχου το[ῦ] <Ου>ασεου Νεβουλα, στρατη[γήσαντα τῆς κολωνείας]
2 [καὶ ἀγορανομήσαντα ἐπι]σήμως καὶ φιλοτείμω[ς] ὡς ἐπὶ πᾶσιν μεμαρτυρῆσθαι ὑπό τε τοῦ πατρῴου θεοῦ καὶ τῆς
3 [κρατίστης βουλῆς καὶ τοῦ λαμ]προτάτου ἡγουμένου, κα[ὶ] Ουασεω πατρὶ αὐτοῦ πάσας λειτουργίας ἐκτελέσαντι, τειμῆς καὶ μνή-
4 [μης χάριν].

1 ṣlmy' 'ln tlt' dy ywlys 'wrlys mlkw br wsḥw br mlkw br wsḥw nbwl' dy 'bdt lh bwl'? wdmws [b'sṭrṭgwt' dy]
2 qlny' wbrbnšqwth dy špr lhwn wḥsr lhwn mn kysh w'l hnn shd lh 'lh' [w]skrt lh mdyth wshd lh [nhyr' hgmn' wlwsḥw 'bwh]
3 dy špr bkl 'ḥydw klh lmdyth lyqrh byrḥ ṭbt [šnt ...]

PAT 1416 **Inv 10 118** **n. d.**
Prov: Palmyra, outside Agora. Loc: Palmyra, A 1066. *Dedicatory. On crater fragment.* Bib: *Pl V, 7.*

1 [..] 'rṣw [...]

PAT 1417 **Inv 10 119** **A.D. 214**
Prov: Palmyra, Agora. Loc: Palmyra, *in situ*, S 200. *Honorific. On double console.* Bib: *Pl VIII,*

5.

1 Θαιμ[ην] Αλ[αφ]αθα
2 Βαραθο[υς] Αλλαταιου καὶ Αλαφα-
3 θαν υἱὸν [α]ὐτοῦ,
4 ʼΙουλία Αὐρηλία Αγγη
5 τὸν πατέρα καὶ τὸν
6 ἀδελφόν, τιμῆς καὶ
7 μνήμης χάριν,
8 ἔτους ζκφʹ, Λώου, μετὰ
9 τὴν τε[λε]υτήν.

1 ṣlmyʾ ʾln trwyhwn dy
2 tymʾ wdy ḥlptʾ brh
3 br ḥlptʾ brʿth ʾlṭy
4 dy ʾqymt lhyn btr
5 mwthn ḥgʾ brth dy
6 tymʾ wʾḥth <dy> ḥlptʾ
7 lyqrhyn byrḥ ṭbt šnt
8 5.100+20+5

PAT 1418 **Inv 10 123** **n. d.**
Prov: Palmyra, Agora, W corner. Loc: Palmyra, A 979. *Unclassified. On plinth fragment of console.*

1 [...]wn š[nt ...]

PAT 1419 **Inv 10 124** **A.D. 150**
Prov: Palmyra, Agora, rampart. Loc: Palmyra, nos. A 975+A 976. *Honorific. On wall console.* Bib: *Pl IV, 2a, b.*

1 Νε[ση Αλ]α τοῦ Νεση τοῦ Αλα συνο[διάρχην]
2 ἡ σ[υνκα]ταβᾶσα μετʼ αὐτοῦ συνο<δ>ία εἰς [ʼΟλο-]
3 γασίαν, μηνὶ Περιτίῳ τοῦ
4 αξυʹ ἔτους, τειμῆς <κ>αὶ εὐχα-
5 ριστεί<α>ς ἕνεκεν.

1 ṣlmʾ dnh
2 dy <n>šʾ br ḥlʾ br nšʾ ḥlʾ dy
3 ʿbdw lh bny šyrtʾ dy nḥtw
4 ʿmh mn tdmwr lʾlgšyʾ bdyl
5 [dy špr l]hwn wʿdrnwn bkl [ṣbw]
6 klh lyqrh byrḥ [š]bṭ šnt 4.100+60+1

PAT 1420 **Inv 10 126** **n. d.**
Prov: Palmyra, Agora (from a pit). Loc: Palmyra, (Museum) S 2338. *Honorific. On column console (painted).* Bib: *Pl III, 4.*

1 lṣlm ywlys ʾwrlys
2 lšmš br tymw

PAT 1421 **Inv 10 127** **A.D. 86**
Prov: Palmyra, Agora (from a pit). Loc: Palmyra, A 1901. *Honorific. On console.* Bib: *Pl IV, 6.*

1 [ἡ βο]υλὴ Ιαρ[αιον Ζαβδιλα φιλόπατριν καὶ
2 [φιλότειμ]ον εὐνοίας καὶ σπου
3 [δῆς ἕνεκεν ἧς ε]νδέδεικται πρὸς
4 [τοὺς ἐμπό]ρους, τειμῆς χάριν
5 [ἔτους ζϘτʹ μην]ὸς Γορπιαί[ου].

1 bwlʾ lyrḥy br zbdlʾ qr[..]
2 lḥšbn ḥpy<ṭ>wtʾ wḥšʾ ṭb[ʾ]
3 dy ʾšt<k>ḥ lh lwt tgryʾ
4 lyqrh byrḥ ʾlwl
5 šnt 3.100+80+10+5+2

Line 2 *ḥpy<ṭ>wtʾ*: conjecture of Hillers for *ḥpywtʾ*; see Glossary.

PAT 1422 **Inv 10 128** **n. d.**
Prov: Palmyra, Agora (from a pit). Loc: Palmyra, S 2342=A 1105. *Honorific. On console fragment.* Bib: *Pl VIII, 6.*

1 [Τιβέριον Κλαύδιον ....]
2 ἔπαρχον σπείρης πρώτης Αὐγούς-
3 της Θρακῶν ἱππέων καὶ χειλίαρχον
4 λεγέωνος ἑκκαιδεκάτης Φλαουίας
5 Φίρμης καὶ ἔπαρχον εἴλης πρώτης
6 [Οὐλπί]ας δρομαδαρίων Παλμυρη-
7 [νῶν καί πολείτη]ν τῆς Παλμυρη-
8 [ν]ῶν πόλεως, Μᾶρκος Οὔλπιος
9 Αιρανου υἱός, Σεργία, Ιαραιος, τὸν
10 ἑαυτοῦ φίλον [........]

1 ṣ?lm[h] dnh dy ṭbrys qlwdys py[......]
2 ʾlʾ drmdryʾ b[...]gr[.]yn[.]d[y ʾqym]
3 lh mr?q?[s] ʾl?pys [y]rḥy br ḥyr[n ʾbgr]
4 [rḥmh lyqrh byr]ḥ? ʾb šn[t ....]

PAT 1423 **Inv 10 129** **A.D. 108**

Prov: Palmyra, Agora (from a pit). Loc: Palmyra, (Museum) S 2343. *Honorific. On console.* Bib: *Pl III, 3.*

1 [ἡ βουλὴ καὶ ὁ δῆμος]
2 Γάιον ʼΙούλιον Ελαβηλου υἱόν,
3 Φαβία, Αιρανην, εὐσεβῆ καὶ φιλό-
4 τειμον πολείτην, τειμῆς ἕνεκεν, ἔτους ιθυʹ, μηνὸς Ξανδικοῦ.

1 ṣlmʾ dnh dy gʾys ywlys ḥyrn
2 br ʾlhbl dy ʿbdt lh bwlʾ
3 wdms lyqrh byrḥ nysn
4 šnt 4.100+10+5+4

PAT 1424 **Inv 10 130** **n. d.**

Prov: Palmyra, Agora (from a pit). Loc: Palmyra, (Museum) S 2351. *Honorific. On console.* Bib: *Pl III, 6.*

1 Γάιον Λικίνιον Φλαβιανόν Βυρρου υ[ἱόν],
2 Σεργία, Μαλιχον, Ζεβειδας, Αβδας
3 καὶ Αβδαασθωρης οἱ Νεσα του Αθη-
4 [ακαβου τὸν] ἑαυτῶν εὐεργέτην
5 τειμῆς ἕνεκεν.

1 [ṣlm]ʾ dnh dy gʾys
2 [lqn]ys plwynws br bwrpʾ srgyʾ
3 [mlkw] dy ʾqy[mw lh zbydʾ wʿbdy]
4 [wʿ]bdʿstwr bny n[šʾ ʿtʿ]qb
5 lyqrh [.....]

PAT 1425 **Inv 10 131** **A.D. 81**

Prov: Palmyra, Agora (from a pit). Loc: Palmyra, (Museum) S 2352. *Honorific. On console.* Bib: *Pl III, 8*; Déd p 234.

1 Μαλιχον Λισαμσου τοῦ Ελ[α-]
2 βηλου τοῦ Ααβει, Αγρουδηνοὶ τει-
3 μῆς ἕνεκεν, ἔτους β(ϙ)τʹ μηνὸς Λώο[υ].

1 ṣlmʾ dnh dy mlkw br lšmš br
2 ḥnbl br brʿth ʾʿby dy ʾqymw
3 lh bny ʿgrwd lyqrh bdyl dy špr
4 lhwn byrḥ ʾb šnt 3.100+80+10+2

PAT 1426 **Inv 10 132** **n. d.**

Prov: Palmyra, Agora, debris. Loc: Palmyra, A 989. *Unclassified. On fragment.* Bib: *Pl V, 8.*

1 [... rḥym md]y$^{?}$th [.....]
2 [.... byrḥ] sy$^{?}$[wn šnt ...]

PAT 1426.02 **Inv 10 140** **n. d.**

Prov: Palmyra, Agora, debris. Loc: Palmyra Museum A 1090. *Unclassified. On fragment.*

1 ḥbl

PAT 1427 **Inv 10 141** **n. d.**

Prov: Palmyra, Agora, debris. Loc: Palmyra Museum. *Funerary. On relief fragment.*

1 [...]r/d b$^{?}$r b$^{?}$l[...]

PAT 1428 **Inv 10 144** **n. d.**

Prov: Palmyra, Agora, S corner. Loc: Palmyra, (Museum) S 2140. *Unclassified. On architectural fragments.* Bib: *Drawing*; Déd p 143; Sta ʼ49c pp 61-62, Pl III, 2, 3.

1 [...]zby lʿglbwl wmlkbl [...]

Line 1 *wmlkbl*: with Déd :: Inv *wmlkbwl*

PAT 1429 **Inv 10 145** **A.D. (30+)**

Prov: Palmyra, Agora, reemployed in buttress. Loc: Palmyra, *in situ*, S 2312. *Dedicatory. On stone block.* Bib: *Pl VI, 8*; Sta ʼ49c pp 44-46, Pl III, 1.

(above; series of two-line texts)
1 ṣlm mlkw br bl[ʿ]qb
2 br ʾbynt
3 ṣlm ʿth [. brt]
4 nšʾ br mtʾ ʾtth
5 ṣlm blʿqb br
6 ḥyrn blʿqb
7 ṣlm blʿqb br
8 mlkw br blʿqb

9 ṣlm mqym[w]
10 br mlkw
(below)
1 [byrḥ ... šnt 3.100+*x*+]40+2 ḥmnʾ dnh ʿbdw wqrbw mlkw br blʿqb br m[ykʾ ...]
2 [.....] mn pḥd bny zmrʾ lšdrpʾ wldʿnt ʾlhyʾ ṭb[yʾ ....]

PAT 1430 **Inv 11 1** **A.D. 235**
Prov: Palmyra. Loc: Palmyra, A 538. *Dedicatory. On altar.* Bib: *Pl I.*

1 bryk šmh lʿlmʾ
2 ʿbd wmwdʾ
3 yrḥblʾ wbrḥwm
4 ʾʿylm wʾqmʾ
5 ʾtʿm dy qrw
6 lrḥmnʾ wʿnnwn
7 ʿn lhwn byrḥ
8 nysn šnt 5.100+40+5+1

PAT 1431 **Inv 11 2** **A.D. 137**
Prov: Palmyra. Loc: Palmyra, A 29. *Dedicatory. On altar.* Bib: *Pl I.*

1 lbryk šmh lʿlmʾ
2 ʿbd lšmšy br tymʾ
3 lšmšy ʿl ḥyy zbydʾ
4 brh byrḥ nysn šnt
5 4.100+40+5+3

PAT 1432 **Inv 11 3** **A.D. 138**
Prov: Palmyra. Loc: Palmyra, A 837. *Dedicatory. On altar.*

1 [..] wḥyy b[......]
2 [. ʿ]lmʾ wldkrn [.....]
3 [..]h wʿbšy brh
4 [šn]t 4.100+40+10 [......]

PAT 1433 **Inv 11 4** **A.D. 139**
Prov: Palmyra, reemployed. Loc: Palmyra, A 532. *Dedicatory. On altar.* Bib: *Pl I.*

1 dkrn lbryk šmh
2 lʿlmʾ qrb ʿbny
3 ʿl ḥywhy wʿl ḥyy zbd[ʾ]
4 bnwh lʿlmʾ byrḥ
5 ʾlwl šnt 4.100+40+10

PAT 1434 **Inv 11 5** **A.D. 165**
Prov: Palmyra. Loc: Palmyra, A 525. *Dedicatory. On altar.* Bib: *Pl I.*

1 lbryk šmh
2 lʿlmʾ ʿbdt tdʾl brt
3 ḥry bss br mʿn[w]
4 br ʾrqṭws byr[ḥ]
5 šbṭ šnt 4.100
6 +60+10+5+1

PAT 1435 **Inv 11 6** **A.D. 182**
Prov: Palmyra. Loc: Palmyra, A 470. *Dedicatory. On altar.*

1 lbryk šmh lʿlmʾ ʿbd
2 krsmʾ br ḥ[.......]
3 zbdʿth br [.......]
4 ʿbd ʿltʾ dh[......]
5 dkrn lbryk šmh lʿlmʾ
6 ʿl ḥywhy wḥyy bnw[hy]
7 wḥyy ʾḥwhy wlḥyy bny
8 bˀyˀtʾˀ klhwn byrḥ ʾdr
9 šnt 4.100+80+10+3
10 dˀkˀyˀr l[..]wmˀ[.........]
11 [...] bṭb

PAT 1436 **Inv 11 7** **n. d.**
Prov: Palmyra. Loc: Palmyra, A 573. *Dedicatory. On altar.* Bib: IP 74. Bib: *Pl III.*

1 [lbry]k šmh lʿlmʾ
2 [ʿbd] šlmlt br tymʾ [...]
3 knwnyn trn ʿl ḥywh[y wḥyy]
4 ʾḥyh wʿl ḥyy bnw[hy byrḥ]
5 nysn šnt 4[....]

PAT 1437 **Inv 11 8** **n. d.**
Prov: Palmyra. Loc: Palmyra, A 246. *Dedicatory. On altar.* Bib: *Pl I.*

1 lb[ryk šmh]

2 lʿ[lmʾ rḥ]
3 [mn]ʾ wṭbʾ [ʿbd]
4 [....] br zb[d]ʾ w[...]
5 [....]ʿl ḥywh wḥyʾ
6 byth klh [by]r[ḥ ...]
7 šnt 5.100+[....]

PAT 1438 **Inv 11 9** **n. d.**
Prov: Palmyra. Loc: Palmyra, A 248. *Dedicatory. On altar.* Bib: *Pl II.*

1 bryk šmh lʿlmʾ ṭbʾ wrḥmnʾ
2 [ʿ]bd ʿltʾ dh w[mw]dʾ gdyʾ b[r]
3 [yr]ḥy [br] gdʾ lbryk šmh lʿlm[ʾ]
4 [ṭb]ʾ wrḥ[m]nʾ [ʿl ḥy]wh wḥy[...]
5 [šnt] 5.100+[.....]

PAT 1439 **Inv 11 10** **A.D. 205**
Prov: Palmyra. Loc: Palmyra, A 286. *Dedicatory. On altar.* Bib: *Pl I.*

1 [......]mw[...]nʾ
2 [.....]h$^{?}$ ʿl ḥyʾ
3 mlkw br lšmš byr$^{?}$ḥ$^{?}$
4 ʾyr šnt 5.100+10+5+1

PAT 1440 **Inv 11 11** **A.D. 213**
Prov: Palmyra, reemployed in Arab fortification. Loc: Palmyra, A 1157. *Dedicatory. On altar.* Bib: *Pl I.*

1 ʿltʾ d[h dy]
2 ʿbd ʿgy[lw br]
3 tymrṣw b[r]
4 ḥdʾ qrb
5 [lr]ḥmnʾ wlʾ[lhʾ]
6 ṭbʾ wsk[rʾ]
7 wmwdʾ dy q[rh
8 w]ʿynh wʾdnʾh
9 byrḥ ṭbt šnt
10 5.100+20+4

line 4: *ḥdʾ* (for *ḥm*ʾ) with Stark PN p 120

PAT 1441 **Inv 11 12** **A.D. 214**
Prov: Palmyra. Loc: Palmyra, A 390+A 391. *Dedicatory. On altar fragments.* Bib: *Pl II.*

1 byrḥ šbṭ šnt
2 5.100+20+5 qrb
3 [ʿg]ylw br zbdbwl br
4 [.....]
5 [.....]
6 wml$^{?}$kbl ʾlhyʾ ʿl
7 ḥywhy wḥyy bnwhy
8 [wlḥyy] ʾḥwhy

PAT 1442 **Inv 11 13** **A.D. 219**
Prov: Palmyra, reemployed in Arab fortification. Loc: Palmyra, A 1159. *Dedicatory. On altar.*

1 [bryk š]mh lʿ[lmʾ]
2 [ṭbʾ] wrḥm[nʾ]
3 [wt]y$^{?}$rʾ ʿbd wmw[dʾ]
4 [ḥ]yrn ṭlyʾ dy [....]
5 ydʾ br mʿyʾ ʿl
6 ḥywh wḥyʾ bnʾ
7 mrwhy byrḥ sywn
8 šnt 5.100+20+10

PAT 1443 **Inv 11 14** **A.D. 221**
Prov: Palmyra. Loc: Palmyra, A 255. *Dedicatory. On altar.*

1 [bryk] šm[h]
2 [......]
3 [......]
4 [......] b$^{?}$rsmy$^{?}$ʾ
5 [ʿl] ḥywhy wḥyʾ
6 šlmlt ʾmh
7 byrḥ ʾyr š[nt]
8 5.100+20+10+2

PAT 1444 **Inv 11 15** **A.D. (239)**
Prov: Palmyra. Loc: Palmyra, A 549. *Dedicatory. On altar.* Bib: *Pl I.*

1 b[r]yk šmh lʿlmʾ
2 ʿbd gdʾ wmwdʾ br
3 ḥlpʾ ʿl ḥywh wḥyʾ
4 bnwhw gdh dy sy[wn]
5 šnt 5.100+40+10+[.]

PAT 1445 **Inv 11 16** **A.D. 217**
Prov: Palmyra, reemployed. Loc: Palmyra, A 377. *Dedicatory. On altar.* Bib: *Pl III.*

1 bryk šmh lʿlmʾ ṭb[ʾ]
2 wrḥmnʾ ʿbd wmwdʾ
3 bwnʾ ʿgʾ gbyns ʿl ḥy[wh]
4 wḥyʾ bny byth dy qr lh
5 wʿnyh šnt 5.100+20+5+2
6 byrḥ ʾb

PAT 1446 **Inv 11 17** **A.D. 246**
Prov: Palmyra. Loc: Palmyra, A 289. *Dedicatory. On altar.* Bib: *Pl II.*

1 [bryk] šmh lʿlmʾ
2 [ʿbd] lrḥmnʾ
3 [....]t br
4 [....]ʾ ʿl ḥyʾ
5 [bny] byth klhwn
6 [dy] qrw lh
7 wʿnnwn šnt
8 5.100+40+10+5+2

PAT 1447 **Inv 11 19** **A.D. 256**
Prov: Palmyra. Loc: Palmyra, A 438. *Dedicatory. On altar.*

1 [b]ryk šmh l[ʿlmʾ ṭbʾ]
2 r?ḥ?mnʾ ʿbd w?m?wdʾ
3 [...] br zbwdw br ʿbʾ
4 [l]ḥyw wlḥ?yʾ ʾḥwh?y?
5 qr lh wʿnyh š[nt]
6 5.100+60+5+3

PAT 1448 **Inv 11 20** **A.D. 263**
Prov: Palmyra. Loc: Palmyra, A 273. *Dedicatory. On altar.* Bib: *Pl IV.*

1 lbryk šmh lʿlmʾ
2 rḥmnʾ ṭbʾ wtyrʾ
3 ʿltʾ dnh ʿbd wmwdʾ
4 [y]rḥbwlʾ br yrḥbwlʾ
5 ʿrgʾ ʿl ḥyʾ ʾbwhy
6 wbny byth klhwn
7 lʿlmʾ byrḥ sywn
8 šnt 5.100+60+10+4

PAT 1449 **Inv 11 21** **n. d.**
Prov: Palmyra. Loc: Palmyra, A 241. *Dedicatory. On altar.* Bib: *Pl II.*

(On frame)
1 mwdyʾ rmʾ lrḥ[mnʾ]
2 b[...]
(On back)
1 [...].mʾ
2 [...]b?ṭbt
3 [...].hm.

PAT 1450 **Inv 11 22** **n. d.**
Prov: Palmyra. Loc: Palmyra, A 242. *Dedicatory. On altar.* Bib: *Pl III.*

1 {brlky}<lbryk>
2 šmh {llʿmʾ}<lʿlmʾ>
3 ʿbd mzbnʾ
4 br bʿly

PAT 1451 **Inv 11 24** **n. d.**
Prov: Palmyra. Loc: Palmyra, A 270. *Dedicatory. On altar.* Bib: *Pl II.*

1 dkrn ṭb lbryk šmh
2 lʿlmʾ ʿbdt tqym
3 ʿl ḥyyh wḥyy bnyh

PAT 1452 **Inv 11 25** **n. d.**
Prov: Palmyra. Loc: Palmyra, A 274. *Dedicatory. On altar.* Bib: *Pl III.*

1 [..................]
2 [.]wmwdʾ ḥyrn br bryky br ḥyrn
3 wbnʾ byth klhwn byrḥ ʾl[wl šnt ...]

PAT 1453 **Inv 11 26** **n. d.**
Prov: Palmyra. Loc: Palmyra, A 302. *Dedicatory. On altar fragment.* Bib: *Pl II.*

1 šgd/rʾ lrḥ
2 mnʾ ṭbʾ dqr
3 lh wʿnyh

PAT 1454 **Inv 11 27** **n. d.**

Prov: Palmyra. Loc: Palmyra, A 374. *Dedicatory. On altar fragment.* Bib: *Pl III.*

1 [bryk šm]h lʿlmʾ ṭbʾ
2 [wrḥmnʾ] wtyrʾ ʿltʾ dh
3 [ʿbd ...]h$^{?}$ zbdʾ br ḥyrn
4 [... ʿl ḥ]ywhy wḥyʾ [...]

PAT 1455 **Inv 11 28** **n. d.**

Prov: Palmyra. Loc: Palmyra, A 375. *Dedicatory. On altar.* Bib: *Pl IV.*

1 [..]md/rʾ dnh ldkrn qdm
2 bryk šmh ʿbd zbydʾ [br]
3 š$^{?}$gʾ ʾklb lḥywhy wḥ[yʾ]
4 [ʾ]ḥwhy wḥyy tymlt br [...]

PAT 1456 **Inv 11 30** **n. d.**

Prov: Palmyra. Loc: Palmyra, A 431. *Dedicatory. On altar.* Bib: *Pl V.*

1 bryk šmh lʿlmʾ
2 [ṭ]bʾ wrḥmnʾ ʿbd
3 [w]mwdʾ yrḥbwlʾ
4 [br] ydyʿbl dy [...]

PAT 1457 **Inv 11 31** **n. d.**

Prov: Palmyra. Loc: Palmyra, A 433. *Dedicatory. On altar.* Bib: *Pl V*; Déd p 25.

1 bryk šmh lʿlmʾ
2 rḥmnʾ ʿbd wmwd[ʾ]
3 [..]wbd/rʾ br syw[.]ʾ
4 [.....]ḥy[......]

PAT 1458 **Inv 11 32** **n. d.**

Prov: Palmyra. Loc: Palmyra, A 439. *Dedicatory. On altar.* Bib: *Pl III.*

1 bryk šmh
2 lʿlm[ʾ ʿ]lt[ʾ]
3 dnh ʿbd
4 [.]ln[.....]
5 br bsʾ nḥ$^{?}$twmʾ
6 ʿl ḥy[why wḥyʾ]
7 bnyhy

line 5: *nḥ$^{?}$twmʾ* for *nhtwmʾ* of editor; see Glossary s.v.

PAT 1459 **Inv 11 33** **n. d.**

Prov: Palmyra. Loc: Palmyra, A 466. *Dedicatory. On altar.* Bib: *Pl III.*

1 šmʿwn$^{?}$ b$^{?}$r$^{?}$
2 [y]rḥy šmʿ[wn]
3 ʿbd ʿltʾ
4 d$^{?}$h lʿglbwl
5 w$^{?}$mlkbl ʿl
6 ḥyʾ dbnwh

PAT 1460 **Inv 11 34** **n. d.**

Prov: Palmyra. Loc: Palmyra, A 504. *Dedicatory. On altar.* Bib: *Pl IV.*

(Face A of altar)
1 lbryk šmh l[ʿlmʾ]
2 ʿbd wmwdʾ zb[ydʾ br]
3 zbydʾ br zb[ydʾ]
4 lḥyʾ bnyh [....]
5 20+10+2 byr[ḥ ....]
(Face B)
1' [...]bl
2' [...]wḥyʾ bny[h]

PAT 1461 **Inv 11 35** **n. d.**

Prov: Palmyra. Loc: Palmyra, A 508. *Dedicatory. On altar.* Bib: *Pl IV.*

1 [...] br tym$^{?}$lt
2 [...] dy qr$^{??}$ lh$^{?}$
3 [...]wb[.]q
4 [...] wšlwm
5 ʾḥwh

PAT 1462 **Inv 11 36** **n. d.**

Prov: Palmyra. Loc: Palmyra, A 510. *Dedicatory. On altar.* Bib: *Pl V.*

1 bryk šmh lʿlmʾ
2 ṭbʾ wrḥmnʾ ʿbd
3 [wmw]dʾ zbdbwl br

4 [.........]whbʾ ʿl ḥˀyˀwhy
5 [........... b]yrḥ
6 [..........]45

Line 6: Writing of number not legible on photo.

PAT 1463 **Inv 11 37** **n. d.**
Prov: Palmyra. Loc: Palmyra, A 528. *Dedicatory. On altar.* Bib: *Pl IV.*

1 mwdʾ ʿnnw
2 lrḥmnʾ
3 kl ywm dy
4 qr lh
5 [......] šnt
6 [...]+20+5

PAT 1464 **Inv 11 38** **n. d.**
Prov: Palmyra. Loc: Palmyra, A 530. *Dedicatory. On altar.* Bib: *Pl V.*

1 [b]ryk šmh lʿlmʾ
2 ṭbʾ wrḥmnʾ
3 wskrʾ mwdʾ
4 šlmn br mryʾ

PAT 1465 **Inv 11 39** **n. d.**
Prov: Palmyra. Loc: Palmyra, A 558. *Dedicatory. On altar fragment.* Bib: *Pl V.*

1 [ʿ]ltʾ dh ʿbd
2 mzbnʾ br y[rḥ]y [b]r
3 šmʿwn lbryk šˀmh
4 lʿlm[ʾ rḥmn]ʾ ṭbʾ

PAT 1466 **Inv 11 40** **n. d.**
Prov: Palmyra. Loc: Palmyra, A 709. *Dedicatory. On altar fragment.* Bib: *Pl IV.*

1 bryk šmh
2 lʿlmh ṭbʾ
3 wrḥmnʾ ʿbd
4 [..... ʿg]lylw
5 [........]

PAT 1467 **Inv 11 41** **n. d.**
Prov: Palmyra. Loc: Palmyra, A 914. *Dedicatory. On altar.* Bib: *Pl V.*

1 mwdʾ ʿgylw br mqym

PAT 1468 **Inv 11 42** **n. d.**
Prov: Palmyra. Loc: Palmyra, A 924. *Dedicatory. On altar fragment.* Bib: *Pl V.*

1 ʿbd ʿbnrgl br ḥry
2 lšmš br ḥyrn glʾ
3 [lbryk] šmh lʿlmʾ
4 [.....]

PAT 1469 **Inv 11 44** **n. d.**
Prov: Palmyra, reemployed in Arab fortification. Loc: Palmyra, A 1155. *Dedicatory. On altar.* Bib: *Pl VI.*

1 [....]
2 whrqlʾ b[r ..]
3 wmrtynʾ bnh[..]
4 kl ywm

PAT 1470 **Inv 11 45** **n. d.**
Prov: Palmyra, reemployed in Arab fortification. Loc: Palmyra, A 1158. *Dedicatory. On altar fragment.*

1 [....]ʾ
2 [....] wḥyʾ
3 [by]rḥ ṭbt šnt
4 [.....]+3

PAT 1471 **Inv 11 46** **n. d.**
Prov: Palmyra, reemployed in Arab fortification. Loc: Palmyra, A 1160. *Dedicatory. On altar.*

1 ʿltʾ dh qrb
2 lwqys lmnwt
3 [lw]qys ḥn[...]

PAT 1472 **Inv 11 47** **A.D. 139**
Prov: Palmyra, reemployed in Arab fortification. Loc: Palmyra, A 1161. *Dedicatory. On altar fragment.* Bib: *Pl VI.*

1 lb[.]y
2 ʿlṭʾ ʿb[d ....]
3 ʿl ḥyy bn[wh byrḥ]
4 ṭbt šnt 4.100+40+10

PAT 1473 **Inv 11 48** **n. d.**
Prov: Palmyra, reemployed in Arab fortification. Loc: Palmyra, A 1162. *Dedicatory. On altar fragment.*

1 ʿbdw w[....]
2 yrḥy b[r ...]
3 mlkw b[r ...]

PAT 1474 **Inv 11 49** **n. d.**
Prov: Palmyra. Loc: Palmyra, A 290. *Funerary. On stele fragment.* Bib: *Pl VI.*

1 [...] ʿtʿqb br
2 [...]wl šmʿwn
3 [...] br bwlzbd

PAT 1475 **Inv 11 50** **n. d.**
Prov: Palmyra. Loc: Palmyra, A 411. *Funerary. On relief fragment.* Bib: *Pl VI.*

1 ḥbl brtʾ b r t ʾmʾ ʾt?t?h
2 mlkw br yrḥy sgʾ
line 1 *brtʾ b r t*: with Stark PN

PAT 1476 **Inv 11 51** **n. d.**
Prov: Palmyra. Loc: Palmyra, A 244. *Funerary. On stone fragment.*

1 [..] br rpʾ[...]

PAT 1477 **Inv 11 52** **n. d.**
Prov: Palmyra. Loc: Palmyra, A 257. *Funerary. On stele fragment.* Bib: *Pl VI.*

1 šlmt
2 brt
3 tymw
4 lšmš

PAT 1478 **Inv 11 53** **n. d.**
Prov: Palmyra. Loc: Palmyra, A 298. *Funerary. On relief.* Bib: *Pl VI.*

1 yrḥy br
2 šḥry
3 ḥbl

PAT 1479 **Inv 11 54** **n. d.**
Prov: Palmyra. Loc: Palmyra, A 352. *Funerary. On relief fragment.* Bib: *Pl VII.*

1 [m]q?ymw
2 br ʿlybwl
3 br tymr?[ṣw]

PAT 1480 **Inv 11 55** **n. d.**
Prov: Palmyra. Loc: Palmyra, A 363. *Funerary. On stele fragment.* Bib: *Pl VII.*

1 ḥbl
2 mlʾ br
3 šmʿwn
4 br mlkw
5 gʿlw/gʿly

PAT 1481 **Inv 11 56** **n. d.**
Prov: Palmyra. Loc: Palmyra, A 369. *Funerary. On plinth.* Bib: *Pl VI.*

1 [...]y? br mlkw b?r?
2 [...]ʾ byrḥ nysn šnt 4.100+[...]
3 br ḥyrn bʿlh wydyʿbl b[....]

PAT 1482 **Inv 11 57** **n. d.**
Prov: Palmyra. Loc: Palmyra, A 379. *Funerary. On relief fragment.* Bib: *Pl VII.*

1 bwlyʾ ʿmt

PAT 1483 **Inv 11 58** **n. d.**
Prov: Palmyra. Loc: Palmyra, A 403. *Funerary.*
On relief. Bib: *Pl VII.*

1 šlmt
2 brt
3 tymʾ
4 ḥbl

PAT 1484 **Inv 11 59** **n. d.**
Prov: Palmyra. Loc: Palmyra, A 408. *Funerary.*
On relief. Bib: *Pl IX.*

1 ʿtnwry
2 br ḥyrn
3 br ʿtnwry

PAT 1485 **Inv 11 60** **n. d.**
Prov: Palmyra. Loc: Palmyra, A 416. *Funerary.*
On statue base. Bib: *Pl VII.*

1 [..]ʿdy br šky ḥbl

PAT 1486 **Inv 11 61** **n. d.**
Prov: Palmyra. Loc: Palmyra, A 841. *Funerary.*
On fragment. Bib: *Pl VII.*

1 z?bdʾ [br]
2 [ḥ]yrn mlkʾl
3 ḥbl

PAT 1487 **Inv 11 62** **n. d.**
Prov: Palmyra. Loc: Palmyra, A 857. *Funerary.*
On relief fragment.

1 gmlt
2 brt
3 ngmw
4 ḥbl

PAT 1488 **Inv 11 63** **n. d.**
Prov: Palmyra. Loc: Palmyra, A 858. *Funerary.*
On relief. Bib: *Pl VII.*

(On right of head)
1 šlmt
2 brt
3 mky
4 ḥbl
(On left)
1 ḥbl
2 ʿlybʿl brh [...]

PAT 1489 **Inv 11 64** **n. d.**
Prov: Palmyra. Loc: Palmyra, A 896. *Funerary.*
On relief fragment.

1 [ṣ]lm ʿbdbl
2 [y]rḥbwlʾ ḥbl

PAT 1490 **Inv 11 65** **n. d.**
Prov: Palmyra. Loc: Palmyra, A 918. *Funerary.*
On relief fragment. Bib: *Pl VII.*

1 whblt br
2 b?lʿqb br
3 [n]š ḥbl

PAT 1491 **Inv 11 66** **n. d.**
Prov: Palmyra. Loc: Palmyra, A 840. *Dedicatory.*
On relief fragment. Bib: *Pl VII.*

1 ʾšr
2 gnyʾ
3 ʿbd
4 mlk[w]
5 s[....]

PAT 1492 **Inv 11 67** **n. d.**
Prov: Palmyra. Loc: Palmyra, A 915. *Dedicatory.*
On cornice fragment. Bib: *Pl VIII.*

1 [...]tn?yḥʾ dnh ʿbd zbydʾ q[...]
2 [...] wzbdbwl wnwrbl wgdyʾ wtybw[l ..]
line 2: *zbdbwl* with Stark PN p 120

PAT 1493 **Inv 11 68** **n. d.**
Prov: Palmyra. Loc: Palmyra, A 309. *Dedicatory.*
On plinth fragment. Bib: Déd p 103. Bib: *Pl XIII.*

1 [....] ʾlhʾ dkmr[...]
2 [....]4.100[.......]

PAT 1494 **Inv 11 69** **n. d.**
Prov: Palmyra. Loc: Palmyra, A 890. *Dedicatory. On fragment.* Bib: *Pl IX*; Déd p 262.

1 [...] ʿgylw br yʿt br y[...]
2 [.....]bwl ʾtt b[......]

PAT 1495 **Inv 11 70** **n. d.**
Prov: Palmyra. Loc: Palmyra, A 807. *Dedicatory. On fragment.* Bib: *Pl VIII.*

1 [...] brh m?[...]
2 [....] mšrytʾ [...]
3 [....] wbny bnyhwn [...]
4 [......] šbʿtʾ šnt [....]

PAT 1496 **Inv 11 71** **n. d.**
Prov: Palmyra. Loc: Palmyra, A 712. *Dedicatory. On console fragment?.* Bib: *Pl .*

1 [...τει]μῆς χάριν

1 ṣlm rpbwl [...]
2 ʿbd lh rp[bwl ..]
3 lyqrh bnysn šn[t ..]

PAT 1497 **Inv 11 72** **n. d.**
Prov: Palmyra. Loc: Palmyra, A 362. *Dedicatory. On statuette base.*

1 ḥyrn br ydy[....]

PAT 1498 **Inv 11 73** **n. d.**
Prov: Palmyra. Loc: Palmyra, A 912. *Dedicatory. On stone block.* Bib: *Pl VIII*; Déd p 233.

1 byrḥ šbt š[nt ..]
2 qrb brʿth br [...]
3 dy mn bny ʿgrwd [...]
4 [ʿ]glbw]l wlmlkbl ʿl[ḥyʾ ...]
lines 3-4: with Stark PN p 120

PAT 1499 **Inv 11 74** **n. d.**
Prov: Palmyra. Loc: Palmyra, A 761. *Dedicatory. On base relief fragment.* Bib: *Pl IX.*

1 dkrn ṭb lbl wly[rḥybwl]
2 wʿglbwl ʿbd bny b[....]

PAT 1500 **Inv 11 75** **n. d.**
Prov: Palmyra. Loc: Palmyra, A 865. *Dedicatory, bit of inscription, and graffito. On plaster.*

(Inscription)
1' [...]mlwk[...]
(Graffito)
1 dkyr ʿgylw br
2 ḥyrn bṭb šlm

PAT 1501 **Inv 11 76** **n. d.**
Prov: Palmyra. Loc: Palmyra, A 278. *Dedicatory. On column fragment.* Bib: *Pl VIII.*

1 [.]dkyr
2 mtbwl br[..]
3 bys[..]
line 2: with Stark PN p 120

PAT 1502 **Inv 11 77** **n. d.**
Prov: Palmyra. Loc: Palmyra, A 931. *Dedicatory. On stone fragment.* Bib: *Pl VIII.*

1 brykyn
2 ʾln klhwn
3 ḥggw rbʾn
4 qymy wwhby
5 wzbdbwl
line 4: *qymy* with Starcky '66 p 616

PAT 1503 **Inv 11 78** **n. d.**
Prov: Palmyra. Loc: Palmyra, A 803. *Dedicatory. On frame fragment.* Bib: *Pl IX*; Déd p 176.

1 [......]wtʿ[...]
2 [z]bdbwl brʾ ʿl ḥywhy
3 lmrby[...]
4 y[..]
Text after Milik (Déd), who restores still

more

PAT 1504 **Inv 11 79** **n. d.**

Prov: Palmyra. Loc: Palmyra, A 435. *Dedicatory. On column fragment.* Bib: *Pl VIII*; Déd p 38, pl IV, 1.

1 byrḥ šbṭ [šnt 3.100+*x*+ qrb]
2 ymlkw br zb[dʾ .. dy mn bny]
3 kmrʾ ʿmwd[ʾ.]
4 lʿglbwl wm[lkbl .. ʿl ḥywhy]
5 wḥyy bnwh[y...]

Text after Déd p 38.

PAT 1505 **Inv 11 80** **n. d.**

Prov: Palmyra. Loc: Palmyra, A 445. *Dedicatory. On stone block.* Bib: *Pl IX*; Déd p 1 and pl I, 1.

1 [ṣ]lmyʾ ʾ$^?$ln[...]
2 ʿlyšʾ wdynʾ [...]
3 bwlnʾ ʾywn[.. ʿglbwl]
4 wmlkbl wbny [...]
5 [..]ntʾ dy ḥr[....]
6 [..]yhwʾ bgnw[...]

PAT 1506 **Inv 11 81** **A.D. 79**

Prov: Palmyra. Loc: Palmyra, A 523. *Dedicatory. On stone block.* Bib: *Pl X*; Déd p 234.

1 ṣlmyʾ ʾln wkpyhn wb/s[...]
2 wbnʾ mqymw br mqym[w ..]
3 lyqr mqymw ʾbwhy wʾ[...]
4 byrḥ ʾb šnt 3.100+80+10+[..]
5 rbʾ br zbdbw ʿrymʾ ṣlm z[...]
6 mlkw brh ṣlm bwrpʾ brh [...]

Text restored more fully Déd p 234.

PAT 1507 **Inv 11 82** **n. d.**

Prov: Palmyra. Loc: Palmyra, A 280. *Dedicatory. On fragment.* Bib: *Pl X.*

1 [...]y dy m$^?$n$^?$[...]
2 [..] br zbdbwl [..]
3 [.]rt wʾytybl [...]
4 [..]wd wnšʾ br zbdbwl [..]

PAT 1508 **Inv 11 83** **n. d.**

Prov: Palmyra. Loc: Palmyra, A 751. *Dedicatory. On console fragment.* Bib: *Pl X*; Déd p 31 and pl II, 2; Gaw '73a p 35.

1 [ṣ]lmyʾ ʾln trwyhwn ʿbd [...]
2 [....] wbny khnbw lm[...]
3 [........]ly$^?$ q[.......]

Text restored more fully Déd p 31.

PAT 1509 **Inv 11 85** **n. d.**

Prov: Palmyra. Loc: Palmyra, A 895. *Dedicatory. On door lintel.* Bib: *Pl XIII*; Déd p 75 and pl VII, 2.

1 [.....]ln dy [.....]bwl bny mqymw br tybwl dy [mt]q$^?$rh
2 [...]lhn ʿglbwl wmlkbl wbny kmrʾ lyqrhwn šlm

PAT 1510 **Inv 11 86** **n. d.**

Prov: Palmyra. Loc: Palmyra, A 447. *Dedicatory. On statue base.* Bib: *Pl XI.*

1 [ṣ]lmʾ dnh dy y[......]mn$^{ʾ?}$
2 mn bny kmrʾ d[y ʾ]qymw lh b[ny ..]
3 [.... byrḥ] šbṭ šnt 3.100[+20$^?$ (or +10$^?$)]

PAT 1511 **Inv 11 87** **n. d.**

Prov: Palmyra. Loc: Palmyra, A 839. *Dedicatory. On relief fragment.* Bib: *Pl X*; Syr '33 6; Déd p 172.

1 byrḥ tšry šnt 2+[.].100
2 +20+10 mṣbʾ dnh nṣb y[dyʿbl]
3 br nʿbʾ br ydyʿ[bl ......]
4 ʾštrʾ wqrb [............]
5 dnh [.........]

PAT 1512 **Inv 11 88** **n. d.**

Prov: Palmyra, Temple of Bel, wall T. Loc: Palmyra, A 949. *Honorific. On gypsum blocks.* Bib: *Pl X.*

1 [ṣlmʾ] dnh lmlkw br ʿgylw dy [m]tqrh br

2 ʾʿry dy mn bny mʿz[yn] šlm

PAT 1513 **Inv 11 89** **n. d.**

Prov: Palmyra, Temple of Bel, wall T. Loc: Palmyra, A 948. *Honorific. On gypsum fragment.* Bib: *Pl XII.*

1 km?ryʾ
2 dy mn bny

Other traces of letters on block, perhaps *dkyr*

PAT 1514 **Inv 11 90** **n. d.**

Prov: Palmyra, Temple of Bel, wall T. Loc: Palmyra, A 945. *Honorific. On stone fragment.* Bib: *Pl XII.*

1 bny kmrʾ

PAT 1515 **Inv 11 91** **n. d.**

Prov: Palmyra, Temple of Bel, wall T. Loc: Palmyra, A 946. *Honorific. On stone block.* Bib: *Pl XII.*

1 dkyr spr
2 [..]1.100+40
3 dkyr

Separate lines, not connected text.

PAT 1516 **Inv 11 92** **n. d.**

Prov: Palmyra, Temple of Bel, wall T. Loc: Palmyra, A 953. *Honorific. On stone block.* Bib: *Pl XI.*

1 l?ṣlm šʾylʾ b[r n]wrbl
2 br ʾqmt dy mn bny mʿzyn

PAT 1517 **Inv 11 93** **n. d.**

Prov: Palmyra, Temple of Bel, wall T. Loc: Palmyra, A 950. *Honorific. On statue-base fragment.* Bib: *Pl X.*

1 [...] lbny [...]

PAT 1518 **Inv 11 94** **n. d.**

Prov: Palmyra, Temple of Bel, wall T. Loc: Palmyra, A 954. *Unclassified. On fragment.* Bib: *Pl XII.*

1 [...] b?r mrywn
2 [...]zn br ydy[...]
3 [.....]m?bl[...]
4 [............]

PAT 1519 **Inv 11 95** **n. d.**

Prov: Palmyra, Temple of Bel, wall T. Loc: Palmyra, A 958. *Honorific. On stone block.* Bib: *Pl XI.*

1 lmlkw ḥyrn lṣlm

PAT 1520 **Inv 11 96** **n. d.**

Prov: Palmyra, Temple of Bel, wall T. Loc: Palmyra, A 962. *Honorific. On column fragment.*

1 bny zgwg

PAT 1521 **Inv 11 97** **n. d.**

Prov: Palmyra, Temple of Bel, wall T. Loc: Palmyra, A 951. *Unclassified. On stone fragment.* Bib: *Pl XII*; Déd p 308 and pl I, 2.

1 br
2 ḥnb[l]
3 tymrṣw
4 ʾply[...]
5 zbdlh br
6 br blʿq[b]yʾ
4032002 dy mn bny

PAT 1522 **Inv 11 98** **n. d.**

Prov: Palmyra, Temple of Bel, wall T. Loc: Palmyra, A 952. *Unclassified. On stone block.* Bib: *Pl XI.*

(Above)
1 lbwrpʾ ʿgylw lṣlm
(Below)
1 lṣlm rpbwl
2 br ʾhwd

Line (Above) 1: text damaged.

PAT 1523 **Inv 11 99** **n. d.**
Prov: Palmyra, Temple of Bel, wall T. Loc: Palmyra, A 943. *Dedicatory. On stone block.* Bib: Sta StudLdV '56 p 516 3. Bib: *Pl XIII.*

1 qrb tbrʾ br zbdlh
2 wmqym mqym br zbdbwl ʾšʿd
3 lbl blḥmwn wmnwt

PAT 1524 **Inv 11 100** **A.D. 44**
Prov: Palmyra, Temple of Bel, wall T. Loc: Palmyra, A 959. *Honorific. On stone block.* Bib: *Pl XIII*; Sta StudLdV '56 p 514, 2; RosAH 1; Déd p 31 and pl II, 3.

1 byrḥ tšry šnt 2.100
2 +60+5+4 ʾqym[w] kmryʾ
3 dy bl ṣlmʾ dnh lgrymy
4 br nbwzbd dy mn pḥd
5 bny khnbw

PAT 1525 **Inv 12 1** **A.D. 144**
Prov: Palmyra, Valley of Tombs, Hypogeum. Loc: Palmyra, *in situ. Funerary: Foundation. On door lintel.* Bib: *Pl I.*

1 mʿrtʾ dh ʿbdw nwrbl wmqymw wḥyrn bny mlkw br
2 nwrbl ʾqml lhwn wlbnyhwn wlbny bnyhwn lʿlmʾ
3 byrḥ knwn šnt 4.100+40+10+5+1

PAT 1526 **Inv 12 2** **A.D. 239**
Prov: Palmyra, Valley of Tombs, Hypogeum of Bolbarak. Loc: Palmyra, 1795/6644. *Funerary. On sarcophagus (banquet).* Sarcophagus of Bolbarak:: Inv 12 2-13. Bib: *Pl I, II*; SFP 195 fig 247.

1 ṣlmʾ dnh dy bwlbrk
2 br mqymw bwlbrk
3 dy ʿbd ʾksdrʾ wtmlʾ
4 dqdmwhy nysn šnt 5.100+40+10

PAT 1527 **Inv 12 3** **n. d.**
Prov: Palmyra, Valley of Tombs, Hypogeum of Bolbarak. Loc: Palmyra, 1795/6644. *Funerary. On sarcophagus (banquet).* Sarcophagus of Bolbarak: Inv 12 2-13. Bib: *Pl I, 2,3*; SFP 195 fig 247.

1 ʾtʾ brt gdʾ ʾmh

PAT 1528 **Inv 12 4** **n. d.**
Prov: Palmyra, Valley of Tombs, Hypogeum of Bolbarak. Loc: Palmyra, 1795/6644. *Funerary. On sarcophagus (banquet).* Sarcophagus of Bolbarak: Inv 12 2-13. Bib: *Pl II, 4*; SFP 195 fig 247.

1 mqymw
2 brh

PAT 1529 **Inv 12 5** **n. d.**
Prov: Palmyra, Valley of Tombs, Hypogeum of Bolbarak. Loc: Palmyra, 1795/6644. *Funerary. On sarcophagus (banquet).* Sarcophagus of Bolbarak: Inv 12 2-13. Bib: *Pl I, 2-11*; SFP 195 fig 247.

1 šlmt brt bwrpʾ ʾtt bwlbrk

PAT 1530 **Inv 12 6** **n. d.**
Prov: Palmyra, Valley of Tombs, Hypogeum of Bolbarak. Loc: Palmyra, 1795/6644. *Funerary. On sarcophagus (banquet).* Sarcophagus of Bolbarak: Inv 12 2-13. Bib: *Pl II, 6*; SFP 195 fig 247.

1 ʾmtdʿth (or: ʾmtrʿth) brt bwlbrk
2 ʾtt bwlbrk

PAT 1531 **Inv 12 7** **n. d.**
Prov: Palmyra, Valley of Tombs, Hypogeum of Bolbarak. Loc: Palmyra, 1796/6645. *Funerary. On sarcophagus (kliné).* Sarcophagus of Bolbarak: Inv 12 2-13. Bib: *Pl II, 7-11*; SFP 195 fig 247.

1 whblt
2 brh

PAT 1532 **Inv 12 8** **n. d.**
Prov: Palmyra, Valley of Tombs, Hypogeum of Bolbarak. Loc: Palmyra, 1796/6645. *Funerary. On sarcophagus (kliné).* Sarcophagus of Bolbarak: Inv 12 2-13. Bib: *Pl II, 7-11*; SFP 195 fig 247.

1 ʾtʾ
2 brth

PAT 1533 **Inv 12 9** **n. d.**
Prov: Palmyra, Valley of Tombs, Hypogeum of Bolbarak. Loc: Palmyra, 1796/6645. *Funerary. On sarcophagus (kliné).* Sarcophagus of Bolbarak: Inv 12 2-13. Bib: *Pl II, 7-11*; SFP 195 fig 247.

1 bwlbrk
2 brh

PAT 1534 **Inv 12 10** **n. d.**
Prov: Palmyra, Valley of Tombs, Hypogeum of Bolbarak. Loc: Palmyra, 1796/6645. *Funerary. On sarcophagus (kliné).* Sarcophagus of Bolbarak: Inv 12 2-13. Bib: *Pl II, 7-11*; SFP 195 fig 247.

1 ʾmtnny
2 brth

PAT 1535 **Inv 12 11** **n. d.**
Prov: Palmyra, Valley of Tombs, Hypogeum of Bolbarak. Loc: Palmyra, 1796/6645. *Funerary. On sarcophagus (kliné).* Sarcophagus of Bolbarak: Inv 12 2-13. Bib: *Pl II, 7-11*; SFP 195 fig 247.

1 šlmt
2 brth

PAT 1536 **Inv 12 12** **n. d.**
Prov: Palmyra, Valley of Tombs, Hypogeum of Bolbarak. Loc: Palmyra, 1790/6639. *Funerary. On relief.* Tomb of Bolbarak: Inv 12 2-13. Bib: *Pl III, 12*; SFP 190 fig 158.

(On left)
1 šlʾ
2 brt
3 mlkw
4 ʾtt
5 ʿgylw
6 blbrk
7 ḥbl
(On right)
1 ʾmt
2 brth
3 ḥbl

PAT 1537 **Inv 12 13** **n. d.**
Prov: Palmyra, Valley of Tombs, Hypogeum of Bolbarak. Loc: Palmyra, 1788/6637. *Funerary. On relief.* Tomb of Bolbarak: Inv 12 2-13. Bib: *Pl III, 13*; SFP 188 fig 159.

(On left)
1 ḥbl
2 ʿtw/y
3 brt
4 l[š]mš
5 ʾtt
6 ʿgylw
7 blbrk
(On right)
1 ʾqmt brt[h]
2 ḥbl

PAT 1538 **Inv 12 15** **n. d.**
Prov: Palmyra, Valley of Tombs, near Hypogeum of Shalamallat. Loc: Palmyra, A 1259. *Funerary. On stone slab.* Bib: *Pl II, 15.*

1 šl[..] brt
2 mqymw br
3 bgš ʾtt
4 ʿbdy br
5 ʿtnwry ḥyrn
6 ḥbl

PAT 1539 **Inv 12 22** **A.D. 18**
Prov: Palmyra, Great Colonnade (section A), among debris N-W of Nympée A. Loc: Palmyra, A 1392. *Dedicatory. On column drum.* Bib: *Pl IV.*

1 byrḥ ʾlwl šnt 2.100+
2 80+10+3 qrb blšwry

3 br mqymw dy mn bny zmrʾ
4 ʿmwdʾ dnh lṣbs wʾnhyt
5 ʾlhyʾ ʿl ḥywhy wḥyy
6 bnwhy wʾḥwhy

PAT 1540 **Inv 12 23** **A.D. 219**
Prov: Palmyra, Great Colonnade (section A), among debris N-W of Nympée A. Loc: Palmyra, *in situ. Dedicatory. On stone block.* Bib: *Pl V, 18, 23*; restoration of Greek and combination with Aramaic text (=Inv 12 23) Déd p 242; Inv 3 1; AAS '65 Pl 4; Inv 12 18.

1 Τὴν στοὰν τῶν ὀκτὼ κ[ειόνων...] κείονας ἀνέστησεν,
2 περιὼν μετ' αὐτὸν δὲ 'Ιου[λ. Αὐρ ....ᾠκοδ]όμησε[ν καὶ ἐτέλεσεν σὺν τοῖς ὑπε]ρῴοις πᾶσιν καὶ τῇ τῆς
3 στοᾶς στέγῃ καὶ παντὶ κ[όσμῳ καὶ ἀφιέρωσεν τῇ πατρί]δι, ἔτους λφ' μηνὸς Λώου.

1 [...b]r nbwzʾ brbrh
2 [...]wdnb tṣbyth klh w
3 qdš mgdʾ lmdyth
4 šnt 5.100+20+10

PAT 1541 **Inv 12 24** **n. d.**
Prov: Palmyra, Great Colonnade (section A). Loc: Palmyra, A 1393. *Dedicatory. On stone blocks and architectural fragments.* Bib: *Pl VII, 24.*

1 [...ḥ]mnyʾ mgd nsʾ br nbwzbd nsʾ ʾḥmr wʾqym[...]

PAT 1542 **Inv 12 25** **n. d.**
Prov: Palmyra, Great Colonnade (section A), reemployed in later building. Loc: Palmyra, A 1382. *Funerary. On stone block.* Bib: *Pl VII, 25.*

1 rhbt brt
2 [n?]ṣʿy ʾtth

PAT 1543 **Inv 12 26** **n. d.**
Prov: Palmyra, Great Colonnade (section A), reemployed in later building, S Portico. Loc: Palmyra, A 1246. *Funerary. On klinè.* Bib: *Pl VI.*

(On right edge of couch)
1 bt ʿlm d[...]
(By busts, right to left: a.)
1 [...]ʾ
2 brh dy
3 lšmš
4 bnh
(b.)
1 ʿst[wrgʾ brh]
2 dy lšmš
3 bnh
(c.)
1 [...]
2 brh dy
3 lšmš
4 bnh
(d.)
1 š[... brh]
2 d[y] lšmš
3 bnh
(e.)
1 mqymw brh
2 dy lšmš
3 bnh

PAT 1544 **Inv 12 28** **n. d.**
Prov: Palmyra, Great Colonnade (section A), S Portico. Loc: Palmyra, *in situ. Unclassified. On stone block.* Bib: *Pl VII, 28.*

1 [...]br mqymw ʾrʾš[...]

PAT 1545 **Inv 12 30** **n. d.**
Prov: Palmyra, Great Colonnade (section A). Loc: Palmyra, A 1262. *Dedicatory. On altar fragment.* Bib: *Pl VII, 30.*

1 ʿltʾ dh wmṭ[ltʾ...]
2 br ʾwpmʾ [...]
3 ʾlhyʾ ṭb[yʾ...]
4 bnwhy wʾḥ[wh byrḥ]
5 tšry šnt [...]

PAT 1546 **Inv 12 31** **A.D. 209**
Prov: Palmyra, among debris, Tetrapylon square.

Loc: Palmyra, 1263. *Dedicatory. On altar fragment.* Bib: *Pl VII, 31.*

1 [dkr]n ṭb qdm bryk
2 šmh lʿlmʾ ṭbʾ
3 wrḥmnʾ nṣbtʾ dh
4 wʿltʾ ʿbd šmʿwn
5 br mʿn br šmʿwn
6 ḥmʾ byrḥ nysn šnt 5.100+20

PAT 1547 **Inv 12 32** **n. d.**
Prov: Palmyra, Great Colonnade (section B), N Portico. Loc: Palmyra, 1249. *Dedicatory. On altar.* Bib: *Pl VIII, 32.*

1 [....] dy qrb nb/š[...]
2 [....]l [..] ʾlhyʾ
3 [ṭ]by?ʾ wskryʾ [...]
4 [....]

PAT 1548 **Inv 12 33** **A.D. 115**
Prov: Palmyra, Great Colonnade (section B), N Portico. Loc: Palmyra, *in situ. Dedicatory. On stone pillar.* Bib: *Pl VIII, 33.*

1 ʼΙούλιο]ς Μάξιμος
2 [....]
3 Θεῷ ἐπηκ[ό]ῳ

1 ʿbd gys ywlys mksyms qṭrywnʾ dy mn lgywnʾ dy
2 [...] bʾdr šnt 4.100+20+5+1

PAT 1549 **Inv 12 34** **A.D. 239**
Prov: Palmyra, Great Colonnade (section B), N Portico, W of Nymphée B. Loc: Palmyra, 1260. *Dedicatory. On altar.* Bib: *Pl VIII, 34.*

1 bryk šmh lʿlmʾ
2 ʿbd wmwdʾ ʿltʾ
3 dnh ʿgylw br mlwkʾ
4 wyrḥy ʾḥy ʿl ḥyyhwn
5 wḥyʾ bnyhwn byrḥ
6 ʾdr šnt 5.100+40+10

PAT 1550 **Inv 12 35** **A.D. 51**
Prov: Palmyra, Great Colonnade (section B), N Portico. Loc: Palmyra, 1261. *Honorific. On stone block.* Bib: *Pl IX, 35*; cf C3923 = Inv 9 8; Déd p 154.

1 byrḥ sywn šnt 3.100+60+2[...]
2 br pṣyʾl br tymy dy mtqrh ḥ[...]
3 bny tymy dy mtqrh ḥkyšw bn[...]
4 bkl ṣbʾ klh wbnʾ lhn bt q/l[...]

Teixidor offers fuller restoration based on parallel texts (cf "Bib" above).

PAT 1551 **Inv 12 36** **n. d.**
Prov: Palmyra, Great Colonnade (section B), N Portico debris, near Tetrapylon square. Loc: Palmyra, *in situ. Funerary. On lintel.* Bib: *Pl IX, 36.*

1 [..]r/d mlkw br mlkw wsḥw lwsḥw ʾḥwh lh wlbnwh wlbnʾ
2 [bnyhwn ...]

PAT 1552 **Inv 12 38** **n. d.**
Prov: Palmyra, Great Colonnade (section C), wall across Exedra G. Loc: Palmyra, *in situ. Unclassified. On console fragment.* Bib: *Pl IX, 38.*

1 [...]ʾ br tymʾ br blydʿ[...]

PAT 1553 **Inv 12 39** **A.D. 29**
Prov: Palmyra, reemployed in street going from Theatre to Agora. Loc: Palmyra Museum. *Dedicatory. On rim of stone crater.* Bib: *Pl IX, 39.*

1 byrḥ šbṭ šnt 3.100+40 qrbw šmʿwn wlšmš bny tymrṣw br ḥty[ṭ] gbʾtʾ wʿltʾ ʾln lʿglbwl wlmlkbl ʾlhyʾ

PAT 1554 **Inv 12 40** **n. d.**
Prov: Palmyra, reemployed in street going to Temple of Baashamîn. Loc: Palmyra, *in situ. Graffito. On wall.* Bib: *Pl IX, 40.*

1 dkyr gdʾ ngdʾ

2 bṭb

PAT 1555 **Inv 12 41** **n. d.**
Prov: Palmyra, in street to Temple of Baashamîn. Loc: Palmyra Museum. *Dedicatory. On altar.* Bib: *Pl X, 41.*

1 lʾšr šbb[...]
2 mlʾ br ʾbʾ ʿl ḥ[y...]
3 byrḥ ʾyr šnt 4.100[...]

PAT 1556 **Inv 12 43** **A.D. 128**
Prov: Palmyra, in gardens near spring by Jebel Munṭar. Loc: Palmyra, A 1401/8112. *Dedicatory. On altar.* Bib: *Pl X, 43*; Gaw Syr '71 p 408, Pl 24.

1 lbryk šmh lʿlmʾ
2 ʿbd blḥmwn wmnwt
3 mn kys ʿtʿqb br
4 ḥyrn bgmwt byrḥ
5 sywn šnt
6 4.100
7 +20+10+5+4

PAT 1557 **Inv 12 44** **A.D. 206**
Prov: Palmyra, near spring Afqa. Loc: Palmyra Museum. *Dedicatory. On altar.* Bib: *Pl X, 44.*

1 brbnwt ʿynʾ dy ʾḥd
2 yrḥbwl ʾlhʾ tymw
3 br lšmš br tymw br
4 bwlḥʾ ʿbd ʿltʾ dh
5 ʿl ḥyʾ ʾbwhy wḥywhy
6 wḥyy bnwhy byrḥ ʾb
7 šnt 5.100+10+5+2

PAT 1558 **Inv 12 45** **A.D. 243**
Prov: Palmyra, near spring Afqa. Loc: Palmyra Museum. *Dedicatory. On stone slab.* Bib: *Pl X, 45.*

1 sm?k?ʾ dnh?[...]ʾ
2 lbryk šmh lʿ[l]mʾ rḥmnʾ
3 ṭbʾ wlwdʾ dy ʾḥdy hyklʾ
4 d[y] bl mlq ʾsyʾ gwyʾ
5 br mqymw br ʿqybʾ lh
6 wlbnwhy wlbny bnwh wlšb
7 ʿṭʾ dy wdʾ lʿlmʾ byrḥ
8 nysn šnt 5.100+40+10+4
9 dkyr qdm rḥmnʾ ṣʿd
10 br nbwzbd ṣʿd rḥmh

PAT 1559 **Inv 12 46** **A.D. 129**
Prov: Palmyra, near spring Afqa. Loc: Palmyra, *in situ. Dedicatory. On altar.* Bib: *Pl X, 46.*

1 [...εὐχὴ]ν ἀ[ν]έθηκαν
2 [.....]ατου Σαλαμα [...]
3 [.....] Ζαβδ<ι>βωλου ὑπὲρ
4 [.....]ν καὶ ἀδελφῶν
5 [μηνὸς Ξαν]δικου

1 [l]bryk šmh lʿlmʾ ṭ?bʾ wr?ḥ?[mnʾ..]
2 [..]twyhn ʿbd šqy br brʿʾ br[..]m[...]
3 br ʿgylw br zbdbwl ʿl ḥyyhwn wḥy[...]
4 wʾḥyhwn byrḥ nysn šnt 4.100+40 (or: 4.100+60) [..]

PAT 1560 **Inv 12 47** **n. d.**
Prov: Palmyra, near spring Afqa. Loc: Palmyra Museum. *Uncertain. On stone fragment.* Bib: *Pl XI, 47*; Du Mesnil '66 p 165.

1 [....]m šbʿṭʾ
2 [.......]ʾ šb[..]

PAT 1561 **Inv 12 48** **A.D. 89**
Prov: Palmyra, Diocletian Camp, Temple of Allat. Loc: Palmyra, *in situ. Dedicatory. On door lintel.* Group: Temple of Allat: Inv 12 48, 49 very similar. Bib: *Pl XI, 48*; Du Mesnil '66 pp 165-70; Teixidor '68 pp 380-82 (see Teixidor '86); Gaw TP p 83.

1 lbl ḥmwn ʿbdw mn kyshwn mqymw br mqymw br zbdbwl ʿrymʾ wyrḥbwlʾ br mlkw br lšmš br ḥnbl ʾʿby hyklʾ dnh wʾsṭwʾ
2 dy šyšʾ dy qdmwhy wʾsṭwʾ dy lʿlmnh wṭṭlylʾ klh wtrʿwhy wšrgbʾ dy nḥšʾ wʾp qrbw hyklʾ dy mnwt wʾsṭwwhy wtṣbyth
3 klh ʿl ḥyyhwn wḥyy bnyhwn wʾḥyhw[n] lʿlmʾ byrḥ ʾyr šnt 4.100

Line 1: with du Mesnil, plate III: ʿrymʾ (aleph omitted in Inv 12 48)

PAT 1562 **Inv 12 49** **A.D. 89**

Prov: Palmyra, Diocletian Camp, Temple of Allat. Loc: Palmyra Museum. *Dedicatory. On console.* Bib: *Pl XI, 49.*

1 [...]
2 [m]q[ymw br zbdbwl]
3 ʿrym[ʾ wyrḥbwlʾ br mlkw br]
4 lšmš br ḥ[nbl ʾʿby hyklʾ dnh w]ʾs[ṭwʾ]
5 dy qdymwhy wʾsṭwʾ dy lʿlmnh w[t]ṭl[ylʾ]
6 klh wmlbnh w šrgbʾ dy nḥš[ʾ why]klʾ
7 dy mnwt wʾsṭwwhy wtṣbyth klh mn
8 kyshwn wtrṣw ṣbwt btʾ
9 byrḥ ʾyr šnt 4.100

Line 5 *qdymwhy*: so Inv 12; pl not very legible, seems to read *qdmwhy*.

PAT 1563 **Inv 12 50** **n. d.**

Prov: Palmyra, Diocletian Camp, Temple of Allat. Loc: Palmyra Museum. *Dedicatory. On gypsum fragment.* Bib: *Pl XI, 50*; du Mesnil '66 p 174.

1 [.......]...[.......]
2 [.......] lbl ḥm[wn...]
3 [.......]why w.[.......]
4 [.......]why š[....]

Text of Inv 12

PAT 1564 **Inv 12 51** **n. d.**

Prov: Palmyra, Temple of Bel, reemployed in foundation. Loc: Palmyra, *in situ. Dedicatory. On stone block.* Bib: *Hand copy p 47, pl XI, 51*; du Mesnil '66 pp 179-85; Gaw TP pp 60-61.

1 hʾ dkrn ṭb
2 ldywn qdm
3 bl

Archaic, from find-spot and script (1st century B.C.)

PAT 1565 **Inv 12 52** **n. d.**

Prov: Palmyra, Temple of Bel. Loc: Palmyra, *in situ. Dedicatory/graffito. On stone block.* Bib: *Pl XII, 52.*

1 tymrṣw br [...]
2 dkyr lšmš br
3 ʿgyl[w]

Line 1 carved; lines 2-3 separate text, graffito.

PAT 1566 **Inv 12 53** **n. d.**

Prov: Palmyra, reemployed in Wall, S of Museum. Loc: Palmyra, A 1400. *Funerary. On stone with moulding.* Bib: *Pl XI, 53.*

1 [ṣl]m bwrpʾ yrḥbwlʾ br bwrpʾ ʿšylt ḥbl

PAT 1567 **Inv 12 54** **n. d.**

Prov: Palmyrene: Al-Maqateʿ, 14 km. N-E of Palmyra. Loc: Palmyra, B 2195. *Dedicatory. On relief.* Bib: *Pl XII, 54*; Bounni '66 pp 313-20.

1 ʿštrt ʿglbwl bl bʿlšmn yrḥbwl

PAT 1568 **Inv 12 55** **A.D. 153**

Prov: Palmyrene, Wadi ʿArafa, Jebel el-ʾAbiad. Loc: Palmyra, 1234. *Dedicatory. On relief.* Bib: *Pl XII, 55*; Bounni '66 pp 316-19; Déd. p 23.

1 [ṣlmʾ dnh dy ʿ]bd šwyrʾ br tymʾ wmlʾ br [..]mlky lbl wlbʿšmn
2 [wlʿglbwl wlml]kbl wlʿštrt wlnmsys wlʾrṣw wlʾbgl ʾlhy ṭbyʾ
3 [wskryʾ ʿl ḥyyh]wn wḥyy bnyhwn byrḥ knwn šnt 4.100+60+4 šlm

PAT 1569 **Inv 12 56** **n. d.**

Prov: Palmyrene, Jebel al-Merah, 75 N-W of Palmyra. Loc: Palmyra, A 1233. *Dedicatory. On relief.* Bib: *Pl XII, 56*; German transl. Jakob-Rost '86, p 71; Photo, German transl.: PGKK p 313 35; Bounni '66 pp 314-16; map, p 315 fig 1; photo, fig2.

1 dkrn ṭb lbl wlyrḥbwl
2 wlʿglbwl wlʾrṣw ʿbd
3 ʾḥyʾ br ḥry khyl[w]
4 wyrḥy ʾḥwhy
5 ʿtw/y

Line 5, on base contains (presumably) name of sculptor.

PAT 1570 **IP 5** **n. d.**
Prov: Qaryatein. Loc: Qaryatein. *Funerary. On relief.*

1 ḥbl

PAT 1571 **IP 10** **n. d.**
Prov: Palmyra. Loc: Palmyra Museum. *Dedicatory. On altar base.*

1 [Διὶ Υ]ΨΙΣΤΩ ΚΑΙ ΕΠΗΚΟΩ ΜΑΝΝΑΙΟΣ ΑΜΜΑΘΟΥ
2 [τοῦ Αδδ]ΟΥΔ?Α?ΝΟΥ ΤΟΥ Φ?ΙΡΜΩΝΟΣ ΥΠΕΡ ΣΩΤΗ
3 [ρίας αὐτοῦ καὶ τῶ]Ν ΤΕΚΝΩΝ ΜΗΝΙ ΠΕΡΕΙΤΙΩ
4 [.........]

1 lbʿl? š?m?n? rbʾ wrḥmnʾ ʿl[t]ʾ? dh wsmkʾ ʿbd
2 [mʿny br] ʿmt br ḥd?w?[dn pr]mw[n] ʿl ḥywhy wḥyy
3 bnwhy byrḥ šbṭ šnt 4?.100+[....]

PAT 1572 **IP 11** **n. d.**
Prov: Palmyra. Loc: Palmyra Museum. *Funerary. On door lintel.*

1 [...]εγγ[...]

1 [...........]wd?[...........]
2 [...]ʾd?[...]bḥ?n?[..]dšmnhdṣ
3 [..............]h[..]ʿndyʾm?n
4 [...]s?l?..]lyqr lhwn wl[...]

PAT 1573 **IP 12bis** **n. d.**
Prov: Palmyra, Funerary Temple 85b (Tomb of Aʿailamī and Zebīdā). Loc: Palmyra Museum. *Funerary. On fragment.* Tomb Group: Watzinger 85b, C4168, C4169, C4243, C4244; Inv 4 9a, (=C4168), Inv 4 9b; IP pp 13-18, nos. 12bis-23.

1 qbrʾ dnh bt ʿlmʾ wʾsṭwʾ[....]
2 byrḥ nysn šnt 4.100+60

PAT 1574 **IP 16** **n. d.**
Prov: Palmyra, Funerary Temple 85b. Loc: Palmyra Museum. *Funerary. On relief base.* Tomb Group: Watzinger 85b, C4168, C4169, C4243, C4244; Inv 4 9a, (=C4168), Inv 4 9b; IP pp 13-18, nos. 12bis-23.

1 [ṣlmʾ] dnh dy mqymw b[r ...]

PAT 1575 **IP 18** **n. d.**
Prov: Palmyra, Funerary Temple 85b. Loc: Palmyra Museum. *Funerary. On moulding fragments.* Tomb Group: Watzinger 85b, C4168, C4169, C4243, C4244; Inv 4 9a, (=C4168), Inv 4 9b; IP pp 13-18, nos. 12bis-23.

(fragment A)
1 [.....] ḥyrn [.....]
(fragment B)
1 [.....] hrmzd [...]

PAT 1576 **IP 20** **n. d.**
Prov: Palmyra, Funerary Temple 85b. Loc: Palmyra Museum. *Funerary. On fragment.* Tomb Group: Watzinger 85b, C4168, C4169, C4243, C4244; Inv 4 9a, (=C4168), Inv 4 9b; IP pp 13-18, nos. 12bis-23.

1 [.....] ḥyrn [.....]

PAT 1577 **IP 21** **n. d.**
Prov: Palmyra, Funerary Temple 85b. Loc: Palmyra Museum. *Funerary. On relief fragment.* Tomb Group: Watzinger 85b, C4168, C4169, C4243, C4244; Inv 4 9a, (=C4168), Inv 4 9b; IP pp 13-18, nos. 12bis-23.

1 ḥbl [.....]
2 ʾmšmš [...]
3 md/r[...]
4 d/r[...]

PAT 1578 **IP 23** **n. d.**
Prov: Palmyra, Funerary Temple 85b. Loc: Palmyra Museum. *Unclassified. On relief fragment.* Tomb Group: Watzinger 85b, C4168,

C4169, C4243, C4244; Inv 4 9a, (=C4168), Inv 4 9b; IP pp 13-18, nos. 12bis-23.

1 [..... t]yms'
2 [..... ty]mḥ'

PAT 1579 **IP 25** **n. d.**

Prov: Palmyra. Loc: Palmyra Museum. *Dedicatory. On cippus fragment.*

1 [l]bryk šmh [l'lm' ṭb']
2 [w]rḥmn' 'lt[' dh 'bd]
3 [m]'ny br yrḥy [br .....]
4 ['l ḥ]ywhy wḥ[yy bnwhy]
5 [...]

PAT 1580 **IP 26** **n. d.**

Prov: Palmyra. Loc: Palmyra Museum. *Funerary. On relief fragment.*

1 [ḥ]bl ty[m']
2 brt ḥyrn
3 'tt zby[d']
4 br mqy[mw]

PAT 1581 **IP 27** **A.D. 189**

Prov: Palmyra. Loc: Palmyra Museum. *Dedicatory. On base fragment.*

1' [.....]
2' ḥy bnwhy
3' byrḥ 'lwl
4' šnt 5.100

PAT 1582 **IP 28** **n. d.**

Prov: Palmyra. Loc: Palmyra Museum. *Unclassified. On fragment.*

1' [.....]
2' byrḥ
3' šbṭ
4' ym 20
5' šnt
6' 20+10

PAT 1583 **IP 33** **n. d.**

Prov: Palmyra, street near Nymphée A. Loc: Palmyra, *in situ. Dedicatory. On column drum.* May = Inv 12 21 see Teixidor ad Inv 12 21 and pl IV, 21; Déd p 243.

1 qrb mlkw br myrn 'lhbl
2 plg' w'lhbl wwhblt br
3 m'ny br 'lhbl plg'

Déd p 243 assumes two copyists' errors (correct readings in duplicate Inv 12 21): l. 1: *myrn* for *ḥyrn*, and l. 2 *br* for *bny*

PAT 1584 **IP 34** **A.D. (70)**

Prov: Palmyra. Loc: Palmyra Museum. *Dedicatory. On column drum.*

1 [.....] šnt 3.100+60+2 (or: 3.100+80+2)
2 ṣlm' dnh dy zbdbwl br 'byhn
3 br zbdbwl br lšmš br mkn'
4 rb' dy mn pḥd bny mtbwl dy
5 'qymw lh tgry' tdmry'
6 dy b'sp[s]nqrṭ klhn spwn
7 [.......]kl ṣbw dnpl'
8 [............]

PAT 1585 **IP 36** **n. d.**

Prov: Palmyra, S of spring Afqa. Loc: Palmyra Museum. *Dedicatory. On column drum.*

1 lṣlmyn lmqymw br
2 mqymw 'rym' wb[n]why
3 qrbw mqymw br mqymw 'rym'
4 wyrḥbwl' br mlkw ''b

PAT 1586 **IP 37** **n. d.**

Prov: Palmyra, N, in ruins of Justinian Wall. Loc: Palmyra Museum. *Dedicatory. On door lintel.*

1 'bd ydy br mqymw br ydy br rmw br ḥl'

PAT 1587 **IP 46** **n. d.**

Prov: Palmyra. Loc: Palmyra Museum. *Funerary. On relief fragment.*

1 [.....]yw[....]

2 [...m]qymw br[...]
3 [....n]wrbl

PAT 1588 **IP 57** **n. d.**
Prov: Palmyra, Wadi eṣ-Ṣarayṣir. Loc: Palmyra Museum. *Unclassified. On column shaft.*

1 k?p?r?y?' dy[...]l br yrḥy z?w?
2 br ydy' br 'wr[...]lt

PAT 1589 **IP 58** **n. d.**
Prov: Palmyra. Loc: Palmyra Museum. *Dedicatory. On column shaft.*

1 qrb tymy br[...]
2 wmlkw br [...]br[...]

PAT 1590 **IP 60** **n. d.**
Prov: Palmyra, N of village. Loc: Palmyra Museum. *Dedicatory. On cippus.*

1 [῾Ηλίῳ] Π[ατ]ΡΩΩ ΚΑΙ ΕΠΗΚΟΩ ΘΕ[ῳ....]

1 [...]šb?r?[...]br[...]bš' 'lh' [..]ṭ[..]
2 mlkbl

PAT 1591 **IP 61** **n. d.**
Prov: Palmyra, spring Afqa. Loc: Palmyra Museum. *Dedicatory. On altar.*

1 [lbr]yk šmh l'lm'
2 [mwd]' yrḥy br ydy[....]

PAT 1592 **IP 62** **n. d.**
Prov: Palmyra, Jebel Munṭar. Loc: Palmyra Museum. *Dedicatory. On altar fragments (not a connected text).*

1 [lbryk šm]h l'lm'
2 dkrn [...]
3 [....] br 'gylw br mlkw
4 [... ']l ḥywhy wḥyy b[nwhy]
5 [....] lšm[š ...]
6 [... byr]ḥ šb[ṭ ...]

7 [....]3 ywm šb['' .....]

PAT 1593 **IP 67** **n. d.**
Prov: Palmyra, W necropolis. Loc: Palmyra Museum. *Funerary. On lamp.* Bib: HNE p 483, pl XLII, 1.

1 'glbwl wmlkbl

PAT 1594 **IP 76** **n. d.**
Prov: Palmyra. Loc: . *Funerary. On relief fragment.*

1 [ḥ]bl 'wydlt
2 [b]r yrḥy nṣr'
May be same as Inv 8 19

PAT 1595 **IP 78** **n. d.**
Prov: Palmyra. Loc: Not known. *Funerary. On relief.*

1 'l'
2 brt
3 'yd'n
4 br yrḥy
5 mqy 'mh
6 w'bwh
7 tnn
8 ḥb
9 l

PAT 1596 **IP 79** **n. d.**
Prov: Palmyra. Loc: Damascus, National Museum, 25. *Funerary. On relief.* Bib: PS 330.

1 ḥbl
2 tyks'
3 brt
4 nṣry br
5 lšmš
6 'ḥyb

PAT 1597 **IP 80** **n. d.**
Prov: Palmyra. Loc: Damascus, National Museum, 30. *Funerary. On relief.* Bib: Ber '38 p 117 and

pl XLII, 4.

1 ḥbl
2 nʿm brt
3 rmy br
4 rpʾl

PAT 1598 **IP 81** **n. d.**
Prov: Palmyra. Loc: Damascus, National Museum, 32. *Funerary. On relief.* Bib: PS 351.

1 ḥbl
2 s?ygʾ
3 brt
4 mlkw
5 dn[...]

PAT 1599 **IP 82** **n. d.**
Prov: Palmyra. Loc: Damascus, National Museum, 34. *Funerary. On relief.*

1 ḥbl mʿny
2 br yrḥbwlʾ

PAT 1600 **IP 83** **n. d.**
Prov: Palmyra. Loc: Damascus, National Museum, 65. *Funerary. On relief.*

1 yrḥy
2 br ḥyrn

PAT 1601 **IP 84** **n. d.**
Prov: Palmyra. Loc: Damascus, National Museum, 245. *Funerary. On relief.* Bib: PS 106, p 102.

1 ḥbl
2 grymy
3 pgʾ
4 wbnwhy
5 ḥbl

PAT 1602 **IP 85** **n. d.**
Prov: Palmyra. Loc: Damascus, National Museum, 246. *Funerary. On relief.* Bib: PS 215.

(On right)
1 mqymw
2 br ʿgylw
3 br zbdʾ
4 ḥbl
(On left)
5 ḥyrn

PAT 1603 **Iraq ’49 p 185** **n. d.**
Prov: Palmyra. Loc: Not known. *Funerary. On relief.* Bib: Sta ’49e, pp 185-86 in Mackay ’49; pl LX, No. 4 and LXI, No. 2; latter a detail photo showing the text.

1 symʾ
2 brt
3 mtb{y}<w>l
4 ḥbl

PAT 1604 **Iraq ’87 p 57** **n. d.**
Prov: Hatra, shrine E of Great Temple. Loc: Not known. *Dedicatory. On stele.*

1 ʾbyhn br
2 ḥry ʾdy
3 ʾlt
4 ʾlt

With Hatran graffiti; apparently not in IH

PAT 1604.5 **JA ’18 p 281** no. 5. **n. d.**
Prov: Palmyra. Loc: Not known. *Funerary. On stele (from squeeze and notes).*

1 rʿtʾ brt
2 ʿgylw br
3 yrḥbwlʾ
4 ḥbl

PAT 1605 **JA ’18 p 282** no. 7 **n. d.**
Prov: Palmyra. Loc: Stanford (CA), Stanford University Museum of Art, 17204 (Leland Stanford Jr. Collection 1884). *Funerary. On relief.* Bib: Parlasca ’90c p 141 no. 13 (photo).

1 ʾmry br

2 ʿgʾ br
3 ʿbdy
4 ḥbl
Collated with museum photo.

PAT 1606 **JA '18 p 295** no. 18 **n.d.**
Prov: Palmyra. Loc: Louvre, AO 26429. *Funerary. On stele.* Bib: Lou 231.

1 ḥbl ḥlyšw
2 br [t]ymḥʾ

PAT 1607 **JA '33 p 230** **n. d.**
Prov: Palmyra. Loc: Palmyra Museum. *Dedicatory. On stone tablet fragment.*

1' [ ]
2' [...]mtb[...]
3' [...]ḥmkt[..]w[....]
4' [...]b dy mn bny [....]
5' [...] lyqrhwn wʾ[....]
6' [...]ln bt bʿlš[mn]
7' [......] wbt brt bl
8' [......]

PAT 1608 **JSS '88 p 171** **A.D. (143)**
Prov: Palmyra, Temple of Allat. Loc: Palmyra Museum. *Dedicatory. On door lintel fragments.* Bib: *Pl I*; Dri 1976b; Gaw '77; Gaw '83 p 61.

(fragments A, B, C, D)
1 [bšnt ..]10+5 qrb tymrṣw [br.......dy bḥm]nʾ ʿtyqʾ wṣl[mtʾ dy n]ḥšʾ dy bḥmnʾ dy lh[.....]
(fragments A. B, C, D)
2 [...p]rʿw wb[yrḥ ... šnt 46 ... bn]h nwsʾ dnh d[y q]dyšʾ wtrʿwhy wprnyn l[ʾlt ...]
Drijvers restores at end *ʾlhtʾ*; better might be *ʾštrʾ* or *ʾštrʾ ṭbtʾ* `the good goddess'

PAT 1609 **Lou 149** **n.d.**
Prov: Palmyra. Loc: Louvre, AO 11450. *Dedicatory. On altar.* Bib: *Photo*; Caubet '90 no. 37.

1 zbdbwl br
2 zbdbwl

3 [...] (illegible)
4 [...] (illegible)
5 lrḥmnʾ
6 bṭb [....]

PAT 1610 **Lou 157** **n.d.**
Prov: Palmyra. Loc: Louvre, AO 28548. *Dedicatory. On altar.* Bib: *Photo.*

1 ʿbd ʿltʾ wmwdn
2 [y]r̊ḥbwlʾ wmhr̊dt
3 bny r̊ʾšmhr̊ lb[l]
4 wlyr̊ḥbwl wʿgl<y>bwl
5 lʿlmʾ ṭbʾ mwdʾ
6 šlmn r̊ḥmh

PAT 1611 **Lou 232** **n.d.**
Prov: Palmyra. Loc: Louvre, AO 26430. *Funerary. On relief.* Bib: PS 473.

1 ḥbl ʿt[...]
2 brt ʾbgr$^{?}$
Text follows Lou; photo almost illegible

PAT 1612 **Lou 239** **A.D 91 or 103**
Prov: Palmyra. Loc: Louvre, AO 29537. *Funerary. On relief fragment.* Bib: *Fig 239.*

1 b$^{?}$tʿʾ brt
2 b$^{?}$rʾ br
3 lšm$^{?}$š dy
4 mtqrh
5 špry ḥb[l]
6 by<r>ḥ ʾdr
7 šnt 4.100
8 [+10?]+2
Stone shows ruling for lines

PAT 1613 **Maarav '87 p 72** no. 4 **n. d.**
Prov: Egypt, Edfu. Loc: Cairo, Egyptian Museum, 64738. *Unclassified. On ostracon.* Bib: *Pl 4*; Aimé-Giron '39 p 38 (No. 113).

1 ḥ$^{?}$d$^{?}$h$^{?}$/h$^{?}$w$^{?}$h$^{?}$ ʾš[. . .]
2 tpḥy ʾtt pkn$^{?}$[. . .]
3 dy ʾtšm

Read by Aimé-Giron as Egyptian Aramaic

PAT 1614 **MélCol p 161** **A.D. 131**

Prov: Palmyra. Loc: Geneva, Musée d'art et d'histoire, 19806. *Funerary: Foundation (lines 1-8) and partnership (9-10, smaller script, later). On stone slab.* Bib: *Fig 1 (photo).*

1 bt ʿlmʾ dnh dy ʿbdw
2 bwlḥʾ br ʿtnwry br
3 ḥyrn mʿlk ʿl ymynʾ
4 wmʿlk ʿl šmlʾ ʿbd
5 ʿtʿqb br yrḥbwlʾ
6 ʿtnwry wyrḥy br tymy
7 br yrḥy lhwn wbnwhn
8 bšnt 4.100+10+5
9 wštp tymʾ br yrḥy bmnth šmʿwn
10 br ḥyrn ddh šnt 4.100+40+3

PAT 1615 **MélDus p 277** **n. d.**

Prov: Palmyra, Agora, near Justinian Wall. Loc: Palmyra, A 618. *Honorific. On stone fragment.* Bib: *Hand copy p 278.*

1 [.....]l dy
2 [....] bšwšn
3 [....] wrwd mlk

Part of Inv 10 114 q.v. for assembled fragments.

PAT 1616 **MélDus p 885** **n. d.**

Prov: Cos (Greece). Loc: Not known. *Dedicatory. On altar.* Bib: *Photo p 884; of squeeze p 885.*

(Below Aramaic)
5 Ραββηλ Αιρα-
6 νου θεῶι Βή-
7 λω<ι> εὐχήν

1 [rb]ʾl br ḥyrn
2 [l]byl tdmryʾ
3 wyrḥbl wʿglbwl
4 dy ʾqym ʿltʾ

PAT 1617 **MélRob** **A.D. 157**

Prov: Palmyra, the Palmyrene?. Loc: Aleppo, private collection. *Dedicatory. On relief.*
Bib: *Photo, fig 2*; Déd pp 21-22.

1 ʿbd mkʿʾ ʿl ḥy zb
2 dh wḥyʾ bnwhy lʾ
3 [l]hy ʾlhʾ ṭbʾ wskrʾ
4 šnt 4.100 +
5 60+5+3
6 byrḥ
7 nysn

Déd p 21 gives substantially different reading of lines 1-3 (from photograph)

1 ʿbd mknʾ[b]r[?] z[?]b[?][...] ʿl ḥy
2 wh wḥyʾ bnwhy lʾr
3 [ṣ]w ʾlhʾ ṭbʾ wskrʾ (final ʾ begins line 4)

PAT 1618 **MUSJ '49 p 46** no. 1 **A.D. 160**

Prov: Palmyrene, desert S-W of Palmyra. Loc: Palmyra Museum. *Funerary. On stele.*
Bib: *Hand copy fig 1 p 45.*

1 npš dnh
2 dy ʿbnr̊gl
3 br̊ ḥr̊ʾ mqy br̊
4 ytmʾ dy bnʾ lh
5 mhr̊dt ʾḥwh
6 wgmlyʾ ḥbr̊h lyqr̊h
7 byr̊ḥ ṭbṭ šnt
8 4.100+60+10+1
9 ḥbl

PAT 1619 **MUSJ '49 p 52** **A.D. 175**

Prov: Palmyra, Damascus Gate. Loc: Palmyra, *in situ. Dedicatory. On altar.*
Bib: *Pl XVI*; CRAIBL '46 pp 391-92.

1 bryk šmh lʿlmʾ ṭbʾ
2 wrḥm[n]ʾ ʿbd ʿlwtʾ ʾln
3 [y]rḥy br ḥlptʾ br yrḥy
4 br ḥlptʾ ʿl ḥywhy wḥyʾ
5 šlʾ brt ḥṭry ʾtt!h
6 wḥy bnwhy wʾḥwhy
7 byrḥ nysn šnt 4.100
8 +80+5+1

Line 5 *ʾtt!h*: for *ʾtth*

PAT 1620 **MUSJ '49 p 56** **n. d.**

Prov: Palmyra. Loc: Palmyra Museum. *Dedicatory. On altar.* Bib: *Pl XVII, 2, 3.*

1 [ʿl]tʾ dh mn ksp ʿnwš[tʾ]

PAT 1621 **MUSJ '61 p 125** no. 1 **n. d.**

Prov: Palmyra, temple of Bel. Loc: Palmyra, A 1121. *Dedicatory. On relief.*
Bib: *Pl XI? (labelled II), XIV of volume, photo and photo of squeeze.*

1 ʿbd wmwdʾ
2 lgdʾ dy gn
3 yʾ wlʾrṣw
4 wrḥm
5 yrḥbwlʾ br
6 ʾ[.]bʾ bnʾ
7 wbʿlw
8 brh

PAT 1622 **MUSJ '61 p 133**

Prov: Palmyrene, Arak, 28 km N-W of Palmyra. Loc: Palmyra, A 1192. *Dedicatory. On altar.*
Bib: *Pl XII (labelled I), XIII of the volume), photo and photo of squeeze.*

1 ʿltʾ dy ʿbd
2 mlkw br̊
3 mr̊bnʾ
4 lyr̊ḥbwl
5 lšqʾ lʾrq?
6 lgdʾ dy qrt[ʾ]
7 lʾlhʾ škr[ʾ]
8 šnt 5.100+20+[.]
9 byrḥ nysn

PAT 1623 **MUSJ '62 p 104** **n. d.**

Prov: Palmyra, S-W Necropolis, Hypogeum of Malku. Loc: Palmyra Museum. *Funerary. On stele.* Group: Ber '35 pp 90-108; Inv 8 60; MUSJ '62 p 104-19.

1 ḥbl
2 ʾprht
3 br ʿgylw

PAT 1624 **MUSJ '62 p 106** **A.D. 214**

Prov: Palmyra, S-W Necropolis, Hypogeum of Malku. Loc: Ny Carlsberg Glyptotek, 3727. *Funerary: Cession. On stone tablet.* Group: see MUSJ '62 p 104.
Bib: *Pl II (XII of volume), 1*; MF Concession no. 18; NyCG 131.

1 byr̊ḥ ʾlwl šnt ḥmš mʾh wʿšr̊yn wḥmš
2 ywlys ʾwr̊lys ydyʿbl dy mtqr̊ʾ mzbnʾ br̊ ywlys
3 ʾwr̊lys ʾnynws ʾšʾlt ktb ydy lywlys br̊ ʾwr̊lys
4 ʿgylw br̊ ʾpr̊ht br̊ ḥr̊y zbdbwl bdyl dy lʾ ydʿ spr̊
5 d mwdʾ hw lywlys ʾwr̊lys ʾgr̊pʾ br̊ ʾgtpws br̊
6 ḥr̊y hlydwr̊s yr̊ḥbwlʾ dy lwt lh br̊bwʿtʾ dy qymʾ
7 btr̊ gwmḥyn tltʾ dy ʾgr̊pʾ mdʿn kl lmṭl dy plg nsb
8 mnth plgh r̊wḥʾ nwyt gmḥwhy tltʾ dy str̊ wlʾ
9 yhʾ šlyṭ lh lmr̊ḥ lʿlwh ʿl r̊bwʿtʾ mdʿn wʾn ṣbʾ
10 dy yʿbd bsṭr̊ʾ dydh ḥwlwh mdʿn yhwʾ bnʾ ʾw
11 ktl dy ḥwr̊ʾ ʾw ḥmr̊yn dy yr̊ḥ lʿlyhwn bh
12 bšṭr̊ʾ ywlys ʾwr̊lys nšʾ br̊ br̊ʿth
13 šhd ywlys ʾwr̊lys yr̊ḥbwlʾ br̊ mlkw
14 šhd

PAT 1625 **MUSJ '66 p 177** no. 1 **A.D. (213)**

Prov: Palmyra. Loc: Not known. *Dedicatory. On altar.* Bib: *Pl I, 1.*

1 dkyr gdʾ br mškw ḥpqws
2 qdm bl wʾrṣw šlm bṭb

3 dkyr gdʾ br mškw
4 [...............]
5 [...............]
6 byrḥ tšry šnt
7 20+5 ʿlth dh
8 qrb mlkw rbḥ?
9 lbl ʾlhʾ ṭb
10 wškr bṭb

Line 8 *rbḥ?*: read *rbʾ?*

PAT 1627 **MUSJ ’66 p 178** no. 2 **n. d.**
Prov: Palmyra. Loc: Not known. *Dedicatory. On relief fragment.* Bib: *Pl I, 2.*

1 [... zb]dbwl lgnyʾ dy mkmn

PAT 1628 **MUSJ ’66 p 178** no. 3 **n. d.**
Prov: Palmyra. Loc: Not known. *Tessera. Terracotta.*

Obv. 1 tymʿmd
2 bwlḥʾ

PAT 1626 **MUSJ ’66 p 178** no. 4 **n. d.**
Prov: Palmyra. Loc: Not known. *Tessera. Terracotta.* Bib: *Pl I, 4, a and b.*

Obv. 1 ʾgn bl
2 bny mknʾ
Rev. 1 bʿlšmn
2 bny mknʾ

PAT 1629 **MUSJ ’66 p 178** no. 5 **n. d.**
Prov: Palmyra. Loc: Louvre, AO 28360. *Dedicatory. On relief.*
Bib: *Pl I, 5*; Lou 153.

(Below figure of eagle)
1 ʿbd zbdʿth br zbydʾ bydʾ

PAT 1630 **MUSJ ’66 p 179** no. 6 **n. d.**
Prov: Palmyra. Loc: Not known. *Funerary. On relief.* Group: MUSJ ’66 p 179 nos. 6, 7. Bib: *Pl II, 6.*

1 mʿnw
2 br mqymw
3 ḥbl

PAT 1631 **MUSJ ’66 p 179** no. 7 **n. d.**
Prov: Palmyra. Loc: Not known. *Funerary. On relief.* Group: MUSJ ’66 p 179 nos. 6, 7. Bib: *Pl II, 7.*

1 bʿltgʾ
2 brt
3 mqymw
4 ḥbl

PAT 1632 **NyCG 47** **n.d.**
Prov: Palmyra. Loc: Ny Carlsberg Glyptotek, 2833. *funerary. On relief.* Bib: *Photo.*

1' [...]l?
2' ḥbl

PAT 1633 **NyCG 62** **A.D. 148 or 248**
Prov: Palmyra. Loc: Ny Carlsberg Glyptotek, 2775. *Funerary. On relief.* Bib: *Photo.*

(On left)
1 mlʾ
2 zʿwrʾ
3 bq?ly
4 gmlyh
5 ywm 5
6 bʾyr
7 ḥbl
(On right)
1 [b]r mlʾ
2 illegible
3 illegible
4 šnt

(On left) line 3: reading from photo, uncertain; (On right) lines 2-3 photo is illegible

PAT 1634 **NyCG 70** **n.d.**
Prov: Palmyra. Loc: Ny Carlsberg Glyptotek, 1043. *Funerary. On relief.* Bib: *Photo.*

1 [ḥb]l

PAT 1635 **NyCG 73** **n.d.**
Prov: Palmyra. Loc: Ny Carlsberg Glyptotek, 2763. *Funerary. On relief.* Bib: *Photo.*

(On right)
1 nwrbl
2 br
3 ʿtykʾ
4 ʾqmʾ
5 brth
(On left)
1 šʿd
2 brh
3 ḥbl

OM '88 p 37 **n. d.**
Prov: Palmyra. Loc: Leiden, Rijksmuseum van Oudheden, B 1977/4.1. *Funerary. On relief.*
Bib: Bastet '79, p 208; Van Rompay '90, p 79.

(On right)
1 ḥbl
2 brt whbʾ
3 šlmt
(Between heads)
1 brt whbʾ
(On left)
1 ʾqmt
2 ḥbl
(On girl's tablet)
1 ʾqmt
2 ḥbl
Collated 7/93

PAT 1637 **Palm III p 238** no. 5 **n. d.**
Prov: Palmyra, Diocletian Camp. Loc: Palmyra. *Tessera. Terracotta.*
Bib: *Pl III, p 194, no 59.*

Obv. 1 mlkbl
2 ʿgl<bwl>

PAT 1638 **Palm IV p 184** no. 3 **n. d.**
Prov: Palmyra, Valley of Tombs, Tower no. 15. Loc: Palmyra, *in situ. Funerary, Graffito. On wall.* Group: Palm IV, p 184 no. 3; RSP nos. 49-50. Bib: *Fig 215.*

1 [...]20+10+4 b[...]
2 10+5+1

PAT 1639 **Palm IV p 190** no. 9 **n. d.**
Prov: Palmyra, Diocletian Camp, W of Great Gate. Loc: Palmyra, CD 41/62. *Unclassified. On stone fragments.* Bib: *Fig. 221.*

1 [...]ln[....]br[....]y ʿty dy[...]
2 [...]hgy[....]w[..]wlyqr[...byrḥ]
3 ʾb šnt 1.100[+ .....]

PAT 1640 **Palm IV p 194** no. 16 **n. d.**
Prov: Palmyra, Diocletian Camp, W of Great Gate. Loc: Palmyra, CD 25/62. *Funerary. On relief fragment.* Bib: *Fig. 137.*

1 [...]y b$^{?}$r[...]

PAT 1641 **Palm IV p 195** no. 18 **n. d.**
Prov: Palmyra, Diocletian Camp, in foundations of Great Gate. Loc: Palmyra. *Funerary. On relief fragment.* Bib: *Fig. 117.*

1 ʾ[......]
2 b$^{?}$[......]

PAT 1642 **Palm V p 117** 13 **n. d.**
Prov: Palmyra, Diocletian Camp, "Temple des Enseignes". Loc: Palmyra, *in situ*, TE 243. *Dedicatory. On altar.* Bib: *Fig. 226.*

1 [...]y$^{?}$ky$^{?}$[...]
2 [...]t$^{?}$ymʾ[...]l$^{?ʾ}$
3 [...]ypṭ[...]
4 [...]brʾ[...]m[...]

PAT 1643 **Palm VIII p 121** no. 22 **n. d.**
Prov: Palmyra, Diocletian Camp, near "Temple des Enseignes". Loc: Palmyra, CD 17/68. *Unclassified. On stone fragments.*

1 [..b]t ḥry[...]

2 [...]b[...]
3 [...]2[?].100+[?][...]

PAT 1644 **Palm VIII p 121** no. 23 **n. d.**
Prov: Palmyra, Diocletian Camp, reemployed in later wall. Loc: Palmyra, CD 1/73. *Dedicatory. On door lintel.* Bib: *Pl C, 229.*

1 qrbt šgl[...]
2 b[ʿ]lh ʾqm[...]

PAT 1645 **Palm VIII p 121** no. 24 **n. d.**
Prov: Palmyra, Diocletian Camp, on surface. Loc: Palmyra, CD 2/73. *Dedicatory. On altar fragment.* Bib: *Pl CI, 230.*

1 [lbryk šm]h lrḥmnʾ
2 [...] ʿgylw
3 [br] wh[...]

PAT 1646 **Palm VIII p 121** no. 25 **n. d.**
Prov: Palmyra, Diocletian Camp, reemployed in later wall. Loc: Palmyra, CD 31/73. *Funerary. On stele fragment.* Bib: *Pl CI, 231.*

1 ṣlm
2 bwnʾ br̊
3 yr̊ḥy br̊ tymr̊ṣw
4 ḥbl

PAT 1647 **Palm VIII p 122** no. 26 **n. d.**
Prov: Palmyra, Diocletian Camp, reemployed in later wall. Loc: Palmyra, CD 46/73. *Funerary. On relief.* Bib: *Pl LXXIX, 166.*

1 hd/rn
2 br ḥk[.]
3 tymḥ[ʾ]
4 mlʾ dky

PAT 1648 **Palm VIII p 122** no. 27 **n. d.**
Prov: Palmyra, Diocletian Camp, reemployed in later wall. Loc: Palmyra, CD 47/73. *Funerary. On relief.* Bib: *Pl LXXXV, 184.*

1 ḥbʾ brt
2 ʿgʾ ʾqml
3 ʾtt tymšʾ
4 br ʾlhšʾ
5 ḥbl

PAT 1649 **Palm VIII p 122** no. 28 **A.D. (89)**
Prov: Palmyra, Diocletian Camp, reemployed in later wall. Loc: Palmyra, CD 56/73. *Funerary. On relief fragment.* Bib: *Pl LXXXII, 175.*

1 [...]
2 brt ʾ[...]
3 ḥbl
4 šlmn brh ḥbl
5 byrḥ ʾb šnt 4.100+[?][..]

PAT 1650 **Palm VIII p 122** no. 29 **n. d.**
Prov: Palmyra, Diocletian Camp, reemployed in later wall. Loc: Palmyra, CD 57/73. *Funerary. On relief fragment.* Bib: *Pl CII, 232.*

1 mkn(?) (or: mlkʾ)? br
2 ḥyrn br̊h

PAT 1651 **Palm VIII p 123** no. 30 **n. d.**
Prov: Palmyra, Diocletian Camp, Forum. Loc: Palmyra, CD 1/76. *Dedicatory. On corner fragment of frame.* Bib: *Pl CII, 233.*

1 [byr]ḥ ʾdr šn[t...]
2 [... ʿ]bd zbd[...]
3 [...dn]h l[...]

PAT 1651.2 **Parl ʾ90b** **n. d.**
Prov: Palmyra. Loc: Private collection. *Funerary. On relief.* Bib: *Photo*, fig 1.

1 [...]ʾtt
2 m[?]qymw br
3 ʿbydʾ ḥbl

Reading from photograph; in line 1 more can be seen, PN of line 3 not certain

PAT 1652 **Parl ’90c p 140** no. 11 **n. d.**
Prov: Palmyra. Loc: Stanford California, Stanford University Museum of Art, no. 17200 (Leland Stanford Jr. Collection 1884). *Funerary. On relief.* Bib: *Photo, fig 11.*

(On right)
1 [...]
2 b$^{?}$[r]nʿm
3 ṭyl
4 [.$^{?}$]š
5 m/qyl
(On left, two illegible lines)

Parlasca cites Degen, “Bolʿaq(eb) ṭwl(?) und in Zeile 3-4 Smwl” (as Jewish name Samuel — improbable, DRH); collated with museum photograph.

PAT 1653 **Parl ’90c p 141** no. 12 **n. d.**
Prov: Palmyra. Loc: Stanford California, Stanford University Museum of Art, no. 17201 (Leland Stanford Jr. Collection 1884). *Funerary. On relief.* Bib: *Photo, fig 12.*

1 ṣlm[tʾ dh]
2 dy ʿ[...]

PAT 1654 **Parl ’90c p 143** no. 18 **n. d.**
Prov: Palmyra. Loc: California, private collection. *Funerary. On relief.* Bib: *Fig 18; Antike und Orient*, Fa. Libresso AG, Zurich, Bibliographie Nr. 10 (1975), fig 17 (reference from Parl ’90c).

1 ʾlkšndr̊ʾ
2 br nr̊qys
3 ḥbl

Reading from photo.

PAT 1655 **Parl ’90c p 143** no. 17 **n. d.**
Prov: Palmyra. Loc: Formerly, Hollywood, California, Stendhal Galleries. *Funerary. On relief.* Bib: *Fig 17.*

1 ʾmyʾ
2 brt
3 grymy
4 ḥbl

Text approximate, following Degen as cited in Parlasca; not readily legible from available photo.

PAT 1656 **PDura 152** **n. d.**
Prov: Dura Europos. Loc: New Haven, Connecticut, Beinecke Library, Yale Univ., Inv. D.Pg. 35. *Uncertain; “Probably a lease” (Welles). On parchment.*
Bib: Welles ’59 p 414, pl LXVIII, 2; Altheim and Stiehl ’53 pp 69-73 fig 18; Henning ’54 479-80.

1 [............]
2 [............]
3 ʾgr̊$^{?}$tʾ.[.......]
4-6 only isolated individual letters can be distinguished on the published plate

Dot on *r* not certain; Welles (quoting Ingholt?) “in line 2, it may be possible to read šlm”; new edition in preparation by E. Cussini

PAT 1657 **PGKK p 306** no. 28 **A.D. 222**
Prov: Palmyra, Temple of Allat, reemployed in foundation. Loc: Palmyra, A 1426. *Funerary: Cession. On stone slab.* Bib: *Photo p 306.*

1 byr̊ḥ qnyn šnt 5.100+20+10+4
2 ʾḥbr̊ ywlys ʾwr̊lys zbdbwl br̊
3 mlkw br̊ lšmš ʾpsk mn gwmḥ[yʾ]
4 ʾln tr̊n bsṭr̊ʾ mʿr̊byʾ dy
5 lʾksdr̊ʾ dnʾ tymnyʾ lywlys
6 ʾwr̊lys mtly br̊ ḥlptʾ br̊
7 dygns lh wlbnwhy wlbnʾ
8 bnwhy lʿlmʾ

Rubricated; date in PGKK erroneous.

PAT 1658 **PGKK p 310** no. 33 **A.D. 213**
Prov: Palmyra. Loc: Palmyra, A 1422. *Dedicatory. On altar.* Bib: *Photo p 311*; Meisterwerke, photo p 42; German transl. p 71.

1 br̊yk šmh lʿlmʾ
2 ṭbʾ wr̊ḥmnʾ ʿbd
3 w$^{?}$mwdʾ šmʿwn br̊
4 [..]šy ʿl ḥywhy wḥyʾ
5 [ʾ]byhy wʾmh wʾḥw[y]
6 byrḥ nysn šnt 5.100+
7 20+4

PAT 1659 **PGKK p 310** no. 32 **(n.d.)**
Prov: Palmyra. Loc: Palmyra, B 2304 (A 143/75). *Dedicatory. On relief.* Bib: *Photo p 32.*

(Beside figure of deity)
1 yrḥbwl
(On lower margin)
2 šky?y br ḥyrn

PAT 1660 **PGSc 8** **n. d.**
Prov: Palmyra. Loc: Private Collection (see note to text). *Funerary. On relief.*

(On left)
1 mrty
2 ʾtth
(On right)
1 zbdbl
2 rbʾ

New York, Sotheby Parke Bernet, May 21, 1977; and again June 10-11, 1983, lot no. 165 (Formerly Yale University Art Gallery).

PAT 1661 **PGSc 12** **n. d.**
Prov: Palmyra. Loc: Chapel Hill N. C., The Ackland Art Museum, no. 79.29.1. *Funerary. On relief.*
Bib: *Photo*; Cussini '92 pp 428-29, figs 3, 4.

1 nʿm ʾtt
2 ḥyrʾ br
3 mlkw
4 ʾšyn
5 ḥbl

PAT 1662 **PGSc 13** **n. d.**
Prov: Palmyra. Loc: New Haven, Connecticut, Yale University Art Gallery, 1930.6. *Funerary. On relief.*

1 ʾbnʾ
2 brt nbwnʾ
3 br ʿnyny
4 ḥbl

Collated

PAT 1663 **PNO no. 1** **n. d.**
Prov: Palmyrene, Khirbet Semrin (Jebel Shaar). Loc: Damascus, National Museum. *Dedicatory. On stone fragment.* Bib: *Pl XLV, 10.*

1 [...] ʿbd l[...]
2 [..] ḥ?yʾ bnwh?[...]

PAT 1664 **PNO no. 2** **n. d.**
Prov: Palmyrene, Khirbet Semrin, Temple of Abgal. Loc: Damascus, National Museum. *Honorary. On statue base.* Group: Temple of Abgal nos. 2-29. Bib: *Pl XLV, 9.*

1 ṣlm ḥnynʾ ʿgylw ʾsry/ʾsdy

PAT 1665 **PNO no. 2 bis** **n. d.**
Prov: Palmyrene, Khirbet Semrin, Temple of Abgal. Loc: Damascus, National Museum. *Honorary. On statue base.* Group: See no. 2 above. Bib: *Pl XLV, 4.*

1 [... ʿgy]lw ʾsd/ry

PAT 1666 **PNO no. 2 ter** **n. d.**
Prov: Palmyrene, Khirbet Semrin, Temple of Abgal. Loc: Damascus, National Museum. *Dedicatory?. On stone.* Group: See no. 2 above. Bib: *Pl XLII, 1.*

1 dkyr
2 ʾbgl
3 wʾḥwhy
4 wbny byth
5 qdm yrḥbwl
6 dy yhb lʾbgl
7 šlṭnʾ bʾtrʾ
8 klh lʿlm
9 wdkyr kl gbr dy
10 ydḥl lʾbg
11 l bṭb ʾdry

Line 11 *ʾdry*: Not visible on pl.

PAT 1667 **PNO no. 3** **A.D. 199**
Prov: Palmyrene, Khirbet Semrin, Temple of Abgal. Loc: Damascus, National Museum. *Dedicatory.*

On relief. Group: See no. 2 above. Bib: *Pl XXI, 1.*

(A)
1 ṣlm ʾbgl br šʿdw
(B)
1 ʿbd ʾbgl br šʿdw hyklʾ
2 lʾbgl ʾlhʾ mwdʾ [ʾ]dr šnt 5.100+10

PAT 1668 **PNO no. 4** **n. d.**
Prov: Palmyrene, Khirbet Semrin, Temple of Abgal, cella. Loc: Damascus, National Museum, no. 5917. *Dedicatory. On statue base.* Group: See no. 2 above. Bib: *Pl XXI, 2.*

1 lʾbgl ʾlhʾ ṭbʾ wskrʾ ʿbd mʿny brʿtʾ

PAT 1669 **PNO no. 5** **n. d.**
Prov: Palmyrene, Khirbet Semrin, Temple of Abgal, cella. Loc: Damascus, National Museum. *Dedicatory. On relief.* Group: See no. 2 above. Bib: *Pl XXI, 3.*

1 lʾbgl gnyʾ
2 ṭbʾ wškrʾ
3 ʿbd
4 bʿly

PAT 1670 **PNO no. 6** **A.D. 154**
Prov: Palmyrene, Khirbet Semrin, Temple of Abgal. Loc: Damascus, National Museum, no. 2842. *Dedicatory. On relief.* Group: See no. 2 above. Bib: *Pl XXII, 1.*

(A. On the plinth)
1 dkrn ṭbʾ ʿbd mqy br ʿzyzw ʿl ḥywhy
2 byrḥ tšry šnt 4.100+60+5+1
(B. To left of rider on right)
1 ʾbgl
2 gnyʾ
3 ṭbʾ
(C. To right of rider on left)
1 ʾšr
2 gnyʾ
3 ṭbʾ
(D. Above head of offerer, (line 1) and (2) on base of altar)
1 smt
2 ʿty

PAT 1671 **PNO no. 7** **n. d.**
Prov: Palmyrene, Khirbet Semrin, Temple of Abgal. Loc: Damascus, National Museum. *Dedicatory. On lintel.* Group: See no. 2 above. Bib: *Pl XXIII, 1.*

(A. On lintel)
1 [..]k?s?? dnh whyklʾ [wttlyl]h wtrʿwh? wtṣbyth klh ʿbd [mn] kysh? ʿg[ʾ]
2 [b]r ḥnynʾ br ʿ?g?y?[lw] lʾbgl wlmʿn ʾlhyʾ ṭbyʾ wškryʾ ʿl ḥywhy
(B. On right of bust on right)
1 qryn
2 ʿgʾ
(C. On left of bust on left)
1 mq[y]
2 ḥnynʾ

PAT 1672 **PNO no. 9** **n. d.**
Prov: Palmyrene, Khirbet Semrin, Temple of Abgal. Loc: Damascus, National Museum. *Unclassified. On stone block fragment.* Group: See no. 2 above. Bib: Hand copy fig 2 p 147.

1 [.........]
2 [.. byr]ḥ sywn šnt 5.100+[...]

PAT 1673 **PNO no. 10** **n. d.**
Prov: Palmyrene, Khirbet Semrin, Temple of Abgal. Loc: Damascus, National Museum. *Dedicatory. On relief fragment.* Group: See no. 2 above. Bib: *Pl XXIII, 4.*

(On right)
1 ʾbgl
(On left)
2 ʿzyzw

PAT 1674 **PNO no. 11** **n. d.**
Prov: Palmyrene, Khirbet Semrin, Temple of Abgal. Loc: Damascus, National Museum. *Dedicatory. On relief fragment.* Group: See no. 2 above. Bib: *Pl XLV,7.*

1 [...]l ʾbgl [...]

PAT 1675 **PNO no. 12** **n. d.**

Prov: Palmyrene, Khirbet Semrin, Temple of Abgal. Loc: Damascus, National Museum. *Dedicatory. On relief fragment.* Group: See no. 2 above. Bib: *Pl XLV, 8.*

1 [....]s ʾwrlys[...]

PAT 1676 **PNO no. 13** **A.D. (212)**

Prov: Palmyrene, Khirbet Semrin, Temple of Abgal. Loc: Damascus, National Museum, no. 5924. *Dedicatory. On altar.* Group: See no. 2 above. Bib: *Pl XXIV, 2.*

1 ʿbd zbdbwl br
2 ʿšrʾ lʾbgl
3 ʾlhʾ ṭbʾ wsk
4 rʾ byrḥ kslwl
5 šnt <5.100>+20+4

PAT 1677 **PNO no. 14** **A.D. 270**

Prov: Palmyrene, Khirbet Semrin, Temple of Abgal. Loc: Damascus, National Museum, no. 5.925. *Dedicatory. On altar.* Group: See no. 2 above. Bib: *Pl XXIV, 3.*

1 ʿltʾ dnh qrb
2 šlmn ṭlyʾ dy
3 ʿgylw kylywn
4 lgnyʾ šʿydʾ
5 dy ndr lhwn
6 dkyr qm?lʾ
7 tym?ʾ šʿdw
8 ʾḥyh byrḥ
9 ʾdr dy šnt 5.100+80+1
10 wgy?n?ʾ bṭb

PAT 1678 **PNO no. 15** **A.D. 252**

Prov: Palmyrene, Khirbet Semrin, Temple of Abgal. Loc: Damascus, National Museum, no. 9023. *Dedicatory. On altar.* Group: See no. 2 above. Bib: *Pl XXIV, 4.*

1 ʿbd ʾbgl
2 br rwlb (or: mwlb) lʾ
3 bgl ʾlhʾ
4 lḥywh šnt
5 5.100+60+4

Pl printed correctly; original written in unsual manner; see comment in PNO.

PAT 1679 **PNO no. 16** **A.D. 214**

Prov: Palmyrene, Khirbet Semrin, Temple of Abgal. Loc: Damascus, National Museum, no. 2844. *Dedicatory. On altar.* Group: See no. 2 above. Bib: *Pl XXIV, 5.*

1 ʿltʾ dh ʾ
2 qrb nbwzbd
3 nḥy lʿglbwl
4 wlmlkbl
5 wlʾbgl gnyʾ
6 ʿl ḥywhy
7 byrḥ šbṭ šn[t]
8 5.100+20+5

PAT 1680 **PNO no. 17** **n. d.**

Prov: Palmyrene, Khirbet Semrin, Temple of Abgal. Loc: Damascus, National Museum. *Dedicatory. On altar.* Group: See no. 2 above. Bib: *Pl XXIV, 6.*

1 dkyr bwlmʾ
2 br ʾḥyʾ
3 qdm ʾbgl
4 g[n]yʾ bṭb

PAT 1681 **PNO no. 18** **n. d.**

Prov: Palmyrene, Khirbet Semrin, Temple of Abgal. Loc: Damascus, National Museum. *Dedicatory. On fragments of altar.* Group: See no. 2 above. Bib: *Pl XLVII, 3, and fig 3, 4 p 150.*

(A)
1' q?r?b m[...]
(B)
1' dkyr [...]
(C)
1' [dkyr]yn wbrykyn

PAT 1682 **PNO no. 19** **n. d.**

Prov: Palmyrene, Khirbet Semrin, Temple of Abgal. Loc: Damascus, National Museum. *Dedicatory. On altar.* Group: See no. 2 above. Bib: *Pl XLVII, 1 a, b.*

1 šyqn
2 šmʿwn
Face B has two illegible lines

PAT 1683 **PNO no. 20** **A.D. 257**

Prov: Palmyrene, Khirbet Semrin, Temple of Abgal. Loc: Damascus, National Museum, no. 5921. *Dedicatory. On stone crater.* Group: See no. 2 above. Bib: *Pl XXV, 1, 2.*

1 qrb šmʿwn br ʾbʾ lʾbgl ʾlhʾ ṭbʾ wškrʾ šnt 5.100+60+5+3 byrḥ qnyn
Inscription on rim

PAT 1684 **PNO no. 21** **A.D. (573 or 578)**

Prov: Palmyrene, Khirbet Semrin, Temple of Abgal. Loc: Damascus, National Museum. *Dedicatory. On fragments of stone crater.* Group: See no. 2 above. Bib: *Pl XXV, 3-6.*

(A, fig C)
1 [...] ʾdynt mlkʾ (space) ʾgnʾ (or: ʾgntʾ)
(B.)
1 blb[ ]y br zby$^{?}$ s$^{?}$[ ]
(C, fig A)
1 b[.. lʾ]bgl ʾlhʾ ṭbʾ šnt 5.100+[.]+3 byr[ḥ ...]
(A) 1: small *t* written above line in *ʾgnʾ*

PAT 1685 **PNO no. 22** **n. d.**

Prov: Palmyrene, Khirbet Semrin, Temple of Abgal. Loc: Damascus, National Museum. *Dedicatory. On stone crater fragments.* Group: See no. 2 above. Bib: *Pl XXVI, 1, 3.*

1 gbʾt[...]

PAT 1686 **PNO no. 23** **n. d.**

Prov: Palmyrene, Khirbet Semrin, Temple of Abgal. Loc: Damascus, National Museum. *Dedicatory. On stone crater fragment.* Group: See no. 2 above. Bib: *Pl XXVI, 6.*

1 [..]y lʾbgl gnyʾ ṭb[ʾ...]

PAT 1687 **PNO no. 24** **n. d.**

Prov: Palmyrene, Khirbet Semrin, Temple of Abgal. Loc: Damascus, National Museum. *Dedicatory. On stone crater fragment.* Group: See no. 2 above. Bib: *Pl XXVI, 5.*

1 [... d]k$^{?}$yr šlmn bṭb[.]

PAT 1688 **PNO no. 25** **n. d.**

Prov: Palmyrene, Khirbet Semrin, Temple of Abgal. Loc: Damascus, National Museum. *Dedicatory. On stone crater fragment.* Group: See no. 2 above. Bib: *Pl XXVI, 2.*

1 [... ʾ]lhʾ ṭbʾ

PAT 1689 **PNO no. 26** **n. d.**

Prov: Palmyrene, Khirbet Semrin, Temple of Abgal. Loc: Damascus, National Museum. *Dedicatory. On stone crater fragment.* Group: See no. 2 above. Bib: *Pl XXVI, 4.*

1 [..b]r$^{?}$ʾty lʾb[gl]

PAT 1690 **PNO no. 27** **n. d.**

Prov: Palmyrene, Khirbet Semrin, Temple of Abgal. Loc: Damascus, National Museum. *Dedicatory. On stone crater fragment.* Group: See no. 2 above.

1 [... l]ʾbgl ʾlhʾ ṭbʾ [...]

PAT 1691 **PNO no. 28** **n. d.**

Prov: Palmyrene, Khirbet Semrin, Temple of Abgal. Loc: Damascus, National Museum. *Dedicatory. On fragment of stone crater.* Group: See no. 2 above. Bib: *Fig 6, p 152.*

1 [..] gbʾ$^{?}$ [...]

PAT 1692 **PNO no. 28 bis** **n. d.**
Prov: Palmyrene, Khirbet Semrin, Temple of Abgal. Loc: Damascus, National Museum. *Dedicatory. On stone fragment.* Group: See no. 2 above. Bib: *Pl XLIII, 6.*

1 dkyr bṭb[...]

PAT 1693 **PNO no. 29** **n. d.**
Prov: Palmyrene, Khirbet Semrin, Temple of Abgal. Loc: Damascus, National Museum. *Dedicatory. On stone crater fragment.* Group: See no. 2 above.

1 lʿbgl ʾ[lhʾ]

PAT 1694 **PNO no. 30** **n. d.**
Prov: Palmyrene, Khirbet Leqteir. Loc: Damascus, National Museum. *Dedicatory. On altar.*

(A)
1' dkyrn bny[...]
(B)
1' ʿmlʾ
Face C illegible

PAT 1695 **PNO no. 31** **n. d.**
Prov: Palmyrene, Khirbet Leqteir. Loc: Damascus, National Museum. *Dedicatory. On stone slab, broken.* Bib: *Pl XLIII, 1.*

1 dkyr yrḥ[y br]
2 yrḥyb[wlʾ]
3 bṭb š[nt]
4 5?.100[..]

PAT 1696 **PNO no. 32** **n. d.**
Prov: Palmyrene, Khirbet Leqteir. Loc: Damascus, National Museum. *Unclassified. On stone block.*

1 [..]ḥmnʾ[..]
2 [..]wbybn[..]
Lines 1, 2 on different faces.

PAT 1697 **PNO no. 33** **n. d.**
Prov: Palmyrene, El-Mekeimle. Loc: Damascus, National Museum. *Dedicatory. On relief.* Bib: *Pl XXVII, 4.*

1 qrb yrḥy lʿbgl
2 ʾlhʾ ṭbʾ

PAT 1698 **PNO no. 34** **n. d.**
Prov: Palmyrene, El-Mekeimle. Loc: Damascus, National Museum. *Dedicatory. On relief.* Bib: *Pl XXVIII, 1.*

(By head)
1 ṣlm zbknʾ
(On plinth)
1 [..]br[..]

PAT 1699 **PNO no. 34bis** **A.D. 228**
Prov: Palmyrene, El-Mekeimle. Loc: El-Mekeimle, *in situ. Dedicatory. On stone.*

1 bṭb
2 šnt
3 5.100+40

PAT 1700 **PNO no. 35** **n. d.**
Prov: Palmyrene, Ras esh-Shaar. Loc: Damascus, National Museum, no. 5069. *Dedicatory. On relief.* Bib: *Pl XXVII, 3.*

A. (On left of god on horseback)
1 ʿbd šmʿwn br
2 mʿn br wrtn
3 lmʿn ʾlhʾ
B. (On right of god on camel)
1 ʿbd šmʿwn
2 br mʿn br wrtn
3 lšʿd ʾlhʾ
C. (On plinth)
1 mṣbyʾ ʾln mʿn wšʿd ʾlhyʾ

PAT 1701 **PNO no. 36** **n. d.**
Prov: Palmyrene, Ras esh-Shaar. Loc: Damascus, National Museum. *Unclassified. On relief fragment.* Bib: *Fig 7, p 155* .

1 [...]n?mḥ[..]

PAT 1702 **PNO no. 37** **A.D. 194**

Prov: Palmyrene, Ras esh-Shaar. Loc: Damascus, National Museum, no. 5070. *Dedicatory. On altar.* Bib: *Pl XXVIII, 4.*

1 ʿltʾ dnh ʿbd
2 ʾlhbl wr̊bʾl
3 [w]mhr̊w bny bwly
4 lmʿnw ʾlhʾ
5 ṭbʾ wskr̊ʾ mwd
6 n lh byr̊ḥ ʾb
7 šnt 5.100+5

PAT 1703 **PNO no. 38** **n. d.**

Prov: Palmyrene, Ras esh-Shaar. Loc: Damascus, National Museum. *Dedicatory. On altar.*
Bib: Abdul-Hak '51 no. 35. Bib: *Pl XXVIII, 6.*

1 šlmt
2 wʾwtqʾ
3 wmqymw
4 mwdy<n> lšlmn
5 wlʾbgl

PAT 1704 **PNO no. 39** **A.D. 191**

Prov: Palmyrene, Khirbet Faruan. Loc: Damascus, National Museum, no. 5215. *Dedicatory. On relief.* Bib: *Pl XXIX, 1.*

1 ʿbd tymʾ br zkyʾ lgnyʾ dy qrytʾ dy bt pṣyʾl ʾlhyʾ ṭbyʾ
2 wskryʾ ʿl ḥywhy whyʾ ʾḥw?hy byrḥ kn[w]n
3 šnt 5.100+3

PAT 1705 **PNO no. 40** **n. d.**

Prov: Palmyrene, Khirbet Faruan. Loc: Damascus, National Museum. *Dedicatory. On relief.* Bib: *Pl XXIX, 3.*

1 [...]r?tlt brt
2 [..ʿ]l ḥyʾ
3 [..] lʾlt

PAT 1706 **PNO no. 41** **n. d.**

Prov: Palmyrene, Khirbet Faruan. Loc: Damascus, National Museum. *Dedicatory. On altar.* Bib: *Pl XXIX, 2.*

1 lgny dy ṣ?ldyḥ?n ʿb[d]
2 brhʾ br ʿgʾ dkrn l[....]
3 mwdʾ

line 2 *brhʾ* with Stark PN p 121 (for *brhn?* of PNO).

PAT 1707 **PNO no. 42** **A.D. 238**

Prov: Palmyrene, Khirbet Faruan. Loc: Damascus, National Museum, 5115. *Dedicatory. On altar.*
Bib: Abdul-Hak '51 no. 50. Bib: *Pl XXVIII, 5.*

1 ʿbd wmwdʾ
2 ʿbdbl lr̊ḥmnʾ
3 ṭbʾ wlgdh dy
4 qr̊ytʾ wlgdʾ
5 dy gnyʾ šnt
6 5.100+40+10

PAT 1708 **PNO no. 43** **n. d.**

Prov: Palmyrene, Khirbet Faruan. Loc: Damascus, National Museum. *Dedicatory. On stone tablet.* Bib: *Pl XLV, 6.*

1 qbtʾ dnh ʿbd
2 nbwzbd br ṣʿdy br
3 mqymw ḥyrn lgnyʾ
4 ʾlhʾ ṭbʾ wškrʾ
5 ʿl ḥywh wḥyʾ bnwh

PAT 1709 **PNO no. 44** **n. d.**

Prov: Palmyrene, Labda. Loc: Damascus, National Museum. *Dedicatory. On relief fragment.* Bib: *Pl XXX, 4.*

1 ʿbd b[.......]

PAT 1710 **PNO no. 45** **n. d.**

Prov: Palmyrene, Khirbet esh-Shteib. Loc: Damascus, National Museum. *Dedicatory. On altar.* Bib: *Pl XXX, 3.*

1 lbryk šmh
2 [lʿl]m[ʾ ʿ]bd šl
3 [mn .....] nḥšṭb

PAT 1711 **PNO no. 46** **n. d.**
Prov: Palmyrene, Khirbet esh-Shteib. Loc: Damascus, National Museum. *Dedicatory. On stone crater fragments.*

1 [..] ʾlhʾ [...]

PAT 1712 **PNO no. 47** **n. d.**
Prov: Palmyrene, Khirbet Wadi es-Suan (Jebel Shaar). Loc: Damascus, National Museum. *Dedicatory. On relief.* Bib: *Pl XXXIV, 4c, 5a; fig 9 p 159.*

(On right face)
1 dkyr ʿwydʾ bṭb
2 br zbdʿy
3 dkyr lšmš br
4 mqymy ʾṣrʿ
5 bṭb k[?]t[?]bʾ
(On left face)
1 [d]kyr ʿnn bṭb
(Front)
1 ʿwyd[?]ʾ[?]
2 dky[?]r bṭb

PAT 1713 **PNO no. 48** **n. d.**
Prov: Palmyrene, Khirbet Wadi es-Suan. Loc: Damascus, National Museum, 5922. *Dedicatory. On altar.* Bib: *Pl XXX, 2.*

1 ʿbd hrms
2 lgnyʾ dy ḥwrtʾ
3 ʾlhyʾ ṭbyʾ
4 wškryʾ

PAT 1714 **PNO no. 49** **n. d.**
Prov: Palmyrene, Madaba. Loc: Damascus, National Museum. *Dedicatory. On stone crater fragment.* Bib: *Pl XXVI, 9.*

1 [..] ʾgn [..]

PAT 1715 **PNO no. 50** **n. d.**
Prov: Palmyrene, Khirbet Ramadan. Loc: Damascus, National Museum. *Dedicatory. On relief.* Bib: *Pl XXXVI, 1.*

1 qrb ʾwṭkʾ lʿglbwl w[lm]lkbl [....]

PAT 1716 **PNO no. 51** **A.D. 149**
Prov: Palmyrene, Khirbet Ramadan. Loc: Damascus, National Museum. *Dedicatory. On stele.* Bib: *Pl XXXV, 1.*

(On right)
1 blḥzy
2 lgd
3 qrytʾ
(On left)
1 šnt
2 4.100
3 +60+1

PAT 1717 **PNO no. 52** **n. d.**
Prov: Palmyrene, Khirbet Ramadan. Loc: Damascus, National Museum. *Dedicatory. On relief fragments.* Bib: *Pl XXXIV, 2.*

1 dkrn ʾlhmnsb[....]
2 wdkyr grmy [...]
3 qdmwh [....]
4 br ʾbyhn

PAT 1718 **PNO no. 52 bis** **n. d.**
Prov: Palmyrene, Khirbet Ramadan. Loc: Damascus, National Museum. *Funerary. On stele.* Bib: *Pl XXXV, 5.*

1 ḥ<bl> tymrṣw ḥ<bl>

On *ḥ<bl>* see Glossary and comment of S(tarcky) PNO ad loc.

PAT 1719 **PNO no. 52 ter** **n. d.**
Prov: Palmyrene, Khirbet es-Sana. Loc: Damascus, National Museum. *Dedicatory. On relief.* Bib: *Pl XXXVI, 3, 4, 5.*

(A)
1 wdkyryn gm[...]
2 [...]by br šwqn[...]
3 lwdʾ dy yrḥ[bwl]

4 dkyryn wbrw[kyn]
5 bš[..]yn[b]ṭ[b]
(B)
1 [d]kyr [....]
2 dy glp ʿlṭʾ
3 lwdʾ dy
4 yrḥbwl
(C)
1 wdky[r ...] (traces of other letters also on C)

PAT 1720 **PNO no. 53** **n. d.**

Prov: Palmyrene, Khirbet es-Sana. Loc: Damascus, National Museum. *Unclassified. On stone block.* Bib: *Fig 10, p 163* .

1 blbw
2 gwbʾ
3 bṭb

PAT 1721 **PNO no. 54** **n. d.**

Prov: Palmyrene, Khirbet Abu Duhur. Loc: Khirbet Abu Duhur, *in situ. Dedicatory. On stone.* Bib: *Pl XLII, 3.*

1 dkyr
2 tymlt
3 br tymrṣw
4 bṭb

With Safaitic inscription, *lmnʿm*$^?$ For Munʿim

PAT 1722 **PNO no. 55** **A.D. 147**

Prov: Palmyrene, Khirbet Abu Duhur. Loc: Damascus, National Museum. *Dedicatory. On stone.* Bib: *Pl XXXVIII, 1.*

(On left, below horseman)
1 wrdn
2 brwqʾ
3 mhrdt
4 ʿmbkrʾ
(On right)
1 ṣlm
2 mqymw
3 y$^?$rḥbwlʾ
(On left, above horseman)
1 dkyr wrdn wbrwqʾ ʿmbkrʾ
(Above temple, to the right)
1 dkyr
2 zʿm/qw br
3 ḥyrn br šḥd/rʾ
4 dyḥr ($^?$: word uncertain) byrḥ ʾb bywm 10+5
5 šnt 4.100+40+10+5+3
6 dkyr mʿyrʾ
(To the right of god's head)
1 b

With drawing depicting a temple with enthroned god, a horseman to the left and a standing man to the right.

PAT 1723 **PNO no. 56** **n. d.**

Prov: Palmyrene, Khirbet Abu Duhur. Loc: Damascus, National Museum. *Dedicatory. On stone block.* Bib: *Pl XLII, 5.*

1 dkyrn ʾlhyʾ
2 šlmn
3 wdkyryn
4 kl mn dhw
5 bd/rn šmk$^?$b$^?$ (-š$^?$n$^?$)
6 gny
7 by mnhm

PAT 1724 **PNO no. 57** **A.D. 262**

Prov: Palmyrene, Khirbet Abu Duhur. Loc: Damascus, National Museum, 3841. *Dedicatory. On relief.* Bib: *Pl XXXVIII, 2.*

1 lyqr mlkʾ ṭbʾ wškrʾ ʿbd glptʾ dnh ʾnʿm wbʿly ʿl ḥyyhwn byrḥ šbṭ šnt 5.100
2 +60+10+3

PAT 1725 **PNO no. 58** **n. d.**

Prov: Palmyrene, Khirbet Abu Duhur. Loc: Khirbet Abu Duhur, *in situ. Unclassified. On stone.*

1 [.....]
2 [.....]
3 mʿny mʿn
4 [.....]
5 [.....]
6 tltyn
7 [.....]
8 dkyrn bny
9 yrḥy

PAT 1726 **PNO no. 59** **n. d.**
Prov: Palmyrene, Khirbet Abu Duhur. Loc: Damascus, National Museum. *Dedicatory. On stele.*

1 dkyr
2 zbydʾ
3 mhrdt
4 bṭb
1 dkyr hrms

PAT 1727 **PNO no. 61** **A.D. 216**
Prov: Palmyrene, Khirbet Marzuqa. Loc: Damascus, National Museum, 9014. *Dedicatory. On relief with lion.* Bib: *Pl XL, 2.*

(On a lion)
1 ʾr̊yʾ dnh
2 ʿbd bwnʾ
3 br̊ ʾmdbw
4 lbʿšmn
5 ṭb wskrʾ
(On the plinth)
1 byrḥ nysn šnt 5.100+20+5+2

PAT 1728 **PNO no. 62** **A.D. (188+)**
Prov: Palmyrene, Khirbet Marzuqa. Loc: Damascus, National Museum. *Dedicatory. On stone crater fragments.* Bib: *Pl XXVI, 10.*

1 [...ṭbʾ wš]krʾ šnt 5.100+[.]

PAT 1729 **PNO no. 63** **n. d.**
Prov: Palmyrene, Weshel. Loc: Damascus, National Museum. *Dedicatory. On stone crater fragments.* Bib: *Pl XXVI, 8.*

1 [....] ʾlhʾ wgd nʾwm? [...]

PAT 1730 **PNO no. 63 ter** **n. d.**
Prov: Palmyrene, Weshel. Loc: Damascus, National Museum. *Unclassified. On pebble.*

1 dkyr ml[....]
Safaitic inscription on other side, "To Wahb son of Kawn, of the Awkat tribe. And he made a mark for ʾanʿam, son of Šakim" PNO p 168

PAT 1731 **PNO no. 64** **n. d.**
Prov: Palmyrene, Tahun el-Masek. Loc: Tahun el-Masek, *in situ. Dedicatory. On stone block.*

1 dkyr ʿrd
2 mwlwmw
3 [...]dly/rly

PAT 1732 **PNO no. 65** **n. d.**
Prov: Palmyrene, Tahun el-Masek. Loc: Tahun el-Masek, *in situ. Dedicatory. On stone block.* Bib: *Pl .*

1 dkyr ʿnbw
2 br ḥyrn

PAT 1733 **PNO no. 66** **n. d.**
Prov: Palmyrene, Tahun el-Masek. Loc: Tahun el-Masek, *in situ. Unclassified. On stone block.*

1 bwṭtn
2 ʿttn
3 bṭb

PAT 1734 **PNO no. 67** **n. d.**
Prov: Palmyrene, Tahun el-Masek. Loc: Tahun el-Masek, *in situ. Dedicatory. On stone block.*

1 dkyr
2 lšmš
3 br šky
4 yrḥy
5 šlm

PAT 1735 **PNO no. 68** **n. d.**
Prov: Uncertain. Loc: Damascus, National Museum. *Dedicatory. On relief.* Bib: *Pl XLIV, 4 (reversed in printing, apparently).*

1 [ʾ]bgl gn[y]ʾ
2 ṭb
3 ʾ

PAT 1736 **PNO no. 69** **A.D. 181**

Prov: Uncertain. Loc: Damascus, National Museum. *Unclassified. On relief fragment.* Bib: *Pl XLII, 7.*

1 [...] šnt 4.100
2 +80+10+1

PAT 1737 **PNO no. 70** **n. d.**

Prov: Uncertain. Loc: Damascus, National Museum. *Dedicatory. On relief fragment.* Bib: *Pl XLII, 6.*

1 [...]
2 wʾhblt br rbʾl

PAT 1738 **PNO no. 71** **n. d.**

Prov: Uncertain. Loc: Damascus, National Museum. *Dedicatory. On relief fragment.* Bib: *Pl XLI, 2.*

1 [...ṣl]mʾ dy[ʿbd]

PAT 1739 **PNO no. 72** **n. d.**

Prov: Uncertain. Loc: Damascus, National Museum. *Dedicatory. On altar.* Bib: *Pl XXX, 5.*

1 ʿltʾ dnh dy
2 [ʿ]bd hr̊ms br
3 ydy lbr̊yk šmh
4 lʿlmʾ ʾlhʾ
5 d/r̊ṭy wrḥmnʾ dy [qr]
6 lh wʿnyh wyh?
7 th w{ʾ}ʿnny br
8 [.]y[....]mdyn

PAT 1740 **PNO no. 73** **n. d.**

Prov: Uncertain. Loc: Damascus, National Museum. *Dedicatory. On altar.* PNO joins (tentatively) with C4022. Bib: *Pl XXVIII, 3.*

1 [mw]dʾ ḥbtʾ wḥgt ʿ[l]
2 [ḥyy r]bʾl br yrḥy yʿt
3 [ʾbwhn w]ʿg[ʾ] br yrḥ[y]
4 [ʾmhn lbr]yk š[mh]

Se C4022 for completion, and Gk?

PAT 1741 **PNO no. 74** **n. d.**

Prov: Uncertain. Loc: Damascus, National Museum. *Dedicatory. On altar.*

1 dkrn rwṣy
2 brt tymʿmd

PAT 1742 **PNO no. 74b** **n. d.**

Prov: Uncertain. Loc: Damascus, National Museum. *Funerary. On stele.*

1 mḥlmw br ryṣw?

PAT 1743 **PNO no. 75** **n. d.**

Prov: Uncertain. Loc: Damascus, National Museum. *Dedicatory. On altar.* Bib: *Pl XLVII, 5.*

1 dk[y]r
2 zbydʾ
3 b[r]
4 y?[..]k?ʾ

PAT 1744 **PNO no. 76** **n. d.**

Prov: Uncertain. Loc: Damascus, National Museum. *Dedicatory. On altar.* Bib: *Pl XLVIII, 2a, b, c.*

A.
1 wd?k?rn ʾ?ḥ?lt
2 mʿn
3 br z?bydʾ
4 [..]
B.
1 dkyrn
2 lšmš ʾbʾ
C.
2 dkyryn
4 mqy[...]
8 ʾlhʾ
9 b?ṭ?b

text C: 9 lines, only these bits legible

PAT 1745 **PNO no. 77** **n. d.**

Prov: Uncertain. Loc: Damascus, National Museum. *Dedicatory. On altar.* Bib: *Pl XLVII,*

2a b.

(A)
1 dkr̊y
2 ʾbyn
3 br̊ hr̊my
4 lṭˀb
(B) 2 lines, not clearly legible from plate.

PAT 1746 **PNO no. 78** **n. d.**
Prov: Uncertain. Loc: Damascus, National Museum. *Unclassified. On stone block.* Bib: *Pl XLII, 2.*

1 dkyr̊n bny
2 qr̊ytʾ
3 wr̊ḥmyhn
4 wnḥšṭb
5 ʾlwr̊ bṭb
6 qdm gnyʾ bṭb

PAT 1747 **PNO no. 79** **n. d.**
Prov: Uncertain. Loc: Damascus, National Museum. *Dedicatory. On stele or relief fragment.* Bib: *Pl XLIII, 3.*

1 nṣb
2 mryʾ
3 br
4 yrḥbwl[ʾ
5 l]mlkbl

PAT 1749 **PS no. 18** p 39 **A.D. 185**
Prov: Palmyra. Loc: Palmyra Museum. *Funerary. On relief.* Bib: *Pl VI no. 1.*

1 [. . . . . .] br
2 [. . . .] bˀyrḥ
3 [. . . . š]nt 4.100+
4 80+10+5+2

PAT 1750 **PS no. 28** p 51 **A.D. 246**
Prov: Palmyra. Loc: Beirut, Musée National. *Funerary. On relief.*
Bib: *Pp 50-51, pl IX no. 3.*

1 5.100+40+10+5+3

PAT 1751 **PS no. 33** p 58 **A.D. 123**
Prov: Palmyra. Loc: Toronto, Royal Ontario Museum, 953x94.1. *Funerary. On relief.*
Bib: *p 58, pl X no. 4; Parlasca 85b, pl 151.*

(On right)
1 tmlk
2 brt ʾwšy
3 br ʾwšy
4 ḥbl
(On left)
1 ywm 2
2 bknwn
3 šnt 4.100
4 +20+10+5
Collated with museum photograph

PAT 1752 **PS no. 39** p 65 **A.D. (149)**
Prov: Palmyra. Loc: Ny Carlsberg Glyptotek, 2794. *Funerary. On relief.*
Bib: *Pp 64-65, pl XII no. 2*; NyCG 6.

1 ḥbl ʾḥʾ
2 brt zbdlh
3 brʿʾ byrḥ
4 šbṭ [4.100]
5 +60

PAT 1753 **PS no. 100** p 101 **n. d.**
Prov: Palmyra. Loc: Private collection, see p 101. *Funerary. On relief.*

1 [.]qynt br mlʾ [...] ḥbl
Text cf. Stark PN p 31

PAT 1754 **PS no. 104** p 101 fn 11 **n. d.**
Prov: Palmyra. Loc: Louvre, AO 1194. *Funerary. On relief.*
Bib: Choix p 124 no. 36; Lou 164.

1 bny br
2 mrd
3 ḥbl

PAT 1755 **PS no. 124** p 104 **n. d.**
Prov: Palmyra. Loc: Damascus, National Museum?. *Funerary. On relief.*

1 ṣlm ʿgʾ br mtny ḥbl
Text cf. Stark PN pp 42-43; possibly same as C4205

PAT 1756 **PS no. 141** p 105 **n. d.**
Prov: Palmyra. Loc: Damascus, National Museum, 33. *Funerary. On relief.*

1 ṣlm zbdlh br bgdn
Text cf. Stark PN p 8

PAT 1757 **PS no. 143** p 106 **n. d.**
Prov: Palmyra. Loc: Damascus, National Museum, 39. *Funerary. On relief.*

1 ḥbl mlkw
Text cf. Stark PN p 33

PAT 1758 **PS no. 148** p 106 **n. d.**
Prov: Palmyra. Loc: Toronto, Royal Ontario Museum, 953x94.2. *Funerary. On relief.*

1 whblt br
2 ymlkw br
3 whblt ḥbl
Collated with museum photograph; cf. Stark PN p 16

PAT 1759 **PS no. 149** p 106 **n. d.**
Prov: Palmyra. Loc: Rome, Museo Barracco di scultura antica, 250. *Funerary. On relief.*
Bib: Déd p 43.

(On right)
1 ḥbl
2 ḥlpwnʾ
3 nšʾ
(On left)
1 br
2 yrḥbwlʾ
Collated.

PAT 1760 **PS no. 167** p 108 **n. d.**
Prov: Palmyra. Loc: Uppsala. *Funerary. On relief.*

1 ḥbyby r[bʾ] br yrḥbwlʾ br nwrbl
Text cf. Stark PN p 20

PAT 1761 **PS no. 174** p 109 **n. d.**
Prov: Palmyra. Loc: Not known. *Funerary. On relief.*

1 zbdbl br gdrṣw ḥbl
Text cf. Stark PN p 17

PAT 1762 **PS no. 192** p 111 **n. d.**
Prov: Palmyra. Loc: Beirut, antiquities dealer (Ingholt ad loc.). *Funerary. On relief.*

1 yrḥy br zbdʿth pgʾ ḥbl
Text cf. Stark PN p 47

PAT 1763 **PS no. 193** p 112 **n. d.**
Prov: Palmyra. Loc: Boston, Museum of Fine Arts, 10.79. *Funerary. On relief.*
Bib: Bibliography, photo, and translation Comstock and Vermeule '76 p 256 no. 399; PS pp 111-12.

1 mqymw
2 br ʾlhbl
3 br ḥyrn
4 [b]r gdnʾ
5 [ḥ]bl
Collated with museum photo

PAT 1764 **PS no. 203** p 113 **n. d.**
Prov: Palmyra. Loc: Toronto, Royal Ontario Museum, 953x94.4. *Funerary. On relief.*

1 ḥbl
2 brnbw
3 br brʿth
4 br brnbw
Collated with museum photograph; cf. Stark PN p 12.

PAT 1765 **PS no. 205** p 113 **n. d.**
Prov: Palmyra. Loc: Not known. *Funerary. On relief.*

1 zbdbwl br yrḥy
Text cf. Stark PN p 17

PAT 1766 **PS no. 209** p 113 **n. d.**
Prov: Palmyra. Loc: Philadelphia, University Museum, B 8906. *Funerary. On relief.*
Bib: Legrain '27 p 347 no. 4.

1 mʿn
2 br brʿʾ
3 br zbdʿth
4 ḥbl
Collated with museum photo

PAT 1767 **PS no. 210** p 113 **n. d.**
Prov: Palmyra. Loc: St. Petersburg, Hermitage Museum (uncertain). *Funerary. On relief.*
Bib: *PS p 113 fn 8*; Ber '38 p 131, pl XLIX, 1.

1 mzbnʾ
2 br yrḥbwlʾ
3 rpbwl bgdn
4 ʿbdt lh
5 ʾnʾ mrbyth
6 ḥbl
Text from pl XLIX, 1; cf. PS p 117 fn 4; cf. Stark PN p 30

PAT 1768 **PS no. 225** p 115 **n. d.**
Prov: Palmyra. Loc: Not known. *Funerary. On relief.*

1 ʿgylw
Text cf. Stark PN p 43

PAT 1769 **PS no. 232** p 117 **n. d.**
Prov: Palmyra. Loc: Not known. *Funerary. On relief.*
Bib: Ber '38 p 131, pl XLVIII, 3.

1 mlkw
2 br ḥ[...]
3 dy rby
4 mkbl
5 ḥbl
Text from pl; cf Stark PN p 34

PAT 1770 **PS no. 234** p 117 **n. d.**
Prov: Palmyra. Loc: Boston, Museum of Fine Arts, 96.682. *Funerary. On relief.*
Bib: Photo and bibliography, Comstock and Vermeule '76 p 255 no. 396.

1 ḥbl
2 [...]ʾ
3 šlmʾ [...]
Prb. not identical to C4221, Stark '71 p 130; collated with museum photograph

PAT 1771 **PS no. 244A** p 118 **n. d.**
Prov: Palmyra. Loc: Belgrade, National Museum. *Funerary. On relief.*

1 ʾmwn br nšʾ ʿgʾ šlmʾ ḥbl

PAT 1772 **PS no. 262** p 120 **n. d.**
Prov: Palmyra. Loc: Philadelphia, University Museum, B 8902. *Funerary. On relief.*
Bib: Legrain '27 p 348, no. 5, Photo p 336.

1 mlkw br
2 mqymw ḥbl
Collated with museum photograph; cf. Stark PN p 34.

PAT 1773 **PS no. 284** p 122 **n. d.**
Prov: Palmyra. Loc: not known. *Funerary. On relief.*

1 ḥbl sgnʾ br mlʾ br tymʾ
Text cf. Stark PN p 40

PAT 1774 **PS no. 307** p 126 **n. d.**
Prov: Palmyra. Loc: Beirut, University Museum. *Funerary. On relief.*

1 ḥbl nšʾ mqy nšʾ
Text cf. Stark PN p 40

PAT 1775 **PS no. 329** p 127 **n. d.**
Prov: Palmyra. Loc: Wroclaw, Muzeum Archidiecezjalnego, 2250. *Funerary. On relief.*
Bib: Gaw 70d.

1 [...]ʾ
2 [ʾ]tt
3 mlʾ
4 ḥbl

PAT 1776 **PS no. 356** p 130 **n. d.**
Prov: Palmyra. Loc: Pittsfield, Mass., Berkshire Museum, 1903.7.4. *Funerary. On relief.*

1 ʾmby
2 brt tybwl
3 twry
4 ḥbl
Collated with museum photo; cf. Stark PN p 5.

PAT 1777 **PS no. 371** p 131 **n. d.**
Prov: Palmyra. Loc: Beirut, Chiha Collection. *Funerary. On relief.* Bib: Sem '74 p 70; pl II, 3.

1 ʾbynʾ brt
2 tyrdt br
3 yrḥy ʾtt
4 mlʾ ḥyrn
5 šqnʾ ḥbl
(On left)
1 mlʾ
2 mlʾ
3 brh
4 ḥbl
Text follows Sem '74 p 70

PAT 1778 **PS no. 377** p 132 **n. d.**
Prov: Palmyra. Loc: Paris, private collection. *Funerary. On relief.*

1 tmʾ brt šmʿwn
Text cf. Stark PN p 56

PAT 1779 **PS no. 394** p 134 **n. d.**
Prov: Palmyra. Loc: Toronto, Royal Ontario Museum, 953x94.3. *Funerary. On relief.*

1 ʾqmʾ
2 brt ḥ[...]
3 ḥbl
Collated with museum photo; cf. Stark PN p 7.

PAT 1780 **PS no. 395** p 135 **n. d.**
Prov: Palmyra. Loc: Not known. *Funerary. On relief.*

1 ʿtd/rn brt bgdn ḥbl
Text cf. Stark PN p 46.

PAT 1781 **PS no. 419** p 138 **n. d.**
Prov: Palmyra. Loc: Philadelphia, University Museum, B 8905. *Funerary. On relief.*
Bib: Legrain '27 p 346 no. 2, Photo p 329.

1 ydyʿt brt
2 syʿwnʾ br
3 tymʾ
4 ḥbl
Collated with museum photo; cf. Stark PN p 34.

PAT 1782 **PS no. 429** p 140 **n. d.**
Prov: Palmyra. Loc: Alexandretta, private collection (?). *Funerary. On relief.*

1 ṣlmt šlmt brt [...] ḥbl [...] brt [...] ḥbl
Text cf. Stark PN p 52

PAT 1783 **PS no. 493** p 149 **n. d.**
Prov: Palmyra. Loc: Amherst Mass., Mead Art Museum, 1942.78. *Funerary. On relief.*
Bib: Chabot '18b pp 289-90, no. 12; hand-copy, from squeeze.

1 ḥbl
2 dʾrm brt
3 zbdʾ
Collated with museum photo; cf. Stark PN pp 14, 84.

PAT 1784 **RB '30 p 536** no. 6 **A.D. 87**
Prov: Palmyra, S-E Necropolis, Hypogeum. Loc:

Palmyra, *in situ. Funerary: Foundation. On door lintel.*
Bib: MF Fondation no. 19.

(A)
1 bt ʿlmʾ dnh ʿbd blḥzy br nwry br zbdbwl ʾʿylmy wnrglzbd
2 wʿgylw bnwhy lyqrhwn wlyqr bnyhwn wlyqr bny ddhwn wldʾ klh dy bny
3 ʾʿylmy byrḥ knwn šnt 3.100+80+10+5+4
(B)
4 wʾp ʿbd whblt br blnwry bwšʾ bt ʿlmʾ lh wlbnwhy wlyqr bny ddh

Line 4 (Cantineau's Texte B) engraved by different hand

PAT 1785 **RB ’30 p 537** no. 7 **A.D. 118**
Prov: Palmyra, S-E Necropolis, Hypogeum. Loc: Palmyra, *in situ. Funerary: Foundation. On door lintel.* Group: Syria ’42 p 80.
Bib: Dupont-Sommer ’42 p 84; MF Fondation no. 37.

1 m$^{?}$ʿ$^{?}$r$^{?}$t$^{?}$ʾ dh ʿbd šmʿwn br bwrpʾ br ʿgylw
2 mṭn wbrpʾ brh wmlkw brh lyqrhwn dy ʿlmʾ
3 byrḥ knwn šnt 4.100+20+10

PAT 1786 **RB ’30 p 538** no. 8 **A.D. 138**
Prov: Palmyra, S-E Necropolis, Hypogeum. Loc: Palmyra, *in situ. Funerary: Foundation. On door lintel.*
Bib: MF Fondation no. 45.

1 mʿrtʾ dh dy bt qbwrʾ ʿbdw ḥyrn br nšʾ tybwl ṣmʾ plgʾ mʿlʾ ʿl šmlʾ wpplys ʾlys tybwl
2 wpplys ʾlys yrḥbwlʾ bny mlkw tybwl ṣmʾ plgʾ mʿlʾ ʿl ymynʾ lhwn wlbnyhwn wlbny bnyhwn
3 lʿlmʾ byrḥ sywn šnt 4.100+40+5+4

PAT 1787 **RB ’30 p 539** no. 9 **A.D. 123**
Prov: Palmyra, S-E Necropolis, Hypogeum. Loc: Palmyra, *in situ. Funerary: Foundation. On door lintel.*
Bib: MF Fondation no. 41.

1 bt qbwrʾ dnh ʿbd lšmšw br mqymw br ḥršw lyqr bt qbwrh
2 lh wlʾḥwhy wlbny ddh klhwn dy mn dy yṣbʾ yḥpr lh mn lgw šṭr mn
3 ʾksdrʾ gwyʾ dy qbyrʾ bh šbʾ ʾḥth wḥnt ʾntth wbtr ʾln mn
4 dy yṣbʾ mn bny ddy yḥpr wytqn lh mqbrtʾ byrḥ knwn šnt 4.100+20+10+5

PAT 1788 **RB ’30 p 540** no. 10 **A.D. 232**
Prov: Palmyra, reemployed in “Source of Sérail”. Loc: Palmyra, *in situ. Funerary: A, Foundation; B, Cession. On door lintel.*
Bib: MF Fondation no. 64.

(A)
1 mʿrtʾ dh dy lšmš br ʿstwrgʾ [b]r lš[mš] b$^{?}$r$^{?}$ [b]ryk$^{?}$y$^{?}$ br l$^{?}$q$^{?}$y$^{?}$ š$^{?}$l$^{?}$mn t$^{?}$l$^{?}$tʾ [..]bw[..]
2 mn mʿrtʾ dh ʾyt llšmš br ʿst[wrg]ʾ [br] lšmš sṭrʾ klh mqblʾ m[..]sʾ dy d[..]
3 wlgw dy [..] ʾksdryn trn mr[..] bywm dn[..] ltymsʾ ʾksdrʾ klh mʿlk t[r]ʿʾ š[mʾ]lʾ$^{?}$ [..]m$^{?}$l$^{?}$[..]
4 [..]wl dy bh lhwn wlbnyhwn wlbny bnyhw[n lʿ]lmʾ b[y]r[ḥ] s$^{?}$y$^{?}$w$^{?}$n šn[t] 5$^{?}$.100+40+4
(B)
1 mn$^{?}$[.] mʿrt[ʾ...]
2 ymnyʾ ʾrḥq [...]
3 br šʿw[d]ʾ m[...]
4 w$^{?}$tw[.....]ʾ[...]
5 y[....]5.100+20+20[+$^{?}$ ...]

PAT 1789 **RB ’30 p 543** no. 12B
Prov: Palmyrene, Gebel ʿAntar, tomb. Loc: Gebel ʿAntar, *in situ. Funerary. On doorpost.*

(B)
1 [......]
2 ḥyrn w$^{?}$tʾ br yh[.....]
3 ṣyḥ$^{?}$wt wdy [...]ml[....]
4 šmʿyn

Perhaps associated with Cantineau's “Texte A”, Greek inscription of cession of A.D. 249.

PAT 1790 **RB ’30 p 545** no. 13
A.D. 101 and 192
Prov: Palmyrene, Gebel ʿAntar. Loc: Gebel

ʿAntar, *in situ. Funerary: A, Foundation; B, Cession. On door lintel.*
Bib: MF Fondation no. 27; Concession no. 26.

(Corresponds to Text B)
1 ἔτους γφʹ, (μ)ηνὸς Πανήμου, ʾΙ[εδεί]-
2 βηλος ʿΗλιοδώρου τοῦ καὶ Λισάμ-
3 σου τοῦ ʾΙεδειβήλου ἔδωκεν [κ]ατά[δ]οσι[ν]
4 τὸ προσῆκον αὐτῷ μέρος τοῦ σπηλαίο[υ]
5 Μεζαββάνᾳ καὶ ʾΙαραίῳ καὶ Ζαβδάθῃ το[ῦ]
6 ʾΑουειδαλλάθου ἀνεψιοῖς αὐτοῦ εἰς τὸ πα[ντ]-
7 ελές

(A)
1 bt ʿlmʾ dnh ʿbdw ydyʿbl br whblt
2 wwhblt br ʿwydlt ʾḥwy bny
3 ydyʿbl br ʾmršʾ dy mn bny mtbwl
4 lhwn wlbnyhwn lyqrhwn dy ʿlmʾ
5 byrḥ nysn šnt 4.100+10+2 [š]l?m?

(B)
1 šnt 5.100+4 byrḥ qnyn ydyʿbl br hlydrws
2 [lš]mš br ydyʿbl yhb mntʾ mnth dy mʿrtʾ
3 [lm]zbnʾ wlyrḥy wlzbdʿtʾ bny ʿwydlt ddh lʿlmʾ

PAT 1791 **RB '30 p 548** no. 14 **A.D. 171**
Prov: Palmyrene, Bazuriyyeh. Loc: Not given in edition. *Funerary: Cession. On stone block.*
Bib: E. Littmann in Wiegand '32 Textband pp 11-12 text and German translation; MF Concession no. 6.

1 byrḥ ʾyr šnt 4.100+80+2
2 šlmʾ brt bwlḥʾ br bwrpʾ bmqmwt ʿgylw br bwr[p]ʾ bʿlh
3 wgnsṭs ydy br kyly mwdyʾ lmlkw br mqymw br ʿgʾ dy mqblʾ
4 mnh ksp dnryn mʾh wʿsryn wtḥwt hln yhbt lh wbʿdt p[l]gwt mnt[ʾ]
5 ʾḥdʾ dydh mn mnwn tlt dy mʿrtʾ dy dqbwrʾ dy hy t[r]n bʾktb[...]
6 mpqyk mn ʾblʾ ʿl šmlk ptyḥʾ lʾpʾ mdnḥʾ bšwtpwt mlkw t[...]
7 wšwtpwt ʿgylw bʿlh wmnt klh tlt ʾmmʾ d[y yh]bt lmlkw wl[...m]nt[ʾ]

PAT 1792 **RSP 1** **n. d.**
Prov: Palmyra, S-E Necropolis, Hypogeum of Ṭaʿai. Loc: Palmyra Museum. *Funerary. On stone tablet fragment.* Group: RSP nos. 1-20.
Bib: Abdul-Hak '52 p 199.

1 [ṣlmyʾ ʾln dy ʿgylw b]r bwrpʾ qsmʾ
2 [dy ʿbd mʿrtʾ dh] byrḥ nysn šnt 4[.100...]
3 [wdy ... ʾtth] wdy bwrpʾ br ʿgylw br bwrpʾ qs[mʾ brh]
4 [wdy ...]ʾm brth wdy ʿgylw brh

PAT 1793 **RSP 2** **n. d.**
Prov: Palmyra, S-E Necropolis, Hypogeum of Ṭaʿai, central gallery. Loc: Damascus, National Museum. *Funerary. On stele.* Group: RSP nos. 1-20.
Bib: Abdul-Hak '52 p 210.

1 ḥbl ydyʿbl
2 ṭʿy br mqymw

PAT 1794 **RSP 3** **n. d.**
Prov: Palmyra, S-E Necropolis, Hypogeum of Ṭaʿai, S exedra. Loc: Damascus, National Museum. *Funerary. On relief.* Group: RSP nos. 1-20.
Bib: Abdul-Hak '52 p 221, pl I, 1.

1 ṣlm
2 nbwlʾ br
3 whblt br
4 ṭʿy ḥbl

PAT 1795 **RSP 4** **n. d.**
Prov: Palmyra, S-E Necropolis, Hypogeum of Ṭaʿai, S exedra. Loc: Damascus, National Museum. *Funerary. On stele.* Group: RSP nos. 1-20.
Bib: Abdul-Hak '52 p 222, pl I, 2.

1 ḥbl ḥyrn
2 br bršmš

PAT 1796 **RSP 5** **n. d.**
Prov: Palmyra, S-E Necropolis, Hypogeum of Ṭaʿai, S exedra. Loc: Damascus, National Museum. *Funerary. On stele.* Group: RSP nos. 1-20.

Bib: Abdul-Hak '52 p 223, pl II, 1.

1 qbwdm/qbwrm brt
2 bwrp' ṭ'y
3 br bwrp'
4 ḥbl

PAT 1797 **RSP 6** **n. d.**
Prov: Palmyra, S-E Necropolis, Hypogeum of Ṭa'ai, S exedra. Loc: Damascus, National Museum. *Funerary. On stele.* Group: RSP nos. 1-20.
Bib: Abdul-Hak '52 p 224, pl II, 1.

1 ḥbl
2 'byšy
3 brt
5 'wydlt
6 ḥbl

PAT 1798 **RSP 7** **n. d.**
Prov: Palmyra, S-E Necropolis, Hypogeum of Ṭa'ai, W exedra. Loc: Damascus, National Museum. *Funerary. On relief.* Group: RSP nos. 1-20.
Bib: Abdul-Hak '52 p 225, pl IV, 1.

1 ṣlm 'g'
2 br bwrp'

PAT 1799 **RSP 8** **n. d.**
Prov: Palmyra, S-E Necropolis, Hypogeum of Ṭa'ai, W exedra. Loc: Damascus, National Museum. *Funerary. On relief.* Group: RSP nos. 1-20.
Bib: Abdul-Hak '52 p 226, pl IV, 2.

1 [...]' br
2 bwrp'
3 ṭ'y
4 ḥbl

PAT 1800 **RSP 9** **n. d.**
Prov: Palmyra, S-E Necropolis, Hypogeum of Ṭa'ai, W exedra. Loc: Damascus, National Museum. *Funerary. On relief.* Group: RSP nos. 1-20.
Bib: Abdul-Hak '52 p 228, pl V, 1.

1 ḥbl bwrp'
2 br 'g'
3 ṭ'y

PAT 1801 **RSP 10** **n. d.**
Prov: Palmyra, S-E Necropolis, Hypogeum of Ṭa'ai, W exedra. Loc: Damascus, National Museum. *Funerary. On relief.* Group: RSP nos. 1-20.
Bib: Abdul-Hak '52 pp 228-29, pl V, 1.

1 mqymw
2 br ṭ'y
3 ḥbl

PAT 1802 **RSP 11** **n. d.**
Prov: Palmyra, S-E Necropolis, Hypogeum of Ṭa'ai, W exedra. Loc: Damascus, National Museum, 18.802. *Funerary. On relief.* Group: RSP nos. 1-20.
Bib: Abdul-Hak '52 pp 233-35, pl II, 2 and pl III of Arabic portion; EblaDam no. 187; Tanabe '86, pl 424.

1 ṣlm ml'
2 br 'g'
3 bwrp'
1 ṣlmt bwly' brt
2 'g' br bwrp'

PAT 1803 **RSP 12** **n. d.**
Prov: Palmyra, S-E Necropolis, Hypogeum of Ṭa'ai, W exedra. Loc: Damascus, National Museum. *Funerary. On relief.* Group: RSP nos. 1-20.
Bib: Abdul-Hak '52 p 235, pl V, 2.

1 'mby
2 brt
3 ml'
4 ḥbl

PAT 1804 **RSP 13** **n. d.**
Prov: Palmyra, S-E Necropolis, Hypogeum of Ṭaʿai, W exedra. Loc: Damascus, National Museum. *Funerary. On relief.* Group: Hypogeum of Ṭaʿai, nos. 1-20.
Bib: Abdul-Hak '52 p 237, pl V, 2.

1 ṭʿy br
2 mqymw
3 br ṭʿy
4 ḥbl

PAT 1805 **RSP 14** **n. d.**
Prov: Palmyra, S-E Necropolis, Hypogeum of Ṭaʿai, W exedra. Loc: Damascus, National Museum. *Funerary. On relief.* Group: RSP nos. 1-20.
Bib: Abdul-Hak '52 p 238, pl VI, 1.

1 bwrpʾ
2 br mqymw
3 br ṭʿy
4 ḥbl

PAT 1806 **RSP 15** **n. d.**
Prov: Palmyra, S-E Necropolis, Hypogeum of Ṭaʿai, W exedra. Loc: Damascus, National Museum. *Funerary. On relief.* Group: Hypogeum of Ṭaʿai, nos. 1-20.
Bib: Abdul-Hak '52 pp 239-40, pl VIII, 2.

1 brtʾ bt
2 mwdlʾ
3 bt mqymw
4 ḥbl

PAT 1807 **RSP 16** **n. d.**
Prov: Palmyra, S-E Necropolis, Hypogeum of Ṭaʿai, W exedra. Loc: Damascus, National Museum, 18.797. *Funerary. On relief.* Group: RSP nos. 1-20.
Bib: Abdul-Hak '52 p 240, pl IX no. 2; bibliography, photos, EblaDam p 296 no. 189; Land des Baal no. 180; Pays du Baal et d'Astarté no. 298.

1 nbwlʾ
2 br mʿnw
3 ṭʿy ḥbl

PAT 1808 **RSP 17** **n. d.**
Prov: Palmyra, S-E Necropolis, Hypogeum of Ṭaʿai, W exedra. Loc: Damascus, National Museum. *Funerary. On relief.* Group: RSP nos. 1-20.
Bib: Abdul-Hak '52 p 241, pl X, 1.

1 [... br bw]rpʾ
2 ṭʿy

PAT 1809 **RSP 18** **n. d.**
Prov: Palmyra, S-E Necropolis, Hypogeum of Ṭaʿai, W exedra. Loc: Damascus, National Museum. *Funerary. On stele.* Group: RSP nos. 1-20.
Bib: Abdul-Hak '52 p 242, pl X, 2.

1 ṭʿy br
2 mqymw
3 ḥbl

PAT 1810 **RSP 19** **n. d.**
Prov: Palmyra, S-E Necropolis, Hypogeum of Ṭaʿai, W exedra. Loc: Damascus, National Museum. *Funerary. On stele.* Group: RSP nos. 1-20.
Bib: Abdul-Hak '52 p 242, pl XI, 1.

2 mqymw br
3 yrḥb
4 wlʾ ṭʿy
5 ḥbl

PAT 1811 **RSP 20** **n. d.**
Prov: Palmyra, S-E Necropolis, Hypogeum of Ṭaʿai, W exedra. Loc: Damascus, National Museum. *Funerary. On relief.* Group: RSP nos. 1-20.
Bib: Abdul-Hak '52 pp 245-46, pl XII, 1.

1 zbdlʾ br zbydʾ
2 zbdlʾ ṭʿy
3 ḥbl

PAT 1812 **RSP 21** **n. d.**

Prov: Palmyra, W Necropolis, Hypogeum of Zabdâ, exedra. Loc: Palmyra, 2047/7222. *Funerary. On relief.* Group: RSP nos. 21-23.
Bib: Palm I 1959 p 219, fig 197; SFP 184 fig 220.

1 ṣlmy’ ’ln dy zbd’ br mqymw bkry wdy
2 bltyḥn brt ’tpny ’tth dy ‘bd bt ‘lm’
3 dnh wbnyn’ dy l‘l dnh wqbyryn lgw mn ṣlmy’
4 ’ln

PAT 1813 **RSP 22** **n. d.**

Prov: Palmyra, W Necropolis, Hypogeum of Zabdâ, exedra. Loc: Palmyra, 2025/7223. *Funerary. On relief.* Group: RSP nos. 21-23.
Bib: Palm I 1959 p 220, fig 199; Tanabe ’86, pl 275; SFP 184 fig 221.

1 bltyḥn
2 ’tth

PAT 1814 **RSP 23** **n. d.**

Prov: Palmyra, W Necropolis, Hypogeum of Zabdâ, N exedra. Loc: Palmyra, 2027/7225. *Funerary. On rilief.* Group: RSP nos. 21-23.
Bib: Palm I 1959 p 220, fig 101; Tanabe ’86, pl 279; SFP 185 fig 41.

1 zbd’
2 br ‘g’
3 ḥbl

PAT 1815 **RSP 24** **A.D. 147**

Prov: Palmyra, W Necropolis, Hypogeum of Šalamallat. Loc: Palmyra, *in situ*. *Funerary: Foundation. On door lintel.* Group: RSP nos. 24-46.
Bib: Bounni ’61 pp 146-49; MF Fondation no. 50.

1 τὸ σπήλαιον τοῦτο ἐπόησε Σαλμαλλαθος Μαλιχου τ<ο>ῦ Διο<ν>υσίου καὶ Ζαβδααθης
2 Ἐ<νν>ιβηλου τοῦ Διο<ν>υσίου ἀ<ν>εψιὸς αὐτοῦ υἱοῖς καὶ υἱω<ν>οῖς μηνὶ Ξανδικῷ ἔτους ηνυ'

1 bt ‘lm’ dnh ‘bd šlmlt br mlkw br dynys lh wlbnwhy wlbny bnwhy
2 wmn btr dy myt šlmlt br mlkw dnh šwtpw ḥnbl br šlmlt br mlkw
3 brh wprštn’ brt tymrṣw br ’tzbd ’tth lzbd‘th br ḥnbl br dynys
4 plgwt m‘rt’ dh lh wlbnwhy wlbny bnwhy lyqrhwn dy ‘lm’ byrḥ nysn šnt 4.100+40+10+5+3

PAT 1816 **RSP 25** **n. d.**

Prov: Palmyra, W Necropolis, Hypogeum of Šalamallat. Loc: Palmyra Museum. *Funerary: Foundation. On stone tablet.* Group: RSP nos. 24-46.
Bib: *Pl I*; Bounni ’61 pp 150-51; MF Fondation no. 50.

1 τὸν ταφ[εῶ]να ῳκοδόμη-
2 σεν Σαλ[μα]λλαθος Μαλιχου
3 τοῦ Διο[νυσίου ἐ]ξ ἰδίων ἐπὶ τοῦ
4 π[ατρὸς αὐτοῦ τ]ελευ[τήσα-]
5 [ν]το<ς> ἔτη λγ' ἑαυτῷ [κ]αὶ υ[ἱοῖς]
6 [κα]ὶ υωνος

1 bt ‘lm’ [dnh ‘bd] šlml[t br mlkw]
2 br d[ynys m]n kysh [..........
3 mn] btr dy myt mlkw [................]
4 šnyn 20+10+3 w‘bd gw[mḥyn ...]
5 dy mn l‘l ktyb lbt ‘[lm’ dnh]
6 mn kysh lh wlbnwhy wl[bny bnwhy]
7 l‘lm’ byrḥ ’yr šnt 3+[1.100 ...]

PAT 1817 **RSP 26** **n. d.**

Prov: Palmyra, W Necropolis, Hypogeum of Šalamallat. Loc: Palmyra Museum. *Funerary. On plaster block.* Group: RSP nos. 24-46.
Bib: *Pl I*; Bounni ’61 pp 151-52.

1 [Θαιμαρσαν Ζα]βδααθους
2 [καὶ Ακμ]ην Μοκι-
3 [μου τοῦ Μον]εμου συνβί-
4 [αν αὐτοῦ] ἔτους γιφ'

1 ṣlm tymr[ṣw br ....]
2 zbd‘th w’[qm’ ... brt]

3 mqymw mnʿ[ym ʾtth ....]

PAT 1818 **RSP 27** **n. d.**
Prov: Palmyra, W Necropolis, Hypogeum of Šalamallat. Loc: Palmyra, 1755/6579. *Funerary. On relief.* Group: RSP nos. 24-46.
Bib: Bounni '61 p 152; Tanabe '86, pl 283; SFP 196 fig 34.

1 ḥbl mlkw br
2 dynys ḥnbl

PAT 1819 **RSP 28** **n. d.**
Prov: Palmyra, W Necropolis, Hypogeum of Šalamallat. Loc: Palmyra, 1764/6588. *Funerary. On relief.* Group: RSP 24-46.
Bib: Bounni '61 p 152; Tanabe '86, pl 284; SFP 197 fig 35.

1 šlmlt br
2 mlkw dynys
3 dy ʿbd mʿrtʾ
4 dh

PAT 1820 **RSP 29** **n. d.**
Prov: Palmyra, W Necropolis, Hypogeum of Šalamallat. Loc: Palmyra, 1771/6595. *Funerary. On relief fragment.* Group: RSP nos. 24-46.
Bib: Bounni '61 p 153; SFP 198 fig 153.

1 [prstn]ʾ
2 [br]t
3 tymrṣw
4 ʿthzb[d]
Illegible from photo

PAT 1821 **RSP 30** **n. d.**
Prov: Palmyra, W Necropolis, Hypogeum of Šalamallat. Loc: Palmyra, 1759/6583. *Funerary. On relief.* Group: RŠP nos. 24-46.
Bib: Bounni '61 p 153; Tanabe '86, pl 328; SFP 199 fig 154.

1 b[...]y
2 [br]t ml
3 [kw d]yns

PAT 1822 **RSP 31** **n. d.**
Prov: Palmyra, W Necropolis, Hypogeum of Šalamallat. Loc: Palmyra, 1754/6578. *Funerary. On relief.* Group: RSP nos. 24-46.
Bib: Bounni '61 p 153; Tanabe '86, pl 286; SFP 201 fig 86.

1 [zb]dʿ[t]h
2 br ḥnbl
3 dynys

PAT 1823 **RSP 32** **n. d.**
Prov: Palmyra, W Necropolis, Hypogeum of Šalamallat. Loc: Palmyra, 1784/6607. *Funerary. On relief.* Group: RSP 24-46.
Bib: Bounni '61 p 154; Tanabe '86, pl 287; SFP 203 fig 37.

1 ḥnbl
2 br zbdʿth
3 br ḥnbl

PAT 1824 **RSP 33** **n. d.**
Prov: Palmyra, W Necropolis, Hypogeum of Šalamallat. Loc: Palmyra, 1783/6606. *Funerary. On relief.* Group: RSP nos. 24-46.
Bib: Bounni '61 p 154; Tanabe '86, pl 288; SFP 202 fig 57.

(On left)
1 [Ι]αραιος
2 Ζαβδαθους
3 τοῦ Ανιβη-
4 λου

(On right)
1 yrḥy
2 br zbdʿth
3 ḥnbl

PAT 1825 **RSP 34** **n. d.**
Prov: Palmyra, W Necropolis, Hypogeum of Šalamallat. Loc: Palmyra, 1750/6574. *Funerary. On relief.* Group: RSP nos. 24-46.
Bib: Bounni '61 p 155; Tanabe '86, pl 289; SFP

204 fig 90.

(Below Palmyrene)
1 Διονυσίος
2 Ζαβδαθους

1 dynys
2 br zbdʿth
3 ḥnbl

PAT 1826 **RSP 35** **n. d.**
Prov: Palmyra, W Necropolis, Hypogeum of Šalamallat. Loc: Palmyra, 1760/6584. *Funerary. On relief.* Group: RSP nos. 24-46.
Bib: Bounni '61 p 155; Tanabe '86, pl 290; SFP 205 fig 91.

(Below Palmyrene)
1 Ζηνόβιος
2 Διονυσίου

1 ḥbl
2 zbdʿth
3 br̊ dynys
4 zbdʿth

PAT 1827 **RSP 36** **n. d.**
Prov: Palmyra, W Necropolis, Hypogeum of Šalamallat. Loc: Palmyra, 1752/6576. *Funerary. On relief.* Group: RSP nos. 24-46.
Bib: Bounni '61 p 156; Tanabe '86, pl 329; SFP 206 fig 187.

1 Μαρθις
2 Θαιμα[ρ-]
3 σου

1 mrty
2 brt ty
3 mrṣw
4 dynys
5 ḥbl

PAT 1828 **RSP 37** **n. d.**
Prov: Palmyra, W Necropolis, Hypogeum of Šalamallat. Loc: Palmyra, 1758-6582. *Funerary. On relief.* Group: RŠP nos. 24-46.
Bib: Bounni '61 p 156; EblaDam no. 191; Tanabe '86, pl 330; SFP 207 fig 176.

(On right)
1 ʾqmt
2 [b]rt
3 ḥyrn br
4 bnr
5 ḥbl
(On left)
1 ʾmh dy
2 nbwzbd
3 bryky

PAT 1829 **RSP 38** **n. d.**
Prov: Palmyra, W Necropolis, Hypogeum of Šalamallat. Loc: Palmyra, 1778/6602. *Funerary. On relief.* Group: RSP nos. 24-46.
Bib: Bounni '61 p 157; SFP 208 fig 89.

1 ṣlm
2 bryky br
3 nbwzbd br
4 [...] b[ryk]y
5 [b]r? d?[y]n?y?s?
6 [......ḥ]bl

PAT 1830 **RSP 39** **n. d.**
Prov: Palmyra, W Necropolis, Hypogeum of Šalamallat. Loc: Palmyra, 1775/6599. *Funerary. On relief.* Group: RSP nos. 24-46.
Bib: Bounni '61 pp 157-58; Tanabe '86, pl 331; SFP 209 fig 160.

(On right)
1 [ʾ]tt bryky
2 br nbwzbd
3 br nbwzbd
(On left)
1 ḥnʾ brt
2 bryky
3 nbwzbd
4 ḥyt šny[n]
5 20+3 ḥbl

PAT 1831 **RSP 40** **n. d.**
Prov: Palmyra, W Necropolis, Hypogeum of Šalamallat. Loc: Palmyra, 1777/6601. *Funerary. On relief.* Group: RSP nos. 24-46.
Bib: *Pl II*; Bounni '61 pp 158-59; Tanabe '86, pl 335; SFP 218 fig 205.

(On right)
1 ṣlmt mzbw
2 brt bryky
3 br mqyn'
4 'tt zbd'
5 br ʿzyzw br
6 br zbd'
7 ḥbl
(On left)
1 qyrl'
2 brh
Line 6 *br*: Gaw {*br*}

PAT 1832 **RSP 41** **n. d.**
Prov: Palmyra, W Necropolis, Hypogeum of Šalamallat. Loc: Palmyra, 1776/6590. *Funerary. On relief.* Group: RSP nos. 24-46.
Bib: Bounni '61 p 159; Tanabe '86, pl 337; SFP 217 fig 181.

1 ʿt'm
2 brt ʿg'
3 šryky
4 ḥbl

PAT 1833 **RSP 42** **n. d.**
Prov: Palmyra, W Necropolis, Hypogeum of Šalamallat. Loc: Palmyra, 1772/6596. *Funerary. On relief.* Group: RSP nos. 24-46.
Bib: Bounni '61 p 160; Tanabe '86, pl 333; SFP 213 fig 202.

1 ṣlmt
2 bʿ' brt
3 ʿtʿqb
4 bt ḥwml
5 ḥbl

PAT 1834 **RSP 43** **n. d.**
Prov: Palmyra, W Necropolis, Hypogeum of Šalamallat. Loc: Palmyra, 1757/6581. *Funerary. On relief.* Group: RSP nos. 24-46.
Bib: Bounni '61 pp 160-61; Tanabe '86, pl 293; SFP 211 fig 113.

1 ḥbl
2 mʿn br
3 [...b]r whby

PAT 1835 **RSP 44** **n. d.**
Prov: Palmyra, W Necropolis, Hypogeum of Šalamallat. Loc: Palmyra, 1756/6580. *Funerary. On relief.* Group: RSP nos. 24-46.
Bib: Bounni '61 p 161; SFP 224 fig 121.

1 ḥbl
2 b[w]ln' br
3 [........]'

PAT 1836 **RSP 45** **n. d.**
Prov: Palmyra, W Necropolis, Hypogeum of Šalamallat. Loc: Palmyra Museum. *Funerary. On relief fragment.* Group: RSP nos. 24-46.
Bib: Bounni '61 pp 161-62.

1 [ṣ]lmt
2 [...]mn'
3 ['t]t
4 [ḥl]ypy
5 [.....]bl
6 [ḥb]l

PAT 1837 **RSP 46** **n. d.**
Prov: Palmyra, W Necropolis, Hypogeum of Šalamallat. Loc: Palmyra, *in situ. Funerary. On various fragments.* Group: RŠP nos. 24-46.
Bib: Bounni '61 p 162.

(Fragments a-e)
a. šḥ
b. [... šl]mlt ḥbl
c. [...]d/rḥ nw[....]
d. [...dy]nys
e. [...]hb[...]

PAT 1838 **RSP 47** **n. d.**
Prov: Palmyra, Valley of Tombs, Tower with Hypogeum no. 19. Loc: Palmyra, T 9/19. *Funerary. On stone fragment.* Group: RSP nos. 47-48.
Bib: Palm III, p 245, fig 280.

1 ṣlmt tml[k ...]
2 m[...] ʾqm[...]

PAT 1839 **RSP 48** **n. d.**
Prov: Palmyra, Valley of Tombs, Tower with Hypogeum no. 19. Loc: Palmyra, T 25/19. *Funerary. On stone fragment.* Group: RSP nos. 47-48.
Bib: Palm III, p 247, fig 282.

1 [. . .] brt yrḥb[wl'...]

PAT 1840 **RSP 49** **n. d.**
Prov: Palmyra, Valley of Tombs, Tower no. 15. Loc: Palmyra, T 10/62. *Funerary. On stone tablet.* Group: Palm IV, p 184 no. 3; RSP nos. 49-50.
Bib: *Pl I*; Palm IV, p 185, no. 4, fig 216..

1 ṣlm ʿgʾ
2 br lšmš br
3 ʾdynh ʾqml
4 ḥbl

PAT 1841 **RSP 50, text A** **n. d.**
Prov: Palmyra, Valley of Tombs, Tower with Hypogeum no. 15. Loc: Palmyra, T 18/62. *Funerary. On relief fragment.* Group: RSP nos. 49, 50.
Bib: *Pl I*; Palm IV, p 186, fig 218, 219.

1 yrḥy br
2 ʾdynt
3 br yrḥy
4 [ḥbl]

PAT 1842 **RSP 50, text B** **n. d.**
Prov: Palmyra, Valley of Tombs, Tower with Hypogeum no. 15. Loc: Palmyra, T 27/62. *Funerary. On relief-fragment.* Group: RSP nos. 49, 50.
Bib: *Pl I*; Palm IV, p 186, fig 218, 219.

1 dstyʾ/rstyʾ
2 brt
3 ʾdynt [br]
4 yrḥy ḥb[l]

PAT 1843 **RSP 51** **A.D. 131**
Prov: Palmyra, S-W Necropolis, Hypogeum of Zabdʿateh. Loc: Palmyra, *in situ. Funerary: Cession. On door lintel.* Group: RSP nos. 51-74.
Bib: *Pl VI (photo of copy)*; As'ad and Taha '65 p 31; Inv 12 14.

1 byrḥ tšry šnt 4.100+40+3 zbn zbdʿth br ḥyrn ykyn
2 mn mnth ʾksdrʾ dy mʿlk ʿl ymynk lbrʿth br
3 mrqs

PAT 1844 **RSP 52** **n. d.**
Prov: Palmyra, S-W Necropolis, Hypogeum of Zabdʿateh. Loc: Palmyra, 2137/7499. *Funerary. On relief.* Group: RSP nos. 51-74.
Bib: As'ad and Taha '65 p 39, no. 1; SFP 163 fig 45.

1 zbdbwl
2 br
3 zbdʿth
4 ʾḥwnʾ
5 ḥbl

PAT 1845 **RSP 53** **n. d.**
Prov: Palmyra, S-W Necropolis, Hypogeum of Zabdʿateh. Loc: Palmyra, 2138/7600. *Funerary. On relief.* Group: RSP nos. 51-74.
Bib: As'ad and Taha '65 p 39, no. 2; SFP 164 fig 62.

1 šmšgrm
2 br
3 zbdlʾ
4 ḥbl

PAT 1846 **RSP 54** **n. d.**

Prov: Palmyra, S-W Necropolis, Hypogeum of Zabdʿateh. Loc: Palmyra, 2139/7601. *Funerary. On relief.* Group: RSP nos. 51-74.
Bib: As'ad and Taha '65 p 40, 3; SFP 165 fig 196.

1 [b]rtʾ bt ḥggw

PAT 1847 **RSP 55** **n. d.**

Prov: Palmyra, S-W Necropolis, Hypogeum of Zabdʿateh. Loc: Palmyra, 2140/7602. *Funerary. On relief.* Group: RSP nos. 51-74.
Bib: As'ad and Taha '65 p 40, no. 4; SFP 166 fig 108.

1 ʿttn
2 br̊
3 qr̊blwn
4 ḥbl

PAT 1848 **RSP 56** **n. d.**

Prov: Palmyra, S-W Necropolis, Hypogeum of Zabdʿateh. Loc: Palmyra, 2141/7603. *Funerary. On relief.* Group: RSP nos. 51-74.
Bib: *Pl II*; PGKK no. 2; As'ad and Taha '65 p 40, no. 5; SFP 167 fig 197.

1 ṣlmt
2 wʾlʾ
3 br̊t r̊pbwl

PAT 1849 **RSP 57** **n. d.**

Prov: Palmyra, S-W Necropolis, Hypogeum of Zabdʿateh. Loc: Palmyra, 2142/7604. *Funerary. On relief.* Group: RSP nos. 51-74.
Bib: *Pl II*; As'ad and Taha '65 p 41, 6; PGKK no. 22; SFP 168 fig 162.

1 tmʾ
2 brt
3 mlk$^{?}$
4 ḥbl

PAT 1850 **RSP 58** **n. d.**

Prov: Palmyra, S-W Necropolis, Hypogeum of Zabdʿateh. Loc: Palmyra, 2143/7605. *Funerary. On relief.* Group: RSP nos. 51-74.
Bib: As'ad and Taha '65 p 41, no. 7; SFP 169 fig 112.

1 ʿttn br
2 q[rb]lwn
3 ḥb[l]

PAT 1851 **RSP 59** **n. d.**

Prov: Palmyra, S-W Necropolis, Hypogeum of Zabdʿateh. Loc: Palmyra, 2144/7606. *Funerary. On relief.* Group: RSP nos. 51-74.
Bib: As'ad and Taha '65 p 41, no. 8; SFP 170 fig 193.

1 ḥbl ʾbnʾ
2 brt qrbl[wn]
3 ʿtt[n brh]
4 ḥbl

line 1: SFP has ḥb<l>, but lamed is perfectly visible from photo

PAT 1852 **RSP 60** **n. d.**

Prov: Palmyra, S-W Necropolis, Hypogeum of Zabdʿateh. Loc: Palmyra, 2145/7607. *Funerary. On relief.* Group: RSP nos. 51-74.
Bib: As'ad and Taha '65 p 42, no. 9; SFP 171 fig 125.

1 ṣlm
2 ḥyrn
3 br
4 [qrb]l$^{?}$w$^{?}$n$^{?}$

PAT 1853 **RSP 61** **n. d.**

Prov: Palmyra, S-W Necropolis, Hypogeum of Zabdʿateh. Loc: Palmyra, 2146/7608. *Funerary. On relief.* Group: RSP nos. 51-74.
Bib: As'ad and Taha '65 p 42, no. 10; SFP 172 fig 109.

1 qrblwn
2 br ʿttn
3 ḥbl

PAT 1854 **RSP 62** **n. d.**

Prov: Palmyra, S-W Necropolis, Hypogeum of Zabdʿateh. Loc: Palmyra, 2147/7609. *Funerary. On relief.* Group: RSP nos. 51-74.

Bib: Asa'd and Taha '65, p 42, no. 11; Meisterwerke no. 87; PGKK no. 20; SFP 173 fig 194.

1 mr̊tʾ
2 br̊t qr̊blwn
3 ḥbl

PAT 1855 **RSP 63** **n. d.**

Prov: Palmyra, S-W Necropolis, Hypogeum of Zabdʿateh. Loc: Palmyra, 2148/7610. *Funerary. On relief.* Group: RSP nos. 51-74.

Bib: *Pl II*; As'ad and Taha '65 p 42; PGKK, no. 21; Tanabe '86, pl 367; SFP 174 fig 42.

1 wls br
2 mrqws
3 ḥbl wtdmwr
4 ʾtth ḥbl
5 mrqws brh
6 ḥbl

PAT 1856 **RSP 64** **n. d.**

Prov: Palmyra, S-W Necropolis, Hypogeum of Zabdʿateh. Loc: Palmyra, 2149/7611. *Funerary. On relief.* Group: RSP nos. 51-74.

Bib: As'ad and Taha '65 p 43, no. 13; SFP 175 fig 190.

1 mrt[ʾ brt]
2 šb[...]
3 yrḥbwlʾ
4 brh ḥbl

PAT 1857 **RSP 65** **n. d.**

Prov: Palmyra, S-W Necropolis, Hypogeum of Zabdʿateh. Loc: Palmyra, 2150/7612. *Funerary. On relief.* Group: RSP nos. 51-74.

Bib: *Pl II*; As'ad and Taha '65 p 43, no. 14; SFP 176 fig 123.

1 lšmš br̊
2 šlmn ḥbl

PAT 1858 **RSP 66** **n. d.**

Prov: Palmyra, S-W Necropolis, Hypogeum of Zabdʿateh. Loc: Palmyra, 2151/7616. *Funerary. On relief.* Group: RSP nos. 51-74.

Bib: As'ad and Taha '65 p 44, no. 15; SFP 177 fig 122.

1 yrḥy br
2 šlmn
3 ḥbl

Photo is illegible

PAT 1859 **RSP 67** **n. d.**

Prov: Palmyra, S-W Necropolis, Hypogeum of Zabdʿateh. Loc: Palmyra, 2152/7614. *Funerary. On relief.* Group: RSP nos. 51-74.

Bib: As'ad and Taha '65 p 44, no. 16; SFP 181 fig 218.

1 ʾṭnyʾ ḥbl

PAT 1860 **RSP 68** **n. d.**

Prov: Palmyra, S-W Necropolis, Hypogeum of Zabdʿateh. Loc: Palmyra, 2153/7615. *Funerary. On relief.* Group: RSP nos. 51-74.

Bib: As'ad and Taha '65 p 44, no. 17; SFP 178 fig 111.

1 zbdʿth
2 br ʿtnwry
3 ḥbl

PAT 1861 **RSP 69** **n. d.**

Prov: Palmyra, S-W Necropolis, Hypogeum of Zabdʿateh. Loc: Palmyra, 2153/7616. *Funerary. On relief.* Group: RSP nos. 51-74.

Bib: As'ad and Taha '65 p 44, no. 18; SFP 179 fig 78.

1 mlkw br̊
2 syʿwnʾ br̊
3 whblt ḥbl

PAT 1862 **RSP 70** **n. d.**

Prov: Palmyra, S-W Necropolis, Hypogeum of

Zabdʿateh. Loc: Palmyra, 2155/7617. *Funerary. On relief.* Group: RSP nos. 51-74.
Bib: As'ad and Taha '65 p 44, no. 19; SFP 180 fig 189.

1 ḥssw
2 ny
3 ḥbl
Text follows SFP, inscription cannot be checked against photo

PAT 1863 **RSP 71** **n. d.**
Prov: Palmyra, S-W Necropolis, Hypogeum of Zabdʿateh. Loc: Palmyra, 2156/7621. *Funerary. On klinè.* Group: RSP nos. 51-74.
Bib: *Pl III*; As'ad and Taha '65 p 45, no. 20; Tanabe '86, pl 427; SFP 181 fig 219.

(On right of woman)
1 mrtʾ
2 ʾmhwn
3 ḥbl
(On right of young girl)
1 bʿšgʾ
2 brth
3 ḥbl
(On left of young boy)
1 ʿbdʿstwr
2 brh
3 ḥbl

PAT 1864 **RSP 72** **n. d.**
Prov: Palmyra, S-W Necropolis, Hypogeum of Zabdʿateh. Loc: Palmyra, 2157/7619. *Funerary. On relief with men holding inscribed cups.* Group: RSP nos. 51-74.
Bib: As'ad and Taha '65 pp 45-46, no. 21; SFP 181 fig 217.

(On cup to the right)
1 mrqws
2 ḥbl
(On cup to the left)
1 wls ḥbl

PAT 1865 **RSP 73** **n. d.**
Prov: Palmyra, S-W Necropolis, Hypogeum of Zabdʿateh. Loc: Palmyra, 2158/7620. *Funerary. On relief.* Group: RSP nos. 51-74.
Bib: As'ad and Taha '65 p 46, no. 22; SFP 182 fig 110.

1 pṣyʾl br
2 syʿwnʾ br
3 whblt ḥbl

PAT 1866 **RSP 74** **n. d.**
Prov: Palmyra, S-W Necropolis, Hypogeum of Zabdʿateh. Loc: Palmyra, 2159/7621. *Funerary. On relief.* Group: RSP nos. 51-74.
Bib: As'ad and Taha '65 p 46, no. 23; SFP 183 fig 124.

1 syʿwnʾ
2 br̊ whblt
3 br̊ mlkw
4 ḥbl

PAT 1867 **RSP 75** **A.D. 89**
Prov: Palmyra, S-W Necropolis, Hypogeum of Bōlḥâ. Loc: Palmyra, *in situ. Funerary. On door lintel.* Group: RSP nos. 75-104.
Bib: As'ad and Taha '68 p 85, fig 2.

1 bt ʿlmʾ dnh ʿbd bwlḥʾ br nbwšwry lh wlbnwhy lʿlmʾ bʾb šnt 4.100

PAT 1868 **RSP 76** **n. d.**
Prov: Palmyra, S-W Necropolis, Hypogeum of Bōlḥâ, main gallery. Loc: Palmyra, *in situ. Funerary. On stele.* Group: RSP nos. 75-104.
Bib: *Pl III*; As'ad and Taha '68 p 93, no. 1; Tanabe '86, pl 217; SFP 95 fig 15.

1 ḥbl ʿg[ʾ]
2 br ḥwrʾ
3 br bwlḥʾ
4 nbwšwry

PAT 1869 **RSP 77** **n. d.**
Prov: Palmyra, S-W Necropolis, Hypogeum of Bōlḥâ, main gallery. Loc: Palmyra, *in situ. Funerary. On stele.* Group: RSP nos. 75-104.

Bib: *Pl III*; As'ad and Taha '68 p 94, no. 2; Tanabe '86, pl 217; SFP 96 fig 2.

(With figures, above)
1 ḥbl ḥyrn bwlḥ'
(On right)
1 bny ny
2 bn'
3 ḥbl
(On left)
1 brt
2 blḥ'
1 ḥbl
(On plinth)
1 nbwšwry br nbwšwry

PAT 1870 **RSP 78** **n. d.**
Prov: Palmyra, S-W Necropolis, Hypogeum of Bōlḥâ. Loc: Palmyra, *in situ. Funerary. On stele.*
Group: RSP nos. 75-104.
Bib: As'ad and Taha '68 p 94, no. 3; Tanabe '86, pl 197; SFP 97 fig 13.

1 ḥbl
2 bwlḥ'
3 br
4 bwlḥ'
5 br
6 bwlḥ'

PAT 1871 **RSP 79** **n. d.**
Prov: Palmyra, S-W Necropolis, Hypogeum of Bōlḥâ. Loc: Palmyra, *in situ. Funerary. On relief.*
Group: RSP nos. 75-104.
Bib: As'ad and Taha '68 p 94, no. 4; Tanabe '86, pl 119; SFP 98 fig 21.

(On left)
1 bwlḥ'
2 br nbwšwry rb'
3 ḥbl
(On right)
1 šnt 10+5

PAT 1872 **RSP 80** **n. d.**
Prov: Palmyra, S-W Necropolis, Hypogeum of Bōlḥâ. Loc: Palmyra, *in situ. Funerary. On relief.*
Group: RSP nos. 75-104.
Bib: *Pl III*; As'ad and Taha '68 p 95, no. 5; Tanabe '86, pl 217; SFP 99 fig 142.

1 ḥbl nybn'
2 brt ydy br
3 nbwšwr dy ʿbd
4 lh bwlḥ' br
5 zbdbwl bʿlh

PAT 1873 **RSP 81** **n. d.**
Prov: Palmyra, S-W Necropolis, Hypogeum of Bōlḥâ. Loc: Palmyra, *in situ. Funerary. On relief.*
Group: RSP nos. 75-104.
Bib: As'ad and Taha '68 p 95, no. 6; Tanabe '86, pl 198; SFP 100 fig 143.

1 bʿdy'
2 brt ḥyrn
3 ḥšš
4 'tt
5 bwlḥ'
6 nbwšwry
7 ḥbl

PAT 1874 **RSP 82** **n. d.**
Prov: Palmyra, S-W Necropolis, Hypogeum of Bōlḥâ. Loc: Palmyra, *in situ. Funerary. On relief.*
Group: RSP nos. 75-104.
Bib: As'ad and Taha '68 p 95, no. 7; Tanabe '86, pl 200; SFP 101 fig 40.

1 nbwšwr
2 br yrḥy
3 br bwlḥ'
4 ḥbl

PAT 1875 **RSP 83** **n. d.**
Prov: Palmyra, S-W Necropolis, Hypogeum of Bōlḥâ. Loc: Palmyra, *in situ. Funerary. On relief.*
Group: RSP nos. 75-104.
Bib: As'ad and Taha '68 p 96, no. 8; Tanabe '86, pl 203; SFP 102 fig 203.

1 ḥl' bt
2 nbwšwr
3 ydy blḥ'

4 ḥbl

PAT 1876 **RSP 84** **n. d.**
Prov: Palmyra, S-W Necropolis, Hypogeum of Bōlḥâ. Loc: Palmyra, *in situ*. *Funerary*. *On relief*.
Group: RSP nos. 75-104.
Bib: *Pl III*; As'ad and Taha '68 p 96, no. 9; Tanabe '86, pl 202; SFP 103 fig 107.

1 ṣlm ydy br̊ yr̊ḥbwlʾ
2 ydy b<r> blšwr̊
3 ḥbl

PAT 1877 **RSP 85** **n. d.**
Prov: Palmyra, S-W Necropolis, Hypogeum of Bōlḥâ. Loc: Palmyra, *in situ*. *Funerary*. *On relief*.
Group: RSP nos. 75-104.
Bib: As'ad and Taha '68 p 96, no. 10; Tanabe '86, pl 194; SFP 104 fig 26.

1 zbdbwl
2 br bwlḥʾ
3 nbwšwry

PAT 1878 **RSP 86** **n. d.**
Prov: Palmyra, S-W Necropolis, Hypogeum of Bōlḥâ. Loc: Palmyra, *in situ*. *Funerary*. *On relief*.
Group: RSP nos. 75-104.
Bib: As'ad and Taha '68 p 97, no. 11; Tanabe '86, pl 195; SFP 105 fig 163.

1 lbnʾ
2 brt yrḥy
3 blḥʾ
4 ḥbl

PAT 1879 **RSP 87** **n. d.**
Prov: Palmyra, S-W Necropolis, Hypogeum of Bōlḥâ. Loc: Palmyra, *in situ*. *Funerary*. *On relief*.
Group: RSP nos. 75-104.
Bib: *Pl III*; As'ad and Taha '68 p 97, no. 12; Tanabe '86, pl 188; SFP 106 fig 127.

1 ḥyr̊n br̊
2 bwlḥʾ
3 nbwšwr̊y

4 ḥbl

PAT 1880 **RSP 88** **A.D. 160**
Prov: Palmyra, S-W Necropolis, Hypogeum of Bōlḥâ. Loc: Palmyra, *in situ*. *Funerary*. *On relief*.
Group: RSP nos. 75-104.
Bib: As'ad and Taha '68 p 97, no. 13; Tanabe '86, pl 205; SFP 107 fig 73.

1 bwlḥʾ br
2 ḥwrʾ nbwšwry
3 ḥbl dy ʿbd
4 lh ḥwrʾ brh
5 bšnt 4.100+60+10+2

PAT 1881 **RSP 89** **n. d.**
Prov: Palmyra, S-W Necropolis, Hypogeum of Bōlḥâ. Loc: Palmyra, *in situ*. *Funerary*. *On relief*.
Group: RSP nos. 75-104.
Bib: As'ad and Taha '68 pp 97-98, no. 14; Tanabe '86, pl 207; SFP 108 fig 106.

1 bwlḥʾ
2 br
3 ḥwrʾ
4 ḥbl

PAT 1882 **RSP 90** **n. d.**
Prov: Palmyra, S-W Necropolis, Hypogeum of Bōlḥâ. Loc: Palmyra, *in situ*. *Funerary*. *On stele*.
Group: RSP nos. 75-104.
Bib: *Pl IV*; As'ad and Taha '68 p 98, no. 15; Tanabe '86, pl 208; SFP 109 fig 16.

1 ḥbl ʿgylw
2 br ḥwrʾ br
3 bwlḥʾ
4 nbwšwry

PAT 1883 **RSP 91** **n. d.**
Prov: Palmyra, S-W Necropolis, Hypogeum of Bōlḥâ. Loc: Palmyra, *in situ*. *Funerary*. *On relief*.
Group: RSP nos. 75-104.
Bib: As'ad and Taha '68 pp 98-99, no. 17; Tanabe '86, pl 204; SFP 111 fig 79.

1 ṣlm
2 ydy br
3 ḥyrn br
4 nbʾ
5 ḥbl

PAT 1884 **RSP 92** **n. d.**
Prov: Palmyra, S-W Necropolis, Hypogeum of Bōlḥâ. Loc: Palmyra, *in situ. Funerary. On relief.*
Group: RSP nos. 75-104.
Bib: As'ad and Taha '68 p 99, no. 18; SFP 112 fig 27.

1 blḥʾ
2 br
3 nbwšwr
4 ḥbl

PAT 1885 **RSP 93** **n. d.**
Prov: Palmyra, S-W Necropolis, Hypogeum of Bōlḥâ. Loc: Palmyra, *in situ. Funerary. On relief.*
Group: RSP nos. 75-104.
Bib: As'ad and Taha '68 p 99, no. 19; Tanabe '86, pl 216; SFP 113 fig 191.

(On left)
1 btʿbdy
2 ḥbl
(On right)
1 ʿgylw
2 brh
3 Alas!

PAT 1886 **RSP 94** **n. d.**
Prov: Palmyra, S-W Necropolis, Hypogeum of Bōlḥâ. Loc: Palmyra, *in situ. Funerary. On relief.*
Group: RSP nos. 75-104.
Bib: As'ad and Taha '68 pp 99-100, no. 20; Tanabe '86, pl 213; SFP 114 fig 94.

1 brʿth
2 br bwlḥʾ
3 ʿg{w}<y>lw
4 nbwšwr
5 ḥbl

PAT 1887 **RSP 95** **n. d.**
Prov: Palmyra, S-W Necropolis, Hypogeum of Bōlḥâ. Loc: Palmyra, *in situ. Funerary. On relief.*
Group: RSP nos. 75-104.
Bib: As'ad and Taha '68 p 100, no. 22; Tanabe '86, pl 215; SFP 116 fig 104.

(On left)
1 ṣlm
2 ʿgylw
3 br
4 qrblʾ
5 ʿgylw
6 ḥbl
(On right)
1 ṣlm
2 ʿgylw
3 br
4 mlkw
5 ʿgylw
6 ḥbl

PAT 1888 **RSP 96** **n. d.**
Prov: Palmyra, S-W Necropolis, Hypogeum of Bōlḥâ. Loc: Palmyra, *in situ. Funerary. On relief.*
Group: RSP nos. 75-104.
Bib: As'ad and Taha '68 p 100, no. 23; Tanabe '86, pl 213; SFP 117 fig 105.

1 ḥbl ʿgylw
2 br̊ zbdbwl
3 dy mtqrʾ
4 qr̊blʾ
5 br̊ nbwšwr̊y
line 3: mtqrʾ, resh seems not dotted

PAT 1889 **RSP 97** **n. d.**
Prov: Palmyra, S-W Necropolis, Hypogeum of Bōlḥâ. Loc: Palmyra, *in situ. Funerary. On relief.*
Group: RSP nos. 75-104.
Bib: As'ad and Taha '68 pp 100-101, no. 24; SFP 118 fig 174.

1 nybnʾ brt
2 blḥʾ
3 br nbwšwr
4 ḥbl

PAT 1890 **RSP 98** **n. d.**
Prov: Palmyra, S-W Necropolis, Hypogeum of Bōlḥâ. Loc: Palmyra, *in situ*. *Funerary*. *On relief fragment*. Group: RSP nos. 75-104.
Bib: As'ad and Taha '68 p 101, no. 25.

1 [...] ḥdwdn
2 br
3 zbdʿtʾ
4 [ḥ]dwdn

PAT 1891 **RSP 99** **n. d.**
Prov: Palmyra, S-W Necropolis, Hypogeum of Bōlḥâ. Loc: Palmyra, *in situ*. *Funerary*. *On stele*. Group: RSP nos. 75-104.
Bib: *Pl IV*; As'ad and Taha '68 p 101, no. 26; Tanabe '86, pl 214; SFP 119 fig 19.

(On left)
1 yr̊ḥy
2 br̊ mlkw
3 ʿgylw
4 ḥbl
(On right, on pedestal)
1 qr̊blʾ br̊
2 mlkw ʿgylw
3 ḥbl

PAT 1892 **RSP 100** **n. d.**
Prov: Palmyra, S-W Necropolis, Hypogeum of Bōlḥâ. Loc: Palmyra, *in situ*. *Funerary*. *On relief*. Group: RSP nos. 75-104.
Bib: As'ad and Taha '68 pp 101-102, no. 27; Tanabe '86, pl 188; SFP 120 fig 231.

(On right of base)
1 ʿgylw
2 br zbdbwl
3 qrblʾ
4 ḥbl
(On couch, left)
1 ṣlm zbdbwl qrblʾ br ʿgylw
2 br zbdbwl nbwšwry ḥbl
(On couch, right)
1 ṣlm bwlḥʾ br ʿgylw br zbdbwl
2 nbwšwr ḥbl

PAT 1893 **RSP 101** **n. d.**
Prov: Palmyra, S-W Necropolis, Hypogeum of Bōlḥâ, N exedra. Loc: Palmyra, *in situ*. *Funerary*. *On klinè sarcophagus*. Group: RSP nos. 75-104.
Bib: As'ad and Taha '68 pp 102-105, no. 28; Tanabe '86, pl 188-189; SFP 120 fig 231-236.

a. (By bust)
1 qrblʾ
2 br mlkw
3 br ʿgylw
b. (By bust)
1 ṣlmt bʿdʾ
2 brt mlkw br
3 ʿgylw
c. (By bust)
1 ṣlmt tmʾ
2 brt ḥwrʾ br
3 bwlḥʾ ḥbl
d. (On couch)
1 ṣlmt ʿtʾ brt nbwdʿ
2 br mqy ʾtt mlkw
e. (On couch)
1 ṣlmʾ dnh dy mlkw br ʿgylw br zbdbwl br bwlḥʾ nbwšwr
f. (On couch)
1 ṣlm ʿgylw br zbdbwl br
2 bwlḥʾ nbwšwr ḥbl
g. (On relief)
1 ṣlm
2 nbwdʿ
3 br mlkw br
4 ʿgylw
h. (On relief)
1 ṣlm ʿgylw
2 br mlkw br
3 ʿgylw

PAT 1894 **RSP 102** **n. d.**
Prov: Palmyra, S-W Necropolis, Hypogeum of Bōlḥâ, N exedra. Loc: Palmyra, *in situ*. *Funerary*. *On sarcophagus*. Group: RSP nos. 75-104.
Bib: As'ad and Taha '68 pp 105-106, no. 29; Tanabe '86, pl 188-189; SFP 120 fig 231-236.

a. (On couch)
1 ṣlm hrms br ḥry mlkw wblḥʾ ʾḥwh
b. (On couch)
1 ṣlmt bʿdyʾ brt bwlḥʾ

2 nbwšwr ʾtt ʿgylw br zbdbwl
c. (On relief)
1 ʿgylw
2 br mlkw
3 br ʿgylw
4 ḥbl
d. (On relief)
1 yrḥy br
2 mlkw br
3 ʿgylw
4 ḥbl

PAT 1895 **RSP 103** **n. d.**

Prov: Palmyra, S-W Necropolis, Hypogeum of Bōlḥâ, S exedra. Loc: Palmyra, *in situ*. *Funerary. On klinè sarcophagus*. Group: RSP nos. 75-104.
Bib: As'ad and Taha '68 pp 106-108, no. 30; Tanabe '86, pl 209-212; SFP 121 fig 246.

a. (By bust)
1 ṣlmt hgʾ
2 bt ʿgylw
b. (By bust)
1 ṣlmt ʾqmʾ bt
2 ʿgʾ ʾqml
3 ʾmh dy
4 nbwšwr
c. (On relief, man to the right)
1 ṣlm ʿgylw br
2 ʿgylw br ʿgylw
3 dy ʿb<d> lh nbwšwr
4 brh btr mwth
5 šnyn štyn
d. (On relief, man to the left)
1 ṣlm nbwšwr
2 br ʿgylw br
3 ʿgylw
e. (On relief, woman)
1 ṣlmt ʾqmʾ
2 bt brʿth

PAT 1896 **RSP 104** **n. d.**

Prov: Palmyra, S-W Necropolis, Hypogeum of Bōlḥâ. Loc: Palmyra, *in situ*. *Funerary: Foundation. On stone tablet.* Group: RSP nos. 75-104.
Bib: *Pl V*.

1 npšʾ dh dy ʿbd[t ...]
2 ḥbtʾ brt zb[... br]
3 ḥnynʾ ʾsry lmlk[w br . . .]
4 ḥlkš bʿlh wlmlk[w br mlkw]
5 brh wlbny ḥryh[wn ...]

PAT 1897 **RSP 105** **n. d.**

Prov: Palmyra, Tomb of Ḥur, reemployed in Byzantine cemetery in garden of Palmyra Museum. Loc: Palmyra, A 1399. *Funerary: with curse. On stele.*
Bib: *Pl VI*; As'ad '68 p 132, pl III; Inv 12 17.

1 gwmḥʾ dny dy ḥwr
2 br pṣyʾl br ʿtʿqb
3 dy mtqrh ḥwr
4 mlʾ wlʾ yptḥh
5 ʾnš lʿlm wqbyrt
6 bh tdmr brt
7 hnʾy br mlkw
8 ʾntth ḥbl
Text of RSP 105

PAT 1898 **RSP 106** **A.D. 190**

Prov: Palmyra, near spring Afqa. Loc: Palmyra, A 1171. *Dedicatory. On altar.*
Bib: al-Hassani and Starcky '53 pp 146-51, pl I, 1.

1 lbryk šmh lʿlmʾ
2 mwdʾ mqymw
3 br ʾwṭkʾ ʿl
4 ḥywhy wḥyʾ
5 bnwhy wʾḥwhy
6 šnt 5.100+2

PAT 1899 **RSP 107** **A.D. 206**

Prov: Palmyra, near spring Afqa. Loc: Palmyra, A 1179. *Dedicatory. On altar.*
Bib: al-Hassani and Starcky '53 pp 148-49, pl I, 2.

1 bryk šmh lʿlmʾ
2 rḥmnʾ ʿl bmʾh
3 [ʿ]bd wmwdʾ tymrṣw
4 [b]r ḥyrn zbdʾ ʿl
5 ḥywhy wḥyʾ
6 bnwhy byrḥ ʾdr
7 šnt 5.100+10+5+2

PAT 1900 **RSP 108** **A.D. 216**
Prov: Palmyra, near spring Afqa. Loc: Palmyra, A 1172. *Dedicatory. On altar.*
Bib: al-Hassani and Starcky '53 pp 149-51, pl I, 3.

1 bryk šmh lʿlmʾ
2 [ṭ]bʾ wrḥmnʾ ʿbd
3 [w]mwdʾ mlk wdms
4 ʾḥyh wbny byth
5 klhwn šnt 5.100
6 +20+5+4

PAT 1901 **RSP 109** **A.D. 218**
Prov: Palmyra, near spring Afqa. Loc: Palmyra, A 1209. *Dedicatory. On altar.*
Bib: al-Hassani and Starcky '53 pp 151-52, pl I, 4.

1 [b]ʾdr šnt 5.100+20+5+4
2 bryk šmh lʿlmʾ
3 ṭbʾ wrḥmnʾ ʿbd
4 [w]mwdʾ mlʾ br
5 ʿgʾ nsʾ rbʾ

PAT 1902 **RSP 110** **A.D. 219**
Prov: Palmyra, near spring Afqa. Loc: Palmyra, A 1207. *Dedicatory. On altar.*
Bib: al-Hassani and Starcky '53 p 152, pl I, 5.

1 bryk šmh lʿlmʾ
2 ṭbʾ wrḥmnʾ ʿbd
3 [w]mwdʾ tymrṣw br
4 bryky ʿl ḥywhy wḥyʾ
5 ʾḥwhy byrḥ ʾb
6 šnt 5.100+20+10

PAT 1903 **RSP 111** **A.D. (223)**
Prov: Palmyra, near spring Afqa. Loc: Palmyra, A 1184. *Dedicatory. On altar.*
Bib: al-Hassani and Starcky '53 pp 152-53, pl I, 6.

1 bryk šmh lʿlmʾ
2 [ṭ]bʾ wskrʾ mwdʾ
3 [...]m br ʿbnrgl ʿl
4 [ḥ]ywh wḥyʾ bnwhy byrḥ
5 [t]šry dy šnt
5.100+20+10+5/5.100+20+10+5+1

PAT 1904 **RSP 112** **A.D. 225**
Prov: Palmyra, near spring Afqa. Loc: Palmyra, A 1205. *Dedicatory. On altar.*
Bib: al-Hassani and Starcky '53 pp 153-54, pl I, 7.

1 mwdʾ zbydʾ br whblt
2 zbydʾ ʾʿky lbryk šmh
3 lʿlmʾ ṭbʾ wrḥmnʾ ʿl
4 ḥywhy wḥyʾ bnwhy
5 wʾḥwhy lʿlmʾ btšry šnt
6 5.100+20+10+5+2

PAT 1905 **RSP 113** **A.D. 231**
Prov: Palmyra, near spring Afqa. Loc: Palmyra, A 1208. *Dedicatory. On altar.*
Bib: al-Hassani and Starcky '53 p 154, pl I, 8.

1 [............]
2 [...yr]ḥy ʿl ḥyyh[wn]
3 [w]ḥyʾ bnyhwn lʿlmʾ
4 byrḥ ʾb dy šnt
5 5.100+40+2

PAT 1906 **RSP 114** **A.D. 239**
Prov: Palmyra, near spring Afqa. Loc: Palmyra, A 1204. *Dedicatory. On altar.*
Bib: al-Hassani and Starcky '53 pp 154-56, pl II, 1.

1 šnt 5.100+40+10+1
2 lbryk šmh
3 ʿbd wmwdʾ
4 lrḥmnʾ dy
5 qr lh wʿny
6 yrḥy br šlmn
7 ʿl ḥywh wḥyʾ
8 ʾbyh wʾḥyh
9 wḥbʾ

PAT 1907 **RSP 115** **A.D. 240**
Prov: Palmyra, near spring Afqa. Loc: Palmyra, A 1175. *Dedicatory. On altar.*
Bib: al-Hassani and Starcky '53 pp 156-58, pl II, 2.

1 lbryk šmh lʿlmʾ
2 ʿltʾ dnh dy ʿbd
3 wmwdʾ yrḥbwlʾ

4 br mqymw ymlʾ
5 wʿwydʾ brh ʿl
6 ḥywh wḥyʾ bnwh
7 wʾḥwh byrḥ ʾyr
8 dy šnt 5.100+40+10+1

PAT 1908 **RSP 116** **A.D. 241**
Prov: Palmyra, near spring Afqa. Loc: Palmyra, A 1174. *Dedicatory. On altar.*
Bib: al-Hassani and Starcky '53 pp 158-59, pl II, 3.

1 bryk šmh lʿlmʾ
2 ṭbʾ wrḥmnʾ ʿbd
3 wmwdʾ mlkʾ wʿtʿy
4 bny ḥggw br mlkw
5 zwzy ʿl ḥyyhwn
6 wḥyʾ bnyhwn
7 byrḥ ʾlwl šnt
8 5.100+40+10+2

PAT 1909 **RSP 117** **A.D. 243**
Prov: Palmyra, near spring Afqa. Loc: Palmyra, A 1176. *Dedicatory. On altar.*
Bib: al-Hassani and Starcky '53 p 159, pl II, 4.

1 bryk šmh lʿlmʾ
2 ṭbʾ wrḥmnʾ ʿbd
3 wmwdʾ ḥyrn br ymlʾ
4 mqymw ʿl ḥywhy
5 wḥyʾ ʾbwhy wddh
6 wʾḥwhy šnt 5.100+40+10+5

PAT 1910 **RSP 118** **A.D. 243**
Prov: Palmyra, near spring Afqa. Loc: Palmyra, A 1206. *Dedicatory. On altar.*
Bib: al-Hassani and Starcky '53 p 160, pl III, 1.

1 bryk šmh lʿlmʾ
2 ṭbʾ wrḥmnʾ ʿbd
3 wmwdʾ mlʾ br
4 [y]hybʾ ʿ?n?n? ʿl
5 ḥywhy wḥyʾ bnwhy
6 šnt 5.100+40+10+5

PAT 1911 **RSP 119** **A.D. 251**
Prov: Palmyra, near spring Afqa. Loc: Palmyra, A 1177. *Dedicatory. On altar.*
Bib: al-Hassani and Starcky '53 pp 160-63, pl III, 2.

1 lbryk šmh lʿlmʾ
2 rḥmnʾ wtyrʾ
3 mwdʾ nʾry br
4 mqymw ṭyṭwylw wʿdʾ
5 ʾtth wbnwh
6 wbnʾ byth klhwn
7 dy qrw lh bʿqʾ
8 wʿnn brwḥʾ ln
9 šnt 5.100+60+2
10 byrḥ nyšn

PAT 1912 **RSP 120** **A.D. 251**
Prov: Palmyra, near spring Afqa. Loc: Palmyra, A 1178. *Dedicatory. On altar.*
Bib: al-Hassani and Starcky '53 p 164, pl III, 3.

1 ʿbd wmwdʾ
2 lrḥmnʾ ṭbʾ
3 yrḥy br ʿgylw
4 br skyy dy qryh
5 wʿnyh byrḥ ʾlwl
6 dy šnt 5.100
7 +60+2

PAT 1913 **RSP 121** **A.D. 256**
Prov: Palmyra, near spring Afqa. Loc: Palmyra, A 1173. *Dedicatory. On altar.*
Bib: al-Hassani and Starcky '57 p 96, pl III, 4.

1 bryk šmh lʿlmʾ rḥmnʾ
2 ṭb[ʾ] wtyrʾ mwdʾ lh
3 lrḥmnʾ ṭbʾ dy qrʾ
4 wʿnʾ lšmš br
5 qrynw br mlʾ wʿbd
6 ʿltʾ dnh byrḥ nysn
7 šnt 5.100+60+5+2

PAT 1914 **RSP 122** **A.D. 251**
Prov: Palmyra, near spring Afqa. Loc: Palmyra, A 1100. *Dedicatory. On altar.*
Bib: al-Hassani and Starcky '57 p 97.

1 [lbryk šmh] lʿlmʾ rḥmnʾ

2 [ṭb]ʾ wtyrʾ ʿbd wmwdʾ
3 [q]ryn br ḥyrn br yrḥbwlʾ
4 [br pnlš]mš qryn ʿl ḥywh
5 [wḥ]yy ʾḥwh byrḥ
6 [nys]n šnt 5.100+60+3

PAT 1915 **RSP 123** **n. d.**
Prov: Palmyra, near spring Afqa. Loc: Palmyra, A 1185. *Dedicatory. On altar.*
Bib: al-Hassani and Starcky '57 pp 97-98, pl I, 9.

1 ʿbdt ʾqmt
2 lbrk šmh
3 [l]ʿlmʾ ʿl
4 [ḥy]h wʿl
5 [ḥyʾ] brh
6 [...........]

PAT 1916 **RSP 124** **n. d.**
Prov: Palmyra, near spring Afqa. Loc: Palmyra, A 1180. *Dedicatory. On altar.*
Bib: *Pl VIII*; al-Hassani and Starcky '57 p 98, pl III, 5.

1 mwdʾ l[......]
2 lrḥmnʾ ʿl
3 [ḥyw]hy wʾtth [w]b[rh]
4 wbrth [.........]
5 dqrw lh [wʿnnwn]

PAT 1917 **RSP 125** **A.D. 162**
Prov: Palmyra, near spring Afqa. Loc: Palmyra, A 1168. *Dedicatory. On altar.*
Bib: al-Hassani and Starcky '57 pp 101-102, pl IV, 1; Sem '73 p 119.

1 Διὶ ὑψίστῳ μεγίστῳ καὶ ἐπηκόῳ Βωλανος Ζηνοβίου
2 τοῦ Αἱρανου τοῦ Μοκιμου τοῦ Μαθθα ἐπιμελητὴς
3 αἱρεθεὶς Ἐφκας πηγῆς ὑπὸ Ἰαριβώλου τοῦ θεοῦ τὸν βω[μὸν]
4 ἐξ ἰδίων ἀνέθηκεν ἔτους δου' μηνὸς Ὑπερβερεταίου κ'.

1 dkrn ṭb lm[rʾ ʿlm] q[rb] bwl[y] br zbydʾ br ḥyrn
2 br mq[ymw mtʾ kdy hwʾ r]b ʿ[yn ʿl] ʾpqʾ wlyq[r...]
3 nnyʾ

PAT 1918 **RSP 126** **A.D. 162**
Prov: Palmyra, near spring Afqa. Loc: Palmyra, A 1167. *Dedicatory. On altar.*
Bib: al-Hassani and Starcky '57 pp 102-111, pl IV, 2.

1 dkrn ṭb lmrʾ ʿlmʾ qrb bwly br zbydʾ
2 br ḥyrn br mqymw mtʾ kdy hwʾ rb ʿyn
3 ʿl ʾpkʾ byrḥ tšry šnt 4.100+60+10+4

PAT 1919 **RSP 127** **A.D. 205**
Prov: Palmyra, near spring Afqa. Loc: Palmyra, A 1169. *Dedicatory. On altar.*
Bib: al-Hassani and Starcky '57 pp 111-14, pl III, 6; Sem '73 p 119.

1 [b]rbnwt ʿynʾ dy bwlḥʾ br ḥyrn br
2 ʿtʿqb ḥwml dy ʾḥd yrḥbwl ʾlhʾ
3 bnʾ bnynʾ dnh dy ʿyn wktlʾ dy qd[m]
4 bt gbʾ wktlʾ dy brʾ wʿbd ktlʾ dy
5 [l]bnʾ byrḥ nysn šnt 5.100+10+5+1
6 wdkyr t[y]mʿʾ br mʿ[.] tymʿʾ blyd[ʿ]
7 [w]ḥyrn b[r] mqym[w mlk]w dy ʾḥd lh bwlḥʾ dnh rb ʿyn
(On right face)
1 wʿbd bwlḥʾ dnh ʿltʾ dh mn kysh ʿl
2 ḥywhy wḥyy bnwhy wʾḥwhy

PAT 1920 **RSP 134** **A.D. (209)**
Prov: Palmyra, Diocletian Camp. Loc: Palmyra, CD 156/60. *Dedicatory. On altar.*
Bib: *Pl VIII*; Palm II, p 248, fig 298.

1 lbryk šmh lʿlmʾ
2 ṭbʾ wrḥmnʾ ʿbd
3 wmwdʾ brny br bʿly
4 ʿbdʿy ʾmry ʿl ḥyh[y]
5 wḥyʾ bny byth klhwn
6 byrḥ knwn šnt [5].100+1

PAT 1921 **RSP 135** **A.D. 236**

Prov: Palmyra, Diocletian Camp, in "Temple des Enseignes". Loc: Palmyra, CD 75/61. *Dedicatory. On stone tablet.*

Bib: Palm III, pp 241-41, no. 11, fig 277.

1 bryk šmh lʿlmʾ ṭb[ʾ]
2 wrḥmnʾ ʿbd wmwdʾ
3 lʿlmʾ whblt br
4 tymrṣw br mlkw ʿl ḥywhy
5 wḥyʾ bnwhy byrḥ nysn ywm 20
6 šnt 5.100+40+5+2

PAT 1922 **RSP 136** **n. d.**

Prov: Palmyra, Diocletian Camp. Loc: Palmyra, CD 96/61. *Dedicatory. On altar fragments.*

Bib: *Pl VII*; Palm III, p 244, no. 14, fig 279.

1 lbryk [šm]h lʿ[lmʾ..........]
2 šmh lmbrkw [ʿl]t) dh
3 ʿbd pplys ʾl[ys] k?h[yly]
4 mʿny br khyly b[r ...ʿl]
5 ḥywh[y] wḥ[y] bnw[hy ...]
6 [byrḥ ... šn]t 4?[.100 ...]

PAT 1923 **RSP 137** **A.D. 188**

Prov: Palmyra, Diocletian Camp, in front of "Temple des Enseignes". Loc: Palmyra, CD 106/62. *Dedicatory. On altar.*

Bib: Palm IV, pp 195-97, no. 19, fig 227.

1 lbryk šmh lʿlmʾ wrḥmnʾ
2 mwdʾ ʾlhbl br brʿth mqymw
3 ʾklb byrḥ tšry šnt 5.100

PAT 1924 **RSP 138** **n. d.**

Prov: Palmyra, Diocletian Camp. Loc: Palmyra, CD 103/62. *Dedicatory. On altar fragment.*

Bib: Palm IV, pp 197, no. 20, fig 228.

1 lbryk šmh lʿlmʾ ṭbʾ
2 wrḥmnʾ ʿbd ʿltʾ dh
3 [...br n]bwzbd mqym[w]
4 [ʿl ḥywhy wḥ]yʾ bnw[hy]

PAT 1925 **RSP 139** **n. d.**

Prov: Palmyra, Diocletian Camp, "Temple des Enseignes". Loc: Palmyra, *in situ*, TE 140. *Dedicatory. On altar.*

Bib: Palm V, pp 112-13, no. 4, fig 109.

1 [m]ʿlt dnh
2 ʿbd yrḥy [...]
3 ʿl ḥywhy wḥy[..]
4 4.100+[...]

PAT 1926 **RSP 140** **n. d.**

Prov: Palmyra, Diocletian Camp, "Temple des Enseignes". Loc: Palmyra, *in situ*, TE 149. *Dedicatory. On altar.*

Bib: Palm V, pp 113-14, no. 5, fig 110.

1 [lbry]yk š[m]h [lʿlm]ʾ
2 [ʿ]bd hrms [br . . .] mlʾ
3 br mlʾ l[. . .ʿl ḥywhy] wḥyy
4 bnwhy by[rḥ t]š[ry] šnt
5 4.100+20+20+[..]

PAT 1927 **RSP 141** **n. d.**

Prov: Palmyra, Diocletian Camp, "Temple des Enseignes". Loc: Palmyra, *in situ*. *Dedicatory. On altar.*

Bib: Palm V, p 116, no. 11, fig 11.

1 ʿmb [...] m[.]wt dy
2 [.....]ḥ [...] ʾḥ[w]h[y byrḥ]
3 ʾlwl ywm [. . .]

PAT 1928 **RSP 142** **A.D. 234**

Prov: Palmyra, Diocletian Camp, "Temple des Enseignes". Loc: Palmyra Museum garden, no. CD 32/63. *Dedicatory. On altar.*

Bib: Palm V, pp 80-81, 114-15, no. 6, fig 90; Déd p 294.

1 [ʿl bryk] šmh lʿ[lmʾ] tymrṣw br nbwzʾ wšlmlt br nbwmr
2 [........]wz pnwn mn šʿtʾ drgzʾ wʿbd ʿmhwn gbwrtʾ byr[ḥ]
3 ʾyr ywm yšrḥʾ/yšdḥʾ šnt 5.100+40+5

PAT 1929 **RSP 143** **A.D. 115**
Prov: Palmyra, Diocletian Camp, reemployed in "Temple des Enseignes". Loc: Palmyra, CD 70/65. *Dedicatory. On altar fragments.*
Bib: Gaw '70 p 314; Gaw '90b pp 103-104, pl 23a (improved translation and comments).

1 byrḥ ʾlwl šnt 4.100+20+5+1 knwnʾ dnh qrb gdrṣw br
2 yrḥy br gdrṣw br ʿty ʿl ḥywhy wḥyy bnwhy wʾḥwh1
3 lmrt bytʾ mṣbʾ dy nṣb mtny br qynw brʿty rbʾ ʾbʾ
4 ʾbwhy dy gdrṣw dnh wlʾlhyʾ klhn dy ytbyn lwth dy
5 [mrt bytʾ ...]ʾ rb bkl ʾtr klh lʿlmʾ
lines 3-4, RSP *ʾbʾ <dy ʾb> ʾbwhy*, rejected in Gaw '90 p 104; line 2, PN *brʿty* in RSP 143; Gaw '90 "fils de ʿAttai"

PAT 1930 **RSP 144** **A.D. (139+)**
Prov: Palmyra, Diocletian Camp, "Temple des Enseignes". Loc: Palmyra, CD 18/66. *Dedicatory. On altar fragment.*
Bib: Gaw '70 p 318.

1 lbryk šmh lʿlm[ʾ]
2 ʿbd lšmšy br lšm[š]
3 br ʾdynt [ʿ]l ḥywhy
4 wḥyy bnwhy byrḥ
5 nys[n] š[nt] 4.100+5+[.] [...]

PAT 1931 **RSP 145** **n. d.**
Prov: Palmyra, Diocletian Camp, Tetrapylon. Loc: Palmyra, CD 140/60. *Dedicatory. On stone tablet fragments.*
Bib: *Pl IV*; Palm II, pp 250-51, no. 12, fig 299.

1 [lbryk šmh lʿlmʾ ṭbʾ]
2 [wrḥm]nʾ mrʾ myt[bʾ..l]
3 dkl ʾḥyd wʿl lkl prys
4 ʿbd ʾns [br] w]hblt ʿl
5 ḥywhy w[ḥyʾ bn]wh[y] byrḥ
6 [. . . . . . .]

PAT 1932 **RSP 146** **n. d.**
Prov: Palmyra, Diocletian Camp, W Portico. Loc: Palmyra, CD 74/61. *Dedicatory. On stone block fragment.*
Bib: Palm III, p 239, no. 10, fig 276.

1 bryky br p[....]
2 ʿl ḥywhy [wḥhyʾ]
3 bnwhy b[yrḥ ...]
4 šnt 5.100+[...] [...]

PAT 1933 **RSP 147** **n. d.**
Prov: Palmyra, Diocletian Camp, reemployed in later construction by Tetrapylon. Loc: Palmyra, CD 36/59. *Dedicatory. On relief fragment.*
Bib: *Pl VIII*; Palm I, pp 116-17, 211-12, no. 6, fig 128; Déd pp 168-69.

1 [m]wdyʾ bbtʾ ʾtth [...]
2 byrḥ šbṭ šnt 4.100+[...]

PAT 1934 **RSP 148** **n. d.**
Prov: Palmyra, Diocletian Camp, reemployed in late construction. Loc: Palmyra, CD 27/59. *Dedicatory. On console.*
Bib: Palm I, p 213, no. 8, fig 232.

1 mwdʾ m[lkw ...]

PAT 1935 **RSP 149** **n. d.**
Prov: Palmyra, Diocletian Camp, Tetrapylon. Loc: Palmyra, CD 102/60. *Dedicatory. On altar.*
Bib: Palm II, pp 245-46, no. 9, fig 296.

1 [.....]
2 mwdyʾ [...]
3 lʾzyʾzʾ[w...]

PAT 1936 **RSP 150** **A.D. (240+)**
Prov: Palmyra, Diocletian Camp, in foundations of Tetrapylon. Loc: Palmyra, CD 129/60. *Dedicatory. On altar, lower part.*
Bib: Palm II, pp 247-48, no. 10, fig 297.

1 [.....]
2 [.....]qʾ wʾtʿm wʾtʿm
3 [...bʾ]lwl šnt 5.100
4 +[..]+40+10+1

PAT 1937 **RSP 151** **n. d.**
Prov: Palmyra, Diocletian Camp, Tetrapylon. Loc: Palmyra, CD 101/60. *Dedicatory. On relief.*
Bib: *Pl IV*; Palm II, pp 251, no. 13, fig 153, 300.

1 ʿ?bʾd?
2 mnʿym
3 lʿzyz ṭbʾ

PAT 1938 **RSP 153** **A.D. 143**
Prov: Palmyra, Diocletian Camp, reemployed in "Temple des Enseignes". Loc: Palmyra, CD 72/65. *Dedicatory. On stone fragment.*
Bib: *Pl VII*; Gaw '70 p 314.

1 [...] klh l[...]
2 [...] bʾsṭ[w]ʾ m[...]
3 [...ʿ]l ḥyy bnyhwn b[...]
4 [...] šnt 4.100+40+10+1+[..]

PAT 1939 **RSP 154** **n. d.**
Prov: Palmyra, Diocletian Camp, reemployed in "Temple des Enseignes". Loc: Palmyra, CD 71/65. *Dedicatory. On stone fragment (of lintel?).*
Bib: Gaw '70 p 316.

1 [...ʿ]bdw bny pṭrt ʾln
2 [...]bmnh mdʿm qdm mr ʾlhʾ

PAT 1940 **RSP 155** **n. d.**
Prov: Palmyra, Diocletian Camp, reemployed in later wall. Loc: Palmyra, CD 40/66. *Dedicatory. On lintel fragment.*

1 [... ʿmwdyʾ ʾ]ln šṭʾ wtṣby[thwn ...]

PAT 1941 **RSP 159** **A.D. 62**
Prov: Palmyra, Diocletian Camp. Loc: Palmyra, CD 69/63. *Honorific. On stone fragment.*
Bib: *Pl VI*; Palm V, pp 111-12, no. 3, fig 108; Déd. pp 79-80, pl V, 2.

1 ṣlm dnh dy zbdlh dy mtqrʾ
2 šḥlph br šmʿwn br ʾyšʾ dy mn
3 bny mʿzyn dy ʾqymw lh ʾlt wbny
4 [n]wrbl lyqrh
5 byrḥ ʾ<d>r šnt 3.100+60+10+3
6 dkyr ḥlypy br yrḥy ʾlhw [g]lwpʾ

PAT 1942 **RSP 160** **A.D. (122)**
Prov: Palmyra, Diocletian Camp, "Temple des Enseignes". Loc: Palmyra, *in situ*, TE 55. *Honorific. On statue base.*
Bib: *Pl VI*; Palm V, p 118, no. 14; Déd. pp 76-77.

1 [...ʾΑ]{γιλ}<γλι>βῶλος καὶ [Μαλ]αχ[βῆλος]
2 [θεοὶ κ]αὶ [Χ]ομαρῆνοι ἀρέσαντα τοῖς θεοῖς
3 [καὶ τ]οῖς [Χ]ομαρῆνοις τ[ειμῆς καὶ εὐ-]
4 σεβεί[ας χάρι]ν.

1 [ṣlmʾ d]nh dy mʿ[ny] br šlmlt br whblt b[r]
2 ʿ[..]ʾ d[y ʾq]y[m]w lh ʿglbwl wmlkbl wbny
3 km[r]ʾ [b]d[yl dy š]pr lʾlhyhn wlhn byrḥ
4 [...šnt 4].100+20+10+4

PAT 1943 **RSP 161** **n. d.**
Prov: Palmyra, Diocletian Camp, reemployed. Loc: Palmyra, CD 38/66. *Honorific. On console.*
Bib: *Pl VI.*

1 [.....]ʾ br zbdʾ ʿg[ylw ... dy] ʿbd
2 lh ʿgylw br mq[ym]w br ʿgylw
3 wʿbd lmlkw br ḥyrn br ʿgylw
4 [ʾyt]ybl bʿlh ṣlm bt bʿl[š]mn
5 [..]l[...]m[.]

PAT 1944 **RSP 162** **n. d.**
Prov: Palmyra, Diocletian Camp, "Temple des Enseignes". Loc: Palmyra, Museum garden. *Honorific. On statue base.*
Bib: Syr '70 p 320.

1 [ṣlmʾ d]nh dy yrḥbwlʾ br ʿwyd[ʾ br ... br]
2 [yrḥbw]lʾ br ḥyrn mḥm myʾ dy [ʾqymw lh]
3 [bny] kmrʾ lyqrh bd[y]l dy m[gd lʿglbwl]
4 [wmlkbl] ʾlhyʾ gntʾ dy mtq[dštʾ]
5 [...... b]yrḥ ʾb šnt 4.100+[...]

PAT 1945 **RSP 163** **A.D. 92 and 240**
Prov: Palmyra, Diocletian Camp, reemployed. Loc:

Palmyra, CD 101/59. *Funerary: Foundation and Cession. On stone tablet.*
Bib: *Pl VI*; Palm I, pp 213-14, no. 9, fig 233; MF Fondation no. 23, Concession no. 43.

(On right)
1 [...]bky[...]
2 [...] br šlmn br tymḥʾ
3 [...] šnt 4.100+4
(On left)
1 ywlyʾ [ʾwr]lyʾ šlʾ br[t] ʾ[....]
2 rḥqt mn ʾksdrʾ šḥymʾ ymyny[ʾ]
3 [d]y mʿl<k> mn bbʾ ʿl šmlk lywlyʾ
4 ʾwrlyʾ tymʾ wlšmš bny ʾwṭkʾ
5 [lhwn wlbnyhwn w]lbny bnyhwn
6 [lʿ]lmʾ [byr]ḥ ʾyr šnt 5.100+40+10+1

PAT 1946 **RSP 164** **n. d.**
Prov: Palmyra, Diocletian Camp. Loc: Palmyra, CD 12/61. *Funerary: Foundation. On stone tablet.*
Bib: *Pl VII*; Palm III, p 235, no. 1, fig 272; MF Fondation no. 21.

1 byrḥ nysn šnt
2 3.100 bt ʿlmʾ
3 [dn]h [ʿb]d mlkw
4 [br lš]mš br
5 [....]w lh
6 ...

PAT 1947 **RSP 165** **A.D. 18**
Prov: Palmyra, Diocletian Camp. Loc: Palmyra, CD 10/63. *Funerary: Foundation. On stone tablet.*
Bib: *Pl VII*; Palm V, pp 110-11, no. 2, fig 107; Déd. no. 268; MF Fondation no. 4.

1 [by]rḥ ʾ[l]wl šnt
2 3.100+20+5+4 qbrʾ dnh
3 dy ʿgylw br ydyʿbl
4 br bwrpʾ dy mn bny
5 [...] dy ʿbd lh
6 [wl]bnwhy

PAT 1948 **RSP 166** **(12) B.C.?**
Prov: Palmyra, Diocletian Camp, reemployed Funerary stone. Loc: Palmyra, A 1481. *Funerary: Foundation. On stone tablet.*
Bib: MF Fondation no. 22; Meisterwerke no. 79; PGKK no. 26.

1 [...] šnt 3.100
2 [ʿbd b]t qbwrʾ dnh
3 [...]ʾ br yrḥbwlʾ br
4 [... dy m]tqrh pšwlʾ
5 [lh wlbnw]hy lyqrhwn
6 šlm

PAT 1949 **RSP 167** **A.D. 138**
Prov: Palmyra, Diocletian Camp, in Hypogeum behind "Temple des Enseignes". Loc: Palmyra Museum. *Funerary: Foundation. On door lintel.*
Bib: Ber '70 p 74, fig 6.

1 mʿrtʾ dh dy bt ʿlmʾ ʿbdw ʿlynʾ br ḥyrn br ʿlynʾ
2 byrḥ knwn šnt 4.100+40+10
See C3951, dedication of statue to ʿAlayneʾ, founder of this tomb.

PAT 1950 **RSP 168** **n. d.**
Prov: Palmyra, Diocletian Camp. Loc: Palmyra, CD 5/59. *Funerary. On relief.*
Bib: Palm I, pp 92, 211, no. 5, fig 99.

1 [m]lkw br
2 [n]bwzbd br
3 mqymw nṣwr
4 ḥbl

PAT 1951 **RSP 169** **n. d.**
Prov: Palmyra, Transversal Colonnade. Loc: Palmyra, CD 63/59. *Funerary. On relief fragment.*
Bib: *Pl II*; Palm I, pp 98, 212, no. 7, fig 107.

1 dkyr mzb[nʾ ...]

PAT 1952 **RSP 170** **A.D. (178+)**
Prov: Palmyra, Diocletian Camp, Tetrapylon. Loc: Palmyra, CD 131/60. *Funerary. On stone tablet fragment.*
Bib: Palm II, p 240, no. 4, fig 291.

1 ḥbl yrḥy

2 br ʿgylw
3 [b]r yrḥy
4 [by]rḥ knw[n]
5 šnt 4.100
6 [+20]+20+20+20+10+[.]

PAT 1953 **RSP 171** **n. d.**

Prov: Palmyra, Diocletian Camp, in Tetrapylon foundations. Loc: Palmyra, CD 123/60. *Funerary. On klinè fragment.*
Bib: Palm II, pp 154, 241-43, no. 5, fig 170, 292-93.

(On right)
1 [bʿl]tgʾ
2 [b]rt
3 [ʾ]bgr
4 [ty]mrṣw
5 ḥbl
(On left)
1 ḥgt
2 brt
3 ʿgyl
4 ʿmr
5 ḥbl

PAT 1954 **RSP 172** **n. d.**

Prov: Palmyra, Diocletian Camp, remployed in later wall W of Tetrapylon. Loc: Palmyra, CD 57/60. *Funerary. On relief.*
Bib: Palm II, pp 193, 243, no. 6, fig 215.

1 [.....]
2 ʾmby
3 mrbt?[ʾ]
4 ḥbl

PAT 1955 **RSP 173** **n. d.**

Prov: Palmyra, Diocletian Camp, in Tetrapylon. Loc: Palmyra, CD 48/60. *Funerary. On stele fragment.*
Bib: Palm II, pp 243-44, no. 7, fig 294.

1 mzbnʾ
2 br nšʾ
3 ḥbl

PAT 1956 **RSP 174** **n. d.**

Prov: Palmyra, Diocletian Camp, by Tetrapylon. Loc: Palmyra, CD 122/60. *Funerary. On relief fragment.*
Bib: Palm II, pp 244-45, no. 8, fig 295.

1' [ ]
2' 60+10+5+2

PAT 1957 **RSP 175** **n. d.**

Prov: Palmyra, Diocletian Camp, reemployed near Tetrapylon. Loc: Palmyra, CD 27/61. *Funerary. On relief fragment.*
Bib: Palm III, pp 131-32, 237, no. 2, fig 180.

1' [ ]
2' brth

PAT 1958 **RSP 176** **n. d.**

Prov: Palmyra, Diocletian Camp, reemployed in later wall. Loc: Palmyra, CD 51/61. *Funerary. On relief fragment.*
Bib: Palm III, pp 134, 237, no. 3, fig 182.

1 nwrbl
2 br lšmš
3 br nwrbl
4 ḥbl

PAT 1959 **RSP 177** **n. d.**

Prov: Palmyra, Diocletian Camp, reemployed in later wall. Loc: Palmyra, CD 58/61. *Funerary. On stele fragment.*
Bib: Palm III, pp 111-12, 238, no. 6, fig 158.

1 nšʾ
2 br nšʾ
3 ḥbl

PAT 1960 **RSP 178** **n. d.**

Prov: Palmyra, Diocletian Camp. Loc: Palmyra, CD 64/61. *Funerary. On stone tablet fragment.*
Bib: *Pl IV*; Palm III, pp 238, no. 7, fig 273.

1 brnbw [br]
2 brnbw [.....]

3 mʿrnʾ/mʿrnʾ ḥb[l]

PAT 1961 **RSP 179** **n. d.**

Prov: Palmyra, Diocletian Camp. Loc: Palmyra, CD 88/61. *Funerary. On stele fragment.*
Bib: Palm III, pp 114, 243, no. 13, fig 160.

1 šm[...]
2 br[...]

PAT 1962 **RSP 180** **n. d.**

Prov: Palmyra, Diocletian Camp. Loc: Palmyra, CD 110/61. *Funerary. On relief.*
Bib: *Pl VIII*; Palm III, pp 138, 245, no. 15, fig 187.

(On right)
1 [. . .]mlq
2 [..]n$^{?}$rʾ
3 ḥyrn
4 ḥbl
(On left)
1 ʿb[d]
2 bwly
3 brh

PAT 1963 **RSP 181** **n. d.**

Prov: Palmyra, Diocletian Camp. Loc: Palmyra, CD 118/61. *Funerary. On relief fragment.*
Bib: Palm III, pp 150, 246, no. 17, fig 200.

1 [ḥ]gt
2 brt
3 yrḥy
4 br
5 nbwzʾ
6 ḥbl

PAT 1964 **RSP 182** **n. d.**

Prov: Palmyra, Diocletian Camp. Loc: Palmyra, CD 114/61. *Funerary. On relief fragment.*
Bib: Palm III, pp 150, 246, no. 18, fig 199.

1 [...]ḥyh[w..]
2 [.5.100]+20+20+10[...]

PAT 1965 **RSP 183** **n. d.**

Prov: Palmyra, Diocletian Camp. Loc: Palmyra, CD 95/61. *Funerary. On relief fragment.*
Bib: Palm III, pp 119, 250, no. 24, fig 167.

1' [ ]
2' [...] br
3' [ ]

PAT 1966 **RSP 184** **n. d.**

Prov: Palmyra, Diocletian Camp. Loc: Palmyra, CD 39/62. *Funerary. On stele fragment.*
Bib: *Pl VII*; Palm IV, p 193, no. 11, fig 223.

1 ḥbl [...]
2 brt glḥ[.]

PAT 1967 **RSP 185** **n. d.**

Prov: Palmyra, Diocletian Camp. Loc: Palmyra, CD 40/62. *Funerary. On relief fragment.*
Bib: Palm IV, p 193, no. 12, fig 224.

1 ḥny$^{?}$[nw br]
2 [m]hrd[t]
3 ḥb[l]

PAT 1968 **RSP 186** **n. d.**

Prov: Palmyra, Diocletian Camp. Loc: Palmyra, CD 32/62. *Funerary. On relief fragment.*
Bib: Palm IV, pp 104, 194, no. 14, fig 140.

1 [.....]
2 ḥbl

PAT 1969 **RSP 187** **n. d.**

Prov: Palmyra, Diocletian Camp. Loc: Palmyra, CD 33/62. *Funerary. On stele fragment.*
Bib: Palm IV, p 194, no. 15, fig 225.

1 br b[...]
2 ḥb[l]

PAT 1970 **RSP 188** **n. d.**

Prov: Palmyra, Diocletian Camp. Loc: Palmyra,

CD 114/62. *Funerary. On relief fragment.*
Bib: *Pl VII*; Palm IV, p 197, no. 21, fig 229.

1 hdy[rt brt]
2 brʿth b[r]
3 rwʿy/dwʿy ḥb[l]

PAT 1971 **RSP 189** **A.D. 192**
Prov: Palmyra, Diocletian Camp. Loc: Palmyra, B 2185. *Funerary. On relief fragment.*
Bib: Palm IV, pp 74, 199, no. 22, fig 108, 230; PGKK, no. 13.

1 byrḥ
2 ʾdr
3 šnt 5.100+3

PAT 1972 **RSP 190** **n. d.**
Prov: Palmyra, Diocletian Camp. Loc: Palmyra, 25/63. *Funerary. On relief fragment.*
Bib: Palm V, pp 69-70, 115, no. 7, fig 79.

1 sbq brt [...]
2 br zbydʾ ḥb[l]

PAT 1973 **RSP 191** **n. d.**
Prov: Palmyra, Diocletian Camp. Loc: Palmyra, B 2211. *Funerary. On stele.*
Bib: Palm V, pp 46-48, 115, no. 8, fig 55; Meisterwerke no. 112; PGKK no. 18.

A. (On right)
1 ḥbl
2 bt
3 mlʾ
B. (On left)
1 brt
2 mtn
3 ʾ

PAT 1974 **RSP 192** **n. d.**
Prov: Palmyra, Diocletian Camp. Loc: Palmyra, CD 42. *Funerary. On relief fragment.*
Bib: Palm V, pp 67-68, 115-16, no. 9, fig 75.

1 tmʾ brt
2 mlʾ br
3 ḥ?[...]

PAT 1975 **RSP 193** **n. d.**
Prov: Palmyra, Diocletian Camp. Loc: Palmyra, CD 67/63. *Funerary. On relief fragment.*
Bib: Palm V, pp 68-69, 116, no. 10, fig 76.

1 [.......]ʾ
2 brt ʿwydʾ
3 ʾḥth
4 ḥbl

PAT 1976 **RSP 194** **n. d.**
Prov: Palmyra, Diocletian Camp, "Temple des Enseignes". Loc: Palmyra, CD 3/65. *Funerary. On relief.*
Bib: *Pl VIII.*

1 brtʾ
2 brt
3 ḥlypy
4 zbdbwl
5 ḥbl

PAT 1977 **RSP 195** **n. d.**
Prov: Palmyra, Diocletian Camp. Loc: Palmyra, CD 35/66. *Funerary. On relief.*
Bib: *Pl IV.*

1 [...]
2 h[...]
3 ʿzyzw
4 bwrʾ

PAT 1978 **RSP 196** **n. d.**
Prov: Palmyra, Diocletian Camp. Loc: Palmyra, CD 47/66. *Funerary. On relief.*
Bib: *Pl VII.*

1 [...]ʾ br
2 [...]br
3 tym[šm]š ḥbl

PAT 1979 **RSP 197** **n. d.**

Prov: Palmyra, Diocletian Camp, reemployed in foundation of “Temple des Enseignes”. Loc: Palmyra, CD 42/67. *Funerary. On relief.*

1 b$^{?}$dn
2 [b]rt
3 [b]wr’
4 ḥbl

PAT 1980 **RSP 198** **n. d.**

Prov: Palmyra, Diocletian Camp, near Hypogeum behind “Temple des Enseignes”. Loc: Palmyra, CD 2/69. *Funerary. On relief.*
Bib: Ber ’70, p 76.

(On right)
1 [...]’
2 [b]r
3 [‘]g[y]lw
4 [srykw]
(On left)
1 [...]
2 b[r]
3 ‘gyl[w]
4 sry[kw]

PAT 1981 **RSP 199** **n. d.**

Prov: Palmyra, Diocletian Camp, in colonnade leading to “Temple des Enseignes”. Loc: Palmyra, CD 18/59. *Legal: Fragment of sacred law. On stone tablet fragments.*
Bib: *Pl VII*; Déd pp 286-87; Sem ’73, pp 115-16.

1 [...] ‘.[...]
2 [...l]wt byt [...]
3 [...]’nš hyk d[y ktyb ...]
4 [...h]n ḥzw ’ḥ[y]dy’ ’[nš ...]
5 [...]lh lwt byt mšḥ’ [...]
6 [...t]hwh ḥṭy’th ‘ ‘yph [...]
7 [mšk]n$^{?}$’ ldy yntn ḥṭy’th ‘ ‘y[ph ...]
8 [yn]tn mškn’ ’w ypr‘ bg$^{?}$[br ...]
9 ypr‘ ḥṭy’th wl’ yn$^{?}$[tn mškn’ ...]
10 yhwn bh bšṭ’ wl’ y[...]
11 ‘l ’ḥydy’ dy yhwn ’[...]
12 mkpṣ ḥmr dy yḥwb ḥ[mr ...]
13 m’ dy y’mrwn tlth š[hdy’ ...]
14 [g]br dy yb‘h ‘l gbr ḥṭ[y’th ...]

PAT 1982 **RSP 200** **n. d.**

Prov: Palmyra, Diocletian Camp. Loc: Palmyra, CD 48/59. *Unclassified. On door lintel fragment.*
Bib: Palm I, p 215, no. 11, fig 235.

1 [...]8

PAT 1983 **RSP 201** **n. d.**

Prov: Palmyra, Diocletian Camp. Loc: Palmyra, CD 47/59. *Unclassified. On relief fragment.*
Bib: Palm I, p 218, no. 12, fig 236.

1 [...]šlmn

PAT 1984 **RSP 202** **n. d.**

Prov: Palmyra, Diocletian Camp. Loc: Palmyra, CD 60/59. *Unclassified. On stone fragment.*
Bib: Palm I, p 218, no. 13, fig 237.

1 [...]l$^{?}$m$^{?}$[...]

PAT 1985 **RSP 203** **n. d.**

Prov: Palmyra, Diocletian Camp. Loc: Palmyra, CD 7/59. *Funerary. On relief fragment.*
Bib: Palm I, p 218, no. 14, fig 238.

1 [...]br[...]
2 [...] ‘lt$^{?}$[’...]

PAT 1986 **RSP 204** **n. d.**

Prov: Palmyra, Diocletian Camp, in Tetrapylon. Loc: Palmyra, CD 84/60. *Honorific. On statue-base fragment.*
Bib: Palm II, pp 251-52, no. 14, fig 301.

1 ṣlm šlmn [...]

PAT 1987 **RSP 205** **n. d.**

Prov: Palmyra, Diocletian Camp, in Tetrapylon. Loc: Palmyra, CD 130/60. *Honorific?. On base fragment.*
Bib: Palm II, p 252, no. 15, fig 302.

1 [...]yly

PAT 1988 **RSP 206** **A.D. 68**
Prov: Palmyra, Diocletian Camp, near Tetrapylon. Loc: Palmyra, CD 46/60. *Unclassified. On stone tablet fragment.*
Bib: Palm II, p 252, no. 16, fig 303; Déd p 285; Sem '73 p 119.

1 [...]n[..]b$^{?}$[.]..]
2 [...]y' w'nt'
3 [...]'y 'nt'
4 [.. šn]t 3.100+80

PAT 1989 **RSP 207** **n. d.**
Prov: Palmyra, Diocletian Camp, in Tetrapylon. Loc: Palmyra, CD 93/60. *Unclassified. On stone fragment.*
Bib: Palm II, p 254, no. 17, fig 304.

1 [...]br[...]

PAT 1990 **RSP 208** **n. d.**
Prov: Palmyra, Diocletian Camp, in Tetrapylon. Loc: Palmyra, CD 16/60. *Funerary?. On stone fragments.*
Bib: Palm II, pp 255-56, no. 18, fig 305-306.

1' [...]br$^{?}$[...]
2' [...]'w[...]

PAT 1991 **RSP 209** **n. d.**
Prov: Palmyra, Diocletian Camp, near Tetrapylon. Loc: Palmyra, CD 14/60. *Funerary. On relief fragment.*
Bib: Palm II, pp 257, no. 19, fig 307.

1' [..........]
2' [...]'wyd'[...]
3' [...........]

PAT 1992 **RSP 210** **n. d.**
Prov: Palmyra, Diocletian Camp, in later house, by main colonnade. Loc: Palmyra, CD 53/61. *Dedicatory. On clay lamp.*
Bib: Palm III, pp 176, 237, no. 4, fig 230.

1 'glbwl wmlkbl

PAT 1993 **RSP 211** **n. d.**
Prov: Palmyra, Diocletian Camp, main colonnade. Loc: Palmyra, CD 65/61. *Unclassified. On stone fragment.*
Bib: Palm III, p 239, no. 8, fig 27.

1 ṣlm blṣ$^{?}$[...]
Incised and painted inscription.

PAT 1994 **RSP 212** **n. d.**
Prov: Palmyra, Diocletian Camp, near main colonnade. Loc: Palmyra, CD 70/61. *Honorific. On console.*
Bib: Palm III, p 239, no. 9, fig 275.

1 [....]brḥ/z
2 [...]zby br mlkw

PAT 1995 **RSP 213** **A.D. 118**
Prov: Palmyra, Diocletian Camp, main colonnade. Loc: Palmyra, CD 86/61. *Honorific. On console.*
Bib: Palm III, pp 242-43, no. 12, fig 278.

1 [...šn]t 4.100+20+10 by[rḥ...]

PAT 1996 **RSP 214** **A.D. 240**
Prov: Palmyra, Diocletian Camp. Loc: Palmyra, CD 132-133/61. *Unclassified. On stone fragments.*
Bib: Palm III, pp 247-49, no. 21, fig 283.

1 [... bw]lḥ' b[y]rḥ '[...š]nt 5.100+20+20+10+1

PAT 1997 **RSP 215** **n. d.**
Prov: Palmyra, Diocletian Camp. Loc: Palmyra, CD 130/61. *Unclassified. On stone fragment.*
Bib: Palm III, p 250, no. 23, fig 285.

1 [...]hwn wy$^{?}$[...]
Incised and painted inscription.

PAT 1998 **RSP 216** **n. d.**
Prov: Palmyra, Diocletian Camp. Loc: Palmyra, CD 45/62. *Honorific. On stone fragment.*
Bib: Palm IV, p 189, no. 8, fig 220.

1 ṣlm᾿ [dnh dy ...]
2 [..]hḥ[...]

PAT 1999 **RSP 217** **n. d.**
Prov: Palmyra, Diocletian Camp. Loc: Palmyra, CD 38/62. *Unclassified. On stone fragment.*
Bib: Palm IV, p 190, no. 10, fig 222.

1 [...]᾿[...]
2 [...]ḥw[...]

PAT 2000 **RSP 218** **n. d.**
Prov: Palmyra, Diocletian Camp. Loc: lost. *Honorific. On console fragment.*
Bib: Palm IV, p 193, no. 13.

1 [ṣlm᾿ d]nh dy mlkw b[r ...]

PAT 2001 **RSP 219** **n. d.**
Prov: Palmyra, Diocletian Camp. Loc: Palmyra, CD 97/62. *Dedicatory. On clay lamp.*
Bib: Palm IV, pp 194-95, no. 17, fig 226, pl I, 5.

1 ῾glbwl wmlkbl

PAT 2002 **RSP 220** **n. d.**
Prov: Palmyra, Diocletian Camp. Loc: Palmyra, CD 29/63. *Unclassified. On stone fragment.*
Bib: Palm V, p 116, no. 12, fig 112.

1 [... b῾]l?tg?[᾿ ...]
Incised and painted inscription.

PAT 2003 **RSP 221** **n. d.**
Prov: Palmyra, Diocletian Camp, "Temple des Enseignes". Loc: Palmyra, CD 14/65. *Unclassified. On stone fragment.*

1 [...]k᾿
2 [...] byrḥ
3 [...]

PAT 2004 **RSP 222** **n. d.**
Prov: Palmyra, Diocletian Camp, "Temple des Enseignes," cella. Loc: Palmyra, CD 239/65. *Unclassified. On stone tablet fragment.*
Bib: *Pl VIII.*

1 [...]t
2 [...]q?sm᾿
3 [.. m]lkbl
4 [... šn]t 3.100+[..]
5 [...]

PAT 2005 **RSP 223** **n. d.**
Prov: Palmyra, Diocletian Camp, "Temple des Enseignes," cella. Loc: Palmyra, CD 240/65. *Unclassified. On stone tablet fragment.*

1 [.. byrḥ] ᾿b šnt
2 3.100+[..]

PAT 2006 **RSP 224** **n. d.**
Prov: Palmyra, Diocletian Camp, "Temple des Enseignes," cella. Loc: Palmyra, CD 241/65. *Unclassified. On stone fragments.*

1 [...]
2 [...] br mlk[w...]

PAT 2007 **RSP 225** **n. d.**
Prov: Palmyra, Diocletian Camp, "Temple des Enseignes". Loc: Palmyra, CD 242/65. *Unclassified. On stone fragment.*

1 [...] tymrṣ[w ...]
2 [...]ḥ[...]

PAT 2008 **RSP 226** **n. d.**
Prov: Palmyra, Diocletian Camp, reemployed in later wall. Loc: Palmyra, CD 29/66. *Unclassified. On console fragment.*

1 [ṣlm᾿ dnh] lmlkw br whbl[t ...]

PAT 2009 **RSP 227** **n. d.**

Prov: Palmyra, Diocletian Camp, "Temple des Enseignes". Loc: Palmyra, CD 13/66. *Unclassified. On stone fragment.*

1 [...]
2 [...] br ḥry
3 [...] ʿltʾ
4 [...]

PAT 2010 **RSP 228** **n. d.**

Prov: Palmyra, Diocletian Camp. Loc: Palmyra, CD 36/66. *Unclassified. On stone fragment.*

1 [...]nʾ
2 [...]bʾ
3 [...] lḥyh mʾ
4 [...]b/dyʾ

PAT 2011 **RSP 229** **n. d.**

Prov: Palmyra, Diocletian Camp, "Temple des Enseignes". Loc: Palmyra, CD 43/66. *Unclassified. On stone fragment.*

1 [...] t?yml[t...]
2 [...]ry br[...]

RTP

A great number of the tesserae from Palmyra (including also bullae) are published in the *Recueil des tessères de Palmyre* of H. Ingholt, H. Seyrig, and J. Starcky, of 1955 (siglum RTP). These are printed here in economical format, omitting repetitious notations. All these inscriptions are brief, all are of the same genre, and only a few are dated or are in any sense bilingual. All are from Palmyra originally; for details as to the present location of the tesserae, many of which are extant in more than one copy, readers should consult RTP. RTP contains plates, and the column "Forme" gives a schematic representation of the various shapes of tesserae, including conical, round, oval, square, diamond-shaped, etc. There are verbal descriptions of any artistic representation a tessera may contain, as well as a rich variety of indices, and "Remarques linguistiques" by A. Caquot (pp. 139-84).

Many of the tesserae in RTP contain no text, hence the series of RTP numbers that follows contains gaps. All but a few of the tesserae and bullae are of terra-cotta; use of any other material (bronze, iron, lead, glass) is explicitly noted below (see RTP p. 191 "Matières" for summary which includes tesserae without Aramaic inscription). General bibliography: du Mesnil, 1944; 1962b (bibliography pp. 14-16; TMP pp. 757-58); Walker 1956 (*StuLdV* 601-2); Dunant, 1959 (*Syr* '59); Dunant '71, *BS III* p. 10; Fellmann and Dunant, '75 *BS VI* p. 113. Teix *MUSJ* '66 p. 178 nos. 3, 4.

PAT 2012 **RTP 3**
Obv. 1 bw[l]ʾ

PAT 2013 **RTP 6**
Obv. 1 qryʾ
Rev. 1 ydyʿbl

PAT 2014 **RTP 7**
Obv. 1 bw[lʾ]
Rev. 1 bwnwr

PAT 2015 **RTP 8**
Obv. 1 krkʾ
Rev. 1 ʿnwštʾ

PAT 2016 **RTP 10**
Obv. 1 kmryʾ dy
2 bl ʾlhʾ
Rev. 1 nšʾ brpʾ

PAT 2017 **RTP 11**
Obv. 1 kmryʾ
2 dy bl
Rev. 1 yrḥy

PAT 2018 **RTP 12**
Obv. 1 kmryʾ dy bl
Rev. 1 šmʿwn br ḥyrn

PAT 2019 **RTP 13**
Déd p 279
Obv. 1 kmryʾ dy [bl]
Rev. 1 [...]ḥ? br ʿg[ʾ]

PAT 2020 **RTP 14**
Obv. 1 kmryʾ dy bl
Rev. 1 ʿgylw tymḥʾ

PAT 2021 **RTP 15**

IP 105
Obv. 1 kmry bl
Rev. 1 yrḥbwl'
2 yrḥbwl' br šby

PAT 2022 **RTP 16**
Obv. 1 [k]mry bl

PAT 2023 **RTP 17**
Obv. 1 kmry bl
Rev. 1 mlkw šm'wn ḥm'

PAT 2024 **RTP 18**
Obv. 1 [k]mry bl

PAT 2025 **RTP 19**
Obv. 1 kmry bl
Rev. 1 lšmš ydy'bl

PAT 2026 **RTP 20**
Obv. 1 kmry
2 bl

PAT 2027 **RTP 21**
Obv. 1 kmry b?l?

PAT 2028 **RTP 22**
Obv. 1 kmry bl
Rev. 1 yrḥbwl'
2 br š?b?y?

PAT 2029 **RTP 23**
Déd p 279
Obv. 1 kmry bl
Rev. 1 mndymn' /mnrymn'
2 [..]'

PAT 2030 **RTP 24**
Obv. 1 kmry bl

PAT 2031 **RTP 25**
Obv. 1 kmry bl

PAT 2032 **RTP 26**
Obv. 1 kmry' dy bl

PAT 2033 **RTP 27**
Déd p 278
Obv. 1 kmry' dy [bl]
Rev. 1 ḥyrn 'tnwry
2 ṣlmy rb mrzḥ'

PAT 2034 **RTP 28**
Obv. 1 [k]mry bl

PAT 2035 **RTP 29**
Obv. 1 [km]ry bl
Rev. 1 [.]lš[..]

PAT 2036 **RTP 30**
Déd p 277
Obv. 1 '[w]yd' br
2 tymrṣw
3 br 'wyd' rb mrzḥ'

PAT 2037 **RTP 31**
Obv. 1 šlmn
2 yrḥbwl'
3 mlkw ''b[y]
4 rb mrzḥ'

PAT 2038 **RTP 32**
A.D. 132
Déd p 238
Obv. 1 bgšw ḥm'
2 rb mrzḥ'
3 šnt 4.100+40+4
On date, see RTP p 201

PAT 2039 **RTP 33**
Obv. 1 bwlḥ' br
2 ḥyrn rb
3 mrzḥ'
Rev. 1 bwlḥ'

PAT 2040 **RTP 34**
Obv. 1 brbnwt
2 mrzḥ' šlmn
3 yrḥbwl'
4 mlkw ''by dy [...]
Rev. 1 šlmn

PAT 2041 **RTP 35**
Déd p 237
Obv. 1 yrḥbwl'
2 lrmn
3 rb mrzḥ[']
Rev. 1 yrḥbwl'

PAT 2042 **RTP 36**
Obv. 1 'nwš[t]'
2 dy bl
3 bwlyd'
4 mhrdt

PAT 2043 **RTP 37**
Obv. 1 hykl'
2 wrbny
3 'wnt'
4 dy bl
Rev. 1 'bd[y]/'bd[']
2 'mry
3 mqymw
4 'g'

PAT 2044 **RTP 38**
Obv. 1 rbny 'wnt'
Rev. 1 yd'w
2 tybwl
3 ḥyrn
4 ṣt'

PAT 2045 **RTP 39**
IP 10; Déd p 284
Obv. 1 'wnt' rš'
Rev. 1 ḥmr mkl wplg

PAT 2046 **RTP 40**
Déd p 286
Obv. 1 bryky
2 šk't'
3 'ḥydy
4 ['w]nt'
Rev. 1 bl

line 3 :: Stark PN ḥyry

PAT 2047 **RTP 41**
Obv. 1 bl

PAT 2048 **RTP 42**
Obv. 1 bl

PAT 2049 **RTP 43**
Obv. 1 bl

PAT 2050 **RTP 44**
Obv. 1 bl
Rev. 1 blḥ[ʾ]

PAT 2051 **RTP 45**
Obv. 1 bl

PAT 2052 **RTP 46**
Obv. 1 bl

PAT 2053 **RTP 47**
Obv. 1 bl

PAT 2054 **RTP 48**
Obv. 1 bl

PAT 2055 **RTP 49**
Obv. 1 bl

PAT 2056 **RTP 50**
Obv. 1 bl

PAT 2057 **RTP 51**
Obv. 1 bl

PAT 2058 **RTP 52**
Obv. 1 bl

PAT 2059 **RTP 53**
Obv. 1 bl m[...]

PAT 2060 **RTP 54**
Obv. 1 bl

PAT 2061 **RTP 55**
Obv. 1 bl

PAT 2062 **RTP 56**
Obv. 1 bl

PAT 2063 **RTP 57**
Obv. 1 bl

PAT 2064 **RTP 58**
Obv. 1 bl

PAT 2065 **RTP 59**
Obv. 1 bl
2 twrʾ
Rev. 1 tymy

PAT 2066 **RTP 60**
Obv. 1 bl
Rev. 1 ʿgylw
2 bwrpʾ
3 qšṭʾ

PAT 2067 **RTP 61**
Obv. 1 bl
Lead

PAT 2068 **RTP 62**
Obv. 1 bl bny
2 bwrʾ

PAT 2069 **RTP 63**
Obv. 1 bl
2 nysn

PAT 2070 **RTP 64**
Obv. 1 bl bny
2 bwrʾ
Rev. 1 tymʿmd
2 bwlḥʾ

PAT 2071 **RTP 65**
Rev. 1 [...]
2 b[...]

PAT 2072 **RTP 66**
Obv. 1 bl bʿltk
2 bny
3 tymrṣw

PAT 2073 **RTP 67**
Obv. 1 bl

PAT 2074 **RTP 68**
Obv. 1 bl

PAT 2075 **RTP 69**
Obv. 1 bl

PAT 2076 **RTP 70**
Obv. 1 [.]d/ryʿy
2 bl
Rev. 1 mkb[l]
2 ʿgylw

PAT 2077 **RTP 71**
Obv. 1 bl

PAT 2078 **RTP 72**
Obv. 1 bl
2 brnbw

PAT 2079 **RTP 73**
Obv. 1 bl
Lead

PAT 2080 **RTP 74**
Obv. 1 bl

PAT 2081 **RTP 75**
Obv. 1 bl

PAT 2082 **RTP 76**
Obv. 1 ʾgn bl

2 bʿltk
Rev. 1 mqymw

PAT 2083 **RTP 77**
Obv. 1 ʾgn bl
2 bʿltk
Rev. 1 bny tymrṣw

PAT 2084 **RTP 78**
Obv. 1 ʾgn bl
2 qšṭʾ
Rev. 1 zbdʿth
2 mtnʾ

PAT 2085 **RTP 79**
Obv. 1 ʾgn bl
2 bny šmwn

PAT 2086 **RTP 80**
IP 88
Obv. 1 ʾgn bl
2 bny gwgʾ

PAT 2087 **RTP 81**
Obv. 1 ʾgn
2 bl
3 bny
4 gwgw

PAT 2088 **RTP 82**
Obv. 1 ʾgn bl bny
2 bwlḥʾ
Rev. 1 mqymw šgʿw

PAT 2089 **RTP 83**
RES 443
Obv. 1 ʾgn bl bny bwlʿʾ

PAT 2090 **RTP 84**
Obv. 1 ʾgn bl
Rev. 1 ʿbsy
2 whblt

PAT 2091 **RTP 85**
Obv. 1 ʾgn bl

PAT 2092 **RTP 86**
Obv. 1 ʾgn bl

PAT 2093 **RTP 87**
Obv. 1 ʾgn bl

PAT 2094 **RTP 88**
Obv. 1 ʾgn
2 bl
3 yrḥy

PAT 2095 **RTP 89**
Obv. 1 ʾgn b[l]

PAT 2096 **RTP 90**
Obv. 1 ʾgn bl

PAT 2097 **RTP 91**
Obv. 1 ʾgn bl
Rev. 1 qšṭʾ

PAT 2098 **RTP 92**
IP 86
Obv. 1 ʾgn bl
Rev. 1 bl
2 ybrk
3 lbny
4 bwdlʾ

PAT 2099 **RTP 93**
Obv. 1 ʾgn bl
2 wʾblʿly
Rev. 1 ḥnktʾ
2 wbny ḥšš

PAT 2100 **RTP 94**
Obv. 1 ʾgn bl
Rev. 1 tymrṣw
2 br šlmn
3 qšṭʾ

PAT 2101 **RTP 95**
Obv. 1 ʾgn bl
Rev. 1 [b]n[y] ydy[ʿb]l

PAT 2102 **RTP 96**
Obv. 1 ʾgn bl
2 bny sknʾ
Rev. 1 [...]
2 bny mzyʾ
3 [...]

PAT 2103 **RTP 97**
Obv. 1 ʾgn bl
2 bny ḥnwr (or: ḥnwd)

PAT 2104 **RTP 98**
Obv. 1 ʾgn bl
Rev. 1 bny
2 ʾʿly
3 šlm

PAT 2105 **RTP 99**
Obv. 1 ʾgn bl bny ʿgrwd

PAT 2106 **RTP 100**
Obv. 1 ʾgn bl
2 bny gwgʾ

PAT 2107 **RTP 101**
Obv. 1 ʾgn bl

PAT 2108 **RTP 102**
Obv. 1 ʾg[n bl]
2 bny t[...]
Rev. 1 [lš]mš
2 [ty]mrṣw

PAT 2109 **RTP 103**
Obv. 1 ʾgn bl
Rev. 1 ʿtnwry
2 bwrpʾ

PAT 2110 **RTP 104**
Obv. 1 [ʾ]gn bl
2 [b]l

PAT 2111 **RTP 105**
Obv. 1 ʾgn bl
Rev. 1 bny
2 mgdt

PAT 2112 **RTP 106**
Obv. 1 ʾgn bl bny qṣmyt
Rev. 1 ʾgn bl bny bḥr

PAT 2113 **RTP 107**
Obv. 1 ʾgn
2 bl bny
3 bwl[ʿ]ʾ

PAT 2114 **RTP 108**
Obv. 1 bl ybrk
2 lbny tymy

PAT 2115 **RTP 109**
Obv. 1 bl ybrk
2 bny ʾʿly

PAT 2116 **RTP 110**
Obv. 1 bl ybrk
2 l[...]
3 [...]
Rev. 1 ʿtnwry
2 zb[db]l

PAT 2117 **RTP 111**
Obv. 1 tgʾ
2 dy bl
3 tymrṣw
4 dyny

PAT 2118 **RTP 112**
Obv. 1 tgʾ
2 [d]y bl

PAT 2119 **RTP 113**
Obv. 1 ḥyrwnʾ
2 dy bl

PAT 2120 **RTP 114**
Obv. 1 bnyn bl

PAT 2121 **RTP 115**
Obv. 1 bnynʾ
2 dy bl
Lead

PAT 2122 **RTP 116**
Obv. 1 bnynʾ
Rev. 1 ʾp[..]

PAT 2123 **RTP 117**
Obv. 1 bnynʾ
2 kʿnyn
3 bl

PAT 2124 **RTP 118**
Rev. 1 mlkw whblt

PAT 2125 **RTP 119**
Obv. 1 nbw
Rev. 1 yrḥbwl ʿglbwl

PAT 2126 **RTP 120**
Rev. 1 whblt

PAT 2127 **RTP 121**
Obv. 1 [ʾ]št[r]

PAT 2128 **RTP 122**
Obv. 1 ʾgn bl
Rev. 1 ʿglbwl

PAT 2129 **RTP 123**
Obv. 1 ʾgn bl
2 bny nwrbl
Rev. 1 ʾlt

PAT 2130 **RTP 124**
Obv. 1 ʾgn bl bny
2 ydyʿbl
Rev. 1 ʿštrt

PAT 2131 **RTP 125**
Obv. 1 ʾgn bl
2 wblʿstr

PAT 2132 **RTP 126**
Obv. 1 bl b[ny]
2 [...]
Rev. 1 [bl]ʿstr

PAT 2133 **RTP 127**
Déd p 169
Obv. 1 bl
2 mkl
Rev. 1 blʿstr nrgl

PAT 2134 **RTP 128**
Obv. 1 ʾgn bl
2 blty
Rev. 1 bny
2 šmwn

PAT 2135 **RTP 129**
Obv. 1 bl
2 blty

PAT 2136 **RTP 130**
Obv. 1 ʾgn bl
2 gd blmʾ

PAT 2137 **RTP 131**
IP 104
Obv. 1 bl
2 gd mšḥʾ

PAT 2138 **RTP 132**
Obv. 1 gd mšḥʾ
Rev. 1 bl
Bronze

PAT 2139 **RTP 133**
Obv. 1 ʾgn
2 bl
3 ḥrtʾ

PAT 2140 **RTP 134**

Obv. 1 ʾgn bl
2 wḥrtʾ
3 wnny
Rev. 1 bl ybrk
2 lbny ḥlʾ

PAT 2141 **RTP 135**
Obv. 1 bl wbny
2 bwnʾ
Rev. 1 mlkbl
2 wgd tymy

PAT 2142 **RTP 136**
Obv. 1 bl
Rev. 1 nbw

PAT 2143 **RTP 137**
Obv. 1 ʾgn bl
2 wnbw
3 bny ʿlyy
Rev. 1 nbw
2 zbdbwl

PAT 2144 **RTP 138**
Obv. 1 ʾgn bl
2 šmš
Rev. 1 bny zbdbwl

PAT 2145 **RTP 139**
Obv. 1 bl
2 šmš

PAT 2146 **RTP 140**
Obv. 1 ʾgn bl
2 wšmš

PAT 2147 **RTP 141**
Obv. 1 ʾgn bl w
2 šmš wbny
3 zbdbwl

PAT 2148 **RTP 142**
Obv. 1 ʾgn bl
Rev. 1 šmš
2 qšṭʾ

PAT 2149 **RTP 143**
Obv. 1 brt bl

PAT 2150 **RTP 144**
Obv. 1 brt bl

PAT 2151 **RTP 145**
Rev. 1 ʿglbwl
2 [.]z[..]
3 gʿl[.]

PAT 2152 **RTP 146**
Obv. 1 ʿglbwl

PAT 2153 **RTP 148**
Obv. 1 [.]wʿd/wʿr[...]

PAT 2154 **RTP 149**
Obv. 1 ʿglbw[l]
Rev. 1 ʿglbwl

PAT 2155 **RTP 150**
Obv. 1 ʿglbwl
2 šlmʾ

PAT 2156 **RTP 151**
Rev. 1 šmšrmʾ

PAT 2157 **RTP 153**
Obv. 1 ʿglbwl
Rev. 1 mʿnw

PAT 2158 **RTP 154**
Obv. 1 ʿglbwl yḥnʾ

PAT 2159 **RTP 155**
Obv. 1 ʿglbwl ml[kb]l

PAT 2160 **RTP 156**
Obv. 1 ʿglbwl
2 mlkbl
Rev. 1 ḥrwṣ
2 ḥyrn

PAT 2161 **RTP 157**
Obv. 1 ʿglbwl
2 mlkbl
Rev. 1 ʿwmy

PAT 2162 **RTP 158**
Obv. 1 ʿglbwl
2 wmlkbl
3 ywm 10+2

PAT 2163 **RTP 159**
Obv. 1 ʿglbwl
2 twrʾ
Rev. 1 mlkbl
2 twrʾ

PAT 2164 **RTP 160**
Déd p 156
Obv. 1 ʿglbwl
2 mlkbl
Rev. 1 m<šḥʾ> 1 ḥ<mrʾ>
1

PAT 2165 **RTP 161**
Déd p 156
Obv. 1 ʿglbwl
2 mlkbl
Rev. 1 m<šḥʾ> 1 ḥ<mrʾ>
1 ʿ<glʾ> 1

PAT 2166 **RTP 163**
Déd p 98
Obv. 1 [.....]

PAT 2167 **RTP 164**
Obv. 1 ʾlt

PAT 2168 **RTP 165**
Obv. 1 ʾlt
2 bny nwrbl

PAT 2169 **RTP 166**

Obv. 1 ʾnhyt

PAT 2170 **RTP 167**
Obv. 1 ʾnhyt
2 ʿnyny
3 tymy

PAT 2171 **RTP 169**
Obv. 1 ʾrṣw
Rev. 1 š[...]

PAT 2172 **RTP 170**
Obv. 1 ʾrṣw

PAT 2173 **RTP 171**
RES 415
Rev. 1 tymrṣ[w] ḥbyby

PAT 2174 **RTP 174**
Rev. 1 tymʿmd tbʿwt

PAT 2175 **RTP 175**
Obv. 1 ʾrṣw
2 rʿyyʾ

PAT 2176 **RTP 176**
Rev. 1 bny
2 ʿbd[.]
3 lrʿyʾ
4 lʾrṣw

PAT 2177 **RTP 177**
Rev. 1 [.]ymʾ[..]

PAT 2178 **RTP 178**
Obv. 1 ʿgylw

PAT 2179 **RTP 179**
Rev. 1 mqymw
2 tymrṣw
3 wtymrṣw
4 nšʾ
5 wzbydʾ
6 [...]w

PAT 2180 **RTP 180**
Rev. 1 ʾrṣw r[bʾ?]

PAT 2181 **RTP 181**
Rev. 1 ʿlyšʾ
2 ʾšqrʾ

PAT 2182 **RTP 182**
Rev. 1 šky[bl]
2 wšlmn
3 wbln[wr]y
4 [w]mqymw

PAT 2183 **RTP 183**
Obv. 1 ʾrṣw
2 rbw
3 ḥyny

PAT 2184 **RTP 184**
IP 91
Obv. 1 ʾrṣw
Rev. 1 t[b]ʿwt/šʿwt
2 bny šlm
3 rbʾ

PAT 2185 **RTP 185**
Rev. 1 tymʾ
2 šlmʾ

PAT 2186 **RTP 186**
Rev. 1 [...]
2 zbdbwl
3 [ʾr]ṣ[w]

PAT 2187 **RTP 187**
Obv. 1 [...]wd/rb
2 [ʾ]r[ṣ]w

PAT 2188 **RTP 188**
Rev. 1 šby
2 yrḥbwlʾ
3 mqymw
4 tymrṣw

PAT 2189 **RTP 189**
Rev. 1 yrḥy brʾ

PAT 2190 **RTP 190**
Obv. 1 rbʾ
2 ʾrṣw

PAT 2191 **RTP 191**
Rev. 1 khylw
2 nbwzbd

PAT 2192 **RTP 192**
Obv. 1 ʾrṣw

PAT 2193 **RTP 193**
Rev. 1 ʾrṣw

PAT 2194 **RTP 194**
Déd p 187
Obv. 1 rbʿ
2 ʾrṣw

PAT 2195 **RTP 195**
Obv. 1 ʾrṣw
2 bny ḥlʾ
Rev. 1 lšmš
2 tymrṣw

PAT 2196 **RTP 196**
Obv. 1 rb
2 [ʾ]rṣw

PAT 2197 **RTP 197**
Déd p 49
Obv. 1 ʾrṣw bl
Rev. 1 tymrṣw
2 wymlkw
3 wšʿdy

(Obv.)1: Stark and others combine as DN *ʾrṣwbl*: Déd p 49: read *ʾrṣw rb[ʾ]*

PAT 2198 **RTP 198**
Rev. 1 ʾštrbd
2 mlktʾ

PAT 2199 **RTP 199**
Obv. 1 ʾštrbd

PAT 2200 **RTP 200**
Obv. 1 bʿltk
2 mlktʾ
Rev. 1 [...]
2 bryk[y ...]

PAT 2201 **RTP 201**
Obv. 1 ʿtrʿth

PAT 2202 **RTP 203**
Obv. 1 bʿlšmn

PAT 2203 **RTP 204**
Obv. 1 bʿlšmn
Rev. 1 mqymw
2 šʿydn

PAT 2204 **RTP 205**
Obv. 1 bʿlšmn

PAT 2205 **RTP 206**
Obv. 1 bʿl[š]m[n]

PAT 2206 **RTP 207**
Obv. 1 [..]zʾ
2 bʿlšmn
Rev. 1 [..]zʾ
2 b[...]

PAT 2207 **RTP 208**
Obv. 1 bʿlšmn
Rev. 1 bʿlšmn

PAT 2208 **RTP 209**
Obv. 1 bʿlšmyn mlkbl

PAT 2209 **RTP 210**
Rev. 1 mqymw
2 mlʾ

PAT 2210 **RTP 211**
Déd p 47
Obv. 1 [...]
2 b[lʿ]str
Rev. 1 gny
2 mny

PAT 2211 **RTP 212**
Obv. 1 bl
2 ḥmwn
3 mqym[w]
4 ʾqt[....]

PAT 2212 **RTP 213**
Obv. 1 bl
2 ḥmwn
Rev. 1 gd
2 ʿgrwd

PAT 2213 **RTP 214**
Obv. 1 (on right) bl (on left) ḥmwn

PAT 2214 **RTP 215**
Obv. 1 blḥmn [...]

PAT 2215 **RTP 216**
Obv. 1 blty

PAT 2216 **RTP 217**
Obv. 1 blty
Rev. 1 yrḥy
2 klbʾ

PAT 2217 **RTP 218**
Obv. 1 blty
Rev. 1 tmwzʾ

PAT 2218 **RTP 219**
Obv. 1 blty
2 blnwry
Rev. 1 tmwzʾ
2 wmnp

PAT 2219 **RTP 220**
Obv. 1 ʾlqnrʿ
Rev. 1 brwq[ʾ]
2 mq[y]

PAT 2220 **RTP 221**
Obv. 1 ʾlqnrʿ
2 š[...]

PAT 2221 **RTP 222**
Obv. 1 ʾlqnrʿ
Rev. 1 ḥyry mlkw

PAT 2222 **RTP 223**
Obv. 1 ʾlqnrʾ
Rev. 1 tymʿmd
2 zbdbl

PAT 2223 **RTP 224**
Rev. 1 gd ʿgrwd

PAT 2224 **RTP 225**
Obv. 1 ḥkym
Rev. 1 gnyʾ

PAT 2225 **RTP 226**
Obv. 1 gnyʾ

PAT 2226 **RTP 227**
Rev. 1 nrgl
2 yrḥy b[r]
3 zbdʾ

PAT 2227 **RTP 233**
RES 1081
Obv. 1 tymrṣw ʿgy[lw]
Rev. 1 ʿtʿqb
2 rbʾ

PAT 2228 **RTP 234**
Rev. 1 mlkw br
2 pgʾ

PAT 2229 **RTP 235**

Rev. 1 bwlḥʾ

PAT 2230 **RTP 236**
Obv. 1 [m]lkw

PAT 2231 **RTP 238**
Obv. 1 ḥrtʾ
2 nny

PAT 2232 **RTP 239**
Obv. 1 ḥrtʾ
Rev. 1 nny
2 ḥggw

PAT 2233 **RTP 240**
Obv. 1 ḥrtʾ wnny

PAT 2234 **RTP 241**
Obv. 1 ḥrt[ʾ]
2 nny

PAT 2235 **RTP 242**
Obv. 1 ḥrtʾ
2 wnny
Rev. 1 tbrkn
2 lmqymw

PAT 2236 **RTP 243**
Obv. 1 [...] lšmš

PAT 2237 **RTP 244**
Obv. 1 yrḥbwl
2 wʿglbwl
Rev. 1 brykyn/brykyʾ
2 tryʾ
Dunant adds: 3 nbw

PAT 2238 **RTP 247**
Obv. 1 yrḥbwl

PAT 2239 **RTP 248**
Obv. 1 mʿnw
2 šʿdw
3 gnyʾ

PAT 2240 **RTP 249**
Obv. 1 mʿnw
2 sṭmʾ
Rev. 1 [šʿ]dw

PAT 2241 **RTP 250**
Rev. 1 dynys
2 ydyʿbl
3 šlmʾ

PAT 2242 **RTP 251**
Obv. 1 mʿnw
Rev. 1 hldrs

PAT 2243 **RTP 252**
Obv. 1 mʿnw
2 t[w]rʾ
3 bny šmʿwn bkl ʿd
šlm

PAT 2244 **RTP 257**
Rev. 1 bwrpʾ

PAT 2245 **RTP 260**
Rev. 1 ʾḥ[..]

PAT 2246 **RTP 261**
Rev. 1 blḥzy šlmn

PAT 2247 **RTP 262**
Obv. 1 mlkbl
Rev. 1 bny
2 tymy

PAT 2248 **RTP 263**
Obv. 1 mlkbl
Rev. 1 bny [...]

PAT 2249 **RTP 264**
Obv. 1 mlkbl
2 ʾkḥtʾ

PAT 2250 **RTP 267**
Rev. 1 ḥyrn
2 yrḥy

PAT 2251 **RTP 270**
Obv. 1 [m]lkbl
2 mntʾ

PAT 2252 **RTP 271**
Obv. 1 mlkbl

PAT 2253 **RTP 272**
Obv. 1 mlkbl wʾlt
2 wbny
3 blnwry
Rev. 1 blnwr mqmw
2 ḥyrn mly

PAT 2254 **RTP 273**
Obv. 1 mlkbl wgd
2 tymy

PAT 2255 **RTP 274**
Obv. 1 mlkbl
2 gd tymy
Rev. 1 yrḥy br
2 bwrpʾ

PAT 2256 **RTP 275**
Obv. 1 mlkbl
2 gd
3 tymy

PAT 2257 **RTP 276**
Obv. 1 mlkbl gd tymy
Rev. 1 bny rbʾl

PAT 2258 **RTP 277**
Obv. 1 mlkbl
2 gd tymy
Rev. 1 bwlḥzy

PAT 2259 **RTP 279**
Obv. 1 mlkbl wgd tymy

PAT 2260 **RTP 280**
Obv. 1 klyn tr[n]
Rev. 1 bwlḥʾ

PAT 2261 **RTP 281**
Obv. 1 mnwt

PAT 2262 **RTP 283**
Rev. 1 mlkw br
2 ydy

PAT 2263 **RTP 284**
Obv. 1 [ḥmr] mkl
2 wplg

PAT 2264 **RTP 285**
Obv. 1 nny
2 škny
3 šyʿt
4 bbl

PAT 2265 **RTP 287**
Obv. 1 nbw
Rev. 1 zbdʿth
2 mtnʾ

PAT 2266 **RTP 288**
Obv. 1 nbw

PAT 2267 **RTP 289**
IP 103
Obv. 1 nbw
2 yrḥbwlʾ

PAT 2268 **RTP 290**
Obv. 1 nb[w]
Rev. 1 nbwlh
2 ḥdwdn

PAT 2269 **RTP 291**
Obv. 1 nbw
Rev. 1 ḥyrn
2 ydʿw

PAT 2270 **RTP 292**
Obv. 1 nbw
2 šbʿtʾ

PAT 2271 **RTP 293**
Obv. 1 nbw
2 zbydʾ
3 ʿlg

PAT 2272 **RTP 294**
Obv. 1 nbw

PAT 2273 **RTP 295**
Déd p 158
Obv. 1 .rw.l. (or: .dw.l.)
Rev. 1 zbdbwl
2 zbydʾ
3 bny
4 ʿlyy
Text after Dunant '59

PAT 2274 **RTP 296**
Obv. 1 nbw
2 brʿth
3 brnbw

PAT 2275 **RTP 297**
Obv. 1 nbw 5+1

PAT 2276 **RTP 298**
Obv. 1 nbw
Rev. 1 gdymy/grymy

PAT 2277 **RTP 299**
Obv. 1 nbw
Rev. 1 zbdbwl
2 [ʿgy]lw

PAT 2278 **RTP 300**
Obv. 1 nbw

PAT 2279 **RTP 301**
Déd p 157
Obv. 1 bny mrzḥ
2 [....]bw
3 nb/ʿb[..]bl
4 k?bd?[..]

PAT 2280 **RTP 302**
Obv. 1 nbw
Rev. 1 yrḥbwlʾ
2 br mtnʾ
3 brʿth

PAT 2281 **RTP 303**
IP 99
Obv. 1 nbw
2 ʾbrykw

PAT 2282 **RTP 304**
Obv. 1 nbw
2 ybrk
Rev. 1 mšmšy pḥdyʾ

PAT 2283 **RTP 305**
Obv. 1 nbw
2 ybrk
Rev. 1 lmtnʾ
2 zbdʿth

PAT 2284 **RTP 306**
IP 90
Obv. 1 qnyt
2 nbw
Rev. 1 nbwzbd
2 mqymw

PAT 2285 **RTP 307**
Obv. 1 nbw
2 qnytʾ

PAT 2286 **RTP 308**
Obv. 1 nbw
2 qnytʾ
Rev. 1 gdymy/grymy
2 nbwlʾ

PAT 2287 **RTP 309**
Obv. 1 qny[t]

2 nbw

PAT 2288 **RTP 311**
IP 96
Obv. 1 zbdbwl
Rev. 1 mqym[w]

PAT 2289 **RTP 312**
Rev. 1 [z]bydʾ

PAT 2290 **RTP 315**
IP 93
Rev. 1 mlkw
2 ḥggw

PAT 2291 **RTP 316**
Rev. 1 t[yml]t
2 br yrḥy

PAT 2292 **RTP 317**
Obv. 1 šdrpʾ

PAT 2293 **RTP 318 bis**
Rev. 1 ʾʿylmy sqḥʾ

PAT 2294 **RTP 321**
Obv. 1 šdrpʾ
Rev. 1 [...]t/ḥ
2 mtny

PAT 2295 **RTP 322**
Obv. 1 mlkw
2 šmʿwn

PAT 2296 **RTP 325**
Obv. 1 šdrpʾ
2 twrʾ

PAT 2297 **RTP 328**
Rev. 1 šdrpʾ
2 mlkw
3 [ty]myʿm[d]

PAT 2298 **RTP 329**
Obv. 1 šdrpʾ
2 dʿnt
Rev. 1 dny
2 ʿbdʾ

PAT 2299 **RTP 330**
Obv. 1 mqy
2 mw

PAT 2300 **RTP 331**
Obv. 1 šʿ[d]w

PAT 2301 **RTP 332**
Rev. 1 bʿltk
2 [šy]ʿlqwm

PAT 2302 **RTP 333**
Déd p 339
Obv. 1 šmš
2 šrn
3 rbʾ

PAT 2303 **RTP 334**
Obv. 1 šmš
2 bny
3 šʿdy

PAT 2304 **RTP 335**
Obv. 1 šmš
Rev. 1 ʿgylw
2 wmškw

PAT 2305 **RTP 336**
Obv. 1 šmš
2 špʾ/šlʾ
3 ḥggw

PAT 2306 **RTP 337**
Obv. 1 blḥzy
2 gnbʾ
Rev. 1 šmš

PAT 2307 **RTP 339**
Obv. 1 šmš dy
2 bny ʿṣr
Rev. 1 tymrṣw mqymw

PAT 2308 **RTP 340**
Obv. 1 šmš

PAT 2309 **RTP 341**
Obv. 1 ʾgn
2 šmš
3 bny
4 šʿdw
Rev. 1 ʿwydʾ
2 wwhblt

PAT 2310 **RTP 342**
Obv. 1 tmwzʾ

PAT 2311 **RTP 344**
Obv. 1 ʿmrʾ/ʿbdʾ

PAT 2312 **RTP 345**
Rev. 1 ʾq[..]wn

PAT 2313 **RTP 350**
Déd p 185
Rev. 1 m<kl> 3

PAT 2314 **RTP 351**
Rev. 1 ʿlyšʾ
2 mlkw

PAT 2315 **RTP 360**
Rev. 1 bryky

PAT 2316 **RTP 361**
Obv. 1 ḥ (on the right)
2 (on the left)y

PAT 2317 **RTP 362**
Rev. 1 lšmš
2 mqymw

PAT 2318 **RTP 363**
Rev. 1 mqymw
2 br ydy

PAT 2319 **RTP 364**
Rev. 1 bny ḥkym

PAT 2320 **RTP 369**
Obv. 1 m[...]
2 ʿb[...]

PAT 2321 **RTP 370**
Rev. 1 whby
2 wmqymw
3 wlšmš

PAT 2322 **RTP 372**
Rev. 1 rbʾl

PAT 2323 **RTP 374**
Obv. Dunant sees traces of: r ... l

PAT 2324 **RTP 375**
Rev. 1 [mq]ymw zbydʾ ḥy[...]

PAT 2325 **RTP 376**
Rev. 1 škyy br w[hb]lt

PAT 2326 **RTP 378**
Obv. 1 mqymw ʿgy[lw]

PAT 2327 **RTP 381**
Obv. 1 šmšgrm
Rev. 1 šmšgrm
2 br nwrbl
3 gynws
4 ḥnynʾ

PAT 2328 **RTP 382**
Obv. 1 ḥnynʾ

PAT 2329 **RTP 383**
Rev. 1 bwlḥʾ
2 šlmʾ

PAT 2330 **RTP 386**
Rev. 1 lšmš

PAT 2331 **RTP 388**
Obv. 1 blḥzy
Rev. 1 blḥzy

PAT 2332 **RTP 391**
Rev. 1 mlkʾl
2 [..]brs/bds

PAT 2333 **RTP 395**
Obv. 1 mqymw
2 ʿlgʾ
3 zbdlh
4 mšy

PAT 2334 **RTP 396**
Rev. 1 mqy ʿlg

PAT 2335 **RTP 398**
Rev. 1 nbwzbd
2 šlmlt

PAT 2336 **RTP 402**
Obv. 1 [.....]tyšḥʾ

PAT 2337 **RTP 406**
Rev. 1 zbydʾ br[...]

PAT 2338 **RTP 407**
Rev. 1 sṭm br
2 zbdbwl
3 zbdʿth

PAT **RTP 411**
Rev. 1 bl[..]

PAT 2340 **RTP 412**
Rev. 1 [...]
2 [..]by[..]
3 mlʾš[...]

PAT 2341 **RTP 419**
Rev. 1 zbdl[h]
2 bwr[pʾ]

PAT 2342 **RTP 420**
Obv. 1 ʾmršʾ
Rev. 1 ʿgylw
2 ʾšqrʾ

PAT 2343 **RTP 421**
Rev. 1 yrḥbwlʾ
2 ʿwydw

PAT 2344 **RTP 424**
Obv. 1 ḥyrʾ
Rev. 1 ʿwydʾ
2 bn[..]mn

PAT 2345 **RTP 425**
Rev. 1 [ʾ]wṭyq[ʾ] / [ʾ]wṭyk[ʾ]

PAT 2346 **RTP 429**
Obv. 1 yrḥy
2 ʿgʾ
Rev. 1 yrḥy
2 ʿgʾ

PAT 2347 **RTP 432**
Obv. 1 mqymw
2 wmlʾ

PAT 2348 **RTP 436**
Rev. 1 bydʾ
2 br b[...]

PAT 2349 **RTP 437**
Obv. 1 ʾgn b<ʿ>ltk

PAT 2350 **RTP 438**

Obv. 1 [..]ḥlny/[..]tbny

PAT 2351 **RTP 439**
Rev. 1 ʾply
2 klbʾ

PAT 2352 **RTP 441**
Rev. 1 yrḥbwlʾ
2 zbydʾ

PAT 2353 **RTP 451**
Rev. 1 tymy br
2 zbdʿth

PAT 2354 **RTP 457**
Rev. 1 lbny
2 ḥšš

PAT 2355 **RTP 461**
Obv. 1 rmšʾ

PAT 2356 **RTP 463**
Obv. 1 bw[n]ʾ br ḥyrn

PAT 2357 **RTP 464**
Rev. 1 pṣgw

PAT 2358 **RTP 465**
Obv. 1 mlkw ḥyrn

PAT 2359 **RTP 466**
Obv. 1 [...] rbʾ

PAT 2360 **RTP 468**
Rev. 1 zbdʾ br
2 mqym[w]

PAT 2361 **RTP 469**
Obv. 1 mlkw br [ʿ]tntn
Rev. 1 ḥmyˀ

PAT 2362 **RTP 472**
Rev. 1 [.]bwl[...]

PAT 2363 **RTP 473**
Rev. 1 ḥggw
2 [z]bdlʾ

PAT 2364 **RTP 474**
Rev. 1 ʿgʾ
2 ʿgʾ

PAT 2365 **RTP 477**
Rev. 1 ʿgylw
2 bwnʾ

PAT 2366 **RTP 480**
Obv. 1 ḥyrn
Rev. 1 sṭm
2 ḥyrn
3 ʾšʿʿ

PAT 2367 **RTP 482**
Obv. 1 [...]
2 br[...]
Rev. 1 ḥyrn
2 mlkw

PAT 2368 **RTP 485**
Obv. 1 ḥyrn
2 ʾdyn[t]
Rev. 1 bwr[..]

PAT 2369 **RTP 486**
Obv. 1 ḥdwdn
Rev. 1 [ḥd]wdn
2 mq[y]

PAT 2370 **RTP 488**
Rev. 1 [m]tnʾ
2 [ḥy]rn

PAT 2371 **RTP 489**
Obv. 1 [...]
Rev. 1 yrḥy

PAT 2372 **RTP 490**
Obv. 1 ḥdwdn
2 mqy
Rev. 1 ḥdwdn

PAT 2373 **RTP 491**
Obv. 1 ḥdwdn
2 mqy
Rev. 1 ḥdwdn

PAT 2374 **RTP 492**
Obv. 1 ḥdwdn
2 mqy
Rev. 1 ḥdwdn
2 mqy

PAT 2375 **RTP 493**
Obv. 1 ʿbʾ
2 yrḥy
Rev. 1 mzbnʾ
2 yrḥy

PAT 2376 **RTP 494**
Rev. 1 šʿdw
2 ʿwydy

PAT 2377 **RTP 495**
Obv. 1 ḥdwdn
2 mqy

PAT 2378 **RTP 500**
Obv. 1 tymʾ
2 [...]

PAT 2379 **RTP 503**
Rev. 1 bny
2 ʾʿly

PAT 2380 **RTP 505**
Obv. 1 [...] rpbwl

PAT 2381 **RTP 506**
Rev. 1 d<bšʾ>/r<bʿyʾ> 2

PAT 2382 **RTP 507**
Obv. 1 ʿbdy
2 br mk
3 gbrʾ
4 ṭbʾ

PAT 2383 **RTP 508**
Rev. 1 mqy
mʿn[w]/mʿn[y]

PAT 2384 **RTP 511**
Obv. 1 hyklʾ

PAT 2385 **RTP 512**
Obv. 1 ḥ tˀ y

PAT 2386 **RTP 516**
Rev. 1 ʿgyl[w]

PAT 2387 **RTP 518**
Rev. 1 pʿl[...]

PAT 2388 **RTP 522**
Obv. 1 bnn
Lead

PAT 2389 **RTP 523**
Obv. 1 mqymw

PAT 2390 **RTP 525**
Obv. 1 byt
2 ḥlyt[ʾ]
Rev. 1 sṭmʾ

PAT 2391 **RTP 526**
Obv. 1 ḥmr
2 plg

PAT 2392 **RTP 533**
Obv. 1 [š]ʿdy

PAT 2393 **RTP 535**
Obv. 1 mlʾ

PAT 2394 **RTP 537**
Obv. 1 ʿgylw
2 ʿgylw
3 ʾšm

PAT 2395 **RTP 541**
Obv. 1 ḥmr

PAT 2396 **RTP 547**
Rev. 1 bryqy
2 yrḥbwl

PAT 2397 **RTP 548**
Obv. 1 bʿltk
Rev. 1 mlkw

PAT 2398 **RTP 549**
Rev. 1 ʿzyzw

PAT 2399 **RTP 550**
Obv. 1 ḥyrʾ
2 šʿdw
Rev. 1 ḥyrʾ
2 šʿdw

PAT 2400 **RTP 551**
Obv. 1 yrḥy
Rev. 1 mlk
2 wsʾ

PAT 2401 **RTP 552**
Rev. 1 yhybʾ

PAT 2402 **RTP 553**
Rev. 1 [..]b[..]

PAT 2403 **RTP 554**
Rev. 1 bryk
2 tym
3 y

PAT 2404 **RTP 555**
Rev. 1 brʿ
2 th

PAT 2405 **RTP 556**
Rev. 1 blydʿ

PAT 2406 **RTP 557**
Rev. 1 yrḥy
2 kyly

PAT 2407 **RTP 561**
Obv. 1 mlkw

PAT 2408 **RTP 562**
Rev. 1 ʿgʾ

PAT 2409 **RTP 563**
Obv. 1 mkl

PAT 2410 **RTP 564**
Rev. 1 plg
2 mkl

PAT 2411 **RTP 565**
Rev. 1 [...]
2 m[...]

PAT 2412 **RTP 566**
Rev. 1 m[...]
2 br [...]

PAT 2413 **RTP 567**
Obv. 1 mhrdt

PAT 2414 **RTP 569**
Obv. 1 plg

PAT 2415 **RTP 570**
Obv. 1 rbʿ

PAT 2416 **RTP 571**
Obv. 1 [r]bʿ

PAT 2417 **RTP 572**
Rev. 1 m ʾ

PAT 2418 **RTP 575**
Rev. 1 yrḥy
2 lšmš

PAT 2419 **RTP 576**
Rev. 1 mqymw
2 ḥyrn

PAT 2420 **RTP 579**
Obv. 1 lšmš
2 mqy

PAT 2421 **RTP 580**
IP 94
Rev. 1 m[q]ymw
2 zbydʾ

PAT 2422 **RTP 581**
Rev. 1 zbydʾ

PAT 2423 **RTP 585**
Obv. 1 šmʿrʾ
Rev. 1 twrʾ

PAT 2424 **RTP 586**
Rev. 1 χαρά
Obv. 1 bny ydyʿbl

PAT 2425 **RTP 590**
Obv. 1 [m]qymw

PAT 2426 **RTP 591**
Rev. 1 [...]y ʿgʾ

PAT 2427 **RTP 592**
Rev. 1 ḥ (on right) y (on left)

PAT 2428 **RTP 595**
Rev. 1 mqymw
2 [m]ndr[s]

PAT 2429 **RTP 610**
Déd p 158
Rev. 1 [...]
2 wn[...]
3 ʾblʿly

PAT 2430 **RTP 613**
Rev. 1 yrḥy b[...]

PAT 2431 **RTP 622**
Obv. 1 ʾbdy
Rev. 1 ʿgʾ

PAT 2432 **RTP 625**
Rev. (on left) 1 [ml]
2 kw
(on right) 1 ḥpr
2 tm?

PAT 2433 **RTP 626**
Obv. 1 zbydʾ

PAT 2434 **RTP 627**
Rev. 1 mq
2 ym
3 w

PAT 2435 **RTP 628**
Obv. 1 ʿw
2 yd

PAT 2436 **RTP 630**
Rev. 1 šlmlt mlkw
2 ḥyrn mʿnw

PAT 2437 **RTP 633**
Rev. 1 ydʿw
2 ʿbdy

PAT 2438 **RTP 638**
Rev. 1 ʾblʿly
2 mqymw
3 tybwl

PAT 2439 **RTP 640**
Obv. 1 [..]ḥmʾ
Rev. 1 yrḥy
2 zbdʿth
3 [b]wrpʾ

PAT 2440 **RTP 641**
Rev. 1 ršy br
2 mlkw

PAT 2441 **RTP 643**
Rev. 1 mlkw
2 ḥyrn
3 bšrʾ

PAT 2442 **RTP 645**
A.D. (108)
Déd p 248
Obv. 1 [...]
2 šn[t] 420[+?..]
On date, see RTP p 201

PAT 2443 **RTP 646**
Rev. 1 ḥyr[n]

PAT 2444 **RTP 647**
Obv. 1 ʿbʾ

PAT 2445 **RTP 650**
Rev. 1 ʿgʾ
2 ʿw[.]
Lead

PAT 2446 **RTP 651**
Obv. 1 mqymw

PAT 2447 **RTP 656**
Rev. 1 [lšm]š
2 [ʿg]ylw

PAT 2448 **RTP 659**
Rev. 1 zbydʾ

PAT 2449 **RTP 660**
Rev. 1 mqymw
2 br ydy

PAT 2450 **RTP 661**
Déd p 278
Obv. 1 mlkw br
2 ḥyrn br ql[..]ʾ

PAT 2451 **RTP 666**
Rev. 1 ḥyrn
2 ʿgylʾ

PAT 2452 **RTP 669**
Obv. 1 ΖΗΝΟΒΙΟΣ
Rev. 1 brʿth zbd[ʾ]

PAT 2453 **RTP 670**
Rev. 1 ʿtnw[r]y
2 ʿgylw

PAT 2454 **RTP 673**
Rev. 1 zbdʾ
2 gmrʾ

PAT 2455 **RTP 674**
Rev. 1 blty
2 wydy

PAT 2456 **RTP 680**
Déd p 150
Rev. 1 ʾgn gdʿtʾ dy bl

PAT 2457 **RTP 682**
Rev. 1 ʿbdšlmʾ
2 ʾrhdwn

PAT 2458 **RTP 684**
Rev. 1 [n$^{?}$]ʿym

PAT 2459 **RTP 687**
Obv. 1 nšʾ
Rev. 1 nšʾ

PAT 2460 **RTP 689**
Déd p 186
Obv. 1 m<kl> 1

PAT 2461 **RTP 690**
Obv. 1 mkl

PAT 2462 **RTP 691**
A.D. 118
Déd p 186
Obv. 1 m<kl> 1
Rev. 1 mlkʾl
2 [šn]t 4.100+20+10
On date, see RTP p 201

PAT 2463 **RTP 692**
Déd p 185
Obv. 1 m<kl> 3

PAT 2464 **RTP 693**
Déd p 185
Obv. 1 m<kl> 4

PAT 2465 **RTP 694**
Déd p 191
Obv. 1 ḥmr mkl wplg
2 qrš bsmk[ʾ]

PAT 2466 **RTP 695**
Déd p 191
Obv. 1 ḥmr mkl wplg
2 qrš bsmk[ʾ]

PAT 2467 **RTP 696**
Déd p 191
Obv. 1 ḥmr mkl wplg
2 [qr]š bsmkʾ
Rev. 1 whblt
2 šmʿ[wn]

PAT 2468 **RTP 697**
Déd p 191, 278
Obv. 1 ḥmr mkl wplg
2 qrš smkʾ
Rev. 1 ʾbb
2 ḥyrn
3 mlkw

PAT 2469 **RTP 698**
Déd p 191
Obv. 1 ḥmr
2 mklw
3 plg
4 qrš
5 bsmkʾ

PAT 2470 **RTP 699**
Déd p 191
Obv. 1 ḥmr
2 mkl
3 wplg
4 qrš
Rev. 1 bwrpʾ

PAT 2471 **RTP 700**
Déd p 191
Obv. 1 ḥmr mkl
2 [w]plg q[r]š
Rev. 1 lqnys brs

PAT 2472 **RTP 701**
Obv. 1 mkl
2 [w]plg
3 ḥmr
4 ḥ[d]t
5 [q]rš

PAT 2473 **RTP 702**
Déd p 191
Obv. 1 mkl
2 wp[l]g
3 ḥdt

PAT 2474 **RTP 703**
Obv. 1 ḥmr plg mkl

PAT 2475 **RTP 704**
Obv. 1 ḥmr plg mkl
Rev. 1 mlkw mqymw ʾgtʾ

PAT 2476 **RTP 705**
Obv. 1 plg p?ʾly

PAT 2477 **RTP 706**
Obv. 1 dmy ḥmrʾ
Rev. 1 šmʿ[r]y

PAT 2478 **RTP 707**
Obv. 1 ʿz[y]
2 ḥmr
3 šmn

PAT 2479 **RTP 708**
Obv. 1 ʿzy ḥmrʾ
2 wšmn
Rev. 1 ʿzy

PAT 2480 **RTP 709**
Obv. 1 ʿgylw
2 kytwt
Rev. 1 mšḥ[ʾ]
2 rbʿ[ʾ]

PAT 2481 **RTP 714**
IP 92
Obv. 1 bʿltk
2 ʿtʿqb

PAT 2482 **RTP 715**
Obv. 1 bʿltk
2 yrḥy ʿbʾ
Rev. 1 bʿltk
2 zbdʾ
3 ydyʿbl

PAT 2483 **RTP 716**
Obv. 1 bʿltk
2 lšmš

PAT 2484 **RTP 717**
Obv. 1 bʿlt[k]

PAT 2485 **RTP 718**
Obv. 1 gdʾ
2 ṭbʾ
3 lbny
4 bwlḥʾ
Rev. 1 ydy
2 ʾmyn

PAT 2486 **RTP 719**
Rev. 1 mʿny

PAT 2487 **RTP 720**
Obv. 1 sṭm[ʾ]
2 mytʾ
3 ywm 5+3
Rev. 1 bly
2 zbydʾ
3 mlkw
4 nṣrlt

PAT 2488 **RTP 721**
Obv. 1 by<wm> 5+2

PAT 2489 **RTP 722**
Rev. 1 tbrk
2 ʿynʾ dh
3 lmgbr
4 dy
5 ʿdr bh

PAT 2490 **RTP 724**
Obv. 1 whblt br
2 šmʿwn

PAT 2491 **RTP 725**
Obv. 1 ʾlhšʾ tymšʾ

PAT 2492 **RTP 727**
Rev. 1 ḥgy

PAT 2493 **RTP 729**
Obv. 1 mlkw ḥyrn

PAT 2494 **RTP 730**
Obv. 1 mlkw
2 bryk[y]
Rev. 1 mlk
3 w bryky

PAT 2495 **RTP 731**
Obv. 1 ʿgy
2 lw
3 kptwt
Rev. 1 šmʿwn
2 kptwt

PAT 2496 **RTP 734**
Obv. 1 zb<dʾ>
2 ty<my>
Rev. 1 zb<dʾ>
2 ml<kw>
See Stark PN "Lexicon": all are abbr

PAT 2497 **RTP 736**
Obv. 1 ḥyrn
2 ʾdynt
Rev. 1 whblt
2 ʾdynt

PAT 2498 **RTP 737**
A.D. 107
Déd p 228
Obv. 1 byrḥ ʾ[d]ʾr/ʾ[y]r šnt 4.100+10+5+4
On date, see RTP p 201

PAT 2499 **RTP 739**
Rev. 1 mzbnʾ
2 tymrṣ[w]

PAT 2500 **RTP 740**
Rev. 1 [ty]mrṣ[w]
2 br tymrṣw

PAT 2501 **RTP 741**
Obv. 1 ḥy<rn> šr<ykw>
Rev. 1 ḥyrn
2 šrykw

PAT 2502 **RTP 742**
Obv. 1 ḥyrn
2 šr

3 ykw
Rev. 1 ḥyrn
2 šr
3 ykw

PAT 2503 **RTP 743**
Obv. 1 mzbnʾ
2 wtymrṣ
Rev. 1 tymrṣw
2 tymrṣw

PAT 2504 **RTP 745**
ReReObv.
1 rbʾl
2 zbydʾ

PAT 2505 **RTP 746**
Obv. 1 bly
2 whblt
Rev. 1 ḥyrn
2 ʾdy[nt]

PAT 2506 **RTP 749**
Rev. 1 qrynw br nbwzbd

PAT 2507 **RTP 752**
IP 97
Rev. 1 sṭm
2 bwnʾ blty

PAT 2508 **RTP 753**
Obv. 1 [ʾr]ṣw
Rev. 1 ḥdwdn

PAT 2509 **RTP 754**
Rev. 1 mlkw br
2 bwrpʾ

PAT 2510 **RTP 756**
Obv. 1 ʿtʿqb
2 ḥyr[n]
Rev. 1 bwrpʾ

PAT 2511 **RTP 758**
Déd p 186
Obv. 1 šbʿʾ
Rev. 1 d<bšʾ> (or: r<bʿyʾ> 2 (or: m<kl>)

PAT 2512 **RTP 759**
Obv. 1 bydʾ
Glass

PAT 2513 **RTP 760**
Obv. 1 [šl]m[lt]
Rev. 1 šlmlt br tymʾ ʿwydy

PAT 2514 **RTP 761**
Obv. 1 ymlkw mqymw
2 ʾqlyš

PAT 2515 **RTP 762**
Obv. 1 ḥyrn[..]
2 [...]

PAT 2516 **RTP 763**
Obv. 1 yrḥbwlʾ mlkw
2 ʾʿby

PAT 2517 **RTP 764**
Obv. 1 [m]lkw [br] t[y]mʾ
Rev. 1 mlkw br tymʾ
2 br ʿšyltʾ

PAT 2518 **RTP 765**
Déd p 279
Obv. 1 whblt mlkw
Rev. 1 whblt
2 br mlkw
3 rpnw

PAT 2519 **RTP 766**
Rev. 1 [ml]kw br mq[y]m[w]
2 [.]š[..]

PAT 2520 **RTP 767**
Obv. 1 šmšgrm
2 nwrbl

PAT 2521 **RTP 770**
Obv. 1 [m]lkw ḥyrn ʾʿb[y]

PAT 2522 **RTP 773**
Obv. 1 nšwm mlkw
2 nšwm

PAT 2523 **RTP 774**
Obv. 1 [n]šwm mlkw

PAT 2524 **RTP 775**
Déd p 253
Obv. 1 zb[d]ʾ
2 ʾlhšʾ
3 ṣʿdy

PAT 2525 **RTP 776**
Obv. 1 lqnys brs

PAT 2526 **RTP 777**
Déd p 279
Obv. 1 [bl]ty tymʿm[d]

PAT 2527 **RTP 778**
Obv. 1 ΙΟΥΛΙΟΣ
2 ΒΑΣΣΟΣ
Rev. 1 nšwm [br zbd]ʾ br mlkw nšwm

PAT 2528 **RTP 779**
Obv. 1 rpbwl yrḥy

PAT 2529 **RTP 780**
Obv. 1 nbw[...]

PAT 2530 **RTP 781**
Obv. 1 [...]ml[..]

PAT 2531 **RTP 783**
Rev. 1 ḥyrʾ

2 yrḥy
3 ʿmrt

PAT 2532 **RTP 785**
A.D. (140)
Déd p 247
Obv. 1 [..] qspryns
2 [..]mw[..]
Rev. 1 šnt
4.100+20+[20+10+2]
On date, see RTP p 104, Déd p 247 :: RTP p 201

PAT 2533 **RTP 786**
Obv. 1 [...]šʾ

PAT 2534 **RTP 787**
Obv. 1 whblt
2 ḥyrn
Rev. 1 whb
2 lt
3 ḥyrn

PAT 2535 **RTP 789**
Déd p 248
Obv. 1 [..]ymʾʿn[.]

PAT 2536 **RTP 791**
Obv. 1 tybwl

PAT 2537 **RTP 792**
Obv. 1 zbydʾ

PAT 2538 **RTP 793**
Obv. 1 bwrʾ

PAT 2539 **RTP 795**
Obv. 1 bwnʾ
Rev. 1 bwrʾ

PAT 2540 **RTP 796**
Obv. 1 ḥy[rn]

PAT 2541 **RTP 797**
Obv. 1 yrḥy
Rev. 1 yrḥy

PAT 2542 **RTP 798**
Obv. 1 yh
2 ybʾ
Rev. 1 yr
2 ḥy

PAT 2543 **RTP 799**
Obv. 1 ḥy<rn>
2 ʿgy<lw>

PAT 2544 **RTP 802**
Obv. 1 ydʿnw
Rev. 1 zbdbwl

PAT 2545 **RTP 804**
Obv. 1 b[w]lmʾ/b[w]lḥʾ
ḥyrn

PAT 2546 **RTP 805**
Obv. 1 zbydʾ
Rev. 1 rpb<wl>

PAT 2547 **RTP 806**
Déd p 265
Obv. 1 prṭnks

PAT 2548 **RTP 807**
RES 1063
Obv. 1 [ʾdy]nt

PAT 2549 **RTP 810**
Obv. (on left) 1 bry
2 kw
(on right) 3 blydʿ

PAT 2550 **RTP 812**
Obv. 1 mʿny
Rev. 1 ḥbʾ

PAT 2551 **RTP 813**
Obv. 1 yhybʾ
Rev. 1 bwrʾ

PAT 2552 **RTP 818**
Rev. 1 q[ry]nw
2 nbwzbd

PAT 2553 **RTP 819**
Rev. 1 zbdʿth
2 mtnʾ
3 ʾnqy

PAT 2554 **RTP 821**
Obv. 1 šlmʾ
2 mlk[w]

PAT 2555 **RTP 822**
Obv. 1 nbwzbd
2 br zbydʾ

PAT 2556 **RTP 825**
Obv. 1 škyy br
2 whblt

PAT 2557 **RTP 828**
Obv. 1 [ʿ]gyl[w]

PAT 2558 **RTP 830**
Obv. 1 zbdlh br zbdʿth
mykʾ
Rev. 1 zbdlh
2 zbdʿth
3 mykʾ

PAT 2559 **RTP 831**
Déd p 278
Obv. 1 mlkw ʿtnw<ry>

PAT 2560 **RTP 835**
Obv. 1 lqnys br[s]

PAT 2561 **RTP 836**
Rev. 1 zbdʿth
2 mtnʾ
Glass

PAT 2562 **RTP 837**
Rev. 1 nšwm
2 br zbd'
3 br mlkw.
4 nšwm

PAT 2563 **RTP 838**
Obv. 1 mlkw
2 w't'qb

PAT 2564 **RTP 840**
Rev. 1 ḥd'

PAT 2565 **RTP 848**
Obv. 1 nš'

PAT 2566 **RTP 850**
Obv. 1 šm
2 'wn
Rev. 1 kp
2 [twt]

PAT 2567 **RTP 851**
Rev. 1 ḥdwdn
2 'wyd'
3 [ḥdwd]n

PAT 2568 **RTP 853**
Rev. 1 ml
2 kw

PAT 2569 **RTP 854**
Obv. 1 šky

PAT 2570 **RTP 855**
Rev. 1 mzbn'
2 nwrbl

PAT 2571 **RTP 858**
Obv. 1 bwrp'
Rev. 1 plyn'

PAT 2572 **RTP 864**
Obv. 1 šm'wn
Rev. 1 kptwt

PAT 2573 **RTP 867**
Obv. 1 kln

PAT 2574 **RTP 870**
Obv. 1 ḥyr[n]
Rev. 1 šryk[w]

PAT 2575 **RTP 871**
Rev. 1 ḥyrn
2 šrykw

PAT 2576 **RTP 874**
Obv. 1 ml
2 [k]w
3 [...]

PAT 2577 **RTP 877**
Obv. 1 bl
2 'qb

PAT 2578 **RTP 881**
Rev. 1 bwn'

PAT 2579 **RTP 884**
Obv. 1 'bd'
2 'yyr
Obv. 2: with Stark PN p 121

PAT 2580 **RTP 885**
Rev. 1 'gylw

PAT 2581 **RTP 887**
Rev. 1 rpb[w]l
2 blḥzy

PAT 2582 **RTP 889**
Rev. 1 tymrṣw

PAT 2583 **RTP 890**
Rev. 1 šm'[w]n

PAT 2584 **RTP 891**
Rev. 1 'bd'
2 br tym'

PAT 2585 **RTP 892**
Obv. 1 r?'' / d?''

PAT 2586 **RTP 893**
Obv. 1 'g'

PAT 2587 **RTP 898**
Obv. 1 [...]wzy

PAT 2588 **RTP 899**
Obv. 1 ml'
Rev. 1 'g'

PAT 2589 **RTP 901**
Rev. 1 rb'l

PAT 2590 **RTP 903**
Rev. 1 bršgl

PAT 2591 **RTP 906**
Rev. 1 bwn'

PAT 2592 **RTP 908**
Obv. 1 ''
2 wy

PAT 2593 **RTP 909**
Obv. 1 bwr
2 '

PAT 2594 **RTP 911**
Rev. 1 rb'l

PAT 2595 **RTP 912**
Rev. 1 mzbn'
2 ṣlm'

PAT 2596 **RTP 913**

Rev. 1 plwy
2 nʾ

PAT 2597 **RTP 914**
Obv. 1 mrnʾ

PAT 2598 **RTP 933**
Rev. 1 zmry
2 bpnyʾ

PAT 2599 **RTP 942**
Rev. 1 [...]
2 qštʾ

PAT 2600 **RTP 951**
Rev. 1 ḥbʾ

PAT 2601 **RTP 954**
Rev. 1 tybwl
2 ḥyrn
3 mndrs

PAT 2602 **RTP 957**
Rev. 1 ḥyrn
2 [...]
3 [...]

PAT 2603 **RTP 964**
Rev. 1 mlkw
2 nšʾ

PAT 2604 **RTP 977**
Obv. 1 bny šzʾ

PAT 2605 **RTP 978**
Obv. 1 yrḥy
2 ʿbšy

PAT 2606 **RTP 979**
Obv. 1 mqymw ʿstwrgʾ

PAT 2607 **RTP 983**
Obv. 1 yrḥy

PAT 2608 **RTP 985**
Obv. 1 bny
2 yšwʿlʾ

PAT 2609 **RTP 986**
Obv. 1 ḥyrn

PAT 2610 **RTP 987**
Obv. 1 drḥlwn
2 ydy mtny

PAT 2611 **RTP 990**
Obv. 1 blkz/blsz
2 tymʿmd
3 bwrpʾ
Lead

PAT 2612 **RTP 991**
Obv. 1 rḥ/rṣ
Rev. 1 yr<ḥy>
Iron

PAT 2613 **RTP 992**
Obv. 1 mlkw
2 tymy
Rev. 1 ʿmt

PAT 2614 **RTP 993**
Obv. 1 šlm bny
2 bwnʾ
Rev. 1 ḥṭrʾ/ḥldʾ
2 brʿth

PAT 2615 **RTP 994**
Obv. 1 yʿqwb

PAT 2616 **RTP 995**
Obv. 1 mlkw
2 zbdbwl
Rev. 1 ʿtnwry
2 zbdbl

PAT 2617 **RTP 996**
IP 100
Obv. 1 ʿtʿqb
2 brʿth
Rev. 1 [...]
2 bl[..]

PAT 2618 **RTP 997**
Obv. 1 zbydʾ
2 ʿštwr
Rev. 1 sṭm
2 ywm
3 ʾʿšr

PAT 2619 **RTP 1045**
Obv. 1 zbdbwl

PAT 2620 **RTP 1056**
Obv. 1 zbdʾ

PAT 2621 **RTP 1090**
Obv. 1 br[..]w

PAT 2622 **RTP 1124**
Obv. 1 myr̊ḥ/tyr̊ḥ

PAT 2623 **RTP 1132**
Obv. 1 bl

PAT 2624 **Sem '50 p 47** **n. d.**
Prov: Palmyrene, Jebel Gattar. Loc: Palmyra, A 1106. *Dedicatory. On relief.*

(above, right)
1 [š]lmn
(above, left)

1 ʾrgyʿ/ʾdgyʿ
(above sacrificer)
1 šlmn br
2 šmʿwn npry/npdy
(dedication)
1 ʿbd
2 šmʿwn
3 npry/npdy
4 lšlmn wlʾrgyʿ/ʾdgyʿ
6 gnyʾ
7 ṭbyʾ
8 wškryʾ

PAT 2625 **Sem '72 p 59** **A.D. (138)**
Prov: Palmyra or Palmyrene. Loc: Beirut: Henri Pharaon Collection. *Dedicatory. On stele.*

1 [...] ιουνυ [..................]ν Μοκι[?][μ]ος κ[αὶ...]
2 [...] βειβο [..................]γοα.[......]αθε
3 [...........]

(Below statues)
a. [m]lkw
b. [...]w
c. [mqymw]
d. mṣ[bt ...]
(Dedication: to right of god's head)
1 mṣbʾ dnh
2 lmnʿym gnyʾ
3 ṭbʾ wškrʾ
4 dyrʾ dy
5 qrytʾ
(On plinth)
6 [byrḥ] tšry šnt 4.100+[40+10]

PAT 2626 **Sem '73 p 121** **n. d.**
Prov: Palmyra. Loc: Paris, Bibliothèque Nationale, Cabinet de Médailles. *Dedicatory. On clay medallion.* Bib: Ing '30a, p 146; PNO, p 167; Nilsson '33 p 162; Seyrig '33c p 247; Février '34b p 12; TMP, pl CCXXIV; TMP p 568, hand-copy fig 272.

1 qrbw
2 [m]dmryʾ
3 mdy ḥš<ʾ>
4 <lb>ʿšmn
5 ʾlhʾ ṭbʾ
6 lḥyyhw<n>
Formerly, Froehner Collection; text after Gaw p 123; see also Glossary s v. *ḥš* and *ḥšḥ*

PAT 2627 **Sem '74 p 68** no. 1 **n. d.**
Prov: Uncertain. Loc: Beirut: Charles Kettaneh Collection. *Funerary. On stele.*

1 šlmt ʾtt
2 ydyʿbl
3 ḥbl

PAT 2628 **Sem '74 p 69** no. 2 **n. d.**
Prov: Uncertain. Loc: Jerusalem, Bible Land Museum, BLMJ 2587. *Funerary. On relief.*

1 lšmš br
2 ʿgylw br
3 ymlkw
4 ḥbl

PAT 2629 **Sem '74 p 72** no. 4 **n. d.**
Prov: Uncertain. Loc: Beirut, Chiha Collection. *Funerary. On relief.*

1 ḥbl
2 mky brt
3 mlʾ zbydʾ

PAT 2630 **Sem '74 p 73** no. 5 **n. d.**
Prov: Uncertain. Loc: Beirut: Henri Pharaon Collection. *Funerary. On relief.*

1 ṣlm ḥyrʾ br
2 rpbwl tybwl
3 šnt 5.100+60
4 +4

PAT 2631 **Sem '77 p 106** **n. d.**
Prov: Palmyra, Diocletian Camp, Temple of Allât. Loc: Palmyra, CD 6/74. *Dedicatory. On votive bronze.* Bib: *Hand copy fig 1, p 106; pl XIII.*

1 mwdʾ
2 ʿbʾ

3 bʿšmn
Below figure of hand

PAT 2632 **Sem '77 p 117** **A.D. 182**
Prov: ʿArqâ (Lebanon) N of Tripoli. Loc: ʿArqâ, private collection. *Dedicatory. On stone block.*

(Upper margin)
1 dkyr blg br mʿyr
(On plaque)
1 byrḥ ʾyr šnt 4.100
2 +80+10+3 ḥgbʾ wmṣbʾ
3 ʿbd whblt br zbydʾ whb
4 lt qmylʾ ltšʿytʾ
5 wrḥmnytʾ ʿl ḥywh wḥyʾ
6 ʾḥwh wbnwh wdkyr qdm ʾln
7 ʾnš ʾnš kd šwʾ mn tnn
8 lšlmyt mynyn mšṭ[rtʾ]
(Lower margin)
9 ʾrbʿʾ

PAT 2633 **Sem '79 p 106** **n. d.**
Prov: Palmyra. Loc: Paris, Emmanuel Koutoulakis Collection. *Funerary. On relief.* Bib: *Pl V.*

1 lšmšw br
2 mqymw ḥršw

PAT 2634 **Sem '86 p 89** **n. d.**
Prov: Palmyra, Valley of Tombs, Umm Belqîs, Tower no. 70. Loc: Palmyra, *in situ. Unclassified. On wall.* Group: C4206, 4207, 4208, Sem '86 p 89. Bib: *Pls. XV (photo), XVI (hand copy).*

1 ʾrbwʿʾ mkyl yrḥ ʾḥd zwzyyn
2 rbwʾn ʾlpyn tryn wmʾtn wtltyn wšt
3 wʾlpyn tšʿh wštmʾh wʾrbʿyn wḥd wmʿyn trtn
4 hwyn slʿyn rbwʾn ḥmš mʾh wḥmšyn wtšʿ wʾlpyn tryn
5 wʾrbʿ mʾh wḥmš wzwz ḥd wmʿyn trtyn hwyn kkryn
6 ʾlpyn tltʾ wšbʿm wʿšryn wslʿʾ wmnyn ʿšrh
7 wšth wslʿyn ḥmš wzwz mʿyn trtn

PAT 2635 **Sem '91 p 84** **n. d.**
Prov: (Palmyra). Loc: Private collection. *Dedicatory. On altar.* Bib: *Fig 1.*

1 bryk šmh lʿl[mʾ]
2 ṭbʾ wrḥmnʾ
3 ʿbd wmwdʾ ntn
4 br wrwd wbltʾ
5 ʾtth dy q[rw]
6 lh wpṣ?[...]

PAT 2636 **Sem '93 p 164** **A.D. 10**
Prov: Palmyra, uncertain. Loc: Palmyra, 1485/8973. *Dedicatory. On stone plaque.* Bib: *Fig 1 p 165.*

1 ktlʾ dnh dy blwyʾ dy
2 gmlyʾ dy lʿl mnh dy blw
3 gbl tdmryʾ klhwn ʿl
4 ʿtntn kptwt br brʿʾ
5 wʿl ymlkw brh dy mn bny
6 mytʾ lyqrhwn šnt
7 3.100+20+3
Word-division of Gawlikowski is given; uncertain in some respects see Glossary s.v. *blw*

PAT 2637 **SFP 1** **n. d.**
Prov: Palmyra, S-E necropolis. Loc: Palmyra, 1238/6330. *Funerary. On bust.* Group: Hypogeum 3 (Sarcophagus of Shoraiku and SFP 1 -3). Bib: *Fig 180.*

1 ṣlmt
2 tmʾ
3 ʾtt
4 šr̊ykw br
5 blḥzy
6 ḥbl
Text above from fig 180; line 1: ṣlmt is read šlmt (PN) by Bounni et al; 2 tmʾ: tymḥʾ is read by Bounni; 4-5: last letters not visible on fig 180

PAT 2638 **SFP 3** no. 5
Prov: Palmyra. Loc: Palmyra, A 1239/6332. *Funerary. On sarcophagus. Fig 239*; for others in this group see Ber '70 p 77 - p 80; Gawlikowski '70a.

1 šlmt brt
2 šrykw
3 ḥbl

Text must be by Makowski or Bounni (inscription numbers in notes of SFP are puzzling at this point); called "illisible" by Gaw Ber '70 p 80

PAT 2639 **SFP 15** **n. d.**
Prov: Palmyra, S-E necropolis, hypogeum no. 4. Loc: Palmyra, A 1240/6405. *Funerary. On stele.* Group: Hypogeum of Ashtor son of Maliku (SFP 4 -18). Bib: *Fig 1.*

1 yrḥy br
2 ʾydʿn ʿbdy
3 ḥbl

line 2 ʾydʿn (from fig 1): gyrḥn read by Bounni in SFP

PAT 2640 **SFP 16** **n. d.**
Prov: Palmyra, S-E necropolis, hypogeum no. 4. Loc: Palmyra, A 1241/6406. *Funerary. On stele.* Group: Hypogeum of Ashtor son of Maliku (SFP 4 -18). Bib: *Fig 5*; Tanabe '86 pl 260.

1 ḥbl
2 ḥyrʾ
3 br zbdlh
4 ḥbl

PAT 2641 **SFP 17** **n. d.**
Prov: Palmyra, S-E necropolis, hypogeum no. 4. Loc: Palmyra, A 1242/6407. *Funerary. On Stele.* Group: Hypogeum of Ashtor son of Maliku (SFP 4 -18). Bib: *Fig 12*; Tanabe '86 pl 270.

1 ḥbl šlwʾ
2 brt ymlʾ

PAT 2642 **SFP 19** **n. d.**
Prov: Palmyra: S-E necropolis, hypogeum no. 5. Loc: Palmyra, *in situ* (SFP p 25). *Funerary. On bust.* Group: Hypogeum of Artaban (SFP 19 - 43). Bib: *Fig 83*; Tanabe '86 pl 236.

1 ḥbl ydy
2 br nṣr
3 br ydy

PAT 2643 **SFP 20** **n. d.**
Prov: Palmyra: S-E necropolis, hypogeum no. 5. Loc: Palmyra, *in situ* (SFP p 25). *Funerary. On bust.* Group: Hypogeum of Artaban (SFP 19 - 43). Bib: *Fig 29*; Tanabe '86 pl 234.

1 šmšgrm br
2 ʿgʾ br ʾrṭbn
3 ḥbl

PAT 2644 **SFP 21** **n. d.**
Prov: Palmyra: S-E necropolis, hypogeum no. 5. Loc: Palmyra, *in situ* (SFP p 25). *Funerary. On bust.* Group: Hypogeum of Artaban (SFP 19 - 43). Bib: *Fig 32*; Tanabe '86 pl 235.

1 ʾrṭbn dy
2 mtqrʾ zbdwn
3 br mlkw br yrḥy
4 nyqʾ ʾpklʾ ṭbʾ
5 dy ʿglbwl wmlkbl

line 4: nyqʾ! :: SFP nydʾ

PAT 2645 **SFP 22** **n. d.**
Prov: Palmyra: S-E necropolis, hypogeum no. 5. Loc: Palmyra, *in situ* (SFP p 25). *Funerary. On bust.* Group: Hypogeum of Artaban (SFP 19 - 43). Bib: *Fig 151*; Tanabe '86 pl 234.

1 ḥbl bʿltgʾ
2 brt ʿgʾ br
3 nṣrʾ ḥbl

line 3: nṣrʾ! ḥby :: SFP nṣr ḥby (but genealogical table SFP p 23 implies nṣr ʾḥby or ʾḥyb)

PAT 2646 **SFP 23** **n. d.**
Prov: Palmyra: S-E necropolis, hypogeum no. 5. Loc: Palmyra, *in situ* (SFP p 25). *Funerary. On bust.* Group: Hypogeum of Artaban (SFP 19 - 43). Bib: *Fig 70.*

1 ṣlmʾ dh dy (?? see note below) šlmlt
2 br ʿgʾ mlkw

3 dy ʿbd lh!
4 šlmlt br
5 ʿbdlt!(?) btr
6 dy myt lyqrh

Inscription illegible from fig 70 of SFP, and transliteration in text (p 28) evidently in error, judging from the accompanying translation; the above text contains our conjectures, as marked.

PAT 2647 **SFP 24** **n. d.**

Prov: Palmyra: S-E necropolis, hypogeum no. 5. Loc: Palmyra, *in situ* (SFP p 25). *Funerary. On bust.* Group: Hypogeum of Artaban (SFP 19 - 43). Bib: *Fig 59.*

1 ABEIBIΩNA
2 KAI NAΣ
3 PAION MAΛ
4 XOY TOY
5 APTABABANOY
6 MNHMHΣ
7 XAPIN

1 ḥbybywn dy
2 mtqrʾ
3 nṣry br
4 mlkw
5 ʾrṭbn
6 ḥbl

Text scarcely legible in fig 59

PAT 2648 **SFP 25** **n. d.**

Prov: Palmyra: S-E necropolis, hypogeum no. 5. Loc: Palmyra, *in situ* (SFP p 25). *Funerary. On bust.* Group: Hypogeum of Artaban (SFP 19 - 43). Bib: *Fig 120.*

1 ʾr̊ṭbn
2 br̊
3 rmnw
4 ḥbl

PAT 2649 **SFP 26** **n. d.**

Prov: Palmyra: S-E necropolis, hypogeum no. 5. Loc: Palmyra, *in situ* (SFP p 25). *Funerary. On bust.* Group: Hypogeum of Artaban (SFP 19 - 43). Bib: *Fig 115.*

(On left) 6 lines illegible

(On right) 6 lines illegible

PAT 2650 **SFP 27** **n. d.**

Prov: Palmyra: S-E necropolis, hypogeum no. 5. Loc: Palmyra, *in situ* (SFP p 25). *Funerary. On bust.* Group: Hypogeum of Artaban (SFP 19 - 43). Bib: *Fig 71.*

1 ḥbl
2 mlkw
3 br ʿgʾ
4 ʾrṭbn

PAT 2651 **SFP 28** **n. d.**

Prov: Palmyra: S-E necropolis, hypogeum no. 5. Loc: Palmyra, *in situ* (SFP p 25). *Funerary. On bust.* Group: Hypogeum of Artaban (SFP 19 - 43). Bib: *Fig 175.*

(On right, 5 lines [SFP p 31], mostly illegible)
. . . KAMNYNA MAΛIXOY APTABABANOY . . .
NA(!?)ΣP . . .ΔK

(On left)
1 ḥbl kmnyn brt mlkw
2 ʾrṭbn ʾtth nṣr

Inscriptions on Fig 175 illegible, text from SFP p 31, scarcely correct in every detail

PAT 2652 **SFP 29** **n. d.**

Prov: Palmyra: S-E necropolis, hypogeum no. 5. Loc: Palmyra, *in situ* (SFP p 25). *Funerary. On bust.* Group: Hypogeum of Artaban (SFP 19 - 43). Bib: *Fig 93.*

(On right, illegible [SFP p 31])

PAT 2653 **SFP 30** **n. d.**

Prov: Palmyra: S-E necropolis, hypogeum no. 5. Loc: Palmyra, *in situ* (SFP p 25). *Funerary. On bust.* Group: Hypogeum of Artaban (SFP 19 - 43).

Bib: *Fig 152*.

1 mrtʾ
2 ʾrṭbn
3 ḥbl

PAT 2654 **SFP 31** **n. d.**
Prov: Palmyra: S-E necropolis, hypogeum no. 5. Loc: Palmyra, *in situ* (SFP p 25). *Funerary. On bust.* Group: Hypogeum of Artaban (SFP 19 - 43). Bib: *Fig 134*.

1 ḥbl
2 brtʾ
3 brt yrḥy
4 mrtʾ
5 brth
6 ḥbl
SFP gives wrong layout of inscription, cf photo

PAT 2655 **SFP 32** **n. d.**
Prov: Palmyra: S-E necropolis, hypogeum no. 5. Loc: Palmyra, *in situ* (SFP p 25). *Funerary. On bust.* Group: Hypogeum of Artaban (SFP 19 - 43). Bib: *Fig 135*; Tanabe '86 pl 233.

1 šlmt brt
2 šmšgrm br
3 blʿqb ʾḥyb

PAT 2656 **SFP 33** **n. d.**
Prov: Palmyra: S-E necropolis, hypogeum no. 5. Loc: Palmyra, *in situ* (SFP p 25). *Funerary. On bust.* Group: Hypogeum of Artaban (SFP 19 - 43). Bib: *Fig 136*; Tanabe '86 pl 233.

1 brtʾ
2 ʿgʾ nṣry
SFP gives wrong layout of inscription, cf photo

PAT 2657 **SFP 34** **n. d.**
Prov: Palmyra: S-E necropolis, hypogeum no. 5. Loc: Palmyra, *in situ* (SFP p 25). *Funerary. On bust.* Group: Hypogeum of Artaban (SFP 19 - 43). Bib: *Fig 25*; Odenthal '82 fig 48.

1 ḥbl
2 mqymw
3 br whby

PAT 2658 **SFP 35** **n. d.**
Prov: Palmyra: S-E necropolis, hypogeum no. 5. Loc: Palmyra, *in situ* (SFP p 25). *Funerary. On bust.* Group: Hypogeum of Artaban (SFP 19 - 43). Bib: *Fig 116*; Odenthal '82 fig 38.

1 ḥbl
2 ʿtnwr̊y br
3 yr̊ḥy zbydʾ

PAT 2659 **SFP 36** **n. d.**
Prov: Palmyra: S-E necropolis, hypogeum no. 5. Loc: Palmyra, *in situ* (SFP p 25). *Funerary. On bust.* Group: Hypogeum of Artaban (SFP 19 - 43). Bib: *Fig 178*.

1 [. . .]
2 [...]nṣry
3 [. . .]
4 [. . .]
5 ḥbl
Inscription not legibile from Fig 178; text from SFP p 34

PAT 2660 **SFP 37** **n. d.**
Prov: Palmyra: S-E necropolis, hypogeum no. 5. Loc: Palmyra, *in situ* (SFP p 25). *Funerary. On bust.* Group: Hypogeum of Artaban (SFP 19 - 43). Bib: *Fig 65*; Odenthal '82 fig 48.

1 ḥbl
2 yr̊ḥy br
3 zbydʾ br
4 yr̊ḥy
5 ʾlpy
Last line not entirely visible on Fig 65

PAT 2661 **SFP 38** **n. d.**
Prov: Palmyra: S-E necropolis, hypogeum no. 5. Loc: Palmyra, *in situ* (SFP p 25). *Funerary. On bust.* Group: Hypogeum of Artaban (SFP 19 - 43). Bib: *Fig 30*.

1 ḥbl ydy
2 br mrtʾ

PAT 2662 **SFP 39** **n. d.**
Prov: Palmyra: S-E necropolis, hypogeum no. 5. Loc: Damascus, Musée de l'Armée (SFP p 25). *Funerary. On bust.* Group: Hypogeum of Artaban (SFP 19 - 43). Bib: *Fig 43*; S. Abdul-Hak '61 p 44 pl 4, 8.

1 ḥbl
2 srʾ
3 br
4 nṣrw

line 2: srʾ seems to be reading of fig 43, cf Stark, PNPI 41, 102; SFP p 36 ṣyrʾ and in translation "Ṣairâ"

PAT 2663 **SFP 40** **n. d.**
Prov: Palmyra: S-E necropolis, hypogeum no. 5. Loc: Palmyra, *in situ* (SFP p 25). *Funerary. On bust.* Group: Hypogeum of Artaban (SFP 19 - 43). Bib: *Fig 117.*

1 mlkw br̊
2 tymr̊ṣw
3 ḥlypy ḥbl
4 yr̊ḥy ʾḥyh

Text at right of head of adult, in 4 vertical lines; line 1: mlkw! :: SFP qrbw; line 4: yr̊ḥy seems probable :: SFP p 36: ...ḥ ʾxwh

PAT 2664 **SFP 41 no. 1** **n. d.**
Prov: Palmyra: S-E necropolis, hypogeum no. 5. Loc: Palmyra, *in situ* (SFP p 25). *Funerary. On sarcophagus with reliefs.* Group: Hypogeum of Artaban (SFP 19 - 43). Bib: *Fig 222-224*; Parlasca '87a p 280, fig 3 p 279; Tanabe '82 pl 229-232.

(with figure reclining on funeral couch)
1 ʿgʾ br ʾrṭbn br
2 ʿgʾ ḥbl dy lʾbwhy
3 wlʾḥwhy ʿl ḥywhy

Texts no. 1 - 10 almost entirely illegible on figures in SFP or Tanabe

PAT 2665 **SFP 41 no. 2** **n. d.**
Prov: Palmyra: S-E necropolis, hypogeum no. 5. Loc: Palmyra, *in situ* (SFP p 25). *Funerary. On sarcophagus with reliefs.* Group: Hypogeum of Artaban (SFP 19 - 43). Bib: *Fig 222-224*; Parlasca '87a p 280, fig 3 p 279; Tanabe '82 pl 229-232.

1 ḥrtbw brt
2 brʾ ʾmh

Texts no. 1 - 10 almost entirely illegible on figures in SFP or Tanabe

PAT 2666 **SFP 41 no. 3** **n. d.**
Prov: Palmyra: S-E necropolis, hypogeum no. 5. Loc: Palmyra, *in situ* (SFP p 25). *Funerary. On sarcophagus with reliefs.* Group: Hypogeum of Artaban (SFP 19 - 43). Bib: *Fig 222-224*; Parlasca '87a p 280, fig 3 p 279; Tanabe '82 pl 229-232.

1 [ʾrṭ]bn br
2 [ʿgʾ ʾ]bwhy

Texts no. 1 - 10 almost entirely illegible on figures in SFP or Tanabe

PAT 2667 **SFP 41 no. 4** **n. d.**
Prov: Palmyra: S-E necropolis, hypogeum no. 5. Loc: Palmyra, *in situ* (SFP p 25). *Funerary. On sarcophagus with reliefs.* Group: Hypogeum of Artaban (SFP 19 - 43). Bib: *Fig 222-224*; Parlasca '87a p 280, fig 3 p 279; Tanabe '82 pl 229-232.

1 brtʾ brt
2 yrḥy brʾ
3 ʾtth

Texts no. 1 - 10 almost entirely illegible on figures in SFP or Tanabe

PAT 2668 **SFP 41 no. 5** **n. d.**
Prov: Palmyra: S-E necropolis, hypogeum no. 5. Loc: Palmyra, *in situ* (SFP p 25). *Funerary. On sarcophagus with reliefs.* Group: Hypogeum of Artaban (SFP 19 - 43). Bib: *Fig 222-224*; Parlasca '87a p 280, fig 3 p 279; Tanabe '82 pl 229-232.

1 ʾrṭbn br
2 yrḥy brʾ

Texts no. 1 - 10 almost entirely illegible on figures in

SFP or Tanabe

PAT 2669 **SFP 41 no. 6** **n. d.**
Prov: Palmyra: S-E necropolis, hypogeum no. 5. Loc: Palmyra, *in situ* (SFP p 25). *Funerary. On sarcophagus with reliefs.* Group: Hypogeum of Artaban (SFP 19 - 43). Bib: *Fig 222-224*; Parlasca '87a p 280, fig 3 p 279; Tanabe '82 pl 229-232.

1 brt' brt
2 ʿg' br[t]h
Texts no. 1 - 10 almost entirely illegible on figures in SFP or Tanabe

PAT 2670 **SFP 41 no. 7** **n. d.**
Prov: Palmyra: S-E necropolis, hypogeum no. 5. Loc: Palmyra, *in situ* (SFP p 25). *Funerary. On sarcophagus with reliefs.* Group: Hypogeum of Artaban (SFP 19 - 43). Bib: *Fig 222-224*; Parlasca '87a p 280, fig 3 p 279; Tanabe '82 pl 229-232.

1 'rṭbn br
2 ʿg' brh
Texts no. 1 - 10 almost entirely illegible on figures in SFP or Tanabe

PAT 2671 **SFP 41 no. 8** **n. d.**
Prov: Palmyra: S-E necropolis, hypogeum no. 5. Loc: Palmyra, *in situ* (SFP p 25). *Funerary. On sarcophagus with reliefs.* Group: Hypogeum of Artaban (SFP 19 - 43). Bib: *Fig 222-224*; Parlasca '87a p 280, fig 3 p 279; Tanabe '82 pl 229-232.

1 ḥbl
2 yrḥy
3 br 'rṭbn
4 br ʿg'
Tanabe '82 fig 231

PAT 2672 **SFP 41 no. 9** **n. d.**
Prov: Palmyra: S-E necropolis, hypogeum no. 5. Loc: Palmyra, *in situ* (SFP p 25). *Funerary. On sarcophagus with reliefs.* Group: Hypogeum of Artaban (SFP 19 - 43). Bib: *Fig 222-224*; Parlasca '87a p 280, fig 3 p 279; Tanabe '82 pl 229-232.

1 ḥbl
2 'rṭbn br
3 yrḥy brh
Legible, Tanabe '82 fig 230

PAT 2673 **SFP 41 no. 10** **n. d.**
Prov: Palmyra: S-E necropolis, hypogeum no. 5. Loc: Palmyra, *in situ* (SFP p 25). *Funerary. On sarcophagus with reliefs.* Group: Hypogeum of Artaban (SFP 19 - 43). Bib: *Fig 222-224*; Parlasca '87a p 280, fig 3 p 279; Tanabe '82 pl 229-232.

1 ḥbl ʿg'
2 br yrḥy
3 'rṭbn brh
Texts no. 1 - 10 almost entirely illegible on figures in SFP or Tanabe

PAT 2674 **SFP 42** **n. d.**
Prov: Palmyra: S-E necropolis, hypogeum no. 5. Loc: Palmyra, *in situ* (SFP p 25). *Funerary. On stele.* Group: Hypogeum of Artaban (SFP 19 - 43). Bib: *Fig 3.*

1 ḥbl dywn br ʿg'
2 br dywn

PAT 2675 **SFP 43** **n. d.**
Prov: Palmyra: S-E necropolis, hypogeum no. 5. Loc: Palmyra, *in situ* (SFP p 25). *Funerary. On sarcophagus.* Group: Hypogeum of Artaban (SFP 19 - 43). Bib: *Fig 227.*

Only traces of inscription remain

PAT 2676 **SFP 122** **n. d.**
Prov: Palmyra: S-E necropolis, hypogeum no. 8. Loc: Palmyra, 1987/7112. *Funerary. On bust.* Group: Hypogeum of Zebida, son of Ogeili, SFP 122-138. Bib: *Fig 96*; Tanabe '82 pl 323.

1 ḥbl
2 šlm'
3 br
4 zbyd'

PAT 2677 **SFP 123** **A.D. 177**
Prov: Palmyra: S-E necropolis, hypogeum no. 8. Loc: Palmyra, 1987/7113. *Funerary. On bust.* Group: Hypogeum of Zebida, son of Ogeili, SFP 122-138. Bib: *Fig 97*; Tanabe '82 pl 308.

1 nbwlʾ
2 br ʿgyly
3 ḥbl šnt
4 4.100+80+
5 5+4 byrḥ
6 tšry

PAT 2678 **SFP 124** **n. d.**
Prov: Palmyra: S-E necropolis, hypogeum no. 8. Loc: Palmyra, 1987/7114. *Funerary. On bust.* Group: Hypogeum of Zebida, son of Ogeili, SFP 122-138. Bib: *Fig 188.*

1 šgl
2 brt
3 ʿgyly
4 ḥbl

PAT 2679 **SFP 125** **n. d.**
Prov: Palmyra: S-E necropolis, hypogeum no. 8. Loc: Palmyra, 1987/7115. *Funerary. On bust.* Group: Hypogeum of Zebida, son of Ogeili, SFP 122-138. Bib: *Fig 171*; Colledge '76a note 362; Tanabe '82 pl 347.

1 ḥbl
2 gpnʾ
3 brt
4 nbwlʾ
5 br šzʾ
6 bgwšy

PAT 2680 **SFP 126** **n. d.**
Prov: Palmyra: S-E necropolis, hypogeum no. 8. Loc: Palmyra, 1987/7116. *Funerary. On bust.* Group: Hypogeum of Zebida, son of Ogeili, SFP 122-138. Bib: *Fig 44*; Colledge '76a note 377; Tanabe '82 pl 321.

1 mlkw
2 br zbdʾ
3 br ʿgyly
4 ḥbl

PAT 2681 **SFP 127** **n. d.**
Prov: Palmyra: S-E necropolis, hypogeum no. 8. Loc: Palmyra, 1987/7117. *Funerary. On bust.* Group: Hypogeum of Zebida, son of Ogeili, SFP 122-138. Bib: *Fig 141*; Colledge '76a note 362; Tanabe '82 pl 346.

1 šlmt brt
2 zbydʾ br
3 ʿgyly ḥbl

PAT 2682 **SFP 128** **n. d.**
Prov: Palmyra: S-E necropolis, hypogeum no. 8. Loc: Palmyra, 1987/7118. *Funerary. On bust.* Group: Hypogeum of Zebida, son of Ogeili, SFP 122-138. Bib: *Fig 185.*

1 ḥbl
2 gpnʾ
3 brt
4 zbydʾ

line 2: gpnʾ! (probable from fig 185) :: SFP ʾpnʾ

PAT 2683 **SFP 129** **n. d.**
Prov: Palmyra: S-E necropolis, hypogeum no. 8. Loc: Palmyra, 1987/7119. *Funerary. On bust.* Group: Hypogeum of Zebida, son of Ogeili, SFP 122-138. Bib: *Fig 186*; Tanabe '82 pl 348.

1 ʾḥtʾ
2 bt
3 ʿttn
4 ḥbl

line 1: ʾḥtʾ :: SFP ʾḥytʾ

PAT 2684 **SFP 130** **n. d.**
Prov: Palmyra: S-E necropolis, hypogeum no. 8. Loc: Palmyra, 1987/7120. *Funerary. On bust.* Group: Hypogeum of Zebida, son of Ogeili, SFP 122-138. Bib: *Fig 192.*

1 šlmt
2 brt

3 šlm'
4 br
5 zbyd'
6 ḥbl

PAT 2685 **SFP 131** **n. d.**
Prov: Palmyra: S-E necropolis, hypogeum no. 8. Loc: Palmyra, 1987/7121. *Funerary. On stele.* Group: Hypogeum of Zebida, son of Ogeili, SFP 122-138. Bib: *Fig 6*; Tanabe '82 pl 262.

1 nbwl'
2 br ʿgylw
3 ḥbl
line 2: ʿgylw :: SFP ʿgyly

PAT 2686 **SFP 132** **n. d.**
Prov: Palmyra: S-E necropolis, hypogeum no. 8. Loc: Palmyra, 1987/7122. *Funerary. On stele.* Group: Hypogeum of Zebida, son of Ogeili, SFP 122-138. Bib: *Fig 7*; Bounni, *L'Art de Palmyre*, p 51 pl 9; Colledge '76a note 197; Tanabe '82 pl 261.

1 yrḥy
2 br ʿgyly

PAT 2687 **SFP 133** **n. d.**
Prov: Palmyra: S-E necropolis, hypogeum no. 8. Loc: Palmyra, 1987/7123. *Funerary. On bust.* Group: Hypogeum of Zebida, son of Ogeili, SFP 122-138. Bib: *Fig 173*; Tanabe '82 pl 349.

1 ḥbl
2 'ḥwt brt
3 yrḥy br
4 zbyd' ḥbl
line 2: 'ḥwt! :: SFP 'ḥyt'

PAT 2688 **SFP 134** **n. d.**
Prov: Palmyra: S-E necropolis, hypogeum no. 8. Loc: Palmyra, 1987/7124. *Funerary. On bust.* Group: Hypogeum of Zebida, son of Ogeili, SFP 122-138. Bib: *Fig 63*; Colledge '76a note 377; Tanabe '82 pl 317.

1 ḥbl
2 yrḥy br zbyd'
3 br ʿgyl[y]
4 'sʿdd
line 4: 's!ʿdd :: SFP 'šʿdd

PAT 2689 **SFP 135** **n. d.**
Prov: Palmyra: S-E necropolis, hypogeum no. 8. Loc: Palmyra, 1987/7125. *Funerary. On bust.* Group: Hypogeum of Zebida, son of Ogeili, SFP 122-138. Bib: *Fig 31*; Colledge '76a p 247; Tanabe '82 pl 315.

1 zbyd' br
2 ʿgyly ḥbl

PAT 2690 **SFP 136** **n. d.**
Prov: Palmyra: S-E necropolis, hypogeum no. 8. Loc: Palmyra, 1987/7126. *Funerary. On bust.* Group: Hypogeum of Zebida, son of Ogeili, SFP 122-138. Bib: *Fig 64*; Colledge '76a notes 362, 377; Tanabe '82 pl 316.

1 ḥbl ʿgyly
2 br zbyd'
3 br ʿgyly
4 'sʿdd
line 4: 'sʿdd SFP 'šʿd

PAT 2691 **SFP 137** **n. d.**
Prov: Palmyra: S-E necropolis, hypogeum no. 8. Loc: Palmyra, 1987/7127. *Funerary. On bust.* Group: Hypogeum of Zebida, son of Ogeili, SFP 122-138. Bib: *Fig 140.*

1 ḥbl
2 mqny
3 brt
4 šlmlt
5 rkl'
line 2: mq!ny :: SFP mkny; line 5: rkl' :: SFP rbl'

PAT 2692 **SFP 138** **n. d.**
Prov: Palmyra: S-E necropolis, hypogeum no. 8. Loc: Palmyra, 1987/7128. *Funerary. On bust.* Group: Hypogeum of Zebida, son of Ogeili, SFP

122-138. Bib: *Fig 157.*

1 ʿḥry brt
2 bryky
3 ḥbl

Text follows SFP, inscription not visible on fig 157

PAT 2693 **SFP 139** **n. d.**
Prov: Palmyra: S-E necropolis, hypogeum no. 9. Loc: Palmyra, 2004. *Funerary. On bust.* Group: Hypogeum of family of Barikay. Bib: *Fig 49.*

1 ḥbl
2 ʿštwr br
3 mlkw

Text follows SFP, inscription not visible on SFP *Fig 49*

PAT 2694 **SFP 140** **n. d.**
Prov: Palmyra: S-E necropolis, hypogeum no. 9. Loc: Palmyra, 2005. *Funerary. On bust.* Group: Hypogeum of family of Barikay. Bib: *Fig 80.*

1 ʿbnrgl
2 br ʾmy
3 ḥbl

PAT 2695 **SFP 141** **n. d.**
Prov: Palmyra: S-E necropolis, hypogeum no. 9. Loc: Palmyra, 2006/7163. *Funerary. On bust.* Group: Hypogeum of family of Barikay. Bib: *Fig 167.*

1 ʿmy
2 brt ḥry
3 zbdʾ
4 mrbyt
5 bryky
6 brʾ

Text follows SFP. *Fig 167* shows bust with inscription broken away

PAT 2696 **SFP 142** **n. d.**
Prov: Palmyra: S-E necropolis, hypogeum no. 9. Loc: Palmyra, 2007 (see note SFP ad loc). *Funerary. On bust.* Group: Hypogeum of family of Barikay. Bib: *Fig 98.*

1 ʿbnbw
2 nwmnws
3 ḥbl

Scarcely visible on SFP *Fig 98*

PAT 2697 **SFP 143** **n. d.**
Prov: Palmyra: S-E necropolis, hypogeum no. 9. Loc: Palmyra, 2008. *Funerary. On bust.* Group: Hypogeum of family of Barikay. Bib: *Fig 137.*

1 ḥnʾ brt
2 lšmš
3 br zbdʾ
4 ḥbl

Text follows SFP, not visible on *Fig 137*

PAT 2698 **SFP 144** **n. d.**
Prov: Palmyra: S-E necropolis, hypogeum no. 9. Loc: Palmyra, 2009. *Funerary. On bust.* Group: Hypogeum of family of Barikay. Bib: *Fig 81.*

1 ḥggw
2 br
3 nwry
4 ḥggw
5 ḥbl

PAT 2699 **SFP 145** **n. d.**
Prov: Palmyra: S-E necropolis, hypogeum no. 9. Loc: Palmyra, 2011. *Funerary. On bust.* Group: Hypogeum of family of Barikay. Bib: *Fig 50.*

1 tymrṣw
2 bryky
3 ḥbl

Scarcely visible on SFP *Fig 50*

PAT 2700 **SFP 146** **n. d.**
Prov: Palmyra: S-E necropolis, hypogeum no. 9. Loc: Palmyra, 2012. *Funerary. On bust.* Group: Hypogeum of family of Barikay. Bib: *Fig 38.*

1 yrḥb
2 wlʾ

3 lšmš
4 ḥbl
SFP describes as having three lines; lines 1-2: yrḥbwlʾ! :: SFP yrḥbwl

PAT 2701 **SFP 147** **n. d.**
Prov: Palmyra: S-E necropolis, hypogeum no. 9. Loc: Palmyra, 2015. *Funerary. On bust.* Group: Hypogeum of family of Barikay. Bib: *Fig 48.*

1 whblt
2 bryky
3 zbydʾ ḥbl

PAT 2702 **SFP 148** **n. d.**
Prov: Palmyra: S-E necropolis, hypogeum no. 9. Loc: Palmyra, 2010. *Funerary. On bust.* Group: Hypogeum of family of Barikay. Bib: *Fig 46.*

1 bryky
2 zbydʾ
3 bryky
4 škybl
5 ḥbl
Text follows SFP, not visible on *Fig 46*

PAT 2703 **SFP 149** **n. d.**
Prov: Palmyra: S-E necropolis, hypogeum no. 9. Loc: Palmyra, 2016. *Funerary. On bust.* Group: Hypogeum of family of Barikay. Bib: *Fig 149.*

(On right)
1 ḥbl
(On left)
1 tmʾ
2 brt
3 bryky
4 zbydʾ
Text follows SFP, not visible on *Fig 149*

PAT 2704 **SFP 150** **n. d.**
Prov: Palmyra: S-E necropolis, hypogeum no. 9. Loc: Palmyra, 2017. *Funerary. On bust.* Group: Hypogeum of family of Barikay. Bib: *Fig 72.*

1 mqymw
2 lšmš
3 ḥbl
Text follows SFP, not visible on *Fig 72*

PAT 2705 **SFP 151** **n. d.**
Prov: Palmyra: S-E necropolis, hypogeum no. 9. Loc: Palmyra, 2013. *Funerary. On bust.* Group: Hypogeum of family of Barikay. Bib: *Fig 28.*

1 yrḥbwlʾ
2 br tymʿmd
3 [...]
4 [...]
5 [...]
Text follows SFP, not visible on *Fig 28*

PAT 2706 **SFP 152** **n. d.**
Prov: Palmyra: S-E necropolis, hypogeum no. 9. Loc: Palmyra, 2018. *Funerary. On bust.* Group: Hypogeum of family of Barikay. Bib: *Fig 150.*

1 ʾqmʾ
2 brt zbydʾ
3 br tymrṣw
4 ʾtt
5 bryky
6 zbydʾ
7 ḥbl
Inscription shows 7 lines :: SFP 6 lines

PAT 2707 **SFP 153** **n. d.**
Prov: Palmyra: S-E necropolis, hypogeum no. 9. Loc: Palmyra Museum (no number given in SFP). *Funerary. On relief, funerary couch.* Group: Hypogeum of family of Barikay. Bib: *Fig 228.*

1 ḥbl [...]
2 ʾqmʾ b[rt]
3 brʾ bryk[y] rʾʾ
4 [s]y d
5 ykn br
6 mqymw
Text follows SFP, not visible on *Fig 228*

PAT 2708 **SFP 154** **n. d.**
Prov: Palmyra: S-E necropolis, hypogeum no. 9.

Loc: Palmyra, 2014. *Funerary. On bust.* Group: Hypogeum of family of Barikay. Bib: *Fig 47.*

1 ḥggw
2 bryky
3 zbyd'

PAT 2709 **SFP 155** **n. d.**
Prov: Palmyra: S-E necropolis, hypogeum no. 9. Loc: Palmyra Museum (no no. given in SFP). *Funerary. On bust.* Group: Hypogeum of family of Barikay. Bib: *Fig 229.*

1' [.....]
2' [br]yky
3' br zbyd'
4' br [...]
Text follows SFP, not visible on *Fig 229*

PAT 2710 **SFP 156** **n. d.**
Prov: Palmyra: S-E necropolis, hypogeum no. 10. Loc: Palmyra, 2023/7200. *Funerary. On stele.* Group: Hypogeum of Taimʿamad (SFP 156-157). Bib: *Fig 4*; Tanabe '82 pl 272.

1 ʿgb' brt rmy
2 br tymn'

PAT 2711 **SFP 157** **n. d.**
Prov: Palmyra: S-E necropolis, hypogeum no. 10. Loc: Palmyra, 2022/7199. *Funerary. On bust.* Group: Hypogeum of Taimʿamad (SFP 156-157). Bib: *Fig 148.*

1 ḥbl
2 'qm' br[t]
3 tymʿmd
4 br mqymw
5 brt ʿgb
line 5: ʿgb' with broken final ' on portrait frame? cf *Fig 148*

PAT 2712 **SFP 159** **n. d.**
Prov: Palmyra. Loc: Palmyra, 2020/7197. *Funerary. On bust.* Group: Hypogeum of Aʿaylami (SFP 158-160). Bib: *Fig 138*; Tanabe '82 pl 353.

1 tm' brt
2 ʿgylw
3 'rqyl

PAT 2713 **Soth 03472 no. 63** **n. d.**
Prov: Palmyra. Loc: Private collection. *Funerary. On relief.* Bib: *Photo,* Sotheby's London, Auction catalog Dec. 13-14, 1990.

1 bʿltg' brt
2 zbyd' br
3 ymlkw
4 ['tt]h

PAT 2714 **Soth 5518 no. 40** **n. d.**
Prov: Palmyra. Loc: J. Paul Getty Museum 88.AA.50. *Funerary. On relief.* Bib: *Photo,* Sotheby's New York, Auction catalog, Nov. 24, 1986; "Acquisitions/1988," *The J. Paul Getty Museum Journal* 17 (1989) "13. Funerary Stele" pp 110-11 (small photo).

1 mqy
2 br mʿny
Reading from photo in Sotheby's catalogue

PAT 2715 **Soth 5722 no. 48** **n. d.**
Prov: Palmyra. Loc: Not known. *Funerary. On relief.* Bib: *Photo,* Sotheby's New York, Auction catalog, June 15, 1988.

1 tdmr brt
2 šml' br
3 šm' ḥbl
Reading from photo in Sotheby's catalogue.

PAT 2716 **Soth 5722 no. 49** **n. d.**
Prov: Palmyra. Loc: New York, private collection. *Funerary. On relief.* Bib: *Photo,* Sotheby's, New York, Auction catalog, June 15, 1988.

1 ḥbl
2 nwrb[l]
3 br

4 [.]wʾšʾ
5 br[.....]
6 š[.]r?[ ]
From photo kindly provided by owner

PAT 2717 **Soth 5722 no. 379** **n. d.**
Prov: Palmyra. Loc: California (private collection). *Funerary. On relief.* Bib: *Photo,* Sotheby's New York, Auction catalog,
June 15, 1988.

1 ʾqmʾ brt
2 mqymw
3 br ḥggw
4 ḥbl
Reading from photo in Sotheby's catalogue

PAT 2718 **Soth 5788 no. 167** **n. d.**
Prov: Palmyra. Loc: Not known (Private Collection). *Funerary. On relief.* Bib: *Photo,* Sotheby's New York, Auction catalog, Dec. 2, 1988.

1 ḥbl
2 yrḥy br
3 zbdbwl
4 zgwg
Reading from photo in Sotheby's catalogue

PAT 2719 **Stieg** **n. d.**
Prov: Palmyra. Loc: Haifa, Stieglitz Collection. *Funerary. On relief.*

1 ḥbl
2 zbydʾ
3 br
4 mqymw
5 ʿrymʾ
Reading from photo provided by K. Parlasca

PAT 2720 **StSc 149** **n.d.**
Prov: Palmyra. Loc: Cambridge, Mass., Harvard University Art Museums, 1908.3. *Funerary. On relief.*

(On left)
1 šm
2 ʿwn
3 brh
(On right, by head of woman)
illegible from photo
(On right, by head of child)
1 ḥyrn
2 brh

PAT 2721 **StSc 151** **n.d.**
Prov: Palmyra. Loc: Cambridge, Mass., Harvard University Art Museums, 593.1941. *Funerary. On relief.*

(On right)
1 mlʾ br
2 mlkw br
3 bgd ḥbl
(On left)
1 mlkw
2 brh
3 ḥbl

PAT 2722 **StudLitt p 64** **n. d.**
Prov: Palmyra. Loc: Frankfurt am Main. *Funerary. On relief.* Bib: *Photo opposite p 65.*

1 mlkw br
2 mlkw
3 šʿd
Line 3 very uncertain, and whole text with relief of female!

PAT 2723 **StudLdV p 512** Starcky **(24 B.C.)**
Prov: Palmyra. Loc: Palmyra Museum. *Dedicatory. On relief fragment.* Bib: *Pl ID.*

1 byrḥ knwn š[nt]
2 [2.100]+80+5+4 ml[.....]
3 qrb mqy[mw ...]
4 br ymlkw t[....dy]
5 mn bny bw[...]
6 lbrt bl w[.....]
7 ʾlhyʾ [ʿl ḥywhy]
8 wḥyy [.....]

PAT 2724 **StudLdV p 601** Walker **n. d.**
Prov: Palmyra. Loc: Private collection. *Tessera. On terracotta.* Bib: *Photo fig 1.*

1 mlkw w
2 ʿtʿqb
cf. RTP no. 838

PAT 2725 **StudPalm '75 p 129** **A.D. 242**
Prov: Palmyra, Valley of Tombs, Jubwel al Husayniyet, Hypogeum of Hermes. Loc: Palmyra, *in situ. Funerary: Cession. On left doorpost.* Group: Inv 4 13, StudPalm '75 p 129. Bib: *Fig 2 p 130*; cf. MF Fondation no. 63.

1 [ywlyʾ ʾwrl]yʾ prymʾ br[t ḥry]
2 [ʾqmʾ br]t ʾnṭykws ḥ[lyp]y
3 [rḥqt lywly]s ʾwrlys zbd[bwl br]
4 k[hy]lw zbdbwl mn ʾtrʾ šḥ[ymʾ]
5 [dy ʾ]myn ʾrbʿ ʿd ktlʾ dy bnʾ
6 y[tr]ʾ mʿlk mn bbʾ šrk ʿl
7 šmlk lh wlbnwh wl[bn]y •
8 bnwh lʿlmʾ byrḥ ʾd[r]
9 šnt 5.100+40+10+3

PAT 2726 **StudPalm '75 p 131** **A.D. 120**
Prov: Palmyra, Camp of Diocletian, Tower of Nabûzabad. Loc: Palmyra, *in situ. Funerary: Foundation. On door lintel.* Bib: *Fig 3, p 132.*

1 τὸ μνη[με]ῖο[ν τού[το ἐις τει]μὴν α[ἰωνίαν
ἔκτισ]εν Ν[εβουσαβαδος τοῦ Νεσα] τοῦ Αλα
[Ρ]ε[φαηλου τοῦ]
2 Αβισσαιο[υ αὐ]τῳ τε καὶ ὑι[οῖς ἀυτο]ῦ καὶ
ὑιωνοῖς καὶ ἐγγόνοις ἐις [το\ παντελε\ς μηνὸς Δίου
)έτους βλυ']

3 qbrʾ [dnh] dy hw dkrn wyqr bt ʿlmʾ bnʾ
nbwzbd br nšʾ br ḥlʾ br rpʾl ʿbšy lh wlbnwhy
wlbny bnwhy byrḥ knwn šnt
4 4.100+20+10+2
With traces of red in inscription

PAT 2727 **StudMiles p 38** **A.D. 95**
Prov: Palmyra, S-W Necropolis, Hypogeum. Loc: Palmyra, *in situ. Funerary: Cession. On door lintel.* Bib: *Pl I.*

1 mʿrtʾ dnh dy gwʾ plgʾ wplgʾ dy bt mtry
wdy bt ʾylyd mʿlyk bbʾ ʿl ymynʾ šqqtʾ
qmytʾ dy bt ʾylyd wdy ʿl smlʾ šqqtʾ
2 qmytʾ dy bt mtry mʿlyk lgw šqqtʾ dy ʿl
ymynʾ dy bt mtry wšqqtʾ dy ʿl smlʾ dy bt
ʾylyd ʾksdrʾ mqblʾ dy trn sṭryʾ mqdš
3 lgwhwn lʿlmʾ byrḥ ṭbt šnt 4.100+5+1

PAT 2728 **StudMiles p 50** no. 1 **A.D. 123**
Prov: Palmyra, S-W Necropolis, Hypogeum of Yarḥibôlâ and Taimoʿamad and Maqqai. Loc: Palmyra, *in situ. Funerary: Foundation. On door lintel.* Group: StudMiles p 50 nos. 1, 2. Bib: *Pl IV.*

1 mʿrtʾ dh ʿbdw [y]rḥbwlʾ br mqy wtymʿmd
br ʿstwrgʾ wmqy br ʿtntn
2 wrpbwl br ʿtʿqb lhwn wlbnyhwn byrḥ ʾdr
šnt 4.100+20+10+4

PAT 2729 **StudMiles p 50** no. 2 **A.D. 243**
Prov: Palmyra, S-W Necropolis, Hypogeum of Yarḥibôlâ, Taimoʿamad and Maqqai. Loc: Palmyra, *in situ. Funerary: Cession. On door-lintel.* Group: StudMiles p 50 nos. 1, 2. Bib: *Pl IV.*

1 šnt 5.100+20+20+10+4
2 ywlyʾ ʾwrlyʾ ʾqmʾ brt
3 rpbwl wbt ʿtʿqb bnt wrdn
4 br rpbwl rḥq lʾwrlys šmʿwn
5 wmzbnʾ wʾsḥq bny yʿqwb
6 ṭkss dy gwmḥyn ʾrbʿʾ mʿlyk
7 bbʾ ʿl smlʾ dy hnwn bʾksdrʾ
8 smlʾ lhwn wlbnyhwn wlbny bnyh
9 wn lyqrhwn lʿlmʾ dy byrḥ qnyn dy [...]
Traces of rubrication

PAT 2730 **Sumer '62 p 63** no. 1 **n. d.**
Prov: Qaʾara (Iraq), 150 Km S of Dura Europos. Loc: Baghdad, Iraq Museum, 51100. *Dedicatory. On stone block.* Bib: Teixidor '63 pp 33-37, pl III.

1 dkyryn wbrykyn
2 ḥṣdyʾ ʾln dy hww

3 ʿm ʾbgr br ḥyrn
4 bqṣṭʾ tnn šlm
5 tymy br tymy br blyhb
6 yrḥy br tymrṣw br šṭʾ
7 mlkw br nbwlʾ br ʾqzmn
8 mqymw mʿzyn krwzʾ
9 ʾbgr br mlʾ br zbdʿth
10 dkyr mhr br ʾtšʿt

Text mostly after Teixidor '63 pp 33-34; line 2: *ḥṣryʾ* in Sumer '62; line 6: *šṭʾ* with Stark PN p 121

PAT 2731 **Sumer '62 p 64** no. 2 **A.D. 128**

Prov: Uncertain. Loc: Baghdad, Iraq Museum, 66457. *Dedicatory. On stone block.* Bib: *Pl 6, fig 10*; Teixidor '63 pp 42-44, pl IV no. 1.

1' Μνησθῇ

1 dkyr ʿgʾ
2 br mlʾ br
3 ʿgylw br
4 tybwl dy
5 mtqrh br
6 ʾḥty ʿd
7 ʿlmʾ šnt
8 [4].100+40

1' Gk text: only this line legible

PAT 2732 **Sumer '64 p 13** no. 1 **A.D. (98)**

Prov: Rijelat Umm-Kubar, Wadi Hauran (Iraq). Loc: Baghdad, Iraq Museum, 67806. *Dedicatory. On stone slab.* Bib: Pl I, no. 1.

1 byrḥ ʾdr š[nt 4.100]
2 +5+4 nṣb zbydʾ br
3 ḥwml bʾsṭrṭyw
4 wrʿʾ tnn bšʿdy [....]
5 šlm gdʾ krzʾ bṭb
6 bʿly mlʾ ʾlhw
7 bṭb

PAT 2733 **Sumer '64 p 14** no. 2 **A.D. 98**

Prov: Rijelat Umm-Kubar, Wadi Hauran (Iraq). Loc: Baghdad, Iraq Museum, 67815. *Unclassified. On stone slab.* Bib: Pl I, no. 2.

1' wḥyrn br šmʿwn
2' br zbydʾ
3' byrḥ ʾdr
4' šnt 4.100+5+4

PAT 2734 **Sumer '64 p 15** no. 3 **n. d.**

Prov: Rijelat Umm-Kubar, Wadi Hauran (Iraq). Loc: Baghdad, Iraq Museum, 67808. *Dedicatory. On stone.* Bib: Pl I, no. 3.

Safaitic: ltymḥʾ wqpn dʾl nʿmn w k? ? l? w bn? ... šnt bn ḥwml slm

1 dkyryn ʾnš br
2 ʾm?y?n wtymḥʾ
3 br tymšʾ[dw]
4 wqwpʾ br šrykw
5 yrḥy dy rʿw tnn
6 šnt zbydʾ ḥwml

PAT 2735 **Sumer '64 p 16** no. 4 **A.D. 98**

Prov: Rijelat Umm-Kubar, Wadi Hauran (Iraq). Loc: Baghdad, Iraq Museum, 67814. *Unclassified. On stone.* Bib: Pl I, no. 4.

1 byrḥ ʾdr
2 šnt 4.100
3 +5+4[...]

PAT 2736 **Sumer '64 p 16** no. 5 **A.D. (98)**

Prov: Rijelat Umm-Kubar, Wadi Hauran (Iraq). Loc: Baghdad, Iraq Museum, 67810. *Dedicatory. On stone.* Bib: Pl II, no. 5.

1 byrḥ ʾdr šnt 4.100+[5+4]
2 zbydʾ br ḥwml hwʾ tnn [...]
3 bny mšknʾ dy tymʾ [...]
4 ḥggw br nšʾ ḥršʾ [...]

5 wʿbdy br zbdbwlʾ š[....]
6 wʿwydʾ ʾd/ʾr[...]
7 wškyy br tlm[...]
8 nbwlʾ yrḥbwl?[ʾ..]

PAT 2737 **Sumer '64 p 17** no. 6 **n. d.**
Prov: Rijelat Umm-Kubar, Wadi Hauran (Iraq). Loc: Baghdad, Iraq Museum, 67809. *Unclassified. On stone slab.* Bib: Pl II, no. 6.

Safaitic: lqpn bn yrḥ dʾl nʿmn l?wdt yʿ?s ... w

1 qwpʾ br šrykw

PAT 2738 **Sumer '64 p 18** no. 8 **A.D. 98**
Prov: Rijelat Umm-Kubar, Wadi Hauran (Iraq). Loc: Baghdad, Iraq Museum, 67811. *Unclassified. On stone slab.* Bib: Pl II, no. 8.

1 šlm
2 byrḥ ʾdr šnt
3 4.100+5+4 dkyryn
4 wbrykyn tymrṣw
5 wḥggw bny tymʾ
6 šwyrʾ wzbydʾ br
7 tymʿmd mškw
8 [w]yrbʾl br tymʾ
9 brykw

PAT 2739 **Sumer '64 p 19** no. 9 **n. d.**
Prov: Rijelat Umm-Kubar, Wadi Hauran (Iraq). Loc: Baghdad, Iraq Museum, 67817. *Unclassified. On stone slab.* Bib: Pl II, no. 9.

1 zbydʾ
2 tymʿmd
3 zbydʾ
4 mškw
5 šlm

PAT 2740 **Sumer '64 p 19** no. 10 **n. d.**
Prov: Rijelat Umm-Kubar, Wadi Hauran (Iraq). Loc: Baghdad, Iraq Museum, 67812. *Unclassified. On stone slab.* Bib: Pl II, no. 10.

1 dkyr yrḥbwlʾ br
2 lšmš br mqymw
3 dy mtqrʾ br
4 ʿzwlt qdm
5 [.]lhyt
6 [..]t[.]

PAT 2741 **Sumer '64 p 20** no. 11 **n. d.**
Prov: Rijelat Umm-Kubar, Wadi Hauran (Iraq). Loc: Baghdad, Iraq Museum, 67807. *Unclassified. On stele.* Bib: Pl III, no. 11.

1 dkyr bryk
2 lšmš br
3 ḥyrn br
4 lšmš br
5 [t]ybwl škybl
6 wḥby br
7 zbydʾ
8 ḥby šlm

PAT 2742 **Sumer '64 p 20** no. 12 **n. d.**
Prov: Rijelat Umm-Kubar, Wadi Hauran (Iraq). Loc: Baghdad, Iraq Museum, 67813. *Unclassified. On stone slab.* Bib: Pl III, no. 12.

1 [dkyr]yn zbdʿth [br]
2 ḥdydw
3 [zbd]ʿth br yrḥy
4 br [ḥ]dydw
4 br d/rd/rhʾ wšʿdw
5 br rbn wʿnnw
6 bṭb

PAT 2743 **Syr '26 p 129** **A.D. 243**
Prov: Palmyra. Loc: Palmyra Museum. *Honorific. On stone block.* Bib: *Pl XXXIV*; Ing '25; Heichelheim '38 p 202; Ros AH no. 13 pp 42-43.

1 [by]rḥ tšry šnt 5.100+40+10+5
2 brbnwt mrzḥwt yrḥy ʾgrpʾ yrḥy
3 ydyʿbl ʿgʾ yʿt dy šmš ʾlhyʾ wytb ʿl
4 qsmʾ štʾ klh wʾsq ḥmrʾ ʿtyqʾ
5 lkmryʾ štʾ klh mn byth wḥmr bzqyn
6 lʾ ʾyty mn mʿrbʾ dkyryn wbrykyn
7 prṭnks wmlkwsʾ bnwhy wʿgylw ktwbʾ
8 wzby br šʿdʾ dy hwʾ ʿl bt dwdʾ
9 wyrḥbwlʾ mmzgnʾ wmsyʿnʾ klhwn

PAT 2744 **Syr '30 pl XL** no. 1 **n. d.**
Prov: Palmyra. Loc: Not known. *Funerary. On relief.*

1 ḥbl
2 šgl brt
3 whblt
4 ʾʿylmy
5 blḥzy

PAT 2745 **Syr '30 pl XL** no. 2 **n. d.**
Prov: Palmyra. Loc: Not known. *Funerary. On relief.*

1 whblt br
2 blnwry dy
3 mtqrh bwly
4 br bwšʾ
5 ḥbl

PAT 2746 **Syr '30 pl XLI** no. 1 "fig 3" **n. d.**
Prov: Palmyra. Loc: Louvre, AO 28381. *Funerary. On relief.* Bib: Caubet '90 no. 33; Lou 237.

1 ḥbl
2 whblt
3 br whblt

PAT 2747 **Syr '30 pl XLI** no. 2 "fig 4" **n. d.**
Prov: Palmyra. Loc: Not known. *Funerary. On relief.*

1 ḥyrn
2 br
3 ndbʾl
4 bwšʾ
5 ḥbl

PAT 2748 **Syr '31 p 127** no. 8 **A.D. (168+)**
Prov: Palmyra, Temple of Bel, reemployed in Arab wall. Loc: Palmyra, *in situ. Funerary. On console.* Bib: *Fig 8, p 127.*

(In upper margin)
1' [...]ης τειμῆς καὶ μνημῆς χάριν

(Upper margin)
1 ṣlmt tmʾ brt nbwzbd br zbdbwl
(Center)
2 šmʿwn dy ʾqymw lh ʾbwh
3 wʾmby ʾmh brt bgrn
4 br mlkw lyqrh ḥbl
(Lower margin)
5 [...]n ywm 10+5+3 šnt 4.100+80

PAT 2749 **Syr '31 p 130** no. 11 **A.D. 48**
Prov: Palmyra, Temple of Bel. Loc: Palmyra Museum. *Dedicatory. On stone fragments.* Bib: *Fig 11.*

(Upper fragment)
1 šnt 3.100+60 mṭlʾ
2 [dh w]ʿmwdyh wšryth wtṭlylh
3 [ʿbd]w ʾwšy br khylw wʾwšy
4 [w...]ʾ bny ḥyrn br ʾwšy
5 [dy mn] bny mytʾ lbw[l]ʿstr
6 [wšdyʾ] ʾlhyʾ ṭbyʾ ʿl ḥyyhwn
(Lower fragment)
7 [.....] bʾyr ywm [....]
8 [....]bt ʾlhyn wbtyn nš[....]
9 [...... bw]lʿstr wšdyʾ
10 lbnynʾ dy ʾlhyʾ

PAT 2750 **Syr '31 p 133** no. 12 **n. d.**
Prov: Palmyra, Temple of Bel. Loc: Palmyra Museum. *Honorific. On console.* Bib: *Fig 12, p 133*; Déd pl IX, 1, 2.

1 ṣlmʾ dnh dy lšmš
2 ḥlypy br ʾtpny dy ʿbdw lh
3 bny tymrṣw [...]bʿltk
4 ʾštrʾ lyqrh

PAT 2751 **Syr '31 p 134** no. 13 **A.D. (133+)**
Prov: Palmyra, Temple of Bel. Loc: Palmyra Museum. *Dedicatory. On altar.* Bib: *Fig 13, p 134.*

1 ʿltʾ dh ʿbd ml[ʾ]
2 br dyny lʿštr[tʾ]

3 ʾštrʾ ṭbtʾ
4 šnt 4.100+40+5+[.]

PAT 2752 **Syr '31 p 135** no. 14 **A.D. 159**
Prov: Palmyra, Temple of Bel. Loc: Palmyra Museum. *Dedicatory. On altar.* Bib: *Fig 14, p 135.*

1 [dkrn] ṭb lšlmt wlʾḥyh gnyʾ
2 [ṭby]ʾ wškryʾ ʿbd rpʾl br
3 [bwl]qʾ br nwrbl ʿl ḥyyhy
4 [wʿl] ḥyy bnwhy byrḥ ʾb
5 šnt 4.100+60+10

PAT 2753 **Syr '31 p 138** no. 17 **n. d.**
Prov: Palmyra. Loc: Palmyra Museum. *Honorific. On stone fragment.* Bib: *Fig 17, p 138.*

1 [...] l[y]qr ʾdynt br ḥyrn whblt [...]
2 [....rš]ʾ dy tdmwr ʿbd ʿgylw b[r
3 [....]ny ḥdwdn ḥdʾ mw[...]dnh[....]
4 [......]wnʾ wmq[...]

PAT 2754 **Syr '31 p 139** no. 18 **n. d.**
Prov: Palmyra, reemployed in later house. Loc: Palmyra Museum. *Honorific. On stone fragment.* Bib: *Fig 18, p 139.*

1 [......d]y mtqrh ʾlksndrws
2 [...... td]mryʾ dy hw ʿbd
3 [....]h lqdmyn wšdrh grmnqs
4 [...... m]lkʾ myšny[ʾ ..]lwt ʾrbz
5 [.....]hʾ mn sṭ[r .....]lyswdy
6 [...... mlk [...]kʾ ršyʾ
7 [.....]wlwt [.....]

PAT 2755 **Syr '33 p 279** (Seyrig) **n. d.**
Prov: Palmyra. Loc: Palmyra Museum. *Dedicatory. On altar.*

1 Διὶ ὑψί[στῳ ...]
2 τοῖς δύο[...]
3 μουθε[...]
4 ουκαι[...]
5 οαιμαη [... Ζαβ]
6 διβώλου [...]

(follows Greek)
7 ʿlmʿ[...]
8 ydwš[...]

PAT 2756 **Syr '33 p 177** Tad 3 **n. d.**
Prov: Palmyra, Temple of Bel, reemployed. Loc: Palmyra Museum. *Honorific. On console fragment.* Bib: *Hand copy.*

1 [...]whl[.]ʾ[...]
2 [....]s dy ʾmry[n] [....]br
3 [....]ḥsy mn kysh [....]ʾ[.]w[...]wʾmn
4 [....] kmryʾ dy bl ʾlhʾ rbʾ wʾp hwh
5 [.... b]ny brkyw wbgrmṭyʾ qdmtʾ slq
6 [....] bnynʾ dy bl ʾlhʾ
7 [.....]ṭ[...]

PAT 2757 **Syr '33 p 179** Tad 4 **A.D. 225**
Prov: Near Aleppo, Umm es-Salabikh. Loc: Damascus, National Museum, 4480. *Unclassified. On relief.* Bib: *Hand copy*; Abdul-Hak and Abdul-Hak, '51 no. 24, photo pl XVI, 1.

1 [.....]dy hw ʾsṭrṭg ʿl ʿnʾ wgmlʾ wḥlpth
kptwt br
2 [.....] wʿdryn wʾšd wʾšd/wʾšr wʾšlm byrḥ
sywn šnt 5.100+20+10+5+1 dkyr mqtlw/mmtlw

PAT 2758 **Syr '33 p 181** Tad 5 **n. d.**
Prov: Khirbet es-Sane (Syria). Loc: Damascus, National Museum, 4834. *Dedicatory. On relief.* Bib: *Hand copy*; Abdul-Hak and Abdul-Hak, '51 no. 7, photo pl XIII, 1.

1 lʾlt wrḥm ʿbd wmwdʾ rbʾl br ʿwydʾ br
ydʿy
2 wdkyr šlmʾ br qsynʾ

PAT 2759 **Syr '33 p 183** Tad 7a **n. d.**
Prov: Palmyra. Loc: Palmyra Museum. *Unclassified. On stone fragment.* Bib: *Hand copy.*

1 [....] bwnʾ br rbʾ[....]
2 [....] dnh dy mn bny myt[...]

3 [....]t ktb bt ʾrkʾ ʾq[...]
4 [....] š[nt] 3?[.100]+80

PAT 2760 **Syr '33 p 184** Tad 7b **n. d.**
Prov: Palmyra. Loc: Palmyra Museum. *Funerary. On door lintel.* Bib: *Hand copy.*

1 [.... qbrʾ dnh bnʾ ...] br yrḥbwlʾ br zbydʾ br ty wlbnwhy wlbny bnwhy lyqrhwn dy ʿlmʾ byrḥ ṭbt šnt 400[...]
2 [....] b?ʾ?mlgyʾ wrmʾ/wdmʾ bt ʾrkʾ mn dy yʿl ltnn swm nkry dy lwʾ mn bnwhy dkryʾ yḥwb lpsqws zwzyn ʾ[lp...]

PAT 2761 **Syr '33 p 185** Tad 8 **A.D. 178**
Prov: Palmyra. Loc: Damascus, National Museum, p 439. *Funerary: Cession. On stone tablet.* Bib: *Hand copy.*

1 dktʾ dh šḥymtʾ dy
2 lgw mn mʿrtʾ rḥqt
3 šlmt brt šḥymw br
4 šḥymw lʿzyzw br ʾdʾ br
5 rbʾl lh wlbnwhy wbnʾ
6 bnwh lʿlmʾ byrḥ tšry
7 šnt 4.100+80+10

PAT 2762 **Syr '33 p 186** Tad 9 **n. d.**
Prov: Palmyra, Temple of Bel. Loc: Palmyra Museum. *Honorific. On column drum.* Bib: *Hand copy.*

1 ṣlmʾ d[y ... br]
2 zbdʿth dy mn p[ḥd]
3 bny mytʾ

PAT 2763 **Syr '33 p 187** Tad 10 **n. d.**
Prov: Palmyra. Loc: Palmyra Museum. *Honorific. On console fragment.* Bib: *Hand copy*; Déd pp 32-33.

A. (Side a)
1 [........]ν φιλο[..........]
2 Σκυθίας ἐν πλοίῳ Βο[...]
3 ἔμποροι συνλαβόμε[νοι ...]
4 [κ]αὶ πάσῃ σπου[δῃ ...]

B. (Side b)
1 dy ʾqym[w ....]
2 dy bʿl[y] bw?p?w?r šlm[...]yl
3 šry lmrbʿʾ mdʿrʾ [...]

Déd pp 32-33 joins Inv 10 95 (Gk) and tentatively Inv 10 91; reconstructs longer text.

PAT 2764 **Syr '33 p 189** Tad 11 **n. d.**
Prov: Palmyrene, Jub al-Qdeym, N of Palmyra. Loc: Palmyra Museum. *Dedicatory. On altar.* Bib: *Hand copy.*

A. (Side a)
1 Διὶ ὑψίστῳ καὶ ἐ[π]ηκό[ῳ]
2 τὸν [βωμὸν ʼI]αρι[βῶ]λης
3 Μαλ[ίχ]ου [το]ῦ [ʼO]γᾶ τ[ο]ῦ
4 [.......]ου [ὑπ]ὲ[ρ ὑ]γίας
5 [ἐποίησ]ε [καὶ ἀνέθηκ[ε]
7 [ἔτ]ους ἐβ[δ]όμου [μηνὸς]
8 [ʼΥπ]ερβερεταίο[υ]

B. (Side b)
1 b[y]rḥ ʾyr ywm 20+5 [...]
2 šnt 4.100+60 [....]
3 [ʿ]ltʾ dnh dy [ʿbd]
4 [wq]rb yrḥb[wlʾ br]
5 [ml]kw br ʿgʾ [br ...]
6 [lbryk] šm[h lʿlmʾ]
7 [.....]

PAT 2765 **Syr '33 p 190** Tad 12a **A.D. 4**
Prov: Palmyra. Loc: Palmyra Museum. *Funerary?. On stone fragment.* Bib: *Hand copy.*

1 byrḥ sywn šnt 3.100+10+5 ʾqymw
2 [m]lkw br ḥlkš qrqpn wʿgylw br [...]
3 [...]ʾzn špyr

PAT 2766 **Syr '36 p 268** Tad 17 **6 B.C.**
Prov: Palmyra. Loc: Palmyra, A 361. *Honorific. On statue base.* Bib: *Hand copy.*

1 byrḥ knwn šnt 3.100+5+1+[1] ʾqymw
2 kmryʾ dy ḥrtʾ ṣlmʾ dnh

3 lʿgylw br ʾydʿn dy mn bny kmrʾ
4 dy ʿbd wqrb hw wbnwhy plgwt
5 [ʿ]ltʾ dh wmšlʾ wbt nḥryʾ w
6 [ʾ]d/rnʾ lḥrtʾ wlnny wlršp ʾlhyʾ

PAT 2767 **Syr '36 p 271** Tad 18 **n. d.**
Prov: Palmyra. Loc: Palmyra, A 314. *Unclassified. On stele.* Bib: *Hand copy.*

1 [...]bqrnʾ mʿrbytʾ
2 [....]lbwl wgd tdmr
3 [..]ʾnwky ʿlʾ ʾʿnšt
4 [...]qmʾ ʾm ʾnwky
5 [...]mʾ ʾqbl ʿlh
6 [...]wmṭ wtwtʾ
7 [.....]bn ʾyš wʾrʿ
8 [...]kz ʾnḥnw bʾrn[..]
9 [.....]ʾšwʿ
10 [...]lylnwd/rz
11 [....] lʿšrt
12 [....] ʿšrt

Aramaic? Milik Déd pp 288-92: Phoenician in Palmyrene script

PAT 2768 **Syr '36 p 274** Tad 19 **n. d.**
Prov: Palmyra, Temple of Bel. Loc: Palmyra, A 285. *Dedicatory. On lintel fragment.* Bib: *Hand copy.*

1 [... m]ṭltʾ ʿmwdyh wšryth [....]
2 [.....b]wl ʾlhʾ ṭbʾ wškrʾ ʿl ḥyyhwn
3 [.....d]y nḥšʾ ʿl ʿmwdʾ dy ʿl bbʾ rbʾ
4 [...]r/dʾ bkl šnʾ ʿd ʿlmʾ lyqrhwn

PAT 2769 **Syr '36 p 280** Tad 20 **A.D. 171**
Prov: Palmyra, Temple of Baalshamîn. Loc: Palmyra, A 306. *Honorific. On column console.* Bib: *Hand copy; photos pl LIII.*

1 [.... ....]
2 ω[......]πο[......... ....]
3 πα[....][ἐ]ν τῷ Καισαρείῳ ἐφ' ἵππον ἀν[δριά]ντα · ἕν δ[ὲ]
4 τῷ τοῦ Βήλου ἱερῷ ἀνδριάντα ὀνομα[τι β]ου[λῆς καὶ]
5 δήμου · καὶ διὰ ψηφισμάτων καὶ ἰσ[...]ρεων ἐ[μαρ-]
6 τύρησαν παρὰ ʾΑουιδίῳ Κασσίῳ τῷ διασημοτάτῳ
7 ὑπά[ρχ]ῳ · αἱ δὲ τ[ῆ]ς π[ό]λε[ω]ς τέσσαρες φυλαὶ ἑκάσ[τη]
8 ἐν ἰ[δίῳ ἱερῷ ἀνδρίαν]τα ἀνήγειρεν τειμῆς καὶ βελτίστου πολιτεύ-
9 [ματος χάριν ....] μηνὸς Δειου.

1 [....]
2 [... yr]ḥbwlʾ [...]
3 [....] lšmš [....]
4 wʾ[.]yn[...]ʾbr[.]lh
5 wʿml bswmh shdt lh bdgm bwlʾ wdms [...]
6 lwt hygmnʾ bqblyn ʾrbʿʾ wʿbd lh [......]
7 ṣlm mrkb swsy ṣlm bt bl[......]
8 nḥš wʾp ʿm yqrʾ dy bwlʾ wdms ʿbd lh [ʾrbʿ]
9 pḥzyʾ pḥz pḥz bt ʾlhyh ṣlm dy nḥš lyqrh bdyl dy špr
10 [.......] byrḥ knwn šnt 4.100+80+3

PAT 2770 **Syr '36 p 346** Tad 21 **A.D. 115**
Prov: Palmyra, Temple of Baalshamîn. Loc: Palmyra, *in situ. Dedicatory. On altar.* Bib: *Hand copy.*

1 [...............]ῳ Μάλιχος κ[..................]
2 [..............] Ἄγεγος οἱ Βωλεμμέου[.........]
3 [.........................]χην ἀνέθηκαν ἔτους ϛκυ'
4 Περειτίου ζ'

1 [l]mrʾ ʿlmʾ qrbw ʿwydw wmlkw wyrḥbwl[ʾ wggw]
2 [bny] bwlmʾ br ʿwydy br bwlmʾ ʾrb/ʾdb ʿl ḥyyhwn wḥ[yy]
3 [b]nyhwn wlyqr bny šʿdʾ šbbyhwn byrḥ šb[ṭ]
4 [šnt] 3+[1].100+20+5+[1]

PAT 2771 **Syr '36 p 348** Tad 22 **A.D. 219**
Prov: Palmyra. Loc: Palmyra, A 277. *Dedicatory. On cippus.* Bib: *Hand copy.*

1 lbryk šmh lʿlmʾ rḥmnʾ ṭbʾ
2 wtyrʾ ʿbd ʿtnwry br tymʿʾ ḥlʾ b[r]
3 ʿtnwry ʿl ḥywhy wḥyʾ bnwhy wlyqr
4 bny pṭrṭʾ byrḥ ʾdr šnt 5.100+20+10

PAT 2772 **Syr '36 p 349** Tad 23 **n. d.**

Prov: Palmyra. Loc: Palmyra, A 372. *Honorific. On stone fragment.* Bib: *Hand copy.*

1 [.....]ʿ[.....]
2 [....]ylwʾ ʾ[....]
3 [...]lbt qsm[ʾ..]
4 [....]tʾ ṭbtʾ[....]
5 [b]nwhy y[...]
6 yln[...]

PAT 2773 **Syr '36 p 350** Tad 24 **n. d.**

Prov: Palmyra. Loc: Palmyra, A 313. *Dedicatory. On statue base.* Bib: *Hand copy.*

1 ṣlm whby br nwrbl
2 br ʾqmt dy mn bny mʿzyn
3 dkyr lšmš

PAT 2774 **Syr '36 p 351** Tad 25 **n. d.**

Prov: Palmyra. Loc: Palmyra, A 304. *Funerary. On stone fragment.* Bib: *Hand copy.*

1 [....]ʾm[....]
2 [....]ʿmt[....]
3 [...]š ʿgylw br lš[mš ....]
4 [..] br khylw br bl[.....]
5 [...]lw br nwrbl ʾqml bw[...]
6 [... b]lʿqb ḥmnwn blmʾ [.....]
7 [...]ql br ʾbb tymʿm[d ...]
8 [.....]rʾyš[yʾ] ḥd [....]
9 [... ʾt[....]wwʾ[....]
10 [...k]l mh dy kšr[....]w lbt ʾ[....]
11 [...]wldwdʾ/dwrʾ dy yrḥbwlʾ l[...]
12 [....]wʾsrw whqymw byny[.....]

PAT 2775 **Syr '36 p 353** Tad 26 **n. d.**

Prov: Palmyra. Loc: Palmyra, A 305. *Unusual, Legal? . On stone fragment.* Bib: *Hand copy.*

1 [.....b]šr wlḥm wm[n........]
2 [......]mh lʾ ygnb wlʾ yḥṭ[p......]
3 [......] bmqymtʾ kl dy ktyb [...]
4 [......] bktbyʾ ʾln ʿbd wqm[......]
5 [......] kmryʾ bd lyt kmryʾ [.....]
6 [.....]wrʾyšyʾ wbd lyt tḥ[.......]
7 [.....]mn dy yʾmr lh ʿbd ḥ[......]
8 [......] mh dy bktbyʾ ʾln ynt[....]
9 [.....]mškn hw ymh byrḥbw[l ....]
10 [.....] q[p]lwhy wysb mšknh [...]
11 [......]yḥwb slʿn[......]

PAT 2776 **Syr '36 p 355** Tad 27 **n. d.**

Prov: Palmyra, S-W Necropolis, Tomb of Three Brothers. Loc: Palmyra, *in situ. Funerary. On lintel.* Group: Ber '38 p 94; C4171-75; Syr '36 p 355 = Tad 27. Bib: *Hand copy*; SFP 162 fig 230; SFP 162 fig 230.

1 mqbr̊tʾ dh ʿbd mlʾ br ṣʿdy br mlʾ lh wlʾdth
2 wlbnwhy wlbnth wlbny bnwhy lʿlmʾ šn!t 4.100+40+10+4

1 *wlʾdth*: sense uncertain; *wlʾrth* not impossible in spite of dotted *r* in *mqbr̊tʾ*; *wlʾḥ!th* yields a known word \`sister'

PAT 2777 **Syr '37 p 31** **n. d.**

Prov: Palmyra. Loc: Damascus, National Museum,

331. *Funerary. On relief.* Bib: *Hand copy Seyrig '37a p 33 fig 20*; Parlasca '85, p 355, pl 150, 1..

1 ḥbl zbdbwl
2 br zgwg br
3 zbdbwl

PAT 2778 **Syr '38 p 76** Tad 29 **A.D. 84**
Prov: Palmyra, Temple of Bel. Loc: Palmyra, *in situ. Honorific. On statue base.* Bib: *Hand copy.*

1 Ἡ βουλὴ Ἄβγαρον Πατρόκλου
2 τοῦ καὶ Ἀστουργᾶ τοῦ Λεκείσου
3 ἀγαθὸν πολείτην καὶ εὔνουν
4 πρὸς τὴν ἴδιαν πατρίδα τιμῆς
5 χάριν ἔτους εϘτ' Δύστρου

1 ṣlmʾ dnh dy ʾbgr br pṭrqls
2 dy mtqrh ʿstwrgʾ br lqyšw
3 dy mn bny mytʾ dy ʾqymw lh bwlʾ
4 lyqrh bdyl dy špr lhwn byrḥ
5 ʾdr šnt 3.100+80+10+5

PAT 2779 **Syr '38 p 78** Tad 31 **A.D. 39**
Prov: Palmyra. Loc: Palmyra, A 622. *Dedicatory. On altar.* Bib: *Hand copy.*

1 Ποσειδῶνι θεῷ

1 byrḥ sywn šnt 3.100+40+10
2 [q]rb mqymw br khylw br zbdbl
3 [dy] mtqrh br zbydy dy mn pḥd bny
4 [gd]ybwl ʿlwtʾ ʾln trtyhn
5 [l]ʾlqwnrʿ ʾlhʾ ṭbʾ

PAT 2780 **Syr '38 p 79** Tad 32 **n. d.**
Prov: Palmyra, Temple of Bel. Loc: Palmyra, A 429. *Dedicatory. On lintel fragment.* Bib: *Photo, hand copy.*

1 [ʿ]ltʾ dh dy ʿb[d] mlkw br ḥyrn
2 [br ..ʾ]gyl[w] lbwlʿstr ʾlhʾ
3 [ʿl ḥywhy] wḥyy bnwhy wʾḥ[w]hy

PAT 2781 **Syr '38 p 80** Tad 33 **A.D. 37**
Prov: Palmyra. Loc: Palmyra, A 847. *Dedicatory. On altar fragment.* Bib: *Hand copy.*

1 [byrḥ] šbṭ šnt 3.100+40+5+3 ʿltʾ
2 [dh.....]ʾtʾ qrbw mlkw [z]bdʿ[th]
3 [....]bny tymʿmd b[r] bwrpʾ zg[wg]
4 [lʿglybwl w]lmlkbl ʾlhyʾ ṭbyʾ
5 [ʿl ḥyyhn wḥyy b]nyhn wʾḥyhn wḥyy tym[ʿmd]
6 [ʾbwhn]

PAT 2782 **Syr '38 p 81** Tad 34 **n. d.**
Prov: Palmyra. Loc: Palmyra, A 415. *Dedicatory. On relief fragment.* Bib: *Hand copy.*

1 [.....]wbl[...]ḥmʾ bnwhy lʿglbw[l]
2 [..... š]nt 3.100+80+[..]

PAT 2783 **Syr '38 p 82** Tad 35 **n. d.**
Prov: Palmyra. Loc: Palmyra, A 123. *Dedicatory. On statuette base.* Bib: *Hand copy.*

1 ʿbd mḥrbzn lšl
2 mt

PAT 2784 **Syr '38 p 153** Tad 36a **A.D. (108)**
Prov: Palmyra, N-W Necropolis, Hypogeum of Yarhai. Loc: Palmyra, A 383. *Funerary: Foundation. On stone tablet.* Group: Syr '38 pp 153-58 = Tad 36 a-g. Bib: *Hand copy;* Amy and Seyrig '36 p 242 no. 12, pl 37 no. 5; MF Fondation 31.

1 byrḥ nysn šnt 1+[2]+1.100+10+5+4
2 bt qbwr[ʾ] dnh
3 ʿbd yrḥy br b[r]yky br
4 [tym]rṣw l[h wl]bnwhy
5 [wlbny bnwhy d]y ʿlmʾ
6 [w]lyqr [bryky] ʾbwhy
7 [w....mʾ...ʾ]ḥy ʾmh

PAT 2785 **Syr '38 p 154** Tad 36b **n. d.**
Prov: Palmyra, N-W Necropolis, Hypogeum of Yarhai. Loc: Palmyra, A 356. *Funerary. On*

stone tablet. Group: Syr '38 p 153-58 = Tad 36 a-g. Bib: *Hand copy*; Amy and Seyrig '36 p 259.

1 [tym]rṣw [....]
2 w[.]qys[....]
3 plgwt [....]
4 lyq[r .....]
5 nysn šnt [....]

PAT 2786 **Syr '38 p 155** Tad 36c **A.D. 241**
Prov: Palmyra, N-W Necropolis, Hypogeum of Yarhai. Loc: Palmyra, A 368. *Funerary: Cession. On stone tablet.* Group: Syr '38 p 153-58 = Tad 36 a-g. Bib: *Hand copy*; Amy and Seyrig '36 p 259-62, pl 48 no. 3.

1 τὸ ἀνατολικὸν πλευρὸν σὺν τῇ ἐν αὐτ-
2 ῷ ὀρυγῇ ψιλῆς ἐξέδρας τῇ(ς τῶ)ν εἰσιόντων
3 τὸ τοῦ σπηλαίου θύρωμα εὐθὺς ἐν εὐω-
4 νύμοις, μέχρι τῆς ἐφεσθηκυίης ἐν κόν-
5 χῃ νείκης παρινῆς τῆς κατὰ μέσον [τῆς]
6 ἄντικρυς ἐξέδρας σὺν τ(α)ῖς ἐπάνω [αὐ]-
7 τῆς ἐν γεισώματι νεκροθήκαις τρε[ῖσι],
8 καὶ τὰς ἐν τῷ αὐτῷ πλευρῷ νεκροθήκ-
9 ας σὺν παντὶ κοσμῷ καὶ δικαίοις ἐξε-
10 χώρησαν Ἰούλιοι Αὐρήλιοι Ἀράνης
11 καὶ Μαλῶχας οἱ Γερμάνου Ἰουλίῳ Αὐ)ρ-
12 ηλίῳ Θεοφίλῳ Θαιμάρσου τοῦ Ζεβεί-
13 δου αὐτῷ τε καὶ υἱοῖς καὶ υἱωνοῖς καὶ
14 ἐγγόνοις εἰς τὸ παντελές. ἔτους βνφ',
15 Λώου.

1 sṭr̊ʾ dnh mdnḥyʾ dy mʿr̊tʾ mʿlyk
2 bbʾ r̊bʾ ʿd nyqʾ dy qymʾ lqblh wtṣbth
3 wqšṭwh r̊ḥq ywlyʾ ʾwr̊lyʾ ḥyr̊n wmlwkʾ
4 bny gr̊mnʾ lywlys ʾwr̊lys typyls br̊ tymr̊ṣw
5 [z]bydʾ lh wlbnʾ bnwh lyqr̊hwn dy
6 ʿlmʾ byr̊ḥ ʾb šnt 5.100+40+10+2

PAT 2787 **Syr '38 p 157** Tad 36d **n. d.**
Prov: Palmyra, N-W Necropolis, Hypogeum of Yarhai. Loc: Palmyra, *in situ. Funerary. On relief.* Group: Syr '38 p 153-58 = Tad 36 a-g. Bib: *Hand copy.*

1 ṣlmt nṣʾ brt typyls
2 ʾtt bwnʾ br tymrṣw
3 ḥbl

line 1 *nṣʾ*: or *nḥʾ* so Stark PN

PAT 2788 **Syr '38 p 157** Tad 36e **n. d.**
Prov: Palmyra, N-W Necropolis, Hypogeum of Yarhai. Loc: Palmyra, A 450. *Funerary. On relief.* Group: Syr '38 p 153-58 = Tad 36 a-g. Bib: *Hand copy.*

1 [ʾ]qmʾ
2 [wn]yny bny
3 [nb]wmʾ
4 ḥbl

PAT 2789 **Syr '38 p 158** Tad 36f **n. d.**
Prov: Palmyra, N-W Necropolis, Hypogeum of Yarhai. Loc: Palmyra, A 384. *Funerary. On relief.* Group: Syr '38 p 153-58 = Tad 36 a-g. Bib: *Hand copy.*

1 wrwd
2 ḥbl

PAT 2790 **Syr '38 p 158** Tad 36g **n. d.**
Prov: Palmyra, N-W Necropolis, Hypogeum of Yarhai. Loc: Palmyra, A 385. *Funerary. On relief.* Group: Syr '38 p 153-58 = Tad 36 a-g. Bib: *Hand copy.*

1 nṣʾ brt
2 yrḥy br
3 bryky ḥbl

PAT 2791 **Syr '38 p 159** Tad 37 **n. d.**
Prov: Palmyra, N-W Necropolis. Loc: Palmyra, A 389. *Honorific. On stele.* Bib: *Hand copy.*

1 dkyr ʿgylw wbnwhy
2 dyhb ʾtrʾ lkptʾ

PAT 2792 **Syr '38 p 159** Tad 38 **n. d.**
Prov: Palmyra, W of Temple of Bel. Loc: Palmyra, A 847. *Funerary. On stone tablet.* Bib: *Hand copy.*

1 ṣlm ʾd/rwnʾ [......]
2 bny šʿdy br [....]
3 [ʾ]qml byrḥ [....]
4 [...].100+70+[...]

PAT 2793 **Syr '42 p 80** **n. d.**
Prov: Palmyra. Loc: Paris, Private collection. *Funerary. On relief.* Group: RB p 537 no. 7. Bib: *Hand copy p 80; pl XXIII.*

1 ḥbl mlkw
2 br šmʿwn
3 bwrpʾ

PAT 2794 **Syr '49 p 36** no. 1 **n. d.**
Prov: Palmyra. Loc: Louvre, AO 19801. *Graffito. On relief.* Group: Syr '49 nos. 1, 2, 4, 5, 7 (Relief of divine triad). Bib: Hand copy; Lou 153.

1 dkyr ḥgwgʾ [br]
2 ʾgyʿ bṭb

PAT 2795 **Syr '49 p 36** no. 2 **n. d.**
Prov: Palmyra. Loc: Louvre, AO 19801. *Graffito. On relief.* Group: Syr '49 nos. 1, 2, 4, 5, 7 (Relief of divine triad). Bib: Hand copy; Lou 153.

1 rpʾl br twpʾ
2 zbdbl bṭb

PAT 2796 **Syr '49 p 38** no. 4 **n. d.**
Prov: Palmyra. Loc: Louvre, AO 19801. *Graffito. On relief.* Group: Syr '49 nos. 1, 2, 4, 5, 7 (Relief of divine triad). Bib: Hand copy; Lou 153.

1 dkyr̊ br̊ʿʾ
2 zbdʿth wbrnbw
3 wzdql dy bt
4 br̊nbw bṭb

PAT 2797 **Syr '49 p 39** no. 5 **n. d.**
Prov: Palmyra. Loc: Louvre, AO 19801. *Graffito. On relief.* Group: Syr '49 nos. 1, 2, 4, 5, 7 (Relief of divine triad). Bib: Hand copy; Lou 153.

1 dkyr br̊ny qd[.]m[.]
2 dy btgʾl ʾlh[ʾ]
3 wšlmʾ dy dšry
4 btbr̊h bṭb

PAT 2798 **Syr '49 p 40** no. 2 **A.D. 228**
Prov: Palmyra (probably). Loc: Paris, Private collection. *Dedicatory. On stone plaque.* Bib: Hand copy.

1 ʿbd mlkw br yrḥy wʿnnw ʾḥwhy lbʿšmn
2 byrḥ ṭbt šnt 5.100+20+10+5+4

Line 1 *lbʿšmn*: final *-mn* written below line

PAT 2799 **Syr '49 p 40** no. 7 **n. d.**
Prov: Palmyra. Loc: Louvre, AO 19801. *Graffito. On relief.* Group: Syr '49 nos. 1, 2, 4, 5, 7 (Relief of divine triad). Bib: *Hand copy*; Lou 153.

1 bryk

PAT 2800 **Syr '49 p 249** no. 53 **n. d.**
Prov: Palmyrene, Jub el-Garrah, 55 km E of Homs. Loc: Damascus, National Museum, 12875. *Dedicatory. On relief.* Bib: *Seyrig and Starcky, Syr '49 pl II*; CatMD 12875.

1 ṣlmʾ dgnyʾ

PAT 2801 **Syr '50 p 137** **A.D. 52**
Prov: Palmyra. Loc: Palmyra, A 1126. *Funerary. On stone tablet.*

1 HAERANES BONNE RABBELI
2 F*(ilius)* PALMIRENUS PHYLES MITHENON
3 SIBI ET SUIS FECIT

1 ἔτους γψτ' μηνὸς ξανδικοῦ
2 Αἱράνης Βωνναίου τοῦ Ραββήλου
3 Παλμυρηνὸς φυλῆς Μειθηνῶν ἑαυτῷ
4 καὶ Βααλθηγα μητρὶ
5 αὐτοῦ εὐνοίας ἕνεκεν καὶ τοῖς ἰδίοις αὐτοῦ.

1 byrḥ nysn šnt 3.100+60+3 qbrʾ dnh dy
2 ḥyrn br bwnʾ br rbʾl br bwnʾ br ʿtntn br

3 tymy tdmryʾ dy mn pḥd bny mytʾ dy bnʾ ʿl
4 bwnʾ ʾbwhy wʿl bʿltgʾ brt blšwry dy mn
5 pḥd bny gdybwl ʾmh wlh wlbnwhy lyqrhwn

PAT 2802 **Syr '59 p 104** no. 2 **n. d.**
Prov: Palmyra, Temple of Baalshamîn. Loc: See Syr '59 p 103. *Tessera. On terracotta.* Bib: *Photo pl XIV.*

1 tgʾ
2 dy bl
3 tymrṣw
4 dyny

PAT 2803 **Syr '59 p 104** no. 3 **n. d.**
Prov: Palmyra, Temple of Baalshamîn. Loc: See Syr '59 p 103. *Tessera. On terracotta.* Bib: *Photo pl XIV.*

1 ʾgn
2 yrḥ
3 bwl

PAT 2804 **Syr '59 p 104** no. 6 **n. d.**
Prov: Palmyra. Loc: See Syr '59 p 103. *Tessera. On terracotta.* Bib: *Photo pl XIV.*

1 nbw
2 šbʿtʾ

PAT 2805 **Syr '59 p 105** no. 9 **n. d.**
Prov: Palmyra. Loc: See Syr '59 p 103. *Tessera. On terracotta.* Bib: *Photo pl XIV.*

1 w?/p?t

PAT 2806 **Syr '59 p 105** no. 10 **n. d.**
Prov: Palmyra. Loc: See Syr '59 p 103. *Tessera. On terracotta.* Bib: *Photo pl XIV.*

1 [..]l

PAT 2807 **Syr '59 p 105** no. 12 **n. d.**
Prov: Palmyra. Loc: See Syr '59 p 103. *Tessera. On terracotta.* Bib: *Photo pl XIV.*

1 mrzḥ
2 bʿltk
3 wtymʾ
4 ywm 5

PAT 2808 **Syr '59 p 105** no. 13 **n. d.**
Prov: Palmyra. Loc: See Syr '59 p 103. *Tessera. On terracotta.* Bib: *Photo pl XIV.*
(Obv.)
1 bʿltk
(Rev.)
1 ʿtnwry
2 bwrpʾ

PAT 2809 **Syr '59 p 106** no. 14 **n. d.**
Prov: Palmyra. Loc: See Syr '59 p 103. *Tessera. On terracotta.* Bib: *Photo pl XIV.*

1 ʿgʾ
2 šmʿwn
1 qštʾ
2 byrtʾ?

PAT 2809.02 **Syr '59 p 107** no. 23 **n. d.**
Prov: Palmyra. Loc: . *Tessera. On terracotta.* Bib: *Photo pl XIV.*

(Rev.)
1 ʿštr[t?]

PAT 2810 **Syr '63 p 48** **n. d.**
Prov: Iraq, near Euphrates (Iraq Petroleum Company Station T-1). Loc: Mosul, Dominican Friars. *Dedicatory. On stone slab.* Bib: *Photo Pl IVc.*

1 dkyr ʾbgr br
2 šlmn br zbdbwl
3 dy ʾtʾ brš
4 qṣtʾ bʾs
5 ṭrṭgwt yrḥy

PAT 2811 **Syr '70 p 413** **n. d.**
Prov: Wadi Miqâṭ, 20 km. from station H 4 of Iraq Petroleum Company. Loc: Not given in edition. *Graffito. On stone.* Bib: *Text and translation* in review of *Oxtoby '68 pp 101-02 and pl XIX.*

1 dkyryn wbrykyn qdm 'lhy
2 tdmr 'n' ṭymrṣw br
3 'gylw wmlkw ml' dy
4 nṭrw tnn šnt dy hww bny
5 ḥgg ḥl/nb/k' ywm 20 bnysn

PAT 2812 **Syr '71 p 420** **A.D. 273**
Prov: Palmyra. Loc: Palmyra Museum. *Honorific. On stone slab.* Bib: *Pl XXIII nos. 1, 2*; cf. IP no. 31; Syr '31 p 117; Inv 9 28; du Mesnil '42-45 pp 76- ..

1 brbnwt mrzḥwt s[p]ṭm[yws] ḥdwdn [snqlṭyq']
2 nhyr' br spṭm[yw]s 'gylw mqy dy 'dr [ḥyl' dy]
3 [']wrlynws qsr [m]r[n]' w'dm[r] 'm wld' [......]
4 [whw]' 'mhwn bdy[r' byrḥ] 'b šnt 5.100+[80+3]
5 [byr]ḥ 'dr d[y] š[nt 584]
6 [wbryk]yn w[hby] br [š''] br 't'qb
7 [.....] '[l] b[w]m'[w..]
8 [...br 't']qb yr[ḥy dy] 'l [...]
9 [w...br] 't'q[b yrḥy] 'l twn' w'g[ylw br...]
10 [dy 'l ']m[wd' w...'l ṭly']
11 [...]
12 [w]yrḥb[wl' br ']gy[lw dy] '[l b]t [nṭr]' [w]šm['
13 [ṭbyt...]

PAT 2813 **Syr '71 p 422** **n. d.**
Prov: Palmyra. Loc: Beirut, Henri Pharaon Collection. *Funerary. On relief.* Bib: *Pl XXIV no. 1.*

(above young man and boy)
1 'lyš' wblšwry
2 bny tymy ḥbl
(above female figure)
3 'ty brt
4 'lyš' 'mhwn
(above another female figure)
5 zqṭrty
6 mrbythn

PAT 2814 **Syr '85 p 57** **A.D. 142**
Prov: Palmyra. Loc: Louvre, AO 28377. *Dedicatory. On altar.* Bib: *Caquot '85, photo fig 1 p 58*; Lou 156.

1 dkrn lbryk šmh
2 'bd zbd'th br
3 ḥggw br br'th
4 'lyb'l 'lt'
5 wšrb' 'l ḥywhy
6 wḥyy bnwhy wḥyy
7 'ḥwhy byrḥ nysn
8 šnt 4.100+40+10+3

PAT 2815 **Syr '85 p 257** no. 13 **A.D. 252**
Prov: Palmyra, Great Colonnade. Loc: Palmyra, *in situ. Honorific. On column.* Bib: *Gaw '85.*

1 Σεπτίμιον 'Οδαίνα[θον Αἱ]ράνου
Ο[ὐαβ]αλλάθ[ου τοῦ Νασώρου] λα[μ]πρότατον
[ἐξαρχον Παλμυ]ρηνῶν 'Ιούλιος Αὐρήλιος
'Αθηακά[βος 'Ο]γήλου Ζαβδιβώ[λου ...] τοῦ καὶ
Κωρα, τὸν φίλον στοργῆς ἕνεκεν, ἔτους γξφ' μηνεὶ
[Ξανδ]ικῷ

1 ṣlm 'spṭmyws '[dynt br ḥyrn] br whblt nṣwr rš[' [tdmw]r nhyr' d'bd lh 't'qb br 'gylw br zbdbwl br mqymw dmqr' qr' rḥmh lyqrhwn brbnwth byrḥ nysn šnt 5.100+60+3

PAT 2816 **Syr '85 p 271** no. 1 **A.D. 86**
Prov: Palmyra, N Wall. Loc: Palmyra, 1467/8774. *Funerary: Foundation. On stone block.* Bib: *As'ad and Teixidor '82 pp 89-96, fig 1*

1 m'rt' dh 'b[d] mlkw br yrḥbwl'
2 br mlkw br nwr'th dy mtqrh br
3 mqy 'l yrḥbwl' 'bwhy w'l tmlk
4 'mh lyqrhn wlh wlbnwhy wl'ḥwhy
5 wlbny ddh lyqrhn dy bt 'lm' byrḥ
6 nysn šnt 3.100+80+10+5+2

PAT 2817 **Syr '85 p 273** no. 2
Prov: Palmyra, N Wall. Loc: Palmyra, 1464/8771. *Funerary: Foundation. On stone block.* Bib: *As'ad and Teixidor '82 pp 89-96, fig 2*

1 Τὸ μνημεῖον σύν τῷ σπηλαίῳ
2 ᾠκο[δό]μησαν Αιεγος καὶ Μοκειμος οἱ
3 Λισαμου τοῦ Θαιμη τοῦ ἐπικαλουμένου
4 Αζαρζειραθου εἴς τε ἑαυτούς καὶ ο[...]αι
5 υἱωνοὺς γέρως χάριν ἔτους ιυ' μηνὸς
[Ξα]νδικος

1 npš' dh wm'rt' 'bdw ḥggw wmqymw bny lšmš
2 br tym' dy mtqrh 'zrzyrt lhwn wlbnyhwn lyqrhn
3 dy 'lm' byrḥ nysn šnt 4.100+10
4 ṣlmy' 'ln dy lšmš br tym' wdy ḥggw wmqymw bnwhy

PAT 2818 **Syr '85 p 274** no. 3 **n. d.**
Prov: Palmyra, N Wall. Loc: Palmyra, 1469/8824. *Funerary. On stone block.* Bib: *As'ad and Teixidor '82 pp 89-96, fig 3.*

1 [.....] m?n?y..[.....]
2 bny mtbwl lh wlb[nwhy]
3 wl'ḥwhy lyqrh[wn ...]
4 'lm' mn kysh w'l[.....]

PAT 2819 **Syr '85 p 274** no. 4 **n. d.**
Prov: Palmyra, N Wall. Loc: Palmyra, 1470/8828. *Funerary. On stone block.* Bib: *As'ad and Teixidor '82 pp 89-96, fig 4.*

1 [Τὸ μν]ημεῖον ἔκτισεν Βωρόφα
2 [Σαμφιγέρ]αμου τοῦ Μαλίχου τοῦ
3 [Σαμψιγέρ]αμου εἰς ταφὴν αἰώνι-
4 [ον ἑαυτο]ῦ καὶ τέκνων τῷ εου' ἔτει

1 npš' dh 'bd bwrp' š[mšgrm]
2 br mlkw br šmšgrm lh w[lbnwhy]
3 lyqrhwn dy 'lm' byrḥ
4 šnt 4.100+60+10
Letters are colored red.

PAT 2820 **Syr '85 p 276** no. 5 **n. d.**
Prov: Palmyra, N Wall. Loc: Palmyra, 1468/8831. *Funerary: Cession. On stone block.* Bib: *As'ad and Teixidor '82 pp 89-96, fig 5.*

1 Τήν ὀρυγήν τοῦ παν[...]
2 ἐξεχώρησεν 'Ιούλιος [Αὐρήλιος ...]
3 Θαιμαρσου τοῦ Ανεινα[ς ...]
4 Αὐρηλία Σαλαμαθι δια[...]
5 Αβδαρσα εἰς τὸ ἐξεῖ[ναι ἀπαλλοτριοῖν ...]
6 τὸ αὐτὸ σπήλεον εἰς [ταφὴν ...]
7 καὶ υἱῶν καὶ υἱων[ῶν καὶ ἐγγόνων εἰς]
8 τὸ παντελές ἔτ[ους ...]

1 [.....] 'wrlys ḥnyn' br
2 [.....] 'wrly' šlmt brt
3 [.....] lh wlbnh
4 [.... šnt] 5.100+40+10
5 [...........] w'wr[ly'..]

PAT 2821 **Syr '85 p 276** no. 6 **n. d.**
Prov: Palmyra, N Wall. Loc: Palmyra, 1452/8642. *Funerary. On stone block.* Bib: *As'ad and Teixidor '82 pp 89-96, fig 6.*

1 ṣlmt' dh dy 'lyt
2 brt yrḥy br šmy
3 'mh
Letters are colored red.

PAT 2822 **Syr '85 p 277** no. 7 **n. d.**
Prov: Palmyra, N Wall. Loc: Palmyra, (no number). *Funerary: Cession. On stone block.* Bib: *As'ad and Teixidor '82 pp 89-96, fig 7.*

1 [.....]'d/r d/r š[......]
2 [...... tš]ry šnt 5.100+[...]
3 [.....]br rb'l br ym[lkw]
4 [... tymr]ṣw bny mqymw [...]
5 [.....]' mqbl' dy y'/h[..]
6 [....lh]wn wlbnyh[wn] [...]

PAT 2823 **Syr '85 p 277** no. 8 **n. d.**
Prov: Palmyra. Loc: Palmyra, 1342/7483. *Funerary: Cession. On stone block.* Bib: *As'ad and Teixidor '82 pp 89-96, fig 8.*

1 ὀπισθό[δομος]
2 ἴσων ἐν α[...]
3 μεσημβρ[ιν...]
4 πλευροῦ σ[ύν...]
5 καὶ υἱωνοῖς [...]
6 ἔτους βνφ' α[...]

1 [.....] ʿbdy ʿbdy br
2 [....b]r ddh rḥq
3 [.....]mq br zbdʾ
4 [.....]ʾrbʿ [....]
5 [...............]

PAT 2824 **Syr '85 p 279** no. 9 **n. d.**
Prov: Palmyra. Loc: Palmyra, no. A 1210/5332. *Dedicatory. On stone block.* Bib: *As'ad and Teixidor '82 pp 89-96, fig 9.*

1 [.....DU]ARUM GUB
2 [..PECUN]IA SUA
3 [..POLLI]ONE II ET APRO II COS

1 [ἔκτι]σεν Λούκιος
2 [....]λῴου τοῦ ζπυ'

1 qbyʾ ʾln tr[yʾ.....]
2 ʾnṭnys q[lsṭrṭs ...]

PAT 2825 **Syr '90 p 186** **n. d.**
Prov: Uncertain. Loc: Private collection. *Dedicatory. On relief.* Bib: *Photo fig 1.*

(On left)
1 ʾlt
2 nmsys
(On right)
1 ʿbʾ?
2 rbʾl?

PAT 2827 **TMP pp 757-58** **n. d.**
Prov: Antioch (probably). Loc: Paris, Bibliothèque Nationale, Cabinet des Médailles. *Tessera. Lead.*

(On obverse)
1 [Σ]ε[π Ζηνοβία] ἡ βασίλισσα

(On reverse)
1 ḥtyʾ or ḥṭyn ?
du Mesnil: connected with a distribution of grain by Zenobia ca. A.D. 268

Trf
Abbr used for the Tariff of Palmyra, text at C3901.

PAT 2828 **Verm '81 p 380** no. 330 **n. d.**
Prov: (Palmyra). Loc: Toledo (OH), Toledo Museum of Art, no. 62.18. *Funerary. On relief.* Bib: *Photos,* Verm '81, pp 380-81, with bibliography; Vermeule '64 p 114; Mackay '49 pl 60 no. 1 and fig 6a.

1 ḥbl
2 ʾmby
3 brt mqy
4 mlʾ lʿš

PAT 2829 **Verm '81 p 382** no. 331 **n. d.**
Prov: (Palmyra). Loc: Cincinnati, Cincinnati Art Museum, no. 1958.257. *Funerary. On relief.* Bib: *Photo.*

1 mlwkʾ
2 br nwrbl
3 ḥbl
Collated with museum photo

PAT 2830 **Verm '81 p 387** no. 336 **n. d.**
Prov: (Palmyra). Loc: Stanford University Museum of Art, no. 17205. *Funerary. On relief.* Bib: *Photo (very unclear).*

1 bnʿm br ʿql
Text illegible on photo in Verm '81 and museum photo; this text a retroversion from "Bon'am son of Aqul" of Vermeule

PAT 2831 **YCS '55 p 131 no. 3** **n. d.**
Prov: Dura Europos, from cistern in Temple of

Atargatis. Loc: Not given in edition. *Dedicatory. On gypsum slab.* Bib: *Pl III 1*; Rostovtzeff '36 pp 202-4; du Mesnil '38a pp 147-52; "Note Additionnelle," by R. Dussaud there..

1 Μαλχίων Σομέσου
2 ἔδωκεν εἰς τὸ ἀνάλω-
3 μα θεῷ ʽΗλίῳ X̶ ρʹ ὑπὲρ σω-
4 τηρίας

1 dkrnʾ ṭbʾ lmlkwn
2 šmyšw mḥybʾ dy qryb
3 mn ʿbdʾ hdyn lšmš ʾlhʾ
4 dnrʾ 100 ʿl ḥywhy lʿlm

Text above follows Ingholt's reading, except for line 3: ʿbdʾ (with du Mesnil), see Glossary

PAT 2832 **YCS '55 p 177** no. 130 **n. d.**
Prov: Dura Europos. Loc: Morris (N.Y.), Frederick A. Godley Collection. *Graffito. On amphora.*

1 Βαρεος

1 brʿ

❖ ❖ ❖ ❖ ❖

GLOSSARY

Most elements of this Glossary will be familiar to users of Semitic lexicons. The following features may call for explanation. **1**. The indication of noun gender, "m" or "f", is sometimes followed by an asterisk, as in *ʾb nm**. This signals that there is explicit *syntactic* evidence for the gender in a passage cited in the Glossary entry, which is correspondingly marked with an asterisk, thus "C4169:1*". Where there is no asterisk, the identification as "m" or "f" is based on morphology or on comparative evidence. **2**. A dagger following an entry means that all the passages with this word found in our corpus of texts have been cited in the article. **3**. At the end of some entries the symbol ▶ is the equivalent of "See also," calling attention to related words, or places where there is further discussion, or relevant bibliography, especially where this supplies encyclopedic information. The Glossary does not, except in special cases, supply information on cognates in other Aramaic dialects or Semitic languages; evidence for etymology, however, is often given. This is done commonly where a word is probably from a non-Semitic language. Since Akkadian is attested from so early a time, and many Aramaic words have been thought to be of Akkadian origin, the critical and authoritative study of S. Kaufman (*AIA*, 1974) is regularly cited, in favor of or against an Akkadian etymology for the Aramaic term in question.

The English translations of Aramaic passages cited are meant as a guide to the sense of the Aramaic, not necessarily to Semitic grammatical features; this is especially evident in frequent use of an English passive verb form where the Aramaic has an active form. This device has been adopted here where it was thought important to preserve the sequence of *elements* mentioned in a text. In many inscriptions the most prominent item is the thing built, donated, or dedicated, etc., and typically the sequence is as in Inv 4 13: *mʿrtʾ dnh . . . ḥpr wbnʾ wṣbt mn kysh ywlys ʾwrlys hrms.* In place of an English rendering which would put the grammatical subject in the most prominent place, as "Julius ... dug, built, and decorated, etc.", we frequently have preferred the transformation to "This hypogeum ... was dug, built, and decorated, at his own expense, by Julius, etc."

ʾb I *nm** 1 father; 2 *ʾbht* forefathers, *ʾbwn rbʾ* ancestor (?); 3 *ʾb ʾb* grandfather (?); 4 *byt ʾb* father's house, clan

s cn *ʾbʾ <dy ʾb> ʾbwhy* see Gaw Syr '70 p 314:3, and ad RSP 143 for the restoration :: Gaw '90b p 104 *ʾbʾ ʾbwhy* "le père, son père"; em *ʾbʾ ʾbwhy* (?) Syr '70 p 314:3 syntax and sense unsatisfactory; sf 3ms *ʾbwh* C4061:6; *ʾbwhy* C4169:1*; *ʾbyh* C3907:8; C4036:3; RSP 114:8; Gaw compares *ʾḥyh* his brother(s) RSP 114:8; 108:4, see RosSpr p 46; *[ʾ]byhy* PGKK p 310 no 33:5; 3fs *ʾbwh* C4067:4; 1pl *ʾbwn* BS III 60:11; 3mpl *ʾbhwn* Inv 8 58, *ʾbwhwn* C4201:2; *ʾbwhn* Inv 10 4b:2; pl sf 3mpl *ʾbhthwn* Inv 8 59:3

1 *ʿl ḥyʾ ʾbwhy wḥywhy wḥyy bnwhy* for the life of his father, and his own life, and the life of his sons *Inv 12 44:5*; *ʿl ḥyʾ ʾbwhy wbny byth klhwn* for the life of his father and all his family *Inv 11 20:5*; *PN dy bnʾ ʾbwhy qbrʾ dnh* PN whose father constructed this tomb *C4169:1*; *PN ʾbwh[wn]* PN, thei[r] father *C4201:2*, Gk *patros* **2** *ʿl ʾbhthwn* on behalf of their forefathers *Inv 8 59:3* Gk *goneusi*; sense 'ancestor' possible in phrase PN *rbʾ ʾbwn rbʾ* PN the elder, our/their ancestor (?) *BS III 60:11*, see Déd 98-99, Gaw '90b p 104, but prb with Dunant BS III pp 76-77 *rbʾ* = PN Rabba, or title 'the elder'; cf Ing '66 pp 471-74 **3** *ʾbʾ <dy ʾb> ʾbwhy dy PN* father [of the] <grand>father of PN Gaw '70 p 314:3 :: ʾbʾ ʾbwhy dy PN the father (ancestor), father of PN Gaw '90 p 104 **4** See *byt ʾb* n phr

▶ PN *ʾbʾ*

ʾb II *nm* Ab (name of month = August)

s ab *ʾb* C3928:5

▶ Appendix CALENDAR

ʾbgl *nm* Abgal (name of deity)

ʾbgl PNO 6 B:1

ʾbgl gnyʾ ṭbʾ Abgal, the good deity *PNO 6 B:1*; *qdm ʾbgl g[n]yʾ* before Abgal, the de[it]y *PNO 17:3*; *wlʾrṣw wlʾbgl ʾlhy ṭbyʾ [wskryʾ]* and for Arsu and for Abgal, the good and [generous] gods *Inv 12 55:2*; *lʾbgl ʾlhʾ ṭbʾ wskrʾ* for Abgal, the good and generous god *PNO 5:1*; *lʾbgl gnyʾ ṭbʾ wškrʾ* for Abgal, the good and generous deity *PNO 5:2*

▶ PN *ʾbgl*; TeixPan pp 58; 80-84; Hof RelAram p 42

ʾbd see *brr* v and *bry* v

ʾbl *nm* doorway (of tomb)
s em *ʾblʾ* RB '30 14:6
mpqyk mn ʾblʾ ʿl šmlk on your left as you go out the doorway
(< Akk *abullu*; AIA 32)†

ʾbn *nf* stone (?)
s em *ʾbnʾ* MUSJ '62 p 106:10
yhw ʾbnʾ Ing: 'let there be stones'; division of words and sense difficult; see at *bnʾ* v
▶ *lbnh* n†

ʾbr *nm* corps, unit of auxiliary troops
s em *ʾbr[ʾ]* BS III 51:3
pršyʾ bʾbr[ʾ] dy gmlʾ wʿnʾ the riders in the corps of Gamla and of Ana
(calque < Lat *ala* 'wing, wing of an army, unit of auxiliaries', Caquot '56 p 77, see *ʾlʾ* n)†

ʾgwr I *nm** tax collector, tax farmer, publican
s em *ʾgwrʾ* Trf(I):11*
dy lʾ yhwʾ gbʾ ʾgwrʾ mn ʾnš mdʿm ytyr that the tax collector should not collect anything in excess from anyone Gk *ton misthoumenon*; see Dessau 1884 pp 492-93
(not < Akk, AIA 33)

ʾgwr II *nm* contract
pl em *ʾgwryʾ* Trf(I):5; cf restoration at Trf:65; *ʾgryʾ* Trf(I):8 CaGr p 57
dy hwʾ mtktb bʾgwryʾ dy mksʾ which was written in the contracts of the tax-farmers *Trf(I):5* Gk *misthōsei*; *wyktb bšṭr ʾgryʾ ḥdtʾ* and let it be written in a new document of contract *Trf(I):8* Gk *misthōsei*; see Piganiol '45 pp 10-11†

ʾgn *nm (or f? see PNO 21)* 1 crater; 2 symposium
s cn *ʾgn* RTP 76; em *ʾgnʾ?* PNO 21:1 (reading *ʾgnt?* possible)
1 *ʾgnʾ? ...* (this) crater (inscribed on a large stone crater) *PNO 21:1*; **2** *ʾgn bl bʿltk* symposium of Bel, Baaltak *RTP 77:1*; on *ʾgn* in Arad inscriptions in sense symposium, see Hillers *ZAH* (forthcoming)
(not < Akk, AIA 33; prior to understanding of *bʿltk* as name of deity, Palm *ʾgn* treated as form of *gnn* v 'to protect' or *gnʾ* v 'to extend oneself': see Caquot, RTP p 143; du Mesnil du Buisson TMP pp 457-59; Déd pp 108-09, 149-50; Gaw ANRW pp 2651-52)

ʾgr *v* G to lease, make a contract; Gt to be drawn up
G pf 3ms *ʾgr* Trf:77; 1cs *ʾgrt* PDura 152:3(? so Ingholt ad loc; see *ʾgrh* n below); Gt pf 3ms *ʾtʾgr* Trf:65
G *[dy] ʾgr bh PN* for which PN contracted (?) **Gt** *hyk ʾ[gwryʾ d]y ʾ[t]ʾgr qdm PN hygmnwnʾ* according to the c[ontracts wh]ich we[re] drawn up before PN the governor;
(not < Akk, AIA 33)†

ʾgr *n* see *ʾgwr* II n

ʾgrh *nf* letter
s em *ʾgrtʾ* Trf:104 Gk *[epis]tolēs*, Trf:121 Gk *epistolēi*; pl em *ʾg[rtʾ]* BS III 45:7 Gk *e[pistol]ais*; *ʾgrtʾ* PDura 152:3 may be noun form; see *ʾgr* v above, and Ingholt ad loc
bʾgrtʾ dy ktb lPN in the letter which he wrote to PN *Trf:104*; *bʾg[rtʾ] wbdy[ṭg]mʾ šhd lh* by let[ters] and by a de[cr]ee (he) testified on his behalf *BS III 45:7*
(prb < Akk *egirtu*; AIA 48)†

ʾdgyʿ *nm/f?* (Or *ʾrgyʿ*; vowels unknown) *name of deity*
ʾdgyʿ Sem '50 p 47:5
(on a stele) *lDN wlʾdgyʿ (or ʾrgyʿ) gnyʾ ṭbyʾ wškryʾ* to Shulman and to *ʾdgyʿ/ʾrgyʿ*, the good and generous deities†

ʾdyʾ *nm* *analysis and meaning uncertain*
ʾdyʾ Inv 8 180:2
PN rḥymʾ ʾdyʾ PN, who loves *ʾdyʾ* ?
(CaGr p 160 connects with *ʾdt* n but latter is

equally obscure)†

ʾdr *nm* Adar (name of month = March)
s ab *ʾdr* Inv 9 28:9
▶ Appendix CALENDAR

ʾdrwn *nm* kind of room: dining room (?); cella (?)
s em *ʾdrwnʾ* CRAIBL '81:7
ḥmnʾ klh hw wʾtrh wʾp ṭll ʾdrwnʾ klh ... the whole chapel, with its precinct, and also the whole ceiling of the dining-room (?; or 'cella'?) *C3917:4*; *dy yg[wr] lmštʾ bʾdrwnʾ* ... who re[clines] at a banquet in the dining-chamber (?; or 'cella'?) *CRAIBL '81:14*; *mwmʾ bʾdrwnʾ wmn dy ymʾ [b]ḥmnʾ yḥwb* ... an oath in/by the cella (?) or whoever swears [by] the shrine shall be liable to ... *CRAIBL '81:11*
(prb < Gk *andrōn* 'men's apartment, banqueting hall', see Starcky Syr '26 pp 55-59 :: Brockelmann LS, CaGr p 154 < Pers *andarōn*)

ʾdrṭ *nm* statue
pl em *ʾdrṭyʾ* Trf:128
ṣlmy nḥšʾ ʾdrṭyʾ bronze images, (that is) statues
(< Gk *andriant-* [nominative s *andrias*] 'statue'); cf Old Syriac inscription (prb 3rd century) *ʾdryṭʾ* 'statue' Dri '72 no. 27:4†

ʾdry *nm? meaning unknown*
ʾdry PNO 2 ter:11-12
kl gbr dy ydḥl lʿbgl bṭb ʾdry every man who pays homage to PN, for good ... (?)†

ʾdt *nf* lady (?)
s sf 3ms *ʾdth* Syr '36 p 355:1
ʿbd PN lh wlʾdth wlbnwhy made by PN ... for himself and for his lady (?) and for his sons
(If not scribal error for *ʾḥ!th* 'his sister', perhaps f of Sem *ʾdn* 'lord', see DISO at *ʾdn*, and Noth '37 col 345-46; Eissfeldt '38 col 489-91)†

ʾw *cj* 1 or; 2 *ʾw* ... *ʾw* either ... or (?)
ʾw Trf:72
1 *dy [y]tʿʿl ʾw yzbn* which is imported or sold *Trf:56*; *dnr ʾw ytyr* a denarius or more *Trf:127*; *ltdmr ʾw ltḥwmyh* to Tadmor or its territory *Trf(II):2-3*; *mt[ʿʿ]l br mn tḥwmʾ ʾw mʾpq* imported from outside the territory or exported *Trf:111* **2** *ʾw ktl dy ḥwrʾ ʾw ḥmryn* either a plastered wall or one of clay *MUSJ '62 p 106:10* (?) :: Ing ad loc.; cf also C4214:1 with word-division of PAT

ʾwdʾ *n* see *wd* n

ʾwṭqrṭwr *nm* emperor
s ab/em *[ʾwṭ]q?rṭwr* Inv 10 102:2, *[ʾw]ṭqrṭwr* Inv 9 26
[ʾwṭ]q?rṭwr ʾṭnyns q[sr] Emperor Antoninus C[aesar] Inv 10 102:2; *[ʾw]ṭqrṭwr qs[r]* [Em]peror Caes[ar ...] Inv 9 26
(< Gk *autokratōr*)†

ʾwyw *nf* agreement (?)
s ab *ʾwyw* CRAIBL '81:7
ʾwyw šṭyrh ʿl[...] an agreement (?) written on [...] *CRAIBL '81:7* Teix: l'accord sera inscrit sur (Teix '81 p 311 cf Syriac *ʾawyūtā* 'agreement', but syntax difficult and different division and reading of text seems preferable, see at *yšṭ* v†

ʾwn *nm** sarcophagus
s em *ʾwnʾ* Ber '70 p 77:1*
(on a sarcophagus) *ʾwnʾ? dnh dy ʿbdw PN* ... this sarcophagus was made by PN ... *Ber '70 p 77:1* (Fig. 8)
(on possible Arab cognate see Gaw Ber '70 p 78; cf *ʾwznʾ* 'sarcophagus' in Old Syriac inscription [2nd-3rd century] Dri '72 no. 35:4)†

ʾwrlyʾ *nm Aurelius, Aurelii*, as title
pl em? *ʾwrlyʾ* Inv 8:58
Compare Gk (with pl *Aurēlioi*) and Aram texts at Inv 8:58; also other occurrences of name may best be interpreted so, as similary *ywlyʾ* and *sptmyʾ*

< Latin Aurelius ▶ *ʾwrlyʾ* PN

ʾḥ *nm** 1 brother; 2 *ʾḥyn bny ʾmʾ* sons of the same mother: half-brothers (?); 3 *br ʾḥ* nephew 4 *ʾḥ ʾm* maternal uncle (reading uncertain); 5 *trn ʾ[ḥy]ʾ qdyšʾ* the Two Holy Brothers (divine title)

s sf 3ms *ʾḥh* C4532:6; *ʾḥwh* Inv 11 35:5; *ʾḥwhw* BS III 67:3; *ʾḥwhy* C4566:7; *ʾḥwy* RB '30 p 545:2; *ʾḥy* Inv 12 34:4; prb at least some of the occurrences of *ʾḥyh* are pl, but note SFP 40:4 and cf *ʾbyh* his father; 3fs *ʾḥh* C4067:4; pl ab *ʾḥyn* Ber '38 p 106:1; pl em *ʾḥyʾ* C4158:2*; pl sf 3ms *ʾḥw* C4024:5; *ʾḥwh* C4018:3; *ʾḥwhy* C3998A:3 Gk pl: *adelphōn*; prb also PNO 39:2 is *ʾḥw?hy* not *ʾḥyhy*; *ʾḥyh* Inv 11 7:4; RSP 108:4; PNO 14:8; see RosSpr p 46; *ʾḥywh* C4029:5; 3mpl *ʾḥwhn* C3995:4; *ʾḥyhwn* C3986:4; *ʾḥyhn* BS III 10:5; in given cases it is often impossible to be sure whether *ʾḥwhy*, *ʾḥwh*, and still other forms, are sg or pl, cf CaGr pp 65-6

1 *ʾḥwhy* his brothers *C3998A:3* Gk *adelphōn*; *dy ʿbd lh PN ʾḥwh* which PN, his brother, made for him *C4284:6*; *ʿl ḥywhy wḥyy bnwhy wʾḥyhy* for his life and the life of his sons and the life of his brother(s) *Inv 1 5:2*; *ʾḥwhy bny PN* his brothers, the sons of PN *BS III 19:4*; *ʾḥd mn ʾrbʿʾ ʾḥyʾ* one of the four brothers *C4158:2** **2** *PN wPN ... ʾḥyn bny ʾmʾ* PN and PN ... brothers, sons of the (same) mother (half-brothers) *Ber '38 p 106:1* note Gk at Inv 4:7a *tois homomētriois autou adelphois* **3** *brh dy ʾḥwhy* son of his brother (his nephew) *C4072:4*; *wḥyy bny [ʾ]ḥwhy* and the life of his [b]rother's sons (nephews) *C4007:5* **4** *[...ʾ]ḥy ʾmh* [bro]thers of his mother = maternal uncles *Syr '38 p 153:7* (but reading uncertain) **5** *wltrn ʾ[ḥy]ʾ qdyšʾ* and to the Two Holy Br[other]s *C4001:3*; *[w]l[trn ʾḥ]yʾ qdšʾ* [and] to the [Two] Holy bro[thers] *C4002:2*; see TeixPan p 41.

▶ PN *ʾḥyʾ*

ʾḥd *v* G 1 to take: a to reserve; b to choose, esp. to choose for a public or sacred service, hence part pass (chosen one >) minister; 2 to possess (?)

G pf 3ms *ʾḥd* Inv 12 44:1; impf 3ms sf 3ms *yḥdnh* BS III 34:4; ptcp act pl cn (?) *ʾḥdy* Inv 12 45:3; ptcp pass s ab *ʾḥyd* CRAIBL '81:9; RSP 145:3 (?); s em *ʾḥydʾ* BS III 70:1; pl ab *ʾḥydyn* BS III 34:2; *ʾḥydyʾ* RSP 199:11; *ʾḥ[y]dyʾ* RSP 199:4; pl cs *ʾḥydy* RTP 40; *ʾḥdy* Inv 12 45:3 (?)

1 a *ʾḥydʾ lPN* reserved for PN *BS III 70:1*; *ʾ[t]r ʾḥyd ...* place reserved ... *BS III 68:1* **1 b** *lmn dy yḥdnh* to whomever he will choose *BS III 34:4*; *PN dy ʾḥd yrḥbwl ʾlhʾ* PN, whom Yarhibol the god chose *RSP 127:2*; (sense 'to seize' favored by Teix ad Inv 12 44 seems unnecessary in view of use of ʾḥd for 'elect to a charge', evident from other passages); *dy yhwʾ ʾḥyd ʿl dhbʾ* who will be elected to be in charge of the gold *CRAIBL '81:9*; *gbr dy yhwʾ ʾḥyd brš[hwn]* a man who will be chosen as [their] head *CRAIBL '81:5*; *wʾḥydyn bh bštʾ dh ʿl ...* and chosen by him in this year to be in charge ... *BS III 34:2*; (part pass) minister: *wlwdʾ dy ʾḥdy hyklʾ* and to the association of ministers (or 'masters') of the temple *Inv 12 45:3* (on this sense see Déd pp 286-87 and Gaw '73b pp 113-24 and Teix ad loc.; reading *ʾḥry* also possible); *ʿl ʾḥydyʾ dy yhwn ...* over the ministers who will be ... *Palm I (1959) 10:9 = RSP 199:11*; *ʾḥydy [ʿw]ntʾ // bl* ministers of [the or]der (on the reverse) Bel *RTP 40* **2** *dkl ʾḥyd* who possesses all (?) *RSP 145:3* Gaw takes as divine title cf Syriac *ʾḥyd kl* 'All-Powerful'; *wlwdʾ dy ʾḥdy (or ʾḥry) hyklʾ* and to the association of masters (or ministers) of the temple *Inv 12 45:3*

▶ *ʾḥydw* n†

ʾḥd *num* see *ḥd* num

ʾḥh *nf* 1 sister; 2 *bt ʾḥth* niece (sister's daughter)

s sf 3ms *ʾḥth* C4462:4; 3fs C3907:5; s (or pl?; see Chabot ad loc.) sf 3mpl *ʾḥthwn* C4018:8; note lack of agreement in gender at C4554:4 *dy ʿbd l[h] PN ʾḥt[h]*. See also CaGr p 40.

1 *PN ʾmh PN ʾḥth* PN, his mother, PN, his sister *BMB '55 p 42:2* **2** *PN ... bt ʾḥth dʾrt ʾtt PN* PN ... niece of PN, the wife of

PN C3907:5

ʾḥydw *nf* office (service for which one is chosen)
s ab *ʾḥydw* Inv 10 115
dy špr bkl ʾḥydw klh lmdyth who did well, in every office, for his city; see Déd p 286 (= exactly Gk *leitourgia*) :: DISO ʿthing, affairʾ
▶ *ʾḥd* v to choose†

ʾḥyr *adj* other; last (?)
pl em *ʾḥyryʾ* so FP I 10:9 :: RSP 199:11 and 4
ʿl ʾḥyryʾ dy yhwn over the other(?)/last(?) who will be RSP 199:11; but prb read *ʾḥydyʾ* and translate ʿover the ministers (French liturges) who will be ...ʾ; see at *ʾḥd* v†

ʾḥr *prep (?; adv?)* after (?); afterward, then (?)
ʾḥr CRAIBL ʾ81:13
wʾḥr šbʿ[....] and after(?) seven(?)[. . .]†

ʾḥrn *pron* 1 other; 2 (adv) in addition (as another thing)
m s ab *ʾḥrn* CRAIBL ʾ81:17; em *ʾḥrnʾ* Ber ʾ35 p 112:4; C3914:4 (CaGr p 134) :: RosSpr p 53 (m pl em); f s em *ʾḥrtʾ* C4199:5; m pl ab *ʾḥrnyn* C4173:2; f pl em *ʾḥrnytʾ* Trf:117
1 *gwmḥ ʾḥrn* another burial niche *Ber ʾ35 p 85:11*; *ʾp bmdyntʾ ʾḥrnytʾ* also in other cities *Trf:117*; *wmdʿn ʾḥrn* and anything else *CRAIBL ʾ81:17*; *ḥdʾ ʿl ymynʾ ... wʾḥrtʾ mqblʾ* one on the right ... and the other facing (you) *C4199:4-5* **2** *ʾḥrnʾ ʿbdw trʿyʾ ʾln šttyhn* in addition they made these six doors *C3914:4*†

ʾyṭlyʾ *nf* Italy
ʾyṭ[lyʾ] Trf:95
ʿmrʾ dy ʾyṭ[lyʾ] Ita[lian] wool†

ʾyṭlyq *adj* Italian
m s em *ʾyṭlyq[ʾ]* Trf:96, *ʾyṭlq[ʾ]* Trf:105, 133
ʿmrʾ ʾyṭlyq[ʾ] Italian wool *Trf:96* Gk *[it]alikōn*; *ita[likon]* (< Gk < Lat *italicus*)†

ʾyṭlq *see Italian ʾyṭlyq adj*

ʾyr *nm* Iyyar (name of month = May)
s ab *ʾyr* C4037:5
▶ Appendix CALENDAR

ʾyš *pron* anyone; (with neg.) no one
m s ab *ʾyš* C4214:1; Syr ʾ36 p 271:7 (prb.)
wlʾḥbwrʾ bh ʾyš or to take anyone as partner in it *C4214:1*; *wlʾ ypth ʾyš* [...] and let no one open [...] *Inv 8 86:2*†

ʾyt *pred* 1 there is, there are (particle predicating existence); 2 *ʾyt l-* belong(s) to
ʾyt Trf:124
1 *bdyl dy ʾyt bhwn tgrtʾ* because there is trade in them *Trf:124*; *btr ʾksdrʾ ... dy ʾyt bgwmḥʾ mqbrn št* behind the exedra ... in which each niche has six burial-places *C4175:7*; **2** *mn mʿrtʾ dh ʾyt lPN* of this tomb, there belongs to PN *RB ʾ30 10A:2*†

ʾkldy see *kldy* adj

ʾksdrʾ *nm* and f** exedra (arcade with niches)
s em *ʾksdrʾ* Inv 4 7b:2; *ʾkšdrʾ* C4171:2; note *mksdrʾ* from the exedra Ber ʾ35 p 107:2; pl abs *ʾksdryn* RB ʾ30 p 540A:3; C4194:5* (m gender), C4175:6* (f gender) see OʾConnor ʾ87 p 365
ʾksdryn trn two exedras *Ber ʾ35 p 110:1* Gk *exedrōn; ʾksdrʾ dnh bt ʿlmʾ dy bgw mʿrtʾ* this exedra, everlasting house, which is inside the tomb Ber ʾ35 p 60
(< Gk *exedra* [L-S ʿhall or arcade furnished with recesses and seatsʾ]; for a plan see e.g. Ing ʾ62 Pl I)

ʾksny *adj* foreign, foreigner
m pl em *ʾksnyʾ* C3959:4
lbny md[yntʾ wl]ʾstr[ṭwmʾ] wlʾksnyʾ dy ʾtʾ ʿmh to the cit[izens and to the] ar[my] and to the foreigners who came with him Gk

xenois
(< Gk *xenos* w suff -*āy*; CaGr pp 114, 155)†

ʾkšdrʾ see *ʾksdrʾ* n

ʾktb *nm ? attestation uncertain*
bʾktb[...] RB '30 14:5†

ʾl *nm* god ([?] only in phrase garden of the gods, sacred garden)
analysis uncertain *ʾlym* BS III 45:12
wʾḥd bgntʾ ʾlym and one (statue) in the sacred garden Gk *[e]n hierō alsei*
(Canaanism? so Caquot 56 pp 77-78, Dunant BS III ad loc., Gaw ANRW pp 2620-21)†

ʾlʾ I *nm** corps (military), unit of auxiliary troops
s em *ʾlʾ* Inv 10 128:2*
ʾlʾ drmdryʾ (prefect of) the camel corps Gk *eiles ... dromadariōn*
(< Lat *ala* or Gk *eilē [ilē]*, both in inscr. from Palmyra, see Seyrig '33b pp 159-63; cf Bertinelli Angeli p 130)
▶ *ʾbr* n†

ʾlʾ II *cj* but, however
ʾlʾ Trf:149
ʾlʾ lʿn dy thwʾ mʿʾl however, for the small cattle that will be imported *Trf:149* Gk *de*; CaGr p 136; *ʾlʾ gbr dy yhwʾ ʾḥyd* but a man who is chosen *CRAIBL ʾ81:5*†

ʾlgšy *nf* Vologesia (near Seleuceia on Tigris)
ʾlgšyʾ C3916:3
mn ʾlgšyʾ from Vologesia Gk *olagasiados*; see Maricq '59; Raschke '78 p 840 fn 780
▶ Appendix MAPS

ʾlh *nm** 1 god; 2 *mrʾ ʾlhʾ* Lord of the Gods (divine title); 3 *ʾlh byt ʾb* god of the father's house (clan); 4 *bt ʾlhʾ* house of god(s), temple
s cn *ʾlh* C3978:7; em *ʾlhʾ* C3932:3; *ʾlhh* BS III 58:2; pl ab *ʾlhyn* Syr '31 p 130:8; cs *ʾlhy* C3903:1; em *ʾlhyʾ* C3930:3; em *ʾlhʾ* (in divine title) RSP 154:2; *ʾlhy* Inv 12 55:2; pl sf 3fs *ʾlhyh* Syr '36 p 280:9 (see Cantineau ad loc., n *pḥz* is f [cf Arab *faḫid*, f]); sf 3mpl *ʾlhyhwn* Inv 9 12:4; *ʾlhyhn* BS III 40:5
1 (often follows DN) *lbʿlšmn ʾlhʾ* to the god Baalshamin *BS III 18:3*; *lḥrtʾ wlnny wlršp ʾlhyʾ* to the gods Herta and Nanay and Reshef *Syr ʾ36 p 286:6*; *[lr]ḥmnʾ wlʾ[lhʾ] ṭbʾ wsk[rʾ]* [to the One who is M]erciful and to the g[od] who is good and gener[ous] *Inv 11 11:5**; *wʿl hnn shd lh ʾlhʾ* and for these things the god gave witness to him *Inv 10 115:2*; *wdḥly ʾlhyʾ* and worshippers of the gods *C3930:3*; *wlʾlhyʾ klhn dy ytbyn lwth* and to all the gods who dwell with her (the Mistress of the Temple) *RSP 143:4*; *lsdrpʾ ʾlhh* to Sadrafa, his god *BS III 58:2*; *lDN wlʾlhy tdmr* to DN and to the gods of Tadmor *C3903:1*; *bmytwytʾ dy ʾlhʾ ʾlksndrws qsr* at the coming of the divine Alexander Caesar (epithet of [deceased] emperor) *C3932:3* **2** *mrʾ ʾlhʾ* Lord of the gods *RSP 154:2* Gaw ad loc. cf Hatra DN *mrlhʾ* **3** *lšmš ʾlh byt ʾbwhn* to Shamash, the god of their father's house *C3978:7* **4** *[ʾ]nšyʾ dy ḥdt bt ʾlh?[ʾ dnh]* the [m]en who renewed [this] house of the gods *Déd p 217:1*; *pḥz pḥz bt ʾlhyh* each tribe in the house of its god *Syr ʾ36 p 280:9*; *wlbt ʾlhyhwn* and to the house of their gods *Inv 9 12:4*; *wlbnynʾ dy ʾlhyʾ* the building of the gods *Syr ʾ31 p 130:10*; *[...]bt ʾlhyn* house of gods *Syr ʾ31 11:8*

ʾlhy *nm* Ilahay (name of deity) ?
ʾ[l]hy MélRob p 373:2; Déd p 21-22: *lʾr[ṣ]w* 'to Arsu'
lʾ[l]hy ʾlhʾ ṭbʾ wskrʾ to I[l]ahay ?, the good and generous god
▶ Hof RelAram p 44†

ʾlwl *nm* Elul (name of month = September)
s ab *ʾlwl* C3925:1; *ʾlyl* C4507:5 (error? or variant pronunciation?)
▶ Appendix CALENDAR

ʾlyl see *ʾlwl* n

ʾln *pron* these (pron dem pl m and f)
with m pl *ʾln* C4173:3*; with f pl C3973:1*; supposed dem pron *ʾlt* of Inv 2 1 (Lidzbarski, Cantineau) is name of deity Allat

gwmḥyʾ ʾln these niches *Ber '35 p 102:1*; *trʿyʾ ʾln* these doors *C3914:4* Gk *tautas*; *ʿlwtʾ ʾln* these altars *MUSJ '49 p 52:2*; *PN wPN ʾln dy* PN and PN, those who *C4173:3*; *wbtr ʾln mn dy* and after these (the aforementioned people), whoever *RB '30 9:3* (RosSpr p 49)

ʾlp *num* thousand
m pl ab *ʾlpyn* Sem '86 p 89:2, 3, 4, 6

rbwʾn ʾlpyn tryn wmʾtn wtltyn wšt interest(?), two thousand and two hundred and thirty six *Sem '86 p 89:2*

ʾlqwnrʿ *nm** Elkonnara (name of deity)
ʾlqwnrʿ Syr '38 p 78:5*; *ʾlqnrʿ* RTP 220, 221, 222, 223

[l]ʾlqwnrʿ ʾlhʾ ṭbʾ to Elkonnara, the good god, Gk *Poseidōn*, cf name of deity in Latin inscr. of Baalbek *Connarus* (IGLS 2743); Gk IGLS 2841 *[k]onnaros,* TeixPan pp 25-26 ('El, creator of the earth' various forms in Hittite(?), Phoenician)

▶ TeixPan pp 25-28; Pope s. v. El WdM p 280; Hof RelAram p 47†

ʾlqnrʿ see *ʾlqwnrʿ* n

ʾlt *nf** Allat (name of deity)
ʾlt C3955:7

šmš wʾlt wrḥm ʾlhyʾ ṭbyʾ Shamash and Allat and Rahim, the good gods *C3955:7*; *tbrk ʾ[lt] mn dy lʾ yšd dm* may A[llat] bless whoever does not shed blood *Dri '82b p 65:1**; Février '31a p 41 cites Gk dedication *athēna allath,* and cf Palm PNs e.g. *whblt* Gk *ouaballathou*

TeixPan esp. 53-64; Gaw ANRW 2636-44; Hof RelAram p 43; Dri '78 pp 331-51

ʾm *nf* mother
s cn *ʾm* C4287:5; em *ʾmʾ* Ber '38 p 106:2; sf 3ms *ʾmh* C4573:1; 3fs *ʾmh* C4365:2; 1pl *ʾmn* Ber '35 p 81 f:1 on reading see Ber '36 p 126; 3mpl *ʾmhwn* C4615:5; *ʾmhn* C3911:11

PN(f) brt PN ʾm PN PN, daughter of PN, mother of PN *C4287:5*; *PN ʾmh* PN, his mother *Inv 11 14:6*; *ʾḥyn bny ʾmʾ* brothers, sons of the (same) mother *Ber '38 p 106:2*; *[...ʾ]ḥy ʾmh* [bro]thers of his mother = maternal uncles *Syr '38 p 153:7* (but reading uncertain); *spṭymyʾ btzby nhyrtʾ mlktʾ ʾmh dy mlk mlkʾ* Septimia Batzabbay, the illustrious, queen, mother of the king of kings *C3971:3* Gk *mētros*

ʾm *adv* also, indeed ([?] reading prb wrong)
[ʾ]m BS III 45:7

wbdy [ʾ]m šhd lh wšbḥh and because [al]so he testified in his behalf and praised him *BS III 45:7*; Dunant compares provisionally *ʾm* also, besides, in Imperial Aram (DISO s.v. *ʾm* III p 16) :: Hillers and Cussini '92 pp 35-37; see *dyṭgmʾ* below.†

ʾm *cj* if (?)
ʾm Syr '36 p 271:4

ʾm ʾnwky (very doubtful, context broken; Cantineau ad loc. speaks of *ʾnwky* as Hebraism; acc. to Déd 288-92 text is Phoenician in Palmyrene script)

▶ *ʾn* cj†

ʾmh *nf** cubit
pl a *[ʾ]myn* StudPalm '75 p 129:5; pl em? *ʾmmʾ* RB '30 p 548:7*

ʾtrʾ šḥ[ymʾ] [dy ʾ]myn ʾrbʿ an unconsecrated place of four [c]ubits *StudPalm '75 p 129:5*; *tlt ʾmmʾ* three cubits (?) *RB '30 p 548:7** (this line of text obscure and form unparalleled in Palmyrene, but see RosSpr p 78 [lit. fn 1] and Dalman '05 pp 196-97) on plural formations of this kind in other Aram dialects†

ʾmlgyʾ *nm ? f ?* contract (?)
(?) *ʾmlgyʾ* Syr '33 p 184:2

[...] b'mlgy' by contract(?); context damaged; sense uncertain
(< Gk *homologia* 'agreement'; in law 'contract'); on *homologia* in Greek law, and in Dura Syriac slave-sale text see Cussini '92a (index, forthcoming revision) and at *ydy* v below†

'mn *nm* master craftsman
s em *'mn'* C4261:4
PN 'mn' PN, the master craftsman *C4258:5*
(< Akk *ummānu;* AIA p 109)

'mr *v* G to say
G impf 3ms *y'mr* Syr '36 p 353:7; 3mp *y'mrwn* RSP 199:13; ptcp m s ab *'mr* C3973:10; pl ab *'mry[n]* Syr '33 p 177:2
dy y'mr who will say *Syr '36 p 353:7*; *kl m'yd 'lwt' 'ln w'mr* anyone who frequents these altars and says *C3973:10*†

'mr *nm* lamb
pl em *'mry'* Trf:42
'mry' lm'[ln wlmpqn] lrš' ḥd 'sr' ḥd lambs for imp[ort or export], each head, one *assarius Trf:42*†

'n *cj* if
'n Trf:149
'n yṣb' mks' yhw' [...] if the tax-collector wishes, let him ... *Trf:149*; *w'n ṣb' dy y'bd* and if he wants to make ... *MUSJ '62 p 106:9*
▶ *hn* cj (DISO has *'n* s.v. *hn*)†

'n' *pron* I
'n' Syr '70 p 413:2
dkyryn wbrykyn qdm 'lhy tdmr 'n' PN wPN may I, PN, and PN be commemorated and blessed before the gods of Tadmor†

'nhyt *nf* Anahita (name of deity)
'nhyt RTP 166, 167
lṣbs w'nhyt 'lhy' for *S-b-s* and Anahita, the gods *Inv 12 22:4*
On this Iranian goddess see Teix ad Inv 12 22; Hof RelAram p 45†

'nwky *pron* I (?)
'nwky Syr '36 p 271:4
'm 'nwky if (?) I (?) (very doubtful, context broken; Cantineau ad loc. speaks of *'nwky* as Hebraism; acc. to Déd pp 288-92 text is Phoenician in Palmyrene script)†

'nwš *nm* men, personnel
s cn *'nwš* Inv 9 12:3 On form (with *w* for *ā) CaGr pp 51-52 :: RosSpr p 27
'qymw lh 'nwš 'nwšt' the men of the treasury erected for him
▶ *'nš* n†

'nḥnw *pron* we (?)
'nḥnw Syr '36 p 271:8
'nḥnw we ? very doubtful, context broken; Cantineau ad loc. and CaGr p 61, n. 1 speaks of *'nwky* and *'nḥnw* as Hebraisms; acc. to Déd pp 288-92 text is Phoenician in Palmyrene script†

'nš *nm** 1 man, pl. personnel; 2 anyone, (with neg) no one; 3 *'nš 'nš* whoever
s ab *'nš* Trf(I):11; s or pl em *'nš'* Inv 9 28:2 pl em *'nšy'* Doura 25:2; *['ʼ]nšy'* Déd p 217:1; sf 3ms *'nšw?h?[y]* C3998(col. 2):3
1 *dkyryn wbrykyn 'nš' dy mhdmryn (cf Gaw Syr '71 pp 413-15)* remembered and blessed be the personnel of the guards *Inv 9 28:2* **2** *mn 'nš* from anyone *Trf(I):11*; *dy l' 'bdh 'nš* which no one has (ever) done *Inv 9 11:6**; *w'nš l' ypth 'lwhy* and let no one open it *C4218:3* **3** *wdkyr qdm 'ln 'nš 'nš* and may there be remembered before these (deities) whoever ... *Sem '77 p 117:7*
▶ *'nwš* n

'nt *pron* you
'nt C4199:4, 7
'l ymyn' kdy 'nt 'll on the right as you enter *C4199:4*†

ʾnth *nf** 1 woman > pron each; 2 wife
s cn *ʾtt* C4151:2; em *ʾtt'* Trf:48; sf 3ms *ʾntth* RSP 105:8 (Gaw ad loc. notes archaism of form); *ʾtth* Inv 11 50:1

1 *dnrʾ ḥd mn ʾttʾ* one denarius from each *Trf:48*; *lʾt[tʾ dn]r* of eac[h, one denarius] *Trf:127* Gk *[he]kastēs* each **2** *PN ʾtt PN* PN wife of PN *C4151:2*; *ḥbl brt mlkw ʾtth* Alas! PN, his wife *Inv 11 50:1*; *dy qbyrʾ bh PN ʾḥth wPN ʾntth* in which is buried PN his sister and PN his wife *RB ʾ30 9:3**; Gaw ad RSP 26 Gk line 3-4, equivalent of *ʾtth* his wife (certainly to be restored in the Palmyrene) is *sunbi[an]* ʿwife'[†]

ʾsṭwʾ *nm** portico
s em *ʾsṭwʾ* C4168:1; pl sf *ʾsṭwwhy* Inv 12 49:7; C3955:4*

qbrʾ dnh bt ʿlmʾ wʾsṭwʾ dqdmwhy this tomb, house of eternity, and the portico in front of it *C4168:1*; *[hy]klʾ dy mnwt wʾsṭwwhy* the temple of Manawat and its porticoes *Inv 12 49:7*; on sense (= Palm *mṭlt*ʾ) see RosSpr p 73 n. 5
(< Gk *stoa*)

ʾsṭrbyl *nm* pinenuts
pl em *ʾsṭrbylyʾ* Trf:114

ʾsṭrbylyʾ wmdy dmʾ lhwn pinenuts and anything similar to them Gk *kōnous* (see Chabot ad loc.)
(< Gk *strobilos* ʿpinecone, pinenut')[†]

ʾsṭrṭg *nm* general
s ab *ʾsṭrṭg* Syr ʾ33 p 179:1; em *ʾsṭrṭgʾ* Déd p 36:2

dy hwʾ ʾsṭrṭg lqlnyʾ who was general of the Colony *C3932:2* Gk *stratēgēsanta*
(< Gk *stratēgos*; see Bertinelli Angeli '70 pp 66-67)

ʾsṭrṭgw *nf* term as general (*strategos*), command, campaign, expedition
s cn *ʾsṭrṭgwt* Syr ʾ63 p 48:5; sf 3ms *ʾsṭrṭgwth* C3934:4; pl ab *ʾsṭrṭgwn* Inv 10 44:4

wšpr lhwn bʾsṭrṭgwth and he did well for them during his term as general *C3934:4* Gk *stra[tēgēsanta]*; *dy špr lhwn bʾsṭrṭgwn šgyʾn* who did well for them in many campaigns *Inv 10 44:4* Gk *stratēgias*
(< Gk *stratēgos* + abstr sf)[†]

ʾsṭrṭwmʾ *nm* army
s em *ʾsṭr[ṭwmʾ]* C3959:4

yhb mšḥʾ lbny md[yntʾ wl]ʾsṭr[ṭwmʾ] wlʾksnyʾ dy ʾtʾ ʿmh he gave oil to the citiz[ens and to the] arm[y] and to the foreigners who came with him Gk *strateumatōn*
(< Gk *strateuma*)[†]

ʾsy *nm* physician, doctor
s em *ʾsyʾ* C4513:2

PN ʾsyʾ PN, the physician *C4513:2*; *PN dy mtqrʾ ʾsyʾ* PN, who is called Doctor *Ber ʾ35 p 99:1*; *PN ʾsyʾ gwyʾ* PN the private (?) physician *Inv 12 45:4*
(< Akk *asû;* AIA p 37)

ʾspsnʾ *nf* Ispasina, Spasinou (Charax)
ʾspsnʾ C3928:3

mn krk ʾspsnʾ from Karak Ispasina *C3928:3* Gk *spasi[nou] charakos*; *Inv 10 107:3* Gk *spasinou charako[s]*
▶ *myšn* n[†]

ʾspsnqrṭ *nf* Aspasinkart
ʾsp[s]nqrṭ IP 34:6

tgryʾ tdmryʾ dy bʾsp[s]nqrṭ the Palmyrene merchants who are in Aspasinkart; see Cantineau ad loc.: perhaps = Persian name of Spasinou Charax, so Déd p 20
▶ *krk* $_{II}$ n[†]

ʾsr *nm** *assarius* (coin; unit of money)
s ab *ʾsr* Trf:105; em *ʾsrʾ* Trf:73*; pl ab *ʾsryn* Trf:47

lršʾ ḥd ʾsrʾ ḥd one *assarius* per head *Trf:42*; *mn dy šqlʾ ʾsryn tmnyʾ* one who charges 8 *assarii* *Trf:49*; *yhb lmdyʾ ʾsr ʾyṭlq[ʾ]* he shall pay an Italia[n] *assarius* per measure *Trf:133*
(< Gk *assarion*, Lat *assarius*)

ʾsr *v* G to bind, obligate self (?)

G pf 3mpl ? *ʾśrw* Syr ʾ36 p 351:11 (Déd p 303:12)

wʾśrw whqymw byny[hn] and they obligated themselves ? and established between [themselves] (context very broken) see Cussini ʾ92a (index, forthcoming revision)†

ʾstrʾ *nf* Istar (variant of Ishtar, name of deity) (?); or: goddess (common noun) (?)

s ab ? em ? *ʾs[t]rʾ* C3985:1 (see Inv 6 1)

... *ʾs[t]rʾ* ... ; most uncertain, context very broken, but ending -ʾ suggests perhaps common n; see Cantineau ad loc.

▶ *ʿštr* n†

ʾʿšr *num* ten ([?] variant form)

m *ʾʿšr* RTP 997

ywm ʾʿšr day ten ?

▶ *ʿšr* num†

ʾp *adv* also

ʾp Trf:103

hyk dy hwʾ ʾp bmdyntʾ ʾḥrnytʾ as it was done also in other cities *Trf:116* Gk *kai*; *ʾp ygbʾ mksʾ* also the tax-collector shall collect *Trf:47*; *wʾp ʾšrw* and also they established *CRAIBL 81:10*; *shd lh yrḥbwl ʾlhʾ wʾp PN* Yarhibol the god and also PN testified for him *C3932:7*; see also Hillers and Cussini ʾ92 35-37

ʾpṭrp *nm* procurator

s em *ʾpṭrpʾ* C3938:2

ʾpṭrpʾ dqnrʾ procurator ducenarius *C3940:1* Gk *epitropon* (procurator receiving a salary of 200,000 sesterces; only in this combination in Palm)

(< Gk *epitropos*)

▶ *dwqnr* n†

ʾpy *prep* according to (followed by unit of measure or money)

ʾpy Trf:102

ʾpy dnr according to the *denarius Trf:102*; *ʾpy ʾsr* according to the *assarius Trf:105, 135*); *[ʾ]py mdyʾ* according to the *modius* [dry measure] *Trf:73*; Gk *eis* and *pros* (Cf Syr *ʿal ʾappay* for; see RosSpr p 84)

▶ *lʾpʾ* prep†

ʾpkl *nm* high religious official, *apkallu*-priest

s em *ʾpklʾ* C3974:2; C4064:5; C4065:4

PN ʾpklʾ dy ʿzyzw PN, priest of (the god) Azizu *C3974:2*; cf IH no. 67:3 *ʾpklʾ rbʾ dʾlhʾ* with bibliography; SFP 21:4 *ʾpklʾ ṭbʾ* the good priest

(< Akk *apkallu* < Sumerian; AIA p 34)†

ʾpmlṭ *nm* curator

s em *ʾpmlṭʾ* C4157:3

ʾpmlṭʾ dy nmšʾ dh curator of this monument

(< Gk *epimelētēs*; Syr *ʾpymlṭws*)

▶ *ʾpmlṭw* n†

ʾpmlṭw *nf** curatorship, term as curator

s cn *ʾpmlṭwt* C3968:2; pl ab *ʾpmlwṭn* C3976:2* read *ʾpmlṭwn!*

bʾpmlṭwt PN in PN's term as curator *C3968:2*; *bʾpmlṭwn! trtn* in two terms as curator *C3976:2*

(< Gk *epimelētēs* + abstr sf)

▶ *ʾpmlṭ* n†

ʾpnrṭṭ *nm* commissioner (Lat. *corrector*)

s ab/em *ʾpnrṭṭʾ* C3971:3

ʾpnrṭṭʾ dy mdnḥʾ klh commissioner for the whole East *C3971:3*; cf *C3946:2 mtqnnʾ dy mdnḥʾ*, Roman title *corrector* designates a special commissioner, appointed from the time of Trajan onward, to supervise the finances of a *libera civitas*; here, title of Odenathus

(< Gk *epanorthōtēs*)†

ʾpqʾ *nf* Afqa (name of spring at Palmyra)

ʾpqʾ RSP 126:3

rb ʿyn ʿl ʾpqʾ curator of the spring Afqa *RSP 126:3*; *125:2* Gk *ephkas*; note cognates already in Ug (*ʾpq*) and Heb†

ʾpr *v* G to distribute food (?)
G inf without *m* ? *ʾpr* CRAIBL '81:15; so Teix
dy hn yḥšḥ ʾpr that if it is necessary to distribute food *CRAIBL '81:15*, so Teix: cf Akk *epēru* 'to feed' (but context broken and difficult, attestation dubious)†

ʾrbʿ *num* four
m s ab *ʾrbʿʾ* C4158:2; *ʾrbwʿʾ* Sem '86 p 89:1 (difficult text); f s ab *ʾrbʿ* Trf:23 (*zq* skin is n f); m s em *ʾrbʿtʾ* C3962:2; f s sf 3mpl *ʾrbʿtyhwn* Inv 10 44:2 cf CaGr p 128
ʾḥd mn ʾrbʿʾ ʾḥyʾ one of the four brothers *C4158:2*; *ʾrbʿ pḥzyʾ* the four tribes *Inv 10 44:3*; *[bzq]yn ʾrbʿ* [in] four goat[skins] *Trf:23*, cf *29*; *ṣlmyʾ ʾln ʾrbʿtyhwn* these four statues *Inv 10 44:2*; *lgywnʾ dy ʾrbʿtʾ* the fourth ? legion C3962:2 see RosSpr p 81 (or 'legion of PN' Lidz ESE II p 291; Chabot ad C3962); *šnt ḥmš mʾh wʾrbʿ* the year five hundred and four *C4199:15*; *ʾrbʿ mʾh* four hundred *Sem '86 p 89:5*

ʾrbʿyn *num* forty
ʾrbʿyn Sem '86 p 89:3
wʾrbʿyn w ḥd and forty-one *Sem '86 p 89:3*

ʾrgbṭ *nm* governor
s em *ʾrgbṭʾ* C3940:2
ʾpṭrpʾ dqnrʾ wʾrgbṭʾ procurator, ducenarius, and governor *C3940:2* Gk *argapetēn*
(< Pers commander of a city Chabot ad C3940; RosSpr pp 96-97; Aram in various spellings)

ʾrgwn *nm* purple
s em *ʾrgwnʾ* Trf:137
[mk]sʾ dy ʾrgwnʾ [ta]x on purple
(< Akk [Babylonian?] *argamannu*; AIA pp 35-36)

ʾrgyʿ see *ʾdgyʿ* n

ʾrwn *nm* box (?)
s em *ʾrwnʾ* BS III 87:1
ʾrwnʾ dnʾ[...] this ? box ? (context damaged and attestation uncertain)†

ʾrḥ *nf** trip
s ab *ʾrḥ* Trf:60*; Ber '38 p 134 Fig 3:3(?)
[lk]l gml lʾrḥ ḥdʾ [for eac]h camel for one trip *Trf:60*†

ʾry *nm** lion
s em *ʾryʾ* PNO 61:1*
ʾryʾ dnh ʿbd PN this lion made by PN (on statue of a lion)†

ʾrkʾ see *byt ʾrkʾ* n phr

ʾrkwn *nm* official, archon
s ab *ʾrkwn* BS III 34:5; pl em *ʾrkwnyʾ* Trf(I):7
dy bwlʾ wdms wʾrkwnyʾ of the Senate and People and the archons *Trf(I):2*; cf *7*, *10* Gk *archontas*
(< Gk *archōn*)†

ʾrʿ *nf* lower part
s cn *ʾrʿ* Ber '34 p 38:10; Syr '36 p 271:7 ?
bʾrʿ gwmḥʾ in the lower part of the niche *Ber '34 p 38:10*
▶ *ʾrq* n†

ʾrṣw *nm* Arsu (name of deity)
s ab *ʾrṣw* Inv 10 118:1
ʾrṣw wmtyʾ Arsu, the camel-rider ? *Doura 47:1 = YCS '55 p 138:1;* see Ing ad loc on epithet; *rbʾ ʾrṣw* great is Arsu *RTP 190; qdm bl wʾrṣw* before Bel and Arsu *MUSJ '66 p 177:2*; *lʾrṣw wlqsmyʾ [w]lbnt ʾl ʾlhyʾ ṭbyʾ* to Arsu and to Kismaya and to the daughters of El, the good gods *CRAIBL '85 p 287:5*
▶ TeixPan esp. pp 69-71; Hof RelAram pp 40-41

ʾrq *nf* Arak ([?] GN); or: earth (?)
s ab ? *ʾrq*? MUSJ '61 p 133:5
lyrḥbwl lšqʾ lʾrq? to (the god) Yarhibol, to

the one who waters Arak ? / the earth ? see Hillers, Notes (forthcoming): possibly archaic spelling of Aram *ʾrqʾ* / *ʾrʿʾ* 'earth', but final *q* not certain
▶ *ʾrʿ* n†

ʾšd I *v* G to pour
G impf 3ms *yšd* Dri '82b p 65:2
mn dy lʾ yšd dm ʿl ḥgbʾ whoever does not shed blood on the shrine†

ʾšd II *v* *sense and reading uncertain*
G pf 3ms ? *ʾšd* / *ʾšr* Syr '33 p 179:2
wʾšd / *wʾšr* and he ... (reading and sense uncertain)
▶ *ʾšr* v†

ʾšr I *v* *sense and reading uncertain*
G pf 3ms ? *ʾšd* / *ʾšr* Syr '33 p 179:2
wʾšd / *wʾšr* and he ... (reading and sense uncertain)
▶ *ʾšd* v†

ʾšr II *nm* Ashar (name of deity)
ʾšr Inv 11 66:1; *ʾšrw* Doura 20:1
ʾbgl gnyʾ ṭbʾ ʾšr gnyʾ ṭbʾ Abgal, the good deity, Ashar, the good deity *PNO 6C:1*
▶ TeixPan pp 81-84 and ad Inv 12 41†

ʾšrw see *ʾšr* n

ʾštr *nf** 1 Ishtar; 2 goddess
[ʾ]št[r] RTP 121; s em *ʾštrʾ* Inv 11 87:4; cf *ʾs[t]rʾ* C3985:1
1 *[ʾ]št[r]* [I]shta[r] *RTP 121* **2** *lʿštr[tʾ] ʾštrʾ ṭbtʾ* to Astar[te], the good goddess *Syr '31 13:3**; *bʿltk ʾštrʾ* Baaltak, the goddess *Syr '31 12:4*; *[l ... ʾš]trʾ ṭbtʾ* [to DN] the good go]ddess *AAS '65 p 90:2* :: Bounni [pour Ish]tar la bonne
(parallels development in Akk of *Ištar* 'Ishtar'(DN) > *ištaru* 'goddess'; perhaps < Akk; see AIA p 60)
▶ TeixPan pp 60-61; *ʾstrʾ* n†

ʾštrbd *nf* Ishtarbad (name of deity)
ʾštrbd RTP 198, 199
ʾštrbd mlktʾ Ishtarbad, the queen *RTP 198* see Caquot RTP p 181
▶ Hof RelAram p 45†

ʾth see *ʾnth* n

ʾty *v* G to come; C to bring
G pf 3ms *ʾtʾ* Syr '63 p 48:3, C3959:3, 4; C pf 3ms *ʾyty* Syr '26 p 129:6; *ʾty* C3932:4 CaGr p 40
G *PN dy ʾtʾ brš* PN, who came at the head of ... *Syr '63 p 48:3* **C** *wḥmr bzqyn lʾ ʾyty mn mʿrbʾ* and he did not bring wine in skins from the west *Syr '26 p 129:6*; *wkdy ʾty lkʾ yt lgynyʾ* and when he brought the legions here *C3932:4*†

ʾtr *nm** 1 place, area; 2 sacred precinct, sanctuary; 3 *ʾtr dy* cj where, place where
s ab *ʾtr* C4011:5; cn *ʾtr* BS III 24:4; em *ʾtrʾ* PNO 2ter:7; s sf 3ms *ʾtrh* C3917:4
1 *mn ʾtrʾ šḥmʾ* from the unconsecrated area *Ber '38 p 110:4**; *dy yhb lʾbgl šlṭnʾ bʾtrʾ klh* who gave Abgal dominion in every place (or: in the whole area) *PNO 2ter:7*; *ʾ[t]r ʾḥyd* place reserved *BS III 68:1* cf Dunant ad loc. cf Gk *topos* seat in theatre inscriptions **2** *[w]lʾlhyʾ klhn dy ytbyn lwth ... bkl ʾtr klh* and to all the gods who live with her (the Mistress of the Temple) ... in the whole temple precinct *RSP 143:5*, on this sense see Gaw ad loc. :: Ing Glossary p 43 in RosAH: place, base; *ḥmnʾ klh hw wʾtrh* the whole chapel and its sacred precinct *C3917:4*
3 *ʾtr dy yhwh* where it will be *BS III 24:4*; see Dunant ad loc.

ʾtrmsyn *nm* *word of uncertain sense*
analysis uncertain *ʾtrmsyn* C4036A:3, C4036B:2
PN ʾtrmsyn ʿl ḥywhy PN, ... , for his life, etc. C4036A:3†

b *prep* 1 in, within, inside; 2 at, by; 3 with (accompanying); 4 with, by (of instrument); 5 by (in oath); 6 *marking object or modifier, with certain verbs* *by* Ber '35 p 86:12 is problematic, see Ing ad loc. (plene writing of *b* ?); sf 3ms *bh* C4214:1; sf 3mp *bhwn* Inv 10 29:4; *bhn* Inv 10 44:5; elided by dissimilation before initial *b-* BS III 45:11 *bt [bʿlšmn]*; on omission of *bh* in Inv 7 6:1 see Cantineau ad loc.

1 *bʾtr* in the place *Trf:131*; *bʾdrwnʾ* in the dining-room *CRAIBL '81:14*; *bʾlgšyʾ* in GN *C3917:3*; *dblgywnʾ* who are in the legion *C3944:5*; *bkl ṣbw klh* in everything *Inv 10 44:6*; *byrḥ ʾb* in the month of Ab *C3924:1*; *bḥywhy* during his life *C4119:6*; *bgrmṭyʾ dy lh* during his term as secretary *Inv 10 39:3*; *bmytwytʾ PN* at the coming of PN (when PN came) *C3932:2*; *wktb ... bgllʾ* and let it be written ... on a stele *Trf(I):9* Gk dative *stēlē* **2** *wqm bršhwn* and he stood at the head of them *C3916:4* **3** *hyklʾ dy DN bqdšwhy* the temple of DN with its sanctuaries *Inv 9 1:5*; *dkyr PN bṭb* may PN be remembered for good *PNO 47:5* **4** *bʾgrtʾ dy ktb* by the letter he wrote *Trf:104* Gk *dia*; *nhryn bmgdyhwn* distinguished by their gifts *C3914:3* Gk *en*; *shdt lh bdgm* gave witness to him by a decree *Syr '36 20:5*; *btwḥyt bwlʾ wdms* by decree of the Senate and People *C3959:1; hw ymh byrḥbwl* he will swear by Yarhibol *Syr '36 26:9*; *bšm bwlʾ [wdm]sʾ* in the name of the Senate [and peop]le *BS III 45:5* Gk *dēmosiois* **6** *šmʿ bqlh* he listened to his voice *C4080:5*; *dy ʿdr bh* he who aided it RTP 722; *[dy] ʾgr bh PN* for [which] PN contracted (?) *Trf:77* (context broken); *lʾḥbwrʾ bh ʾyš* to take anyone as partner in it *C4214:1*; *wštp PN bmnth* and PN has taken as associate in his portion *MélCol p 161:9*

bb *nm** gate, doorway

s em *bbʾ* C4199:9; pl em *bbyʾ* Doura 52:1 ?

dy ʿbd lhn bbʾ wtrʿwhy who made for them the gate and its doors *C3917:3**

(< Akk *bābu*; AIA pp 40-41)

bbl *nf* Babylon

bbl Inv 9 11:4

mdynt bbl the city of Babylon *Inv 9 11:4*; *nny škny šyʿt bbl* DN (and) DN, who accompany Babylon RTP 285†

bgw *prep* inside, within

bgw Ber '35 p 60:1; sf 3ms *bgwh* C4206:2

dy bgw mʿrtʾ which is inside the hypogeum *Ber '35 p 60:1*; *qbrʾ wmʿrtʾ dy bgwh* the tomb and the hypogeum within it *C4206:2*

bgn *nm ? f ? reading and meaning uncertain*: prayer, kind of invocation (?)

bgnw?[...] Inv 11 80:6 perhaps n s ab *bgn* to be read

.yhwʾ bgnw?[...] Inv 11 80:6; Teix ad loc. suggests possibly *bgn* = Syriac and Hatran *bgn*, here in sense ʿprayerʾ; very uncertain†

bd *cj* because

bd Syr '36 26:5, 6

bd lyt kmryʾ ... because (?) there are no priests *Syr '36 26:5*

(prep *b* + *d[y]* Syriac *bad*)

▶ *bdy* cj†

bdy *cj* because

bd[y] BS III 45:8; *wbdy* BS III 45:7 an erroneous reading; see *dyṭgmʾ* n

wbd[y] s[yʿ] šyr[tʾ] and because he h[elped] the carava[n] *BS III 45:8*

(*b* prep + *dy*)

▶ *bd* cj†

bdyl dy *cj* because

bdyl dy Trf:137

bdyl dy špr lhwn because he was good to them *C3916:3*

(*bdyl* < *b* + *dy* + *l*)

▶ Sokoloff '74 p 145; RosSpr pp 86-87; *bdyl kwt* adv

bdyl kwt *adv* accordingly

bdyl kwt Inv 9 11:6

bdyl kwt ʾqymw lh ṣlmʾ dnh accordingly they erected this statue for him *Inv 9 11:6*; cf *C3966:7*; *C3917:6*; *Inv 10 39:4*

(*bdyl* + *kwt*: PJA CPA Syr Sam, extension of Com Sem *k*; RosSpr pp 86-87)

▶ *bdyl dy* cj†

bwl' *nf** Senate, council
s ab/em *bwl'* Inv 10 39:4*
bwl' 'qymt lh ṣlm' dn[h] the Senate erected this statue for him *Inv 10 39:4*; *mn twḥyt bwl' wdmws* by decision of the Senate and People *C3959:1*; *dgm' dy bwl'* a decree of the Senate *Trf(I):1* Gk *boulēs*; *'tḥzy lbwl'* it seemed good to the Senate *Trf(I):7*
(< Gk *boulē*)

bwl'str *nm** Bolastor (name of deity)
bwl'str Syr '38 p 79:2*
lbwl'str 'lh' to Bolastor the god; cf *Syr '31 p 130:5, 9*
▶ *bl'str* n; TeixPan pp 8-9†

bṭl *v* to be of concern
D ptcp pass *mbṭl* Trf(I):10
wyhw' mbṭl l'rkwny' and let it be the concern of the archons Gk *epimeleisthai*†

by *nm** 1 house; 2 *bt 'lm'* eternal home (i.e. tomb); 3 temple; 4 place, *bt qbwr'* burial place; 5 family; 6 *byt 'b* father's house, clan; 7 *bny byt'* family, members of household
s cn *byt* C3978:7; *bt* Syr '36 20:9; em *byt'* C4176B:3; em *bt'* Inv 12 49:8; sf 3ms *byth* C3997:2; sf 3mp *bythwn* C3981:5; pl ab *btyn* Syr '31 p 130:8
1 *wbtyn* ... and houses ... *Syr '31 p 130:8*; see *gb n* for phrase *bt gb'* **2** *qbr' dnh bt 'lm'* this grave, eternal home *C4116:1*; *m'rt' dnh dy bt 'lm' ḥpr wbn' wṣbt ... PN* this burial cave, which is an eternal home, dug, built, and decorated ... by PN *Inv 4 13:1*; Gk renders *bt 'lm' C4192:1* with *aiōnios*; *Inv 4 14:1* (restored) *taphaiōnos*; *RSP 25:7* Gk *taph[eō]na*; cf Old Syriac (2nd-3rd century), Dri '72 no. 45:45 etc.; van der Horst '91 41-44 **3** *bt bl* temple of Bel *C3914:5*; *pḥz bt 'lhyh* (each) tribe in the house of its god *Syr '36 p 346:9*; *lmrt byt' mṣb' dy nṣb PN* to the Lady of the Temple (q. v.), the image erected by PN *RSP 143:3; wtrṣw ṣbwt bt'* and they set straight the affairs of the temple *Inv 12 49:8*; *BS III 45:11-13* Gk *hierō* for *bt* (DN) **4** *wršt' dy byt' wm'rt'* heiress of home and tomb *C4176B:3*; *bt qbwr' dnh 'bdw PN wPN* this burial place was made by PN and PN *C4163:1**; Gk *tapheōna C4160:1*; cf *byt qbwr'* 'tomb' in Old Syriac inscriptions, Dri '72 Glossary p 79; *[b?]t nyḥ'* place of rest ? restoration suggested by Teix ad *Inv 11 67:1*, cf *nyḥ'* Syr '35 p 242 **5** *'l byth* for his family *C3997:2* **6** See *byt 'b* n phr **7** *wlḥyy bny byt' klhwn* and for the life of his whole household *Inv 11 6:8*
▶ *byt 'b* n phr; *byt 'rk'* n phr

byl see *bl* n

bylwṭ *nm** senator
s ab *blwṭ* Inv 10 29:2; em *bylwṭ'* C3937:2*
PN blwṭ b'nṭky' PN, senator in Antioch *Inv 10 29:2* Gk *bouleutēn*; *wbylwṭ' tdmry'* and Senator of Palmyra *C3937:2* Gk *bouleutēn* (< *bouleutēs*)†

byn *v* to determine, decide
C impf 3mp *ybn[w]n* Trf(I):8
dy ybn[w]n md'm dy l' msq bnmws' who are to deter[mine] anything that is not mentioned in the law, Gk *diakreinontas*†

bynwt *prep* between
bynwt Ber '35 p 104:4
mn btr gwmḥ' qdmy' bynwt kpy' behind the first niches, between the two vaulted spaces
(< *byn* prep + *wt*)
▶ *byn* prep†

byny *prep* between
byny Trf(I):7; sf 3mp *bynyhwn* C3915:3; *bnyhwn* ? Ber '38 p 124:9, see *plg* v
byny tgr' lbyny mksy' between the merchants and the tax-collectors *Trf(I):7* Gk *[me]taxu*; *w'bd šlm' bynyhwn* and he made peace between them *C3915:3* cf *Inv 9 13*
▶ *bynwt* prep†

byš *adj* 1 bad; 2 *n* evil, harm
m s ab *byš'* Inv 8 172:1 f s cn *byšt* C4486:3, 7
1 *ḥbl PN son of PN(f) byšt gd'* (here lies) PN, son of PN(f), the unfortunate one! *C4486:3, 7* **2** *mn kl byš' klh* from all harm *Inv 8 172:1*†

byt 'b *n phr m* father's house, clan
byt 'bwhn C3978:7
lšmš 'lh byt 'bwhn to Shamash, the god of their clan *C3978:7*; cf Gk *hēliou patrōou theou* cited Gaw ANRW p 2643
▶ *by* n†

byt 'rk' *n phr m* archives, public records
bt 'rk' Syr '33 p 183:3; p 184:2
ktb bt 'rk' a document in the public records *Syr '33 p 183:3*; *wrm' bt 'rk'* and ... the public records *Syr '33 p 184:2*
(< Gk *ta archeia* 'the archives' [CaGr p 155] cf Syriac *'rkywn* in Dura Slave-Sale text see Cussini '92a (index, forthcoming revision) with citation of Welles '59 and Goldstein '66 :: RosSpr p 91, Gaw '73b p 121 < Gk *archē* 'house of the *archē*', i. e., of the authorities, the archons)
▶ *by* n†

bl *nm* Bel (name of deity)
bl RTP 10; *byl* MélDus p 885:2
dy ḥnk hykl' dy bl wyrḥbwl w'glbwl 'lhy' who dedicated the temple of the gods Bel and Yarhibol and Aglibol *Inv 9 1:4*
▶ TeixPan pp 1-18 *et passim*; Hof RelAram pp 26-33

bl *cj* certainly, indeed
bl C4207:1
bl dkyr PN may PN indeed be commemorated†

blw *nm* revenue, funds
c s *blw* Sem '93 p 164:2; pl em *blwy'* Sem '93 p 164:1
ktl' dnh dy blwy' dy gmly' This wall, (out of) the funds of the (people of) Gamla (the camels?) p 164:1; *dy l'l mnh dy blw gbl tdmry' klhwn 'l PN wPN brh . . . lyqrhwn* the upper part of which is (out of) the funds of the whole people of Tadmor p 164:2; Gaw's interpretation of difficult text differs in some respects†

blwṭ see *bylwṭ* n

blḥmwn *nm* Belham(m)on, name of deity
blḥmwn Inv 11 99:3; *blḥmwn* RTP 215
lbl blḥmwn wmnwt to Bel, Belham(m)on and Manawat *Inv 11 99:3*
▶ TeixPan pp 12-18; Starcky StudLdV pp 516-517; Gaw ANRW p 2624; Hof RelAram pp 47-48

bl'str *nm* Bolastor (name of deity)
s ab *bl'str* RTP 127
'gn bl wbl'str symposium of Bel and Bolastor *RTP 125*
▶ *bwl'str* n; TeixPan pp 8-9, 113-114

blty *nf* Belti
s ab *blty* RTP 218
'gn bl blty symposium of Bel (and) Belti *RTP 128*
▶ PN *blty*; see TeixPan pp 8 ('My Lady'), 57, 88; Hof RelAram p 44

bny *v* to build
G pf 3ms *bn'* C4169:1; 3mp *bnw* C4168:1; pf 3ms sf 3ms *bnhy* Syr '33 p 191:3 ? cf Inv 8 65:2; ptcp m s a *bn'* MUSJ '62 p 106:10; m pl ab *bnn* Ber '38 p 95:9 cf RTP 522 ?; ptcp pass m s ab *bn'* StudPalm '75 p 129:5
dy bn' 'ksdr' dnh who built this exedra *Ber '35 p 64:1*; *yhw' bn'* let him build *MUSJ '62 p 106:10;* for "periphrastic imperative" see e.g. Trf:133 *yhw' yhb* let him give, cf *yhw' pr'* Trf:129, and see Greenfield '69 pp 199-210; Makowski '83 p 176-78; *m'rt' dnh dy bt 'lm' ḥpr wbn' wṣbt ... PN* this tomb, as an eternal resting-place, was dug and built and decorated ... by PN *Inv 4 13:1*;

bn' StudPalm '75 p 131:3 Gk *[ektise]n*
▶ *bnyn* n

bnyn *nm** 1 construction; 2 building
s cn *bnyn* RTP 114; s em *bnyn'* RTP 115
1 *w'[d]r bnyn' dy h[y]kl' dy bl* and he h[el]ped with the construction of the t[em]ple of Bel *Inv 9 11:4*; Chabot RTP p 141 proposes that for tesserae sense is either 'construction', or (like Latin *fabrica*) 'corps charged with the administration of a sacred building'; cf also IH no. 192:2 *lbnyn' d s[gy]l* for the building of Esagil (records a sum paid for the temple building fund, as does no. 191) **2** *bn' bnyn' dnh PN* ... built this building *RSP 127:3** cf Déd p 255
▶ *bn'* v

bnpqyr *nm beneficiarius* (soldier exempt from certain menial duties)
s em *bnpqyr'* C4292:2
ḥbl PN bnpqyr' Alas! PN, the *beneficiarius* (< Lat *beneficiarius*)†

bnt 'l *n phr f* Banat El (Daughters of El), name of deities
[w]lbnt 'l CRAIBL '85 p 287:6
l'rṣw wlqsmy' [w]lbnt 'l 'lhy' ṭby' to Arsu and to Kismaya and to the daughters of El, the good gods†

bʿd *v* to alienate (property)
G pf 1s *bʿdt* RB '30 14:4; G inf *mbʿd'* C4214:1
'w lmbʿd 'w l'ḥbwr' either to alienate or give in partnership *C4214:1* (division of words differs from CIS, see ad loc.)
(cf Arab *bʿd* to be 'distant' ?; CaGr p 78 thinks *bʿr* equally likely, but note semantic parallel *rḥq* 'to be distant' > 'to cede')
▶ *rḥq* v†

bʿy *v* to seek
G impf 3ms *ybʿh* RSP 199:14; Gt impf 3ms *ytbʿ'* Trf:70
dy ybʿh ʿl gbr ḥṭ['] who will inquire about a man who has sin[ned ...] *RSP 199:14*, reading of Déd p 287; *[w]m' dy ytbʿ' ytn [lh]n* [and] when it is requested he will give (it) [to th]em *Trf:70*†

bʿl *nm* 1 husband; 2 owner, master (?)
s sf 3fs *bʿlh* BS III 63:4; pl cs *bʿl[y]* Syr '33 p 187:2(?)
1 *dy ʿbd lh PN bʿlh* which PN, her husband, made for her *C4518A:3* **2** *bʿl[y] bwpwr* masters of GN ? *Syr '33 p 187:2*

bʿlšmyn *nm** Baalshamin, Baashamin (name of deity)
bʿlšmyn RTP 209; *bʿlšmn* RTP 207; *bʿšmn* PNO 61:4*
lbʿšmn ṭb wskr' to Baalshamin, the good and generous *PNO 61:4*; *lbʿlšmn 'lh' ṭb'* to Baalshamin, the good god *C3983:1*
▶ TeixPan index; Gaw ANRW pp 2625-36; Hof RelAram pp 33-38

bʿlšmn see *bʿlšmyn* n

bʿltk *nf* Baaltak (name of deity)
bʿltk RTP 76
'gn bl bʿltk symposium of Bel (and) Baaltak RTP 76; *bʿltk 'štr'* Baaltak, the goddess *Syr '31 p 133:4*
(name < epithet 'Your Lady' Déd p 174)
▶ du Mesnil du Buisson TMP pp 364-67; TeixPan p 57; Hof RelAram pp 46-47

bʿr see *bʿd* v

bʿšmyn see *bʿlšmyn* n

bṣr' *nf* Bosra (main city of Roman province of Arabia)
bṣr' C3944:5
plḥ' dblgywn' dy bṣr' a soldier in the legion of Bosra *C3944:5*
▶ Appendix MAPS†

bqy *v* to seek ([?] attestation dubious)
ptcp m sf 3ms *bq'h* RSP 107:2 or read *bm'h*
rḥmn' ʿl bq'h the merciful to him who

seeks him ? see Gaw ad loc.†

bqr *v* D to inquire
D inf *lmbqrw* CRAIBL '81:18
lmbqrw wlmw[dʿ] to make inquiry and to info[rm]†

br I *nm** 1 son **a** son **b** child **c** son of — : (in n phr for relations) half-brother (?); grandchild; nephew; 2 member of family or other group; 3 *br x years*: *x* years old
s cn *br* Inv 11 12:3; sf 3ms *brh* Inv 11 63B:2; 3fs *brh* C4252B:2; 3mpl *brhwn* C4283:6; pl ab *bnyn* C4227:5; cs *bny* C4214:1; cs *bnʾ* Inv 11 13:6; sf 3ms *bnwh* Inv 11 79:5; *bnwhy* C4571A:3; *bnyh* C3988:3; *bnh* Ber '35 p 112:9; *bnyhw* Ber '35 p 112:10; pl sf 3fs *bnh* C4053:3; 3mpl *bnyhwn* C4121:1; *bnyhn* C4206:2; *bnhw[n]* C4002:5
1 a *PN br PN* PN son of PN *C4182:1*; Gk in genealogies often has patronymic in genitive; *brh* his son *C3920:3* Gk *huios autou*
1 b *wlbnwhy* and for his children *C4112:6* Gaw, MF ad no. 2 pp 184-85 notes that *bnwhy* often should be rendered ʿchildren' in view of those texts that explicitly say *bnwhy dkryʾ* ʿhis male children', as *C4159:6**; note also *bnwhy C3902:2* and elsewhere = Gk *teknōn*
1 c *PN wPN ... ʾḥyn bny ʾmʾ* PN and PN ... brothers, sons of the (same) mother (prb ʿhalf-brothers', cf Hb Gen 20:12; Lev 18:9 etc., unless adoption or other special circumstances is involved) *Ber '38 p 106:2*; *PN br br PN* PN, grandson of PN *C4197:5*; *lbnyn wlbny bnyn dkryn* and for children and grandchildren, males *C4214:1* Gk *huōnois*; *wlyqr bny ddhwn* and in honor of their nephews (sons of their uncle) *RB '30 6:2* **2** *bny bytʾ klhwn* all the members of the family *Inv 11 6:7*; *dy ʿqymw lh bny zbdbwl k[lhw]n* which a[ll] the Bne Zabdibol (members of the Zabdibol tribe) erected for him *C3951:2*; *bny šyrtʾ dy nḥtw ʿmh* the members of the caravan who went down with him *Inv 10 124:3*; *bny mrzḥ* members of the symposium ... *RTP 301*; *yhb mšḥʾ lbny md[yntʾ]* he gave oil to the citi[zens] *C3959:4* Gk *poleitai[s]* **3** *br šnt 4[5] ḥbl* at the age of 45. Alas! *C3908:5*
▶ *brh* n; *br dktʾ* n phr; *br ḥrʾ* n phr

br II *nm* outside, exterior
s em *brʾ* RSP 127:4
wktlʾ dy brʾ and the exterior wall
▶ *lbr mn* prep

br br see *br* n

br dktʾ *n phr m* son of the place ([?] sense uncertain)
br dktʾ Ber '36 p 88:2
PN br dktʾ dy twnʾ son of the place ? of the chamber ? *Ber '36 p 88:2*; Ing ad loc. ʿson of Daketa' (GN), or (preferably) ʿson of purification', i.e. member of a staff concerned with purification (root *dky*); Déd pp 273-74 on basis of possible Hatran *dktʾ* ʿalms-box', proposes ʿalmoner of the cella'. Sense of *twnʾ* here also uncertain.
▶ *dktʾ* n†

brh *nf* 1 daughter; 2 member of a family or group
s cn *brt* C4478:3; *bt* C4380:2; s sf 3ms *brth* C4421:3; pl sf 3ms *bnth* Inv 8 118:2
1 *PN brt PN* PN daughter of PN *C4466:2*
2 *PN b[r]t PN dy mn bnt mytʾ* PN(f) daughter of PN, who is of the daughters of *Mytʾ* (tribal name) *BS III 11:3*; n phr designating social groups of type *br X* are inflected for gender and number; see Hillers, Notes (forthcoming). See Déd pp 258-59 for view that in *brt X*, X is physical father, while in *bt X*, X = name of tribe
▶ *br* n; *br ḥry* n phr; *brt bl* n phr; *bnt ʾl* n phr

brḥ *v* G to bar ([?] attestation uncertain)
G ptcp m s ab/cn ? *brḥ* Doura 39:1
brḥ bb[ʾ] the one who bars the gate ?†

br ḥrʾ *n phr m* freedman; *bt ḥry* freedwoman
m s *br ḥrʾ* C4482:2; *br ḥry* C4385:2; m pl *bny*

ḥryh[wn] RSP 104:5; f s *brt ḥry* Inv 4 13:3; *bt ḥry* C3901:1

hyk [dy] gb[ʾ] PN br ḥry qysr as PN, freedman of Caesar, collected Trf:62 Gk *apeleutheros*; *PN br ḥry PN* PN freedman of PN *C4174:1 wlbny ḥryh[wn]* for their freedmen *RSP 104:5*; *PN bt ḥry PN* PN(f), freedwoman of PN Lat *liberta C3901:1*

br ḥry see *br ḥrʾ* n phr

bry *adj* outer, exterior

m s ab *bryʾ* Ber '35 p 86:12; pl ab *bryyn* Ber '38 p 124:2

sṭr mn gwmḥyn trn bryyn ymnyyn except for two outer niches on the right *Ber '38 p 124:2*†

bry *v* see *brr* v

bryk *adj* blessed

m s ab *bryk* Sumer '64 p 20 no. 11:1; *brk* C4024:1; f s em *bryktʾ* C3976:1; m pl ab *brykyn* Inv 11 77:1; anomalous is *dkyryn wbrw[kyn]* PNO 52 ter:4; m pl em ? *brykyʾ* RTP 244, but *brykyn* is possible reading

dkyr bryk PN remembered (and) blessed be PN *Sumer '64 p 20 no. 11:1*; *lgdʾ dy ʿynʾ bryktʾ* to the Fortune of the blessed spring *C3976:1*

(adj, ptcp pass < *brk v* Com Sem)

⧐ *bryk šmh lʿlmʾ* n; See *brk* v

bryk šmh lʿlmʾ *n phr m* Blessed-Be-His-Name-Forever (frequent euphemistic substitute for name of deity, the "Anonymous God")

bryk šmh lʿlmʾ C4063:2; *brk* etc C4024:1

lbryk šmh lʿlmʾ ṭbʾ wrḥmnʾ ʿbd PN made for Blessed-Be-His-Name-Forever, the good and merciful, by PN *C4085:1**

⧐ TeixPan pp 115-19; Gaw ANRW pp 2631-33; Hof RelAram pp 38-40; du Mesnil du Buisson, '78 pp 777-81

brk *v* D to bless

D impf 3ms *ybrk* RTP 109; 3fs *tbrk* RTP 722; 3fp *tbrkn* RTP 242; inf *lmbrkw* RSP 136:2

nbw ybrk lPN may Nabu bless PN *RTP 305*

⧐ *bryk* adj; *bryk šmh lʿlmʾ* n phr

br mn *prep* **1** (from) outside **2** besides, beyond

br mn Trf:119, 145

1 *mdy yhwʾ mt[ʾʿ]l br mn tḥwmʾ ʾw mʾpq* when it is im[por]ted from outside the territory or exported *Trf:111* **2** *wprns brmnhwn bkl [ṣ]bw klh* and he provided besides these things in every [w]ay *C3915:4 = Inv 9 13:4;* for other suggestions see *brmn n* below †

brmn *nm* affair (?)

s sf 3mpl *brmnhwn* C3915:4

wprns brmnhwn bkl [ṣ]bw klh and he assisted in their affairs ? in every [w]ay *C3915:4 = Inv 9 13:4* but see prep *br mn* above

(for many conjectures on etym., Chabot ad C3915 and DISO s.v. br_{III})†

brr *v* to purify (?); to make profane, to deconsecrate (?)

C pass pf 3ms *ʾbr* ? BS III 60:3; C pf 3ms sf 3ms *ʾbrh* ? BS III 60:5

ptyḥ qbrʾ dnh wʾbr this tomb was opened and purified ? *BS III 60:3*; *wPN ... ptḥh wʾbrh* now PN ... opened it and purified ? it *BS III 60:5*; reading and analysis uncertain (*r* and *d* indistinguishable, hence *ʾbd* etc possible reading); could be from *bry* cf Syriac *bar* 'outside' > 'profane'; see Dunant ad loc.; Teix '86 p 222 (p 444 of *Syr* '49 [1972]); Gaw TP p 18; Hillers, Notes (forthcoming).†

brt ḥry see *br ḥry* n phr

brt bl *n phr f* the Daughter of Bel (title of a deity)

brt bl RTP 143, 144

brt bl the daughter of Bel *RTP 143, 144, StudLdV p 512:6*; *bt brt bl* the house of the daughter of Bel *JA '33 p 230:7*†

brty *adj* Beirutian, of Beirut

m s em *brty'* C4401:3
PN qwlwn brty' PN, colonist of Beirut *C4401:3* Gk *kolōn bērutios*
▶ Appendix MAPS†

bšym *adj* perfumed
m s em *bšym'* Trf(II):13
dy mšḥ' bšym' [dy] mt''l [b]š[typt]' of perfumed oil [which] is imported [in] [alabaster] j[ars]
▶ CaGr p 109†

bt' *prep* between (?)
bt' Ber '35 p 97:1, 98:1 corrected readings of Ingholt Ber '36 p 127 (not *bn'*)
dy bt' qrqsy' which is between ? the arches *Ber '35 p 97:1*; *btr 'ksdr' bt' trn qrqsy'* in back of the exedra between ? two arches *Ber '35 p 98:1*
▶ *byny* prep; *bynwt* prep†

bt 'rk' see *byt 'rk'* n phr

bt bl *n phr m* see *brt bl* n phr

bt ḥry see *br ḥr'* n phr

bt pṣy'l *nf* Beth Phasiel
bt pṣy'l PNO 39:1
dy qryt' dy bt pṣy'l of the town of Beth Phasiel *PNO 39:1*
▶ Appendix MAPS†

btr *prep* 1 behind; 2 after
btr C4175:6; sf 3ms *btrh* C4194:6
1 *btr 'ksdr'* behind the exedra *C4175:6*; *dy mn btr gwmḥ' qdmy'* which is behind the first niche *Ber '35 p 104:3* **2** *btr mwth* after his death *RSP 103:4*; *wbtr 'ln* and after these *RB '30 9:3*
▶ *btr dy* cj

btr *adv* afterward, later
btr Trf:96
lmpqn' btr for export at a later time *Trf:96* Gk *husteron*
▶ *btr* prep†

btr dy *cj* after
btr dy C3920:3, 3927:5
btr dy myt after they died *Inv 10 4B:3*; to be restored in *C3954:2 [btr] dy mytt* after she died
▶ *btr* prep†

gb I *nm* side
s em *gb'* Inv 4 7b:2; PNO 28:1
bsṭr' gb' dy sml' on the wall, the north side *Inv 4 7b:2*†

gb II *nm* ditch, cistern
s em *gb'* RSP 127:4
wktl' dy qd[m] bt gb' and the wall in front of the cistern-house†

gb'h *nf* basin
s em *gb't'* Inv 12 39:1; PNO 22:1
gb't' w'lt' 'ln this basin and altar *Inv 12* (on a basin or crater; so also *PNO 22*, as also possibly *PNO 28* fragment)
(Bou and Teix ad Inv 12 < Akk *gubbû*, *egubbû* 'basin for holy water' [?])†

gbwrh *nf* great deed, mighty deed
pl em *gbwrt'* RSP 142:2
w'bd 'mhwn gbwrt' and did for them great things†

gby *v* G to collect taxes; Gt to be charged
G pf 3ms *gb[']* Trf:62; impf 3ms *ygb'* Trf:50; ptcp act m s ab *gb'* Trf(I):6; pl *gbn* Trf:106; ptcp pass 3ms *gby* Trf(I):14; Gt impf 3ms *[ytg]b'* Trf:69; 3mpl *ytgb[wn] Trf:129*; ptcp m s ab *mtgb'* Trf:149; f pl ab *mtgbyn* Trf(I):5
G *dy l' yhw' gb' 'gwr' mn 'nš md'm ytyr* that the tax-collector should not collect from anyone anything in excess *Trf(I):11*; *whw' gb'* and he would charge *Trf(I):6*; *mks' gby* tax was charged *Trf (I):14* Gk *eprachthē* **Gt** *'tḥzy dy ytgb[wn] hyk [nḥ]š'* it was decided that they should be taxed as bronze *Trf:129*; *hyk bnmws' dnr yhw' mtgb'* according to the

law, a denarius shall be charged *Trf:149*; *whww mtgbyn mn ʿyd'* and they were taxed according to customary rule *Trf(I):5* Gk *eprass[eto]*; Gk throughout the Tariff (Trf) has forms of *prassein* 'to exact payment', or of derivatives *praxin poieisthai*, *paraprassein*

gbl *nm* people
s cn *gbl* C3923:3; Inv 9 12:3
[']qymw lh gbl tdmry' klhn [e]rected for him by all the people of the Palmyrenes Gk *[p]o[lis]* or *[b]o[ulē]*; *Inv 9 12* Gk *dēmos* (perhaps calque of Gk *dēmos* 'district, country' > 'people' [L-S] cf *dms n*)†

gbr *v* to be great (?)
G inf *lmgbr* RTP 722
tbrk ʿyn' dh lmgbr dy ʿdr bh may this spring bless mightily (?) the one who helped with it†

gbr *nm** man
s ab *gbr* PNO 2ter:9*; s em *gbr'* RTP 507
wdkyr kl gbr dy ydḥl lʿbgl bṭb and remembered be every man who fears Abgal, for good†

gd *nm** 1 fortune, luck; 2 Gad, Fortune (name of deity)
s cn *gd* PNO 51:2; s em *gd'* RTP 718*; sf 3ms *gdh* PNO 42:3
1 *byšt gd'* unlucky *C4486:4*; *gd' ṭb' lPN* Good fortune for PN *RTP 718* **2** *wlgd' dy PN* and to the Fortune of Yedi[be]l *BS III 23:3*; *lgd qryt'* to the Fortune of the city *PNO 51:2*; *gd tdmr* the Fortune of Tadmor; *lmlkb[l] wgd tymy wlʿtrʿth 'lh[y'] ṭb[y']* to Malakbel, the Fortune of Taimi, and to Atargatis, the goo[d] god[s] Gk *tychē Taimeios C3927:4*
TeixPan esp. pp 88-100

gd ʿgrwd *n m* Gad ʿAjrud (name of deity)
gd ʿgrwd RTP 213
bl ḥmwn gd ʿgrwd (Obv) Bel Hammon (Rev) Gad ʿAjrud
†

gdʿh *nf* *meaning uncertain*
s em *gdʿt'* RTP 680
'gn gdʿt' dy bl symposium (of ?) the ... ? of Bel; Déd pp 150-51 'barbers' (*grʿt'*), but improbable†

gdʿt' see *gdʿh* n

gw *nm* inside; inner group (?)
s em *gw'* StudMiles p 38:1, ? *gw'* CRAIBL '81:17
ymd mṣʿt gw' he shall measure within the inner group ?
▶ *gwy* adj; *lgw* adv; *gw mn* prep; *lgw mn* prep†

gwy *adj* 1 inner; 2 *n* intimate, counsellor (?)
m s ab ? *gw'* Ber '35 p 102 X:3; em *gwy'* Inv 12 45:4; pl ab *gwyyn* C4174:3; *gwyn* Ber '35 p 102 XI:4; em *gwy'* Ber '35 p 107:3;
1 *gwy'* (these five niches) ... the inner ones; *PN 'sy' gwy'* PN, the personal ? physician *Inv 12 45:4* **2** *ṣlm PN gwy' mhymn'* statue of PN, the trusted counsellor ? *C4239:1*
▶ *gw* n; *mhymn* n

gwmḥ *nm** burial place, niche; grave
s ab *gwmḥ* Ber '35 p 86:11*; em *gwmḥ'* C4227:2; pl ab *gwmḥyn* C4175:5; pl em *gwmḥy'* C4194:6; pl sf 3ms *gwmḥwhy* Ber '38 p 106:4
'yt bgwmḥ' mqbrn št in each niche there are six burials *C4175:7*; *qbr' dnh wgwmḥyn 'rbʿ dy ʿlyt'* this grave and the four niches in the upper chamber *C4212:1*; *gwmḥ' dnh dy PN* this grave is that of PN *RSP 105:1* (inscription from grave, not niche in larger tomb)
(< Akk *kimaḫḫu*; AIA p 64)

gw mn *prep* inside, less than
gw mn Trf:106
wmdy gw mn dnr and what is less than a denarius

▶ *gw* n†

gwr *v* *uncertain reading and analysis*
G impf 3ms *yg[wr]* CRAIBL '81:14
gbr' dy yg[wr] lmšt' b'drwn' a man who p[articipates] ? in the banquet in the dining-hall†

gzz *v* to shear
G inf *lmgz* Trf:147
mt''l' lmdyt' lmgz brought into the city for shearing†

gld *nm* skin, hide
p em *gldy'* Trf:122
'l gldy' dy dgmly['] concerning hides of camels†

glwp *nm** sculptor
s em *glwp'* C3974:4*; *glp'* Doura 47:2 see YCS '55 p 138; Inv 10 110:3; RSP 159:6
dkyr PN glwp' may PN the sculptor be remembered *C3974:4*
▶ *glp* v†

gll *nm* stone slab, stele
s em *gll'* Trf(I):9
wktb 'm nmws' qdmy' bgll' dy lqbl hykl' and be written with the former law on the stele which faces the temple†

glp *v* to carve
G pf 3ms *glp* PNO 52ter:2
dy glp 'lt' who carved the altar
(< Gk *glyphō* 'to carve')
▶ *glwp* n; *glph* n†

glp see *glwp* n

glph *nf* sculpture
s em *glpt'* PNO 57:1 (w. *dnh* see CaGr p 145)
'bd glpt' dnh made this sculpture
▶ *glp* v†

gmw *nf* *meaning uncertain*
s ab ? cn ? *gmwt* Inv 12 43:4
'bd blḥmwn wmnwt mn kys PN bgmwt (on an altar) made by Belhammon and Manawat, at the expense of PN, in ... ? (date follows); Gaw proposed, most improbably, = Gk *gamos*, hence 'at the (sacred) marriage' Syr '71 p 408; rd. *bgm<r>wt* ? cf Akk *ana gamirti*, Syriac *lagmar* completely, in its entirety†

gml *nm** camel
s ab *gml* Trf:120; em *gml'* Trf:61*; pl ab *gmlyn* Trf(I):13; em *gmly'* Trf:118*
l'rb'' ṭ'wnyn dy gmlyn for four camel-loads *Trf(I):13*; *ṭ'wn gml'* a camel-load *Trf(II):8*; *gmly' hn ṭ'ynyn whn sryqyn* camels, whether laden or empty *Trf:118* Gk *kamēlōn*; passim in Tariff (Trf) Gk *kamēlou*, *kamēlikou*

gml' *nf* Gamla (city name = modern Jmela 4 km downstream from Ana)
gml' BS III 51:4; Syr '33 p 179:1
'l 'n' wgml' to Ana and Gamla
▶ Appendix MAPS†

gmly *adj* person of Gamla (?)
pl em *gmly'* Sem '93 p 164:2
ktl' dnh dy blwy' dy gmly' This wall, (out of) the revenues of the (men of) Gamla (?; PN?) p 164:1; sense of whole text problematic, for alternate reading see Gaw ad loc, and above at *blw* n; for dedications at Palmyra by men of the garrison at Gamla cf Syr '33 p 179 (Tad 4) and BS III 51
▶ *gml* n; *blw* n; *gmly'* PN

gmnsyrks *nm* gymnasiarch, superintendent of athletic training
s ab/em *gmnsyrks* Inv 10 102:1
[qr]ṭsṭs wgmnsyrks [... most ex]cellent, and superintendent of athletic training
(< Gk *gymnasiarchos* 'gymnasiarch')†

gn See gnh n

gnb *v* to steal
G impf 3ms *ygnb* Inv 8 86:2

dy ygnb mn bt D[N] any man ... who steals from the house of D[N] *CRAIBL '81:12*

gnh *nf* garden
s em *gnt'* BS III 45:12; pl em *gny'* PNO 42:5
gnt' mtq[dšt'] the conse[crated(?] garden *RSP 162:4; w'ḥd bgnt' 'lym* and one in the *sacred* garden *BS III 45:12* Gk *[e]n hierō alsei;* see also Déd pp 4-8: restores *gnt[' 'lym]* in Inv 11 80:6; *lgdh dy qryt' wlgd' dy gny'* to the Fortune of the town, and to the Fortune of the Gardens; cf *MUSJ 38 p 125:3*†

gny *nm** 1 (tutelary) deity; 2 (name of deity) Genneas or Genius
s ab ? *gny* PNO 41:1; s em *gny'* PNO 5:1*; pl em *gny'* RTP 248
1 *l'bgl gny' ṭb' wškr'* to Abgal, the good and generous deity *PNO 5:1*; *qdm gny'* before Genius (or Genneas; or the deity) *PNO 78:6*; *m'nw š'dw gny'* Maanu, Shaadu, the deities *RTP 248*; (of the dead) *lPN wlPN gny' [ṭby]' wškry'* for PN and PN, the [goo]d and generous deities *Syr '31 14:1* **2** *lgny' 'lh' ṭb' wškr'* to Genneas/Genius, the good and generous god PNO 43:3, 4; on this deity Seyrig and Starcky, Syr '49.
(RosSpr p 92: < Gk *genios* < Lat *genius* :: Seyrig and Starcky Syr '49 pp 254-56: situation complex, a Gk. inscr. Pl XII has *theō gennea patrōō* TeixPan p 77

gnn see *'gn* n

gns *nm** kind, way
s ab *gns* C3966:6; pl em *gnsy'* Trf:68*
mn gnsy' klhwn from all kinds *Trf:68*; *dy klm' gns klh* of any kind *Trf(I):13* Gk *genous*; *[špr l]hn bkl gns klh* he was good to them in every way *C3966:6* Gk *pollois pragmasin*; *Inv 9 11:4*
(< Gk *genos* 'kind')†

gnsṭs *nm* witness, expert witness (?)
s ab ? *gnsṭs* RB '30 14:3
PN bmqmwt PN b'lh wgnsṭs ... mwdy' PN, together with PN, her husband PN and the expert witness ? ... attests
(< Gk *gnōstēs* 'surety, expert witness', RosSpr p 92 :: Cantineau RB '30 548f. posterity)†

gr *nm** 1 client; 2 patron
s ab *gr* C4218:5; *gyr* C3972:4*; s sf *grh* C4035:4; *gyrh* C3973:8
1 *lDN ... dy yh' gyr bh* for DN ... that he may be a client of his *C3972:4*; *'l ḥywh wḥy' bnwh wgrh* for his life and the life of his sons and his client/patron *C4035:4* **2** *l' yhw' lh zr' wgr* may he have no seed or patron *C4218:5*; *gyrh wrḥmh* his patron and friend *C3973:8*
(CaGr pp 116, 153; RosSpr pp 18-19)†

grby *adj* northern
m s em *grbyy'* Ber '35 p 91:2
b'ksdr' grbyy' in the northern exedra

grmṭws *nm* secretary
s ab/em *grmṭws* Trf(I):2
grmṭws dy bwl' secretary of the Senate Gk *grammateōs*
(< Gk *grammateus*)
▶ *grmṭy'* n

grmṭy' *nf* term as secretary, office of secretary
s ab/em *grmṭy'* Inv 10 13:4
bgrmṭy' dydh during his term as secretary Gk *grammatea*
(< Gk *grammateia*)
▶ *grmṭws* n

d *abbr* 1 *d<nr>*, *d<ynr>* n denarius (or pl *d<ynryn>*); 2 *d<bš>* n honey ([?] could be read *r*, [see *r* abbr] sense conjectural)

d see *dy* pron; connecting particle; cj

d' see *dh* pron

dbyḥh *nf* offering (?)
s em *dbyḥtʾ* C4029:4
(PN made this altar) *dbyḥtʾ ʿl ḥy[wh]* as an offering ? for his life†

dbq *v* to be adjacent
G ptcp m pl ab *dbqyn* Ber '35 p 102 XI:4
dbqyn ʿrsʾ (niches) ... adjacent to the mortuary couch†

dbr *v* to conduct (oneself, one's life)
G pf 3ms *dbr* C3932:6
wdbr ʿmrh škytyt and he conducted himself quietly; for Syriac and Gk equivalents see Nöldeke 1878 p 103†

dbš *nm* honey (?)
abbr (s ab?) *d<bš>* ? RTP 758
d<bšʾ> (or: *r<bʿyʾ>*) H(oney?) [or: q(uarters?)]; cf RTP 506†

dgm *nm* decree, decision
s cn *dgm* Syr '36 20:5; em *dgmʾ* Trf(I):1; pl ab *dgmyn* Déd p 13:10
dgmʾ dy bwlʾ Decree of the Senate *Trf(I):1*; *bʾmlgyʾ wd<g>mʾ bt ʾrkʾ* by a contract and decree (conjectural reading) (in) the house of archives *Syr '33 7b:2*
(< Gk *dogma* ʿdecision')
▶ *dmy* v†

dd *nm* uncle
s sf 1s *ddy* RB '30 p 539:4; 3ms *ddh* RB '30 p 536:4; 3mpl *ddhwn* RB '30 p 536:4
wlyqr bny ddh and in honor of his nieces and nephews (children of his uncle) *RB '30 p 536:4*; *ʿl ḥywhy wḥyʾ ʾbwhy wddh* for his life and the life of his father and his uncle *RSP 117:5*

dh *pron* this (dem *fs*)
dh BS III 27:3; *dʾ* ? Inv 11 79:3 (gender disagrees with m *ʿmwd[ʾ]* column, and word order is unusual)
mʿrtʾ dh this hypogeum *C4166:1*; occasional disagreement in gender with n modified: *bt qbwrʾ dh* this tomb *Inv 8 62:1*; *ʾksdrʾ dh* this exedra *Ber '35 p 95:1*, see CaGr p 145
▶ *dnh* pron

dhb *nm* gold
s ab *dhb* C3948:3; s em *dhbʾ* C3945:4
tgmʾ dy qynyʾ ʿbdʾ dhbʾ wkspʾ the guild of smiths, workers in gold and silver *C3945:4*

dhn *nm* fat
s em *dhnʾ* Trf:29, 31, 33
mn ṭʿwn dhnʾ dy bzqyn from a load of fat in skins *Trf:31*†

dwd *nm* kettle
s em (or pl em) *dwdʾ* Syr '26 p 129:7
dy hwʾ ʿl bt dwdʾ who was in charge of the cook-house (house of the kettle [or: kettles]); see *dwr* below; on dwdʾ Syr '36 p 351:11 see *dwrʾ* below†

dwqnr *nm* *ducenarius* (procurator receiving salary of 200,000 sesterces)
s em *dwqnrʾ* C3938:2; *dqnrʾ* C3940:2
PN ʾpṭrpʾ dwqnrʾ PN, the procurator ducenarius *C3938:2*; cf *C3940:2* Gk *doukēnarion*
(< Gk *doukēnarios* < Lat. *ducenarius*)

dwr *nm* household, dwelling
s em (or pl em) *dwrʾ* Syr '36 p 351:11, reading of Déd pp 304, 366-69
wldwrʾ dy DN and to the household of DN
▶ *dd* n†

dwrʾ *nf* Dura (name of city)
dwrʾ Doura 28:1; 19:2
gdʾ dy dwrʾ the Fortune of Dura
▶ Appendix MAPS†

dwrḥlwn *nm* Durahlun (name of deity)
dwrḥlwn BS III 23:3; *drḥlwn* BS III p 10:1; *dwrḥln* BS III 20:2
lbʿlšmn wldwrḥln to Baalshamin and to Durahlun *BS III 20:2*
(< **ḏū* + GN: ʿthe one of Rahle' (on Mt.

Hermon), Starcky, MUSJ 38 pp 131-32, note 4 :: Déd p 96) Dunant BS III, pp 9-10; TeixPan pp 18-25; Gaw ANRW p 2630

dwrḥln see *dwrḥlwn* n

dḥl *v* to fear, reverence, worship
G impf 3ms *ydḥl* PNO 2ter:10; ptcp m s cn *dḥl* Inv 10 62:2; m pl cn *dḥly* C3930:3; *dḥl'* C3914:3
dḥl 'lhy' worshipper of the gods *Inv 10 62:2, cf C3914:3*; *kl gbr dy ydḥl l'bgl* every man who fears Abgal *PNO 2ter:10*

dy (often written d) *pron; connecting particle; cj* 1 *relative pron* a who, which, that; b *dy X* (in titles) the one of X; 2 *connecting particle* of; 3 *cj* that, so that
d C3907:6; *dy* C3940:5
1 a *PN dhw' qym 'l ṭly'* PN, who was in charge of the young men *Inv 9 28:7*; *dqr lh w'nyh* to whom he called and who answered him *Inv 11 26:2*; *dy hw' 'strṭg lqlny'* who was general of the colony *C3932:2*; *kl ywm dy qr lh* whenever he called to him *Inv 11 37:3*; *dy 'bd lh PN brh* That which PN, his son, made for him *C4327:4* **b** *dy X* (in titles) see *dy rb'* s.v. *rb'*; *dy twn'* s.v. *twn'* **2** *'byh dPN* father of PN *C3907:9*; *w'l ḥyh dy sptymy' btzby* and for the life of Septimia Batzabbay *C3971:3*; *ṣlm' dnh dy PN* this statue is of PN *BS III 43:1*; *wlyqr bnwhy dy 'lm'* and in honor of his children, forever *C4130:3*; *byrḥ 'b dy šnt 582* in the month of Ab in the year 582 *C3947:4* **3** *[']tḥzy ly dy* it seemed good to me that ... (introduces indirect discourse) *Trf:131*; (possibly introduces direct discourse) *mwd' hw ... dy lwt lh brbw't* he acknowledges ... I have made him an associate ? in the recess *MUSJ '62 p 106:6*; *yh' šlyṭ gbr' dy yg[wr] lmšt'* the man shall be entitled to take [part] in the banquet *CRAIBL '81:14*; *dy thwyn 'lwt' 'ln 'l bb' rb'* so that these altars should be at the great gate *BS III 24:3*; *dy yh' gyr bh* that he might be his guest *C3972:3*

RosSpr p 51 ; CaGr p 140 See *dyd* connecting particle; *dyl* pron; *bd* cj; *bdy* cj; *bdyl dy* cj; *bdyl kwt* adv; *kdy* cj; *mn dy* cj; *mn dy* pron; *mdy* pron; *btr dy* cj; *hyk dy* cj; *dy rb'* n phr

dyd *connecting particle* 1 *with noun*, of; 2 *with pron sf, possessive pronoun* his, her, etc.
with noun ? *dydqbwr'* RB '30 14:5; sf 3ms *dydh* C4171:2
1 *mnwn tlt dy m'rt' dydqbwr'* three portions of the hypogeum, of the tomb *RB '30 14:5* **2** *bgrmty' dydh* in his term as secretary *Inv 10 13:4*; *šṭr' klh mqbl' tymny' dydh dy 'ksdr'* the whole side of it, of the exedra, facing south *C4171:2*
▶ *dy* pron

dyṭgm' *n* decree
dy[ṭg]m' BS III 45:7
b'g[rt'] wbdy[ṭg]m' šhd lh by let[ters] and by a de[cr]ee (he) testified on his behalf *BS III 45:7* Gk *diatagmati*; see Hillers and Cussini '92†

dyl *pron with pron sf, possessive pronoun* of (him, her, etc.)
sf 3ms *dylh* Inv 10 39:3
w'p bgrmty' dylh and also in his term as secretary
▶ *dy* pron†

dynr *nm** denarius
abbr (s ab) *d* Trf:25; s ab *dynr* Trf:48; *dnr* Trf:102; em ? *dnr'* Trf:48* (prb misdivision, read *dnr 'ḥd* one denarius); pl ab *dynrn* CRAIBL '81:13; *dnryn* C3948:3
mn mn dy šql' dynr from one who charges a denarius *Trf:48*; in Trf frequently Gk *dēnarion*; *dnryn dy dhb 'tyqyn tlt m'h* three hundred old gold denarii *C3948:3**, Gk *chrysa palaia dēnaria*, see Heichelheim '38 p 222; Raschke '78 p 862, fn 882; for abbreviations of amounts of money and commodities, see Aharoni '77 pp 157-64
(< Gk *dēnarion* < Lat. *denarius*)

dyr *nm* community
s em *dyr'* C4501:3
qšyš' dy dyr' the elder of the community *C4501:3*; *dyr' dy qryt'* the community of the town *Sem '72 p 59:4*
Cf IH no. 35:7 *dyr'* 'assembly, community'†

dy rbʿʾ *n phr m* collector of customs ('the one of one fourth', i. e. collector of customs tax of 25 per cent)
s *dy rbʿ* Inv 10 29:2; 113:2
PN blwṭ b'nṭky' dy rbʿ PN, senator in Antioch, customs collector *Inv 10 29:2* Gk *tetartōnēn*; *PN dy rbʿ Inv 10 113:2* Gk *tetartōnē*, Lat. *man(cipi) IIII mer(caturae)* or: *merc(ium adventiciarum)*; see de Laet '49 pp 335-36; Raschke '78 p 781 fn 582
(calque < Gk *tetartōnēs*)†

dk *adj* undefiled, unused
pl ab *dkn* C4174:6
gwmḥyn št' dkn six undefiled burial-niches *Ber '35 p 97:2* (not a dem pron :: RosSpr p 50)

dkh *nf** place
s em *dkt'* Syr '33 p 185:1*
dkt' dh šḥymt' this unconsecrated place Syr '33 p 185:1; *br dkt' dy twn'* son of the place ? of the chamber *Ber '36 p 88:2*; sense of phrase *br dkt'* disputed: 1) GN ? (unidentified); 2) Ing in RosAH: '(consecrated) place [of the chamber]', as a reference to the offspring of hierogamy; 3) Ing "Two Unpublished Tombs ... ," StudMiles pp 37-54, pp 46-47: basic meaning is 'daughter', hence 'son of the Daughter of the Chamber,' or 'son of the Lady of the inner chamber', comparing Middle Persian name of deity Beduxt 'daughter of Bel,' Mandaean Baiduxt; 4) Déd pp 272-74: 'member of association in charge of alms-boxes', citing Hatran evidence, but Aggoula, MUSJ 47 68-80, and IH no. 7 translates Hatran *dkt'* here (if the reading is not actually *dnt'*) 'shop' (boutique); note also IH 254; 282; 284; 5) 'the purified one' so Gaw TP p 79 following Stark†

dkr *adj* male
pl ab *dkryn* Inv 8 58:2; em *dkry'* C4159:6; *dkr'* Ber '35 p 60:2
lh wlbnwhy wlbn' bnwhy dkr' lʿlm' for him and for his children and for his grandchildren, the males, forever *Ber '35 p 60:2*; *C4214:1* Gk *arsesi*

dkr *v* to remember, recall, commemorate
G pf 1 s(?) *dk?ryt* Atiqot '93 p 91:1 but reading difficult; ptcp pass m s ab *dkyr* Inv 9 4a:1; m pl ab *dkyryn* C3973:10; *dkyrn* PNO 56:1
dkyr PN bṭb May PN be remembered for good *Inv 12 40:1*; *dkyr PN qdm DN* May PN be commemorated before DN *PNO 17:1*; *dkyryn wbrykyn 'nš'* May the men be recalled and blessed *Inv 9 28:2*; *dkyrn 'lhy' PN* Remembered be the gods of PN *PNO 56:1*; *wdkyr kl mʿyd ʿlwt' 'ln w'mr dkyryn [h]' 'ln klhwn bṭb* and commemorated be everyone who passes by these altars and says "May all these be remembered for good" *C3973:10*; cf IH nos. 24, 53, 101
▶ *dkrn* n; *zkr* v ?

dkrn *nm** memorial (object which serves to call a person to mind, favorably)
s ab *dkrn* PNO 6A:1*; em *dkrn'* C4123:1
dkrn ṭb' ʿbd PN Memorial for good, made by PN *PNO 6A:1*; *dkrn ṭb lDN* A memorial for good, for DN *C4000:1*; *dkrn ṭb qdm DN* A memorial for good, before DN *Ber '36 p 84:1*; *[ʿ]lt' dh dkrn lDN* this [a]ltar is a memorial for DN *C3993:1*; *dkrn' dnh dy hw yqr bt ʿlm' bn' PN* this memorial, which is an honor, an eternal resting place, was built by PN *C4123:1*
▶ *dkr* v

dkt' see *dkh* n

dm *nm* blood

s ab *dm* Dri '82b p 65:3

mn dy l' yšd dm ʿl ḥgb' whoever does not shed blood on the shrine†

dmws see *dms* n

dmy *v* to be like

G ptcp act m s ab *dm'* Trf:60, 114; m s em or f s ab *dmy'* Trf:91 (broken context)

wmdy dm' lhwn and whatever is like them *Trf:114*; *b'mlgy' wdm' bt 'rk'* by contract, and the house of the archives decided *Syr '33 7b:2* (so Cantineau; for alternate conjecture, see *dgm'* n)

▶ *dmyn* n†

dmyn *nm* price (?)

pl cn *dmy* RTP 706

dmy ḥmr' the price of the wine

▶ *dmy* v†

dmysyt *adv ?* at public expense ?

dmysyt ? (adj ?) C3927:5 (TP p 51 and fig. 8; cf Déd pp 3-4)

... *dmysyt lyqrh* publicly, in his honor so Gaw ad loc., for sense citing Gk *dēmosiois* (in other inscriptions), but text very broken and uncertain, and reading of C3927 *btr dy myt* ('posthumously') is paralleled exactly in *C3920:3*

dms *nm* people

s ab *dms* C3914:1; *dmws* C3938:4; em *[dms]'* BS III 45:5

mn twḥyt bwl' wdmws by decree of the Senate and People *C3959:1* Gk *dēmos*

(< Gk *dēmos*)

dnb *v* *uncertain*

G pf 3ms ? *dnb* Inv 12 23:2; ? *d/rnbt* C4214:1 same as Inv 7 2:1

wdnb tṣbyt' klh and he ... ? the whole decoration *Inv 12 23:2*; see Teix ad loc.; Chabot ad C4214; Cantineau ad Inv 7 2; Déd p 242 and RosSpr p 82: 'to complete'†

dnh *pron* this, pron dem *ms*

dnh C4109:1; *dn'* BS III 87:1

qbr' dn' this grave *C4216:1*; *glpt' dnh* this sculpture *PNO 57:1* (with f noun, as frequently, see CaGr p 145); *b[r]h dy ḥyrn dnh* (after a PN previously given in full) son of this same Hayran *C4114:5-6*

▶ *dh* pron

dny *v* to approach (?)

C pf 3ms sf 3ms *w'dn'h* Inv 11 11:8

q[rh w]ʿynh w'dn'h he called to him and he answered him and approached ? him; see Teix ad loc.†

dnr see *dynr* n

dʿnt *nm* Duanat (name of deity)

dʿnt BS III 58:2

lšdrp' wldʿnt 'lhy' ṭb[y'] to Shadrafa and to Duanat the goo[d] gods *Inv 10 145:2*

(< **d̲ū* + *ʿnt* 'the One of Anat' [GN])

▶ Starcky, Syr '49 44ff., 81ff.; TeixPan pp 67-68; Dunant ad BS III 58; Hof RelAram p 41

dqnr see *dwqnr* n

dqrywn *nm* decurion (member of the Senate of a city)

s em *dqrywn'* Ber '35 p 93:1

lPN dqrywn' to PN, the decurion (member of the Senate)

(< Lat. *decurio, decurionus*)†

drḥlwn see *dwrḥlwn* n

drmdry *adj* of camels

m s em *drmdry'* Inv 10 128:2

'l' drmdry' the camel corps, Gk *dromedariōn*

(< Gk *droma/edarios* < Lat. *dromedarius*)†

h' *pred* behold; here is

h' Inv 8 6:3; *h* Inv 8 8:3

h' dkrn ṭb lPN Here is a good memorial for PN *Inv 12 51:1*; *wh' npš' dh mwly' bšmš*

obscure expression: and here is this monument ... *Inv 8 6:3* (on this phrase see *wly* v); *h' kšr dy [yh]n mksy'* now it is right that the taxes [should] be ... *Trf:105* RosSpr p 82 :: CaGr p 61 pron 3ms *h'*
⧐ *hw* pron

h' 'ln see *hln* pron

hgmwn see *hygmwn* n

hgmn *see hygmwn n*

hdyn *pron* this (?)
hdyn YCS '55 p 131:3
dy qryb mn 'w?b' hdyn lDN who offered of this ... to DN
(unexpected form of pronoun in this corpus; cf Dalman '05 p 111)†

hdryn' *nf* Hadriana (name of Palmyra)
hdryn' Trf(II):1
hdryn' tdmr Hadriana Tadmor *Trf(II):1*
(< emperor's name *Hadrianus*)
⧐ C3959 for visit of Hadrian to Palmyra in 129, and C3902 where Palmyrene dedicator of bilingual inscription has title, in Gk *hadrianos palmyrēnos*†

hw *pron* he
hw C4123:1; *h'* ? Trf:105 CaGr p 61 :: RosSpr p 82: *h'* predicator q.v.
hw w'bwhy he and his father *C4292:7*

hwy *v* to be
G pf 3ms *hw'*; *hwh* Syr '33 p 177:4; 3fs *hwt* Trf(I):3; 3mpl *hww* Trf(I):7; impf 3ms *yh'* Trf:107; *yhw'* Trf:149; *yhwh* BS III 34:5; 3fs *thw'* Trf:94; *thwh* Trf:127; 3mpl *yhwn* RSP 199:10; *yhn* Trf:118; 3fpl *thwyn* BS III 24:3 cf Dunant ad loc., Caquot GLECS 7 pp 77-78 and Huehnergard ZDMG 137 pp 266-277; inf *lmhw'* Trf:77; ptcp f s ab *hwy'* Trf:134 (agrees with *mlḥ'* f); m pl ab *hwyn* Sem '86 p 89:4; *hwn* ? Trf(I):10
PN dy hw' 'sṭrṭg PN who was general *C3932:2*; *w'p mks' [m]lḥ' dy hwy' btdmr* and also the tax on salt which is in Palmyra *Trf:134*

hy *pron* she
hy Trf:128
mdy hy šql' whatever she charges†

hygmwn *nm* consular governor, of consular rank
s em *hgmn'* BS III 45:7; *hygmwn'* Trf:74; *hygmn'* Syr '36 20:6; *hgm[w]n'* C3968:1; pl ab *hgmnyn* Déd p 13:9
[pw]blwqyws mrql[ws] hgmn' Publicius Marcellus, the consular governor *BS III 45:7* Gk *hypatik[ou]*; *q[r]spynws hygmwn'* C[r]ispinus, the consular governor *C3932:4* Gk *hēgēsamenou*; *whgmnyn* and consuls *Déd p 13:9* Gk *hypatikōn*
(< Gk *hēgemōn*)

hygmn see *hygmwn* n

hyk *prep* according to, as
hyk Trf:54
hyk 'yd' according to custom *Trf:136*
⧐ *hyk* cj; *hyk dy* cj

hyk *cj* as, just as
hyk Trf(I):6
hyk bnmws' as is in the law *Trf(I):6*
⧐ *hyk* prep; *hyk dy* cj

hyk dy *cj* as, just as
hyk dy Trf:68
hyk dy ṣbyn as they wish *Ber '38 p 95:9*; *hyk dy 'šr PN* as PN established *Trf:120*
⧐ *hyk* prep; *hyk* cj

hykl *nm** temple
s em *hykl'* BS III 32:1*
dy ḥnk hykl' dy bl who dedicated the temple of Bel *Inv 9 1:4*; *wbn' hykl' wprn'[yn]* and he built the temple and the front hall *C3959:5*; *hykl'* the temple RTP 37
(< Akk *ekallu*; early WSemitic loan, AIA 27)

hymn *v* to believe
quad pf pass 3ms ? *hymn* CRAIBL '81:10; impf pass 3ms ? *wyhym[n]* CRAIBL '81:9

dy hymn bšth who is entrusted for his year's (term)(?) *CRAIBL '81:10* ? so Teix; *dy yhw' 'ḥyd 'l dhb' wyhym[n]* who will be elected to have charge of the gold and will be entrust[ted](?) *CRAIBL '81:9*
▶ *mhymn* adj†

hlk *v* G to go, behave; D to go about
G pf 3ms *hlk* Inv 10 39:3; D ptcp m pl ab *m[h]lkyn* Trf:139
bdyl dy hlk 'mh špr because he behaved well toward him *Inv 10 53:4*; *m[h]lkyn b[md]yt* who [g]o about in [the ci]ty ? *Trf:139*†

hln *pron* these (dem *m pl*)
hln RB '30 14:4; *[h]' 'ln* ? C3973:11
wtḥwt hln yhbt lh and for these (antecedent is denarii) I gave him *RB '30 14:4*; *dkyryn [h]' 'ln klhwn bṭb* may all these ? be remembered for good *C3973:11;* CaGr p 130; RosSpr pp 49-50†

hlss *nm* grove
s ab *hlss* C3968:2 cf RSP 157, Déd pp 7-8
[wmlkbl 'lhy] hlss [and Malakbel the gods of] the grove *C3968:2* Gk *[malach]bēlou theōn hierou also[us ...]*; see Gaw ad loc.; Seyrig '31 p 110; Dunant '56 pp 220-221; see also *gnh* n; *RSP 162:4*
(< Gk *alsos;* on the initial *h* see Bertinelli Angeli '70 p 59)†

hn *cj* 1 if; 2 *hn* ... *whn* whether ... or
hn Trf:127
1 *whn ḥsyr* and if it is less *Trf:127* 2 *hn ṭ'ynyn whn sryqyn* whether loaded or empty *Trf:118*

hnwn *pron* they, these
hnwn Ber '35 p 102 XI:5; *hnn* C4173:2
hnwn wqštyhwn these and their rights *Ber '35 p 102 XI:5*

hpṭyn *nm* centurion's aide
s ab *hpṭyn* C3906:1
PN hpṭyn PN, centurion's aide
(< Lat. *optio*; RosSpr p 36; cf Bertinelli Angeli '70 p 59 for epigraphic parallels to the initial *h* in the Aramaic)†

hpṭyq' *nm* person of consular rank, consul
s em *hpṭyq'* C3945:2
ṣlm spṭmyws 'dynt nhyr' hpṭyq' mrn statue of Septimius Odenathus, the illustrious, consul, our lord
(<Gk *hypatikos* = Lat *consularis*)†

hpk *v* to go around, circulate
G ptcp m pl ab *hpkyn* Trf:57
[mzbn]y nḥty' dy hpkyn bmdyt' [seller]s of garments(?) who go around in the city†

hpq' *nm* equestrian, man of noble rank
s em *hpq'* C3937:1
hpq' wbylwṭ' tdmry' for PN, equestrian and Senator of Tadmor Gk *hippikon*; *C3943:4* Gk *hippeus*
(< Gk *hippikos*)
▶ *hpqws* n†

hpqws *nm* equestrian, man of noble rank
s ab *hpqws* C3940:3; *ḥpqws* ? MUSJ '66 p.177:1, see Teix ad loc. on spelling with *ḥ* :: Déd p 26: PN
PN hpqws br PN PN, equestrian, son of PN *C3940:3* Gk *hippikos*, cf Bertinelli Angeli p 120
(< Gk *hippikos*)
▶ *hpq'* n†

w *cj* 1 and; 2 or
w passim
1 connecting verbs: *yhb w'ḥbr* he gave and ceded *Ber '35 p 77:1*; connecting nouns *bnwhy w'ḥwhy* his sons and his brothers *Inv 12 22:6*; connecting v pf and ptcp: *DN 'bd wmwd' PN* (for) DN, PN made in thanksgiving (made and gives thanks) *C4044:2*; *shd lh DN 'lh' w'p PN* DN, the god, and also PN gave testimony to him *C3932:7*; obscure is *wh'* in the recurring *wh'*

npš' dh ... and behold this monument ... *Inv 8 6:3* and elsewhere; *wl' ypth 'nš l'lm* Now, let no one open (it), ever *RSP 105:4-5*, cf *C4218:3*; *w* ... *w* may have sense 'both ... and' in *wsmyt' dy ksp' wtṣbyth* and the silver standard and its ornament C3902:1; Gk *kai to signon argyroun syn panti kosmō* is unusual with *kai* ... *syn* :: Chabot ad loc., like others, who assumes inscription omits first object donated: 'who gave <X> and the silver etc.' **2** *lṭ'wn' dy ḥṭ' wḥmr' wtbn' w[k]l mdy dm' [lhwn]* a load of wheat or wine or straw or [any]thing like [these] *Trf:59*

wd *nm* friends, group of friends ?
s em *wd'* Inv 12 45:3
lDN wlwd' dy 'ḥdy hykl' d[y] bl for DN and for the friends who are the chosen of the temple of Bel *Inv 12 45:3*; *wlšb't' dy wd'* and for the seven of the friends *Inv 12 45:7*
(< Arab *wadd* 'friends' ?; see Teix '80a pp 61-61; Aggoula, '79 p 116)†

wṭrn *nm* 1 veteran (soldier); 2 veteran slave (slave who has served at least a year in the city)
s ab *wṭrn* Trf:86; em *wṭrn'* Ber '38 p 104:2
1 *PN wṭrn'* PN, the veteran *Ber '38 p 104:2* **2** *mn dy mpq 'lm wṭrn* whoever exports a veteran slave *Trf:86*, cf 83; *wṭr[n] Trf(II):5* Gk *ouetran[a]*
(< Gk *ouet(e)ranos* < Lat. *veteranus*; Ros Sp p 92)†

wld *nm* progeny
s em *wld'* RB '30 6:2
wlyqr bny ddhwn wld' klh dy bny PN and in honor of their nephews, the whole progeny of the sons of PN
(Ros Sp pp 40, 95: not Arab. LW, since it occurs in Heb. and elsewhere in Aram.)†

wly *v* to be adjacent, to accompany (?)
D or C ptcp f s ab *mwly'* Inv 8 6:4; Inv 8 8:4; Inv 8 37B:2; m pl ab *mwln* C4172:2
trn dy mwln the two that are adjacent ? *C4172:2*; *wh' npš' dh mwly' bšmš* and here is this monument accompanying (him) ? in the sun *Inv 8 6:4*; CaGr p 90, RosSpr pp 50 n. 2 and 66 n. 2 adopt a similar grammatical analysis, leaving the sense undetermined; note *dy mwln twpr'* which are close to the cavity ? *C4172:2* :: du Mesnil TMP p 254
(cf Arab. *walâ* to be adjacent ?; S. Kaufman [oral communication] calls attention to Heb *mwl* n and prep; adoption of this etymology might yield a sense not dissimilar to that suggested here)†

wršh *nf* heiress (?)
s em *wršt'* C4176B:3; C4176C:1; C4184:3
PN wršt' PN PN (f) heiress of PN *C4176C:1*; *PN wršt' dy byt' wm'rt'* PN (f) heiress of house and tomb *C4176B:3*; *4184:3* :: RosSpr p 24 (after Lidz ESE II p 275), but *w* as conjunction is here improbable
(CaGr p 150 cf Arab. *waritha*, but this very uncertain)†

zbwn *nm* buyer
s em *zbwn'* Trf(II):6
whn zbwn' ypq 'ly[m]yn and if the buyer exports sla[ve]s†

zbwqh *nf* recess, corner
s em *zbwqt'* Ber '35 p 78:2
m'lyk bb' 'l ymynk bzbwqt' as you enter the door, on your right, in the recess *Ber '35 p 100:6*
(cf Arab. *zābūqatun* 'corners of a house')†

zbn *v* G to buy; D to sell; Dt to be sold
G impf 3ms *yzbn* Trf:133; D pf 3ms *zbn* RSP 51:1; impf 3ms *yzbn* Ber '38 p 133:3; ptcp m s ab *mzbn* Trf:46; m pl cn *[mzbn]y* Trf:57; ptcp pass 3ms ab *mzbn* Trf:136 (or Dt); Dt impf 3ms *yzbn* Trf:56; ptcp f s ab *mtzbn'* Trf:132; ptcp 3ms ab *mzbn* Trf:136 (or D); cf RosSpr pp 56-57, 63, CaGr pp 39, 92
G *mn mn tdmry' yzbn* whoever of the Tadmoreans buys *Trf:133* **D** *mnw dy yzbn 'rb'* whoever sells the security(?) *Ber '38 p 133:3*; *mn dy yhw' yzbn mšḥ' bšym'* whoever sells perfumed oil *Trf:46*; *[mzbn]y nḥty' dy*

hpkyn bmdyt' [seller]s of used clothing who go around the city *Trf:57* Gk *pōl[oun]tes* **Dt** *mn ʿlm wṭr[n] dy yzbn* from a veteran slave who is sold *Trf(II):5*; *dy [y]ṯ'ʿl 'w yzbn* which is imported or is sold *Trf:56*
▶ *zbn* n

zbn I *nm* purchases
pl sf *zbnwhy* C3977B:2
wzbnwhy dy ... and the purchases of ...
▶ *zbn* v†

zbn II *nm** time, period, occasion, occurrence
s ab *zbn* Trf(I):10; pl ab *zbnyn* Trf(I):6; em *zbny'* Trf(I):4*
l'rkwny' dy hwn bzbn zbn to the archons who are in office at any given time *Trf(I):10* Gk *kata kairon*; *zbnyn šgy'n* many times *C3932:5* Gk *pleistakis*, cf Déd p 13 *wbzb[nyn] sgy'n* Gk *en pollois ... kairois*; *bzbny' qdmy'* in former times *Trf(I):4* Gk *[en t]ois palai chronois*; see Schlumberger '37 p 272 fn 1 :: Rostovtzeff '32d p 76
▶ CaGr p 45

zdq *adj* righteous
f s em *zdqt[']* C3947:1
ṣlmt spṭmy' btzby nhyrt' wzdqt['] mlkt' statue of Septimia Batzabbay, the illustrious and righteous, the queen Gk *eusebē*†

zwz *nm** *zuz* (unit of money, coin, equivalent of Attic drachma, denarius)
s ab *zwz* Sem '86 p 89:5*; pl ab *zwzyn* C3934:5
wzwz ḥd and one *zuz Sem '86 p 89:5*; *zwzyn rbw* 10,000 *zuz*'s *C3934:5* Gk *at[tika]s myrias* ten thousand Attic (drachmas)
(< Akk *zūzu*; AIA p 114)

zkw *nf* victory
s sf 3ms *z[kwth]* C3971:1
ʿl ḥ[ywh] wz[kwth dy] PN for the l[ife] and vi[ctory of] Septimius Wahaballat; a probable restoration, see Chabot ad loc.†

zkr *v* to remember ?
G pf 1cs *zkrt* C4093:2
wzkrt and I recalled ? see Chabot ad loc.

zmr *n* singer ?
pl em *zmr'* In 10:145:(below)2
mn pḥd bny zmr' Milik '67 p 556 fn 1: 'guild of singers', cf Déd pp 55-59 but prb simply tribal name, cf also PN *zmry*

znyh *nf* prostitute
pl em *znyt'* Trf:47
'p ygb' mks' mn znyt' also, the tax-collector shall collect from the prostitutes; Gk at line 203 *hetairō[n]*†

zʿwr *adj* 1 small; 2 younger, minor
s em *zʿr'* C3915:4; pl ab *zʿwrn* Inv 10 114:4
1 *bkl [ṣ]bw klh rb' wzʿr'* in every [th]ing, large or small *C3915:4*; *wl' zʿwrn* and not unimportant *Inv 10 114:4* **2** *PN zʿwr'* PN, the younger NyCG 62:2; cf *rb* adj in sense elder†

zʿr see *zʿwr* adj

zq *nm* skin (as container)
pl ab *zqyn* Trf:29
dhn' dy bzqyn fat which is in skins *Trf:29*; *wḥmr bzqyn* and wine in skins *Syr '26:5*

zrʿ *nm* offspring
s ab *zrʿ* C4218:5
ʿd ʿlm' l' yhw' lh zrʿ forever may he have no posterity†

ḥ *abbr* *ḥ<mr> n* wine; *ḥ<bl>* interj Alas!

ḥbl *interj* Alas!
ḥbl C4366:1; *ḥ<bl>* PNO no. 52 bis:1? (see Starcky ad loc)
ḥbl PN Alas! PN (begins funerary inscription) *Inv 8 175:1*; *PN ḥbl* PN. Alas! (concludes funerary inscription) *C3901:1*; (followed by date, as in) *PN ḥbl šnt 542* PN. Alas! The year 542 *C4243:5*; *ḥbl PN wḥbl*

PN Alas! PN, and alas! PN, etc. *Inv 8 63:1* and following
▶ RosSpr p 83

ḥbr *v* D to take as partner (attestation questionable); C to take as partner > to cede
D pf 3mpl *ḥbr* Ber '38 p 106:2 (so Ing, who suggests haplography for <'>*ḥbr*; prb misdivision, read *bny 'm 'ḥbr* [C]); C pf 3ms *'ḥbr* C4195:2; 1s + sf 3ms *'ḥbrth* C4195:6; 3mpl *'ḥbr* Ber '38 p 95:4; inf *l'ḥbwr'* C4214:1

C (D? see above) *PN wPN bny 'm 'ḥbr PN* PN and PN, sons of the same mother, took in partnership PN *Ber '38 p 106:2*; *PN 'ḥbr PN* PN took in partnership PN (i.e. 'PN ceded to PN') *Inv 4 7B:2* Gk *exechōrēsen*; *'ḥbrth mn 'ksdr'* I took him as partner in the exedra *C4195:6*; *PN 'ḥ[br] b'ly[t' dy] qbr' dnh* PN took in partne[rship] in the upp[er part] of this tomb *C4211:1* Gk *koinōnon [proselabe]to*; *'ḥbr PN lPN* PN ceded to PN *PGKK 28:2*; *'ksdr' m'lyk 'l ymynk klh yhb w'ḥbr PN lPN* the exedra as you enter on your right, all of it, PN gave to PN and took him into partnership (i.e. 'ceded to him') *Ber '35 p 76:1*; *'w lmb'd 'w l'ḥbwr' bh 'yš* either to alienate or to take anyone in partnership *C4214:1* (word-division with Chabot CIS :: Cantineau Inv 7 2) Gk *koinōnon autou proslabein*
▶ *ḥbr* n; O'Connor '84; Ing '35 p 76

ḥbr *nm* companion, partner
s sf 3ms *ḥbrh* MUSJ '49 p 46:6

PN 'ḥwh wPN ḥbrh PN, his brother, and PN, his companion; or, with connotation of legal relation: 'partner', cf *ḥbr* v†

ḥgb *nm* shrine
s em *ḥgb'* Dri '82bb p 65:3

tbrk '[lt] mn dy l' yšd dm 'l ḥgb' A[llat] will bless whoever will not shed blood in the shrine *Dri '82b p 65:3*; Dri ad loc. cf Syriac *ḥugbā* temple, shrine; *ḥgb' wmṣb' 'bd PN* the shrine and image made by PN *Sem '77 p 117:2*†

ḥd *num* one
m s ab *'ḥd* C4158:1; *ḥd* Trf:42; f s ab *'ḥd'* RB '30 14:5; *ḥd'* C4199:4

mnt['] 'ḥd' one portio[n] *RB '30 14:5*; *dnr' ḥd* one denarius *Trf:48*; *gwmḥ' ḥd bry'* one outer burial-niche *Ber '35 p 86:11*; *'ḥd mn 'rb' 'ḥy'* one of four brothers *C4158:1*; *'ḥd tnn bt [DN]* one here in the house of [DN] *BS III 45:11* Gk *hen[a]*; (in compound number) *w'rb'yn wḥd* and forty-one *Sem '86 p 89:3*
CaGr pp 40, 124-125; RosSpr p 31

ḥdt *adj* new
m s ab *ḥdt* RTP 702; m s em *ḥdt'* Trf(I):8

mkl wp[l]g ḥdt a measure and a h[al]f, new (wine) *RTP 702*, cf *RTP 701*; *wyktb bštr 'gry' ḥdt'* and let it be written in the new document of contract *Trf(I):8* Gk *tē engista misthōsei*
▶ *ḥdt* v†

ḥdt *v* D 1 to renew, restore; 2 to install
D pf 3ms *ḥdt* C4288:4

D 1 *wḥdt bb' d[nh] PN* and PN restored t[his] gateway *C4197:5*; **2** *dy ḥdt PN* that which PN installed *C4288:4*
▶ *ḥdt* adj

ḥwb *v* to owe
G impf 3ms *yḥwb* Syr '33 p 184:2

mn dy y'l ltnn ... yḥwb lpsqws zwzyn '[lp] whoever brings in here ... shall owe the treasury 1[000] *zuz*'s *Syr '33 p 184:2*; *dy yḥwb ḥty' ddynrn* who owes a penalty of denarii *CRAIBL '81:13*
▶ *ḥyb* adj

ḥwy *v* D to show, make known
D impf 3ms *yḥw* CRAIBL '81:8; ptcp ms *mḥw'* ? Trf:125 (text has *mwḥ'* Nöldeke cj *mḥw'*; see CaGr p 86; but see also *yḥy* v

wmn dy ... yḥw l[...] and whoever ... (?) shall make known ... *CRAIBL '81:8*; *hyk dy nmws' mḥw' (mwḥ')* as the law shows *Trf:125*†

ḥwl *nm meaning uncertain*
analysis uncertain: *ḥwlwh* MUSJ '62 p 106:10
w'n ṣb' dy y'bd bsṭr' dydh ḥwlwh md'n and if he wishes to make on his side *something unconsecrated* (? Ing's rendering, as if from root *ḥwl*)†

ḥws *v* C to spare
C pf 3ms *'ḥ[y]s* Déd p 36:3
wl' 'ḥ[y]s npšh 'l mdyth and he did not sp[a]re himself for his city *Déd p 36:3*†

ḥwr *nm* limestone
s em *ḥwr'* MUSJ '62 p 106:11
ktl dy ḥwr' a wall of limestone†

ḥwrt' *nf* Hawarta (pronunciation and location uncertain)
s em *ḥwrt'* PNO 48:2
lgny' dy ḥwrt' for the genii of Hawarta; for possible identifications, see Ing and Starcky ad loc.†

ḥzy *v* Gt to be decided, be decreed
Gt pf 3ms *'tḥzy* Trf(I):7
'tḥzy lbwl' dy 'rkwny' 'ln wl'šrt' it was decreed by the Senate that the afore-mentioned archons and the Decaprotoi *Trf(I):7* Gk *dedochthai*, on prb of translation see Matthews '84 :: Teix '83b p 238; *'tḥzy dy lkl dy 'll lḥšbn* it was decreed that for everything that is imported for trade *Trf:114* Gk *ed[o]xen*†

ḥṭy *v* to sin
G ptcp 3ms *ḥṭ'* Ber '38 p 133:10, cf line 14; 3mpl ? *ḥṭyw* CRAIBL '81:18 (so apparently Teix 'ont péché')
'l npšh ḥṭ' sins against himself *Ber '38 p 133:10*
▶ *ḥṭy'* n†

ḥṭy' *nf* fine
s ab *ḥṭy'* CRAIBL '81:13; s sf 3ms *ḥṭy'th* RSP 199:6, 7, 9
dy yhwb ḥṭy' ddynrn who owes a fine of denarii *CRAIBL '81:13*, cf 11; *[t]hwh ḥṭy'th ' (= 5) 'yph* his offering in recompense shall be 5 ? times doubled ? *RSP 199:6* (so Gaw); sense of *ḥṭy' TMP p 757:1* (tessera) is uncertain; du Mesnil: 'grain'
▶ *ḥṭy* v†

ḥṭyn *nm (pl)* wheat
pl em *ḥṭ'* Trf:59 (so RosSpr p 76; CaGr p 98 takes as s ab, but note that other items in this list are in the emphatic state
lt'wn' dy ḥṭ' wḥmr' wtbn' w[k]l mdy dm' [lhwn] for a load of wheat or wine or straw or [any]thing like these†

ḥṭr *nm* enclosure wall (?)
s em *ḥṭr'* BS III 19:2
wtpyt' wšryt' dy ḥṭr' and the coping and the entablature of the enclosure wall ? *BS III 19:2*; Dunant ad loc.: 'enceinte, mur de fond' (from PS **ḥẓr* cf Ug *ḥẓr* court, Arab *ḥaẓara* to enclose ?)†

ḥyb *adj* subject to tax, owing
m s ab *ḥyb* Trf:113; f s ab *ḥyb'* Trf:146; m pl ab *ḥybyn* Trf:108; f pl ab *ḥybn* Trf(I):4
'bydn šgyn ḥybn mks' many things subject to tax *Trf(I):4*; *ḥyb kl gml dnr* each camel is subject to tax of a denarius *Trf:119*; *mks l' ḥyb* is not subject to tax *Trf:113*

ḥyṭ *nm* tailor
pl em *ḥyṭ'* Trf:139
wḥyṭ' and tailors [...]†

ḥyy *v* to live
G pf 3ms *ḥy'* C4358:5; 3fs *ḥyt* RSP 39:4
ḥy' šnyn 18 he lived 18 years, i.e. died at the age of 18 *C4358:5*; *PN ḥyt šny[n] 23 ḥbl* PN(f) lived 23 years (i.e. 'died age 23') Alas! *RSP 39:4*
▶ *ḥyyn* n

ḥyyn *nm pl. only* **1** life, lifetime; **2** life, safety, health
pl cs *ḥyy* C3911:10; *ḥy'* C4010:4; *ḥy* C4075:5; abs *ḥy'* Inv 11 33:6; sf 3ms *ḥywhy* C4057:5; *ḥyw* C4009:5; *ḥwh* C4063:6; *ḥyyhy* Syr '31 p 135:3; sf 3fs *ḥyh* C4027:3; *ḥyyh* C3968:3; sf 3mpl *ḥyyhwn* C3978:8;

ḥyyhn C3911:9

1 *dy ʿbd lh bḥywhy* which he made for himself during his life *C4119:6* **2** (extremely common, with variations, in inscriptions asking divine help, or after help received) *ʿl ḥywhy wḥyʾ bnwhy* for his life and the life of his children *C3902:2* Gk *sōtērias*; similar *C3998:3* Gk *hygeias*; *ʿl ḥyʾ ʾbwhy wḥywhy wḥyy bnwhy* for the life of his father and his own life and the life of his sons *Inv 12 44:5*; *ʿl ḥyʾ dbnwh* for the life of his sons *Inv 11 33:6* (construction with *d* unusual); *wʿl ḥyh dy sptymyʾ btzby C3971:5* and for the life of Septimia Batzabbay Gk *[sō]tērias*; *lḥyh wlḥyʾ brth* for her life and the life of her daughter *C4014:5* (prep *l* much less usual in the formula than *ʿl*)

▶ *ḥyy* v

ḥyl see *rb* adj

ḥyrwn *nm* good time, party (?)

s em *ḥyrwnʾ* RTP 113

(on tessera) *ḥyrwnʾ dy bl* party ? of Bel; see Caquot, RTP p 144†

ḥyrtʾ *nf* Hirta

ḥyrtʾ C3973:3

dy hwʾ prš [b]ḥyrtʾ wbmšrytʾ dy ʿnʾ who was a horseman [in] Hirta and in the camp at Ana; name means camp cf Syriac *ḥyrtʾ* camp; Caquot ad loc.: prb al-Hira, in Babylonia

▶ Appendix MAPS†

ḥl *nm* **1** maternal uncle; **2** *bt/bny ḥlh* cousin(s) on mother's side

s sf 3ms *ḥlh* Ber '38 p 104:2

1 *PN ḥlh* PN, his maternal uncle *Ber '38 p 104:2*; cf *C4052:6* **2** *PN wPN bny ḥlh* PN and PN, his cousins *C4206:2*

▶ RosSpr p 95 *ḥlʾ* PN, with same meaning†

ḥly *nf meaning uncertain (PN?)*

s em ? *ḥlyt[ʾ]* RTP 525

byt ḥlyt[ʾ] house of the ... ?†

ḥlph *nf* lieutenant (?)

s sf 3ms *ḥlpth* Syr '33 p 179:1

dy hw ʾstrtgʾ ʿl ʿnʾ wgmlʾ wḥlpth PN who is general in charge of GN and GN, and his lieutenant ? , PN†

ḥlq *nm* portion

s sf 3ms *ḥlqh* Inv 10 54:4

[ ] lḥlqh for his portion (attestation uncertain, context broken)†

ḥm *nm* father-in-law

s sf 3ms *ḥmwhy* Ber '70 p 69:3

PN ddh wḥmwhy PN, his uncle and father-in-law†

ḥmm *v* C to heat

C ptcp m s cn *mḥm* RSP 162:2

PN mḥm myʾ PN, heater of water; cf Gaw ad loc. for similar Gk and Aram titles for man responsible for heating public baths†

ḥmn *nm** chapel

s ab ? *[l]ḥmn* CRAIBL '81:11; em *ḥmnʾ* C3917:3*

ḥmnʾ dnh ʿbdw wqrbw PN [wPN] this chapel was made and offered by PN Inv 10 145:(below)1; see Dri '88a pp 165-179 on sense, formerly often taken (wrongly) as 'incense altar'; see also Del Olmo Lete '84 pp 277-80

(already in Ug *ḥmn* chapel; cf Heb *ḥammān*)

ḥmr *nm** wine

s ab *ḥmr* RTP 701*; em *ḥmrʾ* Syr '26 p 129:4; abbr (s ab or em) *ḥ<mr>* / *ḥ<mrʾ>* RTP 160

ḥmr mkl wplg wine, a measure and a half (on a tessera) *RTP 697*; *wʾsq ḥmrʾ ʿtyqʾ lkmryʾ štʾ klh mn byth wḥmr bzqyn lʾ ʾyty mn mʿrbʾ* and he served old wine to the priests a whole year, from his house, and he did not bring wine in skins from the west *Syr '26 p 129:4-5*

ḥmr *nm* donkey

s ab *ḥmr* Trf:33; em *ḥmrʾ* Trf:37

ṭʿwn ḥmrʾ lmʿln[ʾ] the donkey-load, for

import *Trf:37*

ḥmr *nm meaning uncertain*: element or material of construction, in a tomb
pl ab *ḥmryn* MUSJ '62 p 106:11
yhw' bn' 'w ktl dy ḥwr' 'w ḥmryn he must build either a wall of limestone or ... ?
(cf perhaps JPA *ḥwmr* 'socket' DJPA p 191; Syr *ḥwmrt'* 'socket, joint of a column')†

ḥmš *num* five
m ab *ḥmš'* C3983:1; f ab *ḥmš* Sem '86 p 89:7; cn (in compound num) *ḥmš m'h* Inv 9 29:4; ab (in compound num) *'rb' m'h wḥmš* Sem '86 p 89:5; m em *ḥmšt'* Ber '38 p 95:1
'mwdy' 'ln ḥmš' these five pillars *C3983:1*; *wsl'yn ḥmš* and five *sela*'s *Sem '86 p 89:7*; *byrḥ 'yr ywm ḥmšt'* in the month of Iyyar, the fifth day *Ber '38 p 95:1*; RosSpr p 81: substantivized form regularly used to indicate day of month

ḥmšyn *num* fifty
(in compound) *wḥmšyn* Inv 9 29:4
šnt ḥmš m'h wḥmšyn in the year five hundred and fifty

ḥnw *nf* store, shop
s em *ḥnwt'* Trf:55
[lkl] yr[ḥ] mn ḥnwt' d<ynr> 1 every month from each shop 1 d<enarius>†

ḥny *v* to abide, dwell (?)
G impf 3ms *yḥn'* RTP 154
DN yḥn' may DN dwell ?†

ḥnk *v* to dedicate
pf 3ms *ḥnk* Inv 9 1:4
dy ḥnk hykl' dy DN wDN wDN who dedicated the temple of DN and DN and DN
▶ *ḥnkt'* n†

ḥnkh *nf* dedication
s em *ḥnkt'* RTP 93
'gn DN wPN ḥnkt' symposium of Bel and PN. Dedication.

▶ *ḥnk* v†

ḥnn *adj* gracious
m s em *ḥnn'* C4084:2
lDN rḥmn' wḥnn' wtyr' to DN, the merciful, the gracious, and forgiving†

ḥsy see *ḥsr* v

ḥsyr *adj* less
m s ab *ḥsyr* Trf:127
whn ḥsyr thwh šql' mdy hy šql' and if (she charges) less, she shall pay whatever she charges†

ḥsk *v* to spend, spend on
G pf 3ms *wḥsk* C3932:5; sf 3mpl *ḥsknwn* C3948:3
wḥsk rz'yn šgy'yn and he spent large amounts *C3932:5*; *bdyl dy ḥsknwn nwr dnryn dy dhb* who spent on them a sum ? of denarii of gold *C3948:3*
▶ for similar semantic development, *ḥsr* v†

ḥsr *v* to spend, spend on
pf 3ms *ḥsr* Inv 10 115:2; cf BS III 47:3; prb. also Syr '33 p 177:3 *ḥsr* for Cantineau's *ḥsy* :: Cantineau to consecrate, so also DISO
wḥsr lhwn mn kysh and he spent on them at his own expense *Inv 10 115:2*
▶ *ḥsyr* adj†

ḥpyw *nf meaning uncertain*, text prb wrong
s or pl em *ḥpywt'* Inv 10 127:2
lḥšbn ḥpywt' wḥš' ṭb['] dy 'št<k>ḥ lh in consideration of the ...(?) and good thought fou[n]d in him Gk *eunoias kai spoudēs heneken*; read *ḥpy<ṭ>wt'* zeal, cf Syr *ḥpyṭwt'* = Gk *spoudē*
▶ *ḥpyṭw* n†

ḥpyṭw *nf* zeal, energy (conjectural reading)
s or pl em *ḥpy<ṭ>wt'* Inv 10 127:2
lḥšbn ḥpy<ṭ>wt' wḥš' ṭb['] dy 'št<k>ḥ lh in consideration of the zeal and good thought

fou[n]d in him *Inv 10 127:2* Gk *eunoias kai spoudēs heneken*; see Hillers, Notes (forthcoming), comparing frequent equivalence of Syr *ḥpyṭwt'* = Gk *spoudē*
▶ ḥpyw n†

ḥpqws *n* see *hpqws* n

ḥpr *v* to excavate
G pf 3ms *ḥpr* C4173:3; pl *ḥpr* C4171:1; impf 3ms *yḥpr* RB '30 9:2; ptcp m pl ab *ḥpryn* Ber '38 p 95:9
dy ḥpr wṣbt m'rt' dh who excavated and ornamented this hypogeum *C4173:3*; *m'rt' dnh dy bt 'lm' ḥpr wbn' wṣbt mn kysh PN* this tomb, an eternal dwelling, was excavated and built and ornamented at his own expense by PN *Inv 4 13:1*†

ḥṣd *nm* reaper
pl em *ḥṣdy'* Sumer '62 p 63:2
dkyryn wbrykyn ḥṣdy' 'ln remembered and blessed be these reapers; *ḥsry'* 'settlers' in first publication, see Teix *Syr '63 p 34, fn 2*†

ḥrm *nm* consecrated object (attestation uncertain)
pl em *ḥr[m]'* C3927:3
dy mgd lh ḥr[m]' l'lm' who gave it conse[crated objects] in perpetuity Gk *epidosin* and *thysian* (correspondence uncertain)†

ḥrt' *nf* Herta (name of deity)
ḥrt' RTP 133
kmry' dy ḥrt' the priests of Herta *Syr '36 p 268:2*; *ḥrt' wnny tbrkn lPN* may Herta and Nanay bless PN *RTP 242*
▶ TeixPan pp 111-13; Gaw ANRW pp 2645-46; Hof RelAram p 45

ḥš *nm* good will
s em *ḥš'* Inv 10 127:2
lḥšbn ḥpywt' wḥš' ṭb['] *dy 'št<k>ḥ lh* in consideration of the zeal ? and good will fou[n]d in him; Gk for *ḥpywt'* and *ḥš' ṭb[']* is *eunoias kai spoudēs heneken*, see *ḥpyw* above; Gaw *'73b p 121:3* would read *mdy ḥš<'> <lb> 'šmn* from affection, to DN, but see conjecture, below, s.v. *ḥšḥ* v†

ḥšb *v* Gt to be reckoned, computed
Gt inf *lmtḥšbw* Trf:103
mks' dy qṣb' 'py dnr hyb lmtḥšbw tax on butchers ought to be computed in denarii Gk *lo[geuesthai]*
▶ *ḥšbn* n†

ḥšbn *nm* **1** reckoning, account; **2** *lḥšbn* on account of
s ab/em/cn ? (context broken) *ḥšbn* Trf:75, cf 87 *ḥšb[n]*; cn *lḥšbn* Inv 10 127:2; em *[ḥš]bn'* CRAIBL '81:17
1 *lkl dy 'll lḥšbn tgr'* for anything that comes into the reckoning of the merchants, *or* on account of the merchants (see no. 2 below) *Trf:115* Gk *eis emporeian* **2** *lḥšbn ḥpywt' wḥš' ṭb[']* in consideration of the zeal ? and good will fou[n]d in him *Inv 10 127:2* Gk *heneken*; cf *'l ḥšbn* on account of Syriac Bill of Sale from Dura, Goldstein '66 p 2:13; cf Teix '90 pp 147-49
▶ *ḥšb* v†

ḥšḥ *v* to need, be necessary
G impf 3ms *yḥšḥ* CRAIBL '81:15
hn yḥšḥ if it is necessary CRAIBL '81:15; *qrbw ... mdy ḥš<ḥ> bl'šmn* (sic; read *b'lšmn*) they offered ... what DN needed *Sem '73 p 121:3*, cf Bib Aram Dan 3:16; Ezra 6:9; see Hillers, Notes (forthcoming)
▶ *ḥšḥh* n†

ḥšḥh *nf* need, use (?)
s em *ḥš[ḥ]th* Trf:133
wmn mn tdmry' yzbn lḥš[ḥ]th and whoever of the Palmyrenes sells for his nee[d] ?
▶ *ḥšḥ* v†

ḥškh *nf* darkness, night
s em *ḥškt!'* Ber '36 p 99:3
dy qrth bḥškt!' who invoked him in darkness†

ḥškk *nm* darkness (?)
s em *ḥškk'* Ber '36 p 99:3
dy qrth bḥškk' who invoked him in the darkness ?†

ṭb *adj* good
m s ab *ṭb* C3987:1; em *ṭb'* C3972:3; f s em *ṭbt'* Syr '31 p 134:3; m pl em *ṭby'* C3955:7
dkrn ṭb lbʿlšmn ʿbd PN memorial for good before Baalshamin made by PN *C3987:1*; *PN dkyr bṭb* may PN be remembered for good *Ber '38 p 115 (second graffito):3*; *ʿbd wmwd' lrḥmn' ṭb' PN* made in gratitude to the one who is merciful and good by PN *RSP 120:2*; *dy qrw lh l'lh' wʿnnwn ṭb'* who called on the god and he answered them with good *C4053:7*; *lšdrp' 'lh' ṭb'* to Shadrafa, the good god *C3972:3*; *lbryk šmh lʿlmh ṭb' wrḥmn'* to Blessed-Be-His-Name-Forever, the good and merciful *C4021:1*; *lʿštr[t'] 'štr' ṭbt'* to Astarte, the good goddess *Syr '31 13:3*; *lyqr DN wDN wDN 'lhy' ṭby'* in honor of DN and DN and DN, the good gods *C3955:7*

ṭbḥ *nm* butcher
s em *ṭbḥ'* C4069:2
PN ṭbḥ' PN, the butcher
⊡ *ṭbyt* adv†

ṭbyt *adv* well
ṭbyt Inv 9 28:9
wšmʿ ṭbyt and he hearkened well :: Déd pp 104, 277 'good fortune' or the like
⊡ *ṭb* adj†

ṭbt *nm* Tebet (name of month = January)
ṭbt C3982:1; *ṭbṭ* MUSJ '49 p 46:7
⊡ Appendix CALENDAR

ṭksys *nm* row
s ab/em *ṭksys* C4171:3
ṭksys dy gwmḥyn 'rbʿ a row of four niches
(< Gk *taksis*)

ṭly *nm* **1** child, young person; **2** the younger; **3** servant
s em *ṭly'* C4139:1; pl em *[ṭ]ly'* C4125:1
1 *[ṭ]ly' 'ln bny PN* these children are the sons of PN *C4125:1*; *dhw' qym ʿl ṭly'* who was in charge of the children (or: young people, or: servants) *Inv 9 28:8* **2** *ṣlm PN ṭly' br PN* Statue of PN, the younger, son of PN *C4139:1*, cf *Inv 11 13:4* **3** *PN ṭly' dy PN* PN, servant of PN *PNO 14:2*
⊡ *ṭlyw* n

ṭlyw *nf* youth
s ab *ṭlyw* Ber '36 p 99:6
mn ṭlyw ʿd sybw from youth to old age
⊡ *ṭly* n†

ṭll *v* D to roof over
D pf 3ms *ṭll* C3917:4
w'p ṭll 'drwn' klh and he also provided the ceiling for the whole dining-room
⊡ *ṭṭlyl* n†

ṭm' *nf* *pl* bones
pl cn *ṭm'* C3907:1
npš' dnyḥt ṭm' PN monument for the repose of the bones of PN
(< * *ʿṭm* < * *ʿẓm*)†

ṭʿw *nf* error
pl ab *ṭʿwn* Trf:99
bdyl dy bṭʿwn dy ktb dy ṭʿ' mks['] because of errors of writing which the tax-collector committed Gk *am[ar]tēma*
⊡ *ṭʿy* v†

ṭʿwn *nm** **1** load; **2** weight
s cn *ṭʿwn* Trf:17; em *ṭʿwn'* Trf:36; pl ab *ṭʿwnyn* Trf(I):13
1 *mn ṭʿwn ḥmr [d]y mšḥ b[šy]m'* from a donkey-load [o]f per[fu]med oil *Trf:21*; *ṭʿwn dhn'* a load of fat *Trf:29*; *ṭʿwn qrs* a cart-load *Trf(I):13* **2** *ṣlm bplgwt [ṭʿw]n wṣlmyn trn ṭʿwn* a statue at half its [wei]ght, and two statues at its weight (that is, of one) *Trf:130**, translation problematic, see Matthews JRS '84

p 180 n. 42
▶ *ṭʿn* v

ṭʿy *v* to make a mistake
G pf 3ms *ṭʿʾ* Trf:100
ṭʿwn dy ktb dy ṭʿʾ mks[ʾ] errors of writing which the tax-collector committed
▶ *ṭʿw* n†

ṭʿmh *nf* foodstuffs
pl em *ṭʿmtʾ* Trf:109
lṭʿmtʾ hy<k> bnm[w]sʾ for foodstuffs, accord(ing) to the sta[tu]te Gk *brōtōn*†

ṭʿn *v* to load
G ptcp pass m pl abs *ṭʿynyn* Trf:118
gmlyʾ hn ṭʿynyn whn sryqyn camels whether loaded or not loaded :: Klíma '65
▶ *ṭʿwn* n†

ṭpy *nf architectural term:* coping, i.e. the covering course of a wall (?)
pl em *ṭpytʾ* BS III 19:1; 20:3
ʿmwdyʾ ʾln ʾrbʿʾ wṭpytʾ wšrytʾ dy ḥṭrʾ these four columns and the coping and the entablature of the court *BS III 19:1*; see Dunant ad loc., p 30, and Caquot, GLECS 7 pp 77-78†

y *abbr y<wm>* n day

ybyš *nm* 1 dried goods; 2 dry land
s ab *ybyš* Trf:116; em *ybšʾ* C4047:4; pl ab *yby[šyn]* Trf(II):7
1 *yhwʾ mksʾ hyk lybyš* there shall be a tax as for dried goods *Trf:116* Gk *xērophorton* L-S: 'weight of a cargo of fruit after drying', with reference to this passage **2** *dy qr lh bymʾ wbybšʾ* to whom he called on sea and on dry land *C4047:4*†

yd *nf* 1 hand; 2 hand, care, charge; 3 *ktb yd* ability to write, handwriting
s sf 3ms *[y]dh* C4058:6; 1s *ydy* MUSJ '62 p 106:3; pl sf 3ms *ydwh* C3976:4
1 *[y]dh wrglh* his [h]and and his foot *C4058:6* **2** *dy ʾšlmt ʿl ydwh* which was given into his charge *C3976:4* **3** *ʾšʾlt ktb ydy lPN* I have lent my handwriting to PN *MUSJ '62 p 106:3*†

ydy *v* C 1 to acknowledge; 2 to thank
C pf 3mpl *ʾwdw* Inv 10 114:4; ptcp m s ab *mwdʾ* Inv 11 38:3; f s ab *mwdyʾ* C4020B:2; m pl ab *mwdyn* PNO 38:4; *mwdn* C3981:1; [...]*mdyn* ? PNO 72:8 (so edd., DISO, but not expected at this point in the inscription, and follows lacuna

C 1 (in document of cession) *PN mwdyʾ lPN* PN acknowledges to PN *RB '30 14:3*; cf *mwdynʾ* 'I acknowledge' in Syriac Bill of Sale line 7, Goldstein JNES '66 pp 9-10, see Cussini '92a (index, forthcoming revision); ancient Syriac sale-documents, Teix '90 pp 147, 154 **2** *[zb]nyn wlʾ zʿwryn ʾwdw lbwlʾ...* not a few times they gave thanks ? to the Senate ... (context broken; finite form unique in Palmyrene, sense uncertain) Inv 10 114:4, in Gk note *eu[cha]ristēthēnai auton*; (beginning of inscription) *mwdʾ PN* PN gives thanks *Inv 11 41:1*; *[m]wdʾ lDN PN* PN for DN, in thanksgiving *C4031:1* Gk *euxamenos anethēken*; *DN ... [ʿlt]ʾ dnh ʿbd wmw[dʾ PN]* (for) DN ... , PN made this altar, in thanksgiving *C4066:3* Gk *an[ethēken] eucharist[...]*; *lDN mwdʾ PN* to Blessed-Be-His-Name-Forever PN gives thanks *RSP 137:2*; *mwdʾ PN bʿšmn* PN thanks DN *Sem '77 p 106:1*, see Dri ad loc.; *DN ... ʿbd wmwdʾ PN* DN ... PN made (this), in thanskgiving *C4030:3*; Aram construction with + *w* + ptcp may imitate Gk syntax in use of ptcp instead of finite vb, expected in Aram

ydʿ *v* G to know; C to make known (?)
G pf 3ms *ydʿ* MUSJ '62 p 106:4; C inf *lmw[dʿw]* CRAIBL '81:18
bdyldy lʾ ydʿ spr because he is illiterate *MUSJ '62 p 106:4*; *mlbqrw wlmw[dʿw]* to investigate and to make kn[own] *CRAIBL '81:18*†

yhb *v* to give
G pf 3ms *yhb* Ber '35 p 76:1; 3fs *yhbt* RB '30 14:4;

3mpl *wyhb* Ber '38 p 106:3; ptcp m pl ab *yhbyn* Trf:124

yhb mšḥ' lbny md[ynt'] he donated oil to the citiz[ens] *C3959:3* Gk *para<s>chonta*; *DN dy yhb l'bgl šlṭn'* DN, who gave Abgal dominion *PNO 2ter:6*; *dy yhwn yhbyn mk[s']* they should pay taxes *Trf:124*; *wyhb mn kysh* and he paid out of his own pocket *Inv 9 11:5*; *yhw' yhb lmdy' 'sr 'yṭlq[']* he shall pay one Italian *assarius* for a *modius Trf:133*; *PN yhb mnt' mnth dy m'rt' [lPN]* PN transferred as a part, his portion of the hypogeum [to PN] *RB '30 p 545(B):2* Gk *edōken [k]ata[d]osin* 'paid as an installment'; *'ksdr' ... yhb w'ḥbr PN* the exedra ... PN transferred and ceded *Ber '35 p 76:1*

ywly' *nm* *Julius, Julii,* as title

pl em? *ywly'* Inv 8:58

Compare Gk (with pl *Aurēlioi*) and Aram texts at Inv 8:58; also other occurrences of name may best be interpreted so, as similarly *'wrly'* and *spṭmy'*

< Latin Julius ▶ *ywly'* PN

ywm *nm** day

s ab *ywm* Inv 11 37:3; s ab or cn *ywm* RTP 158; spelling *yym* C4258:6 (cf *syyn* for *sywn* in line 8) is an aberration; C3987:3*; abbr *y<wm>* RTP 721; em *ywm'* CRAIBL '81:3

mwdn kl ywm PN wPN PN and PN give thanks every day *C3981:1*; *ywm 12* the twelfth day *RTP 158*; *byrḥ sywn ywm 18* in the month of Siwan, the 18th day *C4210:4*; *myt ywm 3 bknwn šnt 484* died the 3rd day of Kanun, the year 484 *C4261:5*; *ywm šb't* the seventh day *C3987:3*; *ywm' dy yhwn sm[ky]* on the day when they will recli[ne at table ...] *CRAIBL '81:3*

ywny *adj* Greek

f s ab ? *ywnyt* C4546:4 (a cognomen); pl em *ywny'* C3924:4

wywny' dy bslwky' and the Greeks who are in Seleuceia *C3924:4*; *'mtḥ' brt zbyd' ywnyt* PN, the Greek *C4546:4* (a cognomen, cf *mṣryt* 'the Egyptian' *C4547:4*)†

yḥy *v* C to prescribe, order

C ptcp m s ab ? *mwḥ'* Trf:125

hyk dy nmws' mwḥ' as the law prescribes; so RosSpr p 65 comparing *twḥyt* n 'decree'; others read *mḥw'*

▶ see *ḥw'* v†

yḥl' *nm* onyx (?)

s em *yḥ[l]'* C3956:5

[ṣlm]yn trn dy yḥ[l]' two [statu]es of onyx ?; RosSpr p 97, notes that the Persian origin of *yḥl'* can not be proven, and that meaning 'onyx' is likewise uncertain

(cf rare Syriac *yaḥlā'*)

ym *nm* sea

s em *ym'* C4047:4

dy qr lh bym' wbybš' whose aid they invoked on sea and dry land†

ymy *v* to swear

G pf 3ms *ymh* (with sf ?) Syr '36 26:9; *ym'* CRAIBL '81:11

ymh byrḥbw[l] he has sworn by Yarhibo[l...] *Syr '36 26:9*; *wmn dy ym' [b]ḥmn* and whoever swears [by?] the shrine *CRAIBL '81:11*†

ymyn *nf* right, right hand, side

s em *ymyn'* C4204:2; *ymn'* Ber '35 p 95:1; sf 2ms *ymynk* C4195:7

'l ymyn' on the right side *Ber '35 p 102 X:3*; *gmḥyn tmny' mn ymynk* the eight niches on your right *C4195:7*; *m'lyk bb' dy ymynk wdy smlk* as you enter the door on your right and on your left *Ber '35 p 110:1*; *dy hw pn' lymyn'* which faces right *C4172:2*

▶ *ymyny* adj

ymn *see ymyn n*

ymny *adj* right

m s em *ymny'* Ber '35 p 97:1; pl ab *ymnyyn* Ber '38 p 124:2

mn šṭr' ymny' from the right side *Ber '35 p 97:1*; *gwmḥyn trn bryyn ymnyyn* the two

exterior niches on the right *Ber '38 p 124:2*
▶ *ymyn* n

yqr *v* C to honor
C pf 3fs *'wqrt* C4518A:3
lyqrh dy 'wqrt PN 'ḥwh in her honor, for she honored PN, his brother
▶ *yqr* n†

yqr *nm** 1 honor; 2 gift
s ab *yqr* C4123:1; cn *yqr* C4123:2; em *yqr'* Syr '33 p 280:8; sf 3ms *yqrh* Inv 10 113:3; 3fs *yqrh* C3954:3; 3mpl *yqrhwn* C3930:5; *lyqrhn* C4122:3; 3fpl *yqrhyn* Inv 10 119:7; pl ab *yqryn* BS III 45:6*
1 *dkrn' dnh dy hw yqr bt ʿlm'* this memorial, which is an honor, an eternal dwelling *C4123:1*; *qbr' [dnh] dy hw dkrn wyqr bt ʿlm'* [this] tomb, which is a memorial and an honor, an eternal home *StudPalm '75 p 131:3* Gk *to mnē[me]io[n t]ou[to eis tei]mēn a[iōnian]*; *dy 'qym lh lyqrh* which he set up for him in his honor *Inv 10 113:3*; *lyqrhwn* in their honor *C3930:5*, Gk frequently has *teimēs charin* for *lyqrh* and the like, e.g. C3923; *wyqryn šgy'yn* and many honors *BS III 45:6* **2** *ʿm yqr' dy bwl' wdms* with a gift from the Senate and People *Syr '36 p 280:8* :: Cantineau, ad loc.: 'at the expense of', but Syriac parallel cited is not exact, and 'at the expense of' is frequently expressed in Syriac with *mn kys* X
▶ *yqr* v

yrḥ *nm** month
s ab *yrḥ* Sem '86 p 89:1*; s cn *yrḥ* C3924:1
yrḥ 'ḥd one month Sem '86 p 89:1; *byrḥ 'b šnt 451* in the month of Ab, the year 451 *C4130:6*; Gk often *mēnos*

yrḥbwl *nm** Yarhibol (name of deity)
yrḥbwl C3919:3; *yrḥbl* MélDus p 885:3
yrḥbwl 'lh' Yarhibol, the god *C3932:6**
▶ TeixPan pp 29-34; Gaw ANRW 2616-19; Hof RelAram pp 30-33
▶ *yrḥbwl* and related PN's

yrḥbl see *yrḥbwl* n

yšdḥ *see yšrḥ n*

yšrḥ *nm meaning and reading uncertain*
s em ? *yšrḥ'* RSP 142:3
byr[ḥ] 'yr ywm yšrḥ' šnt 545 in the mont[h] of Iyyar, day(s) of ..., the year 545 *RSP 142:3*; other possible readings: *yšdḥ'* or, with a different division of words (so Gaw) *ywmy šrḥ'*; according to Gaw, Milik's *ywm ʿšrt'* is not a possible reading; in any case, unexplained†

yšṭ *v* to stretch out
C impf 3ms *ywšṭ* CRAIBL '81:7 (Teix divides text otherwise; see *'wyw* n)
'w ywšṭ ydh ʿl [...] or stretches out his hand on/against [...]†

yt *prep object marker*
yt C3932:4
wkdy 'ty lk' yt lgyny' and when he brought the legions here†

ytb *v* 1 to sit, dwell; 2 to preside
pf 3ms *ytb* Syr '26 p 129:3; ptcp m pl ab *ytbyn* RSP 143:4
1 *wl'lhy' klhn dy ytbyn lwth dy [DN]* and to all the gods who dwell with [DN] *RSP 143:4* **2** *PN dy šmš 'lhy' wytb ʿl qsm' šṭ' klh* PN, who served the gods and presided over the divination ? for the whole year *Syr '26 p 129:3*†

ytyr *adj* more
s ab *ytyr* Trf(I):11
mdʿm ytyr anything more, anything in excess *Trf(I):11*; *dnr 'w ytyr* a denarius or more *Trf:127* cf *48*†

k' see *lk'* adv†

kd see *kdy* cj

kdy *cj* when, as
kdy C4199:4; *kd* Trf(I):3
kd hwt bwl' knyš' when the Senate was

assembled *Trf(I):3*; *ḥd' ʿl ymyn' kdy 'nt ʿll* one on the right as you go in *C4199:4*; *kdy lDN wDN* as also to DN and DN *C3981:6*

kwdn *nm* mule
s em *kwdn[']* Trf:39
wlkwdn['] and for a mule
(RosSpr p 90: LW in Aram and in Arab, < Akk *kūdanu, kudannu*, but prb simply cognates)†

kwl *v* C to measure
C impf 3ms + sf 3ms *ykylnh* Trf:73
ykylnh l[mks]' [']py mdy' he shall measure it out to [the tax-collector] according to the *modius*†

kwt See *mtl kwt* adv

kys *nm* money bag, purse, funds s cn *kys* Inv 12 43:3; sf 3ms *kysh* C3902:1; 3mpl *kyshwn* C4201:2
dy 'pq mn kysh npqn rbrbn who paid out of his purse great expenses *Inv 10 44:5*; *ʿbd DN wDN mn kys PN* made by DN and DN at the expense of PN *Inv 12 43:3*; *ʿbd mn kysh PN* made at his own expense by PN *C3902:1*

kkr *nm** talent (?)
pl ab (or dual) *kkryn* Sem '86 p 89:5*
kkryn 'lpyn tlt' wšbʿ m'h wʿšryn two talents, three thousand seven hundred and twenty; the difficult text treats of accounts, so *kkr* talent is appropriate sense; dual *m'tn* two hundred occurs in same text :: Gaw *kkr* refers to unit smaller than denarius, hence LW from Gk *kokkarion* in sense 'grain' (but this rare diminutive [of *kokkos* 'grain, seed'] is not attested, even in Gk, for monetary unit, but only in sense 'pill', acc. to L-S)†

kl *nm* 1 all, every, (the) whole; 2 in divine title *mr' kl* (Lord of all, Lord of) the universe
s ab *kl Trf:115*; cn *kl* Inv 8 172; sf 3ms *klh* C4186:2; 3fs *klh* BS III 3:1; 3mpl *klhwn* Inv 11 6:8; *klhn* C3972:4
1 *wtṣbyth klh* and the ornamentation, all of it *Ber '36 p 84:4*; *mn kl byš' klh* from every kind of evil *Inv 8 172:1*; *kl gbr dy ydḥl DN* every man who fears DN *PNO 2ter:9*; *kl dy ktyb*[...] everything that is written *Syr '36 26:3*; *kl ywm dy qr lh* every time he called to him *Inv 11 37:3*; *wdkyryn kl mn dhw ...* and commemorated be every man who ... *PNO 56:4*; *dy lkl dy ʿll lḥšbn tgr'* that for anything that enters the merchant's reckoning *Trf:115*; *mṭlt' dh klh* this whole portico *BS III 3:1*; *brykyn 'ln klhwn* blessed be all of these *Inv 11 77* **2** *DN mr' kl* DN, lord of the universe *C3998:1*

kl *nm** measure (?)
pl ab *klyn* RTP 280*; *kln* RTP 867
klyn tr[n] PN tw[o] measures. PN *RTP 280*
(from root *kyl* 'to measure' ? [Caquot RTP p 145])†

kldy *adj* (the) Kladian? (perhaps gentilic of tribal name); or: Chaldaean, chaldaean?
m s em *kldy'* Ber '34 p 38:7; perhaps also *'kldy* C4357:5
PN kldy' brh PN, the Kladian, his son *Ber '34 p 38:7*; Déd pp 259-60 relates the term (and the related *'kldy*) to Lat. Claudius, cf also Hajjar '90 p 2255 (but Aram *k* = Lat *c* ?; normal is *q*; see Stark p 138, note *qlwdys* 'Claudius') :: Ing's tentative suggestion Ber '34 p 39 'chaldaean, magician', followed by DISO s.v. *kldy* :: Degen '72 p 212
▶ *'kldy* PN†

klm' *adj* any, every
prb invariable form *klm'* Trf(I):13
ṭʿwn qrs dy klm' gns klh a cart load of any kind at all
(*kl* 'every' + *m'* 'what' [interrogative])†

kmr *nm* priest
pl cn *kmry* RTP 22; em *kmry'* Inv 11 100:2
ʿbdw kmry DN [wDN] made by the priests

of DN [and DN] *C3968:1*; *w'sq ḥmr' 'tyq' lkmry'* and he brought out old wine for the priests *Syr '26 p 129:5*; *kmry' dy bl* the priests of DN *RTP 11*
▶ *kmr'* PN (tribal name) and Déd pp 37-41

knwn I *nm** brazier
s em *knwn'* C3977:4*; pl ab *knwnyn trn* Inv 11 7:3
w'bd knwn' dy nḥš' and he made the bronze brazier *C3952:4*

knwn II *nm* Kanun (name of month = November)
s ab *knwn* C3915:5; *knn* ? Doura 15:5 cf Cantineau Syr '38 p 164 and DISO s. v., who give definition (tentatively) fixation
Kanun, month
▶ Appendix CALENDAR

knš *v* to gather
G ptcp passive f s ab *knyš'* Trf(I):3; Dt ptcp m pl ab *mtknšyn* Trf:132
G *kd hwt bwl' knyš'* when the Senate was assembled *Trf(I):3*; **Dt** *b'tr dy mtknšyn* in the place where they assemble *Trf:132*†

kslw *nm* Kislev (name of month = December; usually *kslwl*)
s ab *kslw* Inv 10 81:5
▶ *kslwl* n; Appendix CALENDAR†

kslwl *nm* Kaslul (name of month = December)
s ab *kslwl* C3939:5
▶ *kslw* n; Appendix CALENDAR

ksp *nm* silver, money
s ab *ksp* RB '30 14:4; cn *ksp* C3994:2; s em *ksp'* C3902:1
mqbl' mnh ksp dnryn m'h w'sryn he has received from him money, 120 denarii *RB '30 14:4*; *'bd' dhb' wksp'* workers in gold and silver *C3945:4*

k'nyn *nm* *meaning and reading uncertain*
pl ab *k'nyn* or *ṭ'nyn* ? RTP 117; see Caquot RTP p 145
bnyn' k'nyn bl the construction ... ? Bel.†

kph *nf* vault, vaulted space, niche
s em *kpt'* C3912:2; pl em *kpy'* Ber '35 p 104:4; sf 3mpl *kpyhn* Inv 11 81:1
qrb kpt' w'rš' PN PN offered a vaulted space and couch *C3912:2* Gk *kamaran* 'vault, vaulted chamber'; *ṣ[lmy' dy] bkpt' dy PN wPN* The s[tatues that are] in the niche are of PN and PN *C4187:1* Gk *psalidi* vault; *ṣlmy' 'ln wkpyhn* these statues and their niches *Inv 11 81:1*

kpṣ *v* *meaning and analysis uncertain*
mkpṣ RSP 199:12
in context with *ḥmr* wine; Gaw '73b) p 116 leaves untranslated, notes possible parallel in Akkadian *kapāṣu* 'contract' (but Semitic usually is *qpṣ*)†

kpr *v* *meaning uncertain*
G pf 3mpl *kprw* Trf:122
'l gldy' dy gmly['] 'p 'ln kprw dy mks l' gbn for came[l] hides, too, they *made exemption* (?), tax is not collected†

kpr *nm* meaning and reading uncertain
pl em *kpry'* IP 57:1
kpry' dy[...] ... which ... ; Cantineau ad loc.: 'tombs', cf Nabataean, where *kbr'* is frequent for *qbr'*; cf Old Syriac (73 C.E.) *kpr* 'tomb' Dri '72 no. 2:7 :: Déd p 178: conjectures different text†

krwz *nm* herald
s em *krz'* Sumer '64 p 13:5; *krwz'* Sumer '62 p 63:8
PN krwz' PN, the herald *Sumer '62 p 63:8*†

krz see *krwz* n

krk I *nm* city
s em *krk'* RTP 8
krk' 'nwšt' The City. The treasury.

(probably related to Gk *charaks* 'fortified camp')
▶ *krk II* n†

krk II *nf* Spasinou Charax (same as Mesene Charax)
s ab *krk 'spsn'* Inv 10 107:3; *krk myšn* Inv 10 81:5; em *krk'* Inv 10 111:3; *krk[']* *dy myšn* Inv 10 112:4

krk 'spsn' Spasinou Charax *C3928:3*; *krk my[šn]* Mesene Charax *Inv 10 40:4*, Gk *spasinou charakos*, cf Cantineau '38 p 76; *mn krk'* from Charax *CIS 3948:3* Gk *[apo] spasinou char[akos]*

kšyr *adj* noble, excellent
m s em *kšyr'* Trf:121

whyk dy 'šr PN kšyr' and as was established by the noble PN Gk *kratistos*
▶ *kšr* v†

kšr *adj* right, proper
m s ab *kšr* Trf:105

dy h' kšr dy [yh]n mksy' 'py 'sr 'yṭlq['] that it is right for taxes to be according to the Italian *assarius Trf:105*; *lmh dy kšr* of that which is right *Syr '36 p 350:10*, reading of Gaw TP p 57, cf Déd pp 303-04†

ktb *v* G to write; Gt to be written
G pf 3ms *ktb* Trf:121; *wktb* Trf(I):9 is of uncertain analyis: passive 3ms ? or error for *w<y>ktb* ? (prb impf. passive); 1s *ktbt* C4214:1; impf passive (?) 3ms *wyktb* Trf(I):8; ptcp passive m s ab *ktyb* Syr '36 p 353:3; Gt ptcp m s ab *mtktb* Trf(I):5

G *b'grt' dy ktb lPN* in the letter which he wrote to PN *Trf:121*; *mdy ktyb mn lṭḥt* what is written below *Trf(I):4* Gk *ta hypotetagmena*; *kl dy ktyb* all that is written *Syr '36 p 353:3*; *wyktb bšṭr 'gry' ḥdt'* and let it be written in a new contract *Trf(I):8* Gk *engrapsai*; *wktb 'm nmws' qdmy'* and let it be written with the former law *Trf(I):9* Gk *engraphēnai*; *wyktb lmd'm' md'm' mksh dy mn 'yd'* and there should be written for each item its customary tax *Trf(I):8* Gk *hypot[a]ksai*; acc. to RosSpr p 56, the forms yktb must be Peal passives, so also DISO :: CaGr pp 81-83, where various alternate explanations are advanced, with references to opinions of earlier scholars **Gt** *dy hw' mtktb b'gwry' dy mks'* which was written in the tax contracts *Trf(I):5* Gk *engraphome[nou]*
▶ *ktwb* n

ktb *nm* writing; *ktb yd* handwriting, ability to write
s ab *ktb* Trf:100; s cn *ktb* MUSJ '62 p 106:3; pl em *ktby' 'ln* Syr '36 p 353:4, 8

bdyl dy bṭ'wn dy ktb dy ṭ'' mks['] because by errors of writing committed by the tax-collect[or] *Trf:100*; *'š'lt ktb ydy lPN* I have put my handwriting at the disposal of PN *MUSJ '62 p 106:3*†

ktwb *nm* scribe
s em *ktwb'* Syr '26 p 129:7; *ktb'* ? PNO 47:5

wPN ktwb' and PN, the scribe *Syr '26 p 129:7*; prb same word at *PNO 47:5 PN bṭb ktb'* PN, for good, the scribe (word-order odd)†

ktl *nm* wall
s ab *ktl* MUSJ '62 p 106:11; em *ktl'* RSP 127:4; sf 3fs *ktlh* BS III 9:1

ktl' dy br' the exterior wall *RSP 127:4*; *ktl' dy [l]bn'* the wall of [b]ricks *RSP 127:4*; *[mṭlt' dh] kl[h] w'mwdyh wktlh wṭṭly[lh]* [this] who[le portico] with it pillars and its wall and its ceili[ng ...] *BS III 9:1*
(not < Akk [so Gaw ad RSP 127], see AIA p 65 s.v. *kutallu*)

l *prep* to, for: 1 to (complementing various verbs): speak to, give to, etc.; 2 to, for (in sense belonging to, of); 3 for (referring to aim, object): in view of, for, unto, with respect to, with reference to; 4 (with passive verbs, the agent): by (if analysis of vb is correct); 5 (with an infinitive): to; 6 (equivalent of *'l*): for, on behalf of; 7 *combining with other prepositions or with conjunctions*
before substantives, etc. *l*; with sf 3ms *lh*; fs *lh*; 1s *ly*;

3mpl *lhwn*; *lhn*; *lhyn* Inv 10 119:4 (scribal error? so Starcky ad loc.); 1pl *ln*

1 to, *complementing various verbs:* speak to, give to, etc. **a** with verbs of saying: *dy y'mr lh* who will say to him *Syr '36 p 353:7*; *shdt lh bdgm bwl' wdms* the Senate and People gave testimony in his behalf by a decree *Syr '36 p 280:5*; *kl ywm dy qr lh* every day he called to him *Inv 11 37:4* **b** with verbs of giving: *wmgd lbwl' zwzyn rbw* and he made a donation of 10,000 *zuz*'s to the Senate *C3934:4*; *yhbt lh* I have given to him *RB '30 14:4* **c** with verbs of dealing, acting towards: *dy ʿbd lh 'rbʿ pḥzy'* which the four tribes made for him *Inv 10 44:3*; *dy rḥqt lh PN* which PN ceded to him *C4199:12* **d** with words denoting what is pleasurable or the reverse: *wl' yqšṭ lmn dy ypthyhy ʿd ʿlm'* and may it not be right with whoever opens it, ever *C4218:6* **e** with verbs expressing motion or direction toward: *wkdy 'ty lk' yt lgyny'* when he brought here the legions *C3932:4*; *lkl dy ʿll lḥšbn tgr'* anything which goes into the merchants' account *Trf:115*; *šyrt' dy nḥtt lkrk'* the caravan that went down to Spasinou Charax *Inv 10 111:2* **f** of time: *wl' ypthh 'nš lʿlm* and let no man open it, ever *RSP 105:5* **g** object of verb: *mwdn lh* thanking him *PNO 37:6*; *mwd' lh lrḥmn' ṭb'* thanks him, the good (and) merciful one *RSP 121:3-4*; *dy lwt lh* that I have taken him as associate ? *MUSJ '62 p 106:6*; *DN wDN tbrkn lPN* may DN and DN bless PN *RTP 242* **h** other kinds of adverbal complementation or modification: *wmdy dm' lhwn* and whatever is like them *Trf:114*; *[m]ks' ḥyb lmhw'* the [ta]x ought to be *Trf:77*; *ḥyb lmtḥšbw* ought to be reckoned *Trf:103*; *wl' yh' šlyṭ lh lmrḥ lʿlwh* and he shall have no right to extend it *MUSJ '62 p 106:9* **2** to, for *in sense* belonging to, of: **a** belonging to, of: *[ṣlm' dnh] lPN* [this statue] belongs to (or: 'is of') PN *RSP 226:1*; *lyqr lhwn* as an honor for them *IP 11:4*; *'ḥyd' lPN* reserved for PN *BS III 70:1*; *l' yhw' lh zrʿ wgr ʿd ʿlm'* may he have no offspring or patron, ever *C4218:4*; *dkrn ṭb lDN wDN* a good commemoration for Asharu and Shaad *Doura 20:1* **b** as periphrasis for the construct state: *'sṭrṭg lqlny'* general of the colony *C3932:2* **3** for *referring to aim, object*, thus: in view of, for, unto, with respect to, with reference to: *dy ʿbd lh bḥywhy lbt ʿlmh* which he made in his lifetime as an eternal home *C4119:6*; *lyqrh* in his honor *C3932:8*; *ytn [lh]n ltšmyš'* it shall be given [to th]em for use *Trf:70*; *lmʿln'* for import *Trf:67*; *l'ṭ[t' dn]r* a [dena]rius per wo[man] *Trf:127*; *lkl rgly [d]<ynryn> 12* for every slave 12 d<enarii> *Trf(II):6*; *ḥty' ddynrn ldhb'* a recompense of denarii, in gold *CRAIBL 81:13*; *wʿnn brwḥ' ln* and he answered us, with relief for us *RSP 119:8* **4** *with passive verbs, the agent*, by: *wyhw' mbṭl l'rkwny'* and let it be of concern to the archons *Trf(I):10* (if *mbṭl* is passive) **5** *with an infinitive, in sense of purpose*, to: *tbrk ʿyn' dh lmgbr* may this spring bless *mightily* (so as to abound) ? *RTP 722*; *bʿmwd' dnh lmqmw ʿlwhy [ṣlm]yn trn* on this pillar, to set up on it two [stat]ues *C3956:4* **6** *equivalent of ʿl*, for, on behalf of: *lḥyh wlḥy' brth* for his life and the life of his daughter *C4014:5*; note esp. *ʿl ḥywhy wḥyy bnw[hy] wḥyy 'ḥwhy wlḥyy bny byt' klhwn* for (*ʿl*) his life and the life of [his] children and the life of his brothers and for (*l*) the life of all his household *Inv 11 6:6-7* **7** combining with other prepositions or with conjunctions: see list after symbol (▶) below.

▶ *'l' cj ('l' l-)*; *hyk* prep *(hyk l-)*; *l'p'* prep; *lgw, lgw mn* prep; *lʿl mn* prep; *lqbl* prep; *lbr mn* prep

l' *adv* no; not

l'; blended with pronoun 3ms *lw'* Syr '33 p 184:2, CaGr p 135, RosSpr p 83

l' 'yty he did not bring *Syr '26 p 129:6*; *pgryn ... l' ḥybyn* corpses ... are not liable to tax *Trf:108*; *dy l' šṭ' ḥmr'* who does not drink wine *C3973:4*; *dy l' yšd dm* whoever does not shed blood *Dri '82b:2*; *w'nš l' ypth ʿlwhy gwmḥ' dnh* and let no one uncover this niche *C4218:3*; *dy lwʾ mn bnwhy dkryʾ* who is not of his male children *Syr '33 p 184:2*

lʾpʾ *prep* towards
lʾpʾ RB '30 14:6; Inv 7 1B:3
ptyḥʾ lʾpʾ mdnḥʾ open towards the east *RB '30 14:6*
(*l*+*ʾpʾ* [pl con] to the face of)
▶ *ʾpy* prep ?†

lbnh *nf* brick (restored)
pl em *[l]bnʾ* RSP 127:5
ktlʾ dy [l]bnʾ a wall of [b]ricks :: Déd p 257
▶ ʾbn n

lbr mn *prep* outside
lbr mn C4172:2
gwmḥyn ʾrbʿʾ dy lbr mn kptʾ four niches outside the vaulted space
▶ *br II n*†

lgw *adv* inside
s ab *lgw* Ber '35 p 82V:1
mn qrqsʾ wlgw from the vault and inside
▶ *gw* n†

lgw mn *prep* inside
lgw mn Syr '33 p 185:2
dy lgw mn mʿrtʾ which is inside the hypogeum
▶ *gw* n†

lgywn *nm* legion
s em *lgywnʾ* C3962:2; pl em *lgynyʾ* C3932:4
wkdy ʾty lkʾ yt lgynyʾ and when he brought here the legions *C3932:4* Gk *ouēksillatiosin* (< Latin *vexillatio* 'troop'); *qṭrywnʾ dy mn lgywnʾ dy ʾrbʿtʾ* centurion in the fourth ? legion *C3962:2*; *dblgywnʾ dy bṣrʾ* who is the legion of Bosra *C3944:5* Gk *leg[eōnos]*
(< Gk *legeōn* < Lat. *legio*)

lwʾ see *lʾ* adv

lwy *v* to make someone a partner (?)
G pf 1s ? *lwt* MUSJ '62 p 106:6
dy lwt lh brbwʿtʾ I have taken him as partner in the recess; Ing ad loc. suggests pael pf 3ms of *lwt v*, derived from prep *lwt*
(Cf perhaps Syriac *lwy* v Pael to accompany; Ethpa. to be made a companion of; cf also DJPA p 279; BJA Jastrow s.v.)†

lwt *prep* toward, directed toward, with
lwt Syr '36 p 280:6, C4058:7; sf 3fs *lwth* RSP 143:4
wḥšʾ ṭb[ʾ] dy ʾšt<k>ḥ lh lwt tgryʾ for kind attention found in him toward the merchants Inv 10 127:3, Gk *pros*; *wlʾlhyʾ klhn dy ytbyn lwth dy [mrt bytʾ]* and for all the gods who dwell with [the Lady of the Temple] *RSP 143:4* Gk *pros*
▶ *lwy* v†

lwt see *lwy* v

lgyn see *lgywn* n

lḥm *nm* bread
s ab *lḥm* C4218:7; Syr '36 26:1
wlḥm wmn lmʾ yšbʿ and may he never have enough bread and water *C4218:7*†

lḥšbn see *ḥšbn* n

lyt *pred* there is not
lyt Syr '36 26:5, 6
bd lyt kmryʾ because there are not any priests ?†

lkʾ *adv* here, hither, to this place
lkʾ C3932:4
wkdy ʾty lkʾ yt lgynyʾ and when he brought here the legions†

lmʾ *adv* not, never
lmʾ C4218:7
wlḥm wmn lmʾ yšbʿ and may he never have enough bread and water
Cf Syriac *lmā* lest, that not†

lmn *nm* port, entrepôt, city
s em *lmn'* Trf(II):1
mks' dy lmn' dy hdryn' tdmr the tax-law of the port, Hadriana Tadmor; see Matthews '84 pp 172, 179 n. 9: = Lat *portus* 'point where a transit tax, *portorium*, was exacted'; Rostovtzeff '32d pp 79-81: Gk *limēn* = 'fiscal district', cf Raschke '78 p 778 n. 566; Brock '75 pp 83-84 'emporium'
(< Gk *limēn* port)
▶ *mḥwz* n†

lʿl I *prep* above
lʿl RSP 21:3; *lʿlwh* MUSJ '62 p 106:9
lʿl dnh above this RSP 21:3
▶ *lʿl adv, lʿl mn prep*

lʿl II *adv* to the top
wtṣbyth klh ʿd lʿl and all the ornamentation, to the top Inv 3 2
lʿl dnh above this RSP 21:3
▶ *lʿl prep, lʿl mn prep*†

lʿl mn *prep* above, over
sf 3ms *lʿl mnh* C3911:3; Inv 12 48:2; 49:5; RSP 21:3
wttlyl' dlʿl mnh and the ceiling that is over it *C3911:3*; *dy lʿl mnh* in the problematic occurrence Sem '93 p 164:2 may have same local sense, but is translated by Gawlikowski as: over and above, beyond that which is due [of tolls]†

lṣḥt *nm meaning and analysis uncertain*
lṣḥt Inv 8 97:2
[...]*lṣḥt ḥbl*†

lqbl *prep* opposite
lqbl Trf(I):10; sf 3ms *lqblh* Syr '38 p 155:2
bgll' dy lqbl hykl' on a stele which is in front of the temple *Trf(I):10*, Gk *antikrus*; *dy qym' lqblh* which stands opposite it *Syr '38 p 155:2*†

lqbl' *adv* opposite
lqbl' Ber '38 p 104:2
mʿlyk bb' lqbl' as you enter the door, opposite†

m *abbr* **1** *m<yl>* mile; **2** *m<kl>* measure; **3** *m<šḥ'>* oil

m' *pron* what, that which; when (?)
m' Trf:70; possibly RSP 228:3; Trf:15
[w]m' dy ytbʿ' ytn [lh]n [and] what is requested will be given to them, or, when it is requested, it etc. *Trf:70*
(interrogative pron with *dy* > compound relative, or cf Syriac *m'd* when)
▶ *mh* pron; *mdy* pron†

m'h *num* hundred
m'h C4174:8
dnryn dy dhb ʿtyqyn tlt m'h three hundred old gold denarii *C3948:4*; *šnt ḥmš m'h wtrtn* the year five hundred and two *C4174:8*

m'tn *num* two hundred
m'tn Sem '86 p 89:2
'lpyn tryn wm'tn wtltyn wšt two thousand and two hundred and thirty-six†

mgd *v* to bestow
G pf 3ms *mgd* Inv 12 24:1
wmgd lbwl' zwzyn rbw and he bestowed on the Senate ten thousand zuz's *C3934:4*
(not < Arab [CaGr p 85], see RosSpr p 95, and Bou and Teix on Inv 12 23, note *mgd* in Syriac theophoric name *mgdl*, cf Dri '72 p 26, no. 36, line 1. Note the name *Magadelos* in Gk at Umm-el-Jimal, cf Wuthnow '35 p 68.)

▶ *mgd* n

mgd *nm* gift
s em *mgd'* C3924:5; s or pl em ? *mgd'* Inv 12 23:3; sf 3mpl *mgdyhwn* C3914:3
wnhryn bmgdyhwn šgy'[y'] and illustrious for their man[y] gifts *C3914:3*; *qdš mgd' lmdyth* consecrated as a gift (or: 'as gifts') to his city *Inv 12 23:3*
▶ *mgd* v†

mgn *adv* gratis
mgn C3936:4
dy ʾsq šyrtʾ mgn mn kysh he led up a caravan gratis, at his own expense†

mdʾ *nm* *modius* (a dry measure, a peck)
s ab *mdʾ* Trf:71; em *mdyʾ* Trf:69, 73
yhwʾ yhb lmdyʾ ʾsr ʾṭlq[ʾ] he shall give per *modius* one Italia[n] *assarius* *Trf:133*
(< Gk *modios* < Lat. *modius*)†

mdd *v* to measure
G impf 3ms *ymd* CRAIBL '81:16, 17
mdʿn dy ymd lgbrʾ anything that he measures out to the man†

mdy *pron* what, that which
mdy Trf:60
ʾšrt mdy ktyb mn lthṭ established what is written below *Trf(I):4*; see also at *ḥš* n above (interrog. pron > compound relative)
▶ *mʾ (mʾ dy)* pron

mdynh *nf** city
s ab ? *[md]yt* Trf:139 (see CaGr p 104); cn *mdynt* Inv 9 11:3; em *mdyntʾ* C3994:1; *mdytʾ* Déd p 36:3; sf 3ms *mdynth* Déd 13:3 *mdyth* Inv 10 54:2; 3mpl *mdythwn* C3930:3; pl em *mdyntʾ* Trf:116*
bmdynt bbl in the city of Babylon *Inv 9 11:3*; *yhb mšḥʾ lbny md[yntʾ wl]ʾstr[ṭwmʾ]* he gave oil to the cit[izens and to [the] arm[y] *C3959:4*; *ʿbdt mdyntʾ lDN* the City (i.e. Tadmor) made (this) for DN *C3994:1*; *rḥymy mdythwn* lovers of their city *C3930:3*

mdmr *nm* guard
pl em *[m]dmryʾ* Sem '73 p 121:2
qrbw [m]dmryʾ offered by the [g]uards
▶ *mhdmr* n†

mdnḥ *nm* **1** east (direction); **2** eastern region
s em *mdnḥʾ* C3971:2
1 *ptyḥʾ lʾpʾ mdnḥʾ* open to the east *RB '30 14:6* **2** *ʾpnrṭʾ dy mdnḥʾ klh* governor of the whole eastern empire *C3971:2*; *mlkʾ wmtqnnʾ dy mdn?ḥʾ klh* king of kings and governor of the whole eastern empire *C3946:2*
▶ *mdnḥy* adj†

mdnḥy *adj* eastern
s em *mdnḥyʾ* C4173:1; pl abs *mdnḥyyn* Ber '38 p 124:6; em *mdnḥyʾ* Ber '35 p 98:2
sṭrʾ dnh mdnḥyʾ this eastern side *Syr '38 p 155:1*
▶ *mdnḥ* n

mdʿm *nm* something, anything; (with *lʾ*) nothing
s ab *mdʿm* Trf(I):11; s em *mdʿmʾ* Trf(I):8
nmwsʾ mdʿm any law *Trf:78*; *mdʿm ytyr* anything in excess *Trf(I):11*, Gk *mēden*; *s[yʿ] šyr[tʾ] dy [sl]qt mn ʾlgšyʾ bmdʿm* he [assis]ted the carav[an] that came up from Vologesia in every way *BS III 45:9*; *bdyl [dy] mdʿm lʾ* [...] so that nothing ... *Trf:90*; *wyktb lmdʿmʾ mdʿmʾ* and let him write for every sort of thing *Trf(I):8*, Gk *hekastō eidei* (Frequently treated as pron by grammarians)

▶ *mdʿn* n

mdʿn *nm** 1 anything; thing; (with *lʾ*) nothing; 2 *bmdʿn dy* in such a way
s ab *mdʿn* CRAIBL '81:16
1 *lmntn lDN mdʿn dy* to give to DN anything that *CRAIBL '81:16*; *[wšpr lm]dyth b[k]l mdʿn* [and he did good to] his [c]ity in e[v]erything *C3959:5*; *wlʾ yhʾ šlyṭ lh lmrḥ lʿlwh ... mdʿn* shall not have the right to widen it ... at all *MUSJ '62 p 106:9*; *wmdʿn ʾḥrn lʾ* and nothing else *CRAIBL '81:17** **2** *bmdʿn dy hwʾ mtktb bʾgwryʾ* in such a way that it was written in the tax-collector's contracts *Trf(I):5*; cf *mdʿn kl lmṭl dy plg nsb* in such a way that ? (or: since ?) that part he has taken as his share *MUSJ '62 p 106:7*
▶ *mdʿm* n

mdʿr *nm* ? *reading and meaning uncertain*

md'r' Syr '33 p 187:3†

mh *pron* (with *dy*) that which
mh Syr '36 26:8; 25:10
mh dy kšr[....] [eve]rything that is proper *Syr '36 25:10*; *mh dy bktby' 'ln* what is in these writings *Syr '36 p 353:8*
▶ *m'* pron†

mhdmr *nm* guard
pl ab *mhdmryn* Inv 9 28:3 reading of Gaw '71 pp 413-15
dkyryn wbrykyn 'nš' dy mhdmryn commemorated and blessed be the personnel of the guards Inv 9 28, according to Gaw '71 pp 413-15 not *mhrqryn* diviners; cf Gaw '73b pp 121-124.
(Gaw Syr '71 p 415: ptcp C of *dmr* to guard)

▶ *mdmr* n†

mhymn *adj* trusty, trusted (?)
s em *mhymn'* C4239:1
ṣlm PN gwy' mhymn' statue of PN, the trusted counsellor ? *C4239:1*; or 'eunuch', or 'treasurer' ? see IH no. 100:2 *mhymn'* 'eunuch (treasurer)' with bibliography†

mhryt *adv* promptly, heartily (?)
mhryt C4047:2
DN mwd' mhryt PN PN thanks DN promptly (or: heartily) ?; RosSpr p 82: perhaps a name of Iranian derivation of which the first part would be *mihr*†

mhrqr see *mhdmr* n

mwṭ *nm* variable amount
s cn *mwṭ* Trf:57
yhn mwṭ mks' they will be (charged) a variable amount of tax Gk *to hikanon* 'what is sufficient'†

mwl see *wly* v

mwly' see *wly* v

mwm' *nf* oath
s ab *mwm'* CRAIBL '81:11
mwm' b'drwn' an oath by the cella ?; Teix ad loc. le serment dans la salle de banquet†

mwt *nm* death
s em *mwt'* Inv 10 53:3; *myt'* ? BS III 35:1 see below); sf 3ms *mwth* RSP 103C:4; sf 3mpl *mwthn* Inv 10 119:5
btr mwt' dy PN 'bwhy after the death of PN, his father *Inv 10 53:3*; *mrt myt' BS III 35:1* Dunant ad loc.: maîtresse de la mort; read prb *mrt b!yt'* Mistress of the Temple
▶ *mrt byt'* n phr†

mwtb *nm* presidency
s sf 3ms *mwtbh* Inv 10 63:3; 106:2
'bdt lh bwl' bmwtbh lyqrh which the Senate made for him, during his presidency, in his honor *Inv 10 63:3*†

mḥwz *nm* city
s sf 3ms *mḥwzh* Inv 10 39:2; 3mpl *mḥwzhwn* Inv 9 12:4
rḥym mḥwzh a lover of his city *Inv 10 39:2*; *špr lhwn wlmḥwzhwn* he did good to them and to their city *Inv 9 12:4*; for discussion and extensive bibliography, see AIA p 68; Amadasi Guzzo '82; Teix '83a (defends sense 'harbor' for Palm.)
▶ *lmn* n†

mḥm *nm* heater (person who heats bath)
s cn *mḥm* RSP 162::2
PN mḥm my' PN, the heater of water
(< *ḥmm* C to heat)
▶ *ḥmm* v†

mḥrmh *nf ?* sacred things
pl ab *[m]ḥr[m]n* C3927:4
w'qm [m]ḥr[m]n lDN wDN wDN and he erected sacred things for DN and DN and DN Gk *anathemata*†

mṭ' *v* to belong
G pf 3ms *mṭ'* C4227:1
mṭ' lPN (this) belongs to PN†

mṭy *n* camel-rider (title of deity) ?
mṭy' Doura 47:1 = YCS '55 p 138:1
'rṣw wmṭy' Arsu, the camel-rider; see Ing ad loc on etymology, iconography, and unusual *w*†

mṭl *cj* because, since; in such a way that (context difficult)
mṭl MUSJ '62 p 106:7
md'n kl lmṭl dy plg nsb in such a way that (or: since) that part he has taken as his share
▶ *mṭl kwt* adv; *md'n* n†

mṭlh *nf** portico
s em *mṭlt'* BS III 1:1*; *mṭlth* BS III 2D:1
mṭlt' dh klh 'mwdyh wšryth wṭṭlylh qrb PN ... lDN this entire portico, its columns and its entablature and its ceiling, was offered by PN ... to DN *BS III 1:1*; *w'bd mṭlt' dh mṣ'yt' klh mn kysh* and built this entire middle portico at his own expense *BS III 40:6**; *wbn' hykl' wprn'[yn wkl mṭl]th k[l]h mn kysh lDN* and he built the temple and the front [hall (pronaos) and al]l its [portic]o, at his own expense, for DN *C3959:6*; on sense see Gaw TP pp 61-62
▶ Dunant '73 p 13 for discussion of sense, in view of archaeology

mṭl kwt *adv* therefore
mṭl kwt C3932:6
mṭl kwt shd lh DN 'lh' therefore DN, the god, testified to him†

myyn *nm* water
pl ab *mn* C4218:7, see RosSpr p 16; em *my'* Trf(II):1; *m[y]* ? (or ab *m[n]* ?) Trf:58
[ltš]myš 'ynn trtn dy m[y] dy bmdyt' [for the u]se of the two springs of wat[er] which are in the city *Trf:58*; *wlḥm wmn lm' yšb'* and may he never have enough food and water *C4218:7*

myl *nm* mile
s ab (abbreviation) *m<yl>* C3971:4
m<yl> 14 m(ile) 14 (on column used as milestone)
(< Lat. *mille* 'mile')†

myn *n* deme, tribe ?
pl ab *mynyn* Sem '77 p 117:8 (?)
lšlmyt mynyn mšṭ[rt'] for the treaty written by the demes, so Aggoula ad loc, but word-division and sense very improbable†

myšn *nf* Mayshan
myšn Inv 10 112:4
[prt] m?yšn Forath Mayshan *Inv 10 112:2*; to be restored in Déd p 13:15 *krk' dy myšn*; *mn krk[']* *dy myšn* Inv 10 112:4 Gk *apo tou charakos*; M. is region near Persian Gulf to which Spasinou Charax belongs; in classical sources Mesene, also Characene; Schlumberger '61 p 258: Gk inscription from Palmyra *Maisēnōn*
▶ Chabot ad C3916, on *prt* and Gk *phoratou*; *myšny* adj; Appendix MAPS†

myšny *adj* of Mayshan
s em *myšny[']* Syr '31 18:4
...myšny['] ... the one of Mayshan
▶ *myšn* n†

myt *v* to die
G pf 3ms *myt* C4261:5; 3fs *mytt* C4258:6; 3mpl *myt* Inv 10 4B:3
ḥy' šnyn 76 myt ywm 4 b'dr <4>73 he lived 76 years; died the 4th of Adar, the year (4)73 *C4562:8*; *btr dy myt* after he died, i.e., posthumously *C3920:3*
▶ *mwt* n

myt see *mwt* n

mytb *nm* throne (reading partially conjectural)
s em *myt[b']* RSP 145:2 conjecture of Gaw
mr' myt[b'] Lord of the Thr[one], epithet of Blessed-Be-His-Name-Forever†

mytwy *nf* coming

s em *mytwyt'* C3932:2

bmytwyt' dy 'lh' 'lksndrws qsr at the coming of the god Alexander Caesar Gk *epidēmia*
(on form see Nöldeke 1870 p 94 and fn 2)†

mkl *nm* measure of wine
s ab *mkl* RTP 704; abbreviated *m<kl>* RTP 689

m' m(easure), o(ne) (?) *RTP 572*; *ḥmr plg mkl* wine, a half of a measure *RTP 704*; *m<kl> 1* one m(easure) *RTP 689*; *ḥmr mkl wplg* wine, a measure and a half *RTP 698* :: Déd p 184 'food'

On abbreviations for amounts of money and commodities see Aharoni '77 pp 157-64

mkmn *nf place name, location unknown*
mkmn MUSJ '66 p 178 no. 2:1

lgny' dy mkmn to the Genii of *Mkmn*†

mks *nm** tax, toll
s ab *mks* Trf:108; em *mks'* Trf:149*; sf 3ms *mksh* Trf(I):9; pl em *mksy'* Trf:105

pgryn dy mšṭdn mks l' ḥybyn carcases cast out are not subject to tax *Trf:108*; *mks' ḥyb'* ... is subject to tax *Trf:146*; *yhwn yhbyn mk[s']* they should pay tax *Trf:124*; *mks' gby* tax is collected *Trf(I):14*; *ḥyb mks'* is subject to tax *Trf:106*; *lkl dy 'll lḥšbn tgr' yhw' mks'* for anything that is entered in the merchant's accounts there shall be tax *Trf:115*; *l' 'mr' 'yṭlyq[']* *[t]hw' pr'' [mk]s[']* *lmpq<n>'* Italia[n] wool [s]hall not be liable to import tax *Trf:97*; *[mzbn]y nḥty' dy hpkyn bmdyt' yhn mwṭ mks'* clothes-vendors who go around the city are not subject to fixed ? tax *Trf:57*; *mks' [m]lḥ'* the salt tax *Trf:134*; *wyktb lmd'm' md'm' mksh dy mn 'yd'* and (there) should be written down for everything whatever its customary tax may be *Trf(I):9*; *kšr dy [yh]n mksy' 'py 'sr 'yṭlq[']* it is right that taxes be according to the Italia[n] *assarius Trf:105*. For this word of common occurrence in the Tariff, Gk uses *telos* toll, tax, and derivatives, or in other idioms, *prassein* to exact (taxes)
(< Akk *miksu*; AIA p 72)

▶ *mks* $_{II}$ n

mks *nm** tax-collector, publican
s em *mks'* Trf:38*; pl em *mksy'* Trf(I):7

bdyl dy bṭ'wn dy ktb dy ṭ'' mks['] by mistakes in writing committed by the tax-collector *Trf:100*; *PN mks'* PN, the tax-collector *C4235:2*; *ygb' mks' mn znyt'* the tax-collector shall collect from prostitutes *Trf:47*; *yhw' pr' lmks'* shall pay to the tax-collector *Trf:80*; *srbnyn hww byny tgr' lbyny mksy'* there were many disputes between the merchants and the tax-collectors *Trf(I):7*. Gk uses the verb *teleō* (Trf(I):6), and *passim* nouns *telōnēs* and *dēmosiōnēs*
(< Akk *mākisu* ? ; AIA p 72)
▶ *mks* $_{I}$ n

mlbn *nm* door-frame
s sf 3ms *mlbnh* Inv 12 49:6

w[t]ṭl[yl'] klh wmlbnh wšrgb' dy nḥš['] and the whole [c]eil[ing] and all its door-frame and the bronze hinges. Teix ad loc. *entrée, encadrement*, cf A. Dupont-Sommer CRAIBL '66 p 189. Note use of *tr'* 'gate' as equivalent in nearly duplicate text Inv 12 48:2; Syriac *mlbn'* has sense 'doorpost', LS p 357; for late Hebrew cognate see Dalman '38 and Jastrow; for Akk see von Soden HWB s.vv. *nalbanu* and *nalbattu*. For fuller discussion see Hillers, Notes (forthcoming).†

mlḥ *nm** salt
s ab *mlḥ* Trf:72; em *mlḥ'* Trf:130

[ml]ḥ ṭb [ytg]b' 'sr' ḥd lmdy' good [sal]t shall be taxed an *assarius* for a *modius Trf:69**; *wml[ḥ' d]y b[m]dyt' wtḥwmyh* and the sal[t tha]t is in the [c]ity and its territory *Trf:64*; *Trf:72* Gk *hala[s]*
▶ *mlyḥ* adj

mlṭ *nm* fleece
s em *mlṭ'* Trf(II):11, 67

mn '[rg]wn' mlṭ' lkl m[šk lm'ln'] *wlm[p]qn'* of p[urp]le(?) wool, for every h[ide, imported] or [ex]ported *Trf(II):11* Gk

mēlōtē[s]
(< Gk *mēlōtē* sheepskin)†

mlyḥ *adj* salted
m pl em *mlyḥy'* Trf:34
mn ṭ'wn n[wny]' mlyḥy' for a load of salted f[ish]
▶ *mlḥ* n†

mlk *nm* king
s cn *mlk* C3946:1; em *mlk'* PNO 21:1; pl em *mlk'* C3946:1
ṣlm sptmyws 'dy[nt] mlk mlk' statue of Septimius Ode[nathus], king of kings *C3946:1*; *'mh dy mlk mlk'* mother of the king of kings *C3971:3* Gk *basileōs*

mlk' *nm* Malka (name of deity)
s em *mlk'* PNO 57:1
lyqr mlk' ṭb' wškr' in honor of Malka, the good and generous
▶ Gaw ANRW p 2643; Hof RelAram p 44†

mlkbwl see *mlkbl* n

mlkbl *nm* Malakbel (name of deity)
mlkbl RTP 157; *mlkbwl* Inv 10 144:1, reading somewhat uncertain, form unique
l'glbwl wlmlkbl 'lhy' to Aglibol and to Malakbel, the gods *Inv 12 39:1*
▶ TeixPan passim; Gaw ANRW passim; Hof RelAram pp 33-38; *mlkbl* PN

mlkh *nf* queen
s em *mlkt'* C3971:3
sptymy' btzby nhyrt' mlkt' Septimia Batzabbay, the illustrious, queen *C3971:3*; *b'ltk mlkt'* Baaltak (a deity), the queen *RTP 200*

mmzgn *nm* one who mixes (?)
s em *mmzgn'* Syr '26 p 129:8
wPN mmzgn' and PN, the one who mixed (the wine)†

mn *pron* who, whoever
mn Trf:80
mn dy yṣb' mn bny ddy yḥpr whoever, of my uncle's sons, wants to, may dig *RB '30 9:3*; *wdkyryn kl mn dhw ...* and commemorated be anyone who ... *PNO 56:4*; *wmn mpq mnhwn* and whoever exports any of them *Trf:35*†

mn *prep* **1** from, out of, as part of, on, at, according to, by, per; **2** in several idiomatic combinations
mn Trf:146; sf 3ms *mnh* C3911:4; 3mpl *mnhwn* Trf:35; scribal error ? *mksdr'* from the exedra Ber '35 p 107:2
1 from, out of *dy slq mn GN* who came up from GN *Inv 10 29:3*; *mpqyk mn 'bl' 'l šmlk* as you go out of the vestibule, on your left *RB '30 14:6*; *mn qrn' dy 'ksdr' dy btr bb' w'd zbwqt'* from the angle of the exedra ... up to ... *Ber '35 p 78:2*; *dy l' yhw' gb' 'gwr' mn 'nš md'm ytyr* that the tax-collector should not collect from anyone anything in excess *Trf(I):11*; *mn kl byš' klh* from every kind of trouble *Inv 8 172:1*; *dy 'qym l[h b]wl' wdmws lyqrh mn rḥm'* which the [S]enate and people erected for [him], out of love *C3935:4*; *dy qryb mn 'bd' hdyn* who offered as part of (the expense of) this work *YCS '55 p 131 no. 3:2-3*; *wmn mn tdmry'* and whoever of the Palmyrenes *Trf:132*; *in sense* of: *'ksdryn trn mn m'rt' dh* two exedras of this tomb *Ber '35 p 110:1*; *gwmḥy' 'ln tlt' mšlmnyn dy mn 'ksdr' mqbl'* these three complete niches which belong to (lit.: are of) the exedra facing (you) *Ber '35 p 82V:1*; *gwmḥyn 'rb'' dy mnhwn smlyn tlt' w'ḥrn' m'rby wsmly* four niches, of which three are to the north and the remaining one to the northwest *Ber '35 p 112:3*; *'ḥd mn 'rb'' 'ḥy' dy bnw qbr' dnh* one of the four brothers who built this tomb *C4158:1*; *dy lw' mn bnwhy dkry'* who is not of his male children *Syr '33 p 184:2*; *dy mn bny mtbwl* who is of the Matibol tribe (the Bani Matibol) *C3975:2*; *in sense* on, at *gmḥyn tmny' mn ymynk 'rb'' wmn smlk 'rb''* eight niches, four on your

right and four on your left *C4195:8*; *mn šṭr' ymny' dy bn' qrqsy' gwmḥyn šṭ'* on the south wall, what is between the *kerkides*, six niches *Ber '35 p 97:1*; *in sense* according to: *whww mtgbyn mn ʿyd'* they taxed according to what was customary *Trf(I):5*; *kd hwt bwl' knyš' mn nmws'* when the Senate was lawfully assembled *Trf(I):3*; *mn twḥyt bwl' wdmws* by the decree of the Senate and People *C3959:1*; *in sense* per: *mn ṭʿwn [dh]n' dy ḥmr lmʿln'* per ass-load of [f]at for import *Trf:33*
2 in several idiomatic combinations: *mn kys* X: at one's expense *ʿbd mn kysh PN* PN had it built at his own expense *C3902:1*; to cede: *rḥq mn* or *'ḥbr mn* *PN wPN rḥq lPN mn gmḥyn ʿrbʿ'* PN and PN have ceded to PN four niches *C4171:1*; *'ḥbr PN mn mʿrt' dh lPN* PN has ceded by partnership this hypogeum to PN *C4194:3*
▶ *gw mn* prep; *lgw mn* prep; *lʿl mn* prep; *sṭr mn* prep; *mn btr dy* cj; *mn dy* cj

mn btr dy *cj* after
mn btr dy RSP 24:2
wmn btr dy myt PN dnh and after this PN died†

mn dy *cj* because
mn dy C3923:3
mn dy špr lhn because he was good to them *C3929:4*; *mn [dy] qm bršhwn* because he stood at their head *C3915:2*

mnh $_{\mathrm{I}}$ *nm* mina
pl ab *mnyn* Sem '86 p 89:6
wmnyn ʿšrh wšth and 16 minas†

mnh $_{\mathrm{II}}$ *nf** part, portion
s cn *mnt* RB '30 14:7; em *mnt'* RTP 270; sf 3ms *mnth* RSP 51:2; pl ab *mnwn* RB '30 p 548:5
yhb mnth mnt' he has given his share as a part (i.e.: installment) *RB '30 p 545:2* Gk *edōken [k]ata[d]osin* ʿgave as an installment'; Déd p 19: ʿgave as a legacy' Gk *kata dosin*, but latter Gk expression also in sense ʿpart, installment'; *wmnt klh tlt 'mm' d[y yh]bt lPN* and the part of the whole, three cubits, [which] she [g]ave to PN *RB '30 14:7*; *yhbt lh wbʿdt p[l]gwt mnt[']* *'ḥd' dydh mn mnwn tlt dy mʿrt'* she has given and ceded to him ha[l]f of the portion, the one belonging to her, of three portions of the cave *RB '30 14:4**; *[m]lkbl mnt'* Malakbel. Portion *RTP 270*

mnw *pron* whoever
mnw Ber '38 p 133:1
mnw dy yzbn ʿrb' dy qdm mʿrt' whoever sells the security ? in front of the hypogeum
(pron *man* ʿwho?' + pron *hû* ʿhe')
▶ *mn* pron†

mnwt *nf* Manawat (name of deity)
s ab *mnwt* Inv 12 49:7
hykl' dy mnwt the temple of Manawat *Inv 12 48:2*; *ʿlt' dh qrb PN lmnwt* this altar offered by PN to Manawat *Inv 11 46:2*
▶ TeixPan pp 12-18; Gaw ANRW p 2624; Hof RelAram p 43

mn lgw *adv* inside
mn lgw RB '30 9:2
yḥpr lh mn lgw let him dig inside†

mn lʿl *adv* above
mn lʿl C4190:5
hyk dy ktyb mn lʿl as is written above *Trf:68*

mn ltḥt *adv* below
mn ltḥt Trf(I):4
mdy ktyb mn ltḥt what is written below Gk *ta hypotetagmena*†

mnʿym *nm* Munim, Monimos (name of deity)
mnʿym Sem '72 p 59:2
mṣb' dnh lmnʿym gny' ṭb' wškr' this stele is for Munim, the good and generous deity

(Arab IV form part)
▶ *mnʿym* PN; Dri '72b, pp 362-365; Gaw ad RSP 151; TeixPan pp 68-69; Gaw ANRW p 2637†

mnp *nm* Manaf (name of deity)
mnp RTP 219
tmwzʾ wmnp Tammuz and Manaf
▶ Hof RelAram p 41†

mn qdm *prep* before
mn qdm BS III 61B:4
dkyryn wbrykyn PN PN mn qdm[...] commemorated and blessed be PN (and?) PN before [name of deity]†

msyʿn *nm* helper, assistant
pl em *msyʿnʾ* Syr '26 p 129:8
wmsyʿnʾ klhwn and all the assistants†

mʿh *nf* coin, obol
pl ab *mʿyn* Sem '86 p 89:5
wzwz ḥd wmʿyn trtyn and one zuz and two obols†

mʿl *nm* entering, going in
s em *mʿlʾ* RB '30 p 358:2; sf 2ms *mʿlk* Ber '35 p 78; *mʿl<k>* RSP 163:3; *mʿlyk* C4204:2 (CaGr p 64); 1pl *mʿln* Ber '35 p 86:10
plgʾ mʿlʾ ʿl ymynʾ the half on the right as one enters *RB '30 p 358:2*; *ʾksdrʾ mʿlk ʿl smlk klh* the whole exedra on the left as one enters *Ber '35 p 77:1*; *sṭrʾ klh dy mʿlk ʿl ymynk* the whole side which is on your right as you go in *Ber '35 p 78:2*; *bʾksdrʾ tymnyʾ mʿlyk ʾksdrʾ ʿl ymynʾ* in the southern exedra, on your right as you enter the exedra *C4204:2*; *bgw mʿrtʾ mʿlyk mn bbʾ ʿl ymynʾ* inside the hypogeum, on your right as you come in the door *Ber '35 p 60:1*; *mʿln ʾksdrʾ ʿl smln* as we enter the exedra on our left *Ber '35 p 86:10*
▶ *mʿlh* n; *mʿln* n; *ʿll* v

mʿlh *nf** vestibule
s em *m[ʿ]ltʾ* Inv 1 5:1
m[ʿ]ltʾ dh klh ʿmwdyh wšryth wttlylh this whole vestibule, its columns, its entablature, and its ceiling
▶ *mʿl* n; *mʿln* n; *ʿll* v†

mʿln *nm* import
s ab *mʿln* Trf:66; em *mʿlnʾ* Trf(II):8
lmʿln ṭʿwn g[m]lʾ d<ynryn> 13 for import, per ca[m]el-load, 13 d(enarii) *Trf:24*; *lmʿlnʾ d<ynryn> 4 wlmpqnʾ d<ynryn> 4* for import, 4 d(enarii) and for export, 4 d(enarii) *Trf:67*
▶ *mʿl* n; *mʿlh* n; *ʿll* v

mʿn *nm* Maan, Maanu (name of deity)
mʿn PNO 7A:2; 35A:3; *mʿnw* RTP 249
lʿbgl wlmʿn ʾlhyʾ ṭbyʾ wškryʾ for Abgal and for Maan, the good and generous gods *PNO 7A:2*; *mṣbyʾ ʾln mʿn wšʿd ʾlhyʾ* these idols are Maan and Shaadu, the gods *PNO 35C:1*
▶ TeixPan pp 81-83; Gaw ANRW p 2637; Hof RelAram p 41†

mʿnw see *mʿn* n

mʿrb *nm* west
s em *mʿrbʾ* Syr '26 p 129:6
wḥmr bzqyn lʾ ʾyty mn mʿrbʾ and he did not bring wine in skins from the west :: Déd p 153 'mixed'
▶ *mʿrby* adj†

mʿrby *adj* **1** western; **2** western part
m s ab *mʿrby* Ber '35 p 112:5; cn *mʿrby* Ber '38 p 110:5; f s em *mʿrbytʾ* C4175:7; m pl abs *mʿrbyyn* Ber '38 p 124:7
1 *gwmḥyn mʿrbyyn štʾ mʿlyk ʾksdrʾ* six niches on the west as you enter the exedra *Ber '38 p 124:7*; *dy mnhwn smlyn tltʾ wʾḥrnʾ mʿrby* of which three are to the north and the other is to the west *Ber '35 p 112:5*; *gwmḥyn tltʾ dkn mʿrbyʾ* three clean niches on the west (note inconcinnity in grammar) *Ber '35 p 98:2* **2** *mʿrby ʾksdrʾ* in the western part of the exedra *Ber '38 p 110:5*

▶ *mʿrb* n

mʿrh *nf** hypogeum
s em *mʿrtʾ* C4199:1*
mʿrtʾ dh bt ʿlmʾ ʿbd PN this hypogeum, an eternal home, was built by PN *Ber ʾ35 p 115:1*; *mʿrtʾ dnh dy bt ʿlmʾ ḥpr wbnʾ wṣbt mn kysh PN* this hypogeum which is an eternal home, was dug and built and decorated at his own expense by PN *Inv 4 13:1*; *qbrʾ dnh wmʿrtʾ dy bnʾ PN* this tomb and hypogeum, built by PN *C4122:1*; *npšʾ dh wmʿrtʾ ʿbdw PN wPN* this monument and tomb made by PN and PN *Syr ʾ85 2:1*, Gk *spēlaiō*; *wrštʾ ... dy bytʾ wmʿrtʾ* heiress(?) of house and hypogeum *C4176C:2*

mpq *nm* going out; exit
s sf 2ms *mpqyk* RB '30 14:6
mpqyk mn ʾblʾ ʿl šmlk as you go out the door on your left
▶ *mʿl* n†

mpqn *nm* export
s ab *mpqn* Trf:66; em *mpqnʾ* Trf:27; *mmpqnʾ* Trf:143 is due to dittography
lmʿlnʾ d<ynryn> 4 wlmpqnʾ d<ynryn> 4 for import 4 d(enarii) and for export 4 d(enarii) *Trf:67*. Gk passim *ekkomisthentos*

mprnsy *nf* guardian, foster-mother
s em *mprnsytʾ* Ber '38 p 124:5
wPN brt ḥry PN mprnsytʾ dy PN brh PN(f), freedwoman of PN, foster-mother of PN, his son†

mṣb *nm** idol; statue, bas-relief
s cn *mṣb* C4064:6; em *mṣbʾ* C3972:1*; pl em *mṣbyʾ* PNO 35C:1
yrḥbwl ʾlhʾ ṭbʾ mṣbʾ dy ʿynʾ Yarhibol, the good god, the idol of the spring *Doura 33:2*; *lmrt bytʾ mṣbʾ dy nṣb PN* (on a votive altar) to the Mistress of the Temple, the idol erected by PN *RSP 143:3; mṣbʾ dnh nṣb PN* (on a stele below bas-relief of god Shadrafa) this idol erected by PN (see Gaw ANRW p 2615; the serpent around the lance is the clue to the identification of the deity in question) *C3972:1*; *mṣbʾ dnh nṣb PN* (on base of bas-relief) this stele set up by PN *Inv 11 87*; *mṣbyʾ ʾln mʿn wšʿd ʾlhyʾ* these images are Maan and Saad, the gods *PNO 35C:1*; *ḥgbʾ wmṣbʾ ʿbd PN lDN* the shrine and image made by PN for DN *Sem ʾ77 p 117:2*; *mṣbʾ* statue (beneath bas-relief) *Doura no. 23:2*, Gk *andrianta*; cf du Mesnil TMP pp 725-26
▶ Gaw MF p 10 note 10; Gaw '90b p 106; *nṣbh* n

mṣbh *nf* idol; statue, bas-relief
pl abs *mṣbt* BS III 45:5
mṣbt bšm bwlʾ [wdm]sʾ statues in the name of the Senate and People, Gk seems to be *andriasi dēmosiois*
▶ *mṣb* n; *nṣbh* n†

mṣʿh *nf* midst (?)
s cn *mṣʿt* CRAIBL '81:17
ymd mṣʿt gwʾ he shall measure within the inner group ?
▶ *mṣʿy* adj†

mṣʿy *adj* middle; central
f s em *mṣʿytʾ* BS III 40:6
wʿbd mṭltʾ dh mṣʿytʾ klh and he built this whole central portico
▶ *mṣʿh* n†

mṣry *adj* Egyptian
f s ab *mṣryt* C4547:5
ḥbl PN mṣryt Alas! PN(f), (the) Egyptian†

mqbrh *nf** tomb
s em *mqbrtʾ* Syr '36 27:1*
yḥpr wytqn lh mqbrtʾ let him dig the tomb and make it ready for himself *RB ʾ30 p 539:4*; *bt mqbrtʾ dh bnʾ PN* this tomb was built by PN *C4170:1*; *mqbrtʾ dh ʿbd PN* this tomb was made by PN *Syr ʾ36 27:1*†

mqymh *nf meaning uncertain*
s em *mqymt'* Syr '36 26:3
[...]bmqymt' kl dy ktyb[...] [...] in perpetuity ? (thus Cantineau ad loc.) all that is written [...]; see also Gaw TP pp 57-58
⯈ *mqmw* n†

mqlw *nf* burnt offering
pl em *[m]qlwt'* C3927:3 see Déd pp 3-4; *mql[wt']* CRAIBL '81:4; *[mql]wt'* C3998:3
dy mgd lh ḥr[m]' lʿlm' w[m]qlwt' because he endowed for it a perpetual distribution of gifts, and [burnt] offerings *C3927:3* see Gaw ad RSP 130 Gk *thysian*; cf *Inv 6 13* (Gk) *[holo]k[a]ust[on] th[ysia]n*; cf Déd pp 3-4; 146-47
(< Akk *maqlūtu* prb; AIA p 70, cf *mqlw* in OffAram AP 33:10=TAD 1 A4.10; see now Lipiński '92, pp 305-11)†

mqmw *nf* place, stead
s cn *mqmwt* RB '30 14:2
PN bmqmwt PN bʿlh PN(f), in the place of PN her husband; see Déd p 304; *mqymh* n†

mrʾ *nm* master, lord (also as title of deity)
s cn *mr'* C3912:1; sf 1pl *mrn* BS III 45:7; 3mpl *mrhwn* C3946:4; pl sf 3ms *mrwhy* Inv 11 13:7
qdm mr' ʾlh' before the Lord of the gods *RSP 154:2*; *lbʿlšmn mr' ʿlm'* to Baalshamin, the Lord of the world *C3912:1*; *[lbryk šm]h lʿlmh mr' kl* [to Blessed-be-his-name-]forever, the Lord of all *C3998:1*; *[l]ʾ[lh' rb'] m[r]' nšmt'* [to the great] g[od], the l[or]d of (all) that have breath *Ber '36 p 99:1*; *why' bn' mrwhy* and the life of the children of his masters *Inv 11 13:7*; *qsr mrn* our lord Caesar *C3938:3*
⯈ *mrh* n; *mr'gr'* n; *ʾlh* n; *mr' kl* s.v. *kl*

mrʾgrʾ *nm* contractor (?)
s em *mr'gr'* C4218:2
PN mr'gr' PN, the contractor (?); specific office designated uncertain; possibly 'head of market' or another office (Cf perhaps Syriac *māre agrā* 'hirer, master' Payne Smith *Syriac Dictionary* p 299; note Akk use of *mār X* in designations of professions)†

mrbyh *nf* foster-mother
s c *mrbyt* SFP 141:4; sf 3ms *mrbyth* C4479:4, PS 210:1; 3mpl *mrbythwn* Inv 8 63:9; *mrbythn* Syr '71 p 422:6; ? *lmrby[t']* Inv 11 78:3 (see Gaw Syr '71 p 423); ? *mrbt[']* RSP 172:2 (reading uncertain)
PN dy ʿbd lh mrbyth PN ḥbl (under relief of boy and his sister) PN, made for him by PN(f), his foster-mother. Alas! *C4479:4*; see Parlasca '82 pp 22 and notes 240-43
⯈ *mrbyn* n†

mrbyn *nm* foster-father
s sf 3ms *mrbynh* C4478:3; Inv 11 78:3 ? *mrby[nh]* so tentatively Teix p 46
ʿb[d] mrbynh lyqrh ma[de] by his foster-father, in his honor; cf in Old Syriac inscription (6 C. E.) *mrbyn'* Dri '72a no. 1:3
⯈ *mrbyh* n†

mrbʿ *nm meaning and analysis uncertain*
s em ? *mrbʿ'* Syr '33 p 187:3 cf Déd pp 32-33
šry lmrbʿ' began ? the ... ; Déd p 33: 'to take the tax of 25%'†

mrh *nf* lady, sovereign
s sf 3mpl *mrthwn* C3947:4
PN wPN ʾqym lmrthwn PN and PN erected to their sovereign (Zenobia) Gk *despoinan*
⯈ *mrt byt'* n phr†

mrzḥ *nm* symposium (religious association for dining)
s ab *mrzḥ* CRAIBL '81:4; cn *mrzḥ* Syr '59 p 105:1; em *mrzḥ'* RTP 27
bny mrzḥ the members of (the) symposium *RTP 301*; *brbnwt mrzḥ' PN* during the term as symposiarch of PN *RTP 34*; *mrzḥ bʿltk wPN* symposium of Baaltak and PN *Syr '59 p 105:1*; *PN rb mrzḥ'* PN, head of the symposium *RTP 33*
⯈ *mrzḥw* n; Hof RelAram pp 28-29

mrzḥw *nf* term as symposiarch, i.e. head of a symposium (following *rbnwt*)
s cn *mrzḥwt* C3970:1; sf 3ms *mrzḥwth* C3919:4
brbnwt mrzḥwt PN during the term as symposiarch of PN *C3970:1*
(double abstract formation, *-ūt* is added to each part of a fixed phrase *rb mrzḥ*)
▶ *mrzḥ* n

mrt byt' *n phr f* the Lady of the Temple (name of deity)
s ab *mrt byt'* C3977A:3
lmrt byt' for the Lady of the Temple *C3977A:3*; *lmrt byt' mṣb' dy nṣb PN* for the Lady of the Temple, the idol erected by PN *RSP 143:3*; *[lb'lšm]n wdrḥl[wn] wmrt b!yt'* [for Baalshami]n and Durahlun and the Lady of the Temple *BS III 35:1*; Lady of *myt'* Death is the reading preserved, according to Dunant, but resulting title is improbable
▶ TeixPan p 24†

mrt myt' see *mrt byt'* n phr

mšḥ *nm* **1** oil; **2** olive tree (?)
s ab *mšḥ* Trf:28; em *mšḥ'* RTP 131; abbreviation *m<šḥ'>* RTP 160
1 *mn dy yhw' mzbn mšḥ' bšym'* anyone who sells perfumed oil *Trf:46*; *'glbwl mlkbl m<šḥ'> 1 ḥ<mr'> 1* Aglibol, Malakbel. 1 o(il), 1 w(ine) *RTP 160*; *byt mšḥ'* house of oil *RSP 199:5* (or anointing, so Gawlikoski '73b p 117); *yhb mšḥ' lbny md[ynt']* he gave unguent to all the citi[zens] *C3959:3* Gk *alimma* (i.e.: *aleimma*) **2** *bl gd mšḥ'* Bel, protective Fortune of the oil, or olive *tree* ? *RTP 131, 132*, so Cantineau, see Caquot RTP p 146, Hof RelAram pp 29-30 :: Gaw '73b p 117

mšk *nm* skin, hide
s ab *mšk* Trf(II):11, 56, 67; em *mšk'* Trf:56
lkl mšk lm'ln' d<ynryn> 4 for every hide imported, 4 d(enarii) *Trf:67*†

mškn *nm* pledge
s em *mškn'* RSP 199:8; sf 3ms *mšknh* Syr '36 26:10
wysb mšknh and he takes his pledge *Syr '36 26:10*, see Déd p 300; *[yn]tn mškn'* and [he] will give the pledge *RSP 199:8*†

mšl *nm* fork (?)
s em *mšl'* Syr '36 17:5
plgwt ['']lt' dh wmšl' wbt nḥry' half of this [al]tar and the fork ? and the slaughtering-place ? :: Déd p 220 'system of water channels'; Gaw TP p 61 leaves untranslated†

mšlm *adj* finishing (?)
m s ab *mšlm* Ber '35 p 93:2
byrḥ 'lwl mšlm šnt 497 in the month of Elul, finishing(?) the year 497, see Ing ad loc. for discussion of calendric implications and difficulties†

mšlmn *adj* complete
m pl ab *mšlmnyn* Ber '35 p 84:1
gwmḥy' 'ln tlt' mšlmnyn these three complete burial-niches *Ber '35 p 82(V):1*†

mšmš *nm* officiant
pl cn *mšmšy* RTP 304
nbw ybrk mšmšy pḥdy' may Nabu bless the tribal officiants†

mšry *nf* camp
s em *mšryt'* Inv 11 70:2
prš [b]ḥyrt' wbmšryt' dy 'n' cavalryman [in] Hirta and in the camp at Ana *C3973:3*†

mtqnn *nm* governor (Gk *epanorthōtēs*, Lat. *corrector* or *restitutor*)
s em *mtqnn'* C3946:2
ṣlm sptmyws 'dy[nt] mlk mlk' wmtqnn' dy mdn?ḥ' klh statue of Septimius Ode[nathus], king of kings and governor of all the eastern empire; on sense in this historical context see Swain '93†

nbw *nm** Nabu (name of deity)
s ab *nbw* RTP 302
nbw ybrk mšmšy pḥdy' may Nabu bless the

tribal officiants *RTP 304**; *ʾgn bl wnbw* symposium of Bel and Nabu *RTP 137*

TeixPan pp 106-11; Gaw ANRW p 2645; Hof RelAram p 44

nbṭy *adj* Nabataean

m s em *nbṭyʾ* C3973:2

PN nbṭyʾ PN, the Nabataean†

nbʿ *v* to offer ([?] analysis and meaning uncertain)

G pf ? *wnbyʿt* C4093:2

wnbyʿt wzkrt and I offered ? and I remembered ?†

ndr *v* to vow

G pf 3ms *ndr* PNO 14:5

PN lgnyʾ šʿydʾ dy ndr lhwn PN to the Helping Genii, that which he vowed to them (i.e. an altar)†

nhwryt *adv* splendidly

nhwryt Inv 10 44:7

wʿbd plṭyʾ šbyḥyt wnhwryt and he conducted his political career in a praiseworthy and splendid way; restored in Déd p 13:4

▶ *nhyr* adj†

nhyr *adj* illustrious

m s em *nhyrʾ* C3945:2; f s em *nhyrtʾ* C3947:1; m pl ab *nhryn* C3914:3

ṣlm spṭmyws ʾdynt nhyrʾ hpṭyqʾ mrn statue of Septimius Odenathus, the illustrious, the consul, our lord *C3945:2*, Gk *lam[protaton]*; *ṣlmt spṭmyʾ btzby nhyrtʾ wzdqt[ʾ] mlktʾ* statue of Septimia Batzabbay, illustrious and pious, the queen *C3947:1* Gk *lamprotatēn*; *ṣlmʾ dnh dy spṭmyws ḥyrn br ʾdynt snqltyqh nhyrʾ wrš tdmwr* this statue is of Septimius Hairan, son of Odenathus, illustrious senator and head of Tadmor *C3944:2* Gk *lamprotaton*; *wrḥymʾ mdythwn wnhryn bmgdyhwn šgyʾ[yʾ]* and lovers of their city and lavish in their many gifts *C3914:3* Gk *philoteimois*

▶ *nhwryt* adv

nwyt *prep ?* as (?); corresponding to (?); next to (?)

nwyt MUSJ '62 p 106:8; Déd p 36:4

plg nsb mnth plgh rwḥʾ nwyt gmḥwhy tltʾ the half he has taken as his share, his half, is a space corresponding to three niches *MUSJ '62 p 106:8*; *nwyt šʾwr pḥzʾ bt ʾlhyhwn* just as ? the rest of the tribes (did) in their temples Déd p 36:4, so Milik :: Ing RosAH glossary: 'next to'†

nwn *nm* fish

pl em *n[wny]ʾ* Trf:34

mn ṭʿwn n[wny]ʾ mlyḥyʾ from a load of smoked f[ish]†

nwr *nm* amount (?)

s cn *nwr̊* C3948:3

bdyl dy ḥsknwn nwr̊ dnryn dy dhb ʿtyqyn tlt mʾh because he spent on them the amount of(?) three hundred old denarii, in gold Gk *analōmatōn*; reading *nwr̊* is certain (not *zwd*) see Cantineau ad Inv 3 28 but etymology and precise sense unexplained

nzly *nf* Nazala (name of town near Qaryatein)

s ab *nzly* C3911:8, 9

PN wPN tdmryʾ [dy] bnzly lʾlhʾ rbʾ dnzly PN and PN, the Tadmoreans [who are] in Nazala, to the great god of Nazala *C3911:8-9*, see Chabot ad loc. on identification, in a Gk inscription *theō megalō nazal[ōn]*†

nḥr *nm* slaughter

pl em *nḥryʾ* Syr '36 17:5

wmšlʾ wbt nḥryʾ and the ... (uncertain word; see *mšl* n) and the place for slaughter†

nḥš *nm* bronze

s ab *nḥš* Syr '36 20:9; em *nḥšʾ* C3952:4

ṣlm dy nḥš a statue (made) of bronze *Syr '36 20:9*; *[ʿl] ṣlmy nḥšʾ ʾdrṭyʾ* [concerning] statues of bronze, (that is,) images *Trf:128*; see Herzig and Schmidt-Colinet '91 p 69, on archaeological evidence

nḥt *v* to go down
G pf 3fs *nḥtt* Inv 10 111:3; 3mpl *nḥtw* Inv 10 124:3; *nḥt* C3933:4
bny šyrt' dy nḥt ʿmh lʾlgšy' the caravaneers who went down with him to Vologesia *C3933:4*†

nḥt *nm* garment
pl em *nḥty'* Trf:57
[mzbn]y nḥty' dy hpkyn bmdyt' itinerant [vendor]s of clothes within the city Gk *himatiopōlai*†

nḥtwm *nm* baker
s em *nḥ!twm'* Inv 11 32:5
PN nḥ!twm' PN, the baker; Stark *Personal Names* pp 39, 99 takes as PN *nhtwm'*, unexplained
(< Akk *nuḫatimmu*; AIA p 79)
▶ Hillers, Notes (forthcoming)†

nṭr *v* to watch, guard
G pf 3mpl *nṭrw* Syr '70 p 413:4; ptcp m pl ab *nṭryn* Doura 39:3 ?, pl con *n[ṭ]ry* Doura 40:2, Milik '67 p 564 fn 3 rejects both readings
dy nṭrw tnn who kept watch here *Syr '70 p 413:4*
▶ *nṭr* n†

nṭr *nm* guard
pl ? em *nṭr'* Inv 9 28:9
dhw' qym ʿl ʿmwd' [or ʿmwr'] wbt nṭr' who was in charge of the columns (or, with Milik, Déd, p 277: inhabitants) and the chamber of the guards
▶ *nṭr* v†

nyḥh *nf* repose
s cn *nyḥt* C3907:1
npš' dnyḥt ṭm' PN monument for the repose of the bones of PN *C3907:1*; cf the consonant sequence *[...]tnyḥ' dnh Inv 11 67:1* and comments of Teix: maison de repos, cf *nyḥ'* in Nabataean-Gk bilingual (*anapauma*) and comments of Milik '58 p 242†

nysn *nm* Nisan (name of month = April)
s ab *nysn* C3919:5
▶ Appendix CALENDAR

nyq' *nf** Nike, statue of Victory
s ab/em *nyq'* Syr '38 p 155:2*
mʿlyk bb' rb' ʿd nyq' dy qym' lqblh as you enter the great gate, up to the statue of Victory which stands before it Gk *neikēs*
▶ PN *nyq'*†

nksyn *nm* property (?); victims (?)
pl sf 3mpl *nksyhwn* C3977B:1
ʾlhy' wnksyhwn ... the gods, and their property ? (or: sacrificial victims ?)†

nkry *adj* alien
m s ab *nkry* Syr '33 p 184:2
mn dy yʿl ltnn swm nkry dy lw' mn bnwhy dkry' whoever brings in here a corpse that does not belong here, which is not of his male descendants†

nmws *nm* law
s em *nmws'* Trf(I):3
kd hwt bwl' knyš' mn nmws' when the Senate was lawfully assembled *Trf(I):3*, Gk *nomimou*; *mks' dy ʿlymt' hyk dy nmws' mwḥ' pšqt* the tax on girls, as shown in the law, I have explained *Trf:125*; *wktb ʿm nmws' qdmy'* and let it be written along with the former law *Trf(I):9*; *bnmws' dy mks' ʿbydn šgyn ḥybn mks' l' ʾsqw* in the tax law many things subject to tax were omitted *Trf(I):4*; *hyk bnmws' whyk dy ʾšr qrblwn kšyr'* as it stands in the law and as the excellent Corbulo confirmed *Trf:120*; *mdʿm dy l' msq bnmws'* anything omitted from the law *Trf(I):8*; *[hyk dy] ktyb bnmws'* [... as it is] written in the law *Trf:87*; Gk passim forms of *nomos*
(< Gk *nomos*)†

nmsys *nf* Nemesis (name of deity)
nmsys Inv 12 55:2; Doura 12:1
wlʿštrt wlnmsys wlʾrṣw and to Astarte and

to Nemesis and to Arsu *Inv 12 55:2* (< Gk name of deity *nemesis*)
▶ TeixPan p 17; Gaw ANRW p 2642†

nmš *nf** monument
s em *nmšʾ* C4157:3
PN ʾpmlṭʾ dy nmšʾ dh PN, curator of this monument
▶ *npš* n†

nny *nf* Nanay (name of deity)
s ab *nny* RTP 238
lḥrtʾ wlnny wlršp ʾlhyʾ for Herta and for Nanay and for Rashap, the gods *Syr ʾ36 17:6*
▶ TeixPan pp 111-113; Gaw ANRW p 2645; Hof RelAram p 45

nsb *v* to take
G pf 3ms *nsb* MUSJ ʼ62 p 106:7; impf 3ms *ysb* C4050:9; ptcp pass m s ab *nsyb* C3977A:4
plg nsb mnth one-half he has taken (as) his portion *MUSJ p 106:7*; *wysb mšknh* and he will take his pledge *Syr ʾ36 26:10*†

npl *v* to be necessary (?) to chance to happen (?)
G ptcp f s ab ? *nplʾ* IP 34:7
kl ṣbw dnplʾ everything necessary ? or: every thing that chances to happen ? see RosSpr p 51, CaGr p 98†

npq *v* C **1** to export; **2** to pay, spend
C pf 3ms *ʾpq* Inv 10 44:5; impf 3ms *ypq* Trf(II):6; ptcp active m s ab *mpq* Trf:81; ptcp pass ms ab *mʾpq* Trf:111, CaGr p 91, RosSpr p 29
1 *whn zbwnʾ ypq ʿly[m]yn* and if the buyer exports sla[v]es *Trf(II):6* Gk *[eks]agētai*; *mt[ʾʿ]l br mn tḥwmʾ ʾw mʾpq* im[por]ted from outside the territory or exported *Trf:111* Gk *eksagētai*
2 *ʾpq mn kysh npqn rbrbn* he spent out of his own pocket great sums *Inv 10 44:5*
▶ *mpqn* n; *npq* n

npqh *nf* expense, sum
pl abs *npqn* Inv 10 44:6
ʾpq mn kysh npqn rbrbn he spent out of his own pocket great sums†

npš *nf** **1** self; **2** tomb, funerary monument; **3** image; **4** uncertain, perhaps same as 2; **5** *bt npšʾ* monument, lit. house which is a monument
s cn *npš* C4597:1; em *npšʾ* Inv 8 64:1; sf 3ms *npšh* Inv 4 13:2
1 *ʿl npšh ḥṭʾ* does wrong to himself *Ber ʾ38 p 133:9*; *lnpšh wlPN* for himself and for PN Inv 4 13:2 Gk *heautō*; *wlʾ ʾḥ[y]s npšh* and he did not spare himself *Déd p 36:3* **2** (on sense tomb, funerary monument, see Gaw MF pp 7-43; van der Horst ʼ91 pp 41-44) *npš dnh dy PN* this tomb belongs to PN *MUSJ ʾ49 p 45:1*; *npšʾ dh wmʿrtʾ ʿbd PN* this monument and hypogeum (were) made by PN *Inv 4 7A:1**; *npšʾ dh ʿbd PN* (on slab) this monument was made by PN *Syr ʾ85 p 274:1* Gk *[mn]ēmeion*; *npšʾ dPN* this monument belongs to PN *Inv 8 64:1*; *npšʾ dnyḥt ṭmʾ PN* monument for the repose of the bones of PN *C3907:1* **3** *npš PN* monument/image of PN *C4597:1*; *npšʾ dnh dy PN* this monument/image belongs to PN *C3908bis:1*; *npšʾ PN dy ʿbd lh PN* this image/monument is PN, made for him by PN C4328:1 (under relief of male figure) **4** *whʾ npšʾ dh mwlyʾ bšmš* obscure phrase, perhaps: and here is this monument, adjacent, in the sun *Inv 8 6:3* **5** *bt npšʾ* and *bnpšʾ* monument, lit. house which is a monument *bnpšʾ dPN* tomb of PN *BethSh p 198:1*; *bt npšʾ dnh dPN* This monument belongs to PN *BethSh p 203:1* according to Gk evidence = *mnēma*; cf *qbwr* n and *bt qbwrʾ* s. v. *by* n
▶ *nmš* n

nṣb *v* to erect
G pf 3ms *nṣb* C3972:2
mṣbʾ dnh nṣb PN PN erected this stele *C3972:2*; *nṣb PN ... [l]DN* PN erected this ... for DN *PNO 79:1*; *lDN mṣbʾ dy nṣb PN* for DN, the stele which PN erected *RSP 143:3*
▶ *mṣb* n; *nṣbh* n

nṣbh *nf** stele
s em *nṣbt'* Inv 12 31:3*
nṣbt' dh w'lt' 'bd PN PN made this stele and altar; cf offering of *'lt'* and *nṣbt'* in Old Syriac inscription (165 C.E.) Dri '72a no. 23:3; cf no. 24:4, 9
▶ *nṣb* v†

nrgl *nm* Nergal (name of deity)
s ab *nrgl* RTP 227
bl'str nrgl Belastor, Nergal *RTP 127*
TeixPan pp 111-114; ANRW p 2646†

nšmh *nf* breathing things, living things
pl em *nšmt'* Ber '36 p 99:1
[l]'[lh' rb'] m[r]' nšmt' [to the great] g[od], l[or]d of living things†

ntyrh *nf* grain or fruit that drops by itself, windfall (?)
f pl em [nt]yrt' Trf:123
'šb[y]' w[nt]yrt' 'tḥzy (about) hay and [things that] drop ? it was decided

ntn *v* to give, pay
G impf 3ms *ytn* Trf:70; *yntn* RSP 199:7; inf *lmntn* CRAIBL '81:16
ytn lkl rgly [d]<ynryn> 12 he shall pay for every individual 12 d(enarii) *Trf(II):6*; *[yn]tn mškn'* he [shall] give a pledge *RSP 199:8*

s *abbr s<l'> n* sela, a coin

sbr *nm* teacher
s em *sbr'* Inv 9 4A:2
dkyr PN sbr' commemorated be PN, the teacher (exact sense uncertain) Gk *kathēgētēs* 'teacher, guide'†

sdq *nm* syndic, public advocate (agent who carried out business of city)
pl em *sdqy'* Trf(I):11
wyhw' mbṭl l'rkwny' dy hwn bzbn zbn w'šrt' wsdqy' and it should be of concern to the archons of any given time and to the Dekaprotoi and the Syndics Gk *syndiko[us]* (< Gk *syndikos* 'public advocate')†

sdrp' see *šdrp* n

shd *v* to testify, give a testimonial
G pf 3ms *shd* C3932:6; 3fs *shdt* Syr '36 p 280:5
mṭl kwt shd lh yrḥbwl 'lh' on this account DN the god gave a testimonial to him *C3932:6*; *shdt lh bdgm bwl' wdms* the Senate and People gave him a testimonial, by a decree Syr '36 p 280:5
▶ *šhd* v

swm *nm* body; self
s ab *swm* Syr '33 p 184:2; sf 3ms *swmh* Syr '36 20:5
mn dy y'l ltnn swm nkry whoever brings in here a dead body that does not belong here *Syr '33 p 184:2*; *w'ml bswmh* and he labored personally *Syr '36 20:5*; see Déd pp 311-312 (< Gk *sōma*)†

swsy *nm* horse
s ab *swsy* Syr '36 20:7
ṣlm mrkb swsy an equestrian statue†

sṭr *nm** side, wall
s em *sṭr'* C4175:5*
sṭr' dnh m'rby' m'lyk bb' 'l smlk this western side, on your left as you enter the door *C4204:1*; *sṭr' klh dy m'lk 'l ymynk* the whole wall as you enter on your right *Ber '35 p 78:1*; *mn sṭr' mdnḥy' dy 'ksdr' tymny'* the east side of the south exedra *C4173:1*
▶ *šṭr* n; *sṭr mn* prep

sṭr mn *prep* except for
sṭr mn Ber '38 p 124:2
sṭr mn gwmḥ' ḥd except for one burial niche *Ber '35 p 86:11*
▶ *sṭr* n; *šṭr mn* prep†

sybw *nf* old age
s ab *sybw* Ber '36 p 99:6
mn ṭlyw 'd sybw from youth to old age†

sywn *nm* Siwan (name of month = June)

s ab *sywn* C4167:1 (spelling *syyn* for *sywn* in C4258:8 [cf *yym* C4258:6] is an aberration)
▶ Appendix CALENDAR

sym *v* to place
G pf 3fs *smt* PNO 6D:1
smt PN placed by PN(f); not s cn of noun *smy* image, see already Ing PNO p 176
▶ *šwm* v†

syʿ *v* to aid
G pf 3ms *syʿ* Inv 10 44:6; *s[yʿ]* BS III 45:8
wsyʿ tgryʾ bkl ṣbw klh and he aided the merchants in every possible way *Inv 10 44:6*†

skr *v* to reward
G pf 3fs *skrt* Inv 10 115:2
[w]skrt lh mdyth [and] the city rewarded him
▶ *skr* adj; *škr* adj†

skr *adj* generous, rewarding
s em *skrʾ* C4013:2; pl em *skryʾ* C3974:1
lʿbgl ʾlhʾ ṭbʾ wskrʾ to Abgal, the good and generous god *PNO 5:1*; *ʾlhyʾ ṭbyʾ wskryʾ* the good and generous gods *PNO 39:2*
▶ *skr* v; *škr* adj

slwkyʾ *nf* Seleuceia (city on Tigris)
s ab *slwkyʾ* C3924:4
wywnyʾ dy bslwkyʾ and the Greeks who are in Seleuceia (note *k* for *kappa*, see Cantineau ad Inv 9 6)
▶ Appendix MAPS†

slʿ *nf* *sela*, a coin
s em *slʿʾ* Sem '86 p 89:6; pl ab *slʿyn* Sem '86 p 86:4*, 7; abbr. *s<lʿyn>* CRAIBL '81:6
s<lʿyn> 3 ṣry ldhbʾ 3 Tyrian *sela*'s of gold *CRAIBL '81:6*; *wslʿyn ḥmš wzwz* and five *sela*'s and a *zuz* *Sem '86 p 89:7*†

slq *v* G to go up; C to bring, to bring up, to enter (in a list)
G pf 3ms *slq* Inv 10 29:3; 3fs *slqt* Inv 10 81:4; 3mpl *slqw* Inv 10 112:4; *slq* C3960:6; C pf 3ms *ʾsq* C3936:4; passive 3mpl *ʾsqw* Trf(I):5, CaGr p 90, RosSpr p 56; ptcp pass m s ab *msq* Trf(I):8
G *bny šyrtʾ dy slq ʿmh mn prt* the members of the caravan who came up with him from GN *C3916:2* Gk *synanabantes*; *C3960:6* Gk *anaban[te]s*, cf *C3948:2*; *tgryʾ dy slq mn krkʾ* the merchants who came up from Charax *Inv 10 29:3*; *šyrtʾ dy slqt mn krk* the caravan which came up from Charax *Inv 10 107:2*
C *dy ʾsq šyrtʾ mgn mn kysh* because he conducted a caravan gratis, at his own expense *C3936:4* Gk *anakomisanta*; *mdʿm dy lʾ msq bnmwsʾ* anything that was not entered in the law *Trf(I):8* Gk *aneilēmenna*; *ʿbydn šgyn ḥybn mksʾ lʾ ʾsqw* many things subject to tax were not entered *Trf(I):5* Gk *anelēmphthē*; *wʾsq ḥmrʾ ʿtyqʾ lkmryʾ štʾ klh* and he brought old wine for the priests a whole year *Syr '26 p 129:4*

smy *nf* image, standard
s cn ? *smt* PNO 6D:1, see *sym v*; em *smytʾ* C3902:1
wsmytʾ dy kspʾ wtṣbyth and the silver standard and its ornamentation *C3902:1* Gk *to signon argyroun*
(<Gk *sēmeion* 'figure, image'; see Downey '92 and cf *smyʾ* in inscriptions of Hatra passim; see Gaw [forthcoming] "Syrian Cults . . . " s.v. Hierapolis)
▶ *w* cj (*w* ... *w*)†

smk *v* to recline (reading partly restored)
G ptcp m pl ab ? *sm[kyn]* CRAIBL '81:3
ywmʾ dy yhwn sm[kyn] when they recline at table
▶ *smk* n†

smk *nm** banquet hall; or couch (?)
s em *smkʾ* BS III 21:1*
ʾl[t]ʾ dh wsmkʾ ʿbd PN this al[t]ar and banquet-hall made by PN *IP 10:1*; *smkʾ dnh ʿbdw wqrbw bny m[rzḥʾ ʾln]* this banquet hall was made and offered by these members of the sy[mposium] *BS III 21:1* (on a couch, see Dunant ad loc., and note Tobit 14:11 Gk

klinē in Qumran Aram text *smk'* Déd p 149; cf Gaw ANRW p 2651 for literature); *ḥmr mkl wplg qrš bsmk[']* wine, a measure and a half, ... in [the] banquet hall *RTP 694*
▶ *smk* v

sml *nm* **1** left; **2** north
s em *sml'* Inv 4 7B:2; sf 2ms *smlk* C4204:1; 1s *smln* Ber '35 p 86:8
1 *m'lyk bb' dy m'rt' 'l sml'* as you enter the door of the hypogeum on the left *Ber '35 p 104:3*; *gmḥyn tmny' mn ymynk 'rb'' wmn smlk 'rb''* eight niches, four on your right and four on your left *C4195:8*; *m'lyk m'rt' dnh 'l smln* as you enter this hypogeum on our (?) left *Ber '35 p 86:8*
2 *pnn lsml'* facing north *Ber '35 p 104:5*
▶ *smly* adj; *šml* n

smly *adj* north, northern
s ab *smly* Ber '35 p 112:5; pl ab *smlyn* Ber '35 p 112:4; pl em *smly'* Ber '38 p 124:1
gwmḥyn 'rb'' dy mnhwn smlyn tlt' w'ḥrn' m'rby wsmly four niches, of which three are to the north and the other to the northwest *Ber '35 p 112:4*; *'ksdr' smly' m'lyk m'rt' 'l ymyn'* the northern exedra as you enter the hypogeum, on the right *Ber '38 p 124:1*
▶ *sml* n; *šml* n

snqlṭyq *nm** senator
s em *snqlṭyqh* C3944:2*; *sqlṭyq'* C4202:1
spṭmyws ḥyrn br 'dynt snqlṭyqh nhyr' wrš tdmwr Septimius Hairan, son of Odenathus, illustrious senator and president of Tadmor *C3944:2*; *brbnwt mrzḥwt PN sqlṭyq'* in the term as symposiarch of PN, the senator *Inv 9 28:1*, cf Syr '71 p 413
(< Gk *sygklētikos* of senatorial rank, Lat. *senatorius*)†

ssṭrṭyn *nm* *sestertius*, sesterce
pl ab *ssṭrṭyn* Trf:71
lkl md' mn nm[ws]' dnh ssṭrṭyn [trn] for every *modius* (dry-measure) according to this law, [two] sesterces
(< Gk *sēstertios* < Lat. *sestertius* 'sesterce')†

sp *nm* praetorium (?)
s em *sp'* C3932:7
w'p PN [rb'] dy sp' PN [chief] of the praetorium ? Gk *eparchou tou hierou praitōriou*, see Bertinelli Angeli p 131, with bibliography; less probable analysis is *sp' v* 'to feed'†

sp' *v* to feed
G ptcp ms ab ? *sp'* C3932:7
dy sp' wrḥym mdth nourisher ?? and lover of his city, so Chabot ad loc.
▶ *sp* n†

spwn *adj* agreed
s ab (invariable) *spwn* Trf:144
hyk dy 'p hww spwn as they also were agreed *Trf:113* Gk *synephōnēsen*, cf *Trf:96*; *klhwn spwn* all of them, with one accord IP 34:6
(< Gk *symphōnos* 'agreed')

spṭmyws *nm* *Septimii* (pl), as title
p em *spṭmyw'* C3947:2
spṭmyw' PN rb ḥyl' rb' wPN rb ḥyl' the Septimii PN, major general, and PN, the general C3947:2-3; cf also *ywly'* n and *'wrly'* n
< Latin Septimius ▶ *spṭmyws* PN

spr *nm* writing
s ab *spr* MUSJ '62 p 106:4
bdyl dy l' yd' spr because he does not know writing (is illiterate); cf in archaic Syriac sale-document, Teix '90 pp 147-48:27 *dspr' l' yd'*; cf *spr'* in Dura-Europos Syriac bill of sale line 22; Frye et al. '55 p 146:22†

srbn *nm* dispute
pl ab *srbnyn* Trf(I):7
'l ṣbwt' 'ln srbnyn hww byny tgr' lbyny mksy' concerning these things there were disputes between the merchants and the tax-

collectors†

sryq *adj* not loaded, empty
m s ab *sryq* Trf:61; pl ab *sryqyn* Trf:118
gmly' hn ṭ'ynyn whn sryqyn camels, whether loaded or not loaded *Trf:118*†

str *v* to hide (?); to destroy (?)
G or D pf 3ms *str* MUSJ '62 p 106:8
gmḥwhy tlt' dy str his three niches which he concealed ? *or* destroyed ?; so Ing ad loc.
▶ *str* n; *šṭr* n†

str *nm* side (?)
s ab *str* MUSJ '62 p 106:8
gmḥwhy tlt' dy str three niches on a side
▶ *sṭr* n; *šṭr n*; *str* v†

ʿ (letter ʿayin) *abbr* 1 *ʿ<gl> n* veal (?); 2 number 5 (?) see *ʿyp* n

ʿbd *v* **1** to do; **2** to make, to build, to erect, to have made, built
G pf 3ms *ʿbd* C4965:1; 3mpl *ʿbd* PNO 57:1; impf 3ms *yʿbd* MUSJ '62 p 106:10; inf *lmʿbd* CRAIBL '81:18
1 *wyhb mn kysh dy l' ʿbdh 'nš* and he gave out of his own pocket, a thing no one ever did *Inv 9 11:5*; *wʿbd ʿmhwn gbwrt'* and he performed a great thing for them *RSP 142:2*; *wlmʿbd ...* and to do/make ... *CRAIBL '81:18* **2** *wʿbd šlm' bynyhwn* and he made peace between them *C3915:3*; *w'n ṣb' dy yʿbd* and if he wishes to make *MUSJ '62 p 106:10*; *dy ʿbd 'ksdr'* who built the exedra *Inv 12 2:3*; *bt qbwr' dnh ʿbd PN* this tomb made by PN *C4160:1* Gk *kateskeuasen*; *qbr' dnh bt ʿlm' [w]tṣbyth kl[h] ʿbdw mn kyshwn PN wPN* this tomb, an eternal home, [and] al[l] its ornamentation, made, at their own expense, by PN and PN *C4201:2* Gk *ōkodomēsan*; *ṣlm' dnh dy PN rb šyrt' dy ʿbdw lh bny šyrt'* this statue is of PN, the caravan leader, erected for him by the members of the caravan *C3948:2*, Gk *anestēsan*; cf *C3902:1* Gk *anethēke*; *C4066:2* Gk prb *an[ethēken]*; *qbr' dnh ʿbd PN* PN made this tomb *Inv 4 12:1*; *npš' dh ʿbd PN* PN made this monument *Syr '85 p 274:1*, Gk *ektisen*; *DN ʿbd PN wmwd'* (for) DN, made by PN, and in thanksgiving *C4035:2*; *ʿbd PN* made by PN (no object expressed in text) *Inv 11 42:1*; *ʿbd glpt' dnh PN wPN* PN and PN made this sculpture *PNO 57:1*; *bryk šmh lʿlm' ṭb' wrḥmn' ʿbd wmwd' PN* (for) Blessed-Be-His-Name-Forever, the good and the merciful, PN made (this), in thanksgiving *C4007:2*; *[lbryk šmh] lʿlm' ṭb' wrḥmn' ʿbd wmwd' [P]N wP[N] brh dy 'ḥwhy* for Blessed-Be-His-Name-Forever, PN and PN, his nephew, made (this) in thanksgiving *C4072:2*; *mṭlt' dh klh ʿmwdyh wšryth wttlylh ʿbd wqrb PN* this entire portico, its columns and its entablature and its ceiling, was made and offered by PN *BS III 3:1*
▶ *ʿbd* n; *ʿbydh* n

ʿbd I *nm* servant
pl cn *ʿbdy* Doura 40:1
ʿl ʿbdy ... for the servants of ? *Doura 40:1* (attestation uncertain)
▶ PN *ʿbdy* and other PN's with *ʿbd*†

ʿbd II *nm* work (attestation uncertain)
s em *ʿbd'* (reading uncertain) YCS '55 p 131:3 reading of du Mesnil '38a p 147
dy qryb mn ʿbd' hdyn lDN who offered of this work ? to DN
▶ *ʿwb'* n†

ʿbydh *nf** thing
pl ab *ʿbydn* Trf(I):4*
bnmws' dy mks' ʿbydn šgyn ḥybn mks' l' 'sqw in the tax law many things subject to tax were not listed
▶ *ʿbd* v†

ʿgl *nm* veal (?)
abbr. (s em) *ʿ<gl'>* RTP 161
m<šḥ'> 1 ḥ<mr'> 1 ʿ<gl'> 1 one o<il>, one w<ine>, one v<eal> Abbr. unusual, restoration conjectural†

ʿglbwl *nm* Aglibol (name of deity)
s ab *ʿglbwl* C3968:1
hykl' dy bl wyrḥbwl wʿglbwl 'lhy' the temple of Bel and Yarhibol and Aglibol, the gods *Inv 9 1:5*
▶ TeixPan *passim*; Gaw ANRW pp 2608-25; Hof RelAram pp 33-38

ʿd *nm* festival
s ab *ʿd* RTP 252
bkl ʿd for the whole festival†

ʿd *prep* up to, until
ʿd C4218:5
ʿd kpt' mqblt' up to the opposite arch ? *C4194:7*; *wtṣbyth klh ʿd lʿl* all of its ornamentation, to the top *Inv 3 2:1*, see Bou and Teix ad Inv 12 19; *mn ṭlyw ʿd sybw* from youth to old age *Ber '36 p 99:6*; *lyqrh wlyqr bnwhy wbny bnwhy ʿd ʿlm'* in his honor, and in honor of his children and grandchildren, forever *C4123:2*

ʿdh *nf* custom
s em *ʿdt'* Trf:54, 107
wmdy gw mn dnr ḥyb mks' hyk ʿdt' whatever is less than a denarius is subject to tax according to custom *Trf:107*†

ʿdn *nm** time
s em *ʿdn'* C3993:2*
lbryk šmh [lʿl]m' wlʿdn' ṭb' to Blessed-Be-His-Name-Forever and to the Good Time†

ʿdr *v* to aid
G pf 3ms *ʿdr* RTP 722; sf 3ms *ʿdrh* C3928:3; 3mpl *ʿdrnwn* Inv 10 124:5; *ʿdrnn* Inv 10 111:4; ptcp m pl ab ? *ʿdryn* Syr '33 p 179:2, context broken, cf RosSpr p 62
bdyl dy ʿdrh bkl ṣbw klh because he helped him in every way *Inv 10 107:4*

ʿwb *nm** porch (very doubtful)
s em *ʿwb'* YCS '55 p 131:3* reading of Ing
dy qryb mn ʿw?b?' hdyn lDN who offered toward this porch ? for DN; Ing cf Heb *ʿāb* I Kg 7:6, architectural term of uncertain sense
▶ *ʿbd* $_{II}$ n

ʿwd *v* to frequent, to come past
C ptcp m s ab *mʿyd* C3973:10; impf 3ms ? *yʿd* CRAIBL '81:8
wdkyr kl mʿyd ʿlwt' 'ln and commemorated be everyone who comes by these altars *C3973:10*†

ʿwnh *nf* service, ritual (?); corps of priests (?)
s em *ʿwnt'* RTP 37, 38, 39, 40
wrbny ʿwnt' dy bl and the leaders of the priesthood of Bel *RTP 37*; see Déd pp 1-2; 92; 283-84, Gaw Sem '73 118-19†

ʿz *nm* goat
s ab *ʿz* Trf:29
bzqyn dy ʿz in goatskins *Trf:98*

ʿzyz see *ʿzyzw* n

ʿzyzw *nm* Azizu (name of deity)
ʿzyzw C3974:2; *ʿzyz* RSP 151:3
lʾrṣw wlʿzyzw 'lhy' ṭby' wskry' ʿbd PN 'pkl' dy ʿzyzw 'lh' ṭb' for Arsu and for Azizu, the good and generous gods, made by PN, priest of Azizu, the good god *C3974:1*; *lʿzyz ṭb'* to Azizu the good *RSP 151:3*
▶ TeixPan pp 68-71; ANRW p 2637; Hof RelAram p 40

ʿyd *nm* custom
s em *ʿyd'* Trf(I):5
whw' gb' hyk bnmws' wbʿyd' and he would collect tax according to law and according to custom *Trf(I):6*

ʿyn *nf** spring of water
s ab *ʿyn* RSP 126:2; s em *ʿyn'* C3976:1*; pl ab *ʿynn* Trf:58; pl em *ʿynt'* Trf(II):1
kdy hw' rb ʿyn ʿl 'pq' when he was curator of the spring for Afqa *RSP 126:2*; *lgd' dy ʿyn' brykt'* to the Fortune of the Blessed Spring *C3976:1*; *[b]rbnwt ʿyn' dy*

PN [during] the term as spring-curator of PN *RSP 127:1*; *[ltš]myš ʿynn trtn dy m[y] dy bmdyt'* [for the u]se of the two springs of wa[ter] that are in the city *Trf:58*

ʿyp *v* to double, multiply (reading uncertain)
G ptcp pass m s ab sf 3fs ? *ʿy[ph]* RSP 199:7
ḥty'th ʿ (= 5) ʿy[ph] his fine will be 5 (times) its double, see Gaw '73b p 116 for this analysis†

ʿyrw *nf meaning uncertain*
s sf 3m/fs *ʿyrwth* Ber '36 p 99:5
bʿyrwth in/by his/her vigilance ?? :: Déd p 183: *ʿydwth* 'his frequenting'†

ʿl *prep* 1 on, upon; 2 on top of, above; 3 at; 4 for, on behalf of; 5 over, in charge of; 6 concerning; 7 against
ʿl C4130:2; *ʿly* C4018:5; sf 3ms ? *ʿlh* Syr '36 p 271:5; *ʿlwhy* C3956:4; *lʿlwh* MUSJ '62 p 106:9; 3mpl *lʿlyhwn* MUSJ '62 p 106:11
1 *mn dy l' yšd dm ʿl ḥgb'* whoever does not shed blood on the shrine ? *Dri '82b p 65:3* **2** *[d]y nḥš' ʿl ʿmwd' dy ʿl bb' rb* [statue of] bronze on top of the pillar by the great gate Syr '36 p 274 (
(Tad 19):3 **3** *kdy 'nt ʿll ʿl šml'* as you enter, on the left *C4199:7*; *dy thwyn ʿlwt' 'ln ʿl bb' rb'* so that these altars should be at the great gate *BS III 24:3* **4** *dy bn' ʿl PN 'bwhy* which he built for PN, his father *Syr '50 p 137:3; ʿl ḥywh wḥy' bnwh* for his life and life of his children *PNO 43:5*; *wl' 'ḥ[y]s npšh ʿl mdyth* and he did not sp[a]re himself on behalf of his city *Déd p 36:4* **5** *rb ʿyn ʿl 'pq'* Spring-curator over Afqa *RSP 126:2*; *dy yhw' 'ḥyd ʿl dhb'* who will be elected official in charge of the gold *CRAIBL '81:9* **6** *zbnyn šgyn ʿl ṣbwt' 'ln srbnyn hww* many times there were disagreements about these things *Trf(I):6* **7** *ʿl npšh ḥṭ'* does wrong against himself *Ber '38 p 133:8*
▶ *lʿl* prep; *mn lʿl* prep

ʿlh *nf** altar
s em *ʿlt'* C3903:1* (with *dh* here as is usual, sometimes with *dnh*, e.g. Inv 12 34:2); pl em *ʿlwt'* C3973:1
ʿlt' dh ʿbd PN PN made this altar (on an altar) *Syr '31 13:1*; *ʿlt' dnh ʿbd wmwd' PN* PN made this altar in thanksgiving *C4029:2*; *ḥmn' dnh wʿlt' dh [ʿ]bdw wqrbw PN wPN* PN and PN made and offered this shrine and altar *C3978:2*

ʿlyh *nf* upper part
s em *ʿlyt'* C4212:1
wgwmḥyn 'rbʿ' dy ʿlyt' and the four niches of the upper part *C4212:1*, cf *ʿly[t']* *C4211:2* Gk *anagai[ō]* upper floor†

ʿlym *nm* slave
s ab *ʿlm* Trf(II):4; sf 3ms *ʿlymh* C4115bis:6; pl ab *ʿly[m]yn* Trf(II):6; pl em *ʿlymy'* Trf(II):2
mn dy mpq ʿlm wtṛn whoever exports a veteran slave (*mancipium veteranum*) *Trf:86*; *ʿlymy' dy mt'ʿlyn ltdmr* slaves that are imported to Palmyra *Trf(II):2*; see Davis and Stuckenbruck '92 266-74 for extended discussion.
▶ *ʿlymh* n

ʿlymh *nf* girl, prostitute
pl em *ʿlymt'* Trf:126
mks' dy ʿlymt' the tax on girls *Trf:125* Gk *hetairō[n]*†

ʿll *v* G to enter, to come in, to go in; C to import; Ct to be imported
G pctp m s ab *ʿll* C4199:7; inf ? *mʿl* C4172:2 (or *mʿl n*); C impf 3ms *yʿl* Syr '33 p 184:2; ptcp active m s ab *mʿl* Trf:80; m pl cn *mʿly* Trf(II):2; pass m s ab *[m]'ʿl* Trf:112; em *m'ʿl'* Trf:149; Ct impf 3ms *[y]t'ʿl* Trf:56; *yt'yʿl* Trf:61; ptcp m s ab *mt'ʿl* Trf(II):14; em *[mt]'ʿl'* Trf:147; pl ab *mt'ʿlyn* Trf:119
G *kdy 'nt ʿll ʿl šml'* as you enter on the left *C4199:7*; *lkl dy ʿll lḥšbn tgr'* anything that enters into the accounts of the merchants *Trf:115*; *mʿl bb' ʿl ymynk* as you enter the gate, on your right *C4172:2* (inf.

?, cf *mʿl n*; on construction see KB³ s.v. *bwʾ* p 76)

C *mn dy yʿl ltnn swm nkry* whoever brings in here a body that does not belong *Syr '33 p 184:2*; *ʾlʾ lʿn dy thwʾ mʾʿlʾ* except for sheep that are imported *Trf:149*; *mn dy mʿl rglyn ltdmr* whoever imports slaves to Palmyra *Trf:80*

Ct *gmlyʾ hn ṭʿynyn whn sryqyn yhn mtʾʿlyn* camels, loaded or empty, that are imported *Trf:119*, Gk *eisachtē;* cf Trf:56 *[y]tʾʿl* Gk *eiskomizont[ōn*

▶ *mʿl* n; *mʿlh* n; *mʿln* n

ʿlm *nm* **1** forever, eternity; in n phr *bt ʿlmʾ* eternal home; *bryk šmh lʿlmʾ* Blessed-Be-His-Name-Forever, name of deity, q.v.; **2** world

s ab *ʿlm* PNO 2ter:8; s em *ʿlmʾ* C4490:1

1 *dy yhb lʿbgl šlṭnʾ bʾtrʾ klh lʿlm* who gave DN (or PN ?) authority in the whole region forever *PNO 2ter:8*; *yhwh dkyr lʿlmʾ* may he be remember[ed] forever *BS III 60:6*; *wlbny bnwhy lyqrhwn ʿd ʿlmʾ* and for his grandchildren, in their honor, forever *C4123bis:4*; *lyqrhn wlyqr bnwhy dy ʿlmʾ* in their honor and in eternal honor of his children *C4130:3*; *wlʾ yqšṭ lmn dy ypthyhy ʿd ʿlmʾ* and may he who opens it never be in the right *C4218:6*; *lhwn wlbnyhwn wlbny bnyhwn lʿlmʾ* for themselves, for their children and for their grandchildren, forever *Ber '38 p 95:10*; *qbrʾ dnʾ bt ʿlmʾ* this grave, an eternal home *C4216:1*; *dkrnʾ dnh dy hw yqr bt ʿlmʾ* this memorial which is the honor of an eternal home *C4123:1* Gk *mnēmeion aiōnion geras*; for the above expressions, Gk *(passim) eis ton aiōna*; *eis to panteles aiōnion*; *aiōnian*; *lbryk šmh lʿlmʾ* to Blessed-Be-His-Name-Forever *C4002:1*; also (once) *bryk šmh lʿlm C4087:2*

2 *lmrʾ ʿlmʾ ṭbʾ wrḥmnʾ mwdʾ PN* PN gives thanks to the Lord of the world, the good and the merciful *C3989:1*; *lbʿlšmn mrʾ ʿlmʾ* for Baalshamin, Lord of the world *C3986:1*

▶ Gaw MF p 169-71; see *bryk šmh lʿlm* n

ʿlm see *ʿlym* n

ʿm *prep* with

ʿm Inv 10 107:3; sf 3ms *ʿmh* C3916:3; 3m pl *ʿmhwn* C3960:7

dy slqt mn GN ʿm PN which went up from GN with PN *Inv 10 107:3*; *wktb ʿm nmwsʾ qdmyʾ* and let it be written with the former law *Trf(I):9*; *bdyl dy hlk ʿmh špr* because he behaved well toward him *Inv 10 53:4*; *wʿbd ʿmhwn gbwrtʾ* and he did mighty things for them *RSP 142:2*; *wʾp ʿm yqrʾ dy bwlʾ wdms* and also with a gift from the Senate and People *Syr '36 20:8*, see Cantineau ad loc.

ʿmwd *nm** column

s em *ʿmwdʾ* C3956:4*; *ʿmdʾ* BS III 20:3; pl ab *ʿmwdyn* C3952:3; em *ʿmwdyʾ* C3984:1; ? *ʿmwdʾ* Inv 9 28:6, 8; sf 3fs *ʿmwdyh* Inv 1 5:1

ʿmdʾ wṭpytʾ wšrytʾ wṭṭlylʾ ʿbd PN the column and the coping and the entablature and the ceiling were made by PN (written on a column; form prb singular, see Dunant ad loc.) *BS III 20:3*

▶ also *ʿmwr* n for ambiguous (*r/d* problem) *ʿmwdʾ* or *ʿmwdʾ* of Inv 9 28:6, 8

ʿmwr *nm* resident, inhabitant (?); or residences (?)

s or pl em *ʿmwrʾ* Inv 9 28:6, 8

PN dy hwʾ ʿl ʿmwrʾ ... wPN dhwʾ qym ʿl ʿmwrʾ PN, who was in charge of the inhabitants (residences ?) ... and PN who was put in charge of the inhabitants (residences ?); see Cantineau ad loc.; Milik, Déd, pp 270-77; DISO

▶ *ʿmwd* n

ʿml *v* to labor

G pf 3ms *ʿml* Syr '36 p 280:5

wʿml bswmh and he labored personally†

ʿmr I *nm* wool

s em *ʿmrʾ* Trf:93, 94, 96

l' ʿmr' ʾyṭlyq[ʾ] [t]hw' prʿʾ [mk]s[ʾ] Italia[n] wool sha[ll] not be charged [ta]x *Trf:96*†

ʿmr II *nm* life, way of life
s sf 3ms *ʿmrh* C3932:6
wdbr ʿmrh škytyt and he conducted his life quietly *C3932:6* Gk *kalōs poleiteusamenon*†

ʿn *nf** small cattle, sheep and goats
s ab *ʿn* Trf:149*; em *ʿn'* Trf:145*
ʾl' lʿn dy thw' mʾl' but for small cattle that are imported *Trf:149*†

ʿnʾ *nf* Ana (name of city)
s ab *ʿn'* C3973:3; BS III 51:4
ʾsṭrṭg ʿl ʿn' wgml' general over Ana and Gamla *Syr ʾ33 p 179:1*
▶ Appendix MAPS†

ʿnwšh *nf* treasury
s em *ʿnwšt'* C3994:3
lDN mn ksp ʿnwšt' bʿnwšt PN wPN for DN, from treasury funds, during the term as treasurer of PN and PN *C3994:3*; see Gaw TP p 14 and Starcky on *MUSJ ʾ49 p 56:1 [dy] ʾqymw lh ʾnwš ʿnwšt'* which the men of the treasury ... erected for him *Inv 9 12:3*; *ʿnwš[t]' dy bl PN wPN* the treasu[ry] of DN. PN and PN *RTP 36*
▶ *ʿnš* v; *ʿnwšw* n

ʿnwšw *nf* term as treasurer
s cn *ʿnwšt* and *ʿnwšwt* C3994:3 (inscription in three copies)
lDN mn ksp ʿnwšt' bʿnwšt PN For DN, from treasury funds, during the term as treasurer of PN Gk *argyrotamiōn*
▶ *ʿnš* v; *ʿnwšh* n†

ʿny *v* to answer
G pf 3ms *ʿn* Inv 11 1:7; sf 3ms *ʿn'* RSP 121:4; *ʿnh* C4047:4; *ʿynh* (sic) Inv 11 11:8, perhaps error for *ʿnyh*; *ʿny* C4092:3; *ʿnyh* C4011:5; *ʿ[ny]hy* C4046:7; 3fs *ʿnh* C4067:3; 1pl *ʿnn* C4048:6, cf RSP 119:8; 3mpl *ʿnnwn* Inv 11 17:7; impf 3ms sf 3ms *yʿnnh* Ber ʾ36 p 99:4
DN dʿnh DN, who answered her *C4067:3*; *dy qrw lh bʿq' wʿnn brwḥ' ln* who called to him in distress, and he answered us with relief for us *RSP 119:7*; *dy qr lh bym' wbybš' wʿnh [bk]l dy qrh* who called to him on sea and dry land and he answered him where[e]ver he called to him *C4047:4*

ʿnš *v* C to fine (?)
C pf 1s ? *ʾʿnšt* Syr ʾ36 18:3
ʾʿnšt I fined ? context broken; no connected sense; linguistic character of text disputed see Déd 288-92
▶ *ʿnwšh* n; *ʿnwšw* n

ʿsr see *ʿšr* num

ʿsryn *num* twenty
ʿsryn C4172:2; *ʿšryn* MUSJ ʾ62 p 106:1
ksp dnryn mʾh wʿsryn one hundred twenty denarii *RB ʾ30 14:4*

ʿq *nm* distress
s em *ʿq'* RSP 119:7; C4100:4
dy qrw lh bʿq' to whom they called in distress *C4100:4*†

ʿqly dy *cj* because (?)
ʿqly dy Inv 10 44:5
ʿqly dy ʾpq mn kysh npqn rbrbn because ? he spent, of his own funds, great sums†

ʿqr *nm* inmost part (?)
s cn ? *ʿqr* C4173:2
wmn gwmḥyn trn dy mn ʿqr twpr' dkn and two unused niches from the inmost part ? of ? (last word of unknown sense) *C4174:5*†

ʿrb *nm* surety (?)
s em *ʿrb'* Ber ʾ38 p 133:4
mnw dy yzbn ʿrb' dy qdm mʿrt' whoever sells a surety ? which is debited to the hypogeum; Milik ʾ67 p 550 and fn 2: ʿgage, caution, hypothèqueʾ :: DISO the thing or document which guaranteed the preservation of the tomb

▶ *qdm* p†

ʿrs *nm* couch
s em *ʿrsʾ* Ber '35 p 102(XI):4; *ʿršʾ* C3912:2
dbqyn ʿrsʾ next to the (funerary) couch *Ber '35 p 102XI:4*; *lDN mrʾ ʿlmʾ qrb kptʾ wʿršʾ PN* PN offered to DN, lord of the world, the vaulted space and the couch *C3912:2* Gk *klinē*; on divine couch, Caquot ad loc. cf Herodotus I 181†

ʿrpn *nm* change, small coins
s ab ? *ʿ[r]pn* Trf:107
ʿ[r]pn yhʾ gbʾ in small coins it shall be collected Gk *pros kerma* 'in coin' (esp. copper money); this equivalence e.g. John 2:15 Gk and Syriac†

ʿrš see *ʿrs* n

ʿšb *nm* hay
pl em *ʿšb[y]ʾ* Trf:123
ʿšb[y]ʾ w[nt]yrtʾ ʾtḥzy (about) hay and [wind]falls ? it was decided†

ʿšr *num* ten
s ab *ʿsrʾ* with m noun Ber '38 p 104:1; *ʿšr* Trf:70 (in compound number 16); *ʿšrh* Sem '86 p 89:6 (in compound number 16)
gwmḥyn ʿsrʾ ten niches *Ber '38 p 104:1*; *lmdyʾ dy qsṭwn ʿšr w[š]t* per *modius* of sixteen *sextarii Trf:70*
▶ *ʿšrh* n†

ʿšrh *nf* the Ten (municipal authorities, Gk *dekaprōtoi*, Lat. *decemprimi*)
s em *ʿšrtʾ* Trf(I):7
ʾtḥzy lbwlʾ dy ʾrkwnyʾ ʾln wlʿšrtʾ it was decided by the Senate of those archons and the Dekaprotoi Gk *d[eka]prōtous*; see Matthews '84 p 174 n. 5; on translation Teix '83b p 238
(Calque of Gk)
▶ IH no. 207:2-3 *bnʾ ʿšrt* members of the Ten (lit.)

ʿšryn see *ʿsryn* num

ʿštrt *nf* Ashtart (name of deity)
s ab *ʿštrt* Inv 12 54:1
lbl wlbʿšmn [wlʿglbwl wlml]kbl wlʿštrt wlnmsys wlʾrṣw wlʾbgl ʾlhy ṭbyʾ [wskryʾ] for DN etc. and for Ashtart and for DN etc., the good and generous gods *Inv 12 55:2*; *lʿštr[t] ʾštrʾ ṭbtʾ* for Ashtart, the good goddess *Syr '31 p 134:2*
(See RosSpr pp 24-25: form is Canaanite, not straightforward Aram form)
▶ TeixPan passim; ANRW pp 2623-2624

ʿtyq *adj* old
m s em *ʿtyqʾ* Syr '26 p 129:4; pl ab *ʿtyqyn* C3948:4
ḥmrʾ ʿtyqʾ old wine *Syr '26 p 129:4*; *dnryn dy dhb ʿtyqyn tlt mʾh* three hundred old gold denarii *C3948:4*, Gk *palaia*; see Buttrey '61

ʿtrʿth *nf* Atargatis (name of deity)
s ab *ʿtrʿth* RTP 201
lmlkb[l] wgd tymy wlʿtrʿth ʾlh[yʾ] ṭb[yʾ] to DN and DN and to Atargatis, [the] good god[s] *C3927:4*; cf *BS III 45:13 [bt ʿtrʿth]* [temple of Atargatis] Gk line 21 *atargateios* (on etymology, Nöldeke 1870 p 92 fn 1; p 109 Nachtrag)
▶ TeixPan pp 71-76; ANRW p 2623†

p *cj* and, that is
p Inv 8 63:3
ḥbl PN wbnwhy pPN brh wḥbl PN brh alas! PN and his children: that is, PN, his son, and alas! PN his son, etc. (there follows an enumeration of the children)†

pgr *nm** carcase
pl ab *pgryn* Trf:108*
pgryn dy mštdn mks lʾ ḥybyn carcases that are cast out are not subject to tax†

pḥd *nm** tribe
s cn *pḥd* C4113:5; *pḥwz* Inv 7 5:1; pl em *pḥdyʾ* RTP 304; *pḥzyʾ* Inv 10 44:3; pl em *pḥzʾ* Déd p 36:5*

PN dy mn pḥd bny PN PN, who is of the tribe of the Bani PN *C4113:5*; *dy ʿbd lh ʾrbʿ pḥzyʾ* which the four tribes made for him *Inv 10 44:3*; *nwyt šʾwr pḥzʾ bt ʾlhyhwn* as also the rest of the tribes in their temples *Déd pp 36:5*
(Forms *pḥzyʾ* and the like show borrowing of Arab *fāḫiḏ* with *z* < Arab. *ḏ*; RosSpr p 94, with reference to Nöldeke)
⊡ Hillers '72 pp 90-92

pḥwz See *pḥd* n

pḥz See *pḥd* n

pṭm *v* to fatten (?)
G pf 3ms ? *pṭ[m]* Inv 6 4:3; restoration uncertain; see Gaw ad RSP 129:3 (same as Inv 6 4:3), on uncertainty of Cantineau's reading (stone damaged since) *[p]ṭmʾ dy pṭm* "... gras. Qu'a engraissé ..."†

pṭply *nm ?* bazaar
s ab ? *pṭply* Trf:53
... wpṭply ... ... and of the bazaars Gk *pantopōl[ei]ōn*
(< Gk *pantopōleion* or *pantopōlēs*)†

pṭrtʾ *nf ? PN ?* sense uncertain: unusual tribal name ?
s or pl em ? *pṭrtʾ* Syr '36 22:4; *pṭrt* RSP 154:1
wlyqr bny pṭrtʾ and in honor of *the sons of pṭrtʾ* *Syr '36 22:4*; *[ʿ]bdw bny pṭrt ʾln* [m]ade by the sons of X *RSP 154:1*, Déd pp 61-62: 'grave superintendents', from etymology: *pṭr* 'to depart' > 'to die'; cf Gaw TP p 34: 'detached, free, exempt'
⊡ Stark PN p 57†

plg *v* to divide, share
G pf 3mpl *plg* Ber '38 p 124:9
wmqblyn gwmḥyn tltʾ dy plg bnyhwn and facing the three niches which they shared between them :: Ing: which are in the middle
⊡ *plg* n; *plgw* n†

plg *nm* half, part
s ab *plg* RTP 526; em *plgʾ* RB '30 p 538:2; sf 3ms *plgh* MUSJ '62 p 106:8
ḥmr plg wine. A half (measure). *RTP 526*; *plg nsb mnth* half he has taken as his portion *MUSJ '62 p 106:7*; *plgʾ wplgʾ* half and half, i. e. as equal partners StudMiles p 38:1, see Cussini '92a (index, forthcoming revision) for Akk equivalents
⊡ *plg* v; *plgw* n

plgw *nf* half, part
s cn *plgwt* RSP 24:4
plgwt mʿrtʾ dh half of this hypogeum
⊡ *plg* v; *plg* n

plhdrw *nf* presidency
s em *plhdrwtʾ* Trf(I):1
bplhdrwtʾ dy PN during the presidency of PN Gk *proedrou*
(< Gk *proedros* president)†

plz *nm* kind of copper or bronze
s em *plzʾ* C3914:4
ʿbdw trʿyʾ ʾln šttyhn dy plzʾ made these six doors of special copper *C3914:4* Gk *auro[chalk]eious* L-S Lexicon p 2055, equivalent of *oreichalkinos*, mountain-copper, i.e. yellow copper ore or metal made of it; Sobernheim '05 p 6: 'brass'†

plḥ *nm* soldier
s em *plḥʾ* C3944:4
PN plḥʾ dblgywnʾ dy bṣrʾ PN, a soldier in the legion of Basra *C3944:4* Gk *stratiōtēs*†

plṭy *nm ?* public life
s em *plṭyʾ* Inv 10 44:7
wʿbd plṭyʾ šbyḥyt wnhwryt and he conducted his public life in a praiseworthy and brilliant way
(< Gk *politeia*)†

plṭyʾ *nm ?* part of tomb interior, corridor
s em ? *plṭyʾ* Ber '35 p 85:7
gwmḥyn tryn dy bplṭyʾ two niches in the

corridor; on sense see O'Connor 1988 p 358
(< Gk *plateia* 'street')

pny *v* G to face; D to deliver
G ptcp m s ab *pn'* C4172:1; m pl ab ? *pnn* C4172:2 (or *pny* adj); D pf 3ms sf 3mpl *pnwn* RSP 142:2
G *mn 'ksdr' smly' dy hw pn' lymyn'* the north exedra, which faces south *C4172:1*
D *pnwn mn š't' drgz'* he delivered them from the hour of wrath *RSP 142:2*
▶ *pny* adj†

pny *nf** side, area
pl ab *pnyn* Ber '38 p 95:6*
w'rhq lhwn mn pnyn trtn dy str' grbyy' wtymny' and ceded to them two areas of the northern and southern sides; cf Déd pp 2-3: restores *p?nt'* in Inv 11 80:5
▶ *pny* v; *pny* adj†

pny *adj* empty
m pl ab *pnn* C4172:2
dy bh gwmhyn pnn 'sryn in which there are twenty empty niches *C4172:2*; perhaps also *Ber '35 p 104:5*; see Bauer cited by Ing '36 p 127
▶ *pny* v†

psl *v* to carve stone (reading and analysis uncertain)
G pf 3ms ? *p[s]l* ARNA p 161:6
p[s]l brh Ca[rv]ed by his son; Starcky notes that 'to carve' is ordinarily *glp* in Palmyrene†

psqws *nm* treasury
s ab *psqws* Syr '33 p 184:2
yhwb lpsqws zwzyn '[lp] he shall owe to the treasury one [thousand] *zuz*'s
(< Gk *phiskos* < Lat. *fiscus*)†

prgmṭt *nm* agent
s em *prgmṭt'* Inv 10 113:4
dy 'qym lh lyqrh PN prgmṭt' which PN, his agent, erected for him in his honor; in this text, agent of a publican, Gk *pragmateutēs*, Latin *actor*
(< Gk *pragmateutēs* 'agent')†

prn' *nm* front hall of a temple
s em *prn'* C3959:6, reading of Déd p 11
wbn' hykl' wprn' and he built the temple and the front hall *C3959:6* Gk *p[ro]naiō*, see Déd p 11
(< Gk *pronaios* front hall of a temple)
▶ *prnyn* n†

prnyn *nm* front hall of temple (?)
s ab ? *[p]rnyn* C3985:3
[p]rnyn wtṣbyth klh the [fr]ont hall and all its ornamentation
(< Gk *pronaos*, *pronaios* front hall of a temple)
▶ *prn'* n†

prns *v* to provide
Quad pf 3ms *prns* C3915:3
wprns brmnhwn and he provided besides these things†

prs *v* to extend (?)
G ptcp pass ? *prys* RSP 145:3
reading and analysis too uncertain for translation; see Gaw ad loc.†

pr' *v* to pay, to be charged
G ptcp m s ab *pr'* Trf:129; f s *pr''* Trf:94; impf 3ms *ypr'* Trf:83
ypr' d<ynryn> 8 (he) shall pay 8 d<enarii> *Trf:83*; *l[' m]ks[...] pr'' thw' 'mr' dy 'yṭ[ly'* Italian wool shall not [be] charged [ta]x *Trf:97*; *wyhw' pr' ṣlm bplgwt [ṭ'w]n* and one statue shall be charged (at the rate of) half [a load] *Trf:129*; at *Trf:149* Gk *opheilesthai*

prš *nm* rider, cavalryman
s ab *prš* C3973:2; pl em *pršy'* BS III 51:3
dy 'qym lh pršy' b'br['] *dy gml' w'n'* erected for him by the riders in (the) wing of Gamla and Ana *BS III 51:3*, acc to Bertinelli Angeli p 72 = Latin *eques*.†

prt *nf* Forat (city on Tigris)
s ab *prt* C3916:3
dy slq ʿmh mn prt wmn ʾlgšyʾ who went up with him from Forat and from Vologesia *C3916:3*; *prt myšn* ... Forat Mayshan *Inv 10 112* Gk *[phor]athōn*; see Raschke '78 p 987 fn 1361
▶ Appendix MAPS†

pšq *v* D to make clear, show
D pf 3ms *pšq* Trf:104; 1s *pšqt* Trf:125
bʾgrtʾ dy ktb lsṭṭyls pšq in the letter he wrote to Statilius he made clear *Trf:104* Gk *diasaphēsantos*†

pṭḥ *v* to open
G pf 3ms sf 3ms *ptḥh* BS III 60:5; impf 3ms *yptḥ* Inv 8 86:2; sf 3ms *yptḥyhy* C4218:6; *yptḥh* RSP 105:4; ptcp pass m s ab *ptyḥ* BS III 60:2, Inv 7 1B:3; f s ab *ptyḥʾ* RB '30 14:6
byrḥ ʾyr šnt 322 ptyḥ qbrʾ dnh in the month of Iyyar, the year 322, this grave was opened *BS III 60:2*†

ṣbw *nf** thing, affair, business
s ab *ṣbw* C3916:4; *ṣbʾ* Inv 12 35:4; pl cn *ṣbwt* Inv 12 49:8; em *ṣbwtʾ* Trf(I):6
šprw lhwn wlʾlhyhwn bkl ṣbw klh they did good to them and to their gods in every thing *C3930:4*, cf *C3928:4* Gk *panti tropō*; *wmṭl kwt zbnyn šgyn ʿl ṣbwtʾ ʾln srbnyn hww* and therefore many times there were disputes about these things *Trf(I):6*; *ṣbwt btʾ* the affairs of the temple *Inv 12 49:8*
▶ *ṣby* v

ṣby *v* to wish
G impf 3ms *yṣbʾ* Trf:149; ptcp m s ab *ṣbʾ* MUSJ '62 p 106:9; pl ab *ṣbyn* Ber '38 p 95:9
mn dy yṣbʾ mn bny ddy yḥpr whoever wishes, of my uncle's children, may dig *RB '30 9:4*; *ʾn yṣbʾ mksʾ* if the publican wishes *Trf:149* Gk *thelē*
▶ *ṣbw* n

ṣbs *nm* name of deity, of uncertain identification and pronunciation
s ab *ṣbs* Inv 12 22:4
lṣbs wʾnhyt ʾlhyʾ for *S-b-s* and for Anahit, the gods; Teix ad loc. tentatively suggests identification with Thracio-Phrygian Sabazios†

ṣbt *v* D to ornament
D pf 3ms *ṣbt* C4173:3
dy ḥpr wṣbt mʿrtʾ dh who excavated and ornamented this hypogeum
▶ *tṣby* n

ṣdyḥ *nm* enterprise (*reading and meaning uncertain)*
pl ab *ṣdyḥyn* Inv 10 44:4; *ṣryḥyn* is also possible reading, but letter is without dot, and in this text *resh* is otherwise dotted
bdyl dy špr lhwn bʾsṭrṭgwn šgyʾn wbṣdyḥyn wšyryn dy slq bhn he did good to them in many campaigns and enterprises (?) and in caravans on which he accompanied them *Inv 10 44:4*; no close literal correspondence of Gk to Aram†

ṣwr *v* to paint
G pf 3mpl *ṣrw* Doura 25:7; ptcp m pl ab *ṣyry[n]* Doura 25:2
dy ṣrw ṣwrtʾ hd[ʾ] who painted thi[s] picture *Doura 25:7*
▶ *ṣwrh* n†

ṣwrh *nf* picture
s em *ṣwrtʾ* Doura 25:7
dy ṣrw ṣwrtʾ hd[ʾ] who painted this picture *Doura 25:7* (accompanies fresco)
▶ *ṣwr* v†

ṣldyḥn *nf* name of place (reading and identification uncertain)
s ab *ṣldyḥn* PNO 41:1
lgny dy ṣldyḥn to the Genius of *ṣldyḥn*†

ṣlm *nm** statue, image
s ab *ṣlm* Inv 11 95:1; cn *ṣlm* C4137:1; em *ṣlmʾ* C3916:1*; pl ab *ṣlmyn* Trf:130*; cn *ṣlmy* Trf:128; em *ṣlmyʾ* C3914:1
ṣlm PN br PN statue of PN, son of PN *Inv*

4 9D:1, statue of a man, common usage; *ṣlm PN brt PN* statue of PN, daughter of PN *Ber '35 p 79C:1*, statue of a woman, less common, but well-attested (*ṣlmh n* is commonly used for statues of women); Gk ordinarily has no explicit equivalent for Aram. *ṣlm'* in these cases; they usually begin instead with the name of the person depicted, but note *ṣlm' dnh* statue C3948:1 Gk *andr[ianta]*; *ṣ[lmy' dy] bkpt' dy PN wPN* the im[ages which are] in the niche are of PN and PN *C4187:1* Gk *eikones*; *w'bd lh [...] ṣlm mrkb swsy* and they made for him [...] an equestrian statue *Syr '36 p 280:7* Gk *ephippon an[dria]nta*; *ṣlm dnh dy PN* this statue is of PN *RSP 159:1*; *lPN lṣlm* for PN, as a statue *Inv 11 95:1*; *ṣlm' dnh dy PN* this statue is of PN *C3916:1*; *'qym[w] kmry' dy bl ṣlm' dnh lPN* the priests of Bel erecte[d] this statue for PN *Inv 11 100:3*; *['l] ṣlmy nḥš' 'drty'* [concerning] bronze statues, images *Trf:128*; *bwl' wdms 'bdw ṣlmy' 'ln trwyhwn lPN* the Senate and People made these two statues for PN *C3930:1*; *wqbyryn lgw mn ṣlmy' 'ln* and are buried below these statues (on a stone funerary relief) *RSP 21:3*

▶ *ṣlmh* n

ṣlmh *nf** statue (of a woman)

s cn *ṣlmt* C4437:1; em *ṣlmt'* C3969:1*

ṣlmt PN brt PN statue of PN, daughter of PN *C4437:1*; *ṣlmt' dh dy PN b[rt PN]* this statue is of PN, daughter of PN *C3969:1*; *ṣlmt' dnh dy PN brt PN* this statue is of PN, daughter of PN *C3954:1*; *ṣlmt'* 'statue of a woman' also in Hatra, IH 5, 30, 34, 37' for occurrences in Old Syriac inscriptions, see Dri '72a no. 42, 59

▶ *ṣlm* n

ṣ'bw *nm* Saabu (name of deity)

s ab *ṣ'b[w]* C3991:3

'bd PN br PN [l]'lh ṣ'b[w] [to] the god Saab[u] *C3991:3*; *dy mqr' gd' [']nbṭ* who is called PN PN, which follows the name of deity in C3991:3 is taken by Chabot as referring, not to the deity, but to the previously-named dedicator of the stone :: Déd p 211: DN 'who is called the Fortune of the Nabataeans'†

ṣry *adj* Tyrian (?)

s ab ? *ṣry* CRAIBL '81:6

s<l'yn> 3 ṣry 3 Tyrian ? s(elas), i. e. drachmas; so Teix but context broken, and grammatical difficulty is evident†

ṣryḥ See *ṣdyḥ* n

qbh *nf** vaulted room; crater (?)

s em *qbt'* PNO 43:1; Ber '36 p 84:3*; pl em ? *qby'* Syr '85 p 279:1

qbt' dnh 'bd PN PN made this vaulted room *PNO 43:1* (on edge of crater, but not necessarily reference to that object :: As'ad and Teix '85 p 84); *'bd qbt' dh wtṣbyth klh* [PN] made this vaulted room and all its ornament *Ber '36 p 84:3*; *qby' 'ln tr[y']* these two vaulted rooms ? *Syr '85 p 279:1*; Lat. apparently transcribes *gub*†

qbwr *nm** grave, tomb

s em *qbwr'* C4160:1*

qbwr' dnh 'bdw PN wPN PN and PN made this tomb *C4163:2*; *mnwn tlt dy m'rt' dy dqbwr'* three parts of the hypogeum, of the tomb *RB '30 14:5*

▶ *qbr* v; *qbr* n

qby' See *qbh* n

qbl *v* G (?; broken context); D **1** to be opposite; **2** to receive; Dt to be received, accepted

G ptcp pass m s ab ? *qbyl* C4050:8, 10; D ptcp m s ab *mqbl* C4199:9; m s em *mqbl'* C4199:8; f s ab *mqbl'* RB '30 14:3; f s em *mqblt'* C4175:7; m pl ab *mqblyn* Ber '38 p 124:8; Dt ptcp m s ab *mtqbl* Trf:136

G *wqbyl l[..]mn'* and was ? by (epithet of deity *rḥmn'* ?) *C4050:8*

D **1** *dy mqbl bb'* which faces the door *C4199:9*; *dy mn 'ksdr' mqbl'* which are of

the exedra opposite *Ber '35 p 82V:1*; see O'Connor '88 p 364 **2** *dy mqbl' mnh ksp dnryn m'h w'sryn* that she received one hundred twenty denarii from him *RB '30 14:3* **Dt** *'py 'sr yhw' mtqbl* it shall be received according to the *assarius* *Trf:136*
▶ *lqbl* prep

qbl *nm** occasion (?)

pl ab *qblyn* Syr '36 20:6*

bqblyn 'rb' on four occasions ? *Syr '36 20:6*
▶ *qbl* v†

qbl See *lqbl* prep

qbr *v* to bury

G pf pass 3ms *qbyr* Ber '34 p 38:9; pf pass 3fs *qbyrt* RSP 105:5; ptcp f s ab *qbyr'* RB '30 9:3 (or pf pass 3fpl ?); ptcp pass m sg ab *qbyryn* RSP 21:3

dy qbyr' bh PN 'ḥth wPN 'ntth in which are buried PN, his sister, and PN, his wife *RB '30 9:3*; *wqbyrt bh PN brt PN 'ntth* and there is buried in it PN, daughter of PN, his wife *RSP 105:5*
▶ *qbr* n; *qbwr* n; *mqbrh* n†

qbr *nm** tomb

s em *qbr'* C4109:1*

qbr' dnh wm'rt' dy bn' PN this tomb, and the hypogeum, is that which PN built *C4122:1* Gk *mnēm[e]ion* and so elsewhere, cf *qbr' dnh C4167:1* Gk *mnēmeion tapheōno[s]*; *C4192:1* Gk *taphos*; *mnth plgh dqbr' wm'rt' dy bgwh* his part, his half of the tomb and the hypogeum within it *C4206:2*
▶ *qbr* v; *qbwr* n; *mqbrh* n

qdym See *qdm* prep

qdyš *adj* holy

m pl em *qdyš'* C4001:3; *qdš'* C4002:2

ltrn '[ḥy]' qdyš' 'bd w[qr]b made and o[ffe]red to the Two Holy Br[other]s *C4001:3*
▶ *qdš* v; *'ḥ* n†

qdm *prep* **1** before, in front of; **2** owed by, debited to

qdm C3973:8; sf 3ms *qdmwhy* C4168:1; *qdmwh* PNO 52:3; *qdymwhy* of Inv 12 49:5 is dubious reading; perhaps text just *qdmwhy*

1 *dkyr PN qdm DN* may PN be remembered before DN *PNO 17:3*
2 *mnw dy yzbn 'rb' dy qdm m'rt'* whoever sells a surety ? which is debited to the hypogeum *Ber '38 p 133:6*; see *'rb n* and Cussini '92a (index, forthcoming revision)
▶ *qdmy* adj

qdmy *adj* **1** first, former; **2** (adv.) in the first place

m s ab *qdmy* Ber '35 p 86:8; em *qdmy'* Trf(I):9; f s em *qdmt'* Syr '33 p 177:5, CaGr p 114; *qmyt'* StudMiles p 38:1-2; m pl ab *qdmyn* C4171:2

1 *'m nmws' qdmy'* with the former law *Trf(I):9*, Gk *prōtou*; *bzbny' qdmy'* in former times *Trf(I):4*, Gk *palai*; *btr qrqs' qdmy'* behind the first pointed arch *Ber '35 p 84:1*
2 *qdmy wtwb* in the first place, and furthermore *Ber '35 p 86:8*
▶ *qdm* prep

qdns *nm** danger

s ab *qdns* BS III 45:9*

[w]šwzbh mn qdns rb d[y] hwt bh and saved it from a great danger in which it found itself Gk *kindynou*; see Hillers and Cussini '92)
(< Gk *kindynos* 'danger')†

qdš *v* D to consecrate; Dt to be consecrated; C to consecrate

D pf 3ms *qdš* Inv 10 24:2; ptcp pass m pl ab *mqdšyn* Ber '38 p 124:3; Dt ptcp f s em *mtq[dšt']* RSP 162:4; C pf 3ms *'qdš* C4162:1; 1s *'qdšt* C4214:1; pass ptcp m s ab *mqdš* StudMiles p 38:2

D *bdyl dy qdš lh PN brh* because he consecrated PN, his son, for him *Inv 10 24:2*; *gwmḥyn trn bryyn ymnyyn mqdšyn* two outer consecrated niches on the right *Ber '38 p 124:3*
Dt *gnt' dy mtq[dšt']* the conse[crate]d garden *RSP 162:4* (reading very uncertain;

could be *mtq[rt']* or something else, see Gaw ad loc.)
C *[qbr]' dnh bn' w'qdš PN* PN built and consecrated this [tomb] *C4162:1* Gk *aphierōsen*, cf *C4214:1 aphierōsa*; *'ksdr' mqbl' ... mqdš* the exedra opposite ... is consecrated *StudMiles p 38:2*
▶ *qdš* n; *qdyš* adj†

qdš *nm* holy thing
pl sf 3ms *qdšwhy* Inv 9 1:5
ḥnk hykl' dy DN wDN wDN 'lhy' bqdšwhy he dedicated the temple of DN and DN and DN, the gods, with its holy things; Gaw '71 p 68: 'on their feast day'; Bou and As'ad '82 p 107 'sanctuaries'
▶ *qdš* v; *qdyš* adj†

qdš *adj* holy (attestation uncertain)
m s ab *qdš (or qrš)* RTP 699
ḥmr mkl wplg qdš wine, a measure and a half, holy ? *RTP 694*; see Fellmann and Dunant '75 p 115; du Mesnil, TMP, p 485; Déd pp 49-50 :: Caquot RTP pp 148-49
▶ *qrš* adj; *qdyš* adj

qwlwn *nm** colonist
s em *qwlwn* C4401:2*
PN qwlwn brty' PN, a colonist of Beirut Gk *kolōn*
(<Gk *kolōn* < Lat. *colonus*)
▶ *qlny'* n†

qwm *v* G **1** to stand; to be erected (G derived from C 1); **2** to be agreed, effected legally (of transfer of property; G derived from C 2); **3** marker of ingressive aspect (before following verb joined by *w*-); **4** *qwm 'l* to be in charge of; C **1** to erect; **2** to establish
G pf 3ms *qm* C3921:2; 3fs *qmt* Ber '35 p 107:9; ptcp m s ab *qym* Inv 9 28:7; f s ab *qym'* Syr '38 p 155:2; C pf 3ms *'qym* C3940:2; *'qm* C3927:3; 3fs *'qymt* C3914:1; 1s *'qymt* Trf:109; 3mpl *'qymw* C3928:2; *'qym* C3922:2; *hqymw* Syr '36 25:11 CaGr p 44; inf *mqmw* C3956:4
G 1 *mn [dy] qm bršhwn w'bd šlm' bynyhwn* because he stood at their head and made peace between them *C3915:2*; *'d nyq' dy qym' lqblh* up to the Victory which stands opposite it *Syr '38 p 155:2*; *qm ṣlm' dnh b[yrḥ]* this statue was erected in the [month of] *C3921:2* **2** *qmt šnt 510 byrḥ sywn* agreed on in the year 590, the month of Siwan *Ber '35 p 107:9*; cf BibHeb *qwm* Gen 23:17, 20; Lev 27:19 **3** *qm wbn' wqrb* he set to work and built and offered *C3966:5* **4** *dhw' qym 'l ṭly'* who was in charge of the youths *Inv 9 28:7*
C 1 *bwl' wdms 'qymt ṣlmy' 'ln trwyhwn* the Senate and People erected these two statues *C3914:1*; *b'mwd' dnh lmqmw 'lwhy [ṣlm]yn trn* on this column, to set on it two [statu]es *C3956:4*; *'qym lh tgr'* the merchants erected for him *C3933:3* Gk *anestēsan*; *ṣlm' dnh ... dy 'qym lh PN* this statue ... which was erected for him by PN *Ber '70 p 66:8*; cf Cantineau *'36 p 278* Gk line 8 *[andrian]ta anēgeiren*
2 *lṭ'mt' hy<k> bnm[w]s' lṭ'wn' 'qymt dy yhw' mtg[b]' dnr* for a load, as it (says) in the law, I have established that it shall be taxed a denarius *Trf:109*, Gk *heistēmi*
▶ *qywm* n

qwpy *nm* part of tomb construction
s em *qwpy'* Ber '38 p 95:7
'd qwpy' dy kpt' up to the ... ? of the vault†

qṭry' *nf* century (Roman military unit)
s ab/em *qṭry'* C3908:4
PN tdmwry' qšṭ' qṭry' mksmws PN, a Palmyrene, a bowman, (in) the century of Maximus Lat. (abbreviated) *c(enturia) Maximi*
(<Lat. *centuria*)
▶ *qṭrywn* n†

qṭrywn *nm* centurion
s em *qṭrywn'* C3962:1; Inv 12 33:1; *qṭryn'* Inv 10 81:2
qṭrywn' dy mn lgywn' dy 'rb't' a centurion of the fourth ? legion *C3962:1*
(<Gk *kentouriōn, kentoriōn, kentyriōn* < Lat.

centurio)
▶ *qṭry'* n†

qywm *nm* patron
s sf 3ms *qywmh* C3940:5, cf C3943:5
lyqr rḥmh wqywmh in honor of his friend and patron *C3940:5* Gk *prostatēn*, cf C3941, C3943 Gk
▶ *qwm* v†

qyny *nm* smith
pl em *qyny'* C3945:3
tgm' dy qyny' the association of smiths
▶ *qnyh* n†

qysr *nm* Caesar
s ab *qysr* Trf:62; *qsr* C3932:3
'p grmnqws qysr also Germanicus Caesar *Trf:103* Gk *kaisaros*; *PN 'pṭrp' dwqnr' dy qsr mrn* PN, governor, ducenarius of our lord Caesar *C3938:3*
(< Gk *kaisar* < Lat. *caesar*)

ql *nm* voice
s sf 3ms *qlh* C4080:5
wšm' bqlh and he heard his voice†

qlny' *nm ?* colony (designation of Palmyra)
s em *qlny'* C3939:4; C3932:2; Inv 10 115:2
'sṭr<t>g' dy qlny' general of the colony *C3939:4* Gk *kolōneias*; *C3942* Gk *mētrokolōneias* mother-colony (Palmyra; see Inv 10 12)
(< Gk *kolōneia*, *kolōneia* < Lat. *colonia*)
▶ *qwlwn* n†

qlsṭr *nm* basket (?); bolt (?) (meaning uncertain)
s em *qlsṭr[']* C3951:5
w'bd qlsṭr[' dy] ksp' qd[m] DN 'lh['] and he made the silver basket(?) before DN, the god
(cf late Heb *qlsṭr n* 'basket' [from Gk *kanastron* 'basket'] ?; or < Gk *kleistron*, *kleithron* 'bar for closing a door' ? See Gaw '70a pp 74-75)†

qmy *adj* see *qdmy* adj

qnyh *nf* association (?)
s cn *qnyt* RTP 306, 309; em *qnyt'* RTP 307, 308
qnyt nbw the association ? of Nabu *RTP 306*; *nbw qnyt'* Nabu, the association ? *RTP 307, 308* :: Déd pp 159-60 'musician'; cf also Dunant BS III pp 66-67 on Gk. *konetōn* (BS III no. 52 line 3); Ing '76 p 133 fn 170; evidence is at best inconclusive†

qnyn *nm* Qinyan (name of month = July)
s ab *qnyn* C4256:2
▶ Appendix CALENDAR

qsṭ *nm* right
pl sf 3mpl *qsṭyhwn* Ber '35 p 104:5
gwmḥy' 'ln trn ... wqsṭyhwn rḥqt ceded these two niches ... and their rights; cf Ber '35 p 110:1 and archaic Syriac sale-document, Teix '90 pp 154-55:8, property is rented with *zdqyh* 'its rights'
▶ *qšṭ* v; *qšṭ II* n†

qsṭwn *nm* *sextarius* (dry measure, approx. 1 pint)
s ab *qsṭwn* Trf:69
[ml]ḥ ṭb [ytg]b' 'sr' ḥd lmdy' dy qsṭwn 'šr w[š]t good [sal]t [shall be ta]xed one assarius per *modius* of [si]xteen *sextarii*
(< Gk *ksestēs*, dry measure < Lat. *sextarius*)†

qsm *nm* distribution (?); divination (?)
s em *qsm'* Syr '26 p 129:4
wytb 'l qsm' šṭ' klh and he supervised the distribution ? (divination ?) a whole year; see Déd p 280
▶ *qsmy'* n; PN *qsm'* †

qsmy' *nm* Kismaya (Destiny), name of deity
qsmy' CRAIBL '85:5
l'rṣw wlqsmy' [w]lbnt 'l 'lhy' ṭby' to

Arsu and to Kismaya and to the daughters of El, the good gods *CRAIBL '85:5*; note remarks of Caquot there p 292
▶ PN *qsm* †

qsr see *qysr* n

qpl *nm reading and meaning uncertain*
pl sf 3ms *q[p]lwhy* Syr '36 26:10
q[p]lwhy its ... †

qṣb *nm* butcher ?; sacrificial victim ?
pl em *qṣb'* Trf:102
mks' dy qṣb' 'py dnr ḥyb lmtḥšbw the tax on butchers ('sacrificial victims') ought to be rendered in denarii Gk for *qṣb'* is *sphaktrou* (a very rare word) '(tax on) sacrificial victims'; see Dessau 1884 p 519: cf Matthews '84, Zahrnt '86 p 283 n. 18†

qṣh *nf* military unit (?); border (?)
s em *qṣt'* Sumer '62 p 63:4
dy 't' brš qṣt' b'sṭrṭgwt PN who came at the head of a unit during the campaign of PN (or: 'to the limit of the border') *Syr '63 p 48:4*; *dy hww 'm PN bqṣt' tnn* who were with PN in the unit here (or: 'at the border') *Sumer '62 p 63:4*; see Starcky, Syr '63 pp 50-51†

qrb *v* D to offer; C (?) to offer
D pf 3ms *qrb* PNO 50:1; 3fs *qrbt* BS III 11:2; 3mpl *qrbw* Inv 12 39:1; *qrb* Inv 11 99:1; C pf 3ms ? *'qrb* PNO 16:2; isolated and suspect reading
D *špr [lhn] [wq]rb lbt 'lhyhn* he was good [to them] [and off]ered to their temple *C3923:4* Gk *didonta*; *qrbw* they offered C3904 Gk *anethēkan*; *'lt' dnh qrb PN* PN offered this altar *PNO 14:1*; *qrb PN lDN* PN offered (this) to DN *PNO 20:1*; *qm wbn' wqrb* he set out and built and offered ... *C3966:5*; *ḥmn' dnh w'lt' dh [']bdw wqrbw PN wPN* PN and PN [m]ade and offered this chapel and this altar *C3978:3*
C *'lt' dh 'qrb PN* PN offered this altar *PNO 16:2* (*aleph* at end of line 1, *qrb* on line 2)

qrṭsṭ *adj* most powerful, distinguished, excellent (title of honor)
m s em *qrṭsṭ'* C3946:4; pl em *qrṭsṭw'* C3947:3
wPN rb ḥyl' dy tdmwr qrṭsṭ' and PN, general of Tadmor, most powerful *C3946:4*; *PN wPN qrṭsṭw'* PN and PN, the most powerful *C3947:3* Gk *hoi kratistoi*
(< Gk *kratistos* 'most powerful')
▶ *qrṭsṭs* adj†

qrṭsṭws *adj* most powerful, distinguished, excellent (title of honor)
s em *qrṭsṭws* C3940:1; *qrṭsṭs* C3942:1
sptmyws wrwd qrṭsṭws 'ptrp' dqnr' w'rgbṭ' Septimius Worod, most powerful, procurator, ducenarius, and governor *C3940:1* Gk *ton kratiston*
(< Gk *kratistos* 'most powerful')
▶ *qrṭsṭ* adj

qrṭsṭs see *qrṭsṭws* adj

qry *v* G to call to (for help); Gt to be called, to be surnamed
G pf 3ms *qr'* RSP 121:3; *qrh* C4047:5; *qr* Inv 11 16:4; sf 3ms *qryh* RSP 120:4; 3fs sf 3ms *qrth* Ber '36 p 99:3; 3mpl *qrw* C4100:3; 1pl *qryny* C4048:6; Gt ptcp m s ab *mtqr'* C3978:5; *mtqrh* C3966:2; *mqr'* C3991:4; *mqrh* Ber '35 p 98:1; em *mtqry'* C4582:4; m pl ab *mtqrn* C4124:2
G *dy qr lh bym' wbybš' w'nh [bk]l dy qrh hw w[bny by]th* to whom he called on sea and dry land and he answered him [ever]y time he called to him, him and the [people of] his [hou]se *C4047:5*; *qrw lh l'lh' w'nnwn* they called to the god and he answered them *C4053:6*
Gt *PN dy mtqr' slwqws* PN, who is called Seleucus *C3934:2*

qryb *adj* relative, relation
m s sf 3ms *qrybh* Ber '35 p 76:1; sf 3mpl *qrybwhy* Ber '35 p 77:2
lPN qrybh to PN, his relative *Ber '35 p 76:1*

▶ *qrb* v†

qryh *nf* town, village
s em *qryt'* PNO 39:1; *qrt[']* MUSJ '61 p 133:6 (reading uncertain); pl (s noun in collective sense) *qry'* Trf:112
mn dy mpq l[qry]' ['w m]''l mn qry' which is exported to the [village]es [or im]ported from the villages *Trf:112* Gk *chōria, [chō]riōn*; *wlgdh dy qryt'* and to the Fortune of the town *PNO 42:4*

qrn *nf* corner
s em *qrn'* Ber '35 p 78:2; cf Syr '36 18:1
mn qrn' dy 'ksdr' from the corner of the exedra *Ber '35 p 78:2*†

qrs *nm* wagon
s ab *qrs* Trf(I):13
ṭ'wn qrs dy klm' gns klh a wagon-load of any kind
(< Lat. *carrus*)†

qrqs *nm* *kerkis*, tympanum, or half-tympanum (Gk *kerkis* 'space between an arch and the horizontal head of a door below'; approximately 'peak of an arch')
s em *qrqs'* Ber '35 p 85:10; pl em *qrqsy'* Ber '35 p 98:1
mn qrqs' wlgw from the peak of the arch and inside *Ber '35 p 82V:1*
(< Gk *kerkis*, 'shuttle' > 'tympanum')

qrš *adj* thick (uncertain; said of wine)
m s ab *qrš (or qdš)* RTP 699
ḥmr mkl wplg qrš wine, a measure and a half, thick ? *RTP 694*; see Caquot RTP p 148-49 :: Déd pp 191-92
▶ *qdš* adj

qrt see *qryh* n

qšṭ *v* to be right (for, *l*)
G impf 3ms *yqšṭ* C4218:5
wl' yqšṭ lmn dy ypthyhy 'd 'lm' and may it never be right for the person who opens it†

qšṭ I *nm* bowman
s em *qšṭ'* C3908:3
PN tdmwry' qšṭ' qṭry' mksmws PN, the Palmyrene, bowman of the century of Maximus *C3908:3* Latin *SAG(ittarius)*; Doura 33:4
▶ *qšt* n

qšṭ II *nm* right (thing); right
s em ? *qšṭ[']* Trf:131; sf 3ms ? *qš[ṭ]h* C4209:3; pl sf 3ms *qšṭwh* Syr '38 p 155:3; 3mpl *qšṭyhwn* Ber '35 p 112:7
qšṭ[' ']tḥzy ly it seemed the right thing to me *Trf:131*; *'ksdryn trn ... wqšṭyhwn rḥq PN* PN cedes two exedras ... with their rights *Ber '35 p 110:1*, Gk *dikaiois*
▶ *qsṭ* n

qšyš *nm* elder, old man
m s em *qšyš'* C4501:2
ṣlm PN qšyš' statue of PN, the elder†

qšt *nm* archer, bowman
s ab *qšt* Inv 8 121:4; s em ? *qšt'* RTP 942; Syr '59 p 106 no. 14
PN qšt ḥbl PN, archer. Alas! *Inv 8 121:4*; Ros apud Cantineau Syr '38 p 166: *qšt* here is PN
▶ *qšṭ* n†

r *abbr* *r<b'>* one fourth

rb *adj* 1 large, great (also as epithet or name of deity); 2 elder; 3 rb *x*: chief of (followed by name of group or thing)
m s ab *rb* BS III 45:9; cn *rb* C3948:2; em *rb'* C4188:2; f s ab *rb'* C3915:4; em *rbt'* C3914:4
1 *bkl [ṣ]bw klh rb' wz'r'* in every [t]hing, great and small *C3915:4*; *'l bb' rb'* at the large gate *Syr '36 19:3*, cf *C3914* Gk *megalē*; *l'lh' rb'* to the great god *C3911:8*; *rb ḥyl' rb'* PN, the chief general *C3946:3*; *C3947:3* Gk *megas*; *rb' 'rsw* the Great One (deity), Arsu *RTP 190* see Milik

Déd p 187 **2** *PN br PN rb'* PN, son of PN the elder *C4288:3*; see Ing '66, pp 471-476: Herod in Josephus xviii not Herod the Great, but Herod the Elder, cf literature cited in Saliby '92 note 7 p 271 ad DaM '92 5:3-5 *br ml' rb'*; cf *z'wr* adj in sense younger, minor **3** *rb ḥyl'* head of army; general *C3947:3* Gk *stratēlatēs*; *rb šwq* agoranomos (head of market, see Bertinelli Angeli p 67) *C3932:5* Gk *agoranomēsanta*; *rb šyrt'* caravan leader *C3936:2* Gk *[a]rchemporon*; *C3948:2* Gk *s[un]odiarchēn*; *rb 'yn* overseer of the spring *RSP 126:2*; *rb mrzḥ'* symposiarch (head of the symposium) *RTP 27*; cf IH passim *rbyt'* 'majordomo'; cf Aggoula '72 59, n. 3.
▶ *rbn* n; *rbnw* n

rb'syr' *nm* Rabasire (name of deity)
s ab *rb'syr'* Trf(I):10
hykl' dy rb'syr' the temple of Rabasire Gk *rabaseirē*†

rbw *num* ten thousand
s ab *rbw* C3934:5
wmgd lbwl' zwzyn rbw and he donated to the Senate ten thousand *zuz*'s†

rbw' *nm* interest (?)
s ab ? *rbw'n* Sem '86 p 89:2, 4
rbw'n 'lpyn tryn wm'tn wtltyn wšt interest ? two thousand and two hundred and thirty-six *Sem '86 p 89:2*†

rbw'h *nf** rectangular space (?)
s em *rbw't'* MUSJ '62 p 106:6, 9*
dy lwt lh brbw't' dy qym' btr gwmḥyn that he has taken him as associate in the rectangular space that stands behind the niches *MUSJ '62 p 106:6*†

rb ḥyl' see *rb* adj

rby *v* D to raise, to bring up
D pf 3ms *rby* PS 232:1
PN br [PN] dy rby PN PN son of [PN], whom PN raised
▶ *mrbyh* n†

rb mrzḥ' see *rb* adj

rbn *nm* chief, leader
pl cn *rbny* RTP 37, 38
wrbny 'wnt' dy bl and the leaders of the priesthood (?) of Bel *RTP 37*
(*rb* and plural forms and derivatives present complex situation in Aram dialects; analysis given here is partial, simplified)
▶ *rb* adj; *rbnw* n†

rbnw *nf* term as head, term as presiding officer
s cn *rbnwt* C3970:1; sf 3ms *rbnwth* Syr '85 p 257:1
brbnwth during his term as chief *Syr '85 p 257:1*; *brbnwt šyrt[']* *[dy PN]* during the term as caravan leader [of PN] *C3928:4* Gk *sunodiarchou*; *brbnwt 'yn'* during the term as supervisor of the spring *Inv 12 44:1*; *brbnwt mrzḥ' PN* during the term as symposiarch of PN *RTP 34*; cf *C3970:1* Gk *su[mposia]rchos*; *brbnwt mrzḥwt PN* during PN's term as symposiarch *Inv 9 28:1*; note that apparently both parts of the term *rb mrzḥ'* are given abstract ending
▶ *rb* adj; *rbn* n

rbnšqw *nf* term as head of market (Gk *agoranomos*)
s sf 3ms *rbnšqwth* Inv 10 115:2
wbrbnšqwth and during his term as *agoranomos*; cf *rb šwq* *C3932:5* Gk *agoranomēsanta*
(calque of Gk *agoranomos*, see Bertinelli Angeli p 68)†

rb' *nm* 1 one fourth; 2 *dy rb''* tax-collector (Gk *tetartōnēs* 'collector of tax of 25 per cent')
s ab *rb'* (s.v.l.) RTP 194; abbr. ? *r<b'y'>* RTP 758; em *rb''* Inv 10 113:2
1 *rb'* one fourth *RTP 194* (s.v.l.) **2** *PN dy rb''* PN, tax-collector *Inv 10 113:2* Gk

tetartōnē
(*dy rbʿʾ* calque < Gk *tetartōnēs*)
▶ *ʾrbʿ* num; *rbwʿ* n; *rbʿw* n

rbʿw *nf* quarter
s cn *rbʿwt* C4206:4
rbʿwt qbrʾ dnh a quarter of this tomb
▶ *ʾrbʿ* num; *rbwʿh* n; *rbʿ* n†

rbʿynʾ See *rb* adj

rbrb *adj* great
m pl ab *rbrbn* Inv 10 44:6; Déd p 13:4
ʾpq mn kysh npqn rbrbn he spent, from his own funds, great sums *Inv 10 44:6*
▶ *rb* adj†

rb šwq see *rb* adj

rb šyrtʾ see *rb* adj

rgz *nm* wrath (?)
s em *rgzʾ* RSP 142:2
pnwn mn šʿtʾ drgzʾ and he rescued them from the time of wrath ?†

rgl *nf* foot
s sf 3ms *rglh* C4058:6
[y]dh wrglh his [han]d and his foot†

rgly *nm* person
s ab *rgly* Trf:81; pl ab *rglyn* Trf:80
ytn lkl rgly [d]<ynryn> 12 he shall pay for every person 12 [d(enarii)] *Trf(II):6* Gk *sōma[tos]*; *mn dy mʿl rglyn ltdmr* whoever imports humans to Palmyra *Trf:80*
▶ *rgl* n

rwḥ *nm* 1 relief; 2 space (?)
s em *rwḥʾ* C4100:5
1 *wʿnnwn brwḥʾ* and he gave them relief *C4100:5* **2** *plg nsb mnth plgh rwḥʾ* the half he has taken as part is the space (sense of sentence unclear) *MUSJ ʾ62 p 106:8*

rwḥyʾ *adj* of Ruhu (tribe or place)
s em *rwḥy[ʾ]* C3973:2
PN nbṭyʾ rwḥyʾ PN, the Nabataean, the Ruhaean†

rzʾ *nm* expenditure
pl ab *rzʾyn* C3932:5
wḥsk rzʾyn šgyʾyn and he made many expenditures Gk *ouk oligōn apheidēsanta chrēmatōn*†

rḥḥ *v* to widen (?)
C inf ? *mrḥ* MUSJ ʾ62 p 106:9
wlʾ yhʾ šlyṭ lh lmrḥ lʿlwh and he shall not be entitled to widen (?) it†

rḥym *adj* 1 loving, lover of; 2 beloved (?)
s cn *rḥym* Inv 10 39:2; *rḥm* C3955:7; em *rḥymʾ* Inv 8 180:2; pl cn *rḥymy* C3930:3; *rḥymʾ* C3914:3
1 *PN rḥym mḥwzh* PN, lover of his city *Inv 10 39:2*; *wrḥymʾ mdythwn* and lovers of their city *C3914:3* Gk *[ph]ilopatrisi*
2 *rḥymʾ* the beloved *Inv 8 180:2* (followed by unknown noun or name; Cantineau ad loc. and CaGr p 160 takes as active in sense)
▶ *rḥm* n; *rḥmn* adj

rḥm I *nm* love, affection
s em *rḥmʾ* C3935:4
dy ʾqym l[h b]wlʾ wdmws lyqrh mn rḥmʾ which the Senate and People erected for him, in his honor, out of affection Gk *eun[oias]* (cf Syriac *raḥmā* affection, favor)
▶ *rḥm* II n; *rḥym* adj; *rḥmn* adj†

rḥm II *nm* friend
s sf 3ms *rḥmh* C3939:4; pl sf 3ms *rḥmwhy* C3960:6; *rḥmwh* C4061:7; 3mpl *rḥmyhn* PNO 78:3
lyqr rḥmh wqywmh in honor of his friend and patron *C3940:5* Gk *philon*; *lḥywh [wḥy]ʾ ʾbwh [wʾḥw]h wrḥmwh* for his life [and the life of] his father [and] his [brother] and his friends *C4061:7*; *PN ... rḥmh* PN, his friend *C3939:4* Gk *ho philos autou*; cf IH 13:3; 36:6 *rḥm* friend

▶ *rḥm* $_{\mathrm{I}}$ n; *rḥmn* adj; *rḥym* adj

rḥm $_{\mathrm{III}}$ *nm* Rahmu (name of deity)
s ab *rḥm* Syr '33 p 181:1; MUSJ '61 p 125:4
[l]b'lšmyn wldwrḥlwn wlrḥm wlgd' dy PN [to] Baalshamin and to Durahlun and to Rahmu and to the Fortune of PN *BS III 23:3*
▶ TeixPan pp 62-64; ANRW pp 2642-43; Hof RelAram p 43[†]

rḥmn *adj* merciful; (in title or epithet of deity) the Merciful One
s em *rḥmn'* C4022:3
dkyr qdm rḥmn' PN may PN be remembered before the Merciful One *Inv 12 45:9*; *lbryk šmh l'lm' rḥmn' ṭb'* for Blessed-Be-His-Name-Forever, the merciful, the good *C4033:2*; *dy qrw lrḥmn' w'nnwn* they called to the Merciful One and he answered them *Inv 11 1:6*; *lb'l šmn rb' w[r]ḥmn'* to Baalshamin, the great and merciful *IP 10:1* Gk *[dii hy]psistō*
▶ *bryk šmh l'lm'* n phr

rḥmny *adj* merciful, in epithet or title of deity
fem pl em *rḥmnyt'* Sem '77 p 117:5
ltš'yt' wrḥmnyt' to the famous ? and merciful ones; Aggoula ad loc. takes as abstract noun 'Mercy'
▶ *rḥmn* adj

rḥq *v* G to withdraw from, cede; C to cede
G pf 3ms *rḥq* Ber '35 p 86:13; 3fs *rḥqt* Ber '35 p 104:5; 1s *rḥqt* Ber '35 p 96:2; 3mpl *rḥq* C4204:2; C pf 3ms *'rḥq* Ber '35 p 88:3
G *gwmḥ' ḥd rḥq PN dnh lPN* this PN ceded one burial niche to PN *Ber '35 p 86:13*; *dy rḥq lh lPN dnh* which they ceded to this PN *C4173:3*; *PN rḥq mn gwmḥyn 'rb''* PN ceded four burial niches *Ber '35 p 112:2*; *PN rḥqt lPN š'r 'ksdr' šḥym'* I PN cede to PN the rest of the unconsecrated exedra *Ber '35 p 96:2*; *[rḥq] C4209:3* Gk *ex[estēsato]*; *rḥq Syr '38 p 155:3* Gk *ekxechōrēsan*, cf Gk Inv 8 68
C *PN 'rḥq lPN* PN cedes to PN *Ber '35 p 88:3*
(transitive sense of G derives from intransitive 'withdraw from [*mn*]' in favor of PN > 'cede to', with or without *mn* as marker of object [property ceded])

rkb See *mrkb* n

rmy *v* to put ([?] reading and meaning uncertain)
G ptcp pass m s ab ? *rm'* Syr '33 p 184:2
wrm' bt 'rk' and put ? in the archives; reading *dm'* possible, or *d<g>m'*
▶ at *dmy* v[†]

r'y *v* to tend sheep
G pf 3ms *r''* Sumer '64 p 13:4; 3mpl *r'w* Sumer '64 p 15:5
dy r'w tnn who tended sheep here *Sumer '64 p 15:5*[†]

r'y' *adj* epithet of god Arsu, meaning uncertain: Shepherd (?); the Favorable One (?)
s em *r'y'* RTP 176; *r'yy'* (?) RTP 175
'rṣw r'yy' Arsu. The Shepherd ? *RTP 176*; *lr'y' l'rṣw* to the Shepherd (?), to Arsu *RTP 175*; see As'ad and Teix '85b p 288 n. 7
▶ TeixPan p 71[†]

rṣp *v* to be established (?)
G ptcp pass m s ab *rṣyp* Trf:101
wbnmws' rṣyp and by law it is established ?[†]

rš *nm* 1 head (of small cattle); 2 leader, presiding person (of group, city)
s cn *rš* Inv 10 29:4; em *rš'* Trf:42; s em (or pl) ? *rš'* RTP 39, cf Syr '85 p 253 1:1 *[rš]'* (probable restoration); sf 3mpl *ršhwn* C3915:3
1 *'mry' lm'[ln wlmpqn] lrš' ḥd 'sr' ḥd* lambs for im[port or for export], for each head, one assarius *Trf:42* **2** *rš šyr'* caravan

leader *Inv 10 29:4* Gk *sunodiarchēn*; *wrš tdmwr* and ruler of Palmyra *C3944:2* Gk *exa[rchon]*; *dy yhwʾ ʾḥyd brš[hwn]* who will be elected to be [their] leader *CRAIBL ʾ81:5*; *dy yhʾ bršhwn* who will be their leader *CRAIBL ʾ81:4*; *wqm bršhwn* and was their leader *C3916:4*
▶ *ršy* adj

ršy *adj* chief, supreme
s em *ršyʾ* Syr ʾ31 18:6
[ml]kʾ ršyʾ supreme [ki]ng (of a king, in a broken text)
▶ *rš* n†

ršp *nm* Resheph (name of deity)
s ab *ršp* Syr ʾ36 17:6
wlnny wlršp ʾlhyʾ and to Nanay and to Resheph, the gods
▶ TeixPan pp 111-113; ANRW p 2647†

šʾwr see *šʾr* n

šʾl *v* C to loan, hire out
C pf 1s *ʾšʾlt* MUSJ ʾ62 p 106:3
ʾšʾlt ktb ydy lPN I have lent my writing to PN†

šʾr *nm* rest, remainder
s cn *šʾr* Ber ʾ35 p 96:2; *šʾwr* Déd p 36:4
nwyt šʾwr pḥzʾ bt ʾlhyhwn as also the rest of the tribes (have done) in the houses of their gods *Déd p 36:4*; *šʾr ʾksdrʾ šḥymʾ* the rest of the unconsecrated exedra *Ber ʾ35 p 96:2*†

šbb *nm* neighbor (?)
pl sf 3mpl *šbbyhwn* Syr ʾ36 21:3; note *šbb*[...] Inv 12 41:1 and Teix ad loc.
wlyqr bny šʿrʾ šbbyhwn and in honor of the Bani Shara, their neighbors *Syr ʾ36 21:3* (= Syriac *šbābāy* neighbor ?; Teix ad Inv 12 41:1 [*šbb* perhaps a divine epithet here] cf tentatively Arab *šbb* youth, etc.)†

šbḥ *v* to praise
G pf 3ms sf 3ms *šbḥh* BS III 45:8
šhd lh wšbḥh he gave testimony to him and praised him Gk (for both verbs) *[teteimē]menon*
▶ *šbyḥyt* adv†

šbṭ *nm* Shebat (name of month = February)
s ab *šbṭ* C3989:4
▶ Appendix CALENDAR

šbyḥyt *adv* in a praiseworthy fashion
šbyḥyt Inv 10 44:7
wʿbd pltyʾ šbyḥyt wnhwryt and he conducted his public career in a praiseworthy and distinguished fashion Gk *endoxōs*
▶ *šbḥ* v†

šbyn *nm* *meaning and word-division most uncertain*
pl sf 3mpl *šbynyhwn* CRAIBL ʾ81:8
wmn dy yʿd šbynyhwn and whoever ... (sense of phrase uncertain; see note to text)†

šbʿ *num* seven
ab with m noun *šbʿʾ* C3952:3; em *šbʿtʾ* C3987:3
ʿmwdyn šbʿʾ seven columns *C3952:3*; *ywm šbʿtʾ* day seven C3987:3

šbʿ *v* to be satisfied, have enough
G impf 3ms *yšbʿ* C4218:7
wlḥm wmn lmʾ yšbʿ and may he never have enough bread and water†

šbʿyn *num* seventy
šbʿyn C4053:5
šnt ḥmš mʾh wšbʿyn wtšʿ the year five hundred seventy-nine†

šbʿtʾ *nf* seventh day (?); group of seven (?)
s em *šbʿtʾ* Inv 12 45:7; BS VI p 114 no. 5:2
nbw šbʿtʾ (on tessera) Nabu. The group of seven (?), or, the seventh day (?) *BS VI p 114 no. 5:2*; *wlšbʿtʾ dy wdʾ Inv 12 45:6* and for the seven of the fellowship; for other

possibilities see Teix ad loc. and Sem ‘80 p 62; Aggoula ‘79 p 116
▶ *šb ʿ* num†

šgyʾ *adj* many
m pl ab *šgyʾyn* BS III 45:6; *šgyʾn* C3949:3; em ? *šgyʾ[yʾ]* C3914:3; f pl ab *šgyʾn* Inv 10 44:4
bʾsṭrṭgwn šgyʾn on many campaigns *Inv 10 44:4*; *bmgdyhwn šgyʾ[yʾ]* by their many gifts *C3914:3* Gk *pollois*

šdy *v* Gt to be thrown out
Gt ptcp m pl ab *mštdn* Trf:108
pgryn dy mštdn mks lʾ ḥybyn carcases that are thrown out are not subject to tax†

šdyʾ *nm* Shadya (name of deity); or, demon (?)
s ab *šdyʾ* Syr ’31 p 130:9; or pl em ?
[bw]lʿstr wšdyʾ [(the god) Bo]lastor and Shadya; or: the demons ? :: Déd p 48†

šdk see *šwr* v

šdr *v* D to send
D pf 3ms sf 3ms *šdrh* Syr ’31 p 139:3
wšdrh grmnqs and Germanicus sent him†

šdrpʾ *nm** Shadrafa (name of deity)
s ab *šdrpʾ* Inv 10 145:2; *sdrpʾ* BS III 58:2
lšdrpʾ ʾlhʾ ṭbʾ to Shadrafa, the good god *C3972:3**; *lsdrpʾ ʾlhh wldʿnt* to Sadrapa, the god, and to Duanat *BS III 58:2*
▶ Starcky ‘49f pp 67-81; Collart ’56 pp 209-215; Caquot ’52 pp 74-88; TeixPan pp 104-105; ANRW pp 2646-47; Hof RelAram pp 43, 47-48

šhd *v* to testify
G pf 3ms *šhd* BS III 45:7
wbdy[tg]mʾ šhd lh and by a decree he gave testimony on his behalf
▶ *šhd* n; *shd* v†

šhd *nm* witness
s ab *šhd* MUSJ ’62 p 106:13, 14
PN šhd PN, witness
▶ *šhd* v; *shd* v†

šwʾ *v* to be equal; to be in agreement (?)
G ptcp m s ab *šwʾ* Sem ’77 p 117:7
word-division and sense of context very uncertain

šwzb *v* to save
Quad pf 3ms sf 3ms *šwzbh* BS III 45:9
[w]šwzbh mn qdns rb [and] saved it from great danger Gk *diasōsanta*†

šwm *v* Gt to be placed (?)
Gt pf 3ms *ʾtšm* Maarav ’87 p 72:3
dy ʾtšm which was placed; brief, difficult inscription
▶ *sym* v†

šwq *nm* market
s ab *šwq* C3932:5
rb šwq head of the market Gk *agoranomēsanta*
▶ *rbnšqw* n†

šwr *v* to pass (?)
G inf sf 2ms *šrk* Ber ’35 p 102XI:5
mʿlyk ʾksdrʾ šrk ʿl smlʾ as you enter the exedra, as you pass on the left; *mʿlk mn bbʾ šrk ʿl šmlk* as you enter from the gate, as you pass on the left *StudPalm ‘75 p 129:6* (O’Connor '88 pp 363-64 tentatively suggests biblical Heb and Arab cognates†

šwšn *nf* Susa
s ab *šwšn* Inv 10 114:7; MélDus p 278:2
bšwšn in Susa *Inv 10 114:7*
▶ Appendix MAPS†

šwtp *v* Quad to make a partner; passive: to be made a partner
Quad pf 3ms *štp* (sic) MélColl p 161:9; 1s *šwtpt* Ber ’35 p 93:1; 3mpl *šwtpw* RSP 24:2; Quad passive ptcp m s ab *mšttp* Trf:79
wštp PN bmnth PN and PN has taken as

associate in his share PN *MélCol p 161:9*; *šwtpt wrḥqt lPN* I have taken PN as associate and ceded (to him) *Ber '35 p 93:1*
(< Akk *šutappu*; AIA p 105)
▶ *šwtpw* n†

šwtpw *nf* association
s cn *šwtpwt* RB '30 p 548 no. 14:6, 7
bšwtpwt PN [...] wšwtpwt PN bʿlh in association with PN, and (in) association with PN, her husband
▶ *šwtp* v†

šḥm *adj* unconsecrated
m s em *šḥym'* Ber '35 p 96:3; RSP 163:2; *šḥm'* Ber '38 p 110:5; f sg em *šḥymt'* Syr '33 p 185:1; m pl em *šḥymy'* Ber '38 p 95:7
š'r 'ksdr' šḥym' the rest of the unconsecrated exedra *Ber '35 p 96:3*; *dkt' dh šḥymt' dy lgw mn mʿrt'* this unconsecrated place inside the hypogeum *Syr '33 p 185:1*; *'tr' šḥ[ym']* an unconsecrated place *StudPalm '75 p 129:4*†

šṭyph *nf* alabaster vessel
s em ? *š[ṭypt]'* Trf(II):14; pl em *š[ṭyp]y'* Trf:20
mšḥ' [bšym' d]y yt'ʿl bš[ṭyp]y' [perfumed] oil [w]hich is imported in al[abaster jar]s *Trf:20*; cf *Trf(II):14* Gk *[alabas]trois*; see Chabot ad loc. (restoration of Reckendorf, cf Syriac šāṭîptā = Gk e.g. at Mark 14:3)†

šṭr *v* to write (attestation dubious)
G ptcp pass f s ab *šṭyrh* CRAIBL '81:7; D ptcp f pl em ? *mšṭ[rt']* Sem '77 p 117:8
G *'wyw šṭyrh ʿl*[...] the agreement is written on ... CRAIBL '81:7, but this reading improbable; see *yšṭ v*
D *mšṭ[rt']* wri[tten] *Sem '77 p 117:8* (uncertain attestation)
▶ *šṭr* n†

šṭr *nm** document
s cn *šṭr* Trf(I):8*
wyktb bšṭr 'gry' ḥdt' and let it be written in a new contract document, Gk *tē eggista misthōsei*; cf archaic Syriac sale-document, Teix '90 p 147-48, lines 6 etc.
▶ *šṭr* v†

šṭr *nm** wall, side
s em *šṭr'* C4171:2*
mn šṭr' grbyy' from the north wall *Ber '35 p 98:1*

šṭr mn *prep* except for
šṭr mn RB '30 9:2
šṭr mn 'ksdr' gwy' except for the interior exedra
▶ *sṭr mn prep*†

šyʿ *v* to accompany
G ptcp f pl cn *šyʿt* RTP 285
nny škny šyʿt bbl DN(f), DN(f), who accompany Babylon
▶ *šyʿ'lqwm* n; *tšʿyt'* n†

šyʿ'lqwm *nm* Shaialqawm (name of deity)
s ab *šyʿ'lqwm* C3973:4, 9; RTP 332
šyʿ'lqwm 'lh' ṭb' Shaialqawm, the good god *C3973:9*
TeixPan pp 85-87; ANRW pp 2637-38; Hof RelAram p 41†

šyrh *nf** caravan
s ab *šyr'* Inv 10 29:4; cn *šyrt* Inv 10 90:3; em *šyrt'* BS III 45:10*; pl ab *šyryn* Inv 10 44:5
dy slq bhwn rš šyr' who went up with them as caravan-leader *Inv 10 29:4*; *[h]nwn bny šyrt' dh ʿbdw lh* they, the members of this caravan, made for him *BS III 45:10* Gk *hē autē synodia*; *rb šyrt'* caravan-leader C3948 Gk *s[un]odiarchēi*, cf *C3916:2* Gk *sunodiarchēn* and Gk paraphrase at C3936 *anakomisanta tēn synodian*

šyš *nm* marble
s em *šyš'* Inv 12 148:2
w'sṭw' dy šyš' dy qdmwhy the marble stoa which is in front of it†

škḥ *v* Gt to be found, to be
Gt pf 3ms *ʾšt<k>ḥ* Inv 10 127:3
dy ʾšt<k>ḥ lh lwt tgryʾ which was found in him toward the merchants†

škytyt *adv* quietly
škytyt C3932:6
wdbr ʿmrh škytyt and he conducted his life quietly, Gk *kalōs*†

škny *nf** Shaknay (name or epithet of deity)
s ab *škny* RTP 285*
nny škny šyʿt bbl Nanay (and) Shaknay, those who accompany Babylon
▶ ANRW p 2645; Hof RelAram p 45†

škr *adj* rewarding, generous (epithet of gods)
m s ab *škr* MUSJ '66 p 177:10; em *škrʾ* C3973:4; pl em *škryʾ* BS III 14:2; *škr[ʾ]* ? MUSJ '62 p 133:7
lbl ʾlhʾ ṭb wškr to Bel, the good and generous god *MUSJ '66 p 177:10*; *lDN lDN lDN lʾlhʾ škr[ʾ]* to DN, to DN, to DN, to [the] generous gods *MUSJ '62 p 133:7*; *lyqr mlkʾ ṭbʾ wškrʾ ʿbd glptʾ dnh* PN made this sculpture in honor of Malka, the good and generous *PNO 57:1*

šlwm *nm* peace (Hebrew form, script is Palmyrene)
s ab *šlwm* BethSh p 199 no. 18:2, see Mazar ad loc.
PN šlwm PN. Peace! Gk inscr. at Beth Shearim have *sallom, salom*
(not Aramaic form historically, of course, but possibly Hebraism within Jewish vocabulary of Aramaic)
▶ *šlm* n†

šlḥ *nm* skin
s em *šlḥʾ* Trf:142
lmʿln šlḥʾ for import, a skin†

šlṭ *v* G to be entitled; C to entitle
G impf 3ms *yšlṭ* CRAIBL '81:10; C pf 3ms sf 3ms *ʾšlṭh* C3956:3
G *[dy l]ʾ yšlṭ ʾnš* [that no] one shall be entitled *CRAIBL '81:10*
C *wʾšlṭh* and he gave him the right *C3956:3*
▶ *šlyṭ* adj; *šlṭn* n†

šlṭn *nm* authority
s em *šlṭnʾ* PNO 2ter:7
dy yhb lʿbgl šlṭnʾ bʾtrʾ klh lʿlm who gave Abgal authority over the whole territory, forever
▶ *šlṭ* v; *šlyṭ* adj†

šlyṭ *adj* entitled, authorized
m s ab *šlyṭ* CRAIBL '81:14
wlʾ yhʾ šlyṭ lh and he shall not be authorized *MUSJ '62 p 106:9*
▶ *šlṭ* v; *šlṭn* n†

šlm *nm* peace
s ab *šlm* C4124:3; em *šlmʾ* Déd p 36:3
dy ʿbd šlmʾ who made peace *Déd p 37:3*; *šlm* peace! (at end of inscription) *BS III 60:11*; *PN šlm lh* PN, peace be upon him! *Inv 4 26B:1*; for Aggoula's *šlmyt* 'treaty' Sem '77 p 117:8 prb a form of *šlm* to be read
▶ *šlm* v

šlm *v* C passive: to be given, to be entrusted
C pf pass 3fs *ʾšlmt* C3976:4, see RosSpr p 56; *wʾšlm* Syr '33 p 179:2 is of uncertain analysis
dy ʾšlmt ʿl ydwh which was entrusted to his keeping *C3976:4*
▶ *šlm* n; *mšlm* adj

šlmn *nm* Shulman (name of deity)
šlmn PNO 38:4
PN wPN mwdyn lšlmn wlʿbgl PN and PN give thanks to Shulman and to Abgal, cf also *Sem '50 p 47*
Etymology discussed TeixPan p 84
▶ Hof RelAram p 44†

šlmt *nf* Shalmat (name of deity)
s ab *šlmt* Syr '38 .p. 82:2; Syr '31 14:1

ʿbd PN lšlmt PN made (this) for Shalmat *Syr ʾ38 p 82:2*; *lšlmt wlʾḥyh gnyʾ [ṭby]ʾ wškryʾ* for Shalmat and for her brothers the [good] and generous deities *Syr ʾ31 14:1*
TeixPan pp 84-85; Hof RelAram p 44†

šlmyt see *šlm* n

šm *nm* name
s cn *šm* BS III 45:5; sf 3ms *šmh* C4028:1
mṣbt bšm bwlʾ [wdm]sʾ statues in the name of the Senate [and Peopl]e *BS III 45:5* Gk *(andriasi) dēmosiois*
⊳ *bryk šmh lʿlmʾ* n phr†

šmʾl see *šml* n

šml *nf* left
s em ? *š[mʾ]lʾ* RB ʾ30 10A:3; *šmlʾ* C4199:7; sf 2ms *šmlk* RB ʾ30 14:6
wmʿlk ʿl šmlʾ as you enter, on the left *MélColl p 161:4*; *mpqyk mn ʾblʾ ʿl šmlk* as you go out the door, on your left *RB ʾ30 14:6*
⊳ *šmly* adj; *sml* n; *smly* adj

šmly *adj* on the left
m s em *šmlyʾ* C4175:6
bsṭrʾ šmlyʾ on the left wall
⊳ *šmʾl* n; *sml* n; *smly* adj†

šmn *nm* oil
s ab *šmn* RTP 707, 708
ḥmrʾ wšmn Wine and oil *RTP 708*†

šmʿ *v* to hear, to attend
G pf 3ms *šmʿ* C4080:5; ptcp m pl ab *šmʿyn* RB ʾ30 12B:4; ptcp pass f s ab ? *šmyʿʾ* C4100:1
wšmʿ bqlh and he heard his voice *C4080:5*; *wšmʿ ṭbyt* and he attended well (to his duty) *Inv 9 28:9* :: Déd pp 104, 277: ʿgood fortuneʾ or the like†

šmš *v* to serve
D pf 3ms *šmš* C3924:5
dy šmš wšpr lhwn who served and did good to them *C3934:3*; *dy šmš ʾlhyʾ* who served the gods *Syr ʾ26 p 129:3*†

šmš I *nm* Shamash (name of deity)
s ab *šmš* C3951:5
lšmš ʾlh byt ʾbwhn to Shamash, the god of their father's house *C3978:6*
TeixPan passim; Hof RelAram p 48

šmš II *nm* sun (?)
s ab *šmš* Inv 8 6:5
whʾ npšʾ dh mwlyʾ bšmš and behold this monument accompanies ? him in the sun ? *Inv 8 8:4*; *Inv 8 37B:2*; sense of phrase probably escapes us†

šnh *nf** year
s ab *šnʾ* Syr ʾ36 p 274:4; cn *šnt* C4163:1; em *šth* CRAIBL ʾ81:10 ?; *štʾ* BS III 34:2*; pl ab *šnyn* C4358:6
bkl šnʾ ʿd ʿlmʾ every year, forever *Syr ʾ36 19:4*; *byrḥ ʾlwl šnt 293* in the month of Elul, the year 293 *Inv 12 22:1*; *šnt 551 lDN* the year 551. To DN *RSP 114:1*; *bšnt 415* in the year 415 *MélColl p 161:8*; *šnt dy hww bny PN [...]* the year when the Bani Haggay were ... *Syr ʾ70 p 413:4*; *štʾ klh* for the whole year *Syr ʾ26 p 129:4*; *bštʾ dh* in that year *BS III 34:2*; *bh bštʾ* in that year *RSP 199:10*; *ḥyʾ šnyn 16* he lived 16 years *C4359:6*; *br šnyn 9* 9 years old *Inv 8 168:4*

šʿd see *šʿdw* n

šʿdw *nm* Shaadu (name of deity)
s ab *šʿdw* RTP 248; *šʿd* PNO 35B:3; reading with *r* instead of *d* is possible, but unlikely, note Doura 20:1, where *r* in *ʾšṙw* has dot, *d* of *šʿd* not dotted
mʿnw šʿdw gnyʾ Maanu, Shaadu, the genii *RTP 248*; *lšʿd ʾlhʾ* to Shaad, the god *PNO 35B:3*
(prb. Arab *saʿd* good fortune)
⊳ TeixPan 82-83; ANRW p 2637; Hof RelAram pp 41, 43

šʿdy *nf* Shaaday
s ab *šʿdy* Sumer ʾ64 p 13:4
wrʿʾ tnn bšʿdy and he tended sheep here

in Shaaday†

šʿh *nf* hour, time
s em *šʿt'* RSP 142:2
pnwn mn šʿt' drgz' he delivered them from the time of wrath(?)†

šʿyd *adj* helpful
pl em *šʿyd'* PNO 14:4
lgny' šʿyd' to the helpful Genii; see Starcky ad loc.†

šʿr see *šʿdw* n

šʿrw see *šʿdw* n

špyr *adj* good, beautiful
s ab *špyr* Syr '33 p 190:3
špyr ... good (broken context)
▶ *špr* v; *špyr* adv†

špr *v* to do good to, to be good to
G pf 3ms *špr* C3933:5; 3mpl *šprw* C3930:4
dy špr bkl 'ḥydw klh lmdyth who did good for his city in every office *Inv 10 115:3*; *mn dy špr lhwn bkl gns klh* because he did good to them in every possible way *Inv 9 11:4*
▶ *špyr* adj; *špyr* adv

špr *adv* well
špr Inv 10 53:4; cf *[špy]r* Inv 10 39:3
bdyl dy hlk ʿmh špr because he behaved well toward him *Inv 10 53:4*
▶ *špr* v; *špyr* adj†

šqy *v* to water
G ptcp m s ab *šq'* MUSJ '61 p 133:5
lyrḥbwl lšq' l'rq to Yarhibol, to the One who gives water to Arq (or: to the earth)
▶ *'rq* n†

šql *v* to receive, to charge
G ptcp f s ab *šql'* Trf:49; f pl ab *šqln* Trf:126
mn znyt' mn mn dy šql' dynr ['w] ytyr from prostitutes, from one who charges a denarius [or] more *Trf:48*

šqqh *nf* narrow street
s ab *šqq'* C4199:7; em *šqqt'* StudMiles p 38:1,2, cf Doura 20:2 *šqqt'* reading of Cantineau Syr '38 p 164; pl ab *šqqn* C4199:3
šqqn trtn ḥd' ʿl ymyn' kdy 'nt ʿll w'ḥrt' mqbl' two aisles, one on the right as you enter and the other opposite *C4199:3*; on sense see Ing StudMiles, p 48
(see AHw *sūqāqû* and von Soden '77 p 196; Aramaism in Akkadian)†

šr *nm* lord (?)
s sf 1pl *šrn* RTP 333
šmš šrn rb' Shamash, our great lord ?†

šrb *nm* brazier (?)
s em *šrb'* Syr '85 p 57:5
ʿlt' wšrb' the altar and brazier ?†

šrgb *nm* hinge or other metal fitting of door
p em *šrgb'* Inv 12 48:2
wtṭlyl' klh wtrʿwhy wšrgb' dy nḥš' and the whole ceiling and its doors and the hinges of bronze *Inv 12 48:2*; *w[t]ṭl[yl'] klh wmlbnh wšrgb' dy nḥš[']* and the whole ce[il]ing and its door-frame and the hinges of bronze *Inv 12 49:6*; see Hillers, Notes (forthcoming); previously undefined, see e. g. Degen 1987 p 29
(Cf JPA *šgm* hinge; Akk *šagammu* ?; see also at *mlbn* n above)†

šry *v* D to begin (?)
D pf 3ms *šry* Syr '33 p 187:3 (context very damaged)
šry lmrbʿ he began ? to ... †

šry *nf* entablature
s em *šryt'* BS III 19:2; sf 3fs *šryth* Inv 1 5:1; 3mpl *šrythwn* BS III 17:2
mʿlt' dh klh ʿmwdyh wšryth wtṭlylh this whole vestibule, its columns, its entablature, and its ceiling *Inv 1 5:1*

šrk see *šwr* v

šrr *v* C to confirm, to establish
C pf 3ms *ʾšr* Trf:120; 3fs *ʾšrt* Trf(I):3; pl *ʾšrw* CRAIBL '81:10, 12; pf passive 3ms *ʾšr* Trf(I):9, CaGr p 90, RosSpr p 56
whyk dy ʾšr qrblwn kšyrʾ bʾgrtʾ dy ktb and as the excellent PN established in the letter he wrote *Trf:120* Gk *esēmiōsato*; *wmdy ʾšr lʾgwrʾ* and when it has been confirmed by the tax-collectors *Trf(I):9* Gk *kyrōthē*†

ššbyn *nm* groomsman
s sf 3ms *ššbynh* Inv 8 137:7
dy ʿbd lh PN ššbynh which PN, his groomsman, made for him
(< Akk *susapinnu*; AIA pp 94, 138 note)†

št *num* six
s with m cn *štt* Ber '38 p 106:4; ab *šth* Sem '86 p 89:7; *štʾ* Ber '35 p 97:2; em *šttʾ* Inv 9 1:6; sf 3mp *šttyhn*; s with fem *št* C4175:8
mqbrn št six burials *C4175:8*; *gwmḥyn štʾ dkn* six unused niches *Ber '35 p 97:2*; *ywm šttʾ bnysn* the sixth day of Nisan *Inv 9 1:6*; *trʿyʾ ʾln šttyhn* these doors, the six of them *C3914:4*; *wštt gwmḥwhy* and its six burial niches *Ber '38 p 106:4*; *ʾlpyn tryn wmʾtn wtltyn wšt* two thousand two hundred and thirty-six *Sem '86 p 89:2*; *lmdyʾ dy qsṭwn ʿšr w[š]t* to a *modius* of [six]teen xestes *Trf:70*; *wmnyn ʿšrh wšth* and sixteen minas *Sem '86 p 89:7*

šty *v* to drink
G ptcp m s ab *štʾ* C3973:5; inf *lmštʾ* CRAIBL '81:14
dy lʾ štʾ ḥmr who does not drink wine *C3973:5*†

štyn *num* sixty
štyn RSP 103C:5
btr mwth šnyn štyn after his death, at sixty years†

tbn *nm* straw
s em *tbnʾ* Trf:59
lṭʿwnʾ dy ḥṭʾ wḥmrʾ wtbnʾ for a load of wheat or wine or straw Gk *achyrōn* ʿchaff, husks'†

tg *nm* crown
s em *tgʾ* RTP 111, 112; Syr '59 p 104:1
tgʾ dy bl crown of Bel *RTP 111*†

tgmʾ *nm* association
s em *tgmʾ* C3945:3
dy ʾqym lh tgmʾ dy qynyʾ which the association of metal-workers erected for him Gk *sunte[leia tōn chrusoch]oōn kai argu[rokopōn]*
(< Gk *tagma* ʿorder, division')†

tgr *nm* merchant
pl em *tgryʾ* Inv 10 40:3; Inv 9 11:3*; *tgrʾ* Trf(I):7
srbnyn hww byny tgrʾ lbyny mksyʾ there were disputes between the merchants and the tax-collectors *Trf(I):7* Gk *enporōn*; *dy ʾqym lh tgrʾ bny šyrtʾ dy nḥt ʿmh lʾlgšyʾ* which the merchants, the members of the caravan that went down with him to GN, erected for him *C3933:3*
(< Akk *tamkaru*; AIA p 107)
▶ *tgrh* n

tgrh *nf* business, trade
s em *tgrtʾ* Trf:124
bdyl dy ʾyt bhwn tgrtʾ because there is trade in them
▶ *tgr* n†

tdmwr *nf* Tadmor, Palmyra
tdmwr C3946:4; *tdmr* Trf:135
mn tdmwr lʾlgšyʾ from Tadmor to Vologesia *Inv 10 124:4*; *nmwsʾ dy mksʾ dy lmnʾ dy hdrynʾ tdmr wʿyntʾ dy myʾ [dy ʾy]ls qysr* the tax law of the port Hadriana Tadmor and the springs of water [of Ae]lius Caesar *Trf(II):1*
On etymology see Gaw '74b p 92; Bron '86 p 96; M. O'Connor 1988b

tdmry *adj* of Tadmor, Palmyrene
m s em *tdmryʾ* C4119:4; pl em *tdmryʾ* Inv 10 114:3

tgry' tdmry' the Palmyrene merchants *Inv 10 114:3*; *PN tdmry'* PN, the Palmyrene *C4119:4*; *gbl tdmry'* the assembly of the Palmyrenes *Inv 9 12:3*; *[l]byl tdmry'* [to] the Palmyrene Bel *MélDuss p 885:2*
▶ *tdmr* n

twb *adv* again; furthermore
twb Ber '35 p 86:8; cf [...]*wtwb* Ber '36 p 99:4
wtwb rḥq lh sṭr' mdnḥy' and furthermore he ceded to him the eastern side *Ber '35 p 86:8*†

twḥy *nf* decree
s cn *twḥyt* C3959:1; Déd p 36:1
mn twḥyt bwl' wdmws by decree of the Senate and People *C3959:1*; *btwḥyt bwl' wdms* by decree of the Senate and People *Inv 10 44:1* Gk *prostagmati*
▶ *yḥy* v†

twn *nm* chamber
s em *twn'* Inv 9 28:6; Syr '71 p 420:9
wPN ʿl twn' PN, in charge of the chamber *Inv 9 28:6*; *PN br dkt' dy twn'* PN, son of the place ? of the chamber *Ber '36 p 88:3*
(See Ing StudMiles p 46, fn 39)
▶ *dkh* n†

twpr *nm* feature of tomb: cavity (?)
s em *twpr'* C4174:6
wtḥwt twpr' dy ptyḥ lʾp' [...] and below the cavity which is open toward ... *Inv 7 1B:3*; *gwmḥyn trn dy mn ʿqr twpr' dkn* the two unused burial niches which are at the bottom of the cavity ? *C4174:6*, cf *C4173:2*; *dy mwln twpr'* which are close to the cavity ? *C4172:2*†

twr *nm* bull, ox (divine title [?]); beef
s em *twr'* RTP 159
bl twr' PN (on tessera) Bel. Beef. (or: The Bull ?) PN. *RTP 59*
▶ Hof RelAram pp 36-37

tḥwm *nm* border; territory
s cn *[tḥw]m* Trf:149; s or pl em *tḥwm'* Trf:72, 111, 119, 145; pl cn *tḥwmy* Déd p 36:3; sf 3fs *tḥwmyh* Trf:64
dy mt'ʿlyn ltdmr ʾw ltḥwmyh which are imported to Palmyra or to its territory *Trf(II):3*†

tḥwt *prep* 1 under; 2 in exchange for
tḥwt RB '30 14:4; *tḥt* Inv 7 1B:3
1 *tḥwt PN* below PN *Ber '34 p 38:13* **2** *wtḥwt hln yhbt lh* and in exchange for these things I have given to him *RB '30 14:4*
▶ *mn ltḥt* adv

tḥt see *tḥwt* prep

ṭṭlyl *nm* ceiling
s em *ṭṭlyl'* C3911:3; sf 3fs *ṭṭlylh* BS III 43:5; 3mpl *ṭṭlylhwn* BS III 19:3; *ṭṭlylhn* C3984:2
mṭlt' dh klh ʿmwdyh wšryth wṭṭlylh this whole portico, its columns and its entablature and its ceiling *BS III 3:1*

tym' *nf* Tayma
s ab *tym'* Sumer '64 p 16(5):3
bny PN dy tym' the Bani PN of Tayma
▶ Appendix MAPS†

tymn see *tymny* adj

tymny *adj* southern
s em *tymny'* C4171:2; *tymn'* Ber '35 p 93:2; pl ab *tymnyyn* C4174:3; em *tymny'* C4171:2; *tymn'* Ber '35 p 107:2: expected form is *tymny'* cf CaGr p 117 for possible parallel (*qdmt'*)
gwmḥy' ʾln ḥmš' tymn' these five southern burial niches *Ber '35 p 106:2*; *bʾksdr' tymn'* in the southern exedra *Ber '35 p 93:2*; *dy ʾkšdr' tymny'* of the southern exedra *C4171:2*

tyr *adj* compassionate
m s em *tyr'* C4028:3
lbryk šmh lʿlm' rḥmn' wtyr' To DN, the merciful and compassionate *RSP 119:2*; *DN*

rḥmnʾ ṭbʾ wtyrʾ DN, the merciful, good, and compassionate *C4038:2*; *lDN rḥmnʾ wḥnnʾ wtyrʾ* to DN, the merciful, kind, and compassionate *C4084:3*
(< Akk *tayyâru* [itself a calque ?]; AIA p 106)

tlt *num* three
with f noun *tlt* RB '30 14:5; m noun *tltʾ* BS III 17:1; *tlth* RSP 199:13
mnwn tlt three parts *RB '30 14:5*; *tlt ʾmmʾ* three cubits ? *RB '30 14:7*; *wgwmḥyn tltʾ* and three burial niches *Ber '35 p 95:1*; *gwmḥyn dkn tltʾ* three unused burial niches *Ber '35 p 99:2*

tltyn *num* thirty
tltyn Sem '86 p 89:2; PNO 58:6
ʾlpyn tryn wmʾtn wtltyn wšt two thousand and two hundred and thirty-six *Sem '86 p 89:2*†

tmwzʾ *nm* Tammuz (name of deity)
s em *tmwzʾ* RTP 218, 219, 342
blty tmwzʾ Belti. Tammuz *RTP 218*
TeixPan p 88; ANRW p 2646; Hof RelAram p 45†

tmlʾ *nf* platform
s em *tmlʾ* Inv 12 2:3
dy ʿbd ʾksdrʾ wtmlʾ who made the exedra and the platform in front of it
(< Gk *thymelē* altar, platform)†

tmny *num* eight
with m noun *tmnyʾ* Trf:49
gmḥyn tmnyʾ eight burial niches *C4173:2*

tnn *adv* here
tnn C3932:3
kdy hwʾ tnn PN when PN was here *C3932:3* Gk *parousia*; *ʾḥd tnn bt [DN]* one here in the temple of [DN] *BS III 45:11* Gk *[e]ntauth[a]*; *mn dy yʿl ltnn swm nkry* whoever brings in here a dead body that does not belong here *Syr '33 p 184:2*
(CaGr p 159; RosSpr pp 82-83)

tṣbw *nf* decoration
s sf 3ms *tṣbwth* C4204:2
wtṣbwth klh and all its decoration
▶ *tṣby* n†

tṣby *nf* decoration
s sf 3ms *tṣbyth* Inv 12 49:7; 3fs *tṣbyth* C4209:3; 3mpl *tṣbythwn* C3952:4
wʾp qrbw hyklʾ dy mnwt wʾsṭwwhy wtṣbyth klh and they also donated the temple of DN and its stoas and all its decoration *Inv 12 48:2*
▶ *tṣbw* n

tqn *v* D to prepare
D (prb, or G) impf 3ms *ytqn* RB '30 9:4
yḥpr wytqn lh mqbrtʾ may dig and prepare for himself a burial place†

tryn *num* 1 two; 2 *dy trtyʾ* a second time
ab with m noun *trn* Trf:130; with f noun *trtn* C4199:4; em *tryʾ* RTP 244; f em *trtyʾ* C3959:2; m sf 3mpl *trwyhwn* C3914:1; *trwyhn* C3931:2; *tryhwn* BS III 10:4; f sf 3mpl *trtyhn* Syr '38 31:4
1 *ṣlmyʾ ʾln trwyhwn* these two statues *C3914:1*; *brykyn tryʾ* blessed be the both of them! *RTP 244*; *mn gwmḥyn tryn* two burial niches *Ber '35 p 85:7*; *trn mʿlyk ʾksdrʾ* two, as you enter the exedra *Ber '35 p 102:3*; *ʿlwtʾ ʾln trtyhn* these two altars *Syr '38 p 78:4*; *[t]rtn ʿlwtʾ ʾln* these [t]wo altars *C3973:1*; *wltrn ʾ[ḥy]ʾ qdyšʾ* and to the two Holy Br[other]s *C4001:3*; *šnt ḥmš mʾh wtrtn* the year five hundred and two *C4174:8* **2** *dy hwʾ grmṭws dy trtyʾ* who was secretary a second time *C3959:2* Gk *to deuteron* CaGr p 129

trʿ *nm* gate, door
s em *t[r]ʿʾ* RB '30 10A:3; pl em *trʿyʾ* C3914:4; sf 3ms *trʿwhy* C3917:3; *trʿwh* PNO 7A:1; ? *trʿw* BS III 39:2
ʿbdw trʿyʾ ʾln šttyhn dy plzʾ dy bbslqʾ rbtʾ made these six doors of special copper in

the great basilica *C3914:4*; *wtr ʿwhy wšrgbʾ dy nḥšʾ* and its doors and the bronze hinges ? *Inv 12 48:2*

trṣ *v* to set right
G pf 3mpl *trṣw* Inv 12 49:8
wtrṣw ṣbwt btʾ and they set right the affairs of the temple†

tškb see *tšbb* PN

tšmyš *nm* use
s cn *[tš]myš* Trf:58; *tšmyšʾ* Trf:70
[ltš]myš ʿynn trtn dy m[y] [for u]se of the two springs of wa[ter] *Trf:58* Gk *chrēseos*; *ytn [lh]n ltšmyšʾ* it shall be given [to th]em for use *Trf:70*; Teix '83b p 243 'administration' in both passages, but Gk seems decisive†

tšʿ *num* nine
with m noun *tšʿʾ* C4229:2; in compound *wtšʿ* C4053:5
gmḥyn tšʿʾ nine burial niches *C4229:2*; *ywm tšʿʾ byrḥ ʾb* the ninth day (day nine) in the month of Ab *C4010:7*; *šnt ḥmš mʾh wšbʿyn wtšʿ* the year five hundred and seventy-nine *C4053:5*

tšʿ *nm* reputation (?)
s em *[t]šʿʾ* C4100:1
[t]šʿʾ ṭbʾ wšmyʿʾ a good and famous reputation ? cf RosSpr p 74 note 2†

tšʿytʾ *nf* divine title or epithet; sense uncertain
s or pl em *tšʿytʾ* Sem '77 p 117:4
ḥgbʾ wmṣbʾ ʿbd PN ltšʿytʾ wrḥmnytʾ the shrine and image made by PN for the . . . and merciful ones;

tšry *nm* Tishri, Tishrin (name of month = October)
s ab *tšry* C4171:3; *tšrn* C4363:7
▶ Appendix CALENDAR

tšrn see *tšry* n

❖ ❖ ❖ ❖ ❖

ENGLISH-ARAMAIC INDEX TO GLOSSARY

This index is intended as a convenience to users of the Glossary; of course not only more information on usage but also more qualification, in the case of words whose attestation is problematic, will be found in the Glossary itself.

Ab (month): **ʾb** $_{II}$
Abgal (DN): **ʾbgl**
abide, dwell (?): **ḥny** *v*
ability to write: **yd**
above: **lʿl mn; mn lʿl**
accompany: **šyʿ** *v*
according to: **ʾpy**
accordingly: **bdyl kwt**
acknowledge: **ydy** *v C*
Adar (month): **ʾdr**
addition (adv; in addition): **ʾḥrn**
adjacent, to be: **dbq** *v*
adjacent, to be, to accompany (?): **wly (mwl, mwly ?)** *v*
affair (?): **brmn**
Afqa: **ʾpqʾ**
after: **btr** ***prep*; btr dy, mn btr dy** ***cj***
afterward: **ʾḥr, btr**
again: **twb**
against: **ʿl**
agent: **prgmṭṭ**
Aglibol (DN): **ʿglbwl**
agreed, effected legally (of transfer of property), to be: **qwm** *v*
agreed: **spwn**
agreement, to be in (?): **šwʾ** *v*
agreement (?): **ʾwyw**
aid: **syʿ; ʿdr** *v*
alabaster vessel: **šṭyph**
Alas!: **ḥbl** *interj*
alien: **nkry**
alienate (property): **bʿd** *v*
all: **kl**
Allat (DN): **ʾlt**
also: **ʾp**
altar: **ʿlh**
amount (?): **nwr**
Ana: **ʿnʾ**
Anahita (DN): **ʾnhyt**
and: **w; p**
answer: **ʿny** *v*
any: **klmʾ**
anyone: **ʾyš; ʾnš**
anything: **mdʿn**
approach (?): **dny** *v*
Arak ([?] GN): **ʾrq**
archer: **qšṭ** $_{I}$**; qšt**
archives: **byt ʾrkʾ**
army: **ʾsṭrṭwmʾ**
Arsu (DN): **ʾrṣw**
as, just as: **hyk; hyk dy**
Ashar (DN): **ʾšr** $_{II}$
Ashtart (DN): **ʿštrt**
Aspasinkart: **ʾspsnqrṭ**
assarius (coin; unit of money): **ʾsr**
association: **qnyh (?); šwtpw; tgmʾ**
at, by: **b; ʿl**
Atargatis (DN): **ʿtrʿth**
authority: **šlṭn**
Azizu (DN): **ʿzyzw**
Baalshamin, Baashamin (DN): **bʿlšmyn**
Baaltak (DN): **bʿltk**
Babylon: **bbl**
bad: **byš**
baker: **nḥtwm**
Banat El (DN): **bnt ʾl**
banquet hall: **smk**
bar, to (?): **brḥ** *v G*
bas-relief: **mṣb, mṣbh, nṣbh**
basin: **gbʾh**
basket (?); bolt (?): **qlsṭr**
bazaar: **pṭply** *nm ?*
be: **hwy** *v*
because: **bd; bdy; bdyl dy; mn dy; ʿqly dy (?)** *cj*
because, since ?, or (in phrase) in such a way that: **mṭl** *cj*
beef: **twr**
before, in front of: **qdm; qdm**
begin (?): **šry** *v D*
behave: **hlk** *v G*
behind: **btr**
behold; here is: **hʾ** *pred*
Beirutian, of Beirut: **brty**
Bel (DN): **bl**
Belham(m)on, name of deity: **blḥmwn**
believe: **hymn** *v*
belong: **mṭʾ** *v*
belong(s) to: **ʾyt** *pred*
belonging to, of (him, her, etc.): **dyl**
beloved (?): **rḥym**
below: **mn ltḥt; tḥwt**
Belti: **blty**
beneficiarius (kind of soldier): **bnpqyr**
besides, beyond: **br mn**
bestow: **mgd** *v*
Beth Phasiel: **bt pṣyʾl**
between: **bynwt; byny; btʾ**
bind, obligate self (?): **ʾsr** *v G*
bless: **brk** *v D*
blessed: **bryk**
Blessed-Be-His-Name-Forever (DN): **bryk šmh lʿlmʾ***
blood: **dm**
body: **swm**
Bolastor (DN): **bwlʿstr; blʿstr**
bolt (?): **qlsṭr**
bones: **ṭmʾ**
border: **tḥwm**
Bosra: **bṣrʾ**
bowman: **qšṭ** $_{I}$**; qšt**
box (?): **ʾrwn**
brazier: **knwn; šrb**
bread: **lḥm**
breathing things, living things: **nšmh**
bring: **ʾty; slq** *v C*
bronze: **nḥš**
brother: **ʾḥ**
build: **bny** *v*
building: **bnyn**
bull, ox (divine title [?]): **twr**
burial place: **gwmḥ**
burnt offering: **mqlw**
bury: **qbr** *v*
business: **tgrh**
but: **ʾlʾ** $_{II}$ *cj*
butcher (?): **ṭbḥ; qṣb**
buy: **zbn** *v G*
buyer: **zbwn**
by (with passive verbs, the agent): **l**
by (in oath): **b**
Caesar: **qysr**
call to (for help): **qry** *v G*
called, surnamed, to be: **qry** *v Gt*
camel: **gml**
camel-rider (DN ?): **mṭy**
camels, of: **drmdry**
camp: **mšry**
caravan: **šyrh**
carcases: **pgr**
carve: **glp; psl (?)** *v*
cede: **rḥq** *v G, C*
ceiling: **ṭṭlyl**
centurion: **qṭrywn**
centurion's aide: **hpṭyn**
century (Roman military unit): **qṭryʾ**
certainly, indeed: **bl**
chamber: **twn**
chapel: **ḥmn**
charge: **šql** *v*
charge of, to be in: **qwm** *v*
charged, to be: **gby** *v Gt*
chief: **rb, rbn**
chief, supreme (adj): **ršy**
child, young person: **ṭly**
choose: **ʾḥd** *v*
cistern: **gb** $_{II}$
city: **krk; mdynh; mḥwz**
client: **gr**
coin: **mʿh**
collect taxes: **gby** *v G*
collector of customs: **dy rbʿʾ**
colonist: **qwlwn**
colony (i.e., Palmyra): **qlnyʾ** *n*
column: **ʿmwd**
come in, go in: **ʿll** *v G*
come: **ʾty** *v G*
coming: **mytwy**
commissioner: **ʾpnrṭṭ**
community: **dyr**
companion, partner: **ḥbr; šbb**
compassionate: **tyr**
complete: **mšlmn**
concern, to be of: **bṭl** *v*
concerning: **ʿl**
conduct (oneself, one's life): **dbr** *v*
confirm, to establish: **šrr** *v C*
consecrate: **qdš** *v C, D*
consecrated, to be: **qdš** *v Dt*
consecrated object (?): **ḥrm**
construction: **bnyn**
consul, person of consular rank: **hpṭyqʾ**
consular governor, of consular rank: **hygmwn**
contract: **ʾgwr; ʾmlgyʾ (?)** $_{II}$

contractor (?): **mrʾgrʾ**
coping, i.e. the covering course of a wall (?): **ṭpy**
copper or bronze (a kind of): **plz**
corner: **qrn**
corps (military): **ʾlʾ** I
corridor (tomb part): **plṭyʾ**
couch: **smk (?); ʿrs**
cousin(s) on mother's side: **ḥl (bny ḥl)**
crater: **ʾgn** *n*
crown: **tg**
cubit: **ʾmh**
curator: **ʾpmlṭ**
curatorship, term as curator: **ʾpmlṭw**
custom: **ʿyd; ʿdh**
danger: **qdns**
darkness (?): **ḥškk**
daughter: **brh**
Daughter of Bel (DN): **brt bl** *n phr f*
day: **ywm; y** *abbr*
death: **mwt**
decided, decreed, to be: **ḥzy** *v Gt*
decoration: **tṣbw; tṣby**
decree; decision: **dgm; dyṭgmʾ; twḥy**
decurion (member of the Senate of a city): **dqrywn**
dedicate: **ḥnk** *v*
dedication: **ḥnkh**
deity: **gny**
deliver: **pny** *v G, D*
deme, tribe (?): **myn**
denarius: **d** *abbr*, **dynr**
destroy (?): **str** *v*
determine, decide: **byn** *v*
die: **myt** *v*
dispute: **srbn**
distress: **ʿq**
distribute food (?): **ʾpr** *v G*
distribution (?): **qsm**
ditch: **gb** II
divide: **plg** *v*
divination (?): **qsm**
do: **ʿbd** *v*
document: **šṭr**
donkey: **ḥmr**
door: **trʿ**
door-frame: **mlbn**
doorway (of tomb): **ʾbl**
double, multiply (?): **ʿyp** *v*
drawn up, to be: **ʾgr** *v Gt*
dried goods: **ybyš**
drink: **šty** *v*
dry land: **ybyš**
Duanat (DN): **dʿnt**
ducenarius (procurator): **dwqnr**
Dura: **dwrʾ**
Durahlun (DN): **dwrḥlwn**
earth (?): **ʾrq**
east (direction): **mdnḥ**
eastern: **mdnḥy**
eastern region: **mdnḥ**
Egyptian: **mṣry**
eight: **tmny** *num*
either ... or (?): **ʾw ... ʾw** *cj*
elder: **rb; qšyš**
Elkonnara (DN): **ʾlqwnrʿ**
Elul (month): **ʾlwl**
emperor: **ʾwṭqrṭwr**
empty: **sryq; pny**
enclosure wall (?): **ḥṭr**
encounter (?): **qbl** *v G*
entablature: **šry**
enter, to come in, to go in: **ʿll** *v G*
entering, going in: **mʿl**
entitle: **šlṭ** *v C*
entitled, authorized: **šlyṭ**
entitled, to be: **šlṭ** *v G*
equal, to be (?): **šwʾ** *v*
equestrian, man of noble rank: **hpqʾ; hpqws**
erect: **qwm** *v C*
erect: **nṣb; qwm** *v*
error: **ṭʿw**
establish: **qwm** *v*
established, to be (?): **rṣp** *v*
eternal home (i.e. tomb): **by**
every: **kl; klmʾ**
evil, harm: **byš**
excavate: **ḥpr** *v*
except for: **sṭr mn; šṭr mn**
exchange for, in exchange for: **tḥwt**
exedra: **ʾksdrʾ**
expenditure: **rzʾ**
expense, sum: **npq**
export: **mpqn**
export: **npq** *v C*
extend (?): **prs** *v*
face: **pny** *v G*
family: **by**
fat: **dhn**
father: **ʾb** I
father's house, clan: **by; byt ʾb**
father-in-law: **ḥm**
fatten (?): **pṭm** *v*
fear, reverence, worship: **dḥl** *v*
feed: **spʾ** *v*
festival: **ʿd**
fifty: **ḥmšyn** *num*
fine (?): **ʿnš** *v C*
fine: **ḥṭyʾ**
finishing (?): **mšlm**
first (in the first place): **qdmy**
first, former: **qdmy**
fish: **nwn**
five: **ḥmš** *num*
fleece: **mlṭ**
foodstuffs: **ṭʿmh**
foot: **rgl**
for, on behalf of: **l; ʿl**
Forat (city on Tigris): **prt**
foreign, foreigner: **ʾksny**
forever, eternity: **ʿlm**
fork (?): **mšl**
fortune, luck: **gd**
forty: **ʾrbʿyn** *num*
foster-father: **mrbyn**
foster-mother: **mrbyh**
found, to be: **škḥ** *v Gt*
four: **ʾrbʿ** *num*
freedman; freedwoman: **br ḥrʾ**
frequent, come past: **ʿwd** *v*
friend: **rḥm** II
friends, group of friends ?: **wd**
from: **mn**
front hall of a temple: **prnʾ; prnyn (?)**
furthermore: **twb**
Gad ʿAjrud (DN): **gd ʿgrwd** *n m*
Gad, Fortune (DN): **gd**
Gamla: **gmlʾ**
garden: **gn; gnh**
garment: **nḥṭ**
gate: **bb; trʿ**
gather: **knš** *v*
general: **ʾsṭrṭg**
generous, rewarding: **skr**
Genius (DN): **gny**
Genneas (DN): **gny**
gift: **yqr; mgd**
girl: **ʿlymh**
give, pay: **yhb; ntn** *v*
given, entrusted, to be: **šlm** *v C passive*
go: **hlk** *v G*
go around, circulate: **hpk** *v*
go down: **nḥt** *v*
go up: **slq** *v G*
go about: **hlk** *v D*
goat: **ʿz**
god: **ʾlh; ʾl (?; in "garden of the gods")**
goddess: **ʿštr**
going out: **mpq**
gold: **dhb**
good will: **ḥš**
good time, party (?): **ḥyrwn**
good, to do; to be good to: **špr** *v*
good, beautiful: **špyr**
good: **ṭb**
governor: **mtqnn; ʾrgbṭ**
gracious: **ḥnn**
grandfather (?): **ʾb (ʾb ʾb s.v. $ʾb_I$)**
gratis: **mgn**
grave: **qbwr; gwmḥ**
great: **rbrb**
great, to be (?): **gbr** *v*
great deed, mighty deed: **gbwrh**
Greek: **ywny**
groomsman: **ššbyn**
grove: **hlss**
guard: **mdmr**
guard: **mhdmr; nṭr**
guardian, foster-mother: **mprnsy**
gymnasiarch: **gmnsyrks**
Hadriana (name of Palmyra): **hdrynʾ**
half, part: **plg; plgw**
hand: **yd**
handwriting: **yd**
Hawarta: **ḥwrtʾ**
hay: **ʿšb**
he: **hw**
head (of small cattle): **rš**
hear, attend: **šmʿ** *v*
heat: **ḥmm** *v C*
heater (person who heats): **mḥm**
heiress: **wršh**
helper, assistant: **msyʿn**
helpful: **šʿyd**
herald: **krwz**
here: **tnn**
here: **lkʾ**
Herta (DN): **ḥrtʾ**
hide (?): **str** *v*
high religious official, priest: **ʾpkl**
hinge: **šrgb**
Hirta: **ḥyrtʾ**
his, her, etc.: **dyd** *connecting particle*
hither, to this place: **lkʾ**

holy thing: **qdš**
holy: **qdyš; qdš**
honey (?): **dbš**
honor: **yqr**
honor: **yqr** *v C*
horse: **swsy**
hour, time: **šʿh**
house: **by**
household, dwelling: **dwr**
however: **ʾlʾ** II *cj*
hundred: **mʾh**
husband: **bʿl**
hypogeum: **mʿrh**
I: **ʾnʾ; ʾnwky (?)**
idol: **mṣb**
if: **ʾn; hn; ʾm (?)** *cj*
Ilahay (DN) ?: **ʾlhy**
illustrious: **nhyr**
image: **npš; smy**
import: **ʿll** *v C*
import: **mʿln**
imported, to be: **ʿll** *v Ct*
in: **b**
inmost part (?): **ʿqr**
inner: **gwy**
inquire: **bqr** *v D*
inside, less than: **gw mn**
inside, within: **bgw; bgw mn; lgw; mn lgw**
inside; inner group (?): **gw**
install: **ḥdt** *v*
interest (?): **rbwʾ**
intimate, counsellor (?): **gwy**
Ishtar (DN): **ʿštr**
Ishtarbad (DN): **ʿštrbd**
Ispasina, Spasinou (Charax): **ʾspsnʾ**
Istar (DN): **ʾstrʾ**
Italian: **ʾyṭlyq**
Italy: **ʾyṭlyʾ**
Iyyar (month): **ʾyr**
Kanun (month): **knwn**
Kaslul (month): **kslwl**
kettle: **dwd**
kind, way: **gns**
king: **mlk**
Kislev (month): **kslw**
Kismaya (DN): **qsmyʾ**
Kladian: **kldy**
know: **ydʿ** *v G*
labor: **ʿml** *v*
lady, sovereign: **mrh; ʾdt (?)**
Lady of the Temple (DN): **mrt bytʾ**
lamb: **ʾmr**
large, great: **rb**
later: **btr**
law: **nmws**
leader: **rbn; rš**
lease, make a contract: **ʾgr** *v G*
left: **šml; sml**
legion: **lgywn**
less: **ḥsyr**
letter: **ʾgrh**
lieutenant (?): **ḥlph**
life, lifetime: **ḥyyn**
life, way of life: **ʿmr** II
like, to be: **dmy** *v*
limestone: **ḥwr**
lion: **ʾry**
live: **ḥyy** *v*
load: **ṭʿn** *v*
load, weight: **ṭʿwn**
loan, hire out: **šʾl** *v C*
lord (?): **šr**
Lord of the Gods (DN): **ʾlh**
love, affection: **rḥm** I
loving, lover of: **rḥym**
lower part: **ʾrʿ**
Maan, Maanu (DN): **mʿn**
make someone a partner (?): **lwy** *v*
make: **ʿbd** *v*
make known (?): **ydʿ** *v C*
make clear, show: **pšq** *v D*
make a mistake: **ṭʿy** *v*
Malakbel (DN): **mlkbl**
male: **dkr**
Malka (DN): **mlkʾ**
man: **ʾnš; gbr**
Manaf (DN): **mnp**
Manawat (DN): **mnwt**
many: **šgyʾ**
marble: **šyš**
market: **šwq**
master, lord (also as DN): **mrʾ**
master craftsman: **ʾmn**
maternal uncle: **ḥl**
Mayshan: **myšn**
Mayshan, of (adj): **myšny**
measure: **mdd** *v*
measure (?): **kl**
measure: **kwl** *v C*
measure of wine: **mkl; m** *abbr*
memorial: **dkrn**
men, personnel: **ʾnwš**
merchant: **tgr**
merciful, in epithet or title of deity: **rḥmn; rḥmny**
middle; central: **mṣʿy**
midst: **mṣʿh**
mile: **myl; m abbr**
military unit (?); border (?): **qṣh**
mina: **mnh** I
minor: **zʿwr**
modius (a dry measure, a peck): **mdʾ**
money: **kys**
month: **yrḥ**
monument: **nmš; npš**
more: **ytyr**
most powerful, distinguished, excellent: **qrṭsṭ; qrṭsṭws**
mother: **ʾm**
mule: **kwdn**
Munim, Monimos (DN): **mnʿym**
Nabataean: **nbṭy**
Nabu (DN): **nbw**
name: **šm**
Nanay (DN): **nny**
narrow street: **šqqh**
Nazala: **nzly**
necessary, to be; to chance to happen (?): **npl** *v*
need, be necessary: **ḥšḥ** *v*
need, use (?): **ḥšḥh**
Nemesis (DN): **nmsys**
nephew: **ʾḥ**
Nergal (DN): **nrgl**
new: **ḥdt**
niche: **gwmḥ**
niece (sister's daughter): **ʾḥh**
Nike, victory: **nyqʾ**
nine: **tšʿ** *num*
Nisan (month): **nysn**
no one: **ʾnš (with neg.); ʾyš (with neg.)**
no; not: **lʾ**
noble, excellent: **kšyr**
north, northern: **sml; smly**
northern: **grby**
not, never: **lmʾ**
oath: **mwmʾ**
obol: **mʿh**
occasion (?): **qbl**
of: **dy (often written d)** *pron; connecting particle; cj*
of (him, her, etc.): **dyl**
of: **dyd** *connecting particle*
offer ([?] analysis and meaning uncertain): **nbʿ** *v*
offer: **qrb** *v D, C (?)*
offering (?): **dbyḥh**
office (service for which one is chosen): **ʾḥydw**
official, archon: **ʾrkwn**
officiant: **mšmš**
offspring: **zrʿ**
oil: **šmn**
oil: **mšḥ**
oil: **m** *abbr*
old age: **sybw**
old: **ʿtyq**
olive tree (?): **mšḥ**
on account of: **ḥšbn**
on the left: **šmly**
on, upon, above: **ʿl, lʿl, lʿl mn**
one: **ḥd** *num*
one fourth: **rbʿ, r** ***abbr***
one who mixes (?): **mmzgn**
onyx (?): **yḥlʾ**
open: **ptḥ** *v*
opposite: **lqblʾ; mwl (wly v)**
opposite, to be: **qbl** *v D*
opposite: **lqbl**
or: **ʾw** *cj*
or: **w** *cj*
ornament: **ṣbt** *v D*
other: **ʾḥrn**
other; last (?): **ʾḥyr**
outer, exterior: **bry**
outside: **lbr mn**
outside, from outside: **br mn**
outside, exterior: **br** II
over: **lʿl mn**
over, in charge of: **ʿl**
owe: **ḥwb** *v*
owed by, debited to: **qdm**
owner, master (?): **bʿl**
paint: **ṣwr** *v*
Palmyrene, of Tadmor: **tdmry**
part, portion: **mnh** II
partner, to make: **šwtp** *v Quad*
patron: **gr; qywm**
pay, spend, be charged: **npq; prʿ** *v*
peace: **šlm; šlwm (?)**
people: **dms; gbl**
perfumed: **bšym**
person: **rgly**
physician: **ʾsy**
picture: **ṣwrh**
pinenuts: **ʾsṭrbyl**
place, area: **ʾtr**
place: **sym** *v*
place, stead: **mqmw; dkh (?)**
placed, to be (?): **šwm** *v Gt*
platform: **tmlʾ**
pledge: **mškn**

porch (?): **ʿwb**
port, entrepôt: **lmn**
portico: **ʾstwʾ; mṭlh**
portion: **ḥlq**
possess (?): **ʾḥd** *v*
pour: **ʾšd** I *v G*
praetorium (?): **sp**
praise: **šbḥ** *v*
praiseworthy way, in a: **šbyḥyt**
prepare: **tqn** *v D*
prescribe, order: **yḥy** *v C*
preside: **ytb** *v*
presidency: **mwtb; plhdrw**
price (?): **dmyn**
priest: **kmr**
procurator: **ʾpṭrp**
profane, deconsecrate (?): **brr** *v*
progeny: **wld**
promptly, heartily (?): **mhryt**
property (?); victims (?): **nksyn**
prostitute: **znyh; ʿlymh**
provide: **prns** *v*
public expense, at (?): **dmysyt**
public life: **plṭy** *nm ?*
purchases: **zbn** I
purify (?): **brr** *v*
purple: **ʾrgwn**
purse, funds: **kys**
Qinyan (month): **qnyn**
quarter: **rbʿw**
queen: **mlkh**
quietly: **škytyt**
Rabasire (DN): **rbʾsyrʾ**
Rahmu (DN): **rḥm** III
raise, to bring up: **rby** *v D*
reaper: **ḥṣd**
receive: **šql** *v*
receive: **qbl** *v*
recess, corner: **zbwqh**
reckoned, computed, to be: **ḥšb** *v Gt*
reckoning, account: **ḥšbn**
recline (?): **smk** *v*
rectangular space (?): **rbwʿh**
relative, relation: **qryb**
relief: **rwḥ**
remember, recall, commemorate: **dkr; zkr (?)** *v*
renew, restore: **ḥdt** *v D*
Renowned One(s) (DN; ?): **tšʿytʾ**
repose: **nyḥh**
reputation (?): **tšʿ**
reserve: **ʾḥd** *v*
Resheph (DN): **ršp**
resident, inhabitant (?): **ʿmwr**
rest, remainder: **šʾr**
reward: **skr** *v*
rewarding, generous (epithet of gods): **škr**
rider: **prš**
right (for,), to be: **qšṭ** *v*
right: **kšr** *adj*
right (thing); right: **qsṭ; qšṭ** II
right: **ymny**
right, right hand, side: **ymyn**
righteous: **zdq**
roof over: **ṭll** *v D*
room (of some kind): **ʾdrwn**
row: **ṭksys**
Ruhu, of (adj): **rwḥyʾ**
Saabu (DN): **ṣʿbw**
sacred precinct, sanctuary: **ʾtr**
sacred things: **mḥrmh** *nf ?*
sacrificial victim (?): **qṣb**
salt: **mlḥ**
salted: **mlyḥ**
sarcophagus: **ʾwn**
satisfied, to be; to have enough: **šbʿ** *v*
save: **šwzb** *v*
say: **ʾmr** *v G*
scribe: **ktwb**
sculptor: **glwp**
sculpture: **glph**
sea: **ym**
second time: **tryn** *num*
secretary: **grmṭws**
seek: **bʿy; bqy (?)** *v*
sela, a coin: **slʿ; s abbr**
Seleuceia (city on Tigris): **slwkyʾ**
self: **npš; swm**
sell: **zbn** *v D*
Senate, council: **bwlʾ**
senator: **bylwṭ; snqlṭyq**
send: **šdr** *v D*
servant: **ṭly; ʿbd**
serve: **šmš** *v*
service, ritual (?); corps of priests (?): **ʿwnh**
sestertius: **sstrṭyn**
set right: **trṣ** *v*
seven: **šbʿ** *num*
seventh day (?); group of seven (?): **šbʿtʾ**
seventy: **šbʿyn** *num*
sextarius (dry measure): **qsṭwn**
Shaaday DN): **šʿdy**
Shaadu (DN): **šʿdw**
Shadrafa (DN): **šdrpʾ**
Shadya (DN); or, demon (?): **šdyʾ**
Shaialqawm (DN): **šyʿʾlqwm**
Shaknay (DN): **škny**
Shalmat (DN): **šlmt**
Shamash (DN): **šmš** I
share: **plg** *v*
she: **hy**
shear: **gzz** *v*
Shebat (month): **šbṭ**
Shepherd (?); Favorable One (?) (divine title): **rʿyʾ**
show, make known: **ḥwy** *v D*
shrine: **ḥgb**
Shulman (DN): **šlmn**
side: **str; sṭr; pny; gb** I
silver, money: **ksp**
sin: **ḥṭy** *v*
singer (?): **zmr**
sister: **ʾḥh**
sit, dwell: **ytb** *v*
Siwan (month): **sywn**
six: **št** *num*
sixty: **štyn** *num*
skin: **gld; zq; mšk; šlḥ**
slaughter: **nḥr**
slave: **ʿlym**
small cattle, sheep and goats: **ʿn**
small coins: **ʿrpn**
small: **zʿwr**
smith: **qyny**
sold, to be: **zbn** *v Dt*
soldier: **plḥ**
something, anything; (with) nothing: **mdʿm**
son: **br** I
son of the place (?): **br dktʾ** *n phr m*
southern: **tymny**
space (?): **rwḥ**
spare: **ḥws** *v C*
Spasinou Charax (same as Mesene Charax): **krk** II
spend, spend on: **ḥsk; ḥsr** *v*
splendidly: **nhwryt**
spring of water: **ʿyn**
stand, to be erected: **qwm** *v G*
statue, image: **ʾdrṭ; ṣlm; ṣlmh**
steal: **gnb** *v*
stele: **gll; nṣbh**
stone (?): **ʾbn**
store, shop: **ḥnw**
straw: **tbn**
stretch out: **yšṭ** *v*
subject to tax, owing: **ḥyb**
sun (?): **šmš** II
surety (?): **ʿrb**
Susa: **šwšn**
swear: **ymy** *v*
symposium: **ʾgn; mrzḥ**
syndic, public advocate (agent who carried out business of city): **sdq**
Tadmor, of (adj): **tdmry**
Tadmor, Palmyra: **tdmwr**
tailor: **ḥyṭ**
take: **ʾḥd; nsb** *v*
take as partner > to cede: **ḥbr** *v C, D*
talent (?): **kkr**
Tammuz (DN): **tmwzʾ**
tax, toll: **mks**
tax collector: **ʾgwr; mks; dy rbʿʾ** I
Tayma: **tymʾ**
teacher: **sbr**
Tebet (month): **ṭbt**
temple: **by; hykl**
ten ([?] variant form): **ʿšr; ʾʿšr** *num*
ten thousand: **rbw** *num*
Ten (municipal authorities): **ʿšrh**
tend sheep: **rʿy** *v*
term as symposiarch: **rbnwt mrzḥw**
term as secretary, office of secretary: **grmṭyʾ**
term as general: **ʾsṭrṭgw**
term as treasurer: **ʿnwšw**
term as head, term as presiding officer: **rbnw**
term as head of market: **rbnšqw**
territory: **tḥwm**
testify: **šhd; shd** *v*
thank: **ydy** *v*
that: **dy, d**
that is: **p** *cj*
that which: **mh**
there is, there are: **ʾyt** *pred*
there is not: **lyt** *pred*
therefore: **mṭl kwt**
these (pron dem pl m and f): **ʾln**
these (dem): **hln; hnwn**
thick (uncertain; said of wine): **qrš**

❖ ❖ ❖ ❖ ❖

PERSONAL NAMES

The standard reference work is J. Stark, *Personal Names in Palmyrene Inscriptions* (Oxford: Clarendon, 1971), cited here as "Stark PN," which contains a "Lexicon" explaining the names and a "Main List" which amounts to a concordance listing all occurrences. Note also, as general works, R. Degen's review of Stark's work, *BO* 29 (1972) 210-16; and J. Teixidor, "Remarques sur l'onomastique palmyrénienne," *Studi epigrafici e linguistici* 8 (1991) 213-23.

In the following name-list, ordinarily just *one* reference for each name is cited, with the symbol "+" if the name occurs 2 — 10 times, and "++" if it occurs more than 10 times; the dagger "†" is used to mark cases where the occurrence cited is unique in our corpus. We do not ordinarily list possible names attested only in a broken form. Names newly attested in the corpus, from texts published after the appearance of Stark's volume, are marked as such; scholarly discussion of such names is frequently to be found at the passage cited here, even where we do not explicitly refer to it. If a Greek or Latin transliteration of a Palmyrene name is found in a bilingual text, we cite at least one such equivalent (in italics); other sources, especially Greek texts other than bilinguals, offer evidence for pronunciation of names, but for practical reasons we do not include such data.

Names of places and deities are included in the Glossary and not here; note that it is not uncommon for humans to bear a name which is also the name for a deity. Names listed as "Tribal Names" in Stark PN are not separated from the rest in our list, but in the citations of these we include *bny* or *bnt* followed by the name, to call attention to this possibility.

ʾb *m* Doura 37:1†
ʾbʾ *m* Ber '35 p 77 III:1+
ʾbb *m* C4374:5+
ʾbbʾ *f* C4462:1+
ʾbbwhy *m* Doura 23:3 *Ababouis*†
ʾbgl *m* PNO no. 3 A:1+
ʾbgr *m* Ber '35 p 107 XIII:6 *C3960 Abgarou*++
ʾbdy *m* RTP 622†
ʾbyhn *m* Ber '35 p 102 X:3+
ʾbyḥy *m* Ber '38 p 114 (sub 20 III: b):1-2†
ʾbyn *m* PNO 77 A:2†
ʾbynʾ *f* PS no. 371:1†
ʾbyʿ *m* C4432:3 Reading of Stark PN for CIS ʾsyʿ†
ʾbyšy *f* Inv 8 12:1+
ʾblʿly *m* RTP 610+
ʾbmrt *m* C3991:2†
ʾbnʾ *f* C4306 B:3+
ʾbnyt *m* C4123 bis:3+
ʾbrwq *m* C3980:6+
ʾbrykw *m* RTP 303†
ʾbrmʾ *m* C4180:4†
ʾgdm *m* Inv 4 7a+
ʾgyʿ *m* Syr '49 p 36 no.1:2†
ʾgrpʾ *m* Ber '35 p 99 VIII:2 *C4209 Agripou*+
ʾgtʾ *m* RTP 704†
ʾgtgls *m* C3912:2 *Agathangelos*†
ʾgtwnʾ *m* Ber '35 p 104 XII:7†
ʾgtpws *m* MUSJ '62 p 106:5†
ʾgtps *m* Ber '35 p 99 VIII:2†
ʾdʾ *m* Syr '33 p 185:4†
ʾdb *m* Syr '36 p 346:2 (or: ʾrb)†
ʾdwnʾ *m* C4121:1 Prob. read ʾrwnʾ q.v.+
ʾdy *m* Iraq '87 p 57:2†
ʾdynh *m* RSP 49:3 Gaw ad loc: reading with *-h* (for normal *t*) is certain. Not in Stark PN.†
ʾdynt *m* C3944:2 *Odainathou; C4202 Odainathos*++
ʾdrynws *m* C4209:2 *Adrianou*†
ʾhwd *m* Inv 10 63:2 *Aeouadou*+
ʾhryʾ *m* Doura 26:2†
ʾwṭykʾ / ʾwṭyqʾ *m* RTP 425†
ʾwṭkʾ *m* C4103:1+
ʾwlʾ *m* BS III 29:5†
ʾwpmʾ *m* Inv 12 30:2 Tx ad loc: = Gk Euphēmos. Not in Stark PN.†
ʾwr *m* C4031:2 *Aur* Abbreviation of ʾwrlys.†
ʾwrlyʾ *m/f* Ber '35 p 88 IX:3 (f); Ber '36 p 124 (21 II):5 (m) *Aurēlios; Ber '35 p 110 II:2 Aurēlia*++
***ʾwrlynws** *m* Syr '71 p 420:3 [ʾ]wrlynws†
ʾwrlys *m* Ber '35 p 60 II:1 *Ber '35 p 110 II:1 Aurēlios*++
ʾwšy *m* C4119:3+
ʾwtqʾ *m* PNO 38:2†
ʾzmd *m* Inv 8 31:4 Stark PN: ʾzmr q.v.†
ʾzmr *m* Inv 8 31:4 Or: ʾzmd.†
ʾzrzyrt *m* C4213 *Syr '85 p 273 (no. 2):2*

Azarzeirathou[+]

ʾḥʾ *f* Ber '38 p 135 (21 IV F):1[+]

ʾḥwt *f* SFP 133:2[†]

ʾḥyʾ *m* Inv 12 56:3 (PNO 17:2)[+]

ʾḥyb *m* IP 79:6[†]

ʾḥybl *m* Inv 4 15b:1[†]

ʾḥyny *m* AAS '53 p 22:2[†]

ʾḥyry *m* RTP 40 So Stark PN, but read ʾḥydy see Glossary ʾḥd v.[†]

ʾḥytwr *m* C4279:4[+]

ʾḥmr *m* Inv 12 24:1[+]

ʾḥmr *m* Inv 12 24:1[+]

ʾḥply *m* C3927:1 *Ao[ph]alein*[†]

ʾḥtʾ *f* C4542:1[+]

ʾḥty *m* Sumer '62 p 64 no. 2:5-6 In name br ʾḥty.[†]

ʾṭykʾ *m* Inv 9 4A:1 *Antiochos*[†]

ʾṭnynys *m* Inv 10 102:2[†]

ʾṭnyʾ *f* RSP 67:1 Gaw ad loc: = Antonia. Not in Stark PN.[†]

ʾydʿn *m* C4581:2 *Ber '70 p 66 (1): Aeidaanou*[+]

ʾyyr *m* RTP 884[†]

ʾyšʾ *m* Inv 10 39:1 *Io[u]sa*[+]

ʾytybl *m* C4197:3[+]

ʾklb *m* Inv 11 28:3[+]

ʾkldy *m* AAS '53 p 24:3 Glossary kldy n.[+]

ʾknby *m* C3986:3[†]

ʾknt *m* Inv 8 22:2[†]

ʾkrn *m* C4391:3[†]

ʾlh *m* C4083:3 ?[†]

ʾlhbl *m* Ber '36 p 99 7:3 *Elabēlou*[++]

ʾlhw *m* C3980:6[+]

ʾlhšmš *m* Doura 25:5[†]

ʾlhšʾ *m* C4121:1 *C4187:1 Elassa*[+]

ʾlwr *m* PNO 78:5[†]

ʾlṭy *m* Inv 10 119:3 *Allataiou*[†]

ʾlys *m* Déd p 36:1, 2; Inv 7 1b; RB '30 p 538:1 (IP 8[+] 2)[+]

ʾlkdrys *m* Inv 4 7b[†]

ʾlksdrs *m* Trf I:2 *Alexandrou*[+]

ʾlksndrws *m* C3932:3 *Alexandrou*[+]

ʾlksndrs *m* Inv 10 112:2 *[A]lexand[rou]*[†]

ʾlkšndr̊ʾ *m* Parl '90 p 143 no. 17:1[†]

ʾlpy *m* C4018:5 At C3961:1 Stark PN ʾlpy; read ʾlpys.[+]

ʾlpys *m* Inv 10 90:1 *Oulpion*[++]

ʾlps *m* C3960:1 *Oulpion*[+]

ʾlqmʾ *m* C4515:1[†]

ʾlqms *m* Trf:78[†]

ʾmʾ *f* Inv 11 50:1[†]

ʾmby *m/f* Inv 8 200 (B):2 (m); Ber '34 p 40 IV:4 (f)[+]

ʾmbkrʾ *m* PNO 55A:4[†]

ʾmbtʾ *f* PS no. 3:2[†]

ʾmdbw *m/f* PNO no. 61:3 (m); Ber '38 p 124:4 (f)[+]

ʾmdy *m* Ber '38 p 106:1[†]

ʾmw *f* Ber '35 p 102 XI:6[+]

ʾmwn *m* PS 244A:1[+]

ʾmy *m* SFP 140:2[†]

ʾmyʾ *f* C4594 A:4[+]

ʾmyn *m* RTP 718[+]

ʾmyt *f* C4428:1[+]

ʾmlyws *m* Inv 10 29:1 *Aimilion*[+]

ʾmṣr *m* C4062:5[†]

ʾmtḥʾ *f* C4151:1[+]

ʾmry *m* JA '18 p 282:1[+]

ʾmrsʿ *m* Inv 4 24:3[+]

ʾmršʾ *m* C3931:2 *Amrisamsou*[+]

ʾmšʾ *m* BethSh p 198 (12):3[†]

ʾmšy *m* Inv 8 17:3[†]

ʾmt *f* Inv 12 12 (right):1[†]

ʾmtʾ *f* Ber '35 p 110 II:2 *Amathē*[++]

ʾmtbl *f* C4081:2[+]

ʾmtbʿl *f* BJPES '47 p 145:1[†]

ʾmtdʿth *f* Inv 12 6:6 Discussed by Tx ad loc: could be read *ʾmtrʿth*. Not in Stark PN.[†]

ʾmtlt *f* C4367:1[+]

ʾmtnny *f* Inv 12 10:1[†]

ʾmtrʿth See ʾmtdʿth[†]

ʾmtšlmʾ *f* Ber '35 p 91 II:2[†]

ʾnʾ *m/f* Ber '38 p 135 (21 IV A):1 (f); Ber '38 p 135 (21 IV B):2 (m)[+]

ʾnbt *m* C39905:2 *Latin ANNVBATHI*[†]

ʾnwbt *m* C3960:5 bny ʾnwbt[†]

ʾnṭwnys *m* Inv 10 113:1 *Gk: Antōniō; Latin: Antonio*[†]

ʾnṭykws *m* StudPalm '75 p 129:2[†]

ʾnṭnys *m* Syr '85 p 279 no. 9:2[†]

ʾnynws *m* MUSJ '62 p 106:3[†]

ʾns *m* RSP 145:4 ʾns[..][†]

ʾnʿm *m* PNO 57[†]

ʾnqyr *m* C3968:3 Gaw ad RSP 157 discusses reading; CIS, Stark PN: *ʾnqy*. Not in Stark PN.[+]

ʾnš *m* Sumer '64 p 15:1[†]

ʾntywkws *m* C3971:7[†]

ʾnṭykys *m* Ber '38 p 110:2[†]

ʾnṭyks *m* Ber '38 p 106:2[+]

ʾswyt *m* Ber '35 p 98 VII:2[†]

ʾsḥq *m* StudMiles p 50 no. 2:5[†]

ʾsyʾ *m* Ber '35 p 86 VIII:4? ʾs[..] Stark PN ʾsy[.].[†]

ʾsʿdd *m* SFP 134:4[†]

ʾspd / ʾspr *m* BS III 17:4[†]

ʾspdyn *m* C4054:2[†]

ʾspdys *m* C4235:2 *Spedios*[†]

ʾspydn *m* C4049:2 [ʾ]spydn[†]

ʾsqlpydʾ *m* Inv 10 29:2 *Asklēpiadēn*[†]

ʾsry *m* PNO 2:1 *Ber '70*

p 66 (1): Asoraiou+

ʾstr *f* BethSh p 206:1†

ʾʿb *m* IP 36:4†

ʾʿby *m* AA '30 p 192:4 *C3963:1 Aabei*++

ʾʿwy *m* RTP 908†

ʾʿwyd *m* C4318:5+

ʾʿylm *m* Inv 11 1:4†

ʾʿylmy *m* AAS '65 p 90:1 *C3930:2 Aailamein*++

ʾʿky *m* RSP 112:2†

ʾʿly *m* RTP 109 bny ʾʿly+

ʾʿry *m* Inv 11 88:2 dy [mt]qrh br ʾʿry q.v.†

ʾpwqḥ *m* C4084:5†

ʾpyn *m* C4003:1†

ʾply *m* RTP 439+

ʾplnys *m* Inv 8 183 A:2+

ʾpsk *m* PGKK p 306 no. 28:3†

ʾprhṭ *m* Ber '35 p 98 VII:2+

ʾṣwly *m* Ber '38 p 120:2†

ʾṣydny / ʾṣyrny *m* Inv 8 11:3†

ʾṣrʿ *m* Inv 8 9:4 dy mtqrh ʾṣrʿ.+

ʾqwpʿ *m* C4031:4 *Akopaou*+

ʾqzmn *m* Sumer '62 p 63 no. 1:7†

ʾqyḥ *m* C3917:1 *Akkeon*+

ʾqlyš *m* C4123bis:2 *Akkaleisou*+

ʾqmʾ *f* C4237 B:1++

ʾqml *m* C4167:1 *Akkim[al]ou; Ber '70 p 71 (5):6 ʾ[qm]l = Aggamalou*?+

ʾqmt *m/f* Ber '35 p 81f:1 (f); Inv 11 92:2 (m) *Ber '36 p 99 7:1 Akamathē*++

ʾrʾwm *m* C4121†

ʾrʾš *m* C4219:3+

ʾrb / ʾdb *m* Syr '36 p 346:2†

ʾrbz *m* Syr '31 p 139 no. 18:4†

ʾrhdwn *m* RTP 682†

ʾrwnʾ *m* C4121:1+

ʾrṭbn *m* C3968:4 *SFP 24:5 Artabanou*+

ʾrsṭyds *m* C4401:1 *Aristeidēs*†

ʾrqṭws *m* Inv 11 5:4†

ʾrqyl *m* SFP 159:3†

ʾrt *f* C3907:6†

ʾšd *m* C4476 A:3+

ʾšdw *m* Inv 8 175:2†

ʾšyn *f* PGSc 12:4 Reading of Cussini '92. Not in Stark PN.†

ʾšlm *m* Syr '33 p 179:2 context difficult; Stark takes as name of deity.†

ʾšm *m* RTP 537†

ʾšʿd *m* Inv 11 99:2†

ʾšʿʿ *m* RTP 480†

ʾšqrʾ *m* RTP 181:2+

ʾšr *m* Doura 21:2†

ʾtʾ *f* Inv 12 3:1+

ʾtm *m* Doura 8:2 bny ʾtm[.]†

ʾtndwrʾ *m* C4084:5†

ʾtndrws *m* C3971:2 ʾtndr[ws]†

ʾtpny *m* C4080:6+

ʾtʿm *m* Inv 11 1:5†

ʾtʿmn *m* C4081:4†

ʾtʿqb *m* C4432:2+

bbʾ *m* Doura 16:1†

bbw *m* Doura 36:1†

bbt *f* C3907:4†

bbtʾ *f* RSP 147:1 See Gaw ad loc for parallels. Not in Stark PN.†

bgd *m* StSc 151 (on right):3†

bgdn *m* C4340:4 *C4402:1 [A]pollo[d]ōros*+

bgwšy *m* SFP 125:6†

bgy *m* Inv 4 7b:2†

bgrn *m* Syr '31 p 127:3 *Inv 8 78:1 [bgr]n = Bogranēs*+

bgrt *m* BMT '55 p 36:2†

bgš *m* C4395:3†

bgšw *m* ARNA p 161:3+

bdn *f* RSP 197:1 bʔdn Gaw ad loc: no plausible explanation for name. Not in Stark PN.†

bwdlʾ *m* RTP 92 bny bwdlʾ†

bwṭʾ *m* C4017:3†

bwṭn *m* C4043:2†

bwṭtn *m* PNO 66:1†

bwlbrk *m* C4122:2 *Bōlbarachou*†

bwlzbd *m* Inv 11 49:3†

bwlḥʾ *m* RTP 82 bny bwlḥʾ *Inv 9 11:2 bōlaa; at C3915:1 for Gk kōma read bōlaa, as conjectured*+

bwlḥʾ *m* Ber '34 p 38 IV:4++

bwlḥzy *m* Ber '35 p 110 II:2 *Bōlazaiou*+

bwly *m* Ber '34 p 42 VI:3+

bwlyʾ *f* RSP 11 (on left):1 Gaw: plene writing of *blyʾ*. Not in Stark PN.†

bwlʾ *f* Inv 11 57:1+

bwlydʾ *m* RTP 36†

bwlmʾ *m* C4206:3+

bwlnʾ Inv 11 80:3†

bwlnwr *m* C4199:6†

bwlʿʾ *m/f* C4394 (right):2 [b]wlʿʾ (m); RTP 83 bny bwlʿʾ†

bwnʾ *m* Ber '35 p 99 VIII:2 *Trf Gk:2 Bōnneous, Syr '50 p 137 Bōnnaiou; Latin: Syr '50 p 137 BONNE* RTP 135 bny bwnʾ.++

bwnwr *m* RTP 7†

bwrʾ *m* RTP 793; RTP 62 bny bwrʾ+

bwrpʾ *m* Ber '34 p 38 IV:2 *C4163:2 Bōrophas*++

bwšʾ *m* C4579:1+

bzy *m* Inv 8 24:2†

bḥr *m* RTP 106 bny bḥr†

bydʾ *m* C3933 *Baida*†

bydn *m* Inv 8 136:3†

bkrw *m* C3907:3†

bkry *m* RSP 21:1 Gaw: reading certain; cites parallels. Not in Stark PN.†

blbw *m* PNO 53:1†

blbrk *m* Inv 12 12:6+

blg *m* Sem '77 p 117 (margin):1†
blḥ' *m* C4560:1⁺
blḥzy *m* C3990:2⁺⁺
blḥy *f* C3911:10†
blṭy *m* C4212:2†
bly *m* Ber '35 p 95 IV:1⁺
bly' *f* C4537 (by female):1†
blyd' *m* C3995:2 *Inv 10 29:4 Bōliadous*⁺
blyd'w *m* Inv 8 109:1†
blyhb *m* Sumer '62 p 63 no. 1:5†
blkz *m* RTP 990 Or read: blsz.†
blm' *m* RTP 130⁺
blnwr *m* RTP 272†
blnwry *m* Syr '30 Pl. XL no.2:2 RTP 272 bny blnwry.⁺
blsz *m* RTP 990 Or read: blkz.†
bl'm *m* Doura 40:4†
bl'qb *m* C4123:1 *C3937:3 Bēlakabos*⁺⁺
blšwr *m* AAS '53 p 24:1 *Inv 10 78:3 [B]ēlsouros*⁺
blšwry *m* AfO '53 p 312:5 *C4124:2 Bēlsourou*⁺⁺
blt' *m/f* C4405 (by girl):1 (f); RTP 752 (m)⁺
bltyḥn *f* C4152:1⁺
bn' *m* Ber '38 p 110 (20 III):4⁺
bnh *m* Inv 12 26 (a):4⁺
bnwr *m* Ber '35 p 115:1 *Bōnnourou*⁺
bnwry *m* C4252 (left):4⁺
bny *m* C4121⁺
bnyh *m* Doura 25:6 If not form of common noun *br*.†
bnkmyn *m* Doura 35:1†
bn'm *m* Verm '81 p 387 no. 336:1†
bnr *m* RSP 37 (on right):4†
bnr' *m* C4331:2†
bs' *m* Ber '35 p 97 VI:1⁺
bsm *m* C4013:3†
bss *m* Inv 11 5:3†
b'' *m/f* ΑΙΩΝ '86a p 246:1 *C4124:3 dy mtqrn bny b'' tou epikaloumenou Baa*⁺
b'd' *f* RSP 101 (b):1†
b'dy' *f* RSP 81:1†
b'yḥw *m* Doura 1:3†
b'lw *m* MUSJ '61 p 125 no.1:7†
b'ly *m* Ber '35 p 93 III:1⁺⁺
b'ltg' *m/f* Ber '38 p 135(21 IV C):1; C4053:2 (f) *Syr '50 p 137:4 Baalthēga*⁺
b'šg' *f* RSP 71 (on right of girl):1 Gaw ad loc: = **b'lšg'*. Not in Stark PN.†
b'šmn *m* Inv 8 162:1†
bpny' *m* RTP 933†
bqy *m* C4517:2†
bqly *m* NyCG 62:3 bq?ly†
br' *m* C4173⁺
br 'ḥty *m* Sumer '62 p 64 no. 2:5-6 dy mtqrh br 'ḥty.†
br ''ry *m* Inv 11 88:2 dy [mt]qrh br ''ry.†
br't' *m* PNO 4†
br b'' *m* C4114:3 dy mtqrh br b''.⁺
brbra *m* Trf:121 *Barbaron (Gk line 197)*†
brdwny *m* Ber '38 p 134:1†
br dkt' *m* Ber '36 p 88:2 See Glossary dkh nf; may be title, not PN.†
brh' *m* PNO 41:2†
brwky *m* BS III 46:3†
brwq' *m* C4311 B:1⁺
br zbydy *m* Syr '38 p 78:3 [dy] mtqrh br zbydy.†
brḥwm *m* Inv 11 1:3†
bry *m* Inv 8 48:2†
bryk *m* RTP 554†
brykw *m* RTP 810†
bryky *m* AAS '65/2:2 *C3931:2 Bareichein*⁺⁺
bryqy *m* RTP 547†
brkh *m* Doura 43:1†
brky *m* C3925:2 *[Bar]chaiou*†
brkyw *m* Syr '33 p 177:5 [b]ny brkyw†
brll *f* C3907:2†
brnbw *m* C3986:2⁺
brny *m* C4542:4⁺
brs *m* RTP 700⁺
brsmy' *m* Ber '38 p 124:4⁺
br' *m* YCS '55 p 177:1 *Bareos*†
br'' *m* Ber '35 p 115:1 *Bareas*⁺⁺
br 'bdbl *m* C3978:5 dy mtqrh br 'bdbl.†
br 'zwlt *m* Sumer '64 p 19:4 dy mtqrh br 'zwlt.†
br'y *m* Inv 10 105:2 *Barath[ous]*†
br't' *m* C3901 *Latin: Barates*†
br'th *m* AA '30 p 192:2⁺⁺
brp' *m* C3996:6⁺
brq *m* C3999:2†
bršgl *m* RTP 903†
bršmš *m* C3911:6⁺
brš'd *m* C4544:1 *C4215 Barsados (lacuna in Aram)*⁺
br š't *m* Inv 9 20:3 *dy [mt]qrh br š't* Gk: [...]thou
brt' *m/f* Inv 4 12:1 (m) (= CaB 3:1??); Inv 11 50:1 (f)⁺
bšr' *m* RTP 643†
bt' *f* Inv 8 10:3⁺
btwhby *f* C4380:1†
btzby *f* C3947:1 *Zēnobias*⁺
btzbyd' *f* C4027:2†
btḥby *f* C4244:2†
btḥw *f* C4518 (right):1†
btḥwml *f* RSP 42:4†
btḥyrn *f* C4568:2†
bty *m/f* Ber '38 p 135 (21 IVE):1 (m); C4383:1 (f)⁺
btml' *f* RSP 191 (on right):2-3†
btmlkw *f* C4175:2⁺
btmrṣw *f* Ber '38 p 135 21 IVA:1
btprmwn *f* Ber '36 p 88 2:4†
bt'' *f* C4178:2⁺
bt'' *m* DuraPR '36 p 170 no. 687†
bt'bdy *f* RSP 93 (on

left):1†
bt'g' *f* C4358:1 (f)+
bt'ty *f* C4431:1†
btšmy' *f* Ber '35 p 80c:1+
bttymrṣw *f* Ber '38 p 135 21 IVB:1
g'ys *m* Inv 10 129:1 *Gaion*+
gb' *m* BS III 39:4†
gbyns *m* Inv 11 16:3†
gbl *f* C4593:1†
gbr' *m* RTP 507†
gd' *m* C3981:2+
gdy' *m* C4076:2++
gdybwl *m* C4231 E:3; C3917:2 bny gdybwl *hoi Gaddeibōlioi*†
gdylt *m* C4092:2†
gdymy *m* RTP 298 Stark PN reads grymy in all occurrences.+
gdrṣw *m* C4027:3 *C4214:3 Gaddar[s]ou*+
gdybwl *m* C3917:2 bny g d y b w l *h o i Gaddeibōlioi*+
gwb' *m* PNO 53:2†
gwg' *m* RTP 80 bny gwg'+
gwgw *m* RTP 81 bny gwgw†
gwr' *m* C3906:1 *Latin: GVRAS*+
gwry *m* C4281:3†
gwrny *m* Inv 10 53:3 *Inv 10 77:3-4 Gouronnaiou*+
gḥynt *m* Inv 8 25:4†
gy *m* C 4024:3 gy?†
gynws *m* RTP 381†
gys *m* Trf:74†
gyr' *m* PS 3:1†
gl' *m* Inv 11 42:2†
glḥ[.] *m* RSP 184:2 glḥ[.]†
glnws *m* Inv 10 113:3 *Galēnos; Latin: GALENVS*†
gml' *m* C3994:5+
gmly' *m* MUSJ '49 p 46:6†
gmlyh *m* NyCG '62:4†
gmlt *f* Inv 11 62:1†
gmr' *m* RTP 673†
gnb' *m* RTP 337†
g'l *m* Inv 8 99:3†
g'lw / g'ly *m* Inv 11 55:5†
gpn *m* Ber '35 p 100 IX:4†
gpn' *f* SFP 125:2†
grb' *m* C3948:2 *Gab[b]a*+
grymy *m* RTP 298 Stark PN prefers grymy to gdymy in all occurrences.+
grmy *m* PNO 52:2†
grmn' *m* Ber '35 p 104 XII:7 *Syr '38 p 155:4 Germanou*+
grmnqws *m* Trf:109 *Trf line 182: Germanikou*†
grmnqs *m* Syr '31 p 139:3†
gtmy *f* C4604 (by female):1†
db *m* Doura 55:1†
dbḥ *m* Ber '38 p 95:5+
ddywn *m* Ber '35 p 102 XI:6+
dwḥy *m* Ber '35 p 60 II:1+
dwmnyn' *f* C4020 A:2+
dw'y / rw'y *m* RSP 188:3†
dwṣy / rwṣy *f* PNO 74:1†
dwr' *m* C4084:3†
dzyṣyḥ *m* C4376:2†
dygns *m* Ber '35 p 102 XI:6†
dywn *m* Ber '35 p 95 III:1+
dyn' *m* Inv 11 80:2†
dyny *m* C4519:2+
dynys *m* C4287:6 *RSP 34:1 Dionysios*++
dk' *m* C4030:5+
dky *m* Palm VIII p 122 no. 26:4 (reading uncertain)†
dkry *m* PNO 77:1†
dkt' *m ?* Ber '36 p 88:2 See Glossary dkh nf; may not be PN.†
dmy *m* C4371:2 etc. With Stark PN read rmy in all occurrences; variant of rm'.†
dms *m* RSP 108:3†
dny *m* C4002:4+
dsty' / rsty' *f* RSP 50 (b):1 Gaw ad loc: perhaps = Gk Dōsithea?. Not in Stark PN.†
d'' *m* RTP 892? Stark PN r''.†
d't' *f* C4291:1 etc. With Stark PN, r't'.+
drm *f* PS no. 493:2 d?rm†
hg' *f* RSP 103 (a):1†
hgy *f* C4469:1+
hgr *f* AfO '53 p 312:1+
hd' *f* C4247:1 (on left)+
hdyr' *f* C4080:3+
hdyrt *f* C4147:1+
hdrynws *m* C3959:3 hdry[nws] *Adrianou*†
hldrs *m* RTP 251†
hlydwrs *m* MUSJ '62 p 106:6†
hlydyrs *m* Ber '35 p 99 VIII:2†
hlydrws *m* RB '30 p 545 B:1 *Hēliodōrou*†
hn'y *m* C4515:5+
hrmz *m* C4074:2†
hrmzd *m* IP 18†
hrmy *m* PNO 77:3†
hrms *m* Ber '35 p 82 V:2 *C4211 (lacuna in Aram): Hermeian*+
hrmsyn' *m* C4016:3†
hrql' *m* Inv 11 44:2†
hrqlyd' *m* C4514:1†
w'l' *f* RSP 56:2 Gaw ad loc cites Nabataean parallels. Not in Stark PN.†
whb' *m* Ber '34 p 42 VI:1++
whby *m* Ber '35 p 91 II:2 *Inv 8 59:3 Ouabaiou*++
whblt *m* C3971:2++
whblth *m* Doura 49:1†
wly *m* Inv 8 168:3†
wls *m* RSP 63:1 Gaw ad loc: perhaps = Valens. Not in Stark PN.†
wsḥw *m* Inv 10 115:1 *Ouaseou*†
w'd / w'r *m* RTP 148†
wrg *m* BS III 63:2†
wrdn *m* Ber '38 p 106:2+
wrwd *m* Ber '36 p 94 4:1 *C3937:1 Ouorōdēn*++
wrtn *m* PNO 35:2+

zb *m* RTP 734 zb<dʾ> or the like Stark PN p 85: an abbr.+
zbʾ *m* C4552:2+
zbd *m* C4070:3+
zbdʾ *m* AAS '53 p 19:5 *C3947:2 Zabdas*++
zbdbw *m* Inv 11 81:5†
zbdbwl *m* Ber '35 p 60 II:1; C3951:2 bny zbdbwl klhwn C3951:2 hoi egg[e]nous Zabdibōleiōn.++
zbdbwlʾ *m* Sumer '64 p 16 no. 5:5†
zbdbl *m* C3997:2++
zbdh *m* MélRob:1†
zbdwn *m* SFP 21:2 dy mtqrʾ zbdwn. Not in Stark PN.†
zbdy *m* C3983:1†
zbdlʾ *m* C3986:3 *C3928:5 Zabdela; C3932:1 Zēnobion ton kai Zabdilan*+
zbdlh *m* C3992:2 *Inv 10 39:1 Zabdilan*++
zbdnbw *m* C3983:1†
zbdʿy *m* Inv 8 7:2+
zbdʿtʾ *m* C4247:5 *Zabdaathous*+
zbdʿth *m* Ber '35 p 59 I:1 *Zabdaathous; RSP 35:2 Zēnobios*++
zbwd *m* C4045:3+
zbwdw *m* Inv 11 19:3†
zby *m* C3946:3 *C3947:3 Zabbaios*+
zbydʾ *m* AfO '53 p 312:2 *C4031:4 Zēnobiou*++
zbydy *m* Syr '38 p 78:3 [dy] mtqrh br zbydy.†
zbknʾ *m* PNO 34:1†
zgwg *m* C4522:3+
zgwg *m* Inv 11 96:1 bny zgwg+
zdql *m* Syr '49 p 38:3†
zwzy *m* RSP 116:5†
zwr *m* C4294:3+
zwrw *m* C4293:5†
zkyʾ *m* PNO 39:1†
zmrʾ *m* Inv 10 145 (below):2 bny zmrʾ+
zmry *m* RTP 933†
zʿmw *m* PNO 55 (above temple):2 Or: zʿqw.†
zʿqw *m* PNO 55 (above temple):2 Or: zʿmw.†
zqʾ *m* Inv 4 4b:1†
zqṭrty *f* Syr '71 p 422:5†
zrzryt *m* Inv 10 24:1 *Zarzirathou*†
ḥbʾ *m/f* Ber '35 p 91 II:1 (m); C4321:1 (f)++
ḥbbt *m* C4399:1†
ḥbwb *m*? Inv 8 152:3 [...] ḥbwb [...].†
ḥbwlʾ *m* C4355:2-3+
ḥby *m* Ber '35 p 102 XI:6+
ḥbybʾ *m* BMB '55 p 34 (3):1†
ḥbyby *m* C3905:1 *Latin: HABIBI*++
ḥbybywn *m* SFP 24:1 *Abeibiōna*†
ḥbn *m* C4571 A:2†
ḥbry *m* C4078:4†
ḥbtʾ *m/f* PNO 73:1 (m); Inv 8 2:1 (f) *Abbatha* See also ḥgt (both names always f except possibly in PNO 73:1).+
ḥbzy *m* C4338:3+
ḥgʾ *f* C4421 B:1 *Inv 10 119:5 Aggē*+
ḥggw *m* C3929:2 *Inv 10 24:1 Agegou; Syr '85 p 273:1 Aiegos (prb for *Agegos)*++
ḥgwgʾ *m* C4473:1+
ḥgwr *m* Ber '34 p 36 III:1+
ḥgy *m* C4211:1+
ḥgt *m/f* C4287:1 Possibly m in PNO 73:1.+
ḥdʾ *m* Inv 11 11:4+
ḥdwdn *m* Ber '36 p 88 2:1 *C3914:2 Addoudanou*++
ḥdydw *m* Sumer '64 p 20 no. 12:2 [ḥ]dydw.†
ḥwml *m* C4122:2+
ḥwr *m* RSP 105:3 dy mtqrh ḥwr†
ḥwrʾ *m* RSP 76:2 Gaw ad loc cites Nabataean parallels. Not in Stark PN.†
ḥṭyṭ *m* Inv 12 39:1 ḥṭy[ṭ]†
ḥṭrʾ *m* RTP 993 *r* could be read *d*.†
ḥṭry *m* AAS '53 p 22:3 C4164:1 bny ḥṭry.+
ḥym *m* Doura 9:2 ḥym?†
ḥyny *m* RTP 183†
ḥyrʾ *m* AAS '53 p 24:2++
ḥyry *m* RTP 222†
ḥyrn *m* AA '32 p 1:1 *Ber '35 p 59 I:3 Airanēn; C3953:1 Hērōdēn ton kai Airanēn, cf. C3940; Latin: Syr '50 p 137:2 HAERANES*++
ḥkym *m* RTP 364 bny ḥkym†
ḥkym *m* RTP 225†
ḥkyšw *m* C3923:2 *dy mtqrh ḥkyšw tou kai Ochchaisou*†
ḥlʾ *m* RTP 134 bny ḥlʾ *C3916:1 Ala*+
ḥldʾ *m* C3993:3+
ḥlh *m* C4206:2 bny ḥlh? Prb common noun *ḥl* "uncle" see Glossary s.v.†
ḥlyʾ *m* C4035:3†
ḥlyw *f* C4442:2†
ḥlypʾ *m* C4530:3+
ḥlypy *m* C3956:2 *Inv 4 13:3 Olaiphei*+
ḥlypt *f* C4460:2+
ḥlyšw *m* JA '18 p 295 no. 18:1†
ḥlyšy *m* Inv 8 62:1†
ḥlkš *m* Syr '33 p 190:2†
ḥll *m* Ber '38 p 104:2++
ḥlpʾ *m* C4198 (Lower):1+
ḥlpw *f* C4289:1†
ḥlpwnʾ *m* C4031:3 *Antipatros ho kai Alaphōnas*+
ḥlptʾ *m* Ber '35 p 84 VI:2 *Inv 10 119:2 Alaphathan*++
ḥmʾ *m* RTP 17++
ḥmy *m* RTP 469†
ḥmyn *m* Ber '38 p 95:5†
ḥmnwn *m* Syr '36 p 351:6†

ḥnʾ *f* C4493:1[+]
ḥnbl *m* AA '30 p 192:3 *RSP 24:2 E<nn>ibēlou; RSP 33:3 Anibēlou*[++]
ḥnwd / ḥnwr *m* RTP 97 bny ḥnwd / ḥnwr[†]
ḥnynʾ *m* AIΩN '86a p 247:1 *Syr '85 p 276 no. 5:1 Aneina[s]*[++]
ḥnynw *m* Inv 10 16:3 *Ona[in]ou*[†]
ḥnyny *m* Inv 7 14[†]
ḥnt *f* RB '30 p 539 no. 9:3[†]
ḥntʾ *m/f* AA '32 p 1:1 (m); C4388:1 (f)[+]
ḥsd *f* C4449:1[†]
ḥss *m* C4038:3[†]
ḥpry *m* Ber '38 p 95 (18 II):3[†]
ḥprtm *m* RTP 625[†]
ḥsswny *f* RSP 70:1-2[†]
ḥrʾ *f* C4615:4[†]
hrbz *m* Doura 48:1[†]
ḥrwṣ *m* RTP 156[†]
ḥršw *m* RB '30 p 539 no. 9:1[+]
ḥrtʾ *f* C4394 (left):2[+]
ḥršʾ *m* C3937:3 *Arsa*[+]
ḥrtbw *f* SFP 41 no. 2:1[†]
ḥšy *m* Inv 8 39:2[†]
ḥšš *m* C3915:1 *Asasou*[+]
ḥšš *m* RTP 93 bny ḥšš[+]
ḥty *m* C3980:5[+]
ṭbrys *m* C3903:2 *Latin (3,4) TI(berius)*[+]
ṭṭys *m* BS III 20:5[†]
ṭyṭwylw *m* RSP 119:4[†]
ṭymwn *m* Inv 4 7a:2[†]
ṭmys *m* C4409:4[+]
ṭms *m* C4410:1[+]
ṭʿy *m* RSP 2:2[++]
ydʾ *m* C3950:1 *Iadēn*[+]
ydbw / yrbw *m* C4491:2[†]
ydy *m* AA '32 p 1:1 *Ber '35 p 59 I:2 Iaddaiou; C3906:1 IIDEI*[++]
ydyʿ *m* Ber '38 p 137 (sub 21 IV):2[+]
ydyʿbl *m* C3959:7 bny ydyʿbl[+]
ydyʿbl *m* Ber '34 p 40 V:2 *Ber '35 p 110 II Iedeibēlos*[++]
ydyʿt *f* C4304:1[†]
ydʿw *m* C4060:2[++]
ydʿy *m* Syr '38 p 181:1[†]
ydʿnw *m* RTP 802[†]
yhybʾ *m* C4030:4[+]
ywl *m* C4031:2 *Iou* Abbreviation of ywlys.[†]
ywlʾ *m* C4206:1 Or read: ywl<y>ʾ.[†]
ywlyʾ *m/f* Ber '35 p 104 XII:6 (m); C4175:2 (f) *Ber '35 p 110 II:2 Ioulia*[++]
ywlyws *m* Ber '35 p 78 IV:1[+]
ywlys *m* Ber '35 p 60 II:1 *Ioulios Ber '35 p 110 II:1*[++]
ykyn *m* RSP 51:1[†]
ymlʾ *m* C4032:3[+]
ymlkw *m* C4123:1 *Iamlichos*[++]
ymlky *m* BS III 71:2[†]
yʿqwb *m* C4029:3[+]
yʿt *m* C4322:6[+]
yʿtw *m* C4324:4 Possible reading only, more likely is yʿt.[†]
yʿty *m* RSP 158:1[+]
yqrwr *m* C4195:5[†]
yrbw / ydbw *m* C4491:2[†]
yrḥbwlʾ *m* Ber '34 p 33 II:1 *C3914:1 Iaribōleous, Iaribōlēi*[++]
yrḥy *m* AIΩN '86a p 246:4 *Ber '70 p 71 (5):7 Iaraiou; Latin Dacia '70 p 405 (lacuna in Aram): IERHEI*[++]
ytmʾ *m* MUSJ '49 p 46:4[†]
yrq *m* Ber '35 p 78 IV:1[+]
yšwʿlʾ *m* RTP 985 bny yšwʿlʾ[†]
kdnny *f* C4517:1[†]
khylw *m* Ber '35 p 85 VII:6 *Inv 10 54:1 Cheilou*[++]
khyly *m* C4462:2[+]
khnbw *m* Inv 11 83:2 bny khnbw[+]
kwmy *m* C4588:1[+]
kyly *m* C4029:3[+]
kylywn *m* PNO 14:3[†]
kytwt *m* C4075:4[+]
klbʾ *m* RTP 217[+]
klby *m* C4527:4[†]
kmyn *m* Doura 54:2[†]
kmnyn *m* SFP 28:1 *Kamnyna*[†]
kmrʾ *m* C3915:2 [bny] kmrʾ *Chomarēnōn* See Déd 37-41 and Glossary s.v. *kmr* n.[++]
kmrʾ *m* C3929:2[†]
knbt *m* C4114:4 bny knbt[†]
kspʾ *f* C4408:1[†]
kʿbw *m* Inv 8 36:1 kʿb[w][†]
kptwt *m* C4173:1[+]
krḥ *m* C4480:4[+]
krystws *m* C4235:2 *Chrysantho[s]*[†]
krsmʾ *m* Inv 11 6:2[†]
lbn *m* Doura 53:1[†]
lbnʾ *f* RSP 86:1 Gaw ad loc cites parallels, including Heb. Not in Stark PN.[†]
lwy *m* C4201:1 *Lēoui*[+]
lwyʾ *f* C4301:1[+]
lwqys *m* Ber '38 p 124 (21 II):4 *Gk: L(oukiō); Latin: L(ucio)*[+]
lwqy *m* Doura 23:3 *Leukiou*[†]
lwqyws *m* C4235:1 [lwqy]ws *Loukios*[+]
lwqlʾ *f* C4401:4 *Loukillēs*[†]
lmlkʾ *m* Ber '35 p 100 IX:3 Perhaps name is the common mlkʾ with preposition repeated, i.e. lywlys ʾwrlys lmlkʾ etc.:: Stark PN.[†]
lʿš *m* Verm '81 p 380 no. 300:4[†]
lqy *m* RB '30 p 540 no. 10:1[†]
lqyšw *m* Syr '38 p 76:2 *Lekeisou*[†]
lqnys *m* RTP 700:1

Likinion. Inv 10 130:2 [lqn]ys+

lrmn *m* RTP 35†

lšmš *m* Ber '35 p 88 IX:4++

lšmšw *m* RB '30 p 539 no. 9:1+

lšmšy *m* C3904:1 *Lisamsou; C3920:2 Lisamsaiou*+

mgdt *m* C3978:6 bny mgdt+

***mgrʾ** *m* C4120 (lacuna in Aram: *bny mgrʾ) *ph[ylē]s Magerēnōn*†

mddy / mrry *m* Ber '73 p 89 204:2†

mdw / mrw *m* Doura 41:2†

mdʿ *m* Ber '73 p 89 204:1†

mhwy *m* C4130:5 dy mtqrh mhwy.+

mhr *m* Sumer '62 p 63 no. 1:10†

mhrdd *m* Inv 9 28:7†

mhrdt *m* PNO 55 (on left):3+

mhrw *m* PNO 37:4†

mwʾlʾ *m* C4601:3+

mwdlʾ *f* RSP 15:2†

mwsʾ *m* Ber '38 p 135 (21 IV D):1†

mzbʾ *f* C4067:1†

mzbw *f* RSP 40:1†

mzbnʾ *m* C4067:1 C4209:2 (lacuna in Aram) *Mezabban[a];* cf Inv 9 26:3++

mzbtʾ *m/f* Inv 8 115:2 (m); C4307:1 (f)+

mzy *m* Inv 8 73:5 Or: qzy.†

mzyʾ *m* RTP 96†

mḥlmw *m* PNO 74b:1†

mḥrbzn *m* Syr '38 p 82:1†

mṭn *m* RB '30 p 537 no. 7:2†

myqṭʾ *m* C4597:3†

mykʾ *m* C4123 bis:3+

mytʾ *m* RTP 720†

myrn *m* IP 33:1 Mistake for ḥyrn, see duplicate text Inv 11 21:1.†

mytʾ *m* C4109 A:5 bny mytʾ; BS III 11:3 bnt mytʾ Latin: Syr '50 p 137:3 *MITHENON*; Gk: Inv 9 20:3 *mithēnōn*+

myšʾ *f* Inv 4 7:3 *Maisa*+

myšn *m* C4007:4†

mk *m* RTP 507†

mkbl *m* PS no. 232:1+

mky *f* Sem '74 p 72 no. 4:2+

mknʾ *m* MUSJ '66 p 178 (no. 4):1;:1+

mknʾ *m* IP 34:3†

mksmws *m* C3908:4 *Latin: MAXIMI; Gk C4401:1 Maximos*+

mksms *m* Inv 10 81:1+

mkʿʾ *m* MélRob:1†

mktš *m* C4063:3†

ml *m* RTP 734 Stark PN: abbr = ml(kw) etc.†

mlʾ *m* AfO '53 p 312:3 *Ber '36 p 99 7:1 Mal[ēs]*++

mlwkʾ *m* AIΩN '86a p 248:1 *C3941:4 (lacuna in Aram): Malōcha*+

mly *m* C4389:3+

mlk *m* RSP 108:3†

mlkʾ *m* Ber '35 p 100 IX:3 *Ber '35 p 110 II:2 Malchē*+

mlkʾl *m* C4372 (middle):2+

mlkbl *m* Ber '34 p 36 III:3-4†

mlkw *m* Ber '34 p 36 III:2 *Ber '35 p 109 (I): Malchou; Latin: Dacia '70 p 405:1 MALCHVS*++

mlkwn *m* YCS '55 p 131 no. 3:1 *Malchiōn*†

mlkwsʾ *m* C4385:2+

mlkt *f* C4581:1†

mlq *m* Inv 12 45:4 Not discussed by Tx ad loc, or by Gaw ad RSP 180. Not in Stark PN.+

mndymnʾ / mnrymnʾ *m* RTP 23†

mndrs *m* RTP 954+

mnʿym *m* RSP 26: *[Mon]emou*+

mʿdnʾ / mʿrnʾ *m* RSP 178:3†

mʿzyn *m* Sumer '62 p 63 no. 1:8†

mʿzyn *m* C3983:2 bny mʿzyn+

mʿyʾ *m* Inv 11 13:5†

mʿynʾ *f* Ber '38 p 124 (21 II):7†

mʿynt *f* C4479 (by female):1†

mʿyrʾ *m* PNO 55 (above temple):6†

mʿytw *m* C4166:2+

mʿyty *m* C3957:2+

mʿn *m* C4199:6+

mʿnʾ *m* C4567:1†

mʿnw *m* RSP 16:2+

mʿny *m* C3964:1 *C3921:1 Mannaiou; C3943:4 Maenaiou*++

mplys *m* C4160:2 mpl[ys] *Mophleou*†

mqlwʾ *m* C4094:2†

mqy *m* Ber '35 p 60 II:1 *C3910:1*++

mqyʾ *m* BS III 51:2†

mqyḥy *m* C4505:1†

mqym *m* Inv 11 41:1+

mqymw *m* AAS '53 p 19:2 *Ber '35 p 110 II:3 Mokimou; Latin C3909:2 MOCIMVS*++

mqymy *m* Inv 8 3:2+

mqymt *m* Inv 8 96:5+

mqynʾ *m* RSP 40:3†

mqmw *m* RTP 272†

mrʾ *f* C4409:2†

mrbnʾ *m* MUSJ '61 p 133:3†

mrd *m* PS no. 104:2†

mrh *f?* C4550:3†

mrwnʾ *m* C4061:3 *Ber '70 p 69 (4):2 dy [mt]qrʾ mrwnʾ ho [kai M]arōnas*+

mryʾ *m* C3944:4†

mrywn *m* C4021:2+

mrym *f* C4023:3†

mrnys *m* Trf:65†

mrnʾ *m* RTP 914†
mrqʾ *m* Ber '35 p 82 V:2†
mrqws *m* C4401:1 *Markos*+
mrqy *m* Inv 8 34†
mrqynws *m* Inv 10:29:1 *Markianon*†
mrqlʾ *m* C4080:4+
***mrqlws** *m* BS III 45:6 mrql[ws] *Mar[kellou]*†
mrqs *m* C3960:1 *Markon*†
mrry / mddy *m* Ber '73 p 89 204:2†
mrtʾ *f* C4335:2†
mrthwn *f* C4238:1+
mrty *f* Ber '35 p 79 c:1 *C3954:1 Marthein*+
mrtynʾ *m* Inv 11 44:3†
mšy *m* RTP 395+
mškw *m* C3994:4++
mšknʾ *m* Sumer '64 p 16 (no. 5):3 bny mšknʾ†
mšlm *m* C3907:7†
mšš *m* BS III 61 (C):1†
mtʾ *m* C4123 bis:3 *C3930:2 Maththa*+
mtbwl *m* C4375:1 mtbwl; C4113:6 bny mtbwl *C3925:3 [b]ny mtbwl Manth(a)bōleiōn*+
mtly *m* PGKK p 306 no. 28:6†
mtnʾ *m* C3980:4++
mtnw *m* C4205:4†
mtny *m* ΑΙΩΝ '86a p 247(2):2++
nʾwm *m* PNO 63:1 gd nʾwm Stark lists with names of deities; see Glossary s.v. *gd* n.†
nʾry *m* RSP 119:3+
nbʾ *m* RSP 91:4 Gaw ad loc: hypocoristic of *nbwšwry*, or combining lines 3-4 read: *brnbʾ*. Not in Stark PN.†
nbwgdy *m* C4231 D:1†
nbwdʿ *m* C4048:2+
nbwzʾ *m* C4249:6+
nbwzbd *m* AAS '65/2 p 127:1 *C4124:1 Nebouzabados*++
nbwydʿ *m* Inv 8 28:1+
nbwlʾ *m* C4249:5 *C4124 (lacuna in Aram) Neboulas*+
nbwlh *m* RTP 290†
nbwmʾ/y *m* Syr '38 p 157:3 [nb]wmʾ; Inv 9 30:2 [nbwmy] *[N]e[b]oumaion at Inv 9 30:2* Text lacunae in both places.+
nbwmwʾ *m* C4206:4? Read prb nbwm<r> wʾ[...]†
nbwmr *m* C4206:2+
nbwnʾ *m* PBSc 13:2†
nbwšwr *m* RSP 80:3+
nbwšwry *m* RSP 75:1+
nbwšy *f* PS no. 3 p 25:2†
nby *m* C4130:2+
ngdʾ / ngrʾ *m* Inv 12 40:1†
ngmw *m* Inv 11 62:3†
ndbʾl *m* Syr '30 Pl. XLI no. 2:3†
nhrʾ *f* C4300:1†
nhtwmʾ *m?* Inv 11 32:5? See Glossary s.v. nḥtwmʾ; prb not PN.†
nwmnws *m* SFP 142:2†
nwrbl *m* AAS '53 p 19:4; RTP 123 bny nwrbl *Ber '38 p 120 (21 I):1 Nourbēlou*++
nwry *m* C3980:7 *Inv 8 58:1 Nour[eos]*+
nwrʿth *m* C4529:3+
nḥʾ *m/f?* Palm IV 4:3 (m); Syr '38 p 157:1 (f)?+
nḥy *m* PNO 16:3†
nḥyʿzyz *m* C4041:3†
nḥštb *m* Ber '35 p 91 II:1+
nybnʾ *m* RSP 77 (on right):1-2†
nyny *m* Syr '38 p 157:2 [.n]yny.†
nynyʾ *m* C4206:1+
nyqʾ *f* C4085:4+
nyqṭwr *m* Doura 29:2†
nnʾ *f* C4541:1†
nsʾ *m* C3916:1 *Nesē*+
nʿbʾ *m* Inv 8 143:2+
nʿm *m/f* C4092:2 (m); IP 80:2 (f)+
nʿmy *f* C4268:1+
nʿmʿyn *m* C4171:1+
nʿry *m* C3917:1 *Noaraiou* [nʿ]ry.†
npry *m* C4204:4+
nṣʾ *f* Syr '38 p 158:1†
nṣwr *m* C4202 *Nasōrou*+
nṣrʾ *m* C4403:1 *Nasrallathe*+
nṣry *m* IP 79:4 *SFP 24:3 Nasraion*†
nṣryḥby *m* C3968:4+
nṣrlt *m* Ber '35 p 109 I:1 *Nasrallathos*+
nqbʾ *m* Ber '38 p 101:2†
nrglzbd *m* RB '30 p 536 (no. 6):1†
nrqys *m* C3996:5+
nšwm *m* C3932:2 *Nassoumou*+
nšm *m* C4062:4+
nšʾ *m* Ber '34 p 33 II:2 *Trf I:3, Gk line 2: Nesa; Latin: Dacia '70 p 405:2 N[E]SES*++
ntn *m* Sem '91 p 84:3†
ntny *m* Inv 8 157:1†
nšry *m* C4085:4+
sbynʾ *m* Ber '38 p 104:2+
sbyns *m* C4084:3†
sbnʾ *m* C4543:2†
sbʾ *m* C4019:4†
sbq *f* RSP 190:1†
sgʾ *m* Inv 11 50:2†
swsʾ *m* C4057:3†
sḥlph *m* RSP 159:2 Gaw ad loc: enigmatic; Milik Déd read *mḥplh*. Not in Stark PN.†
sṭṭyls *m* Trf:104 *Gk line 182 Stateili[on]*†
sṭm *m* RTP 407+
sṭmʾ *m* RTP 525+
sygʾ *f* IP 81:2†
sywd/rʾ *m* Inv 11 31:3 syw[.]ʾ Stark PN sywd/rʾ.†
symʾ *f* Iraq '49 p 185:1†
syʿwnʾ *m* C4300:3+
syʿnʾ *m* C4073:3+

sy'ṭ *f* C4530:1†
syry *m* Ber 1,1338 p 116:1
skyy *m* RSP 120:4†
skn' *m* RTP 96 bny skn'†
slwq' *m* C4048:3+
slwqws *m* C3934:2 *Seleukon*+
slwqs *m* Ber '38 p 104:1+
smy' *m* PS no. 371:5†
ssn *m* Ber '35 p 76 II:1+
sptymy' *f* C3971:3 *Septimias*†
sptymyws *m* C3971:1 *See Gk s.v. spṭmyws*+
spṭmy' *m/f* C3946:2 (m); C3947:1 (f) spṭmy' btzby *C3947:1 Septimian Zēnobian*+
spṭmyw' *m* C3947:2 *Septimioi* Plural, see Glossary s.v..†
spṭmyws *m* C3944:1 *Septimion*+
spṭmys *m* C3939:1 *Septi[mion]*†
spr *m* Inv 11 91:1†
sqḥ' *m* RTP 318 bis†
sr' *f* C4042:3+
sry *m* C4159:2+
sryk' *m* BJPES '47 p 145:2†
srykw *m* C3940:4+
'b' *m* C4033:5+
'bd' *m* AIΩN '86a p 247(3):1++
'bdbl *m* C4110:1+
'bdw *m* C3973:6†
'bdy *m* Ber '35 p 104 XII:8+
'bdlt *m* C4044:3†
'bd'' *m* Ber '34 p 42 VI:2†
'bd'y *m* RSP 134:4†
'bd'swdr *m* Ber '35 p 107 XIII:5†
'bd'stwr *m* C4418:1 *Ber '38 p 120 (21 I):1 Abdaasthō[ro]n*+
'bd'ṭ' *m* C4536:1†
'bd'th *m* Inv 4 7a:3+
'bdṣyr' *m* C4172:1†
'bdšlm' *m* RTP 682†
'bdšmy' *m* Ber '35 p 110 II:1 *Abisamaia*†
'bd[.] *m* RTP 176 bny 'bd[.]†
'bydw *m* C3973:1+
'bnbw *m* SFP 142:1†
'bny *m* Inv 11 4:2†
'bnrgl *m* C4000:3+
'bs' *m* C4368:1†
'bsy *m* Ber '35 p 78 IV:1 *C3916:2 Abisseou*+
'bšy *m* AAS '65/2 p 127:2+
'bšy *m* StudPalm '75 p 131:3 *Abissaio[u]*†
'bšlm' *m* C4198 (lower):2†
'bšmy' *m* Ber '35 p 112 (III):2†
'g' *m* Ber '34 p 33 II:3 *Inv 10 69:1 Oga; C3914:2 Segē (sic), see Chabot ad loc; C3920:2 Ogēlou*++
'gb' *f* SFP 156:1†
'gyl' *m* RTP 666†
'gylw *m* Ber '34 p 40 V:5-6 *Ber '70 p 66 (1):8 Ogēlou*++
'gyly *m* C4532:3†
'glbwl' *m* C3969:3†
'gn' *m* C4587:4 Stark PN gyn' with CIS explained as Latin name. Not in Stark PN.†
'grwd *m* Inv 10 131:3 bny 'grwd *Agroudēnoi*+
'd' *f* RSP 119:4†
'dwn *m* Ber '35 p 104 XII:8†
'dl *m* Inv 9 5a:2†
'dn *m* C4380:2†
'dty *m* BS III 60:4†
'wb *m* C3907:8†
'wd'l *m* C4012:3†
'wdw *m* C3980:3†
'wyd' *m* AIΩN '86a p 246:2++
'wydw *m* Syr '36 p 346:1+
'wydy *m* Inv 8 62:3+
'wydlt *m* Ber '38 p 135 (sub 21 III) a:1+
'wydt *f* Inv 8 117:1†
'wyd *m* C4199:2+
'wmy *m* RTP 157†
'wtn *m* C4361:1†
'zwlt *m* Sumer '64 p 19 (no. 10):4 dy mtqr' br 'zwlt.†
'zy *m* RTP 707 'z[y].+
'zyz *m* C4288:4+
'zyzw *m* C3925:2++
'zyzy *m* C3965:1†
'yb *m* Doura 50:1†
'ḥry *f* SFP 138:1†
'yt' *m* C4461:2+
'l' *f* Ber '34 p 38 IV:14+
'lbn *m* C4001:6+
'lg *m* RTP 293+
'lg' *m* RTP 395†
'ly *m* Inv 8 136:1†
'lybwl *m* Inv 11 54:1†
'lyb'l *m* Inv 8 5:2+
'lyy *m/f* Trf I:3 (m); C4343:2 [']lyy (f) *Olaious*+
'lyy *m* RTP 137 bny 'lyy+
'lyn' *m* C3950:2 *Alainē*+
'lyt *f* C4259 D:1+
'lyš' *m* C4129 (between heads):3 *Inv 10 24:2 Alaisas*+
'mkbr' *m* PNO 55 Extended discussion Stark PN.†
'my *f* SFP 141:1†
'ml' *m* PNO 30†
'mr *m* RSP 171:4†
'mr' *m* RTP 344 Or: 'bd' (uncertain meaning).†
'mrw *m* C3911:5+
'mrt *m/f* C4241:1 (f); RTP 783 (m)+
'mt *m* RTP 992+
'nbw *m* PNO 65:1†
'nyny *m* RTP 167†
'nmw *m* C3973:1†
'nn *m* Ber '35 p 107 XIII:7+
'nnw *m* C3994 A:7

Ananidos+
ʿ**nny** *m* C3994 C:6+
ʿ**stwrgʾ** *m* RTP 979 *Syr '38 p 76:2 Astourga*+
ʿ**sty** *m* C4062:3†
ʿ**ṣr** *m* RTP 339 bny ʿṣr†
ʿ**qby** *m* C4561:6+
ʿ**qybʾ** *m* C4117:1+
ʿ**ql** *m* Verm '81 p 387:1†
ʿ**qrbn** *m* C4450:1†
ʿ**rby** *m* C4044:4+
ʿ**rgʾ** *m* Inv 11 20:5†
ʿ**rgn** *m* C3988:2+
ʿ**rymʾ** *m* Inv 11 81:5+
ʿ**šy** *m* C4099:1†
ʿ**šylt** *m* Inv 12 53†
ʿ**šyltʾ** *m* RTP 764 *Inv 7 5:1 Osailathous*†
ʿ**šrʾ** *m* PNO 13:2†
ʿ**štwr** *m* C4209:3 *Asthōrou*+
ʿ**štwrgʾ** *m* C4199:13+
ʿ**tʾ** *m* Inv 8 107:4 See also brʿtʾ.†
ʿ**tʾm** *f* C3969:12+
ʿ**tdt / ʿtrt** *m* C4596:4†
ʿ**th** *f* Inv 10 145:3†
ʿ**thzbd** *m* RSP 29:4†
ʿ**tw** *f* Inv 12 13:2†
ʿ**tzʾ** *m* Inv 9 7:2†
ʿ**tzbd** *m* RSP 24:3†
ʿ**tḥn** *m* BethSh p 207 (132):2+
ʿ**ty** *m/f* C4526:1 (f); C4227:1 (m)++
ʿ**tykʾ** *m* C4441:3+
ʿ**tyʿqb** *m* C4390:3†
ʿ**tmʾ** *f* C4231 E:1†
ʿ**tnwr** *m* C3911:5†
ʿ**tnwry** *m* Ber '38 p 94 (18I):2++
ʿ**tntn** *m* Ber '35 p 59 I:1 (Gk); Ber '34 p 38 IV:3 *1-2 Athenathanos*++
ʿ**tʿy** *m* C4598:3+
ʿ**tʿy** *m* RSP 116:3 Gaw ad loc: hypocoristic of *ʿtʿqb*. Not in Stark PN.†
ʿ**tʿm** *f* BMB '55 p 38 (8):2†
ʿ**tʿqb** *m* C4116:2 *C4203:2 ʿtʿ[qb] Athēakabou*++
ʿ**trn** *f* C4622:2+
ʿ**tr or ʿtd** *m* Inv 4 14:1 bny ʿtr (or: ʿtd)†
ʿ**tršwry** *m* C4112:4+
ʿ**trt / ʿtdt** *m* C4596:4†
ʿ**tšbʾ** *f* Inv 8 64:2 *Athēsōba*+
ʿ**tšwr** *m* C4526:3+
ʿ**tšʾ** *f* C4341:1†
ʿ**ttn** *m* Ber '35 p 96 V:2+
pgʾ *m* RTP 234+
pwblwqyws *m* BS III 45:6 [pw]blwqyws *Poblikiou*†
pzgʾ *m* C4531:3†
pzl *m* C4595:1 See notes to text.+
pṭrqls *m* Syr '38 p 76:1 *Patroklou*†
pṭrṭʾ *m* Syr '36 p 348:4 bny pṭrṭʾ†
pylʾ *m* C4160:1 *Pheila*+
pkn *m* Maarav '87 p 72 no. 4:2†
plwynʾ *m* RTP 913†
plwynws *m* Inv 10 130:1 *Phlabianon*†
plwys *m* BS III 20:5†
plynʾ *m* C3944:4+
plynws *m* C3944:4 *[Phileino]s*†
plns *m* C4369 (between heads):1†
plpṭr *m* Trf I:2 *Philopatoros*†
plqs *m* C3903:2 *Latin: FELIX*†
pplws *m* Inv 7 1b:2†
pplys *m* RB '30 p 538 (no. 8):1+
pṣʾ *f* C4232 C:1+
pṣgw *m* RTP 464†
pṣyʾ *m* C4220:5†
pṣyʾl *m* C4199:2+
prdš *m* BS III 10:3†
prdšy *m* C4458 bis:1†
prṭnks *m* C4401:4 *Pertinakos*+
prymʾ *f* StudPalm '75 p 129:1†
prmwn *m* C3914:3 *Phirmōnos*+
prnk *m* C3996:3 prn<k> see Stark PN.†
prsqs *m* BS III 20:6†
prštnʾ *f* RSP 24:3 Gaw ad loc: = Pristina.+
pšwlʾ *m* RSP 166:4 [dy m]tqrh pšwlʾ. Not in Stark PN.†
ptyḥb *m* C4446:3†
rwmy *f* C4587:2†
ṣlmʾ *m* RTP 912†
ṣlmy *m* RTP 27†
ṣlt *m* Doura 25:6†
ṣmʾ *m* RB '30 p 538 (no. 8):1+
ṣmy *f* Ber '35 p 88 IX:3†
ṣʿd *m* Inv 12 45:9+
ṣʿdw *m* Inv 4 14:1†
ṣʿdy *m* C4176b:2 *C4187: (lacuna in Aram) Saedei*++
ṣprʾ *m/f* C3950:2 (m); C4276:1 (f) *Sephphera*+
ṣpry *m* C4165:1+
ṣtʾ *m* RTP 38†
qbwdm / qbwrm *f* RSP 5:1†
qbwdʾ *f* C4496 (right):1†
qwpʾ *m* C4198 (lower):1+
qwpyn *m* C4488:5†
qwqʾ *m* Inv 8 198:3†
qwqḥ *m* C4272:3+
qwšy *f* C4048:3†
qzy *m* Inv 8 73:5 Or: mzy.†
qḥzn *m* C3983:1†
qydlʾ / qyrlʾ *m* RSP 40 (on left):1 Reading contains several ambiguities.†
qymw *m* Inv 10 54:1 *Kaiemou*†
qymy *m* Inv 11 77:4†
qynw *m* RSP 143:3+
qysʾ *m* RB '30 11:2†
qlwdys *m* C3903:2 *Latin: CLAVDIVS*†
qlsṭʾ *m* C4565:1+
qlsṭrṭs *m* Inv 10 113:2 *Kallistratō; Latin: Callistrato*+

qlstqs *m* C3962:1†
qlqys *m* Trf:62 *Gk line 93:Kilix*†
qmlʾ *m* ARNA p 161:4+
qmylʾ *m* Sem '77 p 117:4†
qsynʾ *m* C3943:4 *Kassianou*+
qsmʾ *m* RSP 1:1+
qṣmyt *m* RTP 106 bny qṣmyt†
qspryns *m* RTP 785†
qrʾ *m* Syr '85 p 257 no. 13:1 dy mqrʾ qrʾ *Kōra*†
qrblʾ *m* RSP 95 (on left):4 Gaw ad loc: Aramaization of *Kourboulōn* Trf Gk 196. Not in Stark PN.†
qrblwn *m* Trf:121 *Gk line 196 Kourboulōn*†
qrdʾ *m* C4413 (between figures):2+
qryn *m* PNO 7 B:1+
qrynw *m* RTP 749+
qrspynws *m* C3932:4 *Krispeinou*†
qrqpn *m* Syr '33 p 190:2+
qšṭʾ *m* RTP 60+
qšṭy *m* C3987:2†
qšṭʾ *m* RTP 942+
rʾwmʾ *m* C3989:3+
r̊ʾšmhr̊ *m* Lou 157:3†
rbʾ *m* RTP 184 Frequently title: the elder, major see Glossary s.v.+
rbʾl *m* C3975:1 *C4163:3 Rabbēlou; Latin: Syr '50 p 137:2 RABBELI* RTP 276 bny rbʾl.++
rbʾn *m* Inv 11 77:3†
rbbt *m* C3980:4†
rbw *m* RTP 183†
rbwty *m* C4371:2†
rbḥ *m* MUSJ '66 p 177 (no. 1):8†
rbn *m* Sumer '64 p 20 (no. 12):5†
rbnʾ *m* C4015:4†
rbt *m* C3908:2 *Latin: RVBATIS*+
rgynʾ *f* C3901 *Latin: REGINA*†
rdwn *m* C4016:3†
rhbt *f* Inv 12 25:1†
rwḥʾ *f* C4080:7†
rwḥbl *m* Ber '35 p 91 III:2+
rwʿy / dwʿy *m* RSP 188:3†
rwṣy / dwṣy *f* PNO 74:1†
rzyṣyḥ *m* C4376:2†
rysqʾ *m* Ber '35 p 97 VI:1†
ryṣw *m* PNO 74b:1†
rklʾ *m* SFP 137:5†
rmʾ *m* C4257:1+
rmw *m* IP 37:1+
rmy *m* C4371:2+
rmlhʾ *m* C4074:2 [r]mlhʾ.†
rmnw *m* SFP 25:3†
rmnws *m* C4212:2†
rmšʾ *m* RTP 461†
rstyʾ / dstyʾ *f* RSP 50 (b):1†
rstqʾ *m* C4379:3†
rʿʾ *m* RTP 892†
rʿy *m* C3959:2 *Raaiou*+
rʿyʾl BS III 24:1†
rʿtʾ *f* C4291:1+
rʿth *f* C4320:3†
rpʾ *m* C4010:4+
rpʾl *m* C3916:2 *Rephaelou*+
rpbwl *m* C4172:1 *C4203:2 rp[bwl] Rephabōlos*++
rpnw *m* RTP 765†
ršy *m* RTP 641†
šʾylʾ *m* C3934:3 *Seeila*+
šbʾ *m/f* C3927:1 (m); Inv 8 107:2 (f) *Saba*+
šbḥy *f* C4382:1†
šby *m* C4124:1 *Sabeis*++
šbʿʾ *m* RTP 758†
šbʿtʾ *m* RTP 292+
šbty *f* C4048:4+
šgʾ *m* C4574:3+
šgl *f* Ber '35 p 91 II:2++
šgʿw *m* RTP 82†
šgrʾ *m* Inv 11 26:1 Prb this rather than šgdʾ.†
šgry *m* C3994:6+
šdy *m* C4219:2+
šhymw *m* Syr '35 p 185:3+
šwdy *m* Doura 12:1†
šwḥbw *m* Inv 8 33:3†
šwky *m* PGKK p 310 no 32:2†
šwqn[...] *m* PNO 52 ter A:2†
šwyrʾ *m* Inv 8 115:1 *Inv 10 44:3 Seouira*+
šzʾ *m* RTP 977 bny šzʾ+
šḥrʾ *m* PNO 55 (above temple):3 Or: šḥdʾ.+
šḥrw *m* C4234+
šḥry *m* Inv 11 53:2†
šṭʾ *m* C4544:2 [š]ṭʾ.+
šyby *m* Ber '35 p 82 V:2†
šydn *m* C4598:4†
šyʿn *m* C4199:10†
šyqn *m* PNO 19†
šyštʾ *f* C4462:3†
šky *m* Inv 8 180:1+
škybl *m* C4238:2+
škyy *m* C4113:5 *C4134:1 Sochaieis*++
škm *m* Doura 8:3†
škny *m* C4204:3†
škʿtʾ *m* RTP 40†
šlʾ *f* Ber '35 p 82i:1+
šlwʾ *f* SFP 17:1†
šlwm *m/f* C4363:2 (f); C4368:2 (m)+
šlm *m* RTP 184 bny šlm†
šlm *f* Ber '38 p 118†
šlmʾ *m/f* C4197:2 (m); RB '30 p 548 (no. 14):2 *C3943:3 Salmēs*++
šlmwy *m* C4326:3-4+
šlmy *f* C4220:4+
šlmlt *m* C3966:1 *[Salam]allathon*++
šlmn *m* Ber '35 p 100 IX:4++
šlmnʾ *m* C4417:1-2†
šlmny *m* C4198 (lower):2†
šlmt *f* C4019:6 *Syr '85 p 276 no. 5:2 Salamathi*++
šmʾ *m* Soth 5722 no. 48:3†
šmwʾl *m* C4201:2 *Samouēlos*+
šmwn *m* RTP 79+
šmy *m* Inv 8 16:2+
šmyšw *m* YCS '55 p 131 no. 3:2 *Somesou*†
šmlʾ *m* Soth 5722 no.

48:2†

šmʿd or šmʿr *m* Inv 9 16:2 bny šmʿd or šmʿr†

šmʿwʾ *m* Inv 8 49:2†

šmʿwn *m* ΑΙΩΝ '86a p 247 (3):2; RTP 252 bny šmʿwn *C3954:2 Symōnou; Latin: C3909:3 SVMONIS*++

šmʿrʾ *m* RTP 585†

šmʿry *m* RTP 706 šmʿ[r]y.†

šmrpʾ *m* C3929:3 š[m]rpʾ or: š[d]rpʾ.†

šmšgrm *m* C3996:4 *Inv 10 39:1 Samsigeramou*++

šmšy *m* DuraPR '39 p 282 no. 912:5†

šmšrmʾ *m* RTP 151†

špʾ *m* RTP 336 Or: šlʾ.†

šʿʾ *m* Inv 9 28:4†

šʿd *m* ARNA p 161:5+

šʿdʾ *m/f* Syr '26 p 129:7 (m); C4500:1 (f)+

šʿdʾ *m* Syr '36 p 346:3 bny šʿdʾ†

šʿdʾl *m* C4261:1 (on right)+

šʿdw *m* C3919:1++

šʿdw *m* C3920:3; RTP 341 bny šʿdw *C3920:3 Soados*†

šʿdy *m* Ber '35 p 81f:2 RTP 334 bny šʿdy.++

šʿdlt *m* C3973:2+

šʿydn *m* RTP 204†

špylʾ *m* DuraPR '39 p 282 no. 913a†

šʿt *m* Inv 9 20:3 dy [mt]qrʾ br šʿt+

šʿrwnʾ *m* Ber '35 p 102 XI:7+

šʿrnʾ *m* Ber '35 p 95 IV:1+

špry *m* Lou 239:5 dy mtqrh špry†

šqy *m* Inv 12 46:2†

šqn *m* C4306 B:4†

šqnʾ *m* PS no. 371:5 Stark PN reads smyʾ.†

šrykw *m* C3908:2 *C3950:1 Soraichou; Latin: SVRICVS*++

šryky *m* RSP 41:3†

tbll *f* Inv 8 18:1†

tbnn *f* C4503:1†

tbʿwt *m* RTP 174+

tbrʾ *m* Inv 11 99:1†

tdʾl *f* Inv 11 5:2†

tdmwr *f* C4259 B:1+

tdmr *f* AAS '53 p 19:7+

tdrš *m* BethSh p 199 (17):1†

twʾl *f* C4620:2†

twpʾ *m* C4306 B:2+

twry *m* PS no. 356 p 130:1+

tybwl *m* Ber '35 p 76 II:1++

tydwrʾ *m* C4094:3†

tydrws *m* C4209:3 *Theodōrō*†

tyksʾ *f* IP 79:2†

tymʾ *m/f* AAS '65 p 90:2; IP 26:1 ty[mʾ]? Stark ty[mʾ] (f) of Inv 4:13 is to be read prymʾ Gaw '75.++

tymw *m* Ber '38 p 95:5+

tymḥʾ *m* C4130:2 *Ber '70 p 66 (1):9 Thaimaeous*++

tymy *m* AfO '53 p 312:3 *Ber '35 p 59 I:3 Thaimei*++

tymlt *m* C4589:2+

tymnʾ *m* Inv 8 23:1+

tymsʾ *m* Ber '38 p 127:2+

tymʿʾ *m* C4569:3+

tymʿmd *m* C3980:7 *C3994:4 Thaimoamedou*++

tymṣʾ *m* Inv 4 8b:1+

tymrṣw *m* AA '32 p 4:2; RTP 66 bny tymrṣw; note spelling Ber '38 p 135:1 btmrṣw for bt tymrṣw *BS III 45:14 Thaimarsou*++

tymšʾ *m* C4191:4 *C4187:2 (lacuna in Aram) Thai[misa]*+

tymšmš *m* C3919:2 *Ber '70 p 66 (1):8 Thaimisamsou*+

typyls *m* Ber '38 p 104:1+

tyrdt *m* C4598:5+

tlyʾ *m* BMB '55 p 38 (8):3†

tmʾ *m/f* Ber '35 p 107 XIII:4; Inv 8 47:2 (m)++

tmh *f* Inv 8 3:1†

tmlʾ *m* Doura 26:1†

tmlk *f* PS 33 (on right):1+

tmrṣw *m* Ber '38 p 135:1 in combination btmrṣw = bt tymrṣw†

tʿyd/r *f* C4614:1†

tpḥy *f* Maarav '87 p 72 no. 4:2†

tqym *f* Inv 11 24:2†

tšbb *m* Ber '35 p 115:1 *Thosabebou*+

❖ ❖ ❖ ❖ ❖

APPENDIX

THE CALENDAR AND DATING

MONTH	ARAMAIC	GREEK[1]	AN ATTESTATION OF EQUIVALENCE
January	ṭbt	*audunaios*	Inv 10 99, Inv 10 90
February	šbṭ	*peritios*	C3902
March	ʾdr	*dustros*	C3914
April	nysn	*ksandikos*	C3916, cf also C3913 (Tariff)
May	ʾyr	*artemisios**	Inv 4 13 (restored)
June	sywn	*daisios**	? see C3940[2]
July	qnyn	*panēmos*	Inv 10 29
August	ʾb	*lōos*	C3928
September	ʾlwl	*gorpiaios*	C3925
October	tšry	*hyperberetaios*	C3934
November	knwn	*dīos*	C4196, C4187
December	kslwl, kslw	*apellaios*	C3939

This table indicates the equation of Aramaic and Greek months with those of our calendar. In dating texts at Palmyra (without entering into technical complexities and problems involved), a version of the Macedonian calendar was used according to which the Seleucid era starts at Hyperberetaios (Tishri) 1, 312 B.C.

A general detailed introduction to chronological matters is A. Samuel, *Greek and Roman Chronology: Calendars and Years in Classical Antiquity*, in *Muellers Handbuch der Altertumswissenschaft*, Erste Abteilung, Siebenter Teil (Munich: Beck'sche, 1972), especially pp 139-45 (on the Seleucid calendar) and 178-80 (the Macedonian calendar at Palmyra). On the Dura calendar, see the discussion, with bibliography, of Welles in C. Welles, R. Fink, and J. Gilliam, 1959 p 10.

Etymological treatment of the name of the months is found in Kaufman, AIA, pp 114-15. The name *qnyn* is, exceptionally, not of Akkadian origin. The phrase *byrḥ ʾlwl mšlm šnt 4.100+80+10+5+2* Ber '35 p 93:2, with its combination of month-name and "completing(?)," if not a reference to an intercalation, may mark Elul as the end of the year (so Samuel p 178 fn 3 [the inscription is from Palmyra, not Dura]). It may be noted, as of possible significance, that in the sequence of Greek month names on a sundial found in the temple of Bel, Ingholt 1936 pp 112-14, there is a line between *gorpiaios*, "September," and *hyperberetaios* "October;" this is taken by Ingholt as indicating that the year ended with September (p 113).

---

[1] The inflected forms occurring in various texts show some variations in spelling.

[2] At C3940:5 Gk oddly has *ksandikō*, the real equivalent of *sywn* being *daisios*, see Chabot ad loc.

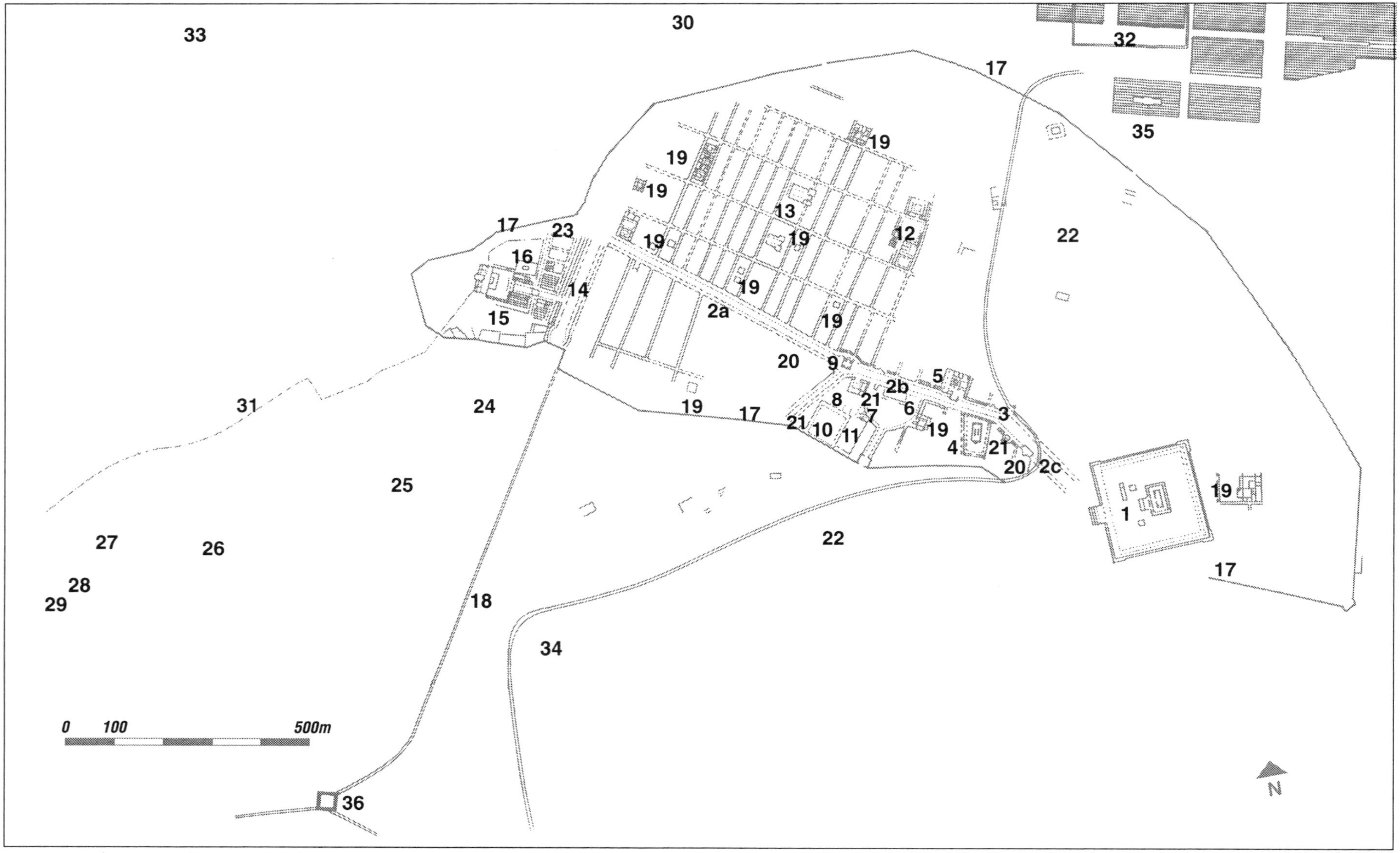

Map 1. Palmyra and environs *(After Starcky and Gawlikowski, Palmyre, Pl III)*

1. Temple of Bel; 2a, 2b, 2c. Great colonnade; 3. Monumental arch; 4. Temple of Nabu; 5. Baths of Diocletian; 6. Theater; 7. Senate; 8. Caesareum; 9. Tetrapylon; 10. Agora; 11. Annex to Agora; 12. Temple of Baalshamin; 13. Byzantine churches; 14. Transverse colonnade; 15. Camp of Diocletian; 16. Temple of Allat; 17. Wall of Diocletian; 18. Ancient wall; 19. Ancient houses; 20. Exedras; 21. Banquet rooms; 22. Honorific columns; 23. Funerary temple; 24. Tomb of Aailemi and Zebeida; 25. Tomb of Yamlichos; 26. Hypogeum of Yarhai; 27. Tomb of Elahbel; 28. Tomb of Atenatan; 29. Tomb called Qasr el-Abyad; 30. Tomb of Marona; 31. Aqueduct; 32. Remains of Roman camp; 33. Arab castle; 34. The spring Afqa; 35. The Museum; 36. Temple of Bel Hammon

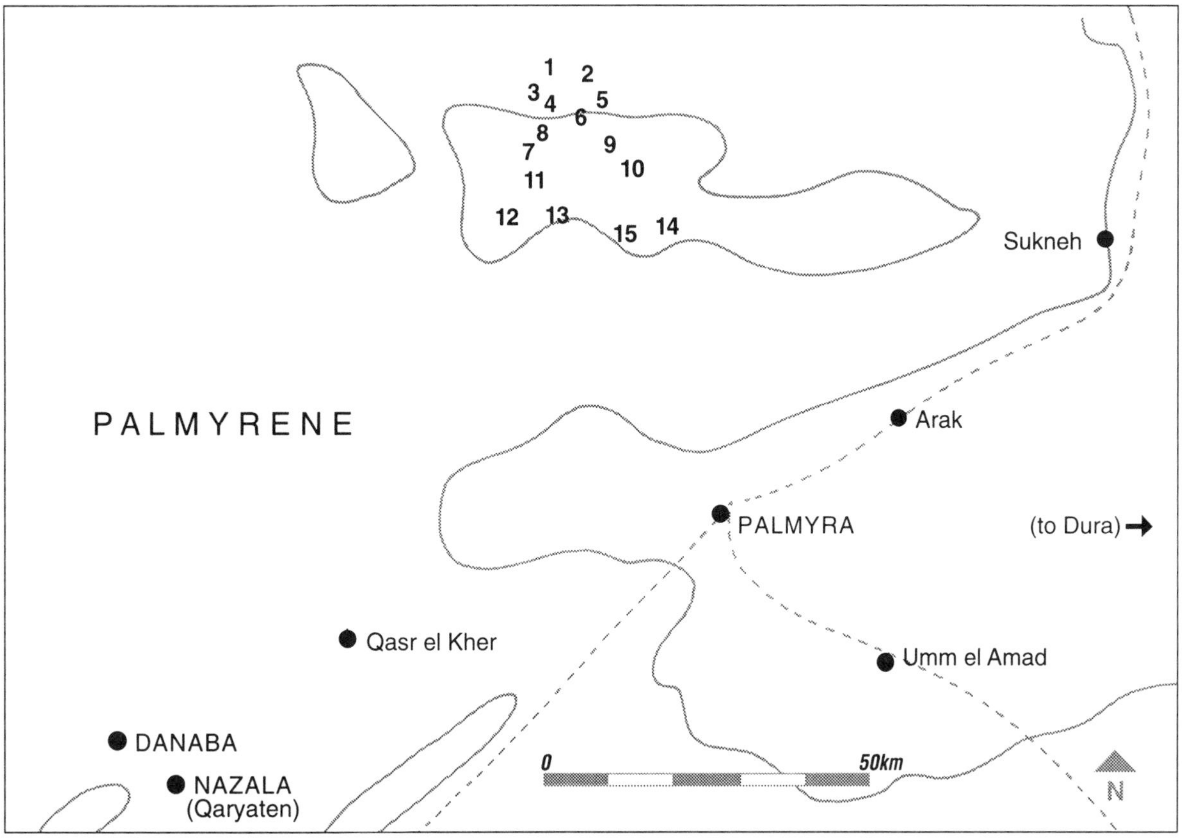

Map 2. The Palmyrene. *Showing area of sites reported in Schlumberger '51,* La Palmyrène du nord-ouest (PNO), *which has detailed map of region p 2, fig. 1, Numbers show approximate location of 1 Khirbet Marzuqa; 2 Kh. Faruan; 3 Kh. Abu Duhur; 4 Labda; 5 Ras esh-Shaar; 6 El-Mekeimle; 7 Kh. Wadi Suan; 8 Kh. Shteib; 9 Kh. Semrin; 10 Kh. Leqteir; 11 Kh. es-Suan 12 Kh. Ramadan; 13 Kh. Madaba; 14 Weshel; 15 Tahun el-Masek*

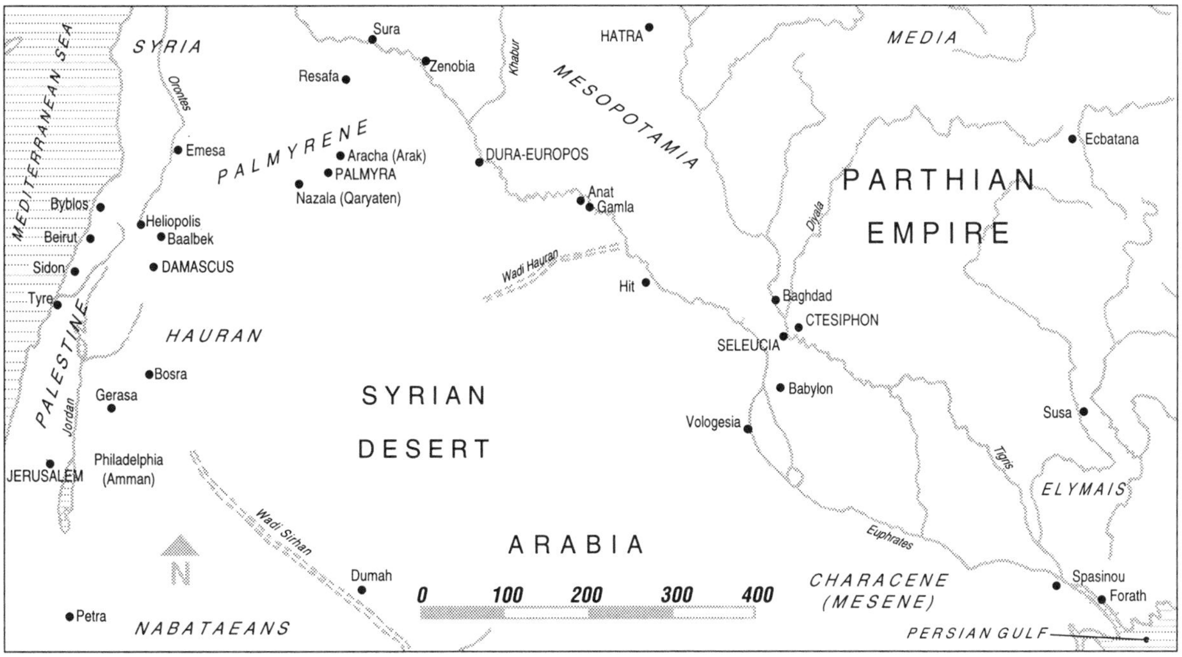

Map 3. Palmyra in the Near East. *(After Starcky and Gawlikowski,* Palmyre, *Pl. 1)*

CONCORDANCES OF TEXT REFERENCES

1. Inv *(Inventaire des inscriptions de Palmyre)* and PAT sigla, including listing of non-Aramaic texts of Inv not included in PAT.

1 1	Gk text
1 2	C3959
1 3	C3958
1 4	C3983
1 5	1 5
2 1	C3966
2 2	C3930
2 3	C3931
3 1	Gk text
3 2	3 2
3 3	Gk text
3 4	Gk text
3 5	Gk text
3 6	C3943
3 7	C3942
3 8	C3941
3 9	C3940
3 10	C3939
3 11	C3938
3 12	C3937
3 13	C3936
3 14	C3934
3 15	C3935
3 16	C3944
3 17	C3945
3 18	Gk text
3 19	C3946
3 20	C3947
3 21	C3933
3 22	C3932
3 23	Gk text
3 24	Gk text
3 25	Inv 3 25
3 26	Gk text
3 27	Gk text
3 28	C3948
3 29	C3949
3 30	Gk text
4 1a	C4206
4 1b	C4207
4 1c	C4208
4 2	C4187
4 3	C4124
4 4a	C4114
4 4b	Inv 4 4b
4 5	C4121
4 6a	C4123bis
4 6b	C4123
4 7a	Inv 4 7a
4 7b	Inv 4 7b
4 8a	Inv 4 8a
4 8b	Inv 4 8b
4 9a	C4168
4 9b	Inv 4 9b
4 9c	Gk text
4 9d	Inv 4 9d
4 9e	Inv 4 9e
4 9f	Gk text
4 10	Gk text
4 11	Gk text
4 12	Inv 4 12
4 13	Inv 4 13
4 14	Inv 4 14
4 15a	Inv 4 15a
4 15b	Inv 4 15b
4 15c	Inv 4 15c
4 16	Inv 4 16
4 17	C4232
4 18a	C4115
4 18b	C4115bis
4 19	C4164
4 20	Gk text
4 21	C4216
4 22	C4192
4 23	C4170
4 24	Inv 4 24
4 25	Inv 4 25
4 26	Inv 4 26
4 27a	C4134
4 27b	C4157
4 27c	C4140
4 27d	C4141
4 27e	C4142
4 27f	C4143
4 27g	C4144
4 27h	C4135
4 27i	C4136
4 27j	C4137
4 27k	C4138
4 27l	C4139
4 27m	C4145
4 27n	C4146
4 27o	C4147
4 27p	C4148
4 27q	C4149
4 27r	C4150
4 27s	C4151
4 27t	C4152
4 27u	C4153
4 27v	C4154
4 27w	C4155
4 27x	C4156
4 27y	C4158
4 27z	Arab text
4 28	C4109
5 1	C3950
5 2	C3951
5 3	C3952
5 4	C3953
5 5	C3954
5 6	C3957
5 7	C3956
5 8	C3955
5 9	C3984
5 10	Inv 5 10
6 1	C3985
6 2	Latin text
6 3	C3988
6 4	Inv 6 4
6 5	C3998
6 6	C3968
6 7	C3967
6 8	Gk text
6 9	C3989
6 10	Gk text
6 11	C3977
6 12	C4102
6 13	Gk text
7 1a	C4162
7 1b	Inv 7 1b
7 2	C4214
7 3	Gk text
7 4	C4201
7 5	Inv 7 5
7 6a	C4122
7 6b	C4236
7 7	Inv 7 7
7 8	C4237
7 9	Inv 7 9
7 10	Inv 7 10
7 11	C4213
7 12	Inv 7 12
7 13	C4212
7 14	Inv 7 14
7 15a, b	C4197
7 15c	Inv 7 15c
8 1-54	Inv 8 1-54
8 55	C4202
8 56	C4113
8 57	C4235
8 58-60	Inv 8 58-60
8 61	C4163
8 62-67	Inv 8 62-67
8 68	Gk text
8 69-79	Inv 8 69-79
8 80	Gk text
8 81-86	Inv 8 81-86
8 87	Gk text
8 88-99	Inv 8 88-99
8 100	C4241
8 101-119	Inv 8 101-119
8 120	Gk text
8 121-159	Inv 8 121-159
8 160	C4125
8 161a	C4126
8 161b	C4127a
8 161c	C4127b
8 162-163	Inv 8 162-163
8 164	Gk text
8 165-192	Inv 8 165-192
8 193	C4239

8 194	C4231
8 195-200	Inv 8 195-200
8 201-218	Non-Aram texts
9 1	Inv 9 1
9 2	Latin text
9 3	Inv 9 3
9 4a, b	Inv 9 4a, b
9 5a	Inv 9 5a
9 5b	Gk text
9 6a	C3924
9 6b	C3925
9 7	Inv 9 7
9 8	C3923
9 9	C3922
9 10	Gk text
9 11-12	Inv 9 11-12
9 13	C3915
9 14a	C3916
9 14b	Inv 9 14b
9 15	C3917
9 16	Inv 9 16
9 17	Gk text
9 18	C3918
9 19	C3919
9 20	Inv 9 20
9 21-24	Gk texts
9 25	C3914
9 26	Inv 9 26
9 27	Gk text
9 28-30	Inv 9 28-30
9 31	C3921
9 32	C3920
9 33-34	Inv 9 33-34
9 35	Gk text
9 35bis	Inv 9 35bis
9 36-54	Non-Aram texts
10 1	Gk text
10 2	Gk text
10 3	Inv 10 3
10 4	Inv 10 4
10 5	Gk text
10 6-8	Inv 10 6-8
10 9-10	Gk texts
10 11-13	Inv 10 11-13
10 14-15	Gk texts
10 16	Inv 10 16
10 17	C3962
10 18-23	Non-Aram texts
10 24	Inv 10 24
10 25-28	Non-Aram texts
10 29	Inv 10 29
10 30-37	Gk texts
10 38-40	Inv 10 38-40
10 41	Gk text
10 42	Inv 10 42
10 43	Gk text
10 44	Inv 10 44
10 45-46	Gk texts
10 47	C3963
10 48	Inv 10 48
10 49	Inv 10 49
10 50-52	Non-Aram texts
10 53	Inv 10 53
10 54	Inv 10 54
10 55	Gk text
10 56	Inv 10 56
10 57	Inv 10 57
10 58-60	Gk texts
10 61-63	Inv 10 61-63
10 64	Gk text
10 65	Inv 10 65
10 66-68	Gk texts
10 69	Inv 10 69
10 70	Inv 10 70
10 71	Gk text
10 72	Inv 10 72
10 73	Gk text
10 74-78	Inv 10 74-78
10 79-80	Gk texts
10 81	Inv 10 81
10 82-84	Gk texts
10 85	Inv 10 85
10 86	Gk text
10 87	C3960
10 88-89	C3960
10 90	Inv 10 90
10 91	Inv 10 91
10 92	Gk text
10 93	Inv 10 93
10 94	Inv 10 94
10 95	Gk text
10 96	Inv 10 96
10 97	Gk text
10 98	Inv 10 98
10 99	Inv 10 99
10 100-101	Non-Aram texts
10 102	Inv 10 102
10 103-104	Gk texts
10 105-107	Inv 10 105-107
10 108-109	Gk texts
10 110-115	Inv 10 110-115
10 116-117	Gk texts
10 118	Inv 10 118
10 119	Inv 10 119
10 120-122	Gk texts
10 123	Inv 10 123
10 124	Inv 10 124
10 125	Gk text
10 126-132	Inv 10 126-132
10 133-139	Gk texts
10 140	Inv 10 140
10 141	Inv 10 141
10 142	Gk text
10 143	C3913
10 144	Inv 10 144
10 145	Inv 10 145
11 1-17	Inv 11 1-17
11 18	C4043
11 19-22	Inv 11 19-22
11 23	C4010
11 24-28	Inv 11 24-28
11 29	C4075
11 30-42	Inv 11 30-42
11 43	Gk text
11 44-83	Inv 11 44-83
11 84	C3969
11 85-100	Inv 11 85-100
12 1-13	Inv 12 1-13
12 14	RSP 51
12 15	Inv 12 15
12 16	C4166
12 17	RSP 105
12 18	Gk text
12 19	Inv 3 2
12 20	Gk text
12 21	IP 33
12 22-26	Inv 12 22-26
12 27	Gk text
12 28	Inv 12 28
12 29	Gk text
12 30-36	Inv 12 30-36
12 37	Gk text
12 38-41	Inv 12 38-41
12 42	Latin text
12 43-56	Inv 12 43-56

2. Texts contained in RSP (*Recueil d'inscriptions palmyréniennes*, Gaw '74c)

Aside from some inscriptions published there for the first time, RSP gathers and re-edits texts that first appeared in various other publications. The following summary list, in alphabetical order, should enable users of this volume who wish to locate these texts to do so without special difficulty.

Abdul-Hak '52a, '52b RSP 1-20
As'ad '68 RSP 105
As'ad and Taha '65 RSP 51-74
As'ad and Taha '68 RSP 75-104
Bounni '61 RSP 24-46
al-Hassani and Starcky '53, '57 RSP 106-127
Michalowski '60 RSP 21-23
Michalowski '62 RSP 49-50
Michalowski '63 RSP 47-48
Michalowski '60, '62, '63, '64, '66 (texts from volumes of *Palmyre: Fouilles Polonaises)* RSP 128-229 (this part of RSP contains also numerous other inscriptions)

3. IP (*Inscriptions palmyréniennes*, Cantineau '30a) and sigla of PAT

1	C4483	23	IP 23	53	Inv 3 25	78-85	IP 78-85
2	C4614	24	Inv 8 144	54-56	Gk texts	86	RTP 92
3	C4486	25-28	IP 25-28	57	IP 57	87	RTP 77
4	C4613	29	Inv 8 169	58	IP 58	88	RTP 80
5	IP 5	30	Inv 1 5	59	Inv 4 16	89	RTP 81
6	Inv 10 39	31	Inv 9 28	60-62	IP 60-62	90	RTP 306
7	Inv 10 40	32	Inv 9 29	63	Inv 7 9	91	RTP 184
8	Inv 10 78	33	IP 33	64	Inv 7 7	92	RTP 714
9	C3960	34	IP 34	65	Inv 7 1a	93	RTP 315
10	IP 10	35	Inv 5 10	66	Inv 8 159	94	RTP 580
11	IP 11	36	IP 36	67	IP 67	95	RTP 821
12	Inv 4 9b	37	IP 37	68	Inv 4 8	96	RTP 311
12bis	IP 12bis	38	C4197	69	Inv 4 10	97	RTP 752
13	Inv 4 9c	39	C4212	70	Inv 4 11	98	RTP 247
14	Gk text	40	Inv 4 13	71	C4216	99	RTP 303
15	Inv 4 9d	41	Inv 4 16	72	Inv 8 68	100	RTP 996
16	IP 16	42-44	Gk texts	73	Gk text	101	RTP 1
17	Inv 4 9e	45	Inv 8 200	74	Inv 11 7	102	RTP 39
18	IP 18	46	IP 46	75	Inv 8 109	103	RTP 289
19	Gk text	47	Inv 3 2	76	IP 76; Inv 8 19$^?$	104	RTP 131
20	IP 20	48	Inv 3 4			105	RTP 15
21	IP 21	49-52	Gk texts	77	Inv 8 65		
22	Inv 8 145						

4. Tad ("Tadmorea" in Cantineau, *Syr* '33, '36, '38) and PAT sigla

1	Inv 9 1	5	Syr '33 p 181	7b	Syr '33 p 184	9	Syr '33 p 186
2	Inv 9 36	6	Inv 11 87	8	Syr '33 p 185	10	Syr '33 p 187
3	Syr '33 p 177	7a	Syr '33 p 183			11	Syr '33 p
4	Syr '33 p 179						

	189
12a	Syr '33 p 190
12b	Inv 8 71
13	C3993
14	RTP 125
15-16	Not texts
17-27	Syr '36 pp 268-355
28a	Inv 10 107
28b	Inv 10 111
29	Syr '38 p 76
30	Inv 10 105
31-38	Syr '38 pp 78-159
39	C4163
40-41	Not texts

5. Lidzbarski, *HNE*, pages and numbers, and plate, if any

457 a. 1, XXXVII, 1	C3915
458 a. 2, XXXIX, 4	C3930
458 a. 3, XXXVII, 2	C3952
458 a. 4, XXXIX, 5	C3948
459 a. 5, XXXVII, 3	C3932
459 a. 6, XXXVII, 4	C3933
460 a. 7, XXXVII, 5	C3934
460 a. 8, XXXVII, 6	C3936
460 a. 9, XXXVII, 7	C3944
461 a. 10, XXXVII, 8	C3939
461 a. 11, XXXVII, 9	C3938
461 a. 12, XXXVIII, 2	C3940
462 a. 13, XXXVIII, 1	C3945
462 a. 14, XXXVIII, 3	C3946
462 a. 15, XXXVIII, 4	C3947
463-73 b., XXXIX, 3	C3913
473 c. 1, XXXVIII, 5	C3983
474 c. 2, XXXVIII, 6	C3978
474 c. 3	C3994
474 c. 4, XL, 2	C3986
474 c. 5, XXXVIII, 8	C3996
475 c. 6, XL, 3	C4014
475 c. 7, XXXVIII, 10	C4027
475 c. 8, XXXVIII, 9	C4029
475 c. 9, XXXVIII, 7	C3981
476 c. 10, XL, 8	C4030
476 c. 11, XL, 5	C3976
476 c. 12, XL, 4	C4051
476 c. 13, XL, 6	C4046
477 c. 14, XL, 1	C3912
477 (Rome) 1, XLII, 9	C3902
477 (Rome) 2, XLII, 10	C3903
478 d. α 1, XL, 11	C4109
478 d. α 2, XL, 9	C4113
478 d. α 3, XL, 10	C4116
478 d. α 4, XXXIX, 1	C4122
478 d. α 5	C4130
479 d. α 6, XL, 12	C4164
479 d. α 7	C4194
479 d. α 8, XL, 7	C4195
479 d. α 9	C4199
480 d. α 10, XXXIX, 2	C4202
480 d. α 11, XLI, 2	C4218
480 d. β 1, XLI, 8	C4403
481 d. β 2, XLI, 3	C4357
481 d. β 3, XLI, 6	C4281
481 d. β 4, XLI, 43	C4283
481 d. β 5, XLI, 5	C4384
481 d. β 6, XLI, 7	C4394
481 d. β 7	C4502
481 d. β 8, XLI, 10	C4501
481 d. β 9, XLI, 9	C4225
481 d. γ 1, XLI, 1	C3905
482 d. γ 2, XLI, 11	C3908
482 d. γ 3, XLI, 12	C3909
482 d. γ 4	C3906
482 d. γ 5, XLI, 13	C3901
483 e. 1-6	tesserae
483 f., XLII, 1	IP 67

6. Museum numbers or locations and PAT sigla. Not included here are inscriptions in private collections or whose museum number is not known to us; often in the "Text" section a general or surmised indication of location is given.

Amherst, Mass.
Mead Art Museum

1942.78	PS no. 493

Baghdad
Iraq Museum

51100	Sumer '62 p 63
66457	Sumer '62 p 64
67806	Sumer '64 p 13
67807	Sumer '64 p 20
67808	Sumer '64 p 15
67809	Sumer '64 p 17
67810	Sumer '64 p 16
67811	Sumer '64 p 18
67812	Sumer '64 p 19
67813	Sumer '64 p 20
67814	Sumer '64 p 16
67815	Sumer '64 p 14
67817	Sumer '64 p 19

Basel
Antikenmuseum

1906/57	C4386

Beirut
American University

Museum
25.1 Ber '34 p 33
32.25 Ber '34 p 36
32.56 Ber '34 p 38
33.12 Ber '34 p 40
2740 C4248
2739 C4254
2733 C4256
2732 C4272
2737 C4275
2734 C4278
30.11 C4317
2738 C4363
2763 C4420
2745 C4564
2742 C4565
2754 C4566
2748 C4567
2753 C4568

Beirut
Musée National
506 BMB '55 p 35
514 BMB '55 p 38
515 BMB '55 p 42
516 C4406
520 Ber '36 p 88
587 BMB '55 p 36
589 BMB '55 p 34
689 BMB '55 p 43
692 BMB '55 p 33
696 BMB '55 p 34
701 BMB '55 p 38
2614 BMB '55 p 30
2625 BMB '55 p 41
2626 BMB '55 p 41

Belgrade
National Museum
PS no. 244A

Berlin
Staatliche Museen, Vorderasiatisches Sammlung
VA 27/65 C4479
VA 47 C4383
VA 50 C4385
VA 51 C4382
VA 2015 C4510
VA 2660 C4301
VA 2661 C4511
VA 3032 C4268
VA 3098 C4540

Bloomington, Indiana
University Art Museum
61.16 C4266

Boston
Museum of Fine Arts
10.79 PS no. 193
96.682 PS no. 234

Brussels
Musées Royaux d'Art et d'Histoire
A 1620 C4257
A. 1621 C4617
O 3633 C4304

Bucharest
Public Museum C3907

Cairo
Egyptian Museum
64738 Maarav '87 p 72

Cambridge, Mass.
Harvard University Art Museums
1908.3 StSc 149
1975.41.116 C4291
593.1941 StSc 151

Canberra
Australian War Memorial
ART 00484 AfO '53 p 312

Chapel Hill, N. C.
The Ackland Art Museum
79.29.1 PGSc 12

Cincinnati
Cincinnati Art Museum
1958.257 Verm '81 p 382

Copenhagen
Ny Carlsberg Glyptotek
1024 C4322
1025 C4365
1027 C4405
1028 C4283
1029 C4318
1030 C4320
1031 C4395
1032 C4285
1033 C4298
1034 C4364
1035 C4400
1036 C4612
1037 C4286
1038 C4360
1039 C4332
1040 C4357
1041 C4361
1042 C4392
1043 NyCG 70
1043 C4611
1044 C4344
1045 C4389
1046 C4280
1049 C4281
1050 C4492
1051 C4494
1052 C4390
1053 C4384
1054 C4393
1055 C4341
1056 C4388
1057 C4354
1058 C4394
1059 C4367
1060 C4391
1061 C4325
1062 C4489
1063 C4380
1064 C4488
1065 C4490
1072 C4493
1073 C4409
1074 C4408
1077 C4495
1078 C4496
1079 C4374bis
1080 C4074
1081 C4008
1135 C4211
1136 C4189
1137 C4188
1138 C4355
1139 C4343
1140 C4366
1146 C4556
1146 C4555
1147 C4133
1155 C4247
1159 C4458
1160 C4458bis
1161 C4089
2763 NyCG 73
2774 C4527
2775 NyCG 62
2776 C4369
2794 PS no. 39
2816 AA '30 p 192
2833 NyCG 47
3727 MUSJ '62 p 106

Damascus
National Museum
2 C4414
7 C4444
5.925 PNO no. 14
9 C4244
10 C4464
12 C4449
15 C4610
18.797 RSP 16
18.802 RSP 11
21 C4473
22 C4243
25 IP 79
26 C4576
30 IP 80
31 C4589
32 IP 81
33 PS no. 141
34 IP 82
39 PS no. 143
65 IP 83
164 (248) C3974
245 IP 84
246 IP 85

331 Syr '37 pp 31, 33 fig 20
2793 (7864) EblaDam p 295
2842 PNO no. 6
2844 PNO no. 16
3841 PNO no. 57
4480 Syr '33 p 179
4522 CatMD
4834 Syr '33 p 181
4947 (10941) CatDam p 123
5069 PNO no. 35
5070 PNO no. 37
5115 PNO no. 42
5215 PNO no. 39
5318 CatMD
5917 PNO no. 5
5921 PNO no. 20
5922 PNO no. 48
5924 PNO no. 13
6340 (15029) C4359
7444 EblaDam p 296
7459 BS III 57
8832 CatMD
9014 PNO no. 61
9023 PNO no. 15
10948 Doura 20
12875 Syr '49 p 249
15020 AAS '53 p 24
15027 AAS '53 p 22
15028 AAS '53 p 19

Musée de l'Armée
(SFP p 25) SFP 39

Dresden
Staatliche Skulpturensammlung
ZV 846 C4300
ZV 845 C4506

Erlangen
Archäologisches Institut der Universität
I 1156 C4461
I 1184 C4569

Geneva
Musée d'Art et d'Histoire
8195 C4265
8191 C4270
8188 C4277
8194 C4309
8194 C4310
8196 C4430
8193 C4431
19806 MélColl p 161

Grenoble
Musée des Beaux Arts,
1582 C4397

Havana
Museo Nacional de l'Havana C4290

Istanbul
Arkeoloji Müzesi
160 C3976
575 T C4517
3703 T C4020
3704 T C4063
3708 T C4077
3711 T? C3929
3712 T C4346
3713 T C4345
3714 T C4348
3715 T C4350
3716 T C4191
3719 T C4347
3725 T C4421
3730 T C4423
3740 T C4512
3741 T C4513
3742 T C4195
3743 T C4514
3744 T C4515
3745 T C4422
3746 T C4586
3747 T C4274
3748 T C4516
3749 T C4447
3750 T C4416
3751 T C4518
3753 T C4419
3758 T C4303
3759 T C4131
3783 T C4306
3784 T? C4606
3794 T C4429
3796 T C4601
3801 T C4424
3805 T C4604
3808 T C4534
3816 T C4476
3818 T C4605
3820 T C4600
3821 T C4602
3822 T C4264
3823 T C4603
3824 T? C4590
3824 T C4591
3828 T C4427
3833 T C4622
3837 T C4299
3839 T C4471
3840 T C4616

Jerusalem
Albright Institute
BJPES '47 p 146

Musée biblique de Bethesda
PB 2669 C4276
PB 2670 C4329

Studium Biblicum Franciscanum
C4450, C4451

Bible Land Museum
BLMJ 2587 Sem '74 p 69

Leiden
Rijksmuseum van Oudheden, B 1977/4.1
OM '88 p 37

London
British Museum
(580) C4337
1250 C4118
102612 C4200
104460 C4404
125017 C4509
125019 C4326
125020 C4323
125023 C4581
125024 C4338
125025 C3912
125031 C4580
125032 C4297
125036 C4296
125038 C4282
125048 C4356
125125 C4433
125150 C4507
125156 C4432
125201 C4288
125202 C4324
125203 C4335
125204 C4508
125206 C3972
125695 C4374

Los Angeles
County Museum of Art
M.79.147 (formerly: Minneapolis, Walker Art Center X.1495)
C4570

Mainz
Prinz Johann Georg Sammlung der Universität
721 C4474
835 C4245
834 C4417
833 C4437

Malibu
J. Paul Getty Museum
88.AA.50 Soth 5518 no. 40

Mentana (Rome)
Federico Zeri Collection
AIΩN '86b p 231, AIΩN '86a p 246, AIΩN '86a p 247, AIΩN '86a p 247, AIΩN '86a p 248, C4587

27
1963/7055 DaM '92
28
1965/7057 DaM '92
30
1966/7058 DaM '92
31
1967/7059 DaM '92
32
1968/7060 DaM '92
33
1969/7061 DaM '92
34
1970/7062 DaM '92
35
1971/7063 DaM '92
36
1972/7064 DaM '92
37
1973/7065 DaM '92
38
1974/7066 DaM '92
39
1975/7067 DaM '92
40
1976/7068 DaM '92
41
1977/7069 DaM '92
42
1978/7070 DaM '92
43
1979/7071 DaM '92
44
1980/7072 DaM '92
45
1981/7073 DaM '92
46
1982/7074 DaM '92
47
1983/7075 DaM '92
48
1984/7076 DaM '92
49
1985/7077 DaM '92
50
1986/7078 DaM '92
51
1987/7112 SFP 122
1987/7113 SFP 123
1987/7114 SFP 124
1987/7115 SFP 125
1987/7116 SFP 126
1987/7117 SFP 127
1987/7118 SFP 128
1987/7119 SFP 129
1987/7120 SFP 130
1987/7121 SFP 131
1987/7122 SFP 132
1987/7123 SFP 133
1987/7124 SFP 134
1987/7125 SFP 135
1987/7126 SFP 136
1987/7127 SFP 137
1987/7128 SFP 138
2004 SFP 139
2005 SFP 140
2006/7163 SFP 141
2007 (see note SFP ad loc) SFP 142
2008 SFP 143
2009 SFP 144
2010 SFP 148
2011 SFP 145
2012 SFP 146
2013 SFP 151
2014 SFP 154
2015 SFP 147
2016 SFP 149
2017 SFP 150
2018 SFP 152
2020/7197 SFP 159
2022/7199 SFP 157
2023/7200 SFP 156
2025/7223 RSP 22
2027/7225 RSP 23
2047/7222 RSP 21
2137/7499 RSP 52
2138/7600 RSP 53
2139/7601 RSP 54
2140/7602 RSP 55
2141/7603 RSP 56
2142/7604 RSP 57
2143/7605 RSP 58
2144/7606 RSP 59
2145/7607 RSP 60
2146/7608 RSP 61
2147/7609 RSP 62
2148/7610 RSP 63
2149/7611 RSP 64
2150/7612 RSP 65
2151/7616 RSP 66
2152/7614 RSP 67
2153/7615 RSP 68
2153/7616 RSP 69
2155/7617 RSP 70
2156/7621 RSP 71
2157/7619 RSP 72
2158/7620 RSP 73
2159/7621 RSP 74
218 C4232
220 Inv 9 7
25/63 RSP 190
38 (?) DaM '85 p 44
41 and 45/62 C3967
519 Ber '36 p 99
A 11 Déd p 36
A 26 Inv 9 1
A 34 C3924
A 34 C3925
A 72 Inv 8 32
A 91 Inv 8 51
A 95 Inv 8 91
A 96 Inv 8 92
A 97 Inv 8 93
A 98 Inv 8 69
A 99 Inv 8 62
A 100 Inv 8 66
A 101 Inv 8 94
A 103 Inv 8 95
A 104 Inv 8 96
A 105 Inv 8 59
A 106 Inv 8 63
A 107 Inv 8 97
A 108 Inv 8 98
A 109 Inv 8 99
A 114 Inv 8 104
A 116 Inv 8 106
A 117 Inv 8 107
A 118 Inv 8 108
A 119 Inv 8 109
A 120 Inv 8 110
A 121 Inv 8 111
A 122 Inv 8 112
A 123 Syr '38 p 82
A 124 Inv 8 113
A 125 Inv 8 114
A 126 Inv 8 115
A 128 Inv 8 116
A 129 Inv 8 117
A 130 Inv 8 118
A 131 Inv 8 119
A 134 Inv 8 121
A 135 Inv 8 122
A 136 Inv 8 123
A 137 Inv 8 124
A 138 Inv 8 125
A 139 Inv 8 126
A 140 Inv 8 127
A 141 Inv 8 128
A 142 Inv 8 129
A 143 Inv 8 130
A 144 Inv 8 131
A 145 Inv 8 132
A 146 Inv 8 133
A 147 Inv 8 134
A 148 Inv 8 135
A 149 Inv 8 136
A 150 Inv 8 137
A 151 Inv 8 138
A 152 C4163
A 153 Inv 8 60
A 154 Inv 8 139
A 155 Inv 8 140
A 156 Inv 8 141
A 157 Inv 8 142
A 158 Inv 8 67
A 159 Inv 8 143
A 160 Inv 8 144
A 161 Inv 8 145
A 162 Inv 8 146
A 163 Inv 8 147
A 165 Inv 8 148
A 166 Inv 8 149
A 167 Inv 8 150
A 168 Inv 8 151
A 169 Inv 8 152
A 170 Inv 8 153
A 171 Inv 8 154
A 172 Inv 8 155
A 173 Inv 8 156
A 174 Inv 8 157
A 175 Inv 8 158
A 176 Inv 8 159
A 177 C4125
A 178 Inv 8 192
A 179 Inv 8 162
A 180 Inv 8 72
A 181 Inv 8 163
A 182 Inv 8 74
A 184 Inv 8 165

A 185	Inv 8 166
A 186	Inv 8 167
A 187	Inv 8 168
A 188	Inv 8 169
A 189	C4120
A 189	Inv 8 75
A 190	Inv 8 76
A 191	Inv 8 70
A 192	Inv 8 170
A 193	Inv 8 171
A 194	Inv 8 172
A 195	Inv 8 173
A 196	Inv 8 174
A 197	Inv 8 175
A 198	Inv 8 176
A 199	Inv 8 177
A 200	Inv 8 178
A 201	Inv 8 179
A 202	Inv 8 180
A 203	Inv 8 181
A 204	Inv 8 182
A 205	Inv 8 183
A 206	Inv 8 184
A 207	Inv 8 185
A 208	Inv 8 186
A 209	Inv 8 187
A 210	Inv 8 188
A 211	Inv 8 189
A 212	Inv 8 190
A 213	Inv 8 191
A 215	C4126
A 215	C4127b
A 215	C4127a
A 217	C4239
A 218	C4231
A 219	Inv 8 195
A 222	Inv 9 30
A 224	Inv 8 196
A 225	Inv 8 197
A 241	Inv 11 21
A 242	Inv 11 22
A 244	Inv 11 51
A 246	Inv 11 8
A 248	Inv 11 9
A 249	C4010
A 255	Inv 11 14
A 255	C4035
A 257	Inv 11 52
A 264	Inv 8 79
A 269	C4101
A 270	Inv 11 24
A 273	Inv 11 20
A 274	Inv 11 25
A 277	Syr '36 p 348
A 278	Inv 11 76
A 280	Inv 11 82
A 281	Ber '36 p 97
A 283	Inv 8 73
A 285	Syr '36 p 274
A 286	Inv 11 10
A 289	Inv 11 17
A 29	Inv 11 2
A 290	Inv 11 49
A 298	Inv 11 53
A 302	Inv 11 26
A 304	Syr '36 p 351
A 305	Syr '36 p 353
A 306	Syr '36 p 280
A 309	Inv 11 68
A 313	Syr '36 p 350
A 314	Syr '36 p 271
A 315	Inv 8 77
A 316	Inv 8 78
A 320	Inv 8 81
A 321	Inv 8 82
A 322	Inv 8 83
A 323	Inv 8 84
A 325	Inv 8 85
A 326	Inv 8 86
A 328	Inv 8 88
A 329	Inv 8 89
A 330	Inv 8 90
A 342	Inv 8 199
A 352	Inv 11 54
A 356	Syr '38 p 154
A 357	C4043
A 361	Syr '36 p 268
A 362	Inv 11 72
A 363	Inv 11 55
A 368	Syr '38 p 155
A 369	Inv 11 56
A 372	Syr '36 p 349
A 374	Inv 11 27
A 375	Inv 11 28
A 377	Inv 11 16
A 379	Inv 11 57
A 38	Inv 8 65
A 383	Syr '38 p 153
A 384	Syr '38 p 158
A 385	Syr '38 p 158
A 389	Syr '38 p 159
A 390+A 391	Inv 11 12
A 403	Inv 11 58
A 408	Inv 11 59
A 411	Inv 11 50
A 415	Syr '38 p 81
A 416	Inv 11 60
A 417	C4075
A 429	Syr '38 p 79
A 431	Inv 11 30
A 433	Inv 11 31
A 435	Inv 11 79
A 438	Inv 11 19
A 439	Inv 11 32
A 445	Inv 11 80
A 447	Inv 11 86
A 450	Syr '38 p 157
A 451	Inv 8 198
A 453	Ber '36 p 94
A 453	C4105ter
A 454	Inv 8 200
A 466	Inv 11 33
A 470	Inv 11 6
A 504	Inv 11 34
A 508	Inv 11 35
A 510	Inv 11 36
A 521	Inv 8 64
A 523	Inv 11 81
A 525	Inv 11 5
A 528	Inv 11 37
A 530	Inv 11 38
A 532	Inv 11 4
A 538	Inv 11 1
A 549	Inv 11 15
A 558	Inv 11 39
A 573	Inv 11 7
A 603	Inv 10 111
A 618	MélDuss p 277
A 618	Inv 10 114
A 621	Inv 10 107
A 622	Syr '38 p 78
A 709	Inv 11 40
A 712	Inv 11 71
A 751	Inv 11 83
A 761	Inv 11 74
A 803	Inv 11 78
A 807	Inv 11 70
A 837	Inv 11 3
A 839	Inv 11 87
A 840	Inv 11 66
A 841	Inv 11 61
A 847	Syr '38 p 80
A 847	Syr '38 p 159
A 857	Inv 11 62
A 858	Inv 11 63
A 865	Inv 11 75
A 890	Inv 11 69
A 895	Inv 11 85
A 896	Inv 11 64
A 912	Inv 11 73
A 914	Inv 11 41
A 915	Inv 11 67
A 918	Inv 11 65
A 924	Inv 11 42
A 931	Inv 11 77
A 943	Inv 11 99
A 945	Inv 11 90
A 946	Inv 11 91
A 948	Inv 11 89
A 949	Inv 11 88
A 950	Inv 11 93
A 951	Inv 11 97
A 952	Inv 11 98
A 953	Inv 11 92
A 954	Inv 11 94
A 958	Inv 11 95
A 959	Inv 11 100
A 962	Inv 11 96
A 964	Inv 10 96
A 966	Inv 10 98
A 968+A 1037+A 1030	Inv 10 99
A 972	Inv 10 12
A 979	Inv 10 123
A 989	Inv 10 132
A 993	Inv 10 16
A 997	Inv 10 77
A 999	Inv 10 65
A 233	Inv 9 35bis
A 1001	Inv 10 76
A 1004	Inv 10 74
A 1005	Inv 10 75
A 1008	Inv 10 70
A 1009	Inv 10 56
A 1013	Inv 10 61
A 1015, A 1003	Inv 10 62
A 1017	Inv 10 72
A 1023	Inv 10 42

A 1033 Inv 10 48
A 1039 Inv 10 49
A 1040 Inv 10 102
A 1054 Inv 10 110
A 1055=A 1070 Inv 10 112
A 1056 Inv 10 85
A 1057 Inv 10 11
A 1057 Inv 10 8
A 1066 Inv 10 118
A 1075 Inv 10 91
A 1076 Inv 10 94
A 1083 Inv 10 93
A 1090 Inv 10 140
A 1100 RSP 122
A 1106 Sem '50 p 47
A 1121 MUSJ '61 p 125
A 1126 Syr '50 p 137
A 1155 Inv 11 44
A 1157 Inv 11 11
A 1158 Inv 11 45
A 1159 Inv 11 13
A 1160 Inv 11 46
A 1161 Inv 11 47
A 1162 Inv 11 48
A 1167 RSP 126
A 1168 RSP 125
A 1169 RSP 127
A 1171 RSP 106
A 1172 RSP 108
A 1173 RSP 121
A 1174 RSP 116
A 1175 RSP 115
A 1176 RSP 117
A 1177 RSP 119
A 1178 RSP 120
A 1179 RSP 107
A 1180 RSP 124
A 1184 RSP 111
A 1185 RSP 123
A 1192 MUSJ '61 p 133
A 1204 RSP 114
A 1205 RSP 112
A 1206 RSP 118
A 1207 RSP 110
A 1208 RSP 113
A 1209 RSP 109
A 1233 Inv 12 56
A 1239/6332 SFP 3
A 1240/6405 SFP 15
A 1241/6406 SFP 16
A 1242/6407 SFP 17
A 1246 Inv 12 26
A 1259 Inv 12 15
A 1262 Inv 12 30
A 1268 BS III 32
A 1269 BS III 84
A 1271 BS III 28
A 1274 BS III 55
A 1275 BS III 90
A 1277 BS III 63
A 1279 BS III 79
A 1280, A 1273 BS III 54
A 1285 BS III 58
A 1285 BS III 41
A 1287 BS III 85
A 1290 + A 1294 BS III 36
A 1291 BS III 88
A 1295 BS III 82
A 1297 BS III 65
A 1298 BS III 67
A 1301 BS III 83
A 1302 BS III 60
A 1303 BS III 27
A 1305 BS III 86
A 1307 BS III 87
A 1309 BS III 66
A 1310 BS III 53
A 1312 BS III 89
A 1382 Inv 12 25
A 1392 Inv 12 22
A 1393 Inv 12 24
A 1399 RSP 105
A 1400 Inv 12 53
A 1401/8112 Inv 12 43
A 1415/8423 DaM '85 p 37
A 1415/8426 DaM '85 p 38
A 1416/8424 DaM '85 p 37
A 1417/8425 DaM '85 p 38
A 1419/8427 DaM '85 p 39
A 1420/8428 DaM '85 p 39
A 1422 PGKK p 310
A 1422/8423 DaM '85 p 39
A 1426 PGKK p 306
A 1441/8599 DaM '85 p 42
A 1453/8646 DaM '85 p 43
A 1454/8654 DaM '85 p 42
A 1460/8690 DaM '85 p 43
A 1465/8772 DaM '85 p 40
A 1472/8840 DaM '85 p 40
A 1473/8841 DaM '85 p 40
A 1474/8842 DaM '85 p 40
A 1475/8843 DaM '85 p 41
A 1475/8843 DaM '85 p 41
A 1481 RSP 166
A 1901 Inv 10 127
A 2471/8710 DaM '85 p 42
B 10/63 AAS '65/2 p 127
B 1864 BS III 56
B 1896 BS III 62
B 1903 BS III 64
B 2185 RSP 189
B 2195 Inv 12 54
B 2211 RSP 191
B 2304 (A 143/75) PGKK p 310
B 7078 EblaDam p 290
CD 1/73 Palm VIII p 121
CD 1/76 Palm VIII p 123
CD 10/63 RSP 165
CD 101/59 RSP 163
CD 101/60 RSP 151
CD 102/60 RSP 149
CD 103/62 RSP 138
CD 106/62 RSP 137
CD 110/61 RSP 180
CD 114/61 RSP 182
CD 114/62 RSP 188
CD 118/61 RSP 181
CD 12/61 RSP 164
CD 122/60 RSP 174
CD 123/60 RSP 171
CD 129/60 RSP 150
CD 13/66 RSP 227
CD 130/60 RSP 205
CD 130/61 RSP 215
CD 131/60 RSP 170
CD 132-133/61 RSP 214
CD 14/60 RSP 209
CD 14/65 RSP 221
CD 140/60 RSP 145
CD 147/75 HomVer
CD 156/60 RSP 134
CD 16/60 RSP 208
CD 17/68 Palm VIII p 121
CD 18/59 RSP 199
CD 18/66 RSP 144
CD 2/69 RSP 198
CD 2/73 Palm VIII p 121
CD 239/65 RSP 222
CD 240/65 RSP 223
CD 241/65 RSP 224
CD 242/65 RSP 225
CD 25/62 Palm IV p 194
CD 27/59 RSP 148
CD 27/61 RSP 175
CD 29/63 RSP 220
CD 29/66 RSP 226
CD 3/65 RSP 194
CD 31/73 Palm VIII p 121
CD 32/62 RSP 186
CD 33/62 RSP 187
CD 35/66 RSP 195
CD 36/59 RSP 147
CD 36/66 RSP 228

CD 38/62 RSP 217
CD 38/66 RSP 161
CD 38/76 HomVer
CD 39/62 RSP 184
CD 40/62 RSP 185
CD 40/66 RSP 155
CD 41/62 Palm IV p 190
CD 42 RSP 192
CD 42/67 RSP 197
CD 43/66 RSP 229
CD 45/62 RSP 216
CD 46/60 RSP 206
CD 46/73 Palm VIII p 122
CD 47/59 RSP 201
CD 47/66 RSP 196
CD 47/73 Palm VIII p 122
CD 48/59 RSP 200
CD 48/60 RSP 173
CD 5/59 RSP 168
CD 51/61 RSP 176
CD 53/61 RSP 210
CD 56/73 Palm VIII p 122
CD 57/60 RSP 172
CD 57/73 Palm VIII p 122
CD 58/61 RSP 177
CD 6/74 Sem '77 p 106
CD 60/59 RSP 202
CD 63/59 RSP 169
CD 64/61 RSP 178
CD 65/61 RSP 211
CD 67/63 RSP 193
CD 69/63 RSP 159
CD 7/59 RSP 203
CD 70/61 RSP 212
CD 70/65 RSP 143
CD 71/65 RSP 154
CD 72/65 RSP 153
CD 74/61 RSP 146
CD 75/61 RSP 135
CD 84/60 RSP 204
CD 86/61 RSP 213
CD 88/61 RSP 179
CD 93/60 RSP 207
CD 95/61 RSP 183
CD 96/61 RSP 136
CD 97/62 RSP 219
entrance Dri '82 p 65
exc no. 109 BS III 7
exc no. 110 BS III 23
exc no. 116 BS III 17
exc no. 123 BS VI p 114
exc no. 128 BS VI p 115
exc no. 13 BS VI p 116
exc no. 133 BS VI p 116
exc no. 134 BS III 45
exc no. 135 BS III 43
exc no. 15 BS III 24
exc no. 156 BS III 35
exc no. 16 BS III 42
exc no. 160 BS III 47
exc no. 19 BS III 51
exc no. 200 BS III 33
exc no. 203 BS III 20
exc no. 216 BS III 70
exc no. 231 BS III 26
exc no. 238 BS VI p 114
exc no. 244 BS VI p 114
exc no. 262 BS III 59
exc no. 27 BS III 12
exc no. 271 BS VI p 113
exc no. 272 BS III 37
exc no. 273 BS III 73
exc no. 277 BS III 11
exc no. 282 BS III 18
exc no. 283 BS III 10
exc no. 287 BS III 14
exc no. 288 BS III 15
exc no. 30 BS III 40
exc no. 302 BS III 4
exc no. 341 BS III 29
exc no. 346 BS III 16
exc no. 36 BS III 9
exc no. 4 BS III 39
exc no. 41 BS III 6
exc no. 42 BS III 3
exc no. 44 BS III 46
exc no. 57 BS III 1
exc no. 76 + 45 BS III 8
exc no. 8 BS III 38
exc no. 85 BS III 69
exc no. 86 BS III 68
exc no. 87 BS III 19
exc no. 87 BS III 72
exc no. 87 BS III 71
exc no. 88 BS III 22
exc no. 89 BS III 21
exc no. 90, 132, 227 (227 = A 1293) BS III 5
exc no. 96, 129, 254, 278, 161 BS III 2
exc no. 99 BS III 34
exc. no. 80 O TG 36 no. 187
garden RSP 162
garden, no. CD 32/63 RSP 142
no. A 1210/5332 Syr '85 p 279
nos. A 975+A 976 Inv 10 124
Room I, S wall C3945
S 1170 Inv 10 54
S 118 (A 969) Inv 10 90
S 1209 Inv 10 69
S 13 (A 633) Inv 10 105
S 1307 Inv 10 39
S 1308 Inv 10 40
S 1494 Inv 10 38
S 1707 C3963
S 1737 Inv 10 29
S 1781 Inv 10 63
S 1782 Inv 10 57
S 1854 Inv 10 106
S 1861 Inv 10 44
S 1872 Inv 10 115
S 1903 Inv 10 81
S 1910 Inv 10 7
S 1911 Inv 10 4
S 1962 Inv 10 6
S 1990 Inv 10 113
S 200 Inv 10 119
S 2140 Inv 10 144
S 2312 Inv 10 145
S 2338 Inv 10 126
S 2342=A 1105 Inv 10 128
S 2343 Inv 10 129
S 2351 Inv 10 130
S 2352 Inv 10 131
S 565 Inv 10 53
S 760 Inv 10 78
T 10/62 RSP 49
T 18/62 RSP 50, text A
T 25/19 RSP 48
T 27/62 RSP 50, text B
T 9/19 RSP 47
TE 1 C3989
TE 140 RSP 139
TE 149 RSP 140
TE 220 C3998
TE 243 Inv 6 4
TE 243 Palm V p 117
TE 320 C3988
TE 55 RSP 160

Paris

Louvre
AO 1144 C4340
AO 1194 PS no. 104
AO 1197 C4289
AO 1555 C4398
AO 1556 C4401
AO 1557 C4321
AO 1558 C4287
AO 1562 C4399
AO 1757 C4284
AO 1758 C4411
AO 1998 C4503
AO 2000 C4501
AO 2067 C4498
AO 2068 C4499
AO 2069 C4497
AO 2093 C4502
AO 2196 C4428
AO 2198 C4500
AO 2199 C4323 bis et ter
AO 2200 C4250

AO 2201 C4251
AO 2203 C4119
AO 2204 C4218
AO 2205 C4112
AO 2398 C4381
AO 2630 C4410
AO 3984 C4588
AO 4085 C4465
AO 4086 C4402
AO 4147 C4538
AO 4148 C4620
AO 4449 C4470
AO 4998 C4027
AO 5000 C4377
AO 5004 C4376
AO 5005 C4331
AO 5006 C4375
AO 5007 C4412
AO 5972 C4457
AO 5991 C4607
AO 7476 C4572
AO 11450 Lou 149
AO 14925 C4621
AO 14926 C4530
AO 19801 Syr '49 p 39
AO 19801 Syr '49 p 36
AO 19801 Syr '49 p 38
AO 19801 Syr '49 p 36
AO 19801 Syr '49 p 40
AO 22253 C4334
AO 22254 C4333
AO 26429 JA '18 p 295
AO 26430 Lou 232
AO 28360 MUSJ '66 p 178
AO 28377 Syr '85 p 57
AO 28381 Syr '30 Pl. XLI
AO 28548 Lou 157
AO 29537 Lou 239

Bibliothèque Nationale, Cabinet des Médailles
TMP pp 757-58
Sem '73 p 121

Institut Catholique, Musée Bible et Terre Sainte Déd p 217

Philadelphia
University Museum
B 8902 PS no. 262
B 8905 PS no. 419
B 8906 PS no. 209

Pittsfield, Mass.
Berkshire Museum
1903.7.3 C4313
1903.7.3 C4315
1903.7.5 C4478
1903.7.4 PS no. 356

Portland
Portland Art Museum
54.1 C4595
54.2 C4535
54.3 C4537

Princeton
The Art Museum, Princeton University
1946-109 C4312

Rome
Museo Capitolino
CE 6715 = NCE 2406 C3902
CE 6721 = NCE 2402 C3903
CE 6707 = NCE 2398 C3904

Museo Nazionale d'Arte orientale, 6011 C4413

Museo Barracco di scultura antica
206 Déd p 43
249 Déd p 43
250 PS no. 149

São Paulo
São Paulo University Museum, 69/3.1 C4293

South Shields, England
Arbeia Roman Fort Museum
TWCMS T 765 C3901

St. Petersburg
Hermitage
4177 C4129
4187 C3913
8839 C4579
8840 C4292
8842 C4575
8843 C4577
8841 C4578
8844 C4574

St. Louis
The St. Louis Art Museum
24:60 C4561

Stanford
Stanford University Museum of Art
17204 (Leland Stanford Jr. Collection 1884) JA '18 p 282
17200 (Leland Stanford Jr. Collection 1884) Parl '90 p 140
17201 (Leland Stanford Jr. Collection 1884) Parl '90 p 141
no. 17205 Verm '81 p 387

Strassburg
Strassburg Museum
S 236 C4545
S 233 C4584
S 234 C4585

University Library
C4014, C4037, C4339, C4378, C4387, C4539, C4619

Tashkent
State University Archaeological Collection EaWe '67

Toledo, Ohio
Toledo Museum of Art
62.18 Verm '81 p 380

Toronto
Royal Ontario Museum
953x94.4 PS no. 203
953x94.2 PS no. 148
953x94.1 PS no. 33
953x94.3 PS no. 394

Vienna
Kunsthistorisches Museum
I 1525 C4349
I 1526 C4351
I 1524 C4352
I 1523 C4353
1503 C4407

Warsaw
Muzeum Narodowe
199576 C4469

Washington
Freer Art Gallery
08.236 C4460

Wroclaw
Muzeum Archidiecezjalnego
2250 PS no. 329

7. Sigla of selected genres of texts

a. Honorific inscriptions: Ber '36 p 88 2; Ber '36 p 94 4; Ber '70 p 66 (1); Ber '70 p 67 (2); BS III 37; BS III 38; BS III 39; BS III 40; BS III 41; BS III 42; BS III 43; BS III 45; BS III 46; BS III 47; BS III 51; BS III 53; BS III 54; BS III 55; C3910; C3914; C3915; C3916; C3917; C3918; C3919; C3920; C3921; C3922; C3923; C3924; C3925; C3926; C3927; C3928; C3929; C3930; C3931; C3932; C3933; C3934; C3935; C3936; C3937; C3938; C3939; C3940; C3941; C3942; C3943; C3944; C3945; C3946; C3947; C3948; C3949; C3950; C3951; C3952; C3953; C3954; C3955; C3956; C3957; C3958; C3959; C3960; C3961; C3962; C3963; C3964; C3965; C3966; C3967; C3968; C3969; C3970; C3971; Déd p 13; Déd p 217; Déd p 36; Doura 25; Inv 10 102; Inv 10 105; Inv 10 106; Inv 10 107; Inv 10 111; Inv 10 112; Inv 10 113; Inv 10 114; Inv 10 115; Inv 10 119; Inv 10 12; Inv 10 124; Inv 10 126; Inv 10 127; Inv 10 128; Inv 10 129; Inv 10 13; Inv 10 130; Inv 10 131; Inv 10 16; Inv 10 24; Inv 10 29; Inv 10 38; Inv 10 39; Inv 10 4; Inv 10 40; Inv 10 42; Inv 10 44; Inv 10 48; Inv 10 49; Inv 10 53; Inv 10 54; Inv 10 57; Inv 10 61; Inv 10 62; Inv 10 63; Inv 10 65; Inv 10 69; Inv 10 74; Inv 10 75; Inv 10 77; Inv 10 78; Inv 10 81; Inv 10 85; Inv 10 90; Inv 10 91; Inv 10 96; Inv 10 98; Inv 10 99; Inv 11 100; Inv 11 88; Inv 11 89; Inv 11 90; Inv 11 91; Inv 11 92; Inv 11 93; Inv 11 95; Inv 11 96; Inv 12 35; Inv 8 200; Inv 9 1; Inv 9 11; Inv 9 12; Inv 9 14b; Inv 9 16; Inv 9 20; Inv 9 26; Inv 9 28; Inv 9 29; Inv 9 30; Inv 9 33; Inv 9 34; Inv 9 4a, 4b; Inv 9 5a; Inv 9 7; MélDuss p 277; PNO no. 2; PNO no. 2 bis; RSP 159; RSP 160; RSP 161; RSP 162; RSP 204; RSP 205; RSP 212; RSP 213; RSP 216; RSP 218; Syr '26 p 129; Syr '31 p 133 no. 12; Syr '31 p 138 no. 17; Syr '31 p 139 no. 18; Syr '33 p 177 Tad 3; Syr '33 p 186 Tad 9; Syr '33 p 187 Tad 10; Syr '36 p 268 Tad 17; Syr '36 p 280 Tad 20; Syr '36 p 349 Tad 23; Syr '38 p 159 Tad 37; Syr '38 p 76 Tad 29; Syr '71 p 420; Syr '85 p 257 no. 13.

b. Funerary inscriptions of foundation of tombs or cession

1) Foundation: AA '32 p 1; Ber '35 p 109 I; Ber '35 p 115; Ber '35 p 59 I; Ber '35 p 60 II; Ber '35 p 75 I; Ber '70 p 69 (4); Ber '70 p 74 (6); C4109; C4112; C4113; C4114; C4115; C4115bis; C4116; C4119; C4120; C4121; C4122; C4123; C4123bis; C4124; C4130; C4134; C4159; C4160; C4161; C4162; C4163; C4164; C4165; C4166; C4167; C4168; C4170; C4192; C4193; C4196; C4197; C4199; C4201; C4202; C4203; C4209; C4215; C4216; C4217; Inv 12 1; Inv 4 12; Inv 4 13; Inv 4 14; Inv 4 25; Inv 4 7a; Inv 4 9b; Inv 7 10; Inv 7 5; Inv 8 58; Inv 8 59; Inv 8 60; Inv 8 62 ; Inv 8 65; MélColl p 161; RB '30 p 536 no. 6; RB '30 p 537 no. 7; RB '30 p 538 no. 8; RB '30 p 539 no. 9; RB '30 p 540 no. 10; RB '30 p 545 no. 13; RSP 104; RSP 163; RSP 164; RSP 165; RSP 166; RSP 167; RSP 24; RSP 25; StudMiles p 50 no. 1; StudPalm '75 p 131; Syr '38 p 153 Tad 36a; Syr '85 p 271 no. 1; Syr '85 p 273 no. 2; TG 36 no. 187 Pl. 15.

2) Cession: Ber '38 p 104 (19); Ber '38 p 106 (20 I); Ber '38 p 109 (20 I bis); Ber '38 p 109 (20 II); Ber '38 p 110 (20 III); Ber '70 p 71 (5); Ber '35 p 100 IX; Ber '35 p 102 X; Ber '35 p 102 XI; Ber '35 p 104 XII; Ber '35 p 107 XIII; Ber '35 p 110 II; Ber '35 p 112 III; Ber '35 p 76 II; Ber '35 p 77 III.; Ber '35 p 78 IV; Ber '35 p 82 V; Ber '35 p 84 VI; Ber '35 p 85 VII; Ber '35 p 86 VIII; Ber '35 p 88 IX; Ber '35 p 91 II; Ber '35 p 93 III; Ber '35 p 95 IV; Ber '35 p 96 V; Ber '35 p 97 VI; Ber '35 p 98 VII; Ber '35 p 99 VIII; Ber '38 p 124 (21 II); Ber '38 p 95 (18 II); C4171; C4172; C4173; C4174; C4175; C4194; C4195; C4204; C4211; Inv 4 7b; Inv 7 15c; Inv 7 1b; Inv 8 69; Inv 8 72; MUSJ '62 p 106; PGKK p 306 no. 28; RB '30 p 540 no. 10; RB '30 p 545 no. 13; RB '30 p 548 no. 14; RSP 51; StudMiles p 38; StudMiles p 50 no. 2; StudPalm '75 p 129; Syr '33 p 185 Tad 8; Syr '38 p 155 Tad 36c; Syr '85 p 276 no. 5; Syr '85 p 277 no. 8; Syr '85 p 277 no. 7.

3) Other: (with curse) C4218; RSP 105; Ber '38 p 133; (unique) BS III 60.

c. Legal texts besides the Tariff (C3913; Trf): CRAIBL '81 p 306; RSP 199.

d. Tesserae not in RTP: BS III p 10; BS VI p 114 (4); BS VI p 114 (6); BS VI p 114 (5); BS VI p 113 (3); BS VI p 116 (16); BS VI p 115 (10); BS VI p 116 (12); MUSJ '66 p 178 no. 3; MUSJ '66 p 178 no. 4; Palm III p 238 no. 5; StudLdV p 601 Walker; Syr '59 p 105 no. 10; Syr '59 p 107 no. 23; Syr '59 p 105 no. 12; Syr '59 p 105 no. 13; Syr '59 p 105 no. 9; Syr '59 p 106 no. 14; Syr '59 p 104 no. 2; Syr '59 p 104 no. 6; Syr '59 p 104 no. 3; TMP pp 757-58.